MODERN POLITICAL THOUGHT

READINGS FROM MACHIAVELLI TO NIETZSCHE

Modern Political Thought
Readings from Machiavelli to Nietzsche

Second Edition

Edited, with Introductions, by
David Wootton

Hackett Publishing Company, Inc.
Indianapolis/Cambridge

For further information, please address:

Hackett Publishing Company, Inc.
P.O. Box 44937
Indianapolis, IN 46244-0937

www.hackettpublishing.com

Cover design by Brian Rak and Abigail Coyle
Interior design by Abigail Coyle
Composition by Agnew's, Inc., and World Composition Services, Inc.

Library of Congress Cataloging-in-Publication Data

Modern political thought : readings from Machiavelli to Nietzsche /
edited, with Introductions, by David Wootton. — 2nd ed.
            p.   cm.
    ISBN-13: 978-0-87220-897-1 (pbk)
    ISBN-13: 978-0-87220-898-8 (cloth)
        1. Political science—History.
        I. Wootton, David, 1952–
            JA83.M64 2007
        320.01—dc22
                    2007031326

CONTENTS

v

COPYRIGHT ACKNOWLEDGMENTS

The translation of Machiavelli reprinted here is from *Selected Political Writings,* translated by David Wootton (Indianapolis: Hackett Publishing Company, 1994), by permission of the publisher.

The translation of Calvin reprinted here is from *Institutes of the Christian Religion*, edited by John T. McNeill (Library of Christian Classics). Used by permission of Westminster John Knox Press and T&T Clark, Ltd.

The translation of Rousseau reprinted here is from *The Basic Political Writings,* translated by Donald A. Cress (Indianapolis: Hackett Publishing Company, 1987), by permission of the publisher.

The translation of Kant reprinted here is from *Perpetual Peace and Other Essays,* translated by Ted Humphrey (Indianapolis: Hackett Publishing Company, 1983), by permission of the publisher.

The translation of Hegel reprinted here is from *Introduction to the Philosophy of History,* translated by Leo Rauch (Indianapolis: Hackett Publishing Company, 1988), by permission of the publisher.

Marx: 'On the Jewish Question', 'Toward a Critique of Hegel's *Philosophy of Right*: Introduction', 'Alienated Labor' from *Economic and Philosophic Manuscripts of 1844*, 'Theses on Feuerbach', and *The German Ideology* translated by Loyd D. Easton and Kurt H. Guddat (Indianapolis: Hackett Publishing Company, 1997), by permission of the publisher.

The Eighteenth Brumaire of Louis Bonaparte, 'Preface to *A Contribution to the Critique of Political Economy*', 'Critique of the Gotha Program' reprinted with the permission of International Publishers Inc., New York.

The translation of Nietzsche reprinted here is from *On the Genealogy of Morality,* translated by Maudemarie Clark and Alan J. Swensen (Indianapolis: Hackett Publishing Company 1998, by permission of the publisher.

ACKNOWLEDGMENTS

I would like to thank Matthew Clayton, Ed Curley, Stuart Elden, Barbara Goodwin, Mark Neocleous, Brian Rak, Gay Weber, and a series of anonymous referees for advice and criticism.

The quotation from Rousseau on p. 367 is taken from Tracy B. Strong, *Jean-Jacques Rousseau: The Politics of the Ordinary* (Thousand Oaks, Cal.: Sage, 1994), pp. 61–62, itself a modified version of Alan Bloom's translation in *Politics and the Arts* (Ithaca: Cornell University Press, 1968), pp. 135–36.

The quotation from Nietzsche on p. 863 is taken from Friedrich Nietzsche, *The Will to Power,* translated by Walter Kaufmann and R. J. Hollingdale (New York: Vintage Books, 1968), pp. 364–65.

INTRODUCTION

This reader provides an introduction to modern political philosophy from Machiavelli (1513) to Nietzsche (1887). Most of the works reprinted here have long been recognized as central to the history of political philosophy: Machiavelli, Hobbes, Locke, Rousseau, Mill. Like any such selection, this one also reflects contemporary interests and preoccupations: Nietzsche seems a much more important political philosopher now than he did thirty years ago, and Mill's *The Subjection of Women* seems a much more important text. Adding one text in a reader such as this means dropping another; Marxism is the obvious casualty of the last twenty years, and though I have included an extensive selection from Marx himself, I have excluded Luxemburg, Lenin, and Trotsky, to name three for whom space might once have been found.

In selecting the texts, I have been conscious of the fact that most students are introduced to modern political thought in the course of a one-semester course. This volume therefore represents an idealized semester's reading: Instructors will want to drop one or more of the selections in order to make the program more manageable. I hoped the book would be shorter than it is, but it did not seem to me that there would be any general agreement about which texts could best be dropped: While one course may pass lightly over Hobbes in order to spend time on Locke, another will skim Rousseau in order to give time to Hume, Smith, and Burke. My hope is that nearly all instructors will find their most urgent needs satisfied by the present selection.

While there is in practice fairly general agreement about which texts students should read, we noticeably lack any satisfactory account of how the modern list of 'classic' texts came to be put together. Instead we have accounts of the changing reputations of individual thinkers, such as Machiavelli, over time, and proposed solutions to particular problems, such as why Locke has always seemed more important in America than in England. But when, where, and why did political theory crystallize into a discipline in which these particular texts were accepted as canonical? Alas, political scientists, philosophers, and historians of ideas have been much less self-conscious about questions of canon-formation than literary critics. But it is worth pausing to note that the canon is more diverse than one might fear, yet also less representative than one might hope. More diverse, in that the texts which are accepted as classics do not simply represent the orthodoxies of liberal, democratic culture: Machiavelli and Hobbes are often made to seem more respectable than they should be, but for century after century they have mainly been read as presenting challenging arguments that must be refuted. Despite the shifting fortunes of Marxism and the continuing disagreement as to whether the works of the 'young' or the 'mature' Marx are the more interesting, Marx's arguments will continue to receive attention, as Rousseau's do. Nevertheless, the canon does not adequately represent the historical evolution of political theorizing. It is far too secular, for one thing (a defect I have sought to remedy by including a chapter from Calvin); moreover it excludes texts which shaped the political thinking of generations, such as Mandeville's *Fable of the Bees,* or Beccaria's *Crimes and Punishments*; and at its heart lie texts which were regarded as insignificant when they were first published (*The Prince, The Second Treatise of Government*), but which came to seem extraordinarily important much later. This selection adopts a critical attitude to the contemporary canon by including three chapters from Smith which, though they may never be canonical, are pedagogically invaluable. But in the main I have accepted the canon for what it is, not sought to reform it.

If there is general agreement about which are the key texts in the history of political philosophy, there is no general agreement about how to read them. Some read them for their relevance to contemporary philosophical debates; others for their enduring wisdom; others in order to understand the development of a particular mode of discourse over time; yet others read them as literature. Different readers are likely to focus on different texts. Contemporary philosophers find Mill more interesting than Machiavelli; followers of Leo Strauss find Machiavelli more interesting than Mill; while Quentin Skinner and John Pocock negotiate the whole question of what distinguishes a classic from a minor text with some unease. Consequently the content of advanced courses designed by members of different schools of thought is bound to differ substantially: It is only at the introductory level that there is widespread agreement on the texts that all students of modern political philosophy need to encounter first. My own introductions to the texts concentrate on historical questions because some historical knowledge is a necessary foundation for any interpretation. Anyone reading Hobbes immediately after Machiavelli (as students often do) needs to have some sense of what has happened in the one hundred and fifty years that separates them. They need to know that the Reformation had transformed political practice and theory, that Galileo had shaken the entrenched supremacy of Aristotelian science, and that Hobbes was contributing to an existing tradition of natural-law theory. About this there can be general agreement, while there is likely to be much less agreement over the relevance to an interpretation of *Leviathan* of Hobbes's translation of Thucydides, the Engagement crisis of 1650, or twentieth-century game theory.

It is worth remarking that the texts that have found their way into the canon have done so because they satisfy a number of very different requirements.

First, they are well written and well argued. Beccaria's *Crimes and Punishments* is a good example of a text that its first readers thought deserved to become a classic, if only it were better written, hence all the revised, reorganized, and heavily annotated editions of Beccaria which promptly appeared.

Second, they simplify the lives of instructors by standing for an intellectual period or a political epoch. So Machiavelli stands for the Renaissance, and few students read More or Montaigne; Rousseau symbolizes the French Revolution, obscuring Siéyès. The one obvious omission among the classic texts is the absence of a text that encapsulates the Reformation: Here Calvin fills the gap.

Third, the classic texts are both philosophically challenging and intriguingly ambiguous. It is fashionable to argue that all texts invite a multitude of interpretations, and one might claim that the range of interpretations surrounding each of the classic texts simply reflects the effort that has gone into their exegesis, but I suspect that ambiguity is a precondition for classic status. There is little disagreement about how to interpret Engels, and little agreement about how to interpret Marx. Yet it is Marx we read, not Engels. Classic texts pose problems that seem almost insoluble. Does Machiavelli favor republicanism or despotism? Is Hobbes an atheist? Is Mill's liberalism consistent with his utilitarianism? These texts invite debate and disputation, and resist a merely passive reading. Which is why each generation in its turn finds reading them not a chore but a pleasure.

On Method

Richard Rorty, J. B. Schneewind and Quentin Skinner (eds.), *Philosophy in History* (Cambridge: Cambridge University Press, 1985)
   Leo Strauss, *Persecution and the Art of Writing* [1952] (Chicago: University of Chicago Press, 1988)
   James Tully (ed.), *Meaning and Context: Quentin Skinner and His Critics* (Princeton: Princeton University Press, 1988)

On Canons

John Guillory, 'Canon', in Frank Letricchia and Thomas McLaughlin (eds.), *Critical Terms for Literary Study* (Chicago: University of Chicago Press, 1990), pp. 233–49

Surveys

There is no good one-volume, single-author survey of our subject. Three works which have stood the test of time and give an account of political theory from Plato to the modern day are:

   Alasdair MacIntyre, *A Short History of Ethics* (London: Routledge and Kegan Paul, 1967)
   Susan Moller Okin, *Women in Western Political Thought* (Princeton: Princeton University Press, 1979)
   Sheldon S. Wolin, *Politics and Vision: Continuity and Innovation in Western Political Thought* (Boston: Little, Brown, 1960)

   A useful collection of essays, again covering ancient as well as modern political theory, is
   John Dunn (ed.), *Democracy: The Unfinished Journey* (Oxford: Oxford University Press, 1992)

1

MACHIAVELLI AND THE RENAISSANCE

Modern political thought begins in the winter of 1513/14, when Niccolò Machiavelli—unemployed, broke, and fresh out of prison—sat down to write *The Prince* on lonely evenings in his rural exile outside Florence. His letter to Francesco Vettori of 10 December 1513 describes the circumstances under which *The Prince* was written, but if we are to grasp why this little book marks a new epoch in the history of ideas, we need to place it in context.

The Renaissance begins, for our purposes, with Francesco Petrarch's discovery in 1345 of a copy of Cicero's letters to Atticus, which had lain moldering and unread for centuries. First, Cicero's letters presented a challenge: Could anyone now write Latin as Cicero had written it? Petrarch set out to learn how to write Latin, not as a living language, transformed by centuries of Christianity and feudalism, but as a language which had to be rediscovered in authentic classical sources. Petrarch was proud of his achievement, proud enough to write letters to Cicero himself, as if he were a contemporary. Second, Cicero's letters provoked thought about time and change. Not only language but also institutions, clothes, currency, weights and measures—everything had changed since Cicero's time. Accurate knowledge of the lost past involved a new sense of change, adaptation, and anachronism, a new historical consciousness. And yet this historical consciousness was directed at restoring the past to life, at learning to think like a Roman, not at demonstrating that it was impossible to step back into the past, that change was irreversible. Third, Cicero's letters invited a questioning of Christian values. Petrarch himself was a devout Christian who read Augustine with as much enthusiasm as he read Cicero, but to rediscover Cicero's world was to learn to think in terms of a set of moral values quite different from those of Christianity, a set of values which stressed pride and courage rather than humility and guilt, citizenship rather than salvation. And in Cicero too one could find a whole series of alternatives to the Aristotelian Christian philosophy—scholasticism—which was taught in the universities of Petrarch's day: Platonism, scepticism, Epicureanism, stoicism took on new life. Above all, Cicero was a republican politician. He wrote his letters from his country retreat because Caesar had driven him out of politics. To learn to think like Cicero was to learn to prefer republics to monarchies, political activity to leisure and contemplation. It was to learn to seek fulfillment in political action, not religious faith, to think of contemplation as an activity undertaken by philosophical laypeople, not pious monks and nuns. At every point Cicero offered an alternative to both the secular and the religious institutions and values of the Middle Ages (even though they themselves had been suffused with Roman influences).

By the time Machiavelli was born, in 1469, the discoveries of Petrarch and his successors had led to the construction of an entirely new educational program, known as humanism. Where the

1

universities stressed the study of Aristotelian philosophy and Christian theology, the humanists (usually outside the universities) concentrated on grammar, rhetoric, history, poetry, and moral philosophy, studied primarily in Latin, but also, for more advanced students, in Greek. Their claim was simple: Such studies prepared laymen for a useful life as civil servants, lawyers, advisers to princes. Men who lacked this education could have no claim to participate in public affairs. This new education also introduced students to the characteristic tensions in humanist thinking: between pagan past and Christian present, republic and monarchy, official business and private leisure. Soon there were innumerable different types of humanist. Some, like Machiavelli's contemporary Etienne Dolet (d. 1546), were such dedicated followers of Cicero that they rejected Christianity; others, like the Florentine Marsilio Ficino (b. 1433), turned from Cicero to Plato and constructed a philosophy compatible both with Christianity and with courtly life; yet others, like Desiderius Erasmus (probably born in the same year as Machiavelli), sought to use humanist techniques to rediscover the authentic message of the Christian Gospels, concealed by centuries of philosophical disputation and anachronistic misinterpretation.

Although his family was poor, Machiavelli received a first-rate humanist education, on the strength of which he was catapulted from obscurity into a senior position in the Florentine civil service in 1498, at the age of twenty-nine. As such, politics was his profession. Machiavelli's Italy may indeed be described as the birthplace of professional politics. Five city-states (Florence, Milan, Naples, Rome, Venice) had been involved in a continuous struggle for dominance for more than a century. In order to be constantly prepared for any eventuality they had invented the institution of the resident ambassador, men sent to observe and analyze every action of a potential friend or enemy. Such men learned a hard-headed realism that went with such a job: As one of them wrote in 1490, "The first duty of an ambassador is exactly the same as that of any other servant of a government, that is, to do, say, advise, and think whatever may best serve the preservation and aggrandizement of his own state." After 1494 their task was immeasurably complicated. In that year Charles VIII of France invaded Italy. His troops overwhelmed all resistance, and for the rest of Machiavelli's life the once-closed world of Italian city-state politics lay a defenseless prey to the invading forces from France, Spain, and Germany. Machiavelli's response to Italian military inadequacy was to advocate that mercenaries (for whom he had unbounded contempt) be replaced by a conscript militia, but the troops he had trained to defend Florence were ignominiously defeated by the Spanish at the battle of Prato in 1512.

Machiavelli melded humanism and professional politics in a quite new way. By immersing himself in ancient history, he hoped to learn why the Romans had been more successful at power politics than anyone before or since. In insisting that 'politics' (as we now call it) must be the study of what worked in practice, Machiavelli was advocating the study of 'statecraft' (*l'arte dello stato*), not 'politics', as it was understood at the time. Since Plato, political philosophy had concerned itself with quite different questions. How should the best state be constructed? How should a just man act? How should a good ruler be educated? Politics was concerned with the definition of the good life (life in a city-state) and was inseparable from moral philosophy. Machiavelli had no interest in the study of politics as that subject was traditionally understood; he read historians instead, since they dealt with success and failure, victory and defeat.

Of course, the line cannot be drawn quite so sharply. Historians were interested in glory and disgrace, as well as success and failure; philosophers had insisted that the good man could achieve practical success. Machiavelli had no doubt that qualities such as courage and piety might be rewarded with success. But for him, success, not morality, was what counted. The important thing about the Romans was that they had defeated their enemies, not that they had lived the good life. Indeed, he believed that, on closer inspection, civil conflict (to take an example of something that had always been regarded as an unmitigated evil) could be seen to have been the precondition for their aggressive foreign policy. Disunity, previously universally condemned, must now be praised. Machiavelli used political professionalism and historical reading to put in question the political philosophy that had been most influential among the humanists, that of Cicero himself. Where Cicero had insisted that honesty was always the best policy, Machiavelli advocated the creative use of deception; where Ciceronians had been preoccupied with the power of words, Machiavelli constantly stressed that violence was the most effective of political tools.

Machiavelli's political theory is born out of humanism and statecraft. These alone make him a 'modern' thinker: secular, scientific, utilitarian. At first sight, one would expect there to be more to it than that. Gutenburg invented printing with movable type around 1450; Columbus, helped by the compass, discovered the New World in 1492; the first battle to be won by artillery was the Battle of Ravenna in 1512. But none of these harbingers of modernity seemed particularly important to Machiavelli. What impressed him was how the problems of politics had remained unchanged for the last two thousand years. Despite the fact that nothing had changed, Machiavelli claimed to be doing something completely new, for he set out to analyze what made for success in politics, so that one could do self-consciously what Roman politicians had done accidentally and instinctively. In the same way, humanists had had to formulate and master the rules of classical Latin, while of course Cicero had learned them without thought in the process of learning to speak. Machiavelli offered a new kind of knowledge.

Second, it is generally assumed that, in order to understand Machiavelli's *Prince*, we must learn to read it in the context of Machiavelli's own experience of Florentine politics. Between 1494 and 1512, when Machiavelli was acquiring his political training, Florentine political life was exceptionally egalitarian and participatory. In 1512 defeat by Spain brought with it the restoration of the Medici family, who thereafter wielded effective power in Florence, even though the institutions of the republic survived in name and there was a continuing pretense of freedom. On 12 February 1513 Machiavelli was arrested and tortured, suspected of plotting against the new regime to restore the republic. Released a month later, he soon began work on *The Prince*, which (it is argued) must be read as the work of a republican politician trying to come to terms with a post-republican age.

This interpretation is plausible but unconvincing. There is no evidence that Machiavelli was committed to republican institutions before 1512, and it is only later in life that he wrote the *Discourses*, in which he argues that republics are superior to monarchies because they find it easier to adapt to changing circumstances. Nor was Machiavelli preoccupied, in the winter of 1513/14, with Florentine politics. The fate of Florence had already been decided. What hung in the balance was his own fate. He desperately needed employment, but he had no prospect of being invited back into the inner circles of power in Florence. However, the same Medici family which now ruled Florence had taken charge in Rome in March 1513, with the election of Giovanni de' Medici as Pope Leo X. Machiavelli's friend Francesco Vettori was the Florentine ambassador to Rome, well-placed to seek employment for him. And there was every expectation that one of the pope's nephews would seek to imitate Cesare Borgia, son of Pope Alexander VI, who, a few years earlier, had tried to carve out an independent kingdom in Italy. In the winter of 1513/14 Machiavelli's eyes were on Rome, not Florence; he was preoccupied with the construction of new states, not with the reform of old ones. It is at this moment of deracination, defeated at home but not without hope of future success abroad, that he wrote *The Prince*. His hope was to persuade the Medici to employ him in their future conquests. In this he failed, and he remained without significant employment until his death in 1527.

Machiavelli's situation was very different in 1517, when he wrote the bulk of the *Discourses*, from what it had been in 1513, when he still hoped that his professional skills might win him employment. By then Machiavelli's friends included discontented republicans, such as Zanobi Buondelmonti and Cosimo Rucellai, who met to discuss politics in the gardens of the Rucellai family. In the *Discourses* Machiavelli is still preoccupied with power and success, but he is now also fascinated by a series of problems which must have obsessed men who longed to restore political freedom to their city. How does one establish a free city? Why do free cities succumb to tyranny? What are the social and political preconditions for freedom? How can one restore freedom once it has been lost? The heroes of the *Discourses* are men like Lycurgus and Romulus, who concentrate power in their own hands, but only in order to establish the preconditions for freedom. The longest chapter is on political assassinations: Buondelmonti was to be condemned to exile after the failure of a plot to murder Cardinal Giulio de' Medici in 1522. If *The Prince* is a handbook for a papal nephew seeking to establish an hereditary monarchy, the *Discourses* is a primer for men who live under tyranny but long for freedom.

So different are Machiavelli's two most famous works that, over the next three centuries, both the most cynical politicians and their most idealistic opponents could turn to him for inspiration. Published in 1532, *The Prince* was placed on the Index in 1559. Apparently universally condemned, it was read everywhere, and the word 'Machiavellist' was soon coined to describe immoral politicians (1581 in France; 1589 in England). 'Reason of state,' as the new, practical science of politics came to be called, dominated political theorizing for the next century. But when the first modern republic was established, in England in 1649, it was to Machiavelli's *Discourses* that James Harrington turned, and in his *Oceana* he offered a new account of the social preconditions for liberty (one much indebted to *Discourses* 1.55) and a new account of the political institutions most likely to preserve freedom (one implicitly critical of *Discourses* 1.4). Algernon Sidney, executed in 1683 for plotting against Charles II, was also a faithful reader of Machiavelli's *Discourses*, and his own posthumously published *Discourses* were to be the text which had the most influence on America's revolutionaries a century later.

Further Reading

The classic book on the Renaissance is Jacob Burckhardt's *Civilization of the Renaissance in Italy* (1860), of which there are many editions. Two writers have shaped recent discussions: Paul Oskar Kristeller (see for example *Renaissance Thought and Its Sources* [New York: Columbia University Press, 1979]) and Hans Baron (*The Crisis of the Early Italian Renaissance* [rev. ed., Princeton: Princeton University Press, 1996). An important, more recent book is Anthony Grafton and Lisa Jardine, *From Humanism to the Humanities* (Cambridge, Mass.: Harvard University Press, 1986).

The best introduction to Renaissance political theory is Quentin Skinner, *The Foundations of Modern Political Thought*, vol. 1 (Cambridge: Cambridge University Press, 1978). More recent is Maurizio Viroli, *From Politics to Reason of State* (Cambridge: Cambridge University Press, 1992).

Again, the best introduction to Machiavelli is Quentin Skinner, *Machiavelli* (Oxford: Oxford University Press, 1981). There are two useful collections of articles: G. Bock, Q. Skinner, and M. Viroli (eds.), *Machiavelli and Republicanism* (Cambridge: Cambridge University Press, 1990) and A. R. Ascoli and V. Kahn (eds.), *Machiavelli and the Discourse of Literature* (Ithaca: Cornell University Press, 1993). Indispensable is Hans Baron, "Machiavelli the Republican Citizen and Author of *The Prince*," in his *In Search of Florentine Civic Humanism* (2 vols., Princeton: Princeton University Press, 1988), 2:101–51.

An important book which begins with Machiavelli and ends with the American Revolution is J.G.A. Pocock's *The Machiavellian Moment* (Princeton: Princeton University Press, 1975). For a discussion of the issues raised by Pocock, see the introduction to D. Wootton (ed.), *Republicanism, Liberty and Commercial Society* (Stanford: Stanford University Press, 1994).

MACHIAVELLI
Letter to Francesco Vettori

To His Excellency the Florentine Ambassador to his Holiness the Pope, and my benefactor, Francesco Vettori, in Rome.

Your Excellency. "Favors from on high are always timely, never late." I say this because I had begun to think I had, if not lost, then mislaid your goodwill, for you had allowed so long to go by without writing to me, and I was in some uncertainty as to what the reason could be. All the explanations I could think of seemed to me worthless, except for the possibility that occurred to me, that you might have stopped writing to me because someone had written to tell you I was not taking proper care of your letters to me; but I knew that I had not been responsible for their being shown to anyone else, with the exception of Filippo and Paolo.

Anyway, I have now received your most recent letter of the 23rd of last month. I was delighted to learn you are fulfilling your official responsibilities without fussing and flapping. I encourage you to carry on like this, for anyone who sacrifices his own convenience in order to make others happy is bound to inconvenience himself, but can't be sure of receiving any thanks for it. And since fortune wants to control everything, she evidently wants to be left a free hand; meanwhile we should keep our own counsel and not get in her way, and wait until she allows human beings to have a say in the course of events. That will be the time for you to work harder, and keep a closer eye on events, and for me to leave my country house and say: "Here I am!"

Since I want to repay your kind gesture, I have no alternative but to describe to you in this letter of mine how I live my life. If you decide you'd like to swap my life for yours, I'll be happy to make a deal.

I am still in my country house: Since my recent difficulties began I have not been, adding them all together, more than twenty days in Florence. Until recently I have been setting bird snares with my own hands. I've been getting up before dawn, making the bird-lime, and setting out with a bundle of cages on my back, so I look like Geta when he comes back from the harbor laden down with Amphitryo's books. I always caught at least two thrushes, but never more than six. This is how I spent September; since then I am sorry to say I have had to give up my rather nasty and peculiar hobby, so I will describe the life I lead now.

I get up in the morning at daybreak and go to a wood of mine where I am having some timber felled. I stay there two hours to check on the work done during the preceding day and to chat to the woodcutters, who are always involved in some conflict, either among themselves or with the neighbors. I could tell you a thousand fine stories about my dealings over this wood, both with Frosino da Panzano and with others who wanted some of the timber. Frosino in particular had them supply some cords without mentioning it to me, and when I asked for payment he wanted to knock off ten lire he said I had owed him for four years, ever since he beat me at cards at Antonio Guicciardini's. I began to cut up rough; I threatened to charge with theft the wagon driver who had fetched the wood. However, Giovanni Machiavelli intervened, and got us to settle our differences. Batista Guicciardini, Filippo Ginori, Tommaso del Bene, and a number of other citizens each bought a cord from me when the cold winds were blowing. I made promises to all of them, and supplied one to Tommaso. But in Florence it turned out to be only half a cord, because there were he, his wife, his servants,

[Reprinted from *Selected Political Writings*, translated by David Wootton (Indianapolis: Hackett Publishing Company, 1994), by permission of the publisher.]

and his sons to stack it: They looked like Gabburra on a Thursday when, assisted by his workmen, he slaughters an ox. Then, realizing I wasn't the one who was getting a good deal, I told the others I had run out of wood. They've all complained bitterly about it; especially Battista, who thinks this is as bad as anything else that has happened as a result of the battle of Prato.

When I leave the wood I go to a spring, and from there to check my bird-nets. I carry a book with me: Dante, or Petrarch, or one of the minor poets, perhaps Tibullus, Ovid, or someone like that. I read about their infatuations and their love affairs, reminisce about my own, and enjoy my reveries for a while. Then I set out on the road to the inn. I chat to those who pass by, asking them for news about the places they come from. I pick up bits and pieces of information, and study the differing tastes and various preoccupations of mankind. It's lunchtime before I know it. I sit down with my family to eat such food as I can grow on my wretched farm or pay for with the income from my tiny inheritance. Once I have eaten I go back to the inn. The landlord will be there, and, usually, the butcher, the miller, and a couple of kiln owners. With them I muck about all day, playing card games. We get into endless arguments and are constantly calling each other names. Usually we only wager a quarter, and yet you could hear us shouting if you were in San Casciano. So, in the company of these bumpkins, I keep my brain from turning moldy, and put up with the hostility fate has shown me. I am happy for fate to see to what depths I have sunk, for I want to know if she will be ashamed of herself for what she has done.

When evening comes, I go back home, and go to my study. On the threshold I take off my work clothes, covered in mud and filth, and put on the clothes an ambassador would wear. Decently dressed, I enter the ancient courts of rulers who have long since died. There I am warmly welcomed, and I feed on the only food I find nourishing, and was born to savor. I am not ashamed to talk to them, and to ask them to explain their actions. And they, out of kindness, answer me. Four hours go by without my feeling any anxiety. I forget every worry. I am no longer afraid

of poverty, or frightened of death. I live entirely through them.

And because Dante says there is no point in studying unless you remember what you have learned, I have made notes of what seem to me the most important things I have learned in my dialogue with the dead, and written a little book *On princedoms* in which I go as deeply as I can into the questions relevant to my subject. I discuss what a principality is, how many types of principality there are, how one acquires them, how one holds onto them, why one loses them. And if any of my little productions have ever pleased you, then this one ought not to displease you; and a ruler, especially a new ruler, ought to be delighted by it. Consequently, I have addressed it to His Highness Giuliano. Filippo Casavecchia has seen it; he can give you a preliminary report, both on the text, and on the discussions I have had with him: though I am still adding to the text and polishing it.

You may well wish, Your Excellency, that I should give up this life, and come and enjoy yours with you. I will do so if I can; what holds me back at the moment is some business that won't take me more than six weeks to finish. Though I am a bit concerned the Soderini family is there, and I will be obliged, if I come, to visit them and socialize with them. My concern is that I might intend my return journey to end at my own house, but find myself instead dismounting at the prison gates. For although this government is well established and solidly based, still it is new, and consequently suspicious, nor is there a shortage of clever fellows who, in order to get a reputation like Pagolo Bertini's, would put me in prison, and leave me to worry about how to get out. I beg you to persuade me this fear is irrational, and then I will make every effort to come and visit you before six weeks are up.

I have discussed my little book with Filippo, asking him whether it was a good idea to present it or not; and if I ought to present it, then whether I should deliver it in person, or whether I should send it through you. My concern is that if I do not deliver it in person Giuliano may not read it; even worse, that chap Ardinghelli may claim the credit for my latest effort. In favor of presenting it is the fact that the wolf is at the door, for my funds are running down, and I cannot continue like this much longer without becoming so poor I lose face. In any case, I would like their lordships, the Medici, to start putting me to use, even if they only assign me some menial task, for if, once I was in their employment, I did not win their favor, I would have only myself to blame. As for my book, if they were to read it, they would see the fifteen years I have spent studying statecraft have not been wasted: I haven't been asleep at my desk or playing cards. Anyone should be keen to employ someone who has had plenty of experience and has learned from the mistakes he made at his previous employers' expense. As for my integrity, nobody should question it: For I have always kept my word, and I am not going to start breaking it now. Someone who has been honest and true for forty-three years, as I have been, isn't going to be able to change character. And that I am honest and true is evident from my poverty.

So: I would like you to write to me again and let me have your opinion on this matter. I give you my regards. Best wishes.

Niccolò Machiavegli in Florence
10 December 1513.

MACHIAVELLI
The Prince

Niccolò Machiavelli to His Magnificence Lorenzo de' Medici

Those who wish to acquire favor with a ruler most often approach him with those among their possessions that are most valuable in their eyes, or that they are confident will give him pleasure. So rulers are often given horses, armor, cloth of gold, precious stones, and similar ornaments that are thought worthy of their social eminence. Since I want to offer myself to your Magnificence, along with something that will symbolize my desire to give you obedient service, I have found nothing among my possessions I value more, or would put a higher price upon, than an understanding of the deeds of great men, acquired through a lengthy experience of contemporary politics and through an uninterrupted study of the classics. Since I have long thought about and studied the question of what makes for greatness, and have now summarized my conclusions on the subject in a little book, it is this I send your Magnificence.

And although I recognize this book is unworthy to be given to Yourself, yet I trust that out of kindness you will accept it, taking account of the fact there is no greater gift I can present to you than the opportunity to understand, after a few hours of reading, everything I have learned over the course of so many years, and have undergone so many discomforts and dangers to discover. I have not ornamented this book with rhetorical turns of phrase, or stuffed it with pretentious and magnificent words, or made use of allurements and embellishments that are irrelevant to my purpose, as many authors do. For my intention has been that my book should be without pretensions, and should

[Reprinted from *Selected Political Writings*, translated by David Wootton (Indianapolis: Hackett Publishing Company, 1994), by permission of the publisher.]

rely entirely on the variety of the examples and the importance of the subject to win approval.

I hope it will not be thought presumptuous for someone of humble and lowly status to dare to discuss the behavior of rulers and to make recommendations regarding policy. Just as those who paint landscapes set up their easels down in the valley in order to portray the nature of the mountains and the peaks, and climb up into the mountains in order to draw the valleys, similarly in order to properly understand the behavior of the lower classes one needs to be a ruler, and in order to properly understand the behavior of rulers one needs to be a member of the lower classes.

I therefore beg your Magnificence to accept this little gift in the spirit in which it is sent. If you read it carefully and think over what it contains, you will recognize it is an expression of my dearest wish, which is that you achieve the greatness your good fortune and your other fine qualities seem to hold out to you. And if your Magnificence, high up at the summit as you are, should occasionally glance down into these deep valleys, you will see I have to put up with the unrelenting malevolence of undeserved ill fortune.

Chapter One: How many types of principality are there? And how are they acquired?

All states, all forms of government that have had and continue to have authority over men, have been and are either republics or principalities. And principalities are either hereditary, when their rulers' ancestors have long been their rulers, or they are new. And if they are new, they are either entirely new, as was Milan for Francesco Sforza, or they are like limbs added on to the hereditary state of the ruler who acquires them, as the kingdom of Naples has been added on to the kingdom of Spain. Those dominions that are acquired by a ruler are either used to living under the rule of one man, or accustomed to being free; and they are either acquired with soldiers belonging to others, or with one's own; either through fortune or through strength [*virtù*].

Chapter Two: On hereditary principalities.

I will leave behind me the discussion of republics, for I have discussed them at length elsewhere. I will concern myself only with principalities. The different types of principality I have mentioned will be the threads from which I will weave my account. I will debate how these different types of principality should be governed and defended.

I maintain, then, it is much easier to hold on to hereditary states, which are accustomed to being governed by the family that now rules them, than it is to hold on to new acquisitions. All one has to do is preserve the structures established by one's forebears, and play for time if things go badly. For, indeed, an hereditary ruler, if he is of no more than normal resourcefulness, will never lose his state unless some extraordinary and overwhelming force appears that can take it away from him; and even then, the occupier has only to have a minor setback, and the original ruler will get back to power.

Let us take a contemporary Italian example: The Duke of Ferrara was able to resist the assaults of the Venetians in '84, and of Pope Julius in 1510, only because his family was long established as rulers of that state. For a ruler who inherits power has few reasons and less cause to give offense; as a consequence he is more popular; and, as long as he does not have exceptional vices that make him hateful, it is to be expected he will naturally have the goodwill of his people. Because the state has belonged to his family from one generation to another, memories of how they came to power, and motives to overthrow them, have worn away. For every change in government creates grievances that those who wish to bring about further change can exploit.

Chapter Three: On mixed principalities.

New principalities are the ones that present problems. And first of all, if the whole of the principality is not new, but rather a new part has been added on to the old, creating a whole one may term "mixed," instability derives first of all from a natural difficulty that is to be found in all new principalities. The problem is that people willingly change their ruler, believing the change will be for the better; and this belief leads them to take up arms against him. But they are mistaken, and they soon find out in practice they have only made things worse. The reason for this, too, is natural and typical: You always have to give offense to those over whom you acquire power when you become a new ruler, both by imposing troops upon them, and by countless other injuries that follow as necessary consequences of the acquisition of power. Thus, you make enemies of all those to whom you have given offense in acquiring power, and in addition you cannot keep the goodwill of those who have put you in power, for you cannot satisfy their aspirations as they thought you would. At the same time you cannot use heavy-handed methods against them, for you are obliged to them. Even if you have an overwhelmingly powerful army, you will have needed the support of the locals to take control of the province. This is why Louis XII of France lost Milan as quickly as he gained it. All that was needed to take it from him the first time were Ludovico's own troops. For those who had opened the gates to him, finding themselves mistaken in their expectations and disappointed in their hopes of future benefit, could not put up with the burdensome rule of a new sovereign.

Of course it is true that, after a ruler has regained power in rebel territories, he is much more likely to hang on to it. For the rebellion gives him an excuse, and he is able to take firmer measures to secure his position, punishing delinquents, checking up on suspects, and taking precautions where needed. So, if the first time the King of France lost Milan all that was needed to throw him out was Duke Ludovico growling on his borders, to throw him out a second time it took the whole world united against him, and the destruction or expulsion from Italy of his armies. We have seen why this was so.

Nevertheless, he lost Milan both times. We have discussed why he was almost bound to lose it the first time; now we must discuss why he managed to lose it the second. What remedies should he have adopted? What can someone in the King of France's position do to hold on to an acquisition more effectively than he did?

Let me start by saying these territories that are newly added on to a state that is already securely in the possession of a ruler are either in the same geographical region as his existing possessions and speak the same language, or they are not. When they are, it is quite straightforward to hold on to them, especially if they are not used to governing themselves. In order to get a secure hold on them one need merely eliminate the surviving members of the family of their previous rulers. In other respects one should keep things as they were, respecting established traditions. If the old territories and the new have similar customs, the new subjects will live quietly. Thus, Burgundy, Brittany, Gascony, and Normandy have for long quietly submitted to France. Although they do not all speak exactly the same language, nevertheless their customs are similar, and they can easily put up with each other. He who acquires neighboring territories in this way, intending to hold on to them, needs to see to two things: First, he must ensure their previous ruler has no heirs; and second, he must not alter their old laws or impose new taxes. If he follows these principles they will quickly become inseparable from his hereditary domains.

But when you acquire territories in a region that has a different language, different customs, and different institutions, then you really have problems, and you need to have great good fortune and great resourcefulness if you are going to hold on to them. One of the best policies, and one of the most effective, is for the new ruler to go and live in his new territories. This will make his grasp on them more secure and more lasting. This is what the Sultan of Turkey has done in Greece. All the other measures he has taken to hold on to that territory would have been worthless

if he had not settled there. For if you are on the spot, you can identify difficulties as they arise, and can quickly take appropriate action. If you are at a distance, you only learn of them when they have become serious, and when it is too late to put matters right. Moreover, if you are there in person, the territory will not be plundered by your officials. The subjects can appeal against their exactions to you, their ruler. As a consequence they have more reason to love you, if they behave themselves, and, if they do not, more reason to fear you. Anyone who wants to attack the territory from without will have to think twice, so that, if you live there, you will be unlucky indeed to lose it.

The second excellent policy is to send colonies to settle in one or two places; they will serve to tie your new subjects down. For it is necessary either to do this, or to garrison your new territory with a substantial army. Colonies do not cost much to run. You will have to lay out little or nothing to establish and maintain them. You will only offend those from whom you seize fields and houses to give to your settlers, and they will be only a tiny minority within the territory. Those whom you offend will be scattered and become poor, so they will be unable to do you any harm. All the rest will remain uninjured, and so ought to remain quiet; at the same time they will be afraid to make a false move, for they will have before them the fate of their neighbors as an example of what may happen to them. I conclude such colonies are economical, reliable, and do not give excessive grounds for resistance; those who suffer by their establishment are in no position to resist, being poor and scattered, as I have said. There is a general rule to be noted here: People should either be caressed or crushed. If you do them minor damage they will get their revenge; but if you cripple them there is nothing they can do. If you need to injure someone, do it in such a way that you do not have to fear their vengeance.

But if, instead of establishing colonies, you rely on an occupying army, it costs a good deal more, for your army will eat up all your revenues from your new territory. As a result, your acquisition will be a loss, not a gain. Moreover, your army will make more enemies than colonies would, for the whole territory will suffer from it, the burden moving from one place to another as the troops are billeted first here, then there. Everybody suffers as a result, and everyone becomes your enemy. And these are enemies who can hurt you, for they remain, even if beaten, in their own homes. In every respect, then, an occupying army is a liability, while colonies are an asset.

In addition, anyone who finds himself with territory in a region with different customs from those of his hereditary possessions should make himself the leader and protector of neighboring powers who are weaker than he is, and should set out to weaken his powerful neighbors. He should also take care no outsider as powerful as himself has any occasion to intervene. Outside powers will always be urged to intervene by those in the region who are discontented, either because their ambitions are unsatisfied, or because they are afraid of the dominant powers. So, long ago, the Aetolians invited the Romans into Greece; and, indeed, in every other region the Romans occupied they were invited by local people. It is in the nature of things that, as soon as a foreign power enters into a region, all the local states that are weak rally to it, for they are driven by the envy they have felt for the state that has exercised predominance over them. As a result, the invader does not have to make any effort at all to win over these lesser states, because they all immediately ally themselves to the territory he has acquired there. He only has to take care they do not become too strong and exercise too much influence. He can easily, with his own troops and his new allies' support, strike down the powerful states, and make himself the arbiter of all the affairs of the region. Anyone who does not see how to play this role successfully will quickly lose what he has gained, and, while he holds it, will have innumerable difficulties and vexations.

The Romans, in the regions they seized, obeyed these principles admirably. They settled colonies; were friendly towards the weaker rulers, without building up their strength; broke the powerful; and did not allow foreign powers to build up support. Let me take just the region of Greece as an example. The Romans favored the Acheans and the Aetolians;

they crushed the Kingdom of Macedon; they expelled Antiochus from the region. Despite the credit the Acheans and the Aetolians had earned with them, they never allowed them to build up any independent power; nor did the blandishments of Philip ever persuade them to treat him as a friend before they had destroyed his power; nor did Antiochus's strength intimidate them into permitting him to retain any territory in that region.

The Romans did in such matters what all wise rulers ought to do. It is necessary not only to pay attention to immediate crises, but to foresee those that will come, and to make every effort to prevent them. For if you see them coming well in advance, then you can easily take the appropriate action to remedy them, but if you wait until they are right on top of you, then the prescription will no longer take effect, because the disease is too far advanced. In this matter it is as doctors say of consumption: In the beginning the disease is easy to cure, difficult to diagnose; but, after a while, if it has not been diagnosed and treated early, it becomes easy to diagnose and hard to cure. So, too, in politics, for if you foresee problems while they are far off (which only a prudent man is able to do) they can easily be dealt with; but, when, because you have failed to see them coming, you allow them to grow to the point that anyone can recognize them, then it is too late to do anything.

The Romans always looked ahead and took action to remedy problems before they developed. They never postponed action in order to avoid a war, for they understood you cannot escape wars, and when you put them off only your opponents benefit. Thus, they wanted to have a war with Philip and Antiochus in Greece, so as not to have one with them in Italy. At the time they could have avoided having a war at all, but this they did not want. They never approved the saying that nowadays is repeated *ad nauseam* by the wise: "Take advantage of the passage of time." Rather they relied on their strength [*virtù*] and prudence, for in time anything can happen, and the passage of time brings good mixed with evil, and evil mixed with good.

But let us return to the kings of France, and let us see whether they followed any of the principles I have outlined. I will discuss Louis, not Charles, for, since Louis held territory in Italy for a longer time, we can have a better understanding of the policies he was following. We will see he did the opposite of what one ought to do in order to hold on to territory in a region unlike one's hereditary lands.

King Louis was brought into Italy by the ambition of the Venetians, who hoped to gain half of the territory of Lombardy as a result of his invasion. I do not want to criticize the king's decision to ally with the Venetians. Since he wanted to get a foothold in Italy, and since he had no friends in that region (rather the opposite, for all the gateways to Italy were closed against him as a result of the actions of King Charles), he was obliged to take what allies he could get. His decision would have been a good one, if he had done everything else right. Now when the king had conquered Lombardy, he at once recovered the reputation Charles had lost for him. Genoa gave itself up and the Florentines became his friends. Everybody came forward to meet him as he advanced and sought his friendship: the Marquis of Mantua, the Duke of Ferrara, Bentivoglio, the Countess of Forlì, the rulers of Faenza, Pesaro, Rimini, Camerino, Piombino, the citizens of Lucca, Pisa, and Siena. Then the Venetians were able to see the risk they had chosen to run; in order to acquire a couple of fortresses in Lombardy, they had made the King of France master of two-thirds of Italy.

Now consider how easy it would have been for the king to preserve his authority in Italy if he had followed the principles I have laid out, and if he had protected and defended all his new friends. They were numerous, weak, and fearful, some afraid of the Church, some of the Venetians, and so had no choice but to remain loyal to him; and with their help he could easily have overwhelmed the surviving great powers. But he had no sooner got to Milan than he did the opposite, coming to the assistance of Pope Alexander so he could occupy the Romagna. He did not realize that by this decision he weakened himself, alienating his friends and those who had flung themselves into his arms; and at the same time strengthened the Church, adding to its already extensive spiritual authority an increased temporal power. And

having made one error he was forced to make another, for, in order to put a stop to Alexander's ambitions, and to prevent his gaining control of Tuscany, he was obliged to march into Italy once more. Nor was he satisfied with having strengthened the Church and thrown away his alliances, but in addition, because he wanted the Kingdom of Naples, he agreed to divide it with the King of Spain. Where he had been all-powerful in Italy, he now shared his power with another, giving ambitious rulers in the region and those who were discontented with him someone to whom they could turn. Where he could have left in the Kingdom of Naples a king who was on his payroll, he threw him out, and replaced him with someone who might aspire to kick out the French.

It is perfectly natural and normal to want to acquire new territory; and whenever men do what will succeed towards this end, they will be praised, or at least not condemned. But when they are not in a position to make gains, and try nevertheless, then they are making a mistake, and deserve condemnation. If the King of France had the military capacity to attack Naples, he should have done so; if he did not have it, he should not have proposed to partition the territory. The division of Lombardy between France and Venice was justified because it gave the French a foothold in Italy; the division of Naples was blameworthy, for it was not justifiable on the same grounds.

Thus, Louis had made the following five mistakes: He wasted his alliance with the lesser states; he increased the strength of one of the more powerful Italian states; he invited an extremely powerful foreign state to intervene in Italy; he did not go and live in Italy; he did not establish settlements there. Even these mistakes might have had no evil consequences while he lived, had he not made a sixth, attacking the Venetians. Had he not strengthened the Church and brought the Spanish into Italy, then it would have been reasonable and appropriate to attack them; but having done what he had done, he should never have given his consent to a policy aimed at their destruction. For as long as they remained powerful, the others would never have been prepared to undertake an attack upon Lombardy. For the Venetians would not have consented to Lombardy's falling into the hands of others, and not themselves; while the others would not have wanted to take Lombardy from the King of France only to give it to the Venetians, and would not have had the courage to try to take it away from both of them.

And if someone were to reply that King Louis allowed Alexander to take the Romagna, and the King of Spain to have the Kingdom of Naples, in order to avoid a war, I would answer as I did above: One should never allow a problem to develop in order to avoid a war, for you end up not avoiding the war, but deferring it to a time that will be less favorable. And if others were to appeal to the promise the king had given to the pope, to help him seize the Romagna in return for the pope's giving him a divorce and making the Bishop of Rouen a cardinal, I would reply with what I will say later on the subject of whether and to what extent rulers should keep their word.

Thus, King Louis lost Lombardy because he did not follow any of the policies others have adopted when they have established predominance within a region and have wanted to hold on to it. There is nothing remarkable about what happened: It is entirely natural and predictable. I spoke about these matters with the Cardinal of Rouen in Nantes, when Valentino (as Cesare Borgia, son of Pope Alexander, was commonly called) was taking possession of the Romagna. The cardinal said to me that the Italians did not understand war; so I told him that the French did not understand politics, for if they did, they would not allow the church to acquire so much power. And in practice we have seen that the strength of the papacy and of the King of Spain within Italy has been brought about by the King of France, and they in turn have been the cause of his own ruin. From this one can draw a general conclusion that will never (or hardly ever) be proved wrong: He who is the cause of someone else's becoming powerful is the agent of his own destruction; for he makes his protegé powerful either through his own skill or through his own strength, and either of these must provoke his protegé's mistrust once he has become powerful.

Chapter Four: Why the kingdom of Darius, which Alexander occupied, did not rebel against his successors after Alexander's death.

When you think of the difficulties associated with trying to hold on to a newly acquired state, you might well be puzzled: Since Alexander the Great had conquered Asia in the space of a few years, and then died when he had scarcely had time to take possession of it, at that point you would expect the whole state to rebel. Nevertheless, Alexander's successors maintained possession of it and had no difficulty in keeping hold of it, beyond the conflicts that sprung up between themselves as a result of their own ambitions. My explanation is that the principalities recorded in history have been governed in two different ways: either by a single individual, and everyone else has been his servant, and they have helped to govern his kingdom as ministers, appointed by his grace and benevolence; or by a monarch together with barons, who, not by concession of the ruler, but by virtue of their noble lineage, hold that rank. Such barons have their own territories and their own subjects: subjects who recognize them as their lords and feel a natural affection for them. In those states that are governed by a single individual and his servants, the sovereign has more authority in his own hands; for in all his territories there is no one recognized as having a right to rule except him alone; and if his subjects obey anyone else, they do so because he is the ruler's minister and representative, and they do not feel any particular loyalty to these subordinate authorities.

In our own day the obvious examples of these two types of ruler are the Sultan of Turkey and the King of France. All the kingdom of Turkey is ruled by a single monarch, and everyone else is his servant. He divides his kingdom into sanjaks, sending administrators, whom he replaces and transfers as he thinks best, to rule them. But the King of France is placed among a multitude of long-established nobles, whose rights are recognized by their subjects and who are loved by them. They have their own inherited privileges, and the king cannot take them away without endangering himself. If you compare these two states, you will realize it would be difficult to seize the sultan's kingdom, but, once you had got control of it, it would be very easy to hold on to it.

It would be difficult to occupy the lands of the sultan for two reasons: The local authorities of that kingdom will not invite you to invade, nor can you hope those around the ruler will rebel, making your task easier. And this for the reasons I have explained. For, since they are all his slaves, and indebted to him, it is harder to corrupt them; and even if you can corrupt them, they are not going to be much use to you, for they cannot command the obedience of the people, as I have explained. Consequently, anyone attacking the sultan must expect to find the Turks united in his defense and must rely more on his own strength than on the disorder of his opponents. But once he has defeated them and has destroyed their forces on the field of battle so completely they cannot muster an army, then he has no one to worry about except the sultan's close relatives. Once he has got rid of them, then there is no one left for him to fear, for there is no one else with influence over the people. Just as the invader, before his victory, had no reason to hope for support, so, after his victory, he has no reason to fear opposition.

The opposite is true in kingdoms governed like that of France. For it is easy to invade them, once one has gained the support of some local noble. For in such kingdoms one can always find malcontents who hope to benefit from innovation. These, as we have seen, can ease your entrance into the state and help you win victory. But then, when you try to hold on to power, you will find the nobility, both those who have been your allies and those you have defeated, present you with an infinity of problems. It simply is not sufficient to kill the ruler and his close relatives, for the rest of the nobility will survive to provide leadership for new insurrections. You cannot win their loyalty or wipe them out, so you will always be in danger of losing your kingdom should anything go wrong.

Now if you ask yourself what sort of state it was Darius ruled, you will see it was similar to that of the sultan. So it was necessary for Alexander, first to take on his forces and seize control of the territory. Once he was victorious, and Darius was dead, Alexander had a firm grip on his new lands, for the reasons I have given. And his successors, if they had stayed united, could have enjoyed them at their leisure; nor was there any resistance to them in that kingdom, apart from their own conflicts with one another. But states that are organized after the French model cannot be held onto, once seized, with such ease. This is why there were frequent rebellions in Spain, France, and Greece against the Romans. For there were many rulers in those territories, and as long as people remembered them, the Romans were always unsure of their grip. Once the memory of these rulers had faded completely away, thanks to the long duration of Roman rule, they became secure in their possession. Even after that, each faction among the Romans, when they fought among themselves, could call on the support of a section of those provinces, depending on the influence they had built up within them. The subjects of these territories, because their former rulers had no heirs, had no loyalties except to Roman leaders. Once you have considered all these matters, you will not be at all surprised at the ease with which Alexander held on to Asia or at the difficulties other conquerors (one might take Pyrrhus as one example among many) have had in keeping control of their acquisitions. The crucial factor in these differing outcomes is not the strength [*virtù*] or weakness of the conqueror but the contrasting character of the societies that have been conquered.

Chapter Five: How you should govern cities or kingdoms that, before you acquired them, lived under their own laws.

When the states one acquires by conquest are accustomed to living under their own laws and in freedom, there are three policies one can follow in order to hold on to them: The first is to lay them waste; the second is to go and live there in person; the third is to let them continue to live under their own laws, make them pay you, and create there an administrative and political elite who will remain loyal to you. For since the elite are the creation of the head of state, its members know they cannot survive without both his friendship and his power, and they know it is in their interest to do everything to sustain it. It is easier to rule a city that is used to being self-governing by employing its own citizens than by other means, assuming you do not wish to destroy it.

Examples are provided by the Spartans and the Romans. The Spartans took Athens and Thebes, establishing oligarchies there. However, they lost them again. The Romans, in order to hold on to Capua, Carthage, and Numantia razed them and never lost them. They sought to govern Greece according to more or less the same policies as those used by Sparta, letting the Greek cities rule themselves and enforce their own laws, but the policy failed, so in the end they were obliged to demolish many cities in that territory in order to hold on to them. The simple truth is there is no reliable way of holding on to a city and the territory around it, short of demolishing the city itself. He who becomes the ruler of a city that is used to living under its own laws and does not knock it down, must expect to be knocked down by it. Whenever it rebels, it will find strength in the language of liberty and will seek to restore its ancient constitution. Neither the passage of time nor good treatment will make its citizens forget their previous liberty. No matter what one does, and what precautions one takes, if one does not scatter and drive away the original inhabitants, one will not destroy the memory of liberty or the attraction of the old institutions. As soon as there is a crisis, they will seek to restore them. This is what happened in Pisa after it had been enslaved by the Florentines for a hundred years.

But when cities or provinces are used to being ruled by a monarch, and one has wiped out his relatives and descendants, then matters are very different. They are used to being obedient. Their old ruler is gone, and they cannot agree among themselves as to who should replace him. They do not know how to rule themselves. The result is that they are slower to take up arms, and it is easier for a new ruler to win them

over and establish himself securely in power. But in former republics there is more vitality, more hatred, more desire for revenge. The memory of their former freedom gives them no rest, no peace. So the best thing to do is to demolish them or to go and live there oneself.

Chapter Six: About new kingdoms acquired with one's own armies and one's own skill [virtù].

No one should be surprised if, in talking about completely new kingdoms (that is, states that are governed by someone who was not a ruler before, and were themselves not previously principalities), I point to the greatest of men as examples to follow. For men almost always walk along the beaten path, and what they do is almost always an imitation of what others have done before. But you cannot walk exactly in the footsteps of those who have gone before, nor is it easy to match the skill [virtù] of those you have chosen to imitate. Consequently, a prudent man will always try to follow in the footsteps of great men and imitate those who have been truly outstanding, so that, if he is not quite as skillful [virtù] as they, at least some of their ability may rub off on him. One should be like an experienced archer, who, trying to hit someone at a distance and knowing the range [virtù] of his bow, aims at a point above his target, not so his arrow will strike the point he is aiming at, but so, by aiming high, he can reach his objective.

I maintain that, in completely new kingdoms, the new ruler has more or less difficulty in keeping hold of power depending on whether he is more or less skillful [virtuoso]. Now you only find yourself in this situation, a private individual only becomes a ruler, if you are either lucky, or skillful [virtù]. Both luck and skill enable you to overcome difficulties. Nevertheless, he who relies least on luck has the best prospect of success. One advantage is common to any completely new sovereign: Because he has no other territories, he has no choice but to come in person and live in his new kingdom. Let us look at those who through their own skill [virtù], and not merely through chance, have become rulers. In my view, the greatest have been Moses, Cyrus, Romulus, Theseus, and others like them.

Obviously, we should not discuss Moses' skill, for he was a mere agent, following the instructions given him by God. So he should be admired, not for his own skill, but for that grace that made him worthy to talk with God. But let us discuss Cyrus and the others who have acquired existing kingdoms or founded new ones. You will find them all admirable. And if you look at the actions and strategies of each one of them, you will find they do not significantly differ from those of Moses, who could not have had a better teacher. If you look at their deeds and their lives, you will find they were dependent on chance only for their first opportunity. They seized their chance to make of it what they wanted. Without that first opportunity their strength [*virtù*] of purpose would never have been revealed. Without their strength [*virtù*] of purpose, the opportunity they were offered would not have amounted to anything.

Thus, it was necessary for Moses to find the people of Israel in Egypt, enslaved and oppressed by the Egyptians, so they, in order to escape from slavery, would be prepared to follow him. It was essential for Romulus to have no future in Alba, it was appropriate he should have been exposed at birth, otherwise he would not have formed the ambition of becoming King of Rome and succeeded in founding that nation. It was necessary that Cyrus should find the Persians hostile to the rule of the Medes, and the Medes weak and effeminate from too much peace. Theseus could not have demonstrated his strength of purpose [*virtù*] if he had not found the Athenians scattered. These opportunities made these men lucky; but it was their remarkable political skill [*virtù*] that enabled them to recognize these opportunities for what they were. Thanks to them their nations were ennobled and blessed with good fortune.

Those who become rulers through strength of purpose [*vie virtuose*], as they did, acquire their kingdoms with difficulty, but they hold on to them with ease. And much of the difficulty they have in getting to power derives from the new institutions and customs they are obliged to establish in order to found their

governments and make them secure. One ought to pause and consider the fact that there is nothing harder to undertake, nothing more likely of failure, nothing more risky to pull off, than to set oneself up as a leader who plans to found a new system of government. For the founder makes enemies of all those who are doing well under the old system, and has only lukewarm support from those who hope to do well under the new one. The weakness of their support springs partly from their fear of their adversaries, who have the law on their side, partly from their own want of faith. For men do not truly believe in new things until they have had practical experience of them. So it is that, whenever those who are enemies of the new order have a chance to attack it, they do so ferociously, while the others defend it half-heartedly. So the new ruler is in danger, along with his supporters.

It is necessary, however, if we are going to make sense of his situation, to find out if our innovator stands on his own feet, or depends on others to prop him up. That is, we need to know if he is obliged to try to obtain his objectives by pleading, or whether he can resort to force. In the first case, he is bound to come to a bad end, and won't achieve anything. But when he can stand on his own feet, and can resort to force, then he can usually overcome the dangers he faces. Thus it is that all armed prophets are victorious, and disarmed ones are crushed. For there is another problem: People are by nature inconstant. It is easy to persuade them of something, but it is difficult to stop them from changing their minds. So you have to be prepared for the moment when they no longer believe: Then you have to force them to believe. Moses, Cyrus, Theseus, and Romulus would not have been able to make their peoples obey their new structures of authority for long if they had been unarmed. This is what happened, in our own day, to Friar Girolamo Savonarola. He and his new constitution were destroyed as soon as the multitude began to stop believing in him. He had no way of stiffening the resolution of those who had been believers or of forcing disbelievers to obey.

Thus the founders of new states have immense difficulties to overcome, and dangers beset their path, dangers they must overcome by skill and strength of purpose [*virtù*]. But, once they have overcome them, and they have begun to be idolized, having got rid of those who were jealous of their superior qualities, they are established, they are powerful, secure, honored, happy.

We have looked at some noble examples, and to them I want to add one less remarkable. Nevertheless, it has some points of similarity to them, and I want it to stand for all the other lesser examples I could have chosen. My example is Hiero of Syracuse. He was a private individual who became ruler of Syracuse. He, too, did not depend on luck once he had been given his opportunity. The people of Syracuse were oppressed and elected him as their military commander; so he deserved to be made their ruler. He was so remarkable [*di tanta virtù*], even before he became a ruler, history records "that he had everything one would look for in a king, except a kingdom." He disbanded the old militia and instituted a new one. Dropped his old friends and chose new ones. Since both his friends and his soldiers were his creatures, he had laid the foundations for constructing any political system he chose. He, too, had difficulties enough to overcome in acquiring power, and few in holding on to it.

Chapter Seven: About new principalities that are acquired with the forces of others and with good luck.

Those who, having started as private individuals, become rulers merely out of good luck, acquire power with little trouble but have a hard time holding on to it. They have no problems on the road to power, because they leap over all the obstacles; but dangers crowd around them once they are in power. I am talking about people who are given a state, either in return for money, or out of the good will of him who hands it over to them. This happened to many individuals in Greece, in the cities of Ionia and the Hellespont, who were made rulers by Darius, who wanted them to hold their cities for his own greater safety and glory. So, too, with those who, having been private

citizens, were made emperors of Rome because they had corrupted the soldiers. Such rulers are entirely dependent on the good will and good fortune of whoever has given them power. Good will and good fortune are totally unreliable and capricious. Such rulers do not know how to hold on to their position and cannot do so. They do not know how, because they have always been private citizens, and only a brilliant and immensely skillful [*di grande virtù*] man is likely to know how to command without having had training and experience. They cannot because they have no troops of their own on whose loyalty and commitment they can count.

Moreover, states that spring up overnight, like all other things in nature that are born and grow in a hurry, cannot have their roots deep in the soil, so they shrivel up in the first drought, blow over in the first storm. Unless, as I have said, those who are suddenly made into rulers are of such extraordinary capacity [*virtù*] they can work out on the spot how to hold on to the gift fortune has unexpectedly handed them; and those preparations the others made before they became rulers, they must find a way of making after the event.

I want to add to the one and the other of these two ways of becoming a ruler, by skill [*virtù*] or by luck, two examples drawn from the events that have occurred in our own lifetimes: the examples of Francesco Sforza and Cesare Borgia. Francesco, by using the right methods and consummate skill [*virtù*], started out as a private citizen and ended up as Duke of Milan. And what he had acquired with painstaking effort, he held on to without trouble. On the other hand Cesare Borgia, who was called Duke Valentino by the common people, acquired his state thanks to the good fortune of his father, and when that came to an end he lost it. This despite the fact he used every technique and did all the things a prudent and skillful [*virtuoso*] man ought to do, to entrench himself in those territories that the arms and fortune of others had acquired for him. For, as I said above, he who does not prepare the foundations first can (in principle), if he is immensely skillful [*virtù*], make up for it later, although the architect will find catching up a painful process, and there is a real danger the building will collapse. So, if we look at all the things Borgia did, we will see he had laid solid foundations for future power. I do not think it irrelevant to discuss his policies, because I cannot think of any better example I could offer a new ruler than that of his actions. And if his strategy did not lead to success, this was not his fault; his failure was due to extraordinary and exceptional hostility on the part of fortune.

Pope Alexander VI, in setting out to make his son the duke into a ruler, was faced with considerable immediate and long-term difficulties. In the first place, he could find no way of making him the lord of any territory, except territory that belonged to the church. And he knew if he took land from the church to give to Cesare, he would have to overcome the opposition of the Duke of Milan, and also of the Venetians, for both Faenza and Rimini were already under Venetian protection. Secondly, he saw the armed forces of Italy, and particularly those he could hope to employ, were under the control of individuals who had reason to fear any increase in papal power. Consequently, he could not regard them as reliable. He could not trust the Orsini, the Colonna, or their associates, but there was no one else to whom he could turn. So it was necessary to break out of this framework, and to bring disorder to the territories of his opponents, so he could safely seize a part of them. This proved easy, for he found the Venetians, for reasons of their own, had decided to invite the French to invade Italy. He not only did not oppose this, but he facilitated it by dissolving the previous marriage of King Louis. So the king marched into Italy, with the help of the Venetians and the consent of Alexander. No sooner was he in Milan than the pope had borrowed forces from him for the attack on the Romagna, which was ceded to him out of fear of the King of France.

So, once Cesare had been made Duke of the Romagna, and the Colonnesi had been beaten, wanting to hang on to his new territories and make further conquests, he was faced with two obstacles. In the first place, his military forces did not appear reliable. In the second, the King of France might oppose him. He had made use of the troops of the Orsini, but they were likely to abandon him, and not only prevent him from making further acquisitions, but take from him what he had already acquired. And the same was true of the king. He had an indication of how far he could trust the Orsini when, after Faenza had been taken by storm, he attacked Bologna, for he discovered they had no appetite for that battle. And as for the king, he discovered his attitude when, having seized the Duchy of Urbino, he attacked Tuscany, for Louis made him abandon that enterprise. So the duke decided he must no longer depend on the troops and the good fortune of others.

The first thing he did was to weaken the factions of the Orsini and the Colonna in Rome. All the nobles who were allied to these families he won over to himself, making them members of his court, and giving them substantial pensions. He favored them with civil and military appointments appropriate to their standing. Thus, in the course of a few months, their attachment to their factions was dissolved, and they became committed to the duke. Next, he looked for a chance to crush the Orsini, having already defeated the forces of the Colonna family. He soon had his chance and he made the most of it. For the Orsini, having realized late in the day that the growing strength of the duke and the pope would be their ruin, called a meeting at Magione, near Perugia. From that meeting sprang the rebellion of Urbino and the uprisings in the Romagna that almost destroyed the duke; but he overcame all resistance with the help of the French. And, having got back his authority and realizing he could trust neither the French nor other external forces, he decided that, in order to prevent their allying against him, he must deceive them. He so successfully concealed his intentions that the Orsini, represented by Signor Paolo, made peace with him. The duke took every opportunity to ingratiate himself with Paolo, giving him money, clothes, and horses. So the leaders of the Orsini were brought, unsuspecting, to Sinigallia, where they were at his mercy. Having got rid of the leaders and won the allegiance of their followers, the duke could feel he had laid decent foundations for his future power. He had control of all the Romagna and the Duchy of Urbino, and it looked as though he had won over the Romagna and acquired the support of its population, who were beginning to enjoy a new prosperity.

Now, since it is worth paying attention to this question, and since it would be sensible to imitate Cesare's actions, I want to amplify what I have just said. Once the duke had subdued the Romagna, he found it had been under the control of weak nobles, who had rather exploited than governed their subjects and had rather been the source of conflict than of order, with the result the whole province was full of robbers, bandits, and every other type of criminal. So he decided it was necessary, if he was going to make the province peaceful and obedient to his commands, to give it good government. He put Mr. Remiro d'Orco, a man both cruel and efficient, in charge, and gave him absolute power. D'Orco in short order established peace and unity, and acquired immense authority. At that point, the duke decided such unchecked power was no longer necessary, for he feared people might come to hate it. So he established a civil court in the center of the province, placing an excellent judge in charge of it, and requiring every city to appoint a lawyer to represent it before the court. Since he knew the harsh measures of the past had given rise to some enmity towards him, in order to purge the ill-will of the people and win them completely over to him, he wanted to make clear that, if there had been any cruelty, he was not responsible for it, and that his hard-hearted minister should be blamed. He saw his opportunity and exploited it. One morning, in the town square of Cesena, he had Remiro d'Orco's corpse laid out in two pieces, with a chopping board and a bloody knife beside it. This ferocious sight made the people of the Romagna simultaneously happy and dumbfounded.

But let us get back to where we were. I was saying the duke found himself rather powerful and had taken precautions against immediate dangers, for he had built up a military force that he had planned himself and had in large part destroyed neighboring forces that could be a threat to him. So what remained, if he wanted to make further acquisitions, was the problem of the King of France; for he knew the king had, late in the day, realized his policy towards Borgia had been misconceived and would not allow him to make further conquests. So Borgia began to look for new alliances and to prevaricate with the French when they dispatched a force towards the Kingdom of Naples to attack the Spanish who were laying siege to Gaeta. His intention was to protect himself against them, which he would soon have succeeded in doing, if Alexander had gone on living.

These were the policies he pursued with regard to his immediate concerns. But there were future problems he also had to consider. In the first place, he had to worry that a new pope would be hostile to him and would try to take from him what Alexander had given him. He had four ways of trying to deal with this threat. In the first place, he set out to eliminate all the relatives of those rulers whose lands he had seized, to make it difficult for the pope to restore their previous rulers. Second, he sought to acquire the allegiance of the nobility of Rome, as I have explained, so he could use them to restrict the pope's freedom of action. Third, to make as many as possible of the members of the College of Cardinals his allies. Fourth, to acquire so much power, before the pope died, that he would be able on his own to resist a first attack. Of these four policies he had successfully carried out three by the time Alexander died; the fourth he had almost accomplished. Of the rulers he had dispossessed, he murdered as many as he could get his hands on, and only a very few survived. The Roman nobility were his supporters, and he had built up a very large faction in the College of Cardinals. As far as new acquisitions were concerned, he had plans for conquering Tuscany; he already held Perugia and Piombino; and he had taken Pisa under his protection. And, as soon as he would no longer have to worry about the King of France (which was already the case, for the French had already lost the Kingdom of Naples to the Spanish, with the result that both France and Spain were now obliged to try to buy his friendship), he would be free to seize Pisa. After which, Lucca and Siena would quickly give in, partly because they hated the Florentines, and partly because they would have been terrified. The Florentines could have done nothing.

If he had succeeded in all this (and he was on the point of succeeding in the very year Alexander died) he would have acquired so much strength and so much authority he would have become his own master. He would no longer have depended on events outside his control and on the policies of others, but would have been able to rely on his own power and strength [*virtù*]. But Alexander died only five years after Cesare Borgia had unsheathed his sword. He found himself with only his control over the Romagna firmly established, with everything else up in the air, caught between two powerful hostile armies, and dangerously ill. But the duke was so pugnacious and so strong [*virtù*], he so well understood what determines whether one wins or loses, and he had laid such sound foundations within such a short time, that, if he had not had these enemy armies breathing down his neck, or if he had been in good health, he could have overcome every difficulty.

I am justified in claiming he had laid sound foundations, for the Romagna remained loyal to him in his absence for more than a month; in Rome, although he was half dead, he was quite safe, and although the Ballioni, the Vitelli, and the Orsini congregated in Rome, they could not muster a following to attack him; and, if he was not in a position to choose who should be pope, he could at least veto anyone he did not trust. So, if he had been well when Alexander died he would have been able to deal with his problems without difficulty. He told me himself, on the day Julius II was elected, that he had asked himself what he would do if his father died and had been confident he could handle the situation, but that it had never occurred to him that when his father died he himself would be at death's door.

So, now I have surveyed all the actions of the duke, I still cannot find anything to criticize. It seems to me I have been right to present him as an example to be imitated by all those who come to power through good luck and thanks to someone else's military might. For, since he was great-hearted and ambitious, he had no choice as to what to do; and he only failed to achieve his goals because Alexander died too soon, and he himself fell ill. So anyone who decides that the policy to follow when one has newly acquired

power is to destroy one's enemies, to secure some allies, to win wars, whether by force or by fraud, to make oneself both loved and feared by one's subjects, to make one's soldiers loyal and respectful, to wipe out those who can or would want to hurt one, to innovate, replacing old institutions with new practices, to be both harsh and generous, magnanimous and open-handed, to disband disloyal troops and form new armies, to build alliances with other powers, so kings and princes either have to win your favor or else think twice before going against your wishes — anyone who thinks in these terms cannot hope to find, in the recent past, a better model to imitate than Cesare Borgia.

His only mistake was to allow Julius to be elected pope, for there he made a bad choice. The choice was his to make, for as I have said, if he could not choose who should be pope, he could veto anyone he did not like, and he should never have agreed to any cardinal's being elected with whom he had been in conflict in the past, or who, once he had been elected, would have been likely to be afraid of him. For men attack either out of fear or out of hatred. Those who had scores to settle with him included San Piero ad Vincula, Colonna, San Giorgio, Ascanio; all the others, if elected pope, would have had good reason to fear him, with the exception of Rouen and of the Spanish cardinals. The Spanish were his relatives and allies; Rouen was powerful, having the support of the King of France. So the duke's first objective should have been to ensure a Spaniard was elected pope; failing that, he should have agreed to the election of Rouen and vetoed that of San Piero ad Vincula. If he imagined recent gestures of goodwill make the powerful forget old injuries, he was much mistaken. So the duke made a mistake during the election of the pope, and this mistake was, in the end, the cause of his destruction.

Chapter Eight: Of those who come to power through wicked actions.

But since there are two other ways a private citizen can become a ruler, two ways that do not simply

involve the acquisition of power either through fortune or strength [*virtù*], I feel I cannot omit discussion
of them, although one of them can be more fully
treated elsewhere, where I discuss republics. These
are, first, when one acquires power through some
wicked or nefarious action, and second when a private
citizen becomes ruler of his own country because he
has the support of his fellow citizens. Here I will talk
about the first of these two routes to power, and will
use two examples, one ancient, one modern, to show
how it is done. These will be sufficient, I trust, to
provide a model for anyone who has no alternative
options. I do not intend to discuss in detail the rights
and wrongs of such a policy.

Agathocles of Sicily became King of Syracuse, although he was not merely a private citizen, but of
humble and poverty-stricken origins. He was the son
of a potter, and from start to finish lived a wicked
life; nevertheless, his wicked behavior testified to so
much strength [*virtù*] of mind and of body that, when
he joined the army, he was promoted through the
ranks to the supreme command. Having risen so high,
he decided to become the sole ruler and to hold on
to power, which he had originally been granted by
the consent of his fellow citizens, by violence and
without being dependent on anyone else. Having
entered into a conspiracy with a Carthaginian called
Hamilcar, who was commander of a hostile army
serving in Sicily, one morning he called together the
people and the senate of Syracuse, as if he wanted
to discuss matters of government policy, and, at a
prearranged signal, had his soldiers kill all the senators
and the richest citizens. With them out of the way,
he made himself ruler of the city and held power
without any resistance. Although the Carthaginians
twice defeated his armies and even advanced to the
walls of the city, he was not only able to defend his
city, but, leaving part of his army behind to withstand
the siege, he was able to attack the Carthaginians in
Africa with the remainder of his forces. Within a short
time he had forced them to lift the siege and was
threatening to conquer Carthage. In the end they
were obliged to come to terms with him, leaving
Sicily to Agathocles in return for security in Africa.

If you consider Agathocles' bold achievements
[*azioni e virtù*], you will not find much that can be
attributed to luck; for, as I have said, he did not
come to power because he had help from above, but
because he worked his way up from below, climbing
from rank to rank by undergoing infinite dangers and
discomforts until in the end he obtained a monopoly
of power, and then holding on to his position by bold
and risky tactics.

One ought not, of course, to call it *virtù* [virtue or
manliness] to massacre one's fellow citizens, to betray
one's friends, to break one's word, to be without mercy
and without religion. By such means one can acquire
power but not glory. If one considers the manly qualities [*virtù*] Agathocles demonstrated in braving and
facing down danger, and the strength of character he
showed in surviving and overcoming adversity, then
there seems to be no reason why he should be judged
less admirable than any of the finest generals. But on
the other hand, his inhuman cruelty and brutality,
and his innumerable wicked actions, mean it would
be wrong to praise him as one of the finest of men.
It is clear, at any rate, that one can attribute neither
to luck nor to virtue [*virtù*] his accomplishments,
which owed nothing to either.

In our own day, when Alexander VI was pope,
Oliverotto of Fermo, whose father had died a few years
before, was raised by his maternal uncle, Giovanni
Fogliani. As soon as he was old enough he joined
the forces of Paolo Vitelli, so that, with a good military
training, he could pursue a career in the army. When
Paolo died, he signed up with his brother, Vitellozzo.
In a very short time, because he was bright and had
both a strong body and a lively spirit, he became
Vitellozzo's second-in-command. Soon he thought it
to be beneath his dignity to serve under another, and
so he conspired to occupy Fermo, relying on the help
of some citizens of that city who preferred to see their
fatherland enslaved than free, and on the support of
Vitellozzo. He wrote to his uncle, saying that, since
he had been away from home for many years, he
wanted to come to visit him and to see his city, and
so, in a manner of speaking, reacquaint himself with
his inheritance. He said he had only gone to war in

order to acquire honor. So his fellow citizens would be able to see he had not been wasting his time, he wanted to arrive in state, accompanied by a hundred men on horseback, some of them his friends, and others his servants. He asked his uncle to ensure that the inhabitants of Fermo received him with respect: This would not only enhance his own reputation, but that of his uncle, who had raised him.

Giovanni did everything he could for his nephew. He ensured he was greeted by the people of Fermo with every honor, and he put him up in his own house. After a few days had gone by, and he had had time to make the arrangements necessary for the carrying out of his wicked plans, he held a lavish banquet at his uncle's, to which he invited his uncle and the most powerful citizens of Fermo. After the food had been eaten, and the guests had been entertained in all the ways that are customary upon such occasions, Oliverotto deliberately began discussing serious questions, talking about the greatness of Pope Alexander and his son Cesare, and about their undertakings. When his uncle Giovanni and the others picked up the subject, he sprang to his feet, saying such matters should be discussed in a more private place. He withdrew into another room, where Giovanni and all the other leading citizens followed. No sooner had they sat down than soldiers emerged from their hiding places and killed Giovanni along with all the rest. Once the killing was over, Oliverotto got on his horse and took possession of the city, laying siege to the government building. Those in authority were so terrified they agreed to obey him and to establish a new regime of which he was the head. With all those who had something to lose and would have been able to resist him dead, he was able to entrench himself by establishing new civilian and military institutions. Within a year of coming to power, he was not only securely in control of Fermo, but had become a threat to all the cities round about. It would soon have been as difficult to get rid of him as to get rid of Agathocles, had he not allowed himself to be taken in by Cesare Borgia, when, as I have already explained, he got rid of the Orsini and the Vitelli at Sinigallia. Oliverotto was seized at the same time, and, a year after he had killed his uncle, he was strangled along with Vitellozzo from whom he had learned how to be bold [virtù] and how to be wicked.

Perhaps you are wondering how Agathocles and others like him, despite their habitual faithlessness and cruelty, have been able to live safely in their homelands year after year, and to defend themselves against their enemies abroad. Why did their fellow subjects not conspire against them? After all, mere cruelty has not been enough to enable many other rulers to hang on to power even in time of peace, let alone during the turmoil of war. I think here we have to distinguish between cruelty well used and cruelty abused. Well-used cruelty (if one can speak well of evil) one may call those atrocities that are committed at a stroke, in order to secure one's power, and are then not repeated, rather every effort is made to ensure one's subjects benefit in the long run. An abuse of cruelty one may call those policies that, even if in the beginning they involve little bloodshed, lead to more rather than less as time goes by. Those who use cruelty well may indeed find both God and their subjects are prepared to let bygones be bygones, as was the case with Agathocles. Those who abuse it cannot hope to retain power indefinitely.

So the conclusion is: If you take control of a state, you should make a list of all the crimes you have to commit and do them all at once. That way you will not have to commit new atrocities every day, and you will be able, by not repeating your evil deeds, to reassure your subjects and to win their support by treating them well. He who acts otherwise, either out of squeamishness or out of bad judgment, has to hold a bloody knife in his hand all the time. He can never rely on his subjects, for they can never trust him, for he is always making new attacks upon them. Do all the harm you must at one and the same time, that way the full extent of it will not be noticed, and it will give least offense. One should do good, on the other hand, little by little, so people can fully appreciate it.

A ruler should, above all, behave towards his subjects in such a way that, whatever happens, whether for good or ill, he has no need to change his policies.

For if you fall on evil times and are obliged to change course, you will not have time to benefit from the harm you do, and the good you do will do you no good, because people will think you have been forced to do it, and they will not be in the slightest bit grateful to you.

Chapter Nine: Of the citizen-ruler.

But, coming to the alternative possibility, when a private citizen becomes the ruler of his homeland, not through wickedness or some act of atrocity, but through the support of his fellow citizens, so that we may call him a citizen-ruler (remember we are discussing power acquired neither by pure strength [*virtù*] nor mere luck—in this case one needs a lucky cunning), I would point out there are two ways to such power: the support of the populace or the favor of the elite. For in every city one finds these two opposed classes. They are at odds because the populace do not want to be ordered about or oppressed by the elite; and the elite want to order about and oppress the populace. The conflict between these two irreconcilable ambitions has in each city one of three possible consequences: rule by one man, liberty, or anarchy.

Rule by one man can be brought about either by the populace or the elite, depending on whether one or the other of these factions hopes to benefit from it. For if the elite fear they will be unable to control the populace, they begin to build up the reputation of one of their own, and they make him sole ruler in order to be able, under his protection, to achieve their objectives. The populace on the other hand, if they fear they are going to be crushed by the elite, build up the reputation of one of their number and make him sole ruler, in order that his authority may be employed in their defense. He who comes to power with the help of the elite has more difficulty in holding on to power than he who comes to power with the help of the populace, for in the former case he is surrounded by many who think of themselves as his equals, and whom he consequently cannot order about or manipulate as he might wish. He who comes to power with the support of the populace, on the other hand, has it all to himself: There is no one, or hardly anyone, around him who is not prepared to obey. In addition, one cannot honorably give the elite what they want, and one cannot do it without harming others; but this is not true with the populace, for the objectives of the populace are less immoral than those of the elite, for the latter want to oppress, and the former not to be oppressed. Thirdly, if the masses are opposed to you, you can never be secure, for there are too many of them; but the elite, since there are few of them, can be neutralized.

The worst a ruler who is opposed by the populace has to fear is that they will give him no support; but from the elite he has to fear not only lack of support, but worse, that they will attack him. For the elite have more foresight and more cunning; they act in time to protect themselves, and seek to ingratiate themselves with rivals for power. Finally, the ruler cannot get rid of the populace but must live with them; he can, however, get by perfectly well without the members of the elite, being able to make and unmake them each day, and being in a position to give them status or take it away, as he chooses.

In order to clarify the issues, let me point out there are two principal points of view from which one should consider the elite. Either they behave in a way that ties their fortunes to yours, or they do not. Those who tie themselves to you and are not rapacious, you should honor and love; those who do not tie themselves to you are to be divided into two categories. If they retain their independence through pusillanimity and because they are lacking in courage, then you should employ them, especially if they have good judgment, for you can be sure they will help you achieve success so long as things are going well for you, and you can also be confident you have nothing to fear from them if things go badly. But if they retain their independence from you out of calculation and ambition, then you can tell they are more interested in their own welfare than yours. A ruler must protect himself against such people and fear them as much as if they were publicly declared enemies, for you can be sure that, in adversity, they will help to overthrow you.

Anyone who becomes a ruler with the support of the populace ought to ensure he keeps their support; which will not be difficult, for all they ask is not to be oppressed. But anyone who becomes a ruler with the support of the elite and against the wishes of the populace must above all else seek to win the populace over to his side, which will be easy to do if he protects their interests. And since people, when they are well-treated by someone whom they expected to treat them badly, feel all the more obliged to their benefactor, he will find that the populace will quickly become better inclined towards him than if he had come to power with their support. There are numerous ways the ruler can win the support of the populace. They vary so much depending on the circumstances they cannot be reduced to a formula, and, consequently, I will not go into them here. I will simply conclude by saying a ruler needs to have the support of the populace, for otherwise he has nothing to fall back on in times of adversity.

Nabis, ruler of the Spartans, survived an attack by the confederate forces of all Greece, together with an almost invincible Roman army, and successfully defended both his homeland and his own hold on power. All he needed to do, when faced with danger, was neutralize a few; but if he had had the populace opposed to him, this would have been insufficient. Do not think you can rebut my argument by citing the well-worn proverb, "Relying on the people is like building on the sand." This is quite true when a private citizen depends upon them and gives the impression he expects the populace to free him if he is seized by his enemies or by the magistrates. In such a case one can easily find oneself disappointed, as happened to the Gracchi in Rome and to Mr. Giorgio Scali in Florence. But if you are a ruler and you put your trust in the populace, if you can give commands and are capable of bold action, if you are not nonplused by adversity, if you take other necessary precautions, and if through your own courage and your policies you keep up the morale of the populace, then you will never be let down by them, and you will discover you have built on a sound foundation.

The type of one-man rule we are discussing tends to be at risk at the moment of transition from constitu-tional to dictatorial government. Such rulers either give commands in their own name, or act through the officers of state. In the second case, their situation is more dangerous and less secure. For they are entirely dependent on the cooperation of those citizens who have been appointed to the offices of state, who can, particularly at times of crisis, easily deprive them of their power, either by directly opposing them or by simply failing to carry out their instructions. It is too late for the ruler once a crisis is upon him to seize dictatorial authority, for the citizens and the subjects, who are used to obeying the constituted authorities, will not, in such circumstances, obey him, and he will always have, in difficult circumstances, a shortage of people on whom he can rely. For such a ruler cannot expect things to continue as they were when there were no difficulties, when all the citizens are conscious of what the government can do for them. Then everyone flocked round, everyone promised support, everyone was willing to die for him, when there was no prospect of having to do so. But when times are tough, when the government is dependent on its citizens, then there will be few who are prepared to stand by it. One does not learn the danger of such an erosion of support from experience, as the first experience proves fatal. So a wise ruler will seek to ensure that his citizens always, no matter what the circumstances, have an interest in preserving both him and his authority. If he can do this, they will always be faithful to him.

Chapter Ten: How one should measure the strength of a ruler.

There is another factor one should take into account when categorizing rulers: One should ask if a ruler has enough resources to be able, if necessary, to look after himself, or whether he will always be dependent on having alliances with other rulers. In order to clarify this question, I would maintain those rulers can look after themselves who have sufficient reserves, whether of troops or of money, to be able to put together a sound army and face battle against any opponent. On the other hand, I judge those rulers to be dependent on the support of others who could not take the field against any potential enemy, but would be obliged to take shelter behind the walls of their cities and castles, and stay there. We have talked already about those who can look after themselves, and we will have more to say in due course; to those who are in the second situation, all one can do is advise them to build defenseworks and stockpile arms, and to give up all thought of holding the open ground. He who has well fortified his city and who has followed the policies towards his own subjects that I have outlined above and will describe below, can be sure his enemies will think twice before they attack him, for people are always reluctant to undertake enterprises that look as if they will be difficult, and no one thinks it will be easy to attack someone who is well-fortified and has the support of the populace.

The cities of Germany are free to do as they please. They have little surrounding territory, and obey the emperor only when they want. They fear neither him nor any other ruler in their region, for they are so well-fortified everyone thinks it will be tedious and difficult to take them. They all have appropriate moats and ramparts, and more than enough artillery. They always keep in the public stores enough food and drink, and enough firewood, to be able to hold out for a year. Moreover, in order to be able to keep the populace quiet and to guarantee tax revenues, they always keep in stock enough supplies to keep their subjects occupied for a year in those crafts that are the basis of the city's prosperity and provide employment for the bulk of the people. They also emphasize military preparedness and have numerous ordinances designed to ensure this.

A ruler, therefore, who has a well-fortified city, and who does not set out to make enemies, is not going to be attacked; and, suppose someone does attack him, his adversary will have to give up in disgrace. For political circumstances change so fast it is impossible for anyone to keep an army in the field for a year doing nothing but maintaining a siege. And if you are tempted to reply that if the people have property outside the city walls and see it burning, then they will not be able patiently to withstand a siege, and that as time goes by, and their own interests are dam-

aged, they will forget their loyalty to their ruler; then I reply that a ruler who is strong and bold will always be able to overcome such difficulties, sometimes encouraging his subjects to think relief is at hand, sometimes terrifying them with stories of what the enemy will do to them if they concede defeat, sometimes taking appropriate action to neutralize those who seem to him to be agitators. Moreover, it is in the nature of things that the enemy will burn and pillage the countryside when they first arrive, at which time the subjects will still be feeling brave and prepared to undertake their own defense. So the ruler has little to fear, for after a few days, when the subjects are feeling less courageous, the damage will already have been done, and it will be too late to prevent it. Then they will be all the more ready to rally to their ruler, believing him to be in their debt, since they have had their houses burnt and their possessions looted for defending him. It is in men's nature to feel as obliged by the good they do to others, as by the good others do to them. So if you consider all the factors, you will see it is not difficult for a wise ruler to keep his subjects loyal during a siege, both at the beginning and as it continues, providing they are not short of food and of arms.

Chapter Eleven: About ecclesiastical states.

All that remains for us to discuss, at this point, is the ecclesiastical states. As far as they are concerned, all the problems are encountered before one gets possession of them. One acquires them either through strength [virtù] or through luck, but one can hold on to them without either. For they are maintained by their long-established institutions that are rooted in religion. These have developed to such a pitch of strength they can support their rulers in power no matter how they live and behave. Only ecclesiastical rulers have states, but no need to defend them; subjects, but no need to govern them. Their states, though they do not defend them, are not taken from them; their subjects, though they do not govern them, do not resent them, and they neither think of replacing their rulers nor are they in a position to do so. So these are the only rulers who are secure and happy.

But because they are ruled by a higher power, which human intelligence cannot grasp, I will say no more about them; for, since they have been built up and maintained by God, only a presumptuous and rash person would debate about them. Nevertheless, if someone were to ask me how it comes about that the church has acquired so much temporal power, given that, until the papacy of Alexander [VI], the rulers of Italy, and indeed not only those who called themselves rulers, but every baron and lord, no matter how small, regarded the papacy's temporal power as of little significance, while now a King of France trembles at its power, for a pope has kicked him out of Italy and been the ruin of the Venetians: Though the answer to this question is well known, I think it will not be a waste of time to remind you of the main principles.

Before Charles, King of France, invaded Italy, control over this geographical region was divided between the pope, the Republic of Venice, the King of Naples, the Duke of Milan, and the Republic of Florence. These rulers were obliged to have two principal preoccupations: In the first place, they had to make sure no foreign power brought an army into Italy; in the second, they had to make sure none of the Italian powers increased its territory. The powers they were most concerned about were the pope and the Venetians. In order to prevent the Venetians from expanding all the rest had to cooperate, as happened when the Venetians tried to take Ferrara. In order to keep the pope in his place they relied on the nobles of Rome. These were divided into two factions, the Orsini and the Colonna, and so there was always occasion for friction between them. Because both factions were constantly in arms within sight of the pope, their strength kept the pope weak and sickly. Although there was occasionally a pope who had ambitions, Sixtus [IV] for example, yet neither luck nor skill enabled him to free himself of that handicap.

The real cause was the shortness of the popes' lives. On average, a pope lived ten years, which was scarcely enough time to crush one of the factions. Suppose a pope had almost destroyed the Colonna; his successor would prove to be an enemy of the Orsini, would rebuild the power of the Colonna, and would not

have time to crush the Orsini. The result was the temporal power of the pope was not thought by the Italians to be of much importance. Then along came Alexander VI, who, more than all the other popes there have been, demonstrated how much a pope, using both money and arms, could get his own way. It was Alexander who, by making use of Duke Valentino and by taking advantage of the invasion of Italy by the French, brought about all those things I have mentioned above, when discussing the achievements of the duke. Although his objective was not to make the church, but rather the duke, powerful, nevertheless, he did make the church a power to be reckoned with. It was the church that, after he had died and the duke had been destroyed, inherited the results of his labors.

After him came Julius [II]. The church was already powerful, for it had control of the whole of the Romagna, and the barons of Rome had been crushed, and the two factions of Orsini and Colonna had, as a result of the hiding given them by Alexander, been eliminated. Moreover, Julius had opportunities to accumulate money of a sort that had not existed before Alexander. Julius not only took over where Alexander had left off, but made further advances. He planned to acquire Bologna, to destroy the power of the Venetians, and to throw the French out of Italy. He not only laid plans, but he succeeded in everything he undertook. His achievements were all the more admirable in that his goal was to build up the power of the Church, not of any private individual. He kept the factions of the Orsini and the Colonna in the feeble condition in which he had found them. Although they made some efforts to rise again, two things kept them down: in the first place, the new power of the church, which intimidated them; and in the second, the fact none of their number were cardinals, for it is the cardinals who have been at the origin of the conflicts between the factions. These two factions have never behaved themselves at times when they have had cardinals, for the cardinals, both in Rome and outside Rome, foster the factions, and the barons are obliged to come to their support. Thus the ambition of the prelates is the cause of the conflicts and tumults among the nobility.

Now His Holiness Pope Leo [X] has acquired the papacy, along with all its immense temporal power. We may hope, if his predecessors made it a military power to be reckoned with, he, who is so good and has so many virtues [virtù], will not only increase its power, but also make it worthy of respect.

Chapter Twelve: How many types of army are there, and what opinion should one have of mercenary soldiers?

So far I have discussed one by one the various types of one-man rule I listed at the beginning, and I have to some extent described the policies that make each type succeed or fail. I have shown the various techniques employed by numerous individuals who have sought to acquire and to hold on to power. Now my task is to outline the various strategies for offense and defense that are common to all these principalities. I said above it was necessary for a ruler to lay good foundations; otherwise, he is likely to be destroyed. The principal foundations on which the power of all governments is based (whether they be new, long-established, or mixed) are good laws and good armies. And, since there cannot be good laws where there are not good armies, and since where there are good armies, there must be good laws, I will omit any discussion of laws, and will talk about armies.

Let me begin by saying, then, that a ruler defends his state with armies that are made up of his own subjects, or of mercenaries, or of auxiliary forces, or of some combination of these three types. Mercenaries and auxiliaries are both useless and dangerous. Anyone who relies on mercenary troops to keep himself in power will never be safe or secure, for they are factious, ambitious, ill-disciplined, treacherous. They show off to your allies and run away from your enemies. They do not fear God and do not keep faith with mankind. A mercenary army puts off defeat for only so long as it postpones going into battle. In peacetime they pillage you, in wartime they let the enemy do it. This is why: They have no motive or principle for joining up beyond the desire to collect their pay. And what you pay them is not enough to make them want to die for you. They are delighted to be your soldiers when you are not at war; when you are at war, they walk away when they do not run. It should not be difficult to convince you of this, because the sole cause of the present ruin of Italy has been the fact that for many years now the Italians have been willing to rely on mercenaries. It is true that occasionally a ruler seems to benefit from their use, and they boast of their own prowess, but as soon as they face foreign troops their true worth becomes apparent. This is why Charles, King of France, was able to conquer Italy with a piece of chalk; and the person who said we were being punished for our sins spoke the truth. But our sins were not the ones of which he was thinking, but those I have been discussing. Because these were the sins of our rulers, our rulers as well as the common people had to pay the price for them.

I want now to make crystal clear the worthlessness of mercenary armies. Mercenary commanders are either excellent or not. If they are excellent, you cannot trust them, for they will always be looking for ways of increasing their own power, either by turning on you, their employer, or by turning on others whom you want them to leave alone. On the other hand, if they are not first rate [virtuoso], then they will be the ruin of you in the normal course of events. And if you want to reply the same problems will arise whoever makes up the army, whether they are mercenaries or not, I will argue it depends on whether they take their orders from a sovereign or from a republic. A sovereign ought to go to war himself, and be his own general. A republic has to send one of its citizens. If it chooses someone who turns out not to be a successful soldier, it must replace him; if it chooses someone who is successful, it must tie his hands with laws, to ensure he keeps within the limits assigned to him. Experience shows individual sovereigns and republics that arm the masses are capable of making vast conquests; but mercenary troops are always a liability. Moreover, it is harder for a treacherous citizen to suborn an army consisting of his own fellow subjects than one made up of foreigners.

Rome and Sparta were armed and free for many centuries. The Swiss are armed to the teeth and do not have to take orders from anyone. In ancient history, we can take the Carthaginians as an example of the consequences of relying on mercenaries. They were in danger of being oppressed by their mercenary soldiers when the first war with Rome was over, despite the fact they employed their own citizens as commanders. Philip of Macedon was made general of the Theban armies after the death of Epaminondas; and, after he had won the war, he enslaved the Thebans. In modern times, Milan, after Duke Filippo died, employed Francesco Sforza to fight the Venetians. Once he had defeated the enemy at Caravaggio, he joined forces with them to attack the Milanese, his employers. Sforza his father, who was employed by Queen Giovanna of Naples, abandoned her without warning and without defenses. As a consequence, she was obliged to throw herself into the embrace of the King of Aragon in order to hold on to her kingdom. If the Venetians and the Florentines have in the past succeeded in acquiring new territory with mercenary armies, and if their commanders have not seized the conquests for themselves, but have held onto them for their employers, this, I would argue, is because the Florentines have had more than their share of luck. For of the first-rate [*virtuosi*] commanders, whom they would have had reason to fear, some have not been victorious, some have not been in sole command, and some have turned their ambitions elsewhere. It was John Hawkwood who did not win: We cannot know if he would have proved reliable had he been victorious, but no one can deny that if he had won Florence would have been his for the taking. Sforza always had to share command with the Braccheschi, and neither could act for fear of the other. Francesco turned his ambitions to Lombardy; Braccio turned his against the church and the Kingdom of Naples.

But let us look at what happened only a short time ago. The Florentines made Paolo Vitelli their commander. He was a very astute man, and, despite being of modest origin, he had acquired a tremendous reputation. If he had succeeded in taking Pisa, no one can deny the Florentines would have needed his goodwill, for, if he had transferred his support to their enemies, they would have been without defenses; and if they

had managed to keep his support, they would have had no choice but to do as he told them.

Consider next the conquests made by the Venetians. You will see they ran no risks and won magnificent victories as long as they relied on their own troops, which was until they tried to conquer territory on the mainland. When they armed both the nobility and the populace they had a magnificent fighting force [*operorono virtuosissimamente*], but when they began to fight on the mainland they abandoned this sound policy [*questa virtù*], and began to copy the other Italian states. When they began their conquests on the mainland, because they had little territory there, and because their own reputation was fearsome, they had little to fear from their mercenary commanders. But as their conquests extended, as they did under Carmagnola, they began to discover their mistake. They recognized he was a first-rate [*virtuosissimo*] general, and that they had, under his command, defeated the Duke of Milan, but they realized he had lost his taste for war, and concluded they could no longer win with him, because he no longer wanted victory; but they could not dismiss him, or the land they had acquired would go with him. So, in order to neutralize him, they had to kill him. Since then they have employed as commanders of their forces Bartolemeo of Bergamo, Roberto of San Severino, the Count of Pitigliano, and others like them. With such commanders they had reason to fear defeat, not the consequences of victory. And indeed they were defeated at Vailà, where, in one day, they lost all they had acquired with so much effort in eight hundred years. For with mercenary troops one acquires new territory slowly, feebly, after many attempts; but one loses so much so quickly that it seems an act of God.

And, since these examples have been drawn from recent Italian experience, and since Italy has been entirely dependent on mercenary forces for many years, I want to trace the present state of affairs back to its source, so that, having seen the origin and development of the problem, it will be easier to see how to correct it. You need to understand, then, that in modern times, as soon as the authority of the Holy Roman Empire began to be rejected in Italy, and the pope began to acquire greater authority in temporal affairs, Italy began to be divided into a number of different states. Many of the larger cities went to war against the nobility of the surrounding countryside, who had been oppressing them, and who were, at first, supported by the emperor. The Church, on the other hand, favored the cities in order to build up its temporal authority. In many other cities individual citizens established princedoms. So Italy came to be more or less divided up between those who owed allegiance to the papacy and a number of independent republican city states. Since neither the priests nor the citizens of the republics were accustomed to fighting wars, they began to employ foreigners in their armies.

The first to win a reputation for these mercenary troops was Alberigo of Conio in the Romagna. Among those who were trained by him were Braccio and Sforza, who were, at the height of their powers, the arbiters of Italian affairs. After them came all the others who have commanded mercenary forces down to the present time. The outcome of all their prowess [*virtù*] has been that Italy has, in quick succession, been overrun by Charles, plundered by Louis, raped by Ferdinand, and humiliated by the Swiss.

The first objective these mercenary commanders have pursued has been to destroy the reputation of the infantry in order to build up that of their own forces. They did this because they have had no resources of their own, but have been dependent on their contracts. A few infantry would have done little for their reputation, while they could not afford to feed a large number. So they specialized in cavalry, for they could feed a reasonably large number, and with them win respect. It came to the point that in an army of twenty thousand soldiers there would not even be two thousand infantry. In addition, they have done everything they could to free themselves and their troops from trouble and from danger. During skirmishes between opposing forces they did not kill each other: Indeed, they not only took prisoners, but released them without demanding a ransom. They were in no hurry to assault fortifications under cover of darkness, while the defending troops were far from eager to mount sorties against their assailants. When they made camp they did not protect themselves with

trenches or palisades. They passed the winters in barracks. And all these practices were permitted by their standing orders and were invented, as I said, so they could avoid effort and risk: so much so that they have reduced Italy to a despicable slavery.

Chapter Thirteen: About auxiliary troops, native troops, and composite armies.

Auxiliaries are the other sort of useless troops. You rely on auxiliaries when you appeal to another ruler to come with his own armies to assist or defend you. This is what Pope Julius did in recent times, when, having discovered the incompetence of his mercenary troops during the siege of Ferrara, he decided to rely on auxiliaries, and reached an agreement with King Ferdinand of Spain that he would come to his assistance with his men and arms. Auxiliary troops can be useful and good when fighting on their own behalf, but they are almost always a liability for anyone relying on their assistance. For if they lose, it is you who are defeated; if they win, you are their prisoner. There are plenty of examples of this in ancient history, but I do not want to stray from the contemporary case of Pope Julius II; he can have had no idea what he was doing when, in the hope of acquiring Ferrara, he placed himself entirely into the hands of a foreigner. But he was lucky: The outcome was neither defeat nor imprisonment, so he did not have to pay the price for his foolish decision. His auxiliaries were routed at Ravenna, but then the Swiss came along and drove out the victors, so that, contrary to everyone's expectation, including his own, he did not end up either a prisoner of his enemies, who had fled, or of his auxiliaries, for it was not they who had been victorious. Another example: The Florentines, having no troops of their own, brought ten thousand French soldiers to take Pisa. This decision placed them in more danger than at any other time during their troubles. Again, the Emperor of Constantinople, in order to attack his neighbors, brought ten thousand Turks into Greece. They, when the war was over, had no intention of leaving: This was the beginning of Greece's enslavement to the infidels.

He, then, who has no desire to be the victor should use these troops, for they are much more dangerous than mercenaries. If your auxiliaries win you are ruined, for they are united in their obedience to someone else. If your mercenaries win it takes them more time and more favorable circumstances to turn against you, for they are not united among themselves, and it is you who recruited and paid them. If you appoint an outsider to command them, it takes him time to establish sufficient authority to be able to attack you. In short, where mercenaries are concerned the main risk is cowardice; with auxiliaries it is valor [*virtù*].

A wise ruler, therefore, will always avoid using mercenary and auxiliary troops, and will rely on his own forces. He would rather lose with his own troops than win with someone else's, for he will not regard it a true victory if it is won with troops that do not belong to him. I never hesitate to cite Cesare Borgia as a model to be imitated. This duke entered the Romagna with an auxiliary army, for his troops were all Frenchmen, and he used it to take Imola and Forlì. But since he did not feel such troops were reliable, he then switched over to mercenaries, believing that using them involved fewer risks, and so he hired the Orsini and the Vitelli. But in practice he found them unreliable, treacherous, and dangerous, and so he got rid of them and formed his own army. And it is easy to see the differences among these three types of army, for you only have to consider how the duke's reputation changed, depending on whether he was relying on the French alone, on the Orsini and the Vitelli, or on his own troops and his own resources. With each change of policy it increased, but he was only taken seriously when everyone could see he was in complete command of his own forces.

I wanted to stick to examples that are both recent and Italian, but I cannot resist mentioning Hiero of Syracuse, since I have already discussed him above. He, when he was made commander-in-chief by the Syracusans, as I have described, quickly realized their mercenary army was worthless, for it was made up of condottieri like our own Italian armies. He decided he could not risk either keeping them on, or letting them go, so he had them massacred. Thereafter, he went to war with troops of his own, not with other people's soldiers. I also want to remind you of an Old Testament story that is relevant. When David proposed to Saul that he should go and fight with Goliath, the Philistine champion, Saul, in order to give him confidence, dressed him in his own armor. David, having tried it on, rejected it, saying he could not give a good account of himself if he relied on Saul's weapons. He wanted to confront the enemy armed with his sling and his knife.

In short, someone else's armor either falls off, or it weighs you down, or it trips you up. Charles VII, father of King Louis XI, having through good luck and valor [*virtù*] driven the English out of France, recognized that it was essential to have one's own weapons and, so, issued instructions for the establishment of a standing army of cavalry and infantry. Later, his son King Louis abolished the infantry and began to recruit Swiss troops. It was this mistake, imitated by his successors, that was, as we can see from recent events, the cause of the dangers faced by that kingdom. For he built up the reputation of the Swiss while undermining his own military capacity, for he destroyed his own infantry and made his own cavalry dependent on the support of foreign troops, for they, having become accustomed to fighting alongside the Swiss, no longer think they can win without them. The result is the French dare not fight against the Swiss, and without the Swiss they are ineffective against anyone else. So the French armies have been mixed, partly mercenary and partly native. Such a mixed army is much preferable to one made up only of auxiliaries or only of mercenaries, but it is much inferior to one made up entirely of one's own troops. The French example is sufficient to make the point, for the Kingdom of France would be able to overcome any enemy if the foundations laid by Charles VII had been built upon, or even if his instructions had merely been kept in force. But men are foolish, and they embark on something that is attractive in its outward appearance, without recognizing the evil consequences that will follow from it: a point I have already made when talking about consumption.

A ruler who cannot foresee evil consequences before they have time to develop is not truly wise; but few have such wisdom. And if one studies the first destruction of the Roman Empire one discovers it came about as a result of the first recruitment of Gothic soldiers, for from that moment the armies of the Roman Empire began to grow feeble. And all the strength [*virtù*] that ebbed from the Romans accrued to the Goths. I conclude, therefore, that no ruler is secure unless he has his own troops. Without them he is entirely dependent on fortune, having no strength [*virtù*] with which to defend himself in adversity. Wise men have always believed and said that, "Nothing is so fragile as a reputation for strength that does not correspond to one's real capacities." Now one's own troops can be made up out of one's subjects, or one's citizens, or one's dependents: All others are either mercenaries or auxiliaries. And the correct way of organizing one's own troops is easy to find out by looking over the instructions given by the four rulers whose conduct I have approved, or by finding out how Philip, the father of Alexander the Great, and how many other republics and sovereigns levied and trained troops: I have complete confidence in their methods.

Chapter Fourteen: What a ruler should do as regards the militia.

A ruler, then, should have no other concern, no other thought, should pay attention to nothing aside from war, military institutions, and the training of his soldiers. For this is the only field in which a ruler has to excel. It is of such importance [*virtù*] that military prowess not only keeps those who have been born rulers in power, but also often enables men who have been born private citizens to come to power. On the other hand, one sees that when rulers think more about luxuries than about weapons, they fall from power. The prime reason for losing power is neglect of military matters; while being an expert soldier opens the way to the acquisition of power.

Francesco Sforza, because he had troops, became Duke of Milan, having begun life as a private citizen. His descendants, who had no taste for the sweat and dust of a soldier's life, started out as dukes and ended up as private citizens. For, among the other deleterious consequences of not having one's own troops, one comes to be regarded with contempt. There are several types of disgrace a ruler should avoid, as I will explain below. This is one of them. For there is no comparison between a ruler who has his own troops and one who has not. It is not to be expected that someone who is armed should cheerfully obey someone who is defenseless, or that someone who has no weapon should be safe when his employees are armed. For the armed man has contempt for the man without weapons; the defenseless man does not trust someone who can overpower him. The two cannot get on together. So, too, a ruler who does not know how to organize a militia, beyond the other dangers he faces, which I have already described, must recognize that he will not be respected by his troops, and that he cannot trust them.

So a ruler must think only of military matters, and in time of peace he should be even more occupied with them than in time of war. There are two ways he can prepare for war: by thinking and by doing. As far as actions are concerned, he should not only keep his troops in good order and see they are well-trained; he should be always out hunting, thereby accustoming his body to fatigue. He should take the opportunity to study the lie of the land, climbing the mountains, descending into the valleys, crossing the plains, fording rivers, and wading through marshes. He should spare no effort to become acquainted with his own land, and this for two reasons. First, the knowledge will stand him in good stead if he has to defend his state against invasion; second, his knowledge and experience on his own terrain will make it easy for him to understand any other landscape with which he has to become acquainted from scratch. The hills, the valleys, the plains, the rivers, the marshes of, for example, Tuscany have a good deal in common with those of the other regions of Italy. A knowledge of the terrain in one region will make it easy for him to learn about the others. A ruler who lacks this sort of skill does not satisfy the first requirement in a military commander, for it is knowledge of the terrain that enables you to locate the enemy and to get the edge over him when deciding where to camp, in what order to march, how to draw up the troops on the field of battle, and where to build fortifications.

Philopoemon, ruler of the Achaeans, is much praised by the historians, but in particular he is admired because during peacetime he thought about nothing but warfare. When he was out riding in the countryside with his friends, he would often halt and ask: "If the enemy were up on those hills, and we were down here with our army, who would have the better position? How should we advance, following the rule book, to attack him? If we wanted to retreat, how would we set about it? If they were retreating, how would we pursue them?" And so he would invite them to discuss, as they rode along, all the possible eventualities an army may have to face. He listened to their views, he explained his own and backed them up with arguments. Thanks to this continual theorizing he ensured that, if he was at the head of an army, he would be perfectly prepared for anything that might happen.

Such theorizing is not enough. Every ruler should read history books, and in them he should study the actions of admirable men. He should see how they conducted themselves when at war, study why they won some battles and lost others, so he will know what to imitate and what to avoid. Above all he should set himself to imitate the actions of some admirable historical character, as great men have always imitated their glorious predecessors, constantly bearing in mind their actions and their ways of behaving. So, it is said, Alexander the Great took Achilles as his model; Caesar took Alexander; Scipio took Cyrus. If you read the life of Cyrus that was written by Xenophon and then study the life of Scipio you will realize to what extent those qualities that are admired in Scipio derive from Cyrus: His chastity, his affability, his kindness, his generosity, all are modelled upon Cyrus as Xenophon portrays him. A wise ruler will follow these examples. He will never relax during peacetime, but will always be working to take advantage of the opportunities peace presents, so he will be fully prepared when adversity comes. When his luck changes, he must be ready to fight back.

Chapter Fifteen: About those factors that cause men, and especially rulers, to be praised or censured.

Our next task is to consider the policies and principles a ruler ought to follow in dealing with his subjects or with his friends. Since I know many people have written on this subject, I am concerned it may be thought presumptuous for me to write on it as well, especially since what I have to say, as regards this question in particular, will differ greatly from the recommendations of others. But my hope is to write a book that will be useful, at least to those who read it intelligently, and so I thought it sensible to go straight to a discussion of how things are in real life and not waste time with a discussion of an imaginary world. For many authors have constructed imaginary republics and principalities that have never existed in practice and never could; for the gap between how people actually behave and how they ought to behave is so great that anyone who ignores everyday reality in order to live up to an ideal will soon discover he has been taught how to destroy himself, not how to preserve himself. For anyone who wants to act the part of a good man in all circumstances will bring about his own ruin, for those he has to deal with will not all be good. So it is necessary for a ruler, if he wants to hold on to power, to learn how not to be good, and to know when it is and when it is not necessary to use this knowledge.

Let us leave to one side, then, all discussion of imaginary rulers and talk about practical realities. I maintain that all men, when people talk about them, and especially rulers, because they hold positions of authority, are described in terms of qualities that are inextricably linked to censure or to praise. So one man is described as generous, another as a miser [*misero*] (to use the Tuscan term; for "avaricious," in our language, is used of someone who has a rapacious desire to acquire wealth, while we call someone a "miser" when he is unduly reluctant to spend the money he has); one is called open-handed, another tight-fisted; one man is cruel, another gentle; one untrustworthy, another reliable; one effeminate and cowardly, another bold and violent; one sympathetic, another self-important; one promiscuous, another monogamous; one straightforward, another duplicitous; one tough, another easy-going; one serious, another cheerful; one religious, another atheistical; and so on. Now I know everyone will agree that if a ruler could have all the good qualities I have listed and none of the bad ones, then this would be an excellent state of affairs. But one cannot have all the good qualities, nor always act in a praiseworthy fashion, for we do not live in an ideal world. You have to be astute enough to avoid being thought to have those evil qualities that would make it impossible for you to retain power; as for those that are compatible with holding on to power, you should avoid them if you can; but if you cannot, then you should not worry too much if people say you have them. Above all, do not be upset if you are supposed to have those vices a ruler needs if he is going to stay securely in power, for, if you think about it, you will realize there are some ways of behaving that are supposed to be virtuous [*che parrà virtù*], but would lead to your downfall, and others that are supposed to be wicked, but will lead to your welfare and peace of mind.

Chapter Sixteen: On generosity and parsimony.

Let me begin, then, with the qualities I mentioned first. I argue it would be good to be thought generous; nevertheless, if you act in the way that will get you a reputation for generosity, you will do yourself damage. For generosity used skillfully [*virtuosamente*] and practiced as it ought to be, is hidden from sight, and being truly generous will not protect you from acquiring a reputation for parsimony. So, if you want to have a reputation for generosity, you must throw yourself into lavish and ostentatious expenditure. Consequently, a ruler who pursues a reputation for generosity will always end up wasting all his resources; and he will be obliged in the end, if he wants to preserve his reputation, to impose crushing taxes upon the people, to pursue every possible source of income, and to be preoccupied with maximizing his revenues.

This will begin to make him hateful to his subjects, and will ensure no one thinks well of him, for no one admires poverty. The result is his supposed generosity will have caused him to offend the vast majority and to have won favor with few. Anything that goes wrong will destabilize him, and the slightest danger will imperil him. Recognizing the problem, and trying to economize, he will quickly find he has acquired a reputation as a miser.

So we see a ruler cannot seek to benefit from a reputation as generous [*questa virtù del liberale*] without harming himself. Recognizing this, he ought, if he is wise, not to mind being called miserly. For, as time goes by, he will be thought of as growing ever more generous, for people will recognize that as a result of his parsimony he is able to live on his income, maintain an adequate army, and undertake new initiatives without imposing new taxes. The result is he will be thought to be generous towards all those whose income he does not tax, which is almost everybody, and stingy towards those who miss out on handouts, who are only a few. In modern times nobody has succeeded on a large scale except those who have been thought miserly; the others came to nothing. Pope Julius II took advantage of a reputation for generosity in order to win election, but once elected he made no effort to keep his reputation, for he wanted to go to war. The present King of France has fought many wars without having to impose additional taxes on his people, because his occasional additional expenditures are offset by his long-term parsimony. The present King of Spain could not have aspired to, or achieved, so many conquests if he had had a reputation for generosity.

So a ruler should not care about being thought miserly, for it means he will be able to avoid robbing his subjects; he will be able to defend himself; he will not become poor and despicable, and he will not be forced to become rapacious. This is one of those vices that make successful government possible. And if you say: But Caesar rose to power thanks to his generosity, and many others have made their way to the highest positions of authority because they have both been and have been thought to be generous; I reply, either you are already a ruler, or you are on your way to becoming one. If you are already a ruler, generosity is a mistake; if you are trying to become one then you do, indeed, need to be thought of as generous. Caesar was one of those competing to become the ruler of Rome; but if, having acquired power, he had lived longer and had not learned to reduce his expenditures, he would have destroyed his own position. You may be tempted to reply: Many established rulers who have been thought to be immensely generous have been successful in war. But my answer is: Rulers either spend their own wealth and that of their subjects, or that of other people. Those who spend their own and their subjects' wealth should be abstemious; those who spend the wealth of others should seize every opportunity to be generous. Rulers who march with their armies, living off plunder, pillage, and confiscations are spending other people's money, and it is essential they should seem generous, for otherwise their soldiers will not follow them. With goods that belong neither to you nor to your subjects, you can afford to be generous, as Cyrus, Caesar, and Alexander were. Squandering other people's money does not do your reputation any harm, quite the reverse. The problem is with squandering your own. There is nothing so self-defeating as generosity, for the more generous you are, the less you are able to be generous. Generosity leads to poverty and disgrace, or, if you try to escape that, to rapacity and hostility. Among all the things a ruler should try to avoid, he must avoid above all being hated and despised. Generosity leads to your being both. So it is wiser to accept a reputation as miserly, which people despise but do not hate, than to aspire to a reputation as generous, and as a consequence, be obliged to face criticism for rapacity, which people both despise and hate.

Chapter Seventeen: About cruelty and compassion; and about whether it is better to be loved than feared, or the reverse.

Going further down our list of qualities, I recognize every ruler should want to be thought of as compassionate and not cruel. Nevertheless, I have to warn you to be careful about being compassionate. Cesare Borgia was thought of as cruel; but this supposed cruelty of his restored order to the Romagna, united it, rendered it peaceful and law-abiding. If you think about it, you will realize he was, in fact, much more compassionate than the people of Florence, who, in order to avoid being thought cruel, allowed Pistoia to tear itself apart. So a ruler ought not to mind the disgrace of being called cruel, if he keeps his subjects peaceful and law-abiding, for it is more compassionate to impose harsh punishments on a few than, out of excessive compassion, to allow disorder to spread, which leads to murders or looting. The whole community suffers if there are riots, while to maintain order the ruler only has to execute one or two individuals. Of all rulers, he who is new to power cannot escape a reputation for cruelty, for he is surrounded by dangers. Virgil has Dido say:

> Harsh necessity, and the fact my kingdom is
>   new, oblige me to do these things,
> And to mass my armies on the frontiers.

Nevertheless, you should be careful how you assess the situation and should think twice before you act. Do not be afraid of your own shadow. Employ policies that are moderated by prudence and sympathy. Avoid excessive self-confidence, which leads to carelessness, and avoid excessive timidity, which will make you insupportable.

This leads us to a question that is in dispute: Is it better to be loved than feared, or vice versa? My reply is one ought to be both loved and feared; but, since it is difficult to accomplish both at the same time, I maintain it is much safer to be feared than loved, if you have to do without one of the two. For of men one can, in general, say this: They are ungrateful, fickle, deceptive and deceiving, avoiders of danger, eager to gain. As long as you serve their interests, they are devoted to you. They promise you their blood, their possessions, their lives, and their children, as I said before, so long as you seem to have no need of them. But as soon as you need help, they turn against you. Any ruler who relies simply on their promises and makes no other preparations, will be destroyed. For you will find that those whose support you buy, who do not rally to you because they admire your strength of character and nobility of soul, these are people you pay for, but they are never yours, and in the end you cannot get the benefit of your investment. Men are less nervous of offending someone who makes himself lovable, than someone who makes himself frightening. For love attaches men by ties of obligation, which, since men are wicked, they break whenever their interests are at stake. But fear restrains men because they are afraid of punishment, and this fear never leaves them. Still, a ruler should make himself feared in such a way that, if he does not inspire love, at least he does not provoke hatred. For it is perfectly possible to be feared and not hated. You will only be hated if you seize the property or the women of your subjects and citizens. Whenever you have to kill someone, make sure you have a suitable excuse and an obvious reason; but, above all else, keep your hands off other people's property; for men are quicker to forget the death of their father than the loss of their inheritance. Moreover, there are always reasons why you might want to seize people's property; and he who begins to live by plundering others will always find an excuse for seizing other people's possessions; but there are fewer reasons for killing people, and one killing need not lead to another.

When a ruler is at the head of his army and has a vast number of soldiers under his command, then it is absolutely essential to be prepared to be thought cruel; for it is impossible to keep an army united and ready for action without acquiring a reputation for cruelty. Among the extraordinary accomplishments of Hannibal, we may note one in particular: He commanded a vast army, made up of men of many different nations, who were fighting far from home, yet they never mutinied and they never fell out with one another, either when things were going badly, or when things were going well. The only possible explanation for this is that he was known to be harsh and cruel. This, together with his numerous virtues [virtù], meant his soldiers always regarded him with admiration and fear. Without cruelty, his other virtues [virtù] would not have done the job. Those who write about Hannibal without thinking things through both

admire the loyalty of his troops and criticize the cruelty that was its principal cause. If you doubt my claim that his other virtues [virtù] would have been insufficient, take the case of Scipio. He was not only unique in his own day, but history does not record anyone his equal. But his army rebelled against him in Spain. The sole cause of this was his excessive leniency, which meant his soldiers had more freedom than is compatible with good military discipline. Fabius Maximus criticized him for this in the senate and accused him of corrupting the Roman armies. When Locri was destroyed by one of his commanders, he did not avenge the deaths of the inhabitants, and he did not punish his officer's insubordination. He was too easygoing. This was so apparent that one of his supporters in the senate was obliged to excuse him by saying he was no different from many other men, who were better at doing their own jobs than at making other people do theirs. In course of time, had he remained in command without learning from his mistakes, this aspect of Scipio's character would have destroyed his glorious reputation. But, because his authority was subordinate to that of the senate, not only were the consequences of this defect mitigated, but it even enhanced his reputation.

I conclude, then, that, as far as being feared and loved is concerned, since men decide for themselves whom they love, and rulers decide whom they fear, a wise ruler should rely on the emotion he can control, not on the one he cannot. But he must take care to avoid being hated, as I have said.

Chapter Eighteen: How far rulers are to keep their word.

Everybody recognizes how praiseworthy it is for a ruler to keep his word and to live a life of integrity, without relying on craftiness. Nevertheless, we see that in practice, in these days, those rulers who have not thought it important to keep their word have achieved great things, and have known how to employ cunning to confuse and disorientate other men. In the end, they have been able to overcome those who have placed store in integrity.

You should therefore know there are two ways to fight: one while respecting the rules, the other with no holds barred. Men alone fight in the first fashion, and animals fight in the second. But because you cannot always win if you respect the rules, you must be prepared to break them. A ruler, in particular, needs to know how to be both an animal and a man. The classical writers, without saying it explicitly, taught rulers to behave like this. They described how Achilles, and many other rulers in ancient times, were given to Chiron the centaur to be raised, so he could bring them up as he thought best. What they intended to convey, with this story of rulers' being educated by someone who was half beast and half man, was that it is necessary for a ruler to know when to act like an animal and when like a man; and if he relies on just one or the other mode of behavior he cannot hope to survive.

Since a ruler, then, needs to know how to make good use of beastly qualities, he should take as his models among the animals both the fox and the lion, for the lion does not know how to avoid traps, and the fox is easily overpowered by wolves. So you must be a fox when it comes to suspecting a trap, and a lion when it comes to making the wolves turn tail. Those who simply act like a lion all the time do not understand their business. So you see a wise ruler cannot, and should not, keep his word when doing so is to his disadvantage, and when the reasons that led him to promise to do so no longer apply. Of course, if all men were good, this advice would be bad; but since men are wicked and will not keep faith with you, you need not keep faith with them. Nor is a ruler ever short of legitimate reasons to justify breaking his word. I could give an infinite number of contemporary examples to support my argument and to show how treaties and promises have been rendered null and void by the dishonesty of rulers; and he who has known best how to act the fox has come out of it the best. But it is essential to know how to conceal how crafty one is, to know how to be a clever counterfeit and hypocrite. You will find people are so simple-minded and so preoccupied with their immediate concerns, that if you set out to deceive them, you will always find plenty of them who will let themselves be deceived.

Among the numerous recent cases one could mention, there is one of particular interest. Alexander VI had only one purpose, only one thought, which was to take people in, and he always found people who were willing victims. There never has been anyone who was more convincing when he swore an oath, nor has there been anybody who has ever formulated more eloquent oaths and has at the same time been quicker to break them. Nevertheless, he was able to find gulls one after another, whenever he wanted them, for he was a master of this particular skill.

So a ruler need not have all the positive qualities I listed earlier, but he must seem to have them. Indeed, I would go so far as to say that if you have them and never make any exceptions, then you will suffer for it; while if you merely appear to have them, they will benefit you. So you should seem to be compassionate, trustworthy, sympathetic, honest, religious, and, indeed, be all these things; but at the same time you should be constantly prepared, so that, if these become liabilities, you are trained and ready to become their opposites. You need to understand this: A ruler, and particularly a ruler who is new to power, cannot conform to all those rules that men who are thought good are expected to respect, for he is often obliged, in order to hold on to power, to break his word, to be uncharitable, inhumane, and irreligious. So he must be mentally prepared to act as circumstances and changes in fortune require. As I have said, he should do what is right if he can; but he must be prepared to do wrong if necessary.

A ruler must, therefore, take great care that he never carelessly says anything that is not imbued with the five qualities I listed above. He must seem, to those who listen to him and watch him, entirely pious, truthful, reliable, sympathetic, and religious. There is no quality that it is more important he should seem to have than this last one. In general, men judge more by sight than by touch. Everyone sees what is happening, but not everyone feels the consequences. Everyone sees what you seem to be; few have direct experience of who you really are. Those few will not dare speak out in the face of public opinion when that opinion is reinforced by the authority of the state. In the behavior of all men, and particularly of rulers, against whom there is no recourse at law, people judge by the outcome. So if a ruler wins wars and holds on to power, the means he has employed will always be judged honorable, and everyone will praise them. The common man accepts external appearances and judges by the outcome; and when it comes down to it only the masses count; for the elite are powerless if the masses have someone to provide them with leadership. One contemporary ruler, whom it would be unwise to name, is always preaching peace and good faith, and he has not a shred of respect for either; if he had respected either one or the other, he would have lost either his state or his reputation several times by now.

Chapter Nineteen: How one should avoid hatred and contempt.

Because I have spoken of the more important of the qualities I mentioned earlier, I want now to discuss the rest of them briefly under this general heading, that a ruler must take care (I have already referred to this in passing) to avoid those things that will make him an object of hatred or contempt. As long as he avoids these he will have done what is required of him, and he will find having a reputation for any of the other vices will do him no harm at all. You become hateful, above all, as I have said, if you prey on the possessions and the women of your subjects. You should leave both alone. The vast majority of men, so long as their goods and their honor are not taken from them, will live contentedly, so you will only have to contend with the small minority who are ambitious, and there are lots of straightforward ways of keeping them under control. You become contemptible if you are thought to be erratic, capricious, effeminate, pusillanimous, irresolute. You should avoid acquiring such a reputation as a pilot steers clear of the rocks. Make every effort to ensure your actions suggest greatness and endurance, strength of character and of purpose. When it comes

to the private business of your subjects, you should aim to ensure you never have to change your decisions once they have been taken, and that you acquire a reputation that will discourage people from even considering tricking or deceiving you.

A ruler who is thought of in these terms has the sort of reputation he needs; and it is difficult to conspire against someone who is respected in this way, difficult to attack him, because people realize he is on top of his job and has the loyalty of his employees. For rulers ought to be afraid of two things: Within the state, they should fear their subjects; abroad, they should fear other rulers. Against foreign powers, a good army and reliable allies are the only defense; and, if you have a good army, you will always find your allies reliable. And you will find it easy to maintain order at home if you are secure from external threats, provided, that is, conspiracies against you have not undermined your authority. Even if foreign powers do attack, if you have followed my advice and lived according to the principles I have outlined, then, as long as you keep a grip on yourself, you will be able to resist any attack, just as I said Nabis of Sparta was able to. But where your subjects are concerned, when you are not being attacked by foreign powers, you have to be wary of secret conspiracies. The best protection against these is to ensure you are not hated or despised, and the people are satisfied with your rule. It is essential to accomplish this, as I have already explained at length.

Indeed, one of the most effective defenses a ruler has against conspiracies is to make sure he is not generally hated. For conspirators always believe the assassination of the ruler will be approved by the people. If they believe the people will be angered, then they cannot screw up the courage to embark on such an enterprise, for conspirators have to overcome endless difficulties to achieve success. Experience shows the vast majority of conspiracies fail. For a conspirator cannot act alone, and he can only find associates among those whom he believes are discontented. As soon as you tell someone who is discontented what you are planning, you give him the means to satisfy his ambitions, because it is obvious he can expect to be richly rewarded if he betrays you. If he betrays you, his reward is certain; if he keeps faith with you, he faces danger, with little prospect of reward. So, you see, he needs either to be an exceptionally loyal friend or to be a completely intransigent enemy of the ruler, if he is to keep faith with you. So we can sum up as follows: The conspirators face nothing but fear, mutual distrust, and the prospect of punishment, so they lose heart; while the ruler is supported by the authority of his office and by the laws, and protected both by his supporters and by the forces of government. So, if you add to this inbuilt advantage the goodwill of the populace, then it is impossible to find anyone who is so foolhardy as to conspire against you. For in most situations a conspirator has to fear capture before he does the deed; but if the ruler has the goodwill of the people, he has to fear it afterwards as well, for the people will turn on him when the deed is done, and he will have nowhere to hide.

I could give an infinite number of examples to illustrate this, but I will confine myself to one only, a conspiracy that took place during the lifetime of our parents. Mr. Annibale Bentivoglio, grandfather of the present Mr. Annibale, was at the time ruler of Bologna. The Canneschi conspired against him and assassinated him. His only surviving relative was Mr. Giovanni, who was still in the cradle. But as soon as he was killed the people rose up and killed all the Canneschi. This happened because the family of Bentivoglio had, in those days, the goodwill of the people. Their loyalty was such that, there being no surviving member of the family in Bologna who could, now Annibale was dead, take over the government, and they having heard that in Florence there was a member of the family, someone who so far had been nothing more than the son of a blacksmith, the citizens of Bologna came to Florence to fetch him and made him the ruler of their city. He ruled it until Mr. Giovanni was old enough to take office.

I conclude, then, that a ruler need not worry much about conspiracies as long as the people wish him well; but if the people are hostile to him and hate him, then he should fear everything and everyone. States that are well-governed and rulers who are wise make every effort to ensure the elite are not driven to despair, and to satisfy the masses and keep them content; for this is one of the most important tasks a ruler must set himself.

Among the states that are well-ordered and well-ruled at the present time is France. There you will find innumerable good institutions that ensure the freedom of action and security of the king. First among them is the *parlement* and its authority. For whoever set up the government of that country understood the powerful are ambitious and insolent, and judged it necessary they should be bridled so they could be controlled, but on the other hand he recognized the hatred most people have for the powerful, whom they have reason to fear, and the consequent need to reassure and protect the great. So he did not want this to be the responsibility of the king, in order to avoid his alienating the powerful by favoring the people or alienating the people by favoring the powerful, and he established an independent tribunal, whose task it is, without incurring blame for the king, to crush the powerful and defend the weak. This arrangement is as intelligent and prudent as could be, and makes a substantial contribution to the security of the king and the stability of the kingdom. This institution enables us to recognize a significant general principle: Rulers should delegate responsibility for unpopular actions, while taking personal responsibility for those that will win favor. And once again I conclude a ruler should treat the powerful with respect, but at all costs he should avoid being hated by the people.

Many perhaps will think, if they consider the lives and deaths of some of the Roman emperors, that these provide examples contrary to the opinion I have expressed. For it would seem some of them lived exemplary lives and demonstrated great strength [*virtù*] of character, yet they fell from power, or rather they were killed by their retainers, who had conspired against them. Since I want to reply to this objection, I will discuss the characters of some of the emperors, explaining the reasons why they were destroyed, and show they do not tell against my argument. This will primarily involve pointing out factors that would seem significant to anyone who read the history of those times. I will confine myself to discussing all those emperors who came after Marcus Aurelius, up to and including Maximilian: that is, Marcus, his son Commodus, Pertinax, Julian, Severus, his son Antoninus Caracalla, Macrinus, Heliogabulus, Alexander, and Maximilian.

The first thing to be remarked is that, where in most states one only has to contend with the ambition of the great and the effrontery of the populace, the emperors of Rome had to face a third problem: They had to put up with the cruelty and greed of their soldiers. This was so difficult to do that it caused the downfall of many of the emperors, for it was almost impossible to satisfy both the soldiers and the populace. The people loved peace and quiet and, for this reason, liked their rulers to be unassuming; but the soldiers wanted the emperor to be a man of war and liked him to be arrogant, cruel, and rapacious. They wanted him to direct his aggression against the populace, so they could double their income and give free rein to their greed and cruelty. The result was those emperors who did not have a sufficiently intimidating reputation to keep both populace and soldiers in check (either because they did not think such a reputation desirable, or because they were incapable of acquiring it) were always destroyed. Most of them, especially those who acquired power without inheriting it, recognizing the difficulty of pleasing both soldiers and people, concentrated on pleasing the soldiers, thinking it could do little harm to alienate the populace. They had no choice, for, since rulers are bound to be hated by someone, their first concern must be to ensure they are not hated by any significant group; and, if they cannot achieve this, then they must make every possible effort to avoid the hatred of those groups that are most powerful. And so those emperors who had not inherited power and, thus, were in need of particularly strong support, attached themselves to the soldiers rather than to the people; a policy that proved successful or not, depending on whether the particular ruler in question knew how to establish his reputation with the army. For these reasons, then, Marcus, Pertinax, and Alexander, all of whom were unassuming, lovers of justice, haters of cruelty, sympathetic and kind, all came, apart from Marcus, to a tragic end. Marcus alone lived honorably and died peaceably, for he inherited power, and did

not have to repay a debt to either the soldiers or the populace. Moreover, since he had many virtues [*virtù*] that made him widely respected, he was able, during his own lifetime, to keep both groups in their place, and he was never hated or despised. But Pertinax was made emperor against the wishes of the soldiers, who, being accustomed to an unbridled life under Commodus, were unable to tolerate the disciplined way of life Pertinax wanted to impose on them. So he made himself hated, and to this hatred was added contempt, for he was an old man, and so his rule had scarcely begun before he fell from power.

Here we should note one can become hated for the good things one does, as much as for the bad. That is why, as I said above, a ruler who wants to hold on to power is often obliged not to be good, for when some powerful group—whether the populace, the soldiers, or the elite—whose support you feel it is essential to have if you are to survive, is corrupt, then you have to adapt to its tastes in order to satisfy it, in which case doing good will do you harm. But let us turn to Alexander. He was so good that among the other things for which he is praised is the fact that during the fourteen years he retained power, nobody was ever executed at his orders without due trial. Nevertheless, he was thought effeminate, and blamed for being under the influence of his mother, and so he came to be despised, the army conspired against him and killed him.

By contrast, let us consider the qualities of Commodus, of Severus, Antoninus Caracalla, and Maximinus. They were, you will find, in the highest degree bloodthirsty and rapacious. In order to satisfy the soldiery, they did not fail to commit every possible type of crime against the populace; and all of them, with the exception of Severus, came to a bad end. For Severus was such a strong ruler [*in Severo fu tanta virtù*] that, with the support of the army, even though the populace were oppressed by him, he could always rule successfully; for his strength [*virtù*] inspired awe in the minds of both soldiers and people: The people were always to a considerable degree stupefied and astonished by him, while the soldiers were admiring and satisfied. Because his deeds were commendable in a new ruler, I want to pause to point out how well he understood how to play the part both of the fox and of the lion: These are the two styles of action I have maintained a ruler must know how to imitate. Severus, because he knew what a coward Julian the new emperor was, persuaded the army he had under his command in Slavonia that it was a good idea to march on Rome to revenge the death of Pertinax, who had been killed by his praetorian guard. With this excuse, and without displaying any ambition to seize the throne, he set out for Rome; and his army was in Italy before anyone knew it had left its station. When he reached Rome, the senate, out of fear, elected him emperor and had Julian put to death. Severus, having begun like this, faced two problems if he wanted to gain effective control of the whole empire: In Asia there was Niger, commander of the Asiatic armies, who had had himself proclaimed emperor; in the West there was Albinus, who also aspired to power. Because he thought it would be dangerous to take on both of them at once, he decided to attack Niger and deceive Albinus. So he wrote to Albinus saying now that he had been elected emperor by the senate, he wanted to share his authority with him. He offered him the title of Caesar and had the senate appoint him co-ruler. Albinus accepted these proposals at face value. But as soon as Severus had defeated and killed Niger and pacified the eastern empire, he returned to Rome and attacked Albinus in the senate, complaining that he, far from being grateful for the generosity he had been shown, had wickedly sought to assassinate him. Severus claimed to have no choice but to go and punish this ingrate. So he attacked him in France and deprived him of his offices and of his life.

Anyone who examines Severus's actions with care will find he was both a ferocious lion and a cunning fox. He will find he was feared and respected by all, and he was not hated by the armies. So it is no surprise Severus, who had not inherited power, was able to hold on to a vast empire, for his immense reputation was a constant defense against the hatred the populace might otherwise have felt for his exactions. Antoninus his son was also a man whose remarkable abilities inspired awe in the populace and gratitude in the soldiers. For he was a man of war, able to make light

of the most arduous task and contemptuous of delicate food and all other luxuries. This made all his soldiers love him. Nevertheless, his ferocity and cruelty were without parallel. He did not only kill vast numbers of individuals, but, on one occasion, a large part of the population of Rome, and, on another, the whole of Alexandria. So he came to be loathed by everyone, and even his close associates began to fear him, with the result he was killed by a centurion while he was surrounded by his own troops. One should note rulers have no protection against an assassination like this, carried out by a truly determined individual, for anyone who is prepared to die can attack them. But, nevertheless, rulers should not worry unduly about such assassins because they are extremely rare. You should try merely to avoid giving grave injury to anyone you employ who comes close to you in the course of business. Antoninus had done just this, for he had outrageously put to death a brother of the centurion who killed him, and had repeatedly threatened the centurion's own life; yet he employed him as a bodyguard. This was foolhardy, and the disastrous outcome could have been predicted.

Now we come to Commodus, who had no difficulty in holding on to power, because he had inherited it, being the son of Marcus. All he had to do was follow in his father's footsteps, and he would have been satisfactory to both soldiers and populace. But, because he was by nature cruel and brutal, he began to ingratiate himself with the soldiers and to encourage them to be undisciplined, so he would be able to give his own rapacity free rein against the people. On the other hand, he did not maintain his own dignity. Often, when he went to the amphitheater, he came down and fought with the gladiators, and he did other things that were despicable and incompatible with imperial majesty. So he became contemptible in the eyes of his soldiers. He was hated by the people and despised by the soldiers, so there was soon a conspiracy against him and he was killed.

There remains for us to discuss the character of Maximinus. He was a most warlike individual. The armies had been irritated by the feebleness of Alexander, whom I have already discussed, and so, with him out of the way, they elected Maximinus emperor. But he did not hold on to power for long, for there were two things that made him hateful and contemptible. In the first place, he was of the lowest social status, having once been a shepherd in Thrace (a fact known to everyone, and one that made them all regard him with disdain); in the second, when he was elected emperor he had delayed going to Rome and taking possession of the throne, but had acquired a reputation for terrible cruelty because his representatives, in Rome and throughout the empire, had acted with great ferocity. So everybody was worked up with disdain for his humble origins and agitated with hatred arising from their fear of his ferocity. First Africa rebelled, and then the senate and the whole population of Rome; soon all Italy was conspiring against him. His own army turned against him. They were laying siege to Aquileia, but were finding it hard to take the city, to which was added their distaste for his cruelty. Seeing so many united against him, they lost their fear of him and killed him.

I do not want to discuss Heliogabulus, Macrinus, and Julian, for they were entirely contemptible and fell from power quickly. We can now come to the end of this discussion. I would have you note the rulers of our own day do not face in such an acute form the problem of having to adopt policies that involve breaking the law in order to satisfy their soldiers' appetites; for, although you cannot afford entirely to ignore contemporary soldiers, you can handle them easily. Modern rulers do not face standing armies with long experience of ruling and administering provinces, such as the Roman armies had. But if in those days it was more important to give satisfaction to the soldiers than to the populace, that was because the soldiers were more to be feared than the populace. Now all rulers, with the exception of the sultans of Turkey and of Egypt, need to be more concerned to satisfy the populace than the soldiers, for the populace are the greater threat. I make an exception of the ruler of Turkey, for at all times he is surrounded by twelve thousand infantry and fifteen thousand cavalry, on whom depends the security and strength of his government. It is essential for him, more than anything else, to retain their loyalty. Similarly, the Sultan of Egypt is entirely at the mercy of his soldiers, so

that he, too, must keep their loyalty, no matter what the consequences for the populace may be. And one should note the Sultan of Egypt is in a different position from all other rulers; for he is comparable to the Christian pope, who also cannot be described as either a hereditary or a new ruler. For the sons of the old ruler do not inherit his office and remain in power, but the new ruler is elected by a group who have the authority to appoint him. Since this arrangement has long been in existence, you cannot call the sultan a new ruler, for he faces none of the difficulties faced by those who are new to power. Even though he himself is new to power, the principle of succession is long-established, and ensures his authority is acknowledged as unquestioningly as would be the case if he were an hereditary ruler.

Let us return to our subject. I believe everyone should agree in the light of this discussion that hatred and contempt caused the fall of the emperors we have been considering, and will also understand how it comes about that, with one group of them following one line of policy and the other its opposite, in both groups one ruler was successful and the rest were killed. For it was pointless and dangerous for Pertinax and Alexander, who were new rulers, to try to imitate Marcus, who had inherited power; similarly it was a bad mistake for Caracalla, Commodus, and Maximinus to imitate Severus, for they lacked the strength [virtù] that would have been necessary for anyone following in his footsteps. Thus, a new ruler, who has not inherited power, should not follow the example of Marcus, but need not follow that of Severus. He ought to imitate in Severus those features that are essential for him to establish himself securely in power, and in Marcus those features that are effective and win glory for someone who is seeking to preserve a government that has already entrenched itself.

Chapter Twenty: Whether the building of fortresses (and many other things rulers regularly do) is useful or not.

Some rulers, in order to ensure they have a firm grip on power, have disarmed their subjects. Others have divided up the territories over which they rule. Some have positively encouraged opposition to their own authority. Others have set out to win over those who were hostile to them when they first came to power. Some have built fortresses. Others have destroyed them. It is impossible to pass definitive judgment on any of these policies until one considers the particular circumstances that existed in the state where the policy was adopted. Nevertheless, I will talk in general terms in so far as the subject itself permits.

No new ruler, let me point out, has ever disarmed his subjects; on the contrary, when he has found them disarmed, he has always armed them. For, when you arm them, their arms become yours, those who have been hostile to you become loyal, while those who have been loyal remain so, and progress from being your obedient subjects to being your active supporters. Because not every subject can be armed, provided you ensure those who receive arms stand to benefit, you will be more secure in your dealings with the others. When they recognize this diversity of treatment, it will make them all the more obliged to you; while the unarmed will forgive you, for they will recognize it is necessary that those who face more dangers and have more onerous obligations should be better rewarded. But if you take their arms away from those who have been armed, you begin to alienate them. You make it clear you do not trust them, either because you think they are poor soldiers or disloyal. Whichever view they attribute to you, they will begin to hate you. And, since you cannot remain undefended, you will be obliged to rely on mercenary troops, with the consequences we have already discussed. No matter how good they are, they will be unable to defend you against a combination of powerful foreign powers and hostile subjects. So, as I have said, a new ruler who has not inherited power has always formed his own army. There are innumerable examples in history. But when a ruler acquires a new state, which is simply added on to his existing territories, then it is essential to disarm the people, with the sole exception of those who have actively supported you in taking power. And they too, over time, and as opportunity occurs, should be encouraged to become weak and effeminate. You should arrange things so that all the weapons in your new state are in the hands of those of your own troops who were closely associated with you in your old territories.

Our ancestors, particularly those who were thought wise, used to say it was necessary to hold Pistoia by encouraging factional divisions, and Pisa by building fortresses. So, in some of the territory they occupied, they encouraged divisions in order to have better control. This was a sound policy in the days when Italy experienced a balance of power; but I do not think it can be recommended now. For I do not believe any good ever comes of internal conflicts. It is certain that when enemy forces approach you run the risk that divided cities will go over to the other side, for the weaker of the two internal factions will attach itself to the invaders, and the stronger will not be able to retain power against enemies within and without the walls.

The Venetians, following, I believe, the same line of thought as our ancestors, encouraged the division of the cities under their control into the two factions of Guelfs and Ghibellines. Although they never allowed the conflicts between them to go so far as bloodshed, they encouraged these tensions so the inhabitants of these cities would be fully occupied with their own internal disagreements and would not unite against their masters. But history shows this policy did not pay off. For, when they were defeated at Vailà, one of the factions quickly plucked up courage and deprived them of all their territories. Such policies, indeed, imply the ruler is weak, for a robust government would never allow such divisions, since you only benefit from them in time of peace, when they enable you to manage your subjects more easily; when war comes, such a policy proves to be misconceived.

There is no doubt rulers become powerful as they overcome the difficulties they face and the opposition they encounter. So fortune, especially when she wants to make a new ruler powerful (for new rulers have more need of acquiring a reputation than ones who have inherited power), makes him start out surrounded by enemies and endangered by threats, so he can overcome these obstacles and can climb higher on a ladder supplied by his enemies. Therefore, many conclude a wise ruler will, when he has the opportunity, secretly foster opposition to his rule, so that, when he has put down his opponents, he will be in a more powerful position.

Rulers, and especially those who are new to power, have sometimes found there is more loyalty and support to be had from those who were initially believed to be opposed to their rule, than from those whom from the start they could count on. Pandolfo Petrucci, ruler of Siena, governed his state by relying more on those who were supposed to be hostile to him than on his supporters. But we cannot discuss this policy in general terms, because its success depends upon circumstances. I will only say those men who have been hostile when a ruler first acquires power, but who belong to those social groups that need to rely on government support in order to maintain their position, can always be won over by the new ruler with the greatest of ease. And they are all the more obliged to serve him faithfully because they know it is essential for them to undo by their actions the negative assessment that was initially made of them. Thus, the ruler can always get more out of them than out of those who, being all too confident of his goodwill, pay little attention to his interests.

And, since it is relevant to our subject, I do not want to fail to point out to rulers who have recently acquired a state through the support of people living within it, that they should give careful consideration to the motives of those who supported them. If they did not give their support out of natural affection for you, but gave it only because they were not happy with their previous government, you will find you can only retain their loyalty with much trouble and effort, for there is no way in which you will be able to keep them happy. If you think about it and consider the record of ancient and modern history, you will realize it will be much easier for you to win the loyalty of those men who were happy with the previous government and were therefore opposed to your seizure of power, than of those who, because they were unhappy with it, became your allies and encouraged you to take power from it.

Rulers have been accustomed, in order to have a more secure grip on their territories, to build fortresses. They are intended to be a bridle and bit for those who plan to rebel against you, and to provide you with a secure refuge in the event of an unexpected attack. I approve of this policy, for it was used by the Romans. Nevertheless, Mr. Niccolò Vitelli, in our own day, had two fortresses in Città di Castello destroyed so he could hold on to that state. Guido Ubaldo, the Duke of Urbino, when he returned to power, having previously been driven into exile by Cesare Borgia, completely destroyed all the fortresses in his territory. He believed that without them it would be harder to deprive him once again of power. The Bentivogli, when they recovered power in Bologna, adopted the same policy.

We must conclude that fortresses are useful or not, depending on circumstances, and that, if they are useful at one time, they may also do you harm at another. We can identify the relevant factors as follows: A ruler who is more afraid of his subjects than of foreign powers should build fortresses; but a ruler who is more afraid of foreign powers than of his subjects should do without them. The castle of Milan, which was built by Francesco Sforza, has done and will do more damage to the house of Sforza than any other defect in that state. For the best fortress one can have is not being hated by one's subjects; for if you have fortresses, but your subjects hate you, they will not save you, for your subjects, once they have risen in arms, will never be short of foreign allies who will come to their support.

In recent times, there is no evidence that fortresses have been useful to any ruler, except for the Contessa of Forlì, when her husband Count Girolamo died: Because she could take refuge in one she was able to escape the popular uprising, hold out until assistance came from Milan, and retake her state. Circumstances at the time were such that the populace could not get assistance from abroad; but later, even she gained little benefit from her fortresses when Cesare Borgia attacked her, and the populace, still hostile to her, joined forces with the invaders. So, both at first and later, it would have been safer for her not to have been hated by her people than to have fortresses. Consequently, having considered all these factors, I would praise both those who build fortresses and those who do not, but I would criticize anyone who, relying on his fortresses, thought it unimportant that his people hated him.

Chapter Twenty-One: What a ruler should do in order to acquire a reputation.

Nothing does more to give a ruler a reputation than embarking on great undertakings and doing remarkable things. In our own day, there is Ferdinand of Aragon, the present King of Spain. He may be called, more or less, a new ruler, because having started out as a weak ruler he has become the most famous and most glorious of all the kings of Christendom. If you think about his deeds, you will find them all noble, and some of them extraordinary. At the beginning of his reign he attacked Granada, and this undertaking was the basis of his increased power. In the first place, he undertook the reconquest when he had no other problems to face, so he could concentrate upon it. He used it to channel the ambitions of his Castilian barons, who, because they were thinking of the war, were no threat to him at home. Meanwhile, he acquired influence and authority over them without their even being aware of it. He was able to raise money from the church and from his subjects to build up his armies. Thus, this lengthy war enabled him to build up his military strength, which has paid off since. Next, in order to be able to engage in more ambitious undertakings, still exploiting religion, he practiced a pious cruelty, expropriating and expelling from his kingdom the Marranos: an act without parallel and truly despicable. He used religion once more as an excuse to justify an attack on Africa. He then attacked Italy and has recently invaded France. He is always plotting and carrying out great enterprises, which have always kept his subjects bewildered and astonished, waiting to see what their outcome would be. And his deeds have followed one another so closely that he has never left space between one and the next for people to plot uninterruptedly against him.

It is also of considerable help to a ruler if he does remarkable things when it comes to domestic policy, such as those that are reported of Mr. Bernabò of Milan. It is a good idea to be widely talked about, as he was, because, whenever anyone happened to do anything extraordinary, whether good or bad, in civil life, he found an imaginative way to reward or to punish them. Above all a ruler should make every effort to ensure that whatever he does it gains him a reputation as a great man, a person who excels.

Rulers are also admired when they know how to be true allies and genuine enemies: That is, when, without any reservations, they demonstrate themselves to be loyal supporters or opponents of others. Such a policy is always better than one of neutrality. For if two rulers who are your neighbors are at war with each other, they are either so powerful that, if one of them wins, you will have to fear the victor, or they are not. Either way, it will be better for you to take sides and fight a good fight; for, if they are powerful, and you do not take sides, you will still be preyed on by the victor, much to the pleasure and satisfaction of his defeated opponent. You will have no excuse, no defense, no refuge. For whoever wins will not want allies who are unreliable and who do not stand by him in adversity; while he who loses will not offer you refuge, since you were not willing, sword in hand, to share his fate.

The Aetolians invited Antiochus to Greece to drive out the Romans. Antiochus sent an ambassador to the Achaeans, who were allies of the Romans, to encourage them to remain neutral; while the Romans urged them to fight on their side. The ruling council of the Achaeans met to decide what to do, and Antiochus's ambassador spoke in favor of neutrality. The Roman ambassador replied: "As for what they say to you, that it would be sensible to keep out of the war, there is nothing further from your true interests. If you are without credit, without dignity, the victor will claim you as his prize."

It will always happen that he who is not your ally will urge neutrality upon you, while he who is your ally will urge you to take sides. Rulers who are unsure what to do, but want to avoid immediate dangers, generally end up staying neutral and usually destroy themselves by doing so. But when a ruler boldly takes sides, if your ally wins, even if he is powerful, and has the ability to overpower you, he is in your debt and fond of you. Nobody is so shameless as to turn on you in so ungrateful a fashion. Moreover, victories are never so overwhelming that the victor can act without any constraint: Above all, victors still need to appear just. But if, on the other hand, your ally is defeated, he will offer you refuge, will help you as long as he is able, and will share your ill-fortune, in the hope of one day sharing good fortune with you. In the second case, when those at war with each other are insufficiently powerful to give you grounds to fear the outcome, there is all the more reason to take sides, for you will be able to destroy one of them with the help of the other, when, if they were wise, they would be helping each other. The one who wins is at your mercy; and victory is certain for him whom you support.

Here it is worth noting a ruler should never take the side of someone who is more powerful than himself against other rulers, unless necessity compels him to, as I have already implied. For if you win, you are your ally's prisoner; and rulers should do everything they can to avoid being at the mercy of others. The Venetians allied with the King of France against the Duke of Milan, when they could have avoided taking sides; they brought about their own destruction. But when you cannot help but take sides (which is the situation the Florentines found themselves in when the pope and the King of Spain were advancing with their armies to attack Lombardy) then you should take sides decisively, as I have explained. Do not for a moment think any state can always take safe decisions, but rather think every decision you take involves risks, for it is in the nature of things that you cannot take precautions against one danger without opening yourself to another. Prudence consists in knowing how to assess risks and in accepting the lesser evil as a good.

A ruler should also show himself to be an admirer of skill [virtù] and should honor those who are excellent in any type of work. He should encourage his citizens by making it possible for them to pursue their occupations peacefully, whether they are businessmen, farmers, or are engaged in any other activity, making sure they do not hesitate to improve what they own for fear it may be confiscated from them, and they are not discouraged from investing in business for fear of losing their profits in taxes; instead, he should ensure that those who improve and invest are rewarded, as should be anyone whose actions will benefit his city or his government. He should, in addition, at appropriate times of the year, amuse the populace with festivals and public spectacles. Since every city is divided into guilds or neighborhoods, he ought to take account of these collectivities, meeting with them on occasion, showing himself to be generous and understanding in his dealings with them, but at the same time always retaining his authority and dignity, for this he should never let slip in any circumstances.

Chapter Twenty-Two: About those whom rulers employ as advisers.

A ruler's choice as to whom to employ as his advisers is of foremost importance. Rulers get the advisers they deserve, for good rulers choose good ones, bad rulers choose bad. The easiest way of assessing a ruler's ability is to look at those who are members of his inner circle. If they are competent and reliable, then you can be sure he is wise, for he has known both how to recognize their ability and to keep them faithful. But if they are not, you can always make a negative assessment of the ruler; for he has already proved his inadequacy by making a poor choice of adviser.

Nobody who knew Mr. Antonio of Venafro when he was adviser to Pandolfo Petrucci, ruler of Siena, could fail to conclude that Pandolfo was a brilliant man, for how else would he come by such an adviser? For there are three types of brains: One understands matters for itself, one follows the explanations of others, and one neither understands nor follows. The first is best, the second excellent, the third useless. It followed logically that if Pandolfo was not in the first rank, then he was at least in the second. For anyone who can judge the good or evil someone says and does, even if he does not have an original mind, will recognize what his adviser does well and what he does ill, and will encourage the first and correct the second. An adviser cannot hope to deceive such an employer, and will do his best.

But there is one infallible way for a ruler to judge his adviser. When you see your adviser give more thought to his own interests than yours, and recognize everything he does is aimed at his own benefit, then you can be sure such a person will never be a good adviser. You will never be able to trust him, for he who runs a government should never think of his own interests, but always of his ruler's, and should never suggest anything to his ruler that is not in the ruler's interests. On the other hand the ruler, in order to get the best out of his adviser, should consider his adviser's interests, heaping honors on him, enriching him, placing him in his debt, ensuring he receives public recognition, so that he sees that he cannot do better without him, that he has so many honors he desires no more, so much wealth he desires no more, so much status he fears the consequences of political upheaval. When a ruler has good advisers and knows how to treat them, then they can rely on each other; when it is otherwise, either ruler or adviser will suffer.

Chapter Twenty-Three: How sycophants are to be avoided.

I do not want to omit an important subject that concerns a mistake it is difficult for rulers to avoid making, unless they are very wise and good judges of men. My subject is sycophants, who pullulate at court. For men are so easily flattered and are so easily taken in by praise, that it is difficult for them to defend themselves against this plague, and in defending themselves they run the risk of making themselves despicable. For there is no way of protecting oneself against flattery other than by making it clear you do not mind being told the truth; but, when anyone can tell you the truth, then you are not treated with sufficient respect. So a wise ruler ought to find an alternative to flattery and excessive frankness. He ought to choose wise men from among his subjects, and give to them alone freedom to tell him the truth, but only in reply to specific questions he puts to them, not on any subject of their choice. But he ought to ask them about everything, and listen to their replies; then think matters over on his own, in his own way.

His response to each of his advisers and their advice should make it apparent that the more freely they talk, the happier he will be. But he should listen to no one who has not been designated as an adviser, he should act resolutely once he has made up his mind, and he should cling stubbornly to his decisions once they have been taken. He who acts otherwise either is rushed into decisions by flatterers or changes his mind often in response to differing advice. Either way, people will form a poor opinion of him.

I want, on this subject, to refer to an example from recent history. The cleric Luca, an adviser to Maximilian, the present emperor, speaking of his sovereign, said that he did not ask for anyone's advice, and that he never did anything the way he wanted to: which was because he did not follow the principles I have just outlined. For the emperor is a secretive man, he keeps things to himself and never asks anyone's advice. But, when his decisions begin to be discovered, which is when they begin to be put into effect, he begins to be criticized by those who are close to him, and, as one might expect, he is persuaded to change his mind. The result is that he undoes each day what he did the day before; that nobody ever knows what he really wants or intends to do; and that one cannot rely upon his decisions.

A ruler, therefore, should always take advice, but only when he wants to, not when others want him to; he should discourage everybody from giving him advice without being asked; but he should be always asking, and, moreover, he should listen patiently to the answers, provided they are truthful. But if he becomes persuaded someone, for whatever reason, is not telling him the truth, he should lose his temper. There are many who think some rulers who have a reputation for being prudent do not really deserve to be thought so, claiming that the rulers themselves are not wise, but that they merely receive good advice. But without doubt they are mistaken. For this is a general rule without exceptions: A ruler who is not himself wise cannot be given good advice. Unless, I should say, he hands over all decisions to one other person and has the good luck to pick someone quite exceptionally prudent. But such an exceptional arrangement will not last long, for the man who takes all the decisions will soon take power. But a ruler who is not wise, if he takes advice from more than one person, will never get the same advice from everyone, nor will he be able to combine the different proposals into a coherent policy unless he has help. His advisers will each think about his own interests, and he will not be able to recognize their bias or correct it. This is how it has to be, for you will find men are always wicked, unless you give them no alternative but to be good. So we may conclude that good advice, no matter who it comes from, really comes from the ruler's own good judgment, and that the ruler's good judgment never comes from good advice.

Chapter Twenty-Four: Why the rulers of Italy have lost their states.

The policies I have described, if prudently followed, will make a new ruler seem long-established and will rapidly make his power better entrenched than it would be if he had long held office. For the actions of a new ruler are much more closely scrutinized than those of an hereditary ruler; and new rulers, when they are seen to be strong [virtuose], attract much more support and make men more indebted to them than do hereditary rulers. For men are much more impressed by what goes on in the present than by what happened in the past; and when they are satisfied with what is happening now, they are delighted and ask for nothing more. So they will spring to a new ruler's defense, provided he plays his part properly. Thus, he will be doubly glorious: He will have begun a new tradition of government, underpinned and ornamented with good laws, good arms, good allies, and good examples; just as he is doubly shamed who, being born a ruler, has lost power through lack of skill in ruling.

And if you consider those Italian rulers who have lost power in recent years, such as the King of Naples, the Duke of Milan, and others, you will find: First, they all had in common an inadequate military preparation, for the reasons I have discussed above at length; second, you will see that some of them either were

at odds with their own populace or, if they had the support of the populace, did not know how to protect themselves from the elite; for without these defects they would not have lost states that were strong enough to put an army in the field. Philip of Macedon (not the father of Alexander, but the Philip who was defeated by Titus Quintius) did not have a large state in comparison with the territory controlled by the Romans and the Greeks who attacked him; nevertheless, because he was a military man and a ruler who knew how to treat his populace and how to protect himself from the elite, he was able to sustain a war against superior forces for several years; and if, at the end, he lost control of several cities, he nevertheless retained his kingdom.

So our own rulers, each of whom had been in power for many years and then lost it, should not blame fortune but their own indolence. For when times were quiet they never once considered the possibility that they might change (it is a common human failing not to plan ahead for stormy weather while the sun shines). When difficult times did come, they thought of flight not of self-defense. They hoped the populace, irritated by the insolence of their conquerors, would recall them to power. This plan is a good one if there is no alternative policy available; but it is stupid to adopt it when there are alternatives. No one would be happy to trip and fall merely because he thought someone would help him back to his feet. Either no one comes to your assistance; or if someone does, you are the weaker for it, for your strategy for self-defense has been ignominious, and your fate has not been in your own hands. No method of defense is good, certain, and lasting that does not depend on your own decisions and your own strength [virtù].

Chapter Twenty-Five: How much fortune can achieve in human affairs, and how it is to be resisted.

I am not unaware of the fact that many have held and still hold the view that the affairs of this world are so completely governed by fortune and by God that human prudence is incapable of correcting them, with the consequence that there is no way in which what is wrong can be put right. So one may conclude that there is no point in trying too hard; one should simply let chance have its way. This view has come to be more widely accepted in our own day because of the extraordinary variation in circumstances that has been seen and is still seen every day. Nobody could predict such events. Sometimes, thinking this matter over, I have been inclined to adopt a version of this view myself. Nevertheless, since our free will must not be eliminated, I think it may be true that fortune determines one half of our actions, but that, even so, she leaves us to control the other half, or thereabouts. And I compare her to one of those torrential rivers that, when they get angry, break their banks, knock down trees and buildings, strip the soil from one place and deposit it somewhere else. Everyone flees before them, everyone gives way in face of their onrush, nobody can resist them at any point. But although they are so powerful, this does not mean men, when the waters recede, cannot make repairs and build banks and barriers so that, if the waters rise again, either they will be safely kept within the sluices or at least their onrush will not be so unregulated and destructive. The same thing happens with fortune: She demonstrates her power where precautions have not been taken to resist her [*dove non è ordinata virtù a resisterle*]; she directs her attacks where she knows banks and barriers have not been built to hold her. If you think about Italy, which is the location of all these changes in circumstance, and the origin of the forces making for change, you will realize she is a landscape without banks and without any barriers. If proper precautions had been taken [*s'ella fussi reparata da conveniente virtù*], as they were in Germany, Spain, and France, either the flood would not have had the consequences it had, or the banks would not even have been overwhelmed. And what I have said is enough, I believe, to answer the general question of how far one can resist fortune.

But, turning rather to individuals, note we see rulers who flourish one day and are destroyed the next without our being able to see any respect in which they have changed their nature or their attributes. I think the cause of this is, in the first place, the one we have already discussed at length: A ruler who depends entirely on his good fortune will be destroyed when his luck changes. I also think a ruler will flourish if he adjusts his policies as the character of the times changes; and similarly, a ruler will fail if he follows policies that do not correspond to the needs of the times. For we see men, in those activities that carry them towards the goal they all share, which is the acquisition of glory and riches, proceed differently. One acts with caution, while another is headstrong; one is violent, while another relies on skill; one is patient, while another is the opposite: And any one of them, despite the differences in their methods, may achieve his objective. One also sees that of two cautious men, one will succeed, and the other not; and similarly we see that two men can be equally successful though quite different in their behavior, one of them being cautious and the other headstrong. This happens solely because of the character of the times, which either suits or is at odds with their way of proceeding. This is the cause of what I have described: that two men, behaving differently, achieve the same result, and of two other men, who behave in the same way, one will attain his objective and the other will not. This is also the cause of the fact that the sort of behavior that is successful changes from one time to another. Take someone who acts cautiously and patiently. If the times and circumstances develop in such a way that his behavior is appropriate, he will flourish; but if the times and circumstances change, he will be destroyed for he will continue to behave in the same way. One cannot find a man so prudent he knows how to adapt himself to changing circumstances, for he will either be unable to deviate from that style of behavior to which his character inclines him, or, alternatively, having always been successful by adopting one particular style, he will be unable to persuade himself that it is time to change. And so, the cautious man, when it is time to be headstrong, does not know how to act and is destroyed. But, if one knew how to change one's character as times and circumstances change, one's luck would never change.

Pope Julius II always acted impetuously; the style of action was so appropriate to the times and circumstances in which he found himself that the outcome was always successful. Consider his first attack on Bologna, when Mr. Giovanni Bentivoglio was still alive. The Venetians were not happy about it; nor was the King of Spain; he had discussed such an action with the French, who had reached no decision. Nevertheless, because he was ferocious and impetuous, he placed himself personally at the head of his troops. This gesture made the Spanish and the Venetians hesitate and do nothing: the Venetians out of fear, and the Spanish because they wanted to recover the territories they had lost from the Kingdom of Naples. On the other hand, he dragged the King of France along behind him. For the king saw it was too late to turn back, and he wanted an alliance with him in order to weaken the Venetians, so he concluded he could not deny him the support of French troops without giving him obvious grounds for resentment. So Julius, by acting impetuously, achieved something no other pope, no matter how skillful and prudent, had been able to achieve. For, if he had delayed his departure from Rome until everything had been arranged and the necessary alliances had been cemented, as any other pope would have done, he would never have succeeded. The King of France would have found a thousand excuses, and his other allies would have pointed out a thousand dangers. I want to leave aside his other actions, for they were all similar, and they were all successful. He did not live long enough to experience failure. But, if the times had changed so that it was necessary to proceed with caution, he would have been destroyed. He would never have been able to change the style of behavior to which his character inclined him.

I conclude, then, that since fortune changes, and men stubbornly continue to behave in the same way, men flourish when their behavior suits the times and fail when they are out of step. I do think, however, that it is better to be headstrong than cautious, for fortune is a lady. It is necessary, if you want to master her, to beat and strike her. And one sees she more often submits to those who act boldly than to those who proceed in a calculating fashion. Moreover, since she is a lady, she smiles on the young, for they are less cautious, more ruthless, and overcome her with their boldness.

Chapter Twenty-Six: Exhortation to seize Italy and free her from the barbarians.

Having considered all the matters we have discussed, I ask myself whether, in Italy now, we are living through times suitable for the triumph of a new ruler, and if there is an opportunity for a prudent and bold [*virtuoso*] man to take control of events and win honor for himself while benefiting everyone who lives here. It seems to me so many factors come together at the moment to help out a new ruler that I am not sure if there has ever been a more propitious time for such a man. If, as I said, Moses could only demonstrate his greatness [*virtù*] because the people of Israel were slaves in Egypt; if we would never have known what a great man Cyrus was if the Persians had not been oppressed by the Medes; if the remarkable qualities of Theseus only became apparent because the Athenians were scattered abroad; so now, the opportunity is there for some bold Italian to demonstrate his greatness [*virtù*]. For see the conditions to which Italy has been reduced: She is more enslaved than the Jews, more oppressed than the Persians, more defenseless than the Athenians. She has no leader, no organization. She is beaten, robbed, wounded, put to flight: She has experienced every sort of injury. Although so far there has been the occasional hint of exceptional qualities in someone, so that one might think he had been ordained by God to redeem Italy, yet later events have shown, as his career progressed, that he was rejected by fortune. So Italy has remained at death's door, waiting for someone who could bind her wounds and put an end to the sack of Lombardy, to the extortion of Tuscany and of the Kingdom of Naples, someone who could heal her sores which long ago became infected. One can see how she prays to God that he will send her someone who will redeem her from this ill treatment and from the insults of the barbarians. One can see every Italian is ready, everyone is eager to rally to the colors, if only someone will raise them high.

At the moment, there is nowhere Italy can turn in her search for someone to redeem her with more chance of success than to your own illustrious family, which is fortunate and resourceful [*virtù*], is favored by God and by the church (indeed the church is now at its command). The undertaking is straightforward, if you keep in mind the lives and the deeds of the leaders I have mentioned. Of course those men were exceptional and marvelous; but, nevertheless, they were only men, and none of them had as good an opportunity as you have at the moment. For their undertakings were not more just than this one, or easier, nor was God more their ally than he is yours. This is truly just: "A war is just if there is no alternative, and the resort to arms is legitimate if they represent your only hope." These circumstances are ideal; and when circumstances are ideal there can be no great difficulty in achieving success, provided your family copies the policies of those I have recommended as your models. Beyond that, we have already seen extraordinary and unparalleled events. God has already shown his hand: The sea has been divided; a cloud has escorted you on your journey; water has flowed out of the rock; manna has fallen from on high. Everything has conspired to make you great. The rest you must do for yourselves. God does not want to have to do the whole thing, for he likes to leave us our free will so we can lay claim to part of the glory by earning it.

There is no need to be surprised that none of the Italian rulers I have discussed has been able to accomplish what I believe your family can achieve, or to be disheartened if during all the wars that have been fought, all the political upheavals that have taken place, it has seemed as if the Italians have completely lost their capacity to fight and win [*la virtù militare*]. This is simply because the traditional way of doing things in Italy is mistaken, and no one has appeared who has known how to bring about change. Nothing does more to establish the reputation of someone who comes new to power than do the new laws and the new institutions he establishes. These, when they are well thought out and noble in spirit, make a ruler revered and admired. In Italy we have the raw materi-

als: You can do anything you wish with them. Here we have people capable of anything [*virtù grande*], all they need are leaders who know what to do. When it comes to fighting one-on-one the Italians prove themselves to be stronger, quicker, cleverer. But when it comes to the clash of armies, the Italians are hopeless. The cause lies in the inadequacy of the leaders. Those who know what to do are not obeyed, and everyone thinks he knows what to do. So far there has been no one who has known how to establish an authority, based on fortune and ability [*virtù*], such that the others will obey him. This is the reason why, through the whole of the last twenty years, during all the wars that have taken place in that time, not a single army consisting solely of Italians has done well. Twenty years ago the Italians were defeated at Taro; since then at Alexandria, Capua, Genoa, Vailà, Bologna, Mestre.

So, if your illustrious family wants to follow in the footsteps of those excellent men who liberated the nations to which they belonged, you must, before you do anything else, do the one thing that is the precondition for success in any enterprise: Acquire your own troops. You cannot hope to have more faithful, more reliable, or more skillful soldiers. And if each soldier will be good, the army as a whole will be better still, once they see their ruler place himself at their head and discover he treats them with respect and sympathy. It is necessary, though, to get such an army ready, if we are to be able to defend Italy from the foreigners with Italian strength and skill [*con la virtù italica*].

It is true that the Swiss and Spanish infantries are thought to be intimidating; nevertheless, they both have their defects, so a third force could not only stand up to them, but could be confident of beating them. For the Spanish cannot withstand a cavalry charge; and the Swiss have reason to be afraid of infantry, should they come up against any as determined to win as they are. Thus, we have seen that the Spanish cannot withstand an attack by the French cavalry, and we will see in practice that the Swiss can be destroyed by the Spanish infantry. It is true that we have yet to see the Spanish properly defeat the

Swiss, but we have seen an indication of what will happen at the Battle of Ravenna, when the Spanish infantry clashed against the German battalions, for the Germans rely on the same formation as the Swiss. There the Spanish, thanks to their agility and with the help of their bucklers, were able to get underneath the pikes of the Germans and were able to attack them in safety, without the Germans' having any defense. If the cavalry had not driven them off, they would have wiped them out. So, since we know the weakness of each of these infantries, we ought to be able to train a new force that will be able to withstand cavalry and will not be afraid of infantry. To accomplish this we need specially designed weapons and new battle formations. This is the sort of new undertaking that establishes the reputation and importance of a new ruler.

So you should not let this opportunity slip by. Italy, so long enslaved, awaits her redeemer. There are no words to describe with what devotion he would be received in all those regions that have suffered from foreign invasions which have flooded across the land. No words can describe the appetite for revenge, the resolute determination, the spirit of self-sacrifice, the tears of emotion that would greet him. What gates would be closed to him? What community would refuse to obey him? Who would dare be jealous of his success? What Italian would refuse to pledge him allegiance? Everyone is sick of being pushed around by the barbarians. Your family must commit itself to this enterprise. Do it with the confidence and hope with which people embark on a just cause so that, marching behind your banner, the whole nation is ennobled. Under your patronage, may we prove Petrarch right:

Virtue [*virtù*] will take up arms against savagery,
And the battle will be short.
For the courage of old is not yet dead
In Italian hearts.

MACHIAVELLI
Discourses

Niccolò Machiavelli to Zanobi Buondelmonti and Cosimo Rucellai, Greetings

I send you a present which, if it does not measure up to the obligations I have to you, is unquestionably the most valuable thing Niccolò Machiavelli could send you. For in it I have put in words all that I know and all I have learned from an extensive experience of the affairs of the world and endless reading about them. Neither you nor anybody else could ask more of me, so you have no reason to complain if this is all I have given you. Of course you may regret my inadequate intelligence when you find my discussions inadequate, and my poor judgment when, as I often do, I present a mistaken argument. In the circumstances, I am not sure which of us has least reason to be obliged to the other: I to you, who forced me to write a work which I, left to myself, would never have written, or you to me, if, in writing, I have not given you satisfaction. So accept this gift as we accept all gifts from friends, for then we always give more weight to the intention that lies behind the gift than to the quality of the gift itself.

And please believe that my manuscript gives me only one satisfaction, which is when I think that, even if I have been mistaken in many particular matters I discuss, I know that I have not made a mistake in at least one thing: in having chosen you, to whom above all others my *Discourses* are addressed. I feel that in so doing I have expressed some gratitude for the benefits I have received from you. Moreover, I have avoided adopting the normal practice of authors, for they nearly always dedicate their books to some ruler, and, blinded by ambition and avarice, they praise

[Reprinted from *Selected Political Writings*, translated by David Wootton (Indianapolis: Hackett Publishing Company, 1994), by permission of the publisher.]

him as if he had all possible virtuous [*virtuose*] qualities, when they ought to criticize him for having every despicable characteristic. So I, in order to avoid falling into this mistake, have chosen, not princes, but people whose innumerable fine qualities make them worthy to be princes. I have chosen, not rulers who can reward me with titles, honors, and wealth, but private citizens who would reward me if they could. If you want to make sound judgments, you should admire those who are generous in spirit, not those who have the resources to be generous, respect those who know how to rule, not those who have no idea of how to rule, but are in power. Writers praise Hiero of Syracuse more when they describe him while he was still a private citizen than Perseus of Macedon while he was king, for Hiero was fit to be king, even if he had no kingdom, while Perseus had none of the attributes of a true ruler other than a kingdom.

So enjoy this book if you can. You are responsible for what is good in it, and for what is bad. If your judgment is so poor that you continue to enjoy reading me, then I will not fail to complete my commentary on Livy, as I originally promised you I would. Farewell.

BOOK ONE

Preface

Men are by nature envious. It has always been as dangerous to propose new ways of thinking and new institutions as it is to seek unknown oceans and undiscovered continents. People are much quicker to criticize than to praise what others have done. Nevertheless, spurred on by an instinctive desire I have always had to do those things that I believe will further the common good and benefit everybody, I have refused

to be intimidated. I have resolved to set out on a road
no one has travelled before me. My journey may be
tiresome and difficult, but I can hope it will prove
rewarding, at least if people are willing to judge sym-
pathetically the purpose of my labors. If my limited
intelligence, my lack of experience of contemporary
politics, and my inadequate knowledge of classical
history will make my efforts defective and of very
limited use to others, I will at least be pointing out
the way to someone with greater ability [*virtù*], more
analytical skill, and better judgment, someone who
will be capable of achieving what I have aimed at.
Perhaps no one will praise my efforts; in any event,
I do not deserve to be reproached.

Think of the respect in which we hold antiquity.
Often, to take just one example, a single fragment
of an antique statue will be purchased at enormous
expense by someone who wants to look at it every
day. He will give it a place of honor in his house and
allow those who aspire to be sculptors to copy it. The
sculptors then make every effort to do work comparable to it. Think, on the other hand, of the immensely
skillful [*virtuosissime*] deeds the history books record
for us, deeds done by ancient kingdoms and classical
republics, by kings, generals, citizens, legislators, and
others who have worn themselves out for their homelands. These deeds may be admired, but they are
scarcely imitated. Indeed, everybody goes to great
lengths to avoid copying them, even if it only concerns
an insignificant detail. The result is not a trace of the
classical military and political skills [*quella antiqua
virtù*] survives. I cannot help but be both astonished
and dismayed by this. Especially when I notice that
when citizens find themselves caught up in legal
disagreements, or when they fall ill, they always appeal to the legal decisions of the ancients, they always
follow the medical remedies prescribed by them. For
the civil laws are nothing other than decisions handed
down by classical jurists, decisions that have been
codified, and are now taught to lawyers by our own
jurists. Similarly, medicine is simply the experience of
classical doctors, on the basis of which contemporary
doctors make their decisions. Nevertheless, in organizing republics, in administering states, in ruling kingdoms, in training armies and fighting wars, in passing

judgment on subjects, and in planning new conquests, when it comes to all these activities, one does
not find a single ruler or republic who tries to learn
from the ancients.

I do not believe the cause of this is the feebleness
contemporary religion has instilled in the world, nor
the evil consequences that a supercilious indolence
has had for many Christian countries and cities. The
real problem is people do not properly understand
the history books. When they read them they do not
get out of them the meaning that is in them. They
chew on them but do not taste them. The result is
countless people read them and enjoy discovering in
them the great variety of events they record, but never
think of imitating them, presuming it would not be
just difficult but would be simply impossible to do
as the ancients did. As if the heavens, the sun, the
elements, human beings had changed in their movement, organization, and capacities, and were quite
different from what they were in days gone by. My
intent has been to rescue men from this mistake, so
I have decided I must write about all the books of
Livy's history that have survived the ravages of time,
explaining whatever I think is important if one is to
understand them. In doing so, I will draw on my
knowledge of ancient and modern affairs. My hope
is that those who read my comments will be able
without difficulty to draw from them those practical
benefits one ought to expect to gain from the study
of history. Although my undertaking is a difficult one,
nevertheless, helped by those who have encouraged
me to embark on this enterprise, I believe I will have
so much success that anyone coming after me will
only have a little to do before he completes my task.

Chapter One: On the universal origins of any city whatever, and on how Rome began.

Those who read how the city of Rome began, who
established its laws, and how it was organized will
not marvel that so much excellence [*virtù*] was preserved in that city for so many centuries; and that later
it gave birth to the vast empire the Roman republic
eventually controlled. Since I want to talk first about

its birth, I will start by saying all cities are constructed either by men born in the place where the city is built or by foreigners. In the first case, the inhabitants decide to build a city because they have been spread out in many tiny settlements in which they have not felt secure, for each settlement on its own, because of its location and because of the small number of its inhabitants, is incapable of resisting the assaults of an attacker. Nor are they in a position to assemble in joint defense when they see the enemy coming, either because it takes too long, or because, even if they could assemble in time, they would be obliged to abandon many of their settlements and would soon see them plundered by their enemies. So, to avoid these dangers, urged on either by their own individual judgments or by some one member of their group who has greater influence among them, they gather together to live in a single place they have chosen, one that will be more convenient to live in, and that will be easier to defend.

Athens and Venice are among the many cities that originated in this way. Athens, under the leadership of Theseus, was constructed by scattered inhabitants for the sort of reasons I have outlined. Venice was established by numerous little groups who had taken refuge on certain tiny islands at the end of the Adriatic sea. They were trying to escape the wars that continually broke out in Italy in the period following the collapse of the Roman empire as a result of the arrival of new groups of barbarians. They organized themselves, without there being any one individual in overall control, to live according to those laws that were, in their view, most conducive to their preservation. Their enterprise was a success because of the lengthy period of peace the site they had chosen ensured for them, for their lagoon was impenetrable, and the tribes who were invading Italy had no ships with which to attack them. So, from the most humble beginnings, they were able to rise to the eminent position they now occupy.

The second case, when foreigners come and build a city, takes two forms, depending on whether the immigrants are free men or men who owe allegiance to others. In the latter case a republic or a ruler may send out colonists in order to reduce the pressure of population in their existing settlements; or because they have recently conquered new territory and want to defend it effectively and inexpensively (the Romans built many such cities throughout their empire); or such a city may be built by a ruler who does not intend to live there, but to immortalize himself through it, as Alexander did by building Alexandria. Because such cities do not start out free, it rarely happens that they make great strides and come to be regarded as the capital cities of their own countries. It is in this category that we should place the construction of Florence, for (no matter whether it was built by Sulla's soldiers or by the inhabitants of the hilltops of Fiesole, who, given confidence by the long peace that the whole world benefited from under Augustus, came down to live in the plain of the Arno) it was built under Roman rule, nor could it, at the beginning, control any territory beyond what was assigned it at the pleasure of the emperor.

Cities are built by free men when a group of people, either under the command of a ruler or acting on their own, are forced to abandon the land of their birth and to seek new territory because of disease, or hunger, or war. They may occupy the cities that already exist in the territory they conquer, as Moses did, or they may build from scratch, as Aeneas did. It is in this latter case that one can fully appreciate the skill [*virtù*] of the architect as it is reflected in the fate of his city, for the history of the city will be more or less marvelous depending on whether its first founder is more or less skillful [*virtuoso*]. The skill [*virtù*] of the founder can be judged by two things: firstly, by his choice of a site for the construction of the new city; secondly, by the laws he draws up for it.

Men act either out of necessity or free choice. Since it seems that men are the most admirable [*maggior virtù*] where they have the least freedom of choice, one must consider whether it might not be better to choose an infertile region for the construction of a city so that its inhabitants will be forced to be industrious and prevented from being self-indulgent, and so that they will be more united, having less occasion for conflict because of the poverty of their land. We can see this happened at Ragusa, and in many other cities built in similar locations. Such a choice of location would be without doubt wiser and would lead to the best outcome, if men were content to live off their own possessions and did not want to try to get control of the property of others. But since men can only secure themselves by building up power, one must avoid building a city in a barren location, but rather settle the most fertile land, whose fecundity will make possible growth, so one will be able both to defend oneself against attackers and to defeat anyone who stands in the way of one's own power. In order to ensure the location does not lead to self-indulgence, one must design the laws to force people to do what the location does not force them to do. Thus, one should imitate those wise men who have lived in countries that have been delightful and fertile, countries apt to produce lazy men who are incapable of any manly [virtuoso] work. In order to avoid the disadvantages that would result from the delightfulness of the land if it caused self-indulgence, they required all those who were liable to military service to drill, so that by means of such regulations their inhabitants became better soldiers than those living in territory that is naturally harsh and infertile. The Kingdom of Egypt is an example of this: Despite the fact that the country is exceptionally fertile, the artificial necessity imposed by the laws was so effective that Egypt produced the finest men; and if their names had not been lost in antiquity, we would be able to see they deserved more praise than Alexander the Great and many others whose deeds remain fresh in our memory. And if you had examined the state of the sultan, with its regiments of Mamelukes and its Turkish militia, before they were abolished by the Sultan Selim, you would have seen there much drilling of soldiers and would have learned how much the Turks feared the self-indulgence the generosity of their country might induce in them, had they not introduced strict legal penalties to prevent it.

So I conclude it is wiser to choose to settle in a fertile place, provided the consequences of that fertility are kept within due limits by legislation. Deinocrates the architect came to Alexander the Great when Alexander wanted to build a city to magnify his own reputation. He showed him how he could build on Mount Athos: The site, apart from being easily defended,

could be cut away so the new city would have the shape of a human body, which would be a remarkable and extraordinary thing and worthy of Alexander's greatness. But when Alexander asked him what the inhabitants of the city would live on he replied he had not given the matter any thought. Alexander laughed, and, leaving Mount Athos intact, built Alexandria in a place where people would want to settle because of the fecundity of the countryside and the ease of access to the sea and to the Nile.

Let us now consider the construction of Rome. If you take it that Aeneas was its first founder, you will think of it as one of the cities built by foreigners. If you believe it was founded by Romulus, you will think of it as founded by men born in the vicinity. Either way you will agree it was founded in freedom and was not under any outsider's authority. You will also recognize — we will return to this subject later — the extent to which the laws established by Romulus, Numa, and the other early legislators imposed an artificial necessity upon the inhabitants, so the fertility of the site, the ease of access to the sea, the frequent victories of their armies, and the extensive territory that fell under Roman control could not corrupt them even over the course of many centuries. Their laws ensured they had more admirable qualities [virtù] than any other city or republic has ever been able to boast of in its citizens.

The deeds of the Romans that are celebrated in Livy's history occurred either as a result of public or of private decisions and either inside or outside the city. I will begin by discussing those things that happened inside the city and as a result of public decision-making, that I take to be worthy of more detailed discussion, and we will need to explore all the consequences that flowed from them. This first book, or at least this first part, will be taken up with a discussion of these matters.

Chapter Two: On the different types of republic that exist, and on how to categorize the Roman republic.

I want to leave aside any discussion of those cities that were under the authority of outsiders from the beginning, and to discuss only those that began completely free of external domination and were ruled by their own wills from the beginning, whether as republics or as princedoms. These cities, since they began in a variety of ways, have had a variety of constitutions and legal systems. In some, either at the very beginning or soon after their foundation, a single individual wrote all the laws at once — Lycurgus, for example, gave the Spartans their laws — while others acquired their laws by chance, little by little, according to the circumstances, as happened in Rome. We can call fortunate any republic in which there appears a leader so prudent he is able to give them a code of law they have no need to revise, but under which they can live securely. We know the Spartans obeyed the laws of Lycurgus for eight hundred years without corrupting them and without any serious internal conflict. On the other hand, we can call in some degree unfortunate any city that does not chance upon a prudent lawmaker, and is obliged to revise its laws for itself. And among these cities, moreover, those are most unfortunate that are furthest from having the right laws; and those are furthest astray whose constitution is quite unlike the one that would lead them to their true and ideal goal. For it is almost impossible for a city that finds itself in this situation to have enough good luck to be able to sort itself out. Those others that, if they do not have a perfect constitution, yet have started out in the right direction and are in a position to improve, can, as opportunity presents itself, become perfect. But this is certainly true: One never establishes a constitution without encountering danger. For enough men will never agree to a new law that changes the constitution of the city unless they are persuaded it is essential to pass it, and they will only be persuaded of this if they see themselves to be in danger, so it can easily happen that the republic is destroyed before she arrives at a perfect constitution. The republic of Florence is a good example of this: Defeat in the Battle of Arezzo led to her reorganization; defeat in the Battle of Prato in 1512 led to her dissolution.

I want now to discuss the constitution of Rome and the events that made it possible for her to achieve perfection. Some who have written about constitutions say they are of three types, which they call "monarchy," "aristocracy," and "democracy." They say anyone drawing up the constitution of a city must choose from these the one he thinks most appropriate. Others, who are widely thought to be wiser, say there are six types of constitution, of which three are inherently bad and three are inherently good, although even the good ones are so easily corrupted they, too, can quickly become pernicious. The good ones are the three I have already mentioned; the bad ones are three others that derive from these three, and each of which is so like the good constitution it most resembles that it is easy for one to turn into the other. Thus, monarchies easily become tyrannies, aristocracies become oligarchies, and democracies slide into anarchy. The result is that if a lawmaker establishes a constitution for a city that corresponds to one of the three good forms of government it will not last long, for no precaution is sufficient to ensure it will not slip into its opposite, for the good [*la virtute*] and the bad are, when it comes to constitutions, closely related.

These different types of government developed among men by accident. When the world began, it had few inhabitants, and they lived for a while apart from one another as the animals do. As their numbers multiplied they gathered together, and in order to be better able to defend themselves, they began to defer to one among their number who was stronger and braver than the rest. They made him, as it were, their leader and obeyed him. This was the origin of knowledge of those things that are good and honest as opposed to those that are pernicious and evil. For men saw that, if someone harmed his benefactor, his associates despised him and felt compassion for his victim. They learned to think ill of the ungrateful and to approve of those who were grateful. They came to realize the injuries that were done to someone else could equally be done to themselves. In order to avoid such evils, they gathered together to make laws and to lay down punishments for those who broke them: This was the invention of justice. Thereafter, when they had to choose a ruler, they no longer obeyed the strongest, but he who was most prudent and most just.

Later, however, they began to appoint their ruler by hereditary succession, not by election, with the immediate result that power was inherited by men who were inferior to their ancestors. They no longer acted virtuously [*lasciando l'opere virtuose*], but thought rulers were simply there to outdo other men in extravagance, lasciviousness, and in every other type of vice. The result was that rulers began to be hated, and, because they were hated, to be afraid. Because they were afraid, they went on the attack, and before long kings had become tyrants. These rulers faced the possibility of being destroyed. The conspiracies and plots hatched against them were not begun by those who were fearful or weak, but by those who surpassed their fellows in generosity, spiritedness, wealth, and nobility, for such men could no longer tolerate the dishonorable lives of their rulers. The masses then followed the lead provided by the elite and armed themselves against their ruler, and, when they had got rid of him, obeyed the elite as their liberators. The new rulers hated the idea of one-man rule and, so, established themselves collectively in power.

At first, remembering the evils of tyranny, they governed according to the laws they had established, putting their own interests second and the public good first. They directed and protected both public and private matters with great care. In due course, this government was inherited by their sons, who had never seen power change hands, had never suffered under evil government, and who were unwilling to continue treating their fellow subjects as their equals. They gave themselves over to avarice, to ambition, to chasing other men's wives. So aristocracy degenerated into an oligarchy in which the norms of civilized life were flouted. In a short time, the oligarchs suffered the same fate as the tyrants, for the masses became fed up with their government and gave their support to anyone who was planning any sort of resistance to their rule. Soon someone, with the assistance of the masses, was able to destroy them. Since they could still clearly remember one-man rule, and the harm it had done them, when they destroyed oligarchy they had no desire to restore monarchy, but instead established popular rule. This they organized in such a manner that neither the elite nor a powerful individual could have any influence whatsoever.

In the beginning, all states can command a certain amount of respect, so popular government survived for a while, but not for long, especially once the generation that had established it had passed away. It quickly degenerated into anarchy, in which neither private individuals nor public officials could command any respect. Each person did as he chose, with the result that every day innumerable crimes were committed. So, compelled by necessity, or advised by some good man, or desperate to escape from anarchy, they established once more the rule of one man. And from monarchy, step by step, they degenerated once again into anarchy, repeating the sequence I have already described.

This is the cycle through which all states revolve, and power is still passed, as it always has been, from hand to hand. But it rarely happens that the same people return to power, for scarcely a single state has survived long enough to travel several times through this cycle without being destroyed. Usually, while a state is torn apart by internal dissent, and as a result is weakened and deprived of good leadership, it is conquered by a neighboring state better organized than it is. But if this did not happen, then a state could repeat this cycle of constitutions over and over again.

I conclude all these forms of government are pestilential: The three good ones do not last long, and the three bad ones are evil. Those who know how to construct constitutions wisely have identified this problem and have avoided each one of these types of constitution in its pure form, constructing a constitution with elements of each. They have been convinced such a constitution would be more solid and stable, would be preserved by checks and balances, there being present in the one city a monarch, an aristocracy, and a democracy.

Lycurgus is the most admirable of those who have established constitutions of this sort. He constructed the constitution of Sparta so that it gave distinct roles to king, aristocracy, and people, with the result the state survived for eight hundred years, throughout which time his name was revered and the city lived in harmony. Matters turned out differently for Solon, who drew up the constitution of Athens. Because he constructed a democracy, it survived such a short time that before Solon died he saw Athens under the tyranny of Pisistratus. Although forty years later Pisistratus's heirs were driven into exile and freedom was restored, because the Athenians re-established the democratic constitution drawn up by Solon, their freedom lasted no more than a century, despite the fact that in order to preserve it they introduced numerous reforms Solon had not considered. They did their best to control the insolence of the powerful and the license of the masses. Nevertheless, because they did not allow a proper role for one-man rule and for aristocracy, Athens survived, by comparison with Sparta, a very short time.

Let us turn to Rome. Even though Rome did not have a Lycurgus to establish from the beginning a constitution that would enable her to live free for centuries, nevertheless, she underwent so many political crises, because of the conflicts between the people and the senate, that chance eventually brought about something no legislator had been able to accomplish. For if Rome did not have the first type of good fortune, she had the second, and although her first constitution was defective, nevertheless, it did not cause her to turn off the right path that could lead her to perfection.

Romulus and all the other kings of Rome made many excellent laws, ones appropriate for a free state. But their goal was the establishment of a kingdom, not a republic, so when Rome became free she lacked many of the laws free government required, for these they had omitted to decree. And although the kings of Rome lost their power for the reasons and in the way I have outlined, nevertheless, those who threw them out quickly established two consuls who played the same role as the kings, so that they expelled from Rome the name of king but not the authority of kingship. The new republic was ruled by the consuls and the senate, so it was a mixture of only two of the three types of power I have described: of monarchy and aristocracy. It failed to give any authority to the populace.

When the Roman nobility became overbearing, for reasons I will explain later, the people rose up against them, with the result that, in order not to lose all power, the nobles were obliged to concede a share of power to the people. On the other hand, the consuls and the senate retained enough authority to be able to hold on to a share of power in the republic. So the tribunes of the people came to be established, after which the constitution of the republic became more stable, for now all three types of authority had a fair share in power. And fortune was so favorable to Rome that, although she passed from monarchy, to aristocracy, to democracy, going through each of the stages I have described for the reasons I have outlined, nevertheless, the aristocracy never seized all power from the monarchical element; nor did the people ever seize all power from the aristocracy; instead, power was added to power, and the mixture that resulted made for a perfect republic. Rome achieved this perfection because of the conflict between senate and people, as I will show at length in the next two chapters.

Chapter Four: On the tensions between the populace and the Roman senate, which made that republic free and powerful.

It would be wrong not to discuss those popular disorders that occurred in Rome between the death of the Tarquins and the creation of the tribunes. Afterwards, I will say a few things in reply to the many people who say Rome was a disorderly republic, one full of so much confusion that if good luck and military discipline [*virtù militare*] had not made up for its defects, it would have been inferior to every other republic. I cannot deny good luck and the army were causes of Rome's imperial greatness, though it seems to me these people do not realize that where there is a good army there must be a good constitution, and one will nearly always find a good army can make its own good luck.

But let us turn to the other particular characteristics of that city. I maintain those who criticize the clashes between the nobility and the populace attack what was, I would argue, the primary factor making for Rome's continuing freedom. They pay more attention to the shouts and cries that rise from such conflicts than to the good effects that derive from them. They do not take into account the fact that there are two distinct viewpoints in every republic: that of the populace and that of the elite. All the laws made in order to foster liberty result from the tensions between them, as one can easily see was the case in the history of Rome. For from Tarquin to the Gracchi, a period of more than three hundred years, the conflicts that broke out in Rome rarely resulted in men's being sent into exile, and even more rarely led to bloodshed. One cannot judge these conflicts as harmful, or the republic as divided, when over such a long period of time the differences between the parties led to no more than eight or ten citizens' being sent into exile, to a tiny number's being murdered, and indeed to only a few's being fined. Nor can there be any good grounds for calling a republic disorderly when it contains so many examples of individual excellence [virtù], for good individuals cannot exist without good education, and good education cannot exist without good laws, and good laws were the result of those very conflicts many people unthinkingly criticize. Anyone who scrutinizes the outcome of these conflicts will find they never led to exiles or murders that were contrary to the public good but always led to laws and institutions that favored public liberty.

And if someone were to argue the methods employed were extralegal and almost bestial — the people in a mob shouting abuse at the senate, the senate replying in kind, mobs running through the streets, shops boarded up, the entire populace of Rome leaving the city — I would reply such things only frighten those who read about them. Every city ought to have practices that enable the populace to give expression to its aspirations, especially those cities that want to be able to rely on the populace at times of crisis. The city of Rome had a number of practices of this kind. For example, when the populace wanted a law passed, either they demonstrated, as I have described, or they refused to enroll for military service, so that in order to pacify them it was necessary to give them at least part of what they wanted. The demands of a free people are rarely harmful to the cause of liberty, for they are a response either to oppression or to the prospect of oppression. When the populace is mistaken, then there is a remedy to hand in the open-air speech. Some sensible man has to get up and harangue them, showing them how they are wrong. The populace, as Cicero says, although they are ignorant, are capable of recognizing the truth, and it is easy for a man whom they have reason to respect to persuade them to change their mind by telling them the truth.

So people ought to be more sparing in their criticisms of the political system of Rome. If you consider all the good things the Romans achieved, you will have to admit the system that gave rise to such achievements must have been excellent. If popular demonstrations resulted in the creation of the tribunate, they should be praised without reserve, for, beyond giving the populace a role in government, the tribunes were set up to be the guardians of Roman liberty, as the next chapter will show.

Chapter Five: On whether the protection of liberty is best entrusted to the populace or to the elite, and on whether those who want to acquire power or those who want to maintain it are most likely to riot.

Those who have understood how to establish a republic have recognized one of the most urgent tasks is that of identifying a group with an interest in protecting liberty. Depending on whether this task is entrusted to the right group or not, political liberty will be preserved for a longer or a shorter time. Because in every state there is an elite and a populace, the question has been raised as to which group it is best to entrust with the task of protecting liberty. The Spartans and, in modern days, the Venetians have relied on the nobles; but the Romans relied on the populace. So we must ask ourselves which of these republics made the better choice. If we argue from first principles, we will find something to say on either side; but if we look at what happened in practice, we will conclude the nobility are more reliable, for liberty in Sparta and Venice has been longer-lived than in Rome. Let us look at the principles involved and first consider the arguments in favor of Rome's policy.

It would seem one ought to entrust something to people who have no desire to steal it. Now there is no question that if one considers the objectives of the nobles and the non-nobles, one must admit the former are very keen to dominate, and the latter want only not to be dominated. Consequently, the populace have a greater desire to live as free men, having less prospect of seizing power for themselves than the elite has. So if you put the populace in charge of protecting liberty, it is reasonable to believe that they will do a better job, and since they cannot hope to monopolize power themselves, they will ensure nobody else does. On the other hand, if you are defending the Spartan and Venetian policy you will say those who entrust the protection of liberty to the powerful accomplish two good things. In the first place, you satisfy some of the nobility's aspirations, and, because they have a greater role in the state as a result of having this power in their hands, they are more likely to be content. In the second, you take away a measure of authority from the populace, who are restless and insatiable. It is the populace who are responsible for innumerable conflicts and clashes in a republic. Their behavior is likely to make the nobility desperate, which in the long run will have evil consequences. You will cite Rome herself as an example. Because the tribunes of the people could claim to be the guardians of liberty, they were not satisfied with ensuring one consul was chosen from among the populace, but insisted both should be. Next they wanted the censor, the praetor, and all the other officials of the city government to be plebeians. Even this was not enough, for, driven on by the same madness, they began in time to worship those men whom they thought were capable of defeating the nobility. The result was the rise of Marius and the ruin of Rome. And indeed, anyone who balanced one set of arguments against the other would have difficulty making up his mind as to which group he should choose as the guardians of liberty, for he would be unable to decide which human aspiration was more dangerous for a republic: defending a status that has already been acquired, or acquiring a status one does not yet have.

In the end, anyone who examines the pros and cons with care will reach the conclusion that you are either thinking in terms of a republic whose goal is to conquer an empire, as Rome's was, or of one that merely wants to defend itself. If the first, then you must do everything as the Romans did; if the second, then you can copy Venice and Sparta, for the reasons I have already given and for others we will come to in the next chapter.

But let us turn to a discussion of which men are more dangerous to a republic, those who want to acquire new power, or those anxious not to lose the power they have. Marcus Menenius was appointed dictator, and Marcus Fulvius general of the horse. Both of them were plebeians. Their mission was to uncover certain conspiracies against Rome that had been hatched in Capua. The populace also gave them authority to enquire whether there were people in Rome who, out of ambition, were scheming to use extralegal means to be elected to the consulate or to other prestigious offices. The nobility thought the dictator had been given this mandate so he could attack them, and so they spread the word around Rome that it was not the nobles who were driven by ambition to use extralegal means to acquire honors, but the non-nobles. Unable to rely on their own abilities [virtù] or their inherited status, it was they who sought to acquire honors by corrupt means. In particular, they attacked Menenius, the dictator. This charge was so damaging that Menenius, having made a speech in which he protested against the calumnies directed at him by the nobles, resigned the dictatorship, and submitted himself to the judgment of the people. When his case had been considered, he was found to be innocent.

In such cases, it is easy to disagree as to who was the more ambitious, those who wanted to hold on to power or those who wanted to acquire it. For either aspiration can easily be the cause of tremendous conflict. Nevertheless, for the most part such conflicts are caused by those who already have power, for the fear of losing it gives them exactly the same ambitions as those who want to acquire power. Men do not feel they are secure in the possession of their property unless they are constantly acquiring more from someone else. Moreover, those who already have power are in a better position to use their influence and their resources to bring about change. In addition, their improper and self-interested behavior excites in the hearts of the powerless the desire to have power, either in order to take their revenge on their enemies by taking what they have from them, or in order to acquire for themselves that wealth and those honors they see their opponents abusing.

Chapter Nine: On how it is necessary to act alone if you want to draw up the constitution for a new republic from scratch, or reform an old one by completely changing its established laws.

Perhaps some people will think that I have jumped too far ahead in the history of ancient Rome, for I have not yet said anything about the men who drew up the Roman constitution, nor have I discussed those laws that dealt with religion or with military service. Since I do not want to keep those who want to read something about these matters waiting any longer, let me say that many will probably think the founding of Rome presents a bad example, for Romulus, in order to establish constitutional government, first killed his brother and then agreed to the killing of Titus Tatius, the Sabine, who had been elected to share office with him. You might think that the citizens of a state founded in this manner could claim that they were only following the example of their ruler if they attacked those who opposed their wishes while they sought to acquire power and authority. You would be right to think this, so long as you did not stop to consider the reasons that had led him to commit murder.

One ought to recognize this as a general principle: It rarely (if ever) happens that a republic or a kingdom has good institutions from the beginning, or is completely reformed along lines quite different from those on which it was previously organized, unless one person has sole responsibility. So one person alone must decide on the strategy, and he must make all the key decisions. A wise legislator when establishing a republic, if he wants to serve not his own interests but the public good, not to benefit his own heirs but the nation as a whole, should make every effort to

ensure that all power lies in his own hands. A wise man will never criticize someone for an extralegal action undertaken to organize a kingdom or establish a republic. He will agree that if his deed accuses him, its consequences excuse him. When the consequences are good, as were the consequences of Romulus's act, then he will always be excused, for it is those who are violent in order to destroy who should be found guilty, not those who are violent in order to build anew.

A legislator should, however, use care and skill [*virtuoso*] to ensure that the power he has seized is not inherited by a successor; for, since men are more inclined to do evil than good, his successor is likely to use for selfish purposes the power he has been using for the public good. Moreover, one person alone may be best at drawing up plans, but the institutions he has designed will not survive long if they continue to depend on the decisions of one man. They will do better if many share the responsibilities, and if many are concerned to preserve them. For just as it is a bad idea to have many people plan something, for they will not agree about what is best, since there will be many differing opinions among them, so, too, when once they know what is right, they will not be able to agree to act contrary to it. Romulus deserved to be pardoned for the death of his brother and his colleague, for his actions were aimed at the public good and not at self-advancement. This is evident from the fact that he quickly established a senate to whose views he listened and whose advice he took. If you analyze the powers Romulus kept in his own hands, you will find that the only powers he kept were those of commanding the armies once war had been declared and of summoning the senate. This became apparent when Rome acquired freedom by driving out the Tarquins, for the Romans did not alter their established constitution at all, beyond replacing an hereditary monarch with two consuls elected annually. This shows that the original institutions of Rome were better adapted for a constitutional and participatory political system than for an absolute and tyrannical one.

There are an infinite number of examples that could be produced in support of what I have said in this chapter, such as Moses, Lycurgus, Solon, and other founders of monarchies and republics who could, because they had laid claim to a certain personal authority, establish laws aimed at the common good. But I want to leave these aside, as the point is obvious. Let me give only one additional example, not such a well-known one, but worth considering if one wants to establish a good constitution. Agis, King of Sparta, wanted to confine the Spartans within the limits that had been established for them by the laws of Lycurgus. He felt that his city, because it had in some measure deviated from its original constitution, had lost a good deal of its traditional excellence [*antica virtù*] and, with it, much of its strength and power. He had no sooner begun his reforms than he was assassinated by the Spartan ephors on the grounds that he was trying to establish a tyranny. But Cleomenes was appointed king to succeed him, and he developed the same aspirations, for he came across some memoranda and memoirs written by Agis. From them he learned the true opinions and intentions of his predecessor. He recognized that he could not do his country the service he intended if he did not concentrate all power in his own hands, for he thought that human beings were so self-interested that one could not do good to the majority if faced with the opposition of a powerful minority. So he seized on a suitable opportunity and had all the ephors and anyone else in a position to oppose him killed. Then he completely overhauled the laws of Lycurgus. This would probably have given Sparta a new lease on life and established for Cleomenes a reputation as great as that of Lycurgus, if the Macedonians had not been establishing their predominance, and if the other Greek cities had not been incapable of resisting them. For after Cleomenes' reforms, the Spartans were attacked by the Macedonians and discovered that, on their own, they were not strong enough to resist them. Their forces had nowhere to retreat and were defeated. So Cleomenes' plans, although wise and admirable, never came to fruition.

Having considered all these matters, I conclude that in order to establish the constitution of a republic one needs to have sole power; and that Romulus should be forgiven, not blamed, for the deaths of Remus and of Titus Tatius.

Chapter Ten: On how, just as the founders of a republic or a kingdom deserve praise, so the founders of a tyranny should be held in contempt.

Of all the types of men who are praised, it is the heads and founders of religions who are the most highly praised. After them come those who founded either republics or kingdoms. After them, the most famous are those who have commanded armies and have expanded either their own territory or that of their nation. To these we may add authors. These are of different types, and each is celebrated according to its ranking. All other men who are praiseworthy—and there are an infinite number of them—acquire a measure of reputation through their skill or craft. On the other hand, those who destroy religions, undermine kingdoms and republics, are hostile to excellence, to literature, and to all the arts and crafts that are useful or honorable to mankind, these men are infamous and detestable. These are the impious, the violent, the ignorant, the good-for-nothings, the lazy, the base. There never will be anybody so crazy or so wise, so devilish or so saintly, that, offered a choice between the two types of man, will not praise those who deserve to be praised and criticize those who deserve to be criticized. Nevertheless, almost all men, misled by a false idea of what is good and a false notion of what is praiseworthy, slip, either willfully or foolishly, into the ranks of those who deserve more blame than praise. Put in a position where they can win eternal praise by founding either a republic or a kingdom, they become tyrants and do not even realize how much reputation, glory, honor, security, peace of mind, and satisfaction of spirit they are giving up, and how much infamy, vituperation, criticism, danger, and unease they are going to incur.

It is impossible for a private citizen living in a republic, if he reads his history books and makes good use of the records of past events, not to want to live in his homeland as a Scipio rather than a Caesar. If by chance or skill [virtù] he becomes a ruler, he is bound to prefer being an Agesilaus, a Timoleon, a Dion, to being a Nabis, a Phalaris, or a Dionysius. For everyone can see that the latter are held in complete contempt, while the former are immoderately praised. They also see that Timoleon and the others had no less authority in their countries than Dionysius and Phalaris had in theirs, but they had a great deal more security.

There is nobody who is taken in by the glory of Caesar, even when they see him praised in the highest terms by those who write about him; for those who praise him have been corrupted by his success and frightened by the long endurance of the Roman empire. Since the rulers of that empire continued to call themselves Caesars, writers could not discuss Caesar freely. But if you want to know what writers would say about him if they were free to speak their minds, look at what they say about Catiline. Caesar is more to be censured than Catiline; just as he who does evil is more blameworthy than he who merely tries to do it. Look, too, at the praise with which authors refer to Brutus. Afraid to criticize Caesar because of his power, they acclaim his enemy.

If you become an absolute ruler in a republic you should also consider how much more praise, once Rome was ruled by emperors, was awarded to those emperors who abided by the laws and were benevolent than to those who were the opposite. Note that Titus, Nerva, Trajan, Hadrian, Antoninus, and Marcus had no need of praetorian guards or of multitudes of legions to defend themselves, because their own way of life, the good will of the populace, and the love of the senate served to defend them. On the other hand, the entire armies of the eastern and western empires were not large enough to protect Caligula, Nero, Vitellius, and many other wicked rulers against the enemies they had acquired by their foul practices and evil lives. Any ruler who gives due consideration to the history of these emperors will be taught clearly enough which is the way to acquire glory, and which the way to deserve censure; what to do in order to be safe, and what to do to live a life of fear.

Of the first twenty-six emperors, from Caesar to Maximinus, sixteen were assassinated, and ten died of natural causes. It is true that among those who were killed the odd good ruler is to be found, Galba for example, or Pertinax, but their deaths were the result of the corruption among the soldiers they had inherited from their predecessors. Among those who died of natural causes the occasional wicked ruler is to be found—Severus, for example—but these were men of extraordinary good fortune and skill [virtù]: Few men can count on both of these. He will also learn by reading the history of Rome how one should organize a good kingdom, for all the emperors who inherited power, with the exception of Titus, were wicked; those who were appointed to succeed without being blood relatives were all good, for example the five emperors from Nerva to Marcus. When power fell once more into the hands of hereditary rulers, the empire declined once again.

Let our ruler consider the period of time that runs from Nerva to Marcus and compare those rulers with those who went before and those who came after; then let us ask him when he would rather have been born, and over which type of state he would rather rule. When the empire was governed by good men, he will find rulers lived in security, surrounded by their citizens who had nothing to fear, and he will find that the world was peaceable and that justice prevailed. He will see that the senate had its due authority, the magistrates their honors, that the rich citizens were able to enjoy their wealth, and that nobility and virtue [virtù] were admired. Everything was peaceable, and all was right with the world. Rancor, license, corruption, and ambition, for their part, were nowhere to be found. These were golden times, when everyone could hold and defend whatever view he wished. In short, everybody benefited: The prince was treated with reverence and esteem, the people were loving and secure. If he then looks carefully at the periods before and after this one, he will find them horrifying because of the frequent wars, unstable because of the frequent seditions, and full of cruelty during both peace and war. Everywhere he looks he will see rulers murdered, civil wars, international conflicts. He will see Italy afflicted and full of unprecedented misfortunes, her cities ruined and sacked. He will see Rome burned, the Capitol destroyed by her own citizens, the ancient temples desolate, religious ceremonies corrupted, the cities full of adultery. On the seas, ships carry men into exile; the rocks on the shores are stained with blood. In Rome itself innumerable atrocities occur; breeding, wealth, previous honors, and above all virtue [*virtù*] are thought to be capital offenses. Slanderers are rewarded, slaves are bribed to turn against their masters, servants against their employers. Those who are not overwhelmed by their enemies find their own friends will do them down. Then he will really know just how much Rome, Italy, and the whole world owe to Caesar.

Doubtless, if he has blood in his veins, he will be appalled at the thought of imitating the evil times and will burn with an immense desire to copy the good. Truly, if a ruler wants to acquire worldly glory, he ought to want to rule over a corrupt city, not in order to destroy it completely, as Caesar destroyed Rome, but to re-establish it, as Romulus did. In truth, the heavens cannot offer a man a greater opportunity to win glory, nor can men desire any reputation more than this one. If, in order to establish a good constitution for a city, there were no alternative to giving up power, then there would be some excuse for anyone who, in order to hold on to power, failed to introduce a good constitution. But since one can introduce a good constitution and still retain power, there is no excuse for such people at all. So those to whom heaven gives such an opportunity should recognize that they stand at a crossroads: One path leads to security in this life and to glory after death; the other leads to continuous anxiety in this life and to perpetual infamy after death.

Chapter Eleven: On the religion of the Romans.

Rome's first founder was Romulus, and she owed her birth and education to him, as a child is indebted to its father. Nevertheless, fate took the view that the institutions established by Romulus were not ade-

quate for the vast empire that Rome was to have; so it inspired the Roman senate to appoint Numa Pompilius as Romulus's successor, so that those things Romulus had omitted to take care of could be dealt with by Numa. The Romans of his day were completely wild, not domesticated; he wanted to train them to live a sociable life and to practice the arts of peace. So he turned to religion because it is essential for the maintenance of a civilized way of life, and he founded a religion such that for many centuries there was more fear of God in Rome than there has ever been anywhere else. Such piety was of considerable assistance whenever the senate or one of Rome's great leaders undertook any enterprise. If you look over the whole record of Roman history, taking into consideration both the Romans as a community and the behavior of individual citizens, you will find that the citizens of Rome were a good deal more afraid of the consequences of breaking their oaths than of breaking the laws, for they were more afraid of God's power than man's.

This is evident from the cases of Scipio and Manlius Torquatus. After Hannibal had routed the Romans at Cannae many of the citizens gathered together and, despairing of their homeland, resolved to abandon Italy and retreat to Sicily. When Scipio heard this he went to meet them and, with a naked sword in his hand, forced them to swear never to abandon the land of their birth. Lucius Manlius, father of Titus Manlius, who was later called Torquatus, had been accused by Marcus Pomponius, tribune of the people. Before the day of judgment came, Titus went to find Marcus and threatened to kill him if he did not promise to lift the charges against his father. He forced him to swear that he would do so, and Marcus, having sworn out of fear, kept his word. Thus, those citizens who could not be kept in Italy by love of country or fear of the laws were held there by an oath they had been forced to take against their wills; and that tribune set aside the hatred he had for the father, ignored the injury the son had done him, and sacrificed his honor, in order to keep an oath he had been forced to take. The sole cause of this behavior was the religion Numa had established in the city.

Anyone who reads the history of Rome with care will recognize how useful religion was when it came to commanding armies, to inspiring the populace, to keeping men on the straight and narrow, to making criminals ashamed of themselves. So that if one had to debate to which ruler Rome owed more, to Romulus or to Numa, I rather think that Numa would come in first. For where religion is well-established it is easy to introduce military prowess; but where there is military prowess without religion it is hard to introduce piety. One can see that there was no need for Romulus, who was trying to establish the senate and construct other civil and military institutions, to claim that his actions were authorized by God; but this was a claim Numa was obliged to make. He pretended to be on friendly terms with a nymph who advised him on everything before he made recommendations to the people. This came about because he wanted to establish new and unaccustomed institutions in Rome, and he feared his own authority might be insufficient.

Indeed, there has not been a single founder of an exceptional constitution for a nation who has not had recourse to divine authority, for otherwise it would have been impossible for him to win acceptance for his proposals. For there are many fine principles that a wise man will acknowledge but that are not sufficiently self-evident to be accepted by ordinary people. So intelligent men who want to overcome this problem turn to God. This is what Lycurgus did, and Solon, and many others whose objectives were the same as theirs. The Roman populace, astonished at Numa's goodness and wisdom, fell in with every proposal he made. It is certainly true that in those days people were very religious, and that the people with whom Numa had to deal were unsophisticated. This made it much easier for him to accomplish what he set out to do, for he could easily manipulate them in any way he chose. Doubtless anyone who in our own day set out to construct a republic would find it easier to do it among the inhabitants of the mountains, who are completely uncivilized, than he would among those who are accustomed to living in the cities, who are civilized but corrupt. A sculptor finds it easier to make a fine sculpture out of a rough block

of marble than out of one that has been poorly worked on by somebody else.

Taking everything into account, I conclude that the religion introduced by Numa was one of the primary reasons for the success of Rome, for a good religion leads to good institutions, good institutions lead to good fortune, and good fortune ensures the success of everything one undertakes. And, just as religious worship is the foundation of the greatness of a republic, so the neglect of it will bring about its ruin. For where the fear of God is missing, either the state will collapse, or if it is held together it will only be by fear of a ruler who is able to make up for an inadequate religion. And since rulers do not live long, such a state is bound to fail soon, once the force [virtù] holding it together is gone. So those states that depend entirely on the strength [virtù] of a single individual do not last long, for his strength cannot outlive him. It is rare for his successor to be able to take over where he leaves off, as Dante has the good sense to note:

It is rare for human integrity to be inherited.
God wants it this way, so that people will
   turn to him for it.

The best thing for a republic or a monarchy is not to have someone in charge who governs well for as long as he lives; it is better to have someone who organizes the state so that when he dies it will continue without him.

Although it is easier to persuade unrefined men to adopt a new institution or a new belief, this does not mean it is impossible to persuade people who are sophisticated and who pride themselves on being refined to do so. The people of Florence do not think of themselves as either ignorant or unsophisticated; nevertheless, Friar Girolamo Savonarola persuaded them that he talked with God. I do not want to say if I think this was true or not; for one should talk with reverence of such a great man. But I certainly will say that innumerable people believed him, although they had not seen anything extraordinary that might lead them to think it true. His way of life, his doctrine, and his message were enough to make them believe him. No one should despair of being able to achieve things that others have achieved before them, for men, as I said in my preface, are born, live, and die in the same way as they always have done.

Chapter Twelve: On how important it is to give due weight to religion, and on how Italy, having been deprived of faith by the Church of Rome, has been ruined as a consequence.

Those rulers and those republics who want to keep their political systems free of corruption must above all else prevent the ceremonies of their religion from being corrupted and must keep them always in due veneration. For one can have no better indication of the prospective ruin of a society than to see that divine worship is held in contempt. It is easy to see why this is so, since we saw above that religions are established wherever men are born. Every religion grounds its spiritual life in one particular doctrine or practice. The religious life of the pagans was based on the replies given them by their oracles and on the cult of divination and augury. All their other ceremonies, sacrifices, and rites depended on these, for it was easy for them to believe that a god who could foretell the good or evil that was going to happen to you could also determine your fate. It was this belief that gave rise to temples, to sacrifices, to prayers, and to all the other ceremonies with which the gods were venerated. They were authorized by the oracle of Delos, the temple of Jupiter Ammon, and by other celebrated oracles who were universally admired and worshipped. These oracles in time came to speak as they were instructed to by the powerful, and the deception involved was recognized by the populace. Thus, men came to be sceptics and became inclined to overthrow every good institution.

So the rulers of a republic or of a kingdom should uphold the basic principles of the religion to which they are committed. If they do this it will be easy for them to keep their state religious and, as a consequence, law-abiding and united. Everything that happens that fosters religious faith, even if they privately judge it to be false, they should support and encour-

age; the more prudent they are, the more scientific their outlook, the more they should do this. It is because sensible men have adopted this policy that belief in miracles has taken hold, even in religions that we know to be false. For wise men supported them without worrying about the truth of their claims, and their authority served to encourage belief in society as a whole.

There were many such miracles reported in Rome: for example, when the Roman soldiers were sacking the city of Veii some of them entered the temple of Juno. They went up to her statue and said, "Do you want to come to Rome?" Some thought she nodded in response; others heard her say yes. Since these men had a genuine religious faith (Livy's account makes this plain, for he reports that they entered the temple without being raucous, but acting devoutly and full of reverence) they thought they had heard the reply to their question that they had, perhaps, expected. This simple-minded belief was unhesitatingly encouraged and favored by Camillus and by the other rulers of the city.

If, when Christianity first became a state religion, such piety had been encouraged (as the founder of the religion instructed it should be), the Christian states and republics would now be more united and a good deal happier than they are. Nor is there any clearer indication of the decline of Christianity than the fact that those peoples who live closest to Rome, whose Church is the head of our religion, have the least faith. If you look back to the founding principles of Christianity, and contrast them with present practices, you will be bound to conclude that our religion will soon be destroyed or scourged.

Since many are of the view that the welfare of the cities of Italy depends on the Roman church, I want to argue the contrary case, employing those reasons that occur to me. I will appeal to two powerful arguments that, I believe, are compatible with each other. The first is that the wicked examples presented by the papal court have caused the whole of Italy to lose all piety and all religious devotion. This has innumerable unfortunate consequences and is the cause of numerous disorders. For just as respect for religion has a whole range of beneficial consequences, so contempt for religion has a whole range of evil consequences. Thus, we Italians owe this much to our Church and to our clergy: They have made us irreligious and wicked.

But this is not the half of what we owe them, for there is another reason why the Church is the cause of our ruin: the Church has been and still is responsible for keeping Italy divided. In truth, no geographical region has ever been unified or happy if it has not been brought under the political control of a single republic or ruler, as has happened in France and Spain. And the only reason why Italy has not been unified as they have been, the only reason why she does not have a republic or a prince who has been able to acquire control of the whole territory, is the existence of the church. The pope lives in Italy and has a temporal authority there, but he has not been powerful or skillful [virtù] enough to acquire absolute power throughout Italy and make himself her ruler; but on the other hand he has never been so weak that, faced with the prospect of losing his temporal possessions, he has been unable to call on some other state to defend him against whatever power has been on the rise in Italy. There is plenty of evidence for this in the past, for example when the papacy employed Charlemagne to kick out the Lombards, who had become rulers of almost the whole of Italy. In our own day the papacy destroyed the power of the Venetians by obtaining the support of the French; and then got rid of the French with the help of the Swiss. So the church has not been powerful enough to conquer Italy, but has prevented anyone else from conquering her. This is the reason why Italy has never been united under one ruler, but has been divided among numerous princes and rulers, which has resulted in so much division and weakness that she has been reduced to being the victim, not only of powerful foreign states, but of anyone who cares to attack her. We Italians owe all this to our Italian church and to no one else.

If you wanted to have an incontrovertible test of the truth of my argument, you would need to be powerful enough to transport the court of Rome, with its temporal authority, from Italy to Switzerland. For the Swiss are the only people who still live as the ancients did, being uncorrupted in both their religion and their military service. You would see that in a short time the evil habits of the court of Rome would introduce more disorder into the territory of the Swiss than anything else that could ever happen there.

Chapter Seventeen: On how a corrupt people who come to be free can only hold on to their freedom with the greatest of difficulty.

In my view, if the kings of Rome had not been abolished, Rome would in a very short time have become weak and worthless. For if you consider the extent of the corruption that had set in among the kings, you will recognize that if there had been two or three generations of such rulers, then the corruption of the rulers would have infected the body of the nation. Once the society as a whole was corrupt, it would never again have been possible to reform it. But because the head was struck off before the body was infected, it was easy for them to accustom themselves to a free and well-organized political system. One should recognize as an indubitable truth that if a corrupt city, accustomed to one-man rule, acquires freedom and sees its ruler and all his relatives killed, it will never know what to do with its newfound liberty. It would be better for it to have a new ruler step into the shoes of the old. Without a new ruler it will never settle down, unless some individual who combines exceptional goodness with exceptional skill [virtù] keeps freedom alive in its midst; but this freedom will only survive as long as he does.

This is what happened at Syracuse with Dion and Timoleon. They both had the skill [virtù], under differing circumstances, to keep freedom alive in their city while they lived; but as soon as they died the old tyranny was restored. But the best example is that of Rome. When the Tarquins were thrown out the Romans were able to seize and maintain their freedom; but when Caesar was killed, when Gaius Caligula was killed, when Nero was killed, when the whole house of Caesar had been eliminated, at no point were they able so much as to lay claim to freedom, let alone maintain it. Events took a very different course, although all this happened in the same city, simply because, in the days of the Tarquins, the Roman people were not yet corrupt, while in later centuries they were rotten to the core. In the early days, in order to keep themselves firm of purpose and determined to prevent the restoration of the monarchy, all that was necessary was that they should swear that they would never agree to there being a king in Rome; in later centuries the authority and severity of Brutus, backed up by all the legions of the eastern empire, were insufficient to keep them committed to preserving the liberty that he, like the first Brutus, had restored to them. This was the result of the corruption that the faction of Marius had introduced into the populace; Caesar, having put himself at the head of this party, had been able to blind the populace to the fact that they were being enslaved, even as he himself placed the yoke upon their necks.

Although this example from the history of Rome is more important than any other, nevertheless, I would like to introduce some further examples of popular corruption drawn from contemporary history. I would say that nothing that could happen, no matter how destructive and violent, could accustom the peoples of Milan and of Naples to freedom, for those societies are completely corrupt. This was apparent after the death of Filippo Visconti, for although the Milanese sought to re-establish liberty, they could not do so, and had not the least idea of how to maintain it. Rome was therefore extremely lucky that her kings became corrupt quickly, so that they were soon kicked out, before their corruption had spread to the guts of the city. It is because the populace of Rome was not corrupt that the innumerable conflicts that broke out in Rome did not harm but actually helped the republic, for her citizens at least had the right objectives.

So we can draw this conclusion: Where the individuals are not corrupt, conflicts and other crises do no harm; where they are corrupt, the best-planned laws are useless, unless the laws are imposed by someone who uses ruthless methods to make people obey him, until the individuals themselves become good. I do not know if this has ever happened, or if it could ever happen. In practice one finds, as I said just before,

that where a city has gone into decline because the individuals who make it up are corrupt, if it ever happens that it acquires freedom, it happens because of the skill [virtù] of one individual who is present by chance, not because of the strength [virtù] of the population as a whole, which is what is needed to maintain good institutions. As soon as the one leader dies, the city returns to its old habits. This is what happened in Thebes which, because of the skill [virtù] of Epaminondas, was able, so long as he was alive, to maintain a republican structure and to hold down an empire; but, as soon as he died, Thebes returned to its old internal conflicts. The problem is that an individual cannot live long enough to have time to discipline properly a city that has long been spoiled. One leader of exceptional longevity or two skilled [virtuose] leaders succeeding each other are not enough to establish order; but without one or the other, as I have said, there is no hope. By the time you discover this, however, you have undergone many dangers, and much blood has been spilled, and still liberty is not reborn. For this sort of corruption, this sort of incapacity for political freedom, is the result of the social inequality that has developed within the city. In order to restore equality, one would have to use quite exceptional measures. Few know how to use them, or, if they do know, are prepared to face what is involved, as I will explain in greater detail elsewhere.

Chapter Eighteen: On the way to preserve political freedom in a corrupt but free city; or to establish it in a corrupt and unfree city.

I think it is relevant to what we have been discussing, and it would not be out of place, to consider whether one can preserve political freedom in a corrupt but free city, or whether one can establish it in a corrupt and unfree city. On this subject, I say that it is very difficult to do either one or the other; and although it is almost impossible to formulate general rules, for one would have to adjust one's policies in the light of the extent of the corruption, nevertheless, since it is good to think through every problem, I do not want to omit a discussion of this one. Let us assume we are dealing with an extremely corrupt city, so that we can consider the most difficult case. Indeed, the case would seem hopeless, for there are neither laws nor institutions that will serve to restrain a universal corruption. For just as good habits need good laws if they are to survive, so good laws will only be obeyed if the subjects have good habits.

Moreover, the institutions and laws that have been established in a republic at the time of its foundation, when the individuals who made it up were good, are no longer appropriate when they become bad. If the laws of a city are relatively easily changed to take account of changing circumstances, the institutions, on the other hand, never change, or do so only at long intervals. The result is that the new laws are insufficient, because the institutions that remain unchanged distort their impact. In order to make clearer what I mean, let me explain what the institutions of the government, or rather of the state, were in Rome, and then I will outline the laws with which the magistrates held the citizens in check. The fundamental institutions of the state were embodied in the respective powers of the people, the senate, the tribunes, and the consuls; in the ways in which magistrates were chosen and appointed; and in the ways in which legislation was passed. This fundamental constitution changed little or not at all as circumstances changed. What did change were the laws that restricted the actions of citizens, such as the laws on adultery, the laws controlling extravagance, those on political corruption, and many others, which were altered as the citizens became progressively more corrupt. But since the institutions of the state remained unchanged, although they were no longer appropriate once the citizens had become corrupt, the revision of particular laws was insufficient to prevent the progress of corruption; the outcome would have been different if not only the laws had been changed, but the constitution as well.

That I am justified in claiming that such institutions were not the right ones for a corrupt city is particularly apparent if we look at two topics: the election of magistrates and the passage of legislation. The people

of Rome did not give the consulate and the rest of the highest offices in the city except to those who sought them. This system was good at first, for only those citizens who thought themselves worthy of high office stood for election. Since defeat was shameful, each candidate behaved well in the hope of being judged worthy of election. However, this system was disastrous when the city had become corrupt. For then it was not the most virtuous [virtù] but the most powerful who stood for election, and the weak, even if virtuous [virtuosi], were too frightened to run for office. Things degenerated to this point not all at once but bit by bit, as happens with all cases of degeneration. Once the Romans had subdued Africa and Asia, and had compelled almost the whole of Greece to acknowledge their authority, they became confident that no one would conquer them, and they no longer thought they had any enemies of whom they ought to be afraid. This sense of security, this absence of enemies who inspired respect, meant that the people of Rome, in electing consuls, no longer paid attention to competence [virtù], but judged only on the basis of charm. They elected those who were best at flattering Rome's citizens, not those who were best at defeating Rome's enemies. Later, even charm was not enough, and the people sank to the point that they voted for those who had the most patronage to distribute; so that good men, because the system was faulty, never stood a chance.

Similarly, a tribune, or indeed any other citizen, could propose a law to the people. Every citizen then had the right to speak for or against the proposal before a vote was taken. This was a good system, so long as the citizens were good, for it is always a good principle that anyone should be free to put forward a proposal of benefit to the public; it is also a good principle that everyone should be able to express his opinion on the subject, so that the people, when they have heard everyone's opinion, can then make the right decision. But once the citizens became corrupt this system became disastrous, for only the powerful proposed laws, and they did so not in order to further the liberty of all, but only in order to build up their own power. Everyone was too frightened to speak against their proposals, so that the people were either taken in, or else compelled to choose policies that would lead to their own destruction.

If one had wanted to preserve liberty in Rome despite the progress of corruption, it would have been necessary to go beyond passing new laws from time to time and to construct new political institutions. For the institutions and ways of life one needs to establish if men are corrupt are different from those that are appropriate if they are good; if one has different materials with which to work, one must build a quite different structure. But these institutions would either have had to be reformed all at once, as soon as it was realized that as a whole they were no longer appropriate, or else they would have had to be revised little by little, as each particular institution was seen to be in need of reform. Both of these procedures are, in my view, almost impossible to carry out. For if you want to revise institutions little by little and one by one, you need to have some wise man proposing change, someone who sees problems almost before they have developed and catches them at the moment of their birth. In the whole history of a city there might easily prove to be not a single person as wise as this. And even if there were such a person, he would never be able to persuade others to recognize the truth of his arguments, for men who have been used to living in a particular way have no desire to change it, especially when they do not find themselves standing toe-to-toe with a problem, but rather are asked to accept its existence on the basis of someone else's conjectures and hypotheses. On the other hand, if one hopes to change the institutions at a stroke, when everyone has come to recognize that they are defective, then I maintain defects that are easy to recognize are hard to correct. For such reforms, ordinary measures are insufficient, for we are dealing with a situation where the ordinary measures have proved defective. So one has to adopt extraordinary measures, such as resorting to violence and civil war. One's primary goal must be to become sole ruler of the city, so that one can do with it as one pleases. In order to reconstruct the constitution of a city so that it fosters political liberty, one needs to be a man with good intentions; but people who resort to arms in order to seize power in a republic are people whose methods are bad. So you can see that there will hardly ever be an occasion when a good man, using wicked means, but using them in the service of good ends, will want to become sole ruler; or when a wicked man, having become sole ruler, wants to do good. It will not occur to him to use for good the power he has acquired by wicked means.

So I have now explained the difficulties that would have to be overcome if one were to try to preserve liberty in a corrupt city or to attempt to establish it from scratch. These difficulties are, in effect, insuperable. Even if one had the opportunity to carry out reform or revolution, one would have to introduce a constitution that was more monarchical than democratic. For men who were so ill-behaved that they could not be kept in order by the laws would need to be kept in check by a more or less arbitrary authority. If one sought to find some other way of making them good, one would either fail completely, or have to resort to extreme cruelty, as I explained above when discussing Cleomenes. He, in order to be sole ruler, had to kill the ephors, just as Romulus, for the same reason, had to kill both his brother and Titus Tatius the Sabine. They went on to use their power well. But you have to take into account the fact that neither of them was dealing with subjects who were as eaten away with corruption as those we have been discussing in this chapter. So it was not unreasonable for them to hope to build a free state; and they were able to turn their aspirations into reality.

Chapter Fifty-Five: On how easy it is to reach decisions in cities where the multitude is not corrupt; and on how it is impossible to establish one-man rule where there is social equality; and on how it is impossible to establish a republic where there is inequality.

Although we have already discussed at some length what one should expect, be it good or bad, in corrupt cities, nevertheless, I do not think it would be a digression if we considered a debate that took place in the senate over a motion introduced by Camillus. He proposed giving one-tenth of the plunder seized in Veii to the temple of Apollo. Since this plunder had fallen into the hands of the Roman populace, and since there was no other way of knowing what it was worth, the senate passed a decree that everyone should hand over to the treasury one-tenth of the loot that he had seized. This decree was never enforced, for the senate later adopted another proposal, and found a different way of compensating Apollo on behalf of the Roman people. Nevertheless, the very fact that it was passed is an indication of the extent to which the senate had confidence in the trustworthiness of the populace. In their opinion, everyone could be relied on to give an accurate account of all that he owed under the terms of the decree. As for the populace, they did not think for a moment of evading the decree by simply handing over less than they owed; they sought to have it repealed by openly protesting against it.

This example, along with many others that we have already discussed, shows the extent to which the Roman populace had a sense of public duty and of religious obligation, and how justified were those who had confidence in them. It is a simple fact that where such a sense of public duty is not to be found, one is entitled to be pessimistic. There is no point in being optimistic if you live in one of those regions that, in our own day, have become corrupt. Italy is the most far gone of them all; even France and Spain have been infected. If we do not see quite so many disorders in those countries as break out in Italy every day, the reason is not so much that the populace has a sense of public duty, for the truth is that their peoples are for the most part corrupted; rather it is because each has a king who keeps it united, not only because he is a strong leader [*non solamente per la virtù sua*], but because the institutions of those kingdoms are still intact. In the territory of Germany, it is evident that a sense of public duty and of religious obligation is still widespread among the populace; the result is that many self-governing republics survive there. They observe their own laws so well that nobody dares try to invade them from without or to subvert them from within.

In order to show that I am right to claim that the sense of public duty we associate with the ancients still predominates in them, I want to give one example comparable to the one I gave earlier concerning the senate and the Roman populace. In the German republics, it is customary, when they find they need to spend a considerable amount of money on public business, for the appropriate magistrates or councils to impose a tax on the inhabitants of the city of one or two percent of each person's assets. Once a decree has been passed according to whatever procedures are required by the local constitution, each person makes an appearance before the officials assigned to collect the tax, and, having taken an oath to pay what he owes, places in an official chest the sum of money that he, having consulted his conscience, thinks he ought to pay. He himself is the only witness to how much he pays. From this you can get some idea of how far a sense of public duty and of religious obligation is still to be found among these men. One is bound to think that each person pays what he really owes; for if he did not, the tax would not yield as much as they expected, judging by its yield on previous occasions over a long period of time; if it did not yield as much, the public would know they had been defrauded; and if they knew they were being defrauded they would change their method of collecting taxes. Such public spiritedness is all the more to be admired in our day and age because it is so rare.

Indeed, it survives only in Germany, and there are two reasons for this. The first is that the Germans do not have numerous contacts with their neighbors, for their neighbors rarely visit them, and they rarely visit their neighbors. They have been content with the products of the local economy, eating food grown and raised nearby, and dressing in wool from their own sheep. This removes the primary reason for contact with foreigners, and with it, the primary source of all corruption. They have avoided being infected with the customs of the French, the Spanish, or the Italians; and these three nations between them are the source of corruption throughout the world. The second reason is that those republics that have preserved popular sovereignty and resisted corruption do not tolerate any of their citizens to style himself a gentleman, or to live like one. So they maintain among themselves a genuine equality, and they are bitterly hostile to those lords and gentlemen who do exist in their region. If by chance some of them fall into their hands, they regard them as the germs of corruption and the causes of every possible immorality, and kill them.

In order to clarify the meaning of this term "gentleman," let me say that men are called "gentlemen" if they live in luxury without working. Their income arises from their estates, but they do not have to worry about cultivating them or going to any other trouble to make ends meet. Such people are pernicious influences in any republic and, indeed, in any part of the world. But even worse are those who, in addition to being wealthy, have a castle at their disposal and have subjects who obey them. Gentlemen of both types are to be found throughout the kingdom of Naples, in the papal states, in the Romagna, and in Lombardy. This is the reason why no republic has ever been established in those regions, nor any other form of popular sovereignty. For such types of men are totally hostile to a civilized way of life. To want to set up a republic in regions with this sort of social structure is to want the impossible; if one wanted to introduce a new political system in such regions, supposing one had gained control of them, there would be no choice but to establish a monarchy. The reason is as follows: Where the individuals are so corrupt that the laws alone will not restrain them, then you need to establish alongside the laws a force greater than theirs, that is to say, the heavy hand of a king, who can use an absolute and unlimited power to put a halt to the unlimited ambition and corruption of the elite.

This argument is confirmed by the example of Tuscany. There you find that for a long time there have been three republics—Florence, Siena, and Lucca—crammed into a small geographical space. And the other cities of the region are either accustomed to subordination, as is apparent both from the character of their citizens and from their constitutions, or else defend, or at least would like to defend, their liberty. The reason is simple: In that region there are no lords of castles to be found and no (or at any rate very few) gentlemen. There is so much social equality that it would be easy for a wise man with some knowledge of ancient civilizations to establish some form of popular sovereignty. But it has been

their great misfortune that, right down to the present, they have not chanced upon a leader who has been able to do it or has understood how to do it.

From this discussion I draw the following conclusion: Anyone who wants to set up a republic in a place where there is a fair number of gentlemen can only do it if he begins by killing them all. On the other hand, anyone who wants to set up a monarchy or a system of one-man rule in a place where there is a fair amount of social equality will never manage to do it unless he lifts out of that equality many individuals who are ambitious and restless, and makes them into gentlemen in fact if not in name, giving them castles and estates, and giving them control of men and property. Then he will be surrounded by an elite whom he can rely on to uphold his power, while they can rely on him to further their aspirations. As for the rest of the population, they will be obliged to submit to a yoke nothing but force could persuade them to tolerate. This way, those doing the forcing will be more than a match for those being forced, and so people will stay obediently in the ranks assigned to them. The task of making a region suited to monarchy into a republic, or one suited to republican government into a monarchy, is one for somebody of quite exceptional intelligence and force of personality. There have been many who have tried to do it, but very few have known how to carry it out in practice. For the scale of the enterprise is daunting in itself, and it means that often people fail when they have scarcely begun.

I believe that this opinion of mine—that where there are gentlemen one cannot establish a republic—may appear to be contradicted by the history of the Venetian republic, for there only those who are gentlemen are allowed to be elected to office. But my reply is that this example does not tell against me, for the gentlemen of Venice are rather gentlemen in name than in fact. For they do not have large incomes from country estates since their great wealth is founded on commerce and trade. Moreover, none of them has a castle or has any private jurisdiction over other men. In their case the name "gentleman" is a purely honorific title, one that has nothing to do with the factors that determine whether or not you are called a gentleman in any other city. Just as all republics have social distinctions that they refer to by one name or another, so Venice is divided into the gentlemen on the one hand and the populace on the other. They insist that the gentlemen have a monopoly, both in practice and in theory, of all the offices, while the rest are completely excluded from them. This does not lead to conflict in that territory, for the reasons I have explained. So we see that a republic can only be established where there is considerable social equality or where men are made to be equal; by contrast, the rule of one man requires considerable social inequality. If you ignore this principle you get a lopsided construction, and one that will not stand for long.

BOOK TWO

Preface

Men always praise the olden days and criticize the present, but they do not always have good reason for doing so. They are so biased in favor of the past that they do not celebrate only those periods they know about because of the surviving descriptions of them written by men alive at the time; they also, once they have become old, praise the way they remember things having been in their youth. When their praise of the past is mistaken, as it usually is, there are, I think, several reasons why history plays tricks on them.

I believe the first is that we are not told the whole truth about the past. For the most part, people keep quiet about those events it would be shameful to record, while those deeds that will make them seem glorious in the eyes of posterity they portray in the most favorable light possible. Most writers place themselves in the service of victory. In order to make fortune's victories glorious they not only exaggerate the skillful [*virtuosamente*] things the victors did, they even improve on the actions of their enemies, with the result anyone who is born in future ages in either of the territories, either that of the victors or that of the vanquished, has good reason to be amazed at the actions of those men and the character of those times,

and has no choice but to praise them to the skies and to love them.

Secondly, men hate things either out of fear or jealousy. But these two powerful motives for hatred cease to apply as time passes, for what is past can no longer hurt you, and you no longer have reason to be jealous of it. The opposite is true of those things you can still touch and see for yourself. Because you know them through and through, and nothing is hidden from you, you recognize their good features, but at the same time there are many aspects of them that displease you. So you conclude things were much better in the past, even when in reality actions in the present are much more deserving of fame and of glory. I am not talking about scientific and artistic activities, for their qualities are so transparent there is little time can do to take away or add to the reputation that they properly deserve. I am talking, rather, about the manners and morals of men, reports of which are much harder to assess.

I ought to admit that although the habit of praising the past and condemning the present is as widespread as I have said, nevertheless, people are not always mistaken when they think the past superior to the present. Sometimes their judgment is bound to be justified. Human affairs are always changing, and when they change it must be either for better or worse. One sees a city or a territory organized for a constitutional government by some one excellent individual; for a while, thanks to the skill [*virtù*] of this founder, the political system will get steadily better and better. Someone who is born in such a state, if he praises the olden times more than his own day, makes a mistake; and he makes this mistake for the reasons I have explained above. But later generations in this same city or territory, born when things have gone into decline, are not mistaken. Thinking about how these things work, I reached the conclusion that the world is always in the same overall condition. There has always been in it as much good as bad, but both the good and the bad are redistributed from territory to territory.

One can see this from what we know about the ancient monarchies. Good and bad were redistributed among them as manners and morals changed, but the overall condition of the world remained the same. There was only this one difference: Where virtue [*virtù*] had at first been resident in Assyria, it later moved to the Kingdom of the Medes, and then to Persia, until eventually it came to Italy, and to Rome. Since the Roman empire, it is true, there has been no lasting empire, and virtue [*virtù*] has not remained concentrated in one place; nevertheless, you can see it was scattered among many nations, each of whom came to live virtuously [*virtuosamente*]: the Kingdoms of France and Turkey; the Sultanate of Egypt; and now the peoples of Germany. Above all, virtue was to be found among the sect of the Saracens, who accomplished so much, occupied so much territory, and were indeed responsible for the destruction of the Roman empire in the east.

In all these territories, then, and in all such sects, virtue [*virtù*] was to be found after the Romans had gone into decline, and still is to be found in some parts of them that still aspire to greatness; there she is deservedly praised. If you are born in one of these virtuous places and praise the olden days more than the present, you may be making a mistake. But if you are born in Italy or in Greece, and if you have not become (if you are Italian) an admirer of the northerners, or (if you are Greek) a supporter of the Turks, then you are right to criticize your own times and praise the past. For in the past, there were plenty of things that deserved admiration; in the present, there is nothing at all to mitigate unalloyed misery, disgrace, and contempt. Now there is no respect for religion, for the law, or for military service; everything is splattered with filth. These vices are all the more detestable because they are most prevalent among those who hold government office, who order everyone else around, and want to be treated like gods.

But let us get back to our subject. I meant to point out that if men's judgment is unreliable when it comes to judging the relative merits of the present and the distant past in matters where one cannot have such detailed knowledge of the past as one can of the present, this does not explain why old men are poor judges of the relative merits of the times of their youth and their old age, for they have had an equal knowledge and experience of the one and the other.

Or at least they would have if men throughout their lives had the same capacity to make judgments and were governed by the same appetites. But men change as they grow older, even if their circumstances do not; so things look different to them, even if they have in fact stayed the same, for men have different appetites, different pleasures, different preoccupations in old age from the ones they had when young. For men, as they grow older, become weaker, but at the same time more prudent and astute in their judgment. So those things that seemed to them tolerable, even excellent, when they were young, as they grow old seem to them intolerable and wretched. Where they ought to blame their own changing judgment, they blame the changing times.

Moreover, there is another reason: Human appetites are insatiable. It is in man's nature to be able to and to want to desire all things; it is in the nature of circumstances that he can only realize a few of his desires. The result is that men are always finding themselves discontented and discovering themselves to be dissatisfied with what they possess. This makes them have a low opinion of the present, praise the past, and put their hope in the future, even though they have no good reason for thinking things were better or will improve.

I do not know, however, if I deserve to be included among those whose judgment is flawed, though I might be thought to praise the ancient Romans too much and criticize our own times too severely in these discourses. Indeed, if the excellence [*virtù*] that was the norm then, and the inadequacy that is to be found everywhere today, were not as plain as day, then I would express myself more cautiously, for fear I might slip into this error for which I criticize others. But the matter is so obvious anyone can recognize the truth, so that I am entitled to speak frankly and express myself bluntly on the differences between our own times and those of the ancient Romans, in the hope any young men who read what I write will be encouraged to reject the world they live in and will want to try to imitate the ancients, should fortune ever give them the opportunity to do so. For it is a worthy undertaking to teach others how to do those admirable things that you, because of corrupt circumstances and hostile fortune, have been unable to perform. If many acquire the ability to do what is needed, then one, if fortune smiles upon him, may be successful.

Having, in the previous book, talked about the decisions the Romans took in matters relating to the internal affairs of the city, in this book we will discuss those things the Roman populace did in order to expand the territory under their control.

Chapter One: On whether skill [virtù] or good fortune was a more significant factor in the Romans' acquisition of an empire.

Many have been of the opinion—among them Plutarch who is an author whose judgment is always to be respected—that the Roman people, in acquiring an empire, benefited more from good fortune than from skill [virtù]. One of the various reasons they put forward to support this view is that it is evident, they say, from the actions of the Romans themselves that they attributed all their victories to good luck, for they erected more temples to the goddess Fortune than to any other god. It would seem Livy was more or less of this opinion, for it is rare for him, whenever he has a Roman speak about skill [virtù], not to couple skill with luck.

But I do not want to admit the truth of this opinion under any circumstances, and I do not believe there are good arguments to support it. For if there has never been a republic that has made as extensive gains as Rome did, it is also evident there has never been a republic better organized to make gains than Rome was. It was the skill [virtù] of their armies that enabled them to conquer an empire, and it was their way of going about things, which dates back to their first legislator, that enabled them to hold on to what they had conquered, as I will explain at length below, over the course of a number of chapters. Some people say it was good fortune and not skill [virtù] that ensured the Roman people never had to face war against two powerful enemies at the same time. Thus, they only found themselves at war with the Latins, when, if they had not really defeated the Samnites, they

were at least able to call on their support, for in fighting the Latins they were helping the Samnites. They did not campaign against the Tuscans until they had first conquered the Latins and had almost completely crippled the Samnites by defeating them again and again. If two of these powers had allied when they were fresh and undefeated, then without doubt one could reasonably have predicted they would destroy the Roman republic.

But, however it came about, it is true they never had to fight two extremely powerful enemies at one time. It seems the rise of one always caused the decline of another, or the decline of one made possible the rise of another. This is apparent from the chronology of the wars they fought, for, leaving aside those that took place before Rome was seized by the French, one can see that while they were at war with the Aequi and the Volsci, and so long as those tribes remained powerful, nobody else attacked them. Only after they had been subdued did the war with the Samnites begin, and although the Latin tribes rebelled against the Romans before that war was over, nevertheless, when that rebellion took place the Samnites entered into a league with the Romans and sent their troops to help the Romans punish the Latins for their insolence. Once they were subdued, the war against the Samnites began again. When the Samnites had been beaten in battle after battle, the war with the Tuscans began; and when that had been settled, the Samnites rebelled again as a result of the invasion of Italy by Pyrrhus. When he had been forced to retreat into Greece, they began the first war with the Carthaginians; no sooner was this war over, but all the French, on both sides of the Alps, allied against the Romans, until they were defeated and butchered in large numbers between Popolonia and Pisa, where now stands the tower of St. Vincent.

After this war, there was a period of about twenty years when they were not involved in any major conflicts, for they only fought against the Ligurians and against those remnants of the French who held out in Lombardy. This relative peace lasted until the beginning of the Second Carthaginian War in which Italy was embroiled for sixteen years. Having brought this to a glorious conclusion, they found themselves at war with Macedon, and, after that was over, with Antiochus and with Asia. And after they had been victorious in that war there was not a ruler or a republic in the whole world who, either alone or in alliance with others, could hope to defy the Roman armies.

But anyone who considers the chronology of the wars before this final victory and who studies the policies of the Romans will realize they did not simply rely on fortune. They also employed a quite remarkable prudence and skill [virtù]. For if you ask yourself why they were so fortunate the answer will be obvious. It is evident that when a ruler or a people acquire a reputation such that every neighboring prince and people is spontaneously afraid of attacking them and fearful of being attacked by them, then it will always be the case that no state will ever attack them unless it has no alternative.

The result is that the dominant state will have almost a free choice when it comes to deciding with which of its neighbors it wants to fight a war, and will be able, with a little effort, to pacify the others. They, partly out of fear of the dominant power and partly taken in by the techniques it will employ to give them a false sense of security, will be easy to pacify. The other powers who are not immediate neighbors and who do not have dealings with the victim, will regard the whole business as taking place a long way away and think it no concern of theirs. They will keep making this mistake until they are next in line. By which time they have no defense available except to rely on their own troops. But by then their own troops will be inadequate, for the dominant power will have become overwhelmingly strong.

I will not delay to discuss how the Samnites stood by and watched while the Romans defeated the Volsci and the Aequi and, in order to be brief, I will confine myself to the case of the Carthaginians. They were very powerful and widely respected at the time the Romans were fighting against the Samnites and the Tuscans, for they already controlled the whole of Africa along with Sardinia, and Sicily, and part of Spain. Because they were so powerful, and because their territory was some distance from that of the

Romans, it never occurred to them to attack them, or to come to the assistance of the Samnites and the Tuscans. Thus, they behaved as one does if one thinks time is on one's side, allying with the Romans, and trying to win their good will. They did not recognize their mistake until the Romans had conquered all the peoples between themselves and the Carthaginians, and had begun to challenge them for control of Sicily and Spain.

The same thing happened to the French as to the Carthaginians, and the same thing again to Philip, King of Macedon, and to Antiochus. Each one of them believed, while the people of Rome were occupied with one of the others, that Rome's enemies would win, and that there was plenty of time to defend themselves, either through diplomacy or war, against Rome's advancing power. So I am of the view that the good fortune the Romans had in never having to fight against two enemies at the same time is available to any ruler who acts as the Romans did and is as skillful [virtù] as they were.

It would be relevant here for us to explain the policies pursued by the Roman people when occupying newly acquired territory if we had not discussed this question at length in our treatise on princedoms. You will find an extensive discussion of this question there. I will only say this much in passing: The Romans always tried hard when they were acquiring new territory to have the support of an ally who could serve as a ladder over the defenses, or as a gate through the walls, or as an assistant in retaining control once it was acquired. So they used the Capuans to get entry to Samnium, the Camertini to get into Tuscany; the Mamertini helped them in Sicily, the Saguntines in Spain, the Masinissa in Africa, the Aetolians in Greece, the Eumenes and other rulers in Asia, the Massilians and the Aedui in France. They were never short of such allies to assist them in their undertakings and to help them acquire and hold new territories. Governments that systematically follow this policy will find they have less need of good fortune than those who do not.

So that everyone can clearly recognize how much more important skill [virtù] was than good fortune in the acquisition of the Roman empire we will discuss in the next chapter the character of the peoples they had to fight against, and will see just how determined they were to defend their liberty.

Chapter Two: On the peoples the Romans had to fight against, and on their determination in defending their liberty.

Nothing made it harder for the Romans to overcome the peoples immediately around them and, indeed, some in more distant territories, than the love many societies in those times had for liberty. They defended their liberty so stubbornly that they could never have been conquered except by a people of quite exceptional strength [virtù]. For there are many examples that show the dangers these societies were willing to endure in order to defend or recover their liberty; and show, too, the revenge they sought to exact on those who had taken their freedom from them.

One learns, too, from the study of history the losses both peoples and cities suffered as a result of their enslavement. While at the present time there is only one geographical region where one can say there are free cities to be found, in classical times there were numerous peoples in every region who lived in complete liberty. One sees how, in the times we are discussing at the moment in Italy there were nothing but free peoples from the Appennines, which now mark the boundary between Tuscany and Lombardy, right down to the southern tip: the Tuscans, the Romans, the Samnites, and many other societies which lived in that section of the peninsula. Nor is there any report of there being any kings other than those who ruled in Rome, plus Porsenna, King of Tuscany—history does not record how many successors he had. But it is evident that when the Romans went to war with Veii, Tuscany was free. Indeed, the Tuscans were so enamored of liberty and so hated the title of king, that, when the inhabitants of Veii, who had appointed a king to take charge of their defense, asked them for help in resisting the Romans, they decided, after much debate, not to come to their assistance. They argued that, so long as they obeyed a king, there was no point in defending the freedom of people who had already given their freedom away.

It is easy to understand how a people acquires such a love of political freedom, for we see by experience that city-states have never been successful, either in expanding their territory or in accumulating wealth, except when they have been free. And really one is bound to be astonished if one considers the extraordinary accumulation of power and wealth in the hands of Athens in the hundred years that followed her freeing herself from the tyranny of Pisistratus. But it is even more breathtaking to consider the astonishing success of Rome once she had freed herself from her kings. It is easy to work out why, for cities become great by pursuing, not the interests of private individuals, but the interests of the community as a whole. And there is no doubt the public interest is never a guiding principle except in republics. There, everything that furthers the common good is carried out, even if one or two private individuals suffer by it. The vast majority have interests that coincide with the public interest, and so they are able to pursue it, even in face of the resistance of the small minority who suffer by it. But the opposite occurs when a city is under the rule of one man, for usually what serves his interests hurts the city, and what would benefit the city is contrary to his interests.

The result is that as soon as a tyranny is established in a city where once there has been political freedom, the least bad outcome for the inhabitants is that their city ceases to make progress and stops accumulating either power or wealth; but usually, indeed nearly always, they begin to lose what they have won. If by chance it were a competent [virtuoso] tyrant who took power, who had the courage and military strength [virtù] to extend the territory under his control, still his society would not benefit at all from his achievements. He would be the only beneficiary. For he would not be able to reward any of his citizens who are strong and good. He must keep such men in servitude for fear they might be a threat to him. Nor can he make the cities he conquers subordinate to his home city or have them pay tribute to it, for if he makes his own city strong he endangers himself. It is in his interest to keep his state divided into distinct territories and to ensure each city and each province answers to him directly. So, naturally, he is the only one who benefits from his conquests, while his homeland is no better off. If you want to see my opinion confirmed and to read numerous arguments in support of it, read the treatise Xenophon wrote *On Tyranny*.

Thus, it is not at all surprising that in classical times peoples hunted down tyrants with such bitterness and were so enamored of political freedom, and that the very idea of liberty was held in such respect among them. See, for example, what happened when Hieronymus, the nephew of Hiero of Syracuse, was killed in the city of Syracuse. News of his death reached his army, which was not far away. At first they began to form a mob, seizing weapons to go to kill his murderers; but, when they heard that in Syracuse people were crying out "Liberty!," the word itself was enough to mesmerize them, and at once they quieted down, put aside their anger against the tyrannicides, and began to ask themselves how one could institutionalize political freedom in their city.

Again, it is not at all surprising that peoples pursued extraordinary vendettas against individuals who had taken their liberty from them. There are plenty of examples of this. I intend to refer only to one case that happened in Corcyra, a Greek city, at the time of the Peloponnesian War. Greece was divided between two alliances, one of which was led by the Athenians, the other by the Spartans. The result was that in many cities where there were already internal divisions one faction allied itself with the Spartans, the other with the Athenians. In Corcyra the nobles got the upper hand and deprived the populace of their liberty. The popular party, thanks to Athenian assistance, took back control and seized all the nobles, locking them up in a prison big enough to hold them all. From there they took them out in groups of eight or ten at a time, pretending they had been sentenced to exile in different places, and tortured them to death in the public view. When those who were still alive realized what was happening, they decided to do their best to escape such an ignominious death. Arming themselves with whatever they could find, they fought with those who wanted to enter the prison, defending the gateway against them. The populace, hearing the noise of the struggle, came running; they wrecked the upper floors of the building and buried their captives under the rubble. Many other similar events, both horrible and remarkable, took place in Greece. They show people go to greater lengths to take revenge on those who have taken their liberty from them than on those who have merely tried to do so.

You may wonder why, in those classical times, peoples were more in love with liberty than they are now. I think the reason is the same as why men in our day are less strong. In my view, both result from the difference between our upbringing and that of classical times, which is rooted in the difference between our religion and theirs. Because our religion has taught us the truth and the right way to salvation, it makes us less concerned with our reputation in this world. The pagans, on the other hand, were much more concerned with reputation and regarded it as the highest good, with the result their deeds were more savage. There are lots of their institutions that could serve as indications of this—one might begin with a comparison between the magnificence of their religious ceremonies and the simplicity of ours. Ours make a show of refinement rather than magnificence and include no actions that require savagery or courage. Their rituals were full of pomp and ceremony, but in addition they sacrificed numerous animals in ceremonies full of blood and savagery. These were cruel rites, and from them the worshipers learned to be cruel men.

Moreover, classical religion only deified men who had already been heaped with worldly glories, men such as generals of armies and rulers of states. Our religion, by contrast, glorifies men who are humble and contemplative, rather than those who do great deeds. In fact, it regards humility, self-abasement, and contempt for worldly goods as the supreme virtues, while classical religion valorized boldness of spirit, strength of body, and all the other qualities that make men redoubtable. It is true our religion requires that you be strong, but it wants you to demonstrate your strength by undergoing suffering without complaint, rather than by overcoming resistance. This set of values, it would seem, has turned the men of our own day into weaklings and left them unable to defend themselves against the ravages of the wicked. The wicked have no difficulty in handling their fellow men, for they know the average individual wants rather to endure their blows than to strike back, for he hopes to go to heaven.

Although it seems we have all been made effeminate, and God himself allows injustice to flourish, it is of course the fault of the sinful nature of mankind, which has caused them to interpret the teachings of our religion as suits their lazy temperament and not as brave men would have done [*non secondo la virtù*]. For if they had taken into account the fact that our religion allows us to praise and defend our homeland, they would have realized that if we are religious we ought to love and honor our country and to prepare ourselves to be the sort of people who will be capable of defending it. The upbringing we get, and these false interpretations of our religion, have the consequence that there are not so many republics to be found in the world as there were in classical times; nor, it follows, does one find in the peoples of our day as much love of liberty as there was then.

Another, and perhaps better, explanation is that the strength and military might of the Roman empire destroyed all the republics and all the free cities. And although that empire later collapsed, the cities within it were not able to reconstruct political freedom or rebuild institutions that would foster liberty, except in a very few places. Whatever the real cause, the Romans, no matter where they went, found republics allied together, armed to the teeth, and determined to defend their freedom to the end. Which shows that the Roman people, had they not been of exceptional and extreme strength [*virtù*], would never have been able to defeat them.

I want to give one example among them all and will confine myself to the case of the Samnites. It seems astonishing, but they were so powerful and so effective on the battlefield, that they could, as Livy admits, resist the Romans right down to the time of the consul Papirius Cursor, son of the first Papirius, that is, for a period of forty-six years, despite having been defeated on the battlefield again and again, having had their crops destroyed repeatedly, and having their people massacred in their homes. Especially when one sees that their territory, where there were

once so many cities and such a dense population, is now almost uninhabited, while in those days the people were so strong and so well organized it would have been impossible to overcome them, had they not been attacked by troops with the strength [*virtù*] of the Romans.

It is easy to establish where the organization they had then came from, and why we are now disorganized. For it is all the result of the fact that in those days they lived as free men, while now we live as slaves. For all the lands and territories, wherever they may be, that live in freedom experience, as I have already said, immense benefits. There you see denser populations, for men are freer to enter into marriage and keener to do so. People are happy to engender children if they think they will be able to feed them and do not fear their family wealth will be confiscated from them. They are happier if they know they will not only be born free, not slaves, but, if they have the right qualities [*virtù*], they will be able to grow up to share in government. There, people see wealth steadily accumulate, both wealth from agriculture and wealth from industry and commerce. For each person tries hard to build up savings and pile up goods if he believes he will have a chance to enjoy what he has acquired. As a result, men are eager to pursue both private and public benefits, and both types of interest are advanced extraordinarily quickly.

The opposite of all this happens in those countries where the people are enslaved. Then their traditional standard of living diminishes in proportion to the severity of their enslavement. Of all harsh enslavements, the harshest is to be enslaved to a republic: in the first place, because republics are more durable, and you have less hope of escaping from their control; in the second, because the objective of a republic is to weaken and consume all other communities in order to strengthen its own. This is not the objective of an individual ruler who forces you to submit to him, unless he is a barbarian, someone who lays waste the countryside and destroys civilized urban life. Oriental rulers act like this. But if he has normal human sentiments, then in most cases he loves all the cities subjected to him equally and leaves them with their commerce intact and with by far the greater part of their ancient institutions, so that if they cannot advance as they could while they were free, they are not ruined because they are enslaved. Here I am talking about the enslavement cities enter into when they are subjected to a foreign ruler, for I have already discussed above the case of cities subjected to one of their own citizens.

If you think about everything I have said, you will not be astonished at the power the Samnites had when they were free, or at the feeble state they were reduced to when they were enslaved. Livy testifies to this at several points, and particularly in his account of the invasion of Hannibal, where he reports the Samnites were being oppressed by a Roman legion based in Nola. They sent ambassadors to Hannibal to ask him to come to their assistance. During their speech they said they had fought against the Romans for a hundred years, relying on their own soldiers and their own commanders. Many times they had stood firm against two consular armies commanded by both consuls; but now they were reduced to such a low condition they could scarcely defend themselves, even against the insignificant Roman legion that was in Nola.

Chapter Twenty-nine: On how fortune blinds men's minds when she does not want them to thwart her plans.

If you will think sensibly about how people's lives are shaped, you will see that often events and accidents occur against which the heavens were determined we should have no protection. Seeing this sort of thing happened to the Romans, who were so skillful [virtù], pious, and well-organized, it is not surprising that it happens much more often to cities or regions who lack these advantages. Because this subject is a rather good one if one wants to show the influence of the heavens in human affairs, Livy discusses it at length and most eloquently.

He says that, because the heavens had some reason for wanting the Romans to recognize their power, they first made those Fabii who had been sent as

ambassadors to the French make mistakes, with the result that their efforts served to incite the French to make war against the Romans, and then they ensured the Romans fell way below their normal standards when it came to making preparations for war. Fate had ensured that Camillus, who would have been able to handle such a difficult situation singlehandedly, but for whose abilities there was no substitute, had been banished to Ardea. When the French began to march on Rome, the Romans, who had often appointed a dictator when faced with attacks by the Volsci and other hostile neighbors, failed to appoint one to deal with the French. Moreover, when it came to choosing soldiers, they chose poorly and without making any real effort. They were so slow to muster that they were only just in time to block the French advance where it had to cross the river Allia, a mere ten miles from Rome. There the tribunes pitched camp without taking any of the normal precautions. They did not reconnoiter the site, nor did they surround the camp with a ditch and palisade. In fact, they did not employ any precautions, either natural or supernatural. When it came to drawing up the battle lines they spread the ranks out so they were thin and weak. Neither soldiers nor officers lived up to the standards of the Roman army. The battle itself was bloodless, for the Romans fled before they were attacked, the bulk of the army making for Veii, while the rest withdrew to Rome. When they arrived in Rome they did not even stop by their houses but made straight for the Capitol, with the result the senate did not give any thought to defending the city, did not even bother to close the gates, but some of them fled, and others went with the rest into the Capitol. However, when it came to defending the Capitol, they finally began to get organized. They did not hamper the defense by admitting people who would be useless, while they stockpiled all the grain they could collect so they could withstand a siege. Of the vast numbers of those who were useless—the old, women, and children—the majority fled into the surrounding countryside, while the rest remained in Rome at the mercy of the French.

Anyone who read about all the Romans had achieved over the preceding years and then came to read about these events, would be quite incapable of believing these were the same people. When Livy has described this whole series of errors, he concludes with the remark: "So one can see the extent to which fortune will blind men's minds when she does not want them to deflect her onward momentum." This conclusion is as true as could be. It follows that men who regularly encounter extreme adversity or have the habit of success deserve less praise or less blame than one might think. For usually you will find they have been led to either tragedy or triumph because the heavens have pushed them decisively either one way or the other, either making it easy or virtually impossible for them to be able to act effectively [*virtuosamente*].

One thing fortune does is select someone, when she wants him to accomplish great things, who will be sufficiently bold and skillful [*virtù*] to recognize the opportunities she makes for him. In the same way, when she wants to bring about someone's destruction, she chooses a man who will help bring about his own undoing. If there is someone around who might get in her way, then she kills him, or deprives him of all the resources he would need to do any good. You can see this clearly in Livy's account. Fortune, in order to make Rome all the greater and build her up to the power she eventually attained, judged it necessary to give her a nasty shock (I will describe all that happened at length at the beginning of the next book), but did not want, at this point, to destroy her completely. That is why she had Camillus banished, but not killed; had Rome seized by the enemy, but not the Capitol; determined that the Romans did nothing right when it came to defending Rome, but did everything right when it came to defending the Capitol. So that Rome would fall to the enemy, she ensured the bulk of the forces that had been defeated at the Allia would make for Veii, thus destroying any opportunity of defending the city. But in bringing this about she also laid the ground for Rome's liberation. A complete Roman army stood ready at Veii, and Camillus was nearby at Ardea. So they were able to make a determined effort to liberate their homeland under the command of a general whose reputation was not tarnished by defeat but was unblemished.

Perhaps I should add, in support of what I have said, an example from modern history; but I do not think it necessary, for this one example should be sufficient to satisfy anyone, and so I will move on. But I want to repeat that this is absolutely true, and all history testifies to it. Men can help fortune along, but they cannot resist it; they can swim with the tide, but they can never make headway against it. Of course, they should never give up, for they can never know what fortune has in mind. Her path is often crooked, her route obscure. So there is always reason to hope, and if one has hope one will never give up, no matter how hostile fortune may be, no matter how dreadful the situation in which one finds oneself.

BOOK THREE

Chapter One: On how, if you want a [political or religious] movement or a state to survive for long you must repeatedly bring it back to its founding principles.

It is certainly true that everything in the world has a natural life expectancy. But usually creatures live out the full cycle the heavens have determined for them only if they do not abuse their bodies, but keep them in such good shape they either remain unchanged, or if they change it is to get healthier, not weaker. Now my subject is collective bodies, such as republics, political parties, and religious sects, and my claim is that those changes are healthy that bring them back to their founding principles. Consequently, the best constructed organizations, those that will live longest, are those that are organized in such a way they can be frequently reformed; it amounts to the same thing if, for some external reason independent of their structure, reform is thrust upon them. It is clearer than daylight that if organizations are not reformed they cannot survive.

The way to reform an organization is, as I just said, to bring it back to its founding principles. For all political and religious movements, all republics and monarchies must have some good in them at the start. Otherwise, they would not be able to start out with a favorable reputation, nor would they be able to make progress in the early days. But as time goes by, that original goodness becomes corrupted, and, unless something happens that brings them back to first principles, corruption inevitably destroys the organization. Medical doctors say, speaking of the human body, "Everyday it takes in something that, in the end, requires treatment."

This return to founding principles, in the case of states, occurs either through some external accident or through domestic wisdom. As for the first, you can see it was necessary for Rome to fall to the French if she was to have a hope of being reborn; being reborn, she acquired new strength and new skill [virtù], committing herself once again to respect for religion and justice, which, in the old Rome, had begun to be corrupted. This is very evident in Livy's history, when he points out that when they marched out with an army against the French and when they created tribunes with consular authority they did not perform any religious ceremonies. Even more strikingly, not only did they not punish the three Fabii who, contrary to the law of nations, had attacked the French, but they appointed them tribunes. One can reasonably presume the other sound laws that had been introduced by Romulus and by Rome's other wise rulers were increasingly treated with less respect than was reasonable and, indeed, necessary if Rome was to preserve political freedom.

Then this shock came from the outside so that all the institutions of the city could be renewed. It was made evident to the people that it was not only necessary to uphold religion and justice, but also to have respect for good citizens and to place more value on their judgment [virtù] than on the interests they felt they would have to sacrifice if they adopted their policies. And this is, indeed, exactly what happened, for as soon as Rome recovered, they renewed all her old religious ordinances; punished the Fabii for beginning a conflict contrary to the law of nations; and moreover held the judgment [virtù] and goodness of

Camillus in such esteem the senate and everyone else put their jealousy to one side and entrusted to him the leadership of the republic.

So it is necessary, as I have said, that men who live together in any sort of institution regularly take stock of themselves, either as a result of external shocks or of internal factors. As far as this second type of reform is concerned, it best arises either as a result of a legal requirement that the members of an institution frequently take stock, or because one good man appears among them and, by his own example and his skillful [virtuose] policies, has the same effect as such a law. So this improvement takes place in a state, either because of the skill [virtù] of a man, or because of the effect [virtù] of a law.

As far as legal authorities are concerned, the institutions that drew the Roman republic back to its first principles were the tribunes of the people, the censors, together with all those laws that were a barrier to the ambition and the insolence of men. Such laws and institutions have to be given life through the will power [virtù] of an individual citizen who determinedly sets out to enforce the laws despite the powerful opposition of those who seek to ignore them. Among such cases of the laws' being enforced, prior to the sack of Rome by the French, one may note the death of the sons of Brutus, the death of the ten citizens, and that of Maelius the corn dealer. After the sack of Rome, there is the death of Manlius Capitolinus, the death of the son of Manlius Torquatus, the prosecution brought by Papirius Cursor against Fabius, his commander of cavalry, and the charges brought against the Scipios. These cases involved going to extremes and caught people's attention. Whenever such a case occurred, it made men take stock; and as they became less common there was more opportunity for men to become corrupt, and reform became accompanied by ever greater danger and ever increasing conflict. For between two such dramatic legal decisions no more than ten years ought to go by. If the gap is longer men begin to develop bad habits and to break the laws; and if nothing happens to remind them of the penalties and to re-awaken their sense of fear, there are soon so many lawbreakers springing up all over the place that it is no longer possible to punish them without endangering stability.

Those who were in charge of the Florentine state from 1434 to 1494 used to say, when discussing this subject, that it was necessary to retake power every five years, otherwise power would slip away from them. What they meant by "retaking power" was inspiring the same fear and terror in their subjects they had inspired when they first came to power, when they had set out to crush those who had acted badly by the standards of the new system of government. But as the memory of that clampdown faded, people began to be emboldened to attempt innovations and to speak ill of their rulers. So it was necessary to provide a remedy by bringing matters back to first principles.

This reform of governments according to their first principles is sometimes the result of the simple virtue [*virtù*] of one man, without being based on any law that inspires him to act rigorously; such men are so respected and admired that good men want to imitate them, and bad men are ashamed to live according to principles at odds with theirs. The individuals in Roman history who are notable for having had such good effects are Horatius Cocles, Scaevola, Fabricius, the two Decii, Regulus Attilius, along with a few others. By their remarkable and virtuous [*virtuosi*] examples they had almost the same effects on their fellow citizens as good laws and good institutions had. If the individual instances of law enforcement I have mentioned, together with the examples provided by admirable individuals, had occurred at least every ten years in Rome, then it would certainly have been the case that Rome would never have become corrupt. But as both punishments and role models became less frequent, corruption began to spread. After Marcus Regulus there is not a single exemplary individual to be found. It is true the two Catos came along later, but there was such a long gap between Regulus and the first Cato, and then between the first and the second, and they were such isolated instances, that they could not by their own good example have any good effects. This is particularly true of the second Cato, who found the city very generally corrupted and

could not by his own example improve the behavior of his fellow citizens. This is all I need to say about republics.

But we should consider movements. We can see similar reforms are necessary if we take the example of our own religion. If this had not been brought back to first principles by St. Francis and St. Dominic it would have completely died away. They, by living lives of poverty and imitating the life of Christ, renewed religion in the minds of men at a time when they had lost all commitment to it. The new orders they founded were so effective that it is only because of them that the dishonesty of the prelates and of the hierarchy does not destroy the church, for the friars continue to live in poverty and have such influence with the people as a result of hearing confession and preaching that they persuade them it is wrong to criticize evil, and it is right quietly to obey the church authorities, and, if they make mistakes, to leave their punishment to God. And so the clergy do as much harm as they can, for they do not fear a punishment they do not see and in which they do not believe. Thus, this reform movement preserved, and continues to preserve, the Christian religion.

Kingdoms, too, need to renew themselves and to reform their laws so they accord with their original principles. One can see what a good effect this policy has in the Kingdom of France. That kingdom lives according to its laws and respects its institutions more than any other kingdom. These laws and institutions are upheld by the *parlements*, and especially the *Parlement* of Paris. They give them new life every time they enforce them against a prince of the kingdom or condemn the king in one of their judgments. So far, the *parlements* have maintained their role by being determined enforcers of the laws whenever the nobility break them; but should they ever leave first one and then more and more noblemen unpunished, the result would certainly be that they would either have to put things right by provoking a major crisis, or the whole system of government would break down.

One can therefore conclude that there is nothing more essential in any form of communal life, whether of a movement, a kingdom, or a republic, than to restore to it the reputation it had when it was first founded, and to strive to ensure there are either good institutions or good men who can bring this about, so that one is not dependent on having some external intervention before reform can occur. For although an external intervention is sometimes the best remedy, as it proved for Rome, it is so dangerous there are no circumstances in which one should hope for it.

In order to show you how the deeds of individuals made Rome great and had numerous good consequences for that city, I will turn to an account of individual leaders and a commentary on their actions. This third and final section of my commentary on the first ten books of Livy will deal with this subject. And although the kings of Rome did great and remarkable things, nevertheless, since history discusses them at length, I will leave them to one side and will say nothing more about them, except for mentioning one or two things they did in pursuit of their own private interests. I will begin, instead, by talking about Brutus, the father of Roman liberty.

Chapter Seven: On why it happens that some revolutions, when liberty is replaced by servitude, or servitude by liberty, are bloodless, while others are bloody.

Perhaps someone wonders why, of the many revolutions and coups d'état that occur, when political liberty is replaced by tyranny or vice versa, some are bloody, others bloodless. For history records that, in what would appear to be similar political upheavals, sometimes innumerable men are killed, and other times no one is hurt. For example, in the revolution in which monarchy was replaced in Rome by the rule of the consuls, the Tarquins were the only people expelled from the city, and nobody else was hurt at all.

The crucial factor is this: The government that is being overthrown was either created through violence, or was not. If it was established through violence, then the likelihood is that many people suffered by it; and, consequently, when it is brought down those who suffered want their revenge, and this desire for revenge leads to bloodshed and killing. But when the government was established by the common

agreement of the community, working together to make it powerful, then when it is brought down the community has no need to attack anyone except the head of state. This was the case with the government of Rome and the expulsion of the Tarquins, just as it was the case with the government of the Medici in Florence. When they were driven out of power in 1494, they were the only ones who were attacked. Such revolutions, consequently, do not turn out to be very dangerous; but those carried out by people with a desire to exact revenge are extremely dangerous. They have always been enough to appall anyone who reads about them, let alone lives through them. And because history is full of examples that make my point, I will say no more.

Chapter Eight: On how, if you want to overthrow a republic, you ought to take account of its inhabitants.

I have already discussed how a wicked citizen can do no harm, except in a republic that is corrupt. Further evidence in support of this view, beyond what I have already given, is provided by the cases of Spurius Cassius and of Manlius Capitolinus. Spurius was ambitious and wanted to acquire unconstitutional power in Rome. He sought to win the support of the populace by doing numerous things to benefit them, such as sharing out among them the agricultural land the Romans had seized from the Hernici. The senators began to suspect his true motives and reported them to the populace, who became so distrustful of him that when he addressed it, offering to hand over to it the proceeds from the sale of the grain the government had imported from Sicily, it was determined to reject his proposal, for it believed Spurius was trying to buy from its liberty. But if the Roman populace had been corrupt, then it would not have turned the money down and would have allowed him to take a step towards establishing a tyranny, instead of blocking his path.

An even more important example of this is that of Manlius Capitolinus. His case enables us to see how strength [*virtú*] of body and mind, and good works done in favor of the homeland, become worthless once one has demonstrated a disgusting desire to seize power. This desire grew in him, it seems, because he was jealous of the honors received by Camillus. He was so blinded by ambition that, giving no thought to the political culture of the day, paying no attention to the inhabitants of the city, who were not yet ready to give their support to an evil constitution, he set out to provoke demonstrations in Rome against the senate and against the fundamental laws. What happened demonstrates the excellence of that city and the goodness of her inhabitants. For in this case not a single member of the nobility, who usually did not hesitate to come to each other's defense, declared support for him; even among his relatives no one moved a finger to help him. It was customary for an accused man's relatives to appear at his trial looking disheveled and sorrowful, dressed in black as if in mourning, in order to evoke pity for the accused; there were no mourners when Manlius stood trial. The tribunes of the people, who usually gave their support to anything that seemed likely to help the populace, and were especially keen to support anything that seemed likely to harm the nobility, in this case made common cause with the nobility to eliminate a threat to them all. The populace of Rome, which was all too keen to defend its own interests and quick to approve of anything that was disadvantageous to the nobility, had given its backing to Manlius in the past; nevertheless, when the Tribunes charged him, and handed him over to the populace to be judged, the populace, sitting in judgment on the man it had supported, showed no partiality at all as it condemned him to death.

I do not think there is another case in this history book better suited to illustrate the excellence of all the traditions of that republic. Not a single person in that city came to the defense of a citizen who had every good quality [virtú], someone who had done, in public life and in private life, very many admirable deeds. For in each of them the love of country counted for more than anything else, and each of them was more concerned about the present danger Manlius represented than about his past accomplishments. They wanted him to die so they might be free.

Livy says: "So died a man who, if he had not been born in a free city, would have left his mark on history." There are two things to think about here: In the first place, we see the strategies you must employ to achieve glory in a city that is corrupt differ from those that work in a city that still lives in freedom; secondly (but the point is almost the same), men should think about the times they live in and adapt how they behave to the circumstances in which they find themselves, particularly if they are trying to accomplish something important. Those who do not fit in with their times, either because they make the wrong decisions or because their temperaments are unsuited, usually live unhappy lives, and everything they try to do comes out badly. The opposite is true of those who meet the needs of the day.

There is no doubt that we can conclude, from the sentence of Livy I just quoted, that if Manlius had been born in the days of Marius and Sulla, when the Romans were already corrupt, and when they would have been responsive to his ambitions, then his plans would have had as much support and success as those of Marius and Sulla and of all the others who aspired to establish tyrannies after they had been shown the way. By the same token, if Marius and Sulla had been born in the days of Manlius, then they would have been crushed almost before their plots had begun to take shape. For a man's behavior and evil talk can begin to corrupt the inhabitants of a city, but there is no way in which one man can live long enough for him to corrupt them sufficiently to gain the benefits himself. Indeed, even if it were possible for him to live that long, success would be at odds with human nature. Men are impatient, and they cannot put off trying to satisfy their desires for year after year. So they make mistakes in the management of their affairs and especially in trying to obtain the things they greatly desire. Either for lack of patience or because of bad judgment, someone who set out to corrupt his city would try to seize power too soon and would come to a bad end.

If you want to take power in a republic and change its constitution for the worse, you will only succeed if the citizens have long been corrupt, if, little by little, for generation after generation, decay has set in. Now this is bound to happen, as I have explained, whenever the republic is not regularly renewed by the exemplary conduct of good citizens or is not brought back to first principles with new laws. We have seen why Manlius would have left his mark on history if he had been born in a corrupt city. The moral is that citizens who try to accomplish anything in a republic, whether in favor of liberty or of tyranny, ought to give some thought to their fellow inhabitants, and, in the light of their assessment of them, decide whether their undertaking is likely to succeed. It is just as difficult and dangerous to try to free a people who want to live in slavery as it is to try to enslave a people who want to live in freedom. I have just said men in making their plans should take into account the nature of the times and adapt themselves to them. We will discuss this point at greater length in the next chapter.

Chapter Nine: On how you have to change with the times, if you want always to have good fortune.

I have pointed out several times that whether men have good or bad fortune depends on whether they adjust their style of behavior to suit the times. It is evident that some men set about doing what they want impetuously, while others act cautiously and carefully. Both styles are mistaken, for in both one behaves inappropriately, and deviates from the best path. But, as I have said, the mistake is less important and you will still encounter good fortune if the times are suited to your style and if you always act as nature urges you.

Everyone knows how Fabius Maximus proceeded cautiously and carefully, keeping his army out of battle and avoiding any display of Roman audacity. It was his good fortune that his style corresponded well to the needs of the time. For Hannibal was a young man when he marched into Italy, things were going his way, and he had already defeated the Roman armies twice. Since Rome had lost most of her best soldiers and was demoralized, she was extremely lucky to acquire a general whose delay and caution slowed the enemy down. Nor could Fabius have found himself in circumstances better suited to his style, with the result that he was covered in glory. It is evident Fabius acted in this way because it came naturally to him, not because he had made a conscious choice. For when Scipio wanted to invade Africa with the Roman armies in order to bring the war to an end, Fabius was strongly opposed to his plan. He could not break with his past habits and adopt a different style. If it had been left to him, Hannibal would still be in Italy, for he could not recognize that circumstances had changed, and he needed to change his style of warfare. If Fabius had been King of Rome he might well have lost the war, for he would not have known to change his style of behavior as the times changed. But he was born in a republic, where numerous citizens, all with different temperaments, had a say. So, just as they had Fabius to lead them when he was the best man to avoid defeat, so they had Scipio when he was the best man to ensure victory.

One can see a republic should survive longer and should more frequently have fortune on its side, than a monarchy, for a republic can adapt itself more easily to changing circumstances because it can call on citizens of differing characters. Someone who is used to proceeding in a particular way will never change, as I have already pointed out, so it is inevitable that when the times change and become unsuitable for his particular style, he will be ruined.

Piero Soderini, as I have already mentioned on several occasions, always proceeded with kindness and patience. Both he and his country did well while the times favored his style of behavior; but when the circumstances were such that he needed to stop being patient and kind, he did not know how to do it; and he and his country were destroyed. Julius II, during the whole time he was pope, proceeded impatiently and always acted in the heat of the moment; and, since the times suited such behavior, he succeeded in all his undertakings. But in other circumstances, when different policies were needed, he would inevitably have brought about his own downfall, for he would not have changed his style of behavior or pursued different policies.

There are two reasons why we are unable to change when we need to: In the first place, we cannot help being what nature has made us; in the second, if one style of behavior has worked well for us in the past, we cannot be persuaded we would be better off acting differently. The consequence is that one's fortune changes, for the times change, and one's behavior does not. Another consequence is that cities are destroyed, for the institutions of a republic are never modified to suit changing circumstances, as I have pointed out at length already. Change comes too late because it is too difficult to accomplish. In order to bring it about the whole society must feel endangered; it is not enough for just one individual to change his methods.

Since I have mentioned Fabius Maximus, who kept Hannibal at bay, I think I will discuss in the next chapter whether a general who is determined to engage the enemy in battle can be prevented from doing so by his opposite number.

2

HOBBES, THE REFORMATION, AND THE SCIENTIFIC REVOLUTION

Thomas Hobbes was born in 1588, as the English waited anxiously for the Spanish Armada to invade their land. "My mother dear/ did bring forth twins at once, both me and fear," Hobbes wrote in his verse autobiography. In November 1640, as civil war loomed, he fled the country in fear of being arrested by Parliament. Indeed, he was "the first of those that fled." His friend John Aubrey denied he was afraid of the dark, but admitted "his extraordinary timorousness Mr. Hobbes doth very ingenuously confess." Fear was an emotion of which Hobbes had intimate experience, and around it he constructed his political philosophy. In so doing, he was deliberately subverting the aristocratic values of his day. But in order to understand his philosophy, we need to see it as a response to a number of intellectual problems that his generation had inherited from the religious conflicts of the previous century.

In 1517, when Machiavelli was writing the *Discourses*, Martin Luther (1483–1546) nailed his Ninety-five Theses to the door of Wittenberg Cathedral and thereby began the Reformation. From that moment until 1688, when the Catholic James II was driven from the throne of England, religious conflict shaped the actions of most of Europe's politicians and the thinking of all Europe's political theorists. This conflict involved four main groups. Among the radical Reformers, especially the Anabaptists, true Christianity was held to involve the adoption of other-worldly values. Christians must withdraw from secular institutions which relied on power—law courts, armies, governments—and practice mutual love. Above all, religion itself must be voluntary, and differences of religious opinion must be tolerated. In particular, the Anabaptists rejected infant baptism: only consenting adults could choose to dedicate themselves to membership of a Christian community. Throughout Europe, Protestant and Catholic rulers united in hunting down and killing Anabaptists, whose beliefs, they held, were destructive of all political order.

Luther and the Catholics were agreed that it was the duty of the ruler to impose the true religion on his subjects and that rulers, even bad rulers, were a necessary part of God's order. They disagreed about the doctrinal content of true Christianity (Catholics believing in salvation by both faith and works, and so advocating penances such as fasting and pilgrimages, while Lutherans insisted that one could never earn salvation, which came about by faith alone) and about the extent to which the state could control the day-to-day affairs of the Church (Lutherans being prepared to extend greatly the legitimate role of the state), but not about the subject's obligation to obey or the ruler's obligation to defend the true faith.

A second generation of reformers, under the leadership first of Ulrich Zwingli (d. 1531) and then of John Calvin (1509–1564), disagreed with the Lutherans in their interpretation of the central

Christian ceremony, known by Catholics as the Mass, by Protestants as the Eucharist or Holy Communion. Catholics held that during the Mass the bread and wine were transubstantiated (transformed in their true essence) into the body and blood of Christ, even though their outward appearance remained unchanged. Lutherans held that Christ was really (if not materially) present in the bread and wine. Calvinists argued that the ceremony was simply an act of remembrance, a reenactment of the Last Supper. These three views implied three quite different conceptions of authority within the Church, with Catholics at one extreme insisting on the powers of the priesthood and on sacramental authority and Calvinists on the other rejecting elaborate ceremonies and regarding all believers as fundamentally equal. There was thus a natural affinity between Calvinism and representative and participatory forms of government.

The main thrust of both Lutheran and Calvinist teaching was, however, deeply conservative: Though true believers must never compromise the principles of their faith, they must accept established authority without dispute. In practice, it was almost impossible to hold fast to this position when faced with persecution. From the 1520s on, wherever religious minorities found themselves under attack from established and powerful authorities, they sought to justify resistance. First Lutherans, then Calvinists, then Jesuits constructed constitutionalist arguments limiting the powers of rulers and insisting on the rights of the representatives of the nation. By appealing to arguments which were constitutionalist rather than religious, minorities sought to divide their opponents and win space within which to practice their own faith. In developing these arguments, Catholics, although they denied it, imitated Protestant classics, such as the *Defense of Liberty against Tyrants* (1579) by the pseudonymous Junius Brutus, and Protestants also learned from Catholics, above all from the Jesuits Mariana (1536–1624), Suarez (1548–1627), and Bellarmine (1542–1621).

This whole tradition of debate in fact was deeply indebted to medieval precedents. From 1378 to 1417, during the Great Schism, there had been two popes, one based in Rome, the other in Avignon, vying for authority over the Catholic Church. Indeed, after 1409 there were three claimants to the highest office in Christendom. The Council of Constance (1414–17) had claimed authority to sit in judgment on the question and had resolved the conflict by appointing Martin V pope in 1417. Those theologians who had defended the authority of a General Council of the Church to depose a wicked pope had drawn on earlier arguments which had maintained that cathedral chapters could exercise restraining authority over corrupt bishops. It was straightforward to apply conciliarist arguments in a secular context: If wicked popes could be deposed, so could wicked monarchs. If the council represented the whole Church, and so had authority over any individual, even the pope, so the Parliament in England, or the Estates General in France, could be claimed to be the representative of the nation, with authority over any individual ruler.

From 1517 to 1688 radical constitutionalist arguments thus replicated the conciliarist arguments of the later Middle Ages, appealing to the time-worn principles that the whole had authority over the part and that the safety of the community as a whole must take precedence over all else. Like their conciliarist precursors, constitutionalists took the fundamental structure of the constitution for granted. Conciliarists believed the structure of the Church had been ordained by God; their task was simply to interpret that structure so it could cope with the unprecedented crisis of the schism. Constitutionalists likewise assumed that there would always be kings, nobles, and representatives of the commons. They saw their task as being not to devise a radically new constitution but to interpret the powers present in the existing constitution so that it could cope with the crises of tyranny, religious intolerance, and civil war. Both saw representative assemblies not as permanent bodies but as institutions called together in moments of crisis to replace one chief executive by another.

Thus the second consequence of the Reformation crisis was a secularized version of conciliarist arguments; the first had been a reassertion on the part of Protestant rulers of the traditional claims of secular rulers to be independent of papal jurisdiction. Popes claimed, as they had in the Middle Ages, the right to depose heretical rulers. Rulers responded by insisting that they had inherited the authority of the first Christian Roman Emperor, Constantine, who had not hesitated to exercise authority over the bishop of Rome. James I of England (1566–1625) argued that kings were God's lieutenants on earth, and no subject had a right to judge them, while they had a right to exercise authority over the Church. Like Luther, he argued that wicked rulers were sent by God as a punishment for their sinful subjects. Resistance could never be justified. Ordered to perform a wicked action, a subject must merely passively disobey and accept without complaint the consequent punishment.

The divine right of kings theory was a deliberate response, not only to papal claims, but also to constitutionalism. James I, who was king of Scotland as well as England, was threatened both by Catholics (who tried to assassinate him in 1605) and by Presbyterians (as Scottish Calvinists were called), who had consistently sought to limit the powers of the monarchy in Scotland. Hobbes's *Leviathan* was intended to defend many of the central claims made on behalf of royal authority (although Hobbes of course insisted that he was merely trying to find a proper balance between liberty and authority), but to do so by relying not on religious but almost entirely on secular arguments. At the same time, in the second half of the book he set out to attack those aspects of Christian teaching which provided a foundation for claims to an independent religious authority, whether on behalf of pope or presbyter. As we shall see, his revision of Christian doctrine was every bit as systematic as his revision of political theory.

The Reformation had resulted in a long-lasting crisis of authority. Hobbes had constructed the outlines of his political philosophy well before the English Civil War (fought between the Episcopalians and the Puritans, as English Calvinists were called) began in 1642. But he had lived in France while Catholics had been at war with Protestants, and, like all his contemporaries, he was not only familiar with the history of the French Wars of Religion (1562–98) and the Dutch Revolt against Spain (1566–1648) but also had been an anxious observer of the Thirty Years' War in Germany (1618–48), which was primarily a war over religion, Catholic versus Protestant. In defending secular authority against any possible challenger, he was offering new arguments in support of the absolute authority of princes and was seeking to overthrow all the existing arguments for constitutionalism and religious freedom.

Not only had the Reformation exacerbated the long-running dispute over the nature of political authority, Protestants and Catholics could not agree over how to obtain knowledge of religious truth. For Protestants, the ultimate authority was the Bible text; for Catholics, it was the traditional teaching of the Church. Their disputes cast in doubt the nature of knowledge itself. In 1562 the works of the Hellenistic sceptical philosopher Sextus Empiricus had been rediscovered and published, and scepticism, brilliantly expounded in the *Essays* (1576–92) of Michel de Montaigne, soon came to provide the basis of a new political and moral theory, which was expounded by Montaigne's disciple Pierre Charron in his *Of Wisdom* (1601). Charron argued that sceptics, since they did not know where truth lay or who had right and justice on their side, were bound to support the status quo and established authority. To do otherwise would be to risk endangering order for no certain gain. Scepticism thus gave birth to a systematic conservatism in moral and political philosophy, expressed, for example, in the third part of Descartes's *Discourse on Method* (1637), where Descartes outlines the rules he had adopted to guide his life before he had discovered a secure principle on which knowledge could be founded, the *cogito ergo sum.*

The sceptical crisis unleashed by the Reformation was intensified by the opening phases of the scientific revolution. In 1632 the Inquisition condemned Galileo's *Dialogue Concerning the Two Chief World Systems,* but increasingly the simple certainties of Aristotelian science, which, though they had occasionally been questioned, had been dominant for two thousand years—that the sun revolved around the earth, that the heavens were unchanging—were being put in doubt by the astronomical calculations, first of Copernicus, and then of Kepler and Brahe, and those doubts were sharply reinforced by Galileo's discoveries when he pointed a telescope at the heavens. "The new philosophy casts all in doubt" wrote the poet John Donne. It was this pervasive uncertainty for which both Hobbes and Descartes (both of them admirers of Galileo) sought remedies. Independently, both reached the conclusion that knowledge must be founded on a deductive science of nature and that the foundation of such a science must be a strictly materialist account of natural phenomena. For Descartes, commitment to a deductive science was compatible with the belief that experiment was an indispensable tool for discovery. For Hobbes, on the other hand, Euclid's geometry, which he first read around 1630, provided a nonexperimental model for such a deductive science, one whose conclusions no one could dispute. Hobbes's Euclidean paradigm points to another respect in which he parted company with Descartes, for Descartes believed that knowledge must be grounded in distinctions that were divinely ordained, while Hobbes thought of all knowledge as man-made.

The wars of religion and the sceptical crisis provide the broad context for Hobbes's political philosophy. That philosophy was first formulated in 1640 in *The Elements of Law.* But we find hints of Hobbes's mature views in essays published anonymously in 1620 (assuming Hobbes is indeed their author). The striking thing about these essays is that they are evidently the result of a sustained reflection on Machiavellian themes. Where Machiavelli had puzzled in the *Discourses* over how a new republic could be founded, Hobbes was preoccupied with the task of how to constitute an absolute, effective political authority where once there had been constitutional authority and limited powers. Machiavelli's hero had been Rome's founder, Romulus. Hobbes's hero was the first emperor, Augustus. Like Machiavelli, Hobbes recognized that power depended on force and the ability to instill fear.

A second influence was joined to that of Machiavelli before Hobbes's discovery of Euclid, when Hugo Grotius published *On the Law of War and Peace* in 1625. Grotius was contributing to what had been a lively tradition of inquiry within scholastic philosophy, that of analyzing the nature of law: Were rational precepts binding, or did laws have to take the form of commands and be enforced by punishments? and of deciding what laws any rational individual would be bound to accept: Would there be a universally applicable moral law in the absence of the Ten Commandments? But Grotius revolutionized the tradition of natural-law philosophy by seeking to produce arguments which would convince even a sceptic, arguments that even an atheist would have to accept as valid. Following in Grotius's footsteps, Hobbes set out in *The Elements of Law* to provide an account of morality and authority which took nothing for granted, but which, like Euclid's geometry, was entirely dependent on self-evident principles. The most evident of all principles were that men flee pain and death, and that fear is a powerful motivator.

In order to argue from first principles Hobbes constructed an account of what he termed 'the state of nature'. Other theorists had discussed how men must have behaved before states were founded or religious truths revealed, but Hobbes's state of nature is not merely an historical hypothesis. It is a logical account of how any rational person would behave in the absence of knowledge of a life after death (in the absence, that is, of knowledge of rewards and punishments which would outweigh the pleasures and pains of this world) and in the absence of an existing political authority capable of imposing order. As such, it is an account of how men should behave whenever authority collapses. Hobbes sets out to prove that in a state of nature each individual will have interests which conflict with those of every other individual; each will have grounds to fear the other, and everyone therefore will be entitled to attack his neighbors before they have a chance to attack him. Only one thing can prevent continual conflict. Men and women must join together to construct a common authority capable of terrorizing each individual and imposing an order from which all will benefit. By constructing a state, they can cause peaceable behavior to be in everyone's interest, but any attempt to limit the power of the state threatens its authority and opens the way to new conflict. Only when acting in self-defense is anyone entitled to resist the ruler's authority. No one can give up the right to resist as they are taken away to be executed, but we can all agree not to come to a condemned person's assistance.

Hobbes argues that we are under an obligation to seek peace, but that in a state of nature we have no choice but to fight each other, and, when peace becomes possible, it is the result of our own success in constructing what he terms a 'mortal God', the state. There is consequently considerable scope for ambiguity about the status of God and divinely ordained obligations in Hobbes's argument, ambiguity which is exacerbated, not eliminated, by Hobbes's discussion of Christian theology and of, for example, the evidence for miracles in the second half of *Leviathan*. Hobbes's political theory was founded on materialist premises, and his account of Christian doctrine was therefore designed to show that materialism was compatible with Christian faith. Most of his contemporaries were unconvinced. They were persuaded that Hobbes himself was an atheist and that he was engaged in a deliberate attack on Christian faith. When he argued that our obligation to obey God was simply a consequence of God's power over us, they suspected him of simply reversing his account of the ruler as a 'mortal God'; for Hobbes God was nothing but an imaginary immortal sovereign. Some twentieth-century commentators have disputed this, claiming that God is central to the logic of *Leviathan* and that Hobbes's theology is much closer to orthodoxy than it seems. It is hard, though, to see why his contemporaries should have found Hobbes's true purposes so hard to fathom or why, if they were mistaken, Hobbes was unable to clarify the nature of their misunderstanding.

It is not just the secular character of Hobbes's argument which makes it seem modern. The tight logic of Hobbes's argument has delighted modern game theorists, who believe that his account of the state of nature foreshadows twentieth-century analyses of what are termed prisoner's dilemmas, situations in which the rational pursuit of selfish interests leads to outcomes that are disadvantageous for all involved. If two criminals are arrested and each is offered a significantly reduced sentence if he betrays the other (say one year in prison if their accomplice does not testify, six if he does), while they each face a long sentence (ten years) if their accomplice testifies against them and they refuse to cooperate, then each has more to gain by squealing than by staying silent, even if both know that if they both stay silent they will only be convicted of a lesser crime and face only two years in prison. Similarly, in the state of nature, each person will look for an opportunity to attack his neighbor simply out of fear that otherwise his neighbor will attack him first.

Hobbes's mature theory was largely formulated by 1640, but two further developments provide an immediate context for *Leviathan*. In the winter of 1642/43 a small group of radical authors made their own innovation in state-of-nature theory. They argued that, in the face of tyranny, all men and women were restored to the state of nature and to the natural freedoms that went with it. These arguments were taken up by the first modern democrats, the Levellers, who called for a new, written constitution, which would protect inalienable natural rights, such as the right to religious freedom. They thus broke through what had been the unquestioned assumption underlying all previous constitutionalist theorizing. Before 1642 everyone assumed that in the face of tyranny men should seek to restore the traditional constitution which had been briefly infringed, just as the Conciliarists had sought to repair the fabric of Church government. Now, as the English Civil War was being fought, it was for the first time argued that there was no reason why a new generation should be bound by the decisions of its ancestors. In the face of tyranny, they could opt for an entirely new beginning, abolishing monarchy and hereditary nobility and establishing the first representative democracy.

To meet such arguments, Hobbes subtly modified the position he had adopted in the *Elements*. There he had argued that people must join together to establish authority; this act, once completed in the past, would bind their future actions. In *Leviathan*, however, he argues that government depends on the continuing consent of the people. The ruler must represent the people, not merely in the sense that they once chose him, but in the sense that they continue to give their support to him (even if only out of fear). Hobbes thus accepted the Levellers' radical rejection of history. Past decisions are worthless; only present consent can constitute legitimacy.

The outcome of the Civil War was not, however, the democracy for which the Levellers had struggled. Instead, when the king's armies were defeated and the king himself was executed, power was concentrated in the hands of Oliver Cromwell, Parliament's triumphant general. In 1650 Parliament demanded that anyone with any official business to conduct take an oath of loyalty to the new regime, even though such an oath would be in direct conflict with their earlier oaths of loyalty to the king. In 1651 *Leviathan* was published. Hobbes had been in exile in France for a decade, and his arguments in favor of unchecked royal authority had been popular among the royalists gathered there in exile, whose numbers were swollen after the victories of Cromwell's armies. But it was part of the logic of Hobbes's argument that there was no reason why one should respect a traditional authority just because it was long-established. Any authority capable of establishing order by instilling fear was deserving of respect, a claim which Hobbes presented bluntly in *Leviathan*. Soon after his book was published, Hobbes returned to England to make his peace with the new regime. This, combined with the fact that Hobbes now felt free, since there was for the moment no established religion in England, to attack the traditional teachings of the Church of England in a way that he had never done before, caused his former allies to turn against him. After Cromwell's death and the restoration of the monarchy in 1660, Hobbes's views were universally attacked by all respectable intellectuals, and Hobbes himself feared arrest and possibly death, though in fact he was allowed to live out his life in peace.

Machiavellian realism, the wars of religion, the sceptical crisis, Grotius's adaptation of natural-law arguments to meet sceptical challenges, Leveller radicalism, and Cromwell's victory: Each contributed something to *Leviathan*. Each of them helped refine Hobbes's argument that only fear could hold society together and that there should be no limitations placed upon the rights of rulers. In stressing the power of the sword and the inefficacy of mere words, Hobbes was following Machiavelli. In fearing disorder and in seeking to establish a chain of argument in which every link could withstand criticism, Hobbes was responding to religious warfare and the scepticism it had engendered. In insisting that legitimacy must constantly be rebuilt in the present and that Cromwell's power was sufficient to give him the right to rule, Hobbes was responding to the immediate events of the Civil War. But out of these disparate elements he fashioned an argument which still has the power to thrill readers who have never heard of Grotius, readers who remain to the end convinced that Hobbes's argument must be wrong, even though they find it almost impossible to say why.

Further Reading

The classic account of the impact of the Reformation on political thought is to be found in Quentin Skinner's *The Foundations of Modern Political Thought* (2 vols., Cambridge: Cambridge University Press, 1978), vol. 2, which should be supplemented by Q. Skinner, "The Origins of the Calvinist Theory of Revolution" in B. Malament (ed.), *After the Reformation* (Philadelphia: University of Pennsylvania Press, 1980), pp. 309–30. Skinner's book ends in the early seventeenth century. The later period is analyzed in Richard Tuck, *Philosophy and Government, 1572–1651* (Cambridge: Cambridge University Press, 1993). The crucial impact of the French Wars of Religion on political thought is analyzed in Donald Kelley, *The Beginnings of Ideology: Consciousness and Society in the French Reformation* (Cambridge: Cambridge University Press, 1981). The argument that much sixteenth- and seventeenth-century political thought had medieval origins is presented in Brian Tierney, *Religion, Law and the Growth of Constitutional Thought, 1150–1650* (Cambridge: Cambridge University Press, 1982). The impact of scepticism is outlined in Richard Popkin, *The History of Scepticism from Erasmus to Spinoza* (Berkeley: University of California Press, 1979). And the emergence of the first modern rights theories is described in D. Wootton, "From Rebellion to Revolution: the Crisis of the Winter of 1642/3 and the Origins of Civil War Radicalism," *English Historical Review*, vol. 105 (1990), 654–69.

The best introduction to Calvin's political thought is H. M. Höpfl, *The Christian Polity of John Calvin* (Cambridge: Cambridge University Press, 1982).

The best short introduction to Hobbes is Richard Tuck, *Hobbes* (Oxford: Oxford University Press, 1989). A more detailed historical account is to be found in Johann Sommerville, *Thomas Hobbes: Political Ideas in Historical Context* (New York: St. Martin's Press, 1992). Particularly stimulating for its application of game theory to Hobbes is Jean Hampton, *Hobbes and the Social Contract Tradition* (Cambridge: Cambridge University Press, 1986). On Hobbes and the scientific revolution, Steven Shapin and Simon Schaffer, *Leviathan and the Air Pump* (Princeton: Princeton University

Press, 1985) is indispensable. Helpful if one wishes to compare Hobbes's science with Descartes's is Daniel Garber, "Descartes and Experiment in the *Discourse* and *Essays*," in Stephen Voss (ed.), *Essays on the Philosophy and Science of Descartes* (New York: Oxford University Press, 1993), pp. 288–310. A controversial account of Hobbes's religious views is to be found in A. P. Martinich, *The Two Gods of Leviathan* (Cambridge: Cambridge University Press, 1992). For a decisive refutation see Quentin Skinner, *Reason and Rhetoric in the Philosophy of Hobbes* (Cambridge: Cambridge University Press, 1996). What would appear to be Hobbes's first philosophical work is reprinted as *Three Discourses* ed. N. B. Reynolds and A. Saxonhouse (Chicago: University of Chicago Press, 1995). Two classic essays are Keith Thomas, "The Social Origins of Hobbes's Political Thought," in K. C. Brown (ed.), *Hobbes Studies* (Oxford: Blackwell, 1965), pp. 185–236, and Quentin Skinner, "Conquest and Consent: Thomas Hobbes and the Engagement Controversy" in G. E. Aylmer (ed.), *The Interregnum: The Quest for Settlement, 1646–1660* (London: Macmillan, 1972), pp. 79–98.

CALVIN

On Civil Government

(How civil and spiritual government are related, 1–2)
1. Differences between spiritual and civil government

Now, since we have established above that man is under a twofold government, and since we have elsewhere discussed at sufficient length the kind that resides in the soul or inner man and pertains to eternal life, this is the place to say something also about the other kind, which pertains only to the establishment of civil justice and outward morality.

For although this topic seems by nature alien to the spiritual doctrine of faith which I have undertaken to discuss, what follows will show that I am right in joining them, in fact, that necessity compels me to do so. This is especially true since, from one side, insane and barbarous men furiously strive to overturn this divinely established order; while, on the other side, the flatterers of princes, immoderately praising their power, do not hesitate to set them against the rule of God himself. Unless both these evils are checked, purity of faith will perish. Besides, it is of no slight importance to us to know how lovingly God has provided in this respect for mankind, that greater zeal for piety may flourish in us to attest our gratefulness.

First, before we enter into the matter itself, we must keep in mind that distinction which we previously laid down so that we do not (as commonly happens) unwisely mingle these two, which have a completely different nature. For certain men, when they hear that the gospel promises a freedom that acknowledges no king and no magistrate among men, but looks to Christ alone, think that they cannot benefit by their freedom so long as they see any power set up over them. They therefore think that nothing will be safe unless the whole world is reshaped to a new form, where there are neither courts, nor laws, nor magistrates, nor anything which in their opinion restricts their freedom. But whoever knows how to distinguish between body and soul, between this present fleeting life and that future eternal life, will without difficulty know that Christ's spiritual Kingdom and the civil jurisdiction are things completely distinct. Since, then, it is a Jewish vanity to seek and enclose Christ's Kingdom within the elements of this world, let us rather ponder that what Scripture clearly teaches is a spiritual fruit, which we gather from Christ's grace; and let us remember to keep within its own limits all that freedom which is promised and offered to us in him. For why is it that the same apostle who bids us stand and not submit to the "yoke of bondage" [Gal. 5:1] elsewhere forbids slaves to be anxious about their state [I Cor. 7:21], unless it be that spiritual freedom can perfectly well exist along with civil bondage? These statements of his must also be taken in the same sense: In the Kingdom of God "there is neither Jew nor Greek, neither male nor female, neither slave nor free" [Gal. 3:28, Vg.; order changed]. And again, "there is not Jew nor Greek, uncircumcised and circumcised, barbarian, Scythian, slave, freeman; but Christ is all in all" [Col. 3:11 p.]. By these statements he means that it makes no difference what your condition among men may be or under what nation's laws you live, since

"On Civil Government" from John Calvin, *Institutes of the Christian Religion*: Bk. IV, Ch. XX, edited by John T. McNeill (Library of Christian Classics). Used by permission of Westminster John Knox Press and T&T Clark, Ltd.

the Kingdom of Christ does not at all consist in these things.

2. The two "governments" are not antithetical

Yet this distinction does not lead us to consider the whole nature of government a thing polluted, which has nothing to do with Christian men. That is what, indeed, certain fanatics who delight in unbridled license shout and boast: after we have died through Christ to the elements of this world [Col. 2:20], are transported to God's Kingdom, and sit among heavenly beings, it is a thing unworthy of us and set far beneath our excellence to be occupied with those vile and worldly cares which have to do with business foreign to a Christian man. To what purpose, they ask, are there laws without trials and tribunals? But what has a Christian man to do with trials themselves? Indeed, if it is not lawful to kill, why do we have laws and trials? But as we have just now pointed out that this kind of government is distinct from that spiritual and inward Kingdom of Christ, so we must know that they are not at variance. For spiritual government, indeed, is already initiating in us upon earth certain beginnings of the Heavenly Kingdom, and in this mortal and fleeting life affords a certain forecast of an immortal and incorruptible blessedness. Yet civil government has as its appointed end, so long as we live among men, to cherish and protect the outward worship of God, to defend sound doctrine of piety and the position of the church, to adjust our life to the society of men, to form our social behavior to civil righteousness, to reconcile us with one another, and to promote general peace and tranquility. All of this I admit to be superfluous, if God's Kingdom, such as it is now among us, wipes out the present life. But if it is God's will that we go as pilgrims upon the earth while we aspire to the true fatherland, and if the pilgrimage requires such helps, those who take these from man deprive him of his very humanity. Our adversaries claim that there ought to be such great perfection in the church of God that its government should suffice for law. But they stupidly imagine such a perfection as can never be found in a community of men. For since the insolence of evil men is so great, their wickedness so stubborn, that it can

scarcely be restrained by extremely severe laws, what do we expect them to do if they see that their depravity can go scot-free—when no power can force them to cease from doing evil?

(Necessity and divine sanction of civil government, 3–7)
3. The chief tasks and burdens of civil government

But there will be a more appropriate place to speak of the practice of civil government. Now we only wish it to be understood that to think of doing away with it is outrageous barbarity. Its function among men is no less than that of bread, water, sun, and air; indeed, its place of honor is far more excellent. For it does not merely see to it, as all these serve to do, that men breathe, eat, drink, and are kept warm, even though it surely embraces all these activities when it provides for their living together. It does not, I repeat, look to this only, but also prevents idolatry, sacrilege against God's name, blasphemies against his truth, and other public offenses against religion from arising and spreading among the people; it prevents the public peace from being disturbed; it provides that each man may keep his property safe and sound; that men may carry on blameless intercourse among themselves; that honesty and modesty may be preserved among men. In short, it provides that a public manifestation of religion may exist among Christians, and that humanity be maintained among men.

Let no man be disturbed that I now commit to civil government the duty of rightly establishing religion, which I seem above to have put outside of human decision. For, when I approve of a civil administration that aims to prevent the true religion which is contained in God's law from being openly and with public sacrilege violated and defiled with impunity, I do not here, any more than before, allow men to make laws according to their own decision concerning religion and the worship of God.

But my readers, assisted by the very clarity of the arrangement, will better understand what is to be thought of the whole subject of civil government if we discuss its parts separately. These are three: the magistrate, who is the protector and guardian of the laws; the laws, according to which he governs; the people, who are governed by the laws and obey the magistrate.

Let us, then, first look at the office of the magistrate, noting whether it is a lawful calling approved of God; the nature of the office; the extent of its power; then, with what laws a Christian government ought to be governed; and finally, how the laws benefit the people, and what obedience is owed to the magistrate.

4. The magistracy is ordained by God

The Lord has not only testified that the office of magistrate is approved by and acceptable to him, but he also sets out its dignity with the most honorable titles and marvelously commends it to us. To mention a few: Since those who serve as magistrate are called "gods" [Ex. 22:8, Vg.; Ps. 82:1, 6], let no one think that their being so-called is of slight importance. For it signifies that they have a mandate from God, have been invested with divine authority, and are wholly God's representatives, in a manner, acting as his vicegerents. This is no subtlety of mine, but Christ's explanation. "If Scripture," he says, "called them gods to whom the word of God came . . ." [John 10:35.] What is this, except that God has entrusted to them the business of serving him in their office, and (as Moses and Jehoshaphat said to the judges whom they appointed in every city of Judah) of exercising judgment not for man but for God [Deut. 1:16–17; II Chron. 19:6]? To the same purpose is what God's wisdom affirms through Solomon's mouth, that it is his doing "that kings reign, and counselors decree what is just, that princes exercise dominion, and all benevolent judges of the earth" [Prov. 8:14–16]. This amounts to the same thing as to say: it has not come about by human perversity that the authority over all things on earth is in the hands of kings and other rulers, but by divine providence and holy ordinance. For God was pleased so to rule the affairs of men, inasmuch as he is present with them and also presides over the making of laws and the exercising of equity in courts of justice. Paul also plainly teaches this when he lists "ruling" among God's gifts [Rom. 12:8, KJV or RV], which, variously distributed according to the diversity of grace, ought to be used by Christ's

servants for the upbuilding of the church. For even though Paul is there speaking specifically of a council of sober men, who were appointed in the primitive church to preside over the ordering of public discipline (which office is called in the letter to the Corinthians, "governments" [I Cor. 12:28]), yet because we see the civil power serving the same end, there is no doubt that he commends to us every kind of just rule.

But Paul speaks much more clearly when he undertakes a just discussion of this matter. For he states both that power is an ordinance of God [Rom. 13:2], and that there are no powers except those ordained by God [Rom. 13:1]. Further, that princes are ministers of God, for those doing good unto praise; for those doing evil, avengers unto wrath [Rom. 13:3–4]. To this may be added the examples of holy men, of whom some possessed kingdoms, as David, Josiah, and Hezekiah; others, lordships, as Joseph and Daniel; others, civil rule among a free people, as Moses, Joshua, and the judges. The Lord has declared his approval of their offices. Accordingly, no one ought to doubt that civil authority is a calling, not only holy and lawful before God, but also the most sacred and by far the most honorable of all callings in the whole life of mortal men.

5. Against the "Christian" denial or rejection of magistracy

Those who desire to usher in anarchy object that, although in antiquity kings and judges ruled over ignorant folk, yet that servile kind of governing is wholly incompatible today with the perfection which Christ brought with his gospel. In this they betray not only their ignorance but devilish arrogance, when they claim a perfection of which not even a hundredth part is seen in them. But whatever kind of men they may be, the refutation is easy. For where David urges all kings and rulers to kiss the Son of God [Ps. 2:12], he does not bid them lay aside their authority and retire to private life, but submit to Christ the power with which they have been invested, that he alone may tower over all. Similarly, Isaiah, when he promises that kings shall be foster fathers of the church, and queens its nurses [Isa. 49:23], does not deprive them of their honor. Rather, by a noble title he makes them defenders of God's pious worshipers; for that prophecy looks to the coming of Christ. I knowingly pass over very many passages which occur frequently, and especially in the psalms, in which the right of rulers is asserted for them all [Ps. 21; 22; 45; 72; 89; 110; 132]. But most notable of all is the passage of Paul where, admonishing Timothy that prayers be offered for kings in public assembly, he immediately adds the reason: "That we may lead a peaceful life under them with all godliness and honesty" [I Tim. 2:2]. By these words he entrusts the condition of the church to their protection and care.

6. Magistrates should be faithful as God's deputies

This consideration ought continually to occupy the magistrates themselves, since it can greatly spur them to exercise their office and bring them remarkable comfort to mitigate the difficulties of their task, which are indeed many and burdensome. For what great zeal for uprightness, for prudence, gentleness, self-control, and for innocence ought to be required of themselves by those who know that they have been ordained ministers of divine justice? How will they have the brazenness to admit injustice to their judgment seat, which they are told is the throne of the living God? How will they have the boldness to pronounce an unjust sentence, by that mouth which they know has been appointed an instrument of divine truth? With what conscience will they sign wicked decrees by that hand which they know has been appointed to record the acts of God? To sum up, if they remember that they are vicars of God, they should watch with all care, earnestness, and diligence, to represent in themselves to men some image of divine providence, protection, goodness, benevolence, and justice. And they should perpetually set before themselves the thought that "if all are cursed who carry out in deceit the work of God's vengeance" [Jer. 48:10 p.], much more gravely cursed are they who deceitfully conduct themselves in a righteous calling. Therefore, when Moses and Jehoshaphat wished to urge their judges to do their duty, they had nothing more effective to persuade them than what we have

previously mentioned [Deut. 1:16]: "Consider what you do, for you exercise judgment not for man but for the Lord; since he is beside you in giving judgment. Now then, let the fear of the Lord be upon you. Take heed what you do, for there is no perversity with the Lord our God" [II Chron. 19:6–7 p.]. And in another place it is said: "God stood in the assembly of the gods, and holds judgment in the midst of the gods" [Ps. 82:1]. This is to hearten them for their task when they learn that they are deputies of God, to whom they must hereafter render account of the administration of their charge. And this admonition deserves to have great weight with them. For if they commit some fault, they are not only wrongdoers to men whom they wickedly trouble, but are also insulting toward God himself, whose most holy judgments they defile [cf. Isa. 3:14–15]. Again, they have the means to comfort themselves greatly when they ponder in themselves that they are occupied not with profane affairs or those alien to a servant of God, but with a most holy office, since they are serving as God's deputies.

7. The coercive character of magistracy does not hinder its recognition

Those who, unmoved by so many testimonies of Scripture, dare rail against this holy ministry as a thing abhorrent to Christian religion and piety—what else do they do but revile God himself, whose ministry cannot be reproached without dishonor to himself? And these folk do not just reject the magistrates, but cast off God that he may not reign over them. For if the Lord truly said this of the people of Israel because they refused Samuel's rule [I Sam. 8:7], why will it less truly be said today of these who let themselves rage against all governments ordained by God? The Lord said to his disciples that the kings of the Gentiles exercise lordship over Gentiles, but it is not so among the disciples, where he who is first ought to become the least [Luke 22:25–26]; by this saying, they tell us, all Christians are forbidden to take kingdoms or governments. O skillful interpreters! There arose a contention among the disciples over which one would excel the others. To silence this vain ambition, the Lord taught them that their ministry is not like kingdoms, in which one is pre-eminent above the rest. What dishonor, I ask you, does this comparison do to kingly dignity? Indeed, what does it prove at all, except that the kingly office is not the ministry of an apostle? Moreover, among magistrates themselves, although there is a variety of forms, there is no difference in this respect, that we must regard all of them as ordained of God. For Paul also lumps them all together when he says that there is no power except from God [Rom. 13:1]. And that which is the least pleasant of all has been especially commended above the rest, that is, the power of one. This, because it brings with it the common bondage of all (except that one man to whose will it subjects all things), in ancient times could not be acceptable to heroic and nobler natures. But to forestall their unjust judgments, Scripture expressly affirms that it is the providence of God's wisdom that kings reign [cf. Prov. 8:15], and particularly commands us to honor the king [Prov. 24:21; I Peter 2:17].

(Forms of government, and duties of magistrates. Issues of war and taxation, 8–13)
8. The diversity of forms of government

Obviously, it would be an idle pastime for men in private life, who are disqualified from deliberating on the organization of any commonwealth, to dispute over what would be the best kind of government in that place where they live. Also this question admits of no simple solution but requires deliberation, since the nature of the discussion depends largely upon the circumstances. And if you compare the forms of government among themselves apart from the circumstances, it is not easy to distinguish which one of them excels in usefulness, for they contend on such equal terms. The fall from kingdom to tyranny is easy; but it is not much more difficult to fall from the rule of the best men to the faction of a few; yet it is easiest of all to fall from popular rule to sedition. For if the three forms of government which the philosophers discuss be considered in themselves, I will not deny that aristocracy, or a system compounded of aristocracy and democracy, far excels all others: not indeed of itself, but because it is very rare for kings so to control themselves that their will never disagrees

with what is just and right; or for them to have been endowed with such great keenness and prudence, that each knows how much is enough. Therefore, men's fault or failing causes it to be safer and more bearable for a number to exercise government, so that they may help one another, teach and admonish one another; and, if one asserts himself unfairly, there may be a number of censors and masters to restrain his willfulness. This has both been proved by experience, and also the Lord confirmed it by his authority when he ordained among the Israelites an aristocracy bordering on democracy, since he willed to keep them in best condition [Ex. 18:13–26; Deut. 1:9–17] until he should bring forward the image of Christ in David. And, as I freely admit that no kind of government is more happy than one where freedom is regulated with becoming moderation and is properly established on a durable basis, so also I reckon most happy those permitted to enjoy this state; and if they stoutly and constantly labor to preserve and retain it, I grant that they are doing nothing alien to this office. Indeed, the magistrates ought to apply themselves with the highest diligence to prevent the freedom (whose guardians they have been appointed) from being in any respect diminished, far less be violated. If they are not sufficiently alert and careful, they are faithless in office, and traitors to their country.

But if those to whom the Lord has appointed another form of government should transfer this very function to themselves, being moved to desire a change of government — even to think of such a move will not only be foolish and superfluous, but altogether harmful. However, as you will surely find if you fix your eyes not on one city alone, but look around and glance at the world as a whole, or at least cast your sight upon regions farther off, divine providence has wisely arranged that various countries should be ruled by various kinds of government. For as elements cohere only in unequal proportion, so countries are best held together according to their own particular inequality. However, all these things are needlessly spoken to those for whom the will of the Lord is enough. For if it has seemed good to him to set kings over kingdoms, senates or municipal officers over free cities, it is our duty to show ourselves compliant and obedient to whomever he sets over the places where we live.

9. Concern for both Tables of the Law

Now in this place we ought to explain in passing the office of the magistrates, how it is described in the Word of God and the things in which it consists. If Scripture did not teach that it extends to both Tables of the Law, we could learn this from secular writers: for no one has discussed the office of magistrates, the making of laws, and public welfare, without beginning at religion and divine worship. And thus all have confessed that no government can be happily established unless piety is the first concern; and that those laws are preposterous which neglect God's right and provide only for men. Since, therefore, among all philosophers religion takes first place, and since this fact has always been observed by universal consent of all nations, let Christian princes and magistrates be ashamed of their negligence if they do not apply themselves to this concern. And we have already shown that these duties are especially enjoined upon them by God; and it is fitting that they should labor to protect and assert the honor of him whose representatives they are, and by whose grace they govern.

Also, holy kings are greatly praised in Scripture because they restored the worship of God when it was corrupted or destroyed, or took care of religion that under them it might flourish pure and unblemished. But on the contrary, the Sacred History places anarchies among things evil: because there was no king in Israel, each man did as he pleased [Judg. 21:25].

This proves the folly of those who would neglect the concern for God and would give attention only to rendering justice among men. As if God appointed rulers in his name to decide earthly controversies but overlooked what was of far greater importance—that he himself should be purely worshiped according to the prescription of his law. But the passion to alter everything with impunity drives turbulent men to the point of wanting all vindicators of violated piety removed from their midst.

As far as the Second Table is concerned, Jeremiah admonishes kings to "do justice and righteousness," to "deliver him who has been oppressed by force from the hand of the oppressor," not to "grieve or wrong the alien, the widow, and the fatherless" or "shed innocent blood" [Jer. 22:3, cf. Vg.]. The exhortation which we read in Ps. 82 has the same purpose: that they should "give justice to the poor and needy, rescue the destitute and needy, and deliver the poor and needy from the hand of the oppressor" [Ps. 82:3–4]. And Moses commands the leaders whom he had appointed as his representatives to "hear the cases between their brethren, and judge . . . between a man and his brother, and the alien" and "not recognize faces in judgment, and hear small and great alike, and be afraid of no man, for the judgment is God's" [Deut. 1:16–17 p.]. But I pass over such statements as these: that kings should not multiply horses for themselves; nor set their mind upon avarice; nor be lifted up above their brethren; that they should be constant in meditating upon the law of the Lord all the days of their life [Deut. 17:16–19]; that judges should not lean to one side or take bribes [Deut. 16:19]—and like passages which we read here and there in Scripture. For in explaining here the office of magistrates, it is not so much my purpose to instruct the magistrates themselves as to teach others what magistrates are and to what end God has appointed them. We see, therefore, that they are ordained protectors and vindicators of public innocence, modesty, decency, and tranquillity, and that their sole endeavor should be to provide for the common safety and peace of all. Of these virtues David professes that he will be a pattern: when he has been elevated to the royal throne, he will not consent to any crimes, but will detest the impious, slanderers, and the proud, and will seek out from everywhere upright and faithful counselors [Ps. 101, esp. vs. 4, 5, 7, 6].

But since they cannot perform this unless they defend good men from the wrongs of the wicked, and give aid and protection to the oppressed, they have also been armed with power with which severely to coerce the open malefactors and criminals by whose wickedness the public peace is troubled or disturbed [cf. Rom. 13:3]. For from experience we thoroughly agree with the statement of Solon that all commonwealths are maintained by reward and punishment;

take these away and the whole discipline of cities collapses and is dissolved. For the care of equity and justice grows cold in the minds of many, unless due honor has been prepared for virtue; and the lust of wicked men cannot be restrained except by severity and the infliction of penalties. And the prophet has included these two functions, when he bids kings and other rulers execute judgment and justice [Jer. 22:3; cf. ch. 21:12]. Justice, indeed, is to receive into safe-keeping, to embrace, to protect, vindicate, and free the innocent. But judgment is to withstand the boldness of the impious, to repress their violence, to punish their misdeeds.

10. The magistrates' exercise of force is compatible with piety

But here a seemingly hard and difficult question arises: if the law of God forbids all Christians to kill [Ex. 20:13; Deut. 5:17; Matt. 5:21], and the prophet prophesies concerning God's holy mountain (the church) that in it men shall not afflict or hurt [Isa. 11:9; 65:25]—how can magistrates be pious men and shedders of blood at the same time?

Yet if we understand that the magistrate in administering punishments does nothing by himself, but carries out the very judgments of God, we shall not be hampered by this scruple. The law of the Lord forbids killing; but, that murders may not go unpunished, the Lawgiver himself puts into the hand of his ministers a sword to be drawn against all murderers. It is not for the pious to afflict and hurt; yet to avenge, at the Lord's command, the afflictions of the pious is not to hurt or to afflict. Would that this were ever before our minds—that nothing is done here from men's rashness, but all things are done on the authority of God who commands it; and while his authority goes before us, we never wander from the straight path! Unless perhaps restraint is laid upon God's justice, that it may not punish misdeeds. But if it is not right to impose any law upon him, why should we try to reproach his ministers? They do not bear the sword in vain, says Paul, for they are ministers of God to execute his wrath, avengers of wrongdoers [Rom. 13:4]. Therefore, if princes and other rulers recognize that nothing is more acceptable to the Lord than their

obedience, let them apply themselves to this ministry, if, indeed, they are intent on having their piety, righteousness, and uprightness approved of God [cf. II Tim. 2:15].

Moses was impelled by this desire when, realizing that he had been destined by the Lord's power to be liberator of his people, he laid his hand upon the Egyptian [Ex. 2:12; Acts 7:24]. This was the case again, when, by slaying three thousand men in one day, he took vengeance upon the people's sacrilege [Ex. 32:27–28]. David also, when at the end of his life he ordered his son Solomon to kill Joab and Shimei [I Kings 2:5–6, 8–9]. Accordingly, he also includes this among kingly virtues: to destroy the wicked of the land, that all evildoers may be driven out of the city of God [Ps. 101:8]. To this also pertains the praise which is given to Solomon: "You have loved righteousness and hated iniquity" [Ps. 45:7; 44:8, Vg.].

How does Moses' gentle and peaceable nature flame up into such savageness that, sprinkled and dripping with the blood of his brethren, he dashes through the camp to new carnage? How can David, a man of such great gentleness throughout life, as he breathes his last, make that bloody testament, that his son should not allow the hoary heads of Joab and Shimei to go in peace to the grave [I Kings 2:5–6, 8–9]? But both men, by executing the vengeance ordained of God, hallowed by cruelty their hands, which by sparing they would have defiled. "It is an abomination among kings," says Solomon, "to do iniquity, for the throne is established in righteousness." [Prov. 16:12.] Again: "A king who sits on the throne of judgment casts his eyes upon every evildoer" [Prov. 20:8 p.]. Again: "A wise king scatters the evildoers and turns them upon the wheel" [Prov. 20:26 p.]. Again: "Remove the dross from the silver, and a vessel will come forth to the metal caster; remove the impious from the king's sight, and his throne will be established in righteousness" [Prov. 25:4–5, cf. Geneva]. Again: "He who justifies the wicked and he who condemns the righteous are both alike an abomination to the Lord" [Prov. 17:15]. Again: "A rebel seeks evil for himself, and a cruel messenger is sent to him" [Prov. 17:11 p.]. Again: "He who says to the wicked, 'You are righteous,' will be cursed by peoples . . . and nations" [Prov. 24:24 p.]. Now if their true righteousness is to pursue the guilty and the impious with drawn sword, should they sheathe their sword and keep their hands clean of blood, while abandoned men wickedly range about with slaughter and massacre, they will become guilty of the greatest impiety, far indeed from winning praise for their goodness and righteousness thereby!

Begone, now, with that abrupt and savage harshness, and that tribunal which is rightly called the reef of accused men! For I am not one either to favor undue cruelty or think that a fair judgment can be pronounced unless clemency, that best counselor of kings and surest keeper of the kingly throne (as Solomon declares) [Prov. 20:28] is always present—clemency, which by a certain writer of antiquity was truly called the chief gift of princes.

Yet it is necessary for the magistrate to pay attention to both, lest by excessive severity he either harm more than heal; or, by superstitious affectation of clemency, fall into the cruelest gentleness, if he should (with a soft and dissolute kindness) abandon many to their destruction. For during the reign of Nerva it was not without reason said: it is indeed bad to live under a prince with whom nothing is permitted; but much worse under one by whom everything is allowed.

11. On the right of the government to wage war

But kings and people must sometimes take up arms to execute such public vengeance. On this basis we may judge wars lawful which are so undertaken. For if power has been given them to preserve the tranquillity of their dominion, to restrain the seditious stirrings of restless men, to help those forcibly oppressed, to punish evil deeds—can they use it more opportunely than to check the fury of one who disturbs both the repose of private individuals and the common tranquillity of all, who raises seditious tumults, and by whom violent oppressions and vile misdeeds are perpetrated? If they ought to be the guardians and defenders of the laws, they should also overthrow the efforts of all whose offenses corrupt the discipline of the laws. Indeed, if they rightly punish those robbers

whose harmful acts have affected only a few, will they allow a whole country to be afflicted and devastated by robberies with impunity? For it makes no difference whether it be a king or the lowest of the common folk who invades a foreign country in which he has no right, and harries it as an enemy. All such must, equally, be considered as robbers and punished accordingly. Therefore, both natural equity and the nature of the office dictate that princes must be armed not only to restrain the misdeeds of private individuals by judicial punishment, but also to defend by war the dominions entrusted to their safekeeping, if at any time they are under enemy attack. And the Holy Spirit declares such wars to be lawful by many testimonies of Scripture.

12. Restraint and humanity in war

But if anyone object against me that in the New Testament there exists no testimony or example which teaches that war is a thing lawful for Christians, I answer first that the reason for waging war which existed of old still persists today; and that, on the other hand, there is no reason that bars magistrates from defending their subjects. Secondly, I say that an express declaration of this matter is not to be sought in the writing of the apostles; for their purpose is not to fashion a civil government, but to establish the spiritual Kingdom of Christ. Finally, that it is there shown in passing that Christ by his coming has changed nothing in this respect. For if Christian doctrine (to use Augustine's words) condemned all wars, the soldiers asking counsel concerning salvation should rather have been advised to cast away their weapons and withdraw completely from military service. But they were told: "Strike no man, do no man wrong, be content with your wages" [Luke 3:14 p.]. When he taught them to be content with their wages, he certainly did not forbid them to bear arms.

But it is the duty of all magistrates here to guard particularly against giving vent to their passions even in the slightest degree. Rather, if they have to punish, let them not be carried away with headlong anger, or be seized with hatred, or burn with implacable severity. Let them also (as Augustine says) have pity on the common nature in the one whose special fault they are punishing. Or, if they must arm themselves against the enemy, that is, the armed robber, let them not lightly seek occasion to do so; indeed, let them not accept the occasion when offered, unless they are driven to it by extreme necessity. For if we must perform much more than the heathen philosopher required when he wanted war to seem a seeking of peace, surely everything else ought to be tried before recourse is had to arms. Lastly, in both situations let them not allow themselves to be swayed by any private affection, but be led by concern for the people alone. Otherwise, they very wickedly abuse their power, which has been given them not for their own advantage, but for the benefit and service of others.

Moreover, this same right to wage war furnishes the reason for garrisons, leagues, and other civil defenses. Now, I call "garrisons," those troops which are stationed among the cities to defend the boundaries of a country; "leagues," those pacts which are made by neighboring princes to the end that if any trouble should happen in their lands, they may come to one another's aid, and join forces to put down the common enemies of mankind. I call "civil defenses," things used in the art of war.

13. Concerning the right of the government to levy tribute

Lastly, I also wish to add this, that tributes and taxes are the lawful revenues of princes, which they may chiefly use to meet the public expenses of their office; yet they may similarly use them for the magnificence of their household, which is joined, so to speak, with the dignity of the authority they exercise. As we see, David, Hezekiah, Josiah, Jehoshaphat, and other holy kings, also Joseph and Daniel (according to the dignity of their office) were, without offending piety, lavish at public expense, and we read in Ezekiel that a very large portion of the land was assigned to the kings [Ezek. 48:21]. There, although the prophet portrays the spiritual Kingdom of Christ, he seeks the pattern for his picture from a lawful human kingdom.

But he does so in such a way that princes themselves will in turn remember that their revenues are not so much their private chests as the treasuries of the entire people (for Paul so testifies [Rom. 13:6]), which

cannot be squandered or despoiled without manifest injustice. Or rather, that these are almost the very blood of the people, which it would be the harshest inhumanity not to spare. Moreover, let them consider that their imposts and levies, and other kinds of tributes are nothing but supports of public necessity; but that to impose them upon the common folk without cause is tyrannical extortion.

These considerations do not encourage princes to waste and expensive luxury, as there is surely no need to add fuel to their cupidity, already too much kindled of itself. But as it is very necessary that, whatever they venture, they should venture with a pure conscience before God, they must be taught how much is lawful for them, that they may not in impious self-confidence come under God's displeasure. And this doctrine is not superfluous for private individuals in order that they should not let themselves rashly and shamelessly decry any expenses of princes, even if these exceed the common expenditures of the citizens.

(Public law and judicial procedures, as related to Christian duty, 14–21)

14. Old Testament law and the laws of nations

Next to the magistracy in the civil state come the laws, stoutest sinews of the commonwealth, or, as Cicero, after Plato, calls them, the souls, without which the magistracy cannot stand, even as they themselves have no force apart from the magistracy. Accordingly, nothing truer could be said than that the law is a silent magistrate; the magistrate, a living law.

But because I have undertaken to say with what laws a Christian state ought to be governed, this is no reason why anyone should expect a long discourse concerning the best kind of laws. This would be endless and would not pertain to the present purpose and place. I shall in but a few words, and as in passing, note what laws can piously be used before God, and be rightly administered among men.

I would have preferred to pass over this matter in utter silence if I were not aware that here many dangerously go astray. For there are some who deny that a commonwealth is duly framed which neglects the political system of Moses, and is ruled by the common laws of nations. Let other men consider how perilous and seditious this notion is; it will be enough for me to have proved it false and foolish.

We must bear in mind that common division of the whole law of God published by Moses into moral, ceremonial, and judicial laws. And we must consider each of these parts, that we may understand what there is in them that pertains to us, and what does not. In the meantime, let no one be concerned over the small point that ceremonial and judicial laws pertain also to morals. For the ancient writers who taught this division, although they were not ignorant that these two latter parts had some bearing upon morals, still, because these could be changed or abrogated while morals remained untouched, did not call them moral laws. They applied this name only to the first part, without which the true holiness of morals cannot stand, nor an unchangeable rule of right living.

15. Moral, ceremonial, and judicial law distinguished

The moral law (to begin first with it) is contained under two heads, one of which simply commands us to worship God with pure faith and piety; the other, to embrace men with sincere affection. Accordingly, it is the true and eternal rule of righteousness, prescribed for men of all nations and times, who wish to conform their lives to God's will. For it is his eternal and unchangeable will that he himself indeed be worshiped by us all, and that we love one another.

The ceremonial law was the tutelage of the Jews, with which it seemed good to the Lord to train this people, as it were, in their childhood, until the fullness of time should come [Gal. 4:3–4; cf. ch. 3:23–24], in order that he might fully manifest his wisdom to the nations, and show the truth of those things which then were foreshadowed in figures.

The judicial law, given to them for civil government, imparted certain formulas of equity and justice, by which they might live together blamelessly and peaceably.

Those ceremonial practices indeed properly belonged to the doctrine of piety, inasmuch as they kept the church of the Jews in service and reverence to God, and yet could be distinguished from piety itself. In like manner, the form of their judicial laws, although it had no other intent than how best to preserve that very love which is enjoined by God's eternal law, had something distinct from that precept of love. Therefore, as ceremonial laws could be abrogated while piety remained safe and unharmed, so too, when these judicial laws were taken away, the perpetual duties and precepts of love could still remain.

But if this is true, surely every nation is left free to make such laws as it foresees to be profitable for itself. Yet these must be in conformity to that perpetual rule of love, so that they indeed vary in form but have the same purpose. For I do not think that those barbarous and savage laws such as gave honor to thieves, permitted promiscuous intercourse, and others both more filthy and more absurd, are to be regarded as laws. For they are abhorrent not only to all justice, but also to all humanity and gentleness.

16. Unity and diversity of laws

What I have said will become plain if in all laws we examine, as we should, these two things: the constitution of the law, and the equity on which its constitution is itself founded and rests. Equity, because it is natural, cannot but be the same for all, and therefore, this same purpose ought to apply to all laws, whatever their object. Constitutions have certain circumstances upon which they in part depend. It therefore does not matter that they are different, provided all equally press toward the same goal of equity.

It is a fact that the law of God which we call the moral law is nothing else than a testimony of natural law and of that conscience which God has engraved upon the minds of men. Consequently, the entire scheme of this equity of which we are now speaking has been prescribed in it. Hence, this equity alone must be the goal and rule and limit of all laws.

Whatever laws shall be framed to that rule, directed to that goal, bound by that limit, there is no reason why we should disapprove of them, howsoever they may differ from the Jewish law, or among themselves.

God's law forbids stealing. The penalties meted out to thieves in the Jewish state are to be seen in Exodus [Ex. 22:1–4]. The very ancient laws of other nations punished theft with double restitution; the laws which followed these distinguished between theft, manifest and not manifest. Some proceeded to banishment, others to flogging, others finally to capital punishment. False testimony was punished by damages similar and equal to injury among the Jews [Deut. 19:18–21]; elsewhere, only by deep disgrace; in some nations, by hanging; in others, by the cross. All codes equally avenge murder with blood, but with different kinds of death. Against adulterers some nations levy severer, others, lighter punishments. Yet we see how, with such diversity, all laws tend to the same end. For, together with one voice, they pronounce punishment against those crimes which God's eternal law has condemned, namely, murder, theft, adultery, and false witness. But they do not agree on the manner of punishment. Nor is this either necessary or expedient. There are countries which, unless they deal cruelly with murderers by way of horrible examples, must immediately perish from slaughters and robberies. There are ages that demand increasingly harsh penalties. If any disturbance occurs in a commonwealth, the evils that usually arise from it must be corrected by new ordinances. In time of war, in the clatter of arms, all humaneness would disappear unless some uncommon fear of punishment were introduced. In drought, in pestilence, unless greater severity is used, everything will go to ruin. There are nations inclined to a particular vice, unless it be most sharply repressed. How malicious and hateful toward public welfare would a man be who is offended by such diversity, which is perfectly adapted to maintain the observance of God's law?

For the statement of some, that the law of God given through Moses is dishonored when it is abrogated and new laws preferred to it, is utterly vain. For others are not preferred to it when they are more approved, not by a simple comparison, but with regard to the condition of times, place, and nation; or when that law is abrogated which was never enacted for us. For the Lord through the hand of Moses did not give that law to be proclaimed among all nations and to be in force everywhere; but when he had taken the Jewish nation into his safekeeping, defense, and protection, he also willed to be a lawgiver especially to it; and—

as became a wise lawgiver—he had special concern for it in making its laws.

17. Christians may use the law courts, but without hatred and revenge

It now remains for us to examine what we had set in the last place: what usefulness the laws, judgments, and magistrates have for the common society of Christians. To this is also joined another question: how much deference private individuals ought to yield to their magistrates, and how far their obedience ought to go. To very many the office of magistrate seems superfluous among Christians, because they cannot piously call upon them for help, inasmuch as it is forbidden to them to take revenge, to sue before a court, or to go to law. But Paul clearly testifies to the contrary that the magistrate is minister of God for our good [Rom. 13:4]. By this we understand that he has been so ordained of God, that, defended by his hand and support against the wrongdoing and injustices of evil men, we may live a quiet and serene life [I Tim. 2:2]. But if it is to no purpose that he has been given by the Lord for our defense unless we are allowed to enjoy such benefit, it is clear enough that the magistrate may without impiety be called upon and also appealed to.

But here I have to deal with two kinds of men. There are very many who so boil with a rage for litigation that they are never at peace with themselves unless they are quarreling with others. And they carry on their lawsuits with bitter and deadly hatred, and an insane passion to revenge and hurt, and they pursue them with implacable obstinacy even to the ruin of their adversaries. Meanwhile, to avoid being thought of as doing something wrong, they defend such perversity on the pretense of legal procedure. But if one is permitted to go to law with a brother, one is not therewith allowed to hate him, or be seized with a mad desire to harm him, or hound him relentlessly.

18. The Christian's motives in litigation

Such men should therefore understand that lawsuits are permissible if rightly used. There is right use, both for the plaintiff in suing and for the accused in defending himself, if the defendant presents himself on the appointed day and with such exception, as he can, defends himself without bitterness, but only with this intent, to defend what is his by right, and if on the other hand, the plaintiff, undeservedly oppressed either in his person or in his property, puts himself in the care of the magistrate, makes his complaint, and seeks what is fair and good. But he should be far from all passion to harm or take revenge, far from harshness and hatred, far from burning desire for contention. He should rather be prepared to yield his own and suffer anything than be carried away with enmity toward his adversary. On the other hand, where hearts are filled with malice, corrupted by envy, inflamed with wrath, breathing revenge, finally so inflamed with desire for contention, that love is somewhat impaired in them, the whole court action of even the most just cause cannot but be impious. For this must be a set principle for all Christians: that a lawsuit, however just, can never be rightly prosecuted by any man, unless he treat his adversary with the same love and good will as if the business under controversy were already amicably settled and composed. Perhaps someone will interpose here that such moderation is so uniformly absent from any lawsuit that it would be a miracle if any such were found. Indeed, I admit that, as the customs of these times go, an example of an upright litigant is rare; but the thing itself, when not corrupted by the addition of anything evil, does not cease to be good and pure. But when we hear that the help of the magistrate is a holy gift of God, we must more diligently guard against its becoming polluted by our fault.

19. Against the rejection of the judicial process

As for those who strictly condemn all legal contentions, let them realize that they therewith repudiate God's holy ordinance, and one of the class of gifts that can be clean to the clean [Titus 1:15]; unless, perchance, they wish to accuse Paul of a shameful act, since he both repelled the slanders of his accusers, exposing at the same time their craft and malice [Acts 24:12 ff.], and in court claimed for himself the privilege of Roman citizenship [Acts 16:37; 22:1, 25],

and, when there was need, appealed from the unjust judge to the judgment seat of Caesar [Acts 25:10–11].

This does not contradict the fact that all Christians are forbidden to desire revenge, which we banish far away from Christian courts [Lev. 19:18; Matt. 5:39; Deut. 32:35; Rom. 12:19]. For if it is a civil case, a man does not take the right path unless he commits his cause, with innocent simplicity, to the judge as public protector; and he should think not at all of returning evil for evil [Rom. 12:17], which is the passion for revenge. If, however, the action is brought for some capital or serious offense, we require that the accuser be one who comes into court without a burning desire for revenge or resentment over private injury, but having in mind only to prevent the efforts of a destructive man from doing harm to society. For if you remove a vengeful mind, that command which forbids revenge to Christians is not broken.

But, some will object, not only are they forbidden to desire revenge, but they are also bidden to wait upon the hand of the Lord, who promises that he will be present to avenge the oppressed and afflicted [Rom. 12:19]; while those who seek aid from the magistrate, either for themselves or for others, anticipate all the vengeance of the Heavenly Protector. Not at all! For we must consider that the magistrate's revenge is not man's but God's, which he extends and exercises, as Paul says [Rom. 13:4], through the ministry of man for our good.

20. The Christian endures insults, but with amity and equity defends the public interest

We are not in any more disagreement with Christ's words in which he forbids us to resist evil, and commands us to turn the right cheek to him who has struck the left, and to give our cloak to him who has taken away our coat [Matt. 5:39–40]. He indeed wills that the hearts of his people so utterly recoil from any desire to retaliate that they should rather allow double injury to be done them than desire to pay it back. And we are not leading them away from this forbearance. For truly, Christians ought to be a kind of men born to bear slanders and injuries, open to the malice, deceits, and mockeries of wicked men. And not that only, but they ought to bear patiently all these evils. That is, they should have such complete spiritual composure that, having received one offense, they make ready for another, promising themselves throughout life nothing but the bearing of a perpetual cross. Meanwhile, let them also do good to those who do them harm, and bless those who curse them [Luke 6:28; cf. Matt. 5:44], and (this is their only victory) strive to conquer evil with good [Rom. 12:21]. So minded, they will not seek an eye for an eye, a tooth for a tooth, as the Pharisees taught their disciples to desire revenge, but, as we are instructed by Christ, they will so suffer their body to be maimed, and their possessions to be maliciously seized, that they will forgive and voluntarily pardon those wrongs as soon as they have been inflicted upon them [Matt. 5:38 ff.].

Yet this equity and moderateness of their minds will not prevent them from using the help of the magistrate in preserving their own possessions, while maintaining friendliness toward their enemies; or zealous for public welfare, from demanding the punishment of a guilty and pestilent man, who, they know, can be changed only by death. For Augustine truly interprets the purpose of all these precepts. The righteous and godly man should be ready patiently to bear the malice of those whom he desires to become good, in order to increase the number of good men — not to add himself to the number of the bad by a malice like theirs. Secondly, these precepts pertain more to the preparation of the heart which is within than to the work which is done in the open, in order that patience of mind and good will be kept in secret, but that we may openly do what we see may benefit those whom we ought to wish well.

21. Paul condemns a litigious spirit, but not all litigation

But the usual objection — that Paul has condemned lawsuits altogether — is also false [I Cor. 6:5–8]. It can easily be understood from his words that there was an immoderate rage for litigation in the church of the Corinthians — even to the point that they exposed to the scoffing and evilspeaking of the impious the gospel of Christ and the whole religion they professed. Paul first criticized them for disgracing the gospel among believers by the intemperateness of their quar-

rels. Secondly, he rebuked them also for contending in this way among themselves, brethren with brethren. For they were so far from bearing wrongs that they greedily panted after one another's possessions, and without cause assailed and inflicted loss upon one another. Therefore, Paul inveighs against that mad lust to go to law, not simply against all controversies.

But he brands it a fault or weakness for them not to accept the loss of their goods, rather than to endeavor to keep them, even to the point of strife. That is, when they were so easily aroused by every loss, and dashed to the court and to lawsuits over the least causes, he speaks of this as proof that their minds are too prone to anger, and not enough disposed to patience. Christians ought indeed so to conduct themselves that they always prefer to yield their own right rather than go into a court, from which they can scarcely get away without a heart stirred and kindled to hatred of their brother. But when any man sees that without loss of love he can defend his own property, the loss of which would be a heavy expense to him, he does not offend against this statement of Paul, if he has recourse to law. To sum up (as we said at the beginning), love will give every man the best counsel. Everything undertaken apart from love and all disputes that go beyond it, we regard as incontrovertibly unjust and impious.

(Obedience, with reverence, due even unjust rulers, 22–29)
22. Deference

The first duty of subjects toward their magistrates is to think most honorably of their office, which they recognize as a jurisdiction bestowed by God, and on that account to esteem and reverence them as ministers and representatives of God. For you may find some who very respectfully yield themselves to their magistrates and desire somebody whom they can obey, because they know that such is expedient for public welfare; nevertheless, they regard magistrates only as a kind of necessary evil. But Peter requires something more of us when he commands that the king be honored [I Peter 2:17]; as does Solomon when he teaches that God and king are to be feared

[Prov. 24:21]. For Peter, in the word "to honor" includes a sincere and candid opinion of the king. Solomon, yoking the king with God, shows that the king is full of a holy reverence and dignity. There is also that famous saying in Paul: that we should obey "not only because of wrath, but because of conscience" [Rom. 13:5, cf. Vg.]. By this he means that subjects should be led not by fear alone of princes and rulers to remain in subjection under them (as they commonly yield to an armed enemy who sees that vengeance is promptly taken if they resist), but because they are showing obedience to God himself when they give it to them; since the rulers' power is from God.

I am not discussing the men themselves, as if a mask of dignity covered foolishness, or sloth, or cruelty, as well as wicked morals full of infamous deeds, and thus acquired for vices the praise of virtues; but I say that the order itself is worthy of such honor and reverence that those who are rulers are esteemed among us, and receive reverence out of respect for their lordship.

23. Obedience

From this also something else follows: that, with hearts inclined to reverence their rulers, the subjects should prove their obedience toward them, whether by obeying their proclamations, or by paying taxes, or by undertaking public offices and burdens which pertain to the common defense, or by executing any other commands of theirs. "Let every soul," says Paul, "be subject to the higher powers. . . . For he who resists authority, resists what God has ordained." [Rom. 13:1–2, Vg.] "Remind them," he writes to Titus, "to be subject to principalities and powers, to obey magistrates, to be ready for every good work." [Titus 3:1, cf. Vg.] And Peter says, "Be subject to every human creature (or rather, as I translate it, ordinance) for the Lord's sake, whether it be to the king, as supreme, or unto governors who are sent through him to punish evildoers, but to praise doers of good." [I Peter 2:13–14.] Now, in order that they may prove that they are not pretending subjection, but are sincerely and heartily subjects, Paul adds that they should commend to God the safety and prosper-

ity of those under whom they live. "I urge," he says, "that supplications, prayers, intercessions, and thanksgivings be made for all men, for kings, and all that are in authority, that we may lead a quiet and peaceable life, with all godliness and honesty." [I Tim. 2:1–2, cf. Vg.]

Let no man deceive himself here. For since the magistrate cannot be resisted without God being resisted at the same time, even though it seems that an unarmed magistrate can be despised with impunity, still God is armed to avenge mightily this contempt toward himself.

Moreover, under this obedience I include the restraint which private citizens ought to bid themselves keep in public, that they may not deliberately intrude in public affairs, or pointlessly invade the magistrate's office, or undertake anything at all politically. If anything in a public ordinance requires amendment, let them not raise a tumult, or put their hands to the task—all of them ought to keep their hands bound in this respect—but let them commit the matter to the judgment of the magistrate, whose hand alone here is free. I mean, let them not venture on anything without a command. For when the ruler gives his command, private citizens receive public authority. For as the counselors are commonly called the ears and eyes of the prince, so may one reasonably speak of those whom he has appointed by his command to do things, as the hands of the prince.

24. Obedience is also due the unjust magistrate

But since we have so far been describing a magistrate who truly is what he is called, that is, a father of his country, and, as the poet expresses it, shepherd of his people, guardian of peace, protector of righteousness, and avenger of innocence—he who does not approve of such government must rightly be regarded as insane.

But it is the example of nearly all ages that some princes are careless about all those things to which they ought to have given heed, and, far from all care, lazily take their pleasure. Others, intent upon their own business, put up for sale laws, privileges, judgments, and letters of favor. Others drain the common people of their money, and afterward lavish it on insane largesse. Still others exercise sheer robbery, plundering houses, raping virgins and matrons, and slaughtering the innocent.

Consequently, many cannot be persuaded that they ought to recognize these as princes and to obey their authority as far as possible. For in such great disgrace, and among such crimes, so alien to the office not only of a magistrate but also of a man, they discern no appearance of the image of God which ought to have shone in the magistrate; while they see no trace of that minister of God, who had been appointed to praise the good, and to punish the evil [cf. I Peter 2:14, Vg.]. Thus, they also do not recognize as ruler him whose dignity and authority Scripture commends to us. Indeed, this inborn feeling has always been in the minds of men to hate and curse tyrants as much as to love and venerate lawful kings.

25. The wicked ruler a judgment of God

But if we look to God's Word, it will lead us farther. We are not only subject to the authority of princes who perform their office toward us uprightly and faithfully as they ought, but also to the authority of all who, by whatever means, have got control of affairs, even though they perform not a whit of the princes' office. For despite the Lord's testimony that the magistrate's office is the highest gift of his beneficence to preserve the safety of men, and despite his appointment of bounds to the magistrates—he still declares at the same time that whoever they may be, they have their authority solely from him. Indeed, he says that those who rule for the public benefit are true patterns and evidences of this beneficence of his; that they who rule unjustly and incompetently have been raised up by him to punish the wickedness of the people; that all equally have been endowed with that holy majesty with which he has invested lawful power.

I shall proceed no farther until I have added some sure testimonies of this thing. Yet, we need not labor to prove that a wicked king is the Lord's wrath upon the earth [Job 34:30, Vg.; Hos. 13:11; Isa. 3:4; 10:5; Deut. 28:29], for I believe no man will contradict me; and thus nothing more would be said of a king than of a robber who seizes your possessions, of an adulterer who pollutes your marriage bed, or of a murderer who seeks to kill you. For Scripture reckons all such calamities among God's curses.

But let us, rather, pause here to prove this, which does not so easily settle in men's minds. In a very wicked man utterly unworthy of all honor, provided he has the public power in his hands, that noble and divine power resides which the Lord has by his Word given to the ministers of his justice and judgment. Accordingly, he should be held in the same reverence and esteem by his subjects, in so far as public obedience is concerned, in which they would hold the best of kings if he were given to them.

26. Obedience to bad kings required in Scripture

First, I should like my readers to note and carefully observe that providence of God, which the Scriptures with good reason so often recall to us, and its special operation in distributing kingdoms and appointing what kings he pleases. In Daniel, the Lord changes times and successions of times, removes kings and sets them up [Dan. 2:21, 37]. Likewise: "to the end that the living may know that the Most High rules the kingdom of men, and gives it to whom he will" [Dan. 4:17; cf. ch. 4:14, Vg.]. Although Scripture everywhere abounds with such passages, this prophecy particularly swarms with them. Now it is well enough known what kind of king Nebuchadnezzar was, who conquered Jerusalem—a strong invader and destroyer of others. Nevertheless, the Lord declares in Ezekiel that He has given him the land of Egypt for the service he had done him in devastating it [Ezek. 29:19–20]. And Daniel said to him: "You, O king, are a king of kings, to whom the God of heaven has given the kingdom, powerful, mighty, and glorious; to you, I say, he has given also all lands where the sons of men dwell, beasts of the forest and birds of the air: these he has given into your hand and made you rule over them" [Dan. 2:37–38, cf. Vg.]. Again, Daniel says to Nebuchadnezzar's son Belshazzar: "The Most High God gave Nebuchadnezzar, your father, kingship and magnificence, honor and glory; and because of the magnificence that he gave him, all peoples, tribes, and tongues were trembling and fearful before him" [Dan. 5:18–19, cf. Vg.]. When we hear that a king has been ordained by God, let us at once call to mind those heavenly edicts with regard to honoring and fearing a king; then we shall not hesitate to hold a most wicked tyrant in the place where the Lord has deigned to set him. Samuel, when he warned the people of Israel what sort of things they would suffer from their kings, said: "This shall be the right of the king that will reign over you: he will take your sons and put them to his chariot to make them his horsemen and to plow his fields and reap his harvest, and make his weapons. He will take your daughters to be perfumers and cooks and bakers. Finally, he will take your fields, your vineyards, and your best olive trees and will give them to his servants. He will take the tenth of your grain and of your vineyards, and will give it to his eunuchs and servants. He will take your menservants, maidservants, and asses and set them to his work. He will take the tenth of your flocks and you will be his servants" [I Sam. 8:11–17, with omissions; cf. Hebrew]. Surely, the kings would not do this by legal right, since the law trained them to all restraint [Deut. 17:16 ff.]. But it was called a right in relation to the people, for they had to obey it and were not allowed to resist. It is as if Samuel had said: The willfulness of kings will run to excess, but it will not be your part to restrain it; you will have only this left to you: to obey their commands and hearken to their word.

27. The case of Nebuchadnezzar in Jer., ch. 27

But in Jeremiah, especially, there is a memorable passage, which (although rather long) it will not trouble me to quote because it very clearly defines this whole question. "I have made the earth and men, says the Lord, and the animals which are upon the face of the earth, with my great strength and outstretched arm; and I give it to him who is pleasing in my eyes. Now, therefore, I have given all these lands into the hand of Nebuchadnezzar . . . my servant. . . . All the nations and great kings shall serve him . . . , until the time of his own land comes. . . . And it shall be that any nation and kingdom that will not serve the king of Babylon, I shall visit that nation with

sword, famine, and pestilence. . . . Therefore, serve the king of Babylon and live." [Jer. 27:5–8, 17, cf. Vg.] We see how much obedience the Lord willed to be paid to that abominable and cruel tyrant for no other reason than that he possessed the kingship. But it was by heavenly decree that he had been set upon the throne of the kingdom and assumed into kingly majesty, which it would be unlawful to violate. If we have continually present to our minds and before our eyes the fact that even the most worthless kings are appointed by the same decree by which the authority of all kings is established, those seditious thoughts will never enter our minds that a king should be treated according to his merits, and that it is unfair that we should show ourselves subjects to him who, on his part, does not show himself a king to us.

28. General testimonies of Scripture on the sanctity of the royal person

It is vain for anyone to object that that command was peculiar to the Israelites. For we must note with what reason the Lord confirms it: "I have given," he says, "the kingdom to Nebuchadnezzar" [Jer. 27:6, cf. Vg.]. "Therefore, serve him and live." [Jer. 27:17, cf. Vg.] Let us not doubt that we ought to serve him to whom it is evident that the kingdom has been given. And when once the Lord advances any man to kingly rank, he attests to us his determination that he would have him reign. For there are general testimonies of Scripture concerning this. Solomon, in the twenty-eighth chapter of The Proverbs, says: "Because of the iniquity of the land there are many princes" [Prov. 28:2 p.]. Likewise, the twelfth chapter of Job: "He takes away subjection from kings, and girds them again with a girdle" [Job 12:18 p.]. Once this has been admitted, nothing remains but that we should serve and live.

In Jeremiah the prophet, there is also another command of the Lord by which he enjoins his people to seek the peace of Babylon, where they have been sent as captives, and to pray to the Lord on its behalf, for in its peace will be their peace [Jer. 29:7]. Behold, the Israelites, divested of all their possessions, driven from their homes, led away into exile, and cast into pitiable bondage, are commanded to pray for the prosperity of their conqueror—not as we are commanded in other passages to pray for our persecutors [cf. Matt. 5:44], but in order that his kingdom may be preserved safe and peaceful, that under him they too may prosper. So David, already designated king by God's ordination and anointed with his holy oil, when he was persecuted by Saul without deserving it, still regarded the head of his assailant as inviolable, because the Lord had sanctified it with the honor of the kingdom. "The Lord forbid," he said, "that I should do this thing before the Lord, to my lord, the Lord's anointed, to put forth my hand against him, since he is the Lord's anointed." [I Sam. 24:6, cf. Vg.] Again: "My soul has spared you; and I have said, 'I shall not put forth my hand against my lord, for he is the Lord's anointed' " [I Sam. 24:11, cf. Vg.]. Again: "Who will put forth his hand against the anointed of the Lord and be innocent? . . . The Lord lives; unless the Lord strike him, or the day come for him to die, or he fall in battle, the Lord forbid that I should put forth my hand against the Lord's anointed" [I Sam. 26:9–11, cf. Vg.].

29. It is not the part of subjects but of God to vindicate the right

We owe this attitude of reverence and therefore of piety toward all our rulers in the highest degree, whatever they may be like. I therefore the more often repeat this: that we should learn not to examine the men themselves, but take it as enough that they bear, by the Lord's will, a character upon which he has imprinted and engraved an inviolable majesty.

But (you will say) rulers owe responsibilities in turn to their subjects. This I have already admitted. But if you conclude from this that service ought to be rendered only to just governors, you are reasoning foolishly. For husbands are also bound to their wives, and parents to their children, by mutual responsibilities. Suppose parents and husbands depart from their duty. Suppose parents show themselves so hard and intractable to their children, whom they are forbidden to provoke to anger [Eph. 6:4], that by their rigor they tire them beyond measure. Suppose husbands most despitefully use their wives, whom they are commanded to love [Eph. 5:25] and to spare as weaker

vessels [I Peter 3:7]. Shall either children be less obedient to their parents or wives to their husbands? They are still subject even to those who are wicked and undutiful.

Indeed, all ought to try not to "look at the bag hanging from their back," that is, not to inquire about another's duties, but every man should keep in mind that one duty which is his own. This ought particularly to apply to those who have been put under the power of others. Therefore, if we are cruelly tormented by a savage prince, if we are greedily despoiled by one who is avaricious or wanton, if we are neglected by a slothful one, if finally we are vexed for piety's sake by one who is impious and sacrilegious, let us first be mindful of our own misdeeds, which without doubt are chastised by such whips of the Lord [cf. Dan. 9:7]. By this, humility will restrain our impatience. Let us then also call this thought to mind, that it is not for us to remedy such evils; that only this remains, to implore the Lord's help, in whose hand are the hearts of kings, and the changing of kingdoms [Prov. 21:1 p.]. "He is God who will stand in the assembly of the gods, and will judge in the midst of the gods." [Ps. 82:1 p.] Before His face all kings shall fall and be crushed, and all the judges of the earth, that have not kissed his anointed [Ps. 2:10–11], and all those who have written unjust laws to oppress the poor in judgment and to do violence to the cause of the lowly, to prey upon widows and rob the fatherless [Isa. 10:1–2, cf. Vg.].

(Constitutional magistrates, however, ought to check the tyranny of kings; obedience to God comes first, 30–31)

30. When God intervenes, it is sometimes by unwitting agents

Here are revealed his goodness, his power, and his providence. For sometimes he raises up open avengers from among his servants, and arms them with his command to punish the wicked government and deliver his people, oppressed in unjust ways, from miserable calamity. Sometimes he directs to this end the rage of men who intend one thing and undertake another. Thus he delivered the people of Israel from the tyranny of Pharaoh through Moses [Ex. 3:7–10];

from the violence of Chusan, king of Syria, through Othniel [Judg. 3:9]; and from other servitudes through other kings or judges. Thus he tamed the pride of Tyre by the Egyptians, the insolence of the Egyptians by the Assyrians, the fierceness of the Assyrians by the Chaldeans; the arrogance of Babylon by the Medes and Persians, after Cyrus had already subjugated the Medes. The ungratefulness of the kings of Judah and Israel and their impious obstinacy toward his many benefits, he sometimes by the Assyrians, sometimes by the Babylonians, crushed and afflicted—although not all in the same way.

For the first kind of men, when they had been sent by God's lawful calling to carry out such acts, in taking up arms against kings, did not at all violate that majesty which is implanted in kings by God's ordination; but, armed from heaven, they subdued the lesser power with the greater, just as it is lawful for kings to punish their subordinates. But the latter kind of men, although they were directed by God's hand whither he pleased, and executed his work unwittingly, yet planned in their minds to do nothing but an evil act.

31. Constitutional defenders of the people's freedom

But however these deeds of men are judged in themselves, still the Lord accomplished his work through them alike when he broke the bloody scepters of arrogant kings and when he overturned intolerable governments. Let the princes hear and be afraid.

But we must, in the meantime, be very careful not to despise or violate that authority of magistrates, full of venerable majesty, which God has established by the weightiest decrees, even though it may reside with the most unworthy men, who defile it as much as they can with their own wickedness. For, if the correction of unbridled despotism is the Lord's to avenge, let us not at once think that it is entrusted to us, to whom no command has been given except to obey and suffer.

I am speaking all the while of private individuals. For if there are now any magistrates of the people, appointed to restrain the willfulness of kings (as in ancient times the ephors were set against the Spartan

kings, or the tribunes of the people against the Roman consuls, or the demarchs against the senate of the Athenians; and perhaps, as things now are, such power as the three estates exercise in every realm when they hold their chief assemblies), I am so far from forbidding them to withstand, in accordance with their duty, the fierce licentiousness of kings, that, if they wink at kings who violently fall upon and assault the lowly common folk, I declare that their dissimulation involves nefarious perfidy, because they dishonestly betray the freedom of the people, of which they know that they have been appointed protectors by God's ordinance.

32. Obedience to man must not become disobedience to God

But in that obedience which we have shown to be due the authority of rulers, we are always to make this exception, indeed, to observe it as primary, that such obedience is never to lead us away from obedience to him, to whose will the desires of all kings ought to be subject, to whose decrees all their commands ought to yield, to whose majesty their scepters ought to be submitted. And how absurd would it be that in satisfying men you should incur the displeasure of him for whose sake you obey men themselves! The Lord, therefore, is the King of Kings, who, when he has opened his sacred mouth, must alone be heard, before all and above all men; next to him we are subject to those men who are in authority over us, but only in him. If they command anything against him, let it go unesteemed. And here let us not be concerned about all that dignity which the magistrates possess; for no harm is done to it when it is humbled before the singular and truly supreme power of God. On this consideration, Daniel denies that he has committed any offense against the king when he has not obeyed his impious edict [Dan. 6:22-23, Vg.]. For the king had exceeded his limits, and had not only been a wrongdoer against men, but, in lifting up his horns against God, had himself abrogated his power. Conversely, the Israelites are condemned because they were too obedient to the wicked proclamation of the king [Hos. 5:13]. For when Jeroboam molded the golden calves, they, to please him, forsook God's

Temple and turned to new superstitions [I Kings 12:30]. With the same readiness, their descendants complied with the decrees of their kings. The prophet sharply reproaches them for embracing the king's edicts [Hos. 5:11]. Far, indeed, is the pretense of modesty from deserving praise, a false modesty with which the court flatterers cloak themselves and deceive the simple, while they deny that it is lawful for them to refuse anything imposed by their kings. As if God had made over his right to mortal men, giving them the rule over mankind! Or as if earthly power were diminished when it is subjected to its Author, in whose presence even the heavenly powers tremble as suppliants! I know with what great and present peril this constancy is menaced, because kings bear defiance with the greatest displeasure, whose "wrath is a messenger of death" [Prov. 16:14], says Solomon. But since this edict has been proclaimed by the heavenly herald, Peter — "We must obey God rather than men" [Acts 5:29] — let us comfort ourselves with the thought that we are rendering that obedience which the Lord requires when we suffer anything rather than turn aside from piety. And that our courage may not grow faint, Paul pricks us with another goad: That we have been redeemed by Christ at so great a price as our redemption cost him, so that we should not enslave ourselves to the wicked desires of men — much less be subject to their impiety [I Cor. 7:23].

GOD BE PRAISED

Key to Biblical References:
Vg. = Vulgate [Latin]
Geneva = The Geneva Bible (1557–60)
KJV = King James Version (1611)
RV = Revised Version (1881)
p. = paraphrase

HOBBES
Leviathan

THE CONTENTS OF THE CHAPTERS.

To My Most Honor'd Friend
Mr. Francis Godolphin,
Of Godolphin

Honor'd Sir,

Your most worthy brother, Mr. *Sidney Godolphin,* when he lived, was pleased to think my studies something, and otherwise to oblige me, as you know, with

[The text of *Leviathan* reprinted here features modernized spelling and punctuation. Reprinted by arrangement with InteLex, Inc.]

real testimonies of his good opinion, great in themselves, and the greater for the worthiness of his person. For there is not any virtue that disposeth a man, either to the service of God or to the service of his country, to civil society or private friendship, that did not manifestly appear in his conversation, not as acquired by necessity or affected upon occasion, but inherent, and shining in a generous constitution of his nature. Therefore, in honour and gratitude to him, and with devotion to yourself, I humbly dedicate unto you this my discourse of Commonwealth.

I know not how the world will receive it, nor how it may reflect on those that shall seem to favour it. For in a way beset with those that contend, on one side for too great liberty, and on the other side for too much authority, 'tis hard to pass between the points of both unwounded. But yet, methinks, the endeavour to advance the civil power, should not be by the civil power condemned; nor private men, by reprehending it, declare they think that power too great. Besides, I speak not of the men, but (in the abstract) of the seat of power (like to those simple and unpartial creatures in the Roman Capitol, that with their noise defended those within it, not because they were they, but there), offending none, I think, but those without, or such within (if there be any such) as favour them.

That which perhaps may most offend are certain texts of Holy Scripture, alleged by me to other purpose than ordinarily they use to be by others. But I have done it with due submission, and also (in order to my subject) necessarily; for they are the outworks of the enemy, from whence they impugn the civil power. If notwithstanding this, you find my labour generally decried, you may be pleased to excuse yourself, and say, I am a man that love my own opinions, and think all true I say, that I honoured your brother, and honour you, and have presumed on that, to assume the title (without your knowledge) of being, as I am,

SIR,
Your most humble, and most obedient Servant,
THOMAS HOBBES.
Paris, April $^{15}/_{25}$, 1651.

THE INTRODUCTION

Nature (the art whereby God hath made and governs the world) is by the *art* of man, as in many other things, so in this also imitated, that it can make an artificial animal. For seeing life is but a motion of limbs, the beginning whereof is in some principal part within; why may we not say, that all *automata* (engines that move themselves by springs and wheels as doth a watch) have an artificial life? For what is the *heart*, but a *spring*; and the *nerves*, but so many *strings*; and the *joints*, but so many *wheels*, giving motion to the whole body, such as was intended by the artificer? *Art* goes yet further, imitating that rational and most excellent work of nature, *man*. For by art is created that great LEVIATHAN called a COMMONWEALTH, or STATE, (in Latin CIVITAS) which is but an artificial man; though of greater stature and strength than the natural, for whose protection and defence it was intended; and in which, the *sovereignty* is an artificial *soul*, as giving life and motion to the whole body; the *magistrates*, and other *officers* of judicature and execution, artificial *joints*; *reward* and *punishment* (by which fastened to the seat of the sovereignty every joint and member is moved to perform his duty) are the *nerves*, that do the same in the body natural; the *wealth* and *riches* of all the particular members, are the *strength*; *salus populi* (the *people's safety*) its *business*; *counsellors*, by whom all things needful for it to know are suggested unto it, are the *memory*; *equity*, and *laws*, an artificial *reason* and *will*; *concord*, health; *sedition*, sickness; and *civil war*, death. Lastly, the *pacts* and *covenants*, by which the parts of this body politic were at first made, set together, and united, resemble that *fiat*, or the *let us make man*, pronounced by God in the creation.

To describe the nature of this artificial man, I will consider

First, the *matter* thereof, and the *artificer*; both which is *man*.

Secondly, *how*, and by what *covenants* it is made; what are the *rights* and just *power* or *authority* of a sovereign; and what it is that *preserveth* and *dissolveth* it.

Thirdly, what is a *Christian commonwealth*.

Lastly, what is the *kingdom of darkness*.

Concerning the first, there is a saying much usurped of late, that *wisdom* is acquired, not by reading of *books*, but of *men*. Consequently whereunto, those persons, that for the most part can give no other proof of being wise, take great delight to show what they think they have read in men, by uncharitable censures of one another behind their backs. But there is another saying not of late understood, by which they might learn truly to read one another, if they would take the pains; and that is, *nosce teipsum, read thyself*: which was not meant, as it is now used, to countenance, either the barbarous state of men in power, towards their inferiors; or to encourage men of low degree, to a saucy behaviour towards their betters; but to teach us, that for the similitude of the thoughts and passions of one man, to the thoughts and passions of another, whosoever looketh into himself, and considereth what he doth, when he does *think, opine, reason, hope, fear,* &c. and upon what grounds; he shall thereby read and know, what are the thoughts and passions of all other men upon the like occasions. I say the similitude of passions, which are the same in all men, *desire, fear, hope,* &c; not the similitude of the *objects* of the passions, which are the things *desired, feared, hoped,* &c: for these the constitution individual, and particular education, do so vary, and they are so easy to be kept from our knowledge, that the characters of man's heart, blotted and confounded as they are with dissembling, lying, counterfeiting, and erroneous doctrines, are legible only to him that searcheth hearts. And though by men's actions we do discover their design sometimes; yet to do it without comparing them with our own, and distinguishing all circumstances, by which the case may come to be altered, is to decypher without a key, and be for the most part deceived, by too much trust, or by too much diffidence; as he that reads, is himself a good or evil man.

But let one man read another by his actions never so perfectly, it serves him only with his acquaintance, which are but few. He that is to govern a whole nation, must read in himself, not this or that particular man; but mankind: which though it be hard to do, harder than to learn any language or science; yet when I shall have set down my own reading orderly, and perspicu-

ously, the pains left another, will be only to consider, if he also find not the same in himself. For this kind of doctrine admitteth no other demonstration.

PART 1
OF MAN

CHAPTER 1: Of Sense

Concerning the thoughts of man, I will consider them first *singly*, and afterwards in *train*, or dependence upon one another. *Singly*, they are every one a *representation* or *appearance*, of some quality, or other accident of a body without us; which is commonly called an *object*. Which object worketh on the eyes, ears, and other parts of a man's body; and by diversity of working, produceth diversity of appearances.

The original of them all, is that which we call SENSE; (For there is no conception in a man's mind, which hath not at first, totally, or by parts, been begotten upon the organs of sense.) The rest are derived from that original.

To know the natural cause of sense, is not very necessary to the business now in hand; and I have elsewhere written of the same at large. Nevertheless, to fill each part of my present method, I will briefly deliver the same in this place.

The cause of sense, is the external body, or object, which presseth the organ proper to each sense, either immediately, as in the taste and touch; or mediately, as in seeing, hearing, and smelling: which pressure, by the mediation of nerves, and other strings and membranes of the body, continued inwards to the brain and heart, causeth there a resistance, or counterpressure, or endeavour of the heart, to deliver it self: which endeavour, because *outward*, seemeth to be some matter without. And this *seeming*, or, *fancy*, is that which men call *sense*; and consisteth, as to the eye, in a *light*, or *colour figured*; to the ear, in a *sound*; to the nostril, in an *odour*; to the tongue and palate, in a *savour*; and to the rest of the body, in *heat, cold, hardness, softness*, and such other qualities as we discern by *feeling*. All which qualities called *sensible*, are in the object, that causeth them, but so many several motions of the matter, by which it presseth our organs diversely. Neither in us that are pressed, are they any thing else, but divers motions; (for motion produceth nothing but motion.) But their appearance to us is fancy, the same waking, that dreaming. And as pressing, rubbing, or striking the eye, makes us fancy a light; and pressing the ear, produceth a din; so do the bodies also we see, or hear, produce the same by their strong, though unobserved action. For if those colours and sounds were in the bodies, or objects that cause them, they could not be severed from them, as by glasses, and in echoes by reflection, we see they are; where we know the thing we see, is in one place; the appearance in another. And though at some certain distance, the real and very object seem invested with the fancy it begets in us; yet still the object is one thing, the image or fancy is another. So that sense in all cases, is nothing else but original fancy, caused (as I have said) by the pressure, that is, by the motion, of external things upon our eyes, ears, and other organs thereunto ordained.

But the philosophy-schools, through all the universities of Christendom, grounded upon certain texts of *Aristotle*, teach another doctrine; and say, for the cause of *vision*, that the thing seen, sendeth forth on every side a *visible species* (in English) a *visible show*, *apparition*, or *aspect*, or *a being seen*; the receiving whereof into the eye, is *seeing*. And for the cause of *hearing*, that the thing heard, sendeth forth an *audible species*, that is, an *audible aspect*, or *audible being seen*; which entering at the ear, maketh *hearing*. Nay for the cause of *understanding* also, they say the thing understood, sendeth forth *intelligible species*, that is, an *intelligible being seen*; which coming into the understanding, makes us understand. I say not this, as disapproving the use of universities: but because I am to speak hereafter of their office in a commonwealth, I must let you see on all occasions by the way, what things would be amended in them; amongst which the frequency of insignificant speech is one.

CHAPTER 2: Of Imagination

That when a thing lies still, unless somewhat else stir it, it will lie still for ever, is a truth that no man doubts of. But that when a thing is in motion, it will eternally be in motion, unless somewhat else stay it, though

the reason be the same, (namely, that nothing can change it self,) is not so easily assented to. For men measure, not only other men, but all other things, by themselves: and because they find themselves subject after motion to pain, and lassitude, think every thing else grows weary of motion, and seeks repose of its own accord; little considering, whether it be not some other motion, wherein that desire of rest they find in themselves, consisteth. From hence it is, that the schools say, heavy bodies fall downwards, out of an appetite to rest, and to conserve their nature in that place which is most proper for them; ascribing appetite and knowledge of what is good for their conservation, (which is more than man has) to things inanimate, absurdly.

When a body is once in motion, it moveth (unless something else hinder it) eternally; and whatsoever hindreth it, cannot in an instant, but in time, and by degrees quite extinguish it: And as we see in the water, though the wind cease, the waves give not over rolling for a long time after; so also it happeneth in that motion, which is made in the internal parts of a man, then, when he sees, dreams, &c. For after the object is removed, or the eye shut, we still retain an image of the thing seen, though more obscure than when we see it. And this is it, the Latins call *imagination*, from the image made in seeing; and apply the same, though improperly, to all the other senses. But the Greeks call it *fancy*; which signifies *appearance*, and is as proper to one sense, as to another. IMAGINATION therefore is nothing but *decaying sense*; and is found in men, and many other living creatures, as well sleeping, as waking.

The decay of sense in men waking, is not the decay of the motion made in sense; but an obscuring of it, in such manner as the light of the sun obscureth the light of the stars; which stars do no less exercise their virtue, by which they are visible, in the day, than in the night. But because amongst many strokes, which our eyes, ears, and other organs receive from external bodies, the predominant only is sensible; therefore the light of the sun being predominant, we are not affected with the action of the stars. And any object being removed from our eyes, though the impression it made in us remain; yet other objects more present succeeding, and working on us, the imagination of the past is obscured, and made weak, as the voice of a man is in the noise of the day. From whence it followeth, that the longer the time is, after the sight or sense of any object, the weaker is the imagination. For the continual change of man's body destroys in time the parts which in sense were moved: so that distance of time, and of place, hath one and the same effect in us. For as at a great distance of place, that which we look at appears dim, and without distinction of the smaller parts; and as voices grow weak, and inarticulate: so also, after great distance of time, our imagination of the past is weak; and we lose (for example) of cities we have seen, many particular streets, and of actions, many particular circumstances. This *decaying sense*, when we would express the thing itself, (I mean *fancy* itself,) we call *imagination*, as I said before: but when we would express the *decay*, and signify that the sense is fading, old, and past, it is called *memory*. So that *imagination* and *memory* are but one thing, which for divers considerations hath divers names.

Much memory, or memory of many things, is called *experience*. Again, imagination being only of those things which have been formerly perceived by sense, either all at once, or by parts at several times; the former, (which is the imagining the whole object, as it was presented to the sense) is *simple imagination*; as when one imagineth a man, or horse, which he hath seen before. The other is *compounded*; as when from the sight of a man at one time, and of a horse at another, we conceive in our mind a Centaur. So when a man compoundeth the image of his own person, with the image of the actions of another man; as when a man imagines himself a *Hercules* or an *Alexander*, (which happeneth often to them that are much taken with reading of romances) it is a compound imagination, and properly but a fiction of the mind. There be also other imaginations that rise in men, (though waking) from the great impression made in sense: as from gazing upon the sun, the impression leaves an image of the sun before our eyes a long time after; and from being long and vehemently attent upon geometrical figures, a man shall in the dark, (though awake) have the images of lines and angles before his eyes: which kind of fancy hath no

particular name; as being a thing that doth not commonly fall into men's discourse.

The imaginations of them that sleep are those we call *dreams*. And these also (as all other imaginations) have been before, either totally or by parcels in the sense. And because in sense, the brain and nerves, which are the necessary organs of sense, are so benumbed in sleep, as not easily to be moved by the action of external objects, there can happen in sleep no imagination; and therefore no dream, but what proceeds from the agitation of the inward parts of man's body; which inward parts, for the connexion they have with the brain, and other organs, when they be distempered, do keep the same in motion; whereby the imaginations there formerly made, appear as if a man were waking; saving that the organs of sense being now benumbed, so as there is no new object, which can master and obscure them with a more vigorous impression, a dream must needs be more clear, in this silence of sense, than are our waking thoughts. And hence it cometh to pass, that it is a hard matter, and by many thought impossible to distinguish exactly between sense and dreaming. For my part, when I consider that in dreams, I do not often, nor constantly think of the same persons, places, objects, and actions that I do waking; nor remember so long a train of coherent thoughts, dreaming, as at other times; and because waking I often observe the absurdity of dreams, but never dream of the absurdities of my waking thoughts; I am well satisfied, that being awake, I know I dream not; though when I dream I think myself awake.

And seeing dreams are caused by the distemper of some of the inward parts of the body; divers distempers must needs cause different dreams. And hence it is, that lying cold breedeth dreams of fear, and raiseth the thought and image of some fearful object (the motion from the brain to the inner parts, and from the inner parts to the brain being reciprocal;) and that as anger causeth heat in some parts of the body, when we are awake; so when we sleep the over heating of the same parts causeth anger, and raiseth up in the brain the imagination of an enemy. In the same manner, as natural kindness, when we are awake, causeth desire; and desire makes heat in certain other parts of the body; so also, too much heat in those parts, while we sleep, raiseth in the brain an imagination of some kindness shown. In sum, our dreams are the reverse of our waking imaginations; the motion when we are awake, beginning at one end; and when we dream, at another.

The most difficult discerning of a man's dream, from his waking thoughts, is then, when by some accident we observe not that we have slept: which is easy to happen to a man full of fearful thoughts; and whose conscience is much troubled; and that sleepeth, without the circumstances, of going to bed, or putting off his clothes, as one that noddeth in a chair. For he that taketh pains, and industriously lays himself to sleep, in case any uncouth and exorbitant fancy come unto him, cannot easily think it other than a dream. We read of *Marcus Brutus*, (one that had his life given him by *Julius Caesar*, and was also his favourite, and notwithstanding murdered him), how at *Philippi*, the night before he gave battle to *Augustus Caesar*, he saw a fearful apparition, which is commonly related by historians as a vision; but considering the circumstances, one may easily judge to have been but a short dream. For sitting in his tent, pensive and troubled with the horror of his rash act, it was not hard for him, slumbering in the cold, to dream of that which most affrighted him; which fear, as by degrees it made him wake; so also it must needs make the apparition by degrees to vanish; and having no assurance that he slept, he could have no cause to think it a dream, or any thing but a vision. And this is no very rare accident; for even they that be perfectly awake, if they be timorous, and superstitious, possessed with fearful tales, and alone in the dark, are subject to the like fancies; and believe they see spirits and dead men's ghosts walking in churchyards; whereas it is either their fancy only, or else the knavery of such persons, as make use of such superstitious fear, to pass disguised in the night, to places they would not be known to haunt.

From this ignorance of how to distinguish dreams, and other strong fancies, from vision and sense, did arise the greatest part of the religion of the Gentiles in time past, that worshipped satyrs, fawns, nymphs, and the like; and now-a-days the opinion that rude people have of fairies, ghosts, and goblins, and of the power of witches. For as for witches, I think not that their witchcraft is any real power; but yet that they are justly punished, for the false belief they have, that they can do such mischief, joined with their purpose to do it if they can: their trade being nearer to a new religion than to a craft or science. And for fairies, and walking ghosts, the opinion of them has I think been on purpose, either taught, or not confuted, to keep in credit the use of exorcism, of crosses, of holy water, and other such inventions of ghostly men. Nevertheless, there is no doubt, but God can make unnatural apparitions: But that he does it so often, as men need to fear such things, more than they fear the stay, or change, of the course of nature, which he also can stay, and change, is no point of Christian faith. But evil men under pretext that God can do any thing, are so bold as to say any thing when it serves their turn, though they think it untrue; it is the part of a wise man, to believe them no further, than right reason makes that which they say, appear credible. If this superstitious fear of spirits were taken away, and with it, prognostics from dreams, false prophecies, and many other things depending thereon, by which, crafty ambitious persons abuse the simple people, men would be much more fitted than they are for civil obedience.

And this ought to be the work of the schools: but they rather nourish such doctrine. For (not knowing what imagination, or the senses are), what they receive, they teach: some saying, that imaginations rise of themselves, and have no cause; others, that they rise most commonly from the will; and that good thoughts are blown (inspired) into a man by God, and evil thoughts by the Devil; or that good thoughts are poured (infused) into a man by God, and evil ones by the Devil. Some say the senses receive the species of things, and deliver them to the common sense; and the common sense delivers them over to the fancy, and the fancy to the memory, and the memory to the judgment, like handing of things from one to another, with many words making nothing understood.

The imagination that is raised in man (or any other creature indued with the faculty of imagining) by words, or other voluntary signs, is that we generally call *understanding*; and is common to man and beast. For a dog by custom will understand the call, or the rating of his master; and so will many other beasts. That understanding which is peculiar to man, is the understanding not only his will, but his conceptions and thoughts, by the sequel and contexture of the names of things into affirmations, negations, and other forms of speech; and of this kind of understanding I shall speak hereafter.

CHAPTER 3: Of the Consequence or Train of Imaginations

By *Consequence*, or TRAIN of thoughts, I understand that succession of one thought to another, which is called (to distinguish it from discourse in words) *mental discourse*.

When a man thinketh on any thing whatsoever, his next thought after, is not altogether so casual as it seems to be. Not every thought to every thought succeeds indifferently. But as we have no imagination, whereof we have not formerly had sense, in whole, or in parts; so we have no transition from one imagination to another, whereof we never had the like before in our senses. The reason whereof is this. All fancies are motions within us, relics of those made in the sense: and those motions that immediately succeeded one another in the sense, continue also together after sense: insomuch as the former coming again to take place, and be predominant, the latter followeth, by coherence of the matter moved, in such manner, as water upon a plain table is drawn which way any one part of it is guided by the finger. But because in sense, to one and the same thing perceived, sometimes one thing, sometimes another succeedeth, it comes to pass in time, that in the imagining of any thing, there is no certainty what we shall imagine next; only this is certain, it shall be something that succeeded the same before, at one time or another.

This train of thoughts, or mental discourse, is of two sorts. The first is *unguided, without design*, and inconstant; wherein there is no passionate thought, to govern and direct those that follow, to it self, as the end and scope of some desire, or other passion: in which case the thoughts are said to wander, and seem impertinent one to another, as in a dream. Such are commonly the thoughts of men, that are not only without company, but also without care of any thing; though even then their thoughts are as busy as at other times, but without harmony; as the sound which a lute out of tune would yield to any man; or in tune, to one that could not play. And yet in this wild ranging of the mind, a man may oft-times perceive the way of it, and the dependence of one thought upon another. For in a discourse of our present civil war, what could seem more impertinent, than to ask (as one did) what was the value of a Roman penny? Yet the coherence to me was manifest enough. For the thought of the war, introduced the thought of the delivering up the king to his enemies; the thought of that, brought in the thought of the delivering up of Christ; and that again the thought of the 30 pence, which was the price of that treason; and thence easily followed that malicious question, and all this in a moment of time; for thought is quick.

The second is more constant; as being *regulated* by some desire, and design. For the impression made by such things as we desire, or fear, is strong, and permanent, or, (if it cease for a time,) of quick return: so strong it is sometimes, as to hinder and break our sleep. From desire, ariseth the thought of some means we have seen produce the like of that which we aim at; and from the thought of that, the thought of means to that mean; and so continually, till we come to some beginning within our own power. And because the end, by the greatness of the impression, comes often to mind, in case our thoughts begin to wander, they are quickly again reduced into the way: which observed by one of the seven wise men, made him give men this precept, which is now worn out, *Respice finem*; that is to say, in all your actions, look often upon what you would have, as the thing that directs all your thoughts in the way to attain it.

The train of regulated thoughts is of two kinds; one, when of an effect imagined, we seek the causes, or means that produce it: and this is common to man and beast. The other is, when imagining any thing whatsoever, we seek all the possible effects, that can by it be produced; that is to say, we imagine what we can do with it, when we have it. Of which I have not at any time seen any sign, but in man only; for this is a curiosity hardly incident to the nature of any living creature that has no other passion but sensual, such as are hunger, thirst, lust, and anger. In sum, the discourse of the mind, when it is governed by design, is nothing but *seeking*, or the faculty of invention, which the Latins called *sagacitas*, and *solertia*; a hunting out of the causes, of some effect, present or past; or of the effects, of some present or past cause. Sometimes a man seeks what he hath lost; and from that place, and time, wherein he misses it, his mind runs back, from place to place, and time to time, to find where, and when he had it; that is to say, to find some certain, and limited time and place, in which to begin a method of seeking. Again, from thence, his thoughts run over the same places and times, to find what action, or other occasion might make him lose it. This we call *remembrance*, or calling to mind: the Latins call it *reminiscentia*, as it were a *re-conning* of our former actions.

Sometimes a man knows a place determinate, within the compass whereof he is to seek; and then his thoughts run over all the parts thereof, in the same manner as one would sweep a room, to find a jewel; or as a spaniel ranges the field, till he find a scent; or as a man should run over the alphabet, to start a rhyme.

Sometime a man desires to know the event of an action; and then he thinketh of some like action past, and the events thereof one after another; supposing like events will follow like actions. As he that foresees what will become of a criminal, recons what he has seen follow on the like crime before; having this order of thoughts, the crime, the officer, the prison, the judge, and the gallows. Which kind of thoughts, is called *foresight*, and *prudence*, or *providence*; and sometimes *wisdom*; though such conjecture, through the difficulty of observing all circumstances, be very fallacious. But this is certain; by how much one man has more experience of things past, than another; by so much also he is more prudent, and his expectations the seldomer fail him. The *present* only has a being in nature; things *past* have a being in the memory only, but things *to come* have no being at all; the *future* being but a fiction of the mind, applying the sequels of actions past, to the actions that are present; which with most certainty is done by him that has most experience; but not with certainty enough. And though it be called prudence, when the event answereth our expectation; yet in its own nature, it is but presumption. For the foresight of things to come, which is providence, belongs only to him by whose will they are to come. From him only, and supernaturally, proceeds prophecy. The best prophet naturally is the best guesser; and the best guesser, he that is most versed and studied in the matters he guesses at: for he hath most *signs* to guess by.

A *sign* is the event antecedent of the consequent; and contrarily, the consequent of the antecedent, when the like consequences have been observed, before: and the oftener they have been observed, the less uncertain is the sign. And therefore he that has most experience in any kind of business, has most signs, whereby to guess at the future time; and consequently is the most prudent: and so much more prudent than he that is new in that kind of business, as not to be equalled by any advantage of natural and extemporary wit: though perhaps many young men think the contrary.

Nevertheless it is not prudence that distinguisheth man from beast. There be beasts, that at a year old observe more, and pursue that which is for their good, more prudently, than a child can do at ten.

As prudence is a *presumption* of the *future*, contracted from the *experience* of time *past*: so there is a presumption of things past taken from other things (not future but) past also. For he that hath seen by what courses and degrees, a flourishing state hath first come into civil war, and then to ruin; upon the sight of the ruins of any other state, will guess, the like war, and the like courses have been there also. But this conjecture, has the same uncertainty almost with the conjecture of the future; both being grounded only upon experience.

There is no other act of man's mind, that I can remember, naturally planted in him, so as to need no other thing, to the exercise of it, but to be born a man, and live with the use of his five senses. Those other faculties, of which I shall speak by and by, and which seem proper to man only, are acquired, and increased by study and industry; and of most men learned by instruction, and discipline; and proceed all from the invention of words, and speech. For besides sense, and thoughts, and the train of thoughts, the mind of man has no other motion; though by the help of speech, and method, the same faculties may be improved to such a height, as to distinguish men from all other living creatures.

Whatsoever we imagine is *finite*. Therefore there is no idea, or conception of any thing we call *infinite*. No man can have in his mind an image of infinite magnitude; nor conceive infinite swiftness, infinite time, or infinite force, or infinite power. When we say any thing is infinite, we signify only, that we are not able to conceive the ends, and bounds of the things named; having no conception of the thing, but of our own inability. And therefore the name of God is used, not to make us conceive him; (for he is *incomprehensible*; and his greatness, and power are unconceivable;) but that we may honour him. Also because whatsoever (as I said before,) we conceive, has been perceived first by sense, either all at once, or by parts; a man can have no thought, representing any thing, not subject to sense. No man therefore can conceive any thing, but he must conceive it in some place; and indued with some determinate magnitude; and which may be divided into parts; nor that any thing is all in this place, and all in another place at the same time; nor that two, or more things can be in one, and the same place at once: for none of these things ever have, or can be incident to sense; but are absurd speeches, taken upon credit (without any signification at all,) from deceived philosophers, and deceived, or deceiving schoolmen.

CHAPTER 4: Of Speech

The invention of *printing*, though ingenious, compared with the invention of *letters*, is no great matter. But who was the first that found the use of letters, is not known. He that first brought them into *Greece*, men say was *Cadmus*, the son of *Agenor*, king of Phoenicia. A profitable invention for continuing the memory of time past, and the conjunction of mankind, dispersed into so many, and distant regions of the earth; and withal difficult, as proceeding from a watchful observation of the divers motions of the tongue, palate, lips, and other organs of speech; whereby to make as many differences of characters, to remember them. But the most noble and profitable invention of all other, was that of SPEECH, consisting of *names* or *appellations*, and their connexion; whereby men register their thoughts; recall them when they are past; and also declare them one to another for mutual utility and conversation; without which, there had been amongst men, neither commonwealth, nor society, nor contract, nor peace, no more than amongst lions, bears, and wolves. The first author of speech was God himself, that instructed Adam how to name such creatures as he presented to his sight; for the Scripture goeth no further in this matter. But this was sufficient to direct him to add more names, as the experience and use of the creatures should give him occasion; and to join them in such manner by degrees, as to make himself understood; and so by succession of time, so much language might be gotten, as he had found use for; though not so copious, as an orator or philosopher has need of. For I do not find any thing in the Scripture, out of which, directly or by consequence can be gathered, that *Adam* was taught the names of all figures, numbers, measures, colours, sounds, fancies, relations; much less the names of words and speech, as *general, special, affirmative, negative, interrogative, optative, infinitive*, all which are useful; and least of all, of *entity, intentionality, quiddity*, and other insignificant words of the school.

But all this language gotten, and augmented by *Adam* and his posterity, was again lost at the tower of *Babel*, when, by the hand of God, every man was stricken, for his rebellion, with an oblivion of his former language. And being hereby forced to disperse themselves into several parts of the world, it must needs be, that the diversity of tongues that now is, proceeded by degrees from them, in such manner as need (the mother of all inventions) taught them; and in tract of time grew every where more copious.

The general use of speech, is to transfer our mental discourse, into verbal; or the train of our thoughts, into a train of words; and that for two commodities, whereof one is the registering of the consequences of our thoughts; which being apt to slip out of our memory, and put us to a new labour, may again be recalled, by such words as they were marked by. So that the first use of names is to serve for *marks*, or *notes* of remembrance. Another is, when many use the same words, to signify (by their connexion and order,) one to another, what they conceive, or think of each matter; and also what they desire, fear, or have any other passion for. And for this use they are called *signs*. Special uses of speech are these; first, to register, what by cogitation, we find to be the cause of any thing, present or past; and what we find things present or past may produce, or effect: which in sum, is acquiring of arts. Secondly, to show to others that knowledge which we have attained; which is, to counsel and teach one another. Thirdly, to make known to others our wills, and purposes, that we may have the mutual help of one another. Fourthly, to please and delight ourselves and others, by playing with our words, for pleasure or ornament, innocently.

To these uses, there are also four correspondent abuses. First, when men register their thoughts wrong, by the inconstancy of the signification of their words; by which they register for their conceptions, that which they never conceived, and so deceive themselves. Secondly, when they use words metaphorically; that is, in other sense than that they are ordained for; and thereby deceive others. Thirdly, when by words they declare that to be their will, which is not. Fourthly, when they use them to grieve one another: for seeing nature hath armed living creatures, some with teeth, some with horns, and some with hands, to grieve an enemy, it is but an abuse of speech, to grieve him with the tongue, unless it be one whom we are obliged to govern; and then it is not to grieve, but to correct and amend.

The manner how speech serveth to the remembrance of the consequence of causes and effects, consisteth in the imposing of *names*, and the *connexion* of them.

Of names, some are *proper*, and singular to one only thing, as *Peter, John, this man, this tree*: and some are *common* to many things, as *man, horse, tree*; every of which though but one name, is nevertheless the name of divers particular things; in respect of all which together, it is called an *universal*; there being nothing in the world universal but names; for the things named, are every one of them individual and singular.

One universal name is imposed on many things, for their similitude in some quality, or other accident; and whereas a proper name bringeth to mind one thing only, universals recall any one of those many.

And of names universal, some are of more, and some of less extent; the larger comprehending the less large: and some again of equal extent, comprehending each other reciprocally. As for example, the name *body* is of larger signification than the word *man*, and comprehendeth it; and the names *man* and *rational*, are of equal extent, comprehending mutually one another. But here we must take notice, that by a name is not always understood, as in grammar, one only word; but sometimes by circumlocution many words together. For all these words, *he that in his actions observeth the laws of his country*, make but one name, equivalent to this one word, *just*.

By this imposition of names, some of larger, some of stricter signification, we turn the reckoning of the consequences of things imagined in the mind, into a reckoning of the consequences of appellations. For example, a man that hath no use of speech at all, (such as is born and remains perfectly deaf and dumb,) if he set before his eyes a triangle, and by it two right angles, (such as are the corners of a square figure,) he may by meditation compare and find, that the three angles of that triangle, are equal to those two right angles that stand by it. But if another triangle be shown him, different in shape from the former, he cannot know without a new labour, whether the three angles of that also be equal to the same. But he that hath the use of words, when he observes, that such equality was consequent, not to the length of the sides, nor to any other particular thing in his triangle; but only to this, that the sides were straight, and the angles three; and that that was all, for which he named it a triangle; will boldly conclude universally, that such equality of angles is in all triangles whatsoever; and register his invention in these general terms, *every triangle hath its three angles equal to two right angles*. And thus the consequence found in one particular, comes to be registered and remembered, as an universal rule, and discharges our mental reckoning, of time and place, and delivers us from all labour of the mind, saving the first, and makes that which was found true *here*, and *now*, to be true in *all times* and *places*.

But the use of words in registering our thoughts is in nothing so evident as in numbering. A natural fool that could never learn by heart the order of numeral words, as *one*, *two*, and *three*, may observe every stroke of the clock, and nod to it, or say *one*, *one*, *one*, but can never know what hour it strikes. And it seems, there was a time when those names of number were not in use; and men were fain to apply their fingers of one or both hands, to those things they desired to keep account of; and that thence it proceeded, that now our numeral words are but ten, in any nation, and in some but five, and then they begin again. And he that can tell ten, if he recite them out of order, will lose himself, and not know when he has done. Much less will he be able to add, and subtract, and perform all other operations of arithmetic. So that without words there is no possibility of reckoning of numbers; much less of magnitudes, of swiftness, of force, and other things, the reckonings whereof are necessary to the being, or well-being of mankind.

When two names are joined together into a consequence, or affirmation, as thus, *a man is a living creature*; or thus, *if he be a man, he is a living creature*, if the latter name *living creature*, signify all that the former name *man* signifieth, then the affirmation, or consequence is *true*; otherwise *false*. For *true* and *false* are attributes of speech, not of things. And where speech is not, there is neither *truth* nor *falsehood*. *Error* there may be, as when we expect that which shall not be, or suspect what has not been: but in neither case can a man be charged with untruth.

Seeing then that *truth* consisteth in the right ordering of names in our affirmations, a man that seeketh precise *truth* had need to remember what every name he uses stands for, and to place it accordingly; or else he will find himself entangled in words, as a bird in lime twigs, the more he struggles the more belimed. And therefore in geometry, (which is the only science that it hath pleased God hitherto to bestow on mankind,) men begin at settling the significations of their words; which settling of significations they call *definitions*, and place them in the beginning of their reckoning.

By this it appears how necessary it is for any man that aspires to true knowledge, to examine the definitions of former authors; and either to correct them, where they are negligently set down, or to make them himself. For the errors of definitions multiply themselves according as the reckoning proceeds, and lead men into absurdities, which at last they see, but cannot avoid, without reckoning anew from the beginning, in which lies the foundation of their errors. From whence it happens, that they which trust to books do as they that cast up many little sums into a greater, without considering whether those little sums were rightly cast up or not; and at last finding the error visible, and not mistrusting their first grounds, know not which way to clear themselves, but spend time in fluttering over their books; as birds that entering by the chimney, and finding themselves enclosed in a chamber, flutter at the false light of a glass window, for want of wit to consider which way they came in. So that in the right definition of names lies the first use of speech; which is the acquisition of science: and in wrong, or no definitions, lies the first abuse; from which proceed all false and senseless tenets; which make those men that take their instruction from the authority of books, and not from their own meditation, to be as much below the condition of ignorant men, as men endued with true science are above it. For between true science and erroneous doctrines, ignorance is in the middle. Natural sense and imagination are not subject to absurdity. Nature itself cannot err; and as men abound in copiousness of language, so they become more wise, or more mad than ordinary. Nor is it possible without letters for any man to become either excellently wise, or (unless his memory be hurt by disease or ill constitution of organs) excellently foolish. For words are wise men's counters, they do but reckon by them; but they are the money of fools, that value them by the authority of an *Aristotle*, a *Cicero*, or a *Thomas*, or any other doctor whatsoever, if but a man.

Subject to names, is whatsoever can enter into or be considered in an account, and be added one to another to make a sum, or subtracted one from another and leave a remainder. The Latins called accounts of money *rationes*, and accounting *ratiocinatio*; and that which we in bills or books of account call *items*, they call *nomina*, that is *names*; and thence it seems to proceed, that they extended the word *ratio* to the faculty of reckoning in all other things. The Greeks have but one word, λόγος, for both *speech* and *reason*; not that they thought there was no speech without reason, but no reasoning without speech: and the act of reasoning they called *syllogism*, which signifieth summing up of the consequences of one saying to another. And because the same things may enter into account for divers accidents, their names are (to show that diversity) diversly wrested and diversified. This diversity of names may be reduced to four general heads.

First, a thing may enter into account for *matter* or *body*; as *living, sensible, rational, hot, cold, moved, quiet*; with all which names the word *matter*, or *body*, is understood; all such being names of matter.

Secondly, it may enter into account, or be considered, for some accident or quality, which we conceive to be in it; as for *being moved*, for *being so long*, for *being hot*, &c.; and then, of the name of the thing it self, by a little change or wresting, we make a name for that accident, which we consider; and for *living* put into the account *life*; for *moved, motion*; for *hot, heat*; for *long, length*, and the like: and all such names are the names of the accidents and properties by which one matter and body is distinguished from another. These are called *names abstract*, because severed (not from matter, but) from the account of matter.

Thirdly, we bring into account the properties of our own bodies, whereby we make such distinction;

as when any thing is *seen* by us, we reckon not the thing it self, but the *sight*, the *colour*, the *idea* of it in the fancy: and when any thing is *heard*, we reckon it not, but the *hearing* or *sound* only, which is our fancy or conception of it by the ear; and such are names of fancies.

Fourthly, we bring into account, consider, and give names, to *names* themselves, and to *speeches*: For *general, universal, special, equivocal*, are names of names. And *affirmation, interrogation, commandment, narration, syllogism, sermon, oration*, and many other such, are names of speeches. And this is all the variety of names *positive*; which are put to mark somewhat which is in nature, or may be feigned by the mind of man, as bodies that are, or may be conceived to be; or of bodies, the properties that are, or may be feigned to be; or words and speech.

There be also other names, called *negative*, which are notes to signify that a word is not the name of the thing in question; as these words *nothing, no man, infinite, indocible, three want four*, and the like; which are nevertheless of use in reckoning, or in correcting of reckoning, and call to mind our past cogitations, though they be not names of any thing, because they make us refuse to admit of names not rightly used.

All other names are but insignificant sounds; and those of two sorts. One when they are new, and yet their meaning not explained by definition; whereof there have been abundance coined by schoolmen, and puzzled philosophers.

Another, when men make a name of two names, whose significations are contradictory and inconsistent; as this name, an *incorporeal body*, or (which is all one) an *incorporeal substance*, and a great number more. For whensoever any affirmation is false, the two names of which it is composed, put together and made one, signify nothing at all. For example, if it be a false affirmation to say *a quadrangle is round*, the word *round quadrangle* signifies nothing, but is a mere sound. So likewise, if it be false to say that virtue can be poured, or blown up and down, the words *in-poured virtue, in-blown virtue*, are as absurd and insignificant as a *round quadrangle*. And therefore you shall hardly meet with a senseless and insignificant word, that is not made up of some Latin or Greek names. A Frenchman seldom hears our Saviour called by the name of *parole*, but by the name of *verbe* often; yet *verbe* and *parole* differ no more, but that one is Latin, the other French.

When a man, upon the hearing of any speech, hath those thoughts which the words of that speech, and their connexion, were ordained and constituted to signify, then he is said to understand it; *understanding* being nothing else but conception caused by speech. And therefore if speech be peculiar to man (as for aught I know it is,) then is understanding peculiar to him also. And therefore of absurd and false affirmations, in case they be universal, there can be no understanding; though many think they understand then, when they do but repeat the words softly, or con them in their mind.

What kinds of speeches signify the appetites, aversions, and passions of man's mind; and of their use and abuse, I shall speak when I have spoken of the passions.

The names of such things as affect us, that is, which please and displease us, because all men be not alike affected with the same thing, nor the same man at all times, are in the common discourses of men of *inconstant* signification. For seeing all names are imposed to signify our conceptions, and all our affections are but conceptions, when we conceive the same things differently, we can hardly avoid different naming of them. For though the nature of that we conceive, be the same; yet the diversity of our reception of it, in respect of different constitutions of body, and prejudices of opinion, gives every thing a tincture of our different passions. And therefore in reasoning a man must take heed of words; which besides the signification of what we imagine of their nature, have a signification also of the nature, disposition, and interest of the speaker; such as are the names of virtues and vices; for one man calleth *wisdom*, what another calleth *fear*; and one *cruelty*, what another *justice*; one *prodigality*, what another *magnanimity*; and one *gravity*, what another *stupidity*, &c. And therefore such names can never be true grounds of any ratiocination. No more can metaphors, and tropes of speech; but these are less dangerous, because they profess their inconstancy; which the other do not.

CHAPTER 5: Of Reason and Science

When a man *reasoneth*, he does nothing else but conceive a sum total, from *addition* of parcels; or conceive a remainder, from *subtraction* of one sum from another; which (if it be done by words,) is conceiving of the consequence of the names of all the parts, to the name of the whole; or from the names of the whole and one part, to the name of the other part. And though in some things, (as in numbers,) besides *adding* and *subtracting*, men name other operations, as *multiplying* and *dividing*, yet they are the same; for multiplication, is but adding together of things equal; and division, but subtracting of one thing, as often as we can. These operations are not incident to numbers only, but to all manner of things that can be added together, and taken one out of another. For as arithmeticians teach to add and subtract in *numbers*; so the geometricians teach the same in *lines*, *figures* (solid and superficial,) *angles*, *proportions*, *times*, *degrees of swiftness*, *force*, *power*, and the like; the logicians teach the same in *consequences of words*; adding together *two names* to make an *affirmation*, and *two affirmations* to make a *syllogism*; and *many syllogisms* to make a *demonstration*; and from the *sum*, or *conclusion* of a *syllogism*, they subtract one *proposition* to find the other. Writers of politics add together *pactions* to find men's *duties*; and lawyers, *laws* and *facts*, to find what is *right* and *wrong* in the actions of private men. In sum, in what matter soever there is place for *addition* and *subtraction*, there also is place for *reason*; and where these have no place, there *reason* has nothing at all to do.

Out of all which we may define, (that is to say determine,) what that is, which is meant by this word *reason*, when we reckon it amongst the faculties of the mind. For REASON, in this sense, is nothing but *reckoning* (that is, adding and subtracting) of the consequences of general names agreed upon for the *marking* and *signifying* of our thoughts; I say *marking* them when we reckon by ourselves, and *signifying*, when we demonstrate or approve our reckonings to other men.

And as in arithmetic, unpractised men must, and professors themselves may often err, and cast up false;

so also in any other subject of reasoning, the ablest, most attentive, and most practised men may deceive themselves, and infer false conclusions; not but that reason itself is always right reason, as well as arithmetic is a certain and infallible art: but no one man's reason, nor the reason of any one number of men, makes the certainty; no more than an account is therefore well cast up, because a great many men have unanimously approved it. And therefore, as when there is a controversy in an account, the parties must by their own accord, set up for right reason, the reason of some arbitrator, or judge, to whose sentence they will both stand, or their controversy must either come to blows, or be undecided, for want of a right reason constituted by nature; so is it also in all debates of what kind soever. And when men that think themselves wiser than all others, clamour and demand right reason for judge, yet seek no more, but that things should be determined, by no other men's reason but their own, it is as intolerable in the society of men, as it is in play after trump is turned, to use for trump on every occasion, that suite whereof they have most in their hand. For they do nothing else, that will have every of their passions, as it comes to bear sway in them, to be taken for right reason, and that in their own controversies: bewraying their want of right reason, by the claim they lay to it.

The use and end of reason, is not the finding of the sum and truth of one, or a few consequences, remote from the first definitions, and settled significations of names, but to begin at these, and proceed from one consequence to another. For there can be no certainty of the last conclusion, without a certainty of all those affirmations and negations, on which it was grounded and inferred. As when a master of a family, in taking an account, casteth up the sums of all the bills of expense into one sum, and not regarding how each bill is summed up, by those that give them in account; nor what it is he pays for; he advantages himself no more, than if he allowed the account in gross, trusting to every of the accountants' skill and honesty: so also in reasoning of all other things, he that takes up conclusions on the trust of authors, and doth not fetch them from the first items in every reckoning, (which are the significations of names

settled by definitions,) loses his labour; and does not know any thing, but only believeth.

When a man reckons without the use of words, which may be done in particular things, (as when upon the sight of any one thing, we conjecture what was likely to have preceded, or is likely to follow upon it;) if that which he thought likely to follow, follows not, or that which he thought likely to have preceded it, hath not preceded it, this is called *error*; to which even the most prudent men are subject. But when we reason in words of general signification, and fall upon a general inference which is false, though it be commonly called error, it is indeed an *absurdity*, or senseless speech. For error is but a deception, in presuming that somewhat is past, or to come; of which, though it were not past, or not to come, yet there was no impossibility discoverable. But when we make a general assertion, unless it be a true one, the possibility of it is inconceivable. And words whereby we conceive nothing but the sound, are those we call *absurd*, *insignificant*, and *nonsense*. And therefore if a man should talk to me of a *round quadrangle*; or, *accidents of bread in cheese*; or *immaterial substances*; or of *a free subject*; *a free will*; or any *free*, but free from being hindered by opposition, I should not say he were in an error, but that his words were without meaning, that is to say, absurd.

I have said before, (in the second chapter,) that a man did excel all other animals in this faculty, that when he conceived any thing whatsoever, he was apt to inquire the consequences of it, and what effects he could do with it. And now I add this other degree of the same excellence, that he can by words reduce the consequences he finds to general rules, called *theorems*, or *aphorisms*; that is, he can reason, or reckon, not only in number, but in all other things, whereof one may be added unto, or subtracted from another.

But this privilege is allayed by another; and that is, by the privilege of absurdity; to which no living creature is subject, but man only. And of men, those are of all most subject to it, that profess philosophy. For it is most true that Cicero saith of them somewhere; that there can be nothing so absurd, but may be found in the books of philosophers. And the reason is manifest. For there is not one of them that begins his ratiocination from the definitions, or explications of the names they are to use; which is a method that hath been used only in geometry; whose conclusions have thereby been made indisputable.

I. The first cause of absurd conclusions I ascribe to the want of method; in that they begin not their ratiocination from definitions; that is, from settled significations of their words: as if they could cast account, without knowing the value of the numeral words, *one*, *two*, and *three*.

And whereas all bodies enter into account upon divers considerations, (which I have mentioned in the precedent chapter;) these considerations being diversely named, divers absurdities proceed from the confusion, and unfit connexion of their names into assertions. And therefore,

II. The second cause of absurd assertions, I ascribe to the giving of names of *bodies* to *accidents*; or of *accidents* to *bodies*; as they do, that say, *faith is infused*, or *inspired*; when nothing can be *poured*, or *breathed* into any thing, but body; and that, *extension* is *body*; that *phantasms* are *spirits*, &c.

III. The third I ascribe to the giving of the names of the *accidents* of *bodies without us*, to the *accidents* of our *own bodies*; as they do that say, the *colour is in the body*; *the sound is in the air*, &c.

IV. The fourth, to the giving of the names of *bodies* to *names*, or *speeches*; as they do that say, that *there be things universal*; that *a living creature is genus*, or *a general thing*, &c.

V. The fifth, to the giving of the names of *accidents* to *names* and *speeches*; as they do that say, *the nature of a thing is its definition*; *a man's command is his will*; and the like.

VI. The sixth, to the use of metaphors, tropes, and other rhetorical figures, instead of words proper. For though it be lawful to say, (for example) in common speech, *the way goeth, or leadeth hither, or thither*; *the proverb says this or that* (whereas ways cannot go, nor proverbs speak;) yet in reckoning, and seeking of truth, such speeches are not to be admitted.

VII. The seventh, to names that signify nothing; but are taken up, and learned by rote from the schools, as *hypostatical*, *transubstantiate*, *consubstantiate*, *eternal-now*, and the like canting of schoolmen.

To him that can avoid these things it is not easy to fall into any absurdity, unless it be by the length of an account; wherein he may perhaps forget what went before. For all men by nature reason alike, and well, when they have good principles. For who is so stupid, as both to mistake in geometry, and also to persist in it, when another detects his error to him?

By this it appears that reason is not, as sense and memory, born with us; nor gotten by experience only, as prudence is; but attained by industry; first in apt imposing of names; and secondly by getting a good and orderly method in proceeding from the elements, which are names, to assertions made by connexion of one of them to another; and so to syllogisms, which are the connexions of one assertion to another, till we come to a knowledge of all the consequences of names appertaining to the subject in hand; and that is it, men call SCIENCE. And whereas sense and memory are but knowledge of fact, which is a thing past, and irrevocable; *Science* is the knowledge of consequences, and dependence of one fact upon another: by which, out of that we can presently do, we know how to do something else when we will, or the like, another time; because when we see how any thing comes about, upon what causes, and by what manner; when the like causes come into our power, we see how to make it produce the like effects.

Children therefore are not endued with reason at all, till they have attained the use of speech; but are called reasonable creatures, for the possibility apparent of having the use of reason in time to come. And the most part of men, though they have the use of reasoning a little way, as in numbering to some degree; yet it serves them to little use in common life; in which they govern themselves, some better, some worse, according to their differences of experience, quickness of memory, and inclinations to several ends; but specially according to good or evil fortune, and the errors of one another. For as for *science*, or certain rules of their actions, they are so far from it, that they know not what it is. Geometry they have thought conjuring: but for other sciences, they who have not been taught the beginnings and some progress in them, that they may see how they be acquired and generated, are in this point like children, that having no thought of generation, are made believe by the women that their brothers and sisters are not born, but found in the garden.

But yet they that have no *science*, are in better, and nobler condition, with their natural prudence; than men, that by mis-reasoning, or by trusting them that reason wrong, fall upon false and absurd general rules. For ignorance of causes, and of rules, does not set men so far out of their way, as relying on false rules, and taking for causes of what they aspire to, those that are not so, but rather causes of the contrary.

To conclude, the light of human minds is perspicuous words, but by exact definitions first snuffed, and purged from ambiguity; *reason* is the *pace*; increase of *science*, the *way*; and the benefit of mankind, the *end*. And on the contrary, metaphors, and senseless and ambiguous words, are like *ignes fatui*; and reasoning upon them is wandering amongst innumerable absurdities; and their end, contention and sedition, or contempt.

As much experience, is *prudence*; so, is much science *sapience*. For though we usually have one name of wisdom for them both, yet the Latins did always distinguish between *prudentia* and *sapientia*; ascribing the former to experience, the latter to science. But to make their difference appear more clearly, let us suppose one man endued with an excellent natural use and dexterity in handling his arms; and another to have added to that dexterity, an acquired science, of where he can offend, or be offended by his adversary, in every possible posture or guard: the ability of the former, would be to the ability of the latter, as prudence to sapience; both useful; but the latter infallible. But they that trusting only to the authority of books, follow the blind blindly, are like him that, trusting to the false rules of a master of fence, ventures presumptuously upon an adversary, that either kills or disgraces him.

The signs of science are some, certain and infallible; some, uncertain. Certain, when he that pretendeth the science of any thing, can teach the same, that is to say, demonstrate the truth thereof perspicuously to another; uncertain, when only some particular events answer to his pretence, and upon many occasions prove so as he says they must. Signs of prudence are all uncertain; because to observe by experience, and remember all circumstances that may alter the success, is impossible. But in any business, whereof a man has not infallible science to proceed by; to forsake his own natural judgment, and be guided by general sentences read in authors, and subject to many exceptions, is a sign of folly, and generally scorned by the name of pedantry. And even of those men themselves, that in councils of the commonwealth love to show their reading of politics and history, very few do it in their domestic affairs, where their particular interest is concerned; having prudence enough for their private affairs: but in public they study more the reputation of their own wit, than the success of another's business.

CHAPTER 6: Of the Interior Beginnings of Voluntary Motions; Commonly Called the Passions; and the Speeches by Which They Are Expressed

There be in animals, two sorts of *motions* peculiar to them: one called *vital*; begun in generation, and continued without interruption through their whole life; such as are the *course* of the *blood*, the *pulse*, the *breathing*, the *concoction, nutrition, excretion*, &c; to which motions there needs no help of imagination: the other is *animal motion*, otherwise called *voluntary motion*; as to *go*, to *speak*, to *move* any of our limbs, in such manner as is first fancied in our minds. That sense is motion in the organs and interior parts of man's body, caused by the action of the things we see, hear, &c.; and that fancy is but the relics of the same motion, remaining after sense, has been already said in the first and second chapters. And because *going, speaking*, and the like voluntary motions, depend always upon a precedent thought of *whither, which way*, and *what*; it is evident, that the imagination is the first internal beginning of all voluntary motion. And although unstudied men do not conceive any motion at all to be there, where the thing moved is invisible; or the space it is moved in, is (for the shortness of it) insensible; yet that doth not hinder, but that such motions are. For let a space be never so little, that which is moved over a greater space, whereof that little one is part, must first be moved over that. These small beginnings of motion, within the body of man, before they appear in walking, speaking, striking, and other visible actions, are commonly called ENDEAVOUR.

This endeavour, when it is toward something which causes it, is called APPETITE, or DESIRE; the latter, being the general name; and the other, oftentimes restrained to signify the desire of food, namely *hunger* and *thirst*. And when the endeavour is fromward something, it is generally called AVERSION. These words, *appetite* and *aversion*, we have from the *Latins*; and they both of them signify the motions, one of approaching, the other of retiring. So also do the Greek words for the same, which are ὁρμὴ and ἀφορμὴ. For nature itself does often press upon men those truths, which afterwards, when they look for somewhat beyond nature, they stumble at. For the Schools find in mere appetite to go, or move, no actual motion at all: but because some motion they must acknowledge, they call it metaphorical motion; which is but an absurd speech: for though words may be called metaphorical; bodies and motions cannot.

That which men desire, they are also said to LOVE: and to HATE those things for which they have aversion. So that desire and love are the same thing; save that by desire, we always signify the absence of the object; by love, most commonly the presence of the same. So also by aversion, we signify the absence; and by hate, the presence of the object.

Of appetites and aversions, some are born with men; as appetite of food, appetite of excretion, and exoneration, (which may also and more properly be called aversions, from somewhat they feel in their bodies;) and some other appetites, not many. The rest, which are appetites of particular things, proceed from experience, and trial of their effects upon themselves or other men. For of things we know not at all, or believe not to be, we can have no further desire, than to taste and try. But aversion we have for things, not only which we know have hurt us, but also that we do not know whether they will hurt us, or not.

Those things which we neither desire, nor hate, we are said to *contemn*; CONTEMPT being nothing else but an immobility, or contumacy of the heart, in resisting the action of certain things; and proceeding from that the heart is already moved otherwise, by other more potent objects; or from want of experience of them.

And because the constitution of a man's body is in continual mutation, it is impossible that all the same things should always cause in him the same appetites, and aversions: much less can all men consent, in the desire of almost any one and the same object.

But whatsoever is the object of any man's appetite or desire, that is it which he for his part calleth *good*: and the object of his hate and aversion, *evil*; and of his contempt, *vile* and *inconsiderable*. For these words of good, evil, and contemptible, are ever used with relation to the person that useth them: there being nothing simply and absolutely so; nor any common rule of good and evil, to be taken from the nature of the objects themselves; but from the person of the man (where there is no commonwealth;) or, (in a commonwealth,) from the person that representeth it; or from an arbitrator or judge, whom men disagreeing shall by consent set up, and make his sentence the rule thereof.

The Latin tongue has two words, whose significations approach to those of good and evil; but are not precisely the same; and those are *pulchrum* and *turpe*. Whereof the former signifies that, which by some apparent signs promiseth good; and the latter, that which promiseth evil. But in our tongue we have not so general names to express them by. But for *pulchrum* we say in some things, *fair*; in others, *beautiful*, or *handsome*, or *gallant*, or *honourable*, or *comely*, or *amiable*; and for *turpe*, *foul*, *deformed*, *ugly*, *base*, *nauseous*, and the like, as the subject shall require; all which words, in their proper places, signify nothing else but the *mine*, or countenance, that promiseth good and evil. So that of good there be three kinds;

good in the promise, that is *pulchrum*; good in effect, as the end desired, which is called *jucundum, delightful*; and good as the means, which is called *utile, profitable*; and as many of evil: for *evil* in promise, is that they call *turpe*; evil in effect, and end, is *molestum, unpleasant, troublesome*; and evil in the means, *inutile, unprofitable, hurtful*.

As, in sense, that which is really within us, is, (as I have said before,) only motion, caused by the action of external objects, but in apparence; to the sight, light and colour; to the ear, sound; to the nostril, odour, &c.: so, when the action of the same object is continued from the eyes, ears, and other organs to the heart, the real effect there is nothing but motion, or endeavour; which consisteth in appetite, or aversion, to or from the object moving. But the apparence, or sense of that motion, is that we either call *delight*, or *trouble of mind*.

This motion, which is called appetite, and for the apparence of it *delight*, and *pleasure*, seemeth to be a corroboration of vital motion, and a help thereunto; and therefore such things as caused delight, were not improperly called *jucunda, (a juvando,)* from helping or fortifying; and the contrary, *molesta, offensive*, from hindering, and troubling the motion vital.

Pleasure therefore, (or *delight*,) is the apparence, or sense of good; and *molestation* or *displeasure*, the apparence, or sense of evil. And consequently all appetite, desire, and love, is accompanied with some delight more or less; and all hatred and aversion, with more or less displeasure and offence.

Of pleasures or delights, some arise from the sense of an object present; and those may be called *pleasures of sense*, (the word *sensual*, as it is used by those only that condemn them, having no place till there be laws.) Of this kind are all onerations and exonerations of the body; as also all that is pleasant, in the *sight, hearing, smell, taste, or touch*. Others arise from the expectation, that proceeds from foresight of the end, or consequence of things; whether those things in the sense please or displease. And these are *pleasures of the mind* of him that draweth those consequences, and are generally called JOY. In the like manner, displeasures are some in the sense, and called PAIN;

others in the expectation of consequences, and are called GRIEF.

These simple passions called *appetite, desire, love, aversion, hate, joy*, and *grief*, have their names for divers considerations diversified. As first, when they one succeed another, they are diversely called from the opinion men have of the likelihood of attaining what they desire. Secondly, from the object loved or hated. Thirdly, from the consideration of many of them together. Fourthly, from the alteration or succession it self.

For *appetite*, with an opinion of attaining, is called HOPE.

The same, without such opinion, DESPAIR.

Aversion, with opinion of *hurt* from the object, FEAR.

The same, with hope of avoiding that hurt by resistance, COURAGE.

Sudden *courage*, ANGER.

Constant *hope*, CONFIDENCE of ourselves.

Constant *despair*, DIFFIDENCE of ourselves.

Anger for great hurt done to another, when we conceive the same to be done by injury, INDIGNATION.

Desire of good to another, BENEVOLENCE, GOOD WILL, CHARITY. If to man generally, GOOD NATURE.

Desire of riches, COVETOUSNESS: a name used always in signification of blame; because men contending for them, are displeased with one another's attaining them; though the desire in itself, be to be blamed, or allowed, according to the means by which those riches are sought.

Desire of office, or precedence, AMBITION: a name used also in the worse sense, for the reason before mentioned.

Desire of things that conduce but a little to our ends, and fear of things that are but of little hindrance, PUSILLANIMITY.

Contempt of little helps and hindrances, MAGNANIMITY.

Magnanimity, in danger of death or wounds, VALOUR, FORTITUDE.

Magnanimity, in the use of riches, LIBERALITY.

Pusillanimity, in the same, WRETCHEDNESS, MISERABLENESS, or PARSIMONY; as it is liked or disliked.

Love of persons for society, KINDNESS.

Love of persons for pleasing the sense only, NATURAL LUST.

Love of the same, acquired from rumination, that is, imagination of pleasure past, LUXURY.

Love of one singularly, with desire to be singularly beloved, THE PASSION OF LOVE. The same, with fear that the love is not mutual, JEALOUSY.

Desire, by doing hurt to another, to make him condemn some fact of his own, REVENGEFULNESS.

Desire to know why, and how, CURIOSITY; such as is in no living creature but *man:* so that man is distinguished, not only by his reason, but also by this singular passion from other *animals;* in whom the appetite of food, and other pleasures of sense, by predominance, take away the care of knowing causes; which is a lust of the mind, that by a perseverance of delight in the continual and indefatigable generation of knowledge, exceedeth the short vehemence of any carnal pleasure.

Fear of power invisible, feigned by the mind, or imagined from tales publicly allowed, RELIGION; not allowed, SUPERSTITION. And when the power imagined, is truly such as we imagine, TRUE RELIGION.

Fear, without the apprehension of why, or what, PANIC TERROR, called so from the fables, that make *Pan* the author of them; whereas in truth, there is always in him that so feareth, first, some apprehension of the cause, though the rest run away by example, every one supposing his fellow to know why. And therefore this passion happens to none but in a throng, or multitude of people.

Joy, from apprehension of novelty, ADMIRATION; proper to man, because it excites the appetite of knowing the cause.

Joy, arising from imagination of a man's own power and ability, is that exultation of the mind which is called GLORYING: which if grounded upon the experience of his own former actions, is the same with *confidence:* but if grounded on the flattery of others; or only supposed by himself, for delight in the consequences of it, is called VAINGLORY: which name is properly given; because a well grounded *confidence* begetteth attempt; whereas the supposing of power does not, and is therefore rightly called *vain.*

Grief, from opinion of want of power, is called DEJECTION of mind.

The *vain-glory* which consisteth in the feigning or supposing of abilities in ourselves, which we know are not, is most incident to young men, and nourished by the histories, or fictions of gallant persons; and is corrected oftentimes by age, and employment.

Sudden glory, is the passion which maketh those *grimaces* called LAUGHTER; and is caused either by some sudden act of their own, that pleaseth them; or by the apprehension of some deformed thing in another, by comparison whereof they suddenly applaud themselves. And it is incident most to them, that are conscious of the fewest abilities in themselves; who are forced to keep themselves in their own favour, by observing the imperfections of other men. And therefore much laughter at the defects of others, is a sign of pusillanimity. For of great minds, one of the proper works is, to help and free others from scorn; and compare themselves only with the most able.

On the contrary, *sudden dejection*, is the passion that causeth WEEPING; and is caused by such accidents, as suddenly take away some vehement hope, or some prop of their power: and they are most subject to it, that rely principally on helps external, such as are women, and children. Therefore some weep for the loss of friends; others for their unkindness; others for the sudden stop made to their thoughts of revenge, by reconciliation. But in all cases, both laughter, and weeping, are sudden motions; custom taking them both away. For no man laughs at old jests; or weeps for an old calamity.

Grief, for the discovery of some defect of ability, is SHAME, or the passion that discovereth itself in BLUSHING; and consisteth in the apprehension of some thing dishonourable; and in young men, is a sign of the love of good reputation, and commendable: in old men it is a sign of the same; but because it comes too late, not commendable.

The *contempt* of good reputation is called IMPUDENCE.

Grief, for the calamity of another, is PITY; and ariseth from the imagination that the like calamity may befall himself; and therefore is called also COMPASSION, and in the phrase of this present time a FELLOW-FEELING: and therefore for calamity arriving from great wickedness, the best men have the least pity; and for the same calamity, those have least pity, that think themselves least obnoxious to the same.

Contempt, or little sense of the calamity of others, is that which men call CRUELTY; proceeding from security of their own fortune. For, that any man should take pleasure in other men's great harms, without other end of his own, I do not conceive it possible.

Grief, for the success of a competitor in wealth, honour, or other good, if it be joined with endeavour to enforce our own abilities to equal or exceed him, is called EMULATION: but joined with endeavour to supplant, or hinder a competitor, ENVY.

When in the mind of man, appetites, and aversions, hopes, and fears, concerning one and the same thing, arise alternately; and divers good and evil consequences of the doing, or omitting the thing propounded, come successively into our thoughts; so that sometimes we have an appetite to it; sometimes an aversion from it; sometimes hope to be able to do it; sometimes despair, or fear to attempt it; the whole sum of desires, aversions, hopes and fears continued till the thing be either done, or thought impossible, is that we call DELIBERATION.

Therefore of things past, there is no *deliberation*; because manifestly impossible to be changed: nor of things known to be impossible, or thought so; because men know, or think such deliberation vain. But of things impossible, which we think possible, we may deliberate; not knowing it is in vain. And it is called *deliberation*; because it is a putting an end to the *liberty* we had of doing, or omitting, according to our own appetite, or aversion.

This alternate succession of appetites, aversions, hopes and fears, is no less in other living creatures than in man: and therefore beasts also deliberate.

Every *deliberation* is then said to *end*, when that whereof they deliberate, is either done, or thought impossible; because till then we retain the liberty of doing, or omitting, according to our appetite, or aversion.

In *deliberation*, the last appetite, or aversion, immediately adhering to the action, or to the omission thereof, is that we call the WILL; the act, (not the faculty,) of *willing*. And beasts that have *deliberation*, must necessarily also have *will*. The definition of the *will*, given commonly by the Schools, that it is a *rational appetite*, is not good. For if it were, then could there be no voluntary act against reason. For a *voluntary act* is that, which proceedeth from the *will*, and no other. But if instead of a rational appetite, we shall say an appetite resulting from a precedent deliberation, then the definition is the same that I have given here. *Will* therefore *is the last appetite in deliberating*. And though we say in common discourse, a man had a will once to do a thing, that nevertheless he forbore to do; yet that is properly but an inclination, which makes no action voluntary; because the action depends not of it, but of the last inclination, or appetite. For if the intervenient appetites, make any action voluntary; then by the same reason all intervenient aversions, should make the same action involuntary; and so one and the same action, should be both voluntary and involuntary.

By this it is manifest, that not only actions that have their beginning from covetousness, ambition, lust, or other appetites to the thing propounded; but also those that have their beginning from aversion, or fear of those consequences that follow the omission, are *voluntary actions*.

The forms of speech by which the passions are expressed, are partly the same, and partly different from those, by which we express our thoughts. And first, generally all passions may be expressed *indicatively*; as *I love, I fear, I joy, I deliberate, I will, I command*: but some of them have particular expressions by themselves, which nevertheless are not affirmations, unless it be when they serve to make other inferences, besides that of the passion they proceed from. Deliberation is expressed *subjunctively*; which is a speech proper to signify suppositions, with their consequences; as, *if this be done, then this will follow*; and differs not from the language of reasoning, save that reasoning is in general words; but deliberation for the most part is of particulars. The language of desire, and aversion, is *imperative*; as *do this, forbear that*; which when the party is obliged to do, or forbear, is *command*; otherwise *prayer*; or else *counsel*. The language of vain-glory, of indignation, pity and revengefulness, *optative*: but of the desire to know, there is a peculiar expression, called *interrogative*; as, *what is it, when shall it, how is it done*, and *why so?* Other language of the passions I find none: for cursing, swearing, reviling, and the like, do not signify as speech; but as the actions of a tongue accustomed.

These forms of speech, I say, are expressions, or voluntary significations of our passions: but certain signs they be not; because they may be used arbitrarily, whether they that use them, have such passions or not. The best signs of passions present, are either in the countenance, motions of the body, actions, and ends, or aims, which we otherwise know the man to have.

And because in deliberation, the appetites, and aversions, are raised by foresight of the good and evil consequences, and sequels of the action whereof we deliberate; the good or evil effect thereof dependeth on the foresight of a long chain of consequences, of which very seldom any man is able to see to the end. But for so far as a man seeth, if the good in those consequences be greater than the evil, the whole chain is that which writers call *apparent*, or *seeming good*. And contrarily, when the evil exceedeth the good, the whole is *apparent*, or *seeming evil*: so that he who hath by experience, or reason, the greatest and surest prospect of consequences, deliberates best himself; and is able when he will, to give the best counsel unto others.

Continual success in obtaining those things which a man from time to time desireth, that is to say, continual prospering, is that men call FELICITY; I mean the felicity of this life. For there is no such thing as perpetual tranquillity of mind, while we live here; because life itself is but motion, and can never be without desire, nor without fear, no more than without sense. What kind of felicity God hath ordained to them that devoutly honour Him, a man shall no sooner know, than enjoy; being joys, that

now are as incomprehensible, as the word of schoolmen *beatifical vision* is unintelligible.

The form of speech whereby men signify their opinion of the goodness of any thing, is PRAISE. That whereby they signify the power and greatness of any thing, is MAGNIFYING. And that whereby they signify the opinion they have of a man's felicity, is by the Greeks called μακαρισμός, for which we have no name in our tongue. And thus much is sufficient for the present purpose, to have been said of the PASSIONS.

CHAPTER 7: Of the Ends, or Resolutions of Discourse

Of all *discourse*, governed by desire of knowledge, there is at last an *end*, either by attaining, or by giving over. And in the chain of discourse, wheresoever it be interrupted, there is an end for that time.

If the discourse be merely mental, it consisteth of thoughts that the thing will be, and will not be, or that it has been, and has not been, alternately. So that wheresoever you break off the chain of a man's discourse, you leave him in a presumption of *it will be*, or, *it will not be*; or *it has been*, or, *has not been*. All which is *opinion*. And that which is alternate appetite, in deliberating concerning good and evil; the same is alternate opinion, in the enquiry of the truth of *past*, and *future*. And as the last appetite in deliberation, is called the *will*; so the last opinion in search of the truth of past, and future, is called the JUDGMENT, or *resolute* and *final sentence* of him that *discourseth*. And as the whole chain of appetites alternate, in the question of good, or bad, is called *deliberation*; so the whole chain of opinions alternate, in the question of true, or false, is called DOUBT.

No discourse whatsoever, can end in absolute knowledge of fact, past, or to come. For, as for the knowledge of fact, it is originally, sense; and ever after, memory. And for the knowledge of consequence, which I have said before is called science, it is not absolute, but conditional. No man can know by discourse, that this, or that, is, has been, or will be; which is to know absolutely: but only, that if this be, that is; if this has been, that has been; if this shall be, that shall be: which is to know conditionally; and that not the consequence of one thing to another; but of one name of a thing, to another name of the same thing.

And therefore, when the discourse is put into speech, and begins with the definitions of words, and proceeds by connexion of the same into general affirmations, and of these again into syllogisms; the end or last sum is called the conclusion; and the thought of the mind by it signified, is that conditional knowledge, or knowledge of the consequence of words, which is commonly called SCIENCE. But if the first ground of such discourse, be not definitions; or if the definitions be not rightly joined together into syllogisms, then the end or conclusion, is again OPINION, namely of the truth of somewhat said, though sometimes in absurd and senseless words, without possibility of being understood. When two, or more men, know of one and the same fact, they are said to be CONSCIOUS of it one to another; which is as much as to know it together. And because such are fittest witnesses of the facts of one another, or of a third; it was, and ever will be reputed a very evil act, for any man to speak against his *conscience*: or to corrupt or force another so to do: insomuch that the plea of conscience, has been always hearkened unto very diligently in all times. Afterwards, men made use of the same word metaphorically, for the knowledge of their own secret facts, and secret thoughts; and therefore it is rhetorically said, that the conscience is a thousand witnesses. And last of all, men, vehemently in love with their own new opinions, (though never so absurd,) and obstinately bent to maintain them, gave those their opinions also that reverenced name of conscience, as if they would have it seem unlawful, to change or speak against them; and so pretend to know they are true, when they know at most, but that they think so.

When a man's discourse beginneth not at definitions, it beginneth either at some other contemplation of his own, and then it is still called opinion; or it beginneth at some saying of another, of whose ability

to know the truth, and of whose honesty in not deceiving, he doubteth not; and then the discourse is not so much concerning the thing, as the person; and the resolution is called BELIEF, and FAITH: *faith, in* the man; *belief,* both *of* the man, and *of* the truth of what he says. So that in belief are two opinions; one of the saying of the man; the other of his virtue. To *have faith in,* or *trust to,* or *believe a man,* signify the same thing; namely, an opinion of the veracity of the man: but to *believe what is said,* signifieth only an opinion of the truth of the saying. But we are to observe that this phrase, *I believe in*; as also the Latin, *credo in*; and the Greek, πιστένω ἔις, are never used but in the writings of divines. Instead of them, in other writings are put, *I believe him; I trust him; I have faith in him; I rely on him*; and in Latin, *credo illi: fido illi:* and in Greek, πιστένω αὐτῷ: and that this singularity of the ecclesiastic use of the word hath raised many disputes about the right object of the Christian faith.

But by *believing in,* as it is in the creed, is meant, not trust in the person; but confession and acknowledgment of the doctrine. For not only Christians, but all manner of men do so believe in God, as to hold all for truth they hear him say, whether they understand it, or not; which is all the faith and trust can possibly be had in any person whatsoever: but they do not all believe the doctrine of the creed.

From whence we may infer, that when we believe any saying whatsoever it be, to be true, from arguments taken, not from the thing it self, or from the principles of natural reason, but from the authority, and good opinion we have, of him that hath said it; then is the speaker, or person we believe in, or trust in, and whose word we take, the object of our faith; and the honour done in believing, is done to him only. And consequently, when we believe that the Scriptures are the word of God, having no immediate revelation from God himself, our belief, faith, and trust is in the church; whose word we take, and acquiesce therein. And they that believe that which a prophet relates unto them in the name of God, take the word of the prophet, do honour to him, and in him trust, and believe, touching the truth of what he

relateth, whether he be a true, or a false prophet. And
so it is also with all other history. For if I should not
believe all that is written by historians, of the glorious
acts of *Alexander*, or *Caesar*; I do not think the ghost
of *Alexander*, or *Caesar*, had any just cause to be
offended; or any body else, but the historian. If *Livy*
say the Gods made once a cow speak, and we believe
it not; we distrust not God therein, but *Livy*. So that
it is evident, that whatsoever we believe, upon no
other reason, than what is drawn from authority of
men only, and their writings; whether they be sent
from God or not, is faith in men only.

CHAPTER 8: Of the Virtues Commonly Called Intellectual; and Their Contrary Defects

Virtue generally, in all sorts of subjects, is somewhat
that is valued for eminence; and consisteth in comparison. For if all things were equally in all men, nothing
would be prized. And by *virtues* INTELLECTUAL,
are always understood such abilities of the mind, as
men praise, value, and desire should be in themselves;
and go commonly under the name of a *good wit*;
though the same word *wit*, be used also, to distinguish
one certain ability from the rest.

These *virtues* are of two sorts; *natural*, and *acquired*.
By natural, I mean not, that which a man hath from
his birth: for that is nothing else but sense; wherein
men differ so little one from another, and from brute
beasts, as it is not to be reckoned amongst virtues.
But I mean, that *wit*, which is gotten by use only, and
experience; without method, culture, or instruction.
This NATURAL WIT, consisteth principally in two
things; *celerity of imagining*, (that is, swift succession
of one thought to another;) and *steady direction* to
some approved end. On the contrary a slow imagination, maketh that defect, or fault of the mind, which
is commonly called DULLNESS, *stupidity*, and
sometimes by other names that signify slowness of
motion, or difficulty to be moved.

And this difference of quickness, is caused by the
difference of men's passions; that love and dislike,
some one thing, some another: and therefore some

men's thoughts run one way, some another; and are
held to, and observe differently the things that pass
through their imagination. And whereas in this succession of men's thoughts, there is nothing to observe
in the things they think on, but either in what they
be *like one another*, or in what they be *unlike*, or *what
they serve for*, or *how they serve to such a purpose*;
those that observe their similitudes, in case they be
such as are but rarely observed by others, are said to
have a *good wit*; by which, in this occasion, is meant
a *good fancy*. But they that observe their differences,
and dissimilitudes; which is called *distinguishing*, and
discerning, and *judging* between thing and thing; in
case, such discerning be not easy, are said to have a
good judgment: and particularly in matter of conversation and business; wherein, times, places, and persons
are to be discerned, this virtue is called DISCRE-
TION. The former, that is, fancy, without the help
of judgment, is not commended as a virtue: but the
latter which is judgment, and discretion, is commended for it self, without the help of fancy. Besides
the discretion of times, places, and persons, necessary
to a good fancy, there is required also an often application of his thoughts to their end; that is to say, to
some use to be made of them. This done; he that
hath this virtue, will be easily fitted with similitudes,
that will please, not only by illustration of his discourse, and adorning it with new and apt metaphors;
but also, by the rarity of their invention. But without
steadiness, and direction to some end, a great fancy
is one kind of madness; such as they have, that entering into any discourse, are snatched from their purpose, by every thing that comes in their thought, into
so many, and so long digressions, and parentheses,
that they utterly lose themselves: which kind of folly,
I know no particular name for: but the cause of it is,
sometimes want of experience; whereby that seemeth
to a man new and rare, which doth not so to others:
sometimes pusillanimity; by which that seems great
to him, which other men think a trifle: and whatsoever
is new, or great, and therefore thought fit to be told,
withdraws a man by degrees from the intended way
of his discourse.

In a good poem, whether it be *epic*, or *dramatic*;
as also in *sonnets*, *epigrams*, and other pieces, both

judgment and fancy are required: but the fancy must be more eminent; because they please for the extravagancy; but ought not to displease by indiscretion.

In a good history, the judgment must be eminent; because the goodness consisteth, in the method, in the truth, and in the choice of the actions that are most profitable to be known. Fancy has no place, but only in adorning the style.

In orations of praise, and in invectives, the fancy is predominant; because the design is not truth, but to honour or dishonour; which is done by noble, or by vile comparisons. The judgment does but suggest what circumstances make an action laudable, or culpable.

In hortatives, and pleadings, as truth, or disguise serveth best to the design in hand; so is the judgment, or the fancy most required.

In demonstration, in counsel, and all rigorous search of truth, judgment does all; except sometimes the understanding have need to be opened by some apt similitude; and then there is so much use of fancy. But for metaphors, they are in this case utterly excluded. For seeing they openly profess deceit; to admit them into counsel, or reasoning, were manifest folly.

And in any discourse whatsoever, if the defect of discretion be apparent, how extravagant soever the fancy be, the whole discourse will be taken for a sign of want of wit; and so will it never when the discretion is manifest, though the fancy be never so ordinary.

The secret thoughts of a man run over all things, holy, profane, clean, obscene, grave, and light, without shame, or blame; which verbal discourse cannot do, farther than the judgment shall approve of the time, place, and persons. An anatomist, or a physician may speak, or write his judgment of unclean things; because it is not to please, but profit: but for another man to write his extravagant, and pleasant fancies of the same, is as if a man, from being tumbled into the dirt, should come and present himself before good company. And it is the want of discretion that makes the difference. Again, in professed remissness of mind, and familiar company, a man may play with the sounds, and equivocal significations of words; and that many times with encounters of extraordinary fancy: but in a sermon, or in public, or before persons unknown, or whom we ought to reverence; there is no gingling of words that will not be accounted folly: and the difference is only in the want of discretion. So that where wit is wanting, it is not fancy that is wanting, but discretion. Judgment therefore without fancy is wit, but fancy without judgment, not.

When the thoughts of a man, that has a design in hand, running over a multitude of things, observes how they conduce to that design; or what design they may conduce unto; if his observations be such as are not easy, or usual, this wit of his is called PRUDENCE; and dependeth on much experience, and memory of the like things, and their consequences heretofore. In which there is not so much difference of men, as there is in their fancies and judgments; because the experience of men equal in age, is not much unequal, as to the quantity; but lies in different occasions; every one having his private designs. To govern well a family, and a kingdom, are not different degrees of prudence; but different sorts of business; no more than to draw a picture in little, or as great, or greater than the life, are different degrees of art. A plain husbandman is more prudent in affairs of his own house, than a privy councillor in the affairs of another man.

To prudence, if you add the use of unjust, or dishonest means, such as usually are prompted to men by fear, or want; you have that crooked wisdom, which is called CRAFT; which is a sign of pusillanimity. For magnanimity is contempt of unjust, or dishonest helps. And that which the Latins call *versutia*, (translated into English, *shifting*,) and is a putting off of a present danger or incommodity, by engaging into a greater, as when a man robs one to pay another, is but a shorter sighted craft, called *versutia*, from *versura*, which signifies taking money at usury for the present payment of interest.

As for *acquired wit*, (I mean acquired by method and instruction,) there is none but reason; which is grounded on the right use of speech, and produceth the sciences. But of reason and science, I have already spoken in the fifth and sixth chapters.

The causes of this difference of wits, are in the passions; and the difference of passions proceedeth, partly from the different constitution of the body, and partly from different education. For if the difference proceeded from the temper of the brain, and the organs of sense, either exterior or interior, there would be no less difference of men in their sight, hearing, or other senses, than in their fancies and discretions. It proceeds therefore from the passions; which are different, not only from the difference of mens' complexions; but also from their difference of customs, and education.

The passions that most of all cause the differences of wit, are principally, the more or less desire of power, of riches, of knowledge, and of honour. All which may be reduced to the first, that is, desire of power. For riches, knowledge, and honour are but several sorts of power.

And therefore, a man who has no great passion for any of these things; but is as men term it indifferent; though he may be so far a good man, as to be free from giving offence; yet he cannot possibly have either a great fancy, or much judgment. For the thoughts are to the desires, as scouts, and spies, to range abroad, and find the way to the things desired: all steadiness of the mind's motion and all quickness of the same, proceeding from thence: for as to have no desire, is to be dead: so to have weak passions, is dullness; and to have passions indifferently for every thing, GIDDINESS, and *distraction*; and to have stronger and more vehement passions for any thing, than is ordinarily seen in others, is that which men call MADNESS.

Whereof there be almost as many kinds, as of the passions themselves. Sometimes the extraordinary and extravagant passion, proceedeth from the evil constitution of the organs of the body, or harm done them; and sometimes the hurt, and indisposition of the organs, is caused by the vehemence, or long continuance of the passion. But in both cases the madness is of one and the same nature.

The passion, whose violence, or continuance, maketh madness, is either great *vain-glory*; which is commonly called *pride*, and *self-conceit*; or great *dejection* of mind.

Pride, subjecteth a man to anger, the excess whereof, is the madness called RAGE and FURY.

And thus it comes to pass that excessive desire of revenge, when it becomes habitual, hurteth the organs, and becomes rage: that excessive love, with jealousy, becomes also rage: excessive opinion of a man's own self, for divine inspiration, for wisdom, learning, form and the like, becomes distraction and giddiness: the same, joined with envy, rage: vehement opinion of the truth of any thing, contradicted by others, rage.

Dejection subjects a man to causeless fears; which is a madness commonly called MELANCHOLY, apparent also in divers manners; as in haunting of solitudes and graves; in superstitious behaviour; and in fearing some one, some another particular thing. In sum, all passions that produce strange and unusual behaviour, are called by the general name of madness. But of the several kinds of madness, he that would take the pains, might enrol a legion. And if the excesses be madness, there is no doubt but the passions themselves, when they tend to evil, are degrees of the same.

(For example,) though the effect of folly, in them that are possessed of an opinion of being inspired, be not visible always in one man, by any very extravagant action, that proceedeth from such passion; yet when many of them conspire together, the rage of the whole multitude is visible enough. For what argument of madness can there be greater, than to clamour, strike, and throw stones at our best friends? Yet this is somewhat less than such a multitude will do. For they will clamour, fight against, and destroy those, by whom all their lifetime before, they have been protected, and secured from injury. And if this be madness in the multitude, it is the same in every particular man. For as in the midst of the sea, though a man perceive no sound of that part of the water next him; yet he is well assured, that part contributes as much to the roaring of the sea, as any other part of the same quantity; so also, though we perceive no great unquietness in one or two men, yet we may be well assured, that their singular passions, are parts of the seditious roaring of a troubled nation. And if there were nothing else that bewrayed their madness; yet that very arrogating such inspiration to themselves, is argument enough. If some man in Bedlam should entertain you with sober discourse; and you desire in taking leave, to know what he were, that you might another time requite his civility; and he should tell you, he were God the Father; I think you need expect no extravagant action for argument of his madness.

This opinion of inspiration, called commonly, private spirit, begins very often, from some lucky finding of an error generally held by others; and not knowing, or not remembering, by what conduct of reason, they came to so singular a truth, (as they think it, though it be many times an untruth they light on,) they presently admire themselves, as being in the special grace of God Almighty, who hath revealed the same to them supernaturally, by his Spirit.

Again, that madness is nothing else, but too much appearing passion, may be gathered out of the effects of wine, which are the same with those of the evil disposition of the organs. For the variety of behaviour in men that have drunk too much, is the same with that of madmen: some of them raging, others loving, others laughing, all extravagantly, but according to their several domineering passions: for the effect of the wine, does but remove dissimulation, and take from them the sight of the deformity of their passions. For, (I believe) the most sober men, when they walk alone without care and employment of the mind, would be unwilling the vanity and extravagance of their thoughts at that time should be publicly seen; which is a confession, that passions unguided, are for the most part mere madness.

The opinions of the world, both in ancient and later ages, concerning the cause of madness, have been two. Some deriving them from the passions; some, from demons, or spirits, either good or bad, which they thought might enter into a man, possess him, and move his organs in such strange and uncouth manner, as madmen use to do. The former sort therefore, called such men, madmen: but the latter, called them sometimes *demoniacs*, (that is, possessed with spirits;) sometimes *enurgumeni*, (that is, agitated or moved with spirits;) and now in *Italy* they are called not only *pazzi*, madmen; but also *spiritati*, men possessed.

There was once a great conflux of people in *Abdera*, a city of the Greeks, at the acting of the tragedy of *Andromeda*, upon an extreme hot day; whereupon, a great many of the spectators falling into fevers, had this accident from the heat, and from the tragedy together, that they did nothing but pronounce iambics, with the names of *Perseus* and *Andromeda*; which, together with the fever, was cured by the coming on of winter; and this madness was thought to proceed from the passion imprinted by the tragedy. Likewise there reigned a fit of madness in another Grecian city, which seized only the young maidens; and caused many of them to hang themselves. This was by most then thought an act of the Devil. But one that suspected, that contempt of life in them, might proceed from some passion of the mind, and supposing they did not contemn also their honour, gave counsel to the magistrates, to strip such as so hanged themselves, and let them hang out naked. This, the story says, cured that madness. But on the other side, the same Grecians, did often ascribe madness to the operation of the Eumenides, or Furies; and sometimes of *Ceres*, *Phoebus*, and other gods; so much did men attribute to phantasms, as to think them aereal living bodies; and generally to call them spirits. And as the Romans in this, held the same opinion with the Greeks, so also did the Jews; for they called madmen prophets, or (according as they thought the spirits good or bad) demoniacs; and some of them called both prophets and demoniacs, madmen; and some called the same man both demoniac, and madman. But for the Gentiles it is no wonder, because diseases and health, vices and virtues, and many natural accidents, were with them termed, and worshipped as demons. So that a man was to understand by demon, as well, (sometimes) an ague, as a devil. But for the Jews to have such opinion, is somewhat strange. For neither *Moses* nor *Abraham* pretended to prophecy by possession of a spirit; but from the voice of God; or by a vision or dream: nor is there any thing in his law, moral or ceremonial, by which they were taught, there was any such enthusiasm, or any possession. When God is said, *Numb.* 11. 25. to take from the spirit that was in *Moses*, and give to the 70 elders, the Spirit of God (taking it for the substance of God) is not divided. The Scriptures, by the Spirit of God in man, mean a man's spirit, inclined to godliness. And where it is said, *Exod.* 28. 3.

whom I have filled with the spirit of wisdom to make garments for Aaron, is not meant a spirit put into them, that can make garments; but the wisdom of their own spirits in that kind of work. In the like sense, the spirit of man, when it produceth unclean actions, is ordinarily called an unclean spirit, and so other spirits, though not always, yet as often as the virtue or vice so styled, is extraordinary, and eminent. Neither did the other prophets of the old Testament pretend enthusiasm; or, that God spake in them; but to them, by voice, vision, or dream; and the *burthen of the Lord* was not possession, but command. How then could the Jews fall into this opinion of possession? I can imagine no reason, but that which is common to all men; namely, the want of curiosity to search natural causes; and their placing felicity in the acquisition of the gross pleasures of the senses, and the things that most immediately conduce thereto. For they that see any strange, and unusual ability, or defect in a man's mind; unless they see withal, from what cause it may probably proceed, can hardly think it natural; and if not natural, they must needs think it supernatural, and then what can it be, but that either God or the Devil is in him? And hence it came to pass, when our Saviour (*Mark* 3. 21.) was compassed about with the multitude, those of the house doubted he was mad, and went out to hold him: but the Scribes said he had *Beelzebub,* and that was it, by which he cast out devils; as if the greater madman had awed the lesser. And that (*John* 10. 20.) some said, *he hath a devil, and is mad*; whereas others holding him for a prophet, said, *these are not the words of one that hath a devil.* So in the old Testament he that came to anoint *Jehu,* 2 *Kings* 9. 11. was a prophet; but some of the company asked *Jehu, what came that madman for?* So that in sum, it is manifest, that whosoever behaved himself in extraordinary manner, was thought by the Jews to be possessed either with a good, or evil spirit; except by the Sadducees, who erred so far on the other hand, as not to believe there were at all any spirits, (which is very near to direct atheism;) and thereby perhaps the more provoked others, to term such men demoniacs, rather than madmen.

But why then does our Saviour proceed in the curing of them, as if they were possessed; and not as if they were mad? To which I can give no other kind of answer, but that which is given to those that urge the Scripture in like manner against the opinion of the motion of the earth. The Scripture was written to shew unto men the kingdom of God, and to prepare their minds to become his obedient subjects; leaving the world, and the philosophy thereof, to the disputation of men, for the exercising of their natural reason. Whether the earth's, or sun's motion make the day, and night; or whether the exorbitant actions of men, proceed from passion, or from the devil, (so we worship him not) it is all one, as to our obedience, and subjection to God Almighty; which is the thing for which the Scripture was written. As for that our Saviour speaketh to the disease, as to a person; it is the usual phrase of all that cure by words only, as Christ did, (and enchanters pretend to do, whether they speak to a devil or not.) For is not Christ also said (*Matt.* 8. 26.) to have rebuked the winds? Is not he said also (*Luke* 4. 39.) to rebuke a fever? Yet this does not argue that a fever is a devil. And whereas many of those devils are said to confess Christ; it is not necessary to interpret those places otherwise, than that those madmen confessed him. And whereas our Saviour (*Matt.* 12. 43.) speaketh of an unclean spirit, that having gone out of a man, wandereth through dry places, seeking rest, and finding none, and returning into the same man, with seven other spirits worse than himself; it is manifestly a parable, alluding to a man, that after a little endeavour to quit his lusts, is vanquished by the strength of them; and becomes seven times worse than he was. So that I see nothing at all in the Scripture, that requireth a belief, that demoniacs were any other thing but madmen.

There is yet another fault in the discourses of some men; which may also be numbered amongst the sorts of madness; namely, that abuse of words, whereof I have spoken before in the fifth chapter, by the name of absurdity. And that is, when men speak such words, as put together, have in them no signification at all; but are fallen upon by some, through misunderstanding of the words they have received, and repeat by rote; by others from intention to deceive by obscurity. And this is incident to none but those, that converse in questions of matters incomprehensible, as the School-men; or in questions of abstruse philosophy. The common sort of men seldom speak insignificantly, and are therefore, by those other egregious persons counted idiots. But to be assured their words are without any thing correspondent to them in the mind, there would need some examples; which if any man require, let him take a School-man into his hands and see if he can translate any one chapter concerning any difficult point, as the Trinity; the Deity; the nature of Christ; transubstantiation; free-will, &c. into any of the modern tongues, so as to make the same intelligible; or into any tolerable Latin, such as they were acquainted withal, that lived when the Latin tongue was vulgar. What is the meaning of these words. *The first cause does not necessarily inflow any thing into the second, by force of the essential subordination of the second causes, by which it may help it to work?* They are the translation of the title of the sixth chapter of *Suarez'* first book, *Of the Concourse, Motion, and Help of God.* When men write whole volumes of such stuff, are they not mad, or intend to make others so? And particularly, in the question of transubstantiation; where after certain words spoken, they that say, the white*ness*, round*ness*, magni*tude*, quali*ty*, corruptibili*ty*, all which are incorporeal, &c. go out of the wafer, into the body of our blessed Saviour, do they not make those *nesses, tudes,* and *ties,* to be so many spirits possessing his body? For by spirits, they mean always things, that being incorporeal, are nevertheless moveable from one place to another. So that this kind of absurdity, may rightly be numbered amongst the many sorts of madness; and all the time that guided by clear thoughts of their worldly lust, they forbear disputing, or writing thus, but lucid intervals. And thus much of the virtues and defects intellectual.

CHAPTER 9: Of the Several Subjects of Knowledge

There are of KNOWLEDGE two kinds; whereof one is *knowledge of fact*: the other *knowledge of the consequence of one affirmation to another*. The former is nothing else, but sense and memory, and is *absolute knowledge*; as when we see a fact doing, or remember it done: and this is the knowledge required in a witness. The latter is called *science*; and is *conditional*; as when we know, that, *if the figure shown be a circle, then any straight line through the center shall divide it into two equal parts.* And this is the knowledge required in a philosopher; that is to say, of him that pretends to reasoning.

The register of *knowledge of fact* is called *history.* Whereof there be two sorts: one called *natural history*; which is the history of such facts, or effects of nature, as have no dependence on man's *will*; such as are the histories of *metals, plants, animals, regions,* and the like. The other, is *civil history*; which is the history of the voluntary actions of men in commonwealths.

The registers of science, are such *books* as contain the *demonstrations* of consequences of one affirmation, to another; and are commonly called *books of philosophy*; whereof the sorts are many, according to the diversity of the matter; and may be divided in such manner as I have divided them in the following table.

CHAPTER 10: Of Power, Worth, Dignity, Honour, and Worthiness

The power *of a man*, (to take it universally,) is his present means, to obtain some future apparent good; and is either *original* or *instrumental*.

Natural power, is the eminence of the faculties of body, or mind: as extraordinary strength, form, prudence, arts, eloquence, liberality, nobility. *Instrumental* are those powers, which acquired by these, or by fortune, are means and instruments to acquire more: as riches, reputation, friends, and the secret working of God, which men call good luck. For the nature of power, is in this point, like to fame, increasing as it proceeds; or like the motion of heavy bodies, which the further they go, make still the more haste.

The greatest of human powers, is that which is compounded of the powers of most men, united by

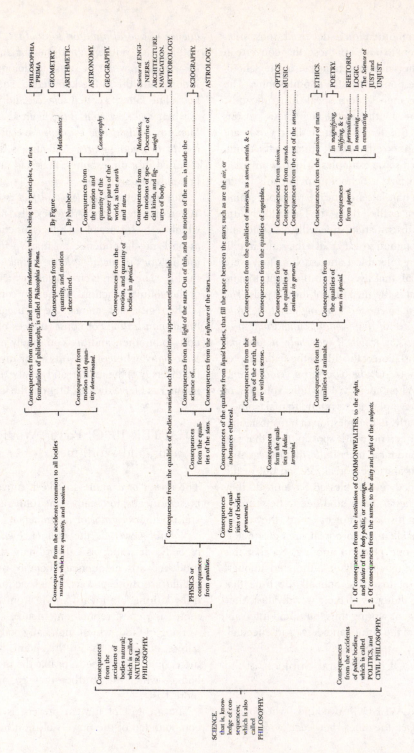

SCIENCE, that is, knowledge of consequences; which is also called PHILOSOPHY.

Consequences from the accidents of bodies natural; which is called NATURAL PHILOSOPHY.

Consequences from quantity, and motion indeterminate; which being the principles, or first foundation of philosophy, is called *Philosophia Prima.* — PHILOSOPHIA PRIMA

Consequences from the accidents common to all bodies natural; which are *quantity,* and *motion.*

Consequences from quantity, and motion determined.

By Figure........ — GEOMETRY
By Number........ — ARITHMETIC.
Mathematics

Consequences from the motion, and quantity of bodies in *special.*

Consequences from the motion and quantity of the greater parts of the world, as the *earth* and *stars.*
Cosmography
ASTRONOMY.
GEOGRAPHY

Consequences from the motions of special kinds, and figures of body.
Mechanics, Doctrine of *weight*
Science of ENGINEERS.
ARCHITECTURE.
NAVIGATION.

PHYSICS or consequences from *qualities.*

Consequences from the qualities of bodies *transient,* such as sometimes appear, sometimes vanish............

Consequences from the qualities of bodies *permanent.*

Consequences from the qualities of the stars.

Consequences from the *light* of the stars. Out of this, and the motion of the sun, is made the science of............
METEOROLOGY.
SCIOGRAPHY.

Consequences from the *influence* of the stars............ — ASTROLOGY.

Consequences of the qualities from *liquid* bodies, that fill the space between the stars; such as are the *air,* or substances ethereal.

Consequences form the qualities of *bodies terrestrial.*

Consequences from the parts of the earth, that are without sense.

Consequences from the qualities of *minerals,* as *stones, metals,* & c.

Consequences from the qualities of *vegetables.*

Consequences from the qualities of animals.

Consequences from the qualities of *animals in general.*

Consequences from *vision*............ — OPTICS.
Consequences from *sounds.*............ — MUSIC.
Consequences from the rest of the *senses.*

Consequences from the qualities of *men in special.*

Consequences from the *passions* of men — ETHICS.

Consequences from *speech.*

In *magnifying, vilifying,* & c — POETRY
In *persuading*............ — RHETORIC.
In *reasoning*............ — LOGIC.
In *contracting*............ — The *Science* of JUST and UNJUST.

Consequences from the accidents of *politic* bodies; which is called POLITICS, and CIVIL PHILOSOPHY.

1. Of consequences from the *institution* of COMMONWEALTHS, to the *rights,* and *duties* of the *body politic,* or sovereign.
2. Of consequences from the same, to the *duty* and *right* of the *subjects.*

consent, in one person, natural, or civil, that has the use of all their powers depending on his will; such as is the power of a commonwealth: or depending on the wills of each particular; such as is the power of a faction or of divers factions leagued. Therefore to have servants, is power; to have friends, is power: for they are strengths united.

Also riches joined with liberality, is power; because it procureth friends, and servants: without liberality, not so; because in this case they defend not; but expose men to envy, as a prey.

Reputation of power, is power; because it draweth with it the adherence of those that need protection.

So is reputation of love of a man's country, (called popularity,) for the same reason.

Also, what quality soever maketh a man beloved, or feared of many; or the reputation of such quality, is power; because it is a means to have the assistance, and service of many.

Good success is power; because it maketh reputation of wisdom, or good fortune; which makes men either fear him, or rely on him.

Affability of men already in power, is increase of power; because it gaineth love.

Reputation of prudence in the conduct of peace or war, is power; because to prudent men, we commit the government of ourselves, more willingly than to others.

Nobility is power, not in all places, but only in those commonwealths, where it has privileges: for in such privileges consisteth their power.

Eloquence is power, because it is seeming prudence.

Form is power; because being a promise of good, it recommendeth men to the favour of women and strangers.

The sciences, are small power; because not eminent; and therefore, not acknowledged in any man; nor are at all, but in a few, and in them, but of a few things. For science is of that nature, as none can understand it to be, but such as in a good measure have attained it.

Arts of public use, as fortification, making of engines, and other instruments of war; because they confer to defence, and victory, are power: and though the true mother of them, be science, namely the mathematics; yet, because they are brought into the light, by the hand of the artificer, they be esteemed (the midwife passing with the vulgar for the mother,) as his issue.

The *value*, or WORTH of a man, is as of all other things, his price; that is to say, so much as would be given for the use of his power: and therefore is not absolute; but a thing dependant on the need and judgment of another. An able conductor of soldiers, is of great price in time of war present, or imminent; but in peace not so. A learned and uncorrupt judge, is much worth in time of peace; but not so much in war. And as in other things, so in men, not the seller, but the buyer determines the price. For let a man (as most men do,) rate themselves at the highest value they can; yet their true value is no more than it is esteemed by others.

The manifestation of the value we set on one another, is that which is commonly called honouring, and dishonouring. To value a man at a high rate, is to *honour* him; at a low rate, is to *dishonour* him. But high, and low, in this case, is to be understood by comparison to the rate that each man setteth on himself.

The public worth of a man, which is the value set on him by the commonwealth, is that which men commonly call DIGNITY. And this value of him by the commonwealth, is understood, by offices of command, judicature, public employment; or by names and titles, introduced for distinction of such value.

To pray to another, for aid of any kind, is to HONOUR; because a sign we have an opinion he has power to help; and the more difficult the aid is, the more is the honour.

To obey, is to honour, because no man obeys them, whom they think have no power to help, or hurt them. And consequently to disobey, is to *dishonour*.

To give great gifts to a man, is to honour him; because it is buying of protection, and acknowledging of power. To give little gifts, is to dishonour; because it is but alms, and signifies an opinion of the need of small helps.

To be sedulous in promoting another's good; also to flatter, is to honour; as a sign we seek his protection or aid. To neglect, is to dishonour.

To give way, or place to another, in any commodity, is to honour; being a confession of greater power. To arrogate, is to dishonour.

To show any sign of love, or fear of another, is to honour; for both to love, and to fear, is to value. To contemn, or less to love or fear, than he expects, is to dishonour; for it is undervaluing.

To praise, magnify, or call happy, is to honour; because nothing but goodness, power, and felicity is valued. To revile, mock, or pity, is to dishonour.

To speak to another with consideration, to appear before him with decency, and humility, is to honour him; as signs of fear to offend. To speak to him rashly, to do any thing before him obscenely, slovenly, impudently, is to dishonour.

To believe, to trust, to rely on another, is to honour him; sign of opinion of his virtue and power. To distrust, or not believe, is to dishonour.

To hearken to a man's counsel, or discourse of what kind soever, is to honour; as a sign we think him wise, or eloquent, or witty. To sleep, or go forth, or talk the while, is to dishonour.

To do those things to another, which he takes for signs of honour, or which the law or custom makes so, is to honour; because in approving the honour done by others, he acknowledgeth the power which others acknowledge. To refuse to do them, is to dishonour.

To agree with in opinion, is to honour; as being a sign of approving his judgment, and wisdom. To dissent, is dishonour, and an upbraiding of error; and (if the dissent be in many things) of folly.

To imitate, is to honour; for it is vehemently to approve. To imitate one's enemy, is to dishonour.

To honour those another honours, is to honour him; as a sign of approbation of his judgment. To honour his enemies, is to dishonour him.

To employ in counsel, or in actions of difficulty, is to honour; as a sign of opinion of his wisdom, or other power. To deny employment in the same cases, to those that seek it, is to dishonour.

All these ways of honouring, are natural; and as well within, as without commonwealths. But in commonwealths, where he, or they that have the supreme authority, can make whatsoever they please, to stand for signs of honour, there be other honours.

A sovereign doth honour a subject, with whatsoever title, or office, or employment, or action, that he himself will have taken for a sign of his will to honour him.

The king of *Persia*, honoured *Mordecai*, when he appointed he should be conducted through the streets in the king's garment, upon one of the king's horses, with a crown on his head, and a prince before him, proclaiming, *thus shall it be done to him that the king will honour*. And yet another king of *Persia*, or the same another time, to one that demanded for some great service, to wear one of the king's robes, gave him leave so to do; but with this addition, that he should wear it as the king's fool; and then it was dishonour. So that of civil honour, the fountain is in the person of the commonwealth, and dependeth on the will of the sovereign; and is therefore temporary, and called *civil honour*; such as are magistracy, offices, titles; and in some places coats and scutcheons painted: and men honour such as have them, as having so many signs of favour in the commonwealth; which favour is power.

Honourable is whatsoever possession, action, or quality, is an argument and sign of power.

And therefore to be honoured, loved, or feared of many, is honourable; as arguments of power. To be honoured of few or none, *dishonourable*.

Dominion, and victory is honourable; because acquired by power; and servitude, for need, or fear, is dishonourable.

Good fortune (if lasting,) honourable, as a sign of the favour of God. Ill fortune, and losses, dishonourable. Riches, are honourable; for they are power. Poverty, dishonourable. Magnanimity, liberality, hope, courage, confidence, are honourable; for they proceed from the conscience of power. Pusillanimity, parsimony, fear, diffidence, are dishonourable.

Timely resolution, or determination of what a man is to do, is honourable; as being the contempt of small difficulties, and dangers. And irresolution, dishonourable; as a sign of too much valuing of little impediments, and little advantages: for when a man has weighed things as long as the time permits, and re-solves not, the difference of weight is but little; and therefore if he resolve not, he overvalues little things, which is pusillanimity.

All actions, and speeches, that proceed, or seem to proceed from much experience, science, discretion, or wit, are honourable; for all these are powers. Actions, or words that proceed from error, ignorance, or folly, dishonourable.

Gravity, as far forth as it seems to proceed from a mind employed on something else, is honourable; because employment is a sign of power. But if it seem to proceed from a purpose to appear grave, it is dishonourable. For the gravity of the former, is like the steadiness of a ship laden with merchandise; but of the latter, like the steadiness of a ship ballasted with sand, and other trash.

To be conspicuous, that is to say, to be known, for wealth, office, great actions, or any eminent good, is honourable; as a sign of the power for which he is conspicuous. On the contrary, obscurity, is dishon-ourable.

To be descended from conspicuous parents, is hon-ourable; because they the more easily attain the aids, and friends of their ancestors. On the contrary, to be descended from obscure parentage, is dishonourable.

Actions proceeding from equity, joined with loss, are honourable; as signs of magnanimity: for magna-nimity is a sign of power. On the contrary, craft, shifting, neglect of equity, is dishonourable.

Covetousness of great riches, and ambition of great honours, are honourable; as signs of power to obtain them. Covetousness, and ambition, of little gains, or preferments, is dishonourable.

Nor does it alter the case of honour, whether an action (so it be great and difficult, and consequently a sign of much power,) be just or unjust: for honour consisteth only in the opinion of power. Therefore the ancient heathen did not think they dishonoured, but greatly honoured the Gods, when they introduced them in their poems, committing rapes, thefts, and other great, but unjust, or unclean acts: insomuch as nothing is so much celebrated in *Jupiter*, as his adulteries; nor in *Mercury*, as his frauds, and thefts:

of whose praises, in a hymn of *Homer*, the greatest is this, that being born in the morning, he had invented music at noon, and before night, stolen away the cattle of *Apollo*, from his herdsmen.

Also amongst men, till there were constituted great commonwealths, it was thought no dishonour to be a pirate, or a highway thief; but rather a lawful trade, not only amongst the Greeks, but also amongst all other nations; as is manifest by the histories of ancient time. And at this day, in this part of the world, private duels are, and always will be honourable, though unlawful, till such time as there shall be honour ordained for them that refuse, and ignominy for them that make the challenge. For duels also are many times effects of courage; and the ground of courage is always strength or skill, which are power; though for the most part they be effects of rash speaking, and of the fear of dishonour, in one, or both the combatants; who engaged by rashness, are driven into the lists to avoid disgrace.

Scutcheons, and coats of arms hereditary, where they have any eminent privileges, are honourable; otherwise not: for their power consisteth either in such privileges, or in riches, or some such thing as is equally honoured in other men. This kind of honour, commonly called gentry, has been derived from the ancient Germans. For there never was any such thing known, where the German customs were unknown. Nor is it now any where in use where the Germans have not inhabited. The ancient Greek commanders, when they went to war, had their shields painted with such devices as they pleased; insomuch as an unpainted buckler was a sign of poverty, and of a common soldier; but they transmit-ted not the inheritance of them. The Romans trans-mitted the marks of their families: but they were the images, not the devices of their ancestors. Amongst the people of *Asia*, *Africa*, and *America*, there is not, nor was ever, any such thing. The Germans only had that custom; from whom it has been derived into *England*, *France*, *Spain*, and *Italy*, when in great numbers they either aided the Romans, or made their own conquests in these western parts of the world.

For *Germany*, being anciently, as all other countries, in their beginnings, divided amongst an infinite number of little lords, or masters of families, that continually had wars one with another; those masters, or lords, principally to the end they might, when they were covered with arms, be known by their followers; and partly for ornament, both painted their armour, or their scutcheon, or coat, with the picture of some beast, or other thing; and also put some eminent and visible mark upon the crest of their helmets. And this ornament both of the arms, and crest, descended by inheritance to their children; to the eldest pure, and to the rest with some note of diversity, such as the old master, that is to say in Dutch, the *Here-alt* thought fit. But when many such families, joined together, made a greater monarchy, this duty of the Herealt, to distinguish scutcheons, was made a private office apart. And the issue of these lords, is the great and ancient gentry; which for the most part bear living creatures, noted for courage, and rapine; or castles, battlements, belts, weapons, bars, palisadoes, and other notes of war; nothing being then in honour, but virtue military. Afterwards, not only kings, but popular commonwealths, gave divers manners of scutcheons, to such as went forth to the war, or returned from it, for encouragement, or recompense to their service. All which, by an observing reader, may be found in such ancient histories, Greek and Latin, as make mention of the German nation and manners, in their times.

Titles of *honour*, such as are duke, count, marquis, and baron, are honourable; as signifying the value set upon them by the sovereign power of the commonwealth: which titles, were in old time titles of office, and command, derived some from the Romans, some from the Germans and French. Dukes, in Latin *duces*, being generals in war: counts, *comites*, such as bare the general company out of friendship, and were left to govern and defend places conquered, and pacified: marquises, *marchiones*, were counts that governed the marches, or bounds of the empire. Which titles of duke, count, and marquis, came into the empire, about the time of *Constantine* the Great, from the customs of the German *militia*. But baron, seems to have been a title of the Gauls, and signifies a great

man; such as were the king's, or prince's men, whom they employed in war about their persons; and seems to be derived from *vir*, to *ber*, and *bar*, that signified the same in the language of the Gauls, that *vir* in Latin; and thence to *bero*, and *baro*: so that such men were called *berones*, and after barones; and (in Spanish) *varones*. But he that would know more particularly the original of titles of honour, may find it, as I have done this, in Mr. Selden's most excellent treatise of that subject. In process of time these offices of honour, by occasion of trouble, and for reasons of good and peaceable government, were turned into mere titles; serving for the most part, to distinguish the precedence, place, and order of subjects in the commonwealth: and men were made dukes, counts, marquises, and barons of places, wherein they had neither possession, nor command: and other titles also, were devised to the same end.

WORTHINESS, is a thing different from the worth, or value of a man; and also from his merit, or desert; and consisteth in a particular power, or ability for that, whereof he is said to be worthy: which particular ability, is usually named FITNESS, or *aptitude*.

For he is worthiest to be a commander, to be a judge, or to have any other charge, that is best fitted, with the qualities required to the well discharging of it; and worthiest of riches, that has the qualities most requisite for the well using of them: any of which qualities being absent, one may nevertheless be a worthy man, and valuable for something else. Again, a man may be worthy of riches, office, and employment, that nevertheless, can plead no right to have it before another; and therefore cannot be said to merit or deserve it. For merit presupposeth a right, and that the thing deserved is due by promise: of which I shall say more hereafter, when I shall speak of contracts.

CHAPTER 11: Of the Difference of Manners

By manners, I mean not here, decency of behaviour; as how one man should salute another, or how a man should wash his mouth, or pick his teeth before company, and such other points of the *small morals*; but those qualities of mankind, that concern their living together in peace, and unity. To which end we are to consider, that the felicity of this life, consisteth not in the repose of a mind satisfied. For there is no such *finis ultimus*, (utmost aim,) nor *summum bonum*, (greatest good,) as is spoken of in the books of the old moral philosophers. Nor can a man any more live, whose desires are at an end, than he, whose senses and imaginations are at a stand. Felicity is a continual progress of the desire, from one object to another; the attaining of the former, being still but the way to the latter. The cause whereof is, that the object of man's desire, is not to enjoy once only, and for one instant of time; but to assure for ever, the way of his future desire. And therefore the voluntary actions, and inclinations of all men, tend, not only to the procuring, but also to the assuring of a contented life; and differ only in the way: which ariseth partly from the diversity of passions, in divers men; and partly from the difference of the knowledge, or opinion each one has of the causes, which produce the effect desired.

So that in the first place, I put for a general inclination of all mankind, a perpetual and restless desire of power after power, that ceaseth only in death. And the cause of this, is not always that a man hopes for a more intensive delight, than he has already attained to; or that he cannot be content with a moderate power: but because he cannot assure the power and means to live well, which he hath present, without the acquisition of more. And from hence it is, that kings, whose power is greatest, turn their endeavours to the assuring it at home by laws, or abroad by wars: and when that is done, there succeedeth a new desire; in some, of fame from new conquest; in others, of ease and sensual pleasure; in others, of admiration, or being flattered for excellence in some art, or other ability of the mind.

Competition of riches, honour, command, or other power, inclineth to contention, enmity, and war: because the way of one competitor, to the attaining of his desire, is to kill, subdue, supplant, or repel the other. Particularly, competition of praise, inclineth to a reverence of antiquity. For men contend with the living, not with the dead; to these ascribing more than due, that they may obscure the glory of the other.

Desire of ease, and sensual delight, disposeth men to obey a common power: because by such desires, a man doth abandon the protection might be hoped for from his own industry, and labour. Fear of death, and wounds, disposeth to the same; and for the same reason. On the contrary, needy men, and hardy, not contented with their present condition; as also, all men that are ambitious of military command, are inclined to continue the causes of war; and to stir up trouble and sedition: for there is no honour military but by war; nor any such hope to mend an ill game, as by causing a new shuffle.

Desire of knowledge, and arts of peace, inclineth men to obey a common power: For such desire, containeth a desire of leisure; and consequently protection from some other power than their own.

Desire of praise, disposeth to laudable actions, such as please them whose judgment they value; for of those men whom we contemn, we contemn also the praises. Desire of fame after death does the same. And though after death, there be no sense of the praise given us on earth, as being joys, that are either swallowed up in the unspeakable joys of Heaven, or extinguished in the extreme torments of hell: yet is not such fame vain; because men have a present delight therein, from the foresight of it, and of the benefit that may redound thereby to their posterity: which though they now see not, yet they imagine; and any thing that is pleasure in the sense, the same also is pleasure in the imagination.

To have received from one, to whom we think ourselves equal, greater benefits than there is hope to requite, disposeth to counterfeit love; but really secret hatred; and puts a man into the estate of a desperate debtor, that in declining the sight of his creditor, tacitly wishes him there, where he might never see him more. For benefits oblige, and obligation is thraldom; and unrequitable obligation, perpetual thraldom; which is to one's equal, hateful. But to have received benefits from one, whom we acknowledge for superior, inclines to love; because the obligation is no new depression: and cheerful acceptation, (which men call *gratitude*,) is such an honour done to the obliger, as is taken generally for retribution. Also to receive benefits, though from an equal, or inferior, as long as there is hope of requital, disposeth to love: for in the intention of the receiver, the obligation is of aid, and service mutual; from whence proceedeth an emulation of who shall exceed in benefiting; the most noble and profitable contention possible; wherein the victor is pleased with his victory, and the other revenged by confessing it.

To have done more hurt to a man, than he can, or is willing to expiate, inclineth the doer to hate the sufferer. For he must expect revenge, or forgiveness; both which are hateful.

Fear of oppression, disposeth a man to anticipate, or to seek aid by society: for there is no other way by which a man can secure his life and liberty.

Men that distrust their own subtlety, are in tumult and sedition, better disposed for victory, than they that suppose themselves wise, or crafty. For these love to consult, the other (fearing to be circumvented,) to strike first. And in sedition, men being always in the precincts of battle, to hold together, and use all advantages of force, is a better stratagem, than any that can proceed from subtlety of wit.

Vain-glorious men, such as without being conscious to themselves of great sufficiency, delight in supposing themselves gallant men, are inclined only to ostentation; but not to attempt: because when danger or difficulty appears, they look for nothing but to have their insufficiency discovered.

Vain-glorious men, such as estimate their sufficiency by the flattery of other men, or the fortune of some precedent action, without assured ground of hope from the true knowledge of themselves, are inclined to rash engaging; and in the approach of danger, or difficulty, to retire if they can: because not seeing the way of safety, they will rather hazard their honour, which may be salved with an excuse; than their lives, for which no salve is sufficient.

Men that have a strong opinion of their own wisdom in matter of government, are disposed to ambition. Because without public employment in council or magistracy, the honour of their wisdom is lost. And therefore eloquent speakers are inclined to ambition; for eloquence seemeth wisdom, both to themselves and others.

Pusillanimity disposeth men to irresolution, and consequently to lose the occasions, and fittest opportunities of action. For after men have been in deliberation till the time of action approach, if it be not then manifest what is best to be done, it is a sign, the difference of motives, the one way and the other, are not great: therefore not to resolve then, is to lose the occasion by weighing of trifles; which is pusillanimity.

Frugality, (though in poor men a virtue,) maketh a man unapt to achieve such actions, as require the strength of many men at once: for it weakeneth their endeavour, which is to be nourished and kept in vigour by reward.

Eloquence, with flattery, disposeth men to confide in them that have it; because the former is seeming wisdom, the latter seeming kindness. Add to them military reputation, and it disposeth men to adhere, and subject themselves to those men that have them. The two former, having given them caution against danger from him; the latter gives them caution against danger from others.

Want of science, that is, ignorance of causes, disposeth, or rather constraineth a man to rely on the advice, and authority of others. For all men whom the truth concerns, if they rely not on their own, must rely on the opinion of some other, whom they think wiser than themselves, and see not why he should deceive them.

Ignorance of the signification of words, which is want of understanding, disposeth men to take on trust, not only the truth they know not; but also the errors; and which is more, the non-sense of them they trust: for neither error nor non-sense, can without a perfect understanding of words, be detected.

From the same it proceedeth, that men give different names, to one and the same thing, from the difference of their own passions: as they that approve a private opinion, call it opinion; but they that mislike it, heresy: and yet heresy signifies no more than private opinion; but has only a greater tincture of choler.

From the same also it proceedeth, that men cannot distinguish, without study and great understanding, between the one action of many men, and many actions of one multitude; as for example, between one action of all the senators of *Rome* in killing *Cataline*, and the many actions of a number of senators in killing *Caesar*; and therefore are disposed to take for the action of the people, that which is a multitude of actions done by a multitude of men, led perhaps by the persuasion of one.

Ignorance of the causes, and original constitution of right, equity, law, and justice, disposeth a man to make custom and example the rule of his actions; in such manner, as to think that unjust which it hath been the custom to punish; and that just, of the impunity and approbation whereof they can produce an example, or (as the lawyers which only use this false measure of justice barbarously call it) a precedent; like little children, that have no other rule of good and evil manners, but the correction they receive from their parents and masters; save that children are constant to their rule, whereas, men are not so; because grown strong, and stubborn, they appeal from custom to reason, and from reason to custom, as it serves their turn; receding from custom when their interest requires it, and setting themselves against reason, as oft as reason is against them: which is the cause, that the doctrine of right and wrong, is perpetually disputed, both by the pen and the sword: whereas the doctrine of lines, and figures, is not so; because men care not, in that subject, what be truth, as a thing that crosses no man's ambition, profit or lust. For I doubt not, but if it had been a thing contrary to any man's right of dominion, or to the interest of men that have dominion, *that the three angles of a triangle, should be equal to two angles of a square*; that doctrine should have been, if not disputed, yet by the burning of all books of geometry, suppressed, as far as he whom it concerned was able.

Ignorance of remote causes, disposeth men to attribute all events, to the causes immediate, and instrumental: for these are all the causes they perceive. And hence it comes to pass, that in all places, men that are grieved with payments to the public, discharge their anger upon the publicans, that is to say, farmers, collectors, and other officers of the public revenue; and adhere to such as find fault with the public government; and thereby, when they have engaged themselves beyond hope of justification, fall also upon the supreme authority, for fear of punishment, or shame of receiving pardon.

Ignorance of natural causes disposeth a man to credulity, so as to believe many times impossibilities: for such know nothing to the contrary, but that they may be true; being unable to detect the impossibility. And credulity, because men love to be hearkened unto in company, disposeth them to lying: so that ignorance it self without malice, is able to make a man both to believe lies, and tell them; and sometimes also to invent them.

Anxiety for the future time, disposeth men to inquire into the causes of things: because the knowledge of them, maketh men the better able to order the present to their best advantage.

Curiosity, or love of the knowledge of causes, draws a man from consideration of the effect, to seek the cause; and again, the cause of that cause; till of necessity he must come to this thought at last, that there is some cause, whereof there is no former cause, but is eternal; which is it men call God. So that it is impossible to make any profound inquiry into natural causes, without being inclined thereby to believe there is one God eternal; though they cannot have any idea of him in their mind, answerable to his nature. For as a man that is born blind, hearing men talk of warming themselves by the fire, and being brought to warm himself by the same, may easily conceive, and assure himself, there is somewhat there, which men call *fire*, and is the cause of the heat he feels; but cannot imagine what it is like; nor have an idea of it in his mind, such as they have that see it: so also, by the visible things of this world, and their admirable order, a man may conceive there is a cause of them, which men call God; and yet not have an idea, or image of him in his mind.

And they that make little, or no inquiry into the natural causes of things, yet from the fear that proceeds from the ignorance it self, of what it is that hath the power to do them much good or harm, are inclined to suppose, and feign unto themselves, several kinds of powers invisible; and to stand in awe of their own imaginations; and in time of distress to invoke them; as also in the time of an expected good success, to give them thanks; making the creatures of their own fancy, their gods. By which means it hath come to pass, that from the innumerable variety of fancy, men have created in the world innumerable sorts of gods. And this fear of things invisible, is the natural seed of that, which every one in himself calleth religion; and in them that worship, or fear that power otherwise than they do, superstition.

And this seed of religion, having been observed by many; some of those that have observed it, have been inclined thereby to nourish, dress, and form it into laws; and to add to it of their own invention, any opinion of the causes of future events, by which they thought they should be best able to govern others, and make unto themselves the greatest use of their powers.

CHAPTER 12: Of Religion

Seeing there are no signs, nor fruit of *religion*, but in man only; there is no cause to doubt, but that the seed of *religion*, is also only in man; and consisteth in some peculiar quality, or at least in some eminent degree thereof, not to be found in other living creatures.

And first, it is peculiar to the nature of man, to be inquisitive into the causes of the events they see, some more, some less; but all men so much, as to be curious in the search of the causes of their own good and evil fortune.

Secondly, upon the sight of any thing that hath a beginning, to think also it had a cause, which determined the same to begin, then when it did, rather than sooner or later.

Thirdly, whereas there is no other felicity of beasts, but the enjoying of their quotidian food, ease, and lusts; as having little or no foresight of the time to come, for want of observation, and memory of the order, consequence, and dependence of the things they see; man observeth how one event hath been produced by another; and remembereth in them antecedence and consequence; and when he cannot assure himself of the true causes of things, (for the causes of good and evil fortune for the most part are invisible,) he supposes causes of them, either such as his own fancy suggesteth; or trusteth to the authority of other men, such as he thinks to be his friends, and wiser than himself.

The two first, make anxiety. For being assured that there be causes of all things that have arrived hitherto, or shall arrive hereafter; it is impossible for a man, who continually endeavoureth to secure himself against the evil he fears, and procure the good he desireth, not to be in a perpetual solicitude of the time to come; so that every man, especially those that are over provident, are in an estate like to that of *Prometheus*. For as *Prometheus*, (which interpreted, is, *the prudent man*,) was bound to the hill *Caucasus*, a place of large prospect, where, an eagle feeding on his liver, devoured in the day, as much as was repaired in the night: so that man, which looks too far before him, in the care of future time, hath his heart all the day long, gnawed on by fear of death, poverty, or other calamity; and has no repose, nor pause of his anxiety, but in sleep.

This perpetual fear, always accompanying mankind in the ignorance of causes, as it were in the dark, must needs have for object something. And therefore when there is nothing to be seen, there is nothing to accuse, either of their good, or evil fortune, but some *power*, or agent *invisible*: in which sense perhaps it was, that some of the old poets said, that the gods were at first created by human fear: which spoken of the gods, (that is to say, of the many gods of the Gentiles) is very true. But the acknowledging of one God, eternal, infinite, and omnipotent, may more easily be derived, from the desire men have to know the causes of natural bodies, and their several virtues, and operations; than from the fear of what was to befall them in time to come. For he that from any effect he seeth come to pass, should reason to the next and immediate cause thereof, and from thence to the cause of that cause, and plunge himself profoundly in the pursuit of causes; shall at last come to this, that there must be (as even the heathen philosophers confessed) one first mover; that is, a first, and an eternal cause of all things; which is that which men mean by the name of God: and all this without thought of their fortune; the solicitude whereof, both inclines to fear, and hinders them from the search of the causes of other things; and thereby gives occasion of feigning of as many gods, as there be men that feign them.

And for the matter, or substance of the invisible agents, so fancied; they could not by natural cogitation, fall upon any other conceit, but that it was the same with that of the soul of man; and that the soul of man, was of the same substance, with that which appeareth in a dream, to one that sleepeth; or in a looking-glass, to one that is awake; which, men not knowing that such apparitions are nothing else but creatures of the fancy, think to be real, and external substances; and therefore call them ghosts; as the Latins called them *imagines*, and *umbrae*, and thought them spirits, that is, thin aerial bodies; and those invisible agents, which they feared, to be like them; save that they appear, and vanish when they please. But the opinion that such spirits were incorporeal, or immaterial, could never enter into the mind of any man by nature; because, though men may put together words of contradictory signification, as *spirit*, and *incorporeal*; yet they can never have the imagination of any thing answering to them: and therefore, men that by their own meditation, arrive to the acknowledgment of one infinite, omnipotent, and eternal God, choose rather to confess he is incomprehensible, and above their understanding, than to define his nature by *spirit incorporeal*, and then confess their definition to be unintelligible: or if they give him such a title, it is not *dogmatically*, with intention to make the divine nature understood; but *piously*, to honour him with attributes, of significations, as remote as they can from the grossness of bodies visible.

Then, for the way by which they think these invisible agents wrought their effects; that is to say, what immediate causes they used, in bringing things to pass, men that know not what it is that we call *causing*, (that is, almost all men) have no other rule to guess by, but by observing, and remembering what they have seen to precede the like effect at some other time, or times before, without seeing between the antecedent and subsequent event, any dependence or connexion at all: and therefore from the like things past, they expect the like things to come; and hope for good or evil luck, superstitiously, from things that have no part at all in the causing of it: as the Athenians did for their war at *Lepanto*, demand another *Phormio*; the Pompeian faction for their war in *Africa*, another *Scipio*; and others have done in divers other occasions since. In like manner they attribute their fortune to a stander by, to a lucky or unlucky place, to words spoken, especially if the name of God be amongst them; as charming and conjuring (the liturgy of witches;) insomuch as to believe, they have power to turn a stone into bread, bread into a man, or any thing into any thing.

Thirdly, for the worship which naturally men exhibit to powers invisible, it can be no other, but such expressions of their reverence, as they would use towards men; gifts, petitions, thanks, submission of body, considerate addresses, sober behaviour, premeditated words, swearing (that is, assuring one another of their promises,) by invoking them. Beyond that reason suggesteth nothing; but leaves them either to rest there; or for further ceremonies, to rely on those they believe to be wiser than themselves.

Lastly, concerning how these invisible powers declare to men the things which shall hereafter come to pass, especially concerning their good or evil fortune in general, or good or ill success in any particular undertaking, men are naturally at a stand; save that using to conjecture of the time to come, by the time past, they are very apt, not only to take casual things, after one or two encounters, for prognostics of the like encounter ever after, but also to believe the like prognostics from other men, of whom they have once conceived a good opinion.

And in these four things, opinion of ghosts, ignorance of second causes, devotion towards what men fear, and taking of things casual for prognostics, consisteth the natural seed of *religion*; which by reason of the different fancies, judgments, and passions of several men, hath grown up into ceremonies so different, that those which are used by one man, are for the most part ridiculous to another.

For these seeds have received culture from two sorts of men. One sort have been they, that have nourished, and ordered them, according to their own invention.

The other have done it, by God's commandment, and direction: but both sorts have done it, with a purpose to make those men that relied on them, the more apt to obedience, laws, peace, charity, and civil society. So that the religion of the former sort, is a part of human politics; and teacheth part of the duty which earthly kings require of their subjects. And the religion of the latter sort is divine politics; and containeth precepts to those that have yielded themselves subjects in the kingdom of God. Of the former sort, were all the founders of commonwealths, and the lawgivers of the Gentiles: of the latter sort, were *Abraham, Moses,* and our *blessed Saviour;* by whom have been derived unto us the laws of the kingdom of God.

And for that part of religion, which consisteth in opinions concerning the nature of powers invisible, there is almost nothing that has a name, that has not been esteemed amongst the Gentiles, in one place or another, a god, or devil; or by their poets feigned to be inanimated, inhabited, or possessed by some spirit or other.

The unformed matter of the world, was a god, by the name of *Chaos.*

The heaven, the ocean, the planets, the fire, the earth, the winds, were so many gods.

Men, women, a bird, a crocodile, a calf, a dog, a snake, an onion, a leek, deified. Besides that, they filled almost all places, with spirits called *demons:* the plains, with *Pan,* and *Panises,* or Satyrs; the woods, with Fawns, and Nymphs; the sea, with Tritons, and other Nymphs; every river, and fountain, with a ghost of his name, and with Nymphs; every house with its *Lares,* or familiars; every man with his *Genius;* hell with ghosts, and spiritual officers, as *Charon, Cerberus,* and the *Furies;* and in the night time, all places with *larvae, lemures,* ghosts of men deceased, and a whole kingdom of fairies and bugbears. They have also ascribed divinity, and built temples to mere accidents, and qualities; such as are time, night, day, peace, concord, love, contention, virtue, honour, health, rust, fever, and the like; which when they prayed for, or against, they prayed to, as if there were ghosts of those names hanging over their heads, and letting fall, or withholding that good, or evil, for, or

against which they prayed. They invoked also their own wit, by the name of *Muses;* their own ignorance, by the name of *Fortune;* their own lust, by the name of *Cupid;* their own rage, by the name *Furies;* their own privy members, by the name of *Priapus,* and attributed their pollutions, to *Incubi,* and *Succubae:* insomuch as there was nothing, which a poet could introduce as a person in his poem, which they did not make either a *god,* or a *devil.*

The same authors of the religion of the Gentiles, observing the second ground for religion, which is men's ignorance of causes; and thereby their aptness to attribute their fortune to causes, on which there was no dependence at all apparent, took occasion to obtrude on their ignorance, instead of second causes, a kind of second and ministerial gods; ascribing the cause of fecundity, to *Venus;* the cause of arts, to *Apollo;* of subtlety and craft, to *Mercury;* of tempests and storms, to *Aeolus;* and of other effects, to other gods; insomuch as there was amongst the heathen almost as great variety of gods, as of business.

And to the worship, which naturally men conceived fit to be used towards their gods, namely, oblations, prayers, thanks, and the rest formerly named; the same legislators of the Gentiles have added their images, both in picture, and sculpture; that the more ignorant sort (that is to say, the most part or generality of the people,) thinking the gods for whose representation they were made, were really included, and as it were housed within them, might so much the more stand in fear of them: and endowed them with lands, and houses, and officers, and revenues, set apart from all other human uses; that is, consecrated, and made holy to those their idols; as caverns, groves, woods, mountains, and whole islands; and have attributed to them, not only the shapes, some of men, some of beasts, some of monsters; but also the faculties, and passions of men and beasts; as sense, speech, sex, lust, generation, (and this not only by mixing one with another, to propagate the kind of gods; but also by mixing with men, and women, to beget mongrel gods, and but inmates of heaven, as *Bacchus, Hercules,* and others;) besides anger, revenge, and other passions of living creatures, and the actions proceeding from them, as fraud, theft, adultery, sodomy, and any vice that may be taken for an effect of power, or a cause of pleasure; and all such vices, as amongst men are taken to be against law, rather than against honour.

Lastly, to the prognostics of time to come; which are naturally, but conjectures upon the experience of time past; and supernaturally, divine revelation; the same authors of the religion of the Gentiles, partly upon pretended experience, partly upon pretended revelation, have added innumerable other superstitious ways of divination; and made men believe they should find their fortunes, sometimes in the ambiguous or senseless answers of the priests at *Delphi, Delos, Ammon,* and other famous oracles; which answers, were made ambiguous by design, to own the event both ways; or absurd, by the intoxicating vapour of the place, which is very frequent in sulphurous caverns: sometimes in the leaves of the Sybils; of whose prophecies (like those perhaps of *Nostradamus*; for the fragments now extant seem to be the invention of later times) there were some books in reputation in the time of the Roman republic: sometimes in the insignificant speeches of madmen, supposed to be possessed with a divine spirit, which possession they called enthusiasm; and these kinds of foretelling events, were accounted theomancy, or prophecy: sometimes in the aspect of the stars at their nativity; which was called horoscopy, and esteemed a part of judiciary astrology: sometimes in their own hopes and fears, called thumomancy, or presage: sometimes in the prediction of witches, that pretended conference with the dead; which is called necromancy, conjuring, and witchcraft; and is but juggling and confederate knavery: sometimes in the casual flight, or feeding of birds; called augury: sometimes in the entrails of a sacrificed beast; which was *aruspicina:* sometimes in dreams: sometimes in croaking of ravens, or chattering of birds: sometimes in the lineaments of the face; which was called metoposcopy; or by palmistry in the lines of the hand; in casual words, called *omina:* sometimes in monsters, or unusual accidents; as eclipses, comets, rare meteors, earthquakes, inundations, uncouth births, and the like, which they called *portenta,* and *ostenta,* because they thought them to portend, or foreshow some great calamity to come; sometimes, in mere lottery, as cross and pile; counting

holes in a sieve; dipping of verses in *Homer,* and *Virgil;* and innumerable other such vain conceits. So easy are men to be drawn to believe any thing, from such men as have gotten credit with them; and can with gentleness, and dexterity, take hold of their fear, and ignorance.

And therefore the first founders, and legislators of commonwealths among the Gentiles, whose ends were only to keep the people in obedience, and peace, have in all places taken care; first, to imprint in their minds a belief, that those precepts which they gave concerning religion, might not be thought to proceed from their own device, but from the dictates of some god, or other spirit; or else that they themselves were of a higher nature than mere mortals, that their laws might the more easily be received: so *Numa Pompilius* pretended to receive the ceremonies he instituted amongst the Romans, from the nymph *Egeria:* and the first king and founder of the kingdom of *Peru,* pretended himself and his wife to be the children of the Sun: and *Mahomet,* to set up his new religion, pretended to have conferences with the Holy Ghost, in form of a dove. Secondly, they have had a care, to make it believed, that the same things were displeasing to the gods, which were forbidden by the laws. Thirdly, to prescribe ceremonies, supplications, sacrifices, and festivals, by which they were to believe, the anger of the gods might be appeased; and that ill success in war, great contagions of sickness, earthquakes, and each man's private misery, came from the anger of the gods, and their anger from the neglect of their worship, or the forgetting, or mistaking some point of the ceremonies required. And though amongst the ancient Romans, men were not forbidden to deny, that which in the poets is written of the pains, and pleasures after this life; which divers of great authority, and gravity in that state have in their *harangues* openly derided; yet that belief was always more cherished, than the contrary.

And by these, and such other institutions, they obtained in order to their end, (which was the peace of the commonwealth,) that the common people in their misfortunes, laying the fault on neglect, or error in their ceremonies, or on their own disobedience to the laws, were the less apt to mutiny against their governors. And being entertained with the pomp, and pastime of festivals, and public games, made in honour of the gods, needed nothing else but bread to keep them from discontent, murmuring, and commotion against the state. And therefore the Romans, that had conquered the greatest part of the then known world, made no scruple of tolerating any religion whatsoever in the city of *Rome* itself, unless it had something in it, that could not consist with their civil government; nor do we read, that any religion was there forbidden, but that of the Jews; who (being the peculiar kingdom of God) thought it unlawful to acknowledge subjection to any mortal king or state whatsoever. And thus you see how the religion of the Gentiles was a part of their policy.

But where God himself, by supernatural revelation, planted religion; there he also made to himself a peculiar kingdom; and gave laws, not only of behaviour towards himself, but also towards one another; and thereby in the kingdom of God, the policy, and laws civil, are a part of religion; and therefore the distinction of temporal, and spiritual domination, hath there no place. It is true, that God is king of all the earth: yet may he be king of a peculiar, and chosen nation. For there is no more incongruity therein, than that he that hath the general command of the whole army, should have withal a peculiar regiment, or company of his own. God is king of all the earth by his power: but of his chosen people, he is king by covenant. But to speak more largely of the kingdom of God, both by nature, and covenant, I have in the following discourse assigned another place.

From the propagation of religion, it is not hard to understand the causes of the resolution of the same into its first seeds, or principles; which are only an opinion of a deity, and powers invisible, and supernatural; that can never be so abolished out of human nature, but that new religions may again be made to spring out of them, by the culture of such men, as for such purpose are in reputation.

For seeing all formed religion, is founded at first, upon the faith which a multitude hath in some one person, whom they believe not only to be a wise man, and to labour to procure their happiness, but also to be a holy man, to whom God himself vouchsafeth to declare his will supernaturally; it followeth necessarily, when they that have the government of religion, shall come to have either the wisdom of those men, their sincerity, or their love suspected; or that they shall be unable to show any probable token of divine revelation; that the religion which they desire to uphold, must be suspected likewise; and (without the fear of the civil sword) contradicted and rejected.

That which taketh away the reputation of wisdom, in him that formeth a religion, or addeth to it when it is already formed, is the enjoining of a belief of contradictories: for both parts of a contradiction cannot possibly be true: and therefore to enjoin the belief of them, is an argument of ignorance; which detects the author in that; and discredits him in all things else he shall propound as from revelation supernatural: which revelation a man may indeed have of many things above, but of nothing against natural reason.

That which taketh away the reputation of sincerity, is the doing or saying of such things, as appear to be signs, that what they require other men to believe, is not believed by themselves; all which doings, or sayings are therefore called scandalous, because they be stumbling blocks, that make men to fall in the way of religion: as injustice, cruelty, profaneness, avarice, and luxury. For who can believe, that he that doth ordinarily such actions as proceed from any of these roots, believeth there is any such invisible power to be feared, as he affrighteth other men withal, for lesser faults?

That which taketh away the reputation of love, is the being detected of private ends: as when the belief they require of others, conduceth or seemeth to conduce to the acquiring of dominion, riches, dignity, or secure pleasure, to themselves only, or specially. For that which men reap benefit by to themselves, they are thought to do for their own sakes, and not for love of others.

Lastly, the testimony that men can render of divine calling, can be no other, than the operation of miracles; or true prophecy, (which also is a miracle;) or extraordinary felicity. And therefore, to those points of religion, which have been received from them that did such miracles; those that are added by such, as approve not their calling by some miracle, obtain no greater belief, than what the custom and laws of the places, in which they be educated, have wrought into them. For as in natural things, men of judgment require natural signs, and arguments; so in supernatural things, they require signs supernatural, (which are miracles,) before they consent inwardly, and from their hearts.

All which causes of the weakening of men's faith, do manifestly appear in the examples following. First, we have the example of the children of Israel; who when *Moses*, that had approved his calling to them by miracles, and by the happy conduct of them out of *Egypt*, was absent but 40 days, revolted from the worship of the true God, recommended to them by him; and setting up (*Exod.* 32. 1, 2.) a golden calf for their god, relapsed into the idolatry of the Egyptians; from whom they had been so lately delivered. And again, after *Moses*, *Aaron*, *Joshua*, and that generation which had seen the great works of God in Israel, (*Judges* 2. 11.) were dead; another generation arose, and served *Baal*. So that miracles failing, faith also failed.

Again, when the sons of *Samuel*, (1 *Sam.* 8. 3.) being constituted by their father judges in *Bersabee*, received bribes, and judged unjustly, the people of Israel refused any more to have God to be their king, in other manner than he was king of other people; and therefore cried out to Samuel, to choose them a king after the manner of the nations. So that justice failing, faith also failed: insomuch, as they deposed their God, from reigning over them.

And whereas in the planting of Christian religion, the oracles ceased in all parts of the Roman empire, and the number of Christians increased wonderfully every day, and in every place, by the preaching of the Apostles, and Evangelists; a great part of that success, may reasonably be attributed, to the contempt, into which the priests of the Gentiles of that time, had brought themselves, by their uncleanness, avarice, and juggling between princes. Also the religion of the church of *Rome*, was partly, for the same cause abolished in *England*, and many other parts of Christendom; insomuch, as the failing of virtue in the pastors, maketh faith fail in the people: and partly from bringing of the philosophy, and doctrine of *Aristotle* into religion, by the Schoolmen; from whence there arose so many contradictions, and absurdities, as brought the clergy into a reputation both of ignorance, and of fraudulent intention; and inclined people to revolt from them, either against the will of their own princes, as in *France* and *Holland*; or with their will, as in *England*.

Lastly, amongst the points by the church of *Rome* declared necessary for salvation, there be so many, manifestly to the advantage of the Pope, and of his spiritual subjects, residing in the territories of other Christian princes, that were it not for the mutual emulation of those princes, they might without war, or trouble, exclude all foreign authority, as easily as it has been excluded in *England*. For who is there that does not see, to whose benefit it conduceth, to have it believed, that a king hath not his authority from Christ, unless a bishop crown him? That a king, if he be a priest, cannot marry? That whether a prince be born in lawful marriage, or not, must be judged by authority from *Rome*? That subjects may be freed from their allegiance, if by the court of *Rome*, the king be judged an heretic? That a king (as *Chilperic* of *France*) may be deposed by a pope (as Pope *Zachary*) for no cause; and his kingdom given to one of his subjects? That the clergy and regulars, in what country soever, shall be exempt from the jurisdiction of their king, in cases criminal? Or who does not see, to whose profit redound the fees of private masses, and vales of purgatory; with other signs of private interest, enough to mortify the most lively faith, if (as I said) the civil magistrate, and custom did not more sustain it, than any opinion they have of the sanctity, wisdom, or probity of their teachers? So that I may attribute all the changes of religion in the world, to one and the same cause; and that is, unpleasing priests; and those not only amongst Catholics, but even in that church that hath presumed most of reformation.

CHAPTER 13: Of the Natural Condition of Mankind as Concerning Their Felicity, and Misery

Nature hath made men so equal, in the faculties of body, and mind; as that though there be found one man sometimes manifestly stronger in body, or of quicker mind than another; yet when all is reckoned together, the difference between man, and man, is not so considerable, as that one man can thereupon claim to himself any benefit, to which another may not pretend, as well as he. For as to the strength of body, the weakest has strength enough to kill the strongest, either by secret machination, or by confederacy with others, that are in the same danger with himself.

And as to the faculties of the mind, (setting aside the arts grounded upon words, and especially that skill of proceeding upon general, and infallible rules, called science; which very few have, and but in few things; as being not a native faculty, born with us; nor attained, (as prudence,) while we look after somewhat else,) I find yet a greater equality amongst men, than that of strength. For prudence, is but experience; which equal time, equally bestows on all men, in those things they equally apply themselves unto. That which may perhaps make such equality incredible, is but a vain conceit of one's own wisdom, which almost all men think they have in a greater degree, than the vulgar; that is, than all men but themselves, and a few others, whom by fame, or for concurring with themselves, they approve. For such is the nature of men, that howsoever they may acknowledge many others to be more witty, or more eloquent, or more learned; yet they will hardly believe there be many so wise as themselves: For they see their own wit at hand, and other men's at a distance. But this proveth rather that men are in that point equal, than unequal. For there is not ordinarily a greater sign of the equal distribution of any thing, than that every man is contented with his share.

From this equality of ability, ariseth equality of hope in the attaining of our ends. And therefore if any two men desire the same thing, which nevertheless they cannot both enjoy, they become enemies;

and in the way to their end, (which is principally their own conservation, and sometimes their delectation only,) endeavour to destroy, or subdue one another. And from hence it comes to pass, that where an invader hath no more to fear, than another man's single power; if one plant, sow, build, or possess a convenient seat, others may probably be expected to come prepared with forces united, to dispossess, and deprive him, not only of the fruit of his labour, but also of his life, or liberty. And the invader again is in the like danger of another.

And from this diffidence of one another, there is no way for any man to secure himself, so reasonable, as anticipation; that is, by force, or wiles, to master the persons of all men he can, so long, till he see no other power great enough to endanger him: and this is no more than his own conservation requireth, and is generally allowed. Also because there be some, that taking pleasure in contemplating their own power in the acts of conquest, which they pursue farther than their security requires; if others, that otherwise would be glad to be at ease within modest bounds, should not by invasion increase their power, they would not be able, long time, by standing only on their defence, to subsist. And by consequence, such augmentation of dominion over men, being necessary to a man's conservation, it ought to be allowed him.

Again, men have no pleasure, (but on the contrary a great deal of grief) in keeping company, where there is no power able to over-awe them all. For every man looketh that his companion should value him, at the same rate he sets upon himself: and upon all signs of contempt, or undervaluing, naturally endeavours, as far as he dares (which amongst them that have no common power to keep them in quiet, is far enough to make them destroy each other), to extort a greater value from his contemners, by damage; and from others, by the example.

So that in the nature of man, we find three principal causes of quarrel. First, competition; secondly, diffidence; thirdly, glory.

The first, maketh men invade for gain; the second, for safety; and the third, for reputation. The first use violence, to make themselves masters of other men's persons, wives, children, and cattle; the second, to defend them; the third, for trifles, as a word, a smile, a different opinion, and any other sign of undervalue, either direct in their persons, or by reflection in their kindred, their friends, their nation, their profession, or their name.

Hereby it is manifest, that during the time men live without a common power to keep them all in awe, they are in that condition which is called war; and such a war, as is of every man, against every man. For WAR, consisteth not in battle only, or the act of fighting; but in a tract of time, wherein the will to contend by battle is sufficiently known: and therefore the notion of *time*, is to be considered in the nature of war; as it is in the nature of weather. For as the nature of foul weather, lieth not in a shower or two of rain; but in an inclination thereto of many days together: so the nature of war, consisteth not in actual fighting; but in the known disposition thereto, during all the time there is no assurance to the contrary. All other time is PEACE.

Whatsoever therefore is consequent to a time of war, where every man is enemy to every man; the same is consequent to the time, wherein men live without other security, than what their own strength, and their own invention shall furnish them withal. In such condition, there is no place for industry; because the fruit thereof is uncertain: and consequently no culture of the earth; no navigation, nor use of the commodities that may be imported by sea; no commodious building; no instruments of moving, and removing such things as require much force; no knowledge of the face of the earth; no account of time; no arts; no letters; no society; and which is worst of all, continual fear, and danger of violent death; and the life of man, solitary, poor, nasty, brutish, and short.

It may seem strange to some man, that has not well weighed these things; that nature should thus dissociate, and render men apt to invade, and destroy one another: and he may therefore, not trusting to this inference, made from the passions, desire perhaps to have the same confirmed by experience. Let him therefore consider with himself, when taking a journey, he arms himself, and seeks to go well accompanied; when going to sleep, he locks his doors; when even in his house he locks his chests; and this when he knows there be laws, and public officers, armed, to revenge all injuries shall be done him; what opinion he has of his fellow subjects, when he rides armed; of his fellow citizens, when he locks his doors; and of his children, and servants, when he locks his chests. Does he not there as much accuse mankind by his actions, as I do by my words? But neither of us accuse man's nature in it. The desires, and other passions of man, are in themselves no sin. No more are the actions, that proceed from those passions, till they know a law that forbids them: which till laws be made they cannot know: nor can any law be made, till they have agreed upon the person that shall make it.

It may peradventure be thought, there was never such a time, nor condition of war as this; and I believe it was never generally so, over all the world: but there are many places, where they live so now. For the savage people in many places of *America*, except the government of small families, the concord whereof dependeth on natural lust, have no government at all; and live at this day in that brutish manner, as I said before. Howsoever, it may be perceived what manner of life there would be, where there were no common power to fear; by the manner of life, which men that have formerly lived under a peaceful government, use to degenerate into, in a civil war.

But though there had never been any time, wherein particular men were in a condition of war one against another; yet in all times, kings, and persons of sovereign authority, because of their independency, are in continual jealousies, and in the state and posture of gladiators; having their weapons pointing, and their eyes fixed on one another; that is, their forts, garrisons, and guns upon the frontiers of their kingdoms; and continual spies upon their neighbours; which is a posture of war. But because they uphold thereby, the industry of their subjects; there does not follow from it, that misery, which accompanies the liberty of particular men.

To this war of every man against every man, this also is consequent; that nothing can be unjust. The notions of right and wrong, justice and injustice have there no place. Where there is no common power, there is no law: where no law, no injustice.

and fraud, are in war the two cardinal virtues. Justice, and injustice are none of the faculties neither of the body, nor mind. If they were, they might be in a man that were alone in the world, as well as his senses, and passions. They are qualities, that relate to men in society, not in solitude. It is consequent also to the same condition, that there be no propriety, no dominion, no *mine* and *thine* distinct; but only that to be every man's, that he can get; and for so long, ✳ as he can keep it. And thus much for the ill condition, which man by mere nature is actually placed in; though with a possibility to come out of it, consisting partly in the passions, partly in his reason.

The passions that incline men to peace, are fear of death; desire of such things as are necessary to commodious living; and a hope by their industry to obtain them. And reason suggesteth convenient articles of peace, upon which men may be drawn to agreement. These articles, are they, which otherwise are called the Laws of Nature: whereof I shall speak more particularly, in the two following chapters.

CHAPTER 14: Of the First and Second Natural Laws, and of Contracts

The RIGHT OF NATURE, which writers commonly call *jus naturale*, is the liberty each man hath, to use his own power, as he will himself, for the preservation of his own nature; that is to say, of his own life; and consequently, of doing any thing, which in his own judgment, and reason, he shall conceive to be the aptest means thereunto.

By LIBERTY, is understood, according to the proper signification of the word, the absence of external impediments: which impediments, may oft take away part of a man's power to do what he would; but ͡annot hinder him from using the power left him, ⸺ing as his judgment, and reason shall dictate

‸TURE, (*lex naturalis*,) is a precept, ‸t by reason, by which a man ‸h is destructive of his ‸ of preserving the same;

and to omit that, by which he thinketh it may be best preserved. For though they that speak of this subject, use to confound *jus*, and *lex*, *right* and *law*; yet they ought to be distinguished; because RIGHT, consisteth in liberty to do, or to forbear; whereas LAW, determineth, and bindeth to one of them: so that law, and right, differ as much, as obligation, and liberty; which in one and the same matter are inconsistent.

And because the condition of man, (as hath been declared in the precedent chapter) is a condition of war of every one against every one; in which case every one is governed by his own reason; and there is nothing he can make use of, that may not be a help unto him, in preserving his life against his enemies; it followeth, that in such a condition, every man has a right to every thing; even to one another's body. And therefore, as long as this natural right of every man to every thing endureth, there can be no security to any man, (how strong or wise soever he be,) of living out the time, which nature ordinarily alloweth men to live. And consequently it is a precept, or general rule of reason, *that every man, ought to endeavour peace, as far as he has hope of obtaining it; and when he cannot obtain it, that he may seek, and use, all helps, and advantages of war.* The first branch of which rule, containeth the first, and fundamental law of nature; which is, *to seek peace, and follow it.* The second, the sum of the right of nature; which is, *by all means we can, to defend ourselves.*

From this fundamental law of nature, by which men are commanded to endeavour peace, is derived this second law; *that a man be willing, when others are so too, as far-forth, as for peace, and defence of himself he shall think it necessary, to lay down this right to all things; and be contented with so much liberty against other men, as he would allow other men against himself.* For as long as every man holdeth this right, of doing any thing he liketh; so long are all men in the condition of war. But if other men will not lay down their right, as well as he; then there is no reason for any one, to divest himself of his: for that were to expose himself to prey, (which no man is bound to) rather than to dispose himself to peace. This is that law of the Gospel; *whatsoever you require that others should do to you, that do ye to them*. And that law of all men, *quod tibi fieri non vis, alteri ne feceris*.

To *lay down* a man's *right* to any thing, is to *divest* himself of the *liberty*, of hindering another of the benefit of his own right to the same. For he that renounceth, or passeth away his right, giveth not to any other man a right which he had not before; because there is nothing to which every man had not right by nature: but only standeth out of his way, that he may enjoy his own original right, without hindrance from him; not without hindrance from another. So that the effect which redoundeth to one man, by another man's defect of right, is but so much diminution of impediments to the use of his own right original.

Right is laid aside, either by simply renouncing it; or by transferring it to another. By *simply* RE-NOUNCING; when he cares not to whom the benefit thereof redoundeth. By TRANSFERRING; when he intendeth the benefit thereof to some certain person, or persons. And when a man hath in either manner abandoned, or granted away his right; then is he said to be OBLIGED, or BOUND, not to hinder those, to whom such right is granted, or abandoned, from the benefit of it: and that he *ought*, and it is his DUTY, not to make void that voluntary act of his own: and that such hindrance is INJUSTICE, and INJURY, as being *sine jure*; the right being before renounced, or transferred. So that *injury*, or *injustice*, in the controversies of the world, is somewhat like to that, which in the disputations of scholars is called *absurdity*. For as it is there called an absurdity, to contradict what one maintained in the beginning: so in the world, it is called injustice, and injury, voluntarily to undo that, which from the beginning he had voluntarily done. The way by which a man either simply renounceth, or transferreth his right, is a declaration, or signification, by some voluntary and sufficient sign, or signs, that he doth so renounce, or transfer; or hath so renounced, or transferred the same, to him that accepteth it. And these signs are either words only, or actions only; or (as it happeneth most often) both words, and actions. And the same are

the BONDS, by which men are bound, and obliged: bonds, that have their strength, not from their own nature, (for nothing is more easily broken than a man's word,) but from fear of some evil consequence upon the rupture.

Whensoever a man transferreth his right, or renounceth it; it is either in consideration of some right reciprocally transferred to himself; or for some other good he hopeth for thereby. For it is a voluntary act: and of the voluntary acts of every man, the object is some *good to himself*. And therefore there be some rights, which no man can be understood by any words, or other signs, to have abandoned, or transferred. As first a man cannot lay down the right of resisting them, that assault him by force, to take away his life; because he cannot be understood to aim thereby, at any good to himself. The same may be said of wounds, and chains, and imprisonment; both because there is no benefit consequent to such patience; as there is to the patience of suffering another to be wounded, or imprisoned: as also because a man cannot tell, when he seeth men proceed against him by violence, whether they intend his death or not. And lastly the motive, and end for which this renouncing, and transferring of right is introduced, is nothing else but the security of a man's person, in his life, and in the means of so preserving life, as not to be weary of it. And therefore if a man by words, or other signs, seem to despoil himself of the end, for which those signs were intended; he is not to be understood as if he meant it, or that it was his will; but that he was ignorant of how such words and actions were to be interpreted.

The mutual transferring of right, is that which men call CONTRACT.

There is difference between transferring of right to the thing; and transferring, or tradition, that is, delivery of the thing it self. For the thing may be delivered together with the translation of the right; as in buying and selling with ready money; or exchange of goods or lands: and it may be delivered some time after

Again, one of the contractors, may deliver the th
contracted for on his part, and leave the oth
perform his part at some determinate time aft

in the mean time be trusted; and then the contract on his part, is called PACT, or COVENANT: or both parts may contract now, to perform hereafter: in which cases, he that is to perform in time to come, being trusted, his performance is called *keeping of promise*, or faith; and the failing of performance (if it be voluntary) *violation of faith*.

When the transferring of right, is not mutual; but one of the parties transferreth, in hope to gain thereby friendship, or service from another, or from his friends; or in hope to gain the reputation of charity, or magnanimity; or to deliver his mind from the pain of compassion; or in hope of reward in heaven; this is not contract, but GIFT, FREE-GIFT, GRACE: which words signify one and the same thing.

Signs of contract, are either *express*, or *by inference*. Express, are words spoken with understanding of what they signify: and such words are either of the time *present*, or *past*; as, *I give, I grant, I have given, I have granted, I will that this be yours*: or of the future; as, *I will give, I will grant*: which words of the future are called PROMISE.

Signs by inference, are sometimes the consequence of words; sometimes the consequence of silence; sometimes the consequence of actions; sometimes the consequence of forbearing an action: and generally a sign by inference, of any contract, is whatsoever sufficiently argues the will of the contractor.

Words alone, if they be of the time to come, and contain a bare promise, are an insufficient sign of a free-gift and therefore not obligatory. For if they be of the time to come, as, *tomorrow I will give*, they are a sign I have not given yet, and consequently that my right is not transferred, but remaineth till I transfer it by some other act. But if the words be of the time present, or past, as, *I have given, or do give to be* *~~livered tomorrow~~*, then is my tomorrow's right given ~~day; and that by the virtue of the words,~~ ~~were no other argument of my will.~~ ~~eat difference in the signification of~~ ~~tuum esse cras~~, and *cras dabo*; ~~hat this be thine tomorrow,~~ ~~ow: for the word~~ *I will*, ~~signifies an act of~~ ~~it signifies a promise~~

of an act of the will to come: and therefore the former words, being of the present, transfer a future right; the latter, that be of the future, transfer nothing. But if there be other signs of the will to transfer a right, besides words; then, though the gift be free, yet may the right be understood to pass by words of the future: as if a man propound a prize to him that comes first to the end of a race, the gift is free; and though the words be of the future, yet the right passeth: for if he would not have his words so be understood, he should not have let them run.

In contracts, the right passeth, not only where the words are of the time present, or past, but also where they are of the future: because all contract is mutual translation, or change of right; and therefore he that promiseth only, because he hath already received the benefit for which he promiseth, is to be understood as if he intended the right should pass: for unless he had been content to have his words so understood, the other would not have performed his part first. And for that cause, in buying, and selling, and other acts of contract, a promise is equivalent to a covenant; and therefore obligatory.

He that performeth first in the case of a contract, is said to MERIT that which he is to receive by the performance of the other; and he hath it as *due*. Also when a prize is propounded to many, which is to be given to him only that winneth; or money is thrown amongst many, to be enjoyed by them that catch it; though this be a free gift; yet so to win, or so to catch, is to *merit*, and to have it as DUE. For the right is transferred in the propounding of the prize, and in throwing down the money; though it be not determined to whom, but by the event of the contention. But there is between these two sorts of merit, this difference, that in contract, I merit by virtue of my own power, and the contractor's need; but in this case of free gift, I am enabled to merit only by the benignity of the giver: in contract, I merit at the contractor's hand that he should depart with his right; in this case of gift, I merit not that the giver should part with his right; but that when he has parted with it, it should be mine, rather than another's. And this I think to be the meaning of that distinction of the Schools, between *meritum congrui*, and *meritum condigni.* For God Almighty, having promised Paradise to those men (hoodwinked with carnal desires,) that can walk through this world according to the precepts, and limits prescribed by him; they say, he that shall so walk, shall merit Paradise *ex congruo.* But because no man can demand a right to it, by his own righteousness, or any other power in himself, but by the free grace of God only; they say, no man can merit Paradise *ex condigno.* This I say, I think is the meaning of that distinction; but because disputers do not agree upon the signification of their own terms of art, longer than it serves their turn; I will not affirm any thing of their meaning: only this I say; when a gift is given indefinitely, as a prize to be contended for, he that winneth meriteth, and may claim the prize as due.

If a covenant be made, wherein neither of the parties perform presently, but trust one another; in the condition of mere nature, (which is a condition of war of every man against every man,) upon any reasonable suspicion, it is void: but if there be a common power set over them both, with right and force sufficient to compel performance, it is not void. For he that performeth first, has no assurance the other will perform after; because the bonds of words are too weak to bridle men's ambition, avarice, anger, and other passions, without the fear of some coercive power; which in the condition of mere nature, where all men are equal, and judges of the justness of their own fears, cannot possibly be supposed. And therefore he which performeth first, does but betray himself to his enemy; contrary to the right (he can never abandon) of defending his life, and means of living.

But in a civil estate, where there is a power set up to constrain those that would otherwise violate their faith, that fear is no more reasonable; and for that cause, he which by the covenant is to perform first, is obliged so to do.

The cause of fear, which maketh such a covenant invalid, must be always something arising after the covenant made; as some new fact, or other sign of the will not to perform: else it cannot make the covenant void. For that which could not hinder a man from promising, ought not to be admitted as a hindrance of performing.

He that transferreth any right, transferreth the means of enjoying it, as far as lieth in his power. As he that selleth land, is understood to transfer the herbage, and whatsoever grows upon it; nor can he that sells a mill turn away the stream that drives it. And they that give to a man the right of government in sovereignty, are understood to give him the right of levying money to maintain soldiers; and of appointing magistrates for the administration of justice.

To make covenants with brute beasts, is impossible; because not understanding our speech, they understand not, nor accept of any translation of right; nor can translate any right to another: and without mutual acceptation, there is no covenant.

To make covenant with God, is impossible, but by mediation of such as God speaketh to, either by revelation supernatural, or by his lieutenants that govern under him, and in his name: for otherwise we know not whether our covenants be accepted, or not. And therefore they that vow any thing contrary to any law of nature, vow in vain; as being a thing unjust to pay such vow. And if it be a thing commanded by the law of nature, it is not the vow, but the law that binds them.

The matter, or subject of a covenant, is always something that falleth under deliberation; (for to covenant, is an act of the will; that is to say an act, and the last act, of deliberation;) and is therefore always understood to be something to come; and which is judged possible for him that covenanteth, to perform.

And therefore, to promise that which is known to be impossible, is no covenant. But if that prove impossible afterwards, which before was thought possible, the covenant is valid, and bindeth, (though not to the thing it self,) yet to the value; or, if that also be impossible, to the unfeigned endeavour of performing as much as is possible: for to more no man can be obliged.

Men are freed of their covenants two ways; by performing; or by being forgiven. For performance, is the natural end of obligation; and forgiveness, th restitution of liberty; as being a retransferring of t right, in which the obligation consisted.

Covenants entered into by fear, in the con of mere nature, are obligatory. For examp covenant to pay a ransom, or service for my life, to an enemy; I am bound by it. For it is a contract, wherein one receiveth the benefit of life; the other is to receive money, or service for it; and consequently, where no other law (as in the condition, of mere nature) forbiddeth the performance, the covenant is valid. Therefore prisoners of war, if trusted with the payment of their ransom, are obliged to pay it: and if a weaker prince, make a disadvantageous peace with a stronger, for fear; he is bound to keep it; unless (as hath been said before) there ariseth some new, and just cause of fear, to renew the war. And even in commonwealths, if I be forced to redeem myself from a thief by promising him money, I am bound to pay it, till the civil law discharge me. For whatsoever I may lawfully do without obligation, the same I may lawfully covenant to do through fear: and what I lawfully covenant, I cannot lawfully break.

A former covenant, makes void a later. For a man that hath passed away his right to one man today, hath it not to pass tomorrow to another: and therefore the later promise passeth no right, but is null.

A covenant not to defend myself from force, by force, is always void. For (as I have showed before) no man can transfer, or lay down his right to save himself from death, wounds, and imprisonment, (the avoiding whereof is the only end of laying down any right, and therefore the promise of not resisting force, in no covenant transferreth any right; nor is obliging. For though a man may covenant thus, *unless I do so, or so, kill me*; he cannot covenant thus, *unless I do so, or so, I will not resist you, when you come to kill me*. For man by nature chooseth the lesser evil, which is danger of death in resisting; rather than the greater, which is certain and present death in not resisting. And this is granted to be true by all men, in that they ⸺d criminals to execution, and prison, with armed ⸺ otwithstanding that such criminals have con-⸺ he law, by which they are condemned.

⸺o accuse one self, without assurance ⸺ise invalid. For in the condition ⸺ an is judge, there is no place ⸺ civil state, the accusation ⸺ which being force, a ⸺ The same is also true,

of the accusation of those, by whose condemnation a man falls into misery; as of a father, wife, or benefactor. For the testimony of such an accuser, if it be not willingly given, is presumed to be corrupted by nature; and therefore not to be received: and where a man's testimony is not to be credited, he is not bound to give it. Also accusations upon torture, are not to be reputed as testimonies. For torture is to be used but as means of conjecture, and light, in the further examination, and search of truth: and what is in that case confessed, tendeth to the ease of him that is tortured, not to the informing of the torturers: and therefore ought not to have the credit of a sufficient testimony: for whether he deliver himself by true, or false accusation, he does it by the right of preserving his own life.

The force of words, being (as I have formerly noted) too weak to hold men to the performance of their covenants; there are in man's nature, but two imaginable helps to strengthen it. And those are either a fear of the consequence of breaking their word; or a glory, or pride in appearing not to need to break it. This latter is a generosity too rarely found to be presumed on, especially in the pursuers of wealth, command, or sensual pleasure; which are the greatest part of mankind. The passion to be reckoned upon, is fear; whereof there be two very general objects: one, the power of spirits invisible; the other, the power of those men they shall therein offend. Of these two, though the former be the greater power, yet the fear of the latter is commonly the greater fear. The fear of the former is in every man, his own religion: which hath place in the nature of man before civil society. The latter hath not so; at least not place enough, to keep men to their promises; because in the condition of mere nature, the inequality of power is not discerned, but by the event of battle. So that before the time of civil society, or in the interruption thereof by war, there is nothing can strengthen a covenant of peace agreed on, against the temptations of avarice, ambition, lust, or other strong desire, but the fear of that invisible power, which they every one worship as God; and fear as a revenger of their perfidy. All therefore that can be done between two men not subject to civil power, is to put one another to swear by the God he feareth: which *swearing*, or OATH, is a *form of speech, added to a promise; by which he that promiseth, signifieth, that unless he perform, he renounceth the mercy of his God, or calleth to him for vengeance on himself.* Such was the heathen form, *Let* Jupiter *kill me else, as I kill this beast.* So is our form, *I shall do thus, and thus, so help me God.* And this, with the rites and ceremonies, which every one useth in his own religion, that the fear of breaking faith might be the greater.

By this it appears, that an oath taken according to any other form, or rite, than his, that sweareth, is in vain; and no oath: and that there is no swearing by any thing which the swearer thinks not God. For though men have sometimes used to swear by their kings, for fear, or flattery; yet they would have it thereby understood, they attributed to them divine honour. And that swearing unnecessarily by God, is but prophaning of his name: and swearing by other things, as men do in common discourse, is not swearing, but an impious custom, gotten by too much vehemence of talking.

It appears also, that the oath adds nothing to the obligation. For a covenant, if lawful, binds in the sight of God, without the oath, as much as with it: if unlawful, bindeth not at all; though it be confirmed with an oath.

CHAPTER 15: Of Other Laws of Nature

From that law of nature, by which we are obliged to transfer to another, such rights, as being retained, hinder the peace of mankind, there followeth a third; which is this, *that men perform their covenants made:* without which, covenants are in vain, and but empty words; and the right of all men to all things remaining, we are still in the condition of war.

And in this law of nature, consisteth the fountain and original of JUSTICE. For where no covenant hath preceded, there hath no right been transferred, and every man has right to every thing; and consequently, no action can be unjust. But when a covenant is made, then to break it is *unjust:* and the definition of INJUSTICE, is no other than *the not performance of covenant.* And whatsoever is not unjust, is *just.*

But because covenants of mutual trust, where there is a fear of not performance on either part, (as hath been said in the former chapter,) are invalid; though the original of justice be the making of covenants; yet injustice actually there can be none, till the cause of such fear be taken away; which while men are in the natural condition of war, cannot be done. Therefore before the names of just, and unjust can have place, there must be some coercive power, to compel men equally to the performance of their covenants, by the terror of some punishment, greater than the benefit they expect by the breach of their covenant; and to make good that propriety, which by mutual contract men acquire, in recompense of the universal right they abandon: and such power there is none before the erection of a commonwealth. And this is also to be gathered out of the ordinary definition of justice in the Schools: for they say, that *justice is the constant will of giving to every man his own.* And therefore where there is no *own,* that is, no propriety, there is no injustice; and where there is no coercive power erected, that is, where there is no commonwealth, there is no propriety; all men having right to all things: therefore where there is no commonwealth, there nothing is unjust. So that the nature of justice, consisteth in keeping of valid covenants: but the validity of covenants begins not but with the constitution of a civil power, sufficient to compel men to keep them: and then it is also that propriety begins.

The fool hath said in his heart, there is no such thing as justice; and sometimes also with his tongue; seriously alleging, that every man's conservation, and contentment, being committed to his own care, there could be no reason, why every man might not do what he thought conduced thereunto: and therefore also to make, or not make; keep, or not keep covenants, was not against reason, when it conduced to one's benefit. He does not therein deny, that there be covenants; and that they are sometimes broken, sometimes kept; and that such breach of them may be called injustice, and the observance of them justice: but he questioneth, whether injustice, taking away the fear of God, (for the same fool hath said in his heart there is no God,) may not sometimes with that reason, which dictateth to every m own good; and particularly then, when it conduceth to such a benefit, as shall put a man in a condition, to neglect not only the dispraise, and revilings, but also the power of other men. The kingdom of God is gotten by violence: but what if it could be gotten by unjust violence? were it against reason so to get it, when it is impossible to receive hurt by it? and if it be not against reason, it is not against justice; or else justice is not to be approved for good. From such reasoning as this, successful wickedness hath obtained the name of virtue: and some that in all other things have disallowed the violation of faith; yet have allowed it, when it is for the getting of a kingdom. And the heathen that believed, that *Saturn* was deposed by his son *Jupiter*, believed nevertheless the same *Jupiter* to be the avenger of injustice: somewhat like to a piece of law in *Coke's Commentaries on Littleton*; where he says, if the right heir of the crown be attainted of treason; yet the crown shall descend to him, and *eo instante* the attainder be void: from which instances a man will be very prone to infer; that when the heir apparent of a kingdom, shall kill him that is in possession, though his father; you may call it injustice, or by what other name you will; yet it can never be against reason, seeing all the voluntary actions of men tend to the benefit of themselves; and those actions are most reasonable, that conduce most to their ends. This specious reasoning is nevertheless false.

For the question is not of promises mutual, where there is no security of performance on either side; as when there is no civil power erected over the parties promising; for such promises are no covenants: but either where one of the parties has performed already; or where there is a power to make him perform; there is the question whether it be against reason, that is, ~~against~~ the benefit of the other to perform, or not. ~~I~~ say it is not against reason. For the manifestation ~~where~~ we are to consider; first, that when a man ~~doth a thing, which~~ notwithstanding any thing can ~~be foreseen, and~~ reckoned on, tendeth to his own ~~destruction, howsoever~~ some accident which he ~~could not expect, arriving~~ may turn it to his benefit; ~~yet such event doth not make~~ it reasonably or wisely ~~done. Secondly, that in a cond~~ition of war, wherein

every man to every man, for want of a common power to keep them all in awe, is an enemy, there is no man can hope by his own strength, or wit, to defend himself from destruction, without the help of confederates; where every one expects the same defence by the confederation, that any one else does: and therefore he which declares he thinks it reason to deceive those that help him, can in reason expect no other means of safety, than what can be had from his own single power. He therefore that breaketh his covenant, and consequently declareth that he thinks he may with reason do so, cannot be received into any society, that unite themselves for peace and defence, but by the error of them that receive him; nor when he is received, be retained in it, without seeing the danger of their error; which errors a man cannot reasonably reckon upon as the means of his security: and therefore if he be left, or cast out of society, he perisheth; and if he live in society, it is by the errors of other men, which he could not foresee, nor reckon upon; and consequently against the reason of his preservation; and so, as all men that contribute not to his destruction, forbear him only out of ignorance of what is good for themselves.

As for the instance of gaining the secure and perpetual felicity of heaven, by any way; it is frivolous: there being but one way imaginable; and that is not breaking, but keeping of covenant.

And for the other instance of attaining sovereignty by rebellion; it is manifest, that though the event follow, yet because it cannot reasonably be expected, but rather the contrary; and because by gaining it so, others are taught to gain the same in like manner, the attempt thereof is against reason. Justice therefore, that is to say, keeping of covenant, is a rule of reason, by which we are forbidden to do any thing destructive to our life; and consequently a law of nature.

There be some that proceed further; and will not have the law of nature, to be those rules which conduce to the preservation of man's life on earth; but to the attaining of an eternal felicity after death; to which they think the breach of covenant may conduce; and consequently be just and reasonable; (such are they that think it a work of merit to kill, or depose, or rebel against, the sovereign power constituted over them by their own consent.) But because there is no natural knowledge of man's estate after death; much less of the reward that is then to be given to breach of faith; but only a belief grounded upon other men's saying, that they know it supernaturally, or that they know those, that knew them, that knew others, that knew it supernaturally; breach of faith cannot be called a precept of reason, or nature.

Others, that allow for a law of nature, the keeping of faith, do nevertheless make exception of certain persons; as heretics, and such as use not to perform their covenant to others: and this also is against reason. For if any fault of a man, be sufficient to discharge our covenant made; the same ought in reason to have been sufficient to have hindered the making of it.

The names of just, and injust, when they are attributed to men, signify one thing; and when they are attributed to actions, another. When they are attributed to men, they signify conformity, or inconformity of manners, to reason. But when they are attributed to actions, they signify the conformity, or inconformity to reason, not of manners, or manner of life, but of particular actions. A just man therefore, is he that taketh all the care he can, that his actions may be all just: and an unjust man, is he that neglecteth it. And such men are more often in our language styled by the names of righteous, and unrighteous; than just, and unjust; though the meaning be the same. Therefore a righteous man, does not lose that title, by one, or a few unjust actions, that proceed from sudden passion, or mistake of things, or persons: nor does an unrighteous man, lose his character, for such actions, as he does, or forbears to do, for fear: because his will is not framed by the justice, but by the apparent benefit of what he is to do. That which gives to human actions the relish of justice, is a certain nobleness or gallantness of courage, (rarely found,) by which a man scorns to be beholding for the contentment of his life, to fraud, or breach of promise. This justice of the manners, is that which is meant, where justice is called a virtue; and injustice a vice.

But the justice of actions denominates men, not just, but *guiltless*: and the injustice of the same, (which is also called injury,) gives them but the name of *guilty*.

Again, the injustice of manners, is the disposition, or aptitude to do injury; and is injustice before it proceed to act; and without supposing any individual person injured. But the injustice of an action, (that is to say injury,) supposeth an individual person injured; namely him, to whom the covenant was made: and therefore many times the injury is received by one man, when the damage redoundeth to another. As when the master commandeth his servant to give money to a stranger; if it be not done, the injury is done to the master, whom he had before covenanted to obey; but the damage redoundeth to the stranger, to whom he had no obligation; and therefore could not injure him. And so also in commonwealths, private men may remit to one another their debts; but not robberies or other violences, whereby they are endamaged; because the detaining of debt, is an injury to themselves; but robbery and violence, are injuries to the person of the commonwealth.

Whatsoever is done to a man, conformable to his own will signified to the doer, is no injury to him. For if he that doeth it, hath not passed away his original right to do what he please, by some antecedent covenant, there is no breach of covenant; and therefore no injury done him. And if he have; then his will to have it done being signified, is a release of that covenant: and so again there is no injury done him.

Justice of actions, is by writers divided into *commutative*, and *distributive*: and the former they say consisteth in proportion arithmetical; the latter in proportion geometrical. Commutative therefore, they place in the equality of value of the things contracted for; and distributive, in the distribution of equal benefit, to men of equal merit. As if it were injustice to sell dearer than we buy; or to give more to a man than he merits. The value of all things contracted for, is measured by the appetite of the contractors: and therefore the just value, is that which they be contented to give. And merit, (besides that which is by covenant, where the performance on one part, meriteth the performance of the other part, and falls under justice commutative, not distributive,) is not due by justice; but is rewarded of grace only. And therefore this distinction, in the sense wherein it useth to be expounded, is not right. To speak properly, commutative justice, is the justice of a contractor; that is, a performance of covenant, in buying, and selling; hiring, and letting to hire; lending, and borrowing; exchanging, bartering, and other acts of contract.

And distributive justice, the justice of an arbitrator; that is to say, the act of defining what is just. Wherein, (being trusted by them that make him arbitrator,) if he perform his trust, he is said to distribute to every man his own: and this is indeed just distribution, and may be called, (though improperly,) distributive justice; but more properly equity; which also is a law of nature, as shall be shown in due place.

As justice dependeth on antecedent covenant; so does GRATITUDE depend on antecedent grace; that is to say, antecedent free-gift: and is the fourth law of nature; which may be conceived in this form, *that a man which receiveth benefit from another of mere grace, endeavour that he which giveth it, have no reasonable cause to repent him of his good will.* For no man giveth, but with intention of good to himself; because gift is voluntary; and of all voluntary acts, the object is to every man his own good; of which if men see they shall be frustrated, there will be no beginning of benevolence, or trust; nor consequently of mutual help; nor of reconciliation of one man to another; and therefore they are to remain still in the condition of *war;* which is contrary to the first and fundamental law of nature, which commandeth men to *seek peace.* The breach of this law, is called *ingratitude;* and hath the same relation to grace, that injustice hath to obligation by covenant.

A fifth law of nature, is COMPLAISANCE; that is to say, *that every man strive to accommodate himself to the rest.* For the understanding whereof, we may consider, that there is in men's aptness to society, a diversity of nature, rising from their diversity of affections; not unlike to that we see in stones brought together for building of an edifice. For as that stone which by the asperity, and irregularity of figure, takes more room from others, than itself fills; and for the hardness, cannot be easily made plain, and thereby hindereth the building, is by the builders cast away as unprofitable, and troublesome: so also, a man that by asperity of nature, will strive to retain those things which to himself are superfluous, and to others necessary; and for the stubbornness of his passions, cannot be corrected, is to be left, or cast out of society, as cumbersome thereunto. For seeing every man, not only by right, but also by necessity of nature, is supposed to endeavour all he can, to obtain that which is necessary for his conservation; he that shall oppose himself against it, for things superfluous, is guilty of the war that thereupon is to follow; and therefore doth that, which is contrary to the fundamental law of nature, which commandeth *to seek peace.* The observers of this law, may be called SOCIABLE, (the Latins call them *commodi;*) the contrary, *stubborn, insociable, froward, intractable.*

A sixth law of nature, is this, *that upon caution of the future time, a man ought to pardon the offences past of them that repenting, desire it.* For PARDON, is nothing but granting of peace; which though granted to them that persevere in their hostility, be not peace, but fear; yet not granted to them that give caution of the future time, is sign of an aversion to peace; and therefore contrary to the law of nature.

A seventh is, *that in revenges,* (that is, retribution of evil for evil,) *men look not at the greatness of the evil past, but the greatness of the good to follow.* Whereby we are forbidden to inflict punishment with any other design, than for correction of the offender, or direction of others. For this law is consequent to the next before it, that commandeth pardon, upon security of the future time. Besides, revenge without respect to the example, and profit to come, is a triumph, or glorying in the hurt of another, tending to no end; (for the end is always somewhat to come;) and glorying to no end, is vain-glory, and contrary to reason; and to hurt without reason, tendeth to the introduction of war; which is against the law of nature; and is commonly styled by the name of *cruelty.*

And because all signs of hatred, or contempt, provoke to fight; insomuch as most men choose rather to hazard their life, than not to be revenged; we may in the eighth place, for a law of nature, set down this precept, *that no man by deed, word, countenance, or gesture, declare hatred, or contempt of another.* The breach of which law, is commonly called *contumely.*

The question who is the better man, has no place in the condition of mere nature; where, (as has been shewn before,) all men are equal. The inequality that now is, has been introduced by the laws civil. I know that *Aristotle* in the first book of his *Politics*, for a foundation of his doctrine, maketh men by nature, some more worthy to command, meaning the wiser sort, (such as he thought himself to be for his philosophy;) others to serve, (meaning those that had strong bodies, but were not philosophers as he;) as if master and servant were not introduced by consent of men, but by difference of wit: which is not only against reason; but also against experience. For there are very few so foolish, that had not rather govern themselves, than be governed by others: nor when the wise in their own conceit, contend by force, with them who distrust their own wisdom, do they always, or often, or almost at any time, get the victory. If nature therefore have made men equal, that equality is to be acknowledged: or if nature have made men unequal; yet because men that think themselves equal, will not enter into conditions of peace, but upon equal terms, such equality must be admitted. And therefore for the ninth law of nature, I put this, *that every man acknowledge other for his equal by nature*. The breach of this precept is *pride*.

On this law, dependeth another, *that at the entrance into conditions of peace, no man require to reserve to himself any right, which he is not content should be reserved to every one of the rest*. As it is necessary for all men that seek peace, to lay down certain rights of nature; that is to say, not to have liberty to do all they list: so is it necessary for man's life, to retain some; as right to govern their own bodies; enjoy air, water, motion, ways to go from place to place; and all things else without which a man cannot live, or not live well. If in this case, at the making of peace, men require for themselves, that which they would not have to be granted to others, they do contrary to the precedent law, that commandeth the acknowledgment of natural equality, and therefore also against the law of nature. The observers of this law, are those we call *modest*, and the breakers *arrogant* men. The Greeks call the violation of this law πλεονεξια; that is, a desire of more than their share.

Also if *a man be trusted to judge between man and man*, it is a precept of the law of nature, *that he deal equally between them*. For without that, the controversies of men cannot be determined but by war. He therefore that is partial in judgment, doth what in him lies, to deter men from the use of judges, and arbitrators; and consequently, (against the fundamental law of nature,) is the cause of war.

The observance of this law, from the equal distribution to each man, of that which in reason belongeth to him, is called EQUITY, and (as I have said before) distributive justice: the violation, *acception of persons*, προσωποληψία.

And from this followeth another law, *that such things as cannot be divided, be enjoyed in common, if it can be; and if the quantity of the thing permit, without stint; otherwise proportionably to the number of them that have right*. For otherwise the distribution is unequal, and contrary to equity.

But some things there be, that can neither be divided, nor enjoyed in common. Then, the law of nature, which prescribeth equity, requireth, *that the entire right; or else, (making the use alternate,) the first possession, be determined by lot*. For equal distribution, is of the law of nature; and other means of equal distribution cannot be imagined.

Of *lots* there be two sorts, *arbitrary*, and *natural*. Arbitrary, is that which is agreed on by the competitors: natural, is either *primogeniture*, (which the Greek calls κληρονομία, which signifies, *given by lot*;) or *first seizure*.

And therefore those things which cannot be enjoyed in common, nor divided, ought to be adjudged to the first possessor; and in some cases to the first-born, as acquired by lot.

It is also a law of nature, *that all men that mediate peace, be allowed safe conduct*. For the law that commandeth peace, as the *end*, commandeth intercession, as the *means*; and to intercession the means is safe conduct.

And because, though men be never so willing to observe these laws, there may nevertheless arise questions concerning a man's action; first, whether it were done, or not done; secondly, (if done,) whether against the law, or not against the law; the former whereof, is called a question *of fact*; the latter a question *of right*; therefore unless the parties to the question, covenant mutually to stand to the sentence of another, they are as far from peace as ever. This other, to whose sentence they submit, is called an ARBITRATOR. And therefore it is of the law of nature, *that they that are at controversy, submit their right to the judgment of an arbitrator.*

And seeing every man is presumed to do all things in order to his own benefit, no man is a fit arbitrator in his own cause: and if he were never so fit; yet equity allowing to each party equal benefit, if one be admitted to be judge, the other is to be admitted also; and so the controversy, that is, the cause of war, remains, against the law of nature.

For the same reason no man in any cause ought to be received for arbitrator, to whom greater profit, or honour, or pleasure apparently ariseth out of the victory of one party, than of the other: for he hath taken (though an unavoidable bribe, yet) a bribe; and no man can be obliged to trust him. And thus also the controversy, and the condition of war remaineth, contrary to the law of nature.

And in a controversy of *fact*, the judge being to give no more credit to one, than to the other, (if there be no other arguments,) must give credit to a third; or to a third and fourth; or more: for else the question is undecided, and left to force, contrary to the law of nature.

These are the laws of nature, dictating peace, for a means of the conservation of men in multitudes; and which only concern the doctrine of civil society. There be other things tending to the destruction of particular men; as drunkenness, and all other parts of intemperance; which may therefore also be reckoned amongst those things which the law of nature hath forbidden; but are not necessary to be mentioned, nor are pertinent enough to this place.

And though this may seem too subtle a deduction of the laws of nature, to be taken notice of by all men; whereof the most part are too busy in getting food, and the rest too negligent to understand; yet to leave all men inexcusable, they have been contracted into one easy sum, intelligible, even to the meanest capacity; and that is, *Do not that to another, which*

thou wouldest not have done to thyself; which sheweth him, that he has no more to do in learning the laws of nature, but, when weighing the actions of other men with his own, they seem too heavy, to put them into the other part of the balance, and his own into their place, that his own passions, and self-love, may add nothing to the weight; and then there is none of these laws of nature that will not appear unto him very reasonable.

The laws of nature oblige *in foro interno*; that is to say, they bind to a desire they should take place: but *in foro externo*; that is, to the putting them in act, not always. For he that should be modest, and tractable, and perform all he promises, in such time, and place, where no man else should do so, should but make himself a prey to others, and procure his own certain ruin, contrary to the ground of all laws of nature, which tend to nature's preservation. And again, he that having sufficient security, that others shall observe the same laws towards him, observes them not himself, seeketh not peace, but war; and consequently the destruction of his nature by violence.

And whatsoever laws bind *in foro interno*, may be broken, not only by a fact contrary to the law, but also by a fact according to it, in case a man think it contrary. For though his action in this case, be according to the law; yet his purpose was against the law; which, where the obligation is *in foro interno*, is a breach.

The laws of nature are immutable and eternal; for injustice, ingratitude, arrogance, pride, iniquity, acception of persons, and the rest, can never be made lawful. For it can never be that war shall preserve life, and peace destroy it.

The same laws, because they oblige only to a desire, and endeavour, I mean an unfeigned and constant endeavour, are easy to be observed. For in that they require nothing but endeavour; he that endeavoureth their performance, fulfilleth them; and he that fulfilleth the law, is just.

And the science of them, is the true and only moral philosophy. For moral philosophy is nothing else but the science of what is *good*, and *evil*, in the conversation, and society of mankind. *Good*, and *evil*, are names that signify our appetites, and aversions; which in different tempers, customs, and doctrines of men, are different: and divers men, differ not only in their judgment, on the senses of what is pleasant, and unpleasant to the taste, smell, hearing, touch, and sight; but also of what is conformable, or disagreeable to reason, in the actions of common life. Nay, the same man, in divers times, differs from himself; and one time praiseth, that is, calleth good, what another time he dispraiseth, and calleth evil: from whence arise disputes, controversies, and at last war. And therefore so long a man is in the condition of mere nature, (which is a condition of war,) as private appetite is the measure of good, and evil: and consequently all men agree on this, that peace is good, and therefore also the way, or means of peace, which, (as I have shewed before) are *justice, gratitude, modesty, equity, mercy,* and the rest of the laws of nature, are good; that is to say, *moral virtues*; and their contrary *vices*, evil. Now the science of virtue and vice, is moral philosophy; and therefore the true doctrine of the laws of nature, is the true moral philosophy. But the writers of moral philosophy, though they acknowledge the same virtues and vices; yet not seeing wherein consisted their goodness; nor that they come to be praised, as the means of peaceable, sociable, and comfortable living; place them in a mediocrity of passions: as if not the cause, but the degree of daring, made fortitude; or not the cause, but the quantity of a gift, made liberality.

These dictates of reason, men use to call by the name of laws; but improperly: for they are but conclusions, or theorems concerning what conduceth to the conservation and defence of themselves; whereas law, properly, is the word of him, that by right hath command over others. But yet if we consider the same theorems, as delivered in the word of God, that by right commandeth all things; then are they properly called laws.

CHAPTER 16: Of Persons, Authors, and Things Personated

A person, is he, *whose words or actions are considered, either as his own, or as representing the words or actions of another man, or of any other thing to whom they are attributed, whether truly or by fiction.*

When they are considered as his own, then is he called a *natural person*: and when they are considered as representing the words and actions of another, then is he a *feigned* or *artificial person*.

The word person is Latin: instead whereof the Greeks have πρόσωπον, which signifies the *face*, as *persona* in Latin signifies the *disguise*, or *outward appearance* of a man, counterfeited on the stage; and sometimes more particularly that part of it, which disguiseth the face, as a mask or vizard: and from the stage, hath been translated to any representer of speech and action, as well in tribunals, as theatres. So that a *person*, is the same that an *actor* is, both on the stage and in common conversation; and to *personate*, is to *act*, or *represent* himself, or another; and he that acteth another, is said to bear his person, or act in his name; (in which sense Cicero useth it where he says, *Unus sustineo tres personas; mei, adversarii, et judicis*, I bear three persons; my own, my adversary's, and the judge's;) and is called in divers occasions, diversly; as a *representer*, or *representative*, a *lieutenant*, a *vicar*, an *attorney*, a *deputy*, a *procurator*, an *actor*, and the like.

Of persons artificial, some have their words and actions *owned* by those whom they represent. And then the person is the *actor*; and he that owneth his words and actions, is the AUTHOR: in which case the actor acteth by authority. For that which in speaking of goods and possessions, is called an *owner*, and in Latin *dominus*, in Greek κύριος; speaking of actions, is called author. And as the right of possession, is called dominion; so the right of doing any action, is called AUTHORITY. So that by authority, is always understood a right of doing any act: and *done by authority*, done by commission, or licence from him whose right it is.

From hence it followeth, that when the actor maketh a covenant by authority, he bindeth thereby the author, no less than if he had made it himself; and no less subjecteth him to all the consequences of the same. And therefore all that hath been said formerly, (*chap.* 14) of the nature of covenants between man and man in their natural capacity, is true also when they are made by their actors, representers, or procurators, that have authority from them, so far forth as is in their commission, but no farther.

And therefore he that maketh a covenant with the actor, or representer, not knowing the authority he hath, doth it at his own peril. For no man is obliged by a covenant, whereof he is not author; nor consequently by a covenant made against, or beside the authority he gave.

When the actor doth any thing against the law of nature by command of the author, if he be obliged by former covenant to obey him, not he, but the author breaketh the law of nature: for though the action be against the law of nature; yet it is not his: but contrarily, to refuse to do it, is against the law of nature, that forbiddeth breach of covenant.

And he that maketh a covenant with the author, by mediation of the actor, not knowing what authority he hath, but only takes his word; in case such authority be not made manifest unto him upon demand, is no longer obliged: for the covenant made with the author, is not valid, without his counter-assurance. But if he that so covenanteth, knew beforehand he was to expect no other assurance, than the actor's word; then is the covenant valid; because the actor in this case maketh himself the author. And therefore, as when the authority is evident, the covenant obligeth the author, not the actor; so when the authority is feigned, it obligeth the actor only; there being no author but himself.

There are few things, that are incapable of being represented by fiction. Inanimate things, as a church, an hospital, a bridge, may be personated by a rector, master, or overseer. But things inanimate, cannot be authors, nor therefore give authority to their actors: yet the actors may have authority to procure their maintenance, given them by those that are owners, or governors of those things. And therefore, such things cannot be personated, before there be some state of civil government.

Likewise children, fools, and madmen that have no use of reason, may be personated by guardians, or curators; but can be no authors, (during that time) of any action done by them, longer than (when they shall recover the use of reason) they shall judge the same reasonable. Yet during the folly, he that hath right of governing them, may give authority to the guardian. But this again has no place but in a state civil, because before such estate, there is no dominion of persons.

An idol, or mere figment of the brain, may be personated; as were the gods of the heathen; which by such officers as the state appointed, were personated, and held possessions, and other goods, and rights, which men from time to time dedicated, and consecrated unto them. But idols cannot be authors: for an idol is nothing. The authority proceeded from the state: and therefore before introduction of civil government, the gods of the heathen could not be personated.

The true God may be personated. As he was; first, by Moses; who governed the Israelites, (that were not his, but God's people,) not in his own name, with *hoc dicit Moses*; but in God's name, with *hoc dicit Dominus*. Secondly, by the Son of man, his own Son, our blessed Saviour Jesus Christ, that came to reduce the Jews, and induce all nations into the kingdom of his father; not as of himself, but as sent from his father. And thirdly, by the Holy Ghost, or Comforter, speaking, and working in the Apostles: which Holy Ghost, was a Comforter that came not of himself; but was sent, and proceeded from them both.

A multitude of men, are made *one* person, when they are by one man, or one person, represented; so that it be done with the consent of every one of that multitude in particular. For it is the *unity* of the representer, not the *unity* of the represented, that maketh the person *one*. And it is the representer that beareth the person, and but one person: and *unity*, cannot otherwise be understood in multitude.

And because the multitude naturally is not *one*, but *many*; they cannot be understood for one; but many authors, of every thing their representative saith, or doth in their name; every man giving their common representer, authority from himself in particular; and owning all the actions the representer doth, in case they give him authority without stint: otherwise, when they limit him in what, and how far he shall represent them, none of them owneth more, than they gave him commission to act.

And if the representative consist of many men, the voice of the greater number, must be considered as the voice of them all. For if the lesser number pronounce (for example) in the affirmative, and the greater in the negative, there will be negatives more than enough to destroy the affirmatives; and thereby the excess of negatives, standing uncontradicted, are the only voice the representative hath.

And a representative of even number, especially when the number is not great, whereby the contradictory voices are oftentimes equal, is therefore oftentimes mute, and incapable of action. Yet in some cases contradictory voices equal in number, may determine a question; as in condemning, or absolving, equality of votes, even in that they condemn not, do absolve; but not on the contrary condemn, in that they absolve not. For when a cause is heard; not to condemn, is to absolve: but on the contrary, to say that not absolving, is condemning, is not true. The like it is in a deliberation of executing presently, or deferring till another time: for when the voices are equal, the not decreeing execution, is a decree of dilation.

Or if the number be odd, as three, or more, (men, or assemblies;) whereof every one has by a negative voice, authority to take away the effect of all the affirmative voices of the rest, this number is no representative; because by the diversity of opinions, and interests of men, it becomes oftentimes, and in cases of the greatest consequence, a mute person, and unapt, as for many things else, so for the government of a multitude, especially in time of war.

Of authors there be two sorts. The first simply so called; which I have before defined to be him, that owneth the action of another simply. The second is he, that owneth an action, or covenant of another conditionally; that is to say, he undertaketh to do it, if the other doth it not, at, or before a certain time. And these authors conditional, are generally called SURETIES, in Latin *fidejussores*, and *sponsores*; and particularly for debt, *praedes*; and for appearance before a judge, or magistrate, *vades*.

PART 2
OF COMMONWEALTH

CHAPTER 17: Of the Causes, Generation, and Definition of a Commonwealth

The final cause, end, or design of men, (who naturally love liberty, and dominion over others,) in the introduction of that restraint upon themselves, (in which we see them live in commonwealths,) is the foresight of their own preservation, and of a more contented life thereby; that is to say, of getting themselves out from that miserable condition of war, which is necessarily consequent (as hath been shown), to, the natural passions of men, when there is no visible power to keep them in awe, and tie them by fear of punishment to the performance of their covenants, and observation of those laws of nature set down in the fourteenth and fifteenth chapters.

For the laws of nature (as *justice, equity, modesty, mercy*, and (in sum) *doing to others, as we would be done to*,) of themselves, without the terror of some power, to cause them to be observed, are contrary to our natural passions, that carry us to partiality, pride, revenge, and the like. And covenants, without the sword, are but words, and of no strength to secure a man at all. Therefore notwithstanding the laws of nature, (which every one hath then kept, when he has the will to keep them, when he can do it safely,) if there be no power erected, or not great enough for our security; every man will, and may lawfully rely on his own strength and art, for caution against all other men. And in all places, where men have lived by small families, to rob and spoil one another, has been a trade, and so far from being reputed against the law of nature, that the greater spoils they gained, the greater was their honour; and men observed no other laws therein, but the laws of honour; that is, to abstain from cruelty, leaving to men their lives, and instruments of husbandry. And as small families did then; so now do cities and kingdoms which are but greater families (for their own security) enlarge their dominions, upon all pretences of danger, and fear of invasion, or assistance that may be given to invaders, endeavour as much as they can, to subdue, or weaken their neighbours, by open force, and secret arts, for want of other caution, justly; and are remembered for it in after ages with honour.

Nor is it the joining together of a small number of men, that gives them this security; because in small numbers, small additions on the one side or the other, make the advantage of strength so great, as is sufficient to carry the victory; and therefore gives encouragement to an invasion. The multitude sufficient to confide in for our security, is not determined by any certain number, but by comparison with the enemy we fear; and is then sufficient, when the odds of the enemy is not of so visible and conspicuous moment, to determine the event of war, as to move him to attempt.

And be there never so great a multitude; yet if their actions be directed according to their particular judgments, and particular appetites, they can expect thereby no defence, nor protection, neither against a common enemy, nor against the injuries of one another. For being distracted in opinions concerning the best use and application of their strength, they do not help, but hinder one another; and reduce their strength by mutual opposition to nothing: whereby they are easily, not only subdued by a very few that agree together; but also when there is no common enemy, they make war upon each other, for their particular interests. For if we could suppose a great multitude of men to consent in the observation of justice, and other laws of nature, without a common power to keep them all in awe; we might as well suppose all mankind to do the same; and then there neither would be, nor need to be any civil government, or commonwealth at all; because there would be peace without subjection.

Nor is it enough for the security, which men desire should last all the time of their life, that they be governed, and directed by one judgment, for a limited time; as in one battle, or one war. For though they obtain a victory by their unanimous endeavour against a foreign enemy; yet afterwards, when either they have no common enemy, or he that by one part is held for an enemy, is by another part held for a friend, they must needs by the difference of their interests dissolve, and fall again into a war amongst themselves.

It is true, that certain living creatures, as bees, and ants, live sociably one with another, (which are therefore by *Aristotle* numbered amongst political creatures;) and yet have no other direction, than their particular judgments and appetites; nor speech, whereby one of them can signify to another, what he thinks expedient for the common benefit: and therefore some man may perhaps desire to know, why mankind cannot do the same. To which I answer,

First, that men are continually in competition for honour and dignity, which these creatures are not; and consequently amongst men there ariseth on that ground, envy and hatred, and finally war; but amongst these not so.

Secondly, that amongst these creatures, the common good differeth not from the private; and being by nature inclined to their private, they procure thereby the common benefit. But man, whose joy consisteth in comparing himself with other men, can relish nothing but what is eminent.

Thirdly, that these creatures, having not, (as man) the use of reason, do not see, nor think they see any fault, in the administration of their common business; whereas amongst men, there are very many, that think themselves wiser, and abler to govern the public, better than the rest; and these strive to reform and innovate, one this way, another that way; and thereby bring it into distraction and civil war.

Fourthly, that these creatures, though they have some use of voice, in making known to one another their desires, and other affections; yet they want that art of words, by which some men can represent to others, that which is good, in the likeness of evil; and evil, in the likeness of good; and augment, or diminish the apparent greatness of good and evil; discontenting men, and troubling their peace at their pleasure.

Fifthly, irrational creatures cannot distinguish between *injury*, and *damage*; and therefore as long as they be at ease, they are not offended with their fellows: whereas man is then most troublesome, when he is most at ease: for then it is that he loves to shew his wisdom, and control the actions of them that govern the commonwealth.

Lastly, the agreement of these creatures is natural; that of men, is by covenant only, which is artificial: and therefore it is no wonder if there be somewhat else required (besides covenant) to make their agreement constant and lasting; which is a common power, to keep them in awe, and to direct their actions to the common benefit.

The only way to erect such a common power, as may be able to defend them from the invasion of foreigners, and the injuries of one another, and thereby to secure them in such sort, as that by their own industry, and by the fruits of the earth, they may nourish themselves and live contentedly; is, to confer all their power and strength upon one man, or upon one assembly of men, that may reduce all their wills, by plurality of voices, unto one will: which is as much as to say, to appoint one man, or assembly of men, to bear their person; and every one to own, and acknowledge himself to be author of whatsoever he that so beareth their person, shall act, or cause to be acted, in those things which concern the common peace and safety; and therein to submit their wills, every one to his will, and their judgments, to his judgment. This is more than consent, or concord; it is a real unity of them all, in one and the same person, made by covenant of every man with every man, in such manner, as if every man should say to every man, *I authorise and give up my right of governing myself, to this man, or to this assembly of men, on this condition, that thou give up thy right to him, and authorize all his actions in like manner*. This done, the multitude so united in one person, is called a COMMON-WEALTH, in Latin CIVITAS. This is the generation of that great LEVIATHAN, or rather (to speak more reverently) of that *mortal god*, to which we owe under the *immortal God*, our peace and defence. For by this authority, given him by every particular man in the commonwealth, he hath the use of so much power and strength conferred on him, that by terror thereof, he is enabled to form the wills of them all, to peace at home, and mutual aid against their enemies abroad. And in him consisteth the essence of the commonwealth; which (to define it,) is *one person, of whose acts a great multitude, by mutual covenants one with another, have made themselves every one the author, to the end he may use the strength and means of them all, as he shall think expedient, for their peace and common defence.*

And he that carrieth this person, is called SOVEREIGN, and said to have sovereign power; and every one besides, his SUBJECT.

The attaining to this sovereign power, is by two ways. One, by natural force; as when a man maketh his children, to submit themselves, and their children to his government, as being able to destroy them if they refuse; or by war subdueth his enemies to his will, giving them their lives on that condition. The other, is when men agree amongst themselves, to submit to some man, or assembly of men, voluntarily, on confidence to be protected by him against all others. This latter, may be called a political commonwealth, or commonwealth by *institution*; and the former, a commonwealth by *acquisition*. And first, I shall speak of a commonwealth by institution.

CHAPTER 18: Of the Rights of Sovereigns by Institution

A *commonwealth* is said to be *instituted*, when a *multitude* of men do agree, and *covenant, every one, with every one*, that to whatsoever *man*, or *assembly of men*, shall be given by the major part, the *right* to *present* the person of them all, (that is to say, to be their *representative*;) every one, as well he that *voted for it*, as he that *voted against it*, shall *authorize* all the actions and judgments, of that man, or assembly of men, in the same manner, as if they were his own, to the end, to live peaceably amongst themselves, and be protected against other men.

From this institution of a commonwealth are derived all the *rights*, and *faculties* of him, or them, on whom the sovereign power is conferred by the consent of the people assembled.

First, because they covenant, it is to be understood, they are not obliged by former covenant to any thing repugnant hereunto. And consequently they that have already instituted a commonwealth, being thereby bound by covenant, to own the actions, and judgments of one, cannot lawfully make a new covenant, amongst themselves, to be obedient to any other, in any thing whatsoever, without his permission. And therefore, they that are subjects to a monarch, cannot without his leave cast off monarchy, and return to the confusion of a disunited multitude; nor transfer their person from him that beareth it, to another man, or other assembly of men: for they are bound, every man to every man, to own, and be reputed author of all, that he that already is their sovereign, shall do, and judge fit to be done: so that any one man dissenting, all the rest should break their covenant made to that man, which is injustice: and they have also every man given the sovereignty to him that beareth their person; and therefore if they depose him, they take from him that which is his own, and so again it is injustice. Besides, if he that attempteth to depose his sovereign, be killed, or punished by him for such attempt, he is author of his own punishment, as being by the institution, author of all his sovereign shall do: and because it is injustice for a man to do any thing, for which he may be punished by his own authority, he is also upon that title, unjust. And whereas some men have pretended for their disobedience to their sovereign, a new covenant, made, not with men, but with God; this also is unjust: for there is no covenant with God, but by mediation of somebody that representeth God's person; which none doth but God's lieutenant, who hath the sovereignty under God. But this pretence of covenant with God, is so evident a lie, even in the pretenders' own consciences, that it is not only an act of an unjust, but also of a vile, and unmanly disposition.

Secondly, because the right of bearing the person of them all, is given to him they make sovereign, by covenant only of one to another, and not of him to any of them; there can happen no breach of covenant on the part of the sovereign; and consequently none of his subjects, by any pretence of forfeiture, can be freed from his subjection. That he which is made sovereign maketh no covenant with his subjects beforehand, is manifest; because either he must make it with the whole multitude, as one party to the covenant; or he must make a several covenant with every man. With the whole, as one party, it is impossible;

because as yet they are not one person: and if he make so many several covenants as there be men, those covenants after he hath the sovereignty are void, because what act soever can be pretended by any one of them for breach thereof, is the act both of himself, and of all the rest, because done in the person, and by the right of every one of them in particular. Besides, if any one, or more of them, pretend a breach of the covenant made by the sovereign at his institution; and others, or one other of his subjects, or himself alone, pretend there was no such breach, there is in this case, no judge to decide the controversy; it returns therefore to the sword again; and every man recovereth the right of protecting himself by his own strength, contrary to the design they had in the institution. It is therefore in vain to grant sovereignty by way of precedent covenant. The opinion that any monarch receiveth his power by covenant, that is to say, on condition, proceedeth from want of understanding this easy truth, that covenants being but words and breath, have no force to oblige, contain, constrain, or protect any man, but what it has from the public sword; that is, from the untied hands of that man, or assembly of men that hath the sovereignty, and whose actions are avouched by them all, and performed by the strength of them all, in him united. But when an assembly of men is made sovereign; then no man imagineth any such covenant to have passed in the institution; for no man is so dull as to say, for example, the people of Rome made a covenant with the Romans, to hold the sovereignty on such or such conditions; which not performed, the Romans might lawfully depose the Roman people. That men see not the reason to be alike in a monarchy, and in a popular government, proceedeth from the ambition of some, that are kinder to the government of an assembly, whereof they may hope to participate, than of monarchy, which they despair to enjoy.

Thirdly, because the major part hath by consenting voices declared a sovereign; he that dissented must now consent with the rest; that is, be contented to avow all the actions he shall do, or else justly be destroyed by the rest. For if he voluntarily entered into the congregation of them that were assembled, he sufficiently declared thereby his will, (and therefore tacitly covenanted) to stand to what the major part should ordain: and therefore if he refuse to stand thereto, or make protestation against any of their decrees, he does contrary to his covenant, and therefore unjustly. And whether he be of the congregation, or not; and whether his consent be asked, or not, he must either submit to their decrees, or be left in the condition of war he was in before; wherein he might without injustice be destroyed by any man whatsoever.

Fourthly, because every subject is by this institution author of all the actions, and judgments of the sovereign instituted; it follows, that whatsoever he doth, it can be no injury to any of his subjects; nor ought he to be by any of them accused of injustice. For he that doth any thing by authority from another, doth therein no injury to him by whose authority he acteth: but by this institution of a commonwealth, every particular man is author of all the sovereign doth; and consequently he that complaineth of injury from his sovereign, complaineth of that whereof he himself is author; and therefore ought not to accuse any man but himself; no nor himself of injury; because to do injury to one's self, is impossible. It is true that they that have sovereign power, may commit iniquity; but not injustice, or injury in the proper signification.

Fifthly, and consequently to that which was said last, no man that hath sovereign power can justly be put to death, or otherwise in any manner by his subjects punished. For seeing every subject is author of the actions of his sovereign; he punisheth another, for the actions committed by himself.

And because the end of this institution, is the peace and defence of them all; and whosoever has right to the end, has right to the means; it belongeth of right, to whatsoever man, or assembly that hath the sovereignty, to be judge both of the means of peace and defence; and also of the hindrances, and disturbances of the same; and to do whatsoever he shall think necessary to be done, both beforehand, for the preserving of peace and security, by prevention of discord at home, and hostility from abroad; and, when peace and security are lost, for the recovery of the same. And therefore,

Sixthly, it is annexed to the sovereignty, to be judge of what opinions and doctrines are averse, and what conducing to peace; and consequently, on what occasions, how far, and what, men are to be trusted withal, in speaking to multitudes of people; and who shall examine the doctrines of all books before they be published. For the actions of men proceed from their opinions; and in the well-governing of opinions, consisteth the well-governing of men's actions, in order to their peace, and concord. And though in matter of doctrine, nothing ought to be regarded but the truth; yet this is not repugnant to regulating of the same by peace. For doctrine repugnant to peace, can no more be true, than peace and concord can be against the law of nature. It is true, that in a commonwealth, where by the negligence, or unskilfulness of governors, and teachers, false doctrines are by time generally received; the contrary truths may be generally offensive: Yet the most sudden, and rough busling in of a new truth, that can be, does never break the peace, but only sometimes awake the war. For those men that are so remissly governed, that they dare take up arms, to defend, or introduce an opinion, are still in war; and their condition not peace, but only a cessation of arms for fear of one another; and they live as it were, in the precincts of battle continually. It belongeth therefore to him that hath the sovereign power, to be judge, or constitute all judges of opinions and doctrines, as a thing necessary to peace; thereby to prevent discord and civil war.

Seventhly, is annexed to the sovereignty, the whole power of prescribing the rules, whereby every man may know, what goods he may enjoy, and what actions he may do, without being molested by any of his fellow-subjects; and this is it men call *propriety*. For before constitution of sovereign power (as hath already been shown) all men had right to all things; which necessarily causeth war: and therefore this propriety, being necessary to peace, and depending on sovereign power, is the act of that power, in order to the public peace. These rules of propriety (or *meum* and *tuum*) and of *good*, *evil*, *lawful*, and *unlawful* in the actions of subjects, are the civil laws; that is to say, the laws of each commonwealth in particular; though the name of civil law be now restrained to the ancient civil laws of the city of *Rome*; which being the head of a great part of the world, her laws at that time were in these parts the civil law.

Eighthly, is annexed to the sovereignty, the right of judicature; that is to say, of hearing and deciding all controversies, which may arise concerning law, either civil, or natural; or concerning fact. For without the decision of controversies, there is no protection of one subject, against the injuries of another; the laws concerning *meum* and *tuum* are in vain; and to every man remaineth, from the natural and necessary appetite of his own conservation, the right of protecting himself by his private strength, which is the condition of war; and contrary to the end for which every commonwealth is instituted.

Ninthly, is annexed to the sovereignty, the right of making war and peace with other nations, and commonwealths; that is to say, of judging when it is for the public good, and how great forces are to be assembled, armed, and paid for that end; and to levy money upon the subjects, to defray the expenses thereof. For the power by which the people are to be defended, consisteth in their armies; and the strength of an army, in the union of their strength under one command; which command the sovereign instituted, therefore hath; because the command of the *militia*, without other institution, maketh him that hath it sovereign. And therefore whosoever is made general of an army, he that hath the sovereign power is always generalissimo.

Tenthly, is annexed to the sovereignty, the choosing of all counsellors, ministers, magistrates, and officers, both in peace, and war. For seeing the sovereign is charged with the end, which is the common peace and defence, he is understood to have power to use such means, as he shall think most fit for his discharge.

Eleventhly, to the sovereign is committed the power of rewarding with riches, or honour; and of punishing with corporal, or pecuniary punishment, or with ignominy every subject according to the law he hath formerly made; or if there be no law made, according as he shall judge most to conduce to the encouraging

of men to serve the commonwealth, or deterring of them from doing disservice to the same.

Lastly, considering what values men are naturally apt to set upon themselves; what respect they look for from others; and how little they value other men; from whence continually arise amongst them, emulation, quarrels, factions, and at last war, to the destroying of one another, and diminution of their strength against a common enemy; it is necessary that there be laws of honour, and a public rate of the worth of such men as have deserved, or are able to deserve well of the commonwealth; and that there be force in the hands of some or other, to put those laws in execution. But it hath already been shown, that not only the whole *militia*, or forces of the commonwealth; but also the judicature of all controversies, is annexed to the sovereignty. To the sovereign therefore it belongeth also to give titles of honour; and to appoint what order of place, and dignity, each man shall hold; and what signs of respect, in public or private meetings, they shall give to one another.

These are the rights, which make the essence of sovereignty; and which are the marks, whereby a man may discern in what man, or assembly of men, the sovereign power is placed, and resideth. For these are incommunicable, and inseparable. The power to coin money; to dispose of the estate and persons of infant heirs; to have praeemption in markets; and all other statute prerogatives, may be transferred by the sovereign; and yet the power to protect his subjects be retained. But if he transfer the *militia*, he retains the judicature in vain, for want of execution of the laws: or if he grant away the power of raising money; the *militia* is in vain: or if he give away the government of doctrines, men will be frighted into rebellion with the fear of spirits. And so if we consider any one of the said rights, we shall presently see, that the holding of all the rest will produce no effect, in the conservation of peace and justice, the end for which all commonwealths are instituted. And this division is it, whereof it is said, *a kingdom divided in itself cannot stand*: for unless this division precede, division into opposite armies can never happen. If there had not first been an opinion received of the greatest part of England, that these powers were divided between the

King, and the Lords, and the House of Commons, the people had never been divided and fallen into this civil war; first between those that disagreed in politics; and after between the dissenters about the liberty of religion; which have so instructed men in this point of sovereign right, that there be few now (in *England*,) that do not see, that these rights are inseparable, and will be so generally acknowledged at the next return of peace; and so continue, till their miseries are forgotten; and no longer, except the vulgar be better taught than they have hitherto been.

And because they are essential and inseparable rights, it follows necessarily, that in whatsoever words any of them seem to be granted away, yet if the sovereign power itself be not in direct terms renounced, and the name of sovereign no more given by the grantees to him that grants them, the grant is void: for when he has granted all he can, if we grant back the sovereignty, all is restored, as inseparably annexed thereunto.

This great authority being indivisible, and inseparably annexed to the sovereignty, there is little ground for the opinion of them, that say of sovereign kings, though they be *singulis majores*, of greater power than every one of their subjects, yet they be *universis minores*, of less power than them all together. For if by *all together*, they mean not the collective body as one person, then *all together*, and *every one*, signify the same; and the speech is absurd. But if by *all together*, they understand them as one person, (which person the sovereign bears,) then the power of all together, is the same with the sovereign's power; and so again the speech is absurd: which absurdity they see well enough, when the sovereignty is in an assembly of the people; but in a monarch they see it not; and yet the power of sovereignty is the same in whomsoever it be placed.

And as the power, so also the honour of the sovereign, ought to be greater, than that of any, or all the subjects. For in the sovereignty is the fountain of honour. The dignities of lord, earl, duke, and prince are his creatures. As in the presence of the master, the servants are equal, and without any honour at all; so are the subjects, in the presence of the sovereign. And though they shine some more, some less, when they are out of his sight; yet in his presence, they shine no more than the stars in presence of the sun.

But a man may here object, that the condition of subjects is very miserable; as being obnoxious to the lusts, and other irregular passions of him, or them that have so unlimited a power in their hands. And commonly they that live under a monarch, think it the fault of monarchy; and they that live under the government of democracy, or other sovereign assembly, attribute all the inconvenience to that form of commonwealth; whereas the power in all forms, if they be perfect enough to protect them, is the same; not considering that the estate of man can never be without some incommodity or other; and that the greatest, that in any form of government can possibly happen to the people in general, is scarce sensible, in respect of the miseries, and horrible calamities, that accompany a civil war, or that dissolute condition of masterless men, without subjection to laws, and a coercive power to tie their hands from rapine and revenge: nor considering that the greatest pressure of sovereign governors, proceedeth not from any delight, or profit they can expect in the damage or weakening of their subjects, in whose vigour, consisteth their own strength and glory; but in the restiveness of themselves, that unwillingly contributing to their own defence, make it necessary for their governors to draw from them what they can in time of peace, that they may have means on any emergent occasion, or sudden need, to resist, or take advantage of their enemies. For all men are by nature provided of notable multiplying glasses, (that is their passions and self-love,) through which, every little payment appeareth a great grievance; but are destitute of those prospective glasses, (namely moral and civil science,) to see afar off the miseries that hang over them, and cannot without such payments be avoided.

CHAPTER 19: Of the Several Kinds of Commonwealth by Institution, and of Succession to the Sovereign Power

The difference of commonwealths, consisteth in the difference of the sovereign, or the person representative of all and every one of the multitude. And because the sovereignty is either in one man, or in an assembly of more than one; and into that assembly either every man hath right to enter, or not every one, but certain men distinguished from the rest; it is manifest, there can be but three kinds of commonwealth. For the representative must needs be one man, or more: and if more, then it is the assembly of all, or but of a part. When the representative is one man, then is the commonwealth a MONARCHY: when an assembly of all that will come together, then it is a DEMOC-RACY, or popular commonwealth: when an assembly of a part only, then it is called an ARISTOCRACY. Other kind of commonwealth there can be none: for either one, or more, or all, must have the sovereign power (which I have shown to be indivisible) entire.

There be other names of government, in the histories, and books of policy; as *tyranny*, and *oligarchy*: But they are not the names of other forms of government, but of the same forms misliked. For they that are discontented under *monarchy*, call it *tyranny*; and they that are displeased with *aristocracy*, call it *oligarchy*: so also, they which find themselves grieved under a *democracy*, call it *anarchy*, (which signifies want of government;) and yet I think no man believes, that want of government, is any new kind of government: nor by the same reason ought they to believe, that the government is of one kind, when they like it, and another, when they mislike it, or are oppressed by the governors.

It is manifest, that men who are in absolute liberty, may, if they please, give authority to one man, to represent them every one; as well as give such authority to any assembly of men whatsoever; and consequently may subject themselves, if they think good, to a monarch, as absolutely, as to any other representative. Therefore, where there is already erected a sovereign power, there can be no other representative of the same people, but only to certain particular ends, by the sovereign limited. For that were to erect two sovereigns; and every man to have his person represented by two actors, that by opposing one another, must needs divide that power, which (if men will live in peace) is indivisible; and thereby reduce the multitude into the condition of war, contrary to the end for which all sovereignty is instituted. And therefore as it is absurd, to think that a sovereign assembly, inviting the people of their dominion, to send up their deputies, with power to make known their advice, or desires, should therefore hold such deputies, rather than themselves, for the absolute representative of the people: so it is absurd also, to think the same in a monarchy. And I know not how this so manifest a truth, should of late be so little observed; that in a monarchy, he that had the sovereignty from a descent of 600 years, was alone called sovereign, had the title of Majesty from every one of his subjects, and was unquestionably taken by them for their king, was notwithstanding never considered as their representative; that name without contradiction passing for the title of those men, which at his command were sent up by the people to carry their petitions, and give him (if he permitted it) their advice. Which may serve as an admonition, for those that are the true, and absolute representative of a people, to instruct men in the nature of that office, and to take heed how they admit of any other general representation upon any occasion whatsoever, if they mean to discharge the trust committed to them.

The difference between these three kinds of commonwealth, consisteth not in the difference of power; but in the difference of convenience, or aptitude to produce the peace, and security of the people; for which end they were instituted. And to compare monarchy with the other two, we may observe; first, that whosoever beareth the person of the people, or is one of that assembly that bears it, beareth also his own natural person. And though he be careful in his politic person to procure the common interest; yet he is more, or no less careful to procure the private good of himself, his family, kindred and friends; and for the most part, if the public interest chance to cross the private, he prefers the private: for the passions of men, are commonly more potent than their reason. From whence it follows, that where the public and private interest are most closely united, there is the public most advanced. Now in monarchy, the private interest is the same with the public. The riches, power, and honour of a monarch arise only from the riches, strength and reputation of his subjects. For no king can be rich, nor glorious, nor secure, whose subjects are either poor, or contemptible, or too weak through want, or dissention, to maintain a war against their enemies: whereas in a democracy, or aristocracy, the public prosperity confers not so much to the private fortune of one that is corrupt, or ambitious, as doth many times a perfidious advice, a treacherous action, or a civil war.

Secondly, that a monarch receiveth counsel of whom, when, and where he pleaseth; and consequently may hear the opinion of men versed in the matter about which he deliberates, of what rank or quality soever, and as long before the time of action, and with as much secrecy, as he will. But when a sovereign assembly has need of counsel, none are admitted but such as have a right thereto from the beginning; which for the most part are of those who have been versed more in the acquisition of wealth than of knowledge; and are to give their advice in long discourses, which may, and do commonly excite men to action, but not govern them in it. For the *understanding* is by the flame of the passions, never enlightened, but dazzled: Nor is there any place, or time, wherein an assembly can receive counsel with secrecy, because of their own multitude.

Thirdly, that the resolutions of a monarch, are subject to no other inconstancy, than that of human nature; but in assemblies, besides that of nature, there ariseth an inconstancy from the number. For the absence of a few, that would have the resolution once taken, continue firm, (which may happen by security, negligence, or private impediments,) or the diligent appearance of a few of the contrary opinion, undoes to day, all that was concluded yesterday.

Fourthly, that a monarch cannot disagree with himself, out of envy, or interest; but an assembly may; and that to such a height, as may produce a civil war.

Fifthly, that in monarchy there is this inconvenience; that any subject, by the power of one man, for the enriching of a favourite or flatterer, may be deprived of all he possesseth; which I confess is a great and inevitable inconvenience. But the same may as well happen, where the sovereign power is in an assembly: for their power is the same; and they are as subject to evil counsel, and to be seduced by orators, as a monarch by flatterers; and becoming one another's flatterers, serve one another's covetousness and ambition by turns. And whereas the favourites of monarchs, are few, and they have none else to advance but their own kindred; the favourites of an assembly, are many; and the kindred much more numerous, than of any monarch. Besides, there is no favourite of a monarch, which cannot as well succour his friends, as hurt his enemies: but orators, that is to say, favourites of sovereign assemblies, though they have great power to hurt, have little to save. For to accuse, requires less eloquence (such is man's nature) than to excuse; and condemnation, than absolution more resembles justice.

Sixthly, that it is an inconvenience in monarchy, that the sovereignty may descend upon an infant, or one that cannot discern between good and evil: and consisteth in this, that the use of his power, must be in the hand of another man, or of some assembly of men, which are to govern by his right, and in his name; as curators, and protectors of his person, and authority. But to say there is inconvenience, in putting the use of the sovereign power, into the hand of a man, or an assembly of men; is to say that all government is more inconvenient, than confusion, and civil war. And therefore all the danger that can be pretended, must arise from the contention of those, that for an office of so great honour, and profit, may become competitors. To make it appear, that this inconvenience, proceedeth not from that form of government we call monarchy, we are to consider, that the precedent monarch, hath appointed who shall have the tuition of his infant successor, either expressly by testament, or tacitly, by not controlling the custom in that case received: and then such inconvenience, (if it happen) is to be attributed, not to the monarchy, but to the ambition, and injustice of the subjects; which in all kinds of government, where the people are not well instructed in their duty, and the rights of sovereignty, is the same. Or else the precedent monarch hath not at all taken order for such tuition; and then the law of nature hath provided this sufficient rule, that the tuition shall be in him, that hath by nature most interest in the preservation of the authority of the infant, and to whom least benefit can accrue by his death, or diminution. For seeing every man by nature seeketh his own benefit, and promotion; to put an infant into the power of those, that can promote themselves by his destruction, or damage, is not tuition, but treachery. So that sufficient provision being taken, against all just quarrel, about the government under a child, if any contention arise to the disturbance of the public peace, it is not to be attributed to the form of monarchy, but to the ambition of subjects, and ignorance of their duty. On the other side, there is no great commonwealth, the sovereignty whereof is in a great assembly, which is not, as to consultations of peace, and war, and making of laws, in the same condition, as if the government were in a child. For as a child wants the judgment to dissent from counsel given him, and is thereby necessitated to take the advice of them, or him, to whom he is committed: so an assembly wanteth the liberty, to dissent from the counsel of the major part, be it good, or bad. And as a child has need of a tutor, or protector, to preserve his person and authority: so also (in great commonwealths,) the sovereign assembly, in all great dangers and troubles, have need of *custodes libertatis*; that is of dictators, or protectors of their authority; which are as much as temporary monarchs; to whom for a time, they may commit the entire exercise of their power; and have (at the end of that time) been oftener deprived thereof, than infant kings, by their protectors, regents, or any other tutors.

Though the kinds of sovereignty be, as I have now shown, but three; that is to say, monarchy, where one man has it; or democracy, where the general assembly of subjects hath it; or aristocracy, where it is in an assembly of certain persons nominated, or otherwise distinguished from the rest: yet he that shall consider the particular commonwealths that have been, and are in the world, will not perhaps easily reduce them to three, and may thereby be inclined to think there be other forms, arising from these mingled together. As for example, elective kingdoms; where kings have the sovereign power put into their hands for a time; or kingdoms, wherein the king hath a power limited: which governments, are nevertheless by most writers called monarchy. Likewise if a popular, or aristocratical commonwealth, subdue an enemy's country, and

govern the same, by a president, procurator, or other magistrate; this may seem perhaps at first sight, to be a democratical, or aristocratical government. But it is not so. For elective kings, are not sovereigns, but ministers of the sovereign; nor limited kings sovereigns, but ministers of them that have the sovereign power: nor are those provinces which are in subjection to a democracy, or aristocracy of another commonwealth, democratically, or aristocratically governed, but monarchically.

And first, concerning an elective king, whose power is limited to his life, as it is in many places of Christendom at this day; or to certain years or months, as the dictator's power amongst the Romans; if he have right to appoint his successor, he is no more elective but hereditary. But if he have no power to elect his successor, then there is some other man, or assembly known, which after his decease may elect anew, or else the commonwealth dieth, and dissolveth with him, and returneth to the condition of war. If it be known who have the power to give the sovereignty after his death, it is known also that the sovereignty was in them before: for none have right to give that which they have not right to possess, and keep to themselves, if they think good. But if there be none that can give the sovereignty, after the decease of him that was first elected; then has he power, nay he is obliged by the law of nature, to provide, by establishing his successor, to keep those that had trusted him with the government, from relapsing into the miserable condition of civil war. And consequently he was, when elected, a sovereign absolute.

Secondly, that king whose power is limited, is not superior to him, or them that have the power to limit it; and he that is not superior, is not supreme; that is to say not sovereign. The sovereignty therefore was always in that assembly which had the right to limit him; and by consequence the government not monarchy, but either democracy, or aristocracy; as of old time in *Sparta*; where the kings had a privilege to lead their armies; but the sovereignty was in the *Ephori*.

Thirdly, whereas heretofore the Roman people governed the land of *Judea* (for example) by a president; yet was not *Judea* therefore a democracy; because they were not governed by any assembly, into the which, any of them, had right to enter; nor by an aristocracy; because they were not governed by any assembly, into which, any man could enter by their election: but they were governed by one person, which though as to the people of *Rome* was an assembly of the people, or democracy; yet as to people of *Judea,* which had no right at all of participating in the government, was a monarch. For though where the people are governed by an assembly, chosen by themselves out of their own number, the government is called a democracy, or aristocracy; yet when they are governed by an assembly, not of their own choosing, it is a monarchy; not of *one* man, over another man; but of one people, over another people.

Of all these forms of government, the matter being mortal, so that not only monarchs, but also whole assemblies die, it is necessary for the conservation of the peace of men, that as there was order taken for an artificial man, so there be order also taken, for an artificial eternity of life; without which, men that are governed by an assembly, should return into the condition of war in every age; and they that are governed by one man, as soon as their governor dieth. This artificial eternity, is that which men call the right of *succession.*

There is no perfect form of government, where the disposing of the succession is not in the present sovereign. For if it be in any other particular man, or private assembly, it is in a person subject, and may be assumed by the sovereign at his pleasure; and consequently the right is in himself. And if it be in no particular man, but left to a new choice; then is the commonwealth dissolved; and the right is in him that can get it; contrary to the intention of them that did institute the commonwealth, for their perpetual, and not temporary security.

In a democracy, the whole assembly cannot fail, unless the multitude that are to be governed fail. And therefore questions of the right of succession, have in that form of government no place at all.

In an aristocracy, when any of the assembly dieth, the election of another into his room belongeth to the assembly, as the sovereign, to whom belongeth the choosing of all counsellors and officers. For that which the representative doth, as actor, every one of the subjects doth, as author. And though the sovereign assembly may give power to others, to elect new men, for supply of their court; yet it is still by their authority, that the election is made; and by the same it may (when the public shall require it) be recalled.

The greatest difficulty about the right of succession, is in monarchy: and the difficulty ariseth from this, that at first sight, it is not manifest who is to appoint the successor; nor many times, who it is whom he hath appointed. For in both these cases, there is required a more exact ratiocination, than every man is accustomed to use. As to the question, who shall appoint the successor, of a monarch that hath the sovereign authority; that is to say, who shall determine of the right of inheritance, (for elective kings and princes have not the sovereign power in propriety, but in use only,) we are to consider, that either he that is in possession, has right to dispose of the succession, or else that right is again in the dissolved multitude. For the death of him that hath the sovereign power in propriety, leaves the multitude without any sovereign at all; that is, without any representative in whom they should be united, and be capable of doing any one action at all: and therefore they are incapable of election of any new monarch; every man having equal right to submit himself to such as he thinks best able to protect him; or if he can, protect himself by his own sword, which is a return to confusion, and to the condition of a war of every man against every man, contrary to the end for which monarchy had its first institution. Therefore it is manifest, that by the institution of monarchy, the disposing of the successor, is always left to the judgment and will of the present possessor.

And for the question (which may arise sometimes) who it is that the monarch in possession, hath designed to the succession and inheritance of his power; it is determined by his express words, and testament; or by other tacit signs sufficient.

By express words, or testament, when it is declared by him in his lifetime, *viva voce,* or by writing; as the first emperors of *Rome* declared who should be their heirs. For the word heir does not of itself imply the children, or nearest kindred of a man; but whomsoever a man shall any way declare, he would have to succeed him in his estate. If therefore a monarch declare expressly, that such a man shall be his heir, either by word or writing, then is that man immediately after the decease of his predecessor, invested in the right of being monarch.

But where testament, and express words are wanting, other natural signs of the will are to be followed: whereof the one is custom. And therefore where the custom is, that the next of kindred absolutely succeedeth, there also the next of kindred hath right to the succession; for that, if the will of him that was in possession had been otherwise, he might easily have declared the same in his life time. And likewise where the custom is, that the next of the male kindred succeedeth, there also the right of succession is in the next of the kindred male, for the same reason. And so it is if the custom were to advance the female. For whatsoever custom a man may by a word control, and does not, it is a natural sign he would have that custom stand.

But where neither custom, nor testament hath preceded, there it is to be understood, first, that a monarch's will is, that the government remain monarchical; because he hath approved that government in himself. Secondly, that a child of his own, male, or female, be preferred before any other; because men are presumed to be more inclined by nature, to advance their own children, than the children of other men; and of their own, rather a male than a female; because men, are naturally fitter than women, for actions of labour and danger. Thirdly, where his own issue faileth, rather a brother than a stranger; and so still the nearer in blood, rather than the more remote; because it is always presumed that the nearer of kin, is the nearer in affection; and it is evident that a man receives always, by reflection, the most honour from the greatness of his nearest kindred.

But if it be lawful for a monarch to dispose of the succession by words of contract, or testament, men may perhaps object a great inconvenience: for he may sell, or give his right of governing to a stranger; which, because strangers (that is, men not used to live under the same government, nor speaking the same language) do commonly undervalue one another, may turn to the oppression of his subjects;

which is indeed a great inconvenience: but it proceedeth not necessarily from the subjection to a stranger's government, but from the unskilfulness of the governors, ignorant of the true rules of politics. And therefore the Romans when they had subdued many nations, to make their government digestible, were wont to take away that grievance, as much as they thought necessary, by giving sometimes to whole nations, and sometimes to principal men of every nation they conquered, not only the privileges, but also the name of Romans; and took many of them into the senate, and offices of charge, even in the Roman city. And this was it our most wise king, king *James*, aimed at, in endeavouring the union of his two realms of *England* and *Scotland*. Which if he could have obtained, had in all likelihood prevented the civil wars, which make both those kingdoms, at this present, miserable. It is not therefore any injury to the people, for a monarch to dispose of the succession by will; though by the fault of many princes, it hath been sometimes found inconvenient. Of the lawfulness of it, this also is an argument, that whatsoever inconvenience can arrive by giving a kingdom to a stranger, may arrive also by so marrying with strangers, as the right of succession may descend upon them: yet this by all men is accounted lawful.

CHAPTER 20: Of Dominion Paternal, and Despotical

A *commonwealth by acquisition*, is that, where the sovereign power is acquired by force; and it is acquired by force, when men singly, or many together by plurality of voices, for fear of death, or bonds, do authorize all the actions of that man, or assembly, that hath their lives and liberty in his power.

And this kind of dominion, or sovereignty, differeth from sovereignty by institution, only in this, that men who choose their sovereign, do it for fear of one another, and not of him whom they institute: but in this case, they subject themselves, to him they are afraid of. In both cases they do it for fear: which is to be noted by them, that hold all such covenants, as proceed from fear of death, or violence, void: which if it were true, no man, in any kind of commonwealth, could be obliged to obedience. It is true, that in a commonwealth once instituted, or acquired, promises proceeding from fear of death or violence, are no covenants, nor obliging, when the thing promised is contrary to the laws; but the reason is not, because it was made upon fear, but because he that promiseth, hath no right in the thing promised. Also, when he may lawfully perform, and doth not, it is not the invalidity of the covenant, that absolveth him, but the sentence of the sovereign. Otherwise, whensoever a man lawfully promiseth, he unlawfully breaketh: but when the sovereign, who is the actor, acquitteth him, then he is acquitted by him that extorted the promise, as by the author of such absolution.

But the rights, and consequences of sovereignty, are the same in both. His power cannot, without his consent, be transferred to another: he cannot forfeit it: he cannot be accused by any of his subjects, of injury: he cannot be punished by them: he is judge of what is necessary for peace; and judge of doctrines: he is sole legislator; and supreme judge of controversies; and of the times, and occasions of war, and peace: to him it belongeth to choose magistrates, counsellors, commanders, and all other officers, and ministers; and to determine of rewards, and punishments, honour, and order. The reasons whereof, are the same which are alleged in the precedent chapter, for the same rights, and consequences of sovereignty by institution.

Dominion is acquired two ways; by generation, and by conquest. The right of dominion by generation, is that, which the parent hath over his children; and is called PATERNAL. And is not so derived from the generation, as if therefore the parent had dominion over his child because he begat him; but from the child's consent, either express, or by other sufficient arguments declared. For as to the generation, God hath ordained to man a helper; and there be always two that are equally parents: the dominion therefore over the child, should belong equally to both; and he be equally subject to both, which is impossible; for no man can obey two masters. And whereas some have attributed the dominion to the man only, as being of the more excellent sex; they misreckon in

it. For there is not always that difference of strength, or prudence between the man and the woman, as that the right can be determined without war. In commonwealths, this controversy is decided by the civil law: and for the most part, (but not always) the sentence is in favour of the father; because for the most part commonwealths have been erected by the fathers, not by the mothers of families. But the question lieth now in the state of mere nature; where there are supposed no laws of matrimony; no laws for the education of children; but the law of nature, and the natural inclination of the sexes, one to another, and to their children. In this condition of mere nature, either the parents between themselves dispose of the dominion over the child by contract; or do not dispose thereof at all. If they dispose thereof, the right passeth according to the contract. We find in history that the *Amazons* contracted with the men of the neighbouring countries, to whom they had recourse for issue, that the issue male should be sent back, but the female remain with themselves: so that the dominion of the females was in the mother.

If there be no contract, the dominion is in the mother. For in the condition of mere nature, where there are no matrimonial laws, it cannot be known who is the father, unless it be declared by the mother: and therefore the right of dominion over the child dependeth on her will, and is consequently hers. Again, seeing the infant is first in the power of the mother, so as she may either nourish, or expose it; if she nourish it, it oweth its life to the mother; and is therefore obliged to obey her, rather than any other; and by consequence the dominion over it is hers. But if she expose it, and another find and nourish it, the dominion is in him that nourisheth it. For it ought to obey him by whom it is preserved; because preservation of life being the end, for which one man becomes subject to another, every man is supposed to promise obedience, to him, in whose power it is to save, or destroy him.

If the mother be the father's subject, the child, is in the father's power: and if the father be the mother's subject, (as when a sovereign queen marrieth one of her subjects,) the child is subject to the mother; because the father also is her subject.

If a man and woman, monarchs of two several kingdoms, have a child, and contract concerning who shall have the dominion of him, the right of the dominion passeth by the contract. If they contract not, the dominion followeth the dominion of the place of his residence. For the sovereign of each country hath dominion over all that reside therein.

He that hath the dominion over the child, hath dominion also over the children of the child; and over their children's children. For he that hath dominion over the person of a man, hath dominion over all that is his; without which, dominion were but a title, without the effect.

The right of succession to paternal dominion, proceedeth in the same manner, as doth the right of succession to monarchy; of which I have already sufficiently spoken in the precedent chapter.

Dominion acquired by conquest, or victory in war, is that which some writers call DESPOTICAL, from Δεσπότης, which signifieth a *lord*, or *master*; and is the dominion of the master over his servant. And this dominion is then acquired to the victor, when the vanquished, to avoid the present stroke of death, covenanteth either in express words, or by other sufficient signs of the will, that so long as his life, and the liberty of his body is allowed him, the victor shall have the use thereof, at his pleasure. And after such covenant made, the vanquished is a SERVANT, and not before: for by the word *servant*, (whether it be derived from *servire*, to serve, or from *servare*, to save, which I leave to grammarians to dispute) is not meant a captive, which is kept in prison, or bonds, till the owner of him that took him, or bought him of one that did, shall consider what to do with him: (for such men, (commonly called slaves,) have no obligation at all; but may break their bonds, or the prison; and kill, or carry away captive their master, justly:) but one, that being taken, hath corporal liberty allowed him; and upon promise not to run away, nor to do violence to his master, is trusted by him.

It is not therefore the victory, that giveth the right of dominion over the vanquished, but his own covenant. Nor is he obliged because he is conquered; that is to say, beaten, and taken, or put to flight; but because he cometh in, and submitteth to the victor; nor is

the victor obliged by an enemy's rendering himself, (without promise of life,) to spare him for this his yielding to discretion; which obliges not the victor longer, than in his own discretion he shall think fit.

And that which men do, when they demand (as it is now called) *quarter*, (which the Greeks called Ζωγρία, *taking alive*,) is to evade the present fury of the victor, by submission, and to compound for their life, with ransom, or service: and therefore he that hath quarter, hath not his life given, but deferred till farther deliberation; for it is not an yielding on condition of life, but to discretion. And then only is his life in security, and his service due, when the victor hath trusted him with his corporal liberty. For slaves that work in prisons, or fetters, do it not of duty, but to avoid the cruelty of their task-masters.

The master of the servant, is master also of all he hath; and may exact the use thereof; that is to say, of his goods, of his labour, of his servants, and of his children, as often as he shall think fit. For he holdeth his life of his master, by the covenant of obedience; that is, of owning, and authorizing whatsoever the master shall do. And in case the master, if he refuse, kill him, or cast him into bonds, or otherwise punish him for his disobedience, he is himself the author of the same; and cannot accuse him of injury.

In sum, the rights and consequences of both *paternal* and *despotical* dominion, are the very same with those of a sovereign by institution; and for the same reasons: which reasons are set down in the precedent chapter. So that for a man that is monarch of divers nations, whereof he hath, in one the sovereignty by institution of the people assembled, and in another by conquest, that is by the submission of each particular, to avoid death or bonds; to demand of one nation more than of the other, from the title of conquest, as being a conquered nation, is an act of ignorance of the rights of sovereignty. For the sovereign is absolute over both alike; or else there is no sovereignty at all; and so every man may lawfully protect himself, if he can, with his own sword, which is the condition of war.

By this it appears; that a great family if it be not part of some commonwealth, is of itself, as to the rights of sovereignty, a little monarchy; whether that family consist of a man and his children; or of a man and his servants; or of a man, and his children, and servants together: wherein the father or master is the sovereign. But yet a family is not properly a commonwealth; unless it be of that power by its own number, or by other opportunities, as not to be subdued without the hazard of war. For where a number of men are manifestly too weak to defend themselves united, every one may use his own reason in time of danger, to save his own life, either by flight, or by submission to the enemy, as he shall think best; in the same manner as a very small company of soldiers, surprised by an army, may cast down their arms, and demand quarter, or run away, rather than be put to the sword. And thus much shall suffice; concerning what I find by speculation, and deduction, of sovereign rights, from the nature, need, and designs of men, in erecting of commonwealths, and putting themselves under monarchs, or assemblies, entrusted with power enough for their protection.

Let us now consider what the Scripture teacheth in the same point. To Moses, the children of *Israel* say thus: *Speak thou to us, and we will hear thee; but let not God speak to us, lest we die.* (Exod. 20. 19.) This is absolute obedience to Moses. Concerning the right of kings, God himself by the mouth of Samuel, saith, (1 *Sam.* 8. 11, 12, &c.) *This shall be the right of the king you will have to reign over you. He shall take your sons, and set them to drive his chariots, and to be his horsemen, and to run before his chariots; and gather in his harvest; and to make his engines of war, and instruments of his chariots; and shall take your daughters to make perfumes, to be his cooks, and bakers. He shall take your fields, your vine-yards, and your olive-yards, and give them to his servants. He shall take the tithe of your corn and wine, and give it to the men of his chamber, and to his other servants. He shall take your man-servants, and your maid-servants, and the choice of your youth, and employ them in his business. He shall take the tithe of your flocks; and you shall be his servants.* This is absolute power, and summed up in the last words, *you shall be his servants.* Again, when the people heard what power their king was to have, yet they consented thereto, and say thus, (*verse* 19) *we will be as all other nations, and our king*

shall judge our causes, and go before us, to conduct our wars. Here is confirmed the right that sovereigns have, both to the *militia*, and to all *judicature*; in which is contained as absolute power, as one man can possibly transfer to another. Again, the prayer of king Solomon to God, was this (1 *Kings*, 3. 9): *Give to thy servant understanding, to judge thy people, and to discern between good and evil.* It belongeth therefore to the sovereign to be judge, and to prescribe the rules of *discerning good* and *evil*: which rules are laws; and therefore in him is the legislative power. Saul sought the life of *David*; yet when it was in his power to slay *Saul*, and his servants would have done it, *David* forbad them, saying, (1 *Sam.* 24. 9) *God forbid I should do such an act against my Lord, the anointed of God.* For obedience of servants St. *Paul* saith; (*Col.* 3. 20) *Servants obey your masters in all things*; and, (*Verse* 22) *children obey your parents in all things.* There is simple obedience in those that are subject to paternal, or despotical dominion. Again, (*Matt.* 23. 2, 3) *The Scribes and Pharisees sit in Moses' chair, and therefore all that they shall bid you observe, that observe and do.* There again is simple obedience. And St. *Paul*, (*Titus* 3. 2) *Warn them that they subject themselves to princes, and to those that are in authority, and obey them.* This obedience is also simple. Lastly, our Saviour himself acknowledges, that men ought to pay such taxes as are by kings imposed, where he says, *Give to Caesar that which is Caesar's*; and paid such taxes himself. And that the king's word, is sufficient to take any thing from any subject, when there is need; and that the king is judge of that need: for he himself, as king of the Jews, commanded his disciples to take the ass, and ass's colt to carry him into Jerusalem, saying, (*Matth.* 21. 2, 3) *Go into the village over against you, and you shall find a she ass tied, and her colt with her, untie them, and bring them to me. And if any man ask you, what you mean by it, say the Lord hath need of them: and they will let them go.* They will not ask whether his necessity be a sufficient title; nor whether he be judge of that necessity; but acquiesce in the will of the Lord.

To these places may be added also that of *Genesis*, (*Genesis* 3. 5) *Ye shall be as gods, knowing good and evil.* And *verse* 11. *Who told thee that thou wast naked?*

hast thou eaten of the tree, of which I commanded thee thou shouldest not eat? For the cognizance or judicature of good and evil, being forbidden by the name of the fruit of the tree of knowledge, as a trial of *Adam's* obedience; the devil to inflame the ambition of the woman, to whom that fruit already seemed beautiful, told her that by tasting it, they should be as gods, knowing *good* and *evil.* Whereupon having both eaten, they did indeed take upon them God's office, which is judicature of good and evil; but acquired no new ability to distinguish between them aright. And whereas it is said, that having eaten, they saw they were naked; no man hath so interpreted that place, as if they had been formerly blind, and saw not their own skins: the meaning is plain, that it was then they first judged their nakedness (wherein it was God's will to create them) to be uncomely; and by being ashamed, did tacitly censure God himself. And thereupon God saith, *Hast thou eaten, &c.* as if he should say, doest thou that owest me obedience, take upon thee to judge of my commandments? Whereby it is clearly, (though allegorically,) signified, that the commands of them that have the right to command, are not by their subjects to be censured, nor disputed.

So that it appeareth plainly, to my understanding, both from reason, and Scripture, that the sovereign power, whether placed in one man, as in monarchy, or in one assembly of men, as in popular, and aristocratical commonwealths, is as great, as possibly men can be imagined to make it. And though of so unlimited a power, men may fancy many evil consequences, yet the consequences of the want of it, which is perpetual war of every man against his neighbour, are much worse. The condition of man in this life shall never be without inconveniences; but there happeneth in no commonwealth any great inconvenience, but what proceeds from the subject's disobedience, and breach of those covenants, from which the commonwealth hath its being. And whosoever thinking sovereign power too great, will seek to make it less, must subject himself, to the power, that can limit it; that is to say, to a greater.

The greatest objection is, that of the practice; when men ask, where, and when, such power has by subjects been acknowledged. But one may ask them again, when, or where has there been a kingdom long free from sedition and civil war. In those nations, whose commonwealths have been long-lived, and not been destroyed but by foreign war, the subjects never did dispute of the sovereign power. But howsoever, an argument from the practice of men, that have not sifted to the bottom, and with exact reason weighed the causes, and nature of commonwealths, and suffer daily those miseries, that proceed from the ignorance thereof, is invalid. For though in all places of the world, men should lay the foundation of their houses on the sand, it could not thence be inferred, that so it ought to be. The skill of making, and maintaining commonwealths, consisteth in certain rules, as doth arithmetic and geometry; not (as tennis-play) on practice only: which rules, neither poor men have the leisure, nor men that have had the leisure, have hitherto had the curiosity, or the method to find out.

CHAPTER 21: Of the Liberty of Subjects

LIBERTY, or FREEDOM, signifieth (properly) the absence of opposition; (by opposition, I mean external impediments of motion;) and may be applied no less to irrational, and inanimate creatures, than to rational. For whatsoever is so tied, or environed, as it cannot move, but within a certain space, which space is determined by the opposition of some external body, we say it hath not liberty to go further. And so of all living creatures, whilst they are imprisoned, or restrained, with walls, or chains; and of the water whilst it is kept in by banks, or vessels, that otherwise would spread itself into a larger space, we use to say, they are not at liberty, to move in such manner, as without those external impediments they would. But when the impediment of motion, is in the constitution of the thing itself, we use not to say, it wants the liberty; but the power to move; as when a stone lieth still, or a man is fastened to his bed by sickness.

And according to this proper, and generally received meaning of the word, *a* FREEMAN, *is he, that in those things, which by his strength and wit he is able to do, is not hindered to do what he has a will to.* But when the words *free,* and *liberty,* are applied to any thing but *bodies,* they are abused; for that which is not subject to motion, is not subject to impediment: and therefore, when it is said (for example) the way is free, no liberty of the way is signified, but of those that walk in it without stop. And when we say a gift is free, there is not meant any liberty of the gift, but of the giver, that was not bound by any law, or covenant to give it. So when we *speak freely*, it is not the liberty of voice, or pronunciation, but of the man, whom no law hath obliged to speak otherwise than he did. Lastly, from the use of the word *free-will*, no liberty can be inferred of the will, desire, or inclination, but the liberty of the man; which consisteth in this, that he finds no stop, in doing what he has the will, desire, or inclination to do.

Fear, and liberty are consistent; as when a man throweth his goods into the sea for *fear* the ship should sink, he doth it nevertheless very willingly, and may refuse to do it if he will: it is therefore the action of one that was *free*: so a man sometimes pays his debt, only for *fear* of imprisonment, which because nobody hindered him from detaining, was the action of a man at *liberty*. And generally all actions which men do in commonwealths, for *fear* of the law, are actions, which the doers had *liberty* to omit.

Liberty, and *necessity* are consistent: as in the water, that hath not only *liberty*, but a *necessity* of descending by the channel; so likewise in the actions which men voluntarily do: which, because they proceed from their will, proceed from *liberty*; and yet, because every act of man's will, and every desire, and inclination proceedeth from some cause, and that from another cause, in a continual chain, (whose first link is in the hand of God the first of all causes,) they proceed from *necessity*. So that to him that could see the connexion of those causes, the *necessity* of all men's voluntary actions, would appear manifest. And therefore God, that seeth, and disposeth all things, seeth also that the *liberty* of man in doing what he will, is accompanied with the *necessity* of doing that which God will, and no more, nor less. For though men may do many things, which God does not command, nor is therefore author of them; yet they can have no passion, nor appetite to any thing, of which appetite God's will is not the cause. And did not his will assure the *necessity* of man's will, and consequently of all

that on man's will dependeth, the *liberty* of men would be a contradiction, and impediment to the omnipotence and *liberty* of God. And this shall suffice, (as to the matter in hand) of that natural *liberty*, which only is properly called *liberty*.

But as men, for the attaining of peace, and conservation of themselves thereby, have made an artificial man, which we call a commonwealth; so also have they made artificial chains, called *civil laws*, which they themselves, by mutual covenants, have fastened at one end, to the lips of that man, or assembly, to whom they have given the sovereign power; and at the other end to their own ears. These bonds in their own nature but weak, may nevertheless be made to hold, by the danger, though not by the difficulty of breaking them.

In relation to these bonds only it is, that I am to speak now, of the *liberty* of *subjects*. For seeing there is no commonwealth in the world, wherein there be rules enough set down, for the regulating of all the actions, and words of men, (as being a thing impossible:) it followeth necessarily, that in all kinds of actions, by the laws praetermitted, men have the liberty, of doing what their own reasons shall suggest, for the most profitable to themselves. For if we take liberty in the proper sense, for corporal liberty; that is to say, freedom from chains, and prison, it were very absurd for men to clamour as they do, for the liberty they so manifestly enjoy. Again, if we take liberty, for an exemption from laws, it is no less absurd, for men to demand as they do, that liberty, by which all other men may be masters of their lives. And yet as absurd as it is, this is it they demand; not knowing that the laws are of no power to protect them, without a sword in the hands of a man, or men, to cause those laws to be put in execution. The liberty of a subject, lieth therefore only in those things, which in regulating their actions, the sovereign hath praetermitted: such as is the liberty to buy, and sell, and otherwise contract with one another; to choose their own abode, their own diet, their own trade of life, and institute their children as they themselves think fit; and the like.

Nevertheless we are not to understand, that by such liberty, the sovereign power of life and death, is either abolished, or limited. For it has been already shown, that nothing the sovereign representative can do to a subject, on what pretence soever, can properly be called injustice, or injury; because every subject is author of every act the sovereign doth; so that he never wanteth right to any thing, otherwise, than as he himself is the subject of God, and bound thereby to observe the laws of nature. And therefore it may, and doth often happen in commonwealths, that a subject may be put to death, by the command of the sovereign power; and yet neither do the other wrong: as when *Jephtha* caused his daughter to be sacrificed: in which, and the like cases, he that so dieth, had liberty to do the action, for which he is nevertheless, without injury put to death. And the same holdeth also in a sovereign prince, that putteth to death an innocent subject. For though the action be against the law of nature, as being contrary to equity, (as was the killing of *Uriah*, by *David*;) yet it was not an injury to *Uriah*; but to *God*. Not to *Uriah*, because the right to do what he pleased, was given him by *Uriah* himself: and yet to *God*, because *David* was *God's* subject; and prohibited all iniquity by the law of nature. Which distinction, *David* himself, when he repented the fact, evidently confirmed, saying, *To thee only have I sinned*. In the same manner, the people of *Athens*, when they banished the most potent of their commonwealth for ten years, thought they committed no injustice; and yet they never questioned what crime he had done; but what hurt he would do: nay they commanded the banishment of they knew not whom; and every citizen bringing his oystershell into the market place, written with the name of him he desired should be banished, without actual accusing him, sometimes banished an *Aristides*, for his reputation of justice; and sometimes a scurrilous jester, as *Hyperbolus*, to make a jest of it. And yet a man cannot say, the sovereign people of *Athens* wanted right to banish them; or an *Athenian* the liberty to jest, or to be just.

The liberty, whereof there is so frequent and honourable mention, in the histories, and philosophy of the ancient Greeks, and Romans, and in the writings, and discourse of those that from them have received all their learning in the politics, is not the liberty of particular men; but the liberty of the commonwealth:

which is the same with that, which every man then should have, if there were no civil laws, nor commonwealth at all. And the effects of it also be the same. For as amongst masterless men, there is perpetual war, of every man against his neighbour; no inheritance, to transmit to the son, nor to expect from the father; no propriety of goods, or lands; no security; but a full and absolute liberty in every particular man: so in states, and commonwealths not dependent on one another, every commonwealth, (not every man) has an absolute liberty, to do what it shall judge (that is to say, what that man, or assembly that representeth it, shall judge) most conducing to their benefit. But withal, they live in the condition of a perpetual war, and upon the confines of battle, with their frontiers armed, and cannons planted against their neighbours round about. The *Athenians*, and *Romans* were free; that is, free commonwealths: not that any particular men had the liberty to resist their own representative; but that their representative had the liberty to resist, or invade other people. There is written on the turrets of the city of *Lucca* in great characters at this day, the word LIBERTAS; yet no man can thence infer, that a particular man has more liberty, or immunity from the service of the commonwealth there, than in *Constantinople*. Whether a commonwealth be monarchical, or popular, the freedom is still the same.

But it is an easy thing, for men to be deceived, by the specious name of *liberty*, and for want of judgment to distinguish, mistake that for their private inheritance, and birth right, which is the right of the public only. And when the same error is confirmed by the authority of men in reputation for their writings in this subject, it is no wonder if it produce sedition, and change of government. In these western parts of the world, we are made to receive our opinions concerning the institution, and rights of commonwealths, from *Aristotle*, *Cicero*, and other men, Greeks and Romans, that living under popular states, derived those rights, not from the principles of nature, but transcribed them into their books, out of the practice of their own commonwealths, which were popular; as the grammarians describe the rules of language, out of the practice of the time; or the rules of poetry, out of the poems of *Homer* and *Virgil*. And because the Athenians were taught, (to keep them from desire of changing their government,) that they were free-men, and all that lived under monarchy were slaves; therefore Aristotle puts it down in his *Politics, (lib. 6. cap. 2.) In democracy,* Liberty *is to be supposed: for it is commonly held, that no man is* Free *in any other government.* And as Aristotle; so Cicero, and other writers have grounded their civil doctrine, on the opinions of the Romans, who were taught to hate monarchy, at first, by them that having deposed their sovereign, shared amongst them the sovereignty of *Rome*; and afterwards by their successors. And by reading of these Greek, and Latin authors, men from their childhood have gotten a habit (under a false show of liberty,) of favouring tumults, and of licentious controlling the actions of their sovereigns; and again of controlling those controllers, with the effusion of so much blood; as I think I may truly say, there was never any thing so dearly bought, as these western parts have bought the learning of the Greek and Latin tongues.

To come now to the particulars of the true liberty of a subject; that is to say, what are the things, which though commanded by the sovereign, he may nevertheless, without injustice, refuse to do; we are to consider, what rights we pass away, when we make a commonwealth; or (which is all one,) what liberty we deny ourselves, by owning all the actions (without exception) of the man, or assembly we make our sovereign. For in the act of our *submission*, consisteth both our *obligation*, and our *liberty*; which must therefore be inferred by arguments taken from thence; there being no obligation on any man, which ariseth not from some act of his own; for all men equally, are by nature free. And because such arguments, must either be drawn from the express words, *I authorise all his actions*, or from the intention of him that submitteth himself to his power, (which intention is to be understood by the end for which he so submitteth;) the obligation, and liberty of the subject, is to be derived, either from those words, (or others equivalent;) or else from the end of the institution of sovereignty, namely, the peace of the subjects within themselves, and their defence against a common enemy.

First therefore, seeing sovereignty by institution, is by covenant of every one to every one; and sovereignty by acquisition, by covenants of the vanquished to the victor, or child to the parent; it is manifest, that every subject has liberty in all those things, the right whereof cannot by covenant be transferred. I have shewn before in the 14th chapter, that covenants, not to defend a man's own body, are void. Therefore,

If the sovereign command a man (though justly condemned,) to kill, wound, or maim himself; or not to resist those that assault him; or to abstain from the use of food, air, medicine, or any other thing, without which he cannot live; yet hath that man the liberty to disobey.

If a man be interrogated by the sovereign, or his authority, concerning a crime done by himself, he is not bound (without assurance of pardon) to confess it; because no man (as I have shown in the same chapter) can be obliged by covenant to accuse himself.

Again, the consent of a subject to sovereign power, is contained in these words, *I authorize, or take upon me, all his actions*; in which there is no restriction at all, of his own former natural liberty: for by allowing him to *kill me*, I am not bound to kill myself when he commands me. It is one thing to say, *kill me, or my fellow, if you please*; another thing to say, *I will kill myself, or my fellow*. It followeth therefore, that

No man is bound by the words themselves, either to kill himself, or any other man; and consequently, that the obligation a man may sometimes have, upon the command of the sovereign to execute any dangerous, or dishonourable office, dependeth not on the words of our submission; but on the intention, which is to be understood by the end thereof. When therefore our refusal to obey, frustrates the end for which the sovereignty was ordained; then there is no liberty to refuse: otherwise there is.

Upon this ground, a man that is commanded as a soldier to fight against the enemy, though his sovereign have right enough to punish his refusal with death, may nevertheless in many cases refuse, without injustice; as when he substituteth a sufficient soldier in his place: for in this case he deserteth not the service of the commonwealth. And there is allowance to be made for natural timorousness; not only to women, (of whom no such dangerous duty is expected,) but also to men of feminine courage. When armies fight, there is on one side, or both, a running away; yet when they do it not out of treachery, but fear, they are not esteemed to do it unjustly, but dishonourably. For the same reason, to avoid battle, is not injustice, but cowardice. But he that inrolleth himself a soldier, or taketh imprest money, taketh away the excuse of a timorous nature; and is obliged, not only to go to the battle, but also not to run from it, without his captain's leave. And when the defence of the commonwealth, requireth at once the help of all that are able to bear arms, every one is obliged; because otherwise the institution of the commonwealth, which they have not the purpose, or courage to preserve, was in vain.

To resist the sword of the commonwealth, in defence of another man, guilty, or innocent, no man hath liberty; because such liberty, takes away from the sovereign, the means of protecting us; and is therefore destructive of the very essence of government. But in case a great many men together, have already resisted the sovereign power unjustly, or committed some capital crime, for which every one of them expecteth death, whether have they not the liberty then to join together, and assist, and defend one another? Certainly they have: for they but defend their lives, which the guilty man may as well do, as the innocent. There was indeed injustice in the first breach of their duty; their bearing of arms subsequent to it, though it be to maintain what they have done, is no new unjust act. And if it be only to defend their persons, it is not unjust at all. But the offer of pardon taketh from them, to whom it is offered, the plea of self-defence, and maketh their perseverance in assisting, or defending the rest, unlawful.

As for other liberties, they depend on the silence of the law. In cases where the sovereign has prescribed no rule, there the subject hath the liberty to do, or forbear, according to his own discretion. And therefore such liberty is in some places more, and in some less; and in some times more, in other times less, according as they that have the sovereignty shall think most convenient. As for example, there was a time, when in *England* a man might enter into his own land, (and dispossess such as wrongfully possessed it,) by force. But in aftertimes, that liberty of forcible entry, was taken away by a statute made (by the king,) in parliament. And in some places of the world, men have the liberty of many wives: in other places, such liberty is not allowed.

If a subject have a controversy with his sovereign, of debt, or of right of possession of lands or goods, or concerning any service required at his hands, or concerning any penalty, corporal, or pecuniary, grounded on a precedent law; he hath the same liberty to sue for his right, as if it were against a subject; and before such judges, as are appointed by the sovereign. For seeing the sovereign demandeth by force of a former law, and not by virtue of his power; he declareth thereby, that he requireth no more, than shall appear to be due by that law. The suit therefore is not contrary to the will of the sovereign; and consequently the subject hath the liberty to demand the hearing of his cause; and sentence, according to that law. But if he demand, or take any thing by pretence of his power; there lieth, in that case, no action of law: for all that is done by him in virtue of his power, is done by the authority of every subject, and consequently, he that brings an action against the sovereign, brings it against himself.

If a monarch, or sovereign assembly, grant a liberty to all, or any of his subjects, which grant standing, he is disabled to provide for their safety, the grant is void; unless he directly renounce, or transfer the sovereignty to another. For in that he might openly, (if it had been his will,) and in plain terms, have renounced, or transferred it, and did not; it is to be understood it was not his will; but that the grant proceeded from ignorance of the repugnancy between such a liberty and the sovereign power: and therefore the sovereignty is still retained; and consequently all those powers, which are necessary to the exercising thereof; such as are the power of war, and peace, of judicature, of appointing officers, and councillors, of levying money, and the rest named in the 18th chapter.

The obligation of subjects to the sovereign, is understood to last as long, and no longer, than the power lasteth, by which he is able to protect them. For the right men have by nature to protect themselves, when none else can protect them, can by no covenant be relinquished. The sovereignty is the soul of the commonwealth; which once departed from the body, the members do no more receive their motion from it. The end of obedience is protection; which, wheresoever a man seeth it, either in his own, or in another's sword, nature applieth his obedience to it, and his endeavour to maintain it. And though sovereignty, in the intention of them that make it, be immortal; yet is it in its own nature, not only subject to violent death, by foreign war; but also through the ignorance, and passions of men, it hath in it, from the very institution, many seeds of a natural mortality, by intestine discord.

If a subject be taken prisoner in war; or his person, or his means of life be within the guards of the enemy, and hath his life and corporal liberty given him, on condition to be subject to the victor, he hath liberty to accept the condition; and having accepted it, is the subject of him that took him; because he had no other way to preserve himself. The case is the same, if he be detained on the same terms, in a foreign country. But if a man be held in prison, or bonds, or is not trusted with the liberty of his body; he cannot be understood to be bound by covenant to subjection; and therefore may, if he can, make his escape by any means whatsoever.

If a monarch shall relinquish the sovereignty, both for himself, and his heirs; his subjects return to the absolute liberty of nature; because, though nature may declare who are his sons, and who are the nearest of his kin; yet it dependeth on his own will, (as hath been said in the precedent chapter,) who shall be his heir. If therefore he will have no heir, there is no sovereignty, nor subjection. The case is the same, if he die without known kindred, and without declaration of his heir. For then there can no heir be known, and consequently no subjection be due.

If the sovereign banish his subject; during the banishment, he is not subject. But he that is sent on a message, or hath leave to travel, is still subject; but it is, by contract between sovereigns, not by virtue of the covenant of subjection. For whosoever entereth into another's dominion, is subject to all the laws thereof; unless he have a privilege by the amity of the sovereigns, or by special licence.

If a monarch subdued by war, render himself subject to the victor; his subjects are delivered from their former obligation, and become obliged to the victor. But if he be held prisoner, or have not the liberty of his own body; he is not understood to have given away the right of sovereignty; and therefore his subjects are obliged to yield obedience to the magistrates formerly placed, governing not in their own name, but in his. For, his right remaining, the question is only of the administration; that is to say, of the magistrates and officers; which, if he have not means to name, he is supposed to approve those, which he himself had formerly appointed.

CHAPTER 22: Of Systems Subject, Political, and Private

Having spoken of the generation, form, and power of a commonwealth, I am in order to speak next of the parts thereof. And first of systems, which resemble the similar parts, or muscles of a body natural. By SYSTEMS, I understand any numbers of men joined in one interest, or one business. Of which, some are *regular*, and some *irregular*. *Regular* are those, where one man, or assembly of men, is constituted representative of the whole number. All other are *irregular*.

Of regular, some are *absolute*, and *independent*, subject to none but their own representative: such are only commonwealths; of which I have spoken already in the 5 last precedent chapters. Others are dependent; that is to say, subordinate to some sovereign power, to which every one, as also their representative is *subject*.

Of systems subordinate, some are *political*, and some *private*. *Political*, (otherwise called *bodies politic*, and *persons in law*,) are those, which are made by authority from the sovereign power of the commonwealth. *Private*, are those, which are constituted by subjects amongst themselves, or by authority from a stranger. For no authority derived from foreign power, within the dominion of another, is public there, but private.

And of private systems, some are *lawful*; some *unlawful. Lawful,* are those which are allowed by the commonwealth: all other are *unlawful. Irregular* systems, are those which having no representative, consist only in concourse of people; which if not forbidden by the commonwealth, nor made on evil design, (such as are conflux of people to markets, or shows, or any other harmless end,) are lawful. But when the intention is evil, or (if the number be considerable), unknown, they are unlawful.

In bodies politic, the power of the representative is always limited: and that which prescribeth the limits thereof, is the power sovereign. For power unlimited, is absolute sovereignty. And the sovereign, in every commonwealth, is the absolute representative of all the subjects; and therefore no other, can be representative of any part of them, but so far forth, as he shall give leave. And to give leave to a body politic of subjects, to have an absolute representative to all intents and purposes, were to abandon the government of so much of the commonwealth, and to divide the dominion, contrary to their peace and defence, which the sovereign cannot be understood to do, by any grant, that does not plainly, and directly discharge them of their subjection. For consequences of words, are not the signs of his will, when other consequences are signs of the contrary; but rather signs of error, and misreckoning; to which all mankind is too prone.

The bounds of that power, which is given to the representative of a body politic, are to be taken notice of, from two things. One is their writ, or letters from the sovereign: the other is the law of the commonwealth.

For though in the institution or acquisition of a commonwealth, which is independent, there needs no writing, because the power of the representative has there no other bounds, but such as are set out by the unwritten law of nature; yet in subordinate bodies, there are such diversities of limitation necessary, concerning their businesses, times, and places, as can neither be remembered without letters, nor taken notice of, unless such letters be patent, that they may be read to them, and withal sealed, or testified, with the seals, or other permanent signs of the authority sovereign.

And because such limitation is not always easy, or perhaps possible to be described in writing; the ordinary laws, common to all subjects, must determine, what the representative may lawfully do, in all cases, where the letters themselves are silent. And therefore:

In a body politic, if the representative be one man, whatsoever he does in the person of the body, which is not warranted in his letters, nor by the laws, is his own act, and not the act of the body, nor of any other member thereof besides himself: because further than his letters, or the laws limit, he representeth no man's person, but his own. But what he does according to these, is the act of every one: for of the act of the sovereign every one is author, because he is their representative unlimited; and the act of him that recedes not from the letters of the sovereign, is the act of the sovereign, and therefore every member of the body is author of it.

But if the representative be an assembly; whatsoever that assembly shall decree, not warranted by their letters, or the laws, is the act of the assembly, or body politic, and the act of every one by whose vote the decree was made; but not the act of any man that being present voted to the contrary; nor of any man absent, unless he voted it by procuration. It is the act of the assembly, because voted by the major part; and if it be a crime, the assembly may be punished, as far forth as it is capable, as by dissolution, or forfeiture of their letters (which is to such artificial, and fictitious bodies, capital) or (if the assembly have a common stock, wherein none of the innocent members have propriety,) by pecuniary mulct. For from corporal penalties nature hath exempted all bodies politic. But they that gave not their vote, are therefore innocent, because the assembly cannot represent any man in things unwarranted by their letters, and consequently are not involved in their votes.

If the person of the body politic being in one man, borrow money of a stranger, that is, of one that is not of the same body, (for no letters need limit borrowing, seeing it is left to men's own inclinations to limit lending), the debt is the representative's. For if he should have authority from his letters, to make the members pay what he borroweth, he should have by consequence the sovereignty of them; and therefore the grant were either void, as proceeding from error, commonly incident to human nature, and an insufficient sign of the will of the granter; or if it be avowed by him, then is the representer sovereign, and falleth not under the present question, which is only of bodies subordinate. No member therefore is obliged to pay the debt so borrowed, but the representative himself: because he that lendeth it, being a stranger to the letters, and to the qualification of the body, understandeth those only for his debtors, that are engaged: and seeing the representer can engage himself, and none else, has him only for debtor; who must therefore pay him, out of the common stock (if there be any), or (if there be none) out of his own estate.

If he come into debt by contract, or mulct, the case is the same.

But when the representative is an assembly, and the debt to a stranger; all they, and only they are responsible for the debt, that gave their votes to the borrowing of it, or to the contract that made it due, or to the fact for which the mulct was imposed; because every one of those in voting did engage himself for the payment: for he that is author of the borrowing, is obliged to the payment, even of the whole debt, though when paid by any one, he be discharged.

But if the debt be to one of the assembly, the assembly only is obliged to the payment, out of their common stock (if they have any:) for having liberty of vote, if he vote the money, shall be borrowed, he votes it shall be paid; if he vote it shall not be borrowed, or be absent, yet because in lending, he voteth the borrowing, he contradicteth his former vote, and is obliged by the latter, and becomes both borrower and lender, and consequently cannot demand payment from any particular man, but from the common treasure only; which failing he hath no remedy, nor complaint, but against himself, that being privy to the acts of the assembly, and to their means to pay, and not being enforced, did nevertheless through his own folly lend his money.

It is manifest by this, that in bodies politic subordinate, and subject to a sovereign power, it is sometimes not only lawful, but expedient, for a particular man to make open protestation against the decrees of the representative assembly, and cause their dissent to be registered, or to take witness of it; because otherwise they may be obliged to pay debts contracted, and be responsible for crimes committed by other men. But in a sovereign assembly, that liberty is taken away, both because he that protesteth there, denies their sovereignty; and also because whatsoever is commanded by the sovereign power, is as to the subject (though not so always in the sight of God) justified by the command; for of such command every subject is the author.

The variety of bodies politic, is almost infinite: for they are not only distinguished by the several affairs, for which they are constituted, wherein there is an unspeakable diversity; but also by the times, places, and numbers, subject to many limitations. And as to their affairs, some are ordained for government; as first, the government of a province may be committed to an assembly of men, wherein all resolutions shall depend on the votes of the major part; and then this assembly is a body politic, and their power limited by commission. This word province signifies a charge, or care of business, which he whose business it is, committeth to another man, to be administered for, and under him; and therefore when in one commonwealth there be divers countries, that have their laws distinct one from another, or are far distant in place, the administration of the government being committed to divers persons, those countries where the sovereign is not resident, but governs by commission, are called provinces. But of the government of a province, by an assembly residing in the province itself, there be few examples. The Romans who had the sovereignty of many provinces; yet governed them always by presidents, and praetors; and not by assemblies, as they governed the city of *Rome*, and territories adjacent. In like manner, when there were colonies sent from *England*, to plant *Virginia*, and *Sommer-islands*; though the government of them here, were committed to assemblies in *London*, yet did those assemblies never commit the government under them to any assembly there; but did to each plantation send one governor. For though every man, where he can be present by nature, desires to participate of government; yet where they cannot be present, they are by nature also inclined, to commit the government of their common interest rather to a monarchical, than a popular form of government: which is also evident in those men that have great private estates; who when they are unwilling to take the pains of administering the business that belongs to them, choose rather to trust one servant, than an assembly either of their friends or servants. But howsoever it be in fact, yet we may suppose the government of a province, or colony committed to an assembly: and when it is, that which in this place I have to say, is this; that whatsoever debt is by that assembly contracted; or whatsoever unlawful act is decreed, is the act only of those that assented, and not of any that dissented, or were absent, for the reasons before alleged. Also that an assembly residing out of the bounds of that colony whereof they have the government, cannot execute any power over the persons, or goods of any of the colony, to seize on them for debt, or other duty, in any place without the colony itself, as having no jurisdiction, nor authority elsewhere, but are left to the remedy, which the law of the place alloweth them. And though the assembly have right, to impose a mulct upon any of their members, that shall break the laws they make; yet out of the colony itself, they have no right to execute the same. And that which is said here, of the rights of an assembly, for the government of a province, or a colony, is appliable also to an assembly for the government of a town, an university, or a college, or a church, or for any other government over the persons of men.

And generally, in all bodies politic, if any particular member conceive himself injured by the body itself, the cognizance of his cause belongeth to the sovereign, and those the sovereign hath ordained for judges in such causes, or shall ordain for that particular cause; and not to the body itself. For the whole body is in this case his fellow subject, which in a sovereign assembly, is otherwise: for there, if the sovereign be not judge, though in his own cause, there can be no judge at all.

In a body politic, for the well ordering of foreign traffic, the most commodious representative is an assembly of all the members; that is to say, such a one, as every one that adventureth his money, may be present at all the deliberations, and resolutions of the body, if they will themselves. For proof whereof, we are to consider the end, for which men that are merchants, and may buy and sell, export, and import their merchandise according to their own discretions, do nevertheless bind themselves up in one corporation. It is true, there be few merchants, that with the merchandise they buy at home, can freight a ship, to export it; or with that they buy abroad, to bring it home; and have therefore need to join together in one society; where every man may either participate of the gain, according to the proportion of his adventure; or take his own, and sell what he transports, or imports, at such prices as he thinks fit. But this is no body politic, there being no common representative to oblige them to any other law, than that which is common to all other subjects. The end of their incorporating, is to make their gain the greater; which is done two ways; by sole buying, and sole selling, both at home, and abroad. So that to grant to a company of merchants to be a corporation, or body politic, is to grant them a double monopoly, whereof one is to be sole buyers; another to be sole sellers. For when there is a company incorporate for any particular foreign country, they only export the commodities vendible in that country; which is sole buying at home, and sole selling abroad. For at home there is but one buyer, and abroad but one that selleth: both which is gainful to the merchant, because thereby they buy at home at lower, and sell abroad at higher rates: and abroad there is but one buyer of foreign merchandise, and but one that sells them at home; both which again are gainful to the adventurers.

Of this double monopoly one part is disadvantageous to the people at home, the other to foreigners. For at home by their sole exportation they set what price they please on the husbandry, and handy-works of the people; and by the sole importation, what price they please on all foreign commodities the people have need of; both which are ill for the people. On the contrary, by the sole selling of the native commodities abroad, and sole buying the foreign commodities upon the place, they raise the price of those, and abate the price of these, to the disadvantage of the foreigner: for where but one selleth, the merchandise is the dearer; and where but one buyeth the cheaper. Such corporations therefore are no other than monopolies; though they would be very profitable for a commonwealth, if being bound up into one body in foreign markets they were at liberty at home, every man to buy, and sell at what price he could.

The end then of these bodies of merchants, being not a common benefit to the whole body, (which have in this case no common stock, but what is deducted out of the particular adventures, for building, buying, victualling and manning of ships,) but the particular gain of every adventurer, it is reason that every one be acquainted with the employment of his own; that is, that every one be of the assembly, that shall have the power to order the same; and be acquainted with their accounts. And therefore the representative of such a body must be an assembly, where every member of the body may be present at the consultations, if he will.

If a body politic of merchants, contract a debt to a stranger by the act of their representative assembly, every member is liable by himself for the whole. For a stranger can take no notice of their private laws, but considereth them as so many particular men, obliged every one to the whole payment, till payment made by one dischargeth all the rest: but if the debt be to one of the company, the creditor is debtor for the whole to himself, and cannot therefore demand his debt, but only from the common stock, if there be any.

If the commonwealth impose a tax upon the body, it is understood to be laid upon every member proportionably to his particular adventure in the company. For there is in this case no other common stock, but what is made of their particular adventures.

If a mulct be laid upon the body for some unlawful act, they only are liable by whose votes the act was decreed, or by whose assistance it was executed; for in none of the rest is there any other crime but being of the body; which if a crime, (because the body was ordained by the authority of the commonwealth,) is not his.

If one of the members be indebted to the body, he may be sued by the body; but his goods cannot be taken, nor his person imprisoned by the authority of the body; but only by authority of the commonwealth: for if they can do it by their own authority, they can by their own authority give judgment that the debt is due; which is as much as to be judge in their own cause.

These bodies made for the government of men, or of traffic, be either perpetual, or for a time prescribed by writing. But there be bodies also whose times are limited, and that only by the nature of their business. For example, if a sovereign monarch, or a sovereign assembly, shall think fit to give command to the towns, and other several parts of their territory, to send to him their deputies, to inform him of the condition, and necessities of the subjects, or to advise with him for the making of good laws, or for any other cause, as with one person representing the whole country, such deputies, having a place and time of meeting assigned them, are there, and at that time, a body politic, representing every subject of that dominion; but it is only for such matters as shall be propounded unto them by that man, or assembly, that by the sovereign authority sent for them; and when it shall be declared that nothing more shall be propounded, nor debated by them, the body is dissolved. For if they were the absolute representative of the people, then were it the sovereign assembly; and so there would be two sovereign assemblies, or two sovereigns, over the same people; which cannot consist with their peace. And therefore where there is once a sovereignty, there can be no absolute representation of the people, but by it. And for the limits of how far such a body shall represent the whole people, they are set forth in the writing by which they were sent for. For the people cannot choose their deputies to other intent, than is in the writing directed to them from their sovereign expressed.

Private bodies regular, and lawful, are those that are constituted without letters, or other written authority, saving the laws common to all other subjects. And because they be united in one person representative, they are held for regular; such as are all families, in which the father, or master ordereth the whole family. For he obligeth his children, and servants, as far as the law permitteth, though not further, because none of them are bound to obedience in those actions, which the law hath forbidden to be done. In all other actions, during the time they are under domestic government, they are subject to their fathers, and masters, as to their immediate sovereigns. For the father, and master, being before the institution of commonwealth, absolute sovereigns in their own families, they lose afterward no more of their authority, than the law of the commonwealth taketh from them.

Private bodies regular, but unlawful, are those that unite themselves into one person representative, without any public authority at all; such as are the corporations of beggars, thieves and gipsies, the better to order their trade of begging, and stealing; and the corporations of men, that by authority from any foreign person, unite themselves in another's dominion, for the easier propagation of doctrines, and for making a party, against the power of the commonwealth.

Irregular systems, in their nature, but leagues, or sometimes mere concourse of people, without union to any particular design, not by obligation of one to another, but proceeding only from a similitude of wills and inclinations, become lawful, or unlawful, according to the lawfulness, or unlawfulness of every particular man's design therein: and his design is to be understood by the occasion.

The leagues of subjects, (because leagues are commonly made for mutual defence,) are in a commonwealth (which is no more than a league of all the subjects together) for the most part unnecessary, and savour of unlawful design; and are for that cause unlawful, and go commonly by the name of factions, or conspiracies. For a league being a connexion of men by covenants, if there be no power given to any one man, or assembly (as in the condition of mere nature) to compel them to performance, is so long only valid, as there ariseth no just cause of distrust: and therefore leagues between commonwealths, over whom there is no human power established, to keep them all in awe, are not only lawful, but also profitable for the time they last. But leagues of the subjects of one and the same commonwealth, where every one may obtain his right by means of the sovereign power, are unnecessary to the maintaining of peace and justice, and (in case the design of them be evil, or unknown to the commonwealth) unlawful. For all

uniting of strength by private men, is, if for evil intent, unjust; if for intent unknown, dangerous to the public, and unjustly concealed.

If the sovereign power be in a great assembly, and a number of men, part of the assembly, without authority, consult apart, to contrive the guidance of the rest; this is a faction, or conspiracy unlawful, as being a fraudulent seducing of the assembly for their particular interest. But if he, whose private interest is to be debated and judged in the assembly, make as many friends as he can; in him it is no injustice; because in this case he is no part of the assembly. And though he hire such friends with money, (unless there be an express law against it,) yet it is not injustice. For sometimes, (as men's manners are,) justice cannot be had without money; and every man may think his own cause just, till it be heard, and judged.

In all commonwealths, if a private man entertain more servants, than the government of his estate, and lawful employment he has for them requires, it is faction, and unlawful. For having the protection of the commonwealth, he needeth not the defence of private force. And whereas in nations not thoroughly civilized, several numerous families have lived in continual hostility, and invaded one another with private force; yet it is evident enough, that they have done unjustly; or else that they had no commonwealth.

And as factions for kindred, so also factions for government of religion, as of Papists, Protestants, &c. or of state, as patricians, and plebeians of old time in *Rome*, and of aristocraticals and democraticals of old time in *Greece*, are unjust, as being contrary to the peace and safety of the people, and a taking of the sword out of the hand of the sovereign.

Concourse of people, is an irregular system, the lawfulness, or unlawfulness, whereof dependeth on the occasion, and on the number of them that are assembled. If the occasion be lawful, and manifest, the concourse is lawful; as the usual meeting of men at church, or at a public show, in usual numbers: for if the numbers be extraordinarily great, the occasion is not evident; and consequently he that cannot render a particular and good account of his being amongst them, is to be judged conscious of an unlawful, and tumultuous design. It may be lawful for a thousand men, to join in a petition to be delivered to a judge, or magistrate; yet if a thousand men come to present it, it is a tumultuous assembly; because there needs but one or two for that purpose. But in such cases as these, it is not a set number that makes the assembly unlawful, but such a number, as the present officers are not able to suppress, and bring to justice.

When an unusual number of men, assemble against a man whom they accuse; the assembly is an unlawful tumult; because they may deliver their accusation to the magistrate by a few, or by one man. Such was the case of St. *Paul* at *Ephesus*; where *Demetrius*, and a great number of other men, brought two of *Paul's* companions before the magistrate, saying with one voice, *Great is Diana of the Ephesians*; which was their way of demanding justice against them for teaching the people such doctrine, as was against their religion, and trade. The occasion here, considering the laws of that people, was just; yet was their assembly judged unlawful, and the magistrate reprehended them for it, in these words (*Acts* 19. 40.) *If Demetrius and the other workmen can accuse any man, of any thing, there be pleas, and deputies, let them accuse one another. And if you have any other thing to demand, your case may be judged in an assembly lawfully called. For we are in danger to be accused for this day's sedition; because, there is no cause by which any man can render any reason of this concourse of people.* Where he calleth an assembly, whereof men can give no just account, a sedition, and such as they could not answer for. And this is all I shall say concerning *systems*, and assemblies of people, which may be compared (as I said,) to the similar parts of man's body; such as be lawful, to the muscles; such as are unlawful, to wens, biles, and apostems, engendered by the unnatural conflux of evil humours.

CHAPTER 23: Of the Public Ministers of Sovereign Power

In the last chapter I have spoken of the similar parts of a commonwealth: in this I shall speak of the parts organical, which are public ministers.

A PUBLIC MINISTER, is he, that by the sovereign, (whether a monarch, or an assembly,) is employed in any affairs, with authority to represent in that employment, the person of the commonwealth. And whereas every man, or assembly that hath sovereignty, representeth two persons, or (as the more common phrase is) has two capacities, one natural, and another politic, (as a monarch, hath the person not only of the commonwealth, but also of a man; and a sovereign assembly hath the person not only of the commonwealth, but also of the assembly); they that be servants to them in their natural capacity, are not public ministers; but those only that serve them in the administration of the public business. And therefore neither ushers, nor sergeants, nor other officers that wait on the assembly, for no other purpose, but for the commodity of the men assembled, in an aristocracy, or democracy; nor stewards, chamberlains, cofferers, or any other officers of the household of a monarch, are public ministers in a monarchy.

Of public ministers, some have charge committed to them of a general administration, either of the whole dominion, or of a part thereof. Of the whole, as to a protector, or regent, may be committed by the predecessor of an infant king, during his minority, the whole administration of his kingdom. In which case, every subject is so far obliged to obedience, as the ordinances he shall make, and the commands he shall give be in the king's name, and not inconsistent with his sovereign power. Of a part, or province; as when either a monarch, or a sovereign assembly, shall give the general charge thereof to a governor, lieutenant, praefect or viceroy: and in this case also, every one of that province, is obliged to all he shall do in the name of the sovereign, and that not incompatible with the sovereign's right. For such protectors, viceroys, and governors, have no other right, but what depends on the sovereign's will; and no commission that can be given them, can be interpreted for a declaration of the will to transfer the sovereignty, without express and perspicuous words to that purpose. And this kind of public ministers resembleth the nerves, and tendons that move the several limbs of a body natural.

Others have special administration; that is to say, charges of some special business, either at home, or abroad: as at home; first, for the economy of a commonwealth, they that have authority concerning the *treasure*, as tributes, impositions, rents, fines, or whatsoever public revenue, to collect, receive, issue, or take the accounts thereof, are public ministers: ministers, because they serve the person representative, and can do nothing against his command, nor without his authority: public, because they serve him in his political capacity.

Secondly, they that have authority concerning the *militia*; to have the custody of arms, forts, ports; to levy, pay, or conduct soldiers; or to provide for any necessary thing for the use of war, either by land or sea, are public ministers. But a soldier without command, though he fight for the commonwealth, does not therefore represent the person of it; because there is none to represent it to. For every one that hath command, represents it to them only whom he commandeth.

They also that have authority to teach, or to enable others to teach the people their duty to the sovereign power, and instruct them in the knowledge of what is just, and unjust, thereby to render them more apt to live in godliness, and in peace amongst themselves, and resist the public enemy, are public ministers: ministers, in that they do it not by their own authority, but by another's; and public, because they do it (or should do it) by no authority, but that of the sovereign. The monarch, or the sovereign assembly only hath immediate authority from God, to teach and instruct the people; and no man but the sovereign, receiveth his power *Dei gratia* simply; that is to say, from the favour of none but God: all other, receive theirs from the favour and providence of God, and their sovereigns; as in a monarchy *Dei gratia et regis*; or *Dei providentia et voluntate regis*.

They also to whom jurisdiction is given, are public ministers. For in their seats of justice they represent the person of the sovereign; and their sentence, is his sentence; for, (as hath been before declared) all judicature is essentially annexed to the sovereignty; and therefore all other judges are but ministers of him, or them that have the sovereign power. And as controversies are of two sorts, namely of *fact* and of *law*; so are judgments, some of fact, some of law: and consequently in the same controversy, there may be two judges, one of fact, another of law.

And in both these controversies, there may arise a controversy between the party judged, and the judge; which because they be both subjects to the sovereign, ought in equity to be judged by men agreed on by consent of both; for no man can be judge in his own cause. But the sovereign is already agreed on for judge by them both, and is therefore either to hear the cause, and determine it himself, or appoint for judge such as they shall both agree on. And this agreement is then understood to be made between them divers ways; as first, if the defendant be allowed to except against such of his judges, whose interest maketh him suspect them, (for as to the complainant he hath already chosen his own judge), those which he excepteth not against, are judges he himself agrees on. Secondly, if he appeal to any other judge, he can appeal no further; for his appeal is his choice. Thirdly, if he appeal to the sovereign himself, and he by himself, or by delegates which the parties shall agree on, give sentence; that sentence is final: for the defendant is judged by his own judges, that is to say, by himself.

These properties of just and rational judicature considered, I cannot forbear to observe the excellent constitution of the courts of justice, established both for Common, and also for Public Pleas in England. By Common Pleas, I mean those, where both the complainant and defendant are subjects: and by public, (which are also called Pleas of the Crown) those, where the complainant is the sovereign. For whereas there were two orders of men, whereof one was Lords, the other Commons; the Lords had this privilege, to have for judges in all capital crimes, none but Lords; and of them, as many as would be present; which being ever acknowledged as a privilege of favour, their judges were none but such as they had themselves desired. And in all controversies, every subject (as also in civil controversies the Lords) had for judges, men of the country where the matter in controversy lay; against which he might make his exceptions, till at last twelve men without exception being agreed on, they were judged by those twelve. So that having his own judges, there could be nothing alleged by the party, why the sentence should not be final. These public persons, with authority from the sovereign power, either to instruct, or judge the people, are such members of the commonwealth, as may fitly be compared to the organs of voice in a body natural.

Public ministers are also all those, that have authority from the sovereign, to procure the execution of judgments given; to publish the sovereign's commands; to suppress tumults; to apprehend, and imprison malefactors; and other acts tending to the conservation of the peace. For every act they do by such authority, is the act of the commonwealth; and their service, answerable to that of the hands, in a body natural.

Public ministers abroad, are those that represent the person of their own sovereign, to foreign states. Such are ambassadors, messengers, agents, and heralds, sent by public authority, and on public business.

But such as are sent by authority only of some private party of a troubled state, though they be received, are neither public, nor private ministers of the commonwealth; because none of their actions have the commonwealth for author. Likewise, an ambassador sent from a prince, to congratulate, condole, or to assist at a solemnity, though the authority be public; yet because the business is private, and belonging to him in his natural capacity; is a private person. Also if a man be sent into another country, secretly to explore their counsels, and strength; though both the authority, and the business be public; yet because there is none to take notice of any person in him, but his own; he is but a private minister; but yet a minister of the commonwealth; and may be compared to an eye in the body natural. And those that are appointed to receive the petitions or other informations of the people, and are as it were the public ear, are public ministers, and represent their sovereign in that office.

Neither a councillor, nor a council of state, if we consider it with no authority of judicature or command, but only of giving advice to the sovereign when it is required, or of offering it when it is not required, is a public person. For the advice is addressed to the sovereign only, whose person cannot in his own presence, be represented to him, by another. But a body of councillors, are never without some other authority, either of judicature, or of immediate administration: as in a monarchy, they represent the monarch, in delivering his commands to the public ministers: in a democracy, the council, or senate propounds the result of their deliberations to the people, as a council; but when they appoint judges, or hear causes, or give audience to ambassadors, it is in the quality of a minister of the people: and in an aristocracy, the council of state is the sovereign assembly itself; and gives counsel to none but themselves.

CHAPTER 24: Of the Nutrition, and Procreation of a Commonwealth

The Nutrition of a commonwealth consisteth, in the *plenty*, and *distribution* of *materials* conducing to life: in *concoction*, or *preparation*; and, (when concocted) in the *conveyance* of it, by convenient conduits, to the public use.

As for the plenty of matter, it is a thing limited by nature, to those commodities, which from (the two breasts of our common mother) land, and sea, God usually either freely giveth, or for labour selleth to mankind.

For the matter of this nutriment, consisting in animals, vegetals, and minerals, God hath freely laid them before us, in or near to the face of the earth; so as there needeth no more but the labour, and industry of receiving them. Insomuch as plenty dependeth (next to God's favour) merely on the labour and industry of men.

This matter, commonly called commodities, is partly *native*, and partly *foreign*: *native*, that which is to be had within the territory of the commonwealth: *foreign*, that which is imported from without. And because there is no territory under the dominion of one commonwealth, (except it be of very vast extent,) that produceth all things needful for the maintenance, and motion of the whole body; and few that produce not something more than necessary; the superfluous commodities to be had within, become no more superfluous, but supply these wants at home, by importation of that which may be had abroad, either by exchange, or by just war, or by labour: for a man's labour also, is a commodity exchangeable for benefit, as well as any other thing: and there have been commonwealths that having no more territory, than hath served them for habitation, have nevertheless, not only maintained, but also encreased their power, partly by the labour of trading from one place to another, and partly by selling the manufactures, whereof the materials were brought in from other places.

The distribution of the materials of this nourishment, is the constitution of *mine*, and *thine*, and *his*; that is to say, in one word *propriety*; and belongeth in all kinds of commonwealth to the sovereign power. For where there is no commonwealth, there is (as hath been already shown) a perpetual war of every man against his neighbour; and therefore every thing is his that getteth it, and keepeth it by force; which is neither *propriety*, nor *community*; but *uncertainty*. Which is so evident, that even *Cicero*, (a passionate defender of liberty,) in a public pleading, attributeth all propriety to the law civil. *Let the civil law*, saith he, *be once abandoned, or but negligently guarded, (not to say oppressed,) and there is nothing, that any man can be sure to receive from his ancestor, or leave to his children*. And again; *Take away the civil law, and no man knows what is his own, and what another man's*. Seeing therefore the introduction of *propriety* is an effect of commonwealth; which can do nothing but by the person that represents it, it is the act only of the sovereign; and consisteth in the laws, which none can make that have not the sovereign power. And this they well knew of old, who called that Νόμος, (that is to say, *distribution*,) which we call law; and defined justice, by *distributing* to every man *his own*.

In this distribution, the first law, is for division of the land itself: wherein the sovereign assigneth to every man a portion, according as he, and not according as any subject, or any number of them, shall judge agreeable to equity, and the common good. The children of Israel, were a commonwealth in the wilderness; but wanted the commodities of the earth,

till they were masters of the Land of Promise; which afterward was divided amongst them, not by their own discretion, but by the discretion of *Eleazar* the Priest, and *Joshua* their General, who, when there were twelve tribes, making them thirteen by subdivision of the tribe of *Joseph*; made nevertheless but twelve portions of the land; and ordained for the tribe of *Levi* no land; but assigned them the tenth part of the whole fruits; which division was therefore arbitrary. And though a people coming into possession of a land by war, do not always exterminate the ancient inhabitants, (as did the Jews,) but leave to many, or most, or all of them their estates; yet it is manifest they hold them afterwards, as of the victors' distribution; as the people of *England* held all theirs of *William* the *Conqueror*.

From whence we may collect, that the propriety which a subject hath in his lands, consisteth in a right to exclude all other subjects from the use of them; and not to exclude their sovereign, be it an assembly, or a monarch. For seeing the sovereign, that is to say, the commonwealth (whose person he representeth,) is understood to do nothing but in order to the common peace and security, this distribution of lands, is to be understood as done in order to the same: and consequently, whatsoever distribution he shall make in prejudice thereof, is contrary to the will of every subject, that committed his peace, and safety to his discretion, and conscience; and therefore by the will of every one of them, is to be reputed void. It is true, that a sovereign monarch, or the greater part of a sovereign assembly, may ordain the doing of many things in pursuit of their passions, contrary to their own consciences, which is a breach of trust, and of the law of nature; but this is not enough to authorize any subject, either to make war upon, or so much as to accuse of injustice, or any way to speak evil of their sovereign; because they have authorized all his actions, and in bestowing the sovereign power, made them their own. But in what cases the commands of sovereigns are contrary to equity, and the law of nature, is to be considered hereafter in another place.

In the distribution of land, the commonwealth itself, may be conceived to have a portion, and possess, and improve the same by their representative; and that such portion may be made sufficient, to sustain the whole expense to the common peace, and defence necessarily required: Which were very true, if there could be any representative conceived free from human passions, and infirmities. But the nature of men being as it is, the setting forth of public land, or of any certain revenue for the commonwealth, is in vain; and tendeth to the dissolution of government, and to the condition of mere nature, and war, as soon as ever the sovereign power falleth into the hands of a monarch, or of an assembly, that are either too negligent of money, or too hazardous in engaging the public stock, into a long or costly war. Commonwealths can endure no diet: for seeing their expense is not limited by their own appetite, but by external accidents, and the appetites of their neighbours, the public riches cannot be limited by other limits, than those which the emergent occasions shall require. And whereas in *England,* there were by the Conqueror, divers lands reserved to his own use, (besides forests, and chases, either for his recreation, or for preservation of woods,) and divers services reserved on the land he gave his subjects; yet it seems they were not reserved for his maintenance in his public, but in his natural capacity. For he, and his successors did for all that, lay arbitrary taxes on all subjects' land, when they judged it necessary. Or if those public lands, and services, were ordained as a sufficient maintenance of the commonwealth, it was contrary to the scope of the institution; being (as it appeared by those ensuing taxes) insufficient, and (as it appears by the late small revenue of the crown) subject to alienation and diminution. It is therefore in vain, to assign a portion to the commonwealth; which may sell, or give it away; and does sell and give it away when it is done by their representative.

As the distribution of lands at home; so also to assign in what places, and for what commodities, the subject shall traffic abroad, belongeth to the sovereign. For if it did belong to private persons to use their own discretion therein, some of them would be drawn for gain, both to furnish the enemy with means to hurt the commonwealth, and hurt it themselves, by importing such things, as pleasing men's appetites,

be nevertheless noxious, or at least unprofitable to them. And therefore it belongeth to the commonwealth, (that is, to the sovereign only,) to approve, or disapprove both of the places, and matter of foreign traffic.

Further, seeing it is not enough to the sustentation of a commonwealth, that every man have a propriety in a portion of land, or in some few commodities, or a natural property in some useful art, and there is no art in the world, but is necessary either for the being, or well being almost of every particular man; it is necessary, that men distribute that which they can spare, and transfer their propriety therein, mutually one to another, by exchange, and mutual contract. And therefore it belongeth to the commonwealth, (that is to say, to the sovereign,) to appoint in what manner, all kinds of contract between subjects, (as buying, selling, exchanging, borrowing, lending, letting, and taking to hire,) are to be made; and by what words and signs they shall be understood for valid. And for the matter, and distribution of the nourishment, to the several members of the commonwealth, thus much (considering the model of the whole work) is sufficient.

By concoction, I understand the reducing of all commodities, which are not presently consumed, but reserved for nourishment in time to come, to some thing of equal value, and withal so portable, as not to hinder the motion of men from place to place; to the end a man may have in what place soever, such nourishment as the place affordeth. And this is nothing else but gold, and silver, and money. For gold and silver, being (as it happens) almost in all countries of the world highly valued, is a commodious measure of the value of all things else between nations; and money (of what matter soever coined by the sovereign of a commonwealth,) is a sufficient measure of the value of all things else, between the subjects of that commonwealth. By the means of which measures, all commodities, moveable, and immoveable, are made to accompany a man, to all places of his resort, within and without the place of his ordinary residence; and the same passeth from man to man, within the commonwealth; and goes round about, nourishing (as it passeth) every part thereof; in so much as this concoction, is as it were the sanguification of the commonwealth: for natural blood is in like manner made of the fruits of the earth; and circulating, nourisheth by the way, every member of the body of man.

And because silver and gold, have their value from the matter itself; they have first this privilege, that the value of them cannot be altered by the power of one, nor of a few commonwealths; as being a common measure of the commodities of all places. But base money, may easily be enhanced, or abased. Secondly, they have the privilege to make commonwealths move, and stretch out their arms, when need is, into foreign countries; and supply, not only private subjects that travel, but also whole armies with provision. But that coin, which is not considerable for the matter, but for the stamp of the place, being unable to endure change of air, hath its effect at home only; where also it is subject to the change of laws, and thereby to have the value diminished, to the prejudice many times of those that have it.

The conduits, and ways by which it is conveyed to the public use, are of two sorts; one, that conveyeth it to the public coffers; the other, that issueth the same out again for public payments. Of the first sort, are collectors, receivers, and treasurers; of the second are the treasurers again, and the officers appointed for payment of several public or private ministers. And in this also, the artificial man maintains his resemblance with the natural; whose veins receiving the blood from the several parts of the body, carry it to the heart; where being made vital, the heart by the arteries sends it out again, to enliven, and enable for motion all the members of the same.

The procreation, or children of a commonwealth, are those we call *plantations*, or *colonies*; which are numbers of men sent out from the commonwealth, under a conductor, or governor, to inhabit a foreign country, either formerly void of inhabitants, or made void then, by war. And when a colony is settled, they are either a commonwealth of themselves, discharged of their subjection to their sovereign that sent them, (as hath been done by many commonwealths of ancient time,) in which case the commonwealth from which they went, was called their metropolis, or mother, and requires no more of them, than fathers require of the children, whom they emancipate and make free from their domestic government, which is honour, and friendship; or else they remain united to their metropolis, as were the colonies of the people of *Rome*; and then they are no commonwealths themselves, but provinces, and parts of the commonwealth that sent them. So that the right of colonies (saving honour, and league with their metropolis,) dependeth wholly on their licence, or letters, by which their sovereign authorized them to plant.

CHAPTER 25: Of Counsel

How fallacious it is to judge of the nature of things, by the ordinary and inconstant use of words, appeareth in nothing more, than in the confusion of counsels, and commands, arising from the imperative manner of speaking in them both, and in many other occasions besides. For the words *do this*, are the words not only of him that commandeth; but also of him that giveth counsel; and of him that exhorteth; and yet there are but few, that see not, that these are very different things; or that cannot distinguish between them, when they perceive who it is that speaketh, and to whom the speech is directed, and upon what occasion. But finding those phrases in men's writings, and being not able, or not willing to enter into a consideration of the circumstances, they mistake sometimes the precepts of counsellors, for the precepts of them that command; and sometimes the contrary; according as it best agreeth with the conclusions they would infer, or the actions they approve. To avoid which mistakes, and render to those terms of commanding, counselling, and exhorting, their proper and distinct significations, I define them thus.

COMMAND is where a man saith, *do this*, or *do not this*, without expecting other reason than the will of him that says it. From this it followeth manifestly, that he that commandeth, pretendeth thereby his own benefit: for the reason of his command is his own will only, and the proper object of every man's will, is some good to himself.

COUNSEL, is where a man saith, *do*, or *do not this*, and deduceth his reasons from the benefit that arriveth by it to him to whom he saith it. And from this it is evident, that he that giveth counsel, pretendeth only (whatsoever he intendeth) the good of him, to whom he giveth it.

Therefore between counsel and command, one great difference is, that command is directed to a man's own benefit; and counsel to the benefit of another man. And from this ariseth another difference, that a man may be obliged to do what he is commanded; as when he hath covenanted to obey: but he cannot be obliged to do as he is counselled, because the hurt of not following it, is his own; or if he should covenant to follow it, then is the counsel turned into the nature of a command. A third difference between them is, that no man can pretend a right to be of another man's counsel; because he is not to pretend benefit by it to himself: but to demand right to counsel another, argues a will to know his designs, or to gain some other good to himself; which (as I said before) is of every man's will the proper object.

This also is incident to the nature of counsel; that whatsoever it be, he that asketh it, cannot in equity accuse, or punish it: for to ask counsel of another, is to permit him to give such counsel as he shall think best; and consequently, he that giveth counsel to his sovereign, (whether a monarch, or an assembly) when he asketh it, cannot in equity be punished for it, whether the same be conformable to the opinion of the most, or not, so it be to the proposition in debate. For if the sense of the assembly can be taken notice of, before the debate be ended, they should neither ask, nor take any further counsel; for the sense of the assembly, is the resolution of the debate, and end of all deliberation. And generally he that demandeth counsel, is author of it; and therefore cannot punish it; and what the sovereign cannot, no man else can. But if one subject giveth counsel to another, to do any thing contrary to the laws, whether that counsel proceed from evil intention, or from ignorance only, it is punishable by the commonwealth; because ignorance of the law, is no good excuse, where every man is bound to take notice of the laws to which he is subject.

EXHORTATION, and DEHORTATION, is counsel, accompanied with signs in him that giveth it, of vehement desire to have it followed; or to say it more briefly, *counsel vehemently pressed.* For he that exhorteth, doth not deduce the consequences of what he adviseth to be done, and tie himself therein to the rigour of true reasoning; but encourages him he counselleth, to action: as he that dehorteth, deterreth him from it. And therefore they have in their speeches, a regard to the common passions, and opinions of men, in deducing their reasons; and make use of similitudes, metaphors, examples, and other tools of oratory, to persuade their hearers of the utility, honour, or justice of following their advice.

From whence may be inferred, first, that exhortation and dehortation, is directed to the good of him that giveth the counsel, not of him that asketh it, which is contrary to the duty of a counsellor; who (by the definition of counsel) ought to regard, not his own benefit, but his whom he adviseth. And that he directeth his counsel to his own benefit, is manifest enough, by the long and vehement urging, or by the artificial giving thereof; which being not required of him, and consequently proceeding from his own occasions, is directed principally to his own benefit, and but accidentally to the good of him that is counselled, or not at all.

Secondly, that the use of exhortation and dehortation lieth only where a man is to speak to a multitude; because when the speech is addressed to one, he may interrupt him, and examine his reasons more rigorously, than can be done in a multitude; which are too many to enter into dispute, and dialogue with him that speaketh indifferently to them all at once.

Thirdly, that they that exhort and dehort, where they are required to give counsel, are corrupt counsellors, and as it were bribed by their own interest. For though the counsel they give be never so good; yet he that gives it, is no more a good counsellor, than he that giveth a just sentence for a reward, is a just judge. But where a man may lawfully command, as a father in his family, or a leader in an army, his exhortations and dehortations, are not only lawful, but also necessary, and laudable: But then they are no more counsels, but commands; which when they are for execution of sour labour; sometimes necessity, and always humanity requireth to be sweetened in the delivery, by encouragement, and in the tune and phrase of counsel, rather than in harsher language of command.

Examples of the difference between command and counsel, we may take from the forms of speech that express them in Holy Scripture. *Have no other Gods but me; make to thyself no graven image; take not God's name in vain; sanctify the sabbath; honour thy parents; kill not; steal not, &c.* are commands; *because the reason for which we are to obey them, is drawn from the will of God our king, whom we are obliged to obey. But these words, Sell all thou hast; give it to the poor; and follow me,* are counsel; because the reason for which we are to do so, is drawn from our own benefit; which is this, that we shall have *treasure in Heaven.* These words, *Go into the village over against you, and you shall find an ass tied, and her colt; loose her, and bring her to me,* are a command: for the reason of their fact is drawn from the will of their Master: but these words, *Repent and be baptized in the name of Jesus,* are counsel; because the reason why we should so do, tendeth not to any benefit of God Almighty, who shall still be king in what manner soever we rebel; but of ourselves, who have no other means of avoiding the punishment hanging over us for our sins.

As the difference of counsel from command, hath been now deduced from the nature of counsel, consisting in a deducing of the benefit, or hurt that may arise to him that is to be counselled, by the necessary or probable consequences of the action he propoundeth; so may also the differences between *apt,* and *inept* counsellors be derived from the same. For experience, being but memory of the consequences of like actions formerly observed, and counsel but the speech whereby that experience is made known to another; the virtues, and defects of counsel, are the same with the virtues, and defects intellectual: and to the person of a commonwealth, his counsellors serve him in the place of memory, and mental discourse. But with this resemblance of the commonwealth, to a natural man, there is one dissimilitude joined, of great importance; which is, that a natural man receiveth his experience, from the natural objects of sense, which work upon him without passion, or interest of their own; whereas

they that give counsel to the representative person of a commonwealth, may have, and have often their particular ends, and passions, that render their counsels always suspected, and many times unfaithful. And therefore we may set down for the first condition of a good counsellor, *that his ends, and interest, be not inconsistent with the ends and interest of him he counselleth.*

Secondly, because the office of a counsellor, when an action comes into deliberation, is to make manifest the consequences of it, in such manner, as he that is counselled may be truly and evidently informed; he ought to propound his advice, in such form of speech, as may make the truth most evidently appear; that is to say, with as firm ratiocination, as significant and proper language, and as briefly, as the evidence will permit. And therefore *rash, and unevident inferences;* (such as are fetched only from examples, or authority of books, and are not arguments of what is good, or evil, but witnesses of fact, or of opinion,) *obscure, confused, and ambiguous expressions, also all metaphorical speeches, tending to the stirring up of passion,* (because such reasoning, and such expressions, are useful only to deceive, or to lead him we counsel towards other ends than his own) *are repugnant to the office of a counsellor.*

Thirdly, because the ability of counselling proceedeth from experience, and long study; and no man is presumed to have experience in all those things that to the administration of a great commonwealth are necessary to be known, *no man is presumed to be a good counsellor, but in such business, as he hath not only been much versed in, but hath also much meditated on, and considered.* For seeing the business of a commonwealth is this, to preserve the people in peace at home, and defend them against foreign invasion, we shall find, it requires great knowledge of the disposition of mankind, of the rights of government, and of the nature of equity, law, justice, and honour, not to be attained without study; and of the strength, commodities, places, both of their own country, and their neighbours; as also of the inclinations, and designs of all nations that may any way annoy them. And this is not attained to, without much experience. Of which things, not only the whole sum, but every one of the particulars requires the age, and observation of a man in years, and of more than ordinary study. The wit required for counsel, as I have said before (chap. 8.) is judgment. And the differences of men in that point come from different education, of some to one kind of study, or business, and of others to another. When for the doing of any thing, there be infallible rules, (as in engines and edifices, the rules of geometry,) all the experience of the world cannot equal his counsel, that has learnt, or found out the rule. And when there is no such rule, he that hath most experience in that particular kind of business, has therein the best judgment, and is the best counsellor.

Fourthly, to be able to give counsel to a commonwealth, in a business that hath reference to another commonwealth, *it is necessary to be acquainted with the intelligences, and letters* that come from thence, *and with all the records of treaties, and other transactions of state* between them; which none can do, but such as the representative shall think fit. By which we may see, that they who are not called to counsel, can have no good counsel in such cases to obtrude.

Fifthly, supposing the number of counsellors equal, a man is better counselled by hearing them apart, than in an assembly; and that for many causes. First, in hearing them apart, you have the advice of every man; but in an assembly many of them deliver their advice with *aye*, or *no*, or with their hands, or feet, not moved by their own sense, but by the eloquence of another, or for fear of displeasing some that have spoken, or the whole assembly, by contradiction; or for fear of appearing duller in apprehension, than those that have applauded the contrary opinion. Secondly, in an assembly of many, there cannot choose but be some whose interests are contrary to that of the public; and these their interests make passionate, and passion eloquent, and eloquence draws others into the same advice. For the passions of men, which asunder are moderate, as the heat of one brand; in assembly are like many brands, that inflame one another, (especially when they blow one another with orations) to the setting of the commonwealth on fire, under pretence of counselling it. Thirdly, in hearing every man apart, one may examine (when there is

need) the truth, or probability of his reasons, and of the grounds of the advice he gives, by frequent interruptions, and objections; which cannot be done in an assembly, where (in every difficult question) a man is rather astonied, and dazzled with the variety of discourse upon it, than informed of the course he ought to take. Besides, there cannot be an assembly of many, called together for advice, wherein there be not some, that have the ambition to be thought eloquent, and also learned in the politics; and give not their advice with care of the business propounded, but of the applause of their motley orations, made of the divers coloured threds, or shreads of authors; which is an impertinence at least, that takes away the time of serious consultation, and in the secret way of counselling apart, is easily avoided. Fourthly, in deliberations that ought to be kept secret, (whereof there be many occasions in public business,) the counsels of many, and especially in assemblies, are dangerous; and therefore great assemblies are necessitated to commit such affairs to lesser numbers, and of such persons as are most versed, and in whose fidelity they have most confidence.

To conclude, who is there that so far approves the taking of counsel from a great assembly of counsellors, that wisheth for, or would accept of their pains, when there is a question of marrying his children, disposing of his lands, governing his household, or managing his private estate, especially if there be amongst them such as wish not his prosperity? A man that doth his business by the help of many and prudent counsellors, with every one consulting apart in his proper element, does it best, as he that useth able seconds at tennis play, placed in their proper stations. He does next best, that useth his own judgment only; as he that has no second at all. But he that is carried up and down to his business in a framed counsel, which cannot move but by the plurality of consenting opinions, the execution whereof is commonly (out of envy, or interest) retarded by the part dissenting, does it worst of all, and like one that is carried to the ball, though by good players, yet in a wheel-barrow, or other frame, heavy of itself, and retarded also by the inconcurrent judgments, and endeavours of them that drive it; and so much the more, as they be more that set their hands to it; and most of all, when there is one, or more amongst them, that desire to have him lose. And though it be true, that many eyes see more than one; yet it is not to be understood of many counsellors; but then only, when the final resolution is in one man. Otherwise, because many eyes see the same thing in divers lines, and are apt to look asquint towards their private benefit; they that desire not to miss their mark, though they look about with two eyes, yet they never aim but with one; and therefore no great popular commonwealth was ever kept up; but either by a foreign enemy that united them; or by the reputation of some one eminent man amongst them; or by the secret counsel of a few; or by the mutual fear of equal factions; and not by the open consultations of the assembly. And as for very little commonwealths, be they popular, or monarchical, there is no human wisdom can uphold them, longer than the jealousy lasteth of their potent neighbours.

CHAPTER 26: Of Civil Laws

By CIVIL LAWS, I understand the laws, that men are therefore bound to observe, because they are members, not of this, or that commonwealth in particular, but of a commonwealth. For the knowledge of particular laws belongeth to them, that profess the study of the laws of their several countries; but the knowledge of civil law in general, to any man. The ancient law of *Rome* was called their *civil law*, from the word *civitas*, which signifies a commonwealth: and those countries, which having been under the Roman empire, and governed by that law, retain still such part thereof as they think fit, call that part the civil law, to distinguish it from the rest of their own civil laws. But that is not it I intend to speak of here; my design being not to show what is law here, and there; but what is law; as *Plato, Aristotle, Cicero*, and divers others have done, without taking upon them the profession of the study of the law.

And first it is manifest, that law in general, is not counsel, but command; nor a command of any man to any man; but only of him, whose command is addressed to one formerly obliged to obey him. And as for civil law, it addeth only the name of the person

commanding, which is *persona civitatis*, the person of the commonwealth.

Which considered, I define civil law in this manner. CIVIL LAW, *is to every subject, those rules, which the commonwealth hath commanded him, by word, writing, or other sufficient sign of the will, to make use of, for the distinction of right, and wrong; that is to say, of what is contrary, and what is not contrary to the rule.*

In which definition, there is nothing that is not at first sight evident. For every man seeth, that some laws are addressed to all the subjects in general; some to particular provinces; some to particular vocations; and some to particular men; and are therefore laws, to every of those to whom the command is directed; and to none else. As also, that laws are the rules of just, and unjust; nothing being reputed unjust, that is not contrary to some law. Likewise, that none can make laws but the commonwealth; because our subjection is to the commonwealth only: and that commands, are to be signified by sufficient signs; because a man knows not otherwise how to obey them. And therefore, whatsoever can from this definition by necessary consequence be deduced, ought to be acknowledged for truth. Now I deduce from it this that followeth.

1. The legislator in all commonwealths, is only the sovereign, be he one man, as in a monarchy, or one assembly of men, as in a democracy, or aristocracy. For the legislator is he that maketh the law. And the commonwealth only, prescribes, and commandeth the observation of those rules, which we call law: therefore the commonwealth is the legislator. But the commonwealth is no person, nor has capacity to do any thing, but by the representative, (that is, the sovereign;) and therefore the sovereign is the sole legislator. For the same reason, none can abrogate a law made, but the sovereign; because a law is not abrogated, but by another law, that forbiddeth it to be put in execution.

2. The sovereign of a commonwealth, be it an assembly, or one man, is not subject to the civil laws. For having power to make, and repeal laws, he may when he pleaseth, free himself from that subjection, by repealing those laws that trouble him, and making

of new; and consequently he was free before. For he is free, that can be free when he will: nor is it possible for any person to be bound to himself; because he that can bind, can release; and therefore he that is bound to himself only, is not bound.

3. When long use obtaineth the authority of a law, it is not the length of time that maketh the authority, but the will of the sovereign signified by his silence, (for silence is sometimes an argument of consent;) and it is no longer law, than the sovereign shall be silent therein. And therefore if the sovereign shall have a question of right grounded, not upon his present will, but upon the laws formerly made; the length of time shall bring no prejudice to his right; but the question shall be judged by equity. For many unjust actions, and unjust sentences, go uncontrolled a longer time, than any man can remember. And our lawyers account no customs law, but such as are reasonable, and that evil customs are to be abolished: But the judgment of what is reasonable, and of what is to be abolished, belongeth to him that maketh the law, which is the sovereign assembly, or monarch.

4. The law of nature, and the civil law, contain each other, and are of equal extent. For the laws of nature, which consist in equity, justice, gratitude, and other moral virtues on these depending, in the condition of mere nature (as I have said before in the end of the 15th chapter,) are not properly laws, but qualities that dispose men to peace and to obedience. When a commonwealth is once settled, then are they actually laws, and not before; as being then the commands of the commonwealth; and therefore also civil laws: for it is the sovereign power that obliges men to obey them. For in the differences of private men, to declare, what is equity, what is justice, and what is moral virtue, and to make them binding, there is need of the ordinances of sovereign power, and punishments to be ordained for such as shall break them; which ordinances are therefore part of the civil law. The law of nature therefore is a part of the civil law in all commonwealths of the world. Reciprocally also, the civil law is a part of the dictates of nature. For justice, that is to say, performance of covenant, and giving to every man his own, is a dictate of the law of nature. But every subject in a commonwealth,

hath covenanted to obey the civil law, (either one with another, as when they assemble to make a common representative, or with the representative it self one by one, when subdued by the sword they promise obedience, that they may receive life;) and therefore obedience to the civil law is part also of the law of nature. Civil, and natural law are not different kinds, but different parts of law; whereof one part being written, is called civil, the other unwritten, natural. But the right of nature, that is, the natural liberty of man, may by the civil law be abridged, and restrained: nay, the end of making laws, is no other, but such restraint; without the which there cannot possibly be any peace. And law was brought into the world for nothing else, but to limit the natural liberty of particular men, in such manner, as they might not hurt, but assist one another, and join together against a common enemy.

5. If the sovereign of one commonwealth, subdue a people that have lived under other written laws, and afterwards govern them by the same laws, by which they were governed before; yet those laws are the civil laws of the victor, and not of the vanquished commonwealth. For the legislator is he, not by whose authority the laws were first made, but by whose authority they now continue to be laws. And therefore where there be divers provinces, within the dominion of a commonwealth, and in those provinces diversity of laws, which commonly are called the customs of each several province, we are not to understand that such customs have their force, only from length of time; but that they were anciently laws written, or otherwise made known, for the constitutions, and statutes of their sovereigns; and are now laws, not by virtue of the prescription of time, but by the constitutions of their present sovereigns. But if an unwritten law, in all the provinces of a dominion, shall be generally observed, and no iniquity appear in the use thereof; that law can be no other but a law of nature, equally obliging all mankind.

6. Seeing then all laws, written and unwritten, have their authority, and force, from the will of the commonwealth; that is to say, from the will of the representative; which in a monarchy is the monarch, and in other commonwealths the sovereign assembly; a man

may wonder from whence proceed such opinions, as are found in the books of lawyers of eminence in several commonwealths, directly, or by consequence making the legislative power depend on private men, or subordinate judges. As for example, *that the common law, hath no controller but the parliament*; which is true only where a parliament has the sovereign power, and cannot be assembled, nor dissolved, but by their own discretion. For if there be a right in any else to dissolve them, there is a right also to control them, and consequently to control their controllings. And if there be no such right, then the controller of laws is not *parliamentum*, but *rex in parliamento*. And where a parliament is sovereign, if it should assemble never so many, or so wise men, from the countries subject to them, for whatsoever cause; yet there is no man will believe, that such an assembly hath thereby acquired to themselves a legislative power. *Item*, that the two arms of a commonwealth, are *force, and justice; the first whereof is in the king; the other deposited in the hands of the parliament*. As if a commonwealth could consist, where the force were in any hand, which justice had not the authority to command and govern.

7. That law can never be against reason, our lawyers are agreed; and that not the letter, (that is, every construction of it,) but that which is according to the intention of the legislator, is the law. And it is true: but the doubt is of whose reason it is, that shall be received for law. It is not meant of any private reason; for then there would be as much contradiction in the laws, as there is in the Schools; nor yet, (as Sir *Edward Coke* makes it,) an *artificial perfection of reason, gotten by long study, observation, and experience,* (as his was.) For it is possible long study may increase, and confirm erroneous sentences: and where men build on false grounds, the more they build, the greater is the ruin: and of those that study, and observe with equal time, and diligence, the reasons and resolutions are, and must remain discordant: and therefore it is not that *juris prudentia*, or wisdom of subordinate judges; but the reason of this our artificial man the commonwealth, and his command, that maketh law: and the commonwealth being in their representative but one person, there cannot easily arise any

contradiction in the laws; and when there doth, the same reason is able, by interpretation, or alteration, to take it away. In all courts of justice, the sovereign (which is the person of the commonwealth,) is he that judgeth: the subordinate judge, ought to have regard to the reason, which moved his sovereign to make such law, that his sentence may be according thereunto; which then is his sovereign's sentence; otherwise it is his own, and an unjust one.

8. From this, that the law is a command, and a command consisteth in declaration, or manifestation of the will of him that commandeth, by voice, writing, or some other sufficient argument of the same, we may understand, that the command of the commonwealth is law only to those, that have means to take notice of it. Over natural fools, children, or madmen there is no law, no more than over brute beasts; nor are they capable of the title of just, or unjust; because they had never power to make any covenant, or to understand the consequences thereof; and consequently never took upon them to authorize the actions of any sovereign, as they must do that make to themselves a commonwealth. And as those from whom nature, or accident hath taken away the notice of all laws in general; so also every man, from whom any accident, not proceeding from his own default, hath taken away the means to take notice of any particular law, is excused, if he observe it not; and to speak properly, that law is no law to him. It is therefore necessary, to consider in this place, what arguments, and signs be sufficient for the knowledge of what is the law; that is to say, what is the will of the sovereign, as well in monarchies, as in other forms of government.

And first, if it be a law that obliges all the subjects without exception, and is not written, nor otherwise published in such places as they may take notice thereof, it is a law of nature. For whatsoever men are to take knowledge of for law, not upon other men's words, but every one from his own reason, must be such as is agreeable to the reason of all men; which no law can be, but the law of nature. The laws of nature therefore need not any publishing, nor proclamation; as being contained in this one sentence, approved by all the world, *Do not that to another, which thou thinkest unreasonable to be done by another to thyself.*

Secondly, if it be a law that obliges only some condition of men, or one particular man, and be not written, nor published by word, then also it is a law of nature; and known by the same arguments, and signs, that distinguish those in such a condition, from other subjects. For whatsoever law is not written, or some way published by him that makes it law, can be known no way, but by the reason of him that is to obey it; and is therefore also a law not only civil, but natural. For example, if the sovereign employ a public minister, without written instructions what to do; he is obliged to take for instructions the dictates of reason; as if he make a judge, the judge is to take notice, that his sentence ought to be according to the reason of his sovereign, which being always understood to be equity, he is bound to it by the law of nature: or if an ambassador, he is (in all things not contained in his written instructions) to take for instruction that which reason dictates to be most conducing to his sovereign's interest; and so of all other ministers of the sovereignty, public and private. All which instructions of natural reason may be comprehended under one name of *fidelity*; which is a branch of natural justice.

The law of nature excepted, it belongeth to the essence of all other laws, to be made known, to every man that shall be obliged to obey them, either by word, or writing, or some other act, known to proceed from the sovereign authority. For the will of another, cannot be understood, but by his own word, or act, or by conjecture taken from his scope and purpose; which in the person of the commonwealth, is to be supposed always consonant to equity and reason. And in ancient time, before letters were in common use, the laws were many times put into verse; that the rude people taking pleasure in singing, or reciting them, might the more easily retain them in memory. And for the same reason *Solomon* adviseth a man, to bind the ten commandments upon his ten fingers. And for the law which *Moses* gave to the people of Israel at the renewing of the covenant, he biddeth them to teach it their children, by discoursing of it both at home, and upon the way; at going to bed, and at rising from bed; and to write it upon the posts, and doors of their houses; and (*Deut.* 31. 12) to assemble the people, man, woman, and child, to hear it read.

Nor is it enough the law be written, and published; but also that there be manifest signs, that it proceedeth from the will of the sovereign. For private men, when they have, or think they have force enough to secure their unjust designs, and convoy them safely to their ambitious ends, may publish for laws what they please, without, or against the legislative authority. There is therefore requisite, not only a declaration of the law, but also sufficient signs of the author, and authority. The author, or legislator is supposed in every commonwealth to be evident, because he is the sovereign, who having been constituted by the consent of every one, is supposed by every one to be sufficiently known. And though the ignorance, and security of men be such, for the most part, as that when the memory of the first constitution of their commonwealth is worn out, they do not consider, by whose power they use to be defended against their enemies, and to have their industry protected, and to be righted when injury is done them; yet because no man that considers, can make question of it, no excuse can be derived from the ignorance of where the sovereignty is placed. And it is a dictate of natural reason, and consequently an evident law of nature, that no man ought to weaken that power, the protection whereof he hath himself demanded, or wittingly received against others. Therefore of who is sovereign, no man, but by his own fault, (whatsoever evil men suggest,) can make any doubt. The difficulty consisteth in the evidence of the authority derived from him; the removing whereof, dependeth on the knowledge of the public registers, public counsels, public ministers, and public seals; by which all laws are sufficiently verified; verified, I say, not authorized: for the verification, is but the testimony and record; not the authority of the law; which consisteth in the command of the sovereign only.

If therefore a man have a question of injury, depending on the law of nature; that is to say, on common equity; the sentence of the judge, that by commission hath authority to take cognizance of such causes, is a sufficient verification of the law of nature in that individual case. For though the advice of one that professeth the study of the law, be useful for the avoiding of contention; yet it is but advice: it is the judge must tell men what is law, upon the hearing of the controversy.

But when the question is of injury, or crime, upon a written law; every man by recourse to the registers, by himself or others, may (if he will) be sufficiently informed, before he do such injury, or commit the crime, whether it be an injury, or not: nay he ought to do so: for when a man doubts whether the act he goeth about, be just, or unjust; and may inform himself, if he will; the doing is unlawful. In like manner, he that supposeth himself injured, in a case determined by the written law, which he may by himself, or others see and consider; if he complain before he consults with the law, he does unjustly, and bewrayeth a disposition rather to vex other men, than to demand his own right.

If the question be of obedience to a public officer; to have seen his commission, with the public seal, and heard it read; or to have had the means to be informed of it, if a man would, is a sufficient verification of his authority. For every man is obliged to do his best endeavour, to inform himself of all written laws, that may concern his own future actions.

The legislator known; and the laws, either by writing, or by the light of nature, sufficiently published; there wanteth yet another very material circumstance to make them obligatory. For it is not the letter, but the intendment, or meaning; that is to say, the authentic interpretation of the law (which is the sense of the legislator,) in which the nature of the law consisteth; and therefore the interpretation of all laws dependeth on the authority sovereign; and the interpreters can be none but those, which the sovereign, (to whom only the subject oweth obedience) shall appoint. For else, by the craft of an interpreter, the law may be made to bear a sense, contrary to that of the sovereign; by which means the interpreter becomes the legislator.

All laws, written, and unwritten, have need of interpretation. The unwritten law of nature, though it be easy to such, as without partiality, and passion, make use of their natural reason, and therefore leaves the violators thereof without excuse; yet considering there be very few, perhaps none, that in some cases are not blinded by self love, or some other passion; it is now become of all laws the most obscure; and has consequently the greatest need of able interpreters. The written laws, if they be short, are easily misinterpreted, from the divers significations of a word, or two: if long they be more obscure by the divers significations of many words: insomuch as no written law, delivered in few, or many words, can be well understood, without a perfect understanding of the final causes, for which the law was made; the knowledge of which final causes is in the legislator. To him therefore there cannot be any knot in the law, insoluble; either by finding out the ends, to undo it by; or else by making what ends he will, (as *Alexander* did with his sword in the Gordian knot,) by the legislative power; which no other interpreter can do.

The interpretation of the laws of nature, in a commonwealth, dependeth not on the books of moral philosophy. The authority of writers, without the authority of the commonwealth, maketh not their opinions law, be they never so true. That which I have written in this treatise, concerning the moral virtues, and of their necessity, for the procuring, and maintaining peace, though it be evident truth, is not therefore presently law; but because in all commonwealths in the world, it is part of the civil law: For though it be naturally reasonable; yet it is by the sovereign power that it is law: otherwise, it were a great error, to call the laws of nature unwritten law; whereof we see so many volumes published, and in them so many contradictions of one another, and of themselves.

The interpretation of the law of nature, is the sentence of the judge constituted by the sovereign authority, to hear and determine such controversies, as depend thereon; and consisteth in the application of the law to the present case. For in the act of judicature, the judge doth no more but consider, whether the demand of the party, be consonant to natural reason, and equity; and the sentence he giveth, is therefore the interpretation of the law of nature; which interpretation is authentic; not because it is his private sentence; but because he giveth it by authority of the sovereign, whereby it becomes the sovereign's sentence; which is law for that time, to the parties pleading.

But because there is no judge subordinate, nor sovereign, but may err in a judgment of equity; if afterward in another like case he find it more consonant to equity to give a contrary sentence, he is obliged to do it. No man's error becomes his own law; nor obliges him to persist in it. Neither (for the same reason) becomes it a law to other judges, though sworn to follow it. For though a wrong sentence given by authority of the sovereign, if he know and allow it, in such laws as are mutable, be a constitution of a new law, in cases, in which every little circumstance is the same; yet in laws immutable, such as are the laws of nature, they are no laws to the same, or other judges, in the like cases for ever after. Princes succeed one another; and one judge passeth, another cometh; nay, heaven and earth shall pass; but not one title of the law of nature shall pass; for it is the eternal law of God. Therefore all the sentences of precedent judges that have ever been, cannot all together make a law contrary to natural equity: nor any examples of former judges, can warrant an unreasonable sentence, or discharge the present judge of the trouble of studying what is equity (in the case he is to judge,) from the principles of his own natural reason. For example sake, it is against the law of nature, *to punish the innocent*; and innocent is he that acquitteth himself judicially, and is acknowledged for innocent by the judge. Put the case now, that a man is accused of a capital crime, and seeing the power and malice of some enemy, and the frequent corruption and partiality of judges, runneth away for fear of the event, and afterwards is taken, and brought to a legal trial, and maketh it sufficiently appear, he was not guilty of the crime, and being thereof acquitted, is nevertheless condemned to lose his goods; this is a manifest condemnation of the innocent. I say therefore, that there is no place in the world, where this can be an interpretation of a law of nature, or be made a law by the sentences of precedent judges, that had done the same. For he that judged it first, judged unjustly; and no injustice can be a pattern of judgment to succeeding judges. A written law may forbid innocent

men to fly, and they may be punished for flying: but that flying for fear of injury, should be taken for presumption of guilt, after a man is already absolved of the crime judicially, is contrary to the nature of a presumption, which hath no place after judgment given. Yet this is set down by a great lawyer for the common law of *England. If a man,* (saith he) *that is innocent, be accused of felony, and for fear flyeth for the same; albeit he judicially acquitteth himself of the felony; yet if it be found that he fled for the felony; he shall notwithstanding his innocency, forfeit all his goods, chattels, debts, and duties. For as to the forfeiture of them, the law will admit no proof against the presumption in law, grounded upon his flight.* Here you see, *an innocent man judicially acquitted, notwithstanding his innocency,* (when no written law forbad him to fly) after his acquittal, *upon a presumption in law,* condemned to lose all the goods he hath. If the law ground upon his flight a presumption of the fact, (which was capital,) the sentence ought to have been capital: if the presumption were not of the fact, for what then ought he to lose his goods? This therefore is no law of *England;* nor is the condemnation grounded upon a presumption of law, but upon the presumption of the judges. It is also against law, to say that no proof shall be admitted against a presumption of law. For all judges, sovereign and subordinate, if they refuse to hear proof, refuse to do justice: for though the sentence be just, yet the judges that condemn without hearing the proofs offered, are unjust judges; and their presumption is but prejudice; which no man ought to bring with him to the seat of justice, whatsoever precedent judgments, or examples he shall pretend to follow. There be other things of this nature, wherein men's judgments have been perverted, by trusting to precedents: but this is enough to show, that though the sentence of the judge, be a law to the party pleading, yet it is no law to any judge, that shall succeed him in that office.

In like manner, when question is of the meaning of written laws, he is not the interpreter of them, that writeth a commentary upon them. For commentaries are commonly more subject to cavil, than the text; and therefore need other commentaries; and so there will be no end of such interpretation. And therefore unless there be an interpreter authorized by the sovereign, from which the subordinate judges are not to recede, the interpreter can be no other than the ordinary judges, in the same manner, as they are in cases of the unwritten law; and their sentences are to be taken by them that plead, for laws in that particular case; but not to bind other judges, in like cases to give like judgments. For a judge may err in the interpretation even of written laws; but no error of a subordinate judge, can change the law, which is the general sentence of the sovereign.

In written laws, men use to make a difference between the letter, and the sentence of the law: and when by the letter, is meant whatsoever can be gathered from the bare words, it is well distinguished. For the significations of almost all words, are either in themselves, or in the metaphorical use of them, ambiguous; and may be drawn in argument, to make many senses; but there is only one sense of the law. But if by the letter, be meant the literal sense, then the letter, and the sentence or intention of the law, is all one. For the literal sense is that, which the legislator intended, should by the letter of the law be signified. Now the intention of the legislator is always supposed to be equity: for it were a great contumely for a judge to think otherwise of the sovereign. He ought therefore, if the word of the law do not fully authorize a reasonable sentence, to supply it with the law of nature; or if the case be difficult, to respite judgment till he have received more ample authority. For example, a written law ordaineth, that he which is thrust out of his house by force, shall be restored by force: it happens that a man by negligence leaves his house empty, and returning is kept out by force, in which case there is no special law ordained. It is evident, that this case is contained in the same law: for else there is no remedy for him at all; which is to be supposed against the intention of the legislator. Again, the word of the law, commandeth to judge according to the evidence: a man is accused falsely of a fact, which the judge saw himself done by another; and not by him that is accused. In this case neither shall the letter of the law be followed to the condemnation of the innocent, nor shall the judge give sentence against the evidence of the witnesses;

because the letter of the law is to the contrary: but procure of the sovereign that another be made judge, and himself witness. So that the incommodity that follows the bare words of a written law, may lead him to the intention of the law, whereby to interpret the same the better; though no incommodity can warrant a sentence against the law. For every judge of right, and wrong, is not judge of what is commodious, or incommodious to the commonwealth.

The abilities required in a good interpreter of the law, that is to say, in a good judge, are not the same with those of an advocate; namely the study of the laws. For a judge, as he ought to take notice of the fact, from none but the witnesses; so also he ought to take notice of the law, from nothing but the statutes, and constitutions of the sovereign, alleged in the pleading, or declared to him by some that have authority from the sovereign power to declare them; and need not take care beforehand, what he shall judge; for it shall be given him what he shall say concerning the fact, by witnesses; and what he shall say in point of law, from those that shall in their pleadings show it, and by authority interpret it upon the place. The Lords of parliament in *England* were judges, and most difficult causes have been heard and determined by them; yet few of them were much versed in the study of the laws, and fewer had made profession of them: and though they consulted with lawyers, that were appointed to be present there for that purpose; yet they alone had the authority of giving sentence. In like manner, in the ordinary trials of right, twelve men of the common people, are the judges, and give sentence, not only of the fact, but of the right; and pronounce simply for the complainant, or for the defendant; that is to say, are judges not only of the fact, but also of the right: and in a question of crime, not only determine whether done, or not done; but also whether it be *murder, homicide, felony, assault*, and the like, which are determinations of law: but because they are not supposed to know the law of themselves, there is one that hath authority to inform them of it, in the particular case they are to judge of. But yet if they judge not according to that he tells them, they are not subject thereby to any penalty; unless it be made appear, they did it against their consciences, or had been corrupted by reward.

The things that make a good judge, or good interpreter of the laws, are, first, *a right understanding* of that principal law of nature called *equity*; which depending not on the reading of other men's writings, but on the goodness of a man's own natural reason, and meditation, is presumed to be in those most, that have had most leisure, and had the most inclination to meditate thereon. Secondly, *contempt of unnecessary riches, and preferments.* Thirdly, *to be able in judgment to divest himself of all fear, anger, hatred, love, and compassion.* Fourthly, and lastly, *patience to hear; diligent attention in hearing; and memory to retain, digest and apply what he hath heard.*

The difference and division of the laws, has been made in divers manners, according to the different methods, of those men that have written of them. For it is a thing that dependeth not on nature, but on the scope of the writer; and is subservient to every man's proper method. In the Institutions of *Justinian*, we find seven sorts of civil laws.

1. The *edicts, constitutions,* and *epistles of the prince,* that is, of the emperor; because the whole power of the people was in him. Like these, are the proclamations of the kings of *England*.

2. *The decrees of the whole people of Rome,* (comprehending the senate,) when they were put to the question by the *senate.* These were laws, at first, by the virtue of the sovereign power residing in the people; and such of them as by the emperors were not abrogated, remained laws, by the authority imperial. For all laws that bind, are understood to be laws by his authority that has power to repeal them. Somewhat like to these laws, are the acts of parliament in England.

3. *The decrees of the common people,* (excluding the senate,) when they were put to the question by the *tribune* of the people. For such of them as were not abrogated by the emperors, remained laws by the authority imperial. Like to these, were the orders of the House of Commons in *England*.

4. *Senatus consulta,* the *orders of the senate;* because when the people of *Rome* grew so numerous, as it was inconvenient to assemble them; it was thought fit by the emperor, that men should consult the senate, instead of the people: and these have some resemblance with the acts of council.

5. *The edicts of praetors,* and (in some cases) of the *aediles:* such as are the chief justices in the courts of *England*.

6. *Responsa prudentum;* which were the sentences, and opinions of those lawyers, to whom the emperor gave authority to interpret the law, and to give answer to such as in matter of law demanded their advice; which answers, the judges in giving judgment were obliged by the constitutions of the emperor to observe: and should be like the reports of cases judged, if other judges be by the law of *England* bound to observe them. For the judges of the common law of *England*, are not properly judges, but *juris consulti;* of whom the judges, who are either the lords, or twelve men of the country, are in point of law to ask advice.

7. Also, *unwritten customs,* (which in their own nature are an imitation of law,) by the tacit consent of the emperor, in case they be not contrary to the law of nature, are very laws.

Another division of laws, is into *natural* and *positive*. *Natural* are those which have been laws from all eternity; and are called not only *natural*, but also *moral* laws; consisting in the moral virtues, as justice, equity, and all habits of the mind that conduce to peace, and charity; of which I have already spoken in the fourteenth and fifteenth chapters.

Positive, are those which have not been from eternity; but have been made laws by the will of those that have had the sovereign power over others; and are either written, or made known to men, by some other argument of the will of their legislator.

Again, of positive laws, some are *human,* some *divine;* and of human positive laws, some are *distributive,* some *penal. Distributive* are those that determine the rights of the subjects, declaring to every man what it is, by which he acquireth and holdeth a propriety in lands, or goods, and a right or liberty of action: and these speak to all the subjects. *Penal* are those, which declare, what penalty shall be inflicted on those that violate the law; and speak to the ministers and officers ordained for execution. For though every one ought to be informed of the punishments ordained beforehand for their transgression; nevertheless the command is not addressed to the delinquent, (who cannot be supposed will faithfully punish himself,) but to public ministers appointed to see the penalty executed. And these penal laws are for the most part written together with the laws distributive; and are sometimes called judgments. For all laws are general judgments, or sentences of the legislator; as also every particular judgment, is a law to him, whose case is judged.

Divine positive laws (for natural laws being eternal, and universal, are all divine,) are those, which being the commandments of God, (not from all eternity, nor universally addressed to all men, but only to a certain people, or to certain persons,) are declared for such, by those whom God hath authorized to declare them. But this authority of man to declare what be these positive laws of God, how can it be known? God may command a man by a supernatural way, to deliver laws to other men. But because it is of the essence of law, that he who is to be obliged, be assured of the authority of him that declareth it, which we cannot naturally take notice to be from God, *how can a man without supernatural revelation be assured of the revelation received by the declarer?* and *how can he be bound to obey them?* For the first question, how a man can be assured of the revelation of another, without a revelation particularly to himself, it is evidently impossible. For though a man may be induced to believe such revelation, from the miracles they see him do, or from seeing the extraordinary sanctity of his life, or from seeing the extraordinary wisdom, or extraordinary felicity of his actions, all which are marks of God's extraordinary favour; yet they are not assured evidences of special revelation. Miracles are marvellous works: but that which is marvellous to one, may not be so to another. Sanctity may be feigned; and the visible felicities of this world, are most often the work of God by natural, and ordinary causes. And therefore no man can infallibly know by natural reason, that another has had a supernatural revelation of God's will; but only a belief; every one (as the signs thereof shall appear greater, or lesser) a firmer, or a weaker belief.

But for the second, how he can be bound to obey them; it is not so hard. For if the law declared, be not against the law of nature (which is undoubtedly God's law) and he undertake to obey it, he is bound by his own act; bound I say to obey it, but not bound to believe it: for men's belief, and interior cogitations, are not subject to the commands, but only to the operation of God, ordinary, or extraordinary. Faith of supernatural law, is not a fulfilling, but only an assenting to the same; and not a duty that we exhibit to God, but a gift which God freely giveth to whom he pleaseth; as also unbelief is not a breach of any of his laws; but a rejection of them all, except the laws natural. But this that I say, will be made yet clearer, by the examples and testimonies concerning this point in holy Scripture. The covenant God made with *Abraham* (in a supernatural manner) was thus, (*Gen.* 17. 10) *This is the covenant which thou shalt observe between me and thee and thy seed after thee.* *Abraham's* seed had not this revelation, nor were yet in being; yet they are a party to the covenant, and bound to obey what *Abraham* should declare to them for God's law; which they could not be, but in virtue of the obedience they owed to their parents; who (if they be subject to no other earthly power, as here in the case of *Abraham*) have sovereign power over their children and servants. Again, where God saith to *Abraham*, *In thee shall all nations of the earth be blessed; for I know thou wilt command thy children, and thy house after thee to keep the way of the Lord, and to observe righteousness and judgment,* it is manifest, the obedience of his family, who had no revelation, depended on their former obligation to obey their sovereign. At Mount *Sinai Moses* only went up to God; the people were forbidden to approach on pain of death; yet were they bound to obey all that Moses declared to them for God's law. Upon what ground, but on this submission of their own, *Speak thou to us, and we will hear thee; but let not God speak to us, lest we die?* By which two places it sufficiently appeareth, that in a commonwealth, a subject that has no certain and assured revelation particularly to himself concerning the will of God, is to obey for such, the command of the commonwealth: for if men were at liberty, to take for God's commandments, their own dreams, and fancies, or the dreams and fancies of private men; scarce two men would agree upon what is God's commandment; and yet in respect of them, every man would despise the commandments of the commonwealth. I conclude therefore, that in all things not contrary to the moral law, (that is to say, to the law of nature,) all subjects are bound to obey that for divine law, which is declared to be so, by the laws of the commonwealth. Which also is evident to any man's reason; for whatsoever is not against the law of nature, may be made law in the name of them that have the sovereign power; and there is no reason men should be the less obliged by it, when it is propounded in the name of God. Besides, there is no place in the world where men are permitted to pretend other commandments of God, than are declared for such by the commonwealth. Christian states punish those that revolt from Christian religion, and all other states, those that set up any religion by them forbidden. For in whatsoever is not regulated by the commonwealth, it is equity, (which is the law of nature, and therefore an eternal law of God) that every man equally enjoy his liberty.

There is also another distinction of laws, into *fundamental* and *not fundamental*, but I could never see in any author, what a fundamental law signifieth. Nevertheless one may very reasonably distinguish laws in that manner.

For a fundamental law in every commonwealth is that, which being taken away, the commonwealth faileth, and is utterly dissolved; as a building whose foundation is destroyed. And therefore a fundamental law is that, by which subjects are bound to uphold whatsoever power is given to the sovereign, whether a monarch, or a sovereign assembly, without which the commonwealth cannot stand; such as is the power of war and peace, of judicature, of election of officers, and of doing whatsoever he shall think necessary for the public good. Not fundamental is that, the abrogating whereof, draweth not with it the dissolution of the commonwealth; such as are the laws concerning controversies between subject and subject. Thus much of the division of laws.

I find the words *lex civilis*, and *jus civile*, that is to say, *law* and *right civil*, promiscuously used for the same thing, even in the most learned authors; which nevertheless ought not to be so. For *right is liberty*, namely that liberty which the civil law leaves us: but *civil law* is an *obligation*; and takes from us the liberty which the law of nature gave us. Nature gave a right to every man to secure himself by his own strength, and to invade a suspected neighbour, by way of prevention: but the civil law takes away that liberty, in all cases where the protection of the law may be safely stayed for. Insomuch as *lex* and *jus*, are as different as *obligation* and *liberty*.

Likewise *laws* and *charters* are taken promiscuously for the same thing. Yet charters are donations of the sovereign; and not laws, but exemptions from law. The phrase of a law is, *jubeo, injungo, I command*, and *enjoin*: the phrase of a charter is, *dedi, concessi, I have given, I have granted*: but what is given or granted, to a man, is not forced upon him, by a law. A law may be made to bind all the subjects of a commonwealth: a liberty, or charter is only to one man, or some one part of the people. For to say all the people of a commonwealth, have liberty in any case whatsoever; is to say, that in such case, there hath been no law made; or else having been made, is now abrogated.

CHAPTER 27: Of Crimes, Excuses, and Extenuations

A *sin*, is not only a transgression of a law, but also any contempt of the legislator. For such contempt, is a breach of all his laws at once. And therefore may consist, not only in the *commission* of a fact, or in the speaking of words by the laws forbidden, or in the *omission* of what the law commandeth, but also in the *intention*, or purpose to transgress. For the purpose to break the law, is some degree of contempt of him, to whom it belongeth to see it executed. To be delighted in the imagination only, of being possessed of another man's goods, servants, or wife, without any intention to take them from him by force or fraud, is no breach of the law, that saith, *Thou shalt not covet:* nor is the pleasure a man may have in imagining, or dreaming of the death of him, from whose life he expecteth nothing but damage, and displeasure, a sin; but the resolving to put some act in execution, that tendeth thereto. For to be pleased in the fiction of that, which would please a man if it were real, is a passion so adherent to the nature both of man, and every other living creature, as to make it a sin, were to make sin of being a man. The consideration of this, has made me think them too severe, both to themselves, and others, that maintain, that the first motions of the mind, (though checked with the fear of God) be sins. But I confess it is safer to err on that hand, than on the other.

A CRIME, is a sin, consisting in the committing (by deed, or word) of that which the law forbiddeth, or the omission of what it hath commanded. So that every crime is a sin; but not every sin a crime. To intend to steal, or kill, is a sin, though it never appear in word, or fact: for God that seeth the thoughts of man, can lay it to his charge: but till it appear by something done, or said, by which the intention may be argued by a human judge, it hath not the name of crime: which distinction the Greeks observed, in the word ἁμάρτημα, and ἔγκλημα, or ἀιτία; whereof the former, (which is translated *sin*,) signifieth any swerving from the law whatsoever; but the two latter, (which are translated *crime*,) signify that sin only, whereof one man may accuse another. But of intentions, which never appear by any outward act, there is no place for human accusation. In like manner the Latins by *peccatum*, which is *sin*, signify all manner of deviation from the law; but by *crimen*, (which word they derive from *cerno*, which signifies to perceive,) they mean only such sins, as may be made appear before a judge; and therefore are not mere intentions.

From this relation of sin to the law, and of crime to the civil law, may be inferred, first, that where law ceaseth, sin ceaseth. But because the law of nature is eternal, violation of covenants, ingratitude, arrogance, and all facts contrary to any moral virtue, can never cease to be sin. Secondly, that the civil law ceasing, crimes cease: for there being no other law remaining, but that of nature, there is no place for accusation; every man being his own judge, and accused only by his own conscience, and cleared by the uprightness of his own intention. When therefore his intention is right, his fact is no sin: if otherwise, his fact is sin; but not crime. Thirdly, that when the sovereign power ceaseth, crime also ceaseth: for where there is no such power, there is no protection to be had from the law; and therefore every one may protect himself by his own power: for no man in the institution of sovereign power can be supposed to give away the right of preserving his own body; for the safety whereof all sovereignty was ordained. But this is to be understood only of those, that have not themselves contributed to the taking away of the power that protected them: for that was a crime from the beginning.

The source of every crime, is some defect of the understanding; or some error in reasoning; or some sudden force of the passions. Defect in the understanding, is *ignorance*; in reasoning, *erroneous opinion*. Again, ignorance is of three sorts; of the *law*, and of the *sovereign*, and of the *penalty*. Ignorance of the law of nature excuseth no man; because every man that hath attained to the use of reason, is supposed to know, he ought not to do to another, what he would not have done to himself. Therefore into what place soever a man shall come, if he do any thing contrary to that law, it is a crime. If a man come from the *Indies* hither, and persuade men here to receive a new religion, or teach them any thing that tendeth to disobedience of the laws of this country, though he be never so well persuaded of the truth of what he teacheth, he commits a crime, and may be justly punished for the same, not only because his doctrine is false, but also because he does that which he would not approve in another, namely, that coming from hence, he should endeavour to alter the religion there. But ignorance of the civil law, shall excuse a man in a strange country, till it be declared to him; because, till then no civil law is binding.

In the like manner, if the civil law of a man's own country, be not so sufficiently declared, as he may know it if he will; nor the action against the law of nature; the ignorance is a good excuse: in other cases ignorance of the civil law, excuseth not.

Ignorance of the sovereign power, in the place of a man's ordinary residence, excuseth him not; because he ought to take notice of the power, by which he hath been protected there.

Ignorance of the penalty, where the law is declared, excuseth no man: for in breaking the law, which without a fear of penalty to follow, were not a law, but vain words, he undergoeth the penalty, though he know not what it is; because, whosoever voluntarily doth any action, accepteth all the known consequences of it; but punishment is a known consequence of the violation of the laws, in every commonwealth; which punishment, if it be determined already by the law, he is subject to that; if not, then is he subject to arbitrary punishment. For it is reason, that he which does injury, without other limitation than that of his own will, should suffer punishment without other limitation, than that of his will whose law is thereby violated.

But when a penalty, is either annexed to the crime in the law itself, or hath been usually inflicted in the like cases; there the delinquent is excused from a greater penalty. For the punishment foreknown, if not great enough to deter men from the action, is an invitement to it: because when men compare the benefit of their injustice, with the harm of their punishment, by necessity of nature they choose that which appeareth best for themselves: and therefore when they are punished more than the law had formerly determined, or more than others were punished for the same crime; it is the law that tempted, and deceiveth them.

No law, made after a fact done, can make it a crime: because if the fact be against the law of nature, the law was before the fact; and a positive law cannot be taken notice of, before it be made; and therefore cannot be obligatory. But when the law that forbiddeth a fact, is made before the fact be done; yet he that doth the fact, is liable to the penalty ordained after, in case no lesser penalty were made known before, neither by writing, nor by example, for the reason immediately before alleged.

From defect in reasoning, (that is to say, from error,) men are prone to violate the laws, three ways. First, by presumption of false principles: as when men from having observed how in all places, and in all ages, unjust actions have been authorized by the force, and victories of those who have committed them; and that potent men, breaking through the cobweb laws of their country, the weaker sort, and those that have failed in their enterprises, have been esteemed the only criminals; have thereupon taken for principles, and grounds of their reasoning, *that justice is but a vain word: that whatsoever a man can get by his own industry, and hazard, is his own: that the practice of all nations cannot be unjust: that examples of former times are good arguments of doing the like again*; and many more of that kind: which being granted, no act in itself can be a crime, but must be made so (not by the law, but) by the success of them that commit it; and the same fact be virtuous, or vicious, as fortune pleaseth; so that what *Marius* makes a crime, *Sylla* shall make meritorious, and *Caesar*, (the same laws standing) turn again into a crime, to the perpetual disturbance of the peace of the commonwealth.

Secondly, by false teachers, that either misinterpret the law of nature, making it thereby repugnant to the law civil; or by teaching for laws, such doctrines of their own, or traditions of former times, as are inconsistent with the duty of a subject.

Thirdly, by erroneous inferences from true principles; which happens commonly to men that are hasty, and precipitate in concluding, and resolving what to do; such as are they, that have both a great opinion of their own understanding, and believe that things of this nature require not time and study, but only common experience, and a good natural wit; whereof no man thinks himself unprovided: whereas the knowledge, of right and wrong, which is no less difficult, there is no man will pretend to, without great and long study. And of those defects in reasoning, there is none that can excuse (though some of them may extenuate) a crime, in any man, that pretendeth to the administration of his own private business; much less in them that undertake a public charge; because they pretend to the reason, upon the want whereof they would ground their excuse.

Of the passions that most frequently are the causes of crime, one, is vain glory, or a foolish overrating of their own worth; as if difference of worth, were an effect of their wit, or riches, or blood, or some other natural quality, not depending on the will of those that have the sovereign authority. From whence proceedeth a presumption that the punishments ordained by the laws, and extended generally to all subjects, ought not to be inflicted on them, with the same rigour they are inflicted on poor, obscure, and simple men, comprehended under the name of the *vulgar.*

Therefore it happeneth commonly, that such as value themselves by the greatness of their wealth, adventure on crimes, upon hope of escaping punishment, by corrupting public justice, or obtaining pardon by money, or other rewards.

And that such as have multitude of potent kindred; and popular men, that have gained reputation amongst the multitude, take courage to violate the laws, from a hope of oppressing the power, to whom it belongeth to put them in execution.

And that such as have a great, and false opinion of their own wisdom, take upon them to reprehend the actions, and call in question the authority of them that govern, and so to unsettle the laws with their public discourse, as that nothing shall be a crime, but what their own designs require should be so. It happeneth also to the same men, to be prone to all such crimes, as consist in craft, and in deceiving of their neighbours; because they think their designs are too subtle to be perceived. These I say are effects of a false presumption of their own wisdom. For of them that are the first movers in the disturbance of commonwealth, (which can never happen without a civil war,) very few are left alive long enough, to see their new designs established: so that the benefit of their crimes, redoundeth to posterity, and such as would least have wished it: which argues they were not so wise, as they thought they were. And those that deceive upon hope of not being observed, do commonly deceive themselves, (the darkness in which they believe they lie hidden, being nothing else but their own blindness;) and are no wiser than children, that think all hid, by hiding their own eyes.

And generally all vain-glorious men, (unless they be withal timorous,) are subject to anger; as being more prone than others to interpret for contempt, the ordinary liberty of conversation: and there are few crimes that may not be produced by anger.

As for the passions, of hate, lust, ambition, and covetousness, what crimes they are apt to produce, is so obvious to every man's experience and understanding, as there needeth nothing to be said of them, saving that they are infirmities, so annexed to the nature, both of man, and all other living creatures, as that their effects cannot be hindered, but by extraordinary use of reason, or a constant severity in punishing them. For in those things men hate, they find a continual, and unavoidable molestation; whereby either a man's patience must be everlasting, or he must be eased by removing the power of that which molesteth him. The former is difficult; the latter is many times impossible, without some violation of the law. Ambition, and covetousness are passions also that are perpetually incumbent, and pressing; whereas reason is not perpetually present, to resist them: and therefore whensoever the hope of impunity appears, their effects proceed. And for lust, what it wants in the lasting, it hath in the vehemence, which sufficeth to weigh down the apprehension of all easy, or uncertain punishments.

Of all passions, that which inclineth men least to break the laws, is fear. Nay, (excepting some generous natures,) it is the only thing, (when there is apparence of profit or pleasure by breaking the laws,) that makes men keep them. And yet in many cases a crime may be committed through fear.

For not every fear justifies the action it produceth, but the fear only of corporeal hurt, which we call *bodily fear,* and from which a man cannot see how to be delivered, but by the action. A man is assaulted, fears present death, from which he sees not how to escape, but by wounding him that assaulteth him; if he wound him to death, this is no crime; because no man is supposed at the making of a commonwealth, to have abandoned the defence of his life, or limbs, where the law cannot arrive time enough to his assistance. But to kill a man, because from his actions, or his threatenings, I may argue he will kill me when he can, (seeing I have time, and means to demand protection, from the sovereign power,) is a crime. Again, a man receives words of disgrace, or some little injuries, (for which they that made the laws, had assigned no punishment, nor thought it worthy of a man that hath the use of reason, to take notice of,) and is afraid, unless he revenge it, he shall fall into contempt, and consequently be obnoxious to the like injuries from others; and to avoid this, breaks the law, and protects himself for the future, by the terror of his private revenge. This is a crime: for the hurt is not corporeal, but phantastical, and (though in this corner of the world, made sensible by a custom not many years since begun, amongst young and vain men,) so light, as a gallant man, and one that is assured of his own courage, cannot take notice of. Also a man may stand in fear of spirits, either through his own superstition, or through too much credit given to other men, that tell him of strange dreams and visions; and thereby be made believe they will hurt him, for doing, or omitting divers things, which nevertheless, to do, or omit, is contrary to the laws; and that which is so done, or omitted, is not to be excused by this fear; but is a crime. For (as I have shown before in the second chapter) dreams be naturally but the fancies remaining in sleep, after the impressions our senses had formerly received waking; and when men are by any accident unassured they have slept, seem to be real visions; and therefore he that presumes to break the law upon his own, or another's dream, or pretended vision, or upon other fancy of the power of invisible spirits, than is permitted by the commonwealth, leaveth the law of nature, which is a certain offence, and followeth the imagery of his own, or another private man's brain, which he can never know whether it signifieth any thing, or nothing, nor whether he that tells his dream, say true, or lie; which if every private man should have leave to do, (as they must by the law of nature, if any one have it) there could no law be made to hold, and so all commonwealth would be dissolved.

From these different sources of crimes, it appears already, that all crimes are not (as the Stoics of old time maintained) of the same allay. There is place, not only for EXCUSE, by which that which seemed a crime, is proved to be none at all; but also for EXTENUATION, by which the crime, that seemed great, is made less. For though all crimes do equally deserve the name of injustice, as all deviation from a straight line is equally crookedness, which the Stoics rightly observed; yet it does not follow that all crimes are equally unjust, no more than that all crooked lines are equally crooked; which the Stoics not observing, held it as great a crime, to kill a hen, against the law, as to kill one's father.

That which totally excuseth a fact, and takes away from it the nature of a crime, can be none but that, which at the same time, taketh away the obligation of the law. For the fact committed once against the law, if he that committed it be obliged to the law, can be no other than a crime.

The want of means to know the law, totally excuseth: For the law whereof a man has no means to inform himself, is not obligatory. But the want of diligence to inquire, shall not be considered as a want of means; nor shall any man, that pretendeth to reason enough for the government of his own affairs, be supposed to want means to know the laws of nature; because they are known by the reason he pretends to: only children, and madmen are excused from offences against the law natural.

Where a man is captive, or in the power of the enemy (and he is then in the power of the enemy, when his person, or his means of living, is so,) if it be without his own fault, the obligation of the law ceaseth; because he must obey the enemy, or die; and consequently such obedience is no crime: for no man is obliged (when the protection of the law faileth,) not to protect himself, by the best means he can.

If a man, by the terror of present death, be compelled to do a fact against the law, he is totally excused; because no law can oblige a man to abandon his own preservation. And supposing such a law were obligatory; yet a man would reason thus, *If I do it not, I die presently; if I do it, I die afterwards; therefore by doing it, there is time of life gained*; nature therefore compels him to the fact.

When a man is destitute of food, or other thing necessary for his life, and cannot preserve himself any other way, but by some fact against the law; as if in a great famine he take the food by force, or stealth, which he cannot obtain for money, nor charity; or in defence of his life, snatch away another man's sword, he is totally excused, for the reason next before alleged.

Again, facts done against the law, by the authority of another, are by that authority excused against the author; because no man ought to accuse his own fact in another, that is but his instrument: but it is not excused against a third person thereby injured; because in the violation of the law, both the author and actor are criminals. From hence it followeth that when that man, or assembly, that hath the sovereign power, commandeth a man to do that which is contrary to a former law, the doing of it is totally excused: for he ought not to condemn it himself, because he is the author; and what cannot justly be condemned by the sovereign, cannot justly be punished by any other. Besides, when the sovereign commandeth any thing to be done against his own former law, the command, as to that particular fact, is an abrogation of the law.

If that man, or assembly, that hath the sovereign power, disclaim any right essential to the sovereignty, whereby there accrueth to the subject, any liberty inconsistent with the sovereign power, that is to say, with the very being of a commonwealth, if the subject shall refuse to obey the command in any thing, contrary to the liberty granted, this is nevertheless a sin, and contrary to the duty of the subject: for he ought to take notice of what is inconsistent with the sovereignty, because it was erected by his own consent, and for his own defence; and that such liberty as is inconsistent with it, was granted through ignorance of the evil consequence thereof. But if he not only disobey, but also resist a public minister in the execution of it, then it is a crime; because he might have been righted, (without any breach of the peace,) upon complaint.

The degrees of crime are taken on divers scales, and measured, first, by the malignity of the source, or cause: secondly, by the contagion of the example: thirdly, by the mischief of the effect: and fourthly, by the concurrence of times, places, and persons.

The same fact done against the law, if it proceed from presumption of strength, riches, or friends to resist those that are to execute the law, is a greater crime than if it proceed from hope of not being discovered, or of escape by flight: for presumption of impunity by force, is a root, from whence springeth, at all times, and upon all temptations, a contempt of all laws; whereas in the latter case, the apprehension of danger, that makes a man fly, renders him more obedient for the future. A crime which we know to be so, is greater than the same crime proceeding from a false persuasion that it is lawful: for he that committeth it against his own conscience, presumeth on his force, or other power, which encourages him to commit the same again: but he that doth it by error, after the error shewn him, is conformable to the law.

He, whose error proceeds from the authority of a teacher, or an interpreter of the law publicly authorized, is not so faulty, as he whose error proceedeth from a peremptory pursuit of his own principles, and reasoning: for what is taught by one that teacheth by public authority, the commonwealth teacheth, and hath a resemblance of law, till the same authority controlleth it; and in all crimes that contain not in them a denial of the sovereign power, nor are against an evident law, excuseth totally: whereas he that groundeth his actions on his private judgment, ought according to the rectitude, or error thereof, to stand, or fall.

The same fact, if it have been constantly punished in other men, is a greater crime, than if there have been many precedent examples of impunity. For those examples are so many hopes of impunity, given by the sovereign himself: and because he which furnishes a man with such a hope, and presumption of mercy, as encourageth him to offend, hath his part in the offence; he cannot reasonably charge the offender with the whole.

A crime arising from a sudden passion, is not so great, as when the same ariseth from long meditation: for in the former case there is a place for extenuation, in the common infirmity of human nature: but he that doth it with premeditation, has used circumspection, and cast his eye, on the law, on the punishment, and on the consequence thereof to human society; all which in committing the crime, he hath contemned, and postposed to his own appetite. But there is no suddenness of passion sufficient for a total excuse: for all the time between the first knowing of the law, and the commission of the fact, shall be taken for a time of deliberation; because he ought by meditation of the law, to rectify the irregularity of his passions.

Where the law is publicly, and with assiduity, before all the people read and interpreted; a fact done against it, is a greater crime, than where men are left without such instruction, to enquire of it with difficulty, uncertainty, and interruption of their callings, and be informed by private men: for in this case, part of the fault is discharged upon common infirmity; but in the former, there is apparent negligence, which is not without some contempt of the sovereign power.

Those facts which the law expressly condemneth, but the law-maker by other manifest signs of his will tacitly approveth, are less crimes, than the same facts, condemned both by the law and lawmaker. For seeing the will of the law-maker is a law, there appear in this case two contradictory laws; which would totally excuse, if men were bound to take notice of the sovereign's approbation, by other arguments, than are expressed by his command. But because there are punishments consequent, not only to the transgression of his law, but also to the observing of it, he is in part a cause of the transgression, and therefore cannot reasonably impute the whole crime to the delinquent. For example, the law condemneth duels; the punishment is made capital: on the contrary part, he that refuseth duel, is subject to contempt and scorn, without remedy; and sometimes by the sovereign himself thought unworthy to have any charge, or preferment in war. If thereupon he accept duel, considering all men lawfully endeavour to obtain the good opinion of them that have the sovereign power, he ought not in reason to be rigorously punished; seeing part of the fault may be discharged on the punisher: which I say, not as wishing liberty of private revenges, or any other kind of disobedience; but a care in governors, not to countenance any thing obliquely, which directly they forbid. The examples of princes, to those that see them, are, and ever have been, more potent to govern their actions, than the laws themselves. And though it be our duty to do, not what

they do, but what they say; yet will that duty never be performed, till it please God to give men an extraordinary, and supernatural grace to follow that precept.

Again, if we compare crimes by the mischief of their effects, first, the same fact, when it redounds to the damage of many, is greater, than when it redounds to the hurt of few. And therefore, when a fact hurteth, not only in the present, but also, (by example) in the future, it is a greater crime, than if it hurt only in the present: for the former, is a fertile crime, and multiplies to the hurt of many; the latter is barren. To maintain doctrines contrary to the religion established in the commonwealth, is a greater fault, in an authorized preacher, than in a private person: so also is it, to live profanely, incontinently, or do any irreligious act whatsoever. Likewise in a professor of the law, to maintain any point, or do any act, that tendeth to the weakening of the sovereign power, is a greater crime, than in another man: also in a man that hath such reputation for wisdom, as that his counsels are followed, or his actions imitated by many, his fact against the law, is a greater crime, than the same fact in another: for such men not only commit crime, but teach it for law to all other men. And generally all crimes are the greater, by the scandal they give; that is to say, by becoming stumbling-blocks to the weak, that look not so much upon the way they go in, as upon the light that other men carry before them.

Also facts of hostility against the present state of the commonwealth, are greater crimes, than the same acts done to private men: for the damage extends itself to all: such are the betraying of the strengths, or revealing of the secrets of the commonwealth to an enemy; also all attempts upon the representative of the commonwealth, be it a monarch, or an assembly; and all endeavours by word, or deed to diminish the authority of the same, either in the present time, or in succession: which crimes the Latins understand by *crimina laesae majestatis*, and consist in design, or act, contrary to a fundamental law.

Likewise those crimes, which render judgments of no effect, are greater crimes, than injuries done to one, or a few persons; as to receive money to give false judgment, or testimony, is a greater crime, than otherwise to deceive a man of the like, or a greater sum; because not only he has wrong, that falls by such judgments; but all judgments are rendered useless, and occasion ministered to force, and private revenges.

Also robbery, and depeculation of the public treasure, or revenues, is a greater crime, than the robbing, or defrauding of a private man; because to rob the public, is to rob many at once.

Also the counterfeit usurpation of public ministry, the counterfeiting of public seals, or public coin, than counterfeiting of a private man's person, or his seal; because the fraud thereof, extendeth to the damage of many.

Of facts against the law, done to private men, the greater crime, is that, where the damage in the common opinion of men, is most sensible. And therefore

To kill against the law, is a greater crime, than any other injury, life preserved.

And to kill with torment, greater, than simply to kill.

And mutilation of a limb, greater, than the spoiling a man of his goods.

And the spoiling a man of his goods, by terror of death, or wounds, than by clandestine surreption.

And by clandestine surreption, than by consent fraudulently obtained.

And the violation of chastity by force, greater, than by flattery.

And of a woman married, than of a woman not married.

For all these things are commonly so valued; though some men are more, and some less sensible of the same offence. But the law regardeth not the particular, but the general inclination of mankind.

And therefore the offence men take, from contumely, in words, or gesture, when they produce no other harm, than the present grief of him that is reproached, hath been neglected in the laws of the Greeks, Romans, and other both ancient, and modern commonwealths; supposing the true cause of such grief to consist, not in the contumely, (which takes no hold upon men conscious of their own virtue,) but in the pusillanimity of him that is offended by it.

Also a crime against a private man, is much aggravated by the person, time, and place. For to kill one's parent, is a greater crime, than to kill another: for

the parent ought to have the honour of a sovereign, (though he have surrendered his power to the civil law,) because he had it originally by nature. And to rob a poor man, is a greater crime, than to rob a rich man; because it is to the poor a more sensible damage.

And a crime committed in the time or place appointed for devotion, is greater, than if committed at another time or place: for it proceeds from a greater contempt of the law.

Many other cases of aggravation, and extenuation might be added: but by these I have set down, it is obvious to every man, to take the altitude of any other crime proposed.

Lastly, because in almost all crimes there is an injury done, not only to some private men, but also to the commonwealth; the same crime, when the accusation is in the name of the commonwealth, is called public crime: and when in the name of a private man, a private crime; and the pleas according thereunto called public, *judicia publica*, Pleas of the Crown; or Private Pleas. As in an accusation of murder, if the accuser be a private man, the plea is a Private Plea; if the accuser be the sovereign, the plea is a Public Plea.

CHAPTER 28: Of Punishments, and Rewards

A PUNISHMENT, *is an evil inflicted by public authority, on him that hath done, or omitted that which is judged by the same authority to be a transgression of the law; to the end that the will of men may thereby the better be disposed to obedience.*

Before I infer any thing from this definition, there is a question to be answered, of much importance; which is, by what door the right, or authority of punishing in any case, came in. For by that which has been said before, no man is supposed bound by covenant, not to resist violence; and consequently it cannot be intended, that he gave any right to another to lay violent hands upon his person. In the making of a commonwealth, every man giveth away the right of defending another; but not of defending himself. Also he obligeth himself, to assist him that hath the sovereignty, in the punishing of another; but of himself not. But to covenant to assist the sovereign, in doing hurt to another, unless he that so covenanteth have a right to do it himself, is not to give him a right to punish. It is manifest therefore that the right which the commonwealth (that is, he, or they that represent it) hath to punish, is not grounded on any concession, or gift of the subjects. But I have also showed formerly, that before the institution of commonwealth, every man had a right to every thing, and to do whatsoever he thought necessary to his own preservation; subduing, hurting, or killing any man in order thereunto. And this is the foundation of that right of punishing, which is exercised in every commonwealth. For the subjects did not give the sovereign that right; but only in laying down theirs, strengthened him to use his own, as he should think fit, for the preservation of them all: so that it was not given, but left to him, and to him only; and (excepting the limits set him by natural law) as entire, as in the condition of mere nature, and of war of every one against his neighbour.

From the definition of punishment, I infer, first, that neither private revenges, nor injuries of private men, can properly be styled punishment; because they proceed not from public authority.

Secondly, that to be neglected, and unpreferred by the public favour, is not a punishment; because no new evil is thereby on any man inflicted; he is only left in the estate he was in before.

Thirdly, that the evil inflicted by public authority, without precedent public condemnation, is not to be styled by the name of punishment; but of an hostile act; because the fact for which a man is punished, ought first to be judged by public authority, to be a transgression of the law.

Fourthly, that the evil inflicted by usurped power, and judges without authority from the sovereign, is not punishment; but an act of hostility; because the acts of power usurped, have not for author, the person condemned; and therefore are not acts of public authority.

Fifthly, that all evil which is inflicted without intention, or possibility of disposing the delinquent, or (by his example) other men, to obey the laws, is not punishment; but an act of hostility; because without

such an end, no hurt done is contained under that name.

Sixthly, whereas to certain actions, there be annexed by nature, divers hurtful consequences; as when a man in assaulting another, is himself slain, or wounded; or when he falleth into sickness by the doing of some unlawful act; such hurt, though in respect of God, who is the author of nature, it may be said to be inflicted, and therefore a punishment divine; yet it is not contained in the name of punishment in respect of men, because it is not inflicted by the authority of man.

Seventhly, if the harm inflicted be less than the benefit, or contentment that naturally followeth the crime committed, that harm is not within the definition; and is rather the price, or redemption, than the punishment of a crime: because it is of the nature of punishment, to have for end, the disposing of men to obey the law; which end (if it be less than the benefit of the transgression) it attaineth not, but worketh a contrary effect.

Eighthly, if a punishment be determined and prescribed in the law itself, and after the crime committed, there be a greater punishment inflicted, the excess is not punishment, but an act of hostility. For seeing the aim of punishment is not a revenge, but terror; and the terror of a great punishment unknown, is taken away by the declaration of a less, the unexpected addition is no part of the punishment. But where there is no punishment at all determined by the law, there whatsoever is inflicted, hath the nature of punishment. For he that goes about the violation of a law, wherein no penalty is determined, expecteth an indeterminate, that is to say, an arbitrary punishment.

Ninthly, harm inflicted for a fact done before there was a law that forbade it, is not punishment, but an act of hostility: for before the law, there is no transgression of the law: but punishment supposeth a fact judged, to have been a transgression of the law; therefore harm inflicted before the law made, is not punishment, but an act of hostility.

Tenthly, hurt inflicted on the representative of the commonwealth, is not punishment, but an act of hostility: because it is of the nature of punishment, to be inflicted by public authority, which is the authority only of the representative itself.

Lastly, harm inflicted upon one that is a declared enemy, falls not under the name of punishment: because seeing they were either never subject to the law, and therefore cannot transgress it; or having been subject to it, and professing to be no longer so, by consequence deny they can transgress it, all the harms that can be done them, must be taken as acts of hostility. But in declared hostility, all infliction of evil is lawful. From whence it followeth, that if a subject shall by fact, or word, wittingly, and deliberately deny the authority of the representative of the commonwealth (whatsoever penalty hath been formerly ordained for treason,) he may lawfully be made to suffer whatsoever the representative will: For in denying subjection, he denies such punishment as by the law hath been ordained; and therefore suffers as an enemy of the commonwealth; that is, according to the will of the representative. For the punishments set down in the law, are to subjects, not to enemies; such as are they, that having been by their own act subjects, deliberately revolting, deny the sovereign power.

The first, and most general distribution of punishments, is into *divine*, and *human*. Of the former I shall have occasion to speak, in a more convenient place hereafter.

Human, are those punishments that be inflicted by the commandment of man; and are either *corporal*, or *pecuniary*, or *ignominy*, or *imprisonment*, or *exile*, or mixed of these.

Corporal punishment is that, which is inflicted on the body directly, and according to the intention of him that inflicteth it: such as are stripes, or wounds, or deprivation of such pleasures of the body, as were before lawfully enjoyed.

And of these, some be *capital*, some *less* than *capital*. Capital, is the infliction of death; and that either simply, or with torment. Less than capital, are stripes, wounds, chains, and any other corporal pain, not in its own nature mortal. For if upon the infliction of a punishment death follow not in the intention of the inflictor, the punishment is not to be esteemed capital, though the harm prove mortal by an accident

not to be foreseen; in which case death is not inflicted, but hastened.

Pecuniary punishment, is that which consisteth not only in the deprivation of a sum of money, but also of lands, or any other goods which are usually bought and sold for money. And in case the law, that ordaineth such a punishment, be made with design to gather money, from such as shall transgress the same, it is not properly a punishment, but the price of privilege and exemption from the law, which doth not absolutely forbid the fact, but only to those that are not able to pay the money: except where the law is natural, or part of religion; for in that case it is not an exemption from the law, but a transgression of it. As where a law exacteth a pecuniary mulct, of them that take the name of God in vain, the payment of the mulct, is not the price of a dispensation to swear, but the punishment of the transgression of a law indispensable. In like manner if the law impose a sum of money to be paid, to him that has been injured; this is but a satisfaction for the hurt done him; and extinguisheth the accusation of the party injured, not the crime of the offender.

Ignominy, is the infliction of such evil, as is made dishonourable; or the deprivation of such good, as is made honourable by the commonwealth. For there be some things honourable by nature; as the effects of courage, magnanimity, strength, wisdom, and other abilities of body and mind: others made honourable by the commonwealth; as badges, titles, offices, or any other singular mark of the sovereign's favour. The former, (though they may fail by nature, or accident,) cannot be taken away by a law; and therefore the loss of them is not punishment. But the latter, may be taken away by the public authority that made them honourable, and are properly punishments: such are degrading men condemned, of their badges, titles, and offices; or declaring them incapable of the like in time to come.

Imprisonment, is when a man is by public authority deprived of liberty; and may happen from two divers ends; whereof one is the safe custody of a man accused; the other is the inflicting of pain on a man condemned. The former is not punishment; because no man is supposed to be punished, before he be judicially heard, and declared guilty. And therefore whatsoever hurt a man is made to suffer by bonds, or restraint, before his cause be heard, over and above that which is necessary to assure his custody, is against the law of nature. But the latter is punishment, because evil, and inflicted by public authority, for somewhat that has by the same authority been judged a transgression of the law. Under this word imprisonment, I comprehend all restraint of motion, caused by an external obstacle, be it a house, which is called by the general name of a prison; or an island, as when men are said to be confined to it; or a place where men are set to work, as in old time men have been condemned to quarries, and in these times to galleys; or be it a chain, or any other such impediment.

Exile (banishment) is when a man is for a crime, condemned to depart out of the dominion of the commonwealth, or out of a certain part thereof; and during a prefixed time, or for ever, not to return into it: and seemeth not in its own nature, without other circumstances, to be a punishment; but rather an escape, or a public commandment to avoid punishment by flight. And *Cicero* says, there was never any such punishment ordained in the city of *Rome*; but calls it a refuge of men in danger. For if a man banished, be nevertheless permitted to enjoy his goods, and the revenue of his lands, the mere change of air is no punishment; nor does it tend to that benefit of the commonwealth, for which all punishments are ordained, (that is to say, to the forming of men's wills to the observation of the law;) but many times to the damage of the commonwealth. For a banished man, is a lawful enemy of the commonwealth that banished him; as being no more a member of the same. But if he be withal deprived of his lands, or goods, then the punishment lieth not in the exile, but is to be reckoned amongst punishments pecuniary.

All punishments of innocent subjects, be they great or little, are against the law of nature: For punishment is only for transgression of the law, and therefore there can be no punishment of the innocent. It is therefore a violation, first, of that law of nature, which forbiddeth all men, in their revenges, to look at any thing but some future good: For there can arrive no good to the commonwealth, by punishing the innocent.

Secondly, of that, which forbiddeth ingratitude: For seeing all sovereign power, is originally given by the consent of every one of the subjects, to the end they should as long as they are obedient, be protected thereby; the punishment of the innocent, is a rendering of evil for good. And thirdly, of the law that commandeth equity; that is to say, an equal distribution of justice; which in punishing the innocent is not observed.

But the infliction of what evil soever, on an innocent man, that is not a subject, if it be for the benefit of the commonwealth, and without violation of any former covenant, is no breach of the law of nature. For all men that are not subjects, are either enemies, or else they have ceased from being so by some precedent covenants. But against enemies, whom the commonwealth judgeth capable to do them hurt, it is lawful by the original right of nature to make war; wherein the sword judgeth not, nor doth the victor make distinction of nocent, and innocent, as to the time past; nor has other respect of mercy, than as it conduceth to the good of his own people. And upon this ground it is, that also in subjects, who deliberately deny the authority of the commonwealth established, the vengeance is lawfully extended, not only to the fathers, but also to the third and fourth generation not yet in being, and consequently innocent of the fact, for which they are afflicted: because the nature of this offence, consisteth in the renouncing of subjection; which is a relapse into the condition of war, commonly called rebellion; and they that so offend, suffer not as subjects, but as enemies. For *rebellion*, is but war renewed.

Reward, is either of *gift*, or by *contract*. When by contract, it is called *salary*, and *wages*; which is benefit due for service performed, or promised. When of gift, it is benefit proceeding from the *grace* of them that bestow it, to encourage, or enable men to do them service. And therefore when the sovereign of a commonwealth appointeth a salary to any public office, he that receiveth it, is bound in justice to perform his office; otherwise, he is bound only in honour, to acknowledgment, and an endeavour of requital. For though men have no lawful remedy, when they be commanded to quit their private business, to serve the public, without reward or salary; yet they are not bound thereto, by the law of nature, nor by the institution of the commonwealth, unless the service cannot otherwise be done; because it is supposed the sovereign may make use of all their means, insomuch as the most common soldier, may demand the wages of his warfare, as a debt.

The benefits which a sovereign bestoweth on a subject, for fear of some power, and ability he hath to do hurt to the commonwealth, are not properly rewards; for they are not salaries; because there is in this case no contract supposed, every man being obliged already not to do the commonwealth disservice: nor are they graces; because they be extorted by fear, which ought not to be incident to the sovereign power: but are rather sacrifices, which the sovereign (considered in his natural person, and not in the person of the commonwealth) makes, for the appeasing the discontent of him he thinks more potent than himself; and encourage not to obedience, but on the contrary, to the continuance, and increasing of further extortion.

And whereas some salaries are certain, and proceed from the public treasure; and others uncertain, and casual, proceeding from the execution of the office for which the salary is ordained; the latter is in some cases hurtful to the commonwealth; as in the case of judicature. For where the benefit of the judges, and ministers of a court of justice, ariseth for the multitude of causes that are brought to their cognizance, there must needs follow two inconveniences: one, is the nourishing of suits; for the more suits, the greater benefit: and another that depends on that, which is contention about jurisdiction; each court drawing to itself, as many causes as it can. But in offices of execution there are not those inconveniences; because their employment cannot be increased by any endeavour of their own. And thus much shall suffice for the nature of punishment and reward; which are, as it were, the nerves and tendons, that move the limbs and joints of a commonwealth.

Hitherto I have set forth the nature of man, (whose pride and other passions have compelled him to submit himself to government;) together with the great power of his governor, whom I compared to *Levia-*

than, taking that comparison out of the two last verses of the one and fortieth of *Job*; where God having set forth the great power of *Leviathan*, calleth him king of the proud. *There is nothing*, saith he, *on earth, to be compared with him. He is made so as not to be afraid. He seeth every high thing below him; and is king of all the children of pride.* But because he is mortal, and subject to decay, as all other earthly creatures are; and because there is that in heaven, (though not on earth) that he should stand in fear of, and whose laws he ought to obey; I shall in the next following chapters speak of his diseases, and the causes of his mortality; and of what laws of nature he is bound to obey.

CHAPTER 29: Of Those Things That Weaken, or Tend to the Dissolution of a Commonwealth

Though nothing can be immortal, which mortals make; yet, if men had the use of reason they pretend to, their commonwealths might be secured, at least, from perishing by internal diseases. For by the nature of their institution, they are designed to live, as long as mankind, or as the laws of nature, or as justice itself, which gives them life. Therefore when they come to be dissolved, not by external violence, but intestine disorder, the fault is not in men, as they are the *matter*; but as they are the *makers*, and orderers of them. For men, as they become at last weary of irregular jostling, and hewing one another, and desire with all their hearts, to conform themselves into one firm and lasting edifice; so for want, both of the art of making fit laws, to square their actions by, and also of humility, and patience, to suffer the rude and cumbersome points of their present greatness to be taken off, they cannot without the help of a very able architect, be compiled, into any other than a crazy building, such as hardly lasting out their own time, must assuredly fall upon the heads of their posterity.

Amongst the *infirmities* therefore of a commonwealth, I will reckon in the first place, those that arise from an imperfect institution, and resemble the diseases of a natural body, which proceed from a defectuous procreation.

Of which, this is one, *that a man to obtain a kingdom, is sometimes content with less power, than to the peace, and defence of the commonwealth is necessarily required.* From whence it cometh to pass, that when the exercise of the power laid by, is for the public safety to be resumed, it hath the resemblance of an unjust act; which disposeth great numbers of men (when occasion is presented) to rebel; in the same manner as the bodies of children, gotten by diseased parents, are subject either to untimely death, or to purge the ill quality, derived from their vicious conception, by breaking out into biles and scabs. And when kings deny themselves some such necessary power, it is not always (though sometimes), out of ignorance of what is necessary to the office they undertake; but many times out of a hope to recover the same again at their pleasure: Wherein they reason not well; because such as will hold them to their promises, shall be maintained against them by foreign commonwealths; who in order to the good of their own subjects let slip few occasions to *weaken* the estate of their neighbours. So was *Thomas Becket,* archbishop of *Canterbury,* supported against *Henry* the Second, by the Pope; the subjection of ecclesiastics to the commonwealth, having been dispensed with by *William the Conqueror* at his reception, when he took an oath, not to infringe the liberty of the church. And so were the *barons,* whose power was by *William Rufus* (to have their help in transferring the succession from his elder brother, to himself,) increased to a degree, inconsistent with the sovereign power, maintained in their rebellion against *King John,* by the French.

Nor does this happen in monarchy only. For whereas the style of the ancient Roman commonwealth, was, *the senate, and people of Rome;* neither senate, nor people pretended to the whole power; which first caused the seditions, of *Tiberius Gracchus, Caius Gracchus, Lucius Saturninus,* and others; and afterwards the wars between the senate and the people, under *Marius* and *Sylla;* and again under *Pompey* and *Caesar,* to the extinction of their democracy, and the setting up of monarchy.

The people of *Athens* bound themselves but from one only action; which was, that no man on pain of death should propound the renewing of the war for the island of *Salamis;* and yet thereby, if *Solon* had not caused to be given out he was mad, and afterwards in gesture and habit of a madman, and in verse, propounded it to the people that flocked about him, they had had an enemy perpetually in readiness, even at the gates of their city; such damage, or shifts, are all commonwealths forced to, that have their power never so little limited.

In the second place, I observe the *diseases* of a commonwealth, that proceed from the poison of seditious doctrines, whereof one is, *That every private man is judge of good and evil actions.* This is true in the condition of mere nature, where there are no civil laws; and also under civil government, in such cases as are not determined by the law. But otherwise, it is manifest, that the measure of good and evil actions, is the civil law; and the judge the legislator, who is always representative of the commonwealth. From this false doctrine, men are disposed to debate with themselves, and dispute the commands of the commonwealth; and afterwards to obey, or disobey them, as in their private judgments they shall think fit. Whereby the commonwealth is distracted and *weakened.*

Another doctrine repugnant to civil society, is, that *whatsoever a man does against his conscience, is sin;* and it dependeth on the presumption of making himself judge of good and evil. For a man's conscience, and his judgment is the same thing; and as the judgment, so also the conscience may be erroneous. Therefore, though he that is subject to no civil law, sinneth in all he does against his conscience, because he has no other rule to follow but his own reason; yet it is not so with him that lives in a commonwealth; because the law is the public conscience, by which he hath already undertaken to be guided. Otherwise in such diversity, as there is of private consciences, which are but private opinions, the commonwealth must needs be distracted, and no man dare to obey the sovereign power, farther than it shall seem good in his own eyes.

It hath been also commonly taught, *that faith and sanctity, are not to be attained by study and reason, but by supernatural inspiration, or infusion,* which granted, I see not why any man should render a reason of his faith; or why every Christian should not be also a prophet; or why any man should take the law of his country, rather than his own inspiration, for the rule of his action. And thus we fall again into the fault of taking upon us to judge of good and evil; or to make judges of it, such private men as pretend to be supernaturally inspired, to the dissolution of all civil government. Faith comes by hearing, and hearing by those accidents, which guide us into the presence of them that speak to us; which accidents are all contrived by God Almighty; and yet are not supernatural, but only, for the great number of them that concur to every effect, unobservable. Faith and sanctity, are indeed not very frequent; but yet they are not miracles, but brought to pass by education, discipline, correction, and other natural ways, by which God worketh them in his elect, at such time as he thinketh fit. And these three opinions, pernicious to peace and government, have in this part of the world, proceeded chiefly from the tongues, and pens of unlearned divines; who joining the words of Holy Scripture together, otherwise than is agreeable to reason, do what they can, to make men think, that sanctity and natural reason, cannot stand together.

A fourth opinion, repugnant to the nature of a commonwealth, is this, *that he that hath the sovereign power, is subject to the civil laws.* It is true, that sovereigns are all subject to the laws of nature; because such laws be divine, and cannot by any man, or commonwealth be abrogated. But to those laws which the sovereign himself, that is, which the commonwealth maketh, he is not subject. For to be subject to laws, is to be subject to the commonwealth, that is to the sovereign representative, that is to himself; which is not subjection, but freedom from the laws. Which error, because it setteth the laws above the sovereign, setteth also a judge above him, and a power to punish him; which is to make a new sovereign; and again for the same reason a third, to punish the second; and so continually without end, to the confusion, and dissolution of the commonwealth.

A fifth doctrine, that tendeth to the dissolution of a commonwealth, is, *that every private man has an absolute propriety in his goods; such, as excludeth the*

right of the sovereign. Every man has indeed a propriety that excludes the right of every other subject: and he has it only from the sovereign power; without the protection whereof, every other man should have equal right to the same. But if the right of the sovereign also be excluded, he cannot perform the office they have put him into; which is, to defend them both from foreign enemies, and from the injuries of one another; and consequently there is no longer a commonwealth.

And if the propriety of subjects, exclude not the right of the sovereign representative to their goods; much less to their offices of judicature, or execution, in which they represent the sovereign himself.

There is a sixth doctrine, plainly, and directly against the essence of a commonwealth; and it is this, *that the sovereign power may be divided.* For what is it to divide the power of a commonwealth, but to dissolve it; for powers divided mutually destroy each other. And for these doctrines, men are chiefly beholding to some of those, that making profession of the laws, endeavour to make them depend upon their own learning, and not upon the legislative power.

And as false doctrine, so also oftentimes the example of different government in a neighbouring nation, disposeth men to alteration of the form already settled. So the people of the Jews were stirred up to reject God, and to call upon the prophet *Samuel*, for a king after the manner of the nations: so also the lesser cities of *Greece*, were continually disturbed, with seditions of the aristocratical, and democratical factions; one part of almost every commonwealth, desiring to imitate the Lacedemonians; the other, the Athenians. And I doubt not, but many men, have been contented to see the late troubles in *England*, out of an imitation of the Low Countries; supposing there needed no more to grow rich, than to change, as they had done, the form of their government. For the constitution of man's nature, is of itself subject to desire novelty: When therefore they are provoked to the same, by the neighbourhood also of those that have been enriched by it, it is almost impossible for them, not to be content with those that solicit them to change; and love the first beginnings, though they be grieved with the continuance of disorder; like hot bloods, that having gotten the itch, tear themselves with their own nails, till they can endure the smart no longer.

And as to rebellion in particular against monarchy; one of the most frequent causes of it, is the reading of the books of policy, and histories of the ancient Greeks, and Romans; from which, young men, and all others that are unprovided of the antidote of solid reason, receiving a strong, and delightful impression, of the great exploits of war, achieved by the conductors of their armies, receive withal a pleasing idea, of all they have done besides; and imagine their great prosperity, not to have proceeded from the emulation of particular men, but from the virtue of their popular form of government: not considering the frequent seditions, and civil wars, produced by the imperfection of their policy. From the reading, I say, of such books, men have undertaken to kill their kings, because the Greek and Latin writers, in their books and discourses of policy, make it lawful, and laudable, for any man so to do; provided, before he do it, he call him tyrant. For they say not *regicide*, that is, killing of a king, but *tyrannicide*, that is, killing of a tyrant is lawful. From the same books, they that live under a monarch conceive an opinion, that the subjects in a popular commonwealth enjoy liberty; but that in a monarchy they are all slaves. I say, they that live under a monarchy conceive such an opinion; not they that live under a popular government: for they find no such matter. In sum, I cannot imagine, how any thing can be more prejudicial to a monarchy, than the allowing of such books to be publicly read, without present applying such correctives of discreet masters, as are fit to take away their venom: which venom I will not doubt to compare to the biting of a mad dog, which is a disease the physicians call *hydrophobia*, or *fear of water*. For as he that is so bitten, has a continual torment of thirst, and yet abhorreth water; and is in such an estate, as if the poison endeavoured to convert him into a dog: so when a monarchy is once bitten to the quick, by those democratical writers, that continually snarl at that estate; it wanteth nothing more than a strong monarch, which nevertheless out of a certain *tyrannophobia*, or fear of being strongly governed, when they have him, they abhor.

As there have been doctors, that hold there be three souls in a man; so there be also that think there may be more souls, (that is, more sovereigns,) than one, in a commonwealth; and set up a *supremacy* against the *sovereignty*; *canons* against *laws*; and a *ghostly authority* against the *civil*; working on men's minds, with words and distinctions, that of themselves signify nothing, but bewray (by their obscurity) that there walketh (as some think invisibly) another kingdom, as it were a kingdom of fairies, in the dark. Now seeing it is manifest, that the civil power, and the power of the commonwealth is the same thing; and that supremacy, and the power of making canons, and granting faculties, implieth a commonwealth; it followeth, that where one is sovereign, another supreme; where one can make laws, and another make canons; there must needs be two commonwealths, of one and the same subjects; which is a kingdom divided in itself, and cannot stand. For notwithstanding the insignificant distinction of *temporal*, and *ghostly*, they are still two kingdoms, and every subject is subject to two masters. For seeing the *ghostly* power challengeth the right to declare what is sin it challengeth by consequence to declare what is law, (sin being nothing but the transgression of the law;) and again, the civil power challenging to declare what is law, every subject must obey two masters, who both will have their commands be observed as law; which is impossible. Or, if it be but one kingdom, either the *civil*, which is the power of the commonwealth, must be subordinate to the *ghostly*, and then there is no sovereignty but the *ghostly*; or the *ghostly* must be subordinate to the *temporal*, and then there is no *supremacy* but the *temporal*. When therefore these two powers oppose one another, the commonwealth cannot but be in great danger of civil war, and dissolution. For the *civil* authority being more visible, and standing in the clearer light of natural reason, cannot choose but draw to it in all times a very considerable part of the people: and the *spiritual*, though it stand in the darkness of School distinctions, and hard words; yet because the fear of darkness, and ghosts, is greater than other fears, cannot want a party sufficient to trouble, and sometimes to destroy a commonwealth, and this is a disease which not unfitly may be compared to the epilepsy, or falling sickness (which the Jews took to be one kind of possession by spirits) in the body natural. For as in this disease, there is an unnatural spirit, or wind in the head that obstructeth the roots of the nerves, and moving them violently, taketh away the motion which naturally they should have from the power of the soul in the brain, and thereby causeth violent, and irregular motions (which men call convulsions) in the parts; insomuch as he that is seized therewith, falleth down sometimes into the water, and sometimes into the fire, as a man deprived of his senses; so also in the body politic, when the spiritual power, moveth the members of a commonwealth, by the terror of punishments, and hope of rewards (which are the nerves of it,) otherwise than by the civil power (which is the soul of the commonwealth), they ought to be moved; and by strange, and hard words suffocates their understanding, it must needs thereby distract the people, and either overwhelm the commonwealth with oppression, or cast it into the fire of a civil war.

Sometimes also in the merely civil government, there be more than one soul: as when the power of levying money, (which is the nutritive faculty,) has depended on a general assembly; the power of conduct and command, (which is the motive faculty,) on one man; and the power of making laws, (which is the rational faculty,) on the accidental consent, not only of those two, but also of a third; this endangereth the commonwealth, sometimes for want of consent to good laws; but most often for want of such nourishment, as is necessary to life, and motion. For although few perceive, that such government, is not government, but division of the commonwealth into three factions, and call it mixed monarchy; yet the truth is, that it is not one independent commonwealth, but three independent factions; nor one representative person, but three. In the kingdom of God, there may be three persons independent, without breach of unity in God that reigneth; but where men reign, that be subject to diversity of opinions, it cannot be so. And therefore if the king bear the person of the people, and the general assembly bear also the person of the people, and another assembly bear the person of a part of the people, they are not one person, nor one sovereign, but three persons, and three sovereigns.

To what disease in the natural body of man I may exactly compare this irregularity of a commonwealth, I know not. But I have seen a man, that had another man growing out of his side, with an head, arms, breast, and stomach, of his own: if he had had another man growing out of his other side, the comparison might then have been exact.

Hitherto I have named such diseases of a commonwealth, as are of the greatest, and most present danger. There be other, not so great; which nevertheless are not unfit to be observed. As first, the difficulty of raising money, for the necessary uses of the commonwealth; especially in the approach of war. This difficulty ariseth from the opinion, that every subject hath of a propriety in his lands and goods, exclusive of the sovereign's right to the use of the same. From whence it cometh to pass, that the sovereign power, which foreseeth the necessities and dangers of the commonwealth, (finding the passage of money to the public treasure obstructed, by the tenacity of the people,) whereas it ought to extend itself, to encounter, and prevent such dangers in their beginnings, contracteth itself as long as it can, and when it cannot longer, struggles with the people by stratagems of law, to obtain little sums, which not sufficing, he is fain at last violently to open the way for present supply, or perish; and being put often to these extremities, at last reduceth the people to their due temper; or else the commonwealth must perish. Insomuch as we may compare this distemper very aptly to an ague; wherein, the fleshy parts being congealed, or by venomous matter obstructed; the veins which by their natural course empty themselves into the heart, are not (as they ought to be) supplied from the arteries, whereby there succeedeth at first a cold contraction, and trembling of the limbs; and afterwards a hot, and strong endeavour of the heart, to force a passage for the blood; and before it can do that, contenteth itself with the small refreshments of such things as cool for a time, till (if nature be strong enough), it break at last the contumacy of the parts obstructed, and dissipateth the venom into sweat; or (if nature be too weak) the patient dieth.

Again, there is sometimes in a commonwealth, a disease, which resembleth the pleurisy; and that is, when the treasure of the commonwealth, flowing out of its due course, is gathered together in too much abundance in one, or a few private men, by monopolies, or by farms of the public revenues; in the same manner as the blood in a pleurisy, getting into the membrane of the breast, breedeth there an inflammation, accompanied with a fever, and painful stitches.

Also the popularity of a potent subject, (unless the commonwealth have very good caution of his fidelity,) is a dangerous disease; because the people (which should receive their motion from the authority of the sovereign,) by the flattery, and by the reputation of an ambitious man, are drawn away from their obedience to the laws, to follow a man, of whose virtues, and designs they have no knowledge. And this is commonly of more danger in a popular government, than in a monarchy; because an army is of so great force, and multitude, as it may easily be made believe, they are the people. By this means it was, that *Julius Caesar*, who was set up by the people against the senate, having won to himself the affections of his army, made himself master, both of senate and people. And this proceeding of popular, and ambitious men, is plain rebellion; and may be resembled to the effects of witchcraft.

Another infirmity of a commonwealth, is the immoderate greatness of a town, when it is able to furnish out of its own circuit, the number, and expense of a great army: as also the great number of corporations; which are as it were many lesser commonwealths in the bowels of a greater, like worms in the entrails of a natural man. To which may be added, the liberty of disputing against absolute power, by pretenders to political prudence; which though bred for the most part in the lees of the people; yet animated by false doctrines, are perpetually meddling with the fundamental laws, to the molestation of the commonwealth; like the little worms, which physicians call *ascarides*.

We may further add, the insatiable appetite, or Bulimia, of enlarging dominion; with the incurable *wounds* thereby many times received from the enemy; and the *wens*, of ununited conquests, which are many times a burthen, and with less danger lost, than kept; as also the *lethargy* of ease, and *consumption* of riot and vain expense.

Lastly, when in a war (foreign or intestine,) the enemies get a final victory; so as (the forces of the commonwealth keeping the field no longer), there is no farther protection of subjects in their loyalty; then is the commonwealth DISSOLVED, and every man at liberty to protect himself by such courses as his own discretion shall suggest unto him. For the sovereign, is the public soul, giving life and motion to the commonwealth; which expiring, the members are governed by it no more, than the carcase of a man, by his departed (though immortal) soul. For though the right of a sovereign monarch cannot be extinguished by the act of another; yet the obligation of the members may. For he that wants protection, may seek it any where; and when he hath it, is obliged (without fraudulent pretence of having submitted himself out of fear,) to protect his protection as long as he is able. But when the power of an assembly is once suppressed, the right of the same perisheth utterly; because the assembly itself is extinct; and consequently, there is no possibility for the sovereignty to re-enter.

CHAPTER 30: Of the Office of the Sovereign Representative

The office of the sovereign, (be it a monarch, or an assembly,) consisteth in the end, for which he was trusted with the sovereign power, namely the procuration of *the safety of the people*; to which he is obliged by the law of nature, and to render an account thereof to God, the author of that law, and to none but him. But by safety here, is not meant a bare preservation, but also all other contentments of life, which every man by lawful industry, without danger, or hurt to the commonwealth, shall acquire to himself.

And this is intended should be done, not by care applied to individuals, further than their protection from injuries, when they shall complain; but by a general providence, contained in public instruction, both of doctrine, and example; and in the making, and executing of good laws, to which individual persons may apply their own cases.

And because, if the essential rights of sovereignty (specified before in the eighteenth chapter) be taken away, the commonwealth is thereby dissolved, and every man returneth into the condition, and calamity of a war with every other man, (which is the greatest evil that can happen in this life;) it is the office of the sovereign, to maintain those rights entire; and consequently against his duty, first, to transfer to another, or to lay from himself any of them. For he that deserteth the means, deserteth the ends; and he deserteth the means, that being the sovereign, acknowledgeth himself subject to the civil laws; and renounceth the power of supreme judicature; or of making war, or peace by his own authority; or of judging of the necessities of the commonwealth; or of levying money, and soldiers, when, and as much as in his own conscience he shall judge necessary; or of making officers, and ministers both of war and peace; or of appointing teachers, and examining what doctrines are conformable, or contrary to the defence, peace, and good of the people. Secondly, it is against his duty, to let the people be ignorant, or misinformed of the grounds, and reasons of those his essential rights; because thereby men are easy to be seduced, and drawn to resist him, when the commonwealth shall require their use and exercise.

And the grounds of these rights, have the rather need to be diligently, and truly taught; because they cannot be maintained by any civil law, or terror of legal punishment. For a civil law, that shall forbid rebellion (and such is all resistance to the essential rights of sovereignty), is not (as a civil law) any obligation, but by virtue only of the law of nature, that forbiddeth the violation of faith; which natural obligation if men know not, they cannot know the right of any law the sovereign maketh. And for the punishment, they take it but for an act of hostility; which when they think they have strength enough, they will endeavour by acts of hostility, to avoid.

As I have heard some say, that justice is but a word, without substance; and that whatsoever a man can by force, or art, acquire to himself (not only in the condition of war, but also in a commonwealth,) is

his own, which I have already showed to be false: so there be also that maintain, that there are no grounds, nor principles of reason, to sustain those essential rights, which make sovereignty absolute. For if there were, they would have been found out in some place, or other; whereas we see, there has not hitherto been any commonwealth, where those rights have been acknowledged, or challenged. Wherein they argue as ill, as if the savage people of America, should deny there were any grounds, or principles of reason, so to build a house, as to last as long as the materials, because they never yet saw any so well built. Time, and industry, produce every day new knowledge. And as the art of well building, is derived from principles of reason, observed by industrious men, that had long studied the nature of materials, and the divers effects of figure, and proportion, long after mankind began (though poorly) to build: so, long time after men have begun to constitute commonwealths, imperfect, and apt to relapse into disorder, there may principles of reason be found out, by industrious meditation, to make their constitution (excepting by external violence) everlasting. And such are those which I have in this discourse set forth: which whether they come not into the sight of those that have power to make use of them, or be neglected by them, or not, concerneth my particular interest, at this day, very little. But supposing that these of mine are not such principles of reason; yet I am sure they are principles from authority of Scripture; as I shall make it appear, when I shall come to speak of the kingdom of God, (administered by *Moses*,) over the Jews, his peculiar people by covenant.

But they say again, that though the principles be right, yet common people are not of capacity enough to be made to understand them. I should be glad, that the rich, and potent subjects of a kingdom, or those that are accounted the most learned, were no less incapable than they. But all men know, that the obstructions to this kind of doctrine, proceed not so much from the difficulty of the matter, as from the interest of them that are to learn. Potent men, digest hardly any thing that setteth up a power to bridle their affections; and learned men, any thing that discovereth their errors, and thereby lesseneth their authority: whereas the common people's minds, unless they be tainted with dependence on the potent, or scribbled over with the opinions of their doctors, are like clean paper, fit to receive whatsoever by public authority shall be imprinted in them. Shall whole nations be brought to *acquiesce* in the great mysteries of Christian religion, which are above reason; and millions of men be made believe, that the same body may be in innumerable places, at one and the same time, which is against reason; and shall not men be able, by their teaching, and preaching, protected by the law, to make that received, which is so consonant to reason, that any unprejudicated man, needs no more to learn it, than to hear it? I conclude therefore, that in the instruction of the people in the essential rights (which are the natural, and fundamental laws) of sovereignty, there is no difficulty, (whilst a sovereign has his power entire,) but what proceeds from his own fault, or the fault of those whom he trusteth in the administration of the commonwealth; and consequently, it is his duty, to cause them so to be instructed; and not only his duty, but his benefit also, and security, against the danger that may arrive to himself in his natural person, from rebellion.

And (to descend to particulars) the people are to be taught, first, that they ought not to be in love with any form of government they see in their neighbour nations, more than with their own, nor, (whatsoever present prosperity they behold in nations that are otherwise governed than they,) to desire change. For the prosperity of a people ruled by an aristocratical, or democratical assembly, cometh not from aristocracy, nor from democracy, but from the obedience, and concord of the subjects: nor do the people flourish in a monarchy, because one man has the right to rule them, but because they obey him. Take away in any kind of state, the obedience, (and consequently the concord of the people,) and they shall not only not flourish, but in short time be dissolved. And they that go about by disobedience, to do no more than reform the commonwealth, shall find they do thereby destroy it; like the foolish daughters of *Peleus*, (in the fable;) which desiring to renew the youth of their decrepid father, did by the counsel of *Medea*, cut him in pieces, and boil him, together with strange

herbs, but made not of him a new man. This desire of change, is like the breach of the first of God's commandments: for there God says, *Non habebis Deos alienos*; Thou shalt not have the Gods of other nations; and in another place concerning *kings*, that they are *Gods*.

Secondly, they are to be taught, that they ought not to be led with admiration of the virtue of any of their fellow subjects, how high soever he stand, nor how conspicuously soever he shine in the commonwealth; nor of any assembly, (except the sovereign assembly,) so as to defer to them any obedience, or honour, appropriate to the sovereign only, whom (in their particular stations) they represent; nor to receive any influence from them, but such as is conveyed by them from the sovereign authority. For that sovereign, cannot be imagined to love his people as he ought, that is not jealous of them, but suffers them by the flattery of popular men, to be seduced from their loyalty, as they have often been, not only secretly, but openly, so as to proclaim marriage with them *in facie ecclesiciae* by preachers; and by publishing the same in the open streets: which may fitly be compared to the violation of the second of the ten commandments.

Thirdly, in consequence to this, they ought to be informed, how great a fault it is, to speak evil of the sovereign representative, (whether one man, or an assembly of men;) or to argue and dispute his power; or any way to use his name irreverently, whereby he may be brought into contempt with his people, and their obedience (in which the safety of the commonwealth consisteth) slackened. Which doctrine the third commandment by resemblance pointeth to.

Fourthly, seeing people cannot be taught this, nor when it is taught, remember it, nor after one generation past, so much as know in whom the sovereign power is placed, without setting apart from their ordinary labour, some certain times, in which they may attend those that are appointed to instruct them; it is necessary that some such times be determined, wherein they may assemble together, and (after prayers and praises given to God, the sovereign of sovereigns) hear those their duties told them, and the positive laws, such as generally concern them all, read and expounded, and be put in mind of the authority that maketh them laws. To this end had the *Jews* every seventh day, a *sabbath*, in which the law was read and expounded; and in the solemnity whereof they were put in mind, that their king was God; that having created the world in six days, he rested the seventh day; and by their resting on it from their labour, that that God was their king, which redeemed them from their servile, and painful labour in *Egypt*, and gave them a time, after they had rejoiced in God, to take joy also in themselves, by lawful recreation. So that the first table of the commandments, is spent all in setting down the sum of God's absolute power; not only as God, but as king by pact, (in peculiar) of the Jews; and may therefore give light, to those that have sovereign power conferred on them by the consent of men, to see what doctrine they ought to teach their subjects.

And because the first instruction of children, dependeth on the care of their parents; it is necessary that they should be obedient to them, whilst they are under their tuition; and not only so, but that also afterwards (as gratitude requireth,) they acknowledge the benefit of their education, by external signs of honour. To which end they are to be taught, that originally the father of every man was also his sovereign lord, with power over him of life and death; and that the fathers of families, when by instituting a commonwealth, they resigned that absolute power, yet it was never intended, they should lose the honour due unto them for their education. For to relinquish such right, was not necessary to the institution of sovereign power; nor would there be any reason, why any man should desire to have children, or take the care to nourish, and instruct them, if they were afterwards to have no other benefit from them, than from other men. And this accordeth with the fifth commandment.

Again, every sovereign ought to cause justice to be taught, which (consisting in taking from no man what is his,) is as much as to say, to cause men to be taught not to deprive their neighbours, by violence, or fraud, of any thing which by the sovereign authority is theirs. Of things held in propriety, those that are dearest to a man are his own life, and limbs; and in the next degree (in most men,) those that concern conjugal

affection; and after them riches and means of living. Therefore the people are to be taught, to abstain from violence to one another's person, by private revenges; from violation of conjugal honour; and from forcible rapine, and fraudulent surreption of one another's goods. For which purpose also it is necessary they be showed the evil consequences of false judgment, by corruption either of judges or witnesses, whereby the distinction of propriety is taken away, and justice becomes of no effect: all which things are intimated in the sixth, seventh, eighth, and ninth commandments.

Lastly, they are to be taught, that not only the unjust facts, but the designs and intentions to do them, (though by accident hindered,) are injustice; which consisteth in the pravity of the will, as well as in the irregularity of the act. And this is the intention of the tenth commandment, and the sum of the second table; which is reduced all to this one commandment of mutual charity, *thou shalt love thy neighbour as thyself*: as the sum of the first table is reduced to *the love of God*; whom they had then newly received as their king.

As for the means, and conduits, by which the people may receive this instruction, we are to search, by what means so many opinions, contrary to the peace of mankind, upon weak and false principles, have nevertheless been so deeply rooted in them. I mean those, which I have in the precedent chapter specified: as that men shall judge of what is lawful and unlawful, not by the law itself, but by their own consciences; that is to say, by their own private judgments: that subjects sin in obeying the commands of the commonwealth, unless they themselves have first judged them to be lawful: that their propriety in their riches is such, as to exclude the dominion, which the commonwealth hath over the same: that it is lawful for subjects to kill such, as they call tyrants: that the sovereign power may be divided, and the like; which come to be instilled into the people by this means. They whom necessity, or covetousness keepeth attent on their trades, and labour; and they, on the other side, whom superfluity, or sloth carrieth after their sensual pleasures, (which two sorts of men take up the greatest part of mankind,) being diverted from the deep meditation, which the learning of truth, not only in the matter of natural justice, but also of all other sciences necessarily requireth, receive the notions of their duty, chiefly from divines in the pulpit, and partly from such of their neighbours, or familiar acquaintance, as having the faculty of discoursing readily, and plausibly, seem wiser and better learned in cases of law, and conscience, than themselves. And the divines, and such others as make show of learning, derive their knowledge from the universities, and from the schools of law, or from the books, which by men eminent in those schools, and universities have been published. It is therefore manifest, that the instruction of the people, dependeth wholly, on the right teaching of youth in the universities. But are not (may some man say) the universities of *England* learned enough already to do that? or is it you will undertake to teach the universities? Hard questions. Yet to the first, I doubt not to answer; that till towards the latter end of *Henry the Eighth*, the power of the Pope, was always upheld against the power of the commonwealth, principally by the universities; and that the doctrines maintained by so many preachers, against the sovereign power of the king, and by so many lawyers, and others, that had their education there, is a sufficient argument, that though the universities were not authors of those false doctrines, yet they knew not how to plant the true. For in such a contradiction of opinions, it is most certain, that they have not been sufficiently instructed; and it is no wonder, if they yet retain a relish of that subtle liquor, wherewith they were first seasoned, against the civil authority. But to the latter question, it is not fit, nor needful for me to say either aye, or no: for any man that sees what I am doing, may easily perceive what I think.

The safety of the people, requireth further, from him, or them that have the sovereign power, that justice be equally administered to all degrees of people; that is, that as well the rich and mighty, as poor and obscure persons, may be righted of the injuries done them; so as the great, may have no greater hope of impunity, when they do violence, dishonour, or any injury to the meaner sort, than when one of these, does the like to one of them: For in this consisteth equity; to which, as being a precept of the law of nature, a sovereign is as much subject, as any of the meanest of his people. All breaches of the law, are offences against the commonwealth: but there be some, that are also against private persons. Those that concern the commonwealth only, may without breach of equity be pardoned; for every man may pardon what is done against himself, according to his own discretion. But an offence against a private man, cannot in equity be pardoned, without the consent of him that is injured; or reasonable satisfaction.

The inequality of subjects, proceedeth from the acts of sovereign power; and therefore has no more place in the presence of the sovereign; that is to say, in a court of justice, than the inequality between kings, and their subjects, in the presence of the King of kings. The honour of great persons, is to be valued for their beneficence and the aids they give to men of inferior rank, or not at all. And the violences, oppressions, and injuries they do, are not extenuated, but aggravated by the greatness of their persons; because they have least need to commit them. The consequences of this partiality towards the great, proceed in this manner. Impunity maketh insolence; insolence hatred; and hatred, an endeavour to pull down all oppressing and contumelious greatness, though with the ruin of the commonwealth.

To equal justice, appertaineth also the equal imposition of taxes; the equality whereof dependeth not on the equality of riches, but on the equality of the debt, that every man oweth to the commonwealth for his defence. It is not enough, for a man to labour for the maintenance of his life; but also to fight, (if need be,) for the securing of his labour. They must either do as the Jews did after their return from captivity, in re-edifying the temple, build with one hand, and hold the sword in the other; or else they must hire others to fight for them. For the impositions, that are laid on the people by the sovereign power, are nothing else but the wages, due to them that hold the public sword, to defend private men in the exercise of several trades, and callings. Seeing then the benefit that every one receiveth thereby, is the enjoyment of life, which is equally dear to poor and rich; the debt which a poor man oweth them that defend his life, is the same which a rich man oweth for the defence of his; saving that the rich, who have the service of the poor, may be debtors not only for their own persons, but for many more. Which considered, the equality of imposition, consisteth rather in the equality of that which is consumed, than of the riches of the persons that consume the same. For what reason is there, that he which laboureth much, and sparing the fruits of his labour, consumeth little, should be more charged, than he that living idly, getteth little, and spendeth all he gets; seeing the one hath no more protection from the commonwealth, than the other? But when the impositions, are laid upon those things which men consume, every man payeth equally for what he useth: nor is the commonwealth defrauded by the luxurious waste of private men.

And whereas many men, by accident inevitable, become unable to maintain themselves by their labour; they ought not to be left to the charity of private persons; but to be provided for, (as far-forth as the necessities of nature require,) by the laws of the commonwealth. For as it is uncharitableness in any man, to neglect the impotent; so it is in the sovereign of a commonwealth, to expose them to the hazard of such uncertain charity.

But for such as have strong bodies, the case is otherwise: they are to be forced to work; and to avoid the excuse of not finding employment, there ought to be such laws, as may encourage all manner of arts; as navigation, agriculture, fishing, and all manner of manufacture that requires labour. The multitude of poor, and yet strong people still increasing, they are to be transplanted into countries not sufficiently inhabited: where nevertheless, they are not to exterminate those they find there; but constrain them to inhabit closer together, and not range a great deal of ground, to snatch what they find; but to court each little plot with art and labour, to give them their sustenance in due season. And when all the world is overcharged with inhabitants, then the last remedy of all is war; which provideth for every man, by victory, or death.

To the care of the sovereign, belongeth the making of good laws. But what is a good law? By a good law, I mean not a just law: for no law can be unjust. The law is made by the sovereign power, and all that is done by such power, is warranted, and owned by every one of the people; and that which every man will have so, no man can say is unjust. It is in the laws of a commonwealth, as in the laws of gaming: whatsoever the gamesters all agree on, is injustice to none of them. A good law is that, which is *needful*, for the *good of the people*, and withal *perspicuous*.

For the use of laws, (which are but rules authorized) is not to bind the people from all voluntary actions; but to direct and keep them in such a motion, as not to hurt themselves by their own impetuous desires, rashness, or indiscretion; as hedges are set, not to stop travellers, but to keep them in the way. And therefore a law that is not needful, having not the true end of a law, is not good. A law may be conceived to be good, when it is for the benefit of the sovereign; though it be not necessary for the people; but it is not so. For the good of the sovereign and people, cannot be separated. It is a weak sovereign, that has weak subjects; and a weak people, whose sovereign wanteth power to rule them at his will. Unnecessary laws are not good laws; but traps for money: which where the right of sovereign power is acknowledged, are superfluous; and where it is not acknowledged, insufficient to defend the people.

The perspicuity, consisteth not so much in the words of the law itself, as in a declaration of the causes, and motives, for which it was made. That is it, that shows us the meaning of the legislator; and the meaning of the legislator known, the law is more easily understood by few, than many words. For all words, are subject to ambiguity; and therefore multiplication of words in the body of the law, is multiplication of ambiguity: besides it seems to imply, (by too much diligence,) that whosoever can evade the words, is without the compass of the law. And this is a cause of many unnecessary processes. For when I consider how short were the laws of ancient times; and how they grew by degrees still longer; methinks I see a contention between the penners, and pleaders of the law; the former seeking to circumscribe the latter; and the latter to evade their circumscriptions; and that the pleaders have got the victory. It belongeth therefore to the office of a legislator, (such as is in all commonwealths the supreme representative, be it one man, or an assembly,) to make the reason perspicuous, why the law was made; and the body of the law itself, as short, but in as proper, and significant terms, as may be.

It belongeth also to the office of the sovereign, to make a right application of punishments, and rewards. And seeing the end of punishing is not revenge, and discharge of choler; but correction, either of the offender, or of others by his example; the severest punishments are to be inflicted for those crimes, that are of most danger to the public; such as are those which proceed from malice to the government established; those that spring from contempt of justice; those that provoke indignation in the multitude; and those, which unpunished seem authorized, as when they are committed by sons, servants, or favourites of men in authority: For indignation carrieth men, not only against the actors, and authors of injustice; but against all power that is likely to protect them; as in the case of *Tarquin*; when for the insolent act of one of his sons, he was driven out of *Rome*, and the monarchy itself dissolved. But crimes of infirmity; such as are those which proceed from great provocation, from great fear, great need, or from ignorance whether the fact be a great crime, or not, there is place many times for lenity, without prejudice to the commonwealth; and lenity when there is such place for it, is required by the law of nature. The punishment of the leaders, and teachers in a commotion; not the poor seduced people, when they are punished, can profit the commonwealth by their example. To be severe to the people, is to punish that ignorance, which may in great part be imputed to the sovereign, whose fault it was, they were no better instructed.

In like manner it belongeth to the office, and duty of the sovereign, to apply his rewards always so, as there may arise from them benefit to the commonwealth: wherein consisteth their use, and end; and is then done, when they that have well served the commonwealth, are with as little expense of the common treasure, as is possible, so well recompensed, as others thereby may be encouraged, both to serve the same as faithfully as they can, and to study the arts by which they may be enabled to do it better. To buy with money, or preferment, from a popular ambitious subject, to be quiet, and desist from making ill impressions in the minds of the people, has nothing of the nature of reward; (which is ordained not for disservice, but for service past;) nor a sign of gratitude, but of fear: nor does it tend to the benefit, but to the damage of the public. It is a contention with ambition, like that of *Hercules* with the monster *Hydra*, which having many heads, for every one that was vanquished, there grew up three. For in like manner, when the stubbornness of one popular man, is overcome with reward, there arise many more (by the example) that do the same mischief, in hope of like benefit: and as all sorts of manufacture, so also malice encreaseth by being vendible. And though sometimes a civil war, may be deferred, by such ways as that, yet the danger grows still the greater, and the public ruin more assured. It is therefore against the duty of the sovereign, to whom the public safety is committed, to reward those that aspire to greatness by disturbing the peace of their country, and not rather to oppose the beginnings of such men, with a little danger, than after a longer time with greater.

Another business of the sovereign, is to choose good counsellors; I mean such, whose advice he is to take in the government of the commonwealth. For this word counsel, *consilium*, corrupted from *considium*, is of a large signification, and comprehendeth all assemblies of men that sit together, not only to deliberate what is to be done hereafter, but also to judge of facts past, and of law for the present. I take it here in the first sense only: and in this sense, there is no choice of counsel, neither in a democracy, nor aristocracy; because the persons counselling are members of the person counselled. The choice of counsellors therefore is proper to monarchy; in which, the sovereign that endeavoureth not to make choice of those, that in every kind are the most able, dischargeth not his office as he ought to do. The most able counsellors, are they that have least hope of benefit by giving evil counsel, and most knowledge of those things that conduce to the peace, and defence of the commonwealth. It is a hard matter to know who expecteth benefit from public troubles; but the signs that guide to a just suspicion, is the soothing of the people in their unreasonable, or irremediable grievances, by men whose estates are not sufficient to discharge their accustomed expenses and may easily be observed by any one whom it concerns to know it. But to know, who has most knowledge of the public affairs, is yet harder; and they that know them, need them a great deal the less. For to know, who knows the rules almost of any art, is a great degree of the knowledge of the same art; because no man can be assured of the truth of another's rules, but he that is first taught to understand them. But the best signs of knowledge of any art, are, much conversing in it, and constant good effects of it. Good counsel comes not by lot, nor by inheritance; and therefore there is no more reason to expect good advice from the rich, or noble, in matter of state, than in delineating the dimensions of a fortress; unless we shall think there needs no method in the study of the politics, (as there does in the study of geometry,) but only to be lookers on; which is not so. For the politics is the harder study of the two. Whereas in these parts of *Europe*, it hath been taken for a right of certain persons, to have place in the highest council of state by inheritance; it is derived from the conquests of the ancient Germans; wherein many absolute lords joining together to conquer other nations, would not enter into the confederacy, without such privileges, as might be marks of difference in time following, between their posterity, and the posterity of their subjects; which privileges being inconsistent with the sovereign power, by the favour of the sovereign, they may seem to keep; but contending for them as their right, they must needs by degrees let them go, and have at last no further honour, than adhereth naturally to their abilities.

And how able soever be the counsellors in any affair, the benefit of their counsel is greater, when they give every one his advice, and the reasons of it apart, than when they do it in an assembly, by way of orations; and when they have premeditated, than when they speak on the sudden; both because they have more time, to survey the consequences of action; and are less subject to be carried away to contradiction, through envy, emulation, or other passions arising from the difference of opinion.

The best counsel, in those things that concern not other nations, but only the ease, and benefit the subjects may enjoy, by laws that look only inward, is to be taken from the general informations, and complaints of the people of each province, who are best acquainted with their own wants, and ought therefore, when they demand nothing in derogation of the essential rights of sovereignty, to be diligently taken notice of. For without those essential rights, (as I have often before said,) the commonwealth cannot at all subsist.

A commander of an army in chief, if he be not popular, shall not be beloved, nor feared as he ought to be by his army; and consequently cannot perform that office with good success. He must therefore be industrious, valiant, affable, liberal and fortunate, that he may gain an opinion both of sufficiency, and of loving his soldiers. This is popularity, and breeds in the soldiers both desire, and courage, to recommend themselves to his favour; and protects the severity of the general, in punishing (when need is) the mutinous, or negligent soldiers. But this love of soldiers, (if caution be not given of the commander's fidelity,) is a dangerous thing to sovereign power; especially when it is in the hands of an assembly not popular. It belongeth therefore to the safety of the people, both that they be good conductors, and faithful subjects, to whom the sovereign commits his armies.

But when the sovereign himself is popular; that is, reverenced and beloved of his people, there is no danger at all from the popularity of a subject. For soldiers are never so generally unjust, as to side with their captain; though they love him, against their sovereign, when they love not only his person, but also his cause. And therefore those, who by violence have at any time suppressed the power of their lawful sovereign, before they could settle themselves in his place, have been always put to the trouble of contriving their titles, to save the people from the shame of receiving them. To have a known right to sovereign power, is so popular a quality, as he that has it needs no more, for his own part, to turn the hearts of his subjects to him, but that they see him able absolutely to govern his own family: nor, on the part of his enemies, but a disbanding of their armies. For the greatest and most active part of mankind, has never hitherto been well contented with the present.

Concerning the offices of one sovereign to another, which are comprehended in that law, which is commonly called the *law of nations*, I need not say any thing in this place; because the law of nations, and the law of nature, is the same thing. And every sovereign hath the same right, in procuring the safety of his people, that any particular man can have, in procuring the safety of his own body. And the same law, that dictateth to men that have no civil government, what they ought to do, and what to avoid in regard of one another, dictateth the same to commonwealths, that is, to the consciences of sovereign princes, and sovereign assemblies; there being no court of natural justice, but in the conscience only; where not man, but God reigneth; whose laws, (such of them as oblige all mankind,) in respect of God, as he is the author of nature, are *natural*; and in respect of the same God, as he is King of kings, are *laws*. But of the kingdom of God, as King of kings, and as King also of a peculiar people, I shall speak in the rest of this discourse.

CHAPTER 31: Of the Kingdom of God by Nature

That the condition of mere nature, that is to say, of absolute liberty, such as is theirs, that neither are sovereigns, nor subjects, is anarchy, and the condition of war: that the precepts, by which men are guided to avoid that condition, are the laws of nature: that a commonwealth, without sovereign power, is but a word, without substance, and cannot stand: that subjects owe to sovereigns, simple obedience, in all things, wherein their obedience is not repugnant to the laws of God, I have sufficiently proved, in that which I have already written. There wants only, for the entire knowledge of civil duty, to know what are those laws of God. For without that, a man knows not, when he is commanded any thing by the civil power, whether it be contrary to the law of God, or

not: and so, either by too much civil obedience, offends the Divine Majesty, or through fear of offending God, transgresses the commandments of the commonwealth. To avoid both these rocks, it is necessary to know what are the laws divine. And seeing the knowledge of all law, dependeth on the knowledge of the sovereign power; I shall say something in that which followeth, of the KINGDOM OF GOD.

God is king, let the earth rejoice, saith the psalmist. (*Psalm* 96. 1). And again, (*Psalm* 98. 1) *God is king though the nations be angry; and he that sitteth on the cherubims, though the earth be moved.* Whether men will or not, they must be subject always to the divine power. By denying the existence, or providence of God, men may shake off their ease, but not their yoke. But to call this power of God, which extendeth itself not only to man, but also to beasts, and plants, and bodies inanimate, by the name of kingdom, is but a metaphorical use of the word. For he only is properly said to reign, that governs his subjects by his word, and by promise of rewards to those that obey it, and by threatening them with punishment that obey it not. Subjects therefore in the kingdom of God, are not bodies inanimate, nor creatures irrational; because they understand no precepts as his: nor atheists; nor they that believe not that God has any care of the actions of mankind; because they acknowledge no word for his, nor have hope of his rewards, or fear of his threatenings. They therefore that believe there is a God that governeth the world, and hath given precepts, and propounded rewards, and punishments to mankind, are God's subjects; all the rest, are to be understood as enemies.

To rule by words, requires that such words be manifestly made known; for else they are no laws: for to the nature of laws belongeth a sufficient, and clear promulgation, such as may take away the excuse of ignorance; which in the laws of men is but of one only kind, and that is, proclamation, or promulgation by the voice of man. But God declareth his laws three ways; by the dictates of *natural reason*, by *revelation*, and by the *voice* of some *man*, to whom by the operation of miracles, he procureth credit with the rest. From hence there ariseth a triple word of God, *rational, sensible,* and *prophetic:* to which correspondeth a triple hearing; *right reason, sense supernatural,* and *faith.* As for sense supernatural, which consisteth in revelation, or inspiration, there have not been any universal laws so given, because God speaketh not in that manner, but to particular persons, and to divers men divers things.

From the difference between the other two kinds of God's word, *rational,* and *prophetic,* there may be attributed to God, a twofold kingdom, *natural,* and *prophetic:* natural, wherein he governeth as many of mankind as acknowledge his providence, by the natural dictates of right reason; and prophetic, wherein having chosen out one peculiar nation (the Jews) for his subjects, he governed them, and none but them, not only by natural reason, but by positive laws, which he gave them by the mouths of his holy prophets. Of the natural kingdom of God I intend to speak in this chapter.

The right of nature, whereby God reigneth over men, and punisheth those that break his laws, is to be derived, not from his creating them, as if he required obedience, as of gratitude for his benefits; but from his *irresistible power.* I have formerly shown, how the sovereign right ariseth from pact: to show how the same right may arise from nature, requires no more, but to show in what case it is never taken away. Seeing all men by nature had right to all things, they had right every one to reign over all the rest. But because this right could not be obtained by force, it concerned the safety of every one, laying by that right, to set up men (with sovereign authority) by common consent, to rule and defend them: whereas if there had been any man of power irresistible; there had been no reason, why he should not by that power have ruled, and defended both himself, and them, according to his own discretion. To those therefore whose power is irresistible, the dominion of all men adhereth naturally by their excellence of power; and consequently it is from that power, that the kingdom over men, and the right of afflicting men at his pleasure, belongeth naturally to God Almighty; not as Creator, and gracious; but as omnipotent. And though punishment be due for sin only, because by that word is understood

affliction for sin; yet the right of afflicting, is not always derived from men's sin, but from God's power.

This question, *why evil men often prosper, and good men suffer adversity,* has been much disputed by the ancient, and is the same with this of ours, *by what right God dispenseth the prosperities and adversities of this life;* and is of that difficulty, as it hath shaken the faith, not only of the vulgar, but of philosophers, and which is more, of the Saints, concerning the Divine Providence. *How good,* (saith *David*) (*Psalm* 72. 1, 2, 3) *is the God of Israel to those that are upright in heart; and yet my feet were almost gone, my treadings had well-nigh slipt; for I was grieved at the wicked, when I saw the ungodly in such prosperity.* And *Job,* how earnestly does he expostulate with God, for the many afflictions he suffered, notwithstanding his righteousness? This question in the case of *Job,* is decided by God himself, not by arguments derived from *Job's* sin, but his own power. For whereas the friends of *Job* drew their arguments from his affliction to his sin, and he defended himself by the conscience of his innocence, God himself taketh up the matter, and having justified the affliction by arguments drawn from his power, such as this, (*Job* 38. 4) *Where wast thou, when I laid the foundations of the earth,* and the like, both approved Job's innocence, and reproved the erroneous doctrine of his friends. Conformable to this doctrine is the sentence of our Saviour, concerning the man that was born blind, in these words, *Neither hath this man sinned, nor his fathers; but that the works of God might be made manifest in him.* And though it be said, *that death entered into the world by sin,* (by which is meant that if *Adam* had never sinned, he had never died, that is, never suffered any separation of his soul from his body,) it follows not thence, that God could not justly have afflicted him, though he had not sinned, as well as he afflicteth other living creatures, that cannot sin.

Having spoken of the right of God's sovereignty, as grounded only on nature; we are to consider next, what are the Divine laws, or dictates of natural reason; which laws concern either the natural duties of one man to another, or the honour naturally due to our Divine Sovereign. The first are the same laws of nature, of which I have spoken already in the 14th and 15th chapters of this treatise; namely, equity, justice, mercy, humility, and the rest of the moral virtues. It remaineth therefore that we consider, what precepts are dictated to men, by their natural reason only, without other word of God, touching the honour and worship of the Divine Majesty.

Honour consisteth in the inward thought, and opinion of the power, and goodness of another: and therefore to honour God, is to think as highly of his power and goodness, as is possible. And of that opinion, the external signs appearing in the words, and actions of men, are called *worship*; which is one part of that which the Latins understand by the word *cultus*: For *cultus* signifieth properly, and constantly, that labour which a man bestows on any thing, with a purpose to make benefit by it. Now those things whereof we make benefit, are either subject to us, and the profit they yield, followeth the labour we bestow upon them, as a natural effect; or they are not subject to us, but answer our labour, according to their own wills. In the first sense the labour bestowed on the earth, is called *culture*; and the education of children, a *culture* of their minds. In the second sense, where men's wills are to be wrought to our purpose, not by force, but by complaisance, it signifieth as much as courting, that is, a winning of favour by good offices; as by praises, by acknowledging their power, and by whatsoever is pleasing to them from whom we look for any benefit. And this is properly *worship*: in which sense *Publicola*, is understood for a worshipper of the people; and *cultus Dei*, for the worship of God.

From internal honour, consisting in the opinion of power and goodness, arise three passions; *love*, which hath reference to goodness; and *hope*, and *fear*, that relate to power: and three parts of external worship; *praise*, *magnifying*, and *blessing*: the subject of praise, being goodness; the subject of magnifying and blessing, being power, and the effect thereof felicity. Praise, and magnifying are signified both by words, and actions: by words, when we say a man is good, or great: by actions, when we thank him for his bounty, and obey his power. The opinion of the happiness of another, can only be expressed by words.

There be some signs of honour, (both in attributes and actions,) that be naturally so; as amongst attributes, *good*, *just*, *liberal*, and the like; and amongst actions, *prayers*, *thanks*, and *obedience*. Others are so by institution, or custom of men; and in some times and places are honourable; in others, dishonourable; in others indifferent: such as are the gestures in salutation, prayer, and thanksgiving, in different times and places, differently used. The former is *natural*; the latter *arbitrary* worship.

And of arbitrary worship, there be two differences: for sometimes it is a *commanded*, sometimes *voluntary* worship: commanded, when it is such as he requireth, who is worshipped: free, when it is such as the worshipper thinks fit. When it is commanded, not the words, or gesture, but the obedience is the worship. But when free, the worship consists in the opinion of the beholders: for if to them the words, or actions by which we intend honour, seem ridiculous, and tending to contumely; they are no worship; because no signs of honour; and no signs of honour; because a sign is not a sign to him that giveth it, but to him to whom it is made; that is, to the spectator.

Again, there is a *public*, and a *private* worship. Public, is the worship that a commonwealth performeth, as one person. Private, is that which a private person exhibiteth. Public, in respect of the whole commonwealth, is free; but in respect of particular men it is not so. Private, is in secret free; but in the sight of the multitude, it is never without some restraint, either from the laws, or from the opinion of men; which is contrary to the nature of liberty.

The end of worship amongst men, is power. For where a man seeth another worshipped, he supposeth him powerful, and is the readier to obey him; which makes his power greater. But God has no ends: the worship we do him, proceeds from our duty, and is directed according to our capacity, by those rules of honour, that reason dictateth to be done by the weak to the more potent men, in hope of benefit, for fear of damage, or in thankfulness for good already received from them.

That we may know what worship of God is taught us by the light of nature, I will begin with his attributes.

Where, first, it is manifest, we ought to attribute to him *existence*. For no man can have the will to honour that, which he thinks not to have any being.

Secondly, that those philosophers, who said the world, or the soul of the world was God, spake unworthily of him; and denied his existence. For by God, is understood the cause of the world; and to say the world is God, is to say there is no cause of it, that is, no God.

Thirdly, to say the world was not created, but eternal, (seeing that which is eternal has no cause,) is to deny there is a God.

Fourthly, that they who attributing (as they think) ease to God, take from him the care of mankind; take from him his honour: for it takes away men's love, and fear of him; which is the root of honour.

Fifthly, in those things that signify greatness, and power; to say he is *finite*, is not to honour him: for it is not a sign of the will to honour God, to attribute to him less than we can; and finite, is less than we can; because to finite, it is easy to add more.

Therefore to attribute *figure* to him, is not honour; for all figure is finite:

Nor to say we conceive, and imagine, or have an *idea* of him, in our mind: for whatsoever we conceive is finite:

Nor to attribute to him *parts*, or *totality*; which are the attributes only of things finite:

Nor to say he is in this, or that *place*: for whatsoever is in place, is bounded, and finite:

Nor that he is *moved*, or *resteth*: for both these attributes ascribe to him place:

Nor that there be more Gods than one; because it implies them all finite: for there cannot be more than one infinite:

Nor to ascribe to him (unless metaphorically, meaning not the passion but the effect) passions that partake of grief; as *repentance, anger, mercy*: or of want; as *appetite, hope, desire*; or of any passive faculty: for passion, is power limited by somewhat else.

And therefore when we ascribe to God a *will*, it is not to be understood, as that of man, for a *rational appetite*; but as the power, by which he effecteth every thing.

Likewise when we attribute to him *sight*, and other acts of sense; as also *knowledge*, and *understanding*; which in us is nothing else, but a tumult of the mind, raised by external things that press the organical parts of man's body: for there is no such thing in God; and being things that depend on natural causes, cannot be attributed to him.

He that will attribute to God, nothing but what is warranted by natural reason, must either use such negative attributes, as *infinite, eternal, incomprehensible*; or superlatives, as *most high, most great*, and the like; or indefinite, as *good, just, holy, creator*; and in such sense, as if he meant not to declare what he is, (for that were to circumscribe him within the limits of our fancy,) but how much we admire him, and how ready we would be to obey him; which is a sign of humility, and of a will to honour him as much as we can: For there is but one name to signify our conception of his nature, and that is, I AM: and but one name of his relation to us, and that is *God*; in which is contained Father, King, and Lord.

Concerning the actions of divine worship, it is a most general precept of reason, that they be signs of the intention to honour God; such as are, first, *prayers*: For not the carvers, when they made images, were thought to make them gods; but the people that *prayed* to them.

Secondly, *thanksgiving*; which differeth from prayer in divine worship, no otherwise, than that prayers precede, and thanks succeed the benefit; the end both of the one, and the other, being to acknowledge God, for author of all benefits, as well past, as future.

Thirdly, *gifts*; that is to say, *sacrifices*, and *oblations*, (if they be of the best,) are signs of honour: for they are thanksgivings.

Fourthly, *not to swear by any but God*, is naturally a sign of honour: for it is a confession that God only knoweth the heart; and that no man's wit, or strength can protect a man against God's vengeance on the perjured.

Fifthly, it is a part of rational worship, to speak considerately of God; for it argues a fear of him, and fear, is a confession of his power. Hence followeth, that the name of God is not to be used rashly, and to no purpose; for that is as much, as in vain: and it is to no purpose unless it be by way of oath, and by order of the commonwealth, to make judgments certain; or between commonwealths, to avoid war. And that disputing of God's nature is contrary to his honour: for it is supposed, that in this natural kingdom of God, there is no other way to know any thing, but by natural reason; that is, from the principles of natural science; which are so far from teaching us any thing of God's nature, as they cannot teach us our own nature, nor the nature of the smallest creature living. And therefore, when men out of the principles of natural reason, dispute of the attributes of God, they but dishonour him: for in the attributes which we give to God, we are not to consider the signification of philosophical truth; but the signification of pious intention, to do him the greatest honour we are able. From the want of which consideration, have proceeded the volumes of disputation about the nature of God, that tend not to his honour, but to the honour of our own wits, and learning; and are nothing else but inconsiderate, and vain abuses of his sacred name.

Sixthly, in *prayers, thanksgivings, offerings* and *sacrifices*, it is a dictate of natural reason, that they be every one in his kind the best, and most significant of honour. As for example, that prayers and thanksgiving, be made in words and phrases, not sudden, nor light, nor plebeian; but beautiful, and well composed; For else we do not God as much honour as we can. And therefore the heathens did absurdly, to worship images for gods: but their doing it in verse, and with music, both of voice, and instruments, was reasonable. Also that the beasts they offered in sacrifice, and the gifts they offered, and their actions in worshipping, were full of submission, and commemorative of benefits received, was according to reason, as proceeding from an intention to honour him.

Seventhly, reason directeth not only to worship God in secret; but also, and especially, in public, and in the sight of men: For without that, (that which in honour is most acceptable) the procuring others to honour him, is lost.

Lastly, obedience to his laws (that is, in this case to the laws of nature,) is the greatest worship of all.

For as obedience is more acceptable to God than sacrifice; so also to set light by his commandments, is the greatest of all contumelies. And these are the laws of that divine worship, which natural reason dictateth to private men.

But seeing a commonwealth is but one person, it ought also to exhibit to God but one worship; which then it doth, when it commandeth it to be exhibited by private men, publicly. And this is public worship; the property whereof, is to be *uniform:* for those actions that are done differently, by different men, cannot be said to be a public worship. And therefore, where many sorts of worship be allowed, proceeding from the different religions of private men, it cannot be said there is any public worship, nor that the commonwealth is of any religion at all.

And because words (and consequently the attributes of God) have their signification by agreement, and constitution of men; those attributes are to be held significative of honour, that men intend shall so be; and whatsoever may be done by the wills of particular men, where there is no law but reason, may be done by the will of the commonwealth, by laws civil. And because a commonwealth hath no will, nor makes no laws, but those that are made by the will of him, or them that have the sovereign power; it followeth, that those attributes which the sovereign ordaineth, in the worship of God, for signs of honour, ought to be taken and used for such, by private men in their public worship.

But because not all actions are signs by constitution, but some are naturally signs of honour, others of contumely, these latter (which are those that men are ashamed to do in the sight of them they reverence) cannot be made by human power a part of Divine worship; nor the former (such as are decent, modest, humble behaviour) ever be separated from it. But whereas there be an infinite number of actions, and gestures, of an indifferent nature; such of them as the commonwealth shall ordain to be publicly and universally in use, as signs of honour, and part of God's worship, are to be taken and used for such by the subjects. And that which is said in the Scripture, *It is better to obey God than men,* hath place in the kingdom of God by pact, and not by nature.

Having thus briefly spoken of the natural kingdom of God, and his natural laws, I will add only to this chapter a short declaration of his natural punishments. There is no action of man in this life, that is not the beginning of so long a chain of consequences, as no human providence, is high enough, to give a man a prospect to the end. And in this chain, there are linked together both pleasing and unpleasing events; in such manner, as he that will do any thing for his pleasure, must engage himself to suffer all the pains annexed to it; and these pains, are the natural punishments of those actions, which are the beginning of more harm than good. And hereby it comes to pass, that intemperance is naturally punished with diseases; rashness, with mischances; injustice, with the violence of enemies; pride, with ruin; cowardice, with oppression; negligent government of princes, with rebellion; and rebellion, with slaughter. For seeing punishments are consequent to the breach of laws; natural punishments must be naturally consequent to the breach of the laws of nature; and therefore follow them as their natural, not arbitrary effects.

And thus far concerning the constitution, nature, and right of sovereigns; and concerning the duty of subjects, derived from the principles of natural reason. And now, considering how different this doctrine is, from the practice of the greatest part of the world, especially of these western parts, that have received their moral learning from *Rome*, and *Athens*; and how much depth of moral philosophy is required, in them that have the administration of the sovereign power; I am at the point of believing this my labour, as useless, as the commonwealth of *Plato*; For he also is of opinion that it is impossible for the disorders of state, and change of governments by civil war, ever to be taken away, till sovereigns be philosophers. But when I consider again, that the science of natural justice, is the only science necessary for sovereigns, and their principal ministers; and that they need not be charged with the sciences mathematical, (as by *Plato* they are,) further, than by good laws to encourage men to the study of them; and that neither *Plato*, nor any other philosopher hitherto, hath put into

order, and sufficiently or probably proved all the theorems of moral doctrine, that men may learn thereby, both how to govern, and how to obey; I recover some hope, that one time or other, this writing of mine, may fall into the hands of a sovereign, who will consider it himself, (for it is short, and I think clear,) without the help of any interested, or envious interpreter; and by the exercise of entire sovereignty, in protecting the public teaching of it, convert this truth of speculation, into the utility of practice.

PART 3
OF A CHRISTIAN COMMONWEALTH

CHAPTER 32: Of the Principles of Christian Politics

I have derived the rights of sovereign power, and the duty of subjects, hitherto from the principles of nature only; such as experience has found true or consent (concerning the use of words) has made so; that is to say, from the nature of men, known to us by experience, and from definitions (of such words as are essential to all political reasoning) universally agreed on. But in that I am next to handle, which is the nature and rights of a CHRISTIAN COMMONWEALTH, whereof there dependeth much upon supernatural revelations of the will of God, the ground of my discourse must be, not only the natural word of God, but also the prophetical.

Nevertheless, we are not to renounce our senses and experience, nor (that which is the undoubted word of God) our natural reason. For they are the talents which he hath put into our hands to negotiate till the coming again of our blessed Saviour; and therefore not to be folded up in the napkin of an implicit faith, but employed in the purchase of justice, peace, and true religion. For though there be many things in God's word above reason (that is to say, which cannot by natural reason be either demonstrated or confuted), yet there is nothing contrary to it; but when it seemeth so, the fault is either in our unskilful interpretation or erroneous ratiocination.

Therefore, when anything therein written is too hard for our examination, we are bidden to captivate our understanding to the words, and not to labour in sifting out a philosophical truth by logic, of such mysteries as are not comprehensible, nor fall under any rule of natural science. For it is with the mysteries of our religion as with wholesome pills for the sick, which, swallowed whole, have the virtue to cure, but chewed, are for the most part cast up again without effect.

But by the captivity of our understanding is not meant a submission of the intellectual faculty to the opinion of any other man, but of the will to obedience, where obedience is due. For sense, memory, understanding, reason, and opinion are not in our power to change, but always and necessarily such as the things we see, hear, and consider suggest unto us; and therefore are not effects of our will, but our will of them. We then captivate our understanding and reason when we forbear contradiction, when we so speak as (by lawful authority) we are commanded, and when we live accordingly; which, in sum, is trust and faith reposed in him that speaketh, though the mind be incapable of any notion at all from the words spoken.

When God speaketh to man, it must be either immediately or by mediation of another man to whom he had formerly spoken by himself immediately. How God speaketh to a man immediately may be understood by those well enough to whom he hath so spoken; but how the same should be understood by another is hard, if not impossible, to know. For if a man pretend to me that God hath spoken to him supernaturally and immediately, and I make doubt of it, I cannot easily perceive what argument he can produce to oblige me to believe it. It is true that if he be my sovereign, he may oblige me to obedience (so as not by act or word to declare I believe him not), but not to think any otherwise than my reason persuades me. But if one that hath not such authority over me shall pretend the same, there is nothing that exacteth either belief or obedience.

For to say that God hath spoken to him in the Holy Scripture is not to say God hath spoken to him immediately, but by mediation of the prophets, or of the apostles, or of the church, in such manner as he speaks to all other Christian men. To say he hath spoken to him in a dream is no more than to say he dreamed that God spake to him, which is not of force to win belief from any man that knows dreams are for the most part natural and may proceed from former thoughts (and such dreams as that, from self-conceit, and foolish arrogance, and false opinion of a man's own godliness, or other virtue, by which he thinks he hath merited the favour of extraordinary revelation). To say he hath seen a vision, or heard a voice, is to say that he hath dreamed between sleeping and waking; for in such manner a man doth many times naturally take his dream for a vision, as not having well observed his own slumbering. To say he speaks by supernatural inspiration is to say he finds an ardent desire to speak, or some strong opinion of himself, for which he can allege no natural and sufficient reason. So that though God Almighty can speak to a man by dreams, visions, voice, and inspiration, yet he obliges no man to believe he hath so done to him that pretends it, who (being a man) may err, and (which is more) may lie.

How, then, can he to whom God hath never revealed his will immediately (saving by the way of natural reason) know when he is to obey or not to obey his word, delivered by him that says he is a prophet? Of 400 prophets of whom the king of Israel asked counsel concerning the war he made against *Ramoth Gilead* only *Micaiah* was a true one. The prophet that was sent to prophesy against the altar set up by *Jeroboam*, though a true prophet, and that by two miracles done in his presence appears to be a prophet sent from God, was yet deceived by another old prophet that persuaded him, as from the mouth of God, to eat and drink with him. If one prophet deceive another, what certainty is there of knowing the will of God, by other way than that of reason? To which I answer out of the Holy Scripture that there be two marks by which together, not asunder, a true prophet is to be known. One is the doing of miracles; the other is the not teaching any other religion than that which is already established. Asunder (I say) neither of these is sufficient. *If a prophet rise amongst you, or a dreamer of dreams, and shall pretend the doing of a miracle, and the miracle come to pass, if he say, 'Let us follow strange Gods, which thou hast not known,' thou shalt not hearken to him, &c. . . . But that prophet and dreamer of dreams shall be put to death, because he hath spoken to you to revolt from the Lord your God.* In which words two things are to be observed: first, that God will not have miracles alone serve for arguments to approve the prophet's calling, but (as it is in the third verse) for an experiment of the constancy of our adherence to himself. For the works of the *Egyptian* sorcerers, though not so great as those of *Moses*, yet were great miracles. Secondly, that how great soever the miracle be, yet if it tend to stir up revolt against the king, or him that governeth by the king's authority, he that doth such miracle is not to be considered otherwise than as sent to make trial of their allegiance. For these words, *revolt from the Lord your God*, are in this place equivalent to *revolt from your king*. For they had made God their king by pact at the foot of Mount *Sinai*, who ruled them by Moses only; for he only spake with God, and from time to time declared God's commandments to the people. In like manner, after our Saviour Christ had made his disciples acknowledge him for the Messiah (that is to say, for God's anointed, whom the nation of the Jews daily expected for their king, but refused when he came), he omitted not to advertise them of the danger of miracles. *There shall arise* (saith he) *false Christs, and false prophets, and shall do great wonders and miracles, even to the seducing (if it were possible) of the very elect.* By which it appears that false prophets may have the power of miracles; yet are we not to take their doctrine for God's word. St. Paul says further to the Galatians that *if himself or an angel from heaven preach another gospel to them than he had preached, let him be accursed.* That gospel was that Christ was King; so that all preaching against the power of the king received, in consequence to these words, is by St. Paul accursed. For his speech is addressed to those who by his preaching had already received Jesus for the Christ, that is to say, for King of the Jews.

And as miracles without preaching that doctrine which God hath established, so preaching the true doctrine without the doing of miracles is an insuffi-cient argument of immediate revelation. For if a man that teacheth not false doctrine should pretend to be a prophet without showing any miracle, he is never the more to be regarded for his pretence, as is evident by Deut. 18:21–22. *If thou say in thy heart, How shall we know that the word* (of the prophet) *is not that which the Lord hath spoken? When the prophet shall have spoken in the name of the Lord that which shall not come to pass, that is the word which the Lord hath not spoken, but the prophet has spoken it out of the pride of his own heart; fear him not.* But a man may here again ask, When the prophet hath foretold a thing, how shall we know whether it will come to pass or not? For he may foretell it as a thing to arrive after a certain long time, longer than the time of man's life (or indefinitely, that it will come to pass one time or other), in which case this mark of a prophet is unuseful. And therefore the miracles that oblige us to believe a prophet ought to be confirmed by an immediate or a not long deferred event. So that it is manifest that the teaching of the religion which God hath established, and the showing of a present miracle, joined together, were the only marks whereby the Scripture would have a true prophet (that is to say, immediate revelation) to be acknowledged, neither of them being singly sufficient to oblige any other man to regard what he saith.

Seeing therefore miracles now cease, we have no sign left whereby to acknowledge the pretended revelations or inspirations of any private man, nor obligation to give ear to any doctrine farther than it is conformable to the Holy Scriptures, which since the time of our Saviour supply the place and sufficiently recompense the want of all other prophecy, and from which, by wise and learned interpretation and careful ratiocination, all rules and precepts necessary to the knowledge of our duty both to God and man, without enthusiasm or supernatural inspiration, may easily be deduced. And this Scripture is it, out of which I am to take the principles of my discourse concerning the rights of those that are the supreme governors on earth of Christian commonwealths, and of the duty of Christian subjects towards their sovereigns. And to that end I shall speak in the next chapter of the books, writers, scope and authority of the Bible.

CHAPTER 34: Of the Signification of Spirit, Angel, and Inspiration in the Books of Holy Scripture

Seeing the foundation of all true ratiocination is the constant signification of words, which in the doctrine following dependeth not (as in natural science) on the will of the writer, nor (as in common conversation) on vulgar use, but on the sense they carry in the Scripture, it is necessary, before I proceed any further, to determine out of the Bible the meaning of such words as by their ambiguity may render what I am to infer upon them obscure or disputable. I will begin with the words BODY and SPIRIT, which in the language of the Schools are termed *substances, corporeal*, and *incorporeal*.

The word *body*, in the most general acceptation, signifieth that which filleth or occupieth some certain room or imagined place, and dependeth not on the imagination, but is a real part of that we call the *universe*. For the *universe*, being the aggregate of all bodies, there is no real part thereof that is not also *body*, nor anything properly a *body* that is not also part of (that aggregate of all *bodies*) the *universe*. The same also, because bodies are subject to change (that is to say, to variety of appearance to the sense of living creatures) is called *substance* (that is to say, *subject* to various accidents), as: sometimes to be moved, sometimes to stand still; and to seem to our senses sometimes hot, sometimes cold, sometimes of one colour, smell, taste, or sound, sometimes of another. And this diversity of seeming (produced by the diversity of the operation of bodies on the organs of our sense) we attribute to alterations of the bodies that operate and call them *accidents* of those bodies. And according to this acceptation of the word, *substance* and *body* signify the same thing; and therefore, *substance incorporeal* are words which, when they are joined together, destroy one another, as if a man should say an *incorporeal body*.

But in the sense of common people, not all the universe is called body, but only such parts thereof as they can discern by the sense of feeling to resist their force, or by the sense of their eyes to hinder them from a farther prospect. Therefore, in the common

language of men, *air* and *aerial substances* use not to be taken for bodies, but (as often as men are sensible of their effects) are called *wind*, or *breath*, or (because the same are called in the Latin *spiritus*) *spirits* (as when they call that aerial substance which, in the body of any living creature, gives it life and motion *vital* and *animal spirits*). But for those idols of the brain which represent bodies to us where they are not (as in a looking-glass, in a dream, or to a distempered brain waking), they are (as the apostle saith generally of all idols) nothing; nothing at all, I say, there where they seem to be; and in the brain itself, nothing but tumult, proceeding either from the action of the objects or from the disorderly agitation of the organs of our sense. And men that are otherwise employed than to search into their causes know not, of themselves, what to call them, and may therefore easily be persuaded by those whose knowledge they much reverence, some to call them *bodies*, and think them made of air compacted by a power supernatural (because the sight judges them corporeal), and some to call them *spirits* (because the sense of touch discerneth nothing, in the place where they appear, to resist their fingers). So that the proper signification of *spirit* in common speech, is either a subtle, fluid, and invisible body, or a ghost, or other idol or phantasm of the imagination. But for metaphorical significations, there be many; for sometimes it is taken for disposition or inclination of the mind (as when, for the disposition to control the sayings of other men, we say *a spirit of contradiction*; for *a disposition to uncleanness, an unclean spirit*; for *perverseness, a froward spirit*; for *sullenness, a dumb spirit*; and for *inclination to godliness and God's service, the Spirit of God*); sometimes for any eminent ability or extraordinary passion or disease of the mind (as when *great wisdom* is called the *spirit of wisdom*, and *madmen* are said to be *possessed with a spirit*).

Other signification of *spirit* I find nowhere any; and where none of these can satisfy the sense of that word in Scripture, the place falleth not under human understanding, and our faith therein consisteth not in our opinion, but in our submission (as, in all places where God is said to be a *Spirit*, or where by the *Spirit of God* is meant God himself). For the nature of God is incomprehensible; that is to say, we understand nothing of *what he is*, but only *that he is*; and therefore, the attributes we give him are not to tell one another *what he is*, nor to signify our opinion of his nature, but our desire to honour him with such names as we conceive most honourable amongst ourselves.

Gen. 1:2. *The Spirit of God moved upon the face of the waters*. Here if by the *Spirit of God* be meant God himself, then is *motion* attributed to God, and consequently *place*, which are intelligible only of bodies, and not of substances incorporeal; and so the place is above our understanding, that can conceive nothing moved that changes not place or that has not dimension; and whatsoever has dimension is body. But the meaning of those words is best understood by the like place, Gen. 8:1, where when the earth was covered with waters, as in the beginning, God, intending to abate them, and again to discover the dry land, useth the like words: *I will bring my Spirit upon the earth, and the waters shall be diminished*, in which place by *Spirit* is understood a wind (that is an air or *spirit moved*), which might be called (as in the former place) the *Spirit of God*, because it was God's work.

Gen. 41:38. *Pharaoh* calleth the *Wisdom of Joseph* the *Spirit of God*. For *Joseph* having advised him to look out a wise and discreet man, and to set him over the land of Egypt, he saith thus: *Can we find such a man as this is, in whom is the Spirit of God?* And Exod. 28:3, *Thou shalt speak* (saith God) *to all the wise hearted, whom I have filled with the spirit of wisdom, to make Aaron garments, to consecrate him.* Where extraordinary understanding, though but in making garments, as being the *gift* of God, is called the *Spirit* of God. The same is found again, Exod. 31:3–6, and 35:31. And Isaiah 11:2–3, the prophet, speaking of the Messiah, saith: *The Spirit of the Lord shall abide upon him, the spirit of wisdom and understanding, the spirit of counsel and fortitude, and the spirit of the fear of the Lord.* Where manifestly is meant, not so many ghosts, but so many eminent *graces* that God would give him.

In the book of Judges an extraordinary zeal and courage in the defence of God's people is called the *Spirit* of God (as when it excited Othoniel, Gideon, Jephtha, and Sampson to deliver them from servitude, Judges 3:10, 6:34, 11:29, 13:25, 14:6, 14:19). And of *Saul*, upon the news of the insolence of the Ammonites towards the men of Jabesh Gilead, it is said (1 Sam. 11:6) that *The spirit of God came upon Saul, and his anger* (or, as it is in the Latin, *his fury*) *was kindled greatly*. Where it is not probable was meant a ghost, but an extraordinary *zeal* to punish the cruelty of the Ammonites. In like manner, by the *Spirit* of God that came upon Saul, when he was amongst the prophets that praised God in songs and music (1 Sam. 19:[23]), is to be understood, not a ghost, but an unexpected and sudden *zeal* to join with them in their devotion.

The false prophet *Zedekiah* saith to *Micaiah* (1 Kings 22:24): *Which way went the Spirit of the Lord from me to speak to thee?* Which cannot be understood of a ghost, for *Micaiah* declared, before the kings of Israel and Judah, the event of the battle, as from a vision, and not as from a spirit speaking in him.

In the same manner, it appeareth in the books of the Prophets that though they spake by the *spirit* of God, that is to say, by a special grace of prediction, yet their knowledge of the future was not by a ghost within them, but by some supernatural *dream* or *vision*.

Gen. 2:27. It is said: *God made man of the dust of the earth, and breathed into his nostrils* (spiraculum vitae) *the breath of life, and man was made a living soul.* There the *breath of life* inspired by God signifies no more but that God gave him life; and (Job 27:3): *as long as the Spirit of God is in my nostrils* is no more than to say *as long as I live*. So in Ezek. 1:20, *the spirit of life was in the wheels* is equivalent to *the wheels were alive*. And (Ezek. 2:2): *the Spirit entered into me, and set me on my feet*, that is, I *recovered my vital strength*; not that any ghost or incorporeal substance entered into and possessed his body.

In the 11th chap. of Numbers, verse 17: *I will take* (saith God) *of the Spirit, which is upon thee, and will put it upon them, and they shall bear the burden of the people with thee*, that is, upon the seventy elders; whereupon two of the seventy are said to prophecy in the camp; of whom some complained, and Joshua desired Moses to forbid them, which Moses would not do. Whereby it appears that Joshua knew not they had received authority so to do, and prophecied according to the mind of Moses, that is to say, by a *spirit* or *authority* subordinate to his own.

In the like sense we read (Deut. 34:9) that *Joshua was full of the spirit of wisdom, because Moses had laid his hands upon him*, that is, because he was *ordained* by Moses to prosecute the work he had himself begun (namely, the bringing of God's people into the promised land), but prevented by death, could not finish.

In the like sense it is said (Rom. 8:9): *If any man have not the Spirit of Christ, he is none of his*, not meaning thereby the *ghost* of Christ, but a submission to his doctrine. As also (1 John 4:2): *Hereby you shall know the Spirit of God; every spirit that confesseth that Jesus Christ is come in the flesh is of God*, by which is meant the spirit of unfeigned Christianity, or *submission* to that main article of Christian faith, that Jesus is the Christ, which cannot be interpreted of a ghost.

Likewise these words (Luke 4:1): *And Jesus full of the Holy Ghost* (that is, as it is expressed, Matt. 4:1, and Mark 1:12, *of the Holy Spirit*) may be understood for *zeal* to do the work for which he was sent by God the Father; but to interpret it of a ghost is to say that God himself (for so our Saviour was) was filled with God, which is very improper, and insignificant. How we came to translate *spirits* by the word *ghosts*, which signifieth nothing, neither in heaven nor earth, but the imaginary inhabitants of man's brain, I examine not; but this I say, the word *spirit* in the text signifieth no such thing, but either properly a real substance, or metaphorically some extraordinary ability or affection of the mind or of the body.

The disciples of Christ, seeing him walking upon the sea (Matt. 14:26 and Mark 6:49), supposed him to be a *Spirit*, meaning thereby an aerial *body*, and not a phantasm; for it is said they all saw him, which cannot be understood of the delusions of the brain (which are not common to many at once, as visible bodies are, but singular, because of the differences of fancies), but of bodies only. In like manner, where he was taken for a *spirit* by the same apostles (Luke

24:3, 7). So also (Acts 12:15), when St. *Peter* was delivered out of prison, and it would not be believed, but when the maid said he was at the door, they said it was his *angel*, by which must be meant a corporeal substance, or we must say the disciples themselves did follow the common opinion both of Jews and Gentiles, that some such apparitions were not imaginary, but real, and such as needed not the fancy of man for their existence. These the Jews called *spirits* and *angels*, good or bad, as the Greeks called the same by the name of *demons*. And some such apparitions may be real and substantial, that is to say, subtle bodies, which God can form by the same power by which he formed all things, and make use of, as of ministers and messengers (that is to say, angels), to declare his will, and execute the same when he pleaseth, in extraordinary and supernatural manner. But when he hath so formed them, they are substances, endued with dimensions, and take up room, and can be moved from place to place, which is peculiar to bodies; and therefore are not ghosts incorporeal (that is to say, ghosts that are in *no place*; that is to say, that are *nowhere*; that is to say, that seeming to be *somewhat*, are *nothing*). But if corporeal be taken in the most vulgar manner, for such substances as are perceptible by our external senses, then is substance incorporeal a thing not imaginary, but real (namely, a thin substance, invisible, but that hath the same dimensions that are in grosser bodies).

By the name of ANGEL is signified generally, a *messenger*, and most often, *a messenger of God*; and by a messenger of God is signified, anything that makes known his extraordinary presence, that is to say, the extraordinary manifestation of his power, especially by a dream or vision.

Concerning the creation of *angels*, there is nothing delivered in the Scriptures. That they are spirits is often repeated; but by the name of spirit is signified, both in Scripture and vulgarly, both amongst Jews and Gentiles, sometimes thin bodies (as, the air, the wind, the spirits vital and animal of living creatures) and sometimes the images that rise in the fancy in dreams and visions, which are not real substances, nor last any longer than the dream or vision they appear in; which apparitions, though no real substances, but accidents of the brain, yet when God raiseth them supernaturally, to signify his will, they are improperly termed God's messengers (that is to say, his *angels*).

And as the Gentiles did vulgarly conceive the imagery of the brain for things really subsistent without them and not dependent on the fancy, and out of them framed their opinions of *demons*, good and evil, which because they seemed to subsist really they called *substances*, and because they could not feel them with their hands, *incorporeal*, so also the Jews (upon the same ground, without anything in the Old Testament that constrained them thereunto) had generally an opinion (except the sect of the *Sadducees*) that those apparitions (which it pleased God sometimes to produce in the fancy of men, for his own service, and therefore called them his *angels*) were substances, not dependent on the fancy, but permanent creatures of God; whereof those which they thought were good to them, they esteemed the *angels of God*, and those they thought would hurt them, they called *evil angels*, or evil spirits (such as was the spirit of Python and the spirits of madmen, of lunatics, and epileptics; for they esteemed such as were troubled with such diseases, *demoniacs*).

But if we consider the places of the Old Testament where angels are mentioned, we shall find that in most of them there can nothing else be understood by the word *angel* but some image raised (supernaturally) in the fancy, to signify the presence of God in the execution of some supernatural work; and therefore in the rest, where their nature is not expressed, it may be understood in the same manner.

For we read (Gen. 16) that the same apparition is called, not only an *angel*, but *God*, where that which (vs. 7) is called the *angel* of the Lord, in the tenth verse saith to Hagar, *I will multiply thy seed exceedingly*, that is, speaketh in the person of God. Neither was this apparition a fancy figured, but a voice. By which it is manifest that *angel* signifieth there nothing but *God* himself, that caused Hagar supernaturally to apprehend a voice from heaven (or rather, nothing else but a voice supernatural, testifying God's special presence there). Why, therefore, may not the angels that

appeared to Lot, and are called (Gen. 19:[10–12]) *men*, and to whom (though they were two) Lot speaketh (vs. 18) as but to one, and that one as God (for the words are *Lot said unto them, Oh, not so, my Lord*), be understood of images of men supernaturally formed in the fancy, as well as before by angel was understood a fancied voice? When the angel called to Abraham out of heaven, to stay his hand (Gen. 22:11) from slaying Isaac, there was no apparition, but a voice, which nevertheless was called properly enough a messenger or *angel* of God, because it declared God's will supernaturally, and saves the labour of supposing any permanent ghosts. The angels which Jacob saw on the ladder of Heaven (Gen. 28:12) were a vision of his sleep; therefore, only fancy and a dream; yet being supernatural and signs of God's special presence, those apparitions are not improperly called *angels*. The same is to be understood (Gen. 31:11) where Jacob saith thus: *The Angel of the Lord appeared to me in my sleep*. For an apparition made to a man in his sleep is that which all men call a dream, whether such dream be natural or supernatural; and that which there Jacob calleth an *angel* was God himself; for the same angel saith (verse 13) *I am the God of Bethel*.

Also (Exod. 14:[19]) the angel that went before the army of Israel to the Red Sea, and then came behind it, is (verse [24]) the Lord himself; and he appeared not in the form of a beautiful man, but in form (by day) of a *pillar of cloud*, and (by night) in form of a *pillar of fire* [Exod. 13:21]; and yet this pillar was all the apparition and angel promised to Moses (Exod. [33:2]) for the army's guide; for this cloudy pillar is said [Exod. 33:9] to have descended and stood at the door of the Tabernacle, and to have talked with Moses.

There you see motion and speech, which are commonly attributed to angels, attributed to a cloud because the cloud served as a sign of God's presence and was no less an angel than if it had had the form of a man or child of never so great beauty (or with wings, as usually they are painted, for the false instruction of common people). For it is not the shape, but their use, that makes them angels. But their use is to be significations of God's presence in supernatural operations, as when Moses (Exod. 33:14) had desired God to go along with the camp (as he had done always before the making of the golden calf), God did not answer *I will go*, nor *I will send an angel in my stead*, but thus: *My presence shall go with thee*.

To mention all the places in the Old Testament where the name of angel is found would be too long. Therefore, to comprehend them all at once, I say there is no text in that part of the Old Testament which the Church of England holdeth for canonical from which we can conclude, there is or hath been created any permanent thing (understood by the name of *spirit* or *angel*) that hath not quantity, and that may not be by the understanding divided (that is to say, considered by parts, so as one part may be in one place and the next part in the next place to it), and, in sum, which is not (taking body for that which is somewhat or somewhere) corporeal, but in every place the sense will bear the interpretation of angel, for messenger (as John Baptist is called an angel [Matt. 11:10], and Christ the Angel of the Covenant [Mal. 3:1], and as, according to the same analogy, the dove [e.g., Matt. 3:16] and the fiery tongues [Acts 2:3], in that they were signs of God's special presence, might also be called angels). Though we find in Daniel two names of angels, *Gabriel* and *Michael*, yet it is clear out of the text itself (Dan. 12:1) that by *Michael* is meant *Christ* (not as an angel, but as a prince) and that *Gabriel* (as the like apparitions made to other holy men in their sleep) was nothing but a supernatural phantasm by which it seemed to *Daniel* in his dream that, two saints being in talk, one of them said to the other *Gabriel, Let us make this man understand his vision* [Dan. 8:16], for God needeth not to distinguish his celestial servants by names, which are useful only to the short memories of mortals. Nor in the New Testament is there any place out of which it can be proved that angels (except when they are put for such men as God hath made the messengers and ministers of his word or works) are things permanent, and withal incorporeal. That they are permanent may be gathered from the words of our Saviour himself (Matt. 25:41),

where he saith it shall be said to the wicked in the last day: *Go ye cursed into everlasting fire prepared for the Devil and his angels*. Which place is manifest for the permanence of evil angels (unless we might think the name of Devil and his angels may be understood of the Church's adversaries and their ministers), but then it is repugnant to their immateriality (because everlasting fire is no punishment to impatible substances, such as are all things incorporeal). Angels, therefore, are not thence proved to be incorporeal. In like manner, where St. Paul says (1 Cor. 6:3): *Know ye not that we shall judge the angels?* And (2 Pet. 2:4): *For if God spared not the angels that sinned, but cast them down into hell*. And (Jude 1:6): *And the angels that kept not their first estate, but left their own habitation, he hath reserved in everlasting chains under darkness unto the judgment of the last day*, though it prove the permanence of angelical nature, it confirmeth also their materiality. And (Matt. 22:30): *In the resurrection men do neither marry, nor give in marriage, but are as the angels of God in heaven*; but in the resurrection men shall be permanent, and not incorporeal; so, therefore, also are the angels.

There be divers other places out of which may be drawn the like conclusion. To men that understand the signification of these words, *substance* and *incorporeal*, as *incorporeal* is taken, not for subtle body, but for *not body*, they imply a contradiction, insomuch as to say an angel or spirit is (in that sense) an incorporeal substance is to say in effect there is no angel nor spirit at all. Considering, therefore, the signification of the word *angel* in the Old Testament, and the nature of dreams and visions that happen to men by the ordinary way of nature, I was inclined to this opinion, that angels were nothing but supernatural apparitions of the fancy, raised by the special and extraordinary operation of God, thereby to make his presence and commandments known to mankind, and chiefly to his own people. But the many places of the New Testament, and our Saviour's own words (and in such texts wherein is no suspicion of corruption of the Scripture) have extorted from my feeble reason an acknowledgment and belief that there be also angels substantial and permanent. But to believe they be in no place (that is to say, nowhere, that is to say, nothing), as they (though indirectly) say that will have them incorporeal, cannot by Scripture be evinced.

On the signification of the word *spirit* dependeth that of the word INSPIRATION, which must either be taken properly (and then it is nothing but the blowing into a man some thin and subtle air or wind, in such manner as a man filleth a bladder with his breath) or if spirits be not corporeal, but have their existence only in the fancy, then it is nothing but the blowing in of a phantasm (which is improper to say, and impossible; for phantasms are not, but only seem to be somewhat). That word, therefore, is used in the Scripture metaphorically only: as (Gen. 2:7), where it is said that God inspired into man the breath of life, no more is meant than that God gave unto him vital motion. For we are not to think that God made first a living breath, and then blew it into Adam after he was made, whether that breath were real or seeming, but only as it is (Acts 17:25) *that he gave him life, and breath,* that is, made him a living creature. And where it is said (2 Tim. 3:16): *all Scripture is given by inspiration from God* (speaking there of the Scripture of the Old Testament), it is an easy metaphor to signify that God inclined the spirit or mind of those writers to write that which should be useful in teaching, reproving, correcting, and instructing men in the way of righteous living. But where St. Peter (2 Pet. 1:21) saith that *Prophecy came not in old time by the will of man, but the holy men of God spake as they were moved by the Holy Spirit,* by the Holy Spirit is meant the voice of God in a dream or vision supernatural, which is not *inspiration.* Nor when our Saviour, breathing on his disciples, said *Receive the Holy Spirit,* was that breath the Spirit, but a sign of the spiritual graces he gave unto them. And though it be said of many, and of our Saviour himself, that he was full of the Holy *Spirit,* yet that fullness is not to be understood for *infusion* of the substance of God, but for accumulation of his gifts (such as are the gift of sanctity of life, of tongues, and the like, whether attained supernaturally or by study and industry—for in all cases they are the gifts of God). So likewise, where God says (Joel 2:28) *I will pour out my Spirit upon all flesh, and your sons and your daughters shall prophecy, your old men shall dream dreams, and your young men shall see visions,* we are not to understand it in the proper sense, as if his *Spirit* were like water, subject to effusion or infusion; but as if God had promised to give them prophetical dreams and visions. For the proper use of the word *infused,* in speaking of the graces of God, is an abuse of it; for those graces are virtues, not bodies to be carried hither and thither, and to be poured into men as into barrels.

In the same manner, to take *inspiration* in the proper sense, or to say that good *spirits* entered into men to make them prophesy, or evil *spirits* into those that became phrenetic, lunatic, or epileptic, is not to take the word in the sense of the Scripture; for the Spirit there is taken for the power of God, working by causes to us unknown. As also (Acts 2:2), the wind that is there said to fill the house wherein the apostles were assembled on the day of Pentecost is not to be understood for the Holy Spirit, which is the Deity itself, but for an external sign of God's special working on their hearts, to effect in them the internal graces and holy virtues he thought requisite for the performance of their apostleship.

CHAPTER 37: Of Miracles, and their Use

By *miracles* are signified the admirable works of God; and therefore, they are also called *wonders.* And because they are for the most part done for a signification of his commandment, in such occasions as without them men are apt to doubt (following their private natural reasoning) what he hath commanded and what not, they are commonly in Holy Scripture called *signs,* in the same sense as they are called, by the Latins, *ostenta* and *portenta,* from showing and foresignifying that which the Almighty is about to bring to pass.

To understand, therefore, what is a miracle, we must first understand what works they are which men wonder at and call admirable. And there be but two things which make men wonder at any event: the one is, if it be strange, that is to say, such as the like of it hath never, or very rarely, been produced; the other is if, when it is produced, we cannot imagine it to have been done by natural means, but only by the immediate hand of God. But when we see some possible natural cause of it, how rarely soever the like has been done, or if the like have been often done, how impossible soever it be to imagine a natural means thereof, we no more wonder, nor esteem it for a miracle.

Therefore, if a horse or cow should speak, it were a miracle, because both the thing is strange, and the natural cause difficult to imagine. So also were it, to see a strange deviation of nature, in the production of some new shape of a living creature. But when a man or other animal engenders his like, though we know no more how this is done than the other, yet because it is usual, it is no miracle. In like manner, if a man be metamorphosed into a stone or into a pillar, it is a miracle, because strange; but if a piece of wood be so changed, because we see it often, it is no miracle; and yet we know no more by what operation of God the one is brought to pass than the other.

The first rainbow that was seen in the world was a miracle, because the first, and consequently strange; and served for a sign from God, placed in heaven, to assure his people there should be no more universal destruction of the world by water. But at this day, because they are frequent, they are not miracles, neither to them that know their natural causes, nor to them who know them not. Again, there be many rare works produced by the art of man; yet when we know they are done, because thereby we know also the means how they are done, we count them not for miracles, because not wrought by the immediate hand of God, but by mediation of human industry.

Furthermore, seeing admiration and wonder is consequent to the knowledge and experience wherewith men are endued, some more, some less, it followeth that the same thing may be a miracle to one and not to another. And thence it is that ignorant and superstitious men make great wonders of those works which other men, knowing to proceed from nature (which is not the immediate, but the ordinary work of God), admire not at all: as when eclipses of the sun and moon have been taken for supernatural works by the common people, when nevertheless there were others could from their natural causes have foretold the very hour they should arrive; or, as when a man, by confederacy and secret intelligence getting knowledge of the private actions of an ignorant, unwary man, thereby tells him what he has done in former time, it seems to him a miraculous thing; but amongst wise and cautelous men such miracles as those cannot easily be done.

Again, it belongeth to the nature of a miracle that it be wrought for the procuring of credit to God's messengers, ministers, and prophets, that thereby men may know they are called, sent, and employed by God, and thereby be the better inclined to obey them. And therefore, though the creation of the world, and after that the destruction of all living creatures in the universal deluge, were admirable works, yet because they were not done to procure credit to any prophet or other minister of God, they use not to be called miracles. For how admirable soever any work be, the admiration consisteth not in that it could be done, because men naturally believe the Almighty can do all things, but because he does it at the prayer or word of a man. But the works of God in Egypt, by the hand of Moses, were properly miracles, because they were done with intention to make the people of Israel believe that Moses came unto them, not out of any design of his own interest, but as sent from God. Therefore, after God had commanded him to deliver the Israelites from the Egyptian bondage, when he said, *They will not believe me, but will say the Lord hath not appeared unto me*, God gave him power to turn the rod he had in his hand into a serpent, and again to return it into a rod; and by putting his hand into his bosom, to make it leprous, and again by pulling it out to make it whole; to make the children of Israel believe (as it is vs. 5) that the God of their fathers had appeared unto him: and if that were not enough, he gave him power to turn their waters into blood. And when he had done these miracles before the people, it is said (vs. [31]) that *they believed him*. Nevertheless, for fear of Pharaoh, they durst not yet obey him. Therefore, the other works which were done to plague Pharaoh and the Egyptians tended all to make the Israelites believe in Moses, and were properly miracles. In like manner, if we consider all the miracles done by the hand of

Moses and all the rest of the prophets till the captivity, and those of our Saviour and his apostles afterwards, we shall find their end was always to beget or confirm belief that they came not of their own motion, but were sent by God. We may further observe in Scripture that the end of miracles was to beget belief, not universally in all men (elect and reprobate), but in the elect only, that is to say, in such as God had determined should become his subjects. For those miraculous plagues of Egypt had not for end, the conversion of Pharaoh; for God had told Moses before that he would harden the heart of Pharaoh, that he should not let the people go; and when he let them go at last, not the miracles persuaded him, but the plagues forced him to it. So also, of our Saviour it is written (Matt. 13:58) that he wrought not many miracles in his own country, because of their unbelief; and (in Mark 6:5) instead of *He wrought not many*, it is *He could work none*. It was not because he wanted power, which to say were blasphemy against God; nor that the end of miracles was not to convert incredulous men to Christ; for the end of all the miracles of Moses, of the prophets, of our Saviour, and of his apostles was to add men to the church; but it was because the end of their miracles was to add to the church (not all men, but) such as should be saved (that is so say, such as God had elected). Seeing, therefore, our Saviour was sent from his Father, he could not use his power in the conversion of those whom his father had rejected. They that, expounding this place of St. Mark, say that his word *He could not* is put for *He would not*, do it without example in the Greek tongue (where *would not* is put sometimes for *could not*, in things inanimate that have no will, but *could not* for *would not* never), and thereby lay a stumbling block before weak Christians, as if Christ could do no miracles but amongst the credulous.

From that which I have here set down of the nature and use of a miracle, we may define it thus: *A MIRACLE is a work of God (besides his operation by the way of nature, ordained in the creation), done for the making manifest to his elect the mission of an extraordinary minister for their salvation.*

And from this definition we may infer: first, that in all miracles the work done is not the effect of any virtue in the prophet, because it is the effect of the immediate hand of God (that is to say, God hath done it without using the prophet therein as a subordinate cause).

Secondly, that no devil, angel, or other created spirit, can do a miracle. For it must either be by virtue of some natural science or by incantation, that is, by virtue of words. For if the enchanters do it by their own power independent, there is some power that proceedeth not from God, which all men deny; and if they do it by power given them, then is the work not from the immediate hand of God, but natural, and consequently no miracle.

There be some texts of Scripture that seem to attribute the power of working wonders (equal to some of those immediate miracles wrought by God himself) to certain arts of magic and incantation. As, for example, when we read that after the rod of Moses, being cast on the ground, became a serpent, *the magicians of Egypt did the like by their enchantments* (Exod. 7:11); and that after Moses had turned the waters of the Egyptian streams, rivers, ponds, and pools of water into blood, *the magicians of Egypt did so likewise with their enchantments* (Exod. 7:22); and that after Moses had by the power of God brought frogs upon the land, *the magicians also did so with their enchantments* (Exod. 8:7), and brought up frogs upon the land of Egypt. Will not a man be apt to attribute miracles to enchantments (that is to say, to the efficacy of the sound of words), and think the same very well proved out of this and other such places? And yet there is no place of Scripture that telleth us what an enchantment is. If, therefore, enchantment be not, as many think it, a working of strange effects by spells and words, but imposture and delusion, wrought by ordinary means, and so far from supernatural as the impostors need not the study so much as of natural causes, but the ordinary ignorance, stupidity, and superstition of mankind, to do them, those texts that seem to countenance the power of magic, witchcraft, and enchantment must needs have another sense than at first sight they seem to bear.

For it is evident enough that words have no effect but on those that understand them; and then they have no other but to signify the intentions or passions of them that speak, and thereby produce hope, fear, or other passions or conceptions in the hearer. Therefore, when a rod seemeth a serpent, or the waters blood, or any other miracle seemeth done by enchantment, if it be not to the edification of God's people, not the rod, nor the water, nor any other thing is enchanted (that is to say, wrought upon by the words) but the spectator. So that all the miracle consisteth in this: that the enchanter has deceived a man, which is no miracle, but a very easy matter to do.

For such is the ignorance and aptitude to error generally of all men (but especially of them that have not much knowledge of natural causes, and of the nature and interests of men) as by innumerable and easy tricks to be abused. What opinion of miraculous power, before it was known there was a science of the course of the stars, might a man have gained that should have told the people: This hour or day the sun should be darkened? A juggler, by the handling of his goblets and other trinkets (if it were not now ordinarily practised), would be thought to do his wonders by the power at least of the devil. A man that hath practised to speak by drawing in of his breath (which kind of men in ancient time were called *ventriloqui*) and so make the weakness of his voice seem to proceed, not from the weak impulsion of the organs of speech, but from distance of place, is able to make very many men believe it is a voice from Heaven, whatsoever he please to tell them. And for a crafty man that hath enquired into the secrets and familiar confessions that one man ordinarily maketh to another of his actions and adventures past, to tell them him again is no hard matter; and yet there be many that by such means as that obtain the reputation of being conjurers. But it is too long a business to reckon up the several sorts of those men which the Greeks called *Thaumaturgi* (that is to say, workers of things wonderful); and yet these do all they do, by their own single dexterity. But if we look upon the impostures wrought by confederacy, there is nothing how impossible soever to be done, that is impossible to be believed. For two men conspiring, one to seem lame, the other to cure him with a charm, will deceive many; but many conspiring, one to seem lame, another so to cure him, and all the rest to bear witness, will deceive many more.

In this aptitude of mankind to give too hasty belief to pretended miracles, there can be no better, nor I

think any other, caution than that which God hath prescribed, first by Moses (as I have said before in the precedent chapter) in the beginning of the 13th and end of the 18th of Deuteronomy: that we take not any for prophets that teach any other religion than that which God's lieutenant (which at that time was Moses) hath established, nor any (though he teach the same religion) whose prediction we do not see come to pass. Moses, therefore, in his time, and Aaron and his successors in their times, and the sovereign governor of God's people next under God himself, that is to say, the head of the Church in all times, are to be consulted, what doctrine he hath established, before we give credit to a pretended miracle or prophet. And when that is done, the thing they pretend to be a miracle, we must both see it done, and use all means possible to consider whether it be really done; and not only so, but whether it be such as no man can do the like by his natural power, but that it requires the immediate hand of God. And in this also we must have recourse to God's lieutenant, to whom in all doubtful cases, we have submitted our private judgments. For example, if a man pretend that after certain words spoken over a piece of bread, that presently God hath made it not bread, but a god or a man (or both), and nevertheless it looketh still as like bread as ever it did, there is no reason for any man to think it really done, nor consequently to fear him, till he enquire of God, by his vicar or lieutenant, whether it be done or not. If he say not, then followeth that which Moses saith (Deut. 18:22) *he hath spoken it presumptuously, thou shalt not fear him.* If he [the sovereign] say it is done, then he [the subject] is not to contradict it. So also if we see not, but only hear tell of a miracle, we are to consult the lawful Church, that is to say, the lawful head thereof, how far we are to give credit to the relators of it. And this is chiefly the case of men that in these days live under Christian sovereigns. For in these times I do not know one man that ever saw any such wonderous work, done by the charm, or at the word or prayer of a man, that a man endued but with a mediocrity of reason would think supernatural. And the question is no more, whether what we see done be a miracle, [or] whether the miracle we hear or read of were a real work, and not the act of a tongue or pen, but in plain terms, whether the report be true or a lie. In which question we are not every one to make our own private reason or conscience, but the public reason (that is, the reason of God's supreme lieutenant), judge; and indeed we have made him judge already, if we have given him a sovereign power to do all that is necessary for our peace and defence. A private man has always the liberty (because thought is free) to believe or not believe, in his heart, those acts that have been given out for miracles, according as he shall see what benefit can accrue, by men's belief, to those that pretend or countenance them, and thereby conjecture whether they be miracles or lies. But when it comes to confession of that faith, the private reason must submit to the public, that is to say, to God's lieutenant. But who is this lieutenant of God, and head of the Church, shall be considered in its proper place hereafter.

CHAPTER 38: Of the Signification in Scripture of Eternal Life, Hell, Salvation, the World to Come, and Redemption

The maintenance of civil society depending on justice, and justice on the power of life and death (and other less rewards and punishments) residing in them that have the sovereignty of the commonwealth, it is impossible a commonwealth should stand where any other than the sovereign hath a power of giving greater rewards than life, and of inflicting greater punishments than death. Now seeing *eternal life* is a greater reward than the *life present*, and *eternal torment* a greater punishment than the *death of nature*, it is a thing worthy to be well considered, of all men that desire (by obeying authority) to avoid the calamities of confusion and civil war, what is meant in Holy Scripture by *life eternal* and *torment eternal*; and for what offences, and against whom committed, men are to be *eternally tormented*; and for what actions they are to obtain *eternal life*.

And first, we find that Adam was created in such a condition of life as, had he not broken the commandment of God, he had enjoyed it in the paradise of Eden everlastingly. For there was the tree of life,

whereof he was so long allowed to eat as he should forbear to eat of the tree of knowledge of good and evil, which was not allowed him. And therefore, as soon as he had eaten of it, God thrust him out of Paradise *lest he should put forth his hand, and take also of the tree of life, and live for ever.* (Gen. 3:22) By which it seemeth to me (with submission, nevertheless, both in this and in all questions whereof the determination dependeth on the Scriptures, to the interpretation of the Bible authorized by the commonwealth whose subject I am) that Adam, if he had not sinned, had had an eternal life on earth, and that mortality entered upon himself and his posterity by his first sin. (Not that actual death then entered; for Adam then could never have had children, whereas he lived long after, and saw a numerous posterity ere he died. But where it is said *In the day that thou eatest thereof, thou shalt surely die*, it must needs be meant of his mortality and certitude of death.) Seeing, then, eternal life was lost by Adam's forfeiture in committing sin, he that should cancel that forfeiture was to recover thereby that life again. Now Jesus Christ hath satisfied for the sins of all that believe in him; and therefore recovered to all believers that ETERNAL LIFE which was lost by the sin of Adam. And in this sense it is that the comparison of St. Paul holdeth (Rom. 5:18–19): *As by the offence of one, judgment came upon all men to condemnation, even so by the righteousness of one, the free gift came upon all men to justification of life.* Which is again (1 Cor. 15:21–22) more perspicuously delivered in these words: *For since by man came death, by man came also the resurrection of the dead. For as in Adam all die, even so in Christ shall all be made alive.*

Concerning the place wherein men shall enjoy that eternal life which Christ hath obtained for them, the texts next before alleged seem to make it on earth. For if as in Adam all die (that is, have forfeited paradise and eternal life on earth) even so in Christ all shall be made alive, then all men shall be made to live on earth, for else the comparison were not proper. Hereunto seemeth to agree that of the psalmist (Psalm 133:3) *Upon Zion God commanded the blessing, even life for evermore*, for Zion is in Jerusalem, upon earth; as also that of St. John (Rev. 2:7) *To him that over-*

cometh I will give to eat of the tree of life, which is in the midst of the paradise of God. This was the tree of Adam's eternal life; but his life was to have been on earth. The same seemeth to be confirmed again by St. John (Rev. 21:2), where he saith *I John saw the holy city, new Jerusalem, coming down from God out of heaven, prepared as a bride adorned for her husband;* and again (vs. 10) to the same effect, as if he should say, the new Jerusalem, the paradise of God, at the coming again of Christ should come down to God's people from heaven, and not they go up to it from earth. And this differs nothing from that which two men in white clothing (that is, the two angels) said to the apostles that were looking upon Christ ascending (Acts 1:11) *This same Jesus, who is taken up from you into heaven,* shall so come as you have seen him go up into heaven, which soundeth as if they had said he should come down to govern them under his Father, eternally here, and not take them up to govern them in heaven, and is conformable to the restoration of the kingdom of God instituted under Moses, which was a political government of the Jews on earth. Again, that saying of our Saviour (Matt. 22:30) that *in the resurrection they neither marry, nor are given in marriage, but are as the angels of God in heaven* is a description of an eternal life resembling that which we lost in Adam in the point of marriage. For seeing Adam and Eve, if they had not sinned, had lived on earth eternally, in their individual persons, it is manifest they should not continually have procreated their kind. For if immortals should have generated as mankind doth now, the earth in a small time would not have been able to afford them place to stand on. The Jews that asked our Saviour the question, whose wife the woman that had married many brothers should be in the resurrection, knew not what were the consequences of life eternal; and therefore, our Saviour puts them in mind of this consequence of immortality, that there shall be no generation, and consequently no marriage, no more than there is marriage or generation among the angels. The comparison between that eternal life which Adam lost, and our Saviour by his victory over death hath recovered, holdeth also in this: that as Adam lost eternal life by his sin, and yet

lived after it for a time, so the faithful Christian hath recovered eternal life by Christ's passion, though he die a natural death, and remain dead for a time (namely, till the resurrection). For as death is reckoned from the condemnation of Adam, not from the execution, so life is reckoned from the absolution, not from the resurrection of them that are elected in Christ.

That the place wherein men are to live eternally after the resurrection is the heavens, meaning by heaven those parts of the world which are the most remote from earth (as where the stars are, or above the stars, in another higher heaven, called *coelum empyreum,* whereof there is no mention in Scripture nor ground in reason) is not easily to be drawn from any text that I can find. By the Kingdom of Heaven is meant the kingdom of the King that dwelleth in heaven, and his kingdom was the people of Israel, whom he ruled on earth by the prophets his lieutenants (first Moses, and after him, Eleazar and the sovereign priests, till in the days of Samuel they rebelled and would have a mortal man for their king, after the manner of other nations). And when our Saviour Christ, by the preaching of his ministers, shall have persuaded the Jews to return and called the Gentiles to his obedience, then shall there be a new kingdom of heaven, because our king shall then be God, whose throne is heaven, without any necessity evident in the Scripture that man shall ascend to his happiness any higher than God's *footstool,* the earth. On the contrary, we find written (John 3:13) that *no man hath ascended into heaven, but he that came down from heaven, even the son of man, that is in heaven.* Where I observe, by the way, that these words are not, as those which go immediately before, the words of our Saviour, but of St. John himself; for Christ was then not in heaven, but upon the earth. The like is said of David (Acts 2:34) where St. Peter, to prove the ascension of Christ, using the words of the Psalmist (Ps. 16:10), *Thou wilt not leave my soul in hell, nor suffer thine holy one to see corruption,* saith they were spoken (not of David, but) of Christ, and to prove it addeth this reason: *For David is not ascended into heaven.* But to this a man may easily answer, and say that though their bodies were not to ascend till the general day of judgment, yet their souls were in heaven as soon as they were departed from their bodies; which also seemeth to be confirmed by the words of our Saviour (Luke 20:37–38), who, proving the resurrection out of the words of Moses, saith thus: *That the dead are raised, even Moses shewed, at the bush, when he calleth the Lord, the God of Abraham, and the God of Isaac, and the God of Jacob. For he is not a God of the dead, but of the living; for they all live to him.* But if these words be to be understood only of the immortality of the soul, they prove not at all that which our Saviour intended to prove, which was the resurrection of the body (that is to say, the immortality of the man). Therefore, our Saviour meaneth that those patriarchs were immortal, not by a property consequent to the essence and nature of mankind, but by the will of God, that was pleased of his mere grace to bestow *eternal life* upon the faithful. And though at that time the patriarchs and many other faithful men were *dead*, yet (as it is in the text) they *lived to God*, that is, they were written in the Book of Life with them that were absolved of their sins, and ordained to live eternal at the resurrection. That the soul of man is in its own nature eternal, and a living creature independent of the body, or that any mere man is immortal otherwise than by the resurrection in the last day (except Enoch [Heb. 11:5] and Elijah) is a doctrine not apparent in Scripture. The whole of the 14th chapter of *Job*, which is the speech not of his friends, but of himself, is a complaint of this mortality of nature, and yet no contradiction of the immortality at the resurrection. *There is hope of a tree* (saith he, vs. 7) *if it be cast down. Though the root thereof wax old, and the stock thereof die in the ground, yet when it scenteth the water it will bud, and bring forth boughs like a plant. But man dieth, and wasteth away, yea, man giveth up the ghost, and where is he?* And (vs. 12): *Man lieth down, and riseth not, till the heavens be no more.* But when is it, that the heavens shall be no more? St. Peter tells us that it is at the general resurrection. For in his 2nd Epistle (3:7), he saith that *the heavens and the earth that are now, are reserved unto fire against the day of judgment, and perdition of ungodly men*, and (vs. 12): *looking for, and hasting to the coming of God, wherein the heavens shall be on fire, and shall be dissolved, and the elements shall melt with fervent heat. Nevertheless, we, according to the promise, look for new heavens, and a new earth, wherein dwelleth righteousness.* Therefore, when Job saith man riseth not till the heavens be no more, it is all one as if he had said the immortal life (and soul and life, in the Scripture, do usually signify the same thing) beginneth not in man till the resurrection and day of judgment, and hath for cause, not his specifical nature and generation, but the promise. For St. Peter says *We look for new heavens and a new earth* (not from nature) *but from promise*.

Lastly, seeing it hath been already proved out of divers evident places of Scripture (in ch. 35 of this book) that the kingdom of God is a civil commonwealth, where God himself is sovereign, by virtue first of the *Old* and since of the *New* covenant, wherein he reigneth by his vicar or lieutenant, the same places do therefore also prove that after the coming again of our Saviour, in his majesty and glory, to reign actually and eternally, the kingdom of God is to be on earth. But because this doctrine (though proved out of places of Scripture not few, nor obscure) will appear to most men a novelty, I do but propound it, maintaining nothing in this, or any other paradox of religion, but attending the end of that dispute of the sword concerning the authority (not yet amongst my countrymen decided) by which all sorts of doctrine are to be approved or rejected, and whose commands, both in speech and writing, whatsoever be the opinions of private men, must by all men that mean to be protected by their laws be obeyed. For the points of doctrine concerning the kingdom of God have so great influence on the kingdom of man, as not to be determined but by them that under God have the sovereign power.

As the kingdom of God and eternal life, so also God's enemies and their torments after judgment appear by the Scripture to have their place on earth. The name of the place where all men remain till the resurrection, that were either buried or swallowed up of the earth, is usually called in Scripture by words that signify *under ground*, which the Latins read generally *infernus*, and *inferi*, and the Greeks *hades* (that is to say, a place where men cannot see), and containeth as well the grave as any other deeper place. But for the place of the damned after the resurrection, it is not determined, neither in the Old nor New Testament, by any note of situation, but only by the company: as that it shall be where such wicked men were, as God in former times, in extraordinary and miraculous manner, had destroyed from off the face of the earth (as for example, that they are in *Inferno*, in *Tartarus*, or in the bottomless pit, because *Korah*, *Dathan*, and *Abiram* were swallowed up alive into the earth). Not that the writers of the Scripture would have us believe there could be in the globe of the earth (which is not only finite, but also, compared to the height of the stars, of no considerable magnitude) a pit without a bottom—that is, a hole of infinite depth, such as the Greeks in their *demonology* (that is to say, in their doctrine concerning *demons*), and after them the Romans, called *Tartarus*, of which Virgil says: "Bis patet in praeceps, tantum tenditque sub umbras,/Quantus ad aethereum coeli supectus Olympum." ["(*Tartarus* itself) extends down into the depths, under the shadows, twice as far as the distance seen from the earth looking up into the heavens."*] for that is a thing the proportion of earth to heaven cannot bear—but that we should believe them there, indefinitely, where those men are on whom God inflicted that exemplary punishment.

Again, because those mighty men of the earth that lived in the time of Noah, before the flood—which the Greeks called *heroes*, and the Scripture *giants*, and both say were begotten by copulation of the children of God with the children of men—were for their wicked life destroyed by the general deluge, the place of the damned is therefore also sometimes marked out by the company of those deceased giants: as Proverbs 21:16, *That man that wandereth out of the way of understanding, shall remain in the congregation of the giants*; and Job 26:5, *Behold the giants groan under water, and they that dwell with them* (here the place of the damned is under the water); and Isaiah 14:9, *Hell is troubled how to meet thee* (that is, the King of Babylon) *and will displace the giants for thee* (and

here again the place of the damned, if the sense be literal, is to be under water).

Thirdly, because the cities of Sodom and Gomorrah, by the extraordinary wrath of God, were consumed for their wickedness with fire and brimstone, and together with them the country about made a stinking bituminous lake, the place of the damned is sometimes expressed by fire and a fiery lake: as in the Apocalypse, 21:8, *But the timorous, incredulous, and abominable, and murderers, and whoremongers, and sorcerers, and idolaters, and all liars, shall have their part in the lake that burneth with fire and brimstone; which is the second death.* So that it is manifest that hell fire, which is here expressed by metaphor from the real fire of Sodom, signifieth not any certain kind or place of torment, but is to be taken indefinitely, for destruction (as it is in 20:14, where it is said that *death and hell were cast into the lake of fire*, that is to say, were abolished and destroyed, as if after the day of judgment there shall be no more dying, nor no more going into hell, that is, no more going to *Hades* (from which word perhaps our word Hell is derived), which is the same with no more dying).

Fourthly, from the plague of darkness inflicted on the Egyptians (of which it is written (Exod. 10:23) *They saw not one another, neither rose any man from his place for three days; but all the children of Israel had light in their dwellings*), the place of the wicked after judgment is called *utter darkness*, or (as it is in the original) *darkness without*. And so it is expressed (Matt. 22:13) where the king commandeth his servants *to bind hand and foot the man that had not on his wedding garment, and to cast him out*, εἰς τὸ σκότος τὸ ἐξώτερον, [into] *external darkness*, or *darkness without*, which, though translated *utter darkness*, does not signify how great, but where that darkness is to be, namely, without the habitation of God's elect.

Lastly, whereas there was a place near Jerusalem, called the Valley of the Children of Hinnon, in a part whereof, called Tophet, the Jews had committed most grievous idolatry, sacrificing their children to the idol Moloch, and wherein also God had afflicted his enemies with most grievous punishments, and wherein Josiah had burned the priests of Moloch upon their own altars (as appeareth at large in 2 Kings

---

* *Aeneid* VI.578–79, tran. Curley.

23), the place served afterwards to receive the filth and garbage which was carried thither, out of the city, and there used to be fires made, from time to time, to purify the air and take away the stench of carrion. From this abominable place the Jews used ever after to call the place of the damned by the name of *Gehenna*, or *Valley of Hinnon*. And this *Gehenna* is that word which is usually now translated HELL; and from the fires from time to time there burning, we have the notion of everlasting and unquenchable fire.

Seeing now there is none that so interprets the Scripture, as that after the day of judgment the wicked are all eternally to be punished in the Valley of Hinnon, or that they shall so rise again as to be ever after under ground or under water, or that after the resurrection they shall no more see one another, nor stir from one place to another, it followeth, me thinks, very necessarily that that which is thus said concerning hell fire is spoken metaphorically, and that therefore there is a proper sense to be enquired after (for of all metaphors there is some real ground that may be expressed in proper words), both of the place of hell, and the nature of hellish torments and tormenters.

And first, for the tormenters, we have their nature and properties exactly and properly delivered by the names of *the Enemy* (or *Satan*), *the Accuser* (or *Diabolus*), *the Destroyer* (or *Abaddon*). Which significant names (*Satan, Devil, Abaddon*) set not forth to us any individual person, as proper names use to do, but only an office or quality, and are therefore appellatives, which ought not to have been left untranslated (as they are in the Latin and modern Bibles), because thereby they seem to be the proper names of *demons*, and men are the more easily seduced to believe the doctrine of devils, which at that time was the religion of the Gentiles, and contrary to that of Moses, and of Christ.

And because by the *Enemy*, the *Accuser*, and *Destroyer*, is meant the enemy of them that shall be in the kingdom of God, therefore, if the kingdom of God after the resurrection be upon the earth (as in the former chapter I have shewn by Scripture it seems to be), the Enemy and his kingdom must be on earth also. For so also was it in the time before the Jews had deposed God. For God's kingdom was in Pales-

tine, and the nations round about were the kingdoms of the Enemy; and consequently, by *Satan* is meant any earthly enemy of the Church.

The torments of hell are expressed sometimes by *weeping and gnashing of teeth* (as Matt. 8:12), sometimes by *the worm of conscience* (as Isa. 66:24, and Mark 9:44, 46, 48), sometimes by *fire* (as in the place now quoted, *where the worm dieth not, and the fire is not quenched*, and many places beside), sometimes by *shame and contempt* (as Dan. 12:2, *And many of them that sleep in the dust of the earth shall awake, some to everlasting life, and some to shame and everlasting contempt.*) All which places design metaphorically a grief and discontent of mind, from the sight of that eternal felicity in others which they themselves through their own incredulity and disobedience have lost. And because such felicity in others is not sensible but by comparison with their own actual miseries, it followeth that they are to suffer such bodily pains and calamities as are incident to those who not only live under evil and cruel governors, but have also for enemy the eternal king of the saints, God Almighty. And amongst these bodily pains is to be reckoned also to every one of the wicked a second death. For though the Scripture be clear for an universal resurrection, yet we do not read that to any of the reprobate is promised an eternal life. For whereas *St. Paul* (1 Cor. 15:42, 43), to the question concerning what bodies men shall rise with again, saith that *The body is sown in corruption, and is raised in incorruption; it is sown in dishonour, it is raised in glory; it is sown in weakness, it is raised in power*, glory and power cannot be applied to the bodies of the wicked, nor can the name of *second death* be applied to those that can never die but once. And although in metaphorical speech a calamitous life everlasting may be called an everlasting death, yet it cannot well be understood of a *second death*. The fire prepared for the wicked is an everlasting fire, that is to say, the estate wherein no man can be without torture, both of body and mind, after the resurrection, shall endure for ever. And in that sense the fire shall be unquenchable and the torments everlasting. But it cannot thence be inferred that he who shall be cast into that fire, or be tormented with those torments, shall endure and resist them so as to be eternally burnt and tortured, and yet never be destroyed nor die. And though there be many places that affirm everlasting fire, and torments into which men may be cast successively one after another for ever, yet I find none that affirm there shall be an eternal life therein of any individual person, but to the contrary, an everlasting death, which is the second death. *For after death and the grave shall have delivered up the dead which were in them, and every man be judged according to his works, death and the grave shall also be cast into the lake of fire.* (Rev. 20:13–14) This is the second death. Whereby it is evident that there is to be a second death of every one that shall be condemned at the day of judgment, after which he shall die no more.

The joys of life eternal are in Scripture comprehended all under the name of SALVATION, or being saved. To be saved is to be secured, either respectively, against special evils, or absolutely, against all evil (comprehending want, sickness, and death itself). And because man was created in a condition immortal, not subject to corruption, and consequently to nothing that tendeth to the dissolution of his nature, and fell from that happiness by the sin of Adam, it followeth that to be saved from sin is to be saved from all the evil and calamities that sin hath brought upon us. And therefore, in the holy Scripture remission of sin, and salvation from death and misery, is the same thing, as it appears by the words of our Saviour, who, having cured a man sick of the palsy by saying (Matt. 9:2) *Son be of good cheer, thy sins be forgiven thee,* and knowing that the Scribes took for blasphemy that a man should pretend to forgive sins, asked them (vs. 5) *whether it were easier to say, Thy sins be forgiven thee, or, Arise and walk,* signifying thereby that it was all one, as to the saving of the sick, to say *Thy sins are forgiven,* and *Arise and walk,* and that he used that form of speech only to shew he had power to forgive sins. And it is besides evident in reason that, since death and misery were the punishments of sin, the discharge of sin must also be a discharge of death and misery, that is to say, salvation absolute, such as the faithful are to enjoy after the day of judgment, by the power and favour of Jesus Christ, who for that cause is called our SAVIOUR.

Concerning particular salvations, such as are understood (1 Sam. 14:39) *as the Lord liveth that saveth Israel,* that is, from their temporary enemies, and (2 Sam. 22) *Thou art my Saviour, thou savest me from violence,* and (2 Kings 13:5) *God gave the Israelites a Saviour, and so they were delivered from the hand of the Assyrians,* and the like, I need say nothing, there being neither difficulty, nor interest, to corrupt the interpretation of texts of that kind.

But concerning the general salvation, because it must be in the kingdom of heaven, there is great difficulty concerning the place. On one side, by *kingdom* (which is an estate ordained by men for their perpetual security against enemies and want) it seemeth that this salvation should be on earth. For by salvation is set forth unto us, a glorious reign of our king, by conquest, not a safety by escape. And therefore, there where we look for salvation, we must look also for triumph; and before triumph, for victory; and before victory, for battle, which cannot well be supposed shall be in heaven. But how good soever this reason may be, I will not trust to it without very evident places of Scripture. The state of salvation is described at large, Isaiah 33:20–24:

> *Look upon Zion, the city of our solemnities; thine eyes shall see Jerusalem a quiet habitation, a tabernacle that shall not be taken down; not one of the stakes thereof shall ever be removed, neither shall any of the cords thereof be broken.*
>
> *But there the glorious Lord will be unto us a place of broad rivers and streams, wherein shall go no galley with oars; neither shall gallant ship pass thereby.*
>
> *For the Lord is our Judge, the Lord is our lawgiver, the Lord is our king, he will save us.*
>
> *Thy tacklings are loosed; they could not well strengthen their mast; they could not spread the sail: then is the prey of a great spoil divided; the lame take the prey.*
>
> *And the inhabitant shall not say, I am sick; the people that shall dwell therein shall be forgiven their iniquity.*

In which words we have: the place from whence salvation is to proceed, *Jerusalem, a quiet habitation*; the eternity of it, *a tabernacle that shall not be taken down, &c*; the Saviour of it, *the Lord, their judge, their lawgiver, their king, he will save us*; the salvation, the Lord shall be to them as a broad moat of swift waters, &c; the condition of their enemies, their tacklings are loose, their masts weak, the lame shall take the spoil of them; the condition of the saved, The inhabitant shall not say, I am sick; and lastly, all this is comprehended in forgiveness of sin, The people that dwell therein shall be forgiven their iniquity. By which it is evident that salvation shall be on earth, then, when God shall reign (at the coming again of Christ) in Jerusalem; and from Jerusalem shall proceed the salvation of the Gentiles that shall be received into God's kingdom—as is also more expressly declared by the same prophet ([66]:20–21) And they (that is, the Gentiles who had any Jew in bondage) shall bring all your brethren for an offering to the Lord, out of all nations, upon horses, and in chariots, and in litters, and upon mules, and upon swift beasts, to my holy mountain, Jerusalem, saith the Lord, as the children of Israel bring an offering in a clean vessel in to the house of the Lord. And I will also take of them for priests and for Levites, saith the Lord. Whereby it is manifest that the chief seat of God's kingdom (which is the place from whence the salvation of us that were Gentiles shall proceed) shall be Jerusalem. And the same is also confirmed by our Saviour, in his discourse with the woman of Samaria concerning the place of God's worship, to whom he saith (John 4:22) that the Samaritans worshipped they knew not what, but the Jews worshipped what they knew, for salvation is of the Jews (ex Judaeis, that is, begins at the Jews), as if he should say, you worship God, but know not by whom he will save you, as we do, that know it shall be by one of the tribe of Judah, a Jew, not a Samaritan. And therefore also the woman not impertinently answered him again, We know the Messiah shall come. So that which our Saviour saith, Salvation is from the Jews, is the same that Paul says (Rom. 1:16–17) The gospel is the power of God to salvation to every one that believeth; to the Jew first, and also to the Greek. For therein is the righteousness of God revealed from faith to faith; from the faith of the Jew to the faith of the Gentile. In the like sense the prophet Joel, describing the day of Judgment (2:30–31), that God would shew wonders in heaven, and in earth, blood, and fire, and pillars of smoke.

The sun should be turned to darkness, and the moon into blood, before the great and terrible day of the Lord come, he addeth (vs. 32) and it shall come to pass, that whosoever shall call upon the name of the Lord shall be saved. For in Mount Zion and in Jerusalem shall be salvation. And Obadiah (vs. 17) saith the same, Upon Mount Zion shall be deliverance; and there shall be holiness, and the house of Jacob shall possess their possessions, that is, the possessions of the heathen, which possessions he expresseth more particularly in the following verses, by the mount of Esau, the land of the Philistines, the fields of Ephraim, of Samaria, Gilead, and the cities of the south, and concludes with these words: the kingdom shall be the Lord's. All these places are for salvation and the kingdom of God (after the day of judgment) upon earth. On the other side, I have not found any text that can probably be drawn to prove any ascension of the saints into heaven, that is to say, into any coelum empyreum, or other aetherial region, saving that it is called the kingdom of Heaven, which name it may have because God, that was king of the Jews, governed them by his commands, sent to Moses by angels from heaven; and after their revolt, sent his Son from heaven, to reduce them to their obedience; and shall send him thence again, to rule both them and all other faithful men, from the day of judgment, everlastingly—or from that, that the throne of this our great king is in heaven, whereas the earth is but his footstool. But that the subjects of God should have any place as high as his throne, or higher than his footstool, it seemeth not suitable to the dignity of a king, nor can I find any evident text for it in Holy Scripture.

From this that hath been said of the kingdom of God and of salvation, it is not hard to interpret what is meant by the WORLD TO COME. There are three worlds mentioned in Scripture, the old world, the present world, and the world to come. Of the first, St. Peter speaks (2 Pet. 2:5) If God spared not the old world, but saved Noah the eighth person, a preacher of righteousness, bringing the flood upon the world of the ungodly, &c. So the first world was from Adam to the general flood. Of the present world, our Saviour speaks (John 18:36) My kingdom is not of this world. For he came only to teach men the way of salvation, and to renew the kingdom of his Father by his doctrine. Of the world to come, St. Peter speaks (2 Pet. 3:13) *Nevertheless, we according to his promise look for new heavens and a new earth.* This is that WORLD wherein Christ, coming down from heaven in the clouds, with great power and glory, shall send his angels, and shall gather together his elect, from the four winds and from the uttermost parts of the earth, and thenceforth reign over them (under his Father) everlastingly.

Salvation of a sinner supposeth a precedent RE-DEMPTION; for he that is once guilty of sin is obnoxious to the penalty of the same, and must pay (or some other for him) such ransom as he that is offended, and has him in his power, shall require. And seeing the person offended is Almighty God, in whose power are all things, such ransom is to be paid, before salvation can be acquired, as God hath been pleased to require. By this ransom is not intended a satisfaction for sin, equivalent to the offence, which no sinner for himself, nor righteous man can ever be able to make for another; the damage a man does to another he may make amends for by restitution or recompense; but sin cannot be taken away by recompense, for that were to make the liberty to sin a thing vendible. But sins may be pardoned to the repentant, either *gratis* or upon such penalty as God is pleased to accept. That which God usually accepted in the Old Testament was some sacrifice or oblation. To forgive sin is not an act of injustice, though the punishment have been threatened. Even amongst men, though the promise of good bind the promiser, yet threats (that is to say, promises of evil) bind them not; much less shall they bind God, who is infinitely more merciful than men. Our Saviour Christ, therefore, to *redeem* us, did not in that sense satisfy for the sins of men as that his death, of its own virtue, could make it unjust in God to punish sinners with eternal death, but did make that sacrifice and oblation of himself at his first coming, which God was pleased to require for the salvation, at his second coming, of such as in the meantime should repent and believe in him. And though this act of our *redemption* be not always in Scripture called a *sacrifice* and *oblation*, but sometimes a *price*, yet by *price* we are not to

understand anything by the value whereof he could claim right to a pardon for us from his offended Father, but that price which God the Father was pleased in mercy to demand.

CHAPTER 43: Of what is Necessary for a Man's Reception into the Kingdom of Heaven

The most frequent pretext of sedition and civil war, in Christian commonwealths, hath a long time proceeded from a difficulty, not yet sufficiently resolved, of obeying at once both God and man, then when their commandments are one contrary to the other. It is manifest enough that when a man receiveth two contrary commands, and knows that one of them is God's, he ought to obey that and not the other, though it be the command even of his lawful sovereign (whether a monarch or a sovereign assembly) or the command of his father. The difficulty, therefore, consisteth in this: that men, when they are commanded in the name of God, know not, in divers cases, whether the command be from God, or whether he that commandeth do but abuse God's name for some private ends of his own. For as there were, in the Church of the Jews, many false prophets, that sought reputation with the people by feigned dreams and visions, so there have been, in all times in the Church of Christ, false teachers, that seek reputation with the people by fantastical and false doctrines, and by such reputation (as is the nature of ambition) to govern them for their private benefit.

But this difficulty of obeying both God and the civil sovereign on earth, to those that can distinguish between what is *necessary* and what is not *necessary* for their *reception* into the *kingdom of God*, is of no moment. For if the command of the civil sovereign be such as that it may be obeyed without the forfeiture of life eternal, not to obey it is unjust, and the precept of the apostle takes place: *Servants obey your masters in all things*; and, *Children obey your parents in all things*; and the precept of our Saviour: *The Scribes and Pharisees sit in Moses' chair; all, therefore, they shall say, that observe and do.* But if the command be such as cannot be obeyed without being damned to eternal death, then it were madness to obey it, and the counsel of our Saviour takes place (Matt. 10:28): *Fear not those that kill the body, but cannot kill the soul.* All men, therefore, that would avoid both the punishments that are to be in this world inflicted for disobedience to their earthly sovereign, and those that shall be inflicted in the world to come for disobedience to God, have need be taught to distinguish well between what is and what is not necessary to eternal salvation.

All that is NECESSARY *to salvation* is contained in two virtues: *faith in Christ,* and *obedience to laws.* The latter of these, if it were perfect, were enough to us. But because we are all guilty of disobedience to God's law, not only originally in Adam, but also actually by our own transgressions, there is required at our hands now, not only *obedience* for the rest of our time, but also a *remission* of sins for the time past, which remission is the reward of our faith in Christ. That nothing else is necessarily required to salvation is manifest from this: that the kingdom of heaven is shut to none but to sinners (that is to say, to the disobedient, or transgressors of the law); nor to them, in case they repent, and believe all the articles of Christian faith necessary to salvation.

The obedience required at our hands by God, that accepteth in all our actions the will for the deed, is a serious endeavour to obey him, and is called also by all such names as signify that endeavour. And therefore, obedience is sometimes called by the names of *charity* and *love* (because they imply a will to obey, and our Saviour himself maketh our love to God, and to one another, a fulfilling of the whole law [Matt. 22:37–40]); and sometimes by the name of *righteousness* (for righteousness is but the will to give to every one his own—that is to say, the will to obey the laws); and sometimes by the name of *repentance* (because to repent implieth a turning away from sin, which is the same with the return of the will to obedience). Whosoever, therefore, unfeignedly desireth to fulfil the commandments of God, or repenteth him truly of his transgressions, or that loveth God with all his heart, and his neighbour as himself, hath all the obedience necessary to his reception

into the kingdom of God. For if God should require perfect innocence, there could no flesh be saved.

But what commandments are those that God hath given us? Are all those laws which were given to the Jews by the hand of Moses the commandments of God? If they be, why are not Christians taught to obey them? If they be not, what others are so, besides the law of nature? For our Saviour Christ hath not given us new laws, but counsel to observe those we are subject to (that is to say, the laws of nature and the laws of our several sovereigns), nor did he made any new law to the Jews in his sermon on the Mount, but only expounded the laws of Moses, to which they were subject before. The laws of God, therefore, are none but the laws of nature, whereof the principal is that we should not violate our faith, that is, a commandment to obey our civil sovereigns, which we constituted over us by mutual pact one with another. And this law of God, that commandeth obedience to the law civil, commandeth by consequence obedience to all the precepts of the Bible, which (as I have proved in the precedent chapter) is there only law where the civil sovereign hath made it so, and in other places but counsel, which a man at his own peril may without injustice refuse to obey.

Knowing now what is the obedience necessary to salvation, and to whom it is due, we are to consider next, concerning faith, whom and why we believe, and what are the articles or points necessarily to be believed by them that shall be saved. And first, for the person whom we believe, because it is impossible to believe any person before we know what he saith, it is necessary he be one that we have heard speak. The person, therefore, whom Abraham, Isaac, Jacob, Moses and the prophets believed was God himself, that spake unto them supernaturally. And the person whom the apostles and disciples that conversed with Christ believed was our Saviour himself. But of them to whom neither God the father, nor our Saviour ever spake, it cannot be said that the person whom they believed was God. They believed the Apostles, and after them the pastors and doctors of the Church, that recommended to their faith the history of the Old and New Testament. So that the faith of Christians ever since our Saviour's time hath had for foundation, first, the reputation of their pastors, and afterward, the authority of those that made the Old and New Testament to be received for the rule of faith—which none could do but Christian sovereigns, who are therefore the supreme pastors, and the only persons whom Christians now hear speak from God—except such as God speaketh to, in these days, supernaturally. But because there be many false prophets *gone out into the world,* men are to examine such spirits (as St. *John* adviseth us, 1 John 4:1) *whether they be of God, or not.* And therefore, seeing the examination of doctrines belongeth to the supreme pastor, the person which all they that have no special revelation are to believe is (in every commonwealth) the supreme pastor, that is to say, the civil sovereign.

The causes why men believe any Christian doctrine are various. For faith is the gift of God, and he worketh it in each several man by such ways as it seemeth good unto himself. The most ordinary immediate cause of our belief concerning any point of Christian faith is that we believe the Bible to be the word of God. But why we believe the Bible to be the word of God is much disputed, as all questions must needs be that are not well stated. For they make not the question to be, *why we believe it,* but *how we know it,* as if believing and knowing were all one. And thence, while one side ground their knowledge upon the infallibility of the Church, and the other side on the testimony of the private spirit, neither side concludeth what it pretends. For how shall a man know the infallibility of the Church, but by knowing first the infallibility of the Scripture? Or how shall a man know his own private spirit to be other than a belief, grounded upon the authority and arguments of his teachers (or upon a presumption of his own gifts)? Besides, there is nothing in the Scripture from which can be inferred the infallibility of the Church, much less of any particular Church, and least of all, the infallibility of any particular man.

It is manifest, therefore, that Christian men do not know, but only believe the Scripture to be the word of God; and that the means of making them believe which God is pleased to afford men ordinarily is according to the way of nature, that is to say, from their teachers. It is the doctrine of St. Paul, concerning Christian faith in general (*Rom.* 10:17): *Faith cometh by hearing,* that is, by hearing our lawful pastors. He saith also (vss. 14, 15): *How shall they believe in him of whom they have not heard? and how shall they hear without a preacher? and how shall they preach, except they be sent?* Whereby it is evident that the ordinary cause of believing that the Scriptures are the word of God is the same with the cause of the believing of all other articles of our faith: namely, the hearing of those that are by the law allowed and appointed to teach us, as our parents in their houses, and our pastors in the churches. Which also is made more manifest by experience. For what other cause can there be assigned why, in Christian commonwealths, all men (either) believe (or at least profess) the Scripture to be the word of God, and in other commonwealths scarce any, but that in Christian commonwealths they are taught it from their infancy, and in other places they are taught otherwise?

But if teaching be the cause of faith, why do not all believe? It is certain, therefore, that faith is the gift of God, and he giveth it to whom he will. Nevertheless, because to them to whom he giveth it, he giveth it by the means of teachers, the immediate cause of faith is hearing. In a school, where many are taught (and some profit, others profit not), the cause of learning in them that profit is the master; yet it cannot be thence inferred that learning is not the gift of God. All good things proceed from God; yet cannot all that have them say they are inspired. For that implies a gift supernatural and the immediate hand of God—which he that pretends to, pretends to be a prophet, and is subject to the examination of the Church.

But whether men *know,* or *believe,* or *grant* the Scriptures to be the word of God, if, out of such places of them as are without obscurity, I shall show what articles of faith are necessary, and only necessary for salvation, those men must needs know, believe, or grant the same.

The *unum necessarium* (only article of faith which the Scripture maketh simply necessary to salvation) is this: that JESUS IS THE CHRIST. By the name of *Christ* is understood the king which God had before promised, by the prophets of the Old Testament, to send into the world to reign (over the Jews and over such of other nations as should believe in him) under himself eternally and to give them that eternal life which was lost by the sin of Adam. Which, when I have proved out of Scripture, I will further show when and in what sense some other articles may be also called necessary.

For proof that the belief of this article, *Jesus is the Christ,* is all the faith required to salvation, my first argument shall be from the scope of the Evangelists, which was by the description of the life of our Saviour to establish that one article, *Jesus is the Christ.* The sum of St. Matthew's Gospel is this: that Jesus was of the stock of David, born of a Virgin (which are the marks of the true Christ); that the *Magi* came to worship him as King of the Jews; that Herod for the same cause sought to kill him; that John Baptist proclaimed him; that he preached by himself and his apostles that he was that king; that he taught the law, not as a scribe, but as a man of authority; that he cured diseases by his word only, and did many other miracles which were foretold the Christ should do; that he was saluted king when he entered into Jerusalem; that he forewarned them to beware of all others that should pretend to be Christ; that he was taken, accused, and put to death, for saying he was king; that the cause of his condemnation, written on the cross, was JESUS OF NAZARETH, THE KING OF THE JEWS. All which tend to no other end than this: that men should believe that *Jesus is the Christ.* Such, therefore, was the scope of St. Matthew's Gospel. But the scope of all the evangelists (as may appear by reading them) was the same. Therefore, the scope of the whole Gospel was the establishing of that only article. And St. John expressly makes it his conclusion (John 20:31): *These things are written that you may know that Jesus is the Christ, the Son of the living God.*

My second argument is taken from the subject of the sermons of the apostles, both whilst our Saviour lived on earth and after his ascension. The apostles in our Saviour's time were sent (Luke 9:2) to preach the kingdom of God. For neither there, nor Matt. 10:7, giveth he any commission to them other than this: *As ye go, preach, saying, the kingdom of heaven is at hand,* that is, that *Jesus is the Messiah,* the *Christ,*

the *King* which was to come. That their preaching also after his ascension was the same, is manifest out of Acts 17:6, *They drew* (saith St. Luke) *Jason and certain brethren unto the rulers of the city, crying, These that have turned the world upside down are come hither also, whom Jason hath received. And these all do contrary to the decrees of Caesar, saying, that there is another king, one Jesus.* And out of the 2nd and 3rd verses of the same chapter, where it is said that *St. Paul, as his manner was, went in unto them, and three sabbath days reasoned with them out of the Scriptures, opening and alleging that Christ must needs have suffered, and risen again from the dead, and that this Jesus (whom he preached) is Christ.*

The third argument is from those places of Scripture by which all the faith required to salvation is declared to be easy. For if an inward assent of the mind to all the doctrines concerning Christian faith now taught (whereof the greatest part are disputed) were necessary to salvation, there would be nothing in the world so hard as to be a Christian. The thief upon the cross, though repenting, could not have been saved for saying, *Lord remember me when thou comest into thy kingdom,* by which he testified no belief of any other article but this: that *Jesus was the king.* Nor could it be said (as it is, Matt. 11:30) that *Christ's yoke is easy, and his burden light,* nor that *little children believe in him,* as it is Matt. 18:6. Nor could St. Paul have said (1 Cor. 1:21), *It pleased God by the foolishness of preaching, to save them that believe.* Nor could St. Paul himself have been saved, much less have been so great a doctor of the Church so suddenly, that never perhaps thought of transubstantiation, nor purgatory, nor many other articles now obtruded.

The fourth argument is taken from places express, and such as receive no controversy of interpretation: as first, John 5:39, *Search the Scriptures, for in them ye think ye have eternal life; and they are they that testify of me.* Our Saviour here speaketh of the Scriptures only of the Old Testament; for the Jews at that time could not search the Scriptures of the New Testament, which were not written. But the Old Testament hath nothing of Christ but the marks by which men might know him when he came (as that he should descend from David; be born at Bethlehem, and of a Virgin; do great miracles, and the like). Therefore, to believe that this Jesus was He, was sufficient to eternal life; but more than sufficient is not necessary; and consequently no other article is required. Again, (John 11:26) *Whosoever liveth and believeth in me, shall not die eternally.* Therefore, to believe in Christ is faith sufficient to eternal life; and consequently, no more faith than that is necessary. But to believe in Jesus and to believe that Jesus is the Christ is all one, as appeareth in the verses immediately following. For when our Saviour (vs. 26) had said to Martha, *Believest thou this?* she answereth (vs. 27), *Yea, Lord, I believe that thou art the Christ, the Son of God, which should come into the world.* Therefore, this article alone is faith sufficient to life eternal; and more than sufficient is not necessary. Thirdly, John 20:31, *These things are written that ye might believe that Jesus is the Christ, the Son of God, and that believing, ye might have life through his name.* There, to believe that *Jesus is the Christ* is faith sufficient to the obtaining of life; and therefore no other article is necessary. Fourthly, 1 John 4:2, *Every spirit that confesseth that Jesus Christ is come in the flesh is of God.* And 1 John 5:1, *Whosoever believeth that Jesus is the Christ is born of God.* And vs. 5, *Who is he that overcometh the world, but he that believeth that Jesus is the Son of God?* Fifthly, Acts 8:36–37, *See* (saith the Eunuch) *here is water, what doth hinder me to be baptized? And Philip said, if thou believest with all thy heart, thou mayst. And he answered and said, I believe that Jesus Christ is the Son of God.* Therefore this article believed, *Jesus is the Christ,* is sufficient to baptism, that is to say, to our reception into the kingdom of God, and by consequence, only necessary. And generally, in all places where our Saviour saith to any man *Thy faith hath saved thee,* the cause he saith it is some confession, which directly or by consequence implieth a belief that Jesus is the Christ.

The last argument is from the places where this article is made the foundation of faith. For he that holdeth the foundation shall be saved. Which places are first, Matt. 24:23, *If any man shall say unto you, Lo here is Christ, or there, believe it not; for there shall*

arise false Christs, and false prophets, and shall shew great signs and wonders, &c. Here we see this article, *Jesus is the Christ,* must be held, though he that shall teach the contrary should do great miracles. The second place is Gal. 1:8, *Though we, or an angel from heaven, preach any other gospel unto you, than that we have preached unto you, let him be accursed.* But the gospel which Paul and the other apostles preached was only this article, that *Jesus is the Christ.* Therefore, for the belief of this article we are to reject the authority of an angel from heaven, much more of any mortal man, if he teach the contrary. This is, therefore, the fundamental article of Christian faith. A third place is 1 John 4:1, *Beloved, believe not every spirit. Hereby ye shall know the Spirit of God; every spirit that confesseth that Jesus Christ is come in the flesh is of God.* By which it is evident that this article is the measure and rule by which to estimate and examine all other articles; and is, therefore, only fundamental. A fourth is Matt. 16:18, where after St. Peter had professed this article, saying to our Saviour *Thou art Christ the Son of the living God,* our Saviour answered *Thou are Peter, and upon this rock I will build my Church.* From whence I infer that this article is that on which all other doctrines of the Church are built, as on their foundation. A fifth is 1 Cor. 3:11–12, &c.: *Other foundation can no man lay than that which is laid, Jesus is the Christ. Now if any man build upon this foundation [with] gold, silver, precious stones, wood, hay, stubble, every man's work shall be made manifest; for the day shall declare it, because it shall be revealed by fire, and the fire shall try every man's work of what sort it is. If any man's work abide, which he hath built thereupon, he shall receive a reward. If any man's work shall be burnt, he shall suffer loss; but he himself shall be saved, yet so as by fire.* Which words, being partly plain and easy to understand, and partly allegorical and difficult, out of that which is plain may be inferred that pastors that teach this foundation, that *Jesus is the Christ,* though they draw from it false consequences (which all men are sometimes subject to), they may nevertheless be saved—much more, that they may be saved who, being no pastors, but hearers, believe that which is by their lawful pastors taught them. Therefore, the belief of this article is sufficient; and by consequence, there is no other article of faith necessarily required to salvation.

Now for the part which is allegorical, as *that the fire shall try every man's work, and that they shall be saved, but so as by fire* (or *through fire*—for the original is διὰ πυρὸς), it maketh nothing against this conclusion which I have drawn from the other words that are plain. Nevertheless, because upon this place there hath been an argument taken to prove the fire of purgatory, I will also here offer you my conjecture concerning the meaning of this trial of doctrines and saving of men as by fire. The apostle here seemeth to allude to the words of the prophet Zechariah (13:8–9), who, speaking of the restoration of the kingdom of God, saith thus: *Two parts therein shall be cut off, and die, but the third shall be left therein; and I will bring the third part through the fire, and will refine them as silver is refined, and will try them as gold is tried; they shall call on the name of the Lord, and I will hear them.* The day of judgment is the day of the restoration of the kingdom of God; and at that day it is that St. Peter tells us (2 Pet. 3:7, 10, 12) shall be the conflagration of the world, wherein the wicked shall perish, but the remnant which God will save shall pass through that fire unhurt, and be therein (as silver and gold are refined by the fire from their dross) tried, and refined from their idolatry, and be made to call upon the name of the true God. Alluding whereto, St. Paul here saith that the day (that is, the day of judgment, the great day of our Saviour's coming to restore the kingdom of God in Israel) shall try every man's doctrine, by judging which are gold, silver, precious stones, wood, hay, stubble; and then they that have built false consequences on the true foundation shall see their doctrines condemned; nevertheless, they themselves shall be saved, and pass unhurt through this universal fire, and live eternally, to call upon the name of the true and only God. In which sense, there is nothing that accordeth not with the rest of Holy Scripture, or any glimpse of the fire of purgatory.

But a man may here ask whether it be not as necessary to salvation to believe that God is omnipotent, Creator of the world, that Jesus Christ is risen, and that all men else shall rise again from the dead at the last day, as to believe that *Jesus is the Christ.* To which I answer: they are, and so are many more articles; but they are such as are contained in this one, and may be deduced from it, with more or less difficulty. For who is there that does not see that they who believe Jesus to be the Son of the God of Israel, and that the Israelites had for God the Omnipotent Creator of all things, do therein also believe that God is the Omnipotent Creator of all things? Or how can a man believe that Jesus is the king that shall reign eternally, unless he believe him also risen again from the dead? For a dead man cannot exercise the office of a king. In sum, he that holdeth this foundation, *Jesus is the Christ,* holdeth expressly all that he seeth rightly deduced from it, and implicitly all that is consequent thereunto, though he have not skill enough to discern the consequence. And therefore, it holdeth still good that the belief of this one article is sufficient faith to obtain remission of sins to the *penitent,* and consequently to bring them into the kingdom of heaven.

Now that I have shown that all the obedience required to salvation consisteth in the will to obey the law of God (that is to say, in repentance) and all the faith required to the same is comprehended in the belief of this article, *Jesus is the Christ,* I will further allege those places of the Gospel that prove that all that is necessary to salvation is contained in both these joined together. The men to whom St. Peter preached on the day of Pentecost, next after the ascension of our Saviour, asked him and the rest of the apostles, saying (Acts 2:37) *Men and brethren, what shall we do?* To whom St. Peter answered (in the next verse) *Repent, and be baptized every one of you, for the remission of sins, and ye shall receive the gift of the Holy Ghost.* Therefore, repentance and baptism, that is, believing that Jesus is the Christ, is all that is necessary to salvation. Again, our Saviour being asked by a certain ruler (Luke 18:18) *What shall I do to inherit eternal life?* answered (vs. 20) *Thou knowest the commandments, do not commit adultery, do not kill, do not steal, do not bear false witness, honour thy father and thy mother.* Which, when he said he had observed, our Saviour added *Sell all thou hast, give it to the poor, and come and follow me*, which was as much as to say: rely on me that am the king. Therefore, to fulfil the law, and to believe that Jesus is the king, is all that is required to bring a man to eternal life. Thirdly, St. Paul saith (Rom. 1:17) *The just shall live by faith* — not every one, but the *just*. Therefore, faith and justice (that is, the will to be just, or repentance) are all that is necessary to life eternal. And (Mark 1:15) our Saviour preached, saying *The time is fulfilled, and the kingdom of God is at hand, repent and believe the evangel*, that is, the good news that the Christ was come. Therefore, to repent, and to believe that Jesus is the Christ, is all that is required to salvation.

Seeing, then, it is necessary that faith and obedience (implied in the word repentance) do both concur to our salvation, the question by which of the two we are justified is impertinently disputed. Nevertheless, it will not be impertinent to make manifest in what manner each of them contributes thereunto, and in what sense it is said that we are to be justified by the one and by the other. And first, if by righteousness be understood the justice of the works themselves, there is no man that can be saved; for there is none that hath not transgressed the law of God. And therefore, when we are said to be justified by works, it is to be understood of the will, which God doth always accept for the work itself, as well in good as in evil men. And in this sense only it is that a man is called *just* or *unjust*, and that his justice justifies him (that is, gives him the title, in God's acceptation, of *just*, and renders him capable of *living by his faith*, which before he was not). So that justice justifies in that sense in which to *justify* is the same that to *denominate a man just* (and not in the signification of discharging the law, whereby the punishment of his sins should be unjust).

But a man is then also said to be justified when his plea, though in itself insufficient, is accepted, as when we plead our will, our endeavour to fulfil the law, and repent us of our failings, and God accepteth it for the performance itself. And because God accepteth not the will for the deed but only in the faithful, it is therefore faith that makes good our plea. And in this sense it is that faith only justifies. So that *faith* and *obedience* are both necessary to salvation; yet in several senses each of them is said to justify.

Having thus shown what is necessary to salvation, it is not hard to reconcile our obedience to God with our obedience to the civil sovereign, who is either Christian or infidel. If he be a Christian, he alloweth the belief of this article, that *Jesus is Christ* (and of all the articles that are contained in, or are by evident consequence deduced from, it), which is all the faith necessary to salvation. And because he is a sovereign, he requireth obedience to all his own (that is, to all the civil) laws, in which also are contained all the laws of nature (that is, all the laws of God). For besides the laws of nature, and the laws of the Church which are part of the civil law (for the Church that can make laws is the commonwealth), there be no other laws divine. Whosoever, therefore, obeyeth his Christian sovereign is not thereby hindered, neither from believing nor from obeying God. But suppose that a Christian king should from this foundation, *Jesus is the Christ*, draw some false consequences, that is to say, make some superstructions of hay or stubble, and command the teaching of the same. Yet seeing St. Paul says he shall be saved, much more shall he be saved that teacheth them by his command; and much more yet, he that teaches not, but only believes his lawful teacher. And in case a subject be forbidden by the civil sovereign to profess some of those his opinions, upon what just ground can he disobey? Christian kings may err in deducing a consequence, but who shall judge? Shall a private man judge, when the question is of his own obedience? Or shall any man judge but he that is appointed thereto by the Church (that is, by the civil sovereign that representeth it)? Or if the pope or an apostle judge, may he not err in deducing of a consequence? Did not one of the two, St. Peter or St. Paul, err in a superstructure, when St. Paul withstood St. Peter to his face? There can, therefore, be no contradiction between the laws of God and the laws of a Christian commonwealth.

And when the civil sovereign is an infidel, every one of his own subjects that resisteth him sinneth against the laws of God (for such are the laws of nature) and rejecteth the counsel of the apostles, that admonisheth all Christians to obey their princes, and all children and servants to obey their parents and masters in all things. And for their *faith*, it is internal and invisible; they have the license that Naaman had, and need not put themselves into danger for it. But if they do, they ought to expect their reward in heaven, and not complain of their lawful sovereign, much less make war upon him. For he that is not glad of any just occasion of martyrdom has not the faith he professeth, but pretends it only, to set some colour upon his own contumacy. But what infidel king is so unreasonable as, knowing he has a subject that waiteth for the second coming of Christ (after the present world shall be burnt), and intendeth then to obey him (which is the intent of believing that Jesus is the Christ), and in the meantime thinketh himself bound to obey the laws of that infidel king (which all Christians are obliged in conscience to do), to put to death or to persecute such a subject?

And thus much shall suffice concerning the kingdom of God and policy ecclesiastical. Wherein I pretend not to advance any position of my own, but only to show what are the consequences that seem to be deducible from the principles of Christian politics (which are the holy Scriptures), in confirmation of the power of civil sovereigns and the duty of their subjects. And in the allegation of Scripture I have endeavoured to avoid such texts as are of obscure or controverted interpretation, and to allege none but in such sense as is most plain and agreeable to the harmony and scope of the whole Bible, which was written for the re-establishment of the kingdom of God in Christ. For it is not the bare words, but the scope of the writer, that giveth the true light by which any writing is to be interpreted; and they that insist upon single texts, without considering the main design, can derive nothing from them clearly, but rather by casting atoms of Scripture, as dust before men's eyes, make everything more obscure than it is—an ordinary artifice of those that seek not the truth, but their own advantage.

A REVIEW, AND CONCLUSION

From the contrariety of some of the natural faculties of the mind, one to another, as also of one passion to another, and from their reference to conversation, there has been an argument taken, to infer an impossibility that any one man should be sufficiently disposed to all sorts of civil duty. The severity of judgment, they say, makes men censorious, and unapt to pardon the errors and infirmities of other men: and on the other side, celerity of fancy, makes the thoughts less steady than is necessary, to discern exactly between right and wrong. Again, in all deliberations, and in all pleadings, the faculty of solid reasoning, is necessary: for without it, the resolutions of men are rash, and their sentences unjust: and yet if there be not powerful eloquence, which procureth attention and consent, the effect of reason will be little. But these are contrary faculties; the former being grounded upon principles of truth; the other upon opinions already received, true, or false; and upon the passions and interests of men, which are different, and mutable.

And amongst the passions, *courage*, (by which I mean the contempt of wounds, and violent death) inclineth men to private revenges, and sometimes to endeavour the unsettling of the public peace: and *timorousness*, many times disposeth to the desertion of the public defence. Both these they say cannot stand together in the same person.

And to consider the contrariety of men's opinions, and manners in general, it is, they say, impossible to entertain a constant civil amity with all those, with whom the business of the world constrains us to converse: which business, consisteth almost in nothing else but a perpetual contention for honour, riches, and authority.

To which I answer, that these are indeed great difficulties, but not impossibilities: for by education, and discipline, they may be, and are sometimes reconciled. Judgment and fancy may have place in the same man; but by turns; as the end which he aimeth at requireth. As the Israelites in Egypt, were sometimes fastened to their labour of making bricks, and other times were ranging abroad to gather straw: so also may the judgment sometimes be fixed upon one certain consideration, and the fancy at another time wandering about the world. So also reason, and eloquence, (though not perhaps in the natural sciences, yet in the moral) may stand very well together. For wheresoever there is place for adorning and preferring of error, there is much more place for adorning and preferring of truth, if they have it to adorn. Nor is there any repugnancy between fearing the laws, and not fearing a public enemy; nor between abstaining from injury, and pardoning it in others. There is therefore no such inconsistence of human nature, with civil duties, as some think. I have known clearness of judgment, and largeness of fancy; strength of reason, and graceful elocution; a courage for the war, and a fear for the laws, and all eminently in one man; and that was my most noble and honoured friend, Mr. Sidney Godolphin; who hating no man, nor hated of any, was unfortunately slain in the beginning of the late civil war, in the public quarrel, by an undiscerned, and an undiscerning hand.

To the Laws of Nature, declared in Chapter 15, I would have this added, *that every man is bound by nature, as much as in him lieth, to protect in war, the authority, by which he is himself protected in time of peace.* For he that pretendeth a right of nature to preserve his own body, cannot pretend a right of nature to destroy him, by whose strength he is preserved: it is a manifest contradiction of himself. And though this law may be drawn by consequence, from some of those that are there already mentioned; yet the times require to have it inculcated, and remembered.

And because I find by divers English books lately printed, that the civil wars have not yet sufficiently taught men in what point of time it is, that a subject becomes obliged to the conqueror; nor what is conquest; nor how it comes about, that it obliges men to obey his laws: therefore for further satisfaction of men therein, I say, the point of time, wherein a man becomes subject to a conqueror, is that point, wherein having liberty to submit to him, he consenteth, either by express words, or by other sufficient sign, to be his subject. When it is that a man hath the liberty to

submit, I have showed before in the end of Chapter 21; namely, that for him that hath no obligation to his former sovereign but that of an ordinary subject, it is then, when the means of his life is within the guards and garrisons of the enemy; for it is then, that he hath no longer protection from him, but is protected by the adverse party for his contribution. Seeing therefore such contribution is every where, as a thing inevitable, (notwithstanding it be an assistance to the enemy,) esteemed lawful; a total submission, which is but an assistance to the enemy, cannot be esteemed unlawful. Besides, if a man consider that they who submit, assist the enemy but with part of their estates, whereas they that refuse, assist him with the whole, there is no reason to call their submission, or composition an assistance; but rather a detriment to the enemy. But if a man, besides the obligation of a subject, hath taken upon him a new obligation of a soldier, then he hath not the liberty to submit to a new power, as long as the old one keeps the field, and giveth him means of subsistence, either in his armies, or garrisons: for in this case, he cannot complain of want of protection, and means to live as a soldier. But when that also fails, a soldier also may seek his protection wheresoever he has most hope to have it; and may lawfully submit himself to his new master. And so much for the time when he may do it lawfully, if he will. If therefore he do it, he is undoubtedly bound to be a true subject: for a contract lawfully made, cannot lawfully be broken.

By this also a man may understand, when it is, that men may be said to be conquered; and in what the nature of conquest, and the right of a conqueror consisteth: for this submission is it implieth them all. Conquest, is not the victory itself; but the acquisition by victory, of a right, over the persons of men. He therefore that is slain, is overcome, but not conquered: he that is taken, and put into prison, or chains, is not conquered, though overcome; for he is still an enemy, and may save himself if he can: but he that upon promise of obedience, hath his life and liberty allowed him, is then conquered, and a subject; and not before. The Romans used to say, that their general had *pacified* such a *province*, that is to say, in English, *conquered* it; and that the country was *pacified* by victory, when the people of it had promised *imperata facere*, that is, *to do what the Roman people commanded them*: this was to be conquered. But this promise may be either express, or tacit: express, by promise: tacit, by other signs. As for example, a man that hath not been called to make such an express promise, (because he is one whose power perhaps is not considerable;) yet if he live under their protection openly, he is understood to submit himself to the government: but if he live there secretly, he is liable to any thing that may be done to a spy, and enemy of the state. I say not, he does any injustice, (for acts of open hostility bear not that name); but that he may be justly put to death. Likewise, if a man, when his country is conquered, be out of it, he is not conquered, nor subject: but if at his return, he submit to the government, he is bound to obey it. So that *conquest* (to define it) is the acquiring of the right of sovereignty by victory. Which right, is acquired, in the people's submission, by which they contract with the victor, promising obedience, for life and liberty.

In Chapter 29, I have set down for one of the causes of the dissolutions of commonwealths, their imperfect generation, consisting in the want of an absolute and arbitrary legislative power; for want whereof, the civil sovereign is fain to handle the sword of justice unconstantly, and as if it were too hot for him to hold. One reason whereof (which I have not there mentioned) is this, that they will all of them justify the war, by which their power was at first gotten, and whereon (as they think) their right dependeth, and not on the possession. As if, for example, the right of the kings of England did depend on the goodness of the cause of William the Conqueror, and upon their lineal, and directest descent from him; by which means, there would perhaps be no tie of the subjects' obedience to their sovereign at this day in all the world: wherein whilst they needlessly think to justify themselves, they justify all the successful rebellions that ambition shall at any time raise against them, and their successors. Therefore I put down for one of the most effectual seeds of the death of any state, that the conquerors require not only a submission of men's actions to them for the future, but also an approbation of all their actions past; when there is scarce a commonwealth in the world, whose beginnings can in conscience be justified.

And because the name of tyranny, signifieth nothing more, nor less, than the name of sovereignty, be it in one, or many men, saving that they that use the former word, are understood to be angry with them they call tyrants; I think the toleration of a professed hatred of tyranny, is a toleration of hatred to commonwealth in general, and another evil seed, not differing much from the former. For to the justification of the cause of a conqueror, the reproach of the cause of the conquered, is for the most part necessary: but neither of them necessary for the obligation of the conquered. And thus much I have thought fit to say upon the review of the first and second part of this discourse.

In Chapter 35, I have sufficiently declared out of the Scripture, that in the commonwealth of the Jews, God himself was made the sovereign, by pact with the people; who were therefore called his *peculiar people*, to distinguish them from the rest of the world, over whom God reigned not by their consent, but by his own power: and that in this kingdom Moses was God's lieutenant on earth; and that it was he that told them what laws God appointed them to be ruled by. But I have omitted to set down who were the officers appointed to do execution; especially in capital punishments; not then thinking it a matter of so necessary consideration, as I find it since. We know that generally in all commonwealths, the execution of corporal punishments, was either put upon the guards, or other soldiers of the sovereign power; or given to those, in whom want of means, contempt of honour, and hardness of heart, concurred, to make them sue for such an office. But amongst the Israelites it was a positive law of God their sovereign, that he that was convicted of a capital crime, should be stoned to death by the people; and that the witnesses should cast the first stone, and after the witnesses, then the rest of the people. This was a law that designed who were to be the executioners; but not that any one should throw a stone at him before conviction and sentence, where the congregation was judge. The witnesses were nevertheless to be heard before they proceeded to execution, unless the fact were committed in the presence of the congregation itself, or in sight of the lawful judges; for then there needed no other witnesses but the judges themselves. Nevertheless, this manner of proceeding being not thoroughly understood, hath given occasion to a dangerous opinion, that any man may kill another, in some cases, by a right of zeal; as if the executions done upon offenders in the kingdom of God in old time, proceeded not from the sovereign command, but from the authority of private zeal: which, if we consider the texts that seem to favour it, is quite contrary.

First, where the Levites fell upon the people, that had made and worshipped the Golden Calf, and slew three thousand of them; it was by the commandment of Moses, from the mouth of God; as is manifest, *Exod.* 32. 27. And when the son of a woman of Israel had blasphemed God, they that heard it, did not kill him, but brought him before Moses, who put him under custody, till God should give sentence against him; as appears, *Levit.* 25. 11, 12. Again, (*Numb.* 25. 6, 7) when Phinehas killed Zimri and Cosbi, it was not by right of private zeal: their crime was committed in the sight of the assembly; there needed no witness; the law was known, and he the heir apparent to the sovereignty; and which is the principal point, the lawfulness of his act depended wholly upon a subsequent ratification by Moses, whereof he had no cause to doubt. And this presumption of a future ratification, is sometimes necessary to the safety [of] a commonwealth; as in a sudden rebellion, any man that can suppress it by his own power in the country where it begins, without express law or commission, may lawfully do it, and provide to have it ratified, or pardoned, whilst it is in doing, or after it is done. Also *Numb.* 35. 30, it is expressly said, *Whosoever shall kill the murderer, shall kill him upon the word of witnesses:* but witnesses suppose a formal judicature, and consequently condemn that pretence of *jus zelotarum.* The law of Moses concerning him that enticeth to idolatry, that is to say, in the kingdom of God to a renouncing of his allegiance, (*Deut.* 13. 8) forbids to conceal him, and commands the accuser to cause him to be put to death, and to cast the first stone at him; but not to kill him before he be

condemned. And (*Deut.* 17. 4, 5, 6) the process against idolatry is exactly set down: for God there speaketh to the people, as judge, and commandeth them, when a man is accused of idolatry, to enquire diligently of the fact, and finding it true, then to stone him; but still the hand of the witness throweth the first stone. This is not private zeal, but public condemnation. In like manner when a father hath a rebellious son, the law is (*Deut.* 21. 18) that he shall bring him before the judges of the town, and all the people of the town shall stone him. Lastly, by pretence of these laws it was, that St. Stephen was stoned, and not by pretence of private zeal: for before he was carried away to execution, he had pleaded his cause before the high priest. There is nothing in all this, nor in any other part of the Bible, to countenance executions by private zeal; which being oftentimes but a conjunction of ignorance and passion, is against both the justice and peace of a commonwealth.

In chapter 36, I have said, that it is not declared in what manner God spake supernaturally to Moses: not that he spake not to him sometimes by dreams and visions, and by a supernatural voice, as to other prophets: for the manner how he spake unto him from the mercy-seat, is expressly set down *Numbers* 7. 89, in these words, *From that time forward, when Moses entered into the Tabernacle of the congregation to speak with God, he heard a voice which spake unto him from over the mercy-seat, which is over the Ark of the testimony, from between the cherubims he spake unto him.* But it is not declared in what consisted the preeminence of the manner of God's speaking to Moses, above that of his speaking to other prophets, as to Samuel, and to Abraham, to whom he also spake by a voice, (that is, by vision) unless the difference consist in the clearness of the vision. For *face to face,* and *mouth to mouth,* cannot be literally understood of the infiniteness, and incomprehensibility of the Divine nature.

And as to the whole doctrine, I see not yet, but the principles of it are true and proper; and the ratiocination solid. For I ground the civil right of sovereigns, and both the duty and liberty of subjects, upon the known natural inclinations of mankind, and upon the articles of the law of nature; of which no man, that pretends but reason enough to govern his private family, ought to be ignorant. And for the power ecclesiastical of the same sovereigns, I ground it on such texts, as are both evident in themselves, and consonant to the scope of the whole Scripture. And therefore am persuaded, that he that shall read it with a purpose only to be informed, shall be informed by it. But for those that by writing, or public discourse, or by their eminent actions, have already engaged themselves to the maintaining of contrary opinions, they will not be so easily satisfied. For in such cases, it is natural for men, at one and the same time, both to proceed in reading, and to lose their attention, in the search of objections to that they had read before: Of which in a time wherein the interests of men are changed (seeing much of that doctrine, which serveth to the establishing of a new government, must needs be contrary to that which conduced to the dissolution of the old,) there cannot choose but be very many.

In that part which treateth of a Christian commonwealth, there are some new doctrines, which, it may be, in a state where the contrary were already fully determined, were a fault for a subject without leave to divulge, as being an usurpation of the place of a teacher. But in this time, that men call not only for peace, but also for truth, to offer such doctrines as I think true, and that manifestly tend to peace and loyalty, to the consideration of those that are yet in deliberation, is no more, but to offer new wine, to be put into new cask, that both may be preserved together. And I suppose, that then, when novelty can breed no trouble, nor disorder in a state, men are not generally so much inclined to the reverence of antiquity, as to prefer ancient errors, before new and well proved truth.

There is nothing I distrust more than my elocution, which nevertheless I am confident (excepting the mischances of the press) is not obscure. That I have neglected the ornament of quoting ancient poets, orators, and philosophers, contrary to the custom of late time, (whether I have done well or ill in it,) proceedeth from my judgment, grounded on many reasons. For first, all truth of doctrine dependeth either upon *reason*, or upon *Scripture*; both which give credit to many, but never receive it from any writer.

Secondly, the matters in question are not of *fact*, but of *right*, wherein there is no place for *witnesses*. There is scarce any of those old writers, that contradicteth not sometimes both himself and others; which makes their testimonies insufficient. Fourthly, such opinions as are taken only upon credit of antiquity, are not intrinsically the judgment of those that cite them, but words that pass (like gaping) from mouth to mouth. Fifthly, it is many times with a fraudulent design that men stick their corrupt doctrine with the cloves of other men's wit. Sixthly, I find not that the ancients they cite, took it for an ornament, to do the like with those that wrote before them. Seventhly, it is an argument of indigestion, when Greek and Latin sentences unchewed come up again, as they use to do, unchanged. Lastly, though I reverence those men of ancient time, that either have written truth perspicuously, or set us in a better way to find it out ourselves; yet to the antiquity itself I think nothing due: For if we will reverence the age, the present is the oldest. If the antiquity of the writer, I am not sure, that generally they to whom such honour is given, were more ancient when they wrote, than I am that am writing: But if it be well considered, the praise of ancient authors, proceeds not from the reverence of the dead, but from the competition, and mutual envy of the living.

To conclude, there is nothing in this whole discourse, nor in that I writ before of the same subject in Latin, as far as I can perceive, contrary either to the Word of God, or to good manners; or to the disturbance of the public tranquillity. Therefore I think it may be profitably printed, and more profitably taught in the Universities, in case they also think so, to whom the judgment of the same belongeth. For seeing the Universities are the fountains of civil, and moral doctrine, from whence the preachers, and the gentry, drawing such water as they find, use to sprinkle the same (both from the pulpit, and in their conversation) upon the people, there ought certainly to be great care taken, to have it pure, both from the venom of heathen politicians, and from the incantation of deceiving spirits. And by that means the most men, knowing their duties, will be the less subject to serve the ambition of a few discontented persons, in their purposes against the state; and be the less grieved with the contributions necessary for their peace, and defence; and the governors themselves have the less cause, to maintain at the common charge any greater army, than is necessary to make good the public liberty, against the invasions and encroachments of foreign enemies.

And thus I have brought to an end my Discourse of Civil and Ecclesiastical Government, occasioned by the disorders of the present time, without partiality, without application, and without other design, than to set before men's eyes the mutual relation between protection and obedience; of which the condition of human nature, and the laws divine, (both natural and positive) require an inviolable observation. And though in the revolution of states, there can be no very good constellation for truths of this nature to be born under, (as having an angry aspect from the dissolvers of an old government, and seeing but the backs of them that erect a new,) yet I cannot think it will be condemned at this time, either by the public judge of doctrine, or by any that desires the continuance of public peace. And in this hope I return to my interrupted speculation of bodies natural; wherein, (if God give me health to finish it,) I hope the novelty will as much please, as in the doctrine of this artificial body it useth to offend. For such truth, as opposeth no man's profit, nor pleasure, is to all men welcome.

3

JOHN LOCKE, DAVID HUME, AND THE RIGHT OF REVOLUTION

John Locke's *Two Treatises* were published shortly after the English revolution of 1688, in which the Catholic James II was deprived of his throne and the Protestant Dutchman William of Orange, husband to James's daughter Mary, was established in his place. This "Glorious, Bloodless" Revolution gave the English a half-hearted Bill of Rights while preserving the ancient constitution essentially intact.

But, though the *Second Treatise* was published in 1689, it had been written during an earlier crisis which had begun in 1679, over the prospective accession to the throne of Charles II's brother James, the Duke of York, who had declared himself to be a Catholic. This crisis was partly based on the fact that the king was ex officio head of the Church of England, and it was thought to be inconceivable that James as king would not seek to impose Catholicism on his nation. It was also based on the fact that Catholicism seemed to be associated with absolutist government: Across the Channel, in France, Louis XIV had established himself as the most powerful monarch in the world and was actively persecuting his Protestant subjects.

Between 1679 and 1681 the House of Commons, in three separate Parliaments following on three separate elections, called for legislation either to alter the succession ("Exclusion") or to restrict a Catholic ruler's powers in order to render him impotent, but Charles would never agree to such legislation, and after the third Exclusion Parliament had been dissolved, Charles began a campaign to destroy the power base of his opponents. The first victim was Stephen College, executed in Oxford in 1681 for circulating a cartoon in support of the Commons in their conflict with the King. Locke had arranged for College's legal representation and may well have been present at his execution. Charles's real target was Anthony Ashley, Earl of Shaftesbury, who had been a royal minister until 1673, had regained office briefly in 1679, had led the opposition to Charles in the Parliament, and was now imprisoned in London. Locke had been Shaftesbury's close associate since 1667 (when, under Shaftesbury's influence, Locke had abandoned the extremely conservative views of his youth). It was in support of the policy of Exclusion that he had written the *First Treatise* (which attacks divine-right-of-kings arguments, which maintained that monarchs must be absolute and succession must be hereditary, and which he must have finished or abandoned by early 1681), and it was in defense of the radical revolution which seemed to be the only way of preventing James's accession and of protecting the lives of his opponents that Locke wrote the *Second Treatise* some time between 1681 and 1683 (but probably earlier rather than later in this period).

In 1683 the Rye House Plot, an attempt to assassinate Charles, was exposed. Algernon Sidney and other plotters were executed. Locke fled into exile in Holland, where he remained (still in danger from English secret agents) until William invaded England with his army and toppled James (who had inherited the throne in 1685) in 1688. The *Second Treatise* was thus the work not of an armchair philosopher but of someone actively engaged in politics, someone playing for high stakes and prepared to risk his life for his principles.

The *Second Treatise* marks a radical departure from anything Locke had written before, but its arguments are a fairly straightforward adaptation of radical positions that had been presented during the Civil War, and indeed many of Locke's innovations were foreshadowed in a book by a close friend, James Tyrrell, published early in 1681. For convenience we can compare Locke's views with those of Hobbes. Though Hobbes was not the immediate object of his attack (no royalist would admit to holding Hobbesian principles; indeed Hobbes's works were burned by the University of Oxford, perhaps in Locke's presence, just before he fled in 1683), Locke was certainly aware that *Leviathan* was the most powerfully argued contribution to the natural-law tradition. Any radical adaptation of that tradition would have to withstand comparison with Hobbes or at least with Pufendorf (1632–94), who had provided a revision of Hobbes's arguments sufficiently respectable to be discussed in the universities.

Like Hobbes, Locke argued from principles that he believed could be established through natural reason alone. Like Hobbes, he believed governments could have no rights and powers other than those given them by their subjects and that consequently governments were comparable in their rights and powers to individuals in a state of nature. But Locke's account of the state of nature was much more optimistic than Hobbes's. First of all, he believed that there was a genuine law governing behavior in the state of nature: He hoped to argue that one could have knowledge through natural reason of a life after death, in which good would be rewarded and evil punished. Second, he did not believe that there was an irremediable conflict of interests between individuals in a state of nature. Hobbes had been impressed by the competitive passions, such as pride, glory, and self-esteem. Among individuals who see themselves as being in competition, success for one is failure for the others. Although Locke does not deny the importance of such passions, he does not focus his attention upon them. Hobbes thought of most goods as being in limited supply. If there are only two lobsters in the cove, and you catch them, then I must go without. But Locke was impressed at how invested labor could result in increased productivity. If you begin to grow crops on land that has been previously left wild, then you will need less land to support you than before, and I will benefit indirectly from your labor, as there will be more land left for me to hunt over. The notion of economic investment leading to increased productivity is central to Locke's view that conflicts of interest can be moderated. But there is a crucial precondition for this vision of economic progress. Locke believes that individuals in the state of nature can reliably identify what belongs to them and what belongs to others. Only because property has a natural foundation in labor can cooperation replace conflict.

There are, in Locke's view, three fundamental disadvantages about the state of nature. First, individuals often lack the strength required to enforce their rights. Second, the law which governs them in the state of nature is necessarily simple, and open, at least on occasion, to dispute. Murder is wrong; killing in self-defense (or even to punish the guilty) is permissible, but how is one to define self-defense? Third, people make bad judges in their own cases. The whole point of government is that it should provide effective enforcement, comprehensible legislation, and impartial adjudication. This claim is not as innocuous as it seems, for it means that a government which does not set up an independent judiciary is no government at all. A ruler who makes up the law as he goes along or a ruler who decides disputes between himself and his own subjects is no ruler but merely someone in a state of nature with those over whom he rules. By this definition, virtually every government of Locke's own day, including the government of England, which was involved in a campaign to pack juries and so determine the outcome of the trials of Locke's friends, was illegitimate.

Government, in Locke's view, must not only be impartial, it must also be founded in consent. Hobbes had argued (as he was obliged to do) that consent extracted through force was valid. There is little difference between the fear inspired by Hobbes's ruler as he collects taxes and the fear inspired by organized crime as it operates a protection racket. Locke will have none of this. He insists that all human beings are born with a right to freedom and are entitled to freedom once they attain adulthood. Each individual must therefore freely consent to submit to a government, and every individual must consequently have available an alternative to submission. Locke's theory works only if citizenship is voluntary, not hereditary, and there is free land outside the control of any government to which those who wish to retain their independence can retreat. Locke's political theory thus requires an unsettled frontier, for without it there can be no freedom. America is essential to his argument.

Each individual must consent to government; the constitution must represent the choice of the majority; and the majority must consent to taxation. Locke founds government in consent more systematically than any predecessor and in the process makes it clear that any form of hereditary slavery must be illegitimate (though in practice, Locke seems to have had no objection to the slave trade). Moreover, certain rights, such as the right to freedom of religious practice (defended in Locke's *Letter on Toleration,* also published in 1689) are inalienable. Whenever the rights to government by consent, to the impartial rule of law, and to freedom of religion are violated, then tyranny exists, and the relationship between a tyrant and his subjects is no different from that between a bully and his neighbors in the state of nature. Moreover, for Locke resistance is not only a valid but a viable option. First, resistance does not necessitate a return to the state of nature, for a political community may replace its ruler without dissolving into anarchy. Second, even where resistance tears apart the community itself, a return to the state of nature is preferable to submission to tyranny, for a local bully can do less harm than a government with army, police, and prisons at its disposal. Strikingly, Locke does not believe that resistance must be authorized by some official agency. In early 1681 the King had dissolved the Oxford Parliament (Parliament had met in Oxford rather than London that year to escape the plague), and there was no real prospect of Parliament being recalled. So Locke's argument defended the right of private individuals like himself to resist tyranny. Locke's *Second Treatise* is the most sophisticated defense of assassination ever written. In the eyes of Locke's opponents, Locke and his associates were terrorists.

Locke had formulated what has been in its broad outlines the classic view of all those who believe in political liberty (all "liberals," in the vocabulary of the nineteenth century) ever since. There are obvious problems, however, with his argument.

First, he himself was quite incapable of showing how the law of nature could be grounded in reason. His *Essay Concerning Human Understanding,* which was published in 1689 under his own name, whereas the *Letter* and the *Treatises* were anonymous, undermined all the traditional arguments for the immortality of the soul and therefore destroyed the intellectual underpinning of his own argument. Locke held that people necessarily pursue pleasure and flee pain. A moral law which is unaccompanied by sanctions leaves people with no motive for obedience, and since sanctions are not reliably enforced in this life, his concept of natural law depends on an afterlife in which evil is punished and good rewarded. In private Locke seems to have accepted the theology of the Socinians, early Unitarians, who insisted that knowledge of an afterlife came through revelation not reason.

Second, no government has ever accepted that citizenship is purely voluntary (even allowing for Locke's stipulation that consent once given cannot be withdrawn so long as the government does not abuse its trust).

Third, though Locke's arguments imply that almost all the governments of his own day are illegitimate, nevertheless his criteria for legitimacy seem at times broader than one might like. In particular he allows considerable scope for executive power, and, though he requires consent to taxation, he does not stipulate that the legislature must be democratically elected.

Fourth, Locke appears to defend private property on the grounds that everyone benefits and nobody suffers as a result of inequality of property. For this to be true, however, everyone must have access to economic opportunities. Once all the land has been brought under cultivation, there must at least be employment prospects for all. And indeed, in later life, Locke tried to insist, against the bulk of contemporary opinion, that there was no such thing as structural unemployment. The unemployed, in his view, were simply failing to seek work.

Finally, there is a simple gap in Locke's argument: While he insists that no one can be subject to a government to which they have not consented, he never insists that each and every person has a right to become a citizen. It is possible to read Locke as arguing that all individuals should be citizens with equal rights; it is also possible to read him as defending the constitution of England in his own day, when only propertied men had the right to vote and to serve on juries, and the poor and female were disenfranchised.

The arguments of 1681–83, the arguments of Tyrrell, Locke, and Sidney, were to be taken up with enthusiasm by the American revolutionaries in 1776. But, long before then, David Hume (1711–76) had exposed the fragility of Locke's account of the right to revolution. Hume's political philosophy rests on his moral philosophy, and his moral philosophy rests first on a definition of what morality is, and second on a distinction between nature and artifice. Hume, like Hobbes (at least as Hobbes was understood by Hume's contemporaries), held that religious beliefs are contrary to reason. His posthumous *Dialogues Concerning Natural Religion* are the first sustained attempt to subvert the argument from design as a proof of God's existence. There was no point, in Hume's view, in trying to ground morality in a divine law, or in a "natural" law, if that required belief in the immortality of the soul and rewards and punishments after this life.

Take God away, and what foundation for morality is left? Hume pointed out that we straightforwardly approve of those things which give us pleasure and also of those things which are useful to us. We are also naturally prone to share the feelings of our companions. We take pleasure in their pleasures and feel distress at their pains. Thus the good is quite simply whatever is pleasurable or useful to oneself or to others. People naturally approve of whatever benefits them directly. The approval we express for a good meal or a good joke scarcely needs reinforcement. Our approval for whatever benefits others tends to be weak, but we have an interest in joining together to reinforce behavior which is beneficial to others. The approval we express for a parent who sacrifices her interests for the welfare of her children is a socially reinforced expression of our sympathetic involvement in the feelings of the children and of our approval of the parent's ability to take pleasure in their well-being. Morality is the result of this communal reinforcement, reinforcement which leads us to interiorize public disapproval for violent anger or unrestrained selfishness.

Such "natural" virtues—good humor, hard work, self-sacrifice—even if socially reinforced, do not cover the full range of approved social behavior. We require that people keep their promises, respect the property of others, and obey the law. However, there is nothing "natural," in Hume's view, about these types of approved behavior, which he sees as aspects of a purely artificial "justice." (There is of course a natural justice too. There is nothing artificial about anger at someone who has caused you needless pain.)

Take property: Locke had argued that labor gives a title to ownership. But why do I own the apples on the tree in my garden, which I have neither planted nor watered? Why do I own the fish in my pond, which I have never fed? Why do I own this house, which my parents built and left to me, not my brother, in their will? Locke had accepted that it required an artificial convention to make gold and silver the universal medium of exchange. In Hume's view, all property was the result of artificial conventions, ranging from "finders keepers" and "first come, first served" to the legal principle that land below the high-tide mark belongs to the community as a whole.

So too with promises: If I say I expect to meet you for lunch tomorrow and then am unexpectedly called away on business, I have no need to apologize. But if I *promise* to meet you, then I must put my commitment to you ahead of my business. Promises and contracts are devices by which we determine our future behavior on the basis of our present wishes, determine what our behavior will be even if our wishes change. We do this within a framework of unspoken conventions regarding the circumstances under which we can break our promises. After all, if I am robbed and beaten up on the way to meet you for lunch, and I therefore fail to arrive, then I have no need to apologize to you; it is you who must commiserate with me.

Hobbes and Locke had argued that the state was an artificial "person," with rights and obligations. Hume argued that contracts, property, and government were the result of artificial conventions. These conventions did not exist to create artificial replicas of natural objects, however, but were human inventions of institutions, without any analogue in nature. Contracts and governments are machines, not persons. It was evident why these machines had been established. Property, for example, is useful, and without it no advanced economy could function, even if a consequence of property laws is that some people are rendered bankrupt, just as promises make some people liars. But how could such institutions, however useful, originate? No one person had invented the promise, or property, or government, any more than one person had invented language or money. Nor was it obvious that promises came first or that they made property and government possible. Yet if people had not originally promised to obey government, why were they obliged to do so?

Hume argued that artificial justice had evolved slowly over time, just as money, or language, or (for example) clothes must have done. We wear trousers because they protect our legs and because we believe them to be elegant, but no one "invented" trousers, and we have never promised to wear them. For Hume the question of whether a government is legitimate is like the question of whether a person is well dressed. There are two tests, that of function and that of form. Governments have functions to fulfill, and a government that acts unpredictably and partially is dysfunctional, just as city suits are dysfunctional on mountain climbs. But a government does not have to be elected in order to be functional. Just as one society may find a sari more elegant than a skirt, so one may honor the principle of hereditary monarchy while another admires participatory democracy. Either may prove sufficiently functional to serve the purpose at hand.

Depending which side of Hume's argument you stress, you can see him as either a radical or a conservative. Since governments have functions to fulfill, they should be replaced if they fail to fulfill them, if, for example, they fail to protect property and maintain order. But, on the other hand, government is an artificial convention. There is no natural right to inherit property, worship freely, or choose one's rulers, any more than there is a natural law requiring human beings to wear shoes. In general Hume believes that established conventions are so complex and delicate that they deserve respect. We should dress like our neighbors and obey the government they obey. Philosophers may realize that belts are functional while ties are not, but they will wear ties (and select elegant ones) just as their neighbors do, for propriety and elegance depend on such artificial conventions. If the house is on fire, however, only a fool would pause to put on his tie before escaping into the street. Similarly, if a king is mad or bad, respect for hereditary principles should not be an obstacle to replacing him. On the one hand, revolutions are dangerous and have unforeseen consequences. It is usually best to respect the powers that be. But on the other, political systems which are based on liberty tend to foster prosperity and intellectual progress, so that one should opt for liberty where possible.

Hume, by insisting that governments are artificial mechanisms constructed over time, invented most of the arguments of modern conservatism. At the same time, by maintaining that there was nothing sacred about established authority and that the test of government was whether it fostered prosperity and happiness, he laid the foundations of utilitarian radicalism. If both conservatives and radicals can find much to admire in Hume, for liberals he represents a disturbing challenge, for if he is correct, authoritarian governments can be legitimate and rights themselves are not natural but artificial. In abandoning arguments which assumed that nature had been designed to foster moral purposes or that morality itself had been directly decreed by God, Hume was left with little choice but to ground morality and political philosophy in psychology (though he also maintained that one should be very careful indeed about arguing from "is" to "ought"). Thus he employed the principles of Locke's *Essay Concerning Human Understanding* (particularly the fundamental psychological principle of the association of ideas) to destroy the arguments of Locke's *Second Treatise*. Hume himself found much to admire in Machiavelli, Harrington, and Sidney, and American republicans found much to admire in him. But since 1776 conventional political discourse has been based on an uneasy mixture of Lockean and Humean principles, a mixture as unstable as that of oil and water.

Further Reading

Locke

An introduction is to be found in D. Wootton (ed.), *John Locke: Political Writings* (New York: Mentor, 1993). A more detailed historical account is John Marshall, *John Locke: Resistance, Religion and Responsibility* (Cambridge: Cambridge University Press, 1994). Widely influential are Richard Ashcraft, *Revolutionary Politics and Locke's Two Treatises of Government* (Princeton: Princeton University Press, 1986) and James Tully, *An Approach to Political Philosophy: Locke in Contexts*

(Cambridge: Cambridge University Press, 1993). For a close analysis of the text, see Richard Ashcraft, *Locke's Two Treatises of Government* (London: Allen and Unwin, 1987).

Hume

Helpful introductions to the different aspects of Hume's philosophy are to be found in David Norton (ed.), *The Cambridge Companion to Hume* (Cambridge: Cambridge University Press, 1993). On Hume as a political philosopher, see David Miller, *Philosophy and Ideology in Hume's Political Philosophy* (Oxford: Clarendon Press, 1981). For a more detailed historical account, see John B. Stewart, *Opinion and Reform in Hume's Political Philosophy* (Princeton: Princeton University Press, 1992). A brilliant essay is David Gauthier's "David Hume, Contractarian" in his *Moral Dealing* (Ithaca: Cornell University Press, 1990). For a valuable sidelight on the difference between Locke's mode of thinking and Hume's, see Ian Hacking, *The Emergence of Probability* (Cambridge: Cambridge University Press, 1975).

LOCKE

Two Treatises of
Civil Government

PREFACE

READER,

Thou hast here the beginning and end of a discourse concerning government; what fate has otherwise disposed of the papers that should have filled up the middle, and were more than all the rest, it is not worth while to tell thee. These, which remain, I hope are sufficient to establish the throne of our great restorer, our present King William; to make good his title in the consent of the people; which being the only one of all lawful governments, he has more fully and clearly than any prince in Christendom; and to justify to the world the people of England, whose love of their just and natural rights, with their resolution to preserve them, saved the nation when it was on the very brink of slavery and ruin. If these papers have that evidence I flatter myself is to be found in them, there will be no great miss of those which are lost, and my reader may be satisfied without them. For I imagine, I shall have neither the time nor inclination to repeat my pains, and fill up the wanting part of my answer, by tracing Sir Robert again, through all the windings and obscurities which are to be met with in the several branches of his wonderful system. The king, and body of the nation, have since so thoroughly confuted his hypothesis, that I suppose no body hereafter will have either the confidence to appear against our common safety, and be again an advocate for slavery; or the weakness to be deceived with contradictions dressed up in a popular style, and well turned periods. For if any one will be at the pains himself, in those parts which are here untouched, to strip Sir Robert's discourses of the flourish of doubtful expressions, and endeavour to reduce his words to direct, positive, intelligible propositions, and then compare them one with another, he will quickly be satisfied there was never so much glib nonsense put together in well sounding English. If he think it not worth while to examine his works all through, let him make an experiment in that part where he treats of usurpation; and let him try whether he can, with all his skill, make Sir Robert intelligible, and consistent with himself, or common sense. I should not speak so plainly of a gentleman, long since past answering, had not the pulpit, of late years, publicly owned his doctrine, and made it the current divinity of the times. It is necessary those men, who, taking on them to be teachers, have so dangerously misled others, should be openly shewed of what authority this their patriarch is, whom they have so blindly followed; that so they may either retract what upon so ill grounds they have vented, and cannot be maintained; or else justify those principles which they preached up for gospel, though they had no better an author than an English courtier. For I should not have writ against Sir Robert, or taken the pains to shew his mistakes, inconsistencies, and want of (what he so much boasts of, and pretends wholly to build on) scripture-proofs, were there not men amongst us, who, by crying up his books, and espousing his doctrine, save me from the reproach of writing against a dead adversary. They have been so zealous in this point, that, if I have done him any wrong, I cannot hope they should spare me. I wish, where they have done the truth and the public wrong, they would be as ready to redress it, and allow its just weight to this reflection, viz. that there cannot be done a greater mischief to prince and people, than the propagating wrong notions concerning government; that so at last all times might not have reason to complain of the *drum ecclesiastic*. If any one, really concerned for truth, undertake the confutation of my hypothesis, I promise him either to recant my mistake, upon fair conviction; or to answer his difficulties. But he must remember two things,

First, That cavilling here and there, at some expression, or little incident of my discourse, is not an answer to my book.

Secondly, That I shall not take railing for arguments, nor think either of these worth my notice. Though I shall always look on myself as bound to give satisfaction to any one, who shall appear to be conscientiously scrupulous in the point, and shall shew any just grounds for his scruples.

I have nothing more, but to advertise the reader that A. stands for our author. O. for his Observations on Hobbes, Milton, &c. And that a bare quotation of pages always means pages of his *Patriarcha*, edit. 1680.

SECOND TREATISE OF GOVERNMENT

BOOK II

CHAPTER I

1.   It having been shewn in the foregoing discourse,

    1. That Adam had not, either by natural right of fatherhood, or by positive donation from God, any such authority over his children, or dominion over the world, as is pretended:
    2. That if he had, his heirs, yet, had no right to it:
    3. That if his heirs had, there being no law of nature, nor positive law of God, that determines, which is the right heir in all cases that may arise, the right of succession, and consequently of bearing rule, could not have been certainly determined:
    4. That if even that had been determined, yet the knowledge of which is the eldest line of Adam's posterity, being so long since utterly lost, that in the races of mankind and families of the world, there remains not to one above another the least pretence to be the eldest house, and to have the right of inheritance:

All these premises having, as I think, been clearly made out, it is impossible that the rulers now on earth, should make any benefit, or derive any the least shadow of authority from that, which is held to be the fountain of all power, *Adam's private dominion and paternal jurisdiction*; so that he that will not give just occasion to think that all government in the world is the product only of force and violence, and that men live together by no other rules but that of beasts, where the strongest carries it, and so lay a foundation for perpetual disorder and mischief, tumult, sedition, and rebellion (things that the followers of that hypothesis so loudly cry out against) must of necessity find out another rise of government, another original of political power, and another way of designing and knowing the persons that have it, than what Sir Robert Filmer hath taught us.

2.   To this purpose, I think it may not be amiss, to set down what I take to be political power; that the power of a *magistrate* over a subject may be distinguished from that of a *father* over his children, a *master* over his servant, a *husband* over his *wife*, and a *lord* over his slave. All which distinct powers happening sometimes together in the same man, if he be considered under these different relations, it may help us to distinguish these powers one from another, and shew the difference betwixt a ruler of a commonwealth, a father of a family, and a captain of a galley.

3.   *Political power*, then, I take to be a *right* of making laws and penalties of death, and consequently all less penalties for the regulating and preserving of property, and of employing the force of the community, in the execution of such laws, and in the defence of the commonwealth from foreign injury; and all this only for the public good.

CHAPTER II: Of the State of Nature

4.   To understand political power, right, and derive it from its original, we must consider what state all men are naturally in, and that is, a *state of perfect freedom* to order their actions, and dispose of their possessions and persons, as they think fit, within the bounds of the law of nature; without asking leave, or depending upon the will of any other man.

A *state* also of *equality*, wherein all the power and jurisdiction is reciprocal, no one having more than another; there being nothing more evident, than that creatures of the same species and rank, promiscuously born to all the same advantages of nature, and the use of the same faculties, should also be equal one amongst another without subordination or subjection; unless the lord and master of them all should, by any manifest declaration of his will, set one above another, and confer on him, by an evident and clear appointment, an undoubted right to dominion and sovereignty.

5.   This *equality* of men by nature, the judicious Hooker looks upon as so evident in itself, and beyond all question, that he makes it the foundation of that obligation to mutual love amongst men, on which he builds the duties we owe one another, and from whence he derives the great maxims of *justice* and *charity*. His words are, "The like natural inducement hath brought men to know, that it is no less their duty to love others than themselves; for seeing those things which are equal, must needs all have one measure; if I cannot but wish to receive good, even as much at every man's hands, as any man can wish unto his own soul, how should I look to have any part of my desire herein satisfied, unless myself be careful to satisfy the like desire, which is undoubtedly in other men, being of one and the same nature? To have any thing offered them repugnant to this desire, must needs in all respects grieve them as much as me; so that if I do harm, I must look to suffer, there being no reason that others should shew greater measure of love to me, than they have by me shewed unto them: my desire therefore to be loved of my equals in nature, as much as possibly may be, imposeth upon me a natural duty of bearing to themward fully the like affection: From which relation of equality between ourselves and them that are as ourselves, what several rules and canons natural reason hath drawn, for direction of life, no man is ignorant." Eccl. Pol. L. I.

6.   But though this be *a state of liberty*, yet *it is not a state of licence*: though man in that state have an uncontrollable liberty to dispose of his person or possessions, yet he has not liberty to destroy himself, or so much as any creature in his possession, but where some nobler use than its bare preservation calls for it. The *state of nature* has a law of nature to govern it, which obliges every one: And reason, which is that law, teaches all mankind, who will but consult it, that being all *equal and independent*, no one ought to harm another in his life, health, liberty, or possessions. For men being all the workmanship of one omnipotent and infinitely wise Maker; all the servants of one sovereign master, sent into the world by his order, and about his business; they are his property, whose workmanship they are, made to last during his, not another's pleasure. And being furnished with like faculties, sharing all in one community of nature, there cannot be supposed any such subordination among us, that may authorize us to destroy another, as if we were made for one another's uses, as the inferior ranks

of creatures are for ours. Every one, as he is *bound to preserve himself*, and not to quit his station wilfully, so by the like reason, when his own preservation comes not in competition, ought he, as much as he can, *to preserve the rest of mankind*, and may not, unless it be to do justice to an offender, take away or impair the life, or what tends to the preservation of life, the liberty, health, limb, or goods of another.

7. And that all men may be restrained from invading others rights, and from doing hurt to one another, and the law of nature be observed, which willeth the peace and *preservation of all mankind*, the *execution* of the law of nature is, in that state, put into every man's hands, whereby every one has a right to punish the transgressors of that law to such a degree as may hinder its violation. For the *law of nature* would, as all other laws that concern men in this world, be in vain, if there were no body that in the state of nature had a *power to execute* that law, and thereby preserve the innocent and restrain offenders. And if any one in the state of nature may punish another for any evil he has done, every one may do so. For in that *state of perfect equality*, where naturally there is no superiority or jurisdiction of one over another, what any may do in prosecution of that law, every one must needs have a right to do.

8. And thus, in the state of nature, *one man comes by a power over another*; but yet no absolute or arbitrary power, to use a criminal, when he has got him in his hands, according to the passionate heats, or boundless extravagancy of his own will; but only to retribute to him, so far as calm reason and conscience dictate, what is proportionate to his *transgression*; which is so much as may serve for *reparation* and *restraint*. For these two are the only reasons, why one man may lawfully do harm to another, which is that we call *punishment*. In transgressing the law of nature, the offender declares himself to live by another rule than that of reason and common equity, which is that measure God has set to the actions of men, for their mutual security; and so he becomes dangerous to mankind, the tye, which is to secure them from injury and violence, being slighted and broken by him. Which being a trespass against the whole species, and the peace and safety of it, provided for by the law of nature; every man upon this score, by the right he hath to preserve mankind in general, may restrain, or, where it is necessary, destroy things noxious to them, and so may bring such evil on any one, who hath transgressed that law, as may make him repent the doing of it, and thereby deter him, and by his example others, from doing the like mischief. And in this case, and upon this ground, *every man hath a right to punish the offender, and be executioner of the law of nature*.

9. I doubt not but this will seem a very strange doctrine to some men: but before they condemn it, I desire them to resolve me, by what right any prince or state can put to death, or *punish an alien*, for any crime he commits in their country. It is certain their laws, by virtue of any sanction they receive from the promulgated will of the legislative, reach not a stranger. They speak not to him, nor, if they did, is he bound to hearken to them. The legislative authority, by which they are in force over the subjects of that commonwealth, hath no power over him. Those who have the supreme power of making laws in England, France, or Holland, are to an Indian but like the rest of the world, men without authority: And therefore, if by the law of nature every man hath not a power to punish offences against it, as he soberly judges the case to require, I see not how the magistrates of any community can *punish an alien* of another country; since in reference to him, they can have no more power, than what every man naturally may have over another.

10. Besides the crime which consists in violating the law, and varying from the right rule of reason, whereby a man so far becomes degenerate, and declares himself to quit the principles of human nature, and to be a noxious creature, there is commonly injury done to some person or other, and some other man receives damage by his transgression, in which case he who hath received any damage, has besides the right of punishment common to him with other men, a particular right to seek *reparation* from him that has done it. And any other person who finds it just, may also join with him that is injured, and assist him in recovering from the offender so much as may make satisfaction for the harm he has suffered.

11.   From these *two distinct rights*, the one of *punishing* the *crime for restraint*, and preventing the like offence, which right of punishing is in every body; the other of taking reparation, which belongs only to the injured party; comes it to pass that the magistrate, who by being magistrate, hath the common right of punishing put into his hands, can often, where the public good demands not the execution of the law, *remit* the punishment of criminal offences by his own authority, but yet cannot *remit* the satisfaction due to any private man, for the damage he has received. That, he who has suffered the damage has a right to demand in his own name, and he alone can remit: The damnified person has this power of appropriating to himself the goods or service of the offender, *by right of self-preservation*, as every man has a power to punish the crime, to prevent its being committed again, *by the right he has of preserving all mankind*; and doing all reasonable things he can in order to that end: And thus it is, that every man, in the state of nature, has a power to kill a murderer, both to deter others from doing the like injury, which no reparation can compensate, by the example of the punishment that attends it from every body, and also *to secure* men from the attempts of a criminal, who having renounced reason, the common rule and measure, God hath given to mankind, hath by the unjust violence and slaughter he hath committed upon one, declared war against all mankind; and therefore may be destroyed as a *lion* or a *tiger*, one of those wild savage beasts, with whom men can have no society nor security: And upon this is grounded the great law of nature, "Whoso sheddeth man's blood, by man shall his blood be shed." And Cain was so fully convinced, that every one had a right to destroy such a criminal, that after the murder of his brother, he cries out, "Every one that findeth me, shall slay me;" so plain was it writ in the hearts of all mankind.

12.   By the same reason may a man in the state of nature *punish the lesser breaches* of that law. It will perhaps be demanded, with death? I answer, each transgression may be *punished* to that *degree*, and with so much *severity*, as will suffice to make it an ill bargain to the offender, give him cause to repent, and terrify others from doing the like. Every offence

that can be committed in the state of nature, may in the state of nature be also punished equally, and as far forth as it may, in a commonwealth: for though it would be besides my present purpose, to enter here into the particulars of the law of nature, or its *measures of punishment*; yet it is certain there is such a law, and that too, as intelligible and plain to a rational creature, and a studier of that law, as the positive laws of commonwealths, nay possibly plainer; as much as reason is easier to be understood, than the fancies and intricate contrivances of men, following contrary and hidden interests put into words; for so truly are a great part of the *municipal laws* of countries, which are only so far right, as they are founded on the law of nature, by which they are to be regulated and interpreted.

13.   To this strange doctrine, viz. That *in the state of nature every one has the executive power* of the law of nature, I doubt not but it will be objected, that it is unreasonable for men to be judges in their own cases, that self-love will make men partial to themselves and their friends: And on the other side, that ill nature, passion and revenge will carry them too far in punishing others; and hence nothing but confusion and disorder will follow, and that therefore God hath certainly appointed government to restrain the partiality and violence of men. I easily grant, that civil government is the proper remedy for the inconveniencies of the state of nature, which must certainly be great, where men may be judges in their own case, since it is easy to be imagined, that he who was so unjust as to do his brother an injury, will scarce be so just as to condemn himself for it: But I shall desire those who make this objection, to remember, that *absolute monarchs* are but men, and if government is to be the remedy of those evils, which necessarily follow from men's being judges in their own cases, and the state of nature is therefore not to be endured, I desire to know what kind of government that is, and how much better it is than the state of nature, where one man commanding a multitude, has the liberty to be judge in his own case, and may do to all his subjects whatever he pleases, without the least liberty to any one to question or control those who execute his pleasure? and in whatsoever he doth, whether led

by reason, mistake or passion, must be submitted to? Much better it is in the state of nature, wherein men are not bound to submit to the unjust will of another: And if he that judges, judges amiss in his own, or any other case, he is answerable for it to the rest of mankind.

14. It is often asked as a mighty objection, *where are*, or ever were, there any *men in such a state of nature?* To which it may suffice as an answer at present: That since all princes and rulers of *independent* governments, all through the world, are in a state of nature, it is plain the world never was, nor ever will be, without numbers of men in that state. I have named all governors of independent communities, whether they are, or are not, in league with others. For it is not every compact that puts an end to the state of nature between men, but only this one of agreeing together mutually to enter into one community, and make one body politic; other promises and compacts men may make one with another, and yet still be in the state of nature. The promises and bargains for truck, &c. between the two men in the desert island, mentioned by Garcilasso de la Vega, in his history of Peru; or between a Swiss and an Indian, in the woods of America, are binding to them, though they are perfectly in a state of nature, in reference to one another. For truth and keeping of faith belongs to men as men, and not as members of society.

15. To those that say, there were never any men in the state of nature, I will not only oppose the authority of the judicious Hooker, *Eccl. Pol. lib. I. sect. 10*, where he says, "The laws which have been hitherto mentioned," i.e. the laws of nature, "do bind men absolutely, even as they are men, although they have never any settled fellowship, never any solemn agreement amongst themselves what to do or not to do, but for as much as we are not by our selves sufficient to furnish ourselves with competent store of things, needful for such a life, as our nature doth desire, a life fit for the dignity of man; therefore to supply those defects and imperfections which are in us, as living singly and solely by ourselves, we are naturally induced to seek communion and fellowship with others. This was the cause of men's uniting themselves at first in politic societies." But I moreover

affirm, that all men are naturally in that state, and remain so, till by their own consents they make themselves members of some politic society; and I doubt not in the sequel of this discourse to make it very clear.

CHAPTER III: Of the State of War

16. The *state of war* is a state of *enmity* and *destruction:* And therefore declaring by word or action, not a passionate and hasty, but a sedate settled design upon another man's life, *puts him in a state of war* with him against whom he has declared such an intention, and so has exposed his life to the other's power to be taken away by him, or any one that joins with him in his defence, and espouses his quarrel: it being reasonable and just I should have a right to destroy that which threatens me with destruction. For *by the fundamental law of nature, man being to be preserved* as much as possible, when all cannot be preserved, the safety of the innocent is to be preferred: And one may destroy a man who makes war upon him, or has discovered an enmity to his being, for the same reason that he may kill a *wolf* or a *lion*; because such men are not under the ties of the common law of reason, have no other rule, but that of force and violence, and so may be treated as beasts of prey, those dangerous and noxious creatures, that will be sure to destroy him whenever he falls into their power.

17. And hence it is, that he who attempts to get another man into his absolute power, does thereby *put himself into a state of war* with him; it being to be understood as a declaration of a design upon his life. For I have reason to conclude, that he who would get me into his power without my consent, would use me as he pleased when he got me there, and destroy me too when he had a fancy to it; for no body can desire to *have me in his absolute power* unless it be to compel me by force to that which is against the right of my freedom, i.e. make me a slave. To be free from such force is the only security of my preservation; and reason bids me look on him, as an enemy to my preservation, who would take away that freedom which is the fence to it; so that he who makes an *attempt to enslave* me, thereby puts himself

into a state of war with me. He that, in the state of nature, *would take away the freedom* that belongs to any one in that state, must necessarily be supposed to have a design to take away every thing else, that *freedom* being the foundation of all the rest: As he that, in the state of society, would take away the freedom belonging to those of that society or commonwealth, must be supposed to design to take away from them every thing else, and so be looked on as *in a state of war.*

18.   This makes it lawful for a man to *kill a thief,* who has not in the least hurt him, nor declared any design upon his life, any farther, than by the use of force, so to get him in his power, as to take away his money, or what he pleases, from him; because using force, where he has no right, to get me into his power, let his pretence be what it will, I have no reason to suppose, that he, who would *take away my liberty,* would not, when he had me in his power, take away every thing else. And therefore it is lawful for me to treat him as one who has put *himself into a state of war* with me, i.e. kill him if I can; for to that hazard does he justly expose himself, whoever introduces a state of war, and is aggressor in it.

19.   And here we have the plain *difference between the state of nature and the state of war;* which however some men have confounded, are as far distant, as a state of peace, good will, mutual assistance and preservation, and a state of enmity, malice, violence and mutual destruction, are one from another. Men living together according to reason, without a common superior on earth, with authority to judge between them, is *properly the state of nature.* But force, or a declared design of force, upon the person of another, where there is no common superior on earth to appeal to for relief, *is the state of war:* And it is the want of such an appeal gives a man the right of war even against an aggressor, though he be in society and a fellow subject. Thus a *thief,* whom I cannot harm, but by appeal to the law, for having stolen all that I am worth, I may kill, when he sets on me to rob me but of my horse or coat; because the law, which was made for my preservation, where it cannot interpose to secure my life from present force, which, if lost, is capable of no reparation, per-

mits me my own defence, and the right of war, a liberty to kill the aggressor, because the aggressor allows not time to appeal to our common judge, nor the decision of the law, for remedy in a case where the mischief may be irreparable. *Want of a common judge with authority, puts all men in a state of nature: Force without right, upon a man's person, makes a state of war,* both where there is, and is not, a common judge.

20.   But when the actual force is over, the *state of war ceases* between those that are in society, and are equally on both sides subjected to the fair determination of the law; because then there lies open the remedy of appeal for the past injury, and to prevent future harm: but where no such appeal is, as in the state of nature, for want of positive laws, and judges with authority to appeal to, *the state of war once begun, continues* with a right to the innocent party to destroy the other whenever he can, until the aggressor offers peace, and desires reconciliation on such terms as may repair any wrongs he has already done, and secure the innocent for the future: nay, where an appeal to the law, and constituted judges, lies open, but the remedy is denied by a manifest perverting of justice, and a barefaced wresting of the laws to protect or indemnify the violence or injuries of some men, or party of men, *there* it *is* hard to imagine any thing but *a state of war.* For wherever violence is used, and injury done, though by hands appointed to administer justice, it is still violence and injury, however coloured with the name, pretences, or forms of law, the end whereof being to protect and redress the innocent, by an unbiased application of it, to all who are under it; wherever that is not *bona fide* done, *war is made* upon the sufferers, who having no appeal on earth to right them, they are left to the only remedy in such cases, an appeal to heaven.

21.   To avoid this *state of war* (wherein there is no appeal but to heaven, and wherein every the least difference is apt to end, where there is no authority to decide between the contenders) is one great *reason of men's putting themselves into society,* and quitting the state of nature. For where there is an authority, a power on earth, from which relief can be had by *appeal,* there the continuance of the *state of war* is

excluded, and the controversy is decided by that power. Had there been any such court, any superior jurisdiction on earth, to determine the right between Jephthah and the Ammonites, they had never come to a *state of war*: But we see he was forced to appeal to heaven. "The Lord the Judge," says he, "be judge this day, between the children of Israel and the children of Ammon," *Judg.* xi. 27, and then prosecuting, and relying on his appeal, he leads out his army to battle: and therefore in such controversies, where the question is put, *who shall be judge?* it cannot be meant, who shall decide the controversy; every one knows what Jephthah here tells us, that "the Lord the Judge" shall judge. Where there is no judge on earth, the appeal lies to God in heaven. That question then cannot mean, who shall judge? whether another hath put himself in a *state of war* with me, and whether I may, as Jephthah did, *appeal to heaven* in it? of that I myself can only be judge in my own conscience, as I will answer it, at the great day, to the supreme judge of all men.

CHAPTER IV: Of Slavery

22.   The *natural liberty* of man is to be free from any superior power on earth, and not to be under the will or legislative authority of man, but to have only the law of nature for his rule. The *liberty of man*, in society, is to be under no other legislative power, but that established, by consent, in the commonwealth; nor under the dominion of any will, or restraint of any law, but what that legislative shall enact, according to the trust put in it. Freedom then is not what Sir Robert Filmer tells us, O, A. 55. "a liberty for every one to do what he lists, to live as he pleases, and not to be tied by any laws": But *freedom of men under government*, is, to have a standing rule to live by, common to every one of that society, and made by the legislative power erected in it; a liberty to follow my own will in all things, where the rule prescribes not; and not to be subject to the inconstant, uncertain, unknown, arbitrary will of another man: As *freedom of nature* is, to be under no other restraint but the law of nature.

23.   This freedom from absolute, arbitrary power, is so necessary to, and closely joined with a man's preservation, that he cannot part with it, but by what forfeits his preservation and life together. For a man, not having the power of his own life, cannot, by compact, or his own consent, enslave himself to any one, nor put himself under the absolute, arbitrary power of another, to take away his life, when he pleases. No body can give more power than he has himself; and he that cannot take away his own life, cannot give another power over it. Indeed, having by his fault forfeited his own life, by some act that deserves death; he, to whom he has forfeited it, may (when he has him in his power) delay to take it, and make use of him to his own service, and he does him no injury by it. For, whenever he finds the hardship of his slavery outweigh the value of his life, it is in his power, by resisting the will of his master, to draw on himself the death he desires.

24.   This is the perfect condition of *slavery*, which is nothing else, but *the state of war continued, between a lawful conqueror and a captive*. For, if once compact enter between them, and make an agreement for a limited power on the one side, and obedience on the other, the state of war and slavery ceases, as long as the compact endures. For, as has been said, no man can, by agreement, pass over to another that which he hath not in himself, a power over his own life.

I confess, we find among the Jews, as well as other nations, that men did sell themselves; but, it is plain, this was only to *drudgery, not to slavery*. For it is evident, the person sold was not under an absolute, arbitrary, despotical power. For the master could not have power to kill him, at any time, whom, at a certain time, he was obliged to let go free out of his service: and the master of such a servant was so far from having an arbitrary power over his life, that he could not, at pleasure, so much as maim him, but the loss of an eye, or tooth, set him free, *Exod.* xxi.

CHAPTER V: Of Property

25.   Whether we consider natural *reason*, which tells us, that men, being once born, have a right to their preservation, and consequently to meat and drink,

and such other things as nature affords for their subsistence: or *revelation*, which gives us an account of those grants God made of the world to Adam, and to Noah, and his sons, it is very clear, that God, as King David says, *Psal.* cxv. 16, "has given the earth to the children of men," given it to mankind in common. But this being supposed, it seems to some a very great difficulty how any one should ever come to have a *property* in any thing: I will not content myself to answer, that if it be difficult to make out *property*, upon a supposition, that God gave the world to Adam, and his posterity in common; it is impossible that any man, but one universal monarch, should have any property upon a supposition, that God gave the world to Adam, and his heirs in succession, exclusive of all the rest of his posterity. But I shall endeavour to shew, how men might come to have a *property* in several parts of that which God gave to mankind in common, and that without any express compact of all the commoners.

26.　God, who hath given the world to men in common, hath also given them reason to make use of it to the best advantage of life, and convenience. The earth, and all that is therein, is given to men for the support and comfort of their being. And though all the fruits it naturally produces, and beasts it feeds, belong to mankind in common, as they are produced by the spontaneous hand of nature; and no body has originally a private dominion, exclusive of the rest of mankind, in any of them, as they are thus in their natural state: yet being given for the use of men, there must of necessity be *a means to appropriate* them some way or other, before they can be of any use, or at all beneficial to any particular man. The fruit, or venison, which nourishes the wild Indian, who knows no enclosure, and is still a tenant in common, must be his, and so his, i.e. a part of him, that another can no longer have any right to it, before it can do him any good for the support of his life.

27.　Though the earth, and all inferior creatures, be common to all men, yet every man has a property in his own person: this no body has any right to but himself. The labour of his body, and the work of his hands, we may say, are properly his. Whatsoever then he removes out of the state that nature hath provided, and left it in, he hath mixed his labour with, and joined to it something that is his own, and thereby makes it his property. It being by him removed from the common state nature hath placed it in, it hath by this labour something annexed to it, that excludes the common right of other men. For this labour being the unquestionable property of the labourer, no man but he can have a right to what that is once joined to, at least where there is enough, and as good, left in common for others.

28.　He that is nourished by the acorns he picked up under an oak, or the apples he gathered from the trees in the wood, has certainly appropriated them to himself. No body can deny but the nourishment is his. I ask then, when did they begin to be his? When he digested? Or when he eat? Or when he boiled? Or when he brought them home? Or when he picked them up? And it is plain, if the first gathering made them not his, nothing else could. That *labour* put a distinction between them and common: that added something to them more than nature, the common mother of all, had done; and so they became his private right. And will any one say he had no right to those acorns or apples he thus appropriated, because he had not the consent of all mankind to make them his? Was it a robbery thus to assume to himself what belonged to all in common? If such a consent as that was necessary, man had starved, notwithstanding the plenty God had given him. We see in *commons*, which remain so by compact, that it is the taking any part of what is common, and removing it out of the state nature leaves it in, which *begins the property*; without which the common is of no use. And the taking of this or that part does not depend on the express consent of all the commoners. Thus the grass my horse has bit; the turfs my servant has cut; and the ore I have digged in any place, where I have a right to them in common with others, become my *property*, without the assignation or consent of any body. The *labour* that was mine, removing them out of that common state they were in, hath *fixed* my *property* in them.

29.　By making an explicit consent of every commoner necessary to any one's appropriating to himself any part of what is given in common, children or servants could not cut the meat, which their father or master had provided for them in common, without assigning to every one his peculiar part. Though the water running in the fountain be every one's, yet who can doubt, but that in the pitcher is his only who drew it out? His *labour* hath taken it out of the hands of nature, where it was common, and belonged equally to all her children, and *hath* thereby *appropriated* it to himself.

30.   Thus this law of reason makes the deer that Indian's who hath killed it; it is allowed to be his goods, who hath bestowed his labour upon it, though before it was the common right of every one. And amongst those who are counted the civilized part of mankind, who have made and multiplied positive laws to determine *property*, this original law of nature, for the *beginning of property*, in what was before common, still takes place; and by virtue thereof, what fish any one catches in the ocean, that great and still remaining common of mankind; or what ambergreise any one takes up here, is *by* the *labour* that removes it out of that common state nature left it in, *made* his *property*, who takes that pains about it. And even amongst us, the hare that any one is hunting, is thought his who pursues her during the chase. For being a beast that is still looked upon as common, and no man's private possession; whoever has employed so much *labour* about any of that kind, as to find and pursue her, has thereby removed her from the state of nature, wherein she was common, and hath *begun a property*.

31.   It will perhaps be objected to this, that *if gathering the acorns, or other fruits of the earth, &c.* makes a right to them, then any one may engross as much as he will. To which I answer, Not so. The same law of nature, that does by this means give us property, does also *bound* that *property* too. "God has given us all things richly," 1 *Tim*; vi. 17, is the voice of reason confirmed by inspiration. But how far has he given it us? *To enjoy.* As much as any one can make use of to any advantage of life before it spoils, so much he may by his labour fix a property in: whatever is beyond this, is more than his share, and belongs to others. Nothing was made by God for man to spoil or destroy. And thus, considering the plenty

of natural provisions there was a long time in the world, and the few spenders; and to how small a part of that provision the industry of one man could extend itself, and engross it to the prejudice of others; especially keeping within the *bounds*, set by reason, *of* what might serve for his *use*; there could be then little room for quarrels or contentions about property so established.

32.   But the *chief matter of property* being now not the fruits of the earth, and the beasts that subsist on it, but the *earth it self*; as that which takes in, and carries with it all the rest: I think it is plain, that *property* in that too is acquired as the former. *As much land* as a man tills, plants, improves, cultivates, and can use the product of, so much is his *property*. He by his labour does, as it were, enclose it from the common. Nor will it invalidate his right, to say every body else has an equal title to it; and therefore he cannot appropriate, he cannot enclose, without the consent of all his fellow commoners, all mankind. God, when he gave the world in common to all mankind, commanded man also to labour, and the penury of his condition required it of him. God and his reason commanded him to subdue the earth, i.e. improve it for the benefit of life, and therein lay out something upon it that was his own, his labour. He that, in obedience to this command of God, subdued, tilled, and sowed any part of it, thereby annexed to it something that was his *property*, which another had no title to, nor could without injury take from him.

33.   Nor was this *appropriation* of any parcel of *land*, by improving it, any prejudice to any other man, since there was still enough, and as good left; and more than the yet unprovided could use. So that, in effect, there was never the less left for others because of his enclosure for himself. For he that leaves as much as another can make use of, does as good as take nothing at all. No body could think himself injured by the drinking of another man, though he took a good draught, who had a whole river of the same water left him to quench his thirst: And the case of land and water, where there is enough of both, is perfectly the same.

34.   God gave the world to men in common; but since he gave it them for their benefit, and the greatest

conveniences of life they were capable to draw from it, it cannot be supposed he meant it should always remain common and uncultivated. He gave it to the use of the industrious and rational, (and *labour* was to be *his title* to it) not to the fancy or covetousness of the quarrelsome and contentious. He that had as good left for his improvement, as was already taken up, needed not complain, ought not to meddle with what was already improved by another's labour: If he did, it is plain he desired the benefit of another's pains, which he had no right to, and not the ground which God had given him in common with others to labour on, and whereof there was as good left, as that already possessed, and more than he knew what to do with, or his industry could reach to.

35.   It is true, in *land* that is *common* in England, or any other country, where there is plenty of people under government, who have money and commerce, no one can enclose or appropriate any part, without the consent of all his fellow-commoners: Because this is left common by compact, i.e. by the law of the land, which is not to be violated. And though it be common, in respect of some men, it is not so to all mankind, but is the joint property of this country, or this parish. Besides, the remainder, after such enclosure, would not be as good to the rest of the commoners, as the whole was when they could all make use of the whole: whereas in the beginning and first peopling of the great common of the world, it was quite otherwise. The law man was under, was rather for appropriating. God commanded, and his wants forced him to *labour*. That was his *property* which could not be taken from him wherever he had fixed it. And hence subduing or cultivating the earth, and having dominion, we see are joined together. The one gave title to the other. So that God, by commanding to subdue, gave authority so far to *appropriate*: And the condition of human life, which requires labour and materials to work on, necessarily introduces private possessions.

36.   The *measure of property* nature has well set by the extent of men's *labour, and the conveniences of life*: No man's labour could subdue or appropriate all; nor could his enjoyment consume more than a small part; so that it was impossible for any man, this

way, to intrench upon the right of another, or acquire to himself a property, to the prejudice of his neighbour, who would still have room for as good, and as large a possession (after the other had taken out his) as before it was appropriated. This *measure* did confine every man's *possession* to a very moderate proportion, and such as he might appropriate to himself, without injury to any body, in the first ages of the world, when men were more in danger to be lost, by wandering from their company, in the then vast wilderness of the earth, than to be straitened for want of room to plant in. And the same measure may be allowed still without prejudice to any body, as full as the world seems. For supposing a man, or family, in the state they were at first peopling of the world by the children of Adam, or Noah; let him plant in some inland, vacant places of America, we shall find that the *possessions* he could make himself, upon the *measures* we have given, would not be very large, nor, even to this day, prejudice the rest of mankind, or give them reason to complain, or think themselves injured by this man's encroachment, though the race of men have now spread themselves to all the corners of the world, and do infinitely exceed the small number was at the beginning. Nay, the extent of *ground* is of so little value, *without labour*, that I have heard it affirmed, that in Spain itself a man may be permitted to plough, sow, and reap, without being disturbed, upon land he has no other title to, but only his making use of it. But, on the contrary, the inhabitants think themselves beholden to him, who by his industry on neglected and consequently waste land, has increased the stock of corn, which they wanted. But be this as it will, which I lay no stress on; this I dare boldly affirm, that the same *rule of propriety*, (*viz.*) that every man should have as much as he could make use of, would hold still in the world, without straitening any body, since there is land enough in the world to suffice double the inhabitants, had not the *invention of money*, and the tacit agreement of men to put a value on it, introduced (by consent) larger possessions, and a right to them; which, how it has done, I shall by and by shew more at large.

37.   This is certain, that in the beginning, before the desire of having more than man needed had

altered the intrinsic value of things, which depends only on their usefulness to the life of man; or had agreed, *that a little piece of yellow metal*, which would keep without wasting or decay, should be worth a great piece of flesh, or a whole heap of corn; though men had a right to appropriate, by their labour, each one to himself as much of the things of nature as he could use: yet this could not be much, nor to the prejudice of others, where the same plenty was still left to those who would use the same industry. To which let me add, that he who appropriates land to himself by his labour, does not lessen, but increase the common stock of mankind. For the provisions serving to the support of human life, produced by one acre of enclosed and cultivated land, are (to speak much within compass) ten times more than those which are yielded by an acre of land of an equal richness lying waste in common. And therefore he that encloses land, and has a greater plenty of the conveniencies of life from ten acres, than he could have from an hundred left to nature, may truly be said to give ninety acres to mankind. For his labour now supplies him with provisions out of ten acres, which were but the product of an hundred lying in common. I have here rated the improved land very low, in making its product but as ten to one, when it is much nearer an hundred to one. For I ask, whether in the wild woods and uncultivated waste of America, left to nature, without any improvement, tillage, or husbandry, a thousand acres yield the needy and wretched inhabitants as many conveniencies of life, as ten acres of equally fertile land do in Devonshire, where they are well cultivated?

Before the appropriation of land, he who gathered as much of the wild fruit, killed, caught, or tamed, as many of the beasts as he could; he that so employed his pains about any of the spontaneous products of nature, as any way to alter them from the state which nature put them in, *by* placing any of his *labour* on them, did thereby *acquire a propriety in them*: but if they perished, in his possession, without their due use; if the fruits rotted, or the venison putrified, before he could spend it, he offended against the common law of nature, and was liable to be punished; he invaded his neighbour's share, for he had *no right*,

farther than his use called for any of them, and they might serve to afford him conveniencies of life.

38.   The same *measures* governed the *possession of land* too: whatsoever he tilled and reaped, laid up and made use of, before it spoiled, that was his peculiar right; whatsoever he enclosed, and could feed, and make use of, the cattle and product was also his. But if either the grass of his inclosure rotted on the ground, or the fruit of his planting perished without gathering, and laying up, this part of the earth, notwithstanding his inclosure, was still to be looked on as waste, and might be the possession of any other. Thus at the beginning, Cain might take as much ground as he could till, and make it his own land, and yet leave enough to Abel's sheep to feed on; a few acres would serve for both their possessions. But as families increased, and industry enlarged their stocks, their *possessions enlarged* with the need of them; but yet it was commonly *without any fixed property in the ground* they made use of, till they incorporated, settled themselves together, and built cities, and then, by consent, they came in time to set out the *bounds of their distinct territories*, and agree on limits between them and their neighbours; and by laws within themselves settled the *properties* of those of the same society. For we see, that in that part of the world which was first inhabited, and therefore like to be best peopled, even as low down as Abraham's time, they wandered with their flocks, and their herds, which was their substance, freely up and down; and this Abraham did, in a country where he was a stranger. Whence it is plain, that at least a great part of the *land lay in common*; that the inhabitants valued it not, nor claimed property in any more than they made use of. But when there was not room enough in the same place, for their herds to feed together, they by consent, as Abraham and Lot did, *Gen.* xiii. 5. separated and enlarged their pasture, where it best liked them. And for the same reason Esau went from his father, and his brother, and planted in Mount Seir, *Gen.* xxxvi. 6.

39.   And thus, without supposing any private dominion, and property in Adam, over all the *world*, exclusive of all other men, which can no way be proved, nor any one's property be made out from it;

but supposing the *world* given, as it was, to the children of men *in common*, we see how *labour* could make men distinct titles to several parcels of it, for their private uses; wherein there could be no doubt of right, no room for quarrel.

40. Nor is it so strange, as perhaps before consideration it may appear, that the *property of labour* should be able to over-balance the community of land. For it is *labour* indeed that *puts the difference of value* on every thing; and let any one consider what the difference is between an acre of land planted with tobacco or sugar, sown with wheat or barley, and an acre of the same land lying in common, without any husbandry upon it, and he will find, that the improvement of *labour makes* the far greater part of the value. I think it will be but a very modest computation to say, that of the *products* of the earth useful to the life of man, nine tenths are the *effects of labour*: nay, if we will rightly estimate things as they come to our use, and cast up the several expences about them, what in them is purely owing to *nature*, and what to *labour*, we shall find, that in most of them ninety-nine hundredths are wholly to be put on the account of *labour*.

41. There cannot be a clearer demonstration of any thing, than several nations of the Americans are of this, who are rich in land, and poor in all the comforts of life; whom nature having furnished as liberally as any other people, with the materials of plenty, i.e. a fruitful soil, apt to produce in abundance what might serve for food, raiment, and delight; yet *for want of improving it by labour*, have not one hundredth part of the conveniencies we enjoy: and a king of a large and fruitful territory there feeds, lodges, and is clad worse than a day labourer in England.

42. To make this a little clearer, let us but trace some of the ordinary provisions of life, through their several progresses, before they come to our use, and see how much they receive of their *value from human industry*. Bread, wine, and cloth, are things of daily use, and great plenty, yet notwithstanding, acorns, water, and leaves, or skins, must be our bread, drink, and cloathing, did not labour furnish us with these more useful commodities. For whatever bread is more worth than acorns, wine than water, and *cloth* or *silk*,

than leaves, skins, or moss, that is *wholly owing to labour* and *industry*. The one of these being the food and raiment which unassisted nature furnishes us with; the other, provisions which our industry and pains prepare for us, which how much they exceed the other in value, when any one hath computed, he will then see how much *labour makes the far greatest part of the value* of things we enjoy in this world: and the ground which produces the materials, is scarce to be reckoned in, as any, or, at most, but a very small part of it: so little, that even amongst us, land that is left wholly to nature, that hath no improvement of pasturage, tillage, or planting, is called, as indeed it is, *waste*; and we shall find the benefit of it amount to little more than nothing.

This shews how much numbers of men are to be preferred to largeness of dominions; and that the increase of lands, and the right employing of them, is the great art of government: and that prince, who shall be so wise and godlike, as by established laws of liberty to secure protection and encouragement to the honest industry of mankind, against the oppression of power and narrowness of party, will quickly be too hard for his neighbours; but this by the by. To return to the argument in hand.

43. An acre of land, that bears here twenty bushels of wheat, and another in America, which, with the same husbandry, would do the like, are, without doubt, of the same natural intrinsic value: but yet the benefit mankind receives from the one in a year, is worth 5 l. and from the other possibly not worth a penny, if all the profit an Indian received from it were to be valued, and sold here; at least, I may truly say, not one thousandth. It is *labour* then which *puts the greatest part of the value upon land*, without which it would scarcely be worth any thing: it is to that we owe the greatest part of all its useful products; for all that the straw, bran, bread, of that acre of wheat, is more worth than the product of an acre of as good land, which lies waste, is all the effect of labour. For it is not barely the ploughman's pains, the reaper's and thresher's toil, and the baker's sweat is to be counted into the *bread* we eat; the labour of those who broke the oxen, who digged and wrought the iron and stones, who felled and framed the timber

employed about the plough, mill, oven, or any other utensils, which are a vast number requisite to this corn, from its being seed to be sown, to its being made bread, must all be *charged on* the account of *labour*, and received as an effect of that: nature and the earth furnished only the almost worthless materials, as in themselves. It would be a strange *catalogue of things, that industry provided and made use of, about every loaf of bread*, before it came to our use, if we could trace them; iron, wood, leather, bark, timber, stone, bricks, coals, lime, cloth, dying drugs, pitch, tar, masts, ropes, and all the materials made use of in the ship, that brought any of the commodities made use of by any of the workmen, to any part of the work, all which it would be almost impossible, at least too long, to reckon up.

44.   From all which it is evident, that though the things of nature are given in common, yet man, by being master of himself, and *proprietor of his own person, and the actions or labour of it, had still in himself the great foundation of property*; and that, which made up the great part of what he applied to the support or comfort of his being, when invention and arts had improved the conveniencies of life, was perfectly his own, and did not belong in common to others.

45.   Thus *labour*, in the beginning, *gave a right of property*, wherever any one was pleased to employ it upon what was common, which remained a long while the far greater part, and is yet more than mankind makes use of. Men, at first, for the most part, contented themselves with what unassisted nature offered to their necessities: and though afterwards, in some parts of the world, (where the increase of people and stock, with the *use of money*, had made land scarce, and so of some value) the several *communities* settled the bounds of their distinct territories, and by laws within themselves regulated the properties of the private men of their society, and so, by *compact* and agreement, *settled the property* which labour and industry began; and the leagues that have been made between several states and kingdoms, either expressly or tacitly disowning all claim and right to the land in the other's possession, have, by common consent, given up their pretences to their natural common

right, which originally they had to those countries, and so have, by *positive agreement, settled a property* amongst themselves, in distinct parts and parcels of the earth; yet there are still *great tracts of ground* to be found, which (the inhabitants thereof not having joined with the rest of mankind, in the consent of the use of their common money) *lie waste*, and are more than the people who dwell on it do, or can make use of, and so still lie in common. Though this can scarce happen amongst that part of mankind that have consented to the use of money.

46.   The greatest part of *things really useful* to the life of man, and such as the necessity of subsisting made the first commoners of the world look after, as it doth the Americans now, *are* generally things of *short duration*; such as, if they are not consumed by use, will decay and perish of themselves: gold, silver, and diamonds, are things that fancy or agreement hath put the value on, more than real use, and the necessary support of life. Now of those good things which nature hath provided in common, every one had a right, (as hath been said) to as much as he could use, and property in all that he could affect with his labour; all that his *industry* could extend to, to alter from the state nature had put it in, was his. He that *gathered* a hundred bushels of acorns or apples, had thereby a *property* in them, they were his goods as soon as gathered. He was only to look, that he used them before they spoiled, else he took more than his share, and robbed others. And indeed it was a foolish thing, as well as dishonest, to hoard up more than he could make use of. If he gave away a part to any body else, so that it perished not uselessly in his possession, these he also made use of. And if he also bartered away plums, that would have rotted in a week, for nuts that would last good for his eating a whole year, he did no injury; he wasted not the common stock; destroyed no part of the portion of goods that belonged to others, so long as nothing perished uselessly in his hands. Again, if he would give his nuts for a piece of metal, pleased with its colour; or exchange his sheep for shells, or wool for a sparkling pebble or a diamond, and keep those by him all his life, he invaded not the right of others, he might heap up as much of these durable things as he pleased;

the *exceeding of the bounds of* his *just property* not lying in the largeness of his possession, but the perishing of any thing uselessly in it.

47.   And thus *came in the use of money*, some lasting thing that men might keep without spoiling, and that by mutual consent men would take in exchange for the truly useful, but perishable supports of life.

48.   And as different degrees of industry were apt to give men possessions in different proportions, so this *invention of money* gave them the opportunity to continue and enlarge them. For supposing an island, separate from all possible commerce with the rest of the world, wherein there were but an hundred families, but there were sheep, horses, and cows, with other useful animals, wholesome fruits, and land enough for corn for a hundred thousand times as many, but nothing in the island, either because of its commonness, or perishableness, fit to supply the place of *money:* What reason could any one have there to enlarge his possessions beyond the use of his family and a plentiful supply to its *consumption,* either in what their own industry produced, or they could barter for like perishable, useful commodities with others? Where there is not something, both lasting and scarce, and so valuable to be hoarded up, there men will not be apt to enlarge their *possessions of land*, were it never so rich, never so free for them to take. For I ask, what would a man value ten thousand, or an hundred thousand acres of excellent *land*, ready cultivated and well stocked too with cattle, in the middle of the inland parts of America, where he had no hopes of commerce with other parts of the world, to draw *money* to him by the sale of the product? It would not be worth the enclosing, and we should see him give up again to the wild common of nature, whatever was more than would supply the conveniencies of life to be had there for him and his family.

49.   Thus in the beginning all the world was America, and more so than that is now; for no such thing as *money* was any where known. Find out something that hath the *use and value of money* amongst his neighbours, you shall see the same man will begin presently to *enlarge* his possessions.

50.   But since gold and silver, being little useful to the life of man in proportion to food, raiment, and carriage, has its *value* only from the consent of men, whereof *labour* yet *makes*, in great part, the *measure*, it is plain, that men have agreed to a disproportionate and unequal *possession of the earth*, they having, by a tacit and voluntary consent, found out a way how a man may fairly possess more land than he himself can use the product of, by receiving in exchange for the overplus, gold and silver, which may be hoarded up without injury to any one; these metals not spoiling or decaying in the hands of the possessor. This partage of things in an inequality of private possessions, men have made practicable out of the bounds of society, and without compact, only by putting a value on gold and silver, and tacitly agreeing in the use of money. For in governments, the laws regulate the right of property, and the possession of land is determined by positive constitutions.

51.   And thus, I think, it is very easy to conceive, without any difficulty *how labour could at first begin a title of property* in the common things of nature, and how the spending it upon our uses bounded it. So that there could then be no reason of quarrelling about title, nor any doubt about the largeness of possession it gave. Right and conveniency went together; for as a man had a right to all he could employ his labour upon, so he had no temptation to labour for more than he could make use of. This left no room for controversy about the title, nor for encroachment on the right of others; what portion a man carved to himself, was easily seen; and it was useless, as well as dishonest, to carve himself too much, or take more than he needed.

CHAPTER VI: Of Paternal Power

52.   It may perhaps be censured as an impertinent criticism, in a discourse of this nature, to find fault with words and names, that have obtained in the world: and yet possibly it may not be amiss to offer new ones, when the old are apt to lead men into mistakes, as this of *paternal power* probably has done, which seems so to place the power of parents over their children wholly in the *father*, as if the *mother*

had no share in it, whereas, if we consult reason or revelation, we shall find she hath an equal title. This may give one reason to ask, whether this might not be more properly called *parental power*. For whatever obligation nature and the right of generation lays on children, it must certainly bind them equally to both concurrent causes of it. And accordingly we see the positive law of God every where joins them together without distinction, when it commands the obedience of children: "Honour thy father and thy mother," *Exod.* xx. 12. "Whosoever curseth his father or his mother," *Lev.* xx. 9. "Ye shall fear every man his mother and his father," *Lev.* xix. 5. "Children, obey your parents," &c. *Eph.* vi. 1, is the style of the Old and New Testament.

53.   Had but this one thing been well considered, without looking any deeper into the matter, it might perhaps have kept men from running into those gross mistakes they have made, about this power of parents; which, however it might, without any great harshness, bear the name of absolute dominion, and regal authority, when under the title of *paternal power* it seemed appropriated to the father, would yet have sounded but oddly, and in the very name shewn the absurdity, if this supposed absolute power over children had been called *parental*; and thereby have discovered, that it belonged to the *mother* too. For it will but very ill serve the turn of those men, who contend so much for the absolute power and authority of the fatherhood, as they call it, that the mother should have any share in it. And it would have but ill supported the monarchy they contend for, when by the very name it appeared that that fundamental authority, from whence they would derive their government of a single person only, was not placed in one, but two persons jointly. But to let this of names pass.

54.   Though I have said above, chap. ii. "That all men by nature are equal," I cannot be supposed to understand all sorts of *equality: age* or *virtue* may give men a just precedency: *excellency of parts* and *merit* may place others above the common level: *birth* may subject some, and *alliance* or *benefits* others, to pay an observance to those whom nature, gratitude, or other respects, may have made it due; and yet all

this consists with the *equality*, which all men are in, in respect of jurisdiction or dominion one over another; which was the *equality* I there spoke of, as proper to the business in hand, being that *equal right*, that every man hath, *to his natural freedom*, without being subjected to the will or authority of any other man.

55.   *Children*, I confess, are not born in this state of *equality*, though they are born to it. Their parents have a sort of rule and jurisdiction over them, when they come into the world, and for some time after, but it is but a temporary one. The bonds of this subjection are like the swaddling clothes they are wrapt up in, and supported by, in the weakness of their infancy: Age and reason, as they grow up, loosen them, till at length they drop quite off, and leave a man at his own free disposal.

56.   Adam was created a perfect man, his body and mind in full possession of their strength and reason, and so was capable from the first instant of his being to provide for his own support and preservation; and govern his actions according to the dictates of the law of reason which God had implanted in him. From him the world is peopled with his descendants, who are all born infants, weak and helpless, without knowledge or understanding: But to supply the defects of this imperfect state, till the improvement of growth and age hath removed them, Adam and Eve, and after them all *parents* were, by the law of nature, *under an obligation to preserve, nourish, and educate the children*, they had begotten; not as their own workmanship, but the workmanship of their own maker, the Almighty, to whom they were to be accountable for them.

57.   The law, that was to govern Adam, was the same that was to govern all his posterity, the *law of reason*. But his offspring having another way of entrance into the world, different from him, by a natural birth, that produced them ignorant and without the use of *reason*, they were not presently *under that law*; for no body can be under a law, which is not promulgated to him: and this law being promulgated or made known by *reason* only, he that is not come to the use of his *reason*, cannot be said to be *under this law*; and Adam's children, being not presently as

soon as born, *under this law of reason*, were not presently free. For law, in its true notion, *is* not so much the limitation, *as the direction of a free and intelligent agent* to his proper interest, and prescribes no farther than is for the general good of those under that law. Could they be happier without it, the law, as an useless thing, would of it self vanish: and that ill deserves the name of confinement which hedges us in only from bogs and precipices. So that, however it may be mistaken, *the end of law* is not to abolish or restrain, but *to preserve and enlarge freedom*. For in all the states of created beings capable of laws, *where there is no law, there is no freedom*. For liberty is to be free from restraint and violence from others which cannot be where there is no law: but freedom is not, as we are told, "a liberty for every man to do what he lists" (for who could be free, when every other man's humour might domineer over him?) but a liberty to dispose, and order as he lists, his person, actions, possessions, and his whole property, within the allowance of those laws under which he is, and therein not to be subject to the arbitrary will of another, but freely follow his own.

58.   The *power*, then, *that parents have* over their children, arises from that duty which is incumbent on them, to take care of their offspring during the imperfect state of childhood. To inform the mind, and govern the actions of their yet ignorant nonage, till reason shall take its place, and ease them of that trouble, is what the children want, and the parents are bound to. For God having given man an understanding to direct his actions, has allowed him a freedom of will, and liberty of acting, as properly belonging thereunto, within the bounds of that law he is under. But whilst he is in an estate, wherein he has not understanding of his own to direct his will, he is not to have any will of his own to follow: he that understands for him, must will for him too; he must prescribe to his will, and regulate his actions: but when he comes to the estate that made his *father a freeman*, the *son is a freeman* too.

59.   This holds in all the laws a man is under, whether natural or civil. Is a man under the law of nature? *What made him free* of that law? What gave him a free disposing of his property according to

his own will, within the compass of that law? I answer, a state of maturity, wherein he might be supposed capable to know that law, that so he might keep his actions within the bounds of it. When he has acquired that state, he is presumed to know how far that law is to be his guide, and how far he may make use of his *freedom*, and so comes to have it; till then, some body else must guide him, who is presumed to know how far the law allows a liberty. If such a state of reason, such an age of discretion *made him free*, the same shall make his son free too. Is a man under the law of England? *What made him free* of that law? That is, to have the liberty to dispose of his actions and possessions according to his own will within the permission of that law? A capacity of knowing that law. Which is supposed by that law, at the age of one and twenty years, and in some cases sooner. If this made the father free, it shall make the son free too. Till then we see the law allows the son to have no will, but he is to be guided by the will of his father or guardian, who is to understand for him. And if the father die, and fail to substitute a deputy in his trust; if he hath not provided a tutor to govern his son, during his minority, during his want of understanding; the law takes care to do it; some other must govern him, and be a will to him, till he hath *attained to a state of freedom*, and his understanding be fit to take the government of his will. But after that, the father and son are equally free as much as tutor and pupil after nonage: equally subjects of the same law together, without any dominion left in the father over the life, liberty, or estate of his son, whether they be only in the state and under the law of nature, or under the positive laws of an established government.

60.   But if, through defects that may happen out of the ordinary course of nature, any one comes not to such a degree of reason, wherein he might be supposed capable of knowing the law, and so living within the rules of it; he is *never capable of being a free man*, he is never let loose to the disposure of his own will (because he knows no bounds to it, has not understanding, its proper guide) but is continued under the tuition and government of others, all the time his own understanding is incapable of that

charge. And so *lunatics* and *idiots* are never set free from the government of their parents. "Children, who are not as yet come into those years whereat they may have; and innocents which are excluded by a natural defect from ever having; thirdly, madmen, which for the present cannot possibly have the use of right reason to guide themselves; have for their guide the reason that guideth other men, which are tutors over them, to seek and procure their good for them," says Hooker, Eccl. Pol. Lib. I. Sect. 7. All which seems no more than that duty which God and nature has laid on man, as well as other creatures, to preserve their offspring, till they can be able to shift for themselves, and will scarce amount to an instance or proof of parents regal authority.

61.   Thus we are *born free*, as we are born rational; not that we have actually the exercise of either: age, that brings one, brings with it the other too. And thus we see how *natural freedom and subjection to parents* may consist together, and are both founded on the same principle. A *child* is *free* by his father's title, by his father's understanding, which is to govern him till he hath it of his own. The *freedom of a man at years of discretion*, and the *subjection* of a child *to* his parents, whilst yet short of that age, are so consistent, and so distinguishable, that the most blinded contenders for monarchy, *by right of fatherhood*, cannot miss this difference; the most obstinate cannot but allow their consistency. For were their doctrine all true, were the right heir of Adam now known, and by that title settled a monarch in his throne, invested with all the absolute unlimited power, Sir Robert Filmer talks of; if he should die as soon as his heir were born, must not the child, notwithstanding he were never so free, never so much sovereign, be in subjection to his mother and nurse, to tutors and governors, till age and education brought him reason and ability to govern himself and others? The necessities of his life, the health of his body, and the information of his mind, would require him to be directed by the will of others, and not his own; and yet will any one think, that this restraint and subjection were inconsistent with, or spoiled him of, that liberty or sovereignty he had a right to, or gave away his empire to those who had the government of his nonage? This government

over him only prepared him the better and sooner for it. If any body should ask me when my son is of *age to be free?* I shall answer, just when his monarch is of age to govern. "But at what time," says the judicious Hooker, Eccl. Pol. Lib. I. Sect. 6 "a man may be said to have attained so far forth the use of reason, as sufficeth to make him capable of those laws whereby he is then bound to guide his actions: this is a great deal more easy for sense to discern, than for any one by skill and learning to determine."

62.   Commonwealths themselves take notice of, and allow, that there is *a time when men* are to *begin to act like free men*, and therefore till that time require not oaths of fealty, or allegiance, or other public owning of, or submission to, the government of their countries.

63.   The *freedom* then of man, and liberty of acting according to his own will, is *grounded* on his having *reason*, which is able to instruct him in that law he is to govern himself by, and make him know how far he is left to the freedom of his own will. To turn him loose to an unrestrained liberty, before he has reason to guide him, is not the allowing him the privilege of his nature to be free; but to thrust him out amongst brutes, and abandon him to a state as wretched, and as much beneath that of a man, as theirs. This is that which puts the *authority* into the *parents'* hands to govern the *minority* of their children. God hath made it their business to employ this care on their offspring, and hath placed in them suitable inclinations of tenderness and concern to temper this power, to apply it, as his wisdom designed it, to the children's good as long as they should need to be under it.

64.   But what reason can hence advance this care of the *parents* due to their offspring into an *absolute arbitrary dominion* of the father, whose power reaches no farther than, by such a discipline as he finds most effectual, to give such strength and health to their bodies, such vigour and rectitude to their minds, as may best fit his children to be most useful to themselves and others; and, if it be necessary to his condition, to make them work, when they are able, for their own subsistence. But in this power the *mother* too has her share with the *father*.

65. Nay, *this* power so little belongs to the father by any peculiar right of nature, but only as he is guardian of his children, that when he quits his care of them, he loses his power over them, which goes along with their nourishment and education, to which it is inseparably annexed; and it belongs as much to the foster-father of an exposed child, as to the natural father of another. So little power does the bare *act of begetting* give a man over his issue; if all his care ends there, and this be all the title he hath to the name and authority of a father. And what will become of this *paternal power* in that part of the world, where one woman hath more than one husband at a time? or in those parts of America, where, when the husband and wife part, which happens frequently, the children are all left to the mother, follow her, and are wholly under her care and provision? If the father die whilst the children are young, do they not naturally every where owe the same obedience to their mother, during their minority, as to their father were he alive? And will any one say, that the mother hath a legislative power over her children? that she can make standing rules, which shall be of perpetual obligation, by which they ought to regulate all the concerns of their property, and bound their liberty all the course of their lives? or can she enforce the observation of them with capital punishments? For this is the proper *power of the magistrate*, of which the father hath not so much as the shadow. His command over his children is but temporary, and reaches not their life or property: it is but a help to the weakness and imperfection of their nonage, a discipline necessary to their education: and though a father may dispose of his own possessions as he pleases, when his children are out of danger of perishing for want, yet his power extends not to the lives or goods, which either their own industry, or another's bounty has made theirs; nor to their liberty neither, when they are once arrived to the infranchisement of the years of discretion. The *father's empire* then ceases, and can from thence forwards no more dispose of the liberty of his son, than that of any other man: and it must be far from an absolute or perpetual jurisdiction, from which a man may withdraw himself, having licence from divine authority to *leave father and mother, and cleave to his wife*.

66. But though there be a time when a child comes to be as free from subjection to the will and command of his father, as the father himself is free from subjection to the will of any body else, and they are each under no other restraint but that which is common to them both, whether it be the law of nature, or municipal law of their country; yet this freedom exempts not a son from that honour which he ought, by the law of God and nature, to pay his parents. God having made the parents instruments in his great design of continuing the race of mankind, and the occasions of life to their children; as he hath laid on them an obligation to nourish, preserve, and bring up their offspring; so he has laid on the children a perpetual obligation of *honouring their parents*, which containing in it an inward esteem and reverence to be shewn by all outward expressions, ties up the child from any thing that may ever injure or affront, disturb or endanger, the happiness or life of those from whom he received his; and engages him in all actions of defence, relief, assistance, and comfort of those, by whose means he entered into being, and has been made capable of any enjoyments of life. From this obligation no state, no freedom can absolve children. But this is very far from giving parents a power of command over their children, or an authority to make laws and dispose as they please of their lives and liberties. It is one thing to owe honour, respect, gratitude, and assistance; another to require an absolute obedience and submission. The *honour due to parents*, a monarch in his throne owes his mother, and yet this lessens not his authority, nor subjects him to her government.

67. The subjection of a minor places in the father a temporary government, which terminates with the minority of the child: and the *honour due from a child*, places in the parents a perpetual right to respect, reverence, support and compliance too, more or less, as the father's care, cost, and kindness in his education, have been more or less. This ends not with minority, but holds in all parts and conditions of a man's life. The want of distinguishing these two powers, viz. that which the father hath in the right of *tuition*, during minority, and the right of honour all his life, may perhaps have caused a great part of

the mistakes about this matter. For to speak properly of them, the first of these is rather the privilege of children, and duty of parents, than any prerogative of paternal power. The nourishment and education of their children is a charge so incumbent on parents for their children's good, that nothing can absolve them from taking care of it. And though the *power of commanding and chastising* them go along with it, yet God hath woven into the principles of human nature such a tenderness for their offspring, that there is little fear that parents should use their power with too much rigour; the excess is seldom on the severe side, the strong bias of nature drawing the other way. And therefore God Almighty, when he would express his gentle dealing with the Israelites, he tells them, that though he chastened them, "he chastened them as a man chastens his son," *Deut.* viii. 5. i.e. with tenderness and affection, and kept them under no severer discipline than what was absolutely best for them, and had been less kindness to have slackened. This is that power to which children are commanded obedience, that the pains and care of their parents may not be increased, or ill rewarded.

68.   On the other side, *honour* and *support*, all that which gratitude requires to return for the benefits received by and from them, is the indispensable duty of the child, and the proper privilege of the parents. This is intended for the parents' advantage, as the other is for the child's; though education, the parents' duty, seems to have most power, because the ignorance and infirmities of childhood stand in need of restraint and correction; which is a visible exercise of rule, and a kind of dominion. And that duty which is comprehended in the word *honour*, requires less obedience, though the obligation be stronger on grown than younger children. For who can think the command, "Children, obey your parents," requires in a man that has children of his own the same submission to his father, as it does in his yet young children to him; and that by this precept he were bound to obey all his father's commands, if, out of a conceit of authority, he should have the indiscretion to treat him still as a boy?

69.   The first part then of *paternal power*, or rather duty, which is *education*, belongs so to the father, that it terminates at a certain season; when the business of education is over, it ceases of itself, and is also alienable before. For a man may put the tuition of his son in other hands; and he that has made his son an *apprentice* to another, has discharged him, during that time, of a great part of his obedience both to himself and to his mother. But all the *duty of honour*, the other part, remains nevertheless entire to them; nothing can cancel that: It is so inseparable from them both, that the father's authority cannot dispossess the mother of this right, nor can any man discharge his son from *honouring* her that bore him. But both these are very far from a power to make laws, and enforcing them with penalties that may reach estate, liberty, limbs, and life. The power of commanding ends with nonage; and though after that, *honour* and respect, support and defence, and whatsoever gratitude can oblige a man to, for the highest benefits he is naturally capable of, be always due from a son to his parents; yet all this puts no sceptre into the father's hand, no sovereign power of commanding. He has no dominion over his son's property, or actions; nor any right that his will should prescribe to his son's in all things; however it may become his son in many things not very inconvenient to him and his family, to pay a deference to it.

70.   A man may owe *honour* and respect to an ancient, or wise man; defence to his child or friend; relief and support to the distressed; and gratitude to a benefactor, to such a degree, that all he has, all he can do, cannot sufficiently pay it: but all these give no authority, no right to any one, of making laws over him from whom they are owing. And it is plain, all this is due not only to the bare title of father; not only because, as has been said, it is owing to the mother too, but because these obligations to parents, and the degrees of what is required of children, may be varied by the different care and kindness, trouble and expense, which is often employed upon one child more than another.

71.   This shews the reason how it comes to pass, that *parents in societies*, where they themselves are

subjects, retain a *power over their children*, and have as much right to their subjection as those who are in the state of nature. Which could not possibly be, if all political power were only paternal, and that in truth they were one and the same thing. For then, all paternal power being in the prince, the subject could naturally have none of it. But these two *powers, political* and *paternal*, are so perfectly distinct and separate, are built upon so different foundations, and given to so different ends, that every subject that is a father, has as much a paternal power over his children, as the prince has over his: and every prince, that has parents, owes them as much filial duty and obedience, as the meanest of his subjects do to theirs; and cannot therefore contain any part or degree of that kind of dominion which a prince or magistrate has over his subject.

72. Though the obligation on the parents to bring up their children, and the obligation on children to honour their parents, contain all the power on the one hand, and submission on the other, which are proper to this relation, yet there is *another power* ordinary *in the father*, whereby he has a tie on the obedience of his children; which though it be common to him with other men, yet the occasions of shewing it almost constantly happening to fathers in their private families, and the instances of it elsewhere being rare, and less taken notice of, it passes in the world for a part of paternal jurisdiction. And this is the power men generally have to *bestow their estates* on those who please them best. The possession of the father being the expectation and inheritance of the children, ordinarily in certain proportions, according to the law and custom of each country; yet it is commonly in the father's power to bestow it with a more sparing or liberal hand, according as the behaviour of this or that child hath comported with his will and humour.

73. This is no small tie on the obedience of children: and there being always annexed to the enjoyment of land a submission to the government of the country, of which that land is a part; it has been commonly supposed, that a father could *oblige his posterity to that government*, of which he himself was a subject, and that his compact held them; whereas it being only a necessary condition annexed to the land, and the inheritance of an estate which is under that government, reaches only those who will take it on that condition, and so is no natural tie or engagement, but a voluntary submission. For *every man's children* being by nature as free as himself, or any of his ancestors ever were, may, whilst they are in that freedom, choose what society they will join themselves to, what commonwealth they will put themselves under. But if they will enjoy the inheritance of their ancestors, they must take it on the same terms their ancestors had it, and submit to all the conditions annexed to such a possession. By this power indeed fathers oblige their children to obedience to themselves, even when they are past minority, and most commonly too subject them to this or that political power. But neither of these by any peculiar right of fatherhood, but by the reward they have in their hands to enforce and recompence such a compliance; and is no more power than what a Frenchman has over an Englishman, who, by the hopes of an estate he will leave him, will certainly have a strong tie on his obedience: and if, when it is left him, he will enjoy it, he must certainly take it upon the conditions annexed to the *possession of land* in that country where it lies, whether it be France or England.

74. To conclude then, though the father's power of commanding extends no farther than the minority of his children, and to a degree only fit for the discipline and government of that age; and though that honour and respect, and all that which the Latins called piety, which they indispensably owe to their parents all their life-time, and in all estates, with all that support and defence which is due to them, gives the father no power of governing, i.e. making laws and enacting penalties on his children; though by all this he has no dominion over the property or actions of his son; yet it is obvious to conceive how easy it was, in the first ages of the world, and in places still, where the thinness of people gives families leave to separate into unpossessed quarters, and they have room to remove or plant themselves in yet vacant habitations, for the *father of the family* to become the

prince[1] of it; he had been a ruler from the beginning of the infancy of his children: and since without some government it would be hard for them to live together, it was likeliest it should, by the express or tacit consent of the children when they were grown up, be in the father, where it seemed without any change barely to continue; when indeed nothing more was required to it, than the permitting the father to exercise alone, in his family, that executive power of the law of nature, which every free man naturally hath, and by that permission resigning up to him a monarchical power, whilst they remained in it. But that this was not by any *paternal right*, but only by the consent of his children, is evident from hence, that no body doubts, but if a stranger, whom chance or business had brought to his family, had there killed any of his children, or committed any other fact, he might condemn and put him to death, or otherwise punish him, as well as any of his children: which it was impossible he should do by virtue of any paternal authority over one who was not his child, but by virtue of that executive power of the law of nature, which, as a man, he had a right to: and he alone could punish him in his family, where the respect of his children had laid by the exercise of such a power, to give way to the dignity and authority they were willing should remain in him, above the rest of his family.

[1] It is no improbable opinion therefore, which the arch-philosopher was of, "That the chief person in every household was always, as it were, a king: so when numbers of households joined themselves in civil societies together, kings were the first kind of governors amongst them, which is also, as it seemeth, the reason why the name of fathers continued still in them, who, of fathers, were made rulers; as also the ancient custom of governors to do as Melchize-deck, and being kings, to exercise the office of priests, which fathers did, at the first grew perhaps by the same occasion. Howbeit, this is not the only kind of regiment that has been received in the world. The inconveniences of one kind have caused sundry others to be devised; so that in a word, all public regiment of what kind soever, seemeth evidently to have risen from the deliberate advice, consultation and composition between men, judging it convenient and behoveful; there being no impossibility in nature considered by itself, but that man might have lived without any public regiment." Hooker's Eccl. P. L. I. Sect. 10.

75.   Thus it was easy, and almost natural for children, by a tacit, and scarce avoidable consent, to make way for the *father's authority and government*. They had been accustomed in their childhood to follow his direction, and to refer their little differences to him; and when they were men, who fitter to rule them? Their little properties, and less covetousness, seldom afforded greater controversies; and when any should arise, where could they have a fitter umpire than he, by whose care they had every one been sustained and brought up, and who had a tenderness for them all? It is no wonder that they made no distinction betwixt minority and full age; nor looked after one and twenty, or any other age that might make them the free disposers of themselves and fortunes, when they could have no desire to be out of their pupilage. The government they had been under during it, continued still to be more their protection than restraint: and they could no where find a greater security to their peace, liberties, and fortunes, than in the *rule of a father*.

76.   Thus the natural *fathers of families* by an insensible change became the *politic monarchs* of them too: and as they chanced to live long, and leave able and worthy heirs, for several successions, or otherwise; so they laid the foundations of hereditary, or elective kingdoms, under several constitutions and manners, according as chance, contrivance, or occasions happened to mould them. But if princes have their titles in their fathers right, and it be a sufficient proof of the natural *right of fathers* to political authority, because they commonly were those in whose hands we find, *de facto*, the exercise of government: I say, if this argument be good, it will as strongly prove, that all princes, nay princes only, ought to be priests, since it is as certain, that in the beginning, *the father of the family was priest, as that he was ruler in his own household*.

CHAPTER VII: Of Political or Civil Society

77.   God having made man such a creature, that in his own judgment, it was not good for him to be

alone, put him under strong obligations of necessity, convenience, and inclination, to drive him into society, as well as fitted him with understanding and language to continue and enjoy it. The first society was between man and wife, which gave beginning to that between parents and children; to which, in time, that between master and servant came to be added; and though all these might, and commonly did meet together, and make up but one family, wherein the master or mistress of it had some sort of rule proper to a family; each of these, or all together, came short of *political society*, as we shall see, if we consider the different ends, ties, and bounds of each of these.

78.   *Conjugal society* is made by a voluntary compact between man and woman; and though it consist chiefly in such a communion and right in one another's bodies as is necessary to its chief end, procreation; yet it draws with it mutual support and assistance, and a communion of interests too, as necessary not only to unite their care and affection, but also necessary to their common offspring, who have a right to be nourished and maintained by them, till they are able to provide for themselves.

79.   For the end of *conjunction between male and female* being not barely procreation, but the continuation of the species; this conjunction betwixt male and female ought to last, even after procreation, so long as is necessary to the nourishment and support of the young ones, who are to be sustained by those that got them, till they are able to shift and provide for themselves. This rule, which the infinite wise Maker hath set to the works of his hands, we find the inferior creatures steadily obey. In those viviparous animals which feed on grass, the *conjunction between male and female* lasts no longer than the very act of copulation; because the teat of the dam being sufficient to nourish the young, till it be able to feed on grass, the male only begets, but concerns not himself for the female or young, to whose sustenance he can contribute nothing. But in beasts of prey the conjunction lasts longer: because the dam not being able well to subsist herself, and nourish her numerous offspring by her own prey alone, a more laborious, as well as more dangerous way of living, than by feeding on grass; the assistance of the male is necessary to the maintenance of their common family, which cannot subsist till they are able to prey for themselves, but by the joint care of male and female. The same is to be observed in all birds (except some domestic ones, where plenty of food excuses the cock from feeding, and taking care of the young brood), whose young needing food in the nest, the cock and hen continue mates, till the young are able to use their wing, and provide for themselves.

80.   And herein I think lies the chief, if not the only reason, *why the male and female in mankind are tied to a longer conjunction* than other creatures, viz. because the female is capable of conceiving, and *de facto* is commonly with child again, and brings forth too a new birth, long before the former is out of a dependency for support on his parents help, and able to shift for himself, and has all the assistance that is due to him from his parents: whereby the father, who is bound to take care for those he hath begot, is under an obligation to continue in conjugal society with the same woman longer than other creatures, whose young being able to subsist of themselves before the time of procreation returns again, the conjugal bond dissolves of itself, and they are at liberty, till Hymen at his usual anniversary season summons them again to choose new mates. Wherein one cannot but admire the wisdom of the great Creator, who having given to man foresight, and an ability to lay up for the future, as well as to supply the present necessity, hath made it necessary, that *society of man and wife should be more lasting*, than of male and female amongst other creatures; that so their industry might be encouraged, and their interest better united, to make provision and lay up goods for their common issue, which uncertain mixture, or easy and frequent solutions of conjugal society, would mightily disturb.

81.   But though these are ties upon *mankind*, which make the *conjugal bonds* more firm and lasting in man, than the other species of animals; yet it would give one reason to inquire, why this compact, where procreation and education are secured, and inheritance taken care for, may not be made determinable, either by consent, or at a certain time, or upon certain conditions, as well as any other voluntary compacts, there being no necessity in the nature of the thing,

nor to the ends of it, that it should always be for life; I mean, to such as are under no restraint of any positive law, which ordains all such contracts to be perpetual.

82. But the husband and wife, though they have but one common concern, yet having different understandings, will unavoidably sometimes have different wills too; it therefore being necessary that the last determination, i.e. the rule, should be placed somewhere; it naturally falls to the man's share, as the abler and the stronger. But this reaching but to the things of their common interest and property, leaves the wife in the full and free possession of what by contract is her peculiar right, and gives the husband no more power over her life than she has over his. The *power of the husband* being so far from that of an absolute monarch, that the *wife* has in many cases a liberty to separate from him, where natural right or their contract allows it; whether that contract be made by themselves in the state of nature, or by the customs or laws of the country they live in; and the children upon such separation fall to the father's or mother's lot, as such contract does determine.

83. For all the ends of *marriage* being to be obtained under politic government, as well as in the state of nature, the civil magistrate doth not abridge the right or power of either naturally necessary to those ends, viz. procreation and mutual support and assistance whilst they are together; but only decides any controversy that may arise between man and wife about them. If it were otherwise, and that absolute sovereignty and power of life and death naturally belonged to the husband, and were *necessary to the society between man and wife*, there could be no matrimony in any of those countries where the husband is allowed no such absolute authority. But the ends of matrimony requiring no such power in the husband, the condition of conjugal society put it not in him, it being not at all necessary to that state. Conjugal society could subsist and attain its ends without it; nay, community of goods, and the power over them, mutual assistance and maintenance, and other things belonging to conjugal society, might be varied and regulated by that contract which unites man and wife in that society, as far as may consist with

procreation and the bringing up of children till they could shift for themselves; nothing being necessary to any society, that is not necessary to the ends for which it is made.

84. The *society betwixt parents and children*, and the distinct rights and powers belonging respectively to them, I have treated of so largely, in the foregoing chapter, that I shall not here need to say any thing of it. And I think it is plain, that it is far different from a politic society.

85. *Master* and *servant* are names as old as history, but given to those of far different condition; for a free man makes himself a servant to another, by selling him, for a certain time, the service he undertakes to do, in exchange for wages he is to receive: and though this commonly puts him into the family of his master, and under the ordinary discipline thereof: yet it gives the master but a temporary power over him, and no greater than what is contained in the *contract* between them. But there is another sort of servants, which by a peculiar name we call *slaves*, who being captives taken in a just war, are by the right of nature subjected to the absolute dominion and arbitrary power of their masters. These men having, as I say, forfeited their lives, and with it their liberties, and lost their estates; and being in the *state of slavery*, not capable of any property, cannot in that state be considered as any part of *civil society*; the chief end whereof is the preservation of property,

86. Let us therefore consider a *master of a family* with all these subordinate relations of *wife, children, servants*, and *slaves*, united under the domestic rule of a family; which, what resemblance soever it may have in its order, offices, and number too, with a little commonwealth, yet is very far from it, both in its constitution, power, and end: or if it must be thought a monarchy, and the *paterfamilias* the absolute monarch in it, absolute monarchy will have but a very shattered and short power, when it is plain by what has been said before, that the *master of the family* has a very distinct and differently limited power, both as to time and extent, over those several persons that are in it. For excepting the slave (and the family is as much a family, and his power as *paterfamilias* as great, whether there be any slaves in his family or

no) he has no legislative power of life and death over any of them, and none too but what a *mistress of a family* may have as well as he. And he certainly can have no absolute power over the whole family, who has but a very limited one over every individual in it. But how a family, or any other society of men, differ from that which is properly political society, we shall best see by considering wherein political society itself consists.

87.   Man being born, as has been proved, with a title to perfect freedom, and an uncontrolled enjoyment of all the rights and privileges of the law of nature, equally with any other man, or number of men in the world, hath by nature a power, not only to preserve his property, that is, his life, liberty, and estate, against the injuries and attempts of other men; but to judge of and punish the breaches of that law in others, as he is persuaded the offence deserves, even with death itself, in crimes where the heinousness of the fact, in his opinion, requires it. But because no *political* society can be, nor subsist, without having in itself the power to preserve the property, and, in order thereunto, punish the offences of all those of that society; there and there only is *political society*, where every one of the members hath quitted his natural power, resigned it up into the hands of the community in all cases that excludes him not from appealing for protection to the law established by it. And thus all private judgment of every particular member being excluded, the community comes to be umpire by settled standing rules, indifferent, and the same to all parties; and by men having authority from the community, for the execution of those rules, decides all the differences that may happen between any members of that society concerning any matter of right; and punishes those offences which any member hath committed against the society, with such penalties as the law has established, whereby it is easy to discern, who are, and who are not, in *political society* together. Those who are united into one body, and have a common established law and judicature to appeal to, with authority to decide controversies between them, and punish offenders, *are in civil society* one with another: but those who have no such common appeal, I mean on earth, are still in the state of nature, each being, where there is no other, judge for himself, and executioner: which is, as I have before shewed, the perfect *state of nature*.

88.   And thus the commonwealth comes by a power to set down what punishment shall belong to the several transgressions which they think worthy of it, committed amongst the members of that society, (which is the *power of making laws*) as well as it has the power to punish any injury done unto any of its members, by any one that is not of it, (which is the power of war and peace,) and all this for the preservation of the property of all the members of that society, as far as is possible. But though every man who has entered into civil society, and is become a member of any commonwealth, has thereby quitted his power to punish offences against the law of nature, in prosecution of his own private judgment; yet with the judgment of offences, which he has given up to the legislative in all cases, where he can appeal to the magistrate, he has given a right to the commonwealth to employ his force, for the execution of the judgments of the commonwealth whenever he shall be called to it; which indeed are his own judgments, they being made by himself, or his representative. And herein we have the original of the legislative and executive power of civil society, which is to judge by standing laws, how far offences are to be punished, when committed within the commonwealth; and also to determine, by occasional judgments founded on the present circumstances of the fact, how far injuries from without are to be vindicated; and in both these to employ all the force of all the members, when there shall be need.

89.   Whenever therefore any number of men are so united into one society, as to quit every one his executive power of the law of nature, and to resign it to the public, there and there only is a political, or civil society. And this is done, wherever any number of men, in the state of nature, enter into society to make one people, one body politic, under one supreme government; or else when any one joins himself to, and incorporates with any government already made. For hereby he authorizes the society, or, which is all one, the legislative thereof, to make laws for him, as the public good of the society shall require; to the

execution whereof, his own assistance (as to his own degrees) is due. And this puts men out of a state of nature into that of a commonwealth, by setting up a judge on earth, with authority to determine all the controversies, and redress the injuries that may happen to any member of the commonwealth: which judge is the legislative, or magistrate appointed by it. And wherever there are any number of men, however associated, that have no such decisive power to appeal to, there they are still in the state of nature.

90.   Hence it is evident, that absolute monarchy, which by some men is counted the only government in the world, is indeed inconsistent with civil society, and so can be no form of civil government at all; for the end of civil society being to avoid and remedy these inconveniencies of the state of nature, which necessarily follow from every man's being judge in his own case, by setting up a known authority, to which every one of that society may appeal upon any injury received, or controversy that may arise, and which every one of the[2] society ought to obey; wherever any persons are, who have not such an authority to appeal to for the decision of any difference between them, there those persons are still *in the state of nature*. And so is every *absolute prince*, in respect of those who are under his dominion.

91.   For he being supposed to have all, both legislative and executive power in himself alone, there is no judge to be found, no appeal lies open to any one, who may fairly, and indifferently, and with authority decide, and from whose decision relief and redress may be expected of any injury or inconveniency that may be suffered from the prince, or by his order: so that such a man, however intitled, *czar*, or *grand seignior*, or how you please, is as much *in the state of nature*, with all under his dominion, as he is with the rest of mankind. For wherever any two men are,

who have no standing rule, and common judge to appeal to on earth, for the determination of controversies of right betwixt them, there they are still *in the state of*[3] *nature*, and under all the inconveniencies of it, with only this woful difference to the subject, or rather slave of an absolute prince; that whereas in the ordinary state of nature he has a liberty to judge of his right, and, according to the best of his power, to maintain it; now, whenever his property is invaded by the will and order of his monarch, he has not only no appeal, as those in society ought to have, but, as if he were degraded from the common state of rational creatures, is denied a liberty to judge of, or to defend his right; and so is exposed to all the misery and inconveniencies that a man can fear from one, who being in the unrestrained state of nature, is yet corrupted with flattery, and armed with power.

92.   For he that thinks *absolute power purifies men's blood*, and corrects the baseness of human nature, need read but the history of this or any other age, to be convinced of the contrary. He that would have been so insolent and injurious in the woods of America, would not probably be much better in a

---

[2] "The public power of all society is above every soul contained in 'the same society; and the principal use of that power is, to give laws unto all that are under it, which laws in such cases we must obey,' unless there be reason shewed which may necessarily inforce, that the law of reason, or of God, doth enjoin the contrary." Hook. Eccl. Pol. L. I. Sect. 16.

[3] "To take away all such mutual grievances, injuries and wrongs," i.e. such as attend men in the state of nature, "there was no way but only by growing into composition and agreement amongst themselves, by ordaining some kind of government public, and by yielding themselves subject thereunto, that unto whom they granted authority to rule and govern, by them the peace, tranquillity, and happy state of the rest might be procured. Men always knew that where force and injury was offered, they might be defenders of themselves; they knew that however men may seek their own commodity; yet if this were done with injury unto others, it was not to be suffered, but by all men, and all good means to be withstood. Finally, they knew that no man might in reason take upon him to determine his own right, and according to his own determination proceed in maintenance thereof, in as much as every man is towards himself, and them whom he greatly affects, partial; and therefore that strifes and troubles would be endless, except they gave their common consent, all to be ordered by some, whom they should agree upon, without which consent there would be no reason that one man should take upon him to be lord or judge over another." Hooker's Eccl. Pol. L. I. Sect. 10.

throne; where perhaps learning and religion shall be found out to justify all that he shall do to his subjects, and the sword presently silence all those that dare question it. For what the *protection of absolute monarchy* is, what kind of fathers of their countries it makes princes to be, and to what a degree of happiness and security it carries civil society, where this sort of government is grown to perfection; he that will look into the late relation of Ceylon, may easily see.

93. *In absolute monarchies*, indeed, as well as other governments of the world, the subjects have an appeal to the law, and judges to decide any controversies, and restrain any violence that may happen betwixt the subjects themselves, one amongst another. This every one thinks necessary, and believes he deserves to be thought a declared enemy to society and mankind, who should go about to take it away. But whether this be from a true love of mankind and society, and such a charity as we all owe one to another, there is reason to doubt. For this is no more than what every man, who loves his own power, profit, or greatness, may and naturally must do, keep those animals from hurting, or destroying one another, who labour and drudge only for his pleasure and advantage; and so are taken care of, not out of any love the master has for them, but love of himself, and the profit they bring him. For if it be asked, what security, what fence is there, in such a state, *against the violence and oppression of this absolute ruler?* the very question can scarce be borne. They are ready to tell you, that it deserves death only to ask after safety. Betwixt subject and subject, they will grant, there must be measures, laws, and judges, for their mutual peace and security: but as for the ruler he ought to be *absolute*, and is above all such circumstances; because he has power to do more hurt and wrong, it is right when he does it. To ask how you may be guarded from harm, or injury, on that side where the strongest hand is to do it, is presently the voice of faction and rebellion: as if when men quitting the state of nature entered into society, they agreed that all of them but one should be under the restraint of laws, but that he should still retain all the liberty of the state of nature, increased with power, and made licentious by impunity. This is to think, that men are so foolish,

that they take care to avoid what mischiefs may be done them by *pole cats*, or *foxes*; but are content, nay think it safety, to be devoured by *lions*.

94. But whatever flatterers may talk to amuse people's understandings, it hinders not men from feeling; and when they perceive, that any man, in what station soever, is out of the bounds of the civil society which they are of, and that they have no appeal on earth against any harm they may receive from him, they are apt to think themselves in the state of nature, in respect of him whom they find to be so: and to take care, as soon as they can, to have that *safety and security in civil society*, for which it was instituted, and for which only they entered into it. And therefore, though perhaps at first, (as shall be shewed more at large hereafter in the following part of this discourse) some one good and excellent man having got a pre-eminency amongst the rest, had this deference paid to his goodness and virtue, as to a kind of natural authority, that the chief rule, with arbitration of their differences, by a tacit consent devolved into his hands, without any other caution, but the assurance they had of his uprightness and wisdom; yet when time, giving authority, and (as some men would persuade us) sacredness to customs, which the negligent and unforeseen innocence of the first ages began, had brought in successors of another stamp, the people finding their properties not secure under the government, as then it was, (whereas government has no other end but the preservation of [4] property) could never be safe nor at rest, *nor think themselves in civil society*, till the legislature was placed in collective bodies of men, call them senate, parliament, or what

[4] "At the first, when some certain kind of regiment was once appointed, it may be that nothing was then farther thought upon for the manner of governing, but all permitted unto their wisdom and discretion, which were to rule, till by experience they found this for all parts very inconvenient, so as the thing which they had devised for a remedy, did indeed but increase the sore, which it should have cured. They saw, that to live by one man's will, became the cause of all men's misery. This constrained them to come into laws, wherein all men might see their duty beforehand, and know the penalties of transgressing them." Hooker's Eccl. Pol. L. I. Sect. 10.

you please. By which means every single person became subject, equally with other the meanest men, to those laws, which he himself, as part of the legislative, had established; nor could any one, by his own authority, avoid the force of the law, when once made; nor by any pretence of superiority plead exemption, thereby to license his own, or the miscarriages of any of his dependents.[5] *No man in civil society can be exempted from the laws of it.* For if any man may do what he thinks fit, and there be no appeal on earth, for redress or security against any harm he shall do; I ask, whether he be not perfectly still in the state of nature, and so can be *no part or member of that civil society:* unless any one will say, the state of nature and civil society are one and the same thing, which I have never yet found any one so great a patron of anarchy as to affirm.

CHAPTER VIII: Of the Beginning of Political Societies

95.   Men being, as has been said, by nature, all free, equal, and independent, no one can be put out of this estate, and subjected to the political power of another, without his own consent. The only way, whereby any one divests himself of his natural liberty, and puts on the *bonds of civil society*, is by agreeing with other men to join and unite into a community, for their comfortable, safe, and peaceable living one amongst another, in a secure enjoyment of their properties, and a greater security against any, that are not of it. This any number of men may do, because it injures not the freedom of the rest; they are left as they were in the liberty of the state of nature. When any number of men have so *consented to make one community or government*, they are thereby presently incorporated, and make *one body politic*, wherein the *majority* have a right to act and conclude the rest.

96.   For when any number of men have, by the consent of every individual, made a *community*, they have thereby made that *community* one body, with a

power to act as one body, which is only by the will and determination of the majority. For that which acts any community, being only the *consent* of the individuals of it, and it being necessary to that which is one body to move one way; it is necessary the body should move that way whither the greater force carries it, which is the *consent of the majority:* or else it is impossible it should act or continue one body, one community, which the consent of every individual that united into it, agreed that it should; and so every one is bound by that consent to be concluded by the majority. And therefore we see, that in assemblies, impowered to act by positive laws, where no number is set by that positive law which impowers them, the *act of the majority* passes for the act of the whole, and of course determines, as having, by the law of nature and reason, the power of the whole.

97.   And thus every man, by consenting with others to make one body politic under one government, puts himself under an obligation, to every one of that society, to submit to the determination of the majority, and to be concluded by it; or else this *original compact*, whereby he with others incorporate into one society, would signify nothing, and be no compact, if he be left free, and under no other ties than he was in before in the state of nature. For what appearance would there be of any compact? What new engagement if he were no farther tied by any decrees of the society, than he himself thought fit, and did actually consent to? This would be still as great a liberty, as he himself had before his compact, or any one else in the state of nature hath, who may submit himself, and consent to any acts of it if he thinks fit.

98.   For if *the consent of the majority* shall not, in reason, be received as *the act of the whole*, and conclude every individual; nothing but the consent of every individual can make any thing to be the act of the whole: But such a consent is next to impossible ever to be had, if we consider the infirmities of health, and avocations of business, which in a number, though much less than that of a commonwealth, will necessarily keep many away from the public assembly. To which if we add the variety of opinions, and contrariety of interests, which unavoidably happen in all collections of men, the coming into society upon

---

[5] "Civil law, being the act of the whole body politic, doth therefore over-rule each several part of the same body." Hooker, ibid.

such terms would be only like Cato's coming into the theatre, only to go out again. Such a constitution as this would make the mighty *leviathan* of a shorter duration, than the feeblest creatures, and not let it outlast the day it was born in: which cannot be supposed, till we can think, that rational creatures should desire and constitute societies only to be dissolved. For where the majority cannot conclude the rest, there they cannot act as one body, and consequently will be immediately dissolved again.

99. Whosoever therefore out of a state of nature unite into a community, must be understood to give up all the power, necessary to the ends for which they unite into society, to the majority of the community, unless they expressly agreed in any number greater than the majority. And this is done by barely agreeing to *unite into one political society*, which is *all the compact* that is, or needs be, between the individuals, that enter into, or make up a commonwealth. And thus that, which begins and actually *constitutes any political society*, is nothing, but the consent of any number of freemen capable of a majority, to unite and incorporate into such a society. And this is that, and that only, which did, or could give beginning to any lawful government in the world.

100. To this I find two objections made.

First, *That there are no instances to be found in story, of a company of men independent and equal one amongst another, that met together, and in this way began and set up a government.*

Secondly, *It is impossible of right, that men should do so, because all men being born under government, they are to submit to that, and are not at liberty to begin a new one.*

101. To the first there is this to answer, That it is not at all to be wondered, that *history* gives us but a very little account of *men, that lived together in the state of nature.* The inconveniencies of that condition and the love and want of society, no sooner brought any number of them together, but they presently united and incorporated, if they designed to continue together. And if we may not suppose men ever to have been *in the state of nature*, because we hear not much of them in such a state, we may as well suppose the armies of Salmanasser or Xerxes were never chil-

dren, because we hear little of them, till they were men, and embodied in armies. Government is every where antecedent to records, and letters seldom come in amongst a people till a long continuation of civil society has, by other more necessary arts, provided for their safety, ease, and plenty. And then they begin to look after the history of their founders, and search into their original, when they have outlived the memory of it. For it is with commonwealths, as with particular persons, they are commonly *ignorant of their own births and infancies:* and if they know any thing of their original, they are beholden for it to the accidental records that others have kept of it. And those that we have of the beginning of any politics in the world, excepting that of the Jews, where God himself immediately interposed, and which favours not at all paternal dominion, are all either plain instances of such a beginning as I have mentioned, or at least have manifest footsteps of it.

102. He must shew a strange inclination to deny evident matter of fact, when it agrees not with his hypothesis, who will not allow, that the *beginning* of Rome and Venice were by the uniting together of several men free and independent one of another, amongst whom there was no natural superiority or subjection. And if Josephus Acosta's word may be taken, he tells us, that in many parts of America there was no government at all. "There are great and apparent conjectures," says he, "that these men, speaking of those of Peru, for a long time had neither kings nor commonwealths, but lived in troops, as they do this day in Florida, the Cheriquanas, those of Brasil, and many other nations, which have no certain kings, but as occasion is offered, in peace or war, they choose their captains as they please," l. I. c. 25. If it be said, that every man there was born subject to his father, or the head of his family. That the subjection due from a child to a father took not away his freedom of uniting into what political society he thought fit, has been already proved. But be that as it will, these men, it is evident, were actually free; and whatever superiority some politicians now would place in any of them, they themselves claimed it not, but by consent were all equal, till by the same consent they set rulers over themselves. So that their politic societies

all began from a voluntary union, and the mutual agreement of men freely acting in the choice of their governors, and forms of government.

103.   And I hope those who went away from Sparta with Palantus, mentioned by Justin, l. iii. c. 4, will be allowed to have been freemen, *independent* one of another, and to have set up a government over themselves, by their own consent. Thus I have given several examples out of history, of *people free and in the state of nature*, that being met together, incorporated and *began a commonwealth*. And if the want of such instances be an argument to prove that governments were not, nor could not be so begun, I suppose the contenders for paternal empire were better let it alone, than urge it against natural liberty. For if they can give so many instances out of history, of governments begun upon paternal right, I think (though at best an argument from what has been, to what should of right be, has no great force) one might, without any great danger, yield them the cause. But if I might advise them in the case, they would do well not to search too much into the *original of governments*, as they have begun *de facto*; lest they should find, at the foundation of most of them, something very little favourable to the design they promote, and such a power as they contend for.

104.   But to conclude, reason being plain on our side, that men are naturally free, and the examples of history shewing, that the governments of the world, that were begun in peace, had their beginning laid on that foundation, and were *made by the consent of the people*; there can be little room for doubt, either where the right is, or what has been the opinion, or practice of mankind, about the *first erecting of governments*.

105.   I will not deny, that if we look back as far as history will direct us, towards the *original of commonwealths*, we shall generally find them under the government and administration of one man. And I am also apt to believe, that where a family was numerous enough to subsist by itself, and continued entire together, without mixing with others, as it often happens, where there is much land, and few people, the government commonly began *in the father*. For the father having, by the law of nature, the same power with every man else to punish, as he thought fit, any offences against that law, might thereby punish his transgressing children, even when they were men, and out of their pupilage; and they were very likely to submit to his punishment, and all join with him against the offender, in their turns, giving him thereby power to execute his sentence against any transgression, and so in effect make him the law maker, and governour over all that remained in conjunction with his family. He was fittest to be trusted; paternal affection secured their property and interest under his care; and the custom of obeying him, in their childhood, made it easier to submit to him, rather than to any other. If, therefore, they must have one to rule them, as government is hardly to be avoided amongst men that live together; who so likely to be the man as he that was their common father; unless negligence, cruelty, or any other defect of mind or body made him unfit for it? But when either the father died, and left his next heir, for want of age, wisdom, courage, or any other qualities, less fit for rule; or where several families met, and consented to continue together; there, it is not to be doubted, but they used their natural freedom to set up him whom they judged the ablest, and most likely to rule well over them. Conformable hereunto we find the people of America, who (living out of the reach of the conquering swords, and spreading domination of the two great empires of Peru and Mexico) enjoyed their own natural freedom, though, *caeteris paribus*, they commonly prefer the heir of their deceased king; yet, if they find him any way weak, or incapable, they pass him by, and set up the stoutest and bravest man for their ruler.

106.   Thus, though looking back as far as records give us any account of peopling the world, and the history of nations, we commonly find the government to be in one hand; yet it destroys not that which I affirm, viz. that the *beginning of politic society* depends upon the consent of the individuals, to join into, and make one society; who, when they are thus incorporated, might set up what form of government they thought fit. But this having given occasion to men to mistake, and think, that by nature government was monarchical, and belonged to the father; it may

not be amiss here to consider, why people in the beginning generally pitched upon this form; which though perhaps the father's pre-eminency might, in the first institution of some commonwealth give rise to, and place in the beginning the power in one hand; yet it is plain that the reason, that continued the form of *government in a single person*, was not any regard or respect to paternal authority; since all petty monarchies, that is, almost all monarchies, near their original, have been commonly, at least upon occasion, *elective*.

107.   First then, in the beginning of things, the father's government of the childhood of those sprung from him, having accustomed them to the *rule of one man*, and taught them that where it was exercised with care and skill, with affection and love to those under it, it was sufficient to procure and preserve to men all the political happiness they sought for in society. It was no wonder that they should pitch upon, and naturally run into that form of government, which from their infancy they had been all accustomed to; and which, by experience, they had found both easy and safe. To which, if we add, that monarchy being simple, and most obvious to men, whom neither experience had instructed in forms of government, nor the ambition or insolence of empire had taught to beware of the encroachments of prerogative, or the inconveniencies of absolute power, which monarchy in succession was apt to lay claim to, and bring upon them; it was not at all strange, that they should not much trouble themselves to think of methods of restraining any exorbitancies of those to whom they had given the authority over them, and of balancing the power of government, by placing several parts of it in different hands. They had neither felt the oppression of tyrannical dominion, nor did the fashion of the age, nor their possessions, or way of living, (which afforded little matter for covetousness or ambition) give them any reason to apprehend or provide against it; and therefore it is no wonder they put themselves into such a *frame of government*, as was not only, as I said, most obvious and simple, but also best suited to their present state and condition; which stood more in need of defence against foreign invasions and injuries, than of multiplicity of laws. The equality of a

simple poor way of living, confining their desires within the narrow bounds of each man's small property, made few controversies, and so no need of many laws to decide them, or variety of officers to superintend the process, or look after the execution of justice, where there were but few trespasses, and few offenders. Since then those, who liked one another so well as to join into society, cannot but be supposed to have some acquaintance and friendship together, and some trust one in another; they could not but have greater apprehensions of others, than of one another: and therefore their first care and thought cannot but be supposed to be, how to secure themselves against foreign force. It was natural for them to put themselves under a *frame of government* which might best serve to that end, and choose the wisest and bravest man to conduct them in their wars, and lead them out against their enemies, and in this chiefly be their *ruler*.

108.   Thus we see, that the *kings* of the Indians in America, which is still a pattern of the first ages in Asia and Europe, whilst the inhabitants were too few for the country, and want of people and money gave men no temptation to enlarge their possessions of land, or contest for wider extent of ground, are little more than *generals of their armies*; and though they command absolutely in war, yet at home and in time of peace they exercise very little dominion, and have but a very moderate sovereignty; the resolutions of peace and war being ordinarily either in the people, or in a council. Though the war itself, which admits not of plurality of governors, naturally devolves the command into the *king's sole authority*.

109.   And thus, in Israel itself, the *chief business of their judges, and first kings*, seems to have been *to be captains in war*, and leaders of their armies; which (besides what is signified by *going out and in before the people*, which was to march forth to war, and home again at the heads of their forces) appears plainly in the story of Jephthah. The Ammonites making war upon Israel, the Gileadites in fear sent to Jephthah, a bastard of their family whom they had cast off, and article with him, if he will assist them against the Ammonites, to make him their ruler; which they do in these words, "And the people made him head and captain over them," *Judg.* xi. 11. which was, as it

seems, all one as to be judge. "And he judged Israel," *Judg.* xii. 7. that is, was their captain-general, *six years.* So when Jotham upbraids the Shechemites with the obligation they had to Gideon, who had been their judge and ruler, he tells them, "He fought for you, and adventured his life far, and delivered you out of the hands of Midian," *Judg.* ix. 17. Nothing is mentioned of him, but what he did as a *general:* and indeed that is all is found in his history, or in any of the rest of the judges. And Abimelech particularly is called *king,* though at most he was but their *general.* And when, being weary of the ill conduct of Samuel's sons, the children of Israel desired a king, "like all the nations, to judge them, and to go out before them, and to fight their battles," *1 Sam.* viii. 20. God granting their desire, says to Samuel. "I will send thee a man, and thou shalt anoint him to be captain over my people Israel, that he may save my people out of the hands of the Philistines," c. ix. 16. As if the only *business of a king* had been to lead out their armies, and fight in their defence; and accordingly at his inauguration, pouring a vial of oil upon him, declares to Saul, that "the Lord had anointed him to be captain over his inheritance," c. x. 1. And therefore those who, after Saul's being solemnly chosen and saluted *king* by the *tribes* of Mispah, were unwilling to have him their king, made no other objection but this, "How shall this man save us?" v. 27. as if they should have said, this man is unfit to be our *king,* not having skill and conduct enough in war to be able to defend us. And when God resolved to transfer the government to David, it is in these words, "But now thy kingdom shall not continue: the Lord hath sought him a man after his own heart, and the Lord hath commanded him to be captain over his people," c. xiii. 14. As if the whole kingly authority were nothing else but to be their general: and therefore the tribes who had stuck to Saul's family, and opposed David's reign, when they came to Hebron with terms of submission to him, they tell him, amongst other arguments, they had to submit to him as their king, that he was in effect their king in Saul's time, and therefore they had no reason but to receive him as their king now. "Also" (say they,) "in time past, when

Saul was king over us, thou wast he that leddest out, and broughtest in Israel, and the Lord said unto thee, Thou shalt feed my people Israel, and thou shalt be a captain over Israel."

110.   Thus, whether a family by degrees *grew up into a commonwealth*, and the fatherly authority being continued on to the elder son, every one in his turn growing up under it, tacitly submitted to it; and the easiness and equality of it not offending any one, every one acquiesced, till time seemed to have confirmed it, and settled a right of succession by prescription: or whether several families, or the descendants of several families, whom chance, neighbourhood, or business brought together, *uniting into society*, the need of a general, whose conduct might defend them against their enemies in war, and the great confidence the innocence and sincerity of that poor but virtuous age (such as are almost all those which begin governments, that ever come to last in the world), gave men of one another, made the first beginners of commonwealths generally put the rule into one man's hand, without any other express limitation or restraint, but what the nature of the thing and the end of government required: Whichever of those it was that at first put the rule into the hands of a single person, certain it is that no body was entrusted with it but for the public good and safety, and to those ends, in the infancies of commonwealths, those who had it, commonly used it. And unless they had done so, young societies could not have subsisted; without such nursing fathers tender and careful of the public weal, all governments would have sunk under the weakness and infirmities of their infancy, and the prince and the people had soon perished together.

111.   But though the *golden age* (before vain ambition, and *amor sceleratus habendi*, evil concupiscence, had corrupted men's minds into a mistake of true power and honour) had more virtue, and consequently better governors, as well as less vicious subjects; and there was then *no stretching prerogative* on the one side, to oppress the people; nor consequently on the other, any *dispute about privilege*, to lessen or restrain the power of the magistrate; and so no contest betwixt rulers and people about governors or government: yet

when ambition and luxury in future ages[6] would retain and increase the power, without doing the business for which it was given; and, aided by flattery, taught princes to have distinct and separate interests from their people; men found it necessary to examine more carefully the original and rights of government, and to find out ways to *restrain the exorbitancies*, and prevent the abuses of that power, which they having entrusted in another's hands only for their own good, they found was made use of to hurt them.

112.   Thus we may see how probable it is, that people that were naturally free, and by their own consent either submitted to the government of their father, or united together out of different families to make a government, should generally put the *rule into one man's hands*, and choose to be under the conduct of a single person, without so much as by express conditions limiting or regulating his power, which they thought safe enough in his honesty and prudence. Though they never dreamed of monarchy being *jure divino*, which we never heard of among mankind, till it was revealed to us by the divinity of this last age; nor ever allowed paternal power to have a right to dominion, or to be the foundation of all government. And thus much may suffice to shew, that, as far as we have any light from history, we have reason to conclude, that all peaceful beginnings of government have been *laid in the consent of the people*. I say peaceful, because I shall have occasion in another place to speak of conquest, which some esteem a way of beginning of governments.

[6] "At first, when some certain kind of regiment was once approved, it may be nothing was then farther thought upon for the manner of governing, but all permitted unto their wisdom and discretion which were to rule, till by experience they found this for all parts very inconvenient, so as the thing which they had devised for a remedy, did indeed but increase the sore which it should have cured. They saw, that to live by one man's will, became the cause of all men's misery. This constrained them to come unto laws wherein all men might see their duty beforehand, and know the penalties of transgressing them." Hooker's Eccl. Pol. L. I. Sect. 10.

The other objection I find urged against the beginning of polities, in the way I have mentioned, is this, viz.

113.   *That all men being born under government, some or other, it is impossible any of them should ever be free, and at liberty to unite together, and begin a new one, or ever be able to erect a lawful government.*

If this argument be good, I ask, how came so many lawful monarchies into the world? for if any body, upon this supposition, can shew me any one man in any age of the world free to begin a lawful monarchy, I will be bound to shew him ten other *free men* at liberty at the same time to unite and begin a new government under a regal or any other form. It being demonstration, that if any one, *born under the dominion* of another, may be so free as to have a right to command others in a new and distinct empire, every one that is *born under the dominion* of another may be so free too, and may become a ruler, or subject of a distinct separate government. And so by this their own principle, either all men, however born, are free, or else there is but one lawful prince, one lawful government in the world. And then they have nothing to do, but barely to shew us which that is; which when they have done, I doubt not but all mankind will easily agree to pay obedience to him.

114.   Though it be a sufficient answer to their objection, to shew that it involves them in the same difficulties that it doth those they use it against; yet I shall endeavour to discover the weakness of this argument a little farther.

"All men," say they, "are born under government, and therefore they cannot be at liberty to begin a new one. Every one is born a subject to his father, or his prince, and is therefore under the perpetual tie of subjection and allegiance." It is plain mankind never owned nor considered any such natural *subjection that they were born in*, to one or to the other, that tied them, without their own consents, to a subjection to them and their heirs.

115.   For there are no examples so frequent in history, both sacred and profane, as those of men withdrawing themselves, and their obedience from the jurisdiction they were born under, and the family or community they were bred up in, and *setting up*

new governments in other places, from whence sprang all that number of petty commonwealths in the beginning of ages, and which always multiplied as long as there was room enough, till the stronger, or more fortunate, swallowed the weaker; and those great ones again breaking to pieces, dissolved into lesser dominions. All which are so many testimonies against paternal sovereignty, and plainly prove, that it was not the natural right of the father descending to his heirs, that made governments in the beginning, since it was impossible, upon that ground, there should have been so many little kingdoms; all must have been but only one universal monarchy, if men had not been *at liberty to separate themselves* from their families, and the government, be it what it will, that was set up in it, and go and make distinct commonwealths and other governments, as they thought fit.

116.   This has been the practice of the world from its first beginning to this day; nor is it now any more hindrance to the freedom of mankind, that they are *born under constituted and ancient polities*, that have established laws, and set forms of government, than if they were born in the woods, amongst the unconfined inhabitants, that run loose in them. For those who would persuade us, that, *by being born under any government, we are naturally subjects to it*, and have no more any title or pretence to the freedom of the state of nature; have no other reason (bating that of paternal power, which we have already answered) to produce for it, but only, because our fathers or progenitors passed away their natural liberty, and thereby bound up themselves and their posterity to a perpetual subjection to the government which they themselves submitted to. It is true, that whatever engagements or promises any one has made for himself, he is under the obligation of them, but cannot, by any compact whatsoever, bind his children or posterity. For his son, when a man, being altogether as free as the father, any *act of the father can no more give away the liberty of the son*, than it can of any body else: he may indeed annex such conditions to the land he enjoyed as a subject of any commonwealth, as may oblige his son to be of that community, if he will enjoy those possessions which were his father's;

because that estate being his father's property, he may dispose, or settle it, as he pleases.

117.   And this has generally given the occasion to mistake in this matter; because commonwealths not permitting any part of their dominions to be dismembered, nor to be enjoyed by any but those of their community, the son cannot ordinarily enjoy the possessions of his father, but under the same terms his father did, by becoming a member of the society; whereby he puts himself presently under the government he finds there established, as much as any other subject of that commonwealth. And thus *the consent of freemen, born under government, which only makes them members of it*, being given separately in their turns, as each comes to be of age, and not in a multitude together; people take no notice of it, and thinking it not done at all, or not necessary, conclude they are naturally subjects as they are men.

118.   But, it is plain, governments themselves understand it otherwise; they claim *no power over the son, because of that they had over the father*; nor look on children as being their subjects, by their fathers being so. If a subject of England have a child, by an English woman in France, whose subject is he? Not the king of England's; for he must have leave to be admitted to the privileges of it. Nor the king of France's: for how then has his father a liberty to bring him away, and breed him as he pleases? And who ever was judged as a traitor or deserter, if he left, or warred against a country, for being barely born in it of parents that were aliens there? It is plain then, by the practice of governments themselves, as well as by the law of right reasons, that *a child is born a subject of no country or government*. He is under his father's tuition and authority, till he comes to age of discretion; and then he is a freeman, at liberty what government he will put himself under, what body politic he will unite himself to. For if an Englishman's son, born in France, be at liberty, and may do so, it is evident there is no tie upon him by his father's being a subject of this kingdom; nor is he bound up by any compact of his ancestors. And why then hath not his son, by the same reason, the same liberty, though he be born any where else? Since the power that a father

hath naturally over his children is the same, wherever they be born, and the ties of natural obligations are not bounded by the positive limits of kingdoms and commonwealths.

119.   Every man being, as has been shewed, naturally free, and nothing being able to put him into subjection to any earthly power, but only his own consent; it is to be considered, what shall be understood to be a *sufficient declaration* of a man's *consent, to make him subject* to the laws of any government. There is a common distinction of an express and a tacit consent, which will concern our present case. No body doubts but an express consent, of any man entering into any society, makes him a perfect member of that society, a subject of that government. The difficulty is, what ought to be looked upon as a *tacit consent*, and how far it binds, i.e. how far any one shall be looked on to have consented, and thereby submitted to any government, where he has made no expressions of it at all. And to this I say, that every man, that hath any possessions, or enjoyment of any part of the dominions of any government, doth thereby give his *tacit consent*, and is as far forth obliged to obedience to the laws of that government, during such enjoyment, as any one under it; whether this his possession be of land, to him and his heirs for ever, or a lodging only for a week; or whether it be barely travelling freely on the highway: and, in effect, it reaches as far as the very being of any one within the territories of that government.

120.   To understand this the better, it is fit to consider, that every man, when he at first incorporates himself into any commonwealth, he, by his uniting himself thereunto, annexed also, and submits to the community, those possessions which he has, or shall acquire, that do not already belong to any other government. For it would be a direct contradiction, for any one to enter into society with others for the securing and regulating of property, and yet to suppose, his land, whose property is to be regulated by the laws of the society, should be exempt from the jurisdiction of that government, to which he himself, the proprietor of the land, is a subject. By the same act therefore, whereby any one unites his person, which

was before free, to any commonwealth; by the same he unites his possessions, which were before free, to it also: and they become, both of them, person and possession, subject to the government and dominion of that commonwealth, as long as it hath a being. Whoever therefore, from thenceforth, by inheritance, purchase, permission, or otherways, *enjoys any part of the land* so annexed to, and under the government *of that commonwealth, must take it with the condition* it is under; that is, *of submitting to the government of the commonwealth*, under whose jurisdiction it is, as far forth as any subject of it.

121.   But since the government has a direct jurisdiction only over the land, and reaches the possessor of it, (before he has actually incorporated himself in the society) only as he dwells upon, and enjoys that; the obligation any one is under, by virtue of such enjoyment, to *submit to the government, begins and ends with the enjoyment*: so that whenever the owner, who has given nothing but such a tacit consent to the government, will, by donation, sale, or otherwise, quit the said possession, he is at liberty to go and incorporate himself into any other commonwealth; or to agree with others to begin a new one, *in vacuis locis*, in any part of the world they can find free and unpossessed: whereas he, that has once, by actual agreement, and any express declaration, given his *consent* to be of any commonwealth, is perpetually and indispensably obliged to be, and remain unalterably a subject to it, and can never be again in the liberty of the state of nature; unless, by any calamity, the government he was under comes to be dissolved, or else by some public act cuts him off from being any longer a member of it.

122.   But submitting to the laws of any country, living quietly, and enjoying privileges and protection under them, *makes not a man a member of that society*: this is only a local protection and homage due to and from all those, who, not being in a state of war, come within the territories belonging to any government, to all parts whereof the force of its laws extends. But this no more *makes a man a member of that society*, a perpetual subject of that commonwealth, than it would make a man a subject to another, in whose

family he found it convenient to abide for some time, though, whilst he continued in it, he were obliged to comply with the laws, and submit to the government he found there. And thus we see, that foreigners, by living all their lives under another government, and enjoying the privileges and protection of it, though they are bound, even in conscience, to submit to its administration, as far forth as any denison; yet do not thereby come to be *subjects or members of that commonwealth*. Nothing can make any man so, but his actually entering into it by positive engagement, and express promise and compact. This is that, which I think, concerning the beginning of political societies, and that *consent which makes any one a member of any commonwealth*.

CHAPTER IX: Of the Ends of Political Society and Government

123.   If man in the state of nature be so free, as has been said; if he be absolute lord of his own person and possessions, equal to the greatest, and subject to no body, why will he part with his freedom? why will he give up this empire, and subject himself to the dominion and control of any other power? To which it is obvious to answer, that though in the state of nature he hath such a right, yet the enjoyment of it is very uncertain, and constantly exposed to the invasion of others. For all being kings as much as he, every man his equal, and the greater part no strict observers of equity and justice, the enjoyment of the property he has in this state is very unsafe, very unsecure. This makes him willing to quit this condition, which, however free, is full of fears and continual dangers: and it is not without reason, that he seeks out, and is willing to join in society with others, who are already united, or have a mind to unite, for the mutual preservation of their lives, liberties, and estates, which I call by the general name, property.

124.   The great and *chief end*, therefore, of men's uniting into commonwealths, and putting themselves under government, *is the preservation of their property*. To which in the state of nature there are many things wanting.

First, There wants an established, settled, known law, received and allowed by common consent to be the standard of right and wrong, and the common measure to decide all controversies between them. For though the law of nature be plain and intelligible to all rational creatures; yet men being biassed by their interest, as well as ignorant for want of studying it, are not apt to allow of it as a law binding to them in the application of it to their particular cases.

125.   Secondly, In the state of nature there wants *a known and indifferent judge*, with authority to determine all differences according to the established law. For every one in that state being both judge and executioner of the law of nature, men being partial to themselves, passion and revenge is very apt to carry them too far, and with too much heat, in their own cases; as well as negligence, and unconcernedness, to make them too remiss in other men's.

126.   Thirdly, In the state of nature, there often wants power to back and support the sentence when right, and to give it due execution. They who by any injustice offended, will seldom fail, where they are able, by force to make good their injustice; such resistance many times makes the punishment dangerous, and frequently destructive, to those who attempt it.

127.   Thus mankind, notwithstanding all the privileges of the state of nature, being but in an ill condition, while they remain in it, are quickly driven into society. Hence it comes to pass that we seldom find any number of men live any time together in this state. The inconveniencies that they are therein exposed to, by the irregular and uncertain exercise of the power every man has of punishing the transgressions of others, make them take sanctuary under the established laws of government, and therein seek *the preservation of their property*. It is this makes them so willingly give up every one his single power of punishing, to be exercised by such alone, as shall be appointed to it amongst them; and by such rules as the community, or those authorized by them to that purpose, shall agree on. And in this we have the original *right and rise of both the legislative and executive power*, as well as of the governments and societies themselves.

128.   For in the state of nature, to omit the liberty he has of innocent delights, a man has two powers.

The first is to do whatsoever he thinks fit for the preservation of himself and others within the permission of the *law of nature:* by which law, common to them all, he and all the rest of *mankind are one community*, make up one society, distinct from all other creatures. And, were it not for the corruption and viciousness of degenerate men, there would be no need of any other; no necessity that men should separate from this great and natural community, and by positive agreements combine into smaller and divided associations.

The other power a man has in the state of nature, is the *power to punish the crimes* committed against that law. Both these he gives up, when he joins in a private, if I may so call it, or particular politic society, and incorporates into any commonwealth, separate from the rest of mankind.

129.   The first *power, viz. of doing whatsoever he thought fit for the preservation of himself,* and the rest of mankind, *he gives up* to be regulated by laws made by the society, so far forth as the preservation of himself and the rest of that society shall require; which laws of the society in many things confine the liberty he had by the law of nature.

130.   *Secondly,* The *power of punishing he wholly gives up,* and engages his natural force, (which he might before employ in the execution of the law of nature, by his own single authority, as he thought fit) to assist the executive power of the society, as the law thereof shall require. For being now in a new state, wherein he is to enjoy many conveniencies, from the labour, assistance, and society of others in the same community, as well as protection from its whole strength; he is to part also, with as much of his natural liberty, in providing for himself, as the good, prosperity, and safety of the society shall require; which is not only necessary, but just, since the other members of the society do the like.

131.   But though men, when they enter into society, give up the equality, liberty, and executive power they had in the state of nature, into the hands of the society, to be so far disposed of by the legislative, as the good of the society shall require; yet it being only

with an intention in every one the better to preserve himself, his liberty and property; (for no rational creature can be supposed to change his condition with an intention to be worse) the power of the society, or legislative constituted by them, *can never be supposed to extend farther, than the common good;* but is obliged to secure every one's property, by providing against those three defects above mentioned, that made the state of nature so unsafe and uneasy. And so whoever has the legislative or supreme power of any commonwealth, is bound to govern by established standing laws, promulgated and known to the people, and not by extemporary decrees; by indifferent and upright judges, who are to decide controversies by those laws; and to employ the force of the community at home, *only in the execution of such laws*; or abroad to prevent or redress foreign injuries, and secure the community from inroads and invasion. And all this to be directed to no other *end*, but the *peace, safety*, and *public good* of the people.

CHAPTER X: Of the Forms of a Commonwealth

132.   The majority having, as has been shewed, upon men's first uniting into society, the whole power of the community naturally in them, may employ all that power in making laws for the community from time to time, and executing those laws by officers of their own appointing; and then the *form* of the government is a perfect *democracy:* or else may put the power of making laws into the hands of a few select men, and their heirs or successors; and then it is an *oligarchy:* or else into the hands of one man, and then it is a *monarchy:* if to him and his heirs, it is an *hereditary monarchy:* if to him only for life, but upon his death the power only of nominating a successor to return to them; an *elective monarchy.* And so accordingly of these the community may make compounded and mixed forms of government, as they think good. And if the legislative power be at first given by the majority to one or more persons only for their lives, or any limited time, and then the supreme power to revert to them again; when it is so

reverted, the community may dispose of it again anew into what hands they please, and so constitute a new form of government. For the *form of government depending upon the placing* the supreme power, which is the *legislative* (it being impossible to conceive that an inferiour power should prescribe to a superiour, or any but the supreme make laws), according as the power of making laws is placed, such is the *form of the commonwealth*.

133.   By commonwealth, I must be understood all along to mean, not a democracy, or any form of government, but *any independent community*, which the Latins signified by the word *civitas*; to which the word which best answers in our language, is *commonwealth*, and most properly expresses such a society of men, which community or city in English does not. For there may be subordinate communities in government; and city amongst us has quite a different notion from commonwealth: and therefore, to avoid ambiguity, I crave leave to use the word *commonwealth* in that sense, in which I find it used by King *James the first*: and I take it to be its genuine signification; which if any body dislike, I consent with him to change it for a better.

CHAPTER XI: Of the Extent of the Legislative Power

134.   The great end of men's entering into society being the enjoyment of their properties in peace and safety, and the great instrument and means of that being the laws established in that society; the *first and fundamental positive law* of all commonwealths *is the establishing of the legislative* power; as the *first and fundamental natural law*, which is to govern even the legislative itself, *is the preservation of the society*, and (as far as will consist with the public good) of every person in it. This *legislative* is not only *the supreme power* of the commonwealth, but sacred and unalterable in the hands where the community have once placed it; nor can any edict of any body else, in what form soever conceived, or by what power soever backed, have the force and obligation of a law, which has not its *sanction from* that *legislative* which

the public has chosen and appointed; for without this the law could not have that, which is absolutely necessary to its being a *law*,[7] the consent of the society; over whom no body can have a power to make laws, but by their own consent, and by authority received from them; and therefore all the obedience, which by the most solemn ties any one can be obliged to pay, ultimately terminates in this supreme power, and is directed by those laws which it enacts; nor can any oaths to any foreign power whatsoever, or any domestic subordinate power, discharge any member of the society from his *obedience to the legislative*, acting pursuant to their trust; nor oblige him to any obedience contrary to the laws so enacted, or farther than they do allow; it being ridiculous to imagine one can be tied ultimately to obey any power in the society, which is not the supreme.

135.   Though the legislative, whether placed in one or more, whether it be always in being, or only by intervals, though it be the supreme power in every commonwealth; yet,

First, It is *not*, nor can possibly be absolutely *arbitrary* over the lives and fortunes of the people. For it being but the joint power of every member of the society given up to that person, or assembly, which is legislator, it can be no more than those persons had in a state of nature before they entered into

---

[7] "The lawful power of making laws to command whole politic societies of men, belonging so properly unto the same entire societies, that for any prince or potentate of what kind soever upon earth, to exercise the same of himself, and not by express commission immediately and personally received from God, or else by authority derived at the first from their consent, upon whose persons they impose laws, it is no better than mere tyranny. Laws they are not therefore which public approbation hath not made so." Hooker's Eccl. Pol. L. I. Sect. 10. "Of this point therefore we are to note, that sith men naturally have no full and perfect power to command whole politic multitudes of men, therefore utterly without our consent, we could in such sort be at no man's commandment living. And to be commanded we do consent when that society, whereof we be a part, hath at any time before consented, without revoking the same after by the like universal agreement.

  Laws therefore human, of what kind so ever, are available by consent." Ibid.

society, and gave up to the community. For no body can transfer to another more power than he has in himself; and no body has an absolute arbitrary power over himself, or over any other, to destroy his own life, or take away the life or property of another. A man, as has been proved, cannot subject himself to the arbitrary power of another; and having in the state of nature no arbitrary power over the life, liberty, or possession of another, but only so much as the law of nature gave him for the preservation of himself and the rest of mankind; this is all he doth, or can give up to the commonwealth, and by it to the legislative power, so that the legislative can have no more than this. Their power, in the utmost bounds of it, is *limited to the public good* of the society. It is a power, that hath no other end but preservation, and therefore can never[8] have a right to destroy, enslave, or designedly to impoverish the subjects. The obligations of the law of nature cease not in society, but only in many cases are drawn closer, and have by human laws known penalties annexed to them, to enforce their observation. Thus the law of nature stands as an eternal rule to all men, legislators as well as others. The rules that they make for other men's actions, must, as well as their own and other men's actions, be conformable to the law of nature, i.e. to the will of God, of which that is a declaration; and the *fundamental law of nature being the preservation of mankind*, no human sanction can be good or valid against it.

136.   Secondly,[9] The legislative or supreme authority cannot assume to itself a power to rule, by extemporary, arbitrary decrees, but *is bound to dispense justice*, and decide the rights of the subject, *by promulgated, standing laws, and known authorised judges*. For the law of nature being unwritten, and so no-where to be found, but in the minds of men; they who through passion, or interest, shall miscite, or misapply it, cannot so easily be convinced of their mistake, where there is no established judge: and so it serves not, as it ought, to determine the rights, and fence the properties of those that live under it; especially where every one is judge, interpreter, and executioner of it too, and that in his own case: and he that has right on his side, having ordinarily but his own single strength, hath not force enough to defend himself from injuries, or to punish delinquents. To avoid these inconveniencies, which disorder men's properties in the state of nature, men unite into societies, that they may have the united strength of the whole society to secure and defend their properties, and may have standing rules to bound it, by which every one may know what is his. To this end it is that men give up all their natural power to the society which they enter into, and the community put the legislative power into such hands as they think fit: with this trust, that they shall be governed by *declared laws*, or else their peace, quiet, and property will still be at the same uncertainty, as it was in the state of nature.

137.   Absolute arbitrary power, or governing without *settled standing laws*, can neither of them consist with the ends of society and government, which men

---

[8] "Two foundations there are which bear up public societies, the one a natural inclination, whereby all men desire sociable life and fellowship; the other an order, expressly or secretly agreed upon, touching the manner of their union in living together: the latter is that which we call the law of a commonweal, the very soul of a politic body, the parts whereof are by law animated, held together, and set on work in such actions as the common good requireth. Laws politic, ordained for external order and regiment amongst men, are never framed as they should be, unless presuming the will of man to be inwardly obstinate, rebellious, and averse from all obedience to the sacred laws of his nature; in a word, unless presuming man to be, in regard of his depraved mind, little better than a wild beast, they do accordingly provide notwithstanding, so to frame his outward actions, that they be no hindrance unto the common good, for which societies are instituted. Unless they do this, they are not perfect." Hooker's Eccl. Pol. L. I. Sect. 10.

[9] "Human laws are measures in respect of men whose actions they must direct, howbeit such measures they are as have also their higher rules to be measured by, which rules are two, the law of God, and the law of nature; so that laws human must be made according to the general laws of nature, and without contradiction to any positive law of scripture, otherwise they are ill made." Hooker's Eccl. Pol. L. 3. Sect. 9.

"To constrain men to any thing inconvenient doth seem unreasonable." Ibid. L. I. Sect. 10.

would not quit the freedom of the state of nature for, and tie themselves up under, were it not to preserve their lives, liberties, and fortunes, and by *stated rules* of right and property to secure their peace and quiet. It cannot be supposed that they should intend, had they a power so to do, to give to any one, or more, an *absolute arbitrary power* over their persons and estates, and put a force into the magistrate's hand to execute his unlimited will arbitrarily upon them. This were to put themselves into a worse condition than the state of nature, wherein they had a liberty to defend their right against the injuries of others, and were upon equal terms of force to maintain it, whether invaded by a single man, or many in combination. Whereas by supposing they have given up themselves to the absolute arbitrary power and will of a legislator, they have disarmed themselves, and armed him, to make a prey of them when he pleases. He being in a much worse condition, who is exposed to the arbitrary power of one man, who has the command of 100,000, than he that is exposed to the arbitrary power of 100,000 single men; no body being secure, that his will, who has such a command, is better than that of other men, though his force be 100,000 times stronger. And therefore, whatever form the commonwealth is under, the ruling power ought to govern by declared and received laws, and not by extemporary dictates and undetermined resolutions. For then mankind will be in a far worse condition than in the state of nature, if they shall have armed one or a few men with the joint power of a multitude, to force them to obey at pleasure the exorbitant and unlimited decrees of their sudden thoughts, or unrestrained, and till that moment unknown wills, without having any measures set down which may guide and justify their actions; for all the power the government has, being only for the good of the society, as it ought not to be arbitrary and at pleasure, so it ought to be exercised by *established and promulgated laws*; that both the people may know their duty, and be safe and secure within the limits of the law, and the rulers too kept within their bounds, and not to be tempted, by the power they have in their hands, to employ it to such purposes, and by such measures, as they would not have known, and own not willingly.

138.   *Thirdly,* The *supreme power cannot take* from any man part of his property without his own consent. For the preservation of property being the end of government, and that for which men enter into society, it necessarily supposes and requires, that the people should *have property*, without which they must be supposed to lose that, by entering into society, which was the end for which they entered into it; too gross an absurdity for any man to own. *Men* therefore *in society having property*, they have such right to the goods, which by the law of the community are theirs, that no body hath a right to take their substance or any part of it from them, without their own consent; without this they have no property at all. For I have truly no property in that, which another can by right take from me, when he pleases, against my consent. Hence it is a mistake to think, that the *supreme or legislative power* of any commonwealth can do what it will, and dispose of the estates of the subject arbitrarily, or take any part of them at pleasure. This is not much to be feared in governments where the legislative consists, wholly or in part, in assemblies which are variable, whose members, upon the dissolution of the assembly, are subjects under the common laws of their country, equally with the rest. But in governments, where the legislative is in one lasting assembly always in being, or in one man, as in absolute monarchies, there is danger still, that they will think themselves to have a distinct interest from the rest of the community; and so will be apt to increase their own riches and power by taking what they think fit from the people. For a man's property is not at all secure, though there be good and equitable laws to set the bounds of it between him and his fellow subjects, if he who commands those subjects, have power to take from any private man, what part he pleases of his property, and use and dispose of it as he thinks good.

139.   But government, into whatsoever hands it is put, being, as I have before shewed, intrusted with this condition, and *for this end*, that men might have and secure their properties; the prince, or senate, however it may have power to make laws, for the regulating of property between the subjects one amongst another, yet can never have a power to take

to themselves the whole, or any part of the subject's property, without their own consent. For this would be in effect to leave them no property at all. And to let us see, that even absolute power where it is necessary, is not arbitrary by being absolute, but is still limited by that reason, and confined to those ends, which required it in some cases to be absolute, we need look no farther than the common practice of martial discipline. For the preservation of the army, and in it of the whole commonwealth, requires an absolute obedience to the command of every superiour officer, and it is justly death to disobey or dispute the most dangerous or unreasonable of them; but yet we see, that neither the serjeant, that could command a soldier to march up to the mouth of a cannon, or stand in a breach, where he is almost sure to perish, can command that soldier to give him one penny of his money; nor the general, that can condemn him to death for deserting his post, or for not obeying the most desperate orders, can yet, with all his absolute power of life and death, dispose of one farthing of that soldier's estate, or seize one jot of his goods; whom yet he can command any thing, and hang for the least disobedience: because such a blind obedience is necessary to that end, for which the commander has his power, viz. the preservation of the rest; but the disposing of his goods has nothing to do with it.

140.   It is true, governments cannot be supported without great charge, and it is fit every one who enjoys his share of the protection, should pay out of his estate his proportion for the maintenance of it. But still it must be with his own consent, i.e. the consent of the majority, giving it either by themselves, or their representatives chosen by them. For if any one shall claim a *power to lay* and levy *taxes* on the people, by his own authority, and without such consent of the people, he thereby invades the *fundamental law of property*, and subverts the end of government. For what property have I in that, which another may by right take when he pleases, to himself?

141.   *Fourthly,* The *legislative cannot transfer the power of making laws* to any other hands. For it being but a delegated power from the people, they who have it cannot pass it over to others. The people alone can appoint the form of the commonwealth, which is by constituting the legislative, and appointing in whose hands that shall be. And when the people have said, we will submit to rules, and be governed by laws made by such men, and in such forms, no body else can say other men shall make laws for them; nor can the people be bound by any laws, but such as are enacted by those whom they have chosen, and authorized to make laws for them. The power of the legislative being derived from the people by a positive voluntary grant and institution, can be no other than what that positive grant conveyed, which being only to make laws, and not to make legislators, the legislative can have no power to transfer their authority of making laws and place it in other hands.

142.   These are the bounds which the trust, that is put in them by the society and the law of God and nature, have *set to the legislative* power of every commonwealth, in all forms of government.

First, They are to govern by *promulgated established laws*, not to be varied in particular cases, but to have one rule for rich and poor, for the favourite at court, and the countryman at plough.

Secondly, These laws also ought to be designed for no other end ultimately, but *the good of the people*.

Thirdly, They must *not raise taxes* on the *property of the people, without the consent of the people*, given by themselves or their deputies. And this properly concerns only such governments where the legislative is always in being, or at least where the people have not reserved any part of the legislative to deputies, to be from time to time chosen by themselves.

Fourthly, The legislative neither must *nor can transfer the power of making laws* to any body else, or place it any where, but where the people have.

CHAPTER XII: Of the Legislative, Executive, and Federative Power of the Commonwealth

143.   The legislative power is that, which has a right *to direct how the force of the commonwealth* shall be employed for preserving the community and the members of it. But because those laws which are

constantly to be executed, and whose force is always to continue, may be made in a little time; therefore there is no need, that the legislative should be always in being, not having always business to do. And because it may be too great a temptation to human frailty, apt to grasp at power, for the same persons, who have the power of making laws, to have also in their hands the power to execute them, whereby they may exempt themselves from obedience to the laws they make, and suit the law, both in its making and execution, to their own private advantage, and thereby come to have a distinct interest from the rest of the community, contrary to the end of society and government: therefore in well ordered commonwealths, where the good of the whole is so considered, as it ought, the legislative power is put into the hands of divers persons, who, duly assembled, have by themselves, or jointly with others, a power to make laws; which when they have done, being separated again, they are themselves subject to the laws they have made; which is a new and near tie upon them, to take care that they make them for the public good.

144.   But because the laws, that are at once, and in a short time made, have a constant and lasting force, and need a *perpetual execution*, or an attendance thereunto: therefore it is necessary there should be a *power always in being*, which should see to the execution of the laws that are made, and remain in force. And thus the legislative and executive power come often to be separated.

145.   There is another power in every commonwealth, which one may call *natural*, because it is that which answers to the power every man naturally had before he entered into society. For though in a commonwealth, the members of it are distinct persons still in reference to one another, and as such are governed by the laws of the society; yet in reference to the rest of mankind, they make one body, which is, as every member of it before was, still in the state of nature with the rest of mankind. Hence it is, that the controversies that happen between any man of the society with those that are out of it, are managed by the public; and an injury done to a member of their body engages the whole in the reparation of it.

So that, under this consideration, the whole community is one body in the state of nature, in respect of all other states or persons out of its community.

146.   This therefore contains the power of war and peace, leagues and alliances, and all the transactions, with all persons and communities without the commonwealth; and may be called federative, if any one pleases. So the thing be understood, I am indifferent as to the name.

147.   These two powers, executive and federative, though they be really distinct in themselves, yet one comprehending the execution of the municipal laws of the society within itself, upon all that are parts of it; the other the management of the *security and interest of the public without*, with all those that it may receive benefit or damage from; yet they are always almost united. And though this *federative power* in the well or ill management of it be of great moment to the commonwealth, yet it is much less capable to be directed by antecedent, standing, positive laws, than the executive; and so must necessarily be left to the prudence and wisdom of those whose hands it is in, to be managed for the public good. For the laws that concern subjects one amongst another, being to direct their actions, may well enough precede them. But what is to be done in reference to foreigners, depending much upon their actions, and the variation of designs, and interests, must be left in great part to the prudence of those who have this power committed to them, to be managed by the best of their skill, for the advantage of the commonwealth.

148.   Though, as I said, the executive and federative power of every community be really distinct in themselves, yet they are hardly to be separated, and placed at the same time in the hands of distinct persons. For both of them requiring the force of the society for their exercise, it is almost impracticable to place the force of the commonwealth in distinct, and not subordinate hands; or that the executive and federative power should be placed in persons that might act separately, whereby the force of the public would be under different commands: which would be apt some time or other to cause disorder and ruin.

CHAPTER XIII: Of the Subordination of the Powers of the Commonwealth

149. Though in a constituted commonwealth, standing upon its own basis, and acting according to its own nature, that is, acting for the preservation of the community, there can be but *one supreme power*, which is the *legislative*, to which all the rest are and must be subordinate; yet the legislative being only a fiduciary power to act for certain ends, there remains still *in the people a supreme power to remove or alter the legislative*, when they find the legislative act contrary to the trust reposed in them. For all *power given with trust* for the attaining an end, being limited by that end; whenever that end is manifestly neglected or opposed, the trust must necessarily be forfeited, and the power devolve into the hands of those that gave it, who may place it anew where they shall think best for their safety and security. And thus the *community* perpetually *retains a supreme power* of saving themselves from the attempts and designs of any body, even of their legislators, whenever they shall be so foolish, or so wicked, as to lay and carry on designs against the liberties and properties of the subject. For no man, or society of men, having a power to deliver up their preservation, or consequently the means of it, to the absolute will and arbitrary dominion of another; whenever any one shall go about to bring them into such a slavish condition, they will always have a right to preserve what they have not a power to part with; and to rid themselves of those who invade this fundamental, sacred, and unalterable law of self-preservation, for which they entered into society. And thus the community may be said in this respect to be *always the supreme power*, but not as considered under any form of government, because this power of the people can never take place till the government be dissolved.

150. In all cases, whilst the government subsists, the *legislative is the supreme power*. For what can give laws to another, must needs be superiour to him; and since the legislative is no otherwise legislative of the society, but by the right it has to make laws for all the parts, and for every member of the society, prescribing rules to their actions, and giving power of execution, where they are transgressed; the legislative must needs be the supreme, and all other powers, in any members or parts of the society, derived from and subordinate to it.

151. In some commonwealths, where the legislative is not always in being, and the executive is vested in a single person, who has also a share in the legislative; there that single person in a very tolerable sense may also be called supreme; not that he has in himself all the supreme power, which is that of law-making; but because he has in him the supreme execution, from whom all inferiour magistrates derive all their several subordinate powers, or at least the greatest part of them: having also no legislative superiour to him, there being no law to be made without his consent, which cannot be expected should ever subject him to the other part of the legislative, he is properly enough in this sense *supreme*. But yet it is to be observed, that though *oaths of allegiance* and fealty are taken to him, it is not to him as supreme legislator, but as *supreme executor* of the law, made by a joint power of him with others: allegiance being nothing but an *obedience according to law*, which when he violates, he has no right to obedience, nor can claim it otherwise, than as the public person invested with the power of the law; and so is to be considered as the image, phantom, or representative of the commonwealth, acted by the will of the society, declared in its laws; and thus he has no will, no power, but that of the law. But when he quits this representation, this public will, and acts by his own private will, he degrades himself, and is but a single private person without power, and without will, that has no right to obedience; the members owing no obedience but to the public will of the society.

152. The *executive power*, placed any where but in a person that has also a share in the legislative, is visibly subordinate and accountable to it, and may be at pleasure changed and displaced; so that it is not the *supreme executive power* that is exempt from subordination, but the *supreme executive power* vested in one, who having a share in the legislative, has no distinct superiour legislative to be subordinate and

accountable to, farther than he himself shall join and consent; so that he is no more subordinate than he himself shall think fit, which one may certainly conclude will be but very little. Of other ministerial and subordinate powers in a commonwealth, we need not speak, they being so multiplied with infinite variety in the different customs and constitutions of distinct commonwealths, that it is impossible to give a particular account of them all. Only thus much, which is necessary to our present purpose, we may take notice of concerning them, that they have no manner of authority, any of them, beyond what is by positive grant and commission delegated to them, and are all of them accountable to some other power in the commonwealth.

153.   It is not necessary, no, nor so much as convenient, that the *legislative* should be *always in being*. But absolutely necessary that the executive power should; because there is not always need of new laws to be made, but always need of execution of the laws that are made. When the legislative hath put the execution of the laws they make into other hands, they have a power still to resume it out of those hands, when they find cause, and to punish for any maladministration against the laws. The same holds also in regard of the federative power, that and the executive being both *ministerial and subordinate to the legislative*, which, as has been shewed, in a constituted commonwealth is the supreme. The legislative also in this case being supposed to consist of several persons, (for if it be a single person, it cannot but be always in being, and so will, as supreme, naturally have the supreme executive power, together with the legislative) may *assemble, and exercise their legislature*, at the times that either their original constitution, or their own adjournment, appoints, or when they please; if neither of these hath appointed any time, or there be no other way prescribed to convoke them. For the supreme power being placed in them by the people, it is always in them, and they may exercise it when they please, unless by their original constitution they are limited to certain seasons, or by an act of their supreme power they have adjourned to a certain time; and when that time comes, they have a right to assemble and act again.

154.   If the legislative, or any part of it, be made up of representatives chosen for that time by the people, which afterwards return into the ordinary state of subjects, and have no share in the legislature but upon a new choice, this power of choosing must also be exercised by the people, either at certain appointed seasons, or else when they are summoned to it; and in this latter case the power of convoking the legislative is ordinarily placed in the executive, and has one of these two limitations in respect of time: that either the original constitution requires their assembling and acting at certain intervals, and then the executive power does nothing but ministerially issue directions for their electing and assembling according to due forms; or else it is left to his prudence to call them by new elections, when the occasions, or exigencies of the public require the amendment of old, or making of new laws, or the redress or prevention of any inconveniencies, that lie on, or threaten the people.

155.   It may be demanded here, What if the executive power, being possessed of the force of the commonwealth, shall make use of that force to hinder the *meeting* and *acting of the legislative*; when the original constitution, or the public exigencies require it? I say, using force upon the people without authority, and contrary to the trust put in him that does so, is a state of war with the people, who have a right to *reinstate* their *legislative in the exercise* of their power. For having erected a legislative, with an intent they should exercise the power of making laws, either at certain set times, or when there is need of it; when they are hindered by any force from what is so necessary to the society, and wherein the safety and preservation of the people consists, the people have a right to remove it by force. In all states and conditions, the true remedy of force without authority, is to oppose force to it. The use of force without authority, always puts him that uses it into a *state of war*, as the aggressor; and renders him liable to be treated accordingly.

156.   The *power of assembling and dismissing the legislative*, placed in the executive, gives not the executive a superiority over it, but is a fiduciary trust placed in him for the safety of the people, in a case where the uncertainty and variableness of human affairs could not bear a steady fixed rule. For it not

being possible that the first framers of the government should, by any foresight, be so much masters of future events as to be able to prefix so just periods of return and duration to the *assemblies of the legislative*, in all times to come, that might exactly answer all the exigencies of the commonwealth; the best remedy could be found for this defect was to trust this to the prudence of one who was always to be present, and whose business it was to watch over the public good. Constant *frequent meetings of the legislative*, and long continuations of their assemblies, without necessary occasion, could not but be burdensome to the people, and must necessarily in time produce more dangerous inconveniencies, and yet the quick turn of affairs might be sometimes such as to need their present help: any delay of their convening might endanger the public; and sometimes too their business might be so great, that the limited time of their sitting might be too short for their work, and rob the public of that benefit which could be had only from their mature deliberation. What then could be done in this case to prevent the community from being exposed some time or other to eminent hazard, on one side or the other, by fixed intervals and periods, set to the *meeting and acting of the legislative*; but to intrust it to the prudence of some, who being present, and acquainted with the state of public affairs, might make use of this prerogative for the public good? And where else could this be so well placed as in his hands, who was intrusted with the execution of the laws for the same end? Thus supposing the regulation of times for the *assembling and sitting of the legislative* not settled by the original constitution, it naturally fell into the hands of the executive, not as an arbitrary power depending on his good pleasure, but with this trust always to have it exercised only for the public weal, as the occurrences of times and change of affairs might require. Whether *settled periods of their convening*, or *a liberty* left to the prince for *convoking the legislative*, or perhaps a mixture of both, hath the least inconvenience attending it, it is not my business here to inquire; but only to shew, that though the executive power may have the prerogative of *convoking* and *dissolving* such *conventions of the legislative*, yet it is not thereby superiour to it.

157. Things of this world are in so constant a flux, that nothing remains long in the same state. Thus people, riches, trade, power, change their stations, flourishing mighty cities come to ruin, and prove in time neglected desolate corners, whilst other unfrequented places grow into populous countries, filled with wealth and inhabitants. But things not always changing equally, and private interest often keeping up customs and privileges, when the reasons of them are ceased; it often comes to pass, that in governments, where part of the legislative consists of representatives chosen by the people, that in tract of time this representation becomes very unequal and disproportionate to the reasons it was at first established upon. To what gross absurdities the following of custom, when reason has left it, may lead, we may be satisfied, when we see the bare name of a town, of which there remains not so much as the ruins, where scarce so much housing as a sheepcote, or more inhabitants than a shepherd is to be found, sends *as many representatives* to the grand assembly of law-makers, as a whole county numerous in people, and powerful in riches. This strangers stand amazed at, and every one must confess needs a remedy. Though most think it hard to find one; because the constitution of the legislative being the original and supreme act of the society, antecedent to all positive laws in it, and depending wholly on the people, no inferiour power can alter it. And therefore the people, when the legislative is once constituted, having, in such a government as we have been speaking of, no power to act as long as the government stands; this inconvenience is thought incapable of a remedy.

158. *Salus populi suprema lex*, is certainly so just and fundamental a rule, that he, who sincerely follows it, cannot dangerously err. If therefore the executive, who has the power of convoking the legislative, observing rather the true proportion than fashion of representation, regulates not by old custom, but true reason, the *number of members* in all places that have a right to be distinctly represented, which no part of the people, however incorporated, can pretend to, but in proportion to the assistance which it affords to the public; it cannot be judged to have set up a new legislative, but to have restored the old and true

one, and to have rectified the disorders which succession of time had insensibly, as well as inevitably introduced. For it being the interest as well as intention of the people, to have a fair and equal representative; whoever brings it nearest to that, is an undoubted friend to, and establisher of the government, and cannot miss the consent and approbation of the community. Prerogative being nothing but a power in the hands of the prince to provide for the public good, in such cases, which depending upon unforeseen and uncertain occurrences, certain and unalterable laws could not safely direct; whatsoever shall be done manifestly for the good of the people, and the establishing the government upon its true foundations, is, and always will be, just *prerogative*. The power of erecting new corporations, and therewith *new representatives*, carries with it a supposition that in time the *measures of representation* might vary, and those places have a just right to be represented which before had none; and by the same reason, those cease to have a right, and be too inconsiderable for such a privilege, which before had it. It is not a change from the present state, which perhaps corruption or decay has introduced, that makes an inroad upon the government; but the tendency of it to injure or oppress the people, and to set up one part or party, with a distinction from, and an unequal subjection of the rest. Whatsoever cannot but be acknowledged to be of advantage to the society, and people in general, upon just and lasting measures, will always, when done, justify itself; and whenever the people shall choose their *representatives upon* just and undeniably *equal measures*, suitable to the original frame of the government, it cannot be doubted to be the will and act of the society, whoever permitted or caused them so to do.

CHAPTER XIV: Of Prerogative

159.   Where the legislative and executive power are in distinct hands, (as they are in all moderated monarchies and well-framed governments) there the good of the society requires, that several things should be left to the discretion of him that has the executive power. For the legislators not being able to foresee, and provide by laws, for all that may be useful to the

community, the executor of the laws having the power in his hands, has by the common law of nature a right to make use of it for the good of the society, in many cases, where the municipal law has given no direction, till the legislative can conveniently be assembled to provide for it. Many things there are, which the law can by no means provide for; and those must necessarily be left to the discretion of him that has the executive power in his hands, to be ordered by him as the public good and advantage shall require: nay, it is fit that the laws themselves should in some cases give way to the executive power, or rather to this fundamental law of nature and government, viz. That, as much as may be, all the members of the society are to be preserved. For since many accidents may happen, wherein a strict and rigid observation of the laws may do harm; (as not to pull down an innocent man's house to stop the fire, when the next to it is burning) and a man may come sometimes within the reach of the law, which makes no distinction of persons, by an action that may deserve reward and pardon; it is fit the ruler should have a power, in many cases, to mitigate the severity of the law, and pardon some offenders. For the *end of government* being the *preservation of all*, as much as may be, even the guilty are to be spared, where it can prove no prejudice to the innocent.

160.   This power to act according to discretion, for the public good, without the prescription of the law, and sometimes even against it, is that which is called *prerogative*. For since in some governments the lawmaking power is not always in being, and is usually too numerous, and so too slow for the dispatch requisite to execution; and because also it is impossible to foresee, and so by laws to provide for all accidents and necessities that may concern the public, or to make such laws as will do no harm, if they are executed with an inflexible rigour on all occasions, and upon all persons that may come in their way; therefore there is a latitude left to the executive power, to do many things of choice which the laws do not prescribe.

161.   This power, whilst employed for the benefit of the community, and suitably to the trust and ends of the government, *is undoubted prerogative*, and

never is questioned. For the people are very seldom or never scrupulous or nice in the point; they are far from examining prerogative, whilst it is in any tolerable degree employed for the use it was meant; that is, for the good of the people, and not manifestly against it. But if there comes to be a *question* between the executive power and the people, about a thing claimed as a *prerogative*, the tendency of the exercise of such prerogative to the good or hurt of the people will easily decide that question.

162.   It is easy to conceive, that in the infancy of governments, when commonwealths differed little from families in number of people, they differed from them too but little in number of laws: and the governors being as the fathers of them, watching over them, for their good, the government was almost all prerogative. A few established laws served the turn, and the discretion and care of the ruler supplied the rest. But when mistake or flattery prevailed with weak princes to make use of this power for private ends of their own, and not for the public good, the people were fain by express laws to get prerogative determined in those points wherein they found disadvantage from it: and thus declared *limitations of prerogative* were by the people found necessary in cases which they and their ancestors had left, in the utmost latitude, to the wisdom of those princes who made no other but a right use of it; that is, for the good of their people.

163.   And therefore they have a very wrong notion of government, who say, that the people have *encroached upon the prerogative*, when they have got any part of it to be defined by positive laws. For in so doing they have not pulled from the prince any thing that of right belonged to him, but only declared, that that power which they indefinitely left in his or his ancestors hands, to be exercised for their good, was not a thing which they intended him when he used it otherwise. For the end of government being the good of the community, whatsoever alterations are made in it, tending to that end, cannot be an encroachment upon any body, since no body in government can have a right tending to any other end: and those only are encroachments which prejudice or hinder the public good. Those who say otherwise, speak as if the prince had a distinct and separate interest from the good of the community, and was not made for it; the root and source from which spring almost all those evils and disorders which happen in kingly governments. And indeed, if that be so, the people under his government are not a society of rational creatures, entered into a community for their mutual good; they are not such as have set rulers over themselves, to guard and promote that good; but are to be looked on as an herd of inferior creatures under the dominion of a master, who keeps them and works them for his own pleasure or profit. If men were so void of reason, and brutish, as to enter into society upon such terms, prerogative might indeed be, what some men would have it, an arbitrary power to do things hurtful to the people.

164.   But since a rational creature cannot be supposed, when free, to put himself into subjection to another, for his own harm; (though, where he finds a good and wise ruler, he may not perhaps think it either necessary or useful to set precise bounds to his power in all things) prerogative can be nothing but the people's permitting their rulers to do several things, of their own free choice, where the law was silent, and sometimes too against the direct letter of the law, for the public good; and their acquiescing in it when so done. For as a good prince, who is mindful of the trust put into his hands, and careful of the good of his people, cannot have too much prerogative, that is, power to do good; so a weak and ill prince, who would claim that power which his predecessors exercised without the direction of the law, as a prerogative belonging to him by right of his office, which he may exercise at his pleasure, to make or promote an interest distinct from that of the public, gives the people an occasion to claim their right, and limit that power, which, whilst it was exercised for their good, they were content should be tacitly allowed.

165.   And therefore he that will look into the *history of England*, will find, that prerogative was always *largest* in the hands of our wisest and best princes; because the people, observing the whole tendency of their actions to be the public good, contested not what was done without law to that end: or, if any human frailty or mistake (for princes are but men, made as others) appeared in some small declinations

from that end; yet it was visible, the main of their conduct tended to nothing but the care of the public. The people therefore, finding reason to be satisfied with these princes, whenever they acted without, or contrary to the letter of the law, acquiesced in what they did, and without the least complaint, let them enlarge their prerogative as they pleased; judging rightly, that they did nothing herein to the prejudice of their laws, since they acted conformably to the foundation and end of all laws, the public good.

166.   Such God-like princes indeed had some title to arbitrary power by that argument, that would prove absolute monarchy the best government, as that which God himself governs the universe by; because such kings partook of his wisdom and goodness. Upon this is founded that saying, That the reigns of good princes have been always most dangerous to the liberties of their people. For when their successors, managing the government with different thoughts, would draw the actions of those good rulers into precedent, and make them the standard of their prerogative, as if what had been done only for the good of the people was a right in them to do, for the harm of the people, if they so pleased; it has often occasioned contest, and sometimes public disorders, before the people could recover their original right, and get that to be declared not to be prerogative, which truly was never so: since it is impossible that any body in the society should ever have a right to do the people harm; though it be very possible, and reasonable, that the people should not go about to set any bounds to the prerogative of those kings, or rulers, who themselves transgressed not the bounds of the public good. For *prerogative is nothing but the power of doing public good without a rule.*

167.   The power of calling parliaments in England, as to precise time, place, and duration, is certainly a prerogative of the king, but still with this trust, that it shall be made use of for the good of the nation, as the exigencies of the times, and variety of occasions, shall require. For it being impossible to foresee which should always be the fittest place for them to assemble in, and what the best season, the choice of these was left with the executive power, as might be most subservient to the public good, and best suit the ends of parliaments.

168.   The old question will be asked in this matter of prerogative, "But who shall be judge when this power is made a right use of?" I answer: between an executive power in being, with such a prerogative, and a legislative that depends upon his will for their convening, there can be no *judge on earth*; as there can be none between the legislative and the people, should either the executive or the legislative, when they have got the power in their hands, design, or go about to enslave or destroy them. The people have no other remedy in this, as in all other cases where they have no judge on earth, but to *appeal to heaven*. For the rulers, in such attempts, exercising a power the people never put into their hands, (who can never be supposed to consent that any body should rule over them for their harm) do that which they have not a right to do. And where the body of the people, or any single man, is deprived of their right, or is under the exercise of a power without right, and have no appeal on earth, then they have a liberty to appeal to heaven, whenever they judge the cause of sufficient moment. And therefore, *though the people cannot be judge,* so as to have, by the constitution of that society, any superior power to determine and give effective sentence in the case; yet they have, by a law antecedent and paramount to all positive laws of men, reserved that ultimate determination to themselves which belongs to all mankind, where there lies no appeal on earth, viz. to judge, whether they have just cause to make their appeal to heaven. And this judgment they cannot part with, it being out of a man's power so to submit himself to another, as to give him a liberty to destroy him; God and nature never allowing a man so to abandon himself, as to neglect his own preservation: and since he cannot take away his own life, neither can he give another power to take it. Nor let any one think, this lays a perpetual foundation for disorder; for this operates not, till the inconveniency is so great, that the majority feel it, and are weary of it, and find a necessity to have it amended. But this the executive power, or wise princes, never

need come in the danger of: and it is the thing, of all others, they have most need to avoid, as of all others the most perilous.

CHAPTER XV: Of Paternal, Political, and Despotical Power, Considered Together

169.   Though I have had occasion to speak of these separately before, yet the great mistakes of late about government having, as I suppose, arisen from confounding these distinct powers one with another, it may not, perhaps, be amiss to consider them here together.

170.   *First*, then, *Paternal* or *parental power* is nothing but that which parents have over their children, to govern them for the children's good, till they come to the use of reason, or a state of knowledge, wherein they may be supposed capable to understand that rule, whether it be the law of nature, or the municipal law of their country, they are to govern themselves by: capable, I say, to know it, as well as several others, who live as freemen under that law. The affection and tenderness which God hath planted in the breast of parents towards their children, makes it evident that this is not intended to be a severe arbitrary government, but only for the help, instruction, and preservation of their offspring. But happen it as it will, there is, as I have proved, no reason why it should be thought to extend to life and death, at any time, over their children, more than over any body else; neither can there be any pretence why this *parental power* should keep the child, when grown to a man, in subjection to the will of his parents, any farther than having received life and education from his parents, obliges him to respect, honour, gratitude, assistance and support, all his life, to both father and mother. And thus, it is true, the paternal is a natural government, but not at all extending itself to the ends and jurisdictions of that which is political. The *power of the father doth not reach* at all to the *property* of the child, which is only in his own disposing.

171.   *Secondly, Political power* is that power which every man having in the state of nature, has given up into the hands of the society, and therein to the governors, whom the society hath set over itself, with this express or tacit trust, that it shall be employed for their good, and the preservation of their property: now this *power*, which every man has *in the state of nature*, and which he parts with to the society in all such cases where the society can secure him, is to use such means for the preserving of his own property, as he thinks good, and nature allows him; and to punish the breach of the law of nature in others, so as (according to the best of his reason) may most conduce to the preservation of himself, and the rest of mankind. So that the *end and measure of this power*, when in every man's hands in the state of nature, being the preservation of all of his society, that is, all mankind in general; it can have no other *end or measure*, when in the hands of the magistrate, but to preserve the members of that society in their lives, liberties, and possessions; and so cannot be an absolute arbitrary power, over their lives and fortunes, which are as much as possible to be preserved; but a *power to make laws*, and annex such penalties to them, as may tend to the preservation of the whole, by cutting off those parts, and those only, which are so corrupt, that they threaten the sound and healthy, without which no severity is lawful. And this *power has its original only from compact* and agreement, and the mutual consent of those who make up the community.

172.   Thirdly, Despotical power is an absolute, arbitrary power; one man has over another, to take away his life, whenever he pleases. This is a power, which neither nature gives, for it has made no such distinction between one man and another; nor compact can convey. For man not having such an arbitrary power over his own life, cannot give another man such a power over it; but it is *the effect only of forfeiture* which the aggressor makes of his own life, when he puts himself into the state of war with another. For having quitted reason, which God hath given to be the rule betwixt man and man, and the common bond whereby human kind is united into one fellowship and society; and having renounced the way of peace which that teaches, and made use of the force

of war, to compass his unjust ends upon another, where he has no right; and so revolting from his own kind to that of beasts, by making force, which is theirs, to be his rule of right; he renders himself liable to be destroyed by the injured person, and the rest of mankind, that will join with him in the execution of justice, as any other wild beast, or noxious brute, with whom mankind can have neither society nor security.[10] And thus *captives*, taken in a just and lawful war, and such only, are *subject to a despotical power*; which, as it arises not from compact, so neither is it capable of any, but is the state of war continued. For what compact can be made with a man that is not master of his own life? What condition can he perform? And if he be once allowed to be master of his own life, the *despotical arbitrary power* of his master ceases. He that is master of himself, and his own life, has a right too to the means of preserving it; so that, *as soon as compact enters, slavery ceases*, and he so far quits his absolute power, and puts an end to the state of war, who enters into conditions with his captive.

173. Nature gives the first of these, viz. *paternal power, to parents* for the benefit of their children during their minority, to supply their want of ability and understanding how to manage their property. (By property I must be understood here, as in other places, to mean that property which men have in their persons as well as goods.) *Voluntary agreement gives* the second, *viz. political power to governors* for the benefit of their subjects, to secure them in the possession and use of their properties. And *forfeiture gives* the third *despotical power to lords*, for their own benefit, over those who are stripped of all property.

174. He, that shall consider the distinct rise and extent, and the different ends of these several powers, will plainly see, that *paternal power* comes as far short of that of the *magistrate*, as *despotical* exceeds it; and that *absolute dominion*, however placed, is so far from being one kind of civil society, that it is as inconsistent with it, as slavery is with property. *Paternal power* is only where minority makes the child incapable to

manage his property; *political*, where men have property in their own disposal; and *despotical*, over such as have no property at all.

CHAPTER XVI: Of Conquest

175. Though governments can originally have no other rise than that before-mentioned, nor *polities* be *founded* on any thing but *the consent of the people*; yet such have been the disorders ambition has filled the world with, that in the noise of war, which makes so great a part of the history of mankind, *this consent* is little taken notice of: and therefore many have mistaken the force of arms for the consent of the people, and reckon conquest as one of the originals of government. But conquest is as far from setting up any government, as demolishing an house is from building a new one in the place. Indeed, it often makes way for a new frame of a commonwealth, by destroying the former; but, without the consent of the people, can never erect a new one.

176. That the *aggressor*, who puts himself into the state of war with another, and *unjustly invades* another man's right, can, by such an unjust war, *never come to have a right over the conquered*, will be easily agreed by all men, who will not think, that robbers and pirates have a right of empire over whomsoever they have force enough to master; or that men are bound by promises, which unlawful force extorts from them. Should a robber break into my house, and with a dagger at my throat, make me seal deeds to convey my estate to him, would this give him any title? Just such a title, by his sword, has an *unjust conqueror*, who forces me into submission. The injury and the crime are equal, whether committed by the wearer of the crown, or some petty villain. The title of the offender, and the number of his followers, make no difference in the offence, unless it be to aggravate it. The only difference is, great robbers punish little ones, to keep them in their obedience; but the great ones are rewarded with laurels and triumphs; because they are too big for the weak hands of justice in this world, and have the power in their own possession, which should punish offenders. What is my remedy against a robber, that so broke into my house? Appeal

---

[10] Another copy, corrected by Mr. Locke, has it thus, "Noxious brute that is destructive to their being."

to the law for justice. But perhaps justice is denied, or I am crippled and cannot stir, robbed and have not the means to do it. If God has taken away all means of seeking remedy, there is nothing left but patience. But my son, when able, may seek the relief of the law, which I am denied: he or his son may renew his appeal, till he recover his right. But the conquered, or their children, have no court, no arbitrator on earth to appeal to. Then they may appeal, as Jephthah did, to heaven, and repeat their appeal till they have recovered the native right of their ancestors, which was, to have such a legislative over them, as the majority should approve, and freely acquiesce in. If it be objected, this would cause endless trouble; I answer, no more than justice does, where she lies open to all that appeal to her. He that troubles his neighbour without a cause, is punished for it by the justice of the court he appeals to. And he that *appeals to heaven* must be sure he has right on his side; and a right too that is worth the trouble and cost of the appeal, as he will answer at a tribunal that cannot be deceived, and will be sure to retribute to every one according to the mischiefs he hath created to his fellow-subjects; that is, any part of mankind: from whence it is plain, that he that *conquers in an unjust war, can thereby have no title to the subjection and obedience of the conquered.*

177.   But supposing victory favours the right side, let us consider *a conqueror in a lawful war,* and see what power he gets, and over *whom.*

First, it is plain, *he gets no power by his conquest over those that conquered with him.* They that fought on his side cannot suffer by the conquest, but must at least be as much freemen as they were before. And most commonly they serve upon terms, and on conditions to share with their leader, and enjoy a part of the spoil, and other advantages that attended the conquering sword; or at least have a part of the subdued country bestowed upon them. And *the conquering people are not, I hope, to be slaves by conquest,* and wear their laurels only to shew they are sacrifices to their leader's triumph. They that found absolute monarchy upon the title of the sword, make their heroes, who are the founders of such monarchies, arrant Drawcansirs, and forget they had any officers and soldiers that fought on their side in the battles they won, or assisted them in the subduing, or shared in possessing, the countries they mastered. We are told by some, that the English monarchy is founded in the Norman conquest, and that our princes have thereby a title to absolute dominion: which if it were true, (as by the history it appears otherwise) and that William had a right to make war on this island; yet his dominion by conquest could reach no farther than to the Saxons and Britons, that were then inhabitants of this country. The Normans that came with him, and helped to conquer, and all descended from them, are freemen, and no subjects by conquest, let that give what dominion it will. And if I, or any body else, shall claim freedom, as derived from them, it will be very hard to prove the contrary; and it is plain, the law, that has made no distinction between the one and the other, intends not there should be any difference in their freedom or privileges.

178.   But supposing, which seldom happens, that the conquerors and conquered never incorporate into one people, under the same laws and freedom. Let us see next *what power a lawful conqueror has over the subdued;* and that I say is purely despotical. He has an absolute power over the lives of those who by an unjust war have forfeited them; but not over the lives or fortunes of those who engaged not in the war, nor over the possessions even of those who were actually engaged in it.

179.   Secondly, I say then the conqueror gets no power but only over those who have actually assisted, concurred, or consented to that unjust force that is used against him. For the people having given to their governors no power to do an unjust thing, such as is to make an unjust war, (for they never had such a power in themselves) they ought not to be charged as guilty of the violence and injustice that is committed in an unjust war, any farther than they actually abet it; no more than they are to be thought guilty of any violence or oppression their governors should use upon the people themselves, or any part of their fellow-subjects, they having impowered them no more to the one than to the other. Conquerors, it is true, seldom trouble themselves to make the distinction, but they willingly permit the confusion of war

to sweep all together: but yet this alters not the right; for the conqueror's power over the lives of the conquered being only because they have used force to do, or maintain an injustice, he can have that power only over those who have concurred in that force; all the rest are innocent; and he has no more title over the people of that country, who have done him no injury, and so have made no forfeiture of their lives, than he has over any other, who without any injuries or provocations, have lived upon fair terms with him.

180. *Thirdly*, The *power a conqueror gets* over those he overcomes *in a just war, is perfectly despotical*: he has an absolute power over the lives of those, who, by putting themselves in a state of war, have forfeited them; but he has not thereby a right and title to their possessions. This I doubt not but at first sight will seem a strange doctrine, it being so quite contrary to the practice of the world; there being nothing more familiar in speaking of the dominion of countries, than to say such an one conquered it. As if conquest, without any more ado, conveyed a right of possession. But when we consider, that the practice of the strong and powerful, how universal soever it may be, is seldom the rule of right, however it be one part of the subjection of the conquered, not to argue against the conditions cut out to them by the conquering sword.

181. Though in all war there be usually a complication of force and damage, and the aggressor seldom fails to harm the estate, when he uses force against the persons of those he makes war upon; yet it is the use of force only that puts a man into the state of war. For whether by force he begins the injury, or else, having quietly, and by fraud, done the injury, he refuses to make reparation, and by force maintains it, (which is the same thing, as at first to have done it by force) it is the unjust use of force that makes the war. For he that breaks open my house, and violently turns me out of doors; or, having peaceably got in, by force keeps me out; does in effect the same thing; supposing we are in such a state, that we have no common judge on earth, whom I may appeal to, and to whom we are both obliged to submit. For of such I am now speaking. It is the *unjust use of force then, that puts a man into the state of war* with an-

other; and thereby he that is guilty of it makes a forfeiture of his life. For quitting reason, which is the rule given between man and man, and using force, the way of beasts, he becomes liable to be destroyed by him he uses force against as any savage ravenous beast, that is dangerous to his being.

182. But because the miscarriages of the father are no faults of the children, and they may be rational and peaceable, notwithstanding the brutishness and injustice of the father; the father, by his miscarriages and violence, can forfeit but his own life, but involves not his children in his guilt or destruction. His goods, which nature, that willeth the preservation of all mankind as much as is possible, hath made to belong to the children, to keep them from perishing, do still continue to belong to his children. For supposing them not to have joined in the war, either through infancy, absence, or choice, they have done nothing to forfeit them: *nor has the conqueror any right* to take them away, by the bare title of having subdued him that by force attempted his destruction; though perhaps he may have some right to them, to repair the damages he has sustained by the war, and the defence of his own right; which how far it reaches to the possessions of the conquered, we shall see by and by. So that he that *by conquest has a right over a man's person* to destroy him if he pleases, has not thereby a right *over his estate* to possess and enjoy it. For it is the brutal force the aggressor has used, that gives his adversary a right to take away his life, and destroy him if he pleases as a noxious creature; but it is damage sustained that alone gives him title to another man's goods. For, though I may kill a thief that sets on me in the highway, yet I may not (which seems less) take away his money and let him go: this would be robbery on my side. His force, and the state of war he put himself in, made him forfeit his life, but gave me no title to his goods. The *right* then *of conquest extends only to the lives* of those who joined in the war, *not to their estates*, but only in order to make reparation for the damages received, and the charges of the war; and that too with reservation of the right of the innocent wife and children.

183. Let the conqueror have as much justice on his side as could be supposed, he has no right to seize

more than the vanquished could forfeit: his life is at the victor's mercy; and his service and goods he may appropriate, to make himself reparation; but he cannot take the goods of his wife and children: they too had a title to the goods he enjoyed, and their shares in the estate he possessed. For example, I in the state of nature (and all commonwealths are in the state of nature one with another) have injured another man, and refusing to give satisfaction it comes to a state of war, wherein my defending by force what I had gotten unjustly makes me the aggressor. I am conquered: my life, it is true, as forfeit, is at mercy, but not my wife's and children's. They made not the war, nor assisted in it. I could not forfeit their lives; they were not mine to forfeit. My wife had a share in my estate; that neither could I forfeit. And my children also, being born of me, had a right to be maintained out of my labour or substance. Here then is the case: the conqueror has a title to reparation for damages received, and the children have a title to their father's estate for their subsistence. For as to the wife's share, whether her own labour, or compact, gave her a title to it, it is plain, her husband could not forfeit what was hers. What must be done in the case? I answer; the fundamental law of nature being, that all, as much as may be, should be preserved, it follows, that if there be not enough fully to satisfy both, viz. for the conqueror's losses, and children's maintenance, he that hath, and to spare, must remit something of his full satisfaction, and give way to the pressing and preferable title of those who are in danger to perish without it.

184. But supposing the *charge* and *damages of the war* are to be made up to the conqueror, to the utmost farthing; and that the children of the vanquished, spoiled of all their father's goods, are to be left to starve and perish; yet the satisfying of what shall, on this score, be due to the conqueror, will scarce give him a *title to any country he shall conquer.* For the damages of war can scarce amount to the value of any considerable tract of land, in any part of the world, where all the land is possessed, and none lies waste. And if I have not taken away the conqueror's land, which, being vanquished, it is impossible I should; scarce any other spoil I have done

him can amount to the value of mine, supposing it equally cultivated, and of an extent any way coming near what I had over-run of his. The destruction of a year's product or two (for it seldom reaches four or five) is the utmost spoil that usually can be done. For as to money, and such riches and treasure taken away, these are none of nature's goods, they have but a fantastical imaginary value: nature has put no such upon them: they are of no more account by her standard, than the wampompeke of the Americans to an European prince, or the silver money of Europe would have been formerly to an American. And five years product is not worth the perpetual inheritance of land, where all is possessed, and none remains waste, to be taken up by him that is disseized: which will be easily granted, if one do but take away the imaginary value of money, the disproportion being more than between five and five hundred; though, at the same time, half a year's product is more worth than the inheritance, where there being more land than the inhabitants possess and make use of, any one has liberty to make use of the waste: but there conquerors take little care to possess themselves of the *lands of the vanquished.* No damage therefore, that men in the state of nature (as all princes and governments are in reference to one another) suffer from one another, can give a conqueror power to dispossess the posterity of the vanquished, and turn them out of that inheritance which ought to be the possession of them and their descendants to all generations. The conqueror indeed will be apt to think himself master: and it is the very condition of the subdued not to be able to dispute their right. But if that be all, it gives no other title than what bare force gives to the stronger over the weaker. And, by this reason, he that is strongest will have a right to whatever he pleases to seize on.

185. Over those then that joined with him in the war, and over those of the subdued country that opposed him not, and the posterity even of those that did, the conqueror, even in a just war, hath, by his conquest, no *right of dominion:* they are free from any subjection to him, and if their former government be dissolved, they are at liberty to begin and erect another to themselves.

186.   The conqueror, it is true, usually, by the force he has over them, compels them, with a sword at their breasts, to stoop to his conditions, and submit to such a government as he pleases to afford them; but the inquiry is, what right he has to do so? If it be said, they submit by their own consent, then this allows their own *consent* to be *necessary to give the conqueror a title to rule* over them. It remains only to be considered, whether *promises extorted by force, without right,* can be thought consent, and *how far they bind.* To which I shall say, they *bind not at all*; because whatsoever another gets from me by force, I still retain the right of, and he is obliged presently to restore. He that forces my horse from me, ought presently to restore him, and I have still a right to retake him. By the same reason, he that *forced a promise* from me, ought presently to restore it, i.e. quit me of the obligation of it: or I may resume it myself, i.e. choose whether I will perform it. For the law of nature laying an obligation on me only by the rules she prescribes, cannot oblige me by the violation of her rules: such is the extorting any thing from me by force. Nor does it at all alter the case to say, "I gave my promise," no more than it excuses the force, and passes the right, when I put my hand in my pocket and deliver my purse myself to a thief, who demands it with a pistol at my breast.

187.   From all which it follows, that the *government of a conqueror,* imposed by force, on the subdued, against whom he had no right of war, or who joined not in the war against him, where he had right, *has no obligation* upon them.

188.   But let us suppose that all the men of that community, being all members of the same body politic, may be taken to have joined in that unjust war, wherein they are subdued, and so their lives are at the mercy of the conqueror.

189.   I say this concerns not their children who are in their minority. For since a father hath not, in himself, a power over the life or liberty of his child, no act of his can possibly forfeit it. So that the children, whatever may have happened to the fathers, are freemen, and the absolute power of the conqueror reaches no farther than the persons of the men that were subdued by him, and dies with them: and should he govern them as slaves subjected to his absolute arbitrary power, he *has no such right of dominion over their children.* He can have no power over them but by their own consent, whatever he may drive them to say or do; and he has no lawful authority, whilst force, and not choice, compels them to submission.

190.   Every man is born with a double right: *first, a right of freedom to his person,* which no other man has a power over, but the free disposal of it lies in himself. *Secondly, a right,* before any other man, *to inherit with* his brethren his *father's goods.*

191.   By the first of these, a man is *naturally free* from subjection to any government, though he be born in a place under its jurisdiction. But if he disclaim the lawful government of the country he was born in, he must also quit the right that belonged to him by the laws of it, and the possessions there descending to him from his ancestors, if it were a government made by their consent.

192.   By the second, the inhabitants of any country, who are descended, and derive a title to their estates from those who are subdued, and had a government forced upon them against their free consents, *retain a right to the possession of their ancestors,* though they consent not freely to the government, whose hard conditions were by force imposed on the possessors of that country. For, the first *conqueror never having had a title to the land* of that country, the people who are the descendants of, or claim under those who were forced to submit to the yoke of a government by constraint, have always a right to shake it off, and free themselves from the usurpation or tyranny which the sword hath brought in upon them, till their rulers put them under such a frame of government as they willingly and of choice consent to. Who doubts but the Grecian Christians, descendants of the ancient possessors of that country, may justly cast off the Turkish yoke, which they have so long groaned under, whenever they have an opportunity to do it? For no government can have a right to obedience from a people who have not freely consented to it; which they can never be supposed to do, till either they are put in a full state of liberty to choose their

government and governors, or at least till they have such standing laws, to which they have by themselves or their representatives given their free consent; and also till they are allowed their due property, which is, so to be proprietors of what they have, that no body can take away any part of it without their own consent, without which, men under any government are not in the state of freemen, but are direct slaves under the force of war.

193. But granting that the *conqueror* in a just war has a right to the estates, as well as power over the persons of the conquered; which, it is plain, he *hath* not: nothing of absolute power will follow from hence, in the continuance of the government. Because the descendants of these being all freemen, if he grants them estates and possessions to inhabit his country (without which it would be worth nothing) whatsoever he grants them, they have, so far as it is granted, property in. The nature whereof is, that *without a man's own consent, it cannot be taken from him.*

194. Their *persons* are *free* by a native right, and their properties, be they more or less, are *their own, and at their own dispose,* and not at his; or else it is no property. Supposing the conqueror gives to one man a thousand acres, to him and his heirs for ever; to another he lets a thousand acres for his life, under the rent of 50*l.* or 500*l.* per annum, has not the one of these a right to his thousand acres for ever, and the other during his life, paying the said rent? and hath not the tenant for life a property in all that he gets over and above his rent, by his labour and industry during the said term, supposing it to be double the rent? Can any one say, the king, or conqueror, after his grant, may, by his power of conqueror, take away all, or part of the land from the heirs of one, or from the other during his life, he paying the rent? Or can he take away from either the goods or money they have got upon the said land, at his pleasure? If he can, then all free and voluntary contracts cease, and are void in the world; there needs nothing to dissolve them at any time but power enough: and all the grants and *promises* of *men in power* are but mockery and collusion. For can there be any thing more ridiculous than to say, I give you and yours this for ever, and

that in the surest and most solemn way of conveyance can be devised; and yet it is to be understood, that I have a right, if I please, to take it away from you again to-morrow?

195. I will not dispute now, whether princes are exempt from the laws of their country; but this I am sure, they owe subjection to the laws of God and nature. No body, no power, can exempt them from the obligations of that eternal law. Those are so great, and so strong, in the case of *promises*, that omnipotency itself can be tied by them. *Grants, promises,* and *oaths,* are *bonds* that *hold the Almighty*: whatever some flatterers say to princes of the world, who all together, with all their people joined to them, are in comparison of the great God, but as a drop of the bucket, or a dust on the balance, inconsiderable, nothing!

196. The short of the *case in conquest* is this. The conqueror, if he have a just cause, has a despotical right over the persons of all that actually aided, and concurred in the war against him, and a right to make up his damage and cost out of their labour and estates, so he injure not the right of any other. Over the rest of the people, if there were any that consented not to the war, and over the children of the captives themselves, or the possessions of either, he has no power and so can have, *by virtue of conquest, no lawful title* himself *to dominion* over them, or derive it to his posterity; but is an aggressor, if he attempts upon their properties, and thereby puts himself in a state of war against them: and has no better a right of principality, he, nor any of his successors, than Hingar, or Hubba, the Danes, had here in England; or Spartacus had he conquered Italy, would have had; which is to have their yoke cast off, as soon as God shall give those under their subjection courage and opportunity to do it. Thus, notwithstanding whatever title the kings of Assyria had over Judah, by the sword, God assisted Hezekiah to throw off the dominion of that conquering empire. "And the Lord was with Hezekiah, and he prospered; wherefore he went forth, and he rebelled against the king of Assyria, and served him not," *2 Kings,* xviii. 7. Whence it is plain, that shaking off a power, which force, and not right, hath

set over any one, though it hath the name of *rebellion*, yet is no offence before God, but is that which he allows and countenances, though even promises and covenants, when obtained by force, have intervened. For it is very probable, to any one that reads the story of Ahaz and Hezekiah attentively, that the Assyrians subdued Ahaz, and deposed him, and made Hezekiah king in his father's life-time; and that Hezekiah by agreement had done him homage, and paid him tribute all this time.

CHAPTER XVII: Of Usurpation

197.   As conquest may be called a foreign usurpation, so usurpation is a kind of domestic conquest; with this difference, that an usurper can never have right on his side, it being no *usurpation* but where one is got into the *possession of what another has right to*. This, so far as it is *usurpation*, is a change only of persons, but not of the forms and rules of the government; for if the usurper extend his power beyond what of right belonged to the lawful princes, or governors of the commonwealth, it is *tyranny* added to *usurpation*.

198.   In all lawful governments, the designation of the persons, who are to bear rule, is as natural and necessary a part, as the form of the government itself, and is that which had its establishment originally from the people; the anarchy being much alike to have no form of government at all, or to agree, that it shall be monarchical, but to appoint no way to design the person that shall have the power, and be the monarch. Hence all commonwealths, with the form of government established, have rules also of appointing those who are to have any share in the public authority, and settled methods of conveying the right to them. For the anarchy is much alike to have no form of government at all, or to agree that it shall be monarchical, but to appoint no way to know or design the person that shall have the power and be the monarch. Whoever gets into the exercise of any part of the power, by other ways than what the laws of the community have prescribed, hath no right to be obeyed, though the form of the commonwealth be still preserved; since he is not the person the laws

have appointed, and consequently not the person the people have consented to. Nor can such an *usurper*, or any deriving from him, ever have a title, till the people are both at liberty to consent, and have actually consented to allow, and confirm in him the power he hath till then usurped.

CHAPTER XVIII: Of Tyranny

199.   As usurpation is the exercise of power, which another hath a right to, so *tyranny is the exercise of power beyond right*, which no body can have a right to. And this is making use of the power any one has in his hands, not for the good of those who are under it, but for his own private separate advantage. — When the governor, however intitled, makes not the law, but his will, the rule; and his commands and actions are not directed to the preservation of the properties of his people, but the satisfaction of his own ambition, revenge, covetousness, or any other irregular passion.

200.   If one can doubt this to be truth, or reason, because it comes from the obscure hand of a subject, I hope the authority of a king will make it pass with him. King James the first, in his speech to the parliament, 1603, tells them thus: "I will ever prefer the weal of the public, and of the whole commonwealth, in making of good laws and constitutions, to any particular and private ends of mine. Thinking ever the wealth and weal of the commonwealth to be my greatest weal and worldly felicity; a point wherein a lawful king doth directly differ from a tyrant. For I do acknowledge, that the special and greatest point of difference that is between a rightful king and an usurping tyrant, is this, that whereas the proud and ambitious tyrant doth think his kingdom and people are only ordained for satisfaction of his desires and unreasonable appetites, the righteous and just king doth by the contrary acknowledge himself to be ordained for the procuring of the wealth and property of his people." And again, in his speech to the parliament, 1609, he hath these words: "The king binds himself by a double oath to the observation of the fundamental laws of his kingdom; tacitly, as by being a king, and so bound to protect as well the people, as the laws of his kingdom; and expressly, by his oath

at his coronation; so as every just king, in a settled kingdom, is bound to observe that paction made to his people by his laws, in framing his government agreeable thereunto, according to that paction which God made with Noah after the deluge: Hereafter, seed-time and harvest, and cold and heat, and summer and winter, and day and night, shall not cease while the earth remaineth. And therefore a king governing in a settled kingdom, leaves to be a king, and degenerates into a tyrant, as soon as he leaves off to rule according to his laws." And a little after, "Therefore all kings that are not tyrants, or perjured, will be glad to bound themselves within the limits of their laws; and they that persuade them the contrary, are vipers, and pests, both against them and the commonwealth." Thus that learned king, who well understood the notions of things, makes the difference betwixt a *king* and a *tyrant* to consist only in this, that one makes the laws the bounds of his power, and the good of the public the end of his government; the other makes all give way to his own will and appetite.

201. It is a mistake to think this fault is proper only to monarchies; other forms of government are liable to it, as well as that. For wherever the power, that is put in any hands for the government of the people, and the preservation of their properties, is applied to other ends, and made use of to impoverish, harass, or subdue them to the arbitrary and irregular commands of those that have it; there it presently becomes tyranny, whether those that thus use it are one or many. Thus we read of the thirty tyrants at Athens, as well as one at Syracuse; and the intolerable dominion of the decemviri at Rome was nothing better.

202. *Wherever law ends, tyranny begins,* if the law be transgressed to another's harm; and whosoever in authority exceeds the power given him by the law, and makes use of the force he has under his command, to compass that upon the subject, which the law allows not, ceases in that to be a magistrate; and, acting without authority, may be opposed as any other man, who by force invades the right of another. This is acknowledged in subordinate magistrates. He that hath authority to seize my person in the street, may be opposed as a thief and a robber if he endeav-

ours to break into my house to execute a writ, notwithstanding that I know he has such a warrant, and such a legal authority, as will impower him to arrest me abroad. And why this should not hold in the highest, as well as in the most inferiour magistrate, I would gladly be informed. Is it reasonable that the eldest brother, because he has the greatest part of his father's estate, should thereby have a right to take away any of his younger brother's portions? Or, that a rich man, who possessed a whole country, should from thence have a right to seize, when he pleased, the cottage and garden of his poor neighbour? The being rightfully possessed of great power and riches, exceedingly beyond the greatest part of the sons of Adam, is so far from being an excuse, much less a reason for rapine and oppression, which the endamaging another without authority is, that it is a great aggravation of it. For the exceeding the bounds of authority is no more a right in a great, than in a petty officer; no more justifiable in a king than a constable; but is so much the worse in him, in that he has more trust put in him, has already a much greater share than the rest of his brethren, and is supposed, from the advantages of his education, employment, and counsellors, to be more knowing in the measures of right or wrong.

203. May the *commands* then *of a prince be opposed?* may he be resisted as often as any one shall find himself aggrieved, and but imagine he has not right done him? This will unhinge and overturn all polities, and, instead of government and order, leave nothing but anarchy and confusion.

204. To this I answer, that *force* is to be *opposed* to nothing but to unjust and unlawful *force;* whoever makes any opposition in any other case, draws on himself a just condemnation both from God and man; and so no such danger or confusion will follow, as is often suggested. For,

205. *First,* As, in some countries, the person of the prince by the law is sacred; and so, whatever he commands or does, his person is still free from all question or violence, not liable to force, or any judicial censure or condemnation. But yet opposition may be made to the illegal acts of any inferiour officer, or other commissioned by him; unless he will, by actually putting himself into a state of war with his

people, dissolve the government, and leave them to that defence which belongs to every one in the state of nature. For of such things who can tell what the end will be? And a neighbour kingdom has shewed the world an odd example. In all other cases the *sacredness* of the *person exempts him from all inconveniencies*, whereby he is secure, whilst the government stands, from all violence and harm whatsoever; than which there cannot be a wiser constitution. For the harm he can do in his own person not being likely to happen often, nor to extend itself far; nor being able by his single strength to subvert the laws, nor oppress the body of the people, should any prince have so much weakness and ill-nature as to be willing to do it, the inconveniency of some particular mischiefs that may happen sometimes, when a heady prince comes to the throne, are well recompensed by the peace of the public, and security of the government, in the person of the chief magistrate, thus set out of the reach of danger: it being safer for the body that some few private men should be sometimes in danger to suffer, than that the head of the republic should be easily, and upon slight occasions, exposed.

206.   *Secondly*, But this privilege belonging only to the king's person, hinders not, but they may be questioned, opposed, and resisted, who use unjust force, though they pretend a commission from him, which the law authorizes not. As is plain in the case of him that has the king's writ to arrest a man, which is a full commission from the king; and yet he that has it cannot break open a man's house to do it, nor execute this command of the king upon certain days, nor in certain places, though this commission have no such exception in it, but they are the limitations of the law, which if any one transgress, the king's commission excuses him not. For the king's authority being given him only by the law, he cannot impower any one to act against the law, or justify him, by his commission, in so doing. The *commission* or *command of any magistrate, where he has no authority*, being as void and insignificant, as that of any private man. The difference between the one and the other being that the magistrate has some authority so far, and to such ends, and the private man has none at all. For it is not the commission, but the authority,

that gives the right of acting; and *against the laws there can be no authority*. But notwithstanding such resistance, the king's person and authority are still both secured, and so *no danger to governor or government*.

207.   *Thirdly*, supposing a government wherein the person of the chief magistrate is not thus sacred; yet this *doctrine* of the lawfulness of *resisting* all unlawful exercises of his power, *will not* upon every slight occasion endanger him, or *embroil the government*. For where the injured party may be relieved, and his damages repaired by appeal to the law, there can be no pretence for force, which is only to be used where a man is intercepted from appealing to the law. For nothing is to be accounted hostile force, but where it leaves not the remedy of such an appeal. And it is such force alone, that puts him that uses it *into a state of war*, and makes it lawful to resist him. A man with a sword in his hand, demands my purse in the highway, when perhaps I have not twelve-pence in my pocket: this man I may lawfully kill. To another I deliver £100 to hold only whilst I alight, which he refuses to restore me, when I am got up again, but draws his sword to defend the possession of it by force, if I endeavour to retake it. The mischief this man does me is an hundred, or possibly a thousand times more than the other perhaps intended me (whom I killed before he really did me any;) and yet I might lawfully kill the one, and cannot so much as hurt the other lawfully. The reason whereof is plain; because the one using force, which threatened my life, I could not have *time to appeal* to the law to secure it: and when it was gone, it was too late to appeal. The law could not restore life to my dead carcass, the loss was irreparable: which to prevent, the law of nature gave me a right to destroy him, who had put himself into a state of war with me, and threatened my destruction. But in the other case, my life not being in danger, I may have the *benefit of appealing* to the law, and have reparation for my £100 that way.

208.   *Fourthly*, But if the unlawful acts done by the magistrate be maintained (by the power he has got) and the remedy which is due by law, be by the same power obstructed: yet the *right of resisting*, even in such manifest acts of tyranny, will not suddenly,

or on slight occasions, disturb the government. For if it reach no farther than some private men's cases, though they have a right to defend themselves, and to recover by force what by unlawful force is taken from them: yet the right to do so will not easily engage them in a contest, wherein they are sure to perish; it being as impossible for one, or a few oppressed men to *disturb the government*, where the body of the people do not think themselves concerned in it, as for a raving madman, or heady malecontent, to overturn a well-settled state, the people being as little apt to follow the one, as the other.

209.   But if either these illegal acts have extended to the majority of the people; or if the mischief and oppression has lighted only on some few, but in such cases, as the precedent and consequences seem to threaten all; and they are persuaded in their consciences, that their laws, and with them their estates, liberties, and lives are in danger, and perhaps their religion too: how they will be hindered from resisting illegal force, used against them, I cannot tell. This is an *inconvenience*, I confess, that *attends all governments* whatsoever, when the governors have brought it to this pass, to be generally suspected of their people; the most dangerous state which they can possibly put themselves in; wherein they are the less to be pitied, because it is so easy to be avoided; it being as impossible for a governor, if he really means the good of his people, and the preservation of them, and their laws together, not to make them see and feel it, as it is for the father of a family, not to let his children see he loves and takes care of them.

210.   But if all the world shall observe pretences of one kind, and actions of another; arts used to elude the law, and the trust of prerogative, (which is an arbitrary power in some things left in the prince's hand to do good, not harm, to the people) employed contrary to the end for which it was given: if the people shall find the ministers and subordinate magistrates chosen suitable to such ends, and favoured, or laid by, proportionably as they promote or oppose them: if they see several experiments made of arbitrary power, and that religion underhand favoured (though publicly proclaimed against) which is readiest to introduce it; and the operators in it supported, as much

as may be; and when that cannot be done, yet approved still, and liked the better: if a *long train of actions shew the councils* all tending that way; how can a man any more hinder himself from being persuaded in his own mind, which way things are going; or from casting about how to save himself, than he could from believing the captain of the ship he was in, was carrying him, and the rest of the company, to Algiers, when he found him always steering that course, though cross winds, leaks in his ship, and want of men and provisions did often force him to turn his course another way for some time, which he steadily returned to again, as soon as the wind, weather, and other circumstances would let him?

CHAPTER XIX: Of the Dissolution of Government

211.   He that will with any clearness speak of the *dissolution of government*, ought in the first place to distinguish between the *dissolution of the society* and the *dissolution of the government*. That which makes the community, and brings men out of the loose state of nature into *one politic society*, is the agreement which every one has with the rest to incorporate, and act as one body, and so be one distinct commonwealth. The usual, and almost only way whereby *this union is dissolved*, is the inroad of foreign force making a conquest upon them. For in that case, (not being able to maintain and support themselves, as *one entire* and *independent body*) the union belonging to that body which consisted therein, must necessarily cease, and so every one return to the state he was in before, with a liberty to shift for himself, and provide for his own safety, as he thinks fit, in some other society. Whenever the *society is dissolved*, it is certain the government of that society cannot remain. Thus conquerors swords often cut up governments by the roots, and mangle societies to pieces, separating the subdued or scattered multitude from the protection of, and dependence on, that society which ought to have preserved them from violence. The world is too well instructed in, and too forward to allow of, this way of dissolving of governments, to need any more

to be said of it; and there wants not much argument to prove, that where the *society is dissolved*, the government cannot remain; that being as impossible, as for the frame of a house to subsist when the materials of it are scattered and dissipated by a whirlwind, or jumbled into a confused heap by an earthquake.

212.   Besides this overturning from without, *governments are dissolved from within.*

First, When the *legislative* is *altered.* Civil society being a state of peace, amongst those who are of it, from whom the state of war is excluded by the umpirage, which they have provided in their legislative, for the ending all differences that may arise amongst any of them; it is in their legislative, that the members of a commonwealth are united, and combined together into one coherent living body. This *is the soul that gives form, life, and unity* to the commonwealth: from hence the several members have their mutual influence, sympathy, and connexion; and therefore, when the legislative is broken, or dissolved, dissolution and death follows. For, *the essence and union of the society* consisting in having one will, the legislative, when once established by the majority, has the declaring, and as it were keeping of that will. The *constitution of the legislative* is the first and fundamental act of society, whereby provision is made for the *continuation of their union*, under the direction of persons, and bonds of laws, made by persons authorized thereunto, by the consent and appointment of the people; without which no one man, or number of men, amongst them, can have authority of making laws that shall be binding to the rest. When any one, or more, shall take upon them to make laws, whom the people have not appointed so to do, they make laws without authority, which the people are not therefore bound to obey; by which means they come again to be out of subjection, and may constitute to themselves a new legislative, as they think best, being in full liberty to resist the force of those, who without authority would impose any thing upon them. Every one is at the disposure of his own will, when those who had, by the delegation of the society, the declaring of the public will, are excluded from it, and others usurp the place, who have no such authority or delegation.

213.   This being usually brought about by such in the commonwealth who misuse the power they have, it is hard to consider it aright, and know at whose door to lay it, without knowing the form of government in which it happens. Let us suppose then the legislative placed in the concurrence of three distinct persons.

1. A single hereditary person, having the constant, supreme, executive power, and with it the power of convoking and dissolving the other two, within certain periods of time.
2. An assembly of hereditary nobility.
3. An assembly of representatives chosen *pro tempore*, by the people. Such a form of government supposed, it is evident,

214.   First, That when such a single person, or prince, sets up his own arbitrary will in place of the laws, which are the will of the society, declared by the legislative, then the *legislative is changed.* For that being in effect the legislative, whose rules and laws are put in execution, and required to be obeyed; when other laws are set up, and other rules pretended, and enforced, than what the legislative, constituted by the society, have enacted, it is plain that the *legislative is changed.* Whoever introduces new laws, not being thereunto authorized, by the fundamental appointment of the society, or subverts the old, disowns and overturns the power by which they were made, and so sets up a *new legislative.*

215.   Secondly, When the prince hinders the legislative from assembling in its due time, or from acting freely, pursuant to those ends for which it was constituted, the *legislative is altered:* for it is not a certain number of men, no, nor their meeting, unless they have also freedom of debating, and leisure of perfecting, what is for the good of the society, wherein the legislative consists: when these are taken away or altered, so as to deprive the society of the due exercise of their power, the legislative is truly altered. For it is not names that constitute governments, but the use and exercise of those powers that were intended to accompany them; so that he, who takes away the freedom, or hinders the acting of the legislative in its

due seasons, in effect *takes away the legislative*, and *puts an end to the government.*

216. Thirdly, When, by the arbitrary power of the prince, the electors, or ways of election, are altered, without the consent, and contrary to the common interest of the people, there also the *legislative is altered*. For, if others than those whom the society hath authorized thereunto, do choose, or in another way than what the society hath prescribed, those chosen are not the legislative appointed by the people.

217. Fourthly, The delivery also of the people into the subjection of a foreign power, either by the prince, or by the legislative, is certainly a *change of the legislative*, and so a *dissolution of the government.* For the end why people entered into society being to be preserved one intire, free, independent society, to be governed by its own laws; this is lost, whenever they are given up into the power of another.

218. Why, in such a constitution as this, the *dissolution of the government* in these cases is to be imputed to the prince, is evident; because he, having the force, treasure, and offices of the state to employ, and often persuading himself, or being flattered by others, that as supreme magistrate, he is uncapable of control; he alone is in a condition to make great advances toward such changes, under pretence of lawful authority, and has it in his hands to terrify or suppress opposers, as factious, seditious, and enemies to the government: whereas no other part of the legislative, or people, is capable by themselves to attempt any alteration of the legislative, without open and visible rebellion, apt enough to be taken notice of; which, when, it prevails, produces effects very little different from foreign conquest. Besides, the prince in such a form of government having the power of dissolving the other parts of the legislative, and thereby rendering them private persons, they can never in opposition to him, or without his concurrence, alter the legislative by a law, his consent being necessary to give any of their decrees that sanction. But yet, so far as the other parts of the legislative any way contribute to any attempt upon the government, and do either promote, or not, what lies in them, hinder such designs; they are guilty, and partake in this, which is certainly the greatest crime men can be guilty of one towards another.

219. There is one way more whereby such a government may be dissolved, and that is, when he who has the supreme executive power neglects and abandons that charge, so that the laws already made can no longer be put in execution. This is demonstratively to reduce all to anarchy, and so effectually to *dissolve the government.* For laws not being made for themselves, but to be, by their execution, the bonds of the society, to keep every part of the body politic in its due place and function; when that totally ceases, the *government* visibly *ceases*, and the people become a confused multitude, without order or connexion. Where there is no longer the administration of justice, for the securing of men's rights, nor any remaining power within the community to direct the force, or provide for the necessities of the public; there certainly is *no government left*. Where the laws cannot be executed, it is all one as if there were no laws; and a government without laws is, I suppose, a mystery in politics, inconceivable to human capacity, and inconsistent with human society.

220. In these and the like cases, *when the government is dissolved*, the people are at liberty to provide for themselves, by erecting a new legislative, differing from the other, by the change of persons, or form, or both, as they shall find it most for their safety and good. For the *society* can never, by the fault of another, lose the native and original right it has to preserve itself; which can only be done by a settled legislative, and a fair and impartial execution of the laws made by it. But the state of mankind is not so miserable that they are not capable of using this remedy, till it be too late to look for any. To tell *people* they *may provide for themselves*, by erecting a new legislative, when by oppression, artifice, or being delivered over to a foreign power, their old one is gone, is only to tell them, they may expect relief when it is too late, and the evil is past cure. This is in effect no more, than to bid them first be slaves, and then to take care of their liberty; and when their chains are on, tell them, they may act like freemen. This, if barely so, is rather mockery than relief; and men can never be

secure from tyranny, if there be no means to escape it, till they are perfectly under it: And therefore it is, that they have not only a right to get out of it, but to prevent it.

221. There is, therefore, secondly, another way whereby *governments are dissolved*, and that is, when the legislative, or the prince either of them, act contrary to their trust.

First, The *legislative acts against the trust* reposed in them, when they endeavour to invade the property of the subject, and to make themselves, or any part of the community, masters, or arbitrary disposers of the lives, liberties, or fortunes of the people.

222. The reason why men enter into society, is the preservation of their property; and the end why they choose and authorize a legislative, is, that there may be laws made, and rules set, as guards and fences to the properties of all the members of the society: to limit the power, and moderate the dominion, of every part and member of the society. For since it can never be supposed to be the will of the society, that the legislative should have a power to destroy that, which every one designs to secure, by entering into society, and for which the people submitted themselves to legislators of their own making, whenever the *legislators endeavour to take away and destroy the property of the people*, or to reduce them to slavery under arbitrary power, they put themselves into a state of war with the people, who are thereupon absolved from any farther obedience, and are left to the common refuge, which God hath provided for all men, against force and violence. Whensoever therefore the *legislative* shall transgress this fundamental rule of society; and either by ambition, fear, folly or corruption, *endeavour to grasp* themselves, *or put into the hands of any other an absolute power* over the lives, liberties, and estates of the people; by this breach of trust they *forfeit the power*, the people had put into their hands, for quite contrary ends, and it devolves to the people, who have a right to resume their original liberty, and, by the establishment of a new legislative, (such as they shall think fit) provide for their own safety and security, which is the end for which they are in society. What I have said here, concerning the legislative in general, holds true also concerning the supreme executor, who having a double trust put in him, both to have a part in the legislative, and the supreme execution of the law, acts against both, when he goes about to set up his own arbitrary will, as the law of the society. He *acts* also *contrary to his trust*, when he either employs the force, treasure, and offices of the society to corrupt the *representatives*, and gain them to his purposes; or openly pre-engages the *electors*, and prescribes to their choice, such, whom he has by solicitations, threats, promises, or otherwise, won to his designs: and employs them to bring in such, who have promised before-hand, what to vote, and what to enact. Thus to regulate candidates and electors, and new model the ways of election, what is it but to cut up the government by the roots, and poison the very fountain of public security? for the people having reserved to themselves the choice of their *representatives*, as the fence to their properties, could do it for no other end, but that they might always be freely chosen, and so chosen, freely act, and advise, as the necessity of the commonwealth, and the public good should, upon examination and mature debate, be judged to require. This, those who give their votes before they hear the debate, and have weighed the reasons on all sides, are not capable of doing. To prepare such an assembly as this, and endeavour to set up the declared abettors of his own will, for the true representatives of the people, and the law-makers of the society, is certainly as great a *breach of trust*, and as perfect a declaration of a design to subvert the government, as is possible to be met with. To which if one shall add rewards and punishments visibly employed to the same end, and all the arts of perverted law made use of, to take off and destroy all that stand in the way of such a design, and will not comply and consent to betray the liberties of their country, it will be past doubt what is doing. What power they ought to have in the society, who thus employ it contrary to the trust that went along with it in its first institution, is easy to determine; and one cannot but see, that he, who has once attempted any such thing as this, cannot any longer be trusted.

223. To this perhaps it will be said, that the people being ignorant, and always discontented, to lay the foundation of government in the unsteady

opinion and uncertain humour of the people, is to expose it to certain ruin; and *no government will be able long to subsist*, if the people may set up a new legislative, whenever they take offence at the old one. To this I answer, quite the contrary. People are not so easily got out of their old forms as some are apt to suggest. They are hardly to be prevailed with to amend the acknowledged faults in the frame they have been accustomed to. And if there be any original defects, or adventitious ones introduced by time, or corruption: it is not an easy thing to get them changed, even when all the world sees there is an opportunity for it. This slowness and aversion in the people to quit their old constitutions, has in the many revolutions which have been seen in this kingdom, in this and former ages, still kept us to, or, after some interval of fruitless attempts, still brought us back again to, our old legislative of king, lords, and commons: and whatever provocations have made the crown be taken from some of our princes heads, they never carried the people so far as to place it in another line.

224. But it will be said, this *hypothesis* lays a *ferment for* frequent *rebellion*. To which I *answer*,

First, no more than any other *hypothesis*: for when the people are made miserable, and find themselves *exposed to the ill usage of arbitrary power*, cry up their governors as much as you will, for *sons of Jupiter*; let them be sacred or divine, descended, or authorized from heaven; give them out for whom or what you please, the same will happen. *The people generally ill treated*, and contrary to right, will be ready upon any occasion to ease themselves of a burden that sits heavy upon them. They will wish, and seek for the opportunity, which in the change, weakness, and accidents of human affairs, seldom delays long to offer itself. He must have lived but a little while in the world, who has not seen examples of this in his time; and he must have read very little, who cannot produce examples of it in all sorts of governments in the world.

225. *Secondly*, I answer, such *revolutions happen* not upon every little mismanagement in public affairs. *Great mistakes* in the ruling part, many wrong and inconvenient laws, and all the slips of human frailty, will be *borne by the people* without mutiny or murmur. But if a long train of abuses, prevarications and

artifices, all tending the same way, make the design visible to the people, and they cannot but feel what they lie under, and see whither they are going; it is not to be wondered, that they should then rouse themselves, and endeavour to put the rule into such hands which may secure to them the ends for which government was at first erected; and without which, ancient names, and specious forms, are so far from being better, that they are much worse, than the state of nature, or pure anarchy; the inconveniencies being all as great and as near, but the remedy farther off and more difficult.

226. *Thirdly*, I answer, that *this doctrine* of a power in the people of providing for their safety anew, by a new legislative, when their legislators have acted contrary to their trust, by invading their property, is the *best fence against rebellion*, and the probablest means to hinder it. For *rebellion* being an opposition, not to persons, but authority, which is founded only in the constitutions and laws of the government; those, whoever they be, who by force break through, and by force justify their violation of them, are truly and properly *rebels*. For when men, by entering into society and civil government, have excluded force, and introduced laws for the preservation of property, peace, and unity amongst themselves; those who set up force again in opposition to the laws, do *rebellare*, that is, bring back again the state of war, and are properly rebels: Which they who are in power, (by the pretence they have to authority, the temptation of force they have in their hands, and the flattery of those about them) being likeliest to do; the properest way to prevent the evil, is to shew them the danger and injustice of it, who are under the greatest temptation to run into it.

227. In both the forementioned cases, when either the legislative is changed, or the legislators act contrary to the end for which they were constituted, those who are guilty are *guilty of rebellion*; for if any one by force takes away the established legislative of any society, and the laws by them made pursuant to their trust, he thereby takes away the umpirage, which every one had consented to, for a peaceable decision of all their controversies, and a bar to the state of war amongst them. They who remove, or change the

legislative, take away this decisive power, which no body can have but by the appointment and consent of the people; and so destroying the authority which the people did, and no body else can set up, and introducing a power which the people hath not authorized, they actually *introduce a state of war*, which is that of force without authority; and thus by removing the legislative established by the society, (in whose decisions the people acquiesced and united, as to that of their own will) they untie the knot, and *expose the people anew to the state of war*. And if those, who by force take away the legislative, are *rebels*, the *legislators* themselves, as has been shewn, can be no less esteemed so; when they, who were set up for the protection and preservation of the people, their liberties and properties, shall by force invade and endeavour to take them away; and so they putting themselves into a state of war with those who made them the protectors and guardians of their peace, are properly, and with the greatest aggravation, *rebellantes*, rebels.

228.   But if they, who say, "it lays a foundation for rebellion," mean that it may occasion civil wars, or intestine broils, to tell the people they are absolved from obedience when, illegal attempts are made upon their liberties or properties, and may oppose the unlawful violence of those who were their magistrates, when they invade their properties contrary to the trust put in them; and that therefore this doctrine is not to be allowed, being so destructive to the peace of the world: they may as well say, upon the same ground, that honest men may not oppose robbers or pirates, because this may occasion disorder or bloodshed. If any *mischief* come in such cases, it is not to be charged upon him who defends his own right, but *on him that invades* his neighbour's. If the innocent honest man must quietly quit all he has, for peace sake, to him who will lay violent hands upon it, I desire it may be considered, what a kind of peace there will be in the world, which consists only in violence and rapine; and which is to be maintained only for the benefit of robbers and oppressors. Who would not think it an admirable peace betwixt the mighty and the mean, when the lamb, without resistance, yielded his throat to be torn by the imperious

wolf? Polyphemus's den gives us a perfect pattern of such a peace, and such a government, wherein Ulysses and his companions had nothing to do, but quietly to suffer themselves to be devoured. And no doubt Ulysses, who was a prudent man, preached up *passive obedience*, and exhorted them to a quiet submission, by representing to them of what concernment peace was to mankind; and by shewing the inconveniencies might happen, if they should offer to resist Polyphemus, who had now the power over them.

229.   The end of government is the good of mankind: and which is *best for mankind*, that the people should be always exposed to the boundless will of tyranny; or that the rulers should be sometimes liable to be opposed, when they grow exorbitant in the use of their power, and employ it for the destruction, and not the preservation of the properties of their people?

230.   Nor let any one say, that mischief can arise from hence, as often as it shall please a busy head, or turbulent spirit, to desire the alteration of the government. It is true, such men may stir, whenever they please; but it will be only to their own just ruin and perdition. For till the mischief be grown general, and the ill designs of the rulers become visible, or their attempts sensible to the greater part, the people, who are more disposed to suffer than right themselves by resistance, are not apt to stir. The examples of particular injustice or oppression, of here and there an unfortunate man, moves them not. But if they universally have a persuasion, grounded upon manifest evidence, that designs are carrying on against their liberties, and the general course and tendency of things cannot but give them strong suspicions of the evil intention of their governors, who is to be blamed for it? Who can help it, if they, who might avoid it, bring themselves into this suspicion? Are the people to be blamed, if they have the sense of rational creatures, and can think of things no otherwise than as they find and feel them? And is it not rather *their fault*, who put things into such a posture, that they would not have them thought to be as they are? I grant, that the pride, ambition, and turbulency of private men, have sometimes caused great disorders in commonwealths, and factions have been fatal to states and kingdoms. But whether *the mischief* hath *oftener* be-

gun *in the peoples wantonness*, and a desire to cast off the lawful authority of their rulers, or in *the rulers insolence*, and endeavours to get and exercise an arbitrary power over their people; whether oppression, or disobedience, gave the first rise to the disorder; I leave it to impartial history to determine. This I am sure, whoever, either ruler or subject, by force goes about to invade the rights of either prince or people, and lays the foundation for *overturning* the constitution and frame of *any just government*; is highly guilty of the greatest crime, I think, a man is capable of; being to answer for all those mischiefs of blood, rapine, and desolation, which the breaking to pieces of governments bring on a country. And he who does it, is justly to be esteemed the common enemy and pest of mankind, and is to be treated accordingly.

231.   That *subjects* or *foreigners*, attempting by force on the properties of any people, may be resisted with force, is agreed on all hands. But that *magistrates*, doing the same thing, may be *resisted*, hath of late been denied: as if those who had the greatest privileges and advantages by the law, had thereby a power to break those laws, by which alone they were set in a better place than their brethren: whereas their offence is thereby the greater, both as being ungrateful for the greater share they have by the law, and breaking also that trust which is put into their hands by their brethren.

232.   Whosoever uses *force without right*, as every one does in society, who does it without law, puts himself into a *state of war* with those against whom he so uses it; and in that state all former ties are cancelled, all other rights cease, and every one has a right to defend himself, and to *resist the aggressor*. This is so evident, that Barclay himself, that great assertor of the power and sacredness of kings, is forced to confess, that it is lawful for the people, in some cases, to resist their king; and that too in a chapter, wherein he pretends to shew, that the divine law shuts up the people from all manner of rebellion. Whereby it is evident, even by his own doctrine, that, since they may in some cases resist, all resisting of *princes* is not rebellion. His words are these. "Quod siquis dicat, Ergone populus tyrannicae crudelitati & furori jugulum semper praebebit? Ergone multitudo civita-

tes suas fame, ferro, & flamma vastari, seque, conjuges, & liberos fortunae ludibrio & tyranni libidini exponi, inque omnia vitae pericula omnesque miserias & molestias a rege de luci patientur? Num illis quod omni animantium generi est a natura tributum, denegari debet, ut sc. vim vi repellant, seseq; ab injuria tueantur? Huic brevitur responsum sit, Populo universo negari defensionem, quae juris naturalis est, neque ultionem quae praeter naturam est adversus regem concedi debere. Quapropter si rex non in singulares tantum personas aliquot privatum odium exerceat, sed corpus etiam reipublicae, cujus ipse caput est, i.e. totum populum, vel insignem aliquam ejus partem immani & intoleranda saevitia seu tyrannide divexet; populo quidem hoc casu resistendi ac tuendi se ab injuria potestas competit; sed tuendi se tantum, non enim in principem invadendi: & restituendae injuriae illatae, non recedendi a debita reverentia propter acceptam injuriam. Praesentem denique impetum propulsandi non vim praeteritam ulciscendi jus habet. Horum enim alterum a natura est, ut vitam scilicet corpusque tueamur. Alterum vero contra naturam, ut inferior de superiori supplicium sumat. Quod itaque populus malum, antequam factum sit, impedire potest, ne fiat; id postquam factum est, in regem authorem sceleris vindicare non potest: populus igitur hoc amplius quam privatus quispiam habet: quod huic, vel ipsis adversariis judicibus, excepto Buchanano, nullum nisi in patientia remedium superest. Cum ille si intolerabilis tyrannus est (modicum enim ferre omnino debet) resistere cum reverentia possit." Barclay *contra Monarchom.* l. iii. c. 8.

In English thus:

233.   "But if any one should ask, Must the people then always lay themselves open to, the cruelty and rage of tyranny? Must they see their cities pillaged and laid in ashes, their wives and children exposed to the tyrant's lust and fury, and themselves and families reduced by their king to ruin, and all the miseries of want and oppression; and yet sit still? Must men alone be debarred the common privilege of opposing force with force, which nature allows so freely to all other creatures for their preservation from injury? I answer: Self-defence is a part of the law of nature; nor can

it be denied the community, even against the king himself: but to revenge themselves upon him, must by no means be allowed them; it being not agreeable to that law. Wherefore if the king should shew an hatred, not only to some particular persons, but sets himself against the body of the commonwealth, whereof he is the head, and shall, with intolerable ill-usage, cruelly tyrannize over the whole, or a considerable part of the people, in this case the people have a right to resist and defend themselves from injury: but it must be with this caution, that they only defend themselves, but do not attack their prince: they may repair the damages received, but must not for any provocation exceed the bounds of due reverence and respect. They may repulse the present attempt, but must not revenge past violences. For it is natural for us to defend life and limb, but that an inferiour should punish a superiour, is against nature. The mischief which is designed them the people may prevent before it be done; but when it is done, they must not revenge it on the king, though author of the villainy. This therefore is the privilege of the people in general, above what any private person hath; that particular men are allowed by our adversaries themselves (Buchanan only excepted) to have no other remedy but patience; but the body of the people may with reverence resist intolerable tyranny; for, when it is but moderate, they ought to endure it."

234.   Thus far that great advocate of monarchical power allows of *resistance*.

235.   It is true, he has annexed two limitations to it, to no *purpose*:

First, He says, it must be with reverence.

Secondly, It must be without retribution, or punishment; and the reason he gives is, "Because an inferiour cannot punish a superiour."

First, *How to resist force without striking again*, or how to *strike with reverence*, will need some skill to make intelligible. He that shall oppose an assault only with a shield to receive the blows, or in any more respectful posture, without a sword in his hand, to abate the confidence and force of the assailant, will quickly be at an end of his *resistance*, and will find such a defence serve only to draw on himself

the worse usage. This is as ridiculous a way of resisting, as Juvenal thought it of fighting; "ubi tu pulsas, ego vapulo tantum." And the success of the combat will be unavoidably the same he there describes it:

Libertas pauperis haec est:
Pulsatus rogat, & pugnis concisus, adorat,
Ut liceat paucis cum dentibus inde reverti.

This will always be the event of such an imaginary *resistance*, where men may not strike again. He therefore *who may resist, must be allowed to strike*. And then let our author, or any body else, join a knock on the head, or a cut on the face, with as much *reverence* and *respect* as he thinks fit. He that can reconcile blows and reverence, may, for aught I know, deserve for his pains a civil, respectful cudgelling, wherever he can meet with it.

Secondly, as to his second, "An inferiour cannot punish a superiour;" that is true, generally speaking, whilst he is his superiour. But to resist force with force, being the *state of war* that *levels the parties*, cancels all former relation of reverence, respect, and *superiority*: And then the odds that remains, is, that he, who opposes the unjust aggressor, has this *superiority* over him, that he has a right when he prevails, to punish the offender, both for the breach of the peace, and all the evils that followed upon it. Barclay therefore, in another place, more coherently to himself, denies it to be lawful to *resist* a king in any case. But he there assigns two cases, whereby a king may unking himself. His words are,

"Quid ergo, nulline casus incidere possunt quibus populo sese erigere atque in regem impotentius dominantem arma capere & invadere jure suo suaque authoritate liceat? Nulli certe quamdiu rex manet. Semper enim ex divinis id obstat, Regem honorificato; & qui potestati resistit, Dei ordinationi resistit: non alias igitur in eum populo potestas est quam si id committat propter quod ipso jure rex esse desinat. Tunc enim se ipse principatu exuit atque in privatis constituit liber: hoc modo populus & superior efficitur, reverso ad eum sc. jure illo quod ante regem inauguratum in interregno habuit. At sunt paucorum generum commissa ejusmodi quae hunc effectum pariunt. At ego cum plurima animo perlustrem, duo tantam invenio, duos, inquam, casus quibus rex ipso facto ex rege non regem se facit & omni honore & dignitate regali atque in subditos potestate destituit; quorum etiam meminit Winzerus. Horum unus est, Si regnum disperdat, quemadmodum de Nerone fertur, quod is nempe senatum populumque Romanum, atque adeo urbem ipsam ferro flammaque vastare, ac novas sibi sedes quaerere, decrevisset. Et de Caligula, quod palam denunciarit se neque civem neque principem senatui amplius fore, inque animo habuerit interempto utriusque ordinis electissimo quoque Alexandriam commigrare, ac ut populum uno ictu interimeret, unam ei cervicem optavit. Talia cum rex aliquis meditatur & molitur serio, omnem regnandi curam & animum ilico abjicit, ac proinde imperium in subditos amittit, ut dominus servi pro derelicto habiti dominium."

236. "Alter casus est, Si rex in alicujus clientelam se contulit, ac regnum quod liberum a majoribus & populo traditum accepit, alienae ditioni mancipavit. Nam tunc quamvis forte non ea mente id agit populo plane ut incommodet: tamen quia quod praecipuum est regiae dignitatis amisit, ut summus scilicet in regno secundum Deum sit, & solo Deo inferior, atque populum etiam totum ignorantem vel invitum, cujus libertatem sartam & tectam conservare debuit in alterius gentis ditionem & potestatem dedidit, hac velut quadam regni ab alienatione efficit, ut nec quod ipse in regno imperium habuit retineat, nec in eum cui collatum voluit, juris quicquam transferat; atque ita eo facto liberum jam & suae potestatis populum relinquit, cujus rei exemplum unum annales Scotici suppeditant." Barclay *contra Monarchom.* l. iii. c. 16.

Which in English runs thus:

237. "What then, can there no case happen wherein the people may of right, and by their own authority, help themselves, take arms, and set upon their king imperiously domineering over them? None at all, whilst he remains a king. Honour the king, and he that resists the power, resists the ordinance of God; are divine oracles that will never permit it. The people therefore can never come by a power over

him, unless he does something that makes him cease to be a king. For then he divests himself of his crown and dignity, and returns to the state of a private man, and the people become free and superiour, the power which they had in the interregnum, before they crowned him king, devolving to them again. But there are but few miscarriages which bring the matter to this state. After considering it well on all sides, I can find but two. Two cases there are, I say, whereby a king, ipso facto, becomes no king, and loses all power and regal authority over his people; which are also taken notice of by Winzerus.

The first is, If he endeavour to overturn the government, that is, if he have a purpose and design to ruin the kingdom and commonwealth; as it is recorded of Nero, that he resolved to cut off the senate and people of Rome, lay the city waste with fire and sword, and then remove to some other place. And of Caligula, that he openly declared, that he would be no longer a head to the people or senate, and that he had it in his thoughts to cut off the worthiest men of both ranks, and then retire to Alexandria: and he wished that the people had but one neck, that he might dispatch them all at a blow. Such designs as these, when any king harbours in his thoughts, and seriously promotes, he immediately gives up all care and thought of the commonwealth; and consequently forfeits the power of governing his subjects, as a master does the dominion over his slaves whom he hath abandoned."

238. "The other case is, When a king makes himself the dependent of another, and subjects his kingdom which his ancestors left him, and the people put free into his hands, to the dominion of another. For however perhaps it may not be his intention to prejudice the people, yet because he has hereby lost the principal part of regal dignity, viz. to be next and immediately under God supreme in his kingdom; and also because he betrayed or forced his people, whose liberty he ought to have carefully preserved, into the power and dominion of a foreign nation. By this, as it were, alienation of his kingdom, he himself loses the power he had in it before, without transferring any the least right to those on whom he would

have bestowed it; and so by this act sets the people free, and leaves them at their own disposal. One example of this is to be found in the Scotch Annals."

239.   In these cases Barclay, the great champion of absolute monarchy, is forced to allow, that a king may be *resisted*, and *ceases to be a king*. That is, in short, not to multiply cases, in whatsoever he has no authority, there he is no king, and may be resisted. For wheresoever the *authority ceases, the king ceases too*, and becomes like other men who have no *authority*. And these two cases the instances differ little from those above-mentioned, to be destructive to governments, only that he has omitted the principle from which his doctrine flows; and that is, the breach of trust, in not preserving the form of government agreed on, and in not intending the end of government itself, which is the public good and preservation of property. When a king has dethroned himself, and put himself in a state of war with his people, what shall hinder them from prosecuting him who is no king, as they would any other man, who has put himself into a state of war with them; Barclay and those of his opinion would do well to tell us. This farther I desire may be taken notice of out of Barclay, that he says, "The mischief that is designed them, the people may prevent before it be done"; whereby he allows "resistance" when tyranny is but in design. "Such designs as these" (says he) "when any king harbours in his thoughts and seriously promotes, he immediately gives up all care and thought of the commonwealth;" so that, according to him, the neglect of the public good is to be taken as an evidence of such "design," or at least for a sufficient cause of "resistance." And the reason of all, he gives in these words, "Because he betrayed or forced his people, whose liberty he ought carefully to have preserved." What he adds, "into the power and dominion of a foreign nation," signifies nothing, the fault and forfeiture lying in the loss of their "liberty," which he "ought to have preserved," and not in any distinction of the persons to whose dominion they were subjected. The people's right is equally invaded, and their liberty lost, whether they are made slaves to any of their own, or a foreign nation; and

in this lies the injury, and against this only have they the right of defence. And there are instances to be found in all countries, which shew, that it is not the change of nations in the persons of their governors, but the change of government, that gives the offence. Bilson, a bishop of our church, and a great stickler for the power and prerogative of princes, does, if I mistake not, in his treatise of Christian subjection, acknowledge, *that princes may forfeit their power*, and their title to the obedience of their subjects; and if there needed authority in a case where reason is so plain, I could send my reader to Bractan, Fortescue, and the author of the Mirrour, and others, writers that cannot be suspected to be ignorant of our government, or enemies to it. But I thought Hooker alone might be enough to satisfy those men, who relying on him for their ecclesiastical polity, are by a strange fate carried to deny those principles upon which he builds it. Whether they are herein made the tools of cunninger workmen, to pull down their own fabric, they were best look. This I am sure, their civil policy is so new, so dangerous, and so destructive to both rulers and people, that as former ages never could bear the broaching of it; so it may be hoped, those to come, redeemed from the impositions of these Egyptian under taskmasters, will abhor the memory of such servile flatterers, who, whilst it seemed to serve their turn, resolved all government into absolute tyranny, and would have all men born to, what their mean souls fitted them for, slavery.

240.   Here, it is like, the common question will be made, *Who shall be judge*, whether the prince or legislative act contrary to their trust? This, perhaps, ill-affected and factious men may spread amongst the people, when the prince only makes use of his due prerogative. To this I reply, "The people shall be judge;" for who shall be *judge* whether his trustee or deputy acts well, and according to the trust reposed in him, but he who deputes him, and must by having deputed him, have still a power to discard him, when he fails in his trust? If this be reasonable in particular cases of private men, why should it be otherwise in that of the greatest moment, where the welfare of

millions is concerned, and also where the evil, if not prevented, is greater, and the redress very difficult, dear, and dangerous?

241.   But farther, this question, ("Who shall be judge?") cannot mean that there is no judge at all. For where there is no judicature on earth, to decide controversies amongst men, God in heaven is judge. He alone, it is true, is judge of the right. But *every man* is *judge* for himself, as in all other cases, so in this, whether another hath put himself into a state of war with him, and whether he should appeal to the supreme judge, as Jephthah did.

242.   If a controversy arise betwixt a prince and some of the people, in a matter where the law is silent, or doubtful, and the thing be of great consequence, I should think the proper *umpire*, in such a case, should be the body of the *people:* for in cases where the prince hath a trust reposed in him, and is dispensed from the common ordinary rules of the law; there, if any men find themselves aggrieved, and think the prince acts contrary to, or beyond that trust, who so proper to *judge* as the body of the *people*, (who, at first, lodged that trust in him) how far they meant it should extend? But if the prince, or whoever they be in the administration, decline that way of determination, the appeal then lies no where but to heaven; force between either persons, who have no known superior on earth, or which permits no appeal to a judge on earth, being properly a state of war, wherein the appeal lies only to heaven; and in that state the *injured party must judge* for himself, when he will think fit to make use of that appeal, and put himself upon it.

243.   To conclude, The *power that every individual gave the society*, when he entered into it, can never revert to the individuals gain, as long as the society lasts, but will always remain in the community; because without this there can be no community, no commonwealth, which is contrary to the original agreement: so also when the society hath placed the legislative in any assembly of men, to continue in them and their successors, with direction and authority for providing such successors, the *legislative can never revert to the people* whilst that government lasts: Because, having provided a legislative with power to continue for ever, they have given up their political power to the legislative, and cannot resume it. But if they have set limits to the duration of their legislative, and made this supreme power in any person, or assembly, only temporary; or else, when by the miscarriages of those in authority, it is forfeited; upon the forfeiture, or at the determination of the time set, *it reverts to the society*, and the people have a right to act as supreme, and continue the legislative in themselves; or erect a new form, or under the old form place it in new hands, as they think good.

HUME

Of the Original Contract

As no party, in the present age, can well support itself, without a philosophical or speculative system of principles, annexed to its political or practical one; we accordingly find, that each of the factions, into which this nation is divided, has reared up a fabric of the former kind, in order to protect and cover that scheme of actions, which it pursues. The people being commonly very rude builders, especially in this speculative way, and more especially still, when actuated by party-zeal; it is natural to imagine, that their workmanship must be a little unshapely, and discover evident marks of that violence and hurry, in which it was raised. The one party, by tracing up government to the DEITY, endeavour to render it so sacred and inviolate, that it must be little less than sacrilege, however tyrannical it may become, to touch or invade it, in the smallest article. The other party, by founding government altogether on the consent of the PEOPLE, suppose that there is a kind of *original contract*, by which the subjects have tacitly reserved the power of resisting their sovereign, whenever they find themselves aggrieved by that authority, with which they have, for certain purposes, voluntarily entrusted him. These are the speculative principles of the two parties; and these too are the practical consequences deduced from them.

I shall venture to affirm, *That both these* systems *of speculative principles are just; though not in the sense, intended by the parties*: And, *That both the* schemes *of practical consequences are prudent; though not in the extremes, to which each party, in opposition to the other, has commonly endeavoured to carry them.*

That the DEITY is the ultimate author of all government, will never be denied by any, who admit a general providence, and allow, that all events in the universe are conducted by an uniform plan, and di-

[Reprinted from *Essays, Moral, Political, and Literary*.]

rected to wise purposes. As it is impossible for the human race to subsist, at least in any comfortable or secure state, without the protection of government; this institution must certainly have been intended by that beneficent Being, who means the good of all his creatures: And as it has universally, in fact, taken place, in all countries, and all ages; we may conclude, with still greater certainty, that it was intended by that omniscient Being, who can never be deceived by any event or operation. But since he gave rise to it, not by any particular or miraculous interposition, but by his concealed and universal efficacy; a sovereign cannot, properly speaking, be called his vicegerent, in any other sense than every power or force, being derived from him, may be said to act by his commission. Whatever actually happens is comprehended in the general plan or intention of providence; nor has the greatest and most lawful prince any more reason, upon that account, to plead a peculiar sacredness or inviolable authority, than an inferior magistrate, or even an usurper, or even a robber and a pyrate. The same divine superintendant, who, for wise purposes, invested a TITUS or a TRAJAN with authority, did also, for purposes, no doubt, equally wise, though unknown, bestow power on a BORGIA or an ANGRIA. The same causes, which gave rise to the sovereign power in every state, established likewise every petty jurisdiction in it, and every limited authority. A constable, therefore, no less than a king, acts by a divine commission, and possesses an indefeasible right.

When we consider how nearly equal all men are in their bodily force, and even in their mental powers and faculties, till cultivated by education; we must necessarily allow, that nothing but their own consent could, at first, associate them together, and subject them to any authority. The people, if we trace govern-

354

ment to its first origin in the woods and deserts, are the source of all power and jurisdiction, and voluntarily, for the sake of peace and order, abandoned their native liberty, and received laws from their equal and companion. The conditions, upon which they were willing to submit, were either expressed, or were so clear and obvious, that it might well be esteemed superfluous to express them. If this, then, be meant by the *original contract*, it cannot be denied, that all government is, at first, founded on a contract, and that the most ancient rude combinations of mankind were formed chiefly by that principle. In vain, are we asked in what records this charter of our liberties is registered. It was not written on parchment, nor yet on leaves or barks of trees. It preceded the use of writing and all the other civilized arts of life. But we trace it plainly in the nature of man, and in the equality, or something approaching equality, which we find in all the individuals of that species. The force, which now prevails, and which is founded on fleets and armies, is plainly political, and derived from authority, the effect of established government. A man's natural force consists only in the vigour of his limbs, and the firmness of his courage; which could never subject multitudes to the command of one. Nothing but their own consent, and their sense of the advantages resulting from peace and order, could have had that influence.

Yet even this consent was long very imperfect, and could not be the basis of a regular administration. The chieftain, who had probably acquired his influence during the continuance of war, ruled more by persuasion than command; and till he could employ force to reduce the refractory and disobedient, the society could scarcely be said to have attained a state of civil government. No compact or agreement, it is evident, was expressly formed for general submission; an idea far beyond the comprehension of savages: Each exertion of authority in the chieftain must have been particular, and called forth by the present exigencies of the case: The sensible utility, resulting from his interposition, made these exertions become daily more frequent; and their frequency gradually produced an habitual, and, if you please to call it so, a voluntary, and therefore precarious, acquiescence in the people.

But philosophers, who have embraced a party (if that be not a contradiction in terms) are not contented with these concessions. They assert, not only that government in its earliest infancy arose from consent or rather the voluntary acquiescence of the people; but also, that, even at present, when it has attained full maturity, it rests on no other foundation. They affirm, that all men are still born equal, and owe allegiance to no prince or government, unless bound by the obligation and sanction of a *promise*. And as no man, without some equivalent, would forego the advantages of his native liberty, and subject himself to the will of another; this promise is always understood to be conditional, and imposes on him no obligation, unless he meet with justice and protection from his sovereign. These advantages the sovereign promises him in return; and if he fail in the execution, he has broken, on his part, the articles of engagement, and has thereby freed his subject from all obligations to allegiance. Such, according to these philosophers, is the foundation of authority in every government; and such the right of resistance, possessed by every subject.

But would these reasoners look abroad into the world, they would meet with nothing that, in the least, corresponds to their ideas, or can warrant so refined and philosophical a system. On the contrary, we find, every where, princes, who claim their subjects as their property, and assert their independent right of sovereignty, from conquest or succession. We find also, every where, subjects, who acknowledge this right in their prince, and suppose themselves born under obligations of obedience to a certain sovereign, as much as under the ties of reverence and duty to certain parents. These connexions are always conceived to be equally independent of our consent, in PERSIA and CHINA; in FRANCE and SPAIN; and even in HOLLAND and ENGLAND, wherever the doctrines above-mentioned have not been carefully inculcated. Obedience or subjection becomes so familiar, that most men never make any enquiry about its origin or cause, more than about the principle of gravity, resistance, or the most universal laws of nature. Or if curiosity ever move them; as soon as they learn, that they themselves and their ancestors have, for several ages, or from time immemorial, been subject to such a form of government or such a family; they immediately acquiesce, and acknowledge their obligation to allegiance. Were you to preach, in most parts of the world, that political connexions are founded altogether on voluntary consent or a mutual promise, the magistrate would soon imprison you, as seditious, for loosening the ties of obedience; if your friends did not before shut you up as delirious, for advancing such absurdities. It is strange, that an act of the mind, which every individual is supposed to have formed, and after he came to the use of reason too, otherwise it could have no authority; that this act, I say, should be so much unknown to all of them, that, over the face of the whole earth, there scarcely remain any traces or memory of it.

But the contract, on which government is founded, is said to be the *original contract*; and consequently may be supposed too old to fall under the knowledge of the present generation. If the agreement, by which savage men first associated and conjoined their force, be here meant, this is acknowledged to be real; but being so ancient, and being obliterated by a thousand changes of government and princes, it cannot now be supposed to retain any authority. If we would say any thing to the purpose, we must assert, that every particular government, which is lawful, and which imposes any duty of allegiance on the subject, was, at first, founded on consent and a voluntary compact. But besides that this supposes the consent of the fathers to bind the children, even to the most remote generations, (which republican writers will never allow) besides this, I say, it is not justified by history or experience, in any age or country of the world.

Almost all the governments, which exist at present, or of which there remains any record in story, have been founded originally, either on usurpation or conquest, or both, without any pretence of a fair consent, or voluntary subjection of the people. When an artful and bold man is placed at the head of an army or faction, it is often easy for him, by employing, sometimes violence, sometimes false pretences, to establish his dominion over a people a hundred times more numerous than his partizans. He allows no such open communication, that his enemies can know, with certainty, their number or force. He gives them no leisure to assemble together in a body to oppose him. Even all those, who are the instruments of his usurpation, may wish his fall; but their ignorance of each other's intention keeps them in awe, and is the sole cause of his security. By such arts as these, many governments have been established; and this is all the *original contract*, which they have to boast of.

The face of the earth is continually changing, by the encrease of small kingdoms into great empires, by the dissolution of great empires into smaller kingdoms, by the planting of colonies, by the migration of tribes. Is there any thing discoverable in all these events, but force and violence? Where is the mutual agreement or voluntary association so much talked of?

Even the smoothest way, by which a nation may receive a foreign master, by marriage or a will, is not extremely honourable for the people; but supposes them to be disposed of, like a dowry or a legacy, according to the pleasure or interest of their rulers.

But where no force interposes, and election takes place; what is this election so highly vaunted? It is either the combination of a few great men, who decide for the whole, and will allow of no opposition: Or it is the fury of a multitude, that follow a seditious ringleader, who is not known, perhaps, to a dozen among them, and who owes his advancement merely to his own impudence, or to the momentary caprice of his fellows.

Are these disorderly elections, which are rare too, of such mighty authority, as to be the only lawful foundation of all government and allegiance?

In reality, there is not a more terrible event, than a total dissolution of government, which gives liberty to the multitude, and makes the determination or choice of a new establishment depend upon a number, which nearly approaches to that of the body of the people: For it never comes entirely to the whole body of them. Every wise man, then, wishes to see, at the head of a powerful and obedient army, a general, who may speedily seize the prize, and give to the people a master, which they are so unfit to chuse for themselves. So little correspondent is fact and reality to those philosophical notions.

Let not the establishment at the *Revolution* deceive us, or make us so much in love with a philosophical origin to government, as to imagine all others monstrous and irregular. Even that event was far from corresponding to these refined ideas. It was only the succession, and that only in the regal part of the government, which was then changed: And it was only the majority of seven hundred, who determined that change for near ten millions. I doubt not, indeed, but the bulk of those ten millions acquiesced willingly in the determination: But was the matter left, in the least, to their choice? Was it not justly supposed to be, from that moment, decided, and every man punished, who refused to submit to the new sovereign? How otherwise could the matter have ever been brought to any issue or conclusion?

The republic of ATHENS was, I believe, the most extensive democracy, that we read of in history: Yet if we make the requisite allowances for the women, the slaves, and the strangers, we shall find, that that establishment was not, at first, made, nor any law ever voted, by a tenth part of those who were bound to pay obedience to it: Not to mention the islands and foreign dominions, which the ATHENIANS claimed as theirs by right of conquest. And as it is well known, that popular assemblies in that city were always full of licence and disorder, notwithstanding the institutions and laws by which they were checked: How much more disorderly must they prove, where they form not the established constitution, but meet tumultuously on the dissolution of the ancient government, in order to give rise to a new one? How chimerical must it be to talk of a choice in such circumstances?

The ACHAEANS enjoyed the freest and most perfect democracy of all antiquity; yet they employed force to oblige some cities to enter into their league, as we learn from POLYBIUS.

HARRY the IVth and HARRY the VIIth of ENGLAND, had really no title to the throne but a parliamentary election; yet they never would acknowledge it, lest they should thereby weaken their authority. Strange, if the only real foundation of all authority be consent and promise!

It is in vain to say, that all governments are or should be, at first, founded on popular consent, as much as the necessity of human affairs will admit. This favours entirely my pretension. I maintain, that human affairs will never admit of this consent; seldom of the appearance of it. But that conquest or usurpation, that is, in plain terms, force, by dissolving the ancient governments, is the origin of almost all the new ones, which were ever established in the world. And that in the few cases, where consent may seem to have taken place, it was commonly so irregular, so confined, or so much intermixed either with fraud or violence, that it cannot have any great authority.

My intention here is not to exclude the consent of the people from being one just foundation of government where it has place. It is surely the best and most sacred of any. I only pretend, that it has very seldom had place in any degree, and never almost in its full extent. And that therefore some other foundation of government must also be admitted.

Were all men possessed of so inflexible a regard to justice, that, of themselves, they would totally abstain from the properties of others; they had for ever remained in a state of absolute liberty, without subjection to any magistrate or political society: But this is a state of perfection, of which human nature is justly deemed incapable. Again; were all men possessed of so perfect an understanding, as always to know their own interests, no form of government had ever been submitted to, but what was established on consent, and was fully canvassed by every member of the society: But this state of perfection is likewise much superior to human nature. Reason, history, and experience shew us, that all political societies have had an origin much less accurate and regular; and were one to choose a period of time, when the people's consent was the least regarded in public transactions, it would be precisely on the establishment of a new government. In a settled constitution, their inclinations are often consulted; but during the fury of revolutions, conquests, and public convulsions, military force or political craft usually decides the controversy.

When a new government is established, by whatever means, the people are commonly dissatisfied with it, and pay obedience more from fear and necessity, than from any idea of allegiance or of moral obligation. The prince is watchful and jealous, and must carefully guard against every beginning or appearance of insurrection. Time, by degrees, removes all these difficulties, and accustoms the nation to regard, as their lawful or native princes, that family, which, at first, they considered as usurpers or foreign conquerors. In order to found this opinion, they have no recourse to any notion of voluntary consent or promise, which, they know, never was, in this case, either expected or demanded. The original establishment was formed by violence, and submitted to from necessity. The subsequent administration is also supported by power, and acquiesced in by the people, not as a matter of choice, but of obligation. They imagine not, that their consent gives their prince a title: But they willingly consent, because they think, that, from long possession, he has acquired a title, independent of their choice or inclination.

Should it be said, that, by living under the dominion of a prince, which one might leave, every individual has given a *tacit* consent to his authority, and promised him obedience; it may be answered, that such an implied consent can only have place, where a man imagines, that the matter depends on his choice. But where he thinks (as all mankind do who are born under established governments) that by his birth he owes allegiance to a certain prince or certain form of government; it would be absurd to infer a consent or choice, which he expressly, in this case, renounces and disclaims.

Can we seriously say, that a poor peasant or artizan has a free choice to leave his country, when he knows no foreign language or manners, and lives from day to day, by the small wages which he acquires? We may as well assert, that a man, by remaining in a vessel, freely consents to the dominion of the master; though he was carried on board while asleep, and must leap into the ocean, and perish, the moment he leaves her.

What if the prince forbid his subjects to quit his dominions; as in TIBERIUS'S time, it was regarded as a crime in a ROMAN knight that he had attempted to fly to the PARTHIANS, in order to escape the tyranny of that emperor? Or as the ancient MUSCO-VITES prohibited all travelling under pain of death? And did a prince observe, that many of his subjects were seized with the frenzy of migrating to foreign countries, he would doubtless, with great reason and justice, restrain them, in order to prevent the depopulation of his own kingdom. Would he forfeit the allegiance of all his subjects, by so wise and reasonable a law? Yet the freedom of their choice is surely, in that case, ravished from them.

A company of men, who should leave their native country, in order to people some uninhabited region, might dream of recovering their native freedom; but they would soon find, that their prince still laid claim to them, and called them his subjects, even in their new settlement. And in this he would but act conformably to the common ideas of mankind.

The truest *tacit* consent of this kind, that is ever observed, is when a foreigner settles in any country, and is beforehand acquainted with the prince, and government, and laws, to which he must submit: Yet is his allegiance, though more voluntary, much less expected or depended on, than that of a natural born subject. On the contrary, his native prince still asserts a claim to him. And if he punish not the renegade, when he seizes him in war with his new prince's commission; this clemency is not founded on the municipal law, which in all countries condemns the prisoner; but on the consent of princes, who have agreed to this indulgence, in order to prevent reprisals.

Did one generation of men go off the stage at once, and another succeed, as is the case with silk-worms and butterflies, the new race, if they had sense enough to choose their government, which surely is never the case with men, might voluntarily, and by general consent, establish their own form of civil polity, without any regard to the laws or precedents, which prevailed among their ancestors. But as human society is in perpetual flux, one man every hour going out of the world, another coming into it, it is necessary, in order to preserve stability in government, that the new brood should conform themselves to the established constitution, and nearly follow the path which their fathers, treading in the footsteps of theirs, had marked out to them. Some innovations must necessarily have place in every human institution, and it is happy where the enlightened genius of the age give these a direction to the side of reason, liberty, and justice: but violent innovations no individual is entitled to make: they are even dangerous to be attempted by the legislature: more ill than good is ever to be expected from them: and if history affords examples to the contrary, they are not to be drawn into precedent, and are only to be regarded as proofs, that the science of politics affords few rules, which will not admit of some exception, and which may not sometimes be controuled by fortune and accident. The violent innovations in the reign of HENRY VIII. proceeded from an imperious monarch, seconded by the appearance of legislative authority: Those in the reign of CHARLES I. were derived from faction and fanaticism; and both of them have proved happy in the issue: But even the former were long the source of many disorders, and still more dangers; and if the measures of allegiance were to be taken from the latter, a total anarchy must have place in human society, and a final period at once be put to every government.

Suppose, that an usurper, after having banished his lawful prince and royal family, should establish his dominion for ten or a dozen years in any country, and should preserve so exact a discipline in his troops, and so regular a disposition in his garrisons, that no insurrection had ever been raised, or even murmur heard, against his administration: Can it be asserted, that the people, who in their hearts abhor his treason, have tacitly consented to his authority, and promised him allegiance, merely because, from necessity, they live under his dominion? Suppose again their native prince restored, by means of an army, which he levies in foreign countries: They receive him with joy and exultation, and shew plainly with what reluctance they had submitted to any other yoke. I may now ask, upon what foundation the prince's title stands? Not on popular consent surely: For though the people willingly acquiesce in his authority, they never imagine, that their consent made him sovereign. They consent; because they apprehend him to be already, by birth, their lawful sovereign. And as to that tacit consent, which may now be inferred from their living under his dominion,

this is no more than what they formerly gave to the tyrant and usurper.

When we assert, that all lawful government arises from the consent of the people, we certainly do them a great deal more honour than they deserve, or even expect and desire from us. After the ROMAN dominions became too unwieldly for the republic to govern them, the people, over the whole known world, were extremely grateful to AUGUSTUS for that authority, which, by violence, he had established over them; and they shewed an equal disposition to submit to the successor, whom he left them, by his last will and testament. It was afterwards their misfortune, that there never was, in one family, any long regular succession; but that their line of princes was continually broken, either by private assassinations or public rebellions. The *praetorian* bands, on the failure of every family, set up one emperor; the legions in the East a second; those in GERMANY, perhaps, a third: And the sword alone could decide the controversy. The condition of the people, in that mighty monarchy, was to be lamented, not because the choice of the emperor was never left to them; for that was impracticable: But because they never fell under any succession of masters, who might regularly follow each other. As to the violence and wars and bloodshed, occasioned by every new settlement; these were not blameable, because they were inevitable.

The house of LANCASTER ruled in this island about sixty years; yet the partizans of the white rose seemed daily to multiply in ENGLAND. The present establishment has taken place during a still longer period. Have all views of right in another family been utterly extinguished; even though scarce any man now alive had arrived at years of discretion, when it was expelled, or could have consented to its dominion, or have promised it allegiance? A sufficient indication surely of the general sentiment of mankind on this head. For we blame not the partizans of the abdicated family, merely on account of the long time, during which they have preserved their imaginary loyalty. We blame them for adhering to a family, which, we affirm, has been justly expelled, and which, from the moment the new settlement took place, had forfeited all title to authority.

But would we have a more regular, at least a more philosophical, refutation of this principle of an original contract or popular consent; perhaps, the following observations may suffice.

All *moral* duties may be divided into two kinds. The *first* are those, to which men are impelled by a natural instinct or immediate propensity, which operates on them, independent of all ideas of obligation, and of all views, either to public or private utility. Of this nature are, love of children, gratitude to benefactors, pity to the unfortunate. When we reflect on the advantage, which results to society from such humane instincts, we pay them the just tribute of moral approbation and esteem: But the person, actuated by them, feels their power and influence, antecedent to any such reflection.

The *second* kind of moral duties are such as are not supported by any original instinct of nature, but are performed entirely from a sense of obligation, when we consider the necessities of human society, and the impossibility of supporting it, if these duties were neglected. It is thus *justice* or a regard to the property of others, *fidelity* or the observance of promises, become obligatory, and acquire an authority over mankind. For as it is evident, that every man loves himself better than any other person, he is naturally impelled to extend his acquisitions as much as possible; and nothing can restrain him in this propensity, but reflection and experience, by which he learns the pernicious effects of that licence, and the total dissolution of society which must ensue from it. His original inclination, therefore, or instinct, is here checked and restrained by a subsequent judgment or observation.

The case is precisely the same with the political or civil duty of *allegiance*, as with the natural duties of justice and fidelity. Our primary instincts lead us, either to indulge ourselves in unlimited freedom, or to seek dominion over others: And it is reflection only, which engages us to sacrifice such strong passions to the interests of peace and public order. A small degree of experience and observation suffices to teach us, that society cannot possibly be maintained without the authority of magistrates, and that this authority must soon fall into contempt, where exact obedience is not payed to it. The observation of these general and obvious interests is the source of all allegiance, and of that moral obligation, which we attribute to it.

What necessity, therefore, is there to found the duty of *allegiance* or obedience to magistrates on that of *fidelity* or a regard to promises, and to suppose, that it is the consent of each individual, which subjects him to government; when it appears, that both allegiance and fidelity stand precisely on the same foundation, and are both submitted to by mankind, on account of the apparent interests and necessities of human society? We are bound to obey our sovereign, it is said; because we have given a tacit promise to that purpose. But why are we bound to observe our promise? It must here be asserted, that the commerce and intercourse of mankind, which are of such mighty advantage, can have no security where men pay no regard to their engagements. In like manner, may it be said, that men could not live at all in society, at least in a civilized society, without laws and magistrates and judges, to prevent the encroachments of the strong upon the weak, of the violent upon the just and equitable. The obligation to allegiance being of like force and authority with the obligation to fidelity, we gain nothing by resolving the one into the other. The general interests or necessities of society are sufficient to establish both.

If the reason be asked of that obedience, which we are bound to pay to government, I readily answer, *because society could not otherwise subsist*: And this answer is clear and intelligible to all mankind. Your answer is, *because we should keep our word*. But besides, that no body, till trained in a philosophical system, can either comprehend or relish this answer: Besides this, I say, you find yourself embarrassed, when it is asked, *why we are bound to keep our word?* Nor can you give any answer, but what would, immediately, without any circuit, have accounted for our obligation to allegiance.

But *to whom is allegiance due? And who is our lawful sovereign?* This question is often the most difficult of any, and liable to infinite discussions. When people are so happy, that they can answer, *Our present sovereign, who inherits, in a direct line, from ancestors, that have governed us for many ages*; this answer admits of no reply; even though historians, in tracing up to the remotest antiquity, the origin of that royal family, may find, as commonly happens, that its first authority was derived from usurpation and violence. It is confessed, that private justice, or the abstinence from the properties of others, is a most cardinal virtue: Yet reason tells us, that there is no property in durable objects, such as lands or houses, when carefully examined in passing from hand to hand, but must, in some period, have been founded on fraud and injustice. The necessities of human society, neither in private nor public life, will allow of such an accurate enquiry: And there is no virtue or moral duty, but what may, with facility, be refined away, if we indulge a false philosophy, in sifting and scrutinizing it, by every captious rule of logic, in every light or position, in which it may be placed.

The questions with regard to private property have filled infinite volumes of law and philosophy, if in both we add the commentators to the original text; and in the end, we may safely pronounce, that many of the rules, there established, are uncertain, ambiguous, and arbitrary. The like opinion may be formed with regard to the succession and rights of princes and forms of government. Several cases, no doubt, occur, especially in the infancy of any constitution, which admit of no determination from the laws of justice and equity: And our historian RAPIN pretends, that the controversy between EDWARD the Third and PHILIP DE VALOIS was of this nature, and could be decided only by an appeal to heaven, that is, by war and violence.

Who shall tell me, whether GERMANICUS or DRUSUS ought to have succeeded to TIBERIUS, had he died, while they were both alive, without naming any of them for his successor? Ought the right of adoption to be received as equivalent to that of blood, in a nation, where it had the same effect in private families, and had already, in two instances, taken place in the public? Ought GERMANICUS to be esteemed the elder son because he was born before DRUSUS; or the younger, because he was adopted after the birth of his brother? Ought the right of the elder to be regarded in a nation, where he had no advantage in the succession of private families? Ought the ROMAN empire at that time to be deemed hereditary, because of two examples; or ought it, even so early, to be regarded as belonging to the stronger or to the present possessor, as being founded on so recent an usurpation?

COMMODUS mounted the throne after a pretty long succession of excellent emperors, who had acquired their title, not by birth, or public election, but by the fictitious rite of adoption. That bloody debauchee being murdered by a conspiracy suddenly formed between his wench and her gallant, who happened at that time to be *Praetorian Praefect*; these immediately deliberated about choosing a master to human kind, to speak in the style of those ages; and they cast their eyes on PERTINAX. Before the tyrant's death was known, the *Praefect* went secretly to that senator, who, on the appearance of the soldiers, imagined that his execution had been ordered by COMMODUS. He was immediately saluted emperor by the officer and his attendants; chearfully proclaimed by the populace; unwillingly submitted to by the guards; formally recognized by the senate; and passively received by the provinces and armies of the empire.

The discontent of the *Praetorian* bands broke out in a sudden sedition, which occasioned the murder of that excellent prince: And the world being now without a master and without government, the guards thought proper to set the empire formally to sale. JULIAN, the purchaser, was proclaimed by the soldiers, recognized by the senate, and submitted to by the people; and must also have been submitted to by the provinces, had not the envy of the legions begotten opposition and resistance. PESCENNIUS NIGER in SYRIA elected himself emperor, gained the tumultuary consent of his army, and was attended with the secret good will of the senate and people of ROME. ALBINUS in BRITAIN found an equal right to set up his claim; but SEVERUS, who governed PANNONIA, prevailed in the end above both of them. That able politician and warrior, finding his own birth and dignity too much inferior to the imperial crown, professed, at first, an intention only of revenging the death of PERTINAX. He marched as general into ITALY; defeated JULIAN; and without our being able to fix any precise commencement even of the soldiers' consent, he was from necessity acknowledged emperor by the senate and people; and fully established in his violent authority by subduing NIGER and ALBINUS.

Inter haec Gordianus CAESAR (says CAPITOLINUS, speaking of another period) *sublatus a militibus.* Imperator *est appellatus, quia non erat alius in praesenti* [Meanwhile Gordianus Caesar was lifted up by the soldiers and hailed as emperor, there being no one else suitable to hand.] It is to be remarked, that GORDIAN was a boy of fourteen years of age.

Frequent instances of a like nature occur in the history of the emperors; in that of ALEXANDER'S successors; and of many other countries: Nor can any thing be more unhappy than a despotic government of this kind; where the succession is disjointed and irregular, and must be determined, on every vacancy, by force or election. In a free government, the matter is often unavoidable, and is also much less dangerous. The interests of liberty may there frequently lead the people, in their own defence, to alter the succession of the crown. And the constitution, being compounded of parts, may still maintain a sufficient stability, by resting on the aristocratical or democratical members, though the monarchical be altered, from time to time, in order to accommodate it to the former.

In an absolute government, when there is no legal prince, who has a title to the throne, it may safely be determined to belong to the first occupant. Instances of this kind are but too frequent, especially in the eastern monarchies. When any race of princes expires, the will or destination of the last sovereign will be regarded as a title. Thus the edict of LEWIS the XIVth, who called the bastard princes to the succession in case of the failure of all the legitimate princes, would, in such an event, have some authority. Thus the will of CHARLES the Second disposed of the whole SPANISH monarchy. The cession of the ancient proprietor, especially when joined to conquest, is likewise deemed a good title. The general obligation, which binds us to government, is the interest and necessities of society; and this obligation is very strong. The determination of it to this or that particular prince or form of government is frequently more uncertain and dubious. Present possession has considerable authority in these cases, and greater than in private property; because of the disorders which attend all revolutions and changes of government.

We shall only observe, before we conclude, that, though an appeal to general opinion may justly, in the speculative sciences of metaphysics, natural philosophy, or astronomy, be deemed unfair and inconclusive, yet in all questions with regard to morals, as well as criticism, there is really no other standard, by which any controversy can ever be decided. And nothing is a clearer proof, that a theory of this kind is erroneous, than to find, that it leads to paradoxes, repugnant to the common sentiments of mankind, and to the practice and opinion of all nations and all ages. The doctrine, which founds all lawful government on an *original contract*, or consent of the people, is plainly of this kind; nor has the most noted of its partizans, in prosecution of it, scrupled to affirm, *that absolute monarchy is inconsistent with civil society, and so can be no form of civil government at all*; and *that the supreme power in a state cannot take from any man, by taxes and impositions, any part of his property, without his own consent or that of his representatives*. What authority any moral reasoning can have, which leads into opinions so wide of the general practice of mankind, in every place but this single kingdom, it is easy to determine.

The only passage I meet with in antiquity, where the obligation of obedience to government is ascribed to a promise, is in PLATO'S *Crito:* where SOCRATES refuses to escape from prison, because he had tacitly promised to obey the laws. Thus he builds a *tory* consequence of passive obedience, on a *whig* foundation of the original contract.

New discoveries are not to be expected in these matters. If scarce any man, till very lately, ever imagined that government was founded on compact, it is certain, that it cannot, in general, have any such foundation.

The crime of rebellion among the ancients was commonly expressed by the terms νεωτερίζειν, *novas res moliri* [to undertake new things].

4

ROUSSEAU, THE ENLIGHTENMENT, AND THE AGE OF REVOLUTION

Two books mark the birth of the Enlightenment. The first is John Locke's *Essay Concerning Human Understanding* (1689). Locke rejected both Aristotelian teleology and the premises on which Descartes had sought to ground his system of knowledge, in order to construct an empiricist theory of knowledge well-adapted to an age of scientific discovery. By agreeing that it was not inconceivable that matter might think, while maintaining that the universe appeared to be the work of a divine architect, he offered arguments which appealed to both materialist atheists and to deists. By explaining the working of the human mind in terms of the principle of the association of ideas, he appeared to open up the possibility of reforming human nature and transforming society through education and social reform. On Locke's account, it seemed, people were not by nature sinful; vice and crime were the results of defects in their upbringing and environment, which could, in principle, be eliminated. Later philosophers might be highly critical of Locke's achievements, but often their advances were based on choices they had made while picking through Locke's eclectic synthesis. Hume, for example, used Locke's views on probability to undermine his account of causation and turned the association of ideas against Locke's analysis of the self.

For our purposes, though, a second book is more important. It is Pierre Bayle's *Historical and Critical Dictionary,* first published in French, in Amsterdam, in 1697. Bayle's *Dictionary* at first sight appears to be a vast and entirely innocuous work of scholarship. His original project had been to establish the foundations of a reliable historical knowledge by accumulating a list of all the factual errors made by historians, biographers, and bibliographers. Such a work would have been truly perverse, about as useful as a telephone directory which listed only disconnected numbers. But into this arid framework Bayle stuffed an explosive mixture of other ingredients: not only true facts, but also what he termed obscenities (that is, discussions of sex), and, above all, prolonged discussions, buried in the footnotes of the biographical entries for obscure philosophers, of urgent philosophical problems. In the pages of his dictionary Bayle canvassed all the extant objections to Christianity and elaborated a series of alternatives (Manicheism, Pyrrhonism, Spinozism), which he may not have believed in himself, but which he insisted were every bit as rational and sophisticated as any form of Christian faith.

Bayle had himself been baptized a Calvinist, had briefly in his youth been a Catholic convert, and had fled France for Holland in 1681 to escape Louis XIV's persecution of Protestants. Unlike most Protestant refugees, he refused to argue that citizens had a right of resistance in face of tyrannical rulers, but he produced a series of compelling arguments in favor of religious toleration. Above all he exploited the fact that the press was freer in Holland than anywhere else in the world. When his Calvinist coreligionists, for example, condemned his portrait of the Old Testament King David in the *Dictionary*, Bayle meekly revised it, but his publisher reprinted the original article as an appendix so that sales of the second edition would not be adversely affected. French was now replacing Latin as the most widely read language in Europe, and from Holland, as from Switzerland, the works of banned authors could be smuggled not only into the vast French market, but throughout Europe, where every educated person could read them. Censorship, which had played a decisive role in channelling the flow of ideas from 1520 to 1680, became increasingly ineffectual. When Kant, more than a hundred years after the publication of Bayle's *Dictionary*, defined the Enlightenment as obedience to authority combined with the open debate of ideas before the tribunal of public opinion, he was describing an intellectual world first formed by Bayle's great journal, the *Nouvelles de la république des lettres*. It was the authors of Bayle's generation who had first created a "public" which had opinions different from those authorized by the government or the universities and which was so well organized, thanks to its ability to reach across international frontiers, that governments themselves were eventually obliged to defer to it.

If Bayle is the first philosopher to address not his fellow citizens but the republic of letters, it is a disciple of his, Bernard de Mandeville, a medical doctor and an immigrant to England, who demonstrated just how disturbing Bayle's thinking on moral and social questions could be when presented by someone who took pleasure in shocking polite opinion. Much of the political, social, and economic thought of the Enlightenment can be read as an attempt to admit the strength of Mandeville's position without taking on board all his more disturbing conclusions. Mandeville's classic work was a series of lengthy footnotes to a crude satirical poem, *The Fable of the Bees: Or, Private Vices, Publick Benefits* (1723). There he argued that apparently wicked behavior benefited the economy. Where would the brewing industry be without drunkards? Or lacemakers, ribbon-makers, and milliners without the vanity which drove women to choose clothes for their appearance, not their utility? Greed, waste, conspicuous expenditure, extravagance: These were the moral foundations of economic growth and prosperity. A society of true Christians, by contrast, would be poor and, in consequence, quite incapable of mustering the resources required to defend itself against its neighbors. Mandeville did not merely argue that what appeared to be vice was in fact socially beneficial, he also argued that what were generally taken for virtues were usually merely disguised vices. Take modesty, for example: It was Mandeville's observation that well-brought-up young women blushed freely in company when sex was even hinted at, but they did not blush at all if they were listening unobserved to a conversation taking place in the next room. Even blushes, at first sight so natural and unfeigned, were in fact artificial, a learned response, employed to give the appearance of virtue and lay claim to a reputation for modesty. Religious piety, too, was usually intended for public display and was commonly merely a screen for hypocrisy. Everywhere, where other authors saw selfless virtue, Mandeville claimed to trace the workings of a devious vanity.

Mandeville's views are presented here as summarized by Adam Smith in the first edition of *The Theory of Moral Sentiments* (1759) under the heading "Of licentious systems." In fact many of Mandeville's arguments can be traced back beyond Bayle (who always claimed to be an orthodox Calvinist) to a group of strict Catholic moralists, the Jansenists (especially Pierre Nicole), and above all to their close associate, La Rochefoucauld, who had argued in the 1660s and '70s that people were so ineradicably sinful and self-deceiving that much that they took to be virtue was in fact vice and that social life was only possible because vice had been harnessed (as a result of the development of appropriate conventions) to serve public interests. It was love of profit, not charity, that made the miller rise early to grind the corn and kept the innkeeper up late waiting on his guests. There was nothing particularly shocking about these arguments so long as they were presented as being part of an attack upon sin; Mandeville, however, transformed them into what appeared to be an apology for vice. Smith's *Wealth of Nations* (1776), the first great work of economic theory, was a logical development of this tradition of thought; the task he set himself in *The Theory of Moral Sentiments* (and that Hume had also set himself in the *Enquiry Concerning the Principles of Morals*) was that of showing that one could give due weight to self-interest, vanity, and artificial convention without denying that there was a real distinction between moral and immoral behavior, a distinction which derived from the capacity of human beings to identify with the welfare of others through sympathy.

The ghost of Mandeville did not haunt only Smith and Hume: Smith, reviewing Rousseau's *Discourse on the Origins of Inequality* the year after it was published, observed, "whoever reads this . . . work with attention will observe that the second volume of *The Fable of the Bees* has given occasion to the system of Mr. Rousseau." Rousseau, it seemed, had set out to elaborate one of Mandeville's uncompleted projects, that of providing a natural history of morality. How could human beings, who were merely a peculiar species of animal, have invented language, property, political society, and morality—none of which were innate, but all evidently artificial? Hume too had puzzled over this question and, like Rousseau, had insisted that Locke's philosophy provided no adequate answer to it. But there was a fundamental difference between Rousseau and Mandeville, one that cut so deep that, if Smith suspected Rousseau of being a follower of Mandeville, Rousseau could well have replied that it was Hume and Smith who were Mandeville's true allies. Hume and Smith disagreed with Mandeville, in that they maintained that it was possible to be genuinely virtuous and honest within contemporary commercial society, but, like Mandeville, they admired the society that commerce had created. Rousseau, on the other hand, agreed entirely with Mandeville's description of contemporary existence: "everything [is] reduced to appearances, everything becomes factitious and bogus: honor, friendship, and virtue, and often even our vices, about which we eventually find the secret of boasting." Because civilized human beings are vain and competitive (exactly as La Rochefoucauld, Bayle, and Mandeville had claimed), they are, Rousseau believed, only concerned about what others think of them, and therefore are always concerned to have the appearance of virtue, while being quite incapable of doing good for any but the most selfish of reasons.

Where Hume and Smith had defended civilization against Mandeville, who seemed to positively relish the versatility of vice, Rousseau turned in disgust from civilization as Mandeville had portrayed it, in order to try to find an alternative to it. How could one reconstruct virtue, wisdom, and happiness so that they would not be corroded by what Rousseau termed *amour propre,* by which he meant both selfishness and vanity? How could one free human beings from the tyranny expressed by their constant attempt to look good in the eyes of others, and restore to them their independence? Was there any way in which people could live together in communities without being corrupted by competition and its consequences, inequality and hypocrisy?

To these questions Rousseau saw three possible answers. One could try and turn back the clock and return to a simpler society, such as that of ancient Sparta, where true virtue had been admired and commerce despised, where inequality and competition were held in check. But Rousseau was acutely aware that "progress" could not be reversed. Even relatively isolated and disciplined societies, like the Geneva in which he had been raised, were coming increasingly to resemble Paris and London. He and other members of his generation were conscious that modern technology had created a new world: There could be no going back to ancient Rome or Greece. Machiavelli's cyclical view of history was no longer credible in a world where pistols and pocket watches, window panes and chimneys, printed books and newspapers had become commonplace.

The second option was to retreat into a private world. Rousseau, whose first publication, the *Discourse on the Science and the Arts* (1750) had made him a celebrity, had left Paris for a country retreat in 1756, and he increasingly distanced himself from those contemporaries (such as Diderot and Hume) with whom he had previously been on good terms. In his self-imposed isolation Rousseau wrote *Émile,* an account of how a child could be educated to be morally self-reliant and immune to the corrupting pressures of contemporary civilization. A precondition of this, however, was that the child should be brought up in isolation, dependent on things not people. Could one conceive a society in which a young man like Émile would be at home?

At the same time as he was writing *Émile,* Rousseau was working on the *Social Contract* (1762), in which he tried to provide a third solution to the question of how to escape from the corruption of contemporary society. The solution, Rousseau argues, lies in a new sense of community, a commitment to what he terms 'the general will'. The concept of the general will is probably best explained by reference to a question recently posed by John Rawls. Rawls asks what sort of society we would want to establish if we did not know what position we were to hold in that society, if we approached the question while our personal fate was hidden behind "a veil of ignorance." Under such circumstances we might agree, for example, that we would want an efficient police force and an effective IRS, even if we knew there was some chance that we ourselves might prove to be burglars or tax dodgers. With our own circumstances hidden from our sight, we would have to ask what would benefit virtually all members of society and what would serve the interests of the community as a whole. It is something very close to this which Rousseau is referring to when he speaks of the general will and which he distinguishes from the will of each (tax dodgers will want an inefficient tax-collection system) and the will of all (which is not the unanimous will of all, but the aggregate will of all selfish individuals: The majority, who are in work, may well care little about Social Security for the unemployed, whereas, if they were unsure as to which group they would find themselves in, they might be much more sympathetic to arguments for welfare provision).

Rousseau's concept of the general will requires that he draw a sharp distinction between legislation and government. In his view the general will must be based on the common interests of all members of society; it must express itself in legislation which affects all equally; and it must preserve the ultimate authority of the members of the community as a whole. But the members of a community cannot always meet to determine what they want; they must sometimes delegate decision-making. More important, some decisions are inherently divisive. We may agree we will all benefit from a bus service. But is the stop to be placed near my house or yours? Am I going to be able to travel direct to the university without changing, or are you to have this privilege instead? There cannot be answers to such questions which do not involve sacrificing one person's interests in order to benefit someone else, and in Rousseau's view these are consequently questions for government, not for legislation. Rousseau is thus perfectly happy to have a monarch, a commission of experts, or a representative assembly make such decisions (and the bulk of what we think of as 'government' is indeed concerned with such decisions), providing that the sense of belonging to a shared community, in which all share interests which are more important than the interests which divide them, is not undermined. A precondition for such a community is that we really should have extensive common interests. If some of us are very wealthy, while others are very poor, if some have servants, and others are forced to serve, then the sense of community may easily dissolve, and divisive interests may seem more important than common ones.

Rousseau's argument is presented as if his concern is to define the contractual relations between citizens, as if he is writing in the tradition of Hobbes, Pufendorf, and Locke. But the general will is a *moral* rather than a *contractual* relationship. It exists wherever humans recognize important interests in common, wherever they recognize their common humanity or shared citizenship. It may be better expressed in a gesture or a glance than in a contract; indeed Rousseau's most haunting description of what it is to be a citizen occurs in his *Confessions*, when he is describing a scene from his childhood. The militia of Geneva had eaten together after a day of military manoeuvres, and then, spurred on by drums and pipes, had started to dance:

> A dance of men, cheered by a long meal, would seem to present nothing very interesting to see; however, the harmony of five or six hundred men in uniform, holding one another by the hand and forming a long ribbon which wound round around, serpentlike, in cadence and without confusion, with countless turns and returns, countless sorts of figured evolutions, the excellence of the tunes which animated them, the sound of drums, the glare of torches, a certain military pomp in the midst of pleasure, all this created a very lively sensation that could not be experienced coldly. It was late; the women were all in bed; all of them got up. Soon the windows were full of female spectators who gave new zeal to the actors; they could no longer confine themselves to their windows and they came down; the wives came to their husbands, the servants brought wine; even the children, awakened by the noise, ran half-clothed amidst their fathers and mothers. The dance was suspended; now there were only embraces, laughs, toasts, and caresses. There resulted from all this a general emotion that I could not describe but which, in universal gaiety, is quite naturally felt in the midst of all that is dear to us. My father, embracing me, was seized with trembling which I think I still feel and share. "Jean-Jacques," he said to me, "love your country. . . ." [Strong's translation]

Only in a society capable of feeling such a common identity, of responding to such a shared experience, could there be a "general will." Its precondition is that, though there may be "actors" and "spectators," the actors are not in competition with each other, nor are they preoccupied with impressing the spectators.

Both *The Discourse on Inequality* and *The Social Contract* are concerned with the need to overcome the consequences of inequality and competition. It is helpful, I think, to place them alongside two further chapters from Smith's *Theory of Moral Sentiments*. The first, "Of the Origin of Ambition," appeared in the first edition (1759), after Smith had read Rousseau, and presents, as Smith does elsewhere in the *Theory,* a relatively complacent account of the benefits for society (much more marked in Smith's view than the true benefits derived by individuals) which result from competition and inequality. The second, "Of the Corruption of Our Moral Sentiments," first published in 1790, presents a much more anxious account of the disadvantages of inequality.

It would be tempting to see the difference between the two as the result of the French Revolution, but in 1790 this was yet to enter on its radical phase; the slogan of "liberty, equality, fraternity," which owed much to Rousseau, had yet to be raised. Smith's new text provides a measure of the extent to which the idea of equality was making progress, even before the Revolution occurred, thanks to authors such as Beccaria, whose *On Crimes and Punishments* was first published in Italian in 1764 and was soon translated into French and English and read throughout the Old World and the New. Beccaria's book is primarily famous because he opposed torture, both as a way of establishing guilt and as a method of punishment. But in the eyes of his contemporaries, his arguments were particularly shocking because they insisted that all prisoners, no matter what their rank or status, should receive the same punishment. A general who ill-treated a soldier should be punished no differently from a soldier who ill-treated a general (Smith had thought this view ridiculous in 1759). Beccaria rescued egalitarianism from Rousseau's hypothetical societies and argued that it be immediately adopted as a practical principle. Equality seemed much more admirable in 1790 than it had seemed in 1759. The American and French Revolutions reflected this fact, but they were scarcely responsible for it.

It was this development in European culture which provoked Burke's *Reflections,* which, like Smith's chapter on equality, was also written before the French Revolution entered its radical phase. Burke saw the French Revolution as being founded on the false assumption that one could construct a political community on the basis of abstract principles of reason. In his view there was nothing particularly rational about authority, hierarchy, tradition, or, indeed, religion, but unless these were preserved, society would dissolve into a Hobbesian clash of competing wills and interests, until only military force could restore order. In taking this view Burke was attacking not only radicals like Beccaria but also liberal authors such as Smith, for if Smith praised the consequences of inequality, the inequality he admired was not the result of inherited rank or an expression of traditional status; it was the outcome of competition between individuals striving for the fruits of success. Smith was interested in how people deferred to the rich and famous, but he saw no need to insist that they should respect tradition or should regard rank as a privilege rather than a reward for effort. Burke, in defending tradition, was thus attacking a broad spread of Enlightenment opinion, though in doing so he could rely on arguments that had Enlightenment origins. Hume, after all, had insisted that political authority was conventional, not rational, and had argued that it was a natural principle of human psychology that the mere passage of time changed moral relationships. A son might feel with reason that he legitimately owned property which his father had come by under dubious circumstances; a society might come to regard a ruler as legitimate even though he had been regarded as a usurper when he first seized power. Anyone who denied this, Hume thought, would find herself constantly questioning the validity of established institutions.

Burkean conservatism owed a great deal to Hume, but Hume had not felt, as Burke evidently did, that scepticism and rational enquiry were themselves a danger to social stability. Burke sprang to the defense of the Church in France, even though Protestants had normally taken delight in any setback for Catholicism; he defended it not because he was a Catholic (though his Irish background may have made Catholicism seem less alien to him) but because in France the Catholic religion was the established religion and as such was entitled to respect. Rousseau and Burke thus mark two extremes of Enlightenment opinion: one radical, the other conservative, but both opposed to the spirit of competition and commerce which was accepted with equanimity by more moderate figures such as Hume and Smith.

Given the immense range of opinion expressed by Enlightenment philosophers, one may wonder whether there is any straightforward answer to the question "What is Enlightenment?" Kant's famous answer to this question, written in 1784, rightly stresses the fundamental importance of freedom of discussion for the development of enlightened values. Kant's own ruler, Frederick II of Prussia, allowed his subjects a considerable degree of intellectual and religious freedom, so that it was possible for Kant to persuade himself that one could both uphold the motto "Dare to Know!" and insist on the need for unquestioning political obedience. But once the French Revolution had demonstrated that Enlightenment beliefs endangered the old political and social order, the Age of Enlightenment, which Kant had so confidently celebrated, was over. From 1789 until 1917 all political thinkers were obliged to be either for the French Revolution or against it. The nineteenth century was the age of industrial revolution and of the great philosophies of progress—Liberalism, Darwinism, Marxism—but to most politicians and intellectuals the dangers of progress and of liberty now seemed all too apparent. Although we read Bentham, Mill, and Marx, we need to remember that few of their contemporaries agreed with them; most nineteenth-century intellectuals had more sympathy with Burke than with Beccaria. Only after the First World War did arguments which stressed political equality become once more generally respectable. By then a new specter haunted Europe, that of Communism.

Further Reading

There is no one indispensable book on the Enlightenment, and no one book which tells one what one needs to know. Two classic essays are Carl Becker, *The Heavenly City of the Eighteenth-Century Philosophers* (New Haven: Yale University Press, 1932) and Albert Hirschman, *The Passions and the Interests: Political Arguments for Capitalism before Its Triumph* (Princeton: Princeton University Press, 1977).

There is little agreement on the interpretation of Bayle. For one view see David Wootton, "Pierre Bayle, Libertine?" in M. A. Stewart (ed.), *Oxford Studies in the History of Philosophy,* vol. 2 (Oxford: Clarendon Press, 1996). The central importance of Mandeville is brought out by E. J. Hundert, *The Enlightenment's Fable: Bernard Mandeville and the Discovery of Society* (Cambridge: Cambridge University Press, 1994). Cesare Beccaria's *On Crimes and Punishments* is available in a translation by David Young (Indianapolis: Hackett, 1986). Developments in France are well surveyed in Nannerl O. Keohane, *Philosophy and the State in France: The Renaissance to the Enlightenment* (Princeton: Princeton University Press, 1980), while the classic study of England is Leslie Stephen, *History of English Thought in the Eighteenth Century* (2 vols., 1876).

The most important modern book on Rousseau, first published in French in 1957, is Jean Starobinski, *Transparency and Obstruction* (Chicago: University of Chicago Press, 1988). Standard discussions of his political theory, which remain unsuperseded, are Roger Masters, *The Political Philosophy of Rousseau* (Princeton: Princeton University Press, 1958), Judith Shklar, *Men and Citizens: A Study of Rousseau's Social Theory* (Cambridge: Cambridge University Press, 1969), and John Charvet, *The Social Problem in the Philosophy of Rousseau* (Cambridge: Cambridge University Press, 1974).

Among numerous recent works, a postmodern reading is offered by Tracy B. Strong, *Jean-Jacques Rousseau: The Politics of the Ordinary* (Thousand Oaks, Cal.: Sage, 1994).

An excellent short introduction to Burke is C. B. Macpherson, *Burke* (Oxford: Oxford University Press, 1980), and, in the same series, there is D. D. Raphael's judicious *Adam Smith* (Oxford: Oxford University Press, 1985). A helpful introduction to Kant's political philosophy is provided by Wolfgang Kersting's chapter in Paul Guyer (ed.), *The Cambridge Companion to Kant* (Cambridge: Cambridge University Press, 1992). For a famous discussion of Kant's essay, see Michel Foucault, "What is Enlightenment?," in Paul Rabinow (ed.), *The Foucault Reader* (New York, Pantheon Books, 1984).

Rousseau

Discourse on the Origin and Foundations of Inequality among Men

by

Jean-Jacques Rousseau,
Citizen of Geneva

"Not in depraved things but in those well oriented according to nature, are we to consider what is natural."
—Aristotle, *Politics*, II.

To The Republic of Geneva

Magnificent, Most Honored and Sovereign Lords:

Convinced that only a virtuous man may bestow on his homeland those honors which it can acknowledge, I have labored for thirty years to earn the right to offer you public homage. And since this happy occasion supplements to some extent what my efforts have been unable to accomplish, I believed I might be allowed here to give heed to the zeal that urges me on, instead of the right that ought to have given me authorization. Having had the good fortune to be born among you, how could I meditate on the equality which nature has established among men and upon the inequality they have instituted without thinking of the profound wisdom with which both, felicitously combined in this state, cooperate in the manner that most closely approximates the natural law and that is most favorable to society, to the maintenance of public order and to the happiness of private individuals? In searching for the best maxims that good sense could dictate concerning the constitution of a government, I have been so struck on seeing them all in operation in your own, that even if I had not been

[Reprinted from *The Basic Political Writings*, translated by Donald A. Cress (Indianapolis: Hackett Publishing Company, 1987), by permission of the publisher.]

born within your walls, I would have believed myself incapable of dispensing with offering this picture of human society to that people which, of all peoples, seems to me to be in possession of the greatest advantages, and to have best prevented its abuses.

If I had had to choose my birthplace, I would have chosen a society of a size limited by the extent of human faculties, that is to say, limited by the possibility of being well governed, and where, with each being sufficient to his task, no one would have been forced to relegate to others the functions with which he was charged; a state where, with all private individuals being known to one another, neither the obscure maneuvers of vice nor the modesty of virtue could be hidden from the notice and the judgment of the public, and where that pleasant habit of seeing and knowing one another turned love of homeland into love of the citizens rather than into love of the land.

I would have wanted to be born in a country where the sovereign and the people could have but one and the same interest, so that all the movements of the machine always tended only to the common happiness. Since this could not have taken place unless the people and the sovereign were one and the same person, it follows that I would have wished to be born under a democratic government, wisely tempered.

I would have wanted to live and die free, that is to say, subject to the laws in such wise that neither I nor anyone else could shake off their honorable yoke: that pleasant and salutary yoke, which the most arrogant heads bear with all the greater docility, since they are made to bear no other.

I would therefore have wanted it to be impossible for anyone in the state to say that he was above the law and for anyone outside to demand that the state was obliged to give him recognition. For whatever the constitution of a government may be, if a single man is found who is not subject to the law, all the others are necessarily at his discretion.[1] And if there is a national leader and a foreign leader as well, whatever the division of authority they may make, it is impossible for both of them to be strictly obeyed and for the state to be well governed.

I would not have wanted to dwell in a newly constituted republic, however good its laws may be, out of fear that, with the government perhaps constituted otherwise than would be required for the moment and being unsuited to the new citizens or the citizens to the new government, the state would be subject to being overthrown and destroyed almost from its inception. For liberty is like those solid and tasty foods or those full-bodied wines which are appropriate for nourishing and strengthening robust constitutions that are used to them, but which overpower, ruin and intoxicate the weak and delicate who are not suited for them. Once peoples are accustomed to masters, they are no longer in a position to get along without them. If they try to shake off the yoke, they put all the more distance between themselves and liberty, because, in mistaking for liberty an unbridled license which is its opposite, their revolutions nearly always deliver them over to seducers who simply make their chains heavier. The Roman people itself—that model of all free peoples—was in no position to govern itself when it emerged from the oppression of the Tarquins. Debased by slavery and the ignominious labors the Tarquins had imposed on it, at first it was but a stupid rabble that needed to be managed and governed with the greatest wisdom, so that, as it gradually became accustomed to breathe the salutary air of liberty, these souls, enervated or rather brutalized under tyranny, acquired by degrees that severity of mores and that high-spirited courage which eventually made them,

of all the peoples, most worthy of respect. I would therefore have sought for my homeland a happy and tranquil republic, whose antiquity was somehow lost in the dark recesses of time, which had experienced only such attacks as served to manifest and strengthen in its inhabitants courage and love of homeland, and where the citizens, long accustomed to a wise independence, were not only free but worthy of being so.

I would have wanted to choose for myself a homeland diverted by a fortunate impotence from the fierce love of conquest, and protected by an even more fortunate position from the fear of becoming itself the conquest of another state; a free city, situated among several peoples none of whom had any interest in invading it, while each had an interest in preventing the others from invading it themselves; in a word, a republic that did not tempt the ambition of its neighbors and that could reasonably count on their assistance in time of need. It follows that in so fortunate a position, it would have had nothing to fear except from itself; and that, if its citizens were trained in the use of arms, it would have been more to maintain in them that martial fervor and that high-spirited courage that suit liberty so well and whet the appetite for it, than out of the necessity to provide for their defense.

I would have searched for a country where the right of legislation was common to all citizens, for who can know better than they the conditions under which it suits them to live together in a single society? But I would not have approved of plebiscites like those of the Romans where the state's leaders and those most interested in its preservation were excluded from the deliberations on which its safety often depended, and where, by an absurd inconsistency, the magistrates were deprived of the rights enjoyed by ordinary citizens.

On the contrary, I would have desired that, in order to stop the self-centered and ill-conceived projects and the dangerous innovations that finally ruined Athens, no one would have the power to propose new laws according to his fancy; that this right belonged exclusively to the magistrates; that even they used it with such caution that the populace, for its part, was so hesitant about giving its consent to these laws, and that their promulgation could only be done with such solemnity that before the constitution was overturned one had time to be convinced that it is above all the great antiquity of the laws that makes them holy and venerable; that the populace soon holds in contempt those laws that it sees change daily; and that in becoming accustomed to neglect old usages on the pretext of making improvements, great evils are often introduced in order to correct the lesser ones.

Above all, I would have fled, as necessarily ill-governed, a republic where the people, believing it could get along without its magistrates or permit them but a precarious authority, would imprudently have held on to the administration of civil affairs and the execution of its own laws. Such must have been the rude constitution of the first governments immediately emerging from the state of nature, and such too was one of the vices which ruined the republic of Athens.

But I would have chosen that republic where private individuals, being content to give sanction to the laws and to decide as a body and upon the recommendation of their leaders the most important public affairs, would establish respected tribunals, distinguish with care their various departments, annually elect the most capable and most upright of their fellow citizens to administer justice and to govern the state; and where, with the virtue of the magistrates thus bearing witness to the wisdom of the people, they would mutually honor one another. Thus if some fatal misunderstandings were ever to disturb public concord, even those periods of blindness and errors were marked by indications of moderation, reciprocal esteem, and a common respect for the laws: presages and guarantees of a sincere and perpetual reconciliation.

Such, MAGNIFICENT, MOST HONORED, AND SOVEREIGN LORDS, are the advantages that I would have sought in the homeland that I would have chosen for myself. And if in addition providence had joined to it a charming location, a temperate climate, a fertile country and the most delightful appearance there is under the heavens, to complete my happiness I would have desired only to enjoy all these goods in the bosom of that happy homeland, living peacefully in sweet society with my fellow citizens, and practicing toward them (following their own ex-

ample), humanity, friendship, and all the virtues; and leaving behind me the honorable memory of a good man and a decent and virtuous patriot.

If, less happy or too late grown wise, I had seen myself reduced to end an infirm and languishing career in other climates, pointlessly regretting the repose and peace of which an imprudent youth deprived me, I would at least have nourished in my soul those same sentiments I could not have used in my native country; and penetrated by a tender and disinterested affection for my distant fellow citizens, I would have addressed them from the bottom of my heart more or less along the following lines:

My dear fellow citizens, or rather my brothers, since the bonds of blood as well as the laws unite almost all of us, it gives me pleasure to be incapable of thinking of you without at the same time thinking of all the good things you enjoy, and of which perhaps none of you appreciates the value more deeply than I who have lost them. The more I reflect upon your political and civil situation, the less I am capable of imagining that the nature of human affairs could admit of a better one. In all other governments, when it is a question of assuring the greatest good of the state, everything is always limited to imaginary projects, and at most to simple possibilities. As for you, your happiness is complete; it remains merely to enjoy it. And to become perfectly happy you are in need of nothing more than to know how to be satisfied with being so. Your sovereignty, acquired or recovered at the point of a sword, and preserved for two centuries by dint of valor and wisdom, is at last fully and universally recognized. Honorable treaties fix your boundaries, secure your rights and strengthen your repose. Your constitution is excellent, since it is dictated by the most sublime reason and is guaranteed by friendly powers deserving of respect. Your state is tranquil; you have neither wars nor conquerors to fear. You have no other masters but the wise laws you have made, administered by upright magistrates of your own choosing. You are neither rich enough to enervate yourself with softness and to lose in vain delights the taste for true happiness and solid virtues, nor poor enough to need more foreign assistance than your industry procures for you. And this precious liberty, which in large nations is maintained only by exorbitant taxes, costs you almost nothing to pursue.

For the happiness of its citizens and the examples of the peoples, may a republic so wisely and so happily constituted last forever! This is the only wish left for you to make, and the only precaution left for you to take. From here on, it is for you alone, not to bring about your own happiness, your ancestors having saved you the trouble, but to render it lasting by the wisdom of using it well. It is upon your perpetual union, your obedience to the laws, your respect for their ministers that your preservation depends. If there remains among you the slightest germ of bitterness or distrust, hasten to destroy it as a ruinous leaven that sooner or later results in your misfortunes and the ruin of the state. I beg you all to look deep inside your hearts and to heed the secret voice of your conscience. Is there anyone among you who knows of a body that is more upright, more enlightened, more worthy of respect than that of your magistracy? Do not all its members give you the example of moderation, of simplicity of mores, of respect for the laws, and of the most sincere reconciliation? Then freely give such wise chiefs that salutary confidence that reason owes to virtue. Bear in mind that they are of your choice, that they justify it, and that the honors due to those whom you have established in dignity necessarily reflect back upon yourselves. None of you is so unenlightened as to be ignorant of the fact that where the vigor of laws and the authority of their defenders cease, there can be neither security nor freedom for anyone. What then is the point at issue among you except to do wholeheartedly and with just confidence what you should always be obliged to do by a true self-interest, by duty and for the sake of reason? May a sinful and ruinous indifference to the maintenance of the constitution never make you neglect in time of need the wise teachings of the most enlightened and most zealous among you. But may equity, moderation, and the most respectful firmness continue to regulate all your activities and display in you, to the entire universe, the example of a proud and modest people, as jealous of its glory as of its liberty. Above all, beware (and this will be my last counsel) of ever listening to sinister interpretations and venomous speeches, whose secret motives are often more dangerous than the actions that are their object. An entire household awakens and takes warning at the first cries of a good and faithful watchdog who never barks except at the approach of burglars. But people hate the nuisance caused by those noisy animals that continually disturb the public repose and whose continual and ill-timed warnings are not heeded even at the moment when they are necessary.

And you, MAGNIFICENT AND MOST HONORED LORDS, you upright and worthy magistrates of a free people, permit me to offer you in particular my compliments and my respects. If there is a rank in the world suited to conferring honor on those who hold it, it is without doubt the one that is given by talents and virtue, that of which you have made yourselves worthy, and to which your fellow citizens have raised you. Their own merit adds still a new luster to yours. And I that find you, who were chosen by men capable of governing others in order that they themselves may be governed, are as much above other magistrates as a free people; and above all that the one which you have the honor of leading, is, by its enlightenment and reason, above the populace of the other states.

May I be permitted to cite an example of which better records ought to remain, and which will always be near to my heart. I never call to mind without the sweetest emotion the memory of the virtuous citizen to whom I owe my being, and who often spoke to me in my childhood of the respect that was owed you. I still see him living from the work of his hands, and nourishing his soul on the most sublime truths. I see Tacitus, Plutarch and Grotius mingled with the instruments of his craft before him. I see at his side a beloved son receiving with too little profit the tender instruction of the best of fathers. But if the aberrations of foolish youth made me forget such wise lessons for a time, I have the happiness to sense at last that whatever the inclination one may have toward vice, it is difficult for an education in which the heart is involved to remain forever lost.

Such, MAGNIFICENT AND MOST HONORED LORDS, are the citizens and even the simple inhabitants born in the state you govern. Such are those educated and sensible men concerning whom, under the name of workers and people, such base and false ideas are entertained in other nations. My father, I gladly acknowledge, was in no way distinguished among his fellow citizens; he was only what they all are; and such as he was, there was no country where his company would not have been sought after, cultivated, and profitably too, by the most upright men. It does not behoove me, nor, thank heaven, is it necessary to speak to you of the regard which men of that stamp can expect from you: your equals by education as well as by the rights of nature and of birth; your inferiors by their will and by the preference they owe your merit, which they have granted to it, and for which you in turn owe them some sort of gratitude. It is with intense satisfaction that I learn how much, in your dealings with them, you temper with gentleness and cooperativeness the gravity suited to the ministers of the law; how much you repay them in esteem and attention for the obedience and respect they owe you; conduct full of justice and wisdom, suited to putting at a greater and greater distance the memory of unhappy events which must be forgotten so as never to see them again; conduct all the more judicious because this equitable and generous people makes a pleasure out of its duty, because it naturally loves to honor you, and because those who are most zealous in upholding their rights are the ones who are most inclined to respect yours.

It should not be surprising that the leaders of a civil society love its glory and happiness; but, unfortunately for the tranquility of men, that those who consider themselves as the magistrates, or rather as the masters, of a more holy and more sublime homeland manifest some love for the earthly homeland which nourishes them. How sweet it is for me to be able to make such a rare exception in our favor, and to place in the rank of our best citizens those zealous trustees of the sacred dogmas authorized by the laws, those venerable pastors of souls, whose lively and sweet eloquence the better instills the maxims of the Gospel into people's hearts as they themselves always begin by practicing them. Everyone knows the success with which the great art of preaching is cultivated in Geneva. But since people are too accustomed to seeing things said in one way and done in another, few of them know the extent to which the spirit of Christianity, the saintliness of mores, severity to oneself and gentleness to others reign in the body of our ministers. Perhaps

it behooves only the city of Geneva to provide the edifying example of such a perfect union between a society of theologians and of men of letters. It is in large part upon their wisdom and their acknowledged moderation and upon their zeal for the prosperity of the state that I base my hopes for its eternal tranquility. And I note, with a pleasure mixed with amazement and respect, how much they abhor the atrocious maxims of those sacred and barbarous men of whom history provides more than one example, and who, in order to uphold the alleged rights of God—that is to say, their own interests—were all the less sparing of human blood because they hoped their own would always be respected.

Could I forget that precious half of the republic which produces the happiness of the other and whose gentleness and wisdom maintain peace and good mores? Amiable and virtuous women citizens, it will always be the fate of your sex to govern ours. Happy it is when your chaste power, exercised only within the conjugal union, makes itself felt only for the glory of the state and the public happiness! Thus it was that in Sparta women were in command, and thus it is that you deserve to be in command in Geneva. What barbarous man could resist the voice of honor and reason in the mouth of an affectionate wife? And who would not despise vain luxury on seeing your simple and modest attire, which, from the luster it derives from you, seems the most favorable to beauty? It is for you to maintain always, by your amiable and innocent dominion and by your insinuating wit, the love of laws in the state and concord among the citizens; to reunite, by happy marriages, divided families; and above all, to correct, by the persuasive sweetness of your lessons and by the modest graces of your conversation, those extravagances which our young people come to acquire in other countries, whence, instead of the many useful things they could profit from, they bring back, with a childish manner and ridiculous airs adopted among fallen women, nothing more than an admiration for who knows what pretended grandeurs, frivolous compensations for servitude, which will never be worth as much as august liberty. Therefore always be what you are, the chaste guardians of mores and the gentle bonds of peace; and continue to assert on every occasion the rights of the heart and of nature for the benefit of duty and virtue.

I flatter myself that events will not prove me wrong in basing upon such guarantees hope for the general happiness of the citizens and for the glory of the republic. I admit that with all these advantages it will not shine with that brilliance which dazzles most eyes; and the childish and fatal taste for this is the deadliest enemy of happiness and liberty. Let a dissolute youth go elsewhere in search of easy pleasures and lengthy repentances. Let the alleged men of taste admire someplace else the grandeur of palaces, the beauty of carriages, the sumptuous furnishings, the pomp of spectacles, and all the refinements of softness and luxury. In Geneva we will find only men; but such a sight has a value of its own, and those who seek it are well worth the admirers of the rest.

May you all, MAGNIFICENT, MOST HONORED AND SOVEREIGN LORDS, deign to receive with the same goodness the respectful testimonies of the interest I take in your common prosperity. If I were unfortunate enough to be guilty of some indiscreet rapture in this lively effusion of my heart, I beg you to pardon it as the tender affection of a true patriot, and to the ardent and legitimate zeal of a man who envisages no greater happiness for himself than that of seeing all of you happy.

With the most profound respect, I am, MAGNIFICENT, MOST HONORED AND SOVEREIGN LORDS, your most humble and most obedient servant and fellow citizen.

Jean-Jacques Rousseau
Chambéry
12 June 1754

PREFACE

Of all the branches of human knowledge, the most useful and the least advanced seems to me to be that of man;[2] and I dare say that the inscription on the temple at Delphi alone contained a precept more important and more difficult than all the huge tomes of the moralists. Thus I regard the subject of this discourse as one of the most interesting questions that philosophy is capable of proposing, and unhappily for us, one of the thorniest that philosophers can attempt to resolve. For how can the source of the inequality among men be known unless one begins by knowing men themselves? And how will man be successful in seeing himself as nature formed him, through all the changes that the succession of time and things must have produced in his original constitution, and in separating what he derives from his own wherewithal from what circumstances and his progress have added to or changed in his primitive state? Like the statue of Glaucus, which time, sea and storms had disfigured to such an extent that it looked less like a god than a wild beast, the human soul, altered in the midst of society by a thousand constantly recurring causes, by the acquisition of a multitude of bits of knowledge and of errors, by changes that took place in the constitution of bodies, by the constant impact of the passions, has, as it were, changed its appearance to the point of being nearly unrecognizable. And instead of a being active always by certain and invariable principles, instead of that heavenly and majestic simplicity whose mark its author had left on it, one no longer finds anything but the grotesque contrast of passion which thinks it reasons and an understanding in a state of delirium.

What is even more cruel is that, since all the progress of the human species continually moves away from its primitive state, the more we accumulate new knowledge, the more we deprive ourselves of the means of acquiring the most important knowledge of all. Thus, in a sense, it is by dint of studying man that we have rendered ourselves incapable of knowing him.

It is easy to see that it is in these successive changes of the human constitution that we must seek the first origin of the differences that distinguish men, who, by common consensus, are naturally as equal among themselves as were the animals of each species before various physical causes had introduced into certain species the varieties we now observe among some of them. In effect, it is inconceivable that these first changes, by whatever means they took place, should have altered all at once and in the same manner all the individuals of the species. But while some improved or declined and acquired various good or bad qualities which were not inherent in their nature, the others remained longer in their original state. And such was the first source of inequality among men, which it is easier to demonstrate thus in general than to assign with precision its true causes.

Let my readers not imagine, then, that I dare flatter myself with having seen what appears to me so difficult to see. I have begun some lines of reasoning; I have hazarded some guesses, less in the hope of resolving the question than with the intention of clarifying it and of reducing it to its true state. Others will easily be able to go farther on this same route, though it will not be easy for anyone to reach the end of it. For it is no light undertaking to separate what is original from what is artificial in the present nature of man, and to have a proper understanding of a state which no longer exists, which perhaps never existed, which probably never will exist, and yet about which it is necessary to have accurate notions in order to judge properly our own present state. He who would attempt to determine precisely which precautions to take in order to make solid observations on this subject would need even more philosophy than is generally supposed; and a good solution of the following problem would not seem to me unworthy of the Aristotles and Plinys of our century: *What experiments would be necessary to achieve knowledge of natural man? And what are the means of carrying out these experiments in the midst of society?* Far from undertaking to resolve this problem, I believe I have meditated sufficiently on the subject to dare respond in advance that the greatest philosophers will not be too good to direct these experiments, nor the most powerful sovereigns to carry them out. It is hardly reasonable to expect such a combination, especially with the perseverance or rather the succession of understanding and good will needed on both sides in order to achieve success.

These investigations, so difficult to carry out and so little thought about until now, are nevertheless the only means we have left of removing a multitude of difficulties that conceal from us the knowledge of the real foundations of human society. It is this ignorance of the nature of man which throws so much uncertainty and obscurity on the true definition of natural

right. For the idea of right, says M. Burlamaqui, and even more that of natural right, are manifestly ideas relative to the nature of man. Therefore, he continues, the principles of this science must be deduced from this very nature of man, from man's constitution and state.

It is not without surprise and a sense of outrage that one observes the paucity of agreement that prevails among the various authors who have treated it. Among the most serious writers one can hardly find two who are of the same opinion on this point. The Roman jurists—not to mention the ancient philosophers who seem to have done their best to contradict each other on the most fundamental principles—subject man and all other animals indifferently to the same natural law, because they take this expression to refer to the law that nature imposes on itself rather than the law she prescribes, or rather because of the particular sense in which those jurists understood the word "law," which on this occasion they seem to have taken only for the expression of the general relations established by nature among all animate beings for their common preservation. The moderns, in acknowledging under the word "law" merely a rule prescribed to a moral being, that is to say, intelligent, free and considered in his relations with other beings, consequently limit the competence of the natural law to the only animal endowed with reason, that is, to man. But with each one defining this law in his own fashion, they all establish it on such metaphysical principles that even among us there are very few people in a position to grasp these principles, far from being able to find them by themselves. So that all the definitions of these wise men, otherwise in perpetual contradiction with one another, agree on this alone, that it is impossible to understand the law of nature and consequently to obey it without being a great reasoner and a profound metaphysician, which means precisely that for the establishment of society, men must have used enlightenment which develops only with great difficulty and by a very small number of people within the society itself.

Knowing nature so little and agreeing so poorly on the meaning of the word "law," it would be quite difficult to come to some common understanding regarding a good definition of natural law. Thus all those definitions that are found in books have, over and above a lack of uniformity, the added fault of being drawn from several branches of knowledge which men do not naturally have, and from advantages the idea of which they cannot conceive until after having left the state of nature. Writers begin by seeking the rules on which, for the common utility, it would be appropriate for men to agree among themselves; and then they give the name *natural law* to the collection of these rules, with no other proof than the good which presumably would result from their universal observance. Surely this is a very convenient way to compose definitions and to explain the nature of things by virtually arbitrary views of what is seemly.

But as long as we are ignorant of natural man, it is futile for us to attempt to determine the law he has received or which is best suited to his constitution. All that we can see very clearly regarding this law is that, for it to be law, not only must the will of him who is obliged by it be capable of knowing submission to it, but also, for it to be natural, it must speak directly by the voice of nature.

Leaving aside therefore all the scientific books which teach us only to see men as they have made themselves, and meditating on the first and most simple operations of the human soul, I believe I perceive in it two principles that are prior to reason, of which one makes us ardently interested in our well-being and our self-preservation, and the other inspires in us a natural repugnance to seeing any sentient being, especially our fellow man, perish or suffer. It is from the conjunction and combination that our mind is in a position to make regarding these two principles, without the need for introducing that of sociability, that all the rules of natural right appear to me to flow; rules which reason is later forced to reestablish on other foundations, when, by its successive developments, it has succeeded in smothering nature.

In this way one is not obliged to make a man a philosopher before making him a man. His duties toward others are not uniquely dictated to him by the belated lessons of wisdom; and as long as he does not resist the inner impulse of compassion, he will never harm another man or even another sentient being, except in the legitimate instance where, if his preservation were involved, he is obliged to give preference to himself. By this means, an end can also be made to the ancient disputes regarding the participation of animals in the natural law. For it is clear that, lacking intelligence and liberty, they cannot recognize this law; but since they share to some extent in our nature by virtue of the sentient quality with which they are endowed, one will judge that they should also participate in natural right, and that man is subject to some sort of duties toward them. It seems, in effect, that if I am obliged not to do any harm to my fellow man, it is less because he is a rational being than because he is a sentient being: a quality that, since it is common to both animals and men, should at least give the former the right not to be needlessly mistreated by the latter.

This same study of original man, of his true needs and the fundamental principles of his duties, is also the only good means that can be used to remove those multitudes of difficulties which present themselves regarding the origin of moral inequality, the true foundations of the body politic, the reciprocal rights of its members, and a thousand other similar questions that are as important as they are poorly explained.

In considering human society from a tranquil and disinterested point of view it seems at first to manifest merely the violence of powerful men and the oppression of the weak. The mind revolts against the harshness of the former; one is inclined to deplore the blindness of the latter. And since nothing is less stable among men than those external relationships which chance brings about more often than wisdom, and which are called weakness or power, wealth or poverty, human establishments appear at first glance to be based on piles of shifting sand. It is only in examining them closely, only after having cleared away the dust and sand that surround the edifice, that one perceives the unshakeable base on which it is raised and one learns to respect its foundations. Now without a serious study of man, of his natural faculties and their successive developments, one will never succeed in making these distinctions and in separating, in the present constitution of things, what the divine will has done from what human art has pretended to do.

The political and moral investigations occasioned by the important question I am examining are therefore useful in every way; and the hypothetical history of governments is an instructive lesson for man in every respect. In considering what we would have become, left to ourselves, we ought to learn to bless him whose beneficent hand, in correcting our institutions and giving them an unshakeable foundation, has prevented the disorders that must otherwise result from them, and has brought about our happiness from the means that seemed likely to add to our misery.

Learn whom God has ordered you to be, and in what part of human affairs you have been placed.

Notice on the Notes

I have added some notes to this work, following my indolent custom of working in fits and starts. Occasionally these notes wander so far from the subject that they are not good to read with the text. I therefore have consigned them to the end of the Discourse, in which I have tried my best to follow the straightest path. Those who have the courage to begin again will be able to amuse themselves the second time as they beat the bushes and try to run through the notes. There will be little harm done if others do not read them at all.

[Translator's note: These notes are presented on p. 410. Additions to the text, made by Rousseau in the 1782 edition, are translated here and enclosed by brackets.]

QUESTION
Proposed by the Academy of Dijon
What is the Origin of Inequality Among Men, and is it Authorized by the Natural Law?

DISCOURSE ON THE ORIGIN AND FOUNDATIONS OF INEQUALITY AMONG MEN

It is of man that I have to speak, and the question I am examining indicates to me that I am going to be speaking to men, for such questions are not proposed by those who are afraid to honor the truth. I will therefore confidently defend the cause of humanity before the wise men who invite me to do so, and I will not be displeased with myself if I make myself worthy of my subject and my judges.

I conceive of two kinds of inequality in the human species: one which I call natural or physical, because it is established by nature and consists in the difference of age, health, bodily strength, and qualities of mind or soul. The other may be called moral or political inequality, because it depends on a kind of convention and is established, or at least authorized, by the consent of men. This latter type of inequality consists in the different privileges enjoyed by some at the expense of others, such as being richer, more honored, more powerful than they, or even causing themselves to be obeyed by them.

There is no point in asking what the source of natural inequality is, because the answer would be found enunciated in the simple definition of the word. There is still less of a point in asking whether there would not be some essential connection between the two inequalities, for that would amount to asking whether those who command are necessarily better than those who obey, and whether strength of body or mind, wisdom or virtue are always found in the same individuals in proportion to power or wealth. Perhaps this is a good question for slaves to discuss within earshot of their masters, but it is not suitable for reasonable and free men who seek the truth.

Precisely what, then, is the subject of this discourse? To mark, in the progress of things, the moment when, right taking the place of violence, nature was subjected to the law. To explain the sequence of wonders by which the strong could resolve to serve the weak, and the people to buy imaginary repose at the price of real felicity.

The philosophers who have examined the foundations of society have all felt the necessity of returning to the state of nature, but none of them has reached it. Some have not hesitated to ascribe to man in that state the notion of just and unjust, without bothering to show that he had to have that notion, or even that it was useful to him. Others have spoken of the natural right that everyone has to preserve what belongs to him, without explaining what they mean by "belonging." Others started out by giving authority to the stronger over the weaker, and immediately brought about government, without giving any thought to the time that had to pass before the meaning of the words "authority" and "government" could exist among men. Finally, all of them, speaking continually of need, avarice, oppression, desires, and pride, have transferred to the state of nature the ideas they acquired in society. They spoke about savage man, and it was civil man they depicted. It did not even occur to most of our philosophers to doubt that the state of nature had existed, even though it is evident from reading the Holy Scriptures that the first man, having received enlightenment and precepts immediately from God, was not himself in that state; and if we give the writings of Moses the credence that every Christian owes them, we must deny that, even before the flood, men were ever in the pure state of nature, unless they had fallen back into it because of some extraordinary event: a paradox that is quite awkward to defend and utterly impossible to prove.

Let us therefore begin by putting aside all the facts, for they have no bearing on the question. The investigations that may be undertaken concerning this subject should not be taken for historical truths, but only for hypothetical and conditional reasonings, better suited to shedding light on the nature of things than on pointing out their true origin, like those our physicists make everyday with regard to the formation of the world. Religion commands us to believe that since God himself drew men out of the state of nature, they are unequal because he wanted them to be so; but it does not forbid us to form conjectures, drawn solely from the nature of man and the beings that surround him, concerning what the human race could have become, if it had been left to itself. That is what I am asked, and what I propose to examine in this discourse. Since my subject concerns man in general, I will attempt to speak in terms that suit all nations, or rather, forgetting times and places in order to think only of the men to whom I am speaking, I will imagine I am in the Lyceum in Athens, reciting the lessons of my masters, having men like Plato and Xenocrates for my judges, and the human race for my audience.

O man, whatever country you may be from, whatever your opinions may be, listen: here is your history, as I have thought to read it, not in the books of your fellowmen, who are liars, but in nature, who never lies. Everything that comes from nature will be true; there will be nothing false except what I have unintentionally added. The times about which I am going to speak are quite remote: how much you have changed from what you were! It is, as it were, the life of your species that I am about to describe to you according to the qualities you have received, which your education and your habits have been able to corrupt but have been unable to destroy. There is, I feel, an age at which an individual man would want to stop. You will seek the age at which you would want your species to have stopped. Dissatisfied with your present state for reasons that portend even greater grounds for dissatisfaction for your unhappy posterity, perhaps you would like to be able to go backwards in time. This feeling should be a hymn in praise of your first ancestors, the criticism of your contemporaries, and the dread of those who have the unhappiness of living after you.

PART ONE

However important it may be, in order to render sound judgments regarding the natural state of man, to consider him from his origin and to examine him, so to speak, in the first embryo of the species, I will not follow his nature through its successive developments. I will not stop to investigate in the animal kingdom what he might have been at the beginning so as eventually to become what he is. I will not examine whether, as Aristotle thinks, man's elongated nails were not at first hooked claws, whether man was not furry like a bear, and whether, if man walked on all fours,[3] his gaze, directed toward the ground and limited to a horizon of a few steps—did not provide an indication of both the character and the limits of his ideas. On this subject I could form only vague and almost imaginary conjectures. Comparative anatomy has as yet made too little progress; the observations of naturalists are as yet too uncertain for one to be able to establish the basis of solid reasoning on such foundations. Thus, without having recourse to the supernatural knowledge we have on this point, and without taking note of the changes that must have occurred in the internal as well as the external conformation of man, as he applied his limbs to new purposes and nourished himself on new foods, I will suppose him to have been formed from all time as I see him today: walking on two feet, using his hands as we use ours, directing his gaze over all of nature, and measuring with his eyes the vast expanse of the heavens.

When I strip that being, thus constituted, of all the supernatural gifts he could have received and of all the artificial faculties he could have acquired only through long progress; when I consider him, in a word, as he must have left the hands of nature, I see an animal less strong than some, less agile than others, but all in all, the most advantageously organized of all. I see him satisfying his hunger under an oak tree, quenching his thirst at the first stream, finding his bed at the foot of the same tree that supplied his meal; and thus all his needs are satisfied.

When the earth is left to its natural fertility[4] and covered with immense forests that were never mutilated by the axe, it offers storehouses and shelters at every step to animals of every species. Men, dispersed among the animals, observe and imitate their industry, and thereby raise themselves to the level of animal instinct, with the advantage that, whereas each species has only its own instincts, man, who may perhaps have none that belongs to him, appropriates all of them to himself, feeds himself equally well on most of the various foods[5] which the other animals divide among themselves, and consequently finds his sustenance more easily than any of the rest can.

Accustomed from childhood to inclement weather and the rigors of the seasons, acclimated to fatigue, and forced, naked and without arms, to defend their lives and their prey against other ferocious beasts, or to escape them by taking flight, men develop a robust and nearly unalterable temperament. Children enter the world with the excellent constitution of their parents and strengthen it with the same exercises that produced it, thus acquiring all the vigor that the

human race is capable of having. Nature treats them precisely the way the law of Sparta treated the children of its citizens: it renders strong and robust those who are well constituted and makes all the rest perish, thereby differing from our present-day societies, where the state, by making children burdensome to their parents, kills them indiscriminately before their birth.

Since the savage man's body is the only instrument he knows, he employs it for a variety of purposes that, for lack of practice, ours are incapable of serving. And our industry deprives us of the force and agility that necessity obliges him to acquire. If he had had an axe, would his wrists break such strong branches? If he had had a sling, would he throw a stone with so much force? If he had had a ladder, would he climb a tree so nimbly? If he had had a horse, would he run so fast? Give a civilized man time to gather all his machines around him, and undoubtedly he will easily overcome a savage man. But if you want to see an even more unequal fight, pit them against each other naked and disarmed, and you will soon realize the advantage of constantly having all of one's forces at one's disposal, of always being ready for any event, and of always carrying one's entire self, as it were, with one.[6]

Hobbes maintains that man is naturally intrepid and seeks only to attack and to fight. On the other hand, an illustrious philosopher thinks, and Cumberland and Pufendorf also affirm, that nothing is as timid as man in the state of nature, and that he is always trembling and ready to take flight at the slightest sound he hears or at the slightest movement he perceives. That may be the case with regard to objects with which he is not acquainted. And I do not doubt that he is frightened by all the new sights that present themselves to him every time he can neither discern the physical good and evil he may expect from them nor compare his forces with the dangers he must run: rare circumstances in the state of nature, where everything takes place in such a uniform manner and where the face of the earth is not subject to those sudden and continual changes caused by the passions and inconstancy of peoples living together. But since a savage man lives dispersed among the animals and, finding himself early on in a position to measure himself against them, he soon makes the comparison; and, aware that he surpasses them in skillfulness more than they surpass him in strength, he learns not to fear them any more. Pit a bear or a wolf against a savage who is robust, agile, and courageous, as they all are, armed with stones and a hefty cudgel, and you will see that the danger will be at least equal on both sides, and that after several such experiences, ferocious beasts, which do not like to attack one another, will be quite reluctant to attack a man, having found him to be as ferocious as themselves. With regard to animals that actually have more strength than man has skillfulness, he is in the same position as other weaker species, which nevertheless subsist. Man has the advantage that, since he is no less adept than they at running and at finding almost certain refuge in trees, he always has the alternative of accepting or leaving the encounter and the choice of taking flight or entering into combat. Moreover, it appears that no animal naturally attacks man, except in the case of self-defense or extreme hunger, or shows evidence of those violent antipathies toward him that seem to indicate that one species is destined by nature to serve as food for another.

[No doubt these are the reasons why negroes and savages bother themselves so little about the ferocious beasts they may encounter in the woods. In this respect, the Caribs of Venezuela, among others, live in the most profound security and without the slightest inconvenience. Although they are practically naked, says Francisco Coreal, they boldly expose themselves in the forest, armed only with bow and arrow, but no one has ever heard of one of them being devoured by animals.]

There are other, more formidable enemies, against which man does not have the same means of self-defense: natural infirmities, childhood, old age, and illnesses of all kinds—sad signs of our weakness, of which the first two are common to all animals, with the last belonging principally to man living in society. On the subject of childhood, I even observe that a mother, by carrying her child everywhere with her, can feed it much more easily than females of several animal species, which are forced to be continually coming and going, with great fatigue, to seek their food and to suckle or feed their young. It is true that if a woman were to perish, the child runs a considerable risk of perishing with her. But this danger is common to a hundred other species, whose young are for quite some time incapable of going off to seek their nourishment for themselves. And although childhood is longer among us, our lifespan is also longer; thus things are more or less equal in this respect,[7] although there are other rules, not relevant to my subject, which are concerned with the duration of infancy and the number of young.[8] Among the elderly, who are less active and perspire little, the need for food diminishes with the faculty of providing for it. And since savage life shields them from gout and rheumatism, and since old age is, of all ills, the one that human assistance can least alleviate, they eventually die without anyone being aware that they are ceasing to exist, and almost without being aware of it themselves.

With regard to illnesses, I will not repeat the vain and false pronouncements made against medicine by the majority of people in good health. Rather, I will ask whether there is any solid observation on the basis of which one can conclude that the average lifespan is shorter in those countries where the art of medicine is most neglected than in those where it is cultivated most assiduously. And how could that be the case, if we give ourselves more ills than medicine can furnish us remedies? The extreme inequality in our lifestyle: excessive idleness among some, excessive labor among others; the ease with which we arouse and satisfy our appetites and our sensuality; the overly refined foods of the wealthy, which nourish them with irritating juices and overwhelm them with indigestion; the bad food of the poor, who most of the time do not have even that, and who, for want of food, are inclined to stuff their stomachs greedily whenever possible; staying up until all hours, excesses of all kinds, immoderate outbursts of every passion, bouts of fatigue and mental exhaustion; countless sorrows and afflictions which are felt in all levels of society and which perpetually gnaw away at souls: these are the fatal proofs that most of our ills are of our own making, and that we could have avoided nearly all of them by preserving the simple, regular and solitary lifestyle prescribed to us by nature. If nature has destined us to be healthy, I almost dare to affirm that the state of reflection is a state contrary to nature and that the man who meditates is a depraved animal. When one thinks about the stout constitutions of the savages, at least of those whom we have not ruined with our strong liquors; when one becomes aware of the fact that they know almost no illnesses but wounds and old age, one is strongly inclined to believe that someone could easily write the history of human maladies by following the history of civil societies. This at least was the opinion of Plato, who believed that, from certain remedies used or approved by Podalirius and Machaon at the siege of Troy, various illnesses which these remedies should exacerbate were as yet unknown among men. [And Celsus reports that diet, so necessary today, was only an invention of Hippocrates.]

With so few sources of ills, man in the state of nature hardly has any need therefore of remedies, much less of physicians. The human race is in no worse condition than all the others in this respect; and it is easy to learn from hunters whether in their chases they find many sick animals. They find quite a few that have received serious wounds that healed quite nicely, that have had bones or even limbs broken and reset with no other surgeon than time, no other regimen than their everyday life, and that are no less perfectly cured for not having been tormented with incisions, poisoned with drugs, or exhausted with fasting. Finally, however correctly administered medicine may be among us, it is still certain that although a sick savage, abandoned to himself, has nothing to hope for except from nature, on the other hand, he has nothing to fear except his illness. This frequently makes his situation preferable to ours.

Therefore we must take care not to confuse savage man with the men we have before our eyes. Nature treats all animals left to their own devices with a partiality that seems to show how jealous she is of that right. The horse, the cat, the bull, even the ass, are usually taller, and all of them have a more robust constitution, more vigor, more strength, and more courage in the forests than in our homes. They lose half of these advantages in becoming domesticated;

it might be said that all our efforts at feeding them and treating them well only end in their degeneration. It is the same for man himself. In becoming habituated to the ways of society and a slave, he becomes weak, fearful, and servile; his soft and effeminate lifestyle completes the enervation of both his strength and his courage. Let us add that the difference between the savage man and the domesticated man should be still greater than that between the savage animal and the domesticated animal; for while animal and man have been treated equally by nature, man gives more comforts to himself than to the animals he tames, and all of these comforts are so many specific causes that make him degenerate more noticeably.

It is therefore no great misfortune for those first men, nor, above all, such a great obstacle to their preservation, that they are naked, that they have no dwelling, and that they lack all those useful things we take to be so necessary. If they do not have furry skin, they have no need for it in warm countries, and in cold countries they soon learn to help themselves to the skins of animals they have vanquished. If they have but two feet to run with, they have two arms to provide for their defense and for their needs. Perhaps their children learn to walk late and with difficulty, but mothers carry them easily: an advantage that is lacking in other species, where the mother, on being pursued, finds herself forced to abandon her young or to conform her pace to theirs. [It is possible there are some exceptions to this. For example, the animal from the province of Nicaragua which resembles a fox and which has feet like a man's hands, and, according to Coreal, has a pouch under its belly in which the mother places her young when she is forced to take flight. No doubt this is the same animal that is called *tlaquatzin* in Mexico; the female of the species Laët describes as having a similar pouch for the same purpose.] Finally, unless we suppose those singular and fortuitous combinations of circumstances of which I will speak later, and which might very well have never taken place, at any rate it is clear that the first man who made clothing or a dwelling for himself was giving himself things that were hardly necessary, since he had done without them until then and since it is not clear why, as a grown man, he could not endure the kind of life he had endured ever since he was a child.

Alone, idle, and always near danger, savage man must like to sleep and be a light sleeper like animals which do little thinking and, as it were, sleep the entire time they are not thinking. Since his self-preservation was practically his sole concern, his best trained faculties ought to be those that have attack and defense as their principal object, either to subjugate his prey or to prevent his becoming the prey of another animal. On the other hand, the organs that are perfected only by softness and sensuality must remain in a state of crudeness that excludes any kind of refinement in him. And with his senses being divided in this respect, he will have extremely crude senses of touch and taste; those of sight, hearing and smell will have the greatest subtlety. Such is the state of animals in general, and, according to the reports of travellers, such also is that of the majority of savage peoples. Thus we should not be surprised that the Hottentots of the Cape of Good Hope can sight ships with the naked eye as far out at sea as the Dutch can with telescopes; or that the savages of America were as capable of trailing Spaniards by smell as the best dogs could have done; or that all these barbarous nations endure their nakedness with no discomfort, whet their appetites with hot peppers, and drink European liquors like water.

So far I have considered only physical man. Let us now try to look at him from a metaphysical and moral point of view.

In any animal I see nothing but an ingenious machine to which nature has given senses in order for it to renew its strength and to protect itself, to a certain point, from all that tends to destroy or disturb it. I am aware of precisely the same things in the human machine, with the difference that nature alone does everything in the operations of an animal, whereas man contributes, as a free agent, to his own operations. The former chooses or rejects by instinct and the later by an act of freedom. Hence an animal cannot deviate from the rule that is prescribed to it, even when it would be advantageous to do so, while man deviates from it, often to his own detriment.

Thus a pigeon would die of hunger near a bowl filled with choice meats, and so would a cat perched atop a pile of fruit or grain, even though both could nourish themselves quite well with the food they disdain, if they were of a mind to try some. And thus dissolute men abandon themselves to excesses which cause them fever and death, because the mind perverts the senses and because the will still speaks when nature is silent.

Every animal has ideas, since it has senses; up to a certain point it even combines its ideas, and in this regard man differs from an animal only in degree. Some philosophers have even suggested that there is a greater difference between two given men than between a given man and an animal. Therefore it is not so much understanding which causes the specific distinction of man from all other animals as it is his being a free agent. Nature commands every animal, and beasts obey. Man feels the same impetus, but he knows he is free to go along or to resist; and it is above all in the awareness of this freedom that the spirituality of his soul is made manifest. For physics explains in some way the mechanism of the senses and the formation of ideas; but in the power of willing, or rather of choosing, and in the feeling of this power, we find only purely spiritual acts, about which the laws of mechanics explain nothing.

But if the difficulties surrounding all these questions should leave some room for dispute on this difference between man and animal, there is another very specific quality which distinguishes them and about which there can be no argument: the faculty of self-perfection, a faculty which, with the aid of circumstances, successively develops all the others, and resides among us as much in the species as in the individual. On the other hand, an animal, at the end of a few months, is what it will be all its life; and its species, at the end of a thousand years, is what it was in the first of those thousand years. Why is man alone subject to becoming an imbecile? Is it not that he thereby returns to his primitive state, and that, while the animal which has acquired nothing and which also has nothing to lose, always retains its instinct, man, in losing through old age or other accidents all that his *perfectibility* has enabled him to acquire, thus falls even lower than the animal itself? It would be sad for us to be forced to agree that this distinctive and almost unlimited faculty is the source of all man's misfortunes; that this is what, by dint of time, draws him out of that original condition in which he would pass tranquil and innocent days; that this is what, through centuries of giving rise to his enlightenment and his errors, his vices and his virtues, eventually makes him a tyrant over himself and nature.[9] It would be dreadful to be obliged to praise as a beneficent being the one who first suggested to the inhabitant on the banks of the Orinoco the use of boards which he binds to his children's temples, and which assure them of at least part of their imbecility and their original happiness.

Savage man, left by nature to instinct alone, or rather compensated for the instinct he is perhaps lacking by faculties capable of first replacing them and then of raising him to the level of instinct, will therefore begin with purely animal functions.[10] Perceiving and feeling will be his first state, which he will have in common with all animals. Willing and not willing, desiring, and fearing will be the first and nearly the only operations of his soul until new circumstances bring about new developments in it.

Whatever the moralists may say about it, human understanding owes much to the passions, which, by common consensus, also owe a great deal to it. It is by their activity that our reason is perfected. We seek to know only because we desire to find enjoyment; and it is impossible to conceive why someone who had neither desires nor fears would go to the bother of reasoning. The passions in turn take their origin from our needs, and their progress from our knowledge. For one can desire or fear things only by virtue of the ideas one can have of them, or from the simple impulse of nature; and savage man, deprived of every sort of enlightenment, feels only the passion of this latter sort. His desires do not go beyond his physical needs.[11] The only goods he knows in the universe are nourishment, a woman and rest; the only evils he fears are pain and hunger. I say pain and not death because an animal will never know what it is to die;

and knowledge of death and its terrors is one of the first acquisitions that man has made in withdrawing from the animal condition.

Were it necessary, it would be easy for me to support this view with facts and to demonstrate that, among all the nations of the world, the progress of the mind has been precisely proportionate to the needs received by peoples from nature or to those needs to which circumstances have subjected them, and consequently to the passions which inclined them to provide for those needs. I would show the arts coming into being in Egypt and spreading with the flooding of the Nile. I would follow their progress among the Greeks, where they were seen to germinate, grow and rise to the heavens among the sands and rocks of Attica, though never being able to take root on the fertile banks of the Eurotas. I would point out that in general the peoples of the north are more industrious than those of the south, because they cannot get along as well without being so, as if nature thereby wanted to equalize things by giving to their minds the fertility it refuses their soil.

But without having recourse to the uncertain testimony of history, does anyone fail to see that everything seems to remove savage man from the temptation and the means of ceasing to be savage? His imagination depicts nothing to him; his heart asks nothing of him. His modest needs are so easily found at hand, and he is so far from the degree of knowledge necessary to make him desire to acquire greater knowledge, that he can have neither foresight nor curiosity. The spectacle of nature becomes a matter of indifference to him by dint of its becoming familiar to him. It is always the same order, always the same succession of changes. He does not have a mind for marveling at the greatest wonders; and we must not seek in him the philosophy that a man needs in order to know how to observe once what he has seen everyday. His soul, agitated by nothing, is given over to the single feeling of his own present existence, without any idea of the future, however near it may be, and his projects, as limited as his views, hardly extend to the end of the day. Such is, even today, the extent of the Carib's foresight. In the morning he sells his bed of cotton and in the evening he returns in tears to buy it back, for want of having foreseen that he would need it that night.

The more one meditates on this subject, the more the distance from pure sensations to the simplest knowledge increases before our eyes; and it is impossible to conceive how a man could have crossed such a wide gap by his forces alone, without the aid of communication and without the provocation of necessity. How many centuries have perhaps gone by before men were in a position to see any fire other than that from the heavens? How many different risks did they have to run before they learned the most common uses of that element? How many times did they let it go out before they had acquired the art of reproducing it? And how many times perhaps did each of these secrets die with the one who had discovered it? What will we say about agriculture, an art that requires so much labor and foresight, that depends on so many other arts, that quite obviously is practicable only in a society which is at least in its beginning stages, and that serves us not so much to derive from the earth food it would readily provide without agriculture, as to force from it those preferences that are most to our taste? But let us suppose that men multiplied to the point where the natural productions were no longer sufficient to nourish them: a supposition which, it may be said in passing, would show a great advantage for the human species in that way of life. Let us suppose that, without forges or workshops, farm implements had fallen from the heavens into the hands of the savages; that these men had conquered the mortal hatred they all have for continuous work; that they had learned to foresee their needs far enough in advance; that they had guessed how the soil is to be cultivated, grains sown, and trees planted; that they had discovered the arts of grinding wheat and fermenting grapes: all things they would need to have been taught by the gods, for it is inconceivable how they could have picked these things up on their own. Yet, after all this, what man would be so foolish as to tire himself out cultivating a field that will be plundered by the first comer, be it man or beast, who takes a fancy to the crop? And how could each man resolve to spend his life in hard labor, when, the more

necessary to him the fruits of his labor may be, the surer he is of not realizing them? In a word, how could this situation lead men to cultivate the soil as long as it is not divided among them, that is to say, as long as the state of nature is not wiped out?

Were we to want to suppose a savage man as skilled in the art of thinking as our philosophers make him out to be; were we, following their example, to make him a full-fledged philosopher, discovering by himself the most sublime truths, and, by chains of terribly abstract reasoning, forming for himself maxims of justice and reason drawn from the love of order in general or from the known will of his creator; in a word, were we to suppose there was in his mind as much intelligence and enlightenment as he needs, and is in fact found to have dullness and stupidity, what use would the species have for all that metaphysics, which could not be communicated and which would perish with the individual who would have invented it? What progress could the human race make, scattered in the woods among the animals? And to what extent could men mutually perfect and enlighten one another, when, with neither a fixed dwelling nor any need for one another, they would hardly encounter one another twice in their lives, without knowing or talking to one another.

Let us consider how many ideas we owe to the use of speech; how much grammar trains and facilitates the operations of the mind. And let us think of the inconceivable difficulties and the infinite amount of time that the first invention of languages must have cost. Let us join their reflections to the preceding ones, and we will be in a position to judge how many thousands of centuries would have been necessary to develop successively in the human mind the operations of which it was capable.

May I be permitted to consider for a moment the obstacles to the origin of languages. I could be content here to cite or repeat the investigations that the Abbé de Condillac has made on this matter, all of which completely confirm my view, and may perhaps have given me the idea in the first place. But since the way in which this philosopher resolves the difficulties he himself raises concerning the origin of conventional signs shows that he assumed what I question (namely, a kind of society already established among the inventors of language), I believe that, in referring to his reflections, I must add to them my own, in order to present the same difficulties from a standpoint that is pertinent to my subject. The first that presents itself is to imagine how languages could have become necessary; for since men had no communication among themselves nor any need for it, I fail to see either the necessity of this invention or its possibility, if it were not indispensable. I might well say, as do many others, that languages were born in the domestic intercourse among fathers, mothers, and children. But aside from the fact that this would not resolve the difficulties, it would make the mistake of those who, reasoning about the state of nature, intrude into it ideas taken from society. They always see the family gathered in one and the same dwelling, with its members maintaining among themselves a union as intimate and permanent as exists among us, where so many common interests unite them. But the fact of the matter is that in that primitive state, since nobody had houses or huts or property of any kind, each one bedded down in some random spot and often for only one night. Males and females came together fortuitously as a result of chance encounters, occasion, and desire, without there being any great need for words to express what they had to say to one another. They left one another with the same nonchalance.[12] The mother at first nursed her children for her own need; then, with habit having endeared them to her, she later nourished them for their own need. Once they had the strength to look for their food, they did not hesitate to leave the mother herself. And since there was practically no other way of finding one another than not to lose sight of one another, they were soon at the point of not even recognizing one another. It should also be noted that, since the child had all his needs to explain and consequently more things to say to the mother than the mother to the child, it is the child who must make the greatest effort toward inventing a language, and that the language he uses should in large part be of his own making, which multiplies languages as many times as there are individuals to speak them. This tendency was abetted by a nomadic and vagabond life, which

does not give any idiom time to gain a foothold. For claiming that the mother teaches her child the words he ought to use in asking her for this or that is a good way of showing how already formed languages are taught, but it does not tell us how languages are formed.

Let us suppose this first difficulty has been overcome. Let us disregard for a moment the immense space that there must have been between the pure state of nature and the need for languages. And, on the supposition that they are necessary,[13] let us inquire how they might have begun to be established. Here we come to a new difficulty, worse still than the preceding one. For if men needed speech in order to learn to think, they had a still greater need for knowing how to think in order to discover the art of speaking. And even if it were understood how vocal sounds had been taken for the conventional expressions of our ideas, it would still remain for us to determine what could have been the conventional expressions for ideas that, not having a sensible object, could not be indicated either by gesture or by voice. Thus we are scarcely able to form tenable conjectures regarding the birth of this art of communicating thoughts and establishing intercourse between minds, a sublime art which is already quite far from its origin, but which the philosopher still sees at so prodigious a distance from its perfection that there is no man so foolhardy as to claim that it will ever achieve it, even if the sequences of change that time necessarily brings were suspended in its favor, even if prejudices were to be barred from the academies or be silent before them, and even if they were able to occupy themselves with that thorny problem for whole centuries without interruption.

Man's first language, the most universal, the most energetic and the only language he needed before it was necessary to persuade men assembled together, is the cry of nature. Since this cry was elicited only by a kind of instinct in pressing circumstances, to beg for help in great dangers, or for relief of violent ills, it was not used very much in the ordinary course of life, where more moderate feelings prevail. When the ideas of men begin to spread and multiply, and closer communication was established among them, they sought more numerous signs and a more extensive language. They multiplied vocal inflections and combined them with gestures, which, by their nature, are more expressive, and whose meaning is less dependent on a prior determination. They therefore signified visible and mobile objects by means of gestures, and audible ones by imitative sounds. But since a gesture indicates hardly anything more than present or easily described objects and visible actions; since its use is not universal, because darkness or the interposition of a body renders it useless; and since it requires rather than stimulates attention, men finally thought of replacing them with vocal articulations, which, while not having the same relationship to certain ideas, were better suited to represent all ideas as conventional signs. Such a substitution could only be made by a common consent and in a way rather difficult to practice for men whose crude organs had as yet no exercise, and still more difficult to conceive in itself, since that unanimous agreement had to have had a motive, and speech appears to have been necessary in order to establish the use of speech.

We must infer that the first words men used had a much broader meaning in their mind than do those used in languages that are already formed; and that, being ignorant of the division of discourse into its constitutive parts, at first they gave each word the meaning of a whole sentence. When they began to distinguish subject from attribute and verb from noun, which was no mean effort of genius, substantives were at first only so many proper nouns; the [present] infinitive was the only verb tense; and the notion of adjectives must have developed only with considerable difficulty, since every adjective is an abstract word, and abstractions are difficult and not particularly natural operations.

At first each object was given a particular name, without regard to genus and species which those first founders were not in a position to distinguish; and all individual things presented themselves to their minds in isolation, as they are in the spectacle of nature. If one oak tree was called A, another was called B. [For the first idea one draws from two things is that they are not the same; and it often requires quite some time to observe what they have

in common.] Thus the more limited the knowledge, the more extensive becomes the dictionary. The difficulty inherent in all this nomenclature could not easily be alleviated, for in order to group beings under various common and generic denominations, it was necessary to know their properties and their differences. Observations and definitions were necessary, that is to say, natural history and metaphysics, and far more than men of those times could have had.

Moreover, general ideas can be introduced into the mind only with the aid of words, and the understanding grasps them only through sentences. That is one reason why animals cannot form such ideas or even acquire the perfectibility that depends on them. When a monkey moves unhesitatingly from one nut to another, does anyone think the monkey has the general idea of that type of fruit and that he compares its archetype with these two individuals? Undoubtedly not; but the sight of one of these nuts recalls to his memory the sensations he received of the other; and his eyes, modified in a certain way, announce to his sense of taste the modification it is about to receive. Every general idea is purely intellectual. The least involvement of the imagination thereupon makes the idea particular. Try to draw for yourself the image of a tree in general; you will never succeed in doing it. In spite of yourself, it must be seen as small or large, barren or leafy, light or dark; and if you were in a position to see in it nothing but what you see in every tree, this image would no longer resemble a tree. Purely abstract beings are perceived in the same way, or are conceived only through discourse. The definition of a triangle alone gives you the true idea of it. As soon as you behold one in your mind, it is a particular triangle and not some other one, and you cannot avoid making its lines to be perceptible or its plane to have color. It is therefore necessary to utter sentences, and thus to speak, in order to have general ideas. For as soon as the imagination stops, the mind proceeds no further without the aid of discourse. If, then, the first inventors of language could give names only to ideas they already had, it follows that the first substantives could not have been anything but proper nouns.

But when, by means I am unable to conceive, our new grammarians began to extend their ideas and to generalize their words, the ignorance of the inventors must have subjected this method to very strict limitations. And just as they had at first unduly multiplied the names of individual things, owing to their failure to know the genera and species, they later made too few species and genera, owing to their failure to have considered beings in all their differences. Pushing these divisions far enough would have required more experience and enlightenment than they could have had, and more investigations and work than they were willing to put into it. Now if even today new species are discovered everyday that until now had escaped all our observations, just imagine how many species must have escaped the attention of men who judged things only on first appearance! As for primary classes and the most general notions, it is superfluous to add that they too must have escaped them. How, for example, would they have imagined or understood the words "matter," "mind," "substance," "mode," "figure," and "movement," when our philosophers, who for so long have been making use of them, have a great deal of difficulty understanding them themselves; and when, since the ideas attached to these words are purely metaphysical, they found no model of them in nature?

I stop with these first steps, and I implore my judges to suspend their reading here to consider, concerning the invention of physical substantives alone, that is to say, concerning the easiest part of the language to discover, how far language still had to go in order to express all the thoughts of men, assume a durable form, be capable of being spoken in public, and influence society. I implore them to reflect upon how much time and knowledge were needed to discover numbers,[14] abstract words, aorists, and all the tenses of verbs, particles, syntax, the connecting of sentences, reasoning, and the forming of all the logic of discourse. As for myself, being shocked by the unending difficulties and convinced of the almost demonstrable impossibility that languages could have arisen and been established by merely human means, I leave to anyone who would undertake it the discussion of the following difficult problem: which was the more

necessary: an already formed society for the invention of languages, or an already invented language for the establishment of society?

Whatever these origins may be, it is clear, from the little care taken by nature to bring men together through mutual needs and to facilitate their use of speech, how little she prepared them for becoming habituated to the ways of society, and how little she contributed to all that men have done to establish the bonds of society. In fact, it is impossible to imagine why, in that primitive state, one man would have a greater need for another man than a monkey or a wolf has for another of its respective species; or, assuming this need, what motive could induce the other man to satisfy it; or even, in this latter instance, how they could be in mutual agreement regarding the conditions. I know that we are repeatedly told that nothing would have been so miserable as man in that state; and if it is true, as I believe I have proved, that it is only after many centuries that men could have had the desire and the opportunity to leave that state, that would be a charge to bring against nature, not against him whom nature has thus constituted. But if we understand the word *miserable* properly, it is a word which is without meaning or which signifies merely a painful privation and suffering of the body or the soul. Now I would very much like someone to explain to me what kind of misery can there be for a free being whose heart is at peace and whose body is in good health? I ask which of the two, civil or natural life, is more likely to become insufferable to those who live it? We see about us practically no people who do not complain about their existence; many even deprive themselves of it to the extent they are able, and the combination of divine and human laws is hardly enough to stop this disorder. I ask if anyone has ever heard tell of a savage who was living in liberty ever dreaming of complaining about his life and of killing himself. Let the judgment therefore be made with less pride on which side real misery lies. On the other hand, nothing would have been so miserable as savage man, dazzled by enlightenment, tormented by passions, and reasoning about a state different from his own. It was by a very wise providence that the latent faculties he possessed should develop only as the occasion to exercise them presents itself, so that they would be neither superfluous nor troublesome to him beforehand, nor underdeveloped and useless in time of need. In instinct alone, man had everything he needed in order to live in the state of nature; in a cultivated reason, he has only what he needs to live in society.

At first it would seem that men in that state, having among themselves no type of moral relations or acknowledged duties, could be neither good nor evil, and had neither vices nor virtues, unless, if we take these words in a physical sense, we call those qualities that can harm an individual's preservation "vices" in him, and those that can contribute to it "virtues." In that case it would be necessary to call the one who least resists the simple impulses of nature the most virtuous. But without departing from the standard meaning of these words, it is appropriate to suspend the judgment we could make regarding such a situation and to be on our guard against our prejudices, until we have examined with scale in hand whether there are more virtues than vices among civilized men; or whether their virtues are more advantageous than their vices are lethal; or whether the progress of their knowledge is sufficient compensation for ills they inflict on one another as they learn of the good they ought to do; or whether, all things considered, they would not be in a happier set of circumstances if they had neither evil to fear nor good to hope for from anyone, rather than subjecting themselves to a universal dependence and obliging themselves to receive everything from those who do not oblige themselves to give them anything.

Above all, let us not conclude with Hobbes that because man has no idea of goodness he is naturally evil; that he is vicious because he does not know virtue; that he always refuses to perform services for his fellow men he does not believe he owes them; or that, by virtue of the right, which he reasonably attributes to himself, to those things he needs, he foolishly imagines himself to be the sole proprietor of the entire universe. Hobbes has very clearly seen the defect of all modern definitions of natural right, but the consequences he draws from his own definition show that he takes it in a sense that is no less

false. Were he to have reasoned on the basis of the principles he establishes, this author should have said that since the state of nature is the state in which the concern for our self-preservation is the least prejudicial to that of others, that state was consequently the most appropriate for peace and the best suited for the human race. He says precisely the opposite, because he had wrongly injected into the savage man's concern for self-preservation the need to satisfy a multitude of passions which are the product of society and which have made laws necessary. The evil man, he says, is a robust child. It remains to be seen whether savage man is a robust child. Were we to grant him this, what would we conclude from it? That if this man were as dependent on others when he is robust as he is when he is weak, there is no type of excess to which he would not tend: he would beat his mother if she were too slow in offering him her breast; he would strangle one of his younger brothers, should he find him annoying; he would bite someone's leg, should he be assaulted or aggravated by him. But being robust and being dependent are two contradictory suppositions in the state of nature. Man is weak when he is dependent, and he is emancipated from that dependence before he is robust. Hobbes did not see that the same cause preventing savages from using their reason, as our jurists claim, is what prevents them at the same time from abusing their faculties, as he himself maintains. Hence we could say that savages are not evil precisely because they do not know what it is to be good; for it is neither the development of enlightenment nor the restraint imposed by the law, but the calm of the passions and the ignorance of vice which prevents them from doing evil. *So much more profitable to these is the ignorance of vice than the knowledge of virtue is to those.* Moreover, there is another principle that Hobbes failed to notice, and which, having been given to man in order to mitigate, in certain circumstances, the ferocity of his egocentrism or the desire for self-preservation before this egocentrism of his came into being,[15] tempers the ardor he has for his own well-being by an innate repugnance to seeing his fellow men suffer. I do not believe I have any contradiction to fear in granting the only natural virtue that the most excessive detractor of human virtues was forced to recognize. I am referring to pity, a disposition that is fitting for beings that are as weak and as subject to ills as we are; a virtue all the more universal and all the more useful to man in that it precedes in him any kind of reflection, and so natural that even animals sometimes show noticeable signs of it. Without speaking of the tenderness of mothers for their young and of the perils they have to brave in order to protect them, one daily observes the repugnance that horses have for trampling a living body with their hooves. An animal does not go undisturbed past a dead animal of its own species. There are even some animals that give them a kind of sepulchre; and the mournful lowing of cattle entering a slaughterhouse voices the impression they receive of the horrible spectacle that strikes them. One notes with pleasure the author of *The Fable of the Bees*, having been forced to acknowledge man as a compassionate and sensitive being, departing from his cold and subtle style in the example he gives, to offer us the pathetic image of an imprisoned man who sees outside his cell a ferocious animal tearing a child from its mother's breast, mashing its frail limbs with its murderous teeth, and ripping with its claws the child's quivering entrails. What horrible agitation must be felt by this witness of an event in which he has no personal interest! What anguish must he suffer at this sight, being unable to be of any help to the fainting mother or to the dying child?

Such is the pure movement of nature prior to all reflection. Such is the force of natural pity, which the most depraved mores still have difficulty destroying, since everyday one sees in our theaters someone affected and weeping at the ills of some unfortunate person, and who, were he in the tyrant's place, would intensify the torments of his enemy still more; [like the bloodthirsty Sulla, so sensitive to ills he had not caused, or like Alexander of Pherae, who did not dare attend the performance of any tragedy, for fear of being seen weeping with Andromache and Priam, and yet who listened impassively to the cries of so many citizens who were killed everyday on his orders. *Nature, in giving men tears, bears witness that she gave the human race the softest hearts.*] Mandeville has a clear awareness that, with all their mores, men

would never have been anything but monsters, if nature had not given them pity to aid their reason; but he has not seen that from this quality alone flow all the social virtues that he wants to deny in men. In fact, what are generosity, mercy, and humanity, if not pity applied to the weak, to the guilty, or to the human species in general. Benevolence and even friendship are, properly understood, the products of a constant pity fixed on a particular object; for is desiring that someone not suffer anything but desiring that he be happy? Were it true that commiseration were merely a sentiment that puts us in the position of the one who suffers, a sentiment that is obscure and powerful in savage man, developed but weak in man dwelling in civil society, what importance would this idea have to the truth of what I say, except to give it more force? In fact, commiseration will be all the more energetic as the witnessing animal identifies itself more intimately with the suffering animal. Now it is evident that this identification must have been infinitely closer in the state of nature than in the state of reasoning. Reason is what engenders egocentrism, and reflection strengthens it. Reason is what turns man in upon himself. Reason is what separates him from all that troubles him and afflicts him. Philosophy is what isolates him and what moves him to say in secret, at the sight of a suffering man, "Perish if you will; I am safe and sound." No longer can anything but danger to the entire society trouble the tranquil slumber of the philosopher and yank him from his bed. His fellow man can be killed with impunity underneath his window. He has merely to place his hands over his ears and argue with himself a little in order to prevent nature, which rebels within him, from identifying him with the man being assassinated. Savage man does not have this admirable talent, and for lack of wisdom and reason he is always seen thoughtlessly giving in to the first sentiment of humanity. When there is a riot or a street brawl, the populace gathers together; the prudent man withdraws from the scene. It is the rabble, the women of the marketplace, who separate the combatants and prevent decent people from killing one another.

It is therefore quite certain that pity is a natural sentiment, which, by moderating in each individual the activity of the love of oneself, contributes to the mutual preservation of the entire species. Pity is what carries us without reflection to the aid of those we see suffering. Pity is what, in the state of nature, takes the place of laws, mores, and virtue, with the advantage that no one is tempted to disobey its sweet voice. Pity is what will prevent every robust savage from robbing a weak child or an infirm old man of his hard-earned subsistence, if he himself expects to be able to find his own someplace else. Instead of the sublime maxim of reasoned justice, *Do unto others as you would have them do unto you*, pity inspires all men with another maxim of natural goodness, much less perfect but perhaps more useful than the preceding one: *Do what is good for you with as little harm as possible to others*. In a word, it is in this natural sentiment, rather than in subtle arguments, that one must search for the cause of the repugnance at doing evil that every man would experience, even independently of the maxims of education. Although it might be appropriate for Socrates and minds of his stature to acquire virtue through reason, the human race would long ago have ceased to exist, if its preservation had depended solely on the reasonings of its members.

With passions so minimally active and such a salutary restraint, being more wild than evil, and more attentive to protecting themselves from the harm they could receive than tempted to do harm to others, men were not subject to very dangerous conflicts. Since they had no sort of intercourse among themselves; since, as a consequence, they knew neither vanity, nor deference, nor esteem, nor contempt; since they had not the slightest notion of mine and thine, nor any true idea of justice; since they regarded the acts of violence that could befall them as an easily redressed evil and not as an offense that must be punished; and since they did not even dream of vengeance except perhaps as a knee-jerk response right then and there, like the dog that bites the stone that is thrown at him, their disputes would rarely have had bloody consequences, if their subject had been no more sensitive than food. But I see a more dangerous matter that remains for me to discuss.

Among the passions that agitate the heart of man, there is an ardent, impetuous one that renders one sex necessary to the other; a terrible passion which braves all dangers, overcomes all obstacles, and which, in its fury, seems fitted to destroy the human race it is destined to preserve. What would become of men, victimized by this unrestrained and brutal rage, without modesty and self-control, fighting everyday over the object of their passion at the price of their blood?

There must first be agreement that the more violent the passions are, the more necessary the laws are to contain them. But over and above the fact that the disorders and the crimes these passions cause daily in our midst show quite well the insufficiency of the laws in this regard, it would still be good to examine whether these disorders did not come into being with the laws themselves; for then, even if they were capable of repressing them, the least one should expect of them would be that they call a halt to an evil that would not exist without them.

Let us begin by distinguishing between the moral and the physical aspects of the sentiment of love. The physical aspect is that general desire which inclines one sex to unite with another. The moral aspect is what determines this desire and fixes it exclusively on one single object, or which at least gives it a greater degree of energy for this preferred object. Now it is easy to see that the moral aspect of love is an artificial sentiment born of social custom, and extolled by women with so much skill and care in order to establish their hegemony and make dominant the sex that ought to obey. Since this feeling is founded on certain notions of merit or beauty that a savage is not in a position to have, and on comparisons he is incapable of making, it must be almost non-existent for him. For since his mind could not form abstract ideas of regularity and proportion, his heart is not susceptible to sentiments of admiration and love, which, even without its being observed come into being from the application of these ideas. He pays exclusive attention to the temperament he has received from nature, and not the taste [aversion] he has been unable to acquire; any woman suits his purpose.

Limited merely to the physical aspect of love, and fortunate enough to be ignorant of those preferences which stir up the feeling and increase the difficulties in satisfying it, men must feel the ardors of their temperament less frequently and less vividly, and consequently have fewer and less cruel conflicts among themselves. Imagination, which wreaks so much havoc among us, does not speak to savage hearts; each man peacefully awaits the impetus of nature, gives himself over to it without choice, and with more pleasure than frenzy; and once the need is satisfied, all desire is snuffed out.

Hence it is incontestable that love itself, like all other passions, had acquired only in society that impetuous ardor which so often makes it lethal to men. And it is all the more ridiculous to represent savages as continually slaughtering each other in order to satisfy their brutality, since this opinion is directly contrary to experience; and since the Caribs, of all existing peoples, are the people that until now has wandered least from the state of nature, they are the people least subject to jealousy, even though they live in a hot climate which always seems to occasion greater activity in these passions.

As to any inferences that could be drawn, in the case of several species of animals, from the clashes between males that bloody our poultry yards throughout the year, and which make our forests resound in the spring with their cries as they quarrel over a female, it is necessary to begin by excluding all species in which nature has manifestly established, in the relative power of the sexes, relations other than those that exist among us. Hence cockfights do not form the basis for an inference regarding the human species. In species where the proportion is more closely observed, these fights can have for their cause only the scarcity of females in relation to the number of males, or the exclusive intervals during which the female continually rejects the advances of the male, which adds up to the cause just cited. For if each female receives the male for only two months a year, in this respect it is as if the number of females were reduced by five-sixths. Now neither of these two cases is applicable to the human species where the number of females generally surpasses the number of males, and where human females, unlike those of other species, have never been observed to have periods of heat and exclusion, even among savages. Moreover, among several of these animal species, where the entire species goes into heat simultaneously, there comes a terrible moment of common ardor, tumult, disorder and combat: a moment that does not happen in the human species where love is never periodic. Therefore one cannot conclude from the combats of certain animals for the possession of females that the same thing would happen to man in the state of nature. And even if one could draw that conclusion, given that these conflicts do not destroy the other species, one should conclude that they would not be any more lethal for ours. And it is quite apparent that they would wreak less havoc in the state of nature than in society, especially in countries where mores still count for something and where the jealousy of lovers and the vengeance of husbands every day give rise to duels, murders and still worse things; where the duty of eternal fidelity serves merely to create adulterers; and where even the laws of continence and honor necessarily spread debauchery and multiply the number of abortions.

Let us conclude that, wandering in the forests, without industry, without speech, without dwelling, without war, without relationships, with no need for his fellow men, and correspondingly with no desire to do them harm, perhaps never even recognizing any of them individually, savage man, subject to few passions and self-sufficient, had only the sentiments and enlightenment appropriate to that state; he felt only his true needs, took notice of only what he believed he had an interest in seeing; and that his intelligence made no more progress than his vanity. If by chance he made some discovery, he was all the less able to communicate it to others because he did not even know his own children. Art perished with its inventor. There was neither education nor progress; generations were multiplied to no purpose. Since each one always began from the same point, centuries went by with all the crudeness of the first ages; the species was already old, and man remained ever a child.

If I have gone on at such length about the supposition of that primitive condition, it is because, having ancient errors and inveterate prejudices to destroy, I felt I should dig down to the root and show, in the depiction of the true state of nature, how far even natural inequality is from having as much reality and influence in that state as our writers claim.

In fact, it is easy to see that, among the differences that distinguish men, several of them pass for natural ones which are exclusively the work of habit and of the various sorts of life that men adopt in society. Thus a robust or delicate temperament, and the strength or weakness that depend on it, frequently derive more from the harsh or effeminate way in which one has been raised than from the primitive constitution of bodies. The same holds for mental powers; and not only does education make a difference between cultivated minds and those that are not, it also augments the difference among the former in proportion to their culture; for were a giant and a dwarf walking on the same road, each step they both take would give a fresh advantage to the giant. Now if one compares the prodigious diversity of educations and lifestyles in the different orders of the civil state with the simplicity and uniformity of animal and savage life, where all nourish themselves from the same foods, live in the same manner, and do exactly the same things, it will be understood how much less the difference between one man and another must be in the state of nature than in that of society, and how much natural inequality must increase in the human species through inequality occasioned by social institutions.

But even if nature were to affect, in the distribution of her gifts, as many preferences as is claimed, what advantage would the most favored men derive from them, to the detriment of others, in a state of things that allowed practically no sort of relationships among them? Where there is no love, what use is beauty? What use is wit for people who do not speak, and ruse to those who have no dealing with others? I always hear it repeated that the stronger will oppress the weaker. But let me have an explanation of the meaning of the word "oppression." Some will dominate with violence; others will groan, enslaved to all their caprices. That is precisely what I observe among us; but I do not see how this could be said of savage men, to whom it would be difficult even to explain what servitude and domination are. A man could well lay hold of the fruit another has gathered, the game he has killed, the cave that served as his shelter.

But how will he ever succeed in making himself be obeyed? And what can be the chains of dependence among men who possess nothing? If someone chases me from one tree, I am free to go to another; if someone torments me in one place, who will prevent me from going elsewhere? Is there a man with strength sufficiently superior to mine and who is, moreover, sufficiently depraved, sufficiently lazy and sufficiently ferocious to force me to provide for his subsistence while he remains idle? He must resolve not to take his eyes off me for a single instant, to keep me carefully tied down while he sleeps, for fear that I may escape or that I would kill him. In other words, he is obliged to expose himself voluntarily to a much greater hardship than the one he wants to avoid and gives me. After all that, were his vigilance to relax for an instant, were an unforeseen noise to make him turn his head, I take twenty steps into the forest; my chains are broken, and he never sees me again for the rest of his life.

Without needlessly prolonging these details, anyone should see that, since the bonds of servitude are formed merely from the mutual dependence of men and the reciprocal needs that unite them, it is impossible to enslave a man without having first put him in the position of being incapable of doing without another. This being a situation that did not exist in the state of nature, it leaves each person free of the yoke, and renders pointless the law of the strongest.

After having proved that inequality is hardly observable in the state of nature, and that its influence there is almost nonexistent, it remains for me to show its origin and progress in the successive developments of the human mind. After having shown that *perfectibility*, social virtues, and the other faculties that natural man had received in a state of potentiality could never develop by themselves, that to achieve this development they required the chance coming together of several unconnected causes that might never have come into being and without which he would have remained eternally in his primitive constitution, it remains for me to consider and to bring together the various chance happenings that were able to perfect human reason while deteriorating the species, make a being evil while rendering it habituated to the ways of society, and, from so distant a beginning, finally bring man and the world to the point where we see them now.

I admit that, since the events I have to describe could have taken place in several ways, I cannot make a determination among them except on the basis of conjecture. But over and above the fact that these conjectures become reasons when they are the most probable ones that a person can draw from the nature of things and the sole means that a person can have of discovering the truth, the consequences I wish to deduce from mine will not thereby be conjectural, since, on the basis of the principles I have just established, no other system is conceivable that would not furnish me with the same results, and from which I could not draw the same conclusions.

This will excuse me from expanding my reflections on the way in which the lapse of time compensates for the slight probability of events; concerning the surprising power that quite negligible causes may have when they act without interruption; concerning the impossibility, on the one hand, of a person's destroying certain hypotheses, even though, on the other hand, one is not in a position to accord them the level of factual certitude; concerning a situation in which two facts given as real are to be connected by a series of intermediate facts that are unknown or regarded as such, it belongs to history, when it exists, to provide the facts that connect them; it belongs to philosophy, when history is unavailable, to determine similar facts that can connect them; finally, concerning how, with respect to events, similarity reduces the facts to a much smaller number of different classes than one might imagine. It is enough for me to offer these objects to the consideration of my judges; it is enough for me to have seen to it that ordinary readers would have no need to consider them.

PART TWO

The first person who, having enclosed a plot of land, took it into his head to say *this is mine* and found people simple enough to believe him, was the true founder of civil society. What crimes, wars, murders, what miseries and horrors would the human race have been spared, had someone pulled up the stakes or filled in the ditch and cried out to his fellow men: "Do not listen to this impostor. You are lost if you forget that the fruits of the earth belong to all and the earth to no one!" But it is quite likely that by then things had already reached the point where they could no longer continue as they were. For this idea of property, depending on many prior ideas which could only have arisen successively, was not formed all at once in the human mind. It was necessary to make great progress, to acquire much industry and enlightenment, and to transmit and augment them from one age to another, before arriving at this final stage in the state of nature. Let us therefore take things farther back and try to piece together under a single viewpoint that slow succession of events and advances in knowledge in their most natural order.

Man's first sentiment was that of his own existence; his first concern was that of his preservation. The products of the earth provided him with all the help he needed; instinct led him to make use of them. With hunger and other appetites making him experience by turns various ways of existing, there was one appetite that invited him to perpetuate his species; and this blind inclination, devoid of any sentiment of the heart, produced a purely animal act. Once this need had been satisfied, the two sexes no longer took cognizance of one another, and even the child no longer meant anything to the mother once it could do without her.

Such was the condition of man in his nascent stage; such was the life of an animal limited at first to pure sensations, and scarcely profiting from the gifts nature offered him, far from dreaming of extracting anything from her. But difficulties soon presented themselves to him; it was necessary to learn to overcome them. The height of trees, which kept him from reaching their fruits, the competition of animals that sought to feed themselves on these same fruits, the ferocity of those animals that wanted to take his own life: everything obliged him to apply himself to bodily exercises. It was necessary to become agile, fleet-footed and vigorous in combat. Natural arms, which are tree branches and stones, were soon found ready at hand. He learned to surmount nature's obstacles, combat other animals when necessary, fight for his subsistence even with men, or compensate for what he had to yield to those stronger than himself.

In proportion as the human race spread, difficulties multiplied with the men. Differences in soils, climates and seasons could force them to inculcate these differences in their lifestyles. Barren years, long and hard winters, hot summers that consume everything required new resourcefulness from them. Along the seashore and the riverbanks they invented the fishing line and hook, and became fishermen and fish-eaters. In the forests they made bows and arrows, and became hunters and warriors. In cold countries they covered themselves with the skins of animals they had killed. Lightning, a volcano, or some fortuitous chance happening acquainted them with fire: a new resource against the rigors of winter. They learned to preserve this element, then to reproduce it, and finally to use it to prepare meats that previously they devoured raw.

This repeated appropriation of various beings to himself, and of some beings to others, must naturally have engendered in man's mind the perceptions of certain relations. These relationships which we express by the words "large," "small," "strong," "weak," "fast," "slow," "timorous," "bold," and other similar ideas, compared when needed and almost without thinking about it, finally produced in him a kind of reflection, or rather a mechanical prudence which pointed out to him the precautions that were most necessary for his safety.

The new enlightenment which resulted from this development increased his superiority over the other animals by making him aware of it. He trained himself to set traps for them; he tricked them in a thousand different ways. And although several surpassed him in fighting strength or in swiftness in running, of those that could serve him or hurt him, he became in time the master of the former and the scourge of the latter. Thus the first glance he directed upon himself produced within him the first stirring of pride; thus, as yet hardly knowing how to distinguish the ranks, and contemplating himself in the first rank by virtue of his species, he prepared himself from afar to lay claim to it in virtue of his individuality.

Although his fellowmen were not for him what they are for us, and although he had hardly anything more to do with them than with other animals, they were not forgotten in his observations. The conformities that time could make him perceive among them, his female, and himself, made him judge those he did not perceive. And seeing that they all acted as he would have done under similar circumstances, he concluded that their way of thinking and feeling was in complete conformity with his own. And this important truth, well established in his mind, made him follow, by a presentiment as sure as dialectic and more prompt, the best rules of conduct that it was appropriate to observe toward them for his advantage and safety.

Taught by experience that love of well-being is the sole motive of human actions, he found himself in a position to distinguish the rare occasions when common interest should make him count on the assistance of his fellowmen, and those even rarer occasions when competition ought to make him distrust them. In the first case, he united with them in a herd, or at most in some sort of free association, that obligated no one and that lasted only as long as the passing need that had formed it. In the second case, everyone sought to obtain his own advantage, either by overt force, if he believed he could, or by cleverness and cunning, if he felt himself to be the weaker.

This is how men could imperceptibly acquire some crude idea of mutual commitments and of the advantages to be had in fulfilling them, but only insofar as present and perceptible interests could require it, since foresight meant nothing to them, and far from concerning themselves about a distant future, they did not even give a thought to the next day. Were it a matter of catching a deer, everyone was quite aware that he must faithfully keep to his post in order to achieve this purpose; but if a hare happened to pass within reach of one of them, no doubt he would have pursued it without giving it a second thought, and that, having obtained his prey, he cared very little about causing his companions to miss theirs.

It is easy to understand that such intercourse did not require a language much more refined than that of crows or monkeys, which flock together in practically the same way. Inarticulate cries, many gestures, and some imitative noises must for a long time have made up the universal language. By joining to this in each country a few articulate and conventional sounds, whose institution, as I have already said, is not too easy to explain, there were individual languages, but crude and imperfect ones, quite similar to those still spoken by various savage nations today. Constrained by the passing of time, the abundance of things I have to say, and the practically imperceptible progress of the beginnings, I am flying like an arrow over the multitudes of centuries. For the slower events were in succeeding one another, the quicker they can be described.

These first advances enabled man to make more rapid ones. The more the mind was enlightened, the more industry was perfected. Soon they ceased to fall asleep under the first tree or to retreat into caves, and found various types of hatchets made of hard, sharp stones, which served to cut wood, dig up the soil, and make huts from branches they later found it useful to cover with clay and mud. This was the period of a first revolution which formed the establishment of the distinction among families and which introduced a kind of property, whence perhaps there already arose many quarrels and fights. However, since the strongest were probably the first to make themselves lodgings they felt capable of defending, presumably the weak found it quicker and safer to imitate them than to try to dislodge them; and as for those who already had huts, each of them must have rarely sought to appropriate that of his neighbor, less because it did not belong to him than because it was of no use to him, and because he could not seize it without exposing himself to a fierce battle with the family that occupied it.

The first developments of the heart were the effect of a new situation that united the husbands and wives, fathers and children in one common habitation. The habit of living together gave rise to the sweetest sentiments known to men: conjugal love and paternal love. Each family became a little society all the better united because mutual attachment and liberty were its only bonds; and it was then that the first difference was established in the lifestyle of the two sexes, which

until then had had only one. Women became more sedentary and grew accustomed to watch over the hut and the children, while the man went to seek their common subsistence. With their slightly softer life the two sexes also began to lose something of their ferocity and vigor. But while each one separately became less suited to combat savage beasts, on the other hand it was easier to assemble in order jointly to resist them.

In this new state, with a simple and solitary life, very limited needs, and the tools they had invented to provide for them, since men enjoyed a great deal of leisure time, they used it to procure for themselves many types of conveniences unknown to their fathers; and that was the first yoke they imposed on themselves without realizing it, and the first source of evils they prepared for their descendants. For in addition to their continuing thus to soften body and mind (those conveniences having through habit lost almost all their pleasure, and being at the same time degenerated into true needs), being deprived of them became much more cruel than possessing them was sweet; and they were unhappy about losing them without being happy about possessing them.

At this point we can see a little better how the use of speech was established or imperceptibly perfected itself in the bosom of each family; and one can further conjecture how various particular causes could have extended the language and accelerated its progress by making it more necessary. Great floods or earthquakes surrounded the inhabited areas with water or precipices. Upheavals of the globe detached parts of the mainland and broke them up into islands. Clearly among men thus brought together and forced to live together, a common idiom must have been formed sooner than among those who wandered freely about the forests of the mainland. Thus it is quite possible that after their first attempts at navigation, the islanders brought the use of speech to us; and it is at least quite probable that society and languages came into being on islands and were perfected there before they were known on the mainland.

Everything begins to take on a new appearance. Having previously wandered about the forests and having assumed a more fixed situation, men slowly came together and united into different bands, eventually forming in each country a particular nation, united by mores and characteristic features, not by regulations and laws, but by the same kind of life and foods and by the common influence of the climate. Eventually a permanent proximity cannot fail to engender some intercourse among different families. Young people of different sexes live in neighboring huts; the passing intercourse demanded by nature soon leads to another, through frequent contact with one another, no less sweet and more permanent. People become accustomed to consider different objects and to make comparisons. Imperceptibly they acquire the ideas of merit and beauty which produce feelings of preference. By dint of seeing one another, they can no longer get along without seeing one another again. A sweet and tender feeling insinuates itself into the soul and at the least opposition becomes an impetuous fury. Jealousy awakens with love; discord triumphs, and the sweetest passion receives sacrifices of human blood.

In proportion as ideas and sentiments succeed one another and as the mind and heart are trained, the human race continues to be tamed, relationships spread and bonds are tightened. People grew accustomed to gather in front of their huts or around a large tree; song and dance, true children of love and leisure, became the amusement or rather the occupation of idle men and women who had flocked together. Each one began to look at the others and to want to be looked at himself, and public esteem had a value. The one who sang or danced the best, the handsomest, the strongest, the most adroit or the most eloquent became the most highly regarded. And this was the first step toward inequality and, at the same time, toward vice. From these first preferences were born vanity and contempt on the one hand, and shame and envy on the other. And the fermentation caused by these new leavens eventually produced compounds fatal to happiness and innocence.

As soon as men had begun mutually to value one another, and the idea of esteem was formed in their minds, each one claimed to have a right to it, and it was no longer possible for anyone to be lacking it with impunity. From this came the first duties of civility, even among savages; and from this every voluntary wrong became an outrage, because along with the harm that resulted from the injury, the offended party saw in it contempt for his person, which often was more insufferable than the harm itself. Hence each man punished the contempt shown him in a manner proportionate to the esteem in which he held himself; acts of revenge became terrible, and men became bloodthirsty and cruel. This is precisely the stage reached by most of the savage people known to us; and it is for want of having made adequate distinctions among their ideas or of having noticed how far these peoples already were from the original state of nature that many have hastened to conclude that man is naturally cruel, and that he needs civilization in order to soften him. On the contrary, nothing is so gentle as man in his primitive state, when, placed by nature at an equal distance from the stupidity of brutes and the fatal enlightenment of civil man, and limited equally by instinct and reason to protecting himself from the harm that threatens him, he is restrained by natural pity from needlessly harming anyone himself, even if he has been harmed. For according to the axiom of the wise Locke, *where there is no property, there is no injury.*

But it must be noted that society in its beginning stages and the relations already established among men required in them qualities different from those they derived from their primitive constitution; that, with morality beginning to be introduced into human actions, and everyone, prior to the existence of laws, being sole judge and avenger of the offenses he had received, the goodness appropriate to the pure state of nature was no longer what was appropriate to an emerging society; that it was necessary for punishments to become more severe in proportion as the occasions for giving offense became more frequent; and it remained for the fear of vengeance to take the place of the deterrent character of laws. Hence although men had become less forebearing, and although natural pity had already undergone some alteration, this period of the development of human faculties, maintaining a middle position between the indolence of our primitive state and the petulant activity of our egocentrism, must have been the happiest and most durable epoch. The more one reflects on it, the more one finds that this state was the least subject to upheavals and the best for man,[16] and that he must have left it only by virtue of some fatal chance happening that, for the common good, ought never have happened. The example of savages, almost all of whom have been found in this state, seems to confirm that the human race had been made to remain in it always; that this state is the veritable youth of the world; and that all the subsequent progress has been in appearance so many steps toward the perfection of the individual, and in fact toward the decay of the species.

As long as men were content with the rustic huts, as long as they were limited to making their clothing out of skins sewn together with thorns or fish bones, adorning themselves with feathers and shells, painting their bodies with various colors, perfecting or embellishing their bows and arrows, using sharp-edged stones to make some fishing canoes or some crude musical instruments; in a word, as long as they applied themselves exclusively to tasks that a single individual could do and to the arts that did not require the cooperation of several hands, they lived as free, healthy, good and happy as they could in accordance with their nature; and they continued to enjoy among themselves the sweet rewards of independent intercourse. But as soon as one man needed the help of another, as soon as one man realized that it was useful for a single individual to have provisions for two, equality disappeared, property came into existence, labor became necessary. Vast forests were transformed into smiling fields which had to be watered with men's sweat, and in which slavery and misery were soon seen to germinate and grow with the crops.

Metallurgy and agriculture were the two arts whose invention produced this great revolution. For the poet, it is gold and silver; but for the philosopher, it is iron and wheat that have civilized men and ruined the human race. Thus they were both unknown to the savages of America, who for that reason have always remained savages. Other peoples even appear to have remained barbarous, as long as they practiced one of those arts without the other. And perhaps one of the best reasons why Europe has been, if not sooner,

at least more constantly and better governed than the other parts of the world, is that it is at the same time the most abundant in iron and the most fertile in wheat.

It is very difficult to guess how men came to know and use iron, for it is incredible that by themselves they thought of drawing the ore from the mine and performing the necessary preparations on it for smelting it before they knew what would result. From another point of view, it is even less plausible to attribute this discovery to some accidental fire, because mines are set up exclusively in arid places devoid of trees and plants, so that one would say that nature had taken precautions to conceal this deadly secret from us. Thus there remains only the extraordinary circumstance of some volcano that, in casting forth molten metal, would have given observers the idea of imitating this operation of nature. Even still we must suppose them to have had a great deal of courage and foresight to undertake such a difficult task and to have envisaged so far in advance the advantages they could derive from it. This is hardly suitable for minds already better trained than theirs must have been.

As for agriculture, its principle was known long before its practice was established, and it is hardly possible that men, constantly preoccupied with deriving their subsistence from trees and plants, did not rather quickly get the idea of the methods used by nature to grow plant life. But their industry probably did not turn in that direction until very late either because trees, which, along with hunting and fishing, provided their nourishment, had no need of their care; or for want of knowing how to use wheat; or for want of tools with which to cultivate it; or for want of foresight regarding future needs; or, finally, for want of the means of preventing others from appropriating the fruits of their labors. Having become more industrious, it is believable that, with sharp stones and pointed sticks, they began by cultivating some vegetables or roots around their huts long before they knew how to prepare wheat and had the tools necessary for large-scale cultivation. Moreover, to devote oneself to that occupation and to sow the lands, one must be resolved to lose something at first in order to gain a great deal later: a precaution quite far removed from the mind of the savage man, who, as I have said, finds it quite difficult to give thought in the morning to what he will need at night.

The invention of the other arts was therefore necessary to force the human race to apply itself to that of agriculture. Once men were needed in order to smelt and forge the iron, other men were needed in order to feed them. The more the number of workers increased, the fewer hands there were to obtain food for the common subsistence, without there being fewer mouths to consume it; and since some needed foodstuffs in exchange for their iron, the others finally found the secret of using iron to multiply foodstuffs. From this there arose farming and agriculture, on the one hand, and the art of working metals and multiplying their uses, on the other.

From the cultivation of land, there necessarily followed the division of land; and from property once recognized, the first rules of justice. For in order to render everyone what is his, it is necessary that everyone can have something. Moreover, as men began to look toward the future and as they saw that they all had goods to lose, there was not one of them who did not have to fear reprisals against himself for wrongs he might do to another. This origin is all the more natural as it is impossible to conceive of the idea of property arising from anything but manual labor, for it is not clear what man can add, beyond his own labor, in order to appropriate things he has not made. It is labor alone that, in giving the cultivator a right to the product of the soil he has tilled, consequently gives him this right, at least until the harvest, and thus from year to year. With this possession continuing uninterrupted, it is easily transformed into property. When the ancients, says Grotius, gave Ceres the epithet of legislatrix, gave the name Thesmophories to a festival celebrated in her honor, they thereby made it apparent that the division of lands has produced a new kind of right: namely, the right of property, different from that which results from the natural law.

Things in this state could have remained equal, if talents had been equal, and if the use of iron and the consumption of foodstuffs had always been in precise balance. But this proportion, which was not maintained by anything, was soon broken. The strongest did the most work; the most adroit turned theirs to better advantage; the most ingenious found ways to shorten their labor. The farmer had a greater need for iron, or the blacksmith had a greater need for wheat; and in laboring equally, the one earned a great deal while the other barely had enough to live. Thus it is that natural inequality imperceptibly manifests itself together with inequality occasioned by the socialization process. Thus it is that the differences among men, developed by those of circumstances, make themselves more noticeable, more permanent in their effects, and begin to influence the fate of private individuals in the same proportion.

With things having reached this point, it is easy to imagine the rest. I will not stop to describe the successive invention of the arts, the progress of languages, the testing and use of talents, the inequality of fortunes, the use or abuse of wealth, nor all the details that follow these and that everyone can easily supply. I will limit myself exclusively to taking a look at the human race placed in this new order of things.

Thus we find here all our faculties developed, memory and imagination in play, egocentrism looking out for its interests, reason rendered active, and the mind having nearly reached the limit of the perfection of which it is capable. We find here all the natural qualities put into action, the rank and fate of each man established not only on the basis of the quantity of goods and the power to serve or harm, but also on the basis of mind, beauty, strength or skill, on the basis of merit or talents. And since these qualities were the only ones that could attract consideration, he was soon forced to have them or affect them. It was necessary, for his advantage, to show himself to be something other than what he in fact was. Being something and appearing to be something became two completely different things; and from this distinction there arose grand ostentation, deceptive cunning, and all the vices that follow in their wake. On the other hand, although man had previously been free and independent, we find him, so to speak, subject, by virtue of a multitude of fresh needs, to all of nature and particularly to his fellowmen, whose slave in a sense he becomes even in becoming their master;

rich, he needs their services; poor, he needs their help; and being midway between wealth and poverty does not put him in a position to get along without them. It is therefore necessary for him to seek incessantly to interest them in his fate and to make them find their own profit, in fact or in appearance, in working for his. This makes him two-faced and crooked with some, imperious and harsh with others, and puts him in the position of having to abuse everyone he needs when he cannot make them fear them and does not find it in his interests to be of useful service to them. Finally, consuming ambition, the zeal for raising the relative level of his fortune, less out of real need than in order to put himself above others, inspires in all men a wicked tendency to harm one another, a secret jealousy all the more dangerous because, in order to strike its blow in greater safety, it often wears the mask of benevolence; in short, competition and rivalry on the one hand, opposition of interest[s] on the other, and always the hidden desire to profit at the expense of someone else. All these ills are the first effect of property and the inseparable offshoot of incipient inequality.

Before representative signs of wealth had been invented, it could hardly have consisted of anything but lands and livestock, the only real goods men can possess. Now when inheritances had grown in number and size to the point of covering the entire landscape and of all bordering on one another, some could no longer be enlarged except at the expense of others; and the supernumeraries, whom weakness or indolence had prevented from acquiring an inheritance in their turn, became poor without having lost anything, because while everything changed around them, they alone had not changed at all. Thus they were forced to receive or steal their subsistence from the hands of the rich. And from that there began to arise, according to the diverse characters of the rich and the poor, domination and servitude, or violence and thefts. For their part, the wealthy had no sooner known the pleasure of domination, than before long they disdained all others, and using their old slaves to subdue new ones, they thought of nothing but the subjugation and enslavement of their neighbors, like those ravenous wolves which, on having once tasted

human flesh, reject all other food and desire to devour only men.

Thus, when both the most powerful or the most miserable made of their strength or their needs a sort of right to another's goods, equivalent, according to them, to the right of property, the destruction of equality was followed by the most frightful disorder. Thus the usurpations of the rich, the acts of brigandage by the poor, the unbridled passions of all, stifling natural pity and the still weak voice of justice, made men greedy, ambitious and wicked. There arose between the right of the strongest and the right of the first occupant a perpetual conflict that ended only in fights and murders.[17] Emerging society gave way to the most horrible state of war; since the human race, vilified and desolated, was no longer able to retrace its steps or give up the unfortunate acquisitions it had made, and since it labored only toward its shame by abusing the faculties that honor it, it brought itself to the brink of its ruin. *Horrified by the newness of the ill, both the poor man and the rich man hope to flee from wealth, hating what they once had prayed for.*

It is not possible that men should not have eventually reflected upon so miserable a situation and upon the calamities that overwhelm them. The rich in particular must have soon felt how disadvantageous to them it was to have a perpetual war in which they alone paid all the costs, and in which the risk of losing one's life was common to all and the risk of losing one's goods was personal. Moreover, regardless of the light in which they tried to place their usurpations, they knew full well that they were established on nothing but a precarious and abusive right, and that having been acquired merely by force, force might take them away from them without their having any reason to complain. Even those enriched exclusively by industry could hardly base their property on better claims. They could very well say: "I am the one who built that wall; I have earned this land with my labor." In response to them it could be said: "Who gave you the boundary lines? By what right do you claim to exact payment at our expense for labor we did not impose upon you? Are you unaware that a multitude of your brothers perish or suffer from need of what you have in excess, and that you needed explicit and unanimous consent from the human race for you to help yourself to anything from the common subsistence that went beyond your own?" Bereft of valid reasons to justify himself and sufficient forces to defend himself; easily crushing a private individual, but himself crushed by troops of bandits; alone against all and unable on account of mutual jealousies to unite with his equals against enemies united by the common hope of plunder, the rich, pressed by necessity, finally conceived the most thought-out project that ever entered the human mind. It was to use in his favor the very strength of those who attacked him, to turn his adversaries into his defenders, to instill in them other maxims, and to give them other institutions which were as favorable to him as natural right was unfavorable to him.

With this end in mind, after having shown his neighbors the horror of a situation which armed them all against each other and made their possessions as burdensome as their needs, and in which no one could find safety in either poverty or wealth, he easily invented specious reasons to lead them to his goal. "Let us unite," he says to them, "in order to protect the weak from oppression, restrain the ambitious, and assure everyone of possessing what belongs to him. Let us institute rules of justice and peace to which all will be obliged to conform, which will make special exceptions for no one, and which will in some way compensate for the caprices of fortune by subjecting the strong and the weak to mutual obligations. In short, instead of turning our forces against ourselves, let us gather them into one supreme power that governs us according to wise laws, that protects and defends all the members of the association, repulses common enemies, and maintains us in an eternal concord."

Considerably less than the equivalent of this discourse was needed to convince crude, easily seduced men who also had too many disputes to settle among themselves to be able to get along without arbiters, and too much greed and ambition to be able to get along without masters for long. They all ran to chain themselves, in the belief that they secured their liberty, for although they had enough sense to realize the advantages of a political establishment, they did not have enough experience to foresee its dangers. Those most capable of anticipating the abuses were precisely those who counted on profiting from them; and even the wise saw the need to be resolved to sacrifice one part of their liberty to preserve the other, just as a wounded man has his arm amputated to save the rest of his body.

Such was, or should have been, the origin of society and laws, which gave new fetters to the weak and new forces to the rich,[18] irretrievably destroyed natural liberty, established forever the law of property and of inequality, changed adroit usurpation into an irrevocable right, and for the profit of a few ambitious men henceforth subjected the entire human race to labor, servitude and misery. It is readily apparent how the establishment of a single society rendered indispensable that of all the others, and how, to stand head to head against the united forces, it was necessary to unite in turn. Societies, multiplying or spreading rapidly, soon covered the entire surface of the earth; and it was no longer possible to find a single corner in the universe where someone could free himself from the yoke and withdraw his head from the often ill-guided sword which everyone saw perpetually hanging over his own head. With civil right thus having become the common rule of citizens, the law of nature no longer was operative except between the various societies, when, under the name of the law of nations, it was tempered by some tacit conventions in order to make intercourse possible and to serve as a substitute for natural compassion which, losing between one society and another nearly all the force it had between one man and another, no longer resides anywhere but in a few great cosmopolitan souls, who overcome the imaginary barriers that separate peoples, and who, following the example of the sovereign being who has created them, embrace the entire human race in their benevolence.

Remaining thus among themselves in the state of nature, the bodies politic soon experienced the inconveniences that had forced private individuals to leave it; and that state became even more deadly among these great bodies than that state had been among the private individuals of whom they were composed. Whence came the national wars, battles, murders, and reprisals that make nature tremble and offend reason, and all those horrible prejudices that rank the honor of shedding human blood among the virtues. The most decent people learned to consider it one of their duties to kill their fellow men. Finally, men were seen massacring one another by the thousands without knowing why. More murders were committed in a single day of combat and more horrors in the capture of a single city than were committed in the state of nature during entire centuries over the entire face of the earth. Such are the first effects one glimpses of the division of mankind into different societies. Let us return to the founding of these societies.

I know that many have ascribed other origins to political societies, such as conquests by the most powerful, or the union of the weak; and the choice among these causes is indifferent to what I want to establish. Nevertheless, the one I have just described seems to me the most natural, for the following reasons. 1. In the first case, the right of conquest, since it is not a right, could not have founded any other, because the conqueror and conquered peoples always remain in a state of war with one another, unless the nation, returned to full liberty, were to choose voluntarily its conqueror as its leader. Until then, whatever the capitulations that may have been made, since they have been founded on violence alone and are consequently null by this very fact, on this hypothesis there can be neither true society nor body politic, nor any other law than that of the strongest. 2. These words *strong* and *weak* are equivocal in the second case, because in the interval between the establishment of the right of property or of the first occupant and that of political governments, the meaning of these terms is better rendered by the words *poor* and *rich*, because, before the laws, man did not in fact have any other means of placing his equals in subjection except by attacking their goods or by giving them part of his. 3. Since the poor had nothing to lose but their liberty, it would have been utter folly for them to have voluntarily surrendered the only good remaining to them, gaining nothing in return. On the contrary, since the rich men were, so to speak, sensitive in all parts of their goods, it was much easier to do them harm, and

consequently they had to take greater precautions to protect themselves. And finally it is reasonable to believe that a thing was invented by those to whom it is useful rather than by those to whom it is harmful.

Incipient government did not have a constant and regular form. The lack of philosophy and experience permitted only present inconveniences to be perceived, and there was thought of remedying the others only as they presented themselves. Despite all the labors of the wisest legislators, the political state always remained imperfect, because it was practically the work of chance; and, because it had been badly begun, time, in discovering faults and suggesting remedies, could never repair the vices of the constitution. People were continually patching it up, whereas they should have begun by clearing the air and putting aside all the old materials, as Lycurgus did in Sparta, in order to raise a good edifice later on. At first, society consisted merely of some general conventions that all private individuals promised to observe, and concerning which the community became the guarantor for each of them. Experience had to demonstrate how weak such a constitution was, and how easy it was for lawbreakers to escape conviction or punishment for faults of which the public alone was to be witness and judge. The law had to be evaded in a thousand ways; inconveniences and disorders had to multiply continually in order to make them finally give some thought to confiding to private individuals the dangerous trust of public authority, and to make them entrust to magistrates the care of enforcing the observance of the deliberations of the people. For to say that the leaders were chosen before the confederation was brought about and that the ministers of the laws existed before the laws themselves is a supposition that does not allow of serious debate.

It would be no more reasonable to believe that initially the peoples threw themselves unconditionally and for all time into the arms of an absolute master, and that the first means of providing for the common security dreamed up by proud and unruly men was to rush headlong into slavery. In fact, why did they give themselves over to superiors, if not to defend themselves against oppression and to protect their goods, their liberties and their lives, which are, as it were, the constitutive elements of their being? Now, since, in relations between men, the worst that can happen to someone is for him to see himself at the discretion of someone else, would it not have been contrary to good sense to begin by surrendering into the hands of a leader the only things for whose preservation they needed his help? What equivalent could he have offered them for the concession of so fine a right? And if he had dared to demand it on the pretext of defending them, would he not have immediately received the reply given in the fable: "what more will the enemy do to us?" It is therefore incontestable, and it is a fundamental maxim of all political right, that peoples have given themselves leaders in order to defend their liberty and not to enslave themselves. *If we have a prince,* Pliny said to Trajan, *it is so that he may preserve us from having a master.*

[Our] political theorists produce the same sophisms about the love of liberty that [our] philosophers have made about the state of nature. By the things they see they render judgments about very different things they have not seen; and they attribute to men a natural inclination to servitude owing to the patience with which those who are before their eyes endure their servitude, without giving a thought to the fact that it is the same for liberty as it is for innocence and virtue: their value is felt only as long as one has them oneself, and the taste for them is lost as soon as one has lost them. "I know the delights of your country," said Brasidas to a satrap who compared the life of Sparta to that of Persepolis, "but you cannot know the pleasures of mine."

As an unbroken steed bristles his mane, paws the ground with his hoof, and struggles violently at the mere approach of the bit, while a trained horse patiently endures the whip and the spur, barbarous man does not bow his head for the yoke that civilized man wears without a murmur, and he prefers the most stormy liberty to tranquil subjection. Thus it is not by the degradation of enslaved peoples that man's natural dispositions for or against servitude are to be judged, but by the wonders that all free peoples have accomplished to safeguard themselves from oppression. I know that enslaved peoples do nothing but boast of the peace and tranquillity they enjoy in their chains and that *they give the name 'peace' to the most miserable slavery.* But when I see free peoples sacrificing pleasures, tranquillity, wealth, power, and life itself for the preservation of this sole good which is regarded so disdainfully by those who have lost it; when I see animals born free and abhorring captivity break their heads against the bars of their prison; when I see multitudes of utterly naked savages scorn European pleasures and brave hunger, fire, sword and death, simply to preserve their independence, I sense that it is inappropriate for slaves to reason about liberty.

As for paternal authority, from which several have derived absolute government and all society, it is enough, without having recourse to the contrary proofs of Locke and Sidney, to note that nothing in the world is farther from the ferocious spirit of despotism than the gentleness of that authority which looks more to the advantage of the one who obeys than to the utility of the one who commands; that by the law of nature, the father is master of the child as long as his help is necessary for him; that beyond this point they become equals, and the son, completely independent of the father, then owes him merely respect and not obedience; for gratitude is clearly a duty that must be rendered, but not a right that can be demanded. Instead of saying that civil society derives from paternal power, on the contrary it must be said that it is from civil society that this power draws its principal force. An individual was not recognized as the father of several children until the children remained gathered about him. The goods of the father, of which he is truly the master, are the goods that keep his children in a state of dependence toward him, and he can cause their receiving a share in his estate to be consequent upon the extent to which they will have well merited it from him by continuous deference to his wishes. Now, far from having some similar favor to expect from their despot (since they belong to him as personal possessions—they and all they possess—or at least he claims this to be the case), subjects are reduced to receiving as a favor what he leaves them of their goods. He does what is just when he despoils them; he does them a favor when he allows them to live.

In continuing thus to examine facts from the viewpoint of right, no more solidity than truth would be found in the belief that the establishment of tyranny was voluntary; and it would be difficult to show the validity of a contract that would obligate only one of the parties, where all the commitments would be placed on one side with none on the other, and that would turn exclusively to the disadvantage of the one making the commitments. This odious system is quite far removed from being, even today, that of wise and good monarchs, and especially of the kings of France, as may be seen in various places in their edicts, and particularly in the following passage of a famous writing published in 1667 in the name of and by order of Louis XIV: *Let it not be said therefore that the sovereign is not subject to the laws of his state, for the contrary statement is a truth of the law of nations, which flattery has on occasion attacked, but which good princes have always defended as a tutelary divinity of their states. How much more legitimate is it to say, with the wise Plato, that the perfect felicity of a kingdom is that a prince be obeyed by his subjects, that the prince obey the law, and that the law be right and always directed to the public good.* I will not stop to investigate whether, with liberty being the most noble of man's faculties, he degrades his nature, places himself on the level of animals enslaved by instinct, offends even his maker, when he unreservedly renounces the most precious of all his gifts, and allows himself to commit all the crimes he forbids us to commit, in order to please a ferocious or crazed master; nor whether this sublime workman should be more irritated at seeing his finest work destroyed rather than at seeing it dishonored. [I will disregard, if you will, the authority of Barbeyrac, who flatly declares, following Locke, that no one can sell his liberty to the point of submitting himself to an arbitrary power that treats him according to its fancy. *For,* he adds, *this would be selling his own life, of which he is not the master.*] I will merely ask by what right those who have not been afraid of debasing themselves to this degree have been able to subject their posterity to the same ignominy and to renounce for

it goods that do not depend on their liberality, and without which life itself is burdensome to all who are worthy of it.

Pufendorf says that just as one transfers his goods to another by conventions and contracts, one can also divest himself of his liberty in favor of someone. That, it seems to me, is very bad reasoning; for, in the first place, the goods I give away become something utterly foreign to me, and it is a matter of indifference to me whether or not these goods are abused; but it is important to me that my liberty is not abused, and I cannot expose myself to becoming the instrument of crime without making myself guilty of the evil I will be forced to commit. Moreover, since the right of property is merely the result of convention and human institution, every man can dispose of what he possesses as he sees fit. But it is not the same for the essential gifts of nature such as life and liberty, which everyone is allowed to enjoy, and of which it is at least doubtful that one has the right to divest himself. In giving up the one he degrades his being; in giving up the other he annihilates that being insofar as he can. And because no temporal goods can compensate for the one or the other, it would offend at the same time both nature and reason to renounce them, regardless of the price. But even if one could give away his liberty as he does his goods, the difference would be very great for the children who enjoy the father's goods only by virtue of a transmission of his right; whereas, since liberty is a gift they receive from nature in virtue of being men, their parents had no right to divest them of it. Thus, just as violence had to be done to nature in order to establish slavery, nature had to be changed in order to perpetuate this right. And the jurists, who have gravely pronounced that the child of a slave woman is born a slave, have decided, in other words, that a man is not born a man.

Thus it appears certain to me not only that governments did not begin with arbitrary power, which is but their corruption and extreme limit, and which finally brings them back simply to the law of the strongest, for which they were initially to have been the remedy; but also that even if they had begun thus, this power, being illegitimate by its nature, could not have served as a foundation for the rights of society, nor, as a consequence, for the inequality occasioned by social institutions.

Without entering at present into the investigations that are yet to be made into the nature of the fundamental compact of all government, I restrict myself, in following common opinion, to considering here the establishment of the body politic as a true contract between the populace and the leaders it chooses for itself: a contract by which the two parties obligate themselves to observe the laws that are stipulated in it and that form the bonds of their union. Since, with respect to social relations, the populace has united all its wills into a single one, all the articles on which this will is explicated become so many fundamental laws obligating all the members of the state without exception, and one of these regulates the choice and power of the magistrates charged with watching over the execution of the others. This power extends to everything that can maintain the constitution, without going so far as to change it. To it are joined honors that make the laws and their ministers worthy of respect, and, for the ministers personally, prerogatives that compensate them for the troublesome labors that a good administration requires. The magistrate, for his part, obligates himself to use the power entrusted to him only in accordance with the intention of the constituents, to maintain each one in the peaceful enjoyment of what belongs to him, and to prefer on every occasion the public utility to his own interest.

Before experience had shown or knowledge of the human heart had made men foresee the inevitable abuses of such a constitution, it must have seemed all the better because those who were charged with watching over its preservation were themselves the ones who had the greatest interest in it. For since the magistracy and its rights were established exclusively on fundamental laws, were they to be destroyed, the magistracy would immediately cease to be legitimate; the people would no longer be bound to obey them. And since it was not the magistrate but the law that had constituted the essence of the state, everyone would rightfully return to his natural liberty.

The slightest attentive reflection on this point would confirm this by new reasons, and by the nature of the contract it would be seen that it could not be irrevocable. For were there no superior power that could guarantee the fidelity of the contracting parties or force them to fulfill their reciprocal commitments, the parties would remain sole judges in their own case, and each of them would always have the right to renounce the contract as soon as he should find that the other party violated the conditions of the contract, or as soon as the conditions should cease to suit him. It is on this principle that it appears the right to abdicate can be founded. Now to consider, as we are doing, only what is of human institution, if the magistrate, who has all the power in his hands and who appropriates to himself all the advantages of the contract, nevertheless had the right to renounce the authority, a fortiori the populace, which pays for all the faults of the leaders, should have the right to renounce their dependence. But the horrible dissensions, the infinite disorders that this dangerous power would necessarily bring in its wake, demonstrate more than anything else how much need human governments had for a basis more solid than reason alone, and how necessary it was for public tranquillity that the divine will intervened to give to sovereign authority a sacred and inviolable character which took from the subjects the fatal right to dispose of it. If religion had brought about this good for men, it would be enough to oblige them to cherish and adopt it, even with its abuses, since it spares even more blood than fanaticism causes to be shed. But let us follow the thread of our hypothesis.

The various forms of government take their origin from the greater or lesser differences that were found among private individuals at the moment of institution. If a man were eminent in power, virtue, wealth or prestige, he alone was elected magistrate, and the state became monarchical. If several men, more or less equal among themselves, stood out over all the others, they were elected jointly, and there was an aristocracy. Those whose fortune or talents were less disproportionate, and who least departed from the state of nature, kept the supreme administration and formed a democracy. Time made evident which of these forms was the most advantageous to men. Some remained in subjection only to the laws; the others soon obeyed masters. Citizens wanted to keep their liberty; the subjects thought only of taking it away from their neighbors, since they could not endure others enjoying a good they themselves no longer enjoyed. In a word, on the one hand were riches and conquests, and on the other were happiness and virtue.

In these various forms of government all the magistratures were at first elective; and when wealth did not prevail, preference was given to merit, which gives a natural ascendancy, and to age, which gives experience in conducting business and cool-headedness in deliberation. The elders of the Hebrews, the gerontes of Sparta, the senate of Rome, and even the etymology of our word *seigneur* show how much age was respected in former times. The more elections fell upon men of advanced age, the more frequent elections became, and the more their difficulties were made to be felt. Intrigues were introduced; factions were formed; parties became embittered; civil wars flared up. Finally, the blood of citizens was sacrificed to the alleged happiness of the state, and people were on the verge of falling back into the anarchy of earlier times. The ambition of the leaders profited from these circumstances to perpetuate their offices within their families. The people, already accustomed to dependence, tranquillity and the conveniences of life, and already incapable of breaking their chains, consented to let their servitude increase in order to secure their tranquillity. Thus it was that the leaders, having become hereditary, grew accustomed to regard their magistratures as family property, to regard themselves as the proprietors of the state (of which at first they were but the officers), to call their fellow citizens their slaves, to count them like cattle in the number of things that belonged to them, and to call themselves equals of the gods and kings of kings.

If we follow the progress of inequality in these various revolutions, we will find that the first stage was the establishment of the law and of the right of property, the second stage was the institution of the magistracy, and the third and final stage was the transformation of legitimate power into arbitrary power. Thus the class of rich and poor was authorized by the first epoch, that of the strong and the weak by the second, and that of master and slave by the third:

the ultimate degree of inequality and the limit to which all the others finally lead, until new revolutions completely dissolve the government or bring it nearer to its legitimate institution.

To grasp the necessity of this progress, we must consider less the motives for the establishment of the body politic than the form it takes in its execution and the disadvantages that follow in its wake. For the vices that make social institutions necessary are the same ones that make their abuses inevitable. And with the sole exception of Sparta, where the law kept watch chiefly over the education of children, and where Lycurgus established mores that nearly dispensed with having to add laws to them, since laws are generally less strong than passions and restrain men without changing them, it would be easy to prove that any government that always moved forward in conformity with the purpose for which it was founded without being corrupted or altered, would have been needlessly instituted, and that a country where no one eluded the laws and abused the magistrature would need neither magistracy nor laws.

Political distinctions necessarily lend themselves to civil distinctions. The growing inequality between the people and its leaders soon makes itself felt among private individuals, and is modified by them in a thousand ways according to passions, talents and events. The magistrate cannot usurp illegitimate power without producing protégés for himself to whom he is forced to yield some part of it. Moreover, citizens allow themselves to be oppressed only insofar as they are driven by blind ambition; and looking more below than above them, domination becomes more dear to them than independence, and they consent to wear chains in order to be able to give them in turn to others. It is very difficult to reduce to obedience someone who does not seek to command; and the most adroit politician would never succeed in subjecting men who wanted merely to be free. But inequality spreads easily among ambitious and cowardly souls always ready to run the risks of fortune and, almost indifferently, to dominate or serve, according to whether it becomes favorable or unfavorable to them. Thus it is that there must have come a time when the eyes of people were beguiled to such an extent that its leaders merely had to say to the humblest of men, "Be great, you and all your progeny," and he immediately appeared great to everyone as well as in his own eyes, and his descendants were elevated even more in proportion as they were at some remove from him. The more remote and uncertain the cause, the more the effect increased; the more loafers one could count in a family, the more illustrious it became.

If this were the place to go into detail, I would easily explain how [even without government involvement] the inequality of prestige and authority becomes inevitable among private individuals,[19] as soon as they are united in one single society and are forced to make comparisons among themselves and to take into account the differences they discover in the continual use they have to make of one another. These differences are of several sorts, but in general, since wealth, nobility or rank, power and personal merit are the principal distinctions by which someone is measured in society, I would prove that the agreement or conflict of these various forces is the surest indication of a well- or ill-constituted state. I would make it apparent that among these four types of inequality, since personal qualities are the origin of all the others, wealth is the last to which they are ultimately reduced, because it readily serves to buy all the rest, since it is the most immediately useful to well-being and the easiest to communicate. This observation enables one to judge rather precisely the extent to which each people is removed from its primitive institution, and of the progress it has made toward the final stage of corruption. I would note how much that universal desire for reputation, honors, and preferences, which devours us all, trains and compares our talents and strengths; how much it excites and multiplies the passions; and, by making all men competitors, rivals, or rather enemies, how many setbacks, successes and catastrophes of every sort it causes every day, by making so many contenders run the same course. I would show that it is to this ardor for making oneself the topic of conversation, to this furor to distinguish oneself which nearly always keeps us outside ourselves, that we owe what is best and worst among men, our virtues and vices, our sciences and our errors, our

conquerors and our philosophers, that is to say, a multitude of bad things against a small number of good ones. Finally, I would prove that if one sees a handful of powerful and rich men at the height of greatness and fortune while the mob grovels in obscurity and misery, it is because the former prize the things they enjoy only to the extent that the others are deprived of them; and because, without changing their position, they would cease to be happy, if the people ceased to be miserable.

But these details alone would be the subject of a large work in which one would weigh the advantages and the disadvantages of every government relative to the rights of the state of nature, and where one would examine all the different faces under which inequality has appeared until now and may appear in [future] ages, according to the nature of these governments and the upheavals that time will necessarily bring in its wake. We would see the multitude oppressed from within as a consequence of the very precautions it had taken against what menaced it from without. We would see oppression continually increase, without the oppressed ever being able to know where it would end or what legitimate means would be left for them to stop it. We would see the rights of citizens and national liberties gradually die out, and the protests of the weak treated like seditious murmurs. We would see politics restrict the honor of defending the common cause to a mercenary portion of the people. We would see arising from this the necessity for taxes, the discouraged farmer leaving his field, even during peacetime, and leaving his plow in order to gird himself with a sword. We would see the rise of fatal and bizarre rules in the code of honor. We would see the defenders of the homeland sooner or later become its enemies, constantly holding a dagger over their fellow citizens, and there would come a time when we would hear them say to the oppressor of their country: *"If you order me to plunge my sword into my brother's breast or my father's throat, and into my pregnant wife's entrails, I will do so, even though my right hand is unwilling."*

From the extreme inequality of conditions and fortunes, from the diversity of passions and talents, from useless arts, from pernicious arts, from frivolous sciences there would come a pack of prejudices equally contrary to reason, happiness and virtue. One would see the leaders fomenting whatever can weaken men united together by disuniting them; whatever can give society an air of apparent concord while sowing the seeds of real division; whatever can inspire defiance and hatred in the various classes through the opposition of their rights and interests, and can as a consequence strengthen the power that contains them all.

It is from the bosom of this disorder and these upheavals that despotism, by gradually raising its hideous head and devouring everything it had seen to be good and healthy in every part of the state, would eventually succeed in trampling underfoot the laws and the people, and in establishing itself on the ruins of the republic. The times that would precede this last transformation would be times of troubles and calamities; but in the end everything would be swallowed up by the monster, and the peoples would no longer have leader or laws, but only tyrants. Also, from that moment on, there would no longer be any question of mores and virtue, for wherever despotism, *in which decency affords no hope*, reigns, it tolerates no other master. As soon as it speaks, there is neither probity nor duty to consult, and the blindest obedience is the only virtue remaining for slaves.

Here is the final stage of inequality, and the extreme point that closes the circle and touches the point from which we started. Here all private individuals become equals again, because they are nothing. And since subjects no longer have any law other than the master's will, nor the master any rule other than his passions, the notions of good and the principles of justice again vanish. Here everything is returned solely to the law of the strongest, and consequently to a new state of nature different from the one with which we began, in that the one was the state of nature in its purity, and this last one is the fruit of an excess of corruption. Moreover, there is so little difference between these two states, and the governmental contract is so utterly dissolved by despotism, that the despot is master only as long as he is the strongest; and as soon as he can be ousted, he has no cause to protest against violence. The uprising that ends in the strangulation or the dethronement

of a sultan is as lawful an act as those by which he disposed of the lives and goods of his subjects the day before. Force alone maintained him; force alone brings him down. Thus everything happens in accordance with the natural order, and whatever the outcome of these brief and frequent upheavals may be, no one can complain about someone else's injustice, but only of his own imprudence or his misfortune.

In discovering and following thus the forgotten and lost routes that must have led man from the natural state to the civil state; in reestablishing, with the intermediate positions I have just taken note of, those that time constraints on me have made me suppress or that the imagination has not suggested to me, no attentive reader can fail to be struck by the immense space that separates these two states. It is in this slow succession of things that he will see the solution to an infinity of moral and political problems which the philosophers are unable to resolve. He will realize that, since the human race of one age is not the human race of another age, the reason why Diogenes did not find his man is because he searched among his contemporaries for a man who no longer existed. Cato, he will say, perished with Rome and liberty because he was out of place in his age; and this greatest of men merely astonished the world, which five hundred years earlier he would have governed. In short, he will explain how the soul and human passions are imperceptibly altered and, as it were, change their nature; why, in the long run, our needs and our pleasures change their objects; why, with original man gradually disappearing, society no longer offers to the eyes of the wise man anything but an assemblage of artificial men and factitious passions which are the work of all these new relations and have no true foundation in nature. What reflection teaches us on this subject is perfectly confirmed by observation: savage man and civilized man differ so greatly in the depths of their hearts and in their inclinations, that what constitutes the supreme happiness of the one would reduce the other to despair. Savage man breathes only tranquillity and liberty; he wants simply to live and rest easy; and not even the unperturbed tranquillity of the Stoic approaches his profound indifference for any other objects. On the other hand, the citizen is always active and in a sweat, always agitated, and unceasingly tormenting himself in order to seek still more laborious occupations. He works until he dies; he even runs to his death in order to be in a position to live, or renounces life in order to acquire immortality. He pays court to the great whom he hates and to the rich whom he scorns. He stops at nothing to obtain the honor of serving them. He proudly crows about his own baseness and their protection; and proud of his slavery, he speaks with disdain about those who do not have the honor of taking part in it. What a spectacle for the Carib are the difficult and envied labors of the European minister! How many cruel deaths would that indolent savage not prefer to the horror of such a life, which often is not mollified even by the pleasure of doing good. But in order to see the purpose of so many cares, the words *power* and *reputation* would have to have a meaning in his mind; he would have to learn that there is a type of men who place some value on the regard the rest of the world has for them, and who know how to be happy and content with themselves on the testimony of others rather than on their own. Such, in fact, is the true cause of all these differences; the savage lives in himself; the man accustomed to the ways of society is always outside himself and knows how to live only in the opinion of others. And it is, as it were, from their judgment alone that he draws the sentiment of his own existence. It is not pertinent to my subject to show how, from such a disposition, so much indifference for good and evil arises, along with such fine discourse on morality; how, with everything reduced to appearances, everything becomes factitious and bogus: honor, friendship, virtue, and often even our vices, about which we eventually find the secret of boasting; how, in a word, always asking others what we are and never daring to question ourselves on this matter, in the midst of so much philosophy, humanity, politeness, and sublime maxims, we have merely a deceitful and frivolous exterior: honor without virtue, reason without wisdom, and pleasure without happiness. It is enough for me to have proved that this is not the original state of man, and that this is only the spirit of society, and the inequality that

society engenders, which thus change and alter all our natural inclinations.

I have tried to set forth the origin and progress of inequality, the establishment and abuse of political societies, to the extent that these things can be deduced from the nature of man by the light of reason alone, and independently of the sacred dogmas that give to sovereign authority the sanction of divine right. It follows from this presentation that, since inequality is practically non-existent in the state of nature, it derives its force and growth from the development of our faculties and the progress of the human mind, and eventually becomes stable and legitimate through the establishment of property and laws. Moreover, it follows that moral inequality, authorized by positive right alone, is contrary to natural right whenever it is not combined in the same proportion with physical inequality: a distinction that is sufficient to determine what one should think in this regard about the sort of inequality that reigns among all civilized people, for it is obviously contrary to the law of nature, however it may be defined, for a child to command an old man, for an imbecile to lead a wise man, and for a handful of people to gorge themselves on superfluities while the starving multitude lacks necessities.

Rousseau's Notes to
Discourse on the Origin of Inequality

1. Herodotus relates that after the murder of the false Smerdis, the seven liberators of Persia being assembled to deliberate on the form of government they would give the state, Otanes was fervently in support of a republic: an opinion all the more extraordinary in the mouth of a satrap, since, over and above the claim he could have to the empire, a grandee fears more than death a type of government that forces him to respect men. Otanes, as may readily be believed, was not listened to; and seeing that things were progressing toward the election of a monarch, he, who wanted neither to obey nor command, voluntarily yielded to the other rivals his right to the crown, asking as his sole compensation that he and his descendants be free and independent. This was granted him. If Herodotus did not inform us of the restriction that was placed on this privilege, it would be necessary to suppose it, otherwise Otanes, not acknowledging any

sort of law and not being accountable to anyone, would have been all powerful in the state and more powerful than the king himself. But there was hardly any likelihood that a man capable of contenting himself, in similar circumstances, with such a privilege, was capable of abusing it. In fact, there is no evidence that this right ever caused the least trouble in the kingdom, either from wise Otanes or from any of his descendants.

2. From the start I rely with confidence on one of those authorities that are respectable for philosophers, because they come from a solid and sublime reason, which they alone know how to find and perceive.

"Whatever interest we may have in knowing ourselves, I do not know whether we do not have a better knowledge of everything that is not us. Provided by nature with organs uniquely destined for our preservation, we use them merely to receive impressions of external things; we seek merely to extend ourselves outward and to exist outside ourselves. Too much taken with multiplying the functions of our senses and with increasing the external range of our being, we rarely make use of that internal sense which reduces us to our true dimensions, and which separates us from all that is not us. Nevertheless, this is the sense we must use if we wish to know ourselves. It is the only one by which we can judge ourselves. But how can this sense be activated and given its full range? How can our soul, in which it resides, be rid of all the illusions of our mind? We have lost the habit of using it; it has remained unexercised in the midst of the tumult of our bodily sensations; it has been dried out by the fire of our passions; the heart, the mind, the senses, everything has worked against it." *Hist. Nat.*, Vol. IV: *de la Nat. de l'homme*, p. 151.

3. The changes that a long-established habit of walking on two feet could have brought about in the conformation of man, the relations that are still observed between his arms and the forelegs of quadrupeds, and the induction drawn from their manner of walking, could have given rise to doubts about the manner that must have been the most natural to us. All children begin by walking on all fours, and need our example and our lessons to learn to stand upright. There are even savage nations, such as the Hottentots, who, greatly neglecting their children, allow them to walk on their hands for so long that they then have a great deal of trouble getting them to straighten up. The children of the Caribs of the Antilles do the same thing. There are various examples of quadruped men, and I could cite among others that

of the child who was found in 1344 near Hesse, where he had been raised by wolves, and who said afterward at the court of Prince Henry that, had the decision been left exclusively to him, he would have preferred to return to the wolves than to live among men. He had embraced to such an extent the habit of walking like those animals, that wooden boards had to be attached to him to force him to stand upright and maintain his balance on two feet. It was the same with the child who was found in 1694, in the forests of Lithuania, and who lived among bears. He did not give, says M. de Condillac, any sign of reason, walked on his hands and feet, had no language, and formed sounds that bore no resemblance whatever to those of a man. The little savage of Hanover, who was brought to the court of England several years ago, had all sorts of trouble getting himself to walk on two feet. And in 1719, two other savages, who were found in the Pyrenees, ran about the mountains in the manner of quadrupeds. As for the objection one might make that this deprives one of the use of one's hands from which we derive so many advantages, over and above the fact that the example of monkeys shows that the hand can be used quite well in both ways, this would prove only that man can give his limbs a destination more congenial than that of nature, and not that nature has destined man to walk otherwise than it teaches him.

But there are, it seems to me, much better reasons to state in support of the claim that man is a biped. First, if it were shown that he could have originally been formed otherwise than we see him and yet finally become what he is, this would not suffice to conclude that this is how it happened; for, after having shown the possibility of these changes, it would still be necessary, prior to granting them, to demonstrate at least their probability. Moreover, if man's arms seem as if they could have served as legs when needed, it is the sole observation favorable to that system, out of a great number of others which are contrary to it. The chief ones are that the manner in which man's head is attached to his body, instead of directing his view horizontally (as is the case for all other animals and for man himself when he walks upright), would have kept him, while walking on all fours, with his eyes fixed directly on the ground, a situation hardly conducive to the preservation of the individual; that the tail he is lacking, and for which he has no use when walking on two feet, is useful to quadrupeds, and none of them is deprived of one; that the breast of a woman, very well located for a biped who holds her child in her arms, is so poorly located for a quadruped that none has it located in that way; that, since the hind part is of an excessive height in proportion to the forelegs (which causes us to crawl on our knees when walking on all fours), the whole would have made an animal that was poorly proportioned and that walked uncomfortably; that if he had placed his foot as well as his hand down flat, he would have had one less articulation in the hind leg than do other animals, namely the one that joins canon to the tibia; and that by setting down only the tip of the foot, as doubtlessly he would have been forced to do, the tarsus (not to mention the plurality of bones that make it up) appears too large to take the place of the canon, and its articulations with the metatarsus and the tibia too close together to give the human leg in this situation the same flexibility as those of quadrupeds. Since the example of children is taken from an age when natural forces are not yet developed nor the members strengthened, it proves nothing whatever. I might just as well say that dogs are not destined to walk because several weeks after their birth they merely crawl. Particular facts also have little force against the universal practice of all men; even nations that have had no communication with others could not have imitated anything about them. A child abandoned in a forest before he is able to walk, and nourished by some beast, will have followed the example of his nurse in training himself to walk like her. Habit could have given him capabilities he did not have from nature, and just as one-armed men are successful, by dint of exercise, at doing with their feet whatever we do with our hands, he will finally have succeeded in using his hands as feet.

4. Should there be found among my readers a scientist nasty enough to cause me difficulties regarding the supposition of this natural fertility of the earth, I am going to answer him with the following passage:

"As plants derive much more substance from air and water for their sustenance than they do from the earth, it happens that when they rot they return to the earth more than they have derived from it. Moreover, a forest determines the amount of rainwater by stopping vapors. Thus, in a wooded area that was preserved for a long time without being touched, the bed of earth that serves for vegetation would increase considerably. But since animals return to the soil less than they derive from it, and since men take in huge quantities of wood and plants for fire and other uses, it follows that the bed of vegetative earth of an inhabited country must always

diminish and finally become like the terrain of Arabia Petraea, and like that of so many other provinces of the Orient (which in fact is the region that has been inhabited from the most ancient times), where only salt and sand are found. For the fixed salt of plants and animals remains, while all the other parts are volatized." M. de Buffon, *Hist. Nat.*

To this can be added the factual proof based on the quantity of trees and plants of every sort, which filled almost all the uninhabited islands that have been discovered in the last few centuries, and on what history teaches us about the immense forests all over the earth that had to be cut down to the degree that it was populated or civilized. On this I will also make the following three remarks. First, if there is a kind of vegetation that can make up for the loss of vegetative matter which was occasioned by animals, according to M. de Buffon's reasoning, it is above all the wooded areas, where the treetops and the leaves gather and appropriate more water and vapors than do other plants. Second, the destruction of the soil, that is, the loss of the substance that is appropriate for vegetation, should accelerate in proportion as the earth is more cultivated and as the more industrious inhabitants consume in greater abundance its products of every sort. My third and most important remark is that the fruits of trees supply animals with more abundant nourishment than is possible for other forms of vegetation: an experiment I made myself, by comparing the products of two land masses of equal size and quality, the one covered with chestnut trees and the other sown with wheat.

5. Among the quadrupeds, the two most universal distinguishing traits of voracious species are derived, on the one hand, from the shape of the teeth, and, on the other, from the conformation of the intestines. Animals that live solely on vegetation have all flat teeth, like the horse, ox, sheep and hare, but voracious animals have pointed teeth, like the cat, dog, wolf and fox. And as for the intestines, the frugivorous ones have some, such as the colon, which are not found in voracious animals. It appears therefore that man, having teeth and intestines like frugivorous animals, should naturally be placed in that class. And not only do anatomical observations confirm this opinion, but the monuments of antiquity are also very favorable to it. "Dicaearchus," says St. Jerome, "relates in his books on Greek antiquities that under the reign of Saturn, when the earth was still fertile by itself, no man ate flesh, but that all lived on fruits and vegeta-

bles that grew naturally." (*Adv. Jovinian.*, Bk. II) [This opinion can also be supported by the reports of several modern travelers. François Corréal, among others, testifies that the majority of inhabitants of the Lucayes, whom the Spaniards transported to the islands of Cuba, Santo Domingo, and elsewhere, died from having eaten flesh.] From this one can see that I am neglecting several advantageous considerations that I could turn to account. For since prey is nearly the exclusive subject of fighting among carnivorous animals, and since frugivorous animals live among themselves in continual peace, if the human species were of this latter genus, it is clear that it would have had a much easier time subsisting in the state of nature, and much less need and occasion to leave it.

6. All the kinds of knowledge that demand reflection, all those acquired only by the concatenation of ideas and perfected only successively, appear to be utterly beyond the grasp of savage man, owing to the lack of communication with his fellow-men, that is to say, owing to the lack of the instrument which is used for that communication, and to the lack of the needs that make it necessary. His understanding and his industry are limited to jumping, running, fighting, throwing a stone, climbing a tree. But if he knows only those things, in return he knows them much better than we, who do not have the same need for them as he. And since they depend exclusively on bodily exercise and are not capable of any communication or progress from one individual to another, the first man could have been just as adept at them as his last descendants.

The reports of travelers are full of examples of the force and vigor of men of barbarous and savage nations. They praise scarcely less their adroitness and nimbleness. And since eyes alone are needed to observe these things, nothing hinders us from giving credence to what eyewitnesses certify on the matter. I draw some random examples from the first books that fall into my hands.

"The Hottentots," says Kolben, "understand fishing better than the Europeans at the Cape. Their skill is equal when it comes to the net, the hook and the spear, in coves as well as in rivers. They catch fish by hand no less skillfully. They are incomparably good at swimming. Their style of swimming has something surprising about it, something entirely unique to them. They swim with their body upright and their hands stretched out of the water, so that they appear to be walking on land. In the greatest agitation of the sea, when the waves form so

many mountains, they somehow dance on the top of the waves, rising and falling like a piece of cork.

"The Hottentots," says the same author further, "are surprisingly good at hunting, and the nimbleness of their running surpasses the imagination." He is amazed that they did not put their agility to ill use more often, which, however, sometimes happens, as can be judged from the example he gives. "A Dutch sailor," he says, "on disembarking at the Cape, charged a Hottentot to follow him to the city with a roll of tobacco that weighed about twenty pounds. When they were both some distance from the crew, the Hottentot asked the sailor if he knew how to run. Run! answered the Dutchman; yes, very well. Let us see, answered the African. And fleeing with the tobacco, he disappeared almost immediately. The sailor, confounded by such marvelous quickness, did not think of following him, and he never again saw either his tobacco or his porter.

"They have such quick sight and such a sure hand that Europeans cannot go near them. At a hundred paces they will hit with a stone a mark the size of a halfpenny. And what is more amazing, instead of fixing their eyes on the target as we do, they make continuous movements and contortions. It appears that their stone is carried by an invisible hand."

Father du Tertre says about the savages of the Antilles nearly the same things that have just been read about the Hottentots of the Cape of Good Hope. He praises, above all, their accuracy in shooting with their arrows birds in flight and swimming fish, which they then catch by diving for them. The savages of North America are no less famous for their strength and adroitness, and here is an example that will lead us to form a judgment about those qualities in the Indians of South America.

In the year 1746, an Indian from Buenos Aires, having been condemned to the galleys of Cadiz, proposed to the governor that he buy back his liberty by risking his life at a public festival. He promised that by himself he would attack the fiercest bull with no other weapon in his hand but a rope; that he would bring him to the ground, seize him with his rope by whatever part they would indicate, saddle him, bridle him, mount him, and so mounted he would fight two other of the fiercest bulls to be released from the Torillo, and that he would put all of them to death, one after the other, the moment they would command him to do so, and without anyone's help. This was granted him. The Indian kept his word and succeeded in everything he had promised. On the way in which he did it and on the details of the fight, one can consult M. Gautier, *Observations sur l'Histoire Naturelle*, Vol. I (in-12°), p. 262, whence this fact is taken.

7. "The lifespan of horses," says M. de Buffon, "is, as in all other species of animals, proportionate to the length of their growth period. Man, who takes fourteen years to grow, can live six or seven times as long, that is to say, ninety or a hundred years. The horse, whose growth period is four years, can live six or seven times as long, that is to say, twenty-five or thirty years. The examples that could be contrary to this rule are so rare, that they should not even be regarded as an exception from which conclusions can be drawn. And just as large horses achieve their growth in less time than slender horses, they also have a shorter lifespan and are old from the age of fifteen."

8. I believe I see another difference between carnivorous and frugivorous animals still more general than the one I have remarked upon in Note 5, since this one extends to birds. This difference consists in the number of young, which never exceeds two in each litter for the species that lives exclusively on plant life, and which ordinarily exceeds this number for voracious animals. It is easy to know nature's plan in this regard by the number of teats, which is only two in each female of the first species, like the mare, the cow, the goat, the doe, the ewe, etc., and which is always six or eight in the other females, such as the dog, the cat, the wolf, the tigress, etc. The hen, the goose, the duck, which are all voracious birds (as are the eagle, the sparrow hawk, the screech owl), also lay and hatch a large number of eggs, which never happens to the pigeon, the turtle-dove, or to birds that eat nothing but grain, which lay and hatch scarcely more than two eggs at a time. The reason that can be given for this difference is that the animals that live exclusively on grass and plants, remaining nearly the entire day grazing and being forced to spend considerable time feeding themselves, could not be up to the task of nursing several young; whereas the voracious animals, taking their meal almost in an instant, can more easily and more often return to their young and to their hunting, and can compensate for the loss of so large a quantity of milk. There would be many particular observations and reflections to make on all this, but this is not the place to make them, and it is enough for me to have shown in this part the most general system of nature, a system which furnishes a new reason to remove man from the class of carnivorous animals and to place him among the frugivorous species.

9. A famous author, on calculating the goods and evils of human life and comparing the two sums, has found that the latter greatly exceeded the former, and that, all things considered, life was a pretty poor present for man. I am not surprised by his conclusion; he has drawn all of his arguments from the constitution of civil man. Had he gone back as far as natural man, the judgment can be made that he would have found very different results, that he would have realized that man has scarcely any evils other than those he has given himself, and that nature would have been justified. It is not without trouble that we have managed to make ourselves so unhappy. When, on the one hand, one considers the immense labors of men, so many sciences searched into, so many arts invented, and so many forces employed, abysses filled up, mountains razed, rocks broken, rivers made navigable, lands cleared, lakes dug, marshes drained, enormous buildings raised upon the earth, the sea covered with ships and sailors; and when, on the other hand, one searches with a little meditation for the true advantages that have resulted from all this for the happiness of the human species, one cannot help being struck by the astonishing disproportion that obtains between these things, and to deplore man's blindness, which, to feed his foolish pride and who knows what vain sense of self-importance, makes him run ardently after all the miseries to which he is susceptible, and which beneficent nature has taken pains to keep from him.

Men are wicked; a sad and continual experience dispenses us from having to prove it. Nevertheless, man is naturally good; I believe I have demonstrated it. What therefore can have depraved him to this degree, if not the changes that have befallen his constitution, the progress he has made, and the sorts of knowledge he has acquired? Let human society be admired as much as one wants; it will be no less true for it that it necessarily brings men to hate one another to the extent that their interests are at cross-purposes with one another, to render mutually to one another apparent services and in fact do every evil imaginable to one another. What is one to think of an interaction where the reason of each private individual dictates to him maxims directly contrary to those that public reason preaches to the body of society, and where each finds his profit in the misfortune of another? Perhaps there is not a wealthy man whose death is not secretly hoped for by greedy heirs and often by his own children; not a ship at sea whose wreck would not be good news to some merchant; not a firm that a debtor of bad faith would not wish to see burn with all the papers it contains; not a people that does not rejoice at the disasters of its neighbors. Thus it is that we find our advantage in the setbacks of our fellow-men, and that one person's loss almost always brings about another's prosperity. But what is even more dangerous is that public calamities are anticipated and hoped for by a multitude of private individuals. Some want diseases, others death, others war, others famine. I have seen ghastly men weep with the sadness at the likely prospects of a fertile year. And the great and deadly fire of London, which cost the life or the goods of so many unfortunate people, made the fortunes of perhaps more than ten thousand people. I know that Montaigne blames the Athenian Demades for having had a worker punished, who, by selling coffins at a high price, made a great deal from the death of the citizens. But since the reason Montaigne proposes is that everyone would have to be punished, it is evident that it confirms my own. Let us therefore penetrate, through our frivolous demonstration of good will, to what happens at the bottom of our hearts; and let us reflect on what the state of things must be where all men are forced to caress and destroy one another, and where they are born enemies by duty and crooks by interest. If someone answers me by claiming that society is constituted in such a manner that each man gains by serving others, I will reply that this would be very well and good, provided he did not gain still more by harming them. There is no profit, however legitimate, that is not surpassed by one that can be made illegitimately, and wrong done to a neighbor is always more lucrative than services. It is therefore no longer a question of anything but finding the means of being assured of impunity. And this is what the powerful spend all their forces on, and the weak all their ruses.

Savage man, when he has eaten, is at peace with all nature, and the friend of all his fellow-men. Is it sometimes a question of his disputing over his meal? He never comes to blows without having first compared the difficulty of winning with that of finding his sustenance elsewhere. And since pride is not involved in the fight, it is ended by a few swings of the fist. The victor eats; the vanquished is on his way to seek his fortune, and everything is pacified. But for man in society, these are quite different affairs. It is first of all a question of providing for the necessary and then for the superfluous; next

come delights, and then immense riches, and then subjects, and then slaves. He has not a moment's respite. What is most singular is that the less natural and pressing the needs, the more the passions increase and, what is worse, the power to satisfy them; so that after long periods of prosperity, after having swallowed up many treasures and ruined many men, my hero will end by butchering everything until he is the sole master of the universe. Such in brief is the moral portrait, if not of human life, then at least of the secret pretensions of the heart of every civilized man.

Compare, without prejudices, the state of civil man with that of savage man and seek, if you can, how many new doors to suffering and death (other than his wickedness, his needs and his miseries) the former has opened. If you consider the emotional turmoil that consumes us, the violent passions that exhaust and desolate us, the excessive labors with which the poor are overburdened, the still more dangerous softness to which the rich abandon themselves, and which cause the former to die of their needs and the latter of their excesses; if you call to mind the monstrous combinations of foods, their pernicious seasonings, the corrupted foodstuffs, tainted drugs, the knavery of those who sell them, the errors of those who administer them, the poison of the vessels in which they are prepared; if you pay attention to the epidemic diseases engendered by the bad air among the multitudes of men gathered together, to the illnesses occasioned by the effeminacy of our lifestyle, by the coming and going from the inside of our houses to the open air, the use of garments put on or taken off with too little precaution, and all the cares that our excessive sensuality has turned into necessary habits, the neglect or privation of which then costs us our life or our health; if you take into account fires and earthquakes, which, in consuming or turning upside down whole cities, cause their inhabitants to die by the thousands; in a word, if you unite the dangers that all these causes continually gather over our heads, you will realize how dearly nature makes us pay for the scorn we have shown for its lessons.

I will not repeat here what I have said elsewhere about war, but I wish that informed men would, for once, want or dare to give the public the detail of the horrors that are committed in armies by provisions and hospital suppliers. One would see that their not too secret maneuvers, on account of which the most brilliant armies dissolve into less than nothing, cause more soldiers to perish than are cut down by enemy swords.

Moreover, no less surprising is the calculation of the number of men swallowed up by the sea every year, either by hunger, or scurvy, or pirates, or fire, or shipwrecks. It is clear that we must also put to the account of established property, and consequently to that of society, the assassinations, the poisonings, the highway robberies, and even the punishments of these crimes, punishments necessary to prevent greater ills, but which, costing the lives of two or more for the murder of one man, do not fail really to double the loss to the human species. How many are the shameful ways to prevent the birth of men or to fool nature: either by those brutal and depraved tastes which insult its most charming work, tastes that neither savages nor animals ever knew, and that have arisen in civilized countries only as the result of a corrupt imagination; or by those secret abortions, worthy fruits of debauchery and vicious honor; or by the exposure or the murder of a multitude of infants, victims of the misery of their parents or of the barbarous shame of their mothers; or, finally by the mutilation of those unfortunates, part of whose existence and all of whose posterity are sacrificed to vain songs, or what is worse still, to the brutal jealousy of a few men: a mutilation which, in this last case, doubly outrages nature, both by the treatment received by those who suffer it and by the use to which they are destined.

[But are there not a thousand more frequent and even more dangerous cases where paternal rights overtly offend humanity? How many talents are buried and inclinations are forced by the imprudent constraint of fathers! How many men would have distinguished themselves in a suitable station who die unhappy and dishonored in another station for which they have no taste! How many happy but unequal marriages have been broken or disturbed, and how many chaste wives dishonored by this order of conditions always in contradiction with that of nature! How many other bizarre unions formed by interests and disavowed by love and by reason! How many even honest and virtuous couples cause themselves torment because they were ill-matched! How many young and unhappy victims of their parent's greed plunge into vice or pass their sorrowful days in tears, and moan in indissoluble chains which the heart rejects and which gold alone has formed! Happy sometimes are those whose courage and even virtue tear them from life before a barbarous violence forces them into crime or despair. Forgive me, father and mother forever deplorable. I regrettably worsen your sorrows; but may they

serve as an eternal and terrible example to whoever dares, in the name of nature, to violate the most sacred of its rights!

If I have spoken only of those ill-formed relationships that are the result of our civil order, is one to think that those where love and sympathy have presided are themselves exempt from drawbacks?]

What would happen if I were to undertake to show the human species attacked in its very source, and even in the most holy of all bonds, where one no longer dares to listen to nature until after having consulted fortune, and where, with civil disorder confounding virtues and vices, continence becomes a criminal precaution, and the refusal to give life to one's fellow-man an act of humanity? But without tearing away the veil that covers so many horrors, let us content ourselves with pointing out the evil, for which others must supply the remedy.

Let us add to all this that quantity of unwholesome trades which shorten lives or destroy one's health, such as work in mines, various jobs involving the processing of metals, minerals, and especially lead, copper, mercury, cobalt, arsenic, realgar; those other perilous trades which everyday cost the lives of a number of workers, some of them roofers, others carpenters, others masons, others working in quarries; let us bring all of these objects together, I say, and we will be able to see in the establishment and the perfection of societies the reasons for the diminution of the species, observed by more than one philosopher.

Luxury, impossible to prevent among men who are greedy for their own conveniences and for the esteem of others, soon completes the evil that societies have begun; and on the pretext of keeping the poor alive (which it was not necessary to do), luxury impoverishes everyone else, and sooner or later depopulates the state.

Luxury is a remedy far worse than the evil it means to cure; or rather it is itself the worst of all evils in any state, however large or small it may be, and which, in order to feed the hordes of lackeys and wretches it has produced, crushes and ruins the laborer and the citizen—like those scorching south winds that, by covering grass and greenery with devouring insects, take sustenance away from useful animals, and bring scarcity and death to all the places where they make themselves felt.

From society and the luxury it engenders, arise the liberal and mechanical arts, commerce, letters, and all those useless things that make industry flourish, enriching and ruining states. The reason for this decay is quite simple. It is easy to see that agriculture, by its nature, must be the least lucrative of all the arts, because, with its product being of the most indispensable use to all men, its price must be proportionate to the abilities of the poorest. From the same principle can be drawn this rule: that, in general, the arts are lucrative in inverse proportion to their usefulness, and that the most necessary must finally become the most neglected. From this it is clear what must be thought of the true advantages of industry and of the real effect that results from its progress.

Such are the discernible causes of all the miseries into which opulence finally brings down the most admired nations. To the degree that industry and the arts expand and flourish, the scorned farmer, burdened with taxes necessary to maintain luxury and condemned to spend his life between toil and hunger, abandons his fields to go to the cities in search of the bread he ought to be carrying there. The more the capital cities strike the stupid eyes of the people as wonderful, the more it will be necessary to groan at the sight of countrysides abandoned, fields fallow, and main roads jammed with unhappy citizens who have become beggars or thieves, destined to end their misery one day on the rack or on a dung-heap. Thus it is that the state, enriching itself on the one hand, weakens and depopulates itself on the other; and that the most powerful monarchies, after much labor to become opulent and deserted, end by becoming the prey of poor nations which succumb to the deadly temptation to invade them, and which enrich and enfeeble themselves in their turn, until they are themselves invaded and destroyed by others.

Let someone deign to explain to us for once what could have produced those hordes of barbarians which for so many centuries have overrun Europe, Asia and Africa. Was it to the industry of their arts, the wisdom of their laws, the excellence of their civil order that they owed that prodigious population? Would our learned ones be so kind as to tell us why, far from multiplying to that degree, those ferocious and brutal men, without enlightenment, without restraint, without education, did not all kill one another at every moment to argue with one another over their food or game? Let them explain to us how these wretches even had the gall to look right in the eye such capable people as we were, with such fine military discipline, such fine codes, and such wise laws, and why, finally, after society was perfected in the countries of the north, and so many pains were taken there to teach men their mutual duties and the art of living together agreeably and peaceably, nothing more

is seen to come from them like those multitudes of men it produced formerly. I am very much afraid that someone might finally get it into his head to reply to me that all these great things, namely the arts, sciences, and laws, have been very wisely invented by men as a salutary plague to prevent the excessive multiplication of the species, out of fear that this world, which is destined for us, might finally become too small for its inhabitants.

What then! Must we destroy societies, annihilate thine and mine, and return to live in the forests with bears? — a conclusion in the style of my adversaries, which I prefer to anticipate, rather than leave to them the shame of drawing it. Oh you, to whom the heavenly voice has not made itself heard, and who recognize for your species no other destination except to end this brief life in peace; you who can leave in the midst of the cities your deadly acquisitions, your troubled minds, your corrupt hearts and your unbridled desires. Since it depends on you, retake your ancient and first innocence; go into the woods to lose sight and memory of the crimes of your contemporaries, and have no fear of cheapening your species in renouncing its enlightenment in order to renounce its vices. As for men like me, whose passions have forever destroyed their original simplicity, who can no longer feed on grass and acorn[s], nor get by without laws and chiefs; those who were honored in their first father with supernatural lessons; those who will see, in the intention of giving human actions from the beginning a morality they would not have acquired for a long time, the reason for a precept indifferent in itself and inexplicable in any other system; those, in a word, who are convinced that the divine voice called the entire human race to the enlightenment and the happiness of the celestial intelligences; all those latter ones will attempt, through the exercise of virtues they oblige themselves to practice while learning to know them, to merit the eternal reward that they ought to expect for them. They will respect the sacred bonds of the societies of which they are members; they will love their fellow-men and will serve them with all their power; they will scrupulously obey the laws and the men who are their authors and their ministers; they will honor above all the good and wise princes who will know how to prevent, cure or palliate that pack of abuses and evils always ready to overpower us; they will animate the zeal of these worthy chiefs by showing them without fear or flattery the greatness of their task and the rigor of their duty. But they will despise no less for it a constitution that can be maintained only with the help of so many respectable people, who are desired more often than they are obtained, and from which, despite all their care, always arise more real calamities than apparent advantages.

10. Among the men we know, whether by ourselves, or from historians, or from travelers, some are black, others white, others red. Some wear their hair long; others have merely curly wool. Some are almost entirely covered with hair; others do not even have a beard. There have been and perhaps there still are nations of men of gigantic size; and apart from the fable of the Pygmies (which may well be merely an exaggeration), we know that the Laplanders and above all the Greenlanders are considerably below the average size of man. It is even maintained that there are entire peoples who have tails like quadrupeds. And without putting blind faith in the accounts of Herodotus and Ctesias, we can at least draw from them the very likely opinion that had one been able to make good observations in those ancient times when various peoples followed lifestyles differing more greatly among themselves than do those of today, one would have also noted in the shape and posture of the body, much more striking varieties. All these facts, for which it is easy to furnish incontestable proofs, are capable of surprising only those who are accustomed to look solely at the objects that surround them and who are ignorant of the powerful effects of the diversity of climates, air, foods, lifestyle, habits in general, and especially the astonishing force of the same causes when they act continually for long successions of generations. Today, when commerce, voyages and conquests reunite various peoples further, and their lifestyles are constantly approximating one another through frequent communication, it is evident that certain national differences have diminished; and, for example, everyone can take note of the fact that today's Frenchmen are no longer those large, colorless and blond-haired bodies described by Latin historians, although time, together with the mixture of the Franks and the Normans, themselves colorless and blond-haired, should have reestablished what commerce with the Romans could have removed from the influence of the climate in the natural constitution and complexion of the inhabitants. All of these observations on the varieties that a thousand causes can produce and have in fact produced in the human species cause me to wonder whether the various animals similar to men, taken without much scrutiny by travelers for beasts, either because of some differences they noticed in their out-ward structure or simply because these animals did not speak, would not in fact be veritable savage men, whose race, dispersed in the woods during olden times, had not had an occasion to develop any of its virtual faculties, had not acquired any degree of perfection, and was still found in the primitive state of nature. Let us give an example of what I mean.

"There are found in the kingdom of the Congo," says the translator of the *Histoire des Voyages*, "many of those large animals called *orangutans* in the East Indies, which occupy a middle ground between the human species and the baboons. Battel relates that in the forests of Mayomba, in the kingdom of Loango, one sees two kinds of monsters, the larger of which are called *pongos* and the others *enjocos*. The former bear an exact resemblance to man, except they are much larger and very tall. With a human face, they have very deep-set eyes. Their hands, cheeks and ears are without hair, except for their eyebrows, which are very long. Although the rest of their body is quite hairy, the hair is not very thick; the color of the hair is brown. Finally, the only part that distinguishes them from men is their leg, which has no calf. They walk upright, grasping the hair of their neck with their hand. Their retreat is in the woods. They sleep in the trees, and there they make a kind of roof which offers them shelter from the rain. Their foods are fruits or wild nuts; they never eat flesh. The custom of the Negroes who cross the forests is to light fires during the night. They note that in the morning, at their departure, the pongos take their place around the fire, and do not withdraw until it is out; because, for all their cleverness, they do not have enough sense to lay wood on the fire to keep it going.

"They occasionally walk in groups and kill the Negroes who cross the forests. They even fall upon elephants who come to graze in the places they inhabit, and they irritate the elephants so much with punches or with whacks of a stick that they force them howling to take flight. Pongos are never taken alive, because they are so strong that ten men would not be enough to stop them. But the Negroes take a good many young ones after having killed the mother, to whose body the young stick very closely. When one of these animals dies, the others cover its body with a pile of branches or leaves. Purchass adds that, in the conversations he has had with Battel, he had learned from him also that a pongo abducted a little Negro who passed an entire month in the society of these animals, for they do not harm men they take by surprise, at least when these men do not pay any attention to them, as the little Negro had observed. Battel had not described the second species of monster.

"Dapper confirms that the kingdom of the Congo is filled with those animals which in the Indies bear the name orangutans, that is to say, inhabitants of the woods, and which the Africans call *quojas-morros*. This beast, he says, is so similar to man, that it has occurred to some travelers that it could have issued from a woman and a monkey: a myth which even the Negroes reject. One of these animals was transported from the Congo to Holland and presented to the Prince of Orange, Frederick Henry. It was the height of a three-year old child, moderately stocky, but square and well-proportioned, very agile and lively; its legs fleshy and robust; the entire front of the body naked, but the rear covered with black hairs. At first sight, its face resembled that of a man, but it had a flat and turned up nose; its ears were also those of the human species; its breast (for it was a female), was plump, its navel sunken, its shoulders very well joined, its hands divided into fingers and thumbs, its calves and heels fat and fleshy. It often walked upright on its legs; it was capable of lifting and carrying heavy burdens. When it wanted to drink, it took the cover of the pot in one hand, and held the base with the other; afterward it graciously wiped its lips. It lay down to sleep with its head on a cushion, covering itself with such skill that it would have been taken for a man in bed. The Negroes tell strange stories about this animal. They assert not only that it takes women and girls by force, but that it dares to attack armed men. In a word, there is great likelihood that it is the satyr of the ancients. Perhaps Merolla is speaking only of these animals whom he relates that Negroes sometimes lay hold of savage men and women in their hunts."

These species of anthropomorphic animals are again discussed in the third volume of the same *Histoire des Voyages* under the name of *beggos* and *mandrills*. But sticking to the preceding accounts, we find in the description of these alleged monsters striking points of conformity with the human species and lesser differences than those that would be assigned between one man and another. From these pages it is not clear what the reasons are that the authors have for refusing to give the animals in question the name "savage men"; but it is easy to conjecture that it is on account of their stupidity and also because they did not speak — feeble reasons for those who know that although the organ of speech is natural

to man, nevertheless speech itself is not natural to him, and who knows to what point his perfectibility can have elevated civil man above his original state. The small number of lines these descriptions contain can cause us to judge how badly these animals have been observed and with what prejudices they have been viewed. For example, they are categorized as monsters, and yet there is agreement that they reproduce. In one place, Battel says that the pongos kill the Negroes who cross the forests; in another place, Purchass adds that they do not do any harm, even when they surprise them, at least when the Negroes do not fix their gaze upon them. The pongos gather around fires lit by the Negroes upon the Negroes' withdrawal, and withdraw in their turn when the fire is out. There is the fact. Here now is the commentary of the observer: *because, for all their cleverness, they do not have enough sense to lay wood on the fire to keep it going.* I would like to hazard a guess how Battel, or Purchass, his compiler, could have known that the withdrawal of the pongos was an effect of their stupidity rather than their will. In a climate such as Loango, fire is not something particularly necessary for the animals; and if the Negroes light a fire, it is less against the cold than to frighten ferocious beasts. It is therefore a very simple matter that, after having been for some time delighted with the flame or being well warmed, the pongos grow tired of always remaining in the same place and go off to graze, which requires more time than if they ate flesh. Moreover, we know that most animals, man not excluded, are naturally lazy, and that they refuse all sorts of cares which are not absolutely necessary. Finally, it seems very strange that pongos, whose adroitness and strength are praised, the pongos who know how to bury their dead and to make themselves roofs out of branches, should not know how to push fagots into the fire I recall having seen a monkey perform the same maneuver that people deny the pongos can do. It is true that since my ideas were not oriented in this direction, I myself committed the mistake for which I reproach our travelers; I neglected to examine whether the intention of the monkey was actually to sustain the fire or simply, as I believe is the case, to imitate the actions of a man. Whatever the case may be, it is well demonstrated that the monkey is not a variety of man: not only because he is deprived of the faculty of speech, but above all because it is certain that his species does not have the faculty of perfecting itself, which is the specific characteristic of the human species: experiments that do not seem to have been made on the pongos and the orangutan with sufficient care to enable one to draw the same conclusion in their case. However, there would be a means by which, if the orangutan or others were of the human species, even the least sophisticated observers could assure themselves of it by means of demonstration. But beyond the fact that a single generation would not be sufficient for this experiment, it should pass as unworkable, since it would be necessary that what is merely a supposition be demonstrated to be true, before the test that should establish the fact could be innocently tried.

Precipitous judgments, which are not the fruit of an enlightened reason, are prone to be excessive. Without any fanfare, our travelers made into beasts, under the names *pongos, mandrills, orangutans*, the same beings that the ancients, under the names *satyrs, fauns, sylvans*, made into divinities. Perhaps, after more precise investigations it will be found that they are [neither beasts nor gods but] men. Meanwhile, it would seem to me that there is as much reason to defer on this point to Merolla, an educated monk, an eyewitness, and one who, with all his naïveté, did not fail to be a man of wit, as to the merchant Battel, Dapper, Purchass, and the other compilers.

What judgment do we think such observers would have made regarding the child found in 1694, of whom I have spoken before, who gave no indication of reason, walked on his feet and hands, had no language, and made sounds that bore no resemblance whatever to those of a man? It took a long time, continues the same philosopher who provided me with this fact, before he could utter a few words, and then he did it in a barbarous manner. Once he could speak, he was questioned about his first state, but he did not recall it any more than we recall what happened to us in the cradle. If, unhappily* for him, this child had fallen into the hands of our travelers, there can be no doubt that after having observed his silence and stupidity, they would have resolved to send him back to the woods or lock him up in a menagerie; after which they would have spoken eruditely about him in their fine accounts as a very curious beast who looked rather like a man.

For the three or four hundred years since the inhabitants of Europe inundated the other parts of the world and continually published new collections of travels and stories, I am convinced that we know no other men but

[*In the copy of the Discourse *sent to Richard Davenport,* Rousseau inserts here: *or perhaps happily.]*

the Europeans alone. Moreover, it would appear, from the ridiculous prejudices that have not been extinguished even among men of letters, that everybody does hardly anything under the pompous name of "the study of man" except study the men of his country. Individuals may well come and go; it seems that philosophy travels nowhere; moreover, the philosophy of one people is little suited to another. The reason for this is manifest, at least for distant countries. There are hardly more than four sorts of men who make long voyages: sailors, merchants, soldiers, and missionaries. Now we can hardly expect the first three classes to provide good observers; and as for those in the fourth, occupied by the sublime vocation that calls them, even if they were not subject to the prejudices of social position as are all the rest, we must believe that they would not voluntarily commit themselves to investigations that would appear to be sheer curiosity, and which would sidetrack them from the more important works to which they are destined. Besides, to preach the Gospel in a useful manner, zeal alone is needed, and God gives the rest. But to study men, talents are needed which God is not required to give anyone, and which are not always the portion of saints. One does not open a book of voyages where one does not find descriptions of characters and mores. But one is utterly astonished to see that these people who have described so many things have said merely what everyone already knew, that, at the end of the world, they knew how to understand only what it was for them to notice without leaving their street; and that those true qualities which characterize nations and strike eyes made to see have almost always escaped theirs. Whence this fine moral slogan, so bandied about by the philosophizing rabble: that men are everywhere the same; that, since everywhere they have the same passions and the same vices, it is rather pointless to seek to characterize different peoples—which is about as well reasoned as it would be for someone to say that Peter and James cannot be distinguished from one another, because they both have a nose, a mouth and eyes.

Will we never see those happy days reborn when the people did not dabble in philosophizing, but when a Plato, a Thales, a Pythagoras, taken with an ardent desire to know, undertook the greatest voyages merely to inform themselves, and went far away to shake off the yoke of national prejudices, in order to learn to know men by their similarities and their differences, and to acquire those sorts of universal knowledge that are exclusively those of a single century or country, but which, since they are of all times and all places, are, as it were, the common science of the wise?

We admire the splendor of some curious men who, at great expense, made or caused to be made voyages to the Orient with learned men and painters, in order to sketch hovels and to decipher or copy inscriptions. But I have trouble conceiving how, in a century where people take pride in fine sorts of knowledge, there are not to be found two closely united men—rich, one in money, the other in genius, both loving glory and aspiring for immortality—one of whom sacrifices twenty thousand crowns of his goods and the other ten years of his life for a famous voyage around the world, in order to study, not always rocks and plants, but, for once, men and mores, and who, after so many centuries used to measure and examine the house, would finally be of a mind to want to know its inhabitants.

The academicians who have traveled through the northern parts of Europe and the southern parts of America had for their object to visit them more as geometers than as philosophers. Nevertheless, since they were both simultaneously, we cannot regard as utterly unknown the regions that have been seen and described by La Condamine and Maupertuis. The jeweler Chardin, who has traveled like Plato, has left nothing to be said about Persia. China appeared to have been well observed by the Jesuits. Kempfer gives a passable idea of what little he has seen in Japan. Except for these reports, we know nothing about the peoples of the East Indies, who have been visited exclusively by Europeans interested more in filling their purses than their heads. All of Africa and its numerous inhabitants, as unique in character as in color, are yet to be examined. The entire earth is covered with nations of which we know only the names, and we dabble in judging the human race! Let us suppose a Montesquieu, a Buffon, a Diderot, a Duclos, a d'Alembert, a Condillac, or men of that ilk traveling in order to inform their compatriots, observing and describing as they know how to do, Turkey, Egypt, Barbary, the empire of Morocco, Guinea, the land of the Bantus, the interior of Africa and its eastern coastlines, the Malabars, Mogul, the banks of the Ganges, the kingdoms of Siam, Pegu, and Ava, China, Tartary, and especially Japan; then in the other hemisphere, Mexico, Peru, Chile, the straits of Magellan, not to forget the Patagonias true or false, Tucuman, Paraguay (if possible), Brazil; finally the Caribbean Islands, Florida, and all the savage countries—the most important voyage of all and the one that should be embarked upon with the greatest care. Let us suppose that these new Hercules, back from these memorable treks, then wrote at leisure the natural, moral, and political history of what they would have seen; we ourselves would see a new world sally forth from their pen, and we would thus learn to know our own. I say that when such observers will affirm of an animal that it is a man and of another that it is a beast, we will have to believe them. But it would be terribly simpleminded to defer in this to unsophisticated travelers, concerning whom we will sometimes be tempted to put the same question that they dabble at resolving concerning other animals.

11. That appears utterly evident to me and I am unable to conceive whence our philosophers can derive all the passions they ascribe to natural man. With the single exception of the physically necessary which nature itself demands, all our other needs are such merely out of habit (previous to which they were not needs), or by our own desires; and we do not desire what we are not in a position to know. Whence it follows that since savage man desires only the things he knows and knows only those things whose possession is in his power or easily acquired, nothing should be so tranquil as his soul and nothing so limited as his mind.

12. I find in Locke's *Civil Government* an objection which seems to me too specious for me to be permitted to hide it. "Since the purpose of the society between male and female," says this philosopher, "is not merely to procreate, but to continue the species, this society should last, even after procreation, at least as long as it is necessary for the nurture and support of the procreated, that is to say, until they are capable of seeing to their needs on their own. This rule, which the infinite wisdom of the creator has established upon the works of his hands, we see creatures inferior to man observing constantly and strictly. In those animals which live on grass, the society between male and female lasts no longer than each act of copulation, because, the teats of the mother being sufficient to feed the young until they are able to feed on grass, the male is content to beget and no longer mingles with the female or the young, to whose sustenance he has nothing to contribute. But as far as beasts of prey are concerned, the society lasts longer, because, with the mother being unable to see to her own sustenance and at the same time feed her young by means of her prey alone (which is a more

laborious and more dangerous way of taking in nourishment than by feeding on grass), the assistance of the male is utterly necessary for the maintenance of their common family (if one may use that term), which is able to subsist to the point where it can go hunt for prey only through the efforts of the male and the female. We note the same thing in all the birds (with the exception of some domestic birds which are found in places where the continual abundance of nourishment exempts the male from the effort of feeding the young). It is clear that when the young in their nest need food, the male and female bring it to them until the young there are capable of flying and seeing to their own sustenance.

"And, in my opinion, herein lies the principal, if not the only reason why the male and the female in mankind are bound to a longer period of society than is undertaken by other creatures: namely, that the female is capable of conceiving and is ordinarily pregnant again and has a new child long before the previous child is in a position to do without the help of its parents and can take care of itself. Thus, since the father is bound to take care of those he has produced, and to take that care for a long time, he is also under an obligation to continue in conjugal society with the same woman by whom he has had them, and to remain in that society much longer than other creatures, whose young being capable of subsisting by themselves before the time comes for a new procreation, the bond of the male and female breaks of its own accord, and they are both at complete liberty, until such time as that season, which usually solicits the animals to join with one another, obliges them to choose new mates. And here we cannot help admiring the wisdom of the creator, who, having given to man the qualities needed to provide for the future as well as for the present, has willed and has brought it about that the society of man should last longer than that of the male and female among other creatures, so that thereby the industry of man and woman might be stimulated more, and that their interests might be better united, with a view to making provisions for their children and to leaving them their goods — nothing being more to the detriment of the children than an uncertain and vague conjunction, or an easy and frequent dissolution of the conjugal society."*

[*Translator's note: This is a translation of the French rendering of Locke's text.]

The same love of truth which has made me to set forth sincerely this objection, moves me to accompany it with some remarks, if not to resolve it, at least to clarify it.

1. I will observe first that moral proofs do not have great force in matters of physics, and that they serve more to explain existing facts than to establish the real existence of those facts. Now such is the type of proof that M. Locke employs in the passage I have just quoted; for although it may be advantageous to the human species for the union between man and woman to be permanent, it does not follow that it has been thus established by nature; otherwise it would be necessary to say that it also instituted civil society, the arts, commerce, and all that is asserted to be useful to men.

2. I do not know where M. Locke has found that among animals of prey, the society of the male and female lasts longer than does the society of those that live on grass, and that the former assists the latter to feed the young; for it is not manifest that the dog, the cat, the bear, or the wolf recognize their female better than the horse, the ram, the bull, the stag, or all the other quadruped animals do theirs. On the contrary, it seems that if the assistance of the male were necessary to the female to preserve her young, it would be particularly in the species that live only on grass, because a long period of time is needed by the mother to graze, and during that entire interval she is forced to neglect her brood, whereas the prey of a female bear or wolf is devoured in an instant, and, without suffering hunger, she has more time to nurse her young. This line of reasoning is confirmed by an observation upon the relative number of teats and young which distinguishes carnivorous from frugivorous species, and of which I have spoken in Note 8. If this observation is accurate and general, since a woman has only two teats and rarely has more than one child at a time, this is one more strong reason for doubting that the human species is naturally carnivorous. Thus it seems that, in order to draw Locke's conclusion, it would be necessary to reverse completely his reasoning. There is no more solidity in the same distinction when it is applied to birds. For who could be persuaded that the union of the male and the female is more durable among vultures and crows than among turtle-doves? We have two species of domestic birds, the duck and the pigeon, which furnish us with examples directly contrary to the system of this author. The pigeon, which lives solely on grain,

remains united to its female, and they feed their young in common. The duck, whose voraciousness is known, recognizes neither his female nor his young, and provides no help in their sustenance. And among hens, a species hardly less carnivorous, we do not observe that the rooster bothers himself in the least with the brood. And if in the other species the male shares with the female the care of feeding the young, it is because birds, which at first are unable to fly and which the mother cannot nurse, are much less in a position to get along without the help of the father than are quadrupeds, for which the mother's teat is sufficient, at least for a time.

3. There is much uncertainty about the principal fact that serves as a basis for all of M. Locke's reasoning; for in order to know whether, as he asserts, in the pure state of nature the female ordinarily is pregnant again and has a new child long before the preceding one could see to its needs for itself, it would be necessary to perform experiments that M. Locke surely did not perform and that no one is in a position to perform. The continual cohabitation of husband and wife is so near an occasion for being exposed to a new pregnancy that it is very difficult to believe that the chance encounter or the mere impulsion of temperament produced such frequent effects in the pure state of nature as in that of conjugal society: a slowness that would contribute perhaps toward making the children more robust, and that, moreover, might be compensated by the power to conceive, prolonged to a greater age in the women who would have abused it less in their youth. As to children, there are several reasons for believing that their forces and their organs develop much later among us than they did in the primitive state of which I am speaking. The original weakness which they derive from the constitution of the parents, the cares taken to envelop and constrain all of their members, the softness in which they are raised, perhaps the use of milk other than that of their mother, everything contradicts and slows down in them the initial progress of nature. The heed they are forced to pay to a thousand things on which their attention is continually fixed, while no exercise is given to their bodily forces, can also bring about considerable deflection from their growth. Thus, if, instead of first overworking and exhausting their minds in a thousand ways, their bodies were allowed to be exercised by the continual movements that nature seems to demand of them, it is to be believed that they would be in a much

better position to walk and to provide for their needs by themselves.

4. Finally, M. Locke at most proves that there could well be in a man a motive for remaining attached to a woman when she has a child but in no way does he prove that the man must have been attached to her before the childbirth and during the nine months of pregnancy. If a given woman is indifferent to the man during those nine months, if she even becomes unknown to him, why will he help her after childbirth? Why will he help her to raise a child that he does not know belongs to him alone, and whose birth he has neither decided upon nor foreseen? Evidently M. Locke presumes what is in question, for it is not a matter of knowing why the man will remain attached to the woman after childbirth, but why he will be attached to her after conception. Once his appetite is satisfied, the man has no further need for a given woman, nor the woman for a given man. The man does not have the least care or perhaps the least idea of the consequences of his action. The one goes off in one direction, the other in another, and there is no likelihood that at the end of nine months they have the memory of having known one another. For this type of memory, by which one individual gives preference to another for the act of generation, requires, as I prove in the text, more progress or corruption in human understanding than may be supposed in man in the state of animality we are dealing with here. Another woman can therefore satisfy the new desires of the man as congenially as the one he has already known, and another man in the same manner satisfy the woman, supposing she is impelled by the same appetite during the time of pregnancy, about which one can reasonably be in doubt. And if in the state of nature the woman no longer feels the passion of love after the conception of the child, the obstacle to her society with the man thus becomes much greater still, since she then has no further need either for the man who has made her pregnant or for anyone else. There is not, therefore, in the man any reason to seek the same woman, or in the woman any reason to seek the same man. Thus Locke's reasoning falls in ruin, and all the dialectic of this philosopher has not shielded him from the mistake committed by Hobbes and others. They had to explain a fact of the state of nature, that is to say, of a state where men lived in isolation and where a given man did not have any motive for living in proximity to another given man, nor perhaps did a given group of men have a motive for living in

proximity to another given group of men, which is much worse. And they gave no thought to transporting themselves beyond the centuries of society, that is to say, of those times when men always have a reason for living in proximity to one another, and when a given man often has a reason for living in proximity to a given man or woman.

13. I will hold back from embarking on the philosophical reflections that there would be to engage in concerning the advantages and disadvantages of this institution of languages. It is not for me to be permitted to attack vulgar errors; and educated people respect their prejudices too much to abide patiently my alleged paradoxes. Let us therefore allow men to speak, to whom it has not been made a crime to risk sometimes taking the part of reason against the opinion of the multitude. *Nor would anything disappear from the happiness of the human race, if, when the disaster and confusion of so many languages has been cast out, mortals should cultivate one art, and if it should be allowed to explain anything by means of signs, movements and gestures. But now it has been so established that the condition of animals commonly believed to be brutes is considerably better than ours in this respect, inasmuch as they articulate their feelings and their thoughts without an interpreter more readily and perhaps more felicitously than any mortals can, especially if they use a foreign language.* Is. Vossius de Poëmat. Cant. et Viribus Rythmi, p. 66.

14. In showing how ideas of discrete quantity and its relationships are necessary in the humblest of the arts, Plato mocks with good reason the authors of his time who alleged that Palamedes had invented numbers at the siege of Troy, as if, says this philosopher, Agamemnon could have been ignorant until then of how many legs he had. In fact, one senses the impossibility that society and the arts should have arrived at the point where they already were at the time of the siege of Troy, unless men had the use of numbers and arithmetic. But the necessity for knowing numbers, before acquiring other types of knowledge, does not make their invention easier to imagine. Once the names of the numbers are known, it is easy to explain their meaning and to elicit the ideas which these names represent; but in order to invent them, it was necessary, prior to conceiving of these same ideas, to be, as it were, on familiar terms with philosophical meditations, to be trained to consider beings by their essence alone and independently of all other percep-

[*Translator's note: Rousseau here quotes the Latin text.]

tion—a very difficult, very metaphysical, hardly natural abstraction, and yet one without which these ideas could never have been transported from one species or genus to another, nor could numbers have become universal. A savage could consider separately his right leg and his left leg, or look at them together under the indivisible idea of a pair without ever thinking that he had two of them; for the representative idea that portrays for us an object is one thing, and the numerical idea which determines it is another. Even less was he able to count to five. And although, by placing his hands one on top of the other, he could have noticed that the fingers corresponded exactly, he was far from thinking of their numerical equality. He did not know the sum of his fingers any more than that of his hairs. And if, after having made him understand what numbers are, someone had said to him that he had as many fingers as toes, he perhaps would have been quite surprised, in comparing them, to find that this was true.

15. We must not confuse egocentrism with love of oneself, two passions very different by virtue of both their nature and their effects. Love of oneself is a natural sentiment which moves every animal to be vigilant in its own preservation and which, directed in man by reason and modified by pity, produces humanity and virtue. Egocentrism is merely a sentiment that is relative, artificial and born in society, which moves each individual to value himself more than anyone else, which inspires in men all the evils they cause one another, and which is the true source of honor.

With this well understood, I say that in our primitive state, in the veritable state of nature, egocentrism does not exist; for since each particular man regards himself as the only spectator who observes him, as the only being in the universe that takes an interest in him, as the only judge of his own merit, it is impossible that a sentiment which has its source in comparisons that he is not in a position to make could germinate in his soul. For the same reason, this man could not have either hatred or desire for revenge, passions which can arise only from the belief that offense has been received. And since what constitutes the offense is scorn or the intention to harm and not the harm, men who know neither how to appraise nor to compare themselves can do considerable violence to one another when it returns them some advantage for doing it, without ever offending one another. In a word, on seeing his fellow-men hardly otherwise than he would see animals of another species, each man can carry away the prey of the weaker or yield his own to the stronger, viewing these lootings as merely natural events, without the least stirring of insolence or resentment, and without any other passion but the sadness or the joy of a good or bad venture.

16. It is something extremely remarkable that, for the many years that the Europeans torment themselves in order to acclimate the savages of various countries to their lifestyle, they have not yet been able to win over a single one of them, not even by means of Christianity; for our missionaries sometimes turn them into Christians, but never into civilized men. Nothing can overcome the invincible repugnance they have against appropriating our mores and living in our way. If these poor savages are as unhappy as is alleged, by what inconceivable depravity of judgment do they constantly refuse to civilize themselves in imitation of us, or to learn to live happily among us; whereas one reads in a thousand places that the French and other Europeans have voluntarily taken refuge among those nations, and have spent their entire lives there, no longer able to leave so strange a lifestyle; and whereas we even see level-headed missionaries regret with tenderness the calm and innocent days they have spent among those much scorned peoples? If one replies that they do not have enough enlightenment to make a sound judgment about their state and ours, I will reply that the reckoning of happiness is less an affair of reason than of sentiment. Moreover, this reply can be turned against us with still greater force; for there is a greater distance between our ideas and the frame of mind one needed to be in in order to conceive the taste which the savages find in their lifestyle, than between the ideas of savages and those that can make them conceive our lifestyle. In fact, after a few observations it is easy for them to see that all our labors are directed toward but two objects: namely, the conveniences of life for oneself and esteem among others. But what are the means by which we are to imagine the sort of pleasure a savage takes in spending his life alone amidst the woods, or fishing, or blowing into a sorry-looking flute, without ever knowing how to derive a single tone from it and without bothering himself to learn?

Savages have frequently been brought to Paris, London and other cities; people have been eager to display our luxury, our wealth, and all our most useful and curious arts. None of this has ever excited in them anything but a stupid admiration, without the least stirring of covetousness. I recall, among others, the story of a chief of some North Americans who was brought to the court of England about thirty years ago. A thousand things were made to pass before his eye in an attempt to give him some present that could please him, but nothing was found about which he seemed to care. Our weapons seemed heavy and cumbersome to him, our shoes hurt his feet, our clothes restricted him; he rejected everything. Finally, it was noticed that, having taken a wool blanket, he seemed to take some pleasure in wrapping it around his shoulders. You will agree at least, someone immediately said to him, on the usefulness of this furnishing? Yes, he replies, this seems to me to be nearly as good as an animal skin. However, he would not have said that, had he worn them both in the rain.

Perhaps someone will say to me that it is habit which, in attaching everyone to his lifestyle, prevents savages from realizing what is good in ours. And at that rate, it must at least appear quite extraordinary that habit has more force in maintaining the savages in the taste for their misery than the Europeans in the enjoyment of their felicity. But to give to this last objection a reply to which there is not a word to make in reply, without adducing all the young savages that people have tried in vain to civilize, without speaking of the Greenlanders and the inhabitants of Iceland, whom people have tried to raise and feed in Denmark, and all of whom sadness and despair caused to perish, whether from languor or in the sea when they attempted to regain their homeland by swimming back to it, I will be content to cite a single, well-documented example, which I give to the admirers of European civilization to examine.

"All the efforts of the Dutch missionaries at the Cape of Good Hope have never been able to convert a single Hottentot. Van der Stel, Governor of the Cape, having taken one from infancy, had raised him in the principles of the Christian religion and in the practice of the customs of Europe. He was richly clothed; he was taught several languages and his progress corresponded very closely to the care that was taken for his education. Having great hopes for his wit, the Governor sent him to the Indies with a commissioner general who employed him usefully in the affairs of the company. He returned to the Cape after the death of the commissioner. A few days after his return, on a visit he made to some of his Hottentot relatives, he made the decision to strip himself of his European dress in order to clothe himself with a sheepskin. He returned to the fort in this new outfit, carrying a bundle containing his old clothes, and, on presenting them to the Governor, he made the following speech to him: *Please, sir, be so kind as to pay heed to the fact that I forever renounce this clothing. I also renounce the Christian religion for the rest of my life. My resolution is to live and die in the religion, ways and customs of my ancestors. The only favor I ask of you is that you let me keep the necklace and cutlass I am wearing. I will keep them for love of you.* Thereupon, without waiting for Van der Stel's reply, he escaped by taking flight and was never seen again at the Cape." *Histoire des Voyages,* Vol. V, p. 175.

17. One could raise against me the objection that, in such a disorder, men, instead of willfully murdering one another, would have dispersed, had there been no limits to their dispersion. But first, these limits would at least have been those of the world. And if one thinks about the excessive population that results from the state of nature, one will judge that the earth in that state would not have taken long to be covered with men thus forced to keep together. Besides, they would have dispersed, had the evil been rapid, and had it been an overnight change. But they were born under the yoke; they were in the habit of carrying it when they felt its weight, and they were content to wait for the opportunity to shake it off. Finally, since they were already accustomed to a thousand conveniences which forced them to keep together, dispersion was no longer so easy as in the first ages, when, since no one had need for anyone but himself, everyone made his decision without waiting for someone else's consent.

18. Marshal de V*** related that, on one of his campaigns, when the excessive knavery of a provisions supplier had made the army suffer and complain, he gave him a severe dressing down and threatened to have him hanged. "This threat has no effect on me," the knave boldly replied to him, "and I am quite pleased to tell you that nobody hangs a man with a hundred thousand crowns at his disposal." I do not know how it happened, the Marshal added naïvely, but in fact he was not hanged, even though he deserved to be a hundred times over.

19. Distributive justice would still be opposed to this rigorous equality of the state of nature, if it were workable in civil society. And since all the members of the state owe it services proportionate to their talents and forces, the citizens for their part should be distinguished and favored in proportion to their services. It is in this sense that one must understand a passage of Isocrates, in which he praises the first Athenians for having known well how to distinguish which of the two sorts of equality was the more advantageous, one of which consists in portioning out indifferently to all citizens the same advantages, and the other in distributing them according to each one's merit. These able politicians, adds the orator, in banishing that unjust equality that makes no differentiation between wicked and good men, adhered inviolably to that equality which rewards and punishes each according to one's merit. But first, no society has ever existed, regardless of the degree of corruption they could have achieved, in which no differentiation between wicked and good men was made. And in the matter of mores, where the law cannot set a sufficiently precise measurement to serve as a rule for the magistrate, the law very wisely prohibits him from the judgment of persons, leaving him merely the judgment of actions, in order not to leave the fate or the rank of citizens to his discretion. Only mores as pure as those of the ancient Romans could withstand censors; such tribunals would soon have overturned everything among us. It is for public esteem to differentiate between wicked and good men. The magistrate is judge only of strict law [*droit*]; but the populace is the true judge of mores—an upright and even enlightened judge on this point, occasionally deceived but never corrupted. The ranks of citizens ought therefore to be regulated not on the basis of their personal merit, which would be to leave to the magistrate the means of making an almost arbitrary application of the law, but upon the real services which they render to the state and which lend themselves to a more precise reckoning.

ROUSSEAU

On the Social Contract, or Principles of Political Right

By J.-J. Rousseau,
Citizen of Geneva

—foederis aequas
Dicamus leges
—Aeneid, XI

FOREWORD

This little treatise is part of a longer work I undertook some time ago without taking stock of my abilities, and have long since abandoned. Of the various selections that could have been drawn from what had been completed, this is the most considerable, and, it appears to me, the one least unworthy of being offered to the public. The rest no longer exists.

ON THE SOCIAL CONTRACT

BOOK I

I want to inquire whether there can be some legitimate and sure rule of administration in the civil order, taking men as they are and laws as they might be. I will always try in this inquiry to bring together what right permits with what interest prescribes, so that justice and utility do not find themselves at odds with one another.

I begin without demonstrating the importance of my subject. It will be asked if I am a prince or a legislator that I should be writing about politics. I answer that I am neither, and that is why I write about politics. Were I a prince or a legislator, I would not

Reprinted from *The Basic Political Writings*, translated by Donald A. Cress (Indianapolis: Hackett Publishing Company, 1987), by permission of the publisher.

waste my time saying what ought to be done. I would do it or keep quiet.

Born a citizen of a free state and a member of the sovereign, the right to vote is enough to impose upon me the duty to instruct myself in public affairs, however little influence my voice may have in them. Happy am I, for every time I meditate on governments, I always find new reasons in my inquiries for loving that of my country.

CHAPTER I: Subject of the First Book

Man is born free, and everywhere he is in chains. He who believes himself the master of others does not escape being more of a slave than they. How did this change take place? I have no idea. What can render it legitimate? I believe I can answer this question.

Were I to consider only force and the effect that flows from it, I would say that so long as a people is constrained to obey and does obey, it does well. As soon as it can shake off the yoke and does shake it off, it does even better. For by recovering its liberty by means of the same right that stole it, either the populace is justified in getting it back or else those who took it away were not justified in their actions. But the social order is a sacred right which serves as a foundation for all other rights. Nevertheless, this right does not come from nature. It is therefore founded upon conventions. The task at hand is to know what these conventions are. Before coming to that, I ought to substantiate what I just claimed.

CHAPTER II: Of the First Societies

The most ancient of all societies and the only natural one, is that of the family. Even so children remain bound to their father only so long as they need him to take care of them. As soon as the need ceases, the natural bond is dissolved. Once the children are freed from the obedience they owed the father and their father is freed from the care he owed his children, all return equally to independence. If they continue to remain united, this no longer takes place naturally but voluntarily, and the family maintains itself only by means of convention.

This common liberty is one consequence of the nature of man. Its first law is to see to his maintenance; its first concerns are those he owes himself; and, as soon as he reaches the age of reason, since he alone is the judge of the proper means of taking care of himself, he thereby becomes his own master.

The family therefore is, so to speak, the prototype of political societies; the leader is the image of the father, the populace is the image of the children, and, since all are born equal and free, none give up their liberty except for their utility. The entire difference consists in the fact that in the family the love of the father for his children repays him for the care he takes for them, while in the state, where the leader does not have love for his peoples, the pleasure of commanding takes the place of this feeling.

Grotius denies that all human power is established for the benefit of the governed, citing slavery as an example. His usual method of reasoning is always to present fact as a proof of right.[1] A more logical method could be used, but not one more favorable to tyrants.

According to Grotius, it is therefore doubtful whether the human race belongs to a hundred men, or whether these hundred men belong to the human race. And throughout his book he appears to lean toward the former view. This is Hobbes' position as well. On this telling, the human race is divided into herds of cattle, each one having its own leader who guards it in order to devour it.

Just as a herdsman possesses a nature superior to that of his herd, the herdsmen of men who are the leaders, also have a nature superior to that of their peoples. According to Philo, Caligula reasoned thus, concluding quite properly from this analogy that kings were gods, or that the peoples were beasts.

Caligula's reasoning coincides with that of Hobbes and Grotius. Aristotle, before all the others, had also said that men are by no means equal by nature, but that some were born for slavery and others for domination.

Aristotle was right, but he took the effect for the cause. Every man born in slavery is born for slavery; nothing is more certain. In their chains slaves lose everything, even the desire to escape. They love their servitude the way the companions of Ulysses loved their degradation.[2] If there are slaves by nature, it is because there have been slaves against nature. Force has produced the first slaves; their cowardice has perpetuated them.

I have said nothing about King Adam of Emperor Noah, father of three great monarchs who partitioned the universe, as did the children of Saturn, whom some have believed they recognize in them. I hope I will be appreciated for this moderation, for since I am a direct descendent of these princes, and perhaps of the eldest branch, how am I to know whether, after the verification of titles, I might not find myself the legitimate king of the human race? Be that as it may, we cannot deny that Adam was the sovereign of the world, just as Robinson Crusoe was sovereign of his island, so long as he was its sole inhabitant. And the advantage this empire had was that the monarch,

---

[1] "Learned research on public right is often nothing more than the history of ancient abuses, and taking a lot of trouble to study them too closely gets one nowhere." *Treatise on the Interests of France Along With Her Neighbors*, by the Marquis d'Argenson. This is just what Grotius has done.

[2] See a short treatise of Plutarch entitled "That Animals Reason."

securely on his throne, had no rebellions, wars or conspirators to fear.

CHAPTER III: On the Right of the Strongest

The strongest is never strong enough to be master all the time, unless he transforms force into right and obedience into duty. Hence the right of the strongest, a right that seems like something intended ironically and is actually established as a basic principle. But will no one explain this word to me? Force is a physical power; I fail to see what morality can result from its effects. To give in to force is an act of necessity, not of will. At most, it is an act of prudence. In what sense could it be a duty?

Let us suppose for a moment that there is such a thing as this alleged right. I maintain that all that results from it is an inexplicable mish-mash. For once force produces the right, the effect changes places with the cause. Every force that is superior to the first succeeds to its right. As soon as one can disobey with impunity, one can do so legitimately; and since the strongest is always right, the only thing to do is to make oneself the strongest. For what kind of right is it that perishes when the force on which it is based ceases? If one must obey because of force, one need not do so out of duty; and if one is no longer forced to obey one is no longer obliged. Clearly then, this word "right" adds nothing to force. It is utterly meaningless here.

Obey the powers that be. If that means giving in to force, the precept is sound, but superfluous. I reply it will never be violated. All power comes from God—I admit it—but so does every disease. Does this mean that calling in a physician is prohibited? If a brigand takes me by surprise at the edge of a wooded area, is it not only the case that I must surrender my purse, but even that I am in good conscience bound to surrender it, if I were able to withhold it? After all, the pistol he holds is also a power.

Let us then agree that force does not bring about right, and that one is obliged to obey only legitimate powers. Thus my original question keeps returning.

CHAPTER IV: On Slavery

Since no man has a natural authority over his fellow man, and since force does not give rise to any right, conventions therefore remain the basis of all legitimate authority among men.

If, says Grotius, a private individual can alienate his liberty and turn himself into the slave of a master, why could not an entire people alienate its liberty and turn itself into the subject of a king? There are many equivocal words here which need explanation, but let us confine ourselves to the word *alienate*. To alienate is to give or to sell. A man who makes himself the slave of someone else does not give himself; he sells himself, at least for his subsistence. But why does a people sell itself? Far from furnishing his subjects with their subsistence, a king derives his own from them alone, and, according to Rabelais, a king does not live cheaply. Do subjects then give their persons on the condition that their estate will also be taken? I fail to see what remains for them to preserve.

It will be said that the despot assures his subjects of civil tranquility. Very well. But what do they gain, if the wars his ambition drags them into, if his insatiable greed, if the oppressive demands caused by his ministers occasion more grief for his subjects than their own dissensions would have done? What do they gain, if this very tranquility is one of their miseries? A tranquil life is also had in dungeons; is that enough to make them desirable? The Greeks who were locked up in the Cyclops' cave lived a tranquil existence as they awaited their turn to be devoured.

To say that a man gives himself gratuitously is to say something absurd and inconceivable. Such an act is illegitimate and null, if only for the fact that he who commits it does not have his wits about him. To say the same thing of an entire populace is to suppose a populace composed of madmen. Madness does not bring about right.

Even if each person can alienate himself, he cannot alienate his children. They are born men and free. Their liberty belongs to them; they alone have the right to dispose of it. Before they have reached the age of reason, their father can, in their name, stipulate conditions for their maintenance and for their well-being. But he cannot give them irrevocably and unconditionally, for such a gift is contrary to the ends of nature and goes beyond the rights of paternity. For an arbitrary government to be legitimate, it would therefore be necessary in each generation for the people to be master of its acceptance or rejection. But in that event this government would no longer be arbitrary.

Renouncing one's liberty is renouncing one's dignity as a man, the rights of humanity and even its duties. There is no possible compensation for anyone who renounces everything. Such a renunciation is incompatible with the nature of man. Taking away all liberty from his will is tantamount to removing all morality from his actions. Finally, it is a vain and contradictory convention to stipulate absolute authority on one side and a limitless obedience on the other. Is it not clear that no commitments are made to a person from whom one has the right to demand everything? And does this condition alone not bring with it, without equivalent or exchange, the nullity of the act? For what right would my slave have against me, given that all he has belongs to me, and that, since his right is my right, my having a right against myself makes no sense?

Grotius and others derive from war another origin for the alleged right of slavery. Since, according to them, the victor has the right to kill the vanquished, these latter can repurchase their lives at the price of their liberty—a convention all the more legitimate, since it turns a profit for both of them.

But clearly this alleged right to kill the vanquished does not in any way derive from the state of war. Men are not naturally enemies, for the simple reason that men living in their original state of independence do not have sufficiently constant relationships among themselves to bring about either a state of peace or a state of war. It is the relationship between things and not that between men that brings about war. And since this state of war cannot come into existence from simple personal relations, but only from real [proprietary] relations, a private war between one man and another can exist neither in the state of nature,

where there is no constant property, nor in the social state, where everything is under the authority of the laws.

Fights between private individuals, duels, encounters are not acts which produce a state. And with regard to private wars, authorized by the ordinances of King Louis IX of France and suspended by the Peace of God, they are abuses of feudal government, an absurd system if there ever was one, contrary to the principles of natural right and to all sound polity.

War is not therefore a relationship between one man and another, but a relationship between one state and another. In war private individuals are enemies only incidentally: not as men or even as citizens,[3] but as soldiers; not as members of the homeland but as its defenders. Finally, each state can have as enemies only other states and not men, since there can be no real relationship between things of disparate natures.

This principle is even in conformity with the established maxims of all times and with the constant practice of all civilized peoples. Declarations of war are warnings not so much to powers as to their subjects. The foreigner (be he king, private individual, or a people) who robs, kills or detains subjects of another prince without declaring war on the prince,

---

[3] [*At this point the following passage was added to the 1782 edition:* The Romans, who had a better understanding of and a greater respect for the right of war than any other nation, carried their scruples so far in this regard that a citizen was not allowed to serve as a volunteer unless he had expressly committed himself against the enemy and against a specifically named enemy. When a legion in which Cato the Younger first served had been reorganized, Cato the Elder wrote Popilius that if he wanted his son to continue to serve under him, he would have to make him swear the military oath afresh, since, with the first one having been annulled, he could no longer take up arms against the enemy. And this very same Cato wrote his son to take care to avoid going into battle without swearing this military oath afresh. I know the siege of Clusium and other specific cases can be raised as counter-examples to this, but for my part I cite laws and customs. The Romans were the ones who transgressed their laws least often, and are the only ones to have had such noble laws.]

is not an enemy but a brigand. Even in the midst of war a just prince rightly appropriates to himself everything in an enemy country belonging to the public, but respects the person and goods of private individuals. He respects the rights upon which his own rights are founded. Since the purpose of war is the destruction of the enemy state, one has the right to kill the defenders of that state so long as they bear arms. But as soon as they lay down their arms and surrender, they cease to be enemies or instruments of the enemy. They return to being simply men; and one no longer has a right to their lives. Sometimes a state can be killed without a single one of its members being killed. For war does not grant a right that is unnecessary to its purpose. These principles are not those of Grotius. They are not based on the authority of poets. Rather they are derived from the nature of things; they are based on reason.

As to the right of conquest, the only basis it has is the law of the strongest. If war does not give the victor the right to massacre the vanquished peoples, this right (which he does not have) cannot be the basis for the right to enslave them. One has the right to kill the enemy only when one cannot enslave him. The right to enslave him does not therefore derive from the right to kill him. Hence it is an iniquitous exchange to make him buy his life, to which no one has any right, at the price of his liberty. In establishing the right of life and death on the right of slavery, and the right of slavery on the right of life and death, is it not clear that one falls into a vicious circle?

Even if we were to suppose that there were this terrible right to kill everyone, I maintain that neither a person enslaved during wartime nor a conquered people bears any obligation whatever toward its master, except to obey him for as long as it is forced to do so. In taking the equivalent of his life, the victor has done him no favor. Instead of killing him unprofitably he kills him usefully. Hence, far from the victor having acquired any authority over him beyond force, the state of war subsists between them just as before. Their relationship itself is the effect of war, and the usage of the right to war does not suppose any peace treaty. They have made a convention. Fine.

But this convention, far from destroying the state of war, presupposes its continuation.

Thus, from every point of view, the right of slavery is null, not simply because it is illegitimate, but because it is absurd and meaningless. These words, *slavery* and *right*, are contradictory. They are mutually exclusive. Whether it is the statement of one man to another man, or one man to a people, the following sort of talk will always be equally nonsensical. *I make a convention with you which is wholly at your expense and wholly to my advantage; and, for as long as it pleases me, I will observe it and so will you.*

CHAPTER V: That It Is Always Necessary to Return to a First Convention

Even if I were to grant all that I have thus far refuted, the supporters of despotism would not be any better off. There will always be a great difference between subduing a multitude and ruling a society. If scattered men, however many they may be, were successively enslaved by a single individual, I see nothing there but a master and slaves; I do not see a people and its leader. It is, if you will, an aggregation, but not an association. There is neither a public good nor a body politic there. Even if that man had enslaved half the world, he is always just a private individual. His interest, separated from that of others, is never anything but a private interest. If this same man is about to die, after his passing his empire remains scattered and disunited, just as an oak tree dissolves and falls into a pile of ashes after fire has consumed it.

A people, says Grotius, can give itself to a king. According to Grotius, therefore, a people is a people before it gives itself to a king. This gift itself is a civil act; it presupposes a public deliberation. Thus, before examining the act whereby a people chooses a king, it would be well to examine the act whereby a people is a people. For since this act is necessarily prior to the other, it is the true foundation of society.

In fact, if there were no prior convention, then, unless the vote were unanimous, what would become of the minority's obligation to submit to the majority's choice, and where do one hundred who want a master get the right to vote for ten who do not? The law of majority rule is itself an established convention, and presupposes unanimity on at least one occasion.

CHAPTER VI: On the Social Compact

I suppose that men have reached the point where obstacles that are harmful to their maintenance in the state of nature gain the upper hand by their resistance to the forces that each individual can bring to bear to maintain himself in that state. Such being the case, that original state cannot subsist any longer, and the human race would perish if it did not alter its mode of existence.

For since men cannot engender new forces, but merely unite and direct existing ones, they have no other means of maintaining themselves but to form by aggregation a sum of forces that could gain the upper hand over the resistance, so that their forces are directed by means of a single moving power and made to act in concert.

This sum of forces cannot come into being without the cooperation of many. But since each man's force and liberty are the primary instruments of his maintenance, how is he going to engage them without hurting himself and without neglecting the care that he owes himself? This difficulty, seen in terms of my subject, can be stated in the following terms:

"Find a form of association which defends and protects with all common forces the person and goods of each associate, and by means of which each one, while uniting with all, nevertheless obeys only himself and remains as free as before." This is the fundamental problem for which the social contract provides the solution.

The clauses of this contract are so determined by the nature of the act that the least modification renders them vain and ineffectual, that, although perhaps they have never been formally promulgated, they are everywhere the same, everywhere tacitly accepted and acknowledged. Once the social compact is violated, each person then regains his first rights and resumes his natural liberty, while losing the conventional liberty for which he renounced it.

These clauses, properly understood, are all reducible to a single one, namely the total alienation of each associate, together with all of his rights, to the entire community. For first of all, since each person gives himself whole and entire, the condition is equal for everyone; and since the condition is equal for everyone, no one has an interest in making it burdensome for the others.

Moreover, since the alienation is made without reservation, the union is as perfect as possible, and no associate has anything further to demand. For if some rights remained with private individuals, in the absence of any common superior who could decide between them and the public, each person would eventually claim to be his own judge in all things, since he is on some point his own judge. The state of nature would subsist and the association would necessarily become tyrannical or hollow.

Finally, in giving himself to all, each person gives himself to no one. And since there is no associate over whom he does not acquire the same right that he would grant others over himself, he gains the equivalent of everything he loses, along with a greater amount of force to preserve what he has.

If, therefore, one eliminates from the social compact whatever is not essential to it, one will find that it is reducible to the following terms. Each of us places his person and all his power in common under the supreme direction of the general will; and as one we receive each member as an indivisible part of the whole.

At once, in place of the individual person of each contracting party, this act of association produces a moral and collective body composed of as many members as there are voices in the assembly, which receives from this same act its unity, its common *self*, its life and its will. This public person, formed thus by union of all the others formerly took the name *city*,[4] and at present takes the name *republic* or *body*

---

[4] The true meaning of this word is almost entirely lost on modern men. Most of them mistake a town for a city and a townsman for a citizen. They do not know that houses make a town but citizens make a city. Once this mistake cost the Carthaginians dearly. I have not found in my read-

politic, which is called *state* by its members when it is passive, *sovereign* when it is active, *power* when compared to others like itself. As to the associates, they collectively take the name *people*; individually they are called *citizens*, insofar as participants in the sovereign authority, and *subjects*, insofar as they are subjected to the laws of the state. But these terms are often confused and mistaken for one another. It is enough to know how to distinguish them when they are used with absolute precision.

CHAPTER VII: On the Sovereign

This formula shows that the act of association includes a reciprocal commitment between the public and private individuals, and that each individual, contracting, as it were, with himself, finds himself under a twofold commitment: namely as a member of the sovereign to private individuals, and as a member of the state toward the sovereign. But the maxim of civil law that no one is held to commitments made to himself cannot be applied here, for there is a considerable difference between being obligated to oneself, or to a whole of which one is a part.

It must be further noted that the public deliberation that can obligate all the subjects to the sovereign, owing to the two different relationships in which each of them is viewed, cannot, for the opposite reason, obligate the sovereign to itself, and that consequently

---

ing that the title of *citizen* has ever been given to the subjects of a prince, not even in ancient times to the Macedonians or in our own time to the English, although they are closer to liberty than all the others. Only the French adopt this name *citizen* with complete familiarity, since they have no true idea of its meaning, as can be seen from their dictionaries. If this were not the case, they would become guilty of treason for using it. For them, this name expresses a virtue and not a right. When Bodin wanted to speak about our citizens and townsmen, he committed a terrible blunder when he mistook the one group for the other. M. d'Alembert was not in error, and in his article entitled *Geneva* he has carefully distinguished the four orders of men (even five, counting ordinary foreigners) who are in our towns, and of whom only two make up the republic. No other French author I am aware of has grasped the true meaning of the word *citizen*.

it is contrary to the nature of the body politic that the sovereign impose upon itself a law it could not break. Since the sovereign can be considered under but one single relationship, it is then in the position of a private individual contracting with himself. Whence it is apparent that there neither is nor can be any type of fundamental law that is obligatory for the people as a body, not even the social contract. This does not mean that the whole body cannot perfectly well commit itself to another body with respect to things that do not infringe on this contract. For in regard to the foreigner, it becomes a simple being, an individual.

However, since the body politic or the sovereign derives its being exclusively from the sanctity of the contract, it can never obligate itself, not even to another power, to do anything that derogates from the original act, such as alienating some portion of itself or submitting to another sovereign. Violation of the act whereby it exists would be self-annihilation, and whatever is nothing produces nothing.

As soon as this multitude is thus united in a body, one cannot harm one of the members without attacking the whole body. It is even less likely that the body can be harmed without the members feeling it. Thus duty and interest equally obligate the two parties to come to one another's aid, and the same men should seek to combine in this two-fold relationship all the advantages that result from it.

For since the sovereign is formed entirely from the private individuals who make it up, it neither has nor could have an interest contrary to theirs. Hence, the sovereign power has no need to offer a guarantee to its subjects, since it is impossible for a body to want to harm all of its members, and, as we will see later, it cannot harm any one of them in particular. The sovereign, by the mere fact that it exists, is always all that it should be.

But the same thing cannot be said of the subjects in relation to the sovereign, for which, despite their common interest, their commitments would be without substance if it did not find ways of being assured of their fidelity.

In fact, each individual can, as a man, have a private will contrary to or different from the general will that he has as a citizen. His private interest can speak to him in an entirely different manner than the common interest. His absolute and naturally independent existence can cause him to envisage what he owes the common cause as a gratuitous contribution, the loss of which will be less harmful to others than its payment is burdensome to him. And in viewing the moral person which constitutes the state as a being of reason because it is not a man, he would enjoy the rights of a citizen without wanting to fulfill the duties of a subject, an injustice whose growth would bring about the ruin of the body politic.

Thus, in order for the social compact to avoid being an empty formula, it tacitly entails the commitment—which alone can give force to the others—that whoever refuses to obey the general will will be forced to do so by the entire body. This means merely that he will be forced to be free. For this is the sort of condition that, by giving each citizen to the homeland, guarantees him against all personal dependence—a condition that produces the skill and the performance of the political machine, and which alone bestows legitimacy upon civil commitments. Without it such commitments would be absurd, tyrannical and subject to the worst abuses.

CHAPTER VIII: On the Civil State

This passage from the state of nature to the civil state produces quite a remarkable change in man, for it substitutes justice for instinct in his behavior and gives his actions a moral quality they previously lacked. Only then, when the voice of duty replaces physical impulse and right replaces appetite, does man, who had hitherto taken only himself into account, find himself forced to act upon other principles and to consult his reason before listening to his inclinations. Although in this state he deprives himself of several of the advantages belonging to him in the state of nature, he regains such great ones. His faculties are exercised and developed, his ideas are broadened, his feelings are ennobled, his entire soul is elevated to such a height that, if the abuse of this new condition did not often lower his status to beneath the level he left, he ought constantly to bless the happy moment

that pulled him away from it forever and which transformed him from a stupid, limited animal into an intelligent being and a man.

Let us summarize this entire balance sheet so that the credits and debits are easily compared. What man loses through the social contract is his natural liberty and an unlimited right to everything that tempts him and that he can acquire. What he gains is civil liberty and the proprietary ownership of all he possesses. So as not to be in error in these compensations, it is necessary to draw a careful distinction between natural liberty (which is limited solely by the force of the individual involved) and civil liberty (which is limited by the general will), and between possession (which is merely the effect of the force or the right of the first occupant) and proprietary ownership (which is based solely on a positive title).

To the preceding acquisitions could be added the acquisition in the civil state of moral liberty, which alone makes man truly the master of himself. For to be driven by appetite alone is slavery, and obedience to the law one has prescribed for oneself is liberty. But I have already said too much on this subject, and the philosophical meaning of the word *liberty* is not my subject here.

CHAPTER IX: On the Real [i.e., Proprietary] Domain

Each member of the community gives himself to it at the instant of its constitution, just as he actually is, himself and all his forces, including all the goods in his possession. This is not to say that by this act possession changes its nature as it changes hands and becomes property in the hands of the sovereign. Rather, since the forces of the city are incomparably greater than those of a private individual, public possession is by that very fact stronger and more irrevocable, without being more legitimate, at least to strangers. For with regard to its members, the state is master of all their goods in virtue of the social contract, which serves in the state as the basis of all rights. But with regard to other powers, the state is master only in virtue of the right of the first occupant, which it derives from private individuals.

The right of first occupant, though more real than the right of the strongest, does not become a true right until after the establishment of the right of property. Every man by nature has a right to everything he needs; however, the positive act whereby he becomes a proprietor of some goods excludes him from all the rest. Once his lot has been determined, he should limit himself thereto, no longer having any right against the community. This is the reason why the right of the first occupant, so weak in the state of nature, is able to command the respect of every man living in the civil state. In this right, one respects not so much what belongs to others as what does not belong to oneself.

In general, the following rules must obtain in order to authorize the right of the first occupant on any land. First, this land may not already be occupied by anyone. Second, no one may occupy more than the amount needed to subsist. Third, one is to take possession of it not by an empty ceremony, but by working and cultivating it—the only sign of property that ought, in the absence of legal titles, to be respected by others.

In fact, by according to need and work the right of the first occupant, is it not extended as far as it can go? Is it possible to avoid setting limits to this right? Will setting one's foot on a piece of common land be sufficient to claim it at once as one's own? Will having the force for a moment to drive off other men be sufficient to deny them the right ever to return? How can a man or a people seize a vast amount of territory and deprive the entire human race of it except by a punishable usurpation, since this seizure deprives all other men of the shelter and sustenance that nature gives them in common? When Nuñez Balboa stood on the shoreline and took possession of the South Sea and all of South America in the name of crown of Castille, was this enough to dispossess all the inhabitants and to exclude all the princes of the world? On that basis, those ceremonies would be multiplied quite in vain. All the Catholic King had to do was to take possession of the universe all at once from his private room, excepting afterwards from his empire only what already belonged to other princes.

One can imagine how the combined and contiguous lands of private individuals became public territory; and how the right of sovereignty, extending from subjects to the land they occupied, becomes at once real and personal. This places its owners in a greater dependence, turning their very own forces into guarantees of their loyalty. This advantage does not seem to have been fully appreciated by the ancient monarchs, who, calling themselves merely King of the Persians, the Scythians, and the Macedonians, appeared to regard themselves merely as the leaders of men rather than the masters of the country. Today's monarchs more shrewdly call themselves King of France, Spain, England, and so on. In holding the land thus, they are quite sure of holding the inhabitants.

What is remarkable about this alienation is that, in accepting the goods of private individuals, the community is far from despoiling them; rather, in so doing, it merely assures them of legitimate possession, changing usurpation into a true right, and enjoyment into proprietary ownership. In that case, since owners are considered trustees of the public good, and since their rights are respected by all members of the state and maintained with all its force against foreigners, through an advantageous surrender to the public and still more so to themselves, they have, so to speak, acquired all they have given. This paradox is easily explained by the distinction between the rights of the sovereign and those of the proprietor to the same store, as will be seen later.

It can also happen, as men begin to unite before possessing anything and later appropriate a piece of land sufficient for everyone, that they enjoy it in common or divide it among themselves either in equal shares or according to proportions laid down by the sovereign. In whatever way this acquisition is accomplished, each private individual's right to his very own store is always subordinate to the community's right to all, without which there could be neither solidity in the social fabric nor real force in the exercise of sovereignty.

I will end this chapter and this book with a remark that should serve as a basis for every social system. It is that instead of destroying natural equality, the fundamental compact, on the contrary, substitutes a moral and legitimate equality to whatever physical inequality nature may have been able to impose upon men, and that, however, unequal in force or intelligence they may be, men all become equal by convention and by right.[5]

END OF THE FIRST BOOK

BOOK II

CHAPTER I: That Sovereignty Is Inalienable

The first and most important consequence of the principles established above is that only the general will can direct the forces of the state according to the purpose for which it was instituted, which is the common good. For if the opposition of private interests made necessary the establishment of societies, it is the accord of these same interests that made it possible. It is what these different interests have in common that forms the social bond, and, were there no point of agreement among all these interests, no society could exist. For it is utterly on the basis of this common interest that society ought to be governed.

I therefore maintain that since sovereignty is merely the exercise of the general will, it can never be alienated, and that the sovereign, which is only a collective being, cannot be represented by anything but itself. Power can perfectly well be transmitted, but not the will.

In fact, while it is not impossible for a private will to be in accord on some point with the general will, it is impossible at least for this accord to be durable and constant. For by its nature the private will tends toward having preferences, and the general will tends toward equality. It is even more impossible for there

to be a guarantee of this accord even if it ought always to exist. This is not the result of art but of chance. The sovereign may well say, "Right now I want what a certain man wants or at least what he says he wants." But it cannot say, "What this man will want tomorrow I too will want," since it is absurd for the will to tie its hands for the future and since it does not depend upon any will's consenting to anything contrary to the good of the being that wills. If, therefore, the populace promises simply to obey, it dissolves itself by this act, it loses its standing as a people. The very moment there is a master, there no longer is a sovereign, and thenceforward the body politic is destroyed.

This is not to say that the commands of the leaders could not pass for manifestations of the general will, so long as the sovereign, who is free to oppose them, does not do so. In such a case, the consent of the people ought to be presumed on the basis of universal silence. This will be explained at greater length.

CHAPTER II: That Sovereignty Is Indivisible

Sovereignty is indivisible for the same reason that it is inalienable. For either the will is general,[6] or it is not. It is the will of either the people as a whole or of only a part. In the first case, this declared will is an act of sovereignty and constitutes law. In the second case, it is merely a private will, or an act of magistracy. At most it is a decree.

However, our political theorists, unable to divide sovereignty in its principle, divide it in its object. They divide it into force and will, into legislative and executive power, into rights of imposing taxes, of justice and of war, into internal administration and power to negotiate with foreigners. Occasionally they confuse all these parts and sometimes they separate them. They turn the sovereign into a fantastic being made of interconnected pieces. It is as if they built a man out of several bodies, one of which had eyes,

---

[5] Under bad governments this equality is only apparent and illusory. It serves merely to maintain the poor man in his misery and the rich man in his usurpation. In actuality, laws are always useful to those who have possessions and harmful to those who have nothing. Whence it follows that the social state is advantageous to men only insofar as they all have something and none of them has too much.

[6] For a will to be general, it need not always be unanimous; however, it is necessary for all the votes to be counted. Any formal exclusion is a breach of generality.

another had arms, another feet, and nothing more. Japanese sleight-of-hand artists are said to dismember a child before the eyes of spectators, then, throwing all the parts in the air one after the other, they make the child fall back down alive and all in one piece. These conjuring acts of our political theorists are more or less like these performances. After having taken apart the social body by means of a sleight-of-hand worthy of a carnival, they put the pieces back together who knows how.

This error comes from not having formed precise notions of sovereign authority, and from having taken for parts of that authority what were merely emanations from it. Thus, for example, the acts of declaring war and making peace have been viewed as acts of sovereignty, which they are not, since each of these acts is not a law but merely an application of the law, a particular act determining the legal circumstances, as will be clearly seen when the idea attached to the word *law* comes to be defined.

In reviewing the other divisions in the same way, one would find that one is mistaken every time one believes one sees sovereignty divided, and that the rights one takes to be the parts of this sovereignty are all subordinated to it and always presuppose supreme wills which these rights merely put into effect.

It would be impossible to say how much this lack of precision has obscured the decisions of authors who have written about political right when they wanted to judge the respective rights of kings and peoples on the basis of the principles they had established. Anyone can see, in Chapters III and IV of Book I of Grotius, how this learned man and his translator, Barbeyrac, become entangled and caught up in their sophisms, for fear of either saying too much or too little according to their perspectives, and of offending the interests they needed to reconcile. Grotius, taking refuge in France, unhappy with his homeland and desirous of paying court to Louis XIII (to whom his book is dedicated), spares no pain to rob the people of all their rights and to invest kings with them by every possible artifice. This would also have been the wish of Barbeyrac, who dedicated his translation to King George I of England. But unfortunately the expulsion of James II (which he calls an abdication) forced him to be evasive and on his guard and to beat around the bush, in order to avoid making William out to be a usurper. If these two writers had adopted the true principles, all their difficulties would have been alleviated and they would always have been consistent. However, sad to say, they would have told the truth and paid court only to the people. For truth does not lead to fortune, and the populace grants neither ambassadorships, university chairs nor pensions.

CHAPTER III: Whether the General Will Can Err

It follows from what has preceded that the general will is always right and always tends toward the public utility. However, it does not follow that the deliberations of the people always have the same rectitude. We always want what is good for us, but we do not always see what it is. The populace is never corrupted, but it is often tricked, and only then does it appear to want what is bad.

There is often a great deal of difference between the will of all and the general will. The latter considers only the general interest, whereas the former considers private interest and is merely the sum of private wills. But remove from these same wills the pluses and minuses that cancel each other out,[7] and what remains as the sum of the differences is the general will.

If, when a sufficiently informed populace deliberates, the citizens were to have no communication among themselves, the general will would always result from the large number of small differences, and the deliberation would always be good. But when intrigues and partial associations come into being at

---

[7] *Each interest*, says the Marquis d'Argenson, *has different principles. The accord of two private interests is formed in opposition to that of a third.* He could have added that the accord of all the interests is found in the opposition to that of each. If there were no different interests, the common interest, which would never encounter any obstacle, would scarcely be felt. Everything would proceed on its own and politics would cease being an art.

the expense of the large association, the will of each of these associations becomes general in relation to its members and particular in relation to the state. It can be said, then, that there are no longer as many voters as there are men, but merely as many as there are associations. The differences become less numerous and yield a result that is less general. Finally, when one of these associations is so large that it dominates all the others, the result is no longer a sum of minor differences, but a single difference. Then there is no longer a general will, and the opinion that dominates is merely a private opinion.

For the general will to be well articulated, it is therefore important that there should be no partial society in the state and that each citizen make up his own mind.[8] Such was the unique and sublime institution of the great Lycurgus. If there are partial societies, their number must be multiplied and inequality among them prevented, as was done by Solon, Numa and Servius. These precautions are the only effective way of bringing it about that the general will is always enlightened and that the populace is not tricked.

CHAPTER IV: On the Limits of Sovereign Power

If the state or the city is merely a moral person whose life consists in the union of its members, and if the most important of its concerns is that of its own conservation, it ought to have a universal compulsory force to move and arrange each part in the manner best suited to the whole. Just as nature gives each man an absolute power over all his members, the social compact gives the body politic an absolute power over all its members, and it is the same power which,

as I have said, is directed by the general will and bears the name sovereignty.

But over and above the public person, we need to consider the private persons who make it up and whose life and liberty are naturally independent of it. It is, therefore, a question of making a rigorous distinction between the respective rights of the citizens and the sovereign,[9] and between the duties the former have to fulfill as subjects and the natural right they should enjoy as men.

We grant that each person alienates, by the social compact, only that portion of his power, his goods, and liberty whose use is of consequence to the community; but we must also grant that only the sovereign is the judge of what is of consequence.

A citizen should render to the state all the services he can as soon as the sovereign demands them. However, for its part, the sovereign cannot impose on the subjects any fetters that are of no use to the community. It cannot even will to do so, for under the law of reason nothing takes place without a cause, any more than under the law of nature.

The commitments that bind us to the body politic are obligatory only because they are mutual, and their nature is such that in fulfilling them one cannot work for someone else without also working for oneself. Why is the general will always right, and why do all constantly want the happiness of each of them, if not because everyone applies the word *each* to himself and thinks of himself as he votes for all? This proves that the quality of right and the notion of justice it produces are derived from the preference each person gives himself, and thus from the nature of man; that the general will, to be really such, must be general in its object as well as in its essence; that it must derive from all in order to be applied to all; and that it loses its natural rectitude when it tends toward any individual, determinate object. For then, judging what is foreign to us, we have no true principle of equity to guide us.

[8] "It is true," says Machiavelli, "that some divisions are harmful to the republic while others are helpful to it. Those that are accompanied by sects and partisan factions are harmful. Since, therefore, a ruler of a republic cannot prevent enmities from arising within it, he at least ought to prevent them from becoming sects," The History of Florence, Book VII. [Rousseau here quotes the Italian.]

[9] Attentive readers, please do not rush to accuse me of contradiction here. I have been unable to avoid it in my choice of words, given the poverty of the language. But wait.

In effect, once it is a question of a state of affairs or a particular right concerning a point that has not been regulated by a prior, general convention, the issue becomes contentious. It is a suit in which the interested private individuals are one of the parties and the public the other, but in which I fail to see either what law should be followed or what judge should render the decision. In these circumstances it would be ridiculous to want to defer to an express decision of the general will, which can only be the conclusion reached by one of its parts, and which, for the other party, therefore, is merely an alien, particular will, inclined on this occasion to injustice and subject to error. Thus, just as a private will cannot represent the general will, the general will, for its part, alters its nature when it has a particular object; and as general, it is unable to render a decision on either a man or a state of affairs. When, for example, the populace of Athens appointed or dismissed its leaders, decreed that honors be bestowed on one or inflicted penalties on another, and by a multitude of particular decrees, indiscriminately exercised all the acts of government, the people in this case no longer had a general will in the strict sense. It no longer functioned as sovereign but as magistrate. This will appear contrary to commonly held opinions, but I must be given time to present my own.

It should be seen from this that what makes the will general is not so much the number of votes as the common interest that unites them, for in this institution each person necessarily submits himself to the conditions he imposes on others, an admirable accord between interest and justice which bestows on common deliberations a quality of equity that disappears when any particular matter is discussed, for lack of a common interest uniting and identifying the role of the judge with that of the party.

From whatever viewpoint one approaches this principle, one always arrives at the same conclusion, namely that the social compact establishes among the citizens an equality of such a kind that they all commit themselves under the same conditions and should all enjoy the same rights. Thus by the very nature of the compact, every act of sovereignty (that is, every authentic act of the general will) obligates or favors all citizens equally, so that the sovereign knows only the nation as a body and does not draw distinctions between any of those members that make it up. Strictly speaking, then, what is an act of sovereignty? It is not a convention between a superior and an inferior, but a convention of the body with each of its members. This convention is legitimate, because it has the social contract as a basis; equitable, because it is common to all; useful, because it can have only the general good for its object; and solid, because it has the public force and the supreme power as a guarantee. So long as the subjects are subordinated only to such convention, they obey no one but their own will alone. And asking how far the respective rights of the sovereign and the citizens extend is asking how far the latter can commit themselves to one another, each to all and all to each.

We can see from this that the sovereign power, absolute, wholly sacred and inviolable as it is, does not and cannot exceed the limits of general conventions, and that every man can completely dispose of such goods and freedom as has been left to him by these conventions. This results in the fact that the sovereign never has the right to lay more charges on one subject than on another, because in that case the matter becomes particular, no longer within the range of the sovereign's competence.

Once these distinctions are granted, it is so false that there is, in the social contract, any genuine renunciation on the part of private individuals that their situation, as a result of this contract, is really preferable to what it was beforehand; and, instead of an alienation, they have merely made an advantageous exchange of an uncertain and precarious mode of existence for another that is better and surer. Natural independence is exchanged for liberty; the power to harm others is exchanged for their own security; and their force, which others could overcome, for a right which the social union renders invincible. Their life itself, which they have devoted to the state, is continually protected by it; and when they risk their lives for its defense, what are they then doing but returning to the state what they have received from it? What are they doing, that they did not do more frequently and with greater danger in the state of nature, when they would inevitably have to fight battles, defending at the peril of their lives the means of their preservation? It is true that everyone has to fight, if necessary, for the homeland; but it also is the case that no one ever has to fight on his own behalf. Do we not still gain by running, for something that brings about our security, a portion of the risks we would have to run for ourselves once our security is taken away?

CHAPTER V: On the Right of Life or Death

The question arises how private individuals who have no right to dispose of their own lives can transfer to the sovereign this very same right which they do not have. This question seems difficult to resolve only because it is poorly stated. Every man has the right to risk his own life in order to preserve it. Has it ever been said that a person who jumps out a window to escape a fire is guilty of committing suicide? Has this crime ever been imputed to someone who perishes in a storm, unaware of its danger when he embarked?

The social treaty has as its purpose the conservation of the contracting parties. Whoever wills the end also wills the means, and these means are inseparable from some risks, even from some losses. Whoever wishes to preserve his life at the expense of others should also give it up for them when necessary. For the citizen is no longer judge of the peril to which the law wishes he be exposed, and when the prince has said to him, "it is expedient for the state that you should die," he should die. Because it is under this condition alone that he has lived in security up to then, and because his life is not only a kindness of nature, but a conditional gift of the state.

The death penalty inflicted on criminals can be viewed from more or less the same point of view. It is in order to avoid being the victim of an assassin that a person consents to die, were he to become one. According to this treaty, far from disposing of his own life, one thinks only of guaranteeing it. And it cannot be presumed that any of the contracting parties is then planning to get himself hanged.

Moreover, every malefactor who attacks the social right becomes through his transgressions a rebel and a traitor to the homeland; in violating its laws, he ceases to be a member, and he even wages war with it. In that case the preservation of the state is incompatible with his own. Thus one of the two must perish; and when the guilty party is put to death, it is less as a citizen than as an enemy. The legal proceeding and the judgment are the proofs and the declaration that he has broken the social treaty, and consequently that he is no longer a member of the state. For since he has acknowledged himself to be such, at least by his living there, he ought to be removed from it by exile as a violator of the compact, or by death as a public enemy. For such an enemy is not a moral person, but a man, and in this situation the right of war is to kill the vanquished.

But it will be said that the condemnation of a criminal is a particular act. Fine. So this condemnation is not a function of the sovereign. It is a right the sovereign can confer without itself being able to exercise it. All of my opinions are consistent, but I cannot present them all at once.

In addition, frequency of physical punishment is always a sign of weakness or of torpor in the government. There is no wicked man who could not be made good for something. One has the right to put to death, even as an example, only someone who cannot be preserved without danger.

With regard to the right of pardon, or of exempting a guilty party from the penalty decreed by the law and pronounced by the judge, this belongs only to one who is above the judge and the law, that is, to the sovereign. Still its right in this regard is not clearly defined, and the cases in which it is used are quite rare. In a well governed state, there are few punishments, not because many pardons are granted, but because there are few criminals. When a state is in decline, the sheer number of crimes insures impunity. Under the Roman Republic, neither the senate nor the consuls ever tried to grant pardons. The people itself did not do so, even though it sometimes revoked its own judgment. Frequent pardons indicate that transgressions will eventually have no need of them, and everyone sees where that leads. But I feel that my heart murmurs and holds back my pen. Let us leave these questions to be discussed by a just man who has not done wrong and who himself never needed pardon.

CHAPTER VI: On Law

Through the social compact we have given existence and life to the body politic. It is now a matter of giving it movement and will through legislation. For the primitive act whereby this body is formed and united still makes no determination regarding what it should do to preserve itself.

Whatever is good and in conformity with order is such by the nature of things and independently of human conventions. All justice comes from God; he alone is its source. But if we knew how to receive it from so exalted a source, we would have no need for government or laws. Undoubtedly there is a universal justice emanating from reason alone; but this justice, to be admitted among us, ought to be reciprocal. Considering things from a human standpoint, the lack of a natural sanction causes the laws of justice to be without teeth among men. They do nothing but good to the wicked and evil to the just, when the latter observes them in his dealings with everyone while no one observes them in their dealings with him. There must therefore be conventions and laws to unite rights and duties and to refer justice back to its object. In the state of nature where everything is commonly held, I owe nothing to those to whom I have promised nothing. I recognize as belonging to someone else only what is not useful to me. It is not this way in the civil state where all rights are fixed by law.

But what then is a law? So long as we continue to be satisfied with attaching only metaphysical ideas to this word, we will continue to reason without coming to any understanding. And when they have declared what a law of nature is, they will not thereby have a better grasp of what a law of the state is.

I have already stated that there is no general will concerning a particular object. In effect, this particular object is either within or outside of the state. If it is outside of the state, a will that is foreign to it is not general in relation to it. And if this object is within the state, that object is part of it; in that case, a relationship is formed between the whole and its parts which makes two separate beings, one of which is the part, and the other is the whole less that same part. But the whole less a part is not the whole, and so long as this relationship obtains, there is no longer a whole, but rather two unequal parts. Whence it follows that the will of the one is not more general in relation to the other.

But when the entire populace enacts a statute concerning the entire populace, it considers only itself, and if in that case a relationship is formed, it is between the entire object seen from one perspective and the entire object seen from another, without any division of the whole. Then the subject matter about which a statute is enacted is general like the will that enacts it. It is this act that I call a law.

When I say that the object of the laws is always general, I have in mind that the law considers subjects as a body and actions in the abstract, never a man as an individual or a particular action. Thus the law can perfectly well enact a statute to the effect that there be privileges, but it cannot bestow them by name on anyone. The law can create several classes of citizens, and even stipulate the qualifications that determine membership in these classes, but it cannot name specific persons to be admitted to them. It can establish a royal government and a hereditary line of succession, but it cannot elect a king or name a royal family. In a word, any function that relates to an individual does not belong to the legislative power. On this view, it is immediately obvious that it is no longer necessary to ask who is to make the laws, since they are the acts of the general will; nor whether the prince is above the laws, since he is a member of the state; nor whether the law can be unjust, since no one is unjust to himself; nor how one is both free and subject to the laws, since they are merely the record of our own wills.

Moreover, it is apparent that since the law combines the universality of the will and that of the object, what a man, whoever he may be, decrees on his own authority is not a law. What even the sovereign decrees concerning a particular object is no closer to being a law; rather, it is a decree. Nor is it an act of sovereignty but of magistracy.

I therefore call every state ruled by laws a republic, regardless of the form its administration may take. For only then does the public interest govern, and only then is the "public thing" [in Latin: *res publica*] something real. Every legitimate government is republican.[10] I will explain later on what government is.

Strictly speaking, laws are merely the conditions of civil association. The populace that is subjected to the laws ought to be their author. The regulating of the conditions of a society belongs to no one but those who are in association with one another. But how will they regulate these conditions? Will it be by a common accord, by a sudden inspiration? Does the body politic have an organ for making known its will? Who will give it the necessary foresight to formulate acts and to promulgate them in advance, or how will it announce them in time of need? How will a blind multitude, which often does not know what it wants (since it rarely knows what is good for it), carry out on its own an enterprise as great and as difficult as a system of legislation? By itself the populace always wants the good, but by itself it does not always see it. The general will is always right, but the judgment that guides it is not always enlightened. It must be made to see objects as they are, and sometimes as they ought to appear to it. The good path it seeks must be pointed out to it. It must be made safe from the seduction of private wills. It must be given a sense of time and place. It must weigh present, tangible advantages against the danger of distant, hidden evils. Private individuals see the good they reject. The public wills the good that it does not see. Everyone is equally in need of guides. The former must be obligated to conform their wills to their reason; the latter must learn to know what it wants. Then public enlightenment results in the union of the un-

derstanding and the will in the social body; hence the full cooperation of the parts, and finally the greatest force of the whole. Whence there arises the necessity of having a legislator.

CHAPTER VII: On the Legislator

Discovering the rules of society best suited to nations would require a superior intelligence that beheld all the passions of men without feeling any of them; who had no affinity with our nature, yet knew it through and through; whose happiness was independent of us, yet who nevertheless was willing to concern itself with ours; finally, who, in the passage of time, procures for himself a distant glory, being able to labor in one age and find enjoyment in another.[11] Gods would be needed to give men laws.

The same reasoning used by Caligula regarding matters of fact was used by Plato regarding right in defining the civil or royal man he looks for in his dialogue *The Statesman*. But if it is true that a great prince is a rare man, what about a great legislator? The former merely has to follow the model the latter should propose to him. The latter is the engineer who invents the machine; the former is merely the workman who constructs it and makes it run. At the birth of societies, says Montesquieu, it is the leaders of republics who bring about the institution, and thereafter it is the institution that forms the leaders of the republic.

He who dares to undertake the establishment of a people should feel that he is, so to speak, in a position to change human nature, to transform each individual (who by himself is a perfect and solitary whole), into a part of a larger whole from which this individual receives, in a sense, his life and his being; to alter man's constitution in order to strengthen it; to substitute a partial and moral existence for the physical and independent existence we have all received from nature. In a word, he must deny man his own forces

---

[10] By this word I do not have in mind merely an aristocracy or a democracy, but in general every government guided by the general will, which is the law. To be legitimate, the government need not be made indistinguishable from the sovereign, but it must be its minister. Then the monarchy itself is a republic. This will become clear in the next Book.

[11] A people never becomes famous except when its legislation begins to decline. It is not known for how many centuries the institution established by Lycurgus caused the happiness of the Spartans before the rest of Greece took note of it.

in order to give him forces that are alien to him and that he cannot make use of without the help of others. The more these natural forces are dead and obliterated, and the greater and more durable are the acquired forces, the more too is the institution solid and perfect. Thus if each citizen is nothing and can do nothing except in concert with all the others, and if the force acquired by the whole is equal or superior to the sum of the natural forces of all the individuals, one can say that the legislation has achieved the highest possible point of perfection.

The legislator is in every respect an extraordinary man in the state. If he ought to be so by his genius, he is no less so by his office, which is neither magistracy nor sovereignty. This office, which constitutes the republic, does not enter into its constitution. It is a particular and superior function having nothing in common with the dominion over men. For if he who has command over men must not have command over laws, he who has command over the laws must no longer have any authority over men. Otherwise, his laws, ministers of his passions, would often only serve to perpetuate his injustices, and he could never avoid private opinions altering the sanctity of his work.

When Lycurgus gave laws to his homeland, he began by abdicating the throne. It was the custom of most Greek cities to entrust the establishment of their laws to foreigners. The modern republics of Italy often imitated this custom. The republic of Geneva did the same and things worked out well.[12] In its finest age Rome saw the revival within its midst of all the crimes of tyranny and saw itself on the verge of perishing as a result of having united the legislative authority and the sovereign power in the same hands.

Nevertheless, the decemvirs themselves never claimed the right to have any law passed on their

---

[12] Those who view Calvin simply as a theologian fail to grasp the extent of his genius. The codification of our wise edicts, in which he had a large role, does him as much honor as his *Institutes*. Whatever revolution time may bring out in our cult, so long as the love of homeland and of liberty is not extinguished among us, the memory of this great man will never cease to be held sacred.

authority alone. *Nothing we propose*, they would tell the people, *can become law without your consent. Romans, be yourselves the authors of the laws that should bring about your happiness.*

He who frames the laws, therefore, does not or should not have any legislative right. And the populace itself cannot, even if it wanted to, deprive itself of this incommunicable right, because, according to the fundamental compact, only the general will obligates private individuals, and there can never be any assurance that a private will is in conformity with the general will until it has been submitted to the free vote of the people. I have already said this, but it is not a waste of time to repeat it.

Thus we find together in the work of legislation two things that seem incompatible: an undertaking that transcends human force, and, to execute it, an authority that is nil.

Another difficulty deserves attention. The wise men who want to speak to the common masses in the former's own language rather than in the common vernacular cannot be understood by the masses. For there are a thousand kinds of ideas that are impossible to translate in the language of the populace. Overly general perspectives and overly distant objects are equally beyond its grasp. Each individual, in having no appreciation for any other plan of government but the one that relates to his own private interest, finds it difficult to realize the advantages he ought to draw from the continual privations that good laws impose. For an emerging people to be capable of appreciating the sound maxims of politics and to follow the fundamental rules of statecraft, the effect would have to become the cause. The social spirit which ought to be the work of that institution, would have to preside over the institution itself. And men would be, prior to the advent of laws, what they ought to become by means of laws. Since, therefore, the legislator is incapable of using either force or reasoning, he must of necessity have recourse to an authority of a different order, which can compel without violence and persuade without convincing.

This is what has always forced the fathers of nations to have recourse to the intervention of heaven and to credit the gods with their own wisdom, so that the peoples, subjected to the laws of the state as to those of nature and recognizing the same power in the formation of man and of the city, might obey with liberty and bear with docility the yoke of public felicity.

It is this sublime reason, which transcends the grasp of ordinary men, whose decisions the legislator puts in the mouth of the immortals in order to compel by divine authority those whom human prudence could not move.[13] But not everybody is capable of making the gods speak or of being believed when he proclaims himself their interpreter. The great soul of the legislator is the true miracle that should prove his mission. Any man can engrave stone tablets, buy an oracle, or feign secret intercourse with some divinity, or train a bird to talk in his ear, or find other crude methods of imposing his beliefs on the people. He who knows no more than this may perchance assemble a troupe of lunatics, but he will never found an empire and his extravagant work will soon die with him. Pointless sleights-of-hand form a fleeting connection; only wisdom can make it lasting. The Judaic Law, which still exists, and that of the child of Ishmael, which has ruled half the world for ten centuries, still proclaim today the great men who enunciated them. And while pride-ridden philosophy or the blind spirit of factionalism sees in them nothing but lucky impostors, the true political theoretician admires in their institutions that great and powerful genius which presides over establishments that endure.

We should not, with Warburton, conclude from this that politics and religion have a common object among us, but that in the beginning stages of nations the one serves as an instrument of the other.

CHAPTER VIII: On the People

Just as an architect, before putting up a large building, surveys and tests the ground to see if it can bear the weight, the wise teacher does not begin by laying down laws that are good in themselves. Rather he first examines whether the people for whom they are destined are fitted to bear them. For this reason, Plato refused to give laws to the Arcadians and to the Cyrenians, knowing that these two peoples were rich and could not abide equality. For this reason, one finds good laws and evil men in Crete, because Minos had disciplined nothing but a vice-ridden people.

A thousand nations have achieved brilliant earthly success that could never have abided good laws; and even those that could have would have been able to have done so for a very short period of their entire existence. Peoples,[14] like men, are docile only in their youth. As they grow older they become incorrigible. Once customs are established and prejudices have become deeply rooted, it is a dangerous and vain undertaking to want to reform them. The people cannot abide having even their evils touched in order to eliminate them, just like those stupid and cowardly patients who quiver at the sight of a physician.

This is not to say that, just as certain maladies unhinge men's minds and remove from them the memory of the past, one does not likewise sometimes find in the period during which states have existed violent epochs when revolutions do to peoples what certain crises do to individuals, when the horror of the past takes the place of forgetfulness, and when the state, set afire by civil wars, is reborn, as it were, from its ashes and takes on again the vigor of youth as it escapes death's embrace. Such was Sparta at the time of Lycurgus; such was Rome after the Tarquins; and such in our time have been Holland and Switzerland after the expulsion of the tyrants.

But these events are rare. They are exceptions whose cause is always to be found in the particular constitution of the states in question. They cannot take place even twice to the same people, for it can make itself free so long as it is merely barbarous; but

---

[13] *And in truth,* says Machiavelli, *there has never been among a people a single legislator who, in proposing extraordinary laws, did not have recourse to God, for otherwise they would not be accepted, since there are many benefits known to a prudent man that do not have in themselves evident* reasons enabling him to persuade others. Discourses on Titus Livy, Book I, Ch. XI. [Rousseau here quotes the Italian.]

[14] [*In the 1782 edition, this sentence was revised to read:* "Most people, like men. . . ."]

it can no longer do so when civil strength is exhausted. At that point troubles can destroy it with revolutions being unable to reestablish it. And as soon as its chains are broken, it falls apart and exists no longer. Henceforward a master is needed, not a liberator. Free peoples, remember this axiom: Liberty can be acquired, but it can never be recovered.

For nations, as for men, there is a time of maturity that must be awaited before subjecting them to the laws.[15] But the maturity of a people is not always easily recognized; and if it is foreseen, the work is ruined. One people lends itself to discipline at its inception; another, not even after ten centuries. The Russians will never be truly civilized, since they have been civilized too early. Peter had a genius for imitation. He did not have true genius, the kind that creates and makes everything out of nothing. Some of the things he did were good; most of them were out of place. He saw that his people was barbarous; he did not see that it was not ready for civilization. He wanted to civilize it when all it needed was toughening. First he wanted to make Germans and Englishmen, when he should have made Russians. He prevented his subjects from ever becoming what they could have been by persuading them that they were something they are not. This is exactly how a French tutor trains his pupil to shine for a short time in his childhood, and afterwards never to amount to a thing. The Russian Empire would like to subjugate Europe and will itself be subjugated. The Tartars, its subjects or its neighbors, will become its masters and ours. This revolution appears inevitable to me. All the kings of Europe are working in concert to hasten its occurrence.

CHAPTER IX: The People (continued)

Just as nature has set limits to the status of a well-formed man, beyond which there are but giants or dwarfs, so too, with regard to the best constitution of a state, there are limits to the size it can have,

so as not to be too large to be capable of being well governed, nor too small to be capable of preserving itself on its own. In every body politic there is a *maximum* force that it cannot exceed, and which has often fallen short by increasing in size. The more the social bond extends the looser it becomes, and in general a small state is proportionately stronger than a large one.

A thousand reasons prove this maxim. First, administration becomes more difficult over great distances, just as a weight becomes heavier at the end of a longer lever. It also becomes more onerous as the number of administrative levels multiplies, because first each city has its own administration which the populace pays for; each district has its own, again paid for by the people; next each province has one and then the great governments, the satrapies and vice royalties, requiring a greater cost the higher you go, and always at the expense of the unfortunate people. Finally, there is the supreme administration which weights down on everyone. All these surcharges continually exhaust the subjects. Far from being better governed by these different orders, they are worse governed than if there were but one administration over them. Meanwhile, hardly any resources remain for meeting emergencies; and when recourse must be made to them, the state is always on the verge of its ruin.

This is not all. Not only does the government have less vigor and quickness in enforcing the observance of the laws, preventing nuisances, correcting abuses and foreseeing the seditious undertakings that can occur in distant places, but also the populace has less affection for its leaders when it never sees them, for the homeland, which, to its eyes, is like the world, and for its fellow citizens, the majority of whom are foreigners to it. The same laws cannot be suitable to so many diverse provinces which have different customs, live in contrasting climates, and which are incapable of enduring the same form of government. Different laws create only trouble and confusion among the peoples who live under the same rulers and are in continuous communication. They intermingle and intermarry, and, being under the sway of other customs, never know whether their patrimony is actually their own. Talents are hidden; virtues are

---

[15] [*In the 1782 edition, this sentence was revised to read*: "Youth is not childhood. For nations, as for men, maturity must be awaited. . . ."]

unknown; vices are unpunished in this multitude of men who are unknown to one another which the seat of supreme administration brings together in one place. The leaders, overwhelmed with work, see nothing for themselves; clerks govern the state. Finally, the measures that need to be taken to maintain the general authority, which so many distant officials want to avoid or harass, absorb all the public attention. Nothing more remains for the people's happiness, and there barely remains enough for its defense in time of need. And thus a body which is too big for its constitution collapses and perishes, crushed by its own weight.

On the other hand, the state ought to provide itself with a firm foundation to give it solidity, to resist the shocks it is bound to experience, as well as the efforts it will have to make to sustain itself. For all the peoples have a kind of centrifugal force, by which they continually act one against the other and tend to expand at the expense of their neighbors, like Descartes' vortices. Thus the weak risk being soon swallowed up; scarcely any people can preserve itself except by putting itself in a kind of equilibrium with all, which nearly equalizes the pressure on all sides.

It is clear from this that there are reasons for expanding and reasons for contracting, and it is not the least of the political theorist's talents to find, between these and other reasons, the proportion most advantageous to the preservation of the state. In general, it can be said that the former reasons, being merely external and relative, should be subordinated to the latter reasons, which are internal and absolute. A strong, healthy constitution is the first thing one needs to look for, and one should count more on the vigor born of a good government than on the resources furnished by a large territory.

Moreover, there have been states so constituted that the necessity for conquests entered into their very constitution, and that, to maintain themselves, they were forced to expand endlessly. Perhaps they congratulated themselves greatly on account of this happy necessity, which nevertheless showed them, together with the limit of their size, the inevitable moment of their fall.

CHAPTER X: The People (continued)

A body politic can be measured in two ways: namely, by the size of its territory and by the number of its people. And between these measurements there is a relationship suitable for giving the state its true greatness. Men are what make up the state and land is what feeds men. This relationship therefore consists in there being enough land for the maintenance of its inhabitants and as many inhabitants as the land can feed. It is in this proportion that the *maximum* force of a given population size is found. For if there is too much land, its defense is onerous, its cultivation inadequate, and its yield surplus. This is the proximate cause of defensive wars. If there is not enough land, the state finds itself at the discretion of its neighbors for what it needs as a supplement. This is the proximate cause of offensive wars. Any people whose position provides it an alternative merely between commerce and war is inherently weak. It depends on its neighbors; it depends on events. It never has anything but an uncertain and brief existence. Either it conquers and changes the situation, or it is conquered and obliterated. It can keep itself free only by means of smallness or greatness.

No one can provide in mathematical terms a fixed relationship between the size of land and the population size which are sufficient for one another, as much because of the differences in the characteristics of the terrain, its degrees of fertility, the nature of its crops, the influence of its climates, as because of the differences to be noted in the temperaments of the men who inhabit them, some of whom consume little in a fertile country, while others consume a great deal on a barren soil. Again, attention must be given to the greater or lesser fertility of women, to what the country can offer that is more or less favorable to the population, to the number of people that the legislator can hope to bring together through his institutions. Thus, the legislator should not base his judgment on what he sees but on what he foresees. And he should dwell less upon the present state of the population as upon the state it should naturally attain. Finally, there are a thousand situations where the idiosyncracies of a place require or permit the assimilation of more land than appears necessary. Thus, there is considerable expansion in mountainous country, where the natural crops—namely, woods and pastures—demand less work; where experience shows that women are more fertile than on the plains; and where a large amount of sloping soil provides only a very small amount of flat land, the only thing that can be counted on for vegetation. On the other hand, people can draw closer to one another at the seashore, even on rocks and nearly barren sand, because fishing can make up to a great degree for the lack of land crops, since men should be more closely gathered together in order to repulse pirates, and since in addition it is easier to unburden the country of surplus inhabitants by means of colonies.

To these conditions for instituting a people must be added one that cannot be a substitute for any other, but without which all the rest are useless: the enjoyment of the fullness of peace. For the time when a state is organized, like the time when a battalion is formed, is the instant when the body is the least capable of resisting and easiest to destroy. There would be better resistance at a time of absolute disorder than at a moment of fermentation, when each man is occupied with his own position rather than with the danger. Were a war, famine, or sedition to arise in this time of crisis the state inevitably is overthrown.

This is not to say that many governments are not established during such storms; but in these instances it is these governments themselves that destroy the state. Usurpers always bring about or choose these times of trouble to use public terror to pass destructive laws that the people never adopt when they have their composure. The choice of the moment of a government's institution is one of the surest signs by which the work of a legislator can be distinguished from that of a tyrant.

What people, therefore, is suited for legislation? One that, finding itself bound by some union of origin, interest or convention, has not yet felt the true yoke of laws. One that has no custom or superstitions that are deeply rooted. One that does not fear being overpowered by sudden invasion. One that can, without entering into the squabbles of its neighbors, resist each of them single-handed or use the help of one to repel another. One where each member can be known to all, and where there is no need to impose a greater burden on a man than a man can bear. One that can get along without peoples and without which every other people can get along.[16] One that is neither rich nor poor and can be sufficient unto itself; finally, one that brings together the stability of an ancient people and the docility of a new people. What makes the work of legislation trying is not so much what must be established as what must be destroyed. And what makes success so rare is the impossibility of finding the simplicity of nature together with the needs of society. All these conditions, it is true, are hard to find in combination. Hence few well constituted states are to be seen.

In Europe there is still one country capable of receiving legislation. It is the island of Corsica. The valor and constancy with which this brave people has regained and defended its liberty would well merit having some wise man teaching them how to preserve it. I have a feeling that some day that little island will astonish Europe.

CHAPTER XI: On the Various Systems of Legislation

If one enquires into precisely wherein the greatest good of all consists, which should be the purpose of every system of legislation, one will find that it boils down to the two principal objects, *liberty* and *equality*.

---

[16] If there were two neighboring peoples, one being unable to get along without the other, it would be a very tough situation for the former and very dangerous for the latter. In such a case, every wise nation will work very quickly to free the other of its dependency. The republic of Thlascala, enclosed within the Mexican empire, preferred to do without salt, rather than buy it from the Mexicans or even take it from them for nothing. The wise Thlascalans saw the trap hidden beneath this generosity. They kept themselves free, and this small state, enclosed within this great empire, was finally the instrument of its ruin.

Liberty, because all particular dependence is that much force taken from the body of the state; equality, because liberty cannot subsist without it.

I have already said what civil liberty is. Regarding equality, we need not mean by this word that degrees of power and wealth are to be absolutely the same, but rather that, with regard to power, it should transcend all violence and never be exercised except by virtue of rank and laws; and, with regard to wealth, no citizen should be so rich as to be capable of buying another citizen, and none so poor that he is forced to sell himself. This presupposes moderation in goods and credit on the part of the great, and moderation in avarice and covetousness[17] on the part of the lowly.

This equality is said to be a speculative fiction that cannot exist in practice. But if abuse is inevitable, does it follow that it should not at least be regulated? It is precisely because the force of things tends always to destroy equality that the force of legislation should always tend to maintain it.

But these general objects of every good institution should be modified in each country in accordance with the relationships that arise as much from the local situation as from the temperament of the inhabitants. And it is on the basis of these relationships that each people must be assigned a particular institutional system that is the best, not perhaps in itself, but for the state for which it is destined. For example, is the soil barren and unproductive, or the country too confining for its inhabitants? Turn to industry and crafts, whose products you will exchange for the foodstuffs you lack. On the other hand, do you live in rich plains and fertile slopes? Do you lack inhabitants on a good terrain? Put all your effort into agriculture, which increases the number of men, and chase out the crafts that seem only to achieve the depopulation of the country by grouping in a few sectors what

few inhabitants there are.[18] Do you occupy long, convenient coastlines? Cover the sea with vessels; cultivate commerce and navigation. You will have a brilliant and brief existence. Does the sea wash against nothing on your coasts but virtually inaccessible rocks? Remain barbarous and fish-eating. You will live in greater tranquillity, better perhaps and certainly happily. In a word, aside from the maxims common to all, each people has within itself some cause that organizes them in a particular way and renders its legislation proper for it alone. Thus it was that long ago the Hebrews and recently the Arabs have had religion as their main object; the Athenians had letters; Carthage and Tyre, commerce; Rhodes, seafaring; Sparta, war; and Rome, virtue. The author of *The Spirit of the Laws* has shown with a large array of examples the art by which the legislator directs the institution toward each of its objects.

What makes the constitution of a state truly solid and lasting is that proprieties are observed with such fidelity that the natural relations and the laws are always in agreement on the same points, and that the latter serve only to assure, accompany and rectify them. But if the legislator is mistaken about his object and takes a principle different from the one arising from the nature of things (whether the one tends toward servitude and the other toward liberty; the one toward riches, the other toward increased population; the one toward peace, the other toward conquests), the laws will weaken imperceptibly, the constitution will be altered, and the state will not cease being agitated until it is destroyed or changed, and invincible nature has regained her empire.

CHAPTER XII: Classification of the Laws

To set the whole in order or to give the commonwealth the best possible form, there are various relations to consider. First, the action of the entire body

---

[17] Do you therefore want to give constancy to the State? Bring the extremes as close together as possible. Tolerate neither rich men nor beggars. These two estates, which are naturally inseparable, are equally fatal to the common good. From the one come the fomenters of tyranny, and from the other the tyrants. It is always between them that public liberty becomes a matter of commerce. The one buys it and the other sells it.

[18] Any branch of foreign trade, says the Marquis d'Argenson, creates hardly anything more than a false utility for a kingdom in general. It can enrich some private individuals, even some towns, but the nation as a whole gains nothing and the populace is none the better for it.

acting upon itself, that is, the relationship of the whole to the whole, or of the sovereign to the state, and this relationship, as we will see later, is composed of relationships of intermediate terms.

The laws regulating this relationship bear the name political laws, and are also called fundamental laws, not without reason if these laws are wise. For there is only one way of organizing in each state. The people who have found it should stand by it. But if the established order is evil, why should one accept as fundamental, laws that prevent it from being good? Besides, a people is in any case always in a position to change its laws, even the best laws. For if it wishes to do itself harm, who has the right to prevent it from doing so?

The second relation is that of the members to each other or to the entire body. And this relationship should be as small as possible in regard to the former and as large as possible in regard to the latter, so that each citizen would be perfectly independent of all the others and excessively dependent upon the city. This always takes place by the same means, for only the force of the state brings about the liberty of its members. It is from this second relationship that civil laws arise.

We may consider a third sort of relation between man and law, namely that of disobedience and penalty. And this gives rise to the establishment of criminal laws, which basically are not so much a particular kind of law as the sanction for all the others.

To these three sorts of law is added a fourth, the most important of all. It is not engraved on marble or bronze, but in the hearts of citizens. It is the true constitution of the state. Everyday it takes on new forces. When other laws grow old and die away, it revives and replaces them, preserves a people in the spirit of its institution and imperceptibly substitutes the force of habit for that of authority. I am speaking of mores, customs, and especially of opinion, a part of the law unknown to our political theorists but one on which depends the success of all the others; a part with which the great legislator secretly occupies himself, though he seems to confine himself to the particular regulations that are merely the arching of the vault, whereas mores, slower to arise, form in the end its immovable keystone.

Among these various classes, only political laws, which constitute the form of government, are relevant to my subject.

END OF THE SECOND BOOK

BOOK III

Before speaking of the various forms of government, let us try to determine the precise meaning of this word, which has not as yet been explained very well.

CHAPTER I: On Government in General

I am warning the reader that this chapter should be read carefully and that I do not know the art of being clear to those who do not want to be attentive.

Every free action has two causes that come together to produce it. The one is moral, namely the will that determines the act; the other is physical, namely the power that executes it. When I walk toward an object, I must first want to go there. Second, my feet must take me there. A paralyzed man who wants to walk or an agile man who does not want to walk will both remain where they are. The body politic has the same moving causes. The same distinction can be made between force and the will; the one under the name *legislative power* and the other under the name *executive power*. Nothing is done and ought to be done without their concurrence.

We have seen that legislative power belongs to the people and can belong to it alone. On the contrary, it is easy to see, by the principles established above, that executive power cannot belong to the people at large in its role as legislator or sovereign, since this power consists solely of particular acts that are not within the province of the law, nor consequently of the sovereign, none of whose acts can avoid being laws.

Therefore the public force must have an agent of its own that unifies it and gets it working in accordance with the directions of the general will, that serves as a means of communication between the state and the sovereign, and that accomplishes in the public person just about what the union of soul and body accomplishes in man. This is the reason for having government in the state, something often badly confused with the sovereign, of which it is merely the minister.

What then is the government? An intermediate body established between the subjects and the sovereign for their mutual communication, and charged with the execution of the laws and the preservation of liberty, both civil and political.

The members of this body are called magistrates or *kings*, that is to say, *governors*, and the entire body bears the name *prince*.[19] Therefore those who claim that the act by which a people submits itself to leaders is not a contract are quite correct. It is absolutely nothing but a commission, an employment in which the leaders, as simple officials of the sovereign, exercise in its own name the power with which it has entrusted them. The sovereign can limit, modify, or appropriate this power as it pleases, since the alienation of such a right is incompatible with the nature of the social body and contrary to the purpose of the association.

Therefore, I call *government* or supreme administration the legitimate exercise of executive power; I call prince or magistrate the man or the body charged with that administration.

In government one finds the intermediate forces whose relationships make up that of the whole to the whole or of the sovereign to the state. This last relationship can be represented as one between the extremes of a continuous proportion, whose proportional mean is the government. The government receives from the sovereign the orders it gives the people, and, for the state to be in good equilibrium, there must, all things considered, be an equality between the output or the power of the government, taken by itself, and the output or power of the citizens, who are sovereigns on the one hand and subjects on the other.

Moreover, none of these three terms could be altered without the simultaneous destruction of the

proportion. If the sovereign wishes to govern, or if the magistrate wishes to give laws, or if the subjects refuse to obey, disorder replaces rule, force and will no longer act in concert, and thus the state dissolves and falls into despotism or anarchy. Finally, since there is only one proportional mean between each relationship, there is only one good government possible for a state. But since a thousand events can change the relationships of a people, not only can different governments be good for different peoples, but also for the same people at different times.

In trying to provide an idea of the various relationships that can obtain between these two extremes, I will take as an example the number of people, since it is a more easily expressed relationship.

Suppose the state is composed of ten thousand citizens. The sovereign can only be considered collectively and as a body. But each private individual in his position as a subject is regarded as an individual. Thus the sovereign is to the subject as ten thousand is to one. In other words, each member of the state has as his share only one ten-thousandth of the sovereign authority, even though he is totally in subjection to it. If the populace is made up of a hundred thousand men, the condition of the subjects does not change, and each bears equally the entire dominion of the laws, while his vote, reduced to one hundred-thousandth, has ten times less influence in the drafting of them. In that case, since the subject always remains one, the ratio of the sovereign to the subject increases in proportion to the number of citizens. Whence it follows that the larger the state becomes, the less liberty there is.

When I say that the ratio increases, I mean that it places a distance between itself and equality. Thus the greater the ratio is in the sense employed by geometricians, the less relationship there is in the everyday sense of the word. In the former sense, the ratio, seen in terms of quantity, is measured by the quotient; in the latter sense, ratio, seen in terms of identity, is reckoned by similarity.

Now the less relationship there is between private wills and the general will, that is, between mores and the laws, the more repressive force ought to increase.

---

[19] Thus in Venice the College is given the name *Most Serene Prince* even when the Doge is not present.

Therefore, in order to be good, the government must be relatively stronger in proportion as the populace is more numerous.

On the other hand, as the growth of the state gives the trustees of the public authority more temptations and the means of abusing their power, the more the force the government must have in order to contain the people, the more the force the sovereign must have in order to contain the government. I am speaking here not of an absolute force but of the relative force of the various parts of the state.

It follows from this twofold relationship that the continuous proportion between the sovereign, the prince and the people, is in no way an arbitrary idea, but a necessary consequence of the nature of the body politic. It also follows that since one of the extremes, namely the people as subject, is fixed and represented by unity, whenever the doubled ratio increases or decreases, the simple ratio increases or decreases in like fashion, and that as a consequence the middle term is changed. This makes it clear that there is no unique and absolute constitution of government, but that there can be as many governments of differing natures as there are states of differing sizes.

If, in ridiculing this system, someone were to say that in order to find this proportional mean and to form the body of the government, it is necessary merely, in my opinion, to derive the square root of the number of people, I would reply that here I am taking this number only as an example; that the relationships I am speaking of are not measured solely by the number of men, but in general by the quantity of action, which is the combination of a multitude of causes; and that, in addition, if to express myself in fewer words I borrow for the moment the terminology of geometry, I nevertheless am not unaware of the fact that geometrical precision has no place in moral quantities.

The government is on a small scale what the body politic which contains it is on a large scale. It is a moral person endowed with certain faculties, active like the sovereign and passive like the state, and capable of being broken down into other similar relationships whence there arises as a consequence a new proportion and yet again another within this one according to the order of tribunals, until an indivisible middle term is reached; that is, a single leader or supreme magistrate, who can be represented in the midst of this progression as the unity between the series of fractions and that of whole numbers.

Without involving ourselves in this multiplication of terms, let us content ourselves with considering the government as a new body in the state, distinct from the people and sovereign, and intermediate between them.

The essential difference between these two bodies is that the state exists by itself, while the government exists only through the sovereign. Thus the dominant will of the prince is not and should not be anything other than the general will or the law. His force is merely the public force concentrated in him. As soon as he wants to derive from himself some absolute and independent act, the bond that links everything together begins to come loose. If it should finally happen that the prince had a private will more active than that of the sovereign, and that he had made use of some of the public force that is available to him in order to obey this private will, so that there would be, so to speak, two sovereigns—one de jure and the other de facto, at that moment the social union would vanish and the body politic would be dissolved.

However, for the body of the government to have an existence, a real life that distinguishes it from the body of the state, and for all its members to be able to act in concert and to fulfill the purpose for which it is instituted, there must be a particular *self*, a sensibility common to all its members, a force or will of its own that tends toward its preservation. This particular existence presupposes assemblies, councils, a power to deliberate and decide, rights, titles and privileges that belong exclusively to the prince and that render the condition of the magistrate more honorable in proportion as it is more onerous. The difficulties lie in the manner in which this subordinate whole is so organized within the whole, that it in no way alters the general constitution by strengthening its own, that it always distinguishes its particular force, which is intended for its own preservation, from the public force intended for the preservation of the state, and that, in a word, it is always ready to sacrifice the government to the people and not the people to the government.

In addition, although the artificial body of the government is the work of another artificial body and has, in a sense, only a borrowed and subordinate life, this does not prevent it from being capable of acting with more or less vigor or speed, or from enjoying, so to speak, more or less robust health. Finally, without departing directly from the purpose of its institution, it can deviate more or less from it, according to the manner in which it is constituted.

From all these differences arise the diverse relationships that the government should have with the body of the state, according to the accidental and particular relationships by which the state itself is modified. For often the government that is best in itself will become the most vicious, if its relationships are not altered according to the defects of the body politic to which it belongs.

CHAPTER II: On the Principle that Constitutes the Various Forms of Government

In order to lay out the general cause of these differences, a distinction must be made here between the prince and the government, as I had done before between the state and the sovereign.

The body of the magistrates can be made up of a larger or smaller number of members. We have said that the ratio of the sovereign to the subjects was greater in proportion as the populace was more numerous, and by a manifest analogy we can say the same thing about the government in relation to the magistrates.

Since the total force of the government is always that of the state, it does not vary. Whence it follows that the more of this force it uses on its own members, the less that is left to it for acting on the whole populace.

Therefore, the more numerous the magistrates, the weaker the government. Since this maxim is fundamental, let us attempt to explain it more clearly.

We can distinguish in the person of the magistrate three essentially different wills. First, the individual's own will, which tends only to its own advantage. Second, the common will of the magistrates which is uniquely related to the advantage of the prince. This latter can be called the corporate will, and is general in relation to the government, and particular in relation to the state, of which the government forms a part. Third, the will of the people or the sovereign will, which is general both in relation to the state considered as the whole and in relation to the government considered as a part of the whole.

In a perfect act of legislation, the private or individual will should be nonexistent; the corporate will proper to the government should be very subordinate; and consequently the general or sovereign will should always be dominant and the unique rule of all the others.

According to the natural order, on the contrary, these various wills become more active in proportion as they are the more concentrated. Thus the general will is always the weakest, the corporate will has second place, and the private will is first of all, so that in the government each member is first himself, then a magistrate, and then a citizen—a gradation directly opposite to the one required by the social order.

Granting this, let us suppose the entire government is in the hands of one single man. In that case the private will and the corporate will are perfectly united, and consequently the latter is at the highest degree of intensity it can reach. But since the use of force is dependent upon the degree of will, and since the absolute force of the government does not vary one bit, it follows that the most active of governments is that of one single man.

On the other hand, let us suppose we are uniting the government to the legislative authority. Let us make the sovereign the prince and all the citizens that many magistrates. Then the corporate will, confused with the general will, will have no more activity than the latter, and will leave the private will all its force. Thus the government, always with the same absolute force, will have its *minimum* relative force or activity.

These relationships are incontestable, and there are still other considerations that serve to confirm them.

We see, for example, that each magistrate is more active in his body than each citizen is in his, and consequently that the private will has much more influence on the acts of the government than on those of the sovereign. For each magistrate is nearly always charged with the responsibility for some function of government, whereas each citizen, taken by himself, exercises no function of sovereignty. Moreover, the more the state is extended, the more its real force increases, although it does not increase in proportion to its size. But if the state remains the same, the magistrates may well be multiplied without the government acquiring any greater real force, since this force is that of the state, whose size is always equal. Thus the relative force or activity of the government diminishes without its absolute or real force being able to increase.

It is also certain that the execution of public business becomes slower in proportion as more people are charged with the responsibility for it; that in attaching too much importance to prudence, too little importance is attached to fortune, opportunities are missed, and the fruits of deliberation are often lost by dint of deliberation.

I have just proved that the government becomes slack in proportion as the magistrates are multiplied; and I have previously proved that the more numerous the people, the greater should be the increase of repressive force. Whence it follows that the ratio of the magistrate to the government should be the inverse of the ratio of the subjects to the sovereign; that is to say, the more the state increases in size, the more the government should shrink, so that the number of leaders decreases in proportion to the increase in the number of people.

I should add that I am speaking here only about the relative force of the government and not about its rectitude. For, on the contrary, the more numerous the magistrates, the more closely the corporate will approaches the general will, whereas under a single magistrate, the same corporate will is, as I have said, merely a particular will. Thus what can be gained on the one hand is lost on the other, and the art of the legislator is to know how to determine the point at which the government's will and force, always in a reciprocal proportion, are combined in the relationship that is most advantageous to the state.

CHAPTER III: Classification of Governments

We have seen in the previous chapter why the various kinds or forms of government are distinguished by the number of members that compose them. It remains to be seen in this chapter how this classification is made.

In the first place, the sovereign can entrust the government to the entire people or to the majority of the people, so that there are more citizens who are magistrates than who are ordinary private citizens. This form of government is given the name *democracy*.

Or else it can restrict the government to the hands of a small number, so that there are more ordinary citizens than magistrates; and this form is called *aristocracy*.

Finally, it can concentrate the entire government in the hands of a single magistrate from whom all the others derive their power. This third form is the most common and is called *monarchy* or royal government.

It should be noted that all these forms, or at least the first two, can be had in greater or lesser degrees, and even have a rather wide range. For democracy can include the entire populace or be restricted to half. Aristocracy, for its part, can be indeterminately restricted from half the people down to the smallest number. Even royalty can be had in varying levels of distribution. Sparta always had two kings, as required by its constitution; and the Roman Empire is known to have had up to eight emperors at a time, without it being possible to say that the empire was divided. Thus there is a point at which each form of government is indistinguishable from the next, and it is apparent that, under just three names, government can take on as many diverse forms as the state has citizens.

Moreover, since this same government can, in certain respects, be subdivided into other parts, one administered in one way, another in another, there can result from the combination of these three forms a multitude of mixed forms, each of which can be multiplied by all the simple forms.

There has always been a great deal of argument over the best form of government, without considering that each one of them is best in certain cases and the worst in others.

If the number of supreme magistrates in the different states ought to be in inverse ratio to that of the citizens, it follows that in general democratic government is suited to small states, aristocratic government to states of intermediate size, and monarchical government to large ones. This rule is derived immediately from the principle; but how is one to count the multitude of circumstances that can furnish exceptions?

CHAPTER IV: On Democracy

He who makes the law knows better than anyone else how it should be executed and interpreted. It seems therefore to be impossible to have a better constitution than one in which the executive power is united to the legislative power. But this is precisely what renders such a government inadequate in certain respects, since things that should be distinguished are not, and the prince and sovereign, being merely the same person, form, as it were, only a government without a government.

It is not good for the one who makes the laws to execute them, nor for the body of the people to turn its attention away from general perspectives in order to give it particular objects. Nothing is more dangerous than the influence of private interests on public affairs; and the abuse of the laws by the government is a lesser evil than the corruption of the legislator, which is the inevitable outcome of particular perspectives. In such a situation, since the state is being substantially altered, all reform becomes impossible. A people that would never misuse the government would never misuse independence. A people that would always govern well would not need to be governed.

Taking the term in the strict sense, a true democracy has never existed and never will. It is contrary to the natural order that the majority govern and the minority is governed. It is unimaginable that the people would remain constantly assembled to handle public affairs; and it is readily apparent that it could not establish commissions for this purpose without changing the form of administration.

In fact, I believe I can lay down as a principle that when the functions of the government are shared among several tribunals, those with the fewest members sooner or later acquire the greatest authority, if only because of the facility in expediting public business which brings this about naturally.

Besides, how many things that are difficult to unite are presupposed by this government? First, a very small state where it is easy for the people to gather together and where each citizen can easily know all the others. Second, a great simplicity of mores, which prevents the multitude of public business and thorny discussions. Next, a high degree of equality in ranks and fortunes, without which equality in rights and authority cannot subsist for long. Finally, little or no luxury, for luxury either is the effect of wealth or it makes wealth necessary. It simultaneously corrupts both the rich and the poor, the one by possession, the other by covetousness. It sells the homeland to softness and vanity. It takes all its citizens from the state in order to make them slaves to one another, and all of them to opinion.

This is why a famous author has made virtue the principle of the republic. For all these conditions could not subsist without virtue. But owing to his failure to have made the necessary distinctions, this great genius often lacked precision and sometimes clarity. And he did not realize that since the sovereign authority is everywhere the same, the same principle should have a place in every well constituted state, though in a greater or lesser degree, it is true, according to the form of government.

Let us add that no government is so subject to civil wars and internal agitations as a democratic or popular one, since there is none that tends so forcefully and continuously to change its form, or that demands greater vigilance and courage to be maintained in its own form. Above all, it is under this constitution that the citizen ought to arm himself with force and constancy, and to say each day of his life from the bottom of his heart what a virtuous Palatine[20] said in the Diet of Poland: *Better to have liberty fraught with danger than servitude in peace.*

Were there a people of gods, it would govern itself democratically. So perfect a government is not suited to men.

CHAPTER V: On Aristocracy

We have here two very distinct moral persons, namely the government and the sovereign, and consequently two general wills, one in relation to all the citizens, the other only for the members of the administration. Thus, although the government can regulate its internal administration as it chooses, it can never speak to the people except in the name of the sovereign, that is to say, in the name of the populace itself. This is something not to be forgotten.

The first societies governed themselves aristocratically. The leaders of families deliberated among themselves about public affairs. Young people deferred without difficulty to the authority of experience. This is the origin of the words *priests*, *ancients*, *senate* and *elders*. The savages of North America still govern themselves that way to this day, and are very well governed.

But to the extent that inequality occasioned by social institutions came to prevail over natural inequality, wealth or power[21] was preferred to age, and aristocracy became elective. Finally, the transmission of the father's power, together with his goods, to his children created patrician families; the government was made hereditary, and we know of senators who were only twenty years old.

There are therefore three sorts of aristocracy: natural, elective and hereditary. The first is suited only to simple people; the third is the worst of any government. The second is the best; it is aristocracy properly so-called.

In addition to the advantage of the distinction between the two powers, aristocracy has that of the choice of its members. For in popular government all the citizens are born magistrates; however, this type of government limits them to a small number, and they become magistrates only through election,[22] a means by which probity, enlightenment, experience, and all the other reasons for public preference and esteem are so many new guarantees of being well governed.

Furthermore, assemblies are more conveniently held, public business better discussed and carried out with more orderliness and diligence, the reputation of the state is better sustained abroad by venerable senators than by a multitude that is unknown or despised.

In a word, it is the best and most natural order for the wisest to govern the multitude, when it is certain that they will govern for its profit and not for their own. There is no need for multiplying devices uselessly or for doing with twenty thousand men what one hundred hand-picked men can do even better. But it must be noted here that the corporate interest begins to direct the public force in less strict a conformity with the rule of the general will, and that another inevitable tendency removes from the laws a part of the executive power.

With regard to the circumstances that are specifically suitable, a state must not be so small, nor its people so simple and upright that the execution of the laws follows immediately from the public will, as is the case in a good democracy. Nor must a nation be so large that the leaders, scattered about in order

---

[20] The Palatine of Posen, father of the King of Poland, Duke of Lorraine. [Rousseau quotes in Latin the maxim which follows.]

[21] It is clear that among the ancients the word *optimates* does not mean the best, but the most powerful.

[22] It is of great importance that laws should regulate the form of the election of magistrates, for if it is left to the will of the prince, it is impossible to avoid falling into a hereditary aristocracy, as has taken place in the Republics of *Venice* and *Berne*. Thus the former has long been a state in dissolution, while the latter maintains itself through the extreme wisdom of its senate. It is a very honorable and very dangerous exception.

to govern it, can each play the sovereign in his own department, and begin by making themselves independent in order finally to become the masters.

But if aristocracy requires somewhat fewer virtues than popular government, it also demands others that are proper to it, such as moderation among the wealthy and contentment among the poor. For it appears that rigorous equality would be out of place here. It was not observed even in Sparta.

Moreover, if this form of government carries with it a certain inequality of fortune, this is simply in order that in general the administration of public business may be entrusted to those who are best able to give all their time to it, but not, as Aristotle claims, in order that the rich may always be given preference. On the contrary, it is important that an opposite choice should occasionally teach the people that more important reasons for preference are to be found in a man's merit than in his wealth.

CHAPTER VI: On Monarchy

So far, we have considered the prince as a moral and collective person, united by the force of laws, and as the trustee of the executive power in the state. We have now to consider this power when it is joined together in the hands of a natural person, of a real man, who alone has the right to dispose of it in accordance with the laws. Such a person is called a monarch or a king.

In utter contrast with the other forms of administration where a collective entity represents an individual, in this form of administration an individual represents a collective entity; so that the moral unity constituting the prince is at the same time a physical unity, in which all the faculties which are combined by the law in the other forms of administration with such difficulty are found naturally combined.

Thus the will of the people, the will of the prince, the public force of the state, and the particular force of the government, all respond to the same moving agent; all the springs of the machine are in the same hand; everything moves toward the same end; there are no opposing movements which are at cross pur-

poses with one another; and no constitution is imaginable in which a lesser effort produces a more considerable action. Archimedes sitting serenely on the shore and effortlessly launching a huge vessel is what comes to mind when I think of a capable monarch governing his vast states from his private study, and making everything move while appearing himself to be immovable.

But if there is no government that has more vigor, there is none where the private will has greater sway and more easily dominates the others. Everything moves toward the same end, it is true; but this end is not that of public felicity, and the very force of the administration unceasingly operates to the detriment of the state.

Kings want to be absolute, and from a distance one cries out to them that the best way to be so is to make themselves loved by their peoples. This maxim is very noble and even very true in certain respects. Unfortunately it will always be an object of derision in courts. The power that comes from the peoples' love is undoubtedly the greatest, but it is precarious and conditional. Princes will never be satisfied with it. The best kings want to be able to be wicked if it pleases them, without ceasing to be the masters. A political sermonizer might well say to them that since the people's force is their force, their greatest interest is that the people should be flourishing, numerous and formidable. They know perfectly well that this is not true. Their personal interest is first of all that the people should be weak and miserable and incapable of ever resisting them. I admit that, assuming the subjects were always in perfect submission, the interest of the prince would then be for the people to be powerful, so that this power, being his own, would render him formidable in the eyes of his neighbors. But since this interest is merely secondary and subordinate, and since the two suppositions are incompatible, it is natural that the princes should always give preference to the maxim that is the most immediately useful to them. This is the point that Samuel made so forcefully to the Hebrews, and that Machiavelli has made apparent. Under the pretext of teaching kings, he has taught important lessons to the peoples. Machiavelli's *The Prince* is the book of republicans.[23]

We have found, through general relationships, that the monarchy is suited only to large states, and we find this again in examining the monarchy itself. The more numerous the public administration, the more the ratio of the prince to subject diminishes and approaches equality, so that this ratio increases in proportion as the government is restricted, and is at its *maximum* when the government is in the hands of a single man. Then there is too great a distance between the prince and the people, and the state lacks cohesiveness. In order to bring about this cohesiveness, there must therefore be intermediate orders; there must be princes, grandees, and a nobility to fill them. Now none of this is suited to a small state, which is ruined by all these social levels.

But if it is difficult for a large state to be well governed, it is much harder still for it to be well governed by just one man, and everyone knows what happens when the king appoints substitutes.

An essential and inevitable defect, which will always place the monarchical form of government below the republican form, is that in the latter form the public voice hardly ever raises to the highest positions men who are not enlightened and capable and who would not fill their positions with honor. On the other hand, those who attain these positions in monarchies are most often petty bunglers, petty swindlers, petty intriguers, whose petty talents, which cause them to attain high positions at court, serve only to display their incompetence to the public as soon as they reach these positions. The populace is much less often in error in its choice than the prince, and a man of real merit in the ministry is almost as rare as a fool at the head of a republican government. Thus, when by some happy chance one of these men who are born to govern takes the helm of public business in a monarchy that has nearly been sunk by this crowd of fine managers, there is utter amazement at the resources he finds, and his arrival marks an era in the history of the country.

For a monarchical state to be capable of being well governed, its size or extent must be proportionate to the faculties of the one who governs. It is easier to conquer than to rule. With a long enough lever it is possible for a single finger to make the world shake; but holding it in place requires the shoulders of Hercules. However small a state may be, the prince is nearly always too small for it. When, on the contrary, it happens that the state is too small for its leader, which is quite rare, it is still poorly governed, since the leader, always pursuing his grand schemes, forgets the interests of the peoples, making them no less wretched through the abuse of talents he has too much of than does a leader who is limited for want of what he lacks. A kingdom must, so to speak, expand or contract with each reign, depending on the ability of the prince. On the other hand, since the talents of a senate have a greater degree of stability, the state can have permanent boundaries without the administration working any less well.

The most obvious disadvantage of the government of just one man is the lack of that continuous line of succession which forms an unbroken bond of unity in the other two forms of government. When one king dies, another is needed. Elections leave dangerous intervals and are stormy. And unless the citizens have a disinterestedness and integrity that seldom accompanies this form of government, intrigue and corruption enter the picture. It is difficult for one to whom the state has sold itself not to sell it in turn, and reimburse himself at the expense of the weak for the money extorted from him by the powerful. Sooner or later everything becomes venal under such an administration, and in these circumstances, the peace

---

[23] [The following was inserted in the 1782 edition: "Machiavelli was a decent man and a good citizen. But since he was attached to the house of Medici, he was forced during the oppression of his homeland to disguise his love of liberty. The very choice of his execrable hero makes clear enough his hidden intention. And the contrast between the maxims of his book *The Prince* and those of his *Discourses on Titus Livy* and of his *History of Florence* shows that this profound political theorist has until now had only superficial or corrupt readers. The court of Rome has sternly prohibited his book. I can well believe it; it is the court he most clearly depicts."]

enjoyed under kings is worse than the disorders of the interregna.

What has been done to prevent these ills? In certain families, crowns have been made hereditary, and an order of succession has been established which prevents all dispute when kings die. That is to say, by substituting the disadvantage of regencies for that of elections, an apparent tranquillity has been preferred to a wise administration, the risk of having children, monsters, or imbeciles for leaders has been preferred to having to argue over the choice of good kings. No consideration has been given to the fact that in being thus exposed to the risk of the alternative, nearly all the odds are against them. There was a lot of sense in what Dionysius the Younger said in reply to his father, who, while reproaching his son for some shameful action, said "Have I given you such an example?" "Ah," replied the son, "but your father was not king."

When a man has been elevated to command others, everything conspires to deprive him of justice and reason. A great deal of effort is made, it is said, to teach young princes the art of ruling. It does not appear that this education does them any good. It would be better to begin by teaching them the art of obeying. The greatest kings whom history celebrates were not brought up to reign. It is a science one is never less in possession of than after one has learned too much, and that one acquires it better in obeying than in commanding. *For the most useful as well as the shortest method of finding out what is good and what is bad is to consider what you would have wished or not wished to have happened under another prince.*[24]

One result of this lack of coherence is the instability of the royal form of government, which, now regulated by one plan now by another according to the character of the ruling prince or of those who rule for him, cannot have a fixed object for very long or a consistent policy. This variation always causes the state to drift from maxim to maxim, from project to project, and does not take place in the other forms of government, where the prince is always the same.

It is also apparent that in general, if there is more cunning in a royal court, there is more wisdom in a senate; and that republics proceed toward their objectives by means of policies that are more consistent and better followed. On the other hand, each revolution in the ministry produces a revolution in the state, since the maxim common to all ministers and nearly all kings is to do the reverse of their predecessor in everything.

From this same incoherence we derive the solution to a sophism that is very familiar to royalist political theorists. Not only is civil government compared to domestic government and the prince to the father of the family (an error already refuted), but this magistrate is also liberally given all the virtues he might need, and it is always presupposed that the prince is what he ought to be. With the help of this presupposition, the royal form of government is obviously preferable to any other, since it is unquestionably the strongest; and it lacks only a corporate will that is more in conformity with the general will in order to be the best as well.

But if according to Plato,[25] a king by nature is such a rare person, how many times will nature and fortune converge to crown him; and if a royal education necessarily corrupts those who receive it, what is to be hoped from a series of men who have been brought up to reign? Surely then it is deliberate self-deception to confuse the royal form of government with that of a good king. To see what this form of government is in itself, we need to consider it under princes who are incompetent or wicked, for either they come to the throne wicked or incompetent, or else the throne makes them so.

These difficulties have not escaped the attention of our authors, but they have not been troubled by them. The remedy, they say, is to obey without a murmur. God in his anger gives us bad kings, and they must be endured as punishments from heaven. No doubt this sort of talk is edifying, however I do not know but that it belongs more in a pulpit than in a book on political theory. What is to be said of a physician who promises miracles, and whose art

---

[24] Tacitus, *Histories*, Book I. [Rousseau here quotes the Latin.]

[25] *The Statesman.*

consists entirely of exhorting his sick patient to practice patience? It is quite obvious that we must put up with a bad government when that is what we have. The question would be how to find a good one.

CHAPTER VII: On Mixed Government

Strictly speaking, there is no such thing as a simple form of government. A single leader must have subordinate magistrates; a popular government must have a leader. Thus in the distribution of the executive power there is always a gradation from the greater to the lesser number, with the difference that sometimes the greater number depends on the few, and sometimes the few depend on the greater number.

At times the distribution is equal, either when the constitutive parts are in a state of mutual dependence, as in the government of England; or when the authority of each part is independent but imperfect, as in Poland. This latter form is bad, since there is no unity in the government and the state lacks a bond of unity.

Which one is better, a simple or a mixed form of government? A question much debated among political theorists, to which the same reply must be given that I gave above regarding every form of government.

In itself the simple form of government is the best, precisely because it is simple. But when the executive power is not sufficiently dependent upon the legislative power, that is to say, when there is more of a ratio between the prince and the sovereign than between the people and the prince, this defect in the proportion must be remedied by dividing the government; for then all of its parts have no less authority over the subjects, and their division makes all of them together less forceful against the sovereign.

The same disadvantage can also be prevented through the establishment of intermediate magistrates, who, by being utterly separate from the government, serve merely to balance the two powers and to maintain their respective rights. In that case, the government is not mixed; it is tempered.

The opposite difficulty can be remedied by similar means. And when the government is too slack, tribunals can be set up to give it a concentrated focus.

This is done in all democracies. In the first case the government is divided in order to weaken it, and in the second to strengthen it. For the *maximum* of force and weakness are found equally in the simple forms of government, while the mixed forms of government provide an intermediate amount of strength.

CHAPTER VIII: That Not All Forms of Government Are Suited to All Countries

Since liberty is not a fruit of every climate, it is not within the reach of all peoples. The more one meditates on this principle established by Montesquieu, the more one is aware of its truth. The more one contests it, the more occasions there are for establishing it by means of new proofs.

In all the governments in the world, the public person consumes, but produces nothing. Whence therefore does it get the substance it consumes? It is from the labor of its members. It is the surplus of private individuals that produces what is needed by the public. Whence it follows that the civil state can subsist only so long as men's labor produces more than they need.

Now this surplus is not the same in every country in the world. In many countries it is considerable; in others it is moderate; in others it is nil; in still others it is negative.

This ratio depends on the fertility of the climate, the sort of labor the land requires, the nature of its products, the force of its inhabitants, the greater or lesser consumption they need, and many other similar ratios of which it is composed.

On the other hand, not all governments are of the same nature. They are more or less voracious; and the differences are founded on this added principle that the greater the distance the public contributions are from their source, the more onerous they are. It is not on the basis of the amount of the taxes that this burden is to be measured, but on the basis of the path they have to travel in order to return to the hands from which they came. When this circulation is prompt and well established, it is unimportant whether one pays little or a great deal. The populace is always rich and the finances are always in good shape. On the contrary, however little the populace gives, when this small amount does not return, it is soon wiped out by continual giving. The state is never rich and the populace is always destitute.

It follows from this that the greater the distance between the people and the government, the more onerous the taxes become. Thus in a democracy the populace is the least burdened; in an aristocracy it is more so; in a monarchy it bears the heaviest weight. Monarchy, therefore, is suited only to wealthy nations; aristocracy to states of moderate wealth and size; democracy to states that are small and poor.

In fact, the more one reflects on it, the more one finds in it the difference between free and monarchical states. In the former, everything is used for the common utility. In the latter, the public and private forces are reciprocal, the one being augmented by the weakening of the other. Finally, instead of governing subjects in order to make them happy, despotism makes them miserable in order to govern them.

Thus in each climate there are natural causes on the basis of which one can assign the form of government that the force of the climate requires, and can even say what kind of inhabitants it should have. Barren and unproductive lands, where the product is not worth the labor, ought to remain uncultivated and deserted, or peopled only by savages. Places where men's labor yields only what is necessary ought to be inhabited by barbarous peoples; in places such as these all polity would be impossible. Places where the surplus of products over labor is moderate are suited to free peoples. Those where an abundant and fertile soil produces a great deal in return for a small amount of labor require a monarchical form of government, in order that the subject's excess of surplus may be consumed by the prince's luxurious living. For it is better for this excess to be absorbed by the government than dissipated by private individuals. I realize that there are exceptions; but these exceptions themselves prove the rule, in that sooner or later they produce revolutions that restore things to the order of nature.

General laws should always be distinguished from the particular causes that can modify their effect. Even if the entire south were covered with republics and the entire north with despotic states, it would still be no less true that the effect of climate makes despotism suited to hot countries, barbarism to cold countries, and good polity to intermediate regions. I also realize that, while granting the principle, disputes may arise over its application. It could be said that there are cold countries that are very fertile and southern ones that are quite barren. But this poses a difficulty only for those who have not examined the thing in all its relationships. As I have said, it is necessary to take into account those of labor, force, consumption, and so on.

Let us suppose that there are two parcels of land of equal size, one of which yields five units and the other yields ten. If the inhabitants of the first parcel consume four units and the inhabitants of the second consume nine, the excess of the first will be one-fifth and that of the other will be one-tenth. Since the ratio of these two excesses is therefore the inverse of that of the products, the parcel of land that produces only five units will yield a surplus that is double that of the parcel of land that produces ten.

But it is not a question of a double product, and I do not believe that anyone dares, as a general rule, to place the fertility of a cold country even on an equal footing with that of hot countries. Nevertheless, let us assume that this equality does obtain. Let us, if you will, reckon England to be the equal of Sicily, and Poland the equal of Egypt. Further south we have Africa and the Indies; further north we have nothing at all. To achieve this equality of product, what difference must there be in agricultural techniques? In Sicily one needs merely to scratch the soil; in England what efforts it demands to work it! Now where more hands are needed to obtain the same product, the surplus ought necessarily to be less.

Consider too that the same number of men consumes much less in hot countries. The climate demands that a person keep sober in order to be in good health. Europeans wanting to live there just as they do at home would all die of dysentery and indigestion. *We are,* says Chardin, *carnivorous beasts, wolves, in comparison with the Asians. Some attribute the sobriety of the Persians to the fact that their land is less cultivated. On the contrary, I believe that this country is less abundant in commodities because the inhabitants need less. If their frugality, he continues, were an effect of the country's scarcity, only the poor would eat little; however, it is generally the case that everyone does so. And more or less would be eaten in each province according to the fertility of the country; however, the same sobriety is found throughout the kingdom. They take great pride in their lifestyle, saying that one has only to look at their complexions to recognize how far it excels that of the Christians. In fact, the complexion of the Persians is clear. They have fair skin, fine and polished, whereas the complexion of their Armenian subjects, who live in the European style, is coarse and blotchy, and their bodies are fat and heavy.*

The closer you come to the equator, the less people live on. They rarely eat meat; rice, maize, couscous, millet and cassava are their usual diet. In the Indies there are millions of men whose sustenance costs less than a penny a day. In Europe itself we see noticeable differences in appetite between the peoples of the north and the south. A Spaniard will live for eight days on a German's dinner. In countries where men are the most voracious, luxury too turns toward things edible. In England, luxury is shown in a table loaded with meats; in Italy you are regaled on sugar and flowers.

Luxury in clothing also offers similar differences. In the climate where the seasonal changes are sudden and violent, people have better and simpler clothing. In climates where people clothe themselves merely for ornamental purposes, flashiness is more sought after than utility. The clothes themselves are a luxury there. In Naples you see men strolling everyday along the Posilippo decked out in gold-embroidered coats and bare legged. It is the same with buildings; magnificence is the sole consideration when there is nothing to fear from the weather. In Paris or London, people want to be housed warmly and comfortably. In Madrid, there are superb salons, but no windows that close, and people sleep in rat holes.

In hot countries foodstuffs are considerably more substantial and succulent. This is a third difference which cannot help but influence the second. Why do people eat so many vegetables in Italy? Because there they are good, nourishing, and have an excellent flavor. In France, where they are fed nothing but water, they are not nourishing at all, and are nearly counted for nothing at table. Be that as it may, they occupy no less land and cost at least as much effort to cultivate. It is a known fact that the wheats of Barbary, in other respects inferior to those of France, yield far more flour, and that those of France, for their part, yield more wheats than those of the north. It can be inferred from this that a similar gradation in the same direction is generally observed from the equator to the pole. Now is it not a distinct disadvantage to have a smaller quantity of food in an equal amount of produce?

To all these different considerations, I can add one which depends on and strengthens them. It is that hot countries have less of a need for inhabitants than do cold countries, and yet could feed more of them. This produces a double surplus, always to the advantage of despotism. The greater the area occupied by the same number of inhabitants, the more difficult it becomes to revolt, since concerted action cannot be taken promptly and secretly; and it is always easy for the government to discover plots and cut off communications. But the closer together a numerous people is drawn, the less the government can usurp from the sovereign. The leaders deliberate as safely in their rooms as the prince does in his council; and the crowd assembles as quickly in public squares as do troops in their quarters. In this regard, the advantage of a tyrannical government, therefore, is that of acting over great distances. With the help of the points of support it establishes, its force increases with distance like that of levers.[26] On the other hand, the strength of the people acts only when concentrated; it evaporates and is lost as it spreads, like the effect of gunpowder scattered on the ground, which catches fire only

[26] This does not contradict what I said earlier in Book II, Chapter IX, regarding the disadvantages of large states, for there it was a question of the authority of the government over its members, and here it is a question of its force against the subjects. Its scattered members serve it as points of support for acting from a distance upon the people, but it has no support for acting directly on these members themselves. Thus in the one case the length of the lever causes its weakness, and in the other case its force.

one grain at a time. The least populated countries are thus the best suited for tyranny. Ferocious animals reign only in deserts.

CHAPTER IX: On the Signs of a Good Government

When the question arises which one is absolutely the best government, an insoluble question is being raised because it is indeterminate. Or, if you wish, it has as many good answers as there are possible combinations in the absolute and relative positions of peoples.

But if it is asked by what sign it is possible to know that a given people is well or poorly governed, this is another matter, and the question of fact could be resolved.

However, nothing is answered, since each wants to answer it in his own way. The subjects praise public tranquillity; the citizens praise the liberty of private individuals. The former prefers the security of possessions; the latter that of persons. The former has it that the best government is the one that is most severe; the latter maintains that the best government is the one that is mildest. This one wants crimes to be punished, and that one wants them prevented. The former think it a good thing to be feared by their neighbors; the latter prefer to be ignored by them. The one is content so long as money circulates; the other demands that the people have bread. Even if agreement were had on these and similar points, would we be any closer to an answer? Since moral quantities do not allow of precise measurement, even if there were agreement regarding the sign, how could there be agreement regarding the evaluation.

For my part, I am always astonished that such a simple sign is overlooked or that people are of such bad faith as not to agree on it. What is the goal of the political association? It is the preservation and prosperity of its members. And what is the surest sign that they are preserved and prospering? It is their number and their population. Therefore do not go looking elsewhere for this much disputed sign. All other things being equal, the government under which, without external means, without naturaliza-

tions, without colonies, the citizens become populous and multiply the most, is infallibly the best government. That government under which a populace diminishes and dies out is the worst. Calculators, it is now up to you. Count, measure, compare.[27]

CHAPTER X: On the Abuse of Government and Its Tendency to Degenerate

Just as the private will acts constantly against the general will, so the government makes a continual

[27] We should judge on this same principle the centuries that merit preference with respect to the prosperity of the human race. Those in which letters and arts are known to have flourished have been admired too much, without penetrating the secret object of their cultivation, and without considering its devastating effect, *and this was called humanity by the inexperienced, when it was a part of servitude.* [Rousseau here quotes Tacitus, *Agricola*, 21, in Latin.] Will we never see in the maxims of books the crude interest that causes the authors to speak? No. Whatever they may say, when a country is depopulated, it is not true, despite its brilliance, that all goes well; and the fact that a poet has an income of a hundred thousand livres is not sufficient to make his century the best of all. The apparent calm and tranquillity of the leader ought to be less of an object of consideration than the well-being of whole nations and especially of the most populous states. A hailstorm may devastate a few cantons, but it rarely causes famine. Riots and civil wars may greatly disturb the leaders, but they are not the true misfortunes of the people, who may even have a reprieve while people argue over who will tyrannize them. It is their permanent condition that causes real periods of prosperity or calamity. It is when everything remains crushed under the yoke that everything decays. It is then that the leaders destroy them at will, *where they bring about solitude they call it peace.* [Rousseau here quotes Tacitus, *Agricola*, 31, in Latin.] When the quarrels of the great disturbed the kingdom of France, and the Coadjutor of Paris brought with him to the Parliament a knife in his pocket, this did not keep the French people from living happily and in great numbers in a free and decent ease. Long ago, Greece flourished in the midst of the cruelest wars. Blood flowed in waves, and the whole country was covered with men. It seemed, says Machiavelli, that in the midst of murders, proscriptions, and civil wars, our republic became more powerful; the

effort against sovereignty. The more this effort increases, the more the constitution is altered. And since there is here no other corporate will which, by resisting the will of the prince, would create an equilibrium with it, sooner or later the prince must finally oppress the sovereign and break the social treaty. That is the inherent and inevitable vice which, from the birth of the body politic, tends unceasingly to destroy it, just as old age and death destroy the human body.

There are two general ways in which a government degenerates, namely, when it shrinks, or when the state dissolves.

The government shrinks when it passes from a large to a small number, that is to say, from democracy to aristocracy, and from aristocracy to royalty. That is its natural inclination.[28] If it were to go backward from a small number to a large number, it could be said to slacken, but this reverse progression is impossible.

In fact, the government never changes its form except when its exhausted energy leaves it too enfeebled to be capable of preserving what belongs to it. Now if it were to become still more slack while it expanded, its force would become entirely nil; it would be still less likely to subsist. It must therefore wind up and tighten its force in proportion as it gives way; otherwise the state it sustains would fall into ruin.

The dissolution of the state can come about in two ways.

First, when the prince no longer administers the state in accordance with the laws and usurps the sovereign power. In that case a remarkable change takes place, namely that it is not the government but the state that shrinks. I mean that the state as a whole is dissolved, and another is formed inside it, composed exclusively of the members of the government, and which is no longer anything for the rest of the populace but its master and tyrant. So that the instant that the government usurps sovereignty, the social compact is broken, and all ordinary citizens, on recov-

---

virtue of its citizens, their mores, and their independence did more to reinforce it than all its dissensions did to weaken it. A little agitation gives strength to souls, and what truly brings about prosperity for the species is not so much peace as liberty.

[28] The slow formation and the progress of the Republic of Venice in its lagoons offers a notable example of this succession. And it is rather astonishing that after more than twelve hundred years the Venetians seem to be no further than the second stage, which began with *Serrar di Consiglio* in 1198. As for the ancient dukes, for whom the Venetians are reproached, whatever the *squitinio della libertà veneta* may say about them, it has been proved that they were not their sovereigns.

The Roman Republic does not fail to be brought forward as an objection against me, which, it will be said, followed a completely opposite course, passing from monarchy to aristocracy to democracy. I am quite far from thinking of it in this way.

The first establishment of Romulus was a mixed government that promptly degenerated into despotism. For some particular reasons, the state perished before its time, just as one sees a newborn die before reaching manhood. The expulsion of the Tarquins was the true epoch of the birth of the republic. But it did not at first take on a constant form, because in failing to abolish the patriciate, only half the work was completed. For in this way, since hereditary aristocracy, which is the worst of all forms of legitimate administration, remained in conflict with democracy, a form of government that is always uncertain and adrift, it was not determined, as Machiavelli has proved, until the establishment of the tribunes. It was only then that there was a true government and a veritable democracy. In fact, the populace then was not merely sovereign but also magistrate and judge. The senate was merely a subordinate tribunal whose purpose was to temper and concentrate the government; and the consuls themselves, though they were patricians, magistrates, and absolute generals in war, in Rome were merely presidents of the people.

From that point on, the government was also seen to follow its natural inclination and to tend strongly toward aristocracy. With the patriciate having abolished itself, as it were, the aristocracy was no longer in the body of patricians, as it was in Venice and Genoa, but in the body of the senate which was composed of patricians and plebeians, and even in the body of the tribunes when they began to usurp an active power. For words do not affect things, and when the populace has leaders who govern for it, it is always an aristocracy, regardless of the name these leaders bear.

The abuse of aristocracy gave birth to civil wars and the triumvirate. Sulla, Julius Caesar, and Augustus became in fact veritable monarchs, and finally, under the despotism of Tiberius, the state was dissolved. Roman history therefore does not invalidate my principle; it confirms it.

ering by right their natural liberty, are forced but not
obliged to obey.

The same thing happens also when the members
of the government separately usurp the power they
should only exercise as a body. This is no less an
infraction of the laws, and produces even greater disorder. Under these circumstances, there are, so to speak,
as many princes as magistrates, and the state, no less
divided than the government, perishes or changes
its form.

When the state dissolves, the abuse of government,
whatever it is, takes the common name *anarchy*. To
distinguish, democracy degenerates into *ochlocracy*,
aristocracy into *oligarchy*. I would add that royalty
degenerates into *tyranny*, however this latter term is
equivocal and requires an explanation.

In the ordinary sense a tyrant is a king who governs
with violence and without regard for justice and the
laws. In the strict sense, a tyrant is a private individual
who arrogates to himself royal authority without having any right to it. This is how the Greeks understood
the word tyrant. They gave the name indifferently
to good and bad princes whose authority was not
legitimate.[29] Thus *tyrant* and *usurper* are two perfectly
synonymous words.

To give different names to different things, I call
the usurper of royal authority a *tyrant*, and the usurper
of sovereign power a *despot*. The tyrant is someone
who intrudes himself, contrary to the laws, in order
to govern according to the laws. The despot is someone who places himself above the laws themselves.
Thus the tyrant cannot be a despot, but the despot
is always a tyrant.

---

[29] *For all are considered and are called tyrants who use
perpetual power in a city accustomed to liberty.* [Rousseau
here quotes the Latin.] Cornelius Nepos, *Life of Miltiades*.
It is true that Aristotle, *Nicomachean Ethics*, Book XVIII,
Chapter 10, distinguishes between a tyrant and a king, in
that the former governs for his own utility and the latter
governs only for the utility of his subjects. But besides the
fact that generally all the Greek authors used the word tyrant
in another sense, as appears most clearly in Xenophon's
Hiero, it would follow from Aristotle's distinction that there
has not yet been a single king since the beginning of the
world.

CHAPTER XI: On the Death of the Body Politic

Such is the natural and inevitable tendency of the
best constituted governments. If Sparta and Rome
perished, what state can hope to last forever? If we
wish to form a durable establishment, let us then not
dream of making it eternal. To succeed, one must not
attempt the impossible or flatter oneself with giving to
the work of men a solidity that things human do
not allow.

The body politic, like the human body, begins to
die from the very moment of its birth, and carries
within itself the causes of its destruction. But both
can have a constitution that is more or less robust
and suited to preserve them for a longer or shorter
time. The constitution of man is the work of nature;
the constitution of the state is the work of art. It is
not within men's power to prolong their lives; it is
within their power to prolong the life of the state as
far as possible, by giving it the best constitution it can
have. The best constituted state will come to an end,
but later than another, if no unforeseen accident
brings about its premature fall.

The principle of political life is in the sovereign
authority. Legislative power is the heart of the state;
the executive power is the brain, which gives movement to all the parts. The brain can fall into paralysis
and yet the individual may still live. A man may
remain an imbecile and live. But once the heart has
ceased its functions, the animal is dead.

It is not through laws that the state subsists; it is
through legislative power. Yesterday's law does not
obligate today, but tacit consent is presumed from
silence, and the sovereign is taken to be giving incessant confirmation to the laws it does not abrogate
while having the power to do so. Whatever it has once
declared it wants, it always wants, unless it revokes its
declaration.

Why then is so much respect paid to ancient laws?
For just this very reason. We must believe that nothing
but the excellence of the ancient wills that could
have preserved them for so long. If the sovereign
had not constantly recognized them to be salutary, it
would have revoked them a thousand times. This is

why, far from growing weak, the laws continually acquire new force in every well constituted state. The prejudice in favor of antiquity each day renders them more venerable. On the other hand, wherever the laws weaken as they grow old, this proves that there is no longer a legislative power, and that the state is no longer alive.

CHAPTER XII: How the Sovereign Authority Is Maintained

The sovereign, having no other force than legislative power, acts only through the laws. And since the laws are only authentic acts of the general will, the sovereign can act only when the populace is assembled. With the populace assembled, it will be said: what a chimera! It is a chimera today, but two thousand years ago it was not. Have men changed their nature?

The boundaries of what is possible in moral matters are less narrow than we think. It is our weaknesses, our vices and our prejudices that shrink them. Base souls do not believe in great men; vile slaves smile with an air of mockery at the word liberty.

Let us consider what can be done in the light of what has been done. I will not speak of the ancient republics of Greece; however, the Roman Republic was, to my mind, a great state, and the town of Rome was a great town. The last census in Rome gave four thousand citizens bearing arms, and the last census count of the empire gave four million citizens, not counting subjects, foreigners, women, children, and slaves.

What difficulty might not be imagined in frequently calling assemblies of the immense populace of that capital and its environs. Nevertheless, few weeks passed by without the Roman people being assembled, and even several times in one week. It exercised not only the rights of sovereignty but also a part of those of the government. It took care of certain matters of public business; it tried certain cases; and this entire populace was in the public meeting place hardly less often as magistrate than as citizen.

In looking back to the earliest history of nations, one would find that most of the ancient governments, even the monarchical ones such as those of the Macedonians and the Franks, had similar councils. Be that as it may, this lone contestable fact answers every difficulty: arguing from the actual to the possible seems like good logic to me.

CHAPTER XIII: Continuation

It is not enough for an assembled people to have once determined the constitution of the state by sanctioning a body of laws. It is not enough for it to have established a perpetual government or to have provided once and for all for the election of magistrates. In addition to the extraordinary assemblies that unforeseen situations can necessitate, there must be some fixed, periodic assemblies that nothing can abolish or prorogue, so that on a specified day the populace is rightfully convened by law, without the need for any other formal convocation.

But apart from these assemblies which are lawful by their date alone, any assembly of the people that has not been convened by the magistrates appointed for that task and in accordance with the prescribed forms should be regarded as illegitimate, and all that takes place there should be regarded as null, since the order itself to assemble ought to emanate from the law.

As to the question of the greater or lesser frequency of legitimate assemblies, this depends on so many considerations that no precise rules can be given about it. All that can be said is that in general the more force a government has, the more frequently the sovereign ought to show itself.

I will be told that this may be fine for a single town, but what is to be done when the state includes several? Will the sovereign authority be divided, or will it be concentrated in a single town with all the rest made subject to it?

I answer that neither should be done. In the first place, the sovereign authority is simple and one; it cannot be divided without being destroyed. In the second place, a town cannot legitimately be in subjection to another town, any more than a nation can be in subjection to another nation, since the essence of the body politic consists in the harmony of obedience and liberty; and the words *subject* and *sovereign* are identical correlatives, whose meaning is combined in the single word "citizen."

I answer further that it is always an evil to unite several towns in a single city, and that anyone wanting to bring about this union should not expect to avoid its natural disadvantages. The abuses of large states should not be raised as an objection against someone who wants only small ones. But how are small states to be given enough force to resist the large ones, just as the Greek cities long ago resisted a great king, and more recently Holland and Switzerland have resisted the house of Austria?

Nevertheless, if the state cannot be reduced to appropriate boundaries, one expedient still remains: not to allow a fixed capital, to make the seat of government move from one town to another, and to assemble the estates of the country in each of them in their turn.

Populate the territory uniformly, extend the same rights everywhere, spread abundance and life all over. In this way the state will become simultaneously as strong and as well governed as possible. Recall that town walls are made from the mere debris of rural houses. With each palace I see being erected in the capital, I believe I see an entire countryside turned into hovels.

CHAPTER XIV: Continuation

Once the populace is legitimately assembled as a sovereign body, all jurisdiction of the government ceases; the executive power is suspended, and the person of the humblest citizen is as sacred and inviolable as that of the first magistrate, for where those who are represented are found, there is no longer any representative. Most of the tumults that arose in the comitia in Rome were due to ignorance or neglect of this rule. On such occasions the consuls were merely the presidents of the people; the tribunes, ordinary speakers;[30] the senate, nothing at all.

These intervals of suspension, during which the prince recognizes or ought to recognize an actual superior, have always been disturbing to him. And these assemblies of the people, which are the aegis of the body politic and the curb on the government, have at all times been the horror of leaders. Thus they never spare efforts, objections, difficulties, or promises to keep the citizens from having them. When the citizens were greedy, cowardly, and pusillanimous, more enamored of repose than with liberty, they do not hold out very long against the redoubled efforts of the government. Thus it is that, as the resisting force constantly grows, the sovereign authority finally vanishes, and the majority of the cities fall and perish prematurely.

But between the sovereign authority and arbitrary government, there sometimes is introduced an intermediate power about which we must speak.

CHAPTER XV: On Deputies or Representatives

Once public service ceases to be the chief business of the citizens, and they prefer to serve with their wallet rather than with their person, the state is already near its ruin. Is it necessary to march off to battle? They pay mercenary troops and stay at home. Is it necessary to go to the council? They name deputies and stay at home. By dint of laziness and money, they finally have soldiers to enslave the country and representatives to sell it.

The hustle and bustle of commerce and the arts, the avid interest in profits, softness and the love of amenities: these are what change personal services into money. A person gives up part of his profit in order to increase it at leisure. Give money and soon you will be in chains. The word *finance* is a slave's word. It is unknown in the city. In a truly free state the citizens do everything with their own hands and nothing with money. Far from paying to be exempted from their duties, they would pay to fulfill them them-

---

[30] In nearly the same sense as is given this word in English Parliament. The similarity between these activities would have put the consuls and the tribunes in conflict, even if all jurisdiction had been suspended.

selves. Far be it from me to be sharing commonly held ideas. I believe that forced labor is less opposed to liberty than are taxes.

The better a state is constituted, the more public business takes precedence over private business in the minds of the citizens. There even is far less private business, since, with the sum of common happiness providing a more considerable portion of each individual's happiness, less remains for him to look for through private efforts. In a well run city everyone flies to the assemblies; under a bad government no one wants to take a step to get to them, since no one takes an interest in what happens there, for it is predictable that the general will will not predominate, and that in the end domestic concerns absorb everything. Good laws lead to making better laws; bad laws bring about worse ones. Once someone says *what do I care?* about the affairs of state, the state should be considered lost.

The cooling off of patriotism, the activity of private interest, the largeness of states, conquests, the abuse of government: these have suggested the route of using deputies or representatives of the people in the nation's assemblies. It is what in certain countries is called the third estate. Thus the private interest of two orders is given first and second place; the public interest is given merely third place.

Sovereignty cannot be represented for the same reason that it cannot be alienated. It consists essentially in the general will, and the will does not allow of being represented. It is either itself or something else; there is nothing in between. The deputies of the people, therefore, neither are nor can be its representatives; they are merely its agents. They cannot conclude anything definitively. Any law that the populace has not ratified in person is null; it is not a law at all. The English people believes itself to be free. It is greatly mistaken; it is free only during the election of the members of Parliament. Once they are elected, the populace is enslaved; it is nothing. The use the English people makes of that freedom in the brief moments of its liberty certainly warrants their losing it.

The idea of representatives is modern. It comes to us from feudal government, that iniquitous and absurd government in which the human race is degraded and the name of man is in dishonor. In the ancient republics and even in monarchies, the people never had representatives. The word itself was unknown. It is quite remarkable that in Rome where the tribunes were so sacred, no one even imagined that they could usurp the functions of the people, and that in the midst of such a great multitude, they never tried to pass a single plebiscite on their own authority. However, we can size up the difficulties that were sometimes caused by the crowd by what took place in the time of the Gracchi, when part of the citizenry voted from the rooftops.

Where right and liberty are everything, inconveniences are nothing. In the care of this wise people, everything was handled correctly. It allowed its lictors to do what its tribunes would not have dared to do. It had no fear that its lictors would want to represent it.

However, to explain how the tribunes sometimes represented it, it is enough to conceive how the government represents the sovereign. Since the law is merely the declaration of the general will, it is clear that the people cannot be represented in the legislative power. But it can and should be represented in the executive power, which is merely force applied to the law. This demonstrates that, on close examination, very few nations would be found to have laws. Be that as it may, it is certain that, since they have no share in the executive power, the tribunes could never represent the Roman people by the rights of their office, but only by usurping those of the senate.

Among the Greeks, whatever the populace had to do, it did by itself. It was constantly assembled at the public square. It inhabited a mild climate; it was not greedy; its slaves did the work; its chief item of business was its liberty. No longer having the same advantages, how are the same rights to be preserved? Your harsher climates cause you to have more needs;[31] six months out of the year the public square is uninhabi-

---

[31] To adopt in cold countries the luxury and softness of the orientals is to desire to be given their chains; it is submitting to these with even greater necessity than they did.

table; your muted tongues cannot make themselves understood in the open air; you pay more attention to your profits than to your liberty; and you are less fearful of slavery than you are of misery.

What! Can liberty be maintained only with the support of servitude? Perhaps. The two extremes meet. Everything that is not in nature has its drawbacks, and civil society more so than all the rest. There are some unfortunate circumstances where one's liberty can be preserved only at the expense of someone else's, and where the citizen can be perfectly free only if the slave is completely enslaved. Such was the situation in Sparta. As for you, modern peoples, you do not have slaves, but you yourselves are slaves. You pay for their liberty with your own. It is in vain that you crow about that preference. I find more cowardice in it than humanity.

I do not mean by all this that having slaves is necessary, nor that the right of slavery is legitimate, for I have proved the contrary. I am merely stating the reasons why modern peoples who believe themselves free have representatives, and why ancient peoples did not have them. Be that as it may, the moment a people gives itself representatives, it is no longer free; it no longer exists.

All things considered, I do not see that it is possible henceforth for the sovereign to preserve among us the exercise of its rights, unless the city is very small. But if it is very small, will it be subjugated? No. I will show later[32] how the external power of a great people can be combined with the ease of administration and the good order of a small state.

CHAPTER XVI: That the Institution of Government Is Not a Contract

Once the legislative power has been well established, it is a matter of establishing the executive power in the same way. For this latter, which functions only by means of particular acts, not being of the essence

of the former, is naturally separate from it. Were it possible for the sovereign, considered as such, to have the executive power, right and fact would be so completely confounded that we would no longer know what is law and what is not. And the body politic, thus denatured, would soon fall prey to the violence against which it was instituted.

Since the citizens are all equal by the social contract, what everyone should do can be prescribed by everyone. On the other hand, no one has the right to demand that someone else do what he does not do for himself. Now it is precisely this right, indispensable for making the body politic live and move, that the sovereign gives the prince in instituting the government.

Several people have claimed that this act of establishment was a contract between the populace and the leaders it gives itself, a contract by which are stipulated between the two parties the conditions under which the one obliges itself to command and the other to obey. It will be granted, I am sure, that this is a strange way of entering into a social contract! But let us see if this opinion is tenable.

First, the supreme authority cannot be modified any more than it can be alienated; to limit it is to destroy it. It is absurd and contradictory for the sovereign to acquire a superior. To obligate oneself to obey a master is to return to full liberty.

Moreover, it is evident that this contract between the people and some or other persons would be a particular act. Whence it follows that this contract could be neither a law nor an act of sovereignty, and that consequently it would be illegitimate.

It is also clear that the contracting parties would, in relation to one another, be under only the law of nature and without any guarantee of their reciprocal commitments, which is contrary in every way to the civil state. Since the one who has force at his disposal is always in control of its employment, it would come to the same thing if we were to give the name contract to the act of a man who would say to another, "I am giving you all my goods, on the condition that you give me back whatever you wish."

There is only one contract in the state, that of the association, and that alone excludes any other. It is

---

[32] This is what I intended to do in the rest of this work, when in treating external relations I would have come to confederations. An entirely new subject, and its principles have yet to be established.

impossible to imagine any public contract that was not a violation of the first contract.

CHAPTER XVII: On the Institution of the Government

What should be the terms under which we should conceive the act by which the government is instituted? I will begin by saying that this act is complex or composed of two others, namely the establishment of the law and the execution of the law.

By the first, the sovereign decrees that there will be a governing body established under some or other form. And it is clear that this act is a law.

By the second, the people names the leaders who will be placed in charge of the established government. And since this nomination is a particular act, it is not a second law, but merely a consequence of the first and a function of the government.

The problem is to understand how there can be an act of government before a government exists, and how the people, which is only sovereign or subject, can in certain circumstances become prince or magistrate.

Moreover, it is here that we discover one of those remarkable properties of the body politic, by which it reconciles seemingly contradictory operations. For this takes place by a sudden conversion of sovereignty into democracy, so that, without any noticeable change, and solely by a new relation of all to all, the citizens, having become magistrates, pass from general to particular acts, and from the law to its execution.

This change of relation is not a speculative subtlety without exemplification in practice. It takes place everyday in the English Parliament, where the lower chamber on certain occasions turns itself into a committee of the whole in order to discuss better the business of the sovereign court, thus becoming the simple commission of the sovereign court (the latter being what it was the moment before), so that it later reports to itself, as the House of Commons, the result of what it has just settled in the committee of the whole, and deliberates all over again under one title about what it had already settled under another.

The peculiar advantage to democratic government is that it can be established in actual fact by a simple act of the general will. After this, the provisional government remains in power, if this is the form adopted, or establishes in the name of the sovereign the government prescribed by the law; and thus everything is in accordance with the rule. It is not possible to institute the government in any other legitimate way without renouncing the principles established above.

CHAPTER XVIII: The Means of Preventing Usurpations of the Government

From these clarifications, it follows, in confirmation of Chapter XVI, that the act that institutes the government is not a contract but a law; that the trustees of the executive power are not the masters of the populace but its officers; that it can establish and remove them when it pleases; that for them there is no question of contracting, but of obeying; and that in taking on the functions the state imposes on them, they merely fulfill their duty as citizens, without in any way having the right to dispute over the conditions.

Thus, when it happens that the populace institutes a hereditary government, whether it is monarchical within a single family or aristocratic within a class of citizens, this is not a commitment it is entering. It is a provisional form that it gives the administration, until the populace is pleased to order it otherwise.

It is true that these changes are always dangerous, and that the established government should never be touched except when it becomes incompatible with the public good. But this circumspection is a maxim of politics and not a rule of law [droit], and the state is no more bound to leave civil authority to its leaders than it is to leave military authority to its generals.

Again, it is true that in such cases it is impossible to be too careful about observing all the formalities required in order to distinguish a regular and legitimate act from a seditious tumult, and the will of an entire people from the clamor of a faction. And it is here above all that one must not grant anything to odious cases except what cannot be refused according to the full rigor of the law [droit]. And it is also from this obligation that the prince derives a great advantage in preserving his power in spite of the people, without anyone being able to say that he has usurped it. For in appearing to use only his rights, it is quite easy for him to extend them, and under the pretext of public peace, to prevent assemblies destined to reestablish good order. Thus he avails himself of a silence he keeps from being broken, or of irregularities he causes to be committed, to assume that the opinion of those who are silenced by fear is supportive of him, and to punish those who dare to speak. This is how the decemvirs, having been first elected for one year and then continued for another year, tried to retain their power in perpetuity by no longer permitting the comitia to assemble. And it is by this simple means that all the governments of the world, once armed with the public force, sooner or later usurp the public authority.

The periodic assemblies I have spoken of earlier are suited to the prevention or postponement of this misfortune, especially when they have no need for a formal convocation. For then the prince could not prevent them without openly declaring himself a violator of the laws and an enemy of the state.

The opening of these assemblies, which have as their sole object the preservation of the social treaty, should always take place through two propositions which can never be suppressed, and which are voted on separately:

The first: *Does it please the sovereign to preserve the present form of government?*

The second: *Does it please the people to leave its administration to those who are now in charge of it?*

I am presupposing here what I believe I have demonstrated, namely that in the state there is no fundamental law that cannot be revoked, not even the social compact. For if all the citizens were to assemble in order to break this compact by common agreement, no one could doubt that it was legitimately broken. Grotius even thinks that each person can renounce the state of which he is a member and recover his natural liberty and his goods by leaving the country.[33]

But it would be absurd that all the citizens together could not do what each of them can do separately.

END OF THE THIRD BOOK

BOOK IV

CHAPTER I: That the General Will Is Indestructible

So long as several men together consider themselves to be a single body, they have but a single will, which is concerned with their common preservation and the general well-being. Then all the energies of the state are vigorous and simple; its maxims are clear and luminous; there are no entangled, contradictory interests; the common good is clearly apparent everywhere, demanding only good sense in order to be perceived. Peace, union, equality are enemies of political subtleties. Upright and simple men are difficult to deceive on account of their simplicity. Traps and clever pretexts do not fool them. They are not even clever enough to be duped. When, among the happiest people in the world, bands of peasants are seen regulating their affairs of state under an oak tree, and always acting wisely, can one help scorning the refinements of other nations, which make themselves illustrious and miserable with so much art and mystery?

A state thus governed needs very few laws; and in proportion as it becomes necessary to promulgate new ones, this necessity is universally understood. The first to propose them merely says what everybody has already felt; and there is no question of either intrigues or eloquence to secure the passage into law of what each has already resolved to do, once he is sure the others will do likewise.

What misleads argumentative types is the fact that, since they take into account only the states that were badly constituted from the beginning, they are struck by the impossibility of maintaining such an adminis-

---

[33] On the understanding that one does not leave in order to evade one's duty and to be exempt from serving the homeland the moment it needs us. In such circumstances, taking flight would be criminal and punishable; it would no longer be withdrawal, but desertion.

tration. They laugh when they imagine all the foolishness a clever knave or a sly orator could get the people of Paris or London to believe. They do not know that Cromwell would have been sentenced to hard labor by the people of Berne, and the Duc de Beaufort imprisoned by the Genevans.

But when the social bond begins to relax and the state to grow weak, when private interests begin to make themselves felt and small societies begin to influence the large one, the common interest changes and finds opponents. Unanimity no longer reigns in the votes; the general will is no longer the will of all. Contradictions and debates arise, and the best advice does not pass without disputes.

Finally, when the state, on the verge of ruin, subsists only in an illusory and vain form, when the social bond of unity is broken in all hearts, when the meanest interest brazenly appropriates the sacred name of the public good, then the general will becomes mute. Everyone, guided by secret motives, no more express their opinions as citizens than if the state had never existed; and iniquitous decrees having as their sole purpose the private interest are falsely passed under the name of laws.

Does it follow from this that the general will is annihilated or corrupted? No, it is always constant, unalterable and pure; but it is subordinate to other wills that prevail over it. Each man, in detaching his interest from the common interest, clearly sees that he cannot totally separate himself from it; but his share of the public misfortune seems insignificant to him compared to the exclusive good he intends to make his own. Apart from this private good, he wants the general good in his own interest, just as strongly as anyone else. Even in selling his vote for money he does not extinguish the general will in himself; he evades it. The error he commits is that of changing the thrust of the question and answering a different question from the one he was asked. Thus, instead of saying through his vote *it is advantageous to the state*, he says *it is advantageous to this man or that party that this or that view should pass*. Thus the law of the public order in the assemblies is not so much to maintain the general will, as to bring it about that it is always questioned and that it always answers.

I could present here a number of reflections about the simple right to vote in every act of sovereignty, a right that nothing can take away from the citizens; and on the right to state an opinion, to offer proposals, to divide, to discuss, which the government always takes great care to allow only to its members. But this important subject would require a separate treatise, and I cannot say everything in this one.

CHAPTER II: On Voting

It is clear from the preceding chapter that the manner in which general business is taken care of can provide a rather accurate indication of the present state of mores and of the health of the body politic. The more harmony reigns in the assemblies, that is to say, the closer opinions come to unanimity, the more dominant too is the general will. But long debates, dissensions, and tumult betoken the ascendance of private interests and the decline of the state.

This seems less evident when two or more orders enter into its constitution, as had been done in Rome by the patricians and the plebeians, whose quarrels often disturbed the comitia, even in the best of times in the Republic. But this exception is more apparent than real. For then, by the vice inherent in the body politic, there are, as it were, two states in one. What is not true of the two together is true of each of them separately. And indeed even in the most tumultuous times, the plebiscites of the people, when the senate did not interfere with them, always passed quietly and by a large majority of votes. Since the citizens have but one interest, the people had but one will.

At the other extreme of the circle, unanimity returns. It is when the citizens, having fallen into servitude, no longer have either liberty or will. Then fear and flattery turn voting into acclamations. People no longer deliberate; either they adore or they curse. Such was the vile manner in which the senate expressed its opinions under the emperors; sometimes it did so with ridiculous precautions. Tacitus observes that under Otho, the senators, while heaping curses upon Vitellius, contrived at the same time to make a frightening noise, so that, if by chance he became master, he would be unable to know what each of them had said.

From these various considerations there arise the maxims by which the manner of counting votes and comparing opinions should be regulated, depending on whether the general will is more or less easy to know and the state more or less in decline.

There is but one law that by its nature requires unanimous consent. This is the social compact. For civil association is the most voluntary act in the world. Since every man is born free and master of himself, no one can, under any pretext whatever, place another under subjection without his consent. To decide that the son of a slave is born a slave is to decide that he was not a man.

If, therefore, at the time of the social compact, there are opponents to it, their opposition does not invalidate the contract; it merely prevents them from being included in it. They are foreigners among citizens. Once the state is instituted, residency implies consent. To inhabit the territory is to submit to sovereignty.[34]

Aside from this primitive contract, the vote of the majority always obligates all the others. This is a consequence of the contract itself. But it is asked how a man can be both free and forced to conform to wills that are not his own. How can the opponents be both free and be placed in subjection to laws to which they have not consented?

I answer that the question is not put properly. The citizen consents to all the laws, even to those that pass in spite of his opposition, and even to those that punish him when he dares to violate any of them. The constant will of all the members of the state is the general will; through it they are citizens and free.[35]

When a law is proposed in the people's assembly, what is asked of them is not precisely whether they approve or reject, but whether or not it conforms to the general will that is theirs. Each man, in giving his vote, states his opinion on this matter, and the declaration of the general will is drawn from the counting of votes. When, therefore, the opinion contrary to mine prevails, this proves merely that I was in error, and that what I took to be the general will was not so. If my private opinion had prevailed, I would have done something other than what I had wanted. In that case I would not have been free.

This presupposes, it is true, that all the characteristics of the general will are still in the majority. When they cease to be free, there is no longer any liberty regardless of the side one takes.

In showing earlier how private wills were substituted for the general will in public deliberations, I have given an adequate indication of the possible ways of preventing this abuse. I will discuss this again at a later time. With respect to the proportional number of votes needed to declare this will, I have also given the principles on the basis of which it can be determined. The differences of a single vote breaks a tie vote; a single opponent destroys a unanimous vote. But between a unanimous and a tie vote there are several unequal divisions, at any of which this proportionate number can be fixed in accordance with the condition and needs of the body politic.

Two general maxims can serve to regulate these ratios. One, that the more important and serious the deliberations are, the closer the prevailing opinion should be to unanimity. The other, that the more the matter at hand calls for alacrity, the smaller the prescribed difference in the division of opinion should be. In decisions that must be reached immediately, a majority of a single vote should suffice. The first of these maxims seems more suited to the laws, and the second to public business. Be that as it may, it is the combination of the two that establishes the ratios that best help the majority to render its decision.

---

[34] This should always be understood in connection with a free state, for otherwise the family, goods, the lack of shelter, necessity, or violence can keep an inhabitant in a country in spite of himself; and then his sojourn alone no longer presupposes his consent to the contract or to the violation of the contract.

[35] In Genoa, the word *libertas* [liberty] can be read on the front of prisons and on the chains of galley-slaves. This application of the motto is fine and just. Indeed it is only malefactors of all social classes who prevent the citizen from

being free. In a country where all such people were in the galleys, the most perfect liberty would be enjoyed.

CHAPTER III: On Elections

With regard to the elections of the prince and the magistrates, which are, as I have said, complex acts, there are two ways to proceed, namely by choice or by lots. Both of these have been used in various republics, and at present we still see a very complicated mixture of the two in the election of the Doge of Venice.

Voting by lot, says Montesquieu, *is of the essence of democracy*. I agree, but why is this the case? *Drawing lots*, he continues, *is a way of electing that harms no one; it leaves each citizen a reasonable hope of serving the homeland*. These are not reasons.

If we keep in mind that the election of leaders is a function of government and not of the sovereignty, we will see why the method of drawing lots is more in the nature of democracy, where the administration is better in proportion as its acts are less numerous.

In every true democracy the magistrature is not an advantage but a heavy responsibility that cannot justly be imposed on one private individual rather than another. The law alone can impose this responsibility on the one to whom it falls by lot. For in that case, with the condition being equal for all and the choice not depending on any human will, there is no particular application that alters the universality of the law.

In any aristocracy, the prince chooses the prince; the government is preserved by itself, and it is there that voting is appropriate.

The example of the election of the Doge of Venice, far from destroying this distinction, confirms it. This mixed form suits a mixed government. For it is an error to regard the government of Venice as a true aristocracy. For although the populace there has no part in the government, the nobility is itself the people. A multitude of poor Barnabites never came near any magistrature, have nothing to show for their nobility but the vain title of excellency and the right to be present at the grand council. Since this grand council is as numerous as our general council in Geneva, its illustrious members have no more privileges than our single citizens. It is certain that, aside from the extreme disparity between the two republics, the bour-geoisie of Geneva exactly corresponds to the Venetian patriciate. Our natives and inhabitants correspond to the townsmen and people of Venice. Our peasants correspond to the subjects on the mainland. Finally, whatever way one considers this Republic, apart from its size, its government is no more aristocratic than ours. The whole difference lies in the fact that, since we do not have leaders who serve for life, we do not have the same need to draw lots.

Elections by lot would have few disadvantages in a true democracy where, all things being equal both in mores and talents as well as in maxims and fortunes, the choice would become almost indifferent. But I have already said there is no such thing as a true democracy.

When choice and lots are mixed, the former should fill the position requiring special talents, such as military posts. The latter is suited to those positions, such as the responsibilities of judicature, where good sense, justice, and integrity are enough, because in a well constituted state these qualities are common to all the citizens.

Neither the drawing of lots nor voting have any place in a monarchical government. Since the monarch is by right the only prince and sole magistrate, the choice of his lieutenants belongs to him alone. When the Abbé de St. Pierre proposed multiplying the Councils of the King of France and electing the members by ballot, he did not realize that he was proposing to change the form of government.

It remains for me to speak of the manner in which the votes are cast and gathered in the people's assembly. But perhaps in this regard the history of the Roman system of administration will explain more clearly all the maxims I could establish. It is not beneath the dignity of a judicious reader to consider in some detail how public and private business was conducted in a council made of two hundred thousand men.

CHAPTER IV: On the Roman Comitia

We have no especially reliable records of the earliest period of Rome's history. It even appears quite likely that most of the things reported about it are fables.[36] And in general the most instructive part of the annals of peoples, which is the history of their founding, is the part we most lack. Experience teaches us every day the causes that lead to the revolutions of empires. But since peoples are no longer being formed, we have almost nothing but conjecture to explain how they were formed.

The customs we find established attest at the very least to the fact that these customs had an origin. Of the traditions that go back to these origins, those that are supported by the greatest authorities and that are confirmed by the strongest reasons should pass for the most certain. These are the maxims I have tried to follow in attempting to find out how the freest and most powerful people on earth exercised its supreme power.

After the founding of Rome, the new-born Republic, that is, the army of the founder, composed of Albans, Sabines, and foreigners, was divided into three classes, which took the name *tribus* [tribes] by nature of this division. Each of these tribes was divided into ten curiae, and each curia into decuriae, at the head of which were placed leaders called *curiones* and *decuriones*.

Moreover, from each tribe was drawn a body of one hundred horsemen or knights, called a *century*. It is clear from this that these divisions, being hardly necessary in a market-town, originally were exclusively military. But it appears that an instinct for greatness led the small town of Rome to provide itself in advance with a system of administration suited to the capital of the world.

One disadvantage soon resulted from this initial division. With the tribes of the Albans[37] and the Sabines[38] always remaining constant, while that of the

foreigners[39] grew continually, thanks to their perpetual influx, this latter group soon outnumbered the other two. The remedy that Servius found for this dangerous abuse was to change the division and, in place of the division based on race, which he abolished, to substitute another division drawn from the areas of the town occupied by each tribe. In place of the three tribes, he made four. Each of them occupied one of the hills of Rome and bore its name. Thus, in remedying the inequality of the moment, he also prevented it from happening in the future. And in order that this division might not be merely one of localities but of men, he prohibited the inhabitants of one quarter from moving into another, which prevented the races from mingling with one another.

He also doubled the three ancient centuries of horsemen and he added to them twelve others, but always under the old names, a simple and judicious means by which he achieved the differentiation of the body of knights from that of the people, without causing the latter to murmur.

To the four urban tribes, Servius added fifteen others called rural tribes because they were formed from the inhabitants of the countryside, divided into the same number of cantons. Subsequently, the same number of new ones were brought into being, and the Roman people finally found itself divided into thirty-five tribes, a number at which they remained fixed until the end of the Republic.

There resulted from this distinction between the tribes of the city and those of the countryside an effect worth noting, because there is no other example of it, and because Rome owed it both the preservation of its mores and the growth of its empire. One might have thought that the urban tribes soon would have arrogated to themselves power and honors, and wasted no time in vilifying the rural tribes. What took place was quite the opposite. The early Romans' taste for country life is well known. They inherited this taste from the wise founder who united liberty with rural and military labors, and, so to speak, relegated to the town arts, crafts, intrigue, fortune and slavery.

---

[36] The name *Rome*, which presumably comes from *Romulus*, is Greek, and means *force*. The name *Numa* is also Greek, and means *law*. What is the likelihood that the first two kings of that town would have borne in advance names so clearly related to what they did?

[37] Ramnenses.

[38] Tatienses.

[39] Luceres.

Thus, since all the illustrious men in Rome lived in the country and tilled the soil, people became accustomed to look only there for the mainstays of the Republic. Since this condition was that of the worthiest patricians, it was honored by everyone. The simple and laborious life of the townsmen was preferred to the lazy and idle life of the bourgeois of Rome. And someone who would have been merely a miserable proletarian in the town, became a respected citizen as a field worker. It was not without reason, said Varro, that our great-souled ancestors established in the village the nursery of those robust and valiant men who defended them in time of war and nourished them in time of peace. Pliny says positively that the tribes of the fields were honored on account of the men who made them up; on the other hand, cowards whom men wished to vilify were transferred in disgrace to the tribes of the town. When the Sabine Appius Claudius came to settle in Rome, he was decked with honors and inscribed in a rural tribe that later took the name of his family. Finally, freedmen all entered the urban tribes, never the rural ones. And during the entire period of the Republic, there was not a single example of any of these freedmen reaching any magistrature, even if he had become a citizen.

This maxim was excellent, but it was pushed so far that it finally resulted in a change and certainly an abuse in the administration.

First, the censors, after having long arrogated to themselves the right to transfer citizens arbitrarily from one tribe to another, permitted most of them to have themselves inscribed in whatever tribe they pleased. Certainly this permission served no useful purpose and deprived the censorship of one of its greatest resources. Moreover, with the great and the powerful having themselves inscribed in the tribes of the countryside, and the freedmen who had become citizens remaining with the populace in the tribes of the town, the tribes in general no longer had either place or territory. On the contrary, they all found themselves so intermixed that the number of each could no longer be identified except by the registers, so that in this way the idea of the word *tribe* passed from being proprietary to personal, or rather, it became almost a chimera.

In addition, it happened that since the tribes of the town were nearer at hand, they were often the strongest in the comitia, and sold the state to those who deigned to buy the votes of the mob that made them up.

Regarding the curiae, since the founder had created ten curiae in each tribe, the entire Roman people, which was then contained within the town walls, was composed of thirty curiae, each of which had its temples, its gods, its officials, its priests and its feasts called *compitalia*, similar to the *paganalia* later held by the rural tribes.

When Servius established this new division, since this number thirty could not be divided equally among his four tribes, and since he did not want to alter it, the curiae became another division of the inhabitants of Rome, independent of the tribes. But there was no question of the curiae either in the rural tribes or among the people that make them up, for since the tribes had become a purely civil establishment and another system of administration had been introduced for the raising of troops, the military divisions of Romulus were found to be superfluous. Thus, even though every citizen was inscribed in a tribe, there were quite a few who were not inscribed in a curia.

Servius established still a third division which bore no relationship to the two preceding ones and which became, in its effects, the most important of all. He divided the entire Roman people into six classes, which he distinguished neither by place nor by person, but by wealth. Thus the first classes were filled by the rich, the last by the poor, and the middle ones by those who enjoyed a moderate fortune. These six classes were subdivided into one hundred ninety-three other bodies called centuries, and these bodies were divided in such wise that the first class alone contained more than half of them, and the last contained only one. Thus it was that the class with the smallest number of men was the one with the greatest number of centuries, and that the entire last class counted only as a subdivision, even though it alone contained more than half the inhabitants of Rome.

In order that the people might have less of a grasp of the consequences of this last form, Servius feigned giving it a military air. He placed in the second class two centuries of armorers, and two instruments of war in the fourth. In each class, with the exception of the last, he made a distinction between the young and the old, that is to say, between those who were obliged to carry arms and those whose age exempted them by law. This distinction, more than that of wealth, produced the necessity for frequently retaking the census or counting. Finally, he wished the assembly to be held in the Campus Martius, and that all those who were of age to serve should come there with their arms.

The reason he did not follow this same division of young and old in the last division is that the populace of which it was composed was not accorded the honor of bearing arms for the homeland. It was necessary to possess a hearth in order to obtain the right to defend it. And of the innumerable troops of beggars who today grace the armies of kings, there is perhaps no one who would not have been disdainfully chased from a Roman cohort, when the soldiers were the defenders of liberty.

There still is a distinction in the last class between the *proletarians* and those that are called *capite censi*. The former, not completely reduced to nothing, at least gave citizens to the state, sometimes even soldiers in times of pressing need. As for those who possessed nothing at all and could be reckoned only by counting heads, they were reckoned to be absolutely worthless, and Marius was the first who deigned to enroll them.

Without deciding here whether this third method of reckoning was good or bad in itself, I believe I can affirm that it could be made practicable only by the simple mores of the early Romans, their disinterestedness, their taste for agriculture, their dislike for commerce and for the passion for profits. Where is the modern people among whom their devouring greed, their unsettled spirit, their intrigue, their continual displacements, their perpetual revolutions of fortunes could allow such an establishment to last twenty years

without overturning the entire state? It must also be duly noted that the mores and the censorship, which were stronger than this institution, corrected its defects in Rome, and that a rich man found himself relegated to the class of the poor for having made too much of a show of his wealth.

From all this, it is easy to grasp why mention is almost never made of more than five classes, even though there actually were six. The sixth, since it furnished neither soldiers for the army nor voters for the Campus Martius[40] and was of virtually no use in the Republic, was hardly ever counted for anything.

Such were the various divisions of the Roman people. Let us now look at the effect these divisions had on the assemblies. When legitimately convened, these assemblies were called *comitia*. Ordinarily they were held in the Roman forum or in the Campus Martius, and were distinguished as comitia curiata, comitia centuriata, and comitia tributa, according to which of the three forms was the basis on which they were organized. The comitia curiata were based on the institution of Romulus, the comitia centuriata on that of Servius, and the comitia tributa on that of the tribunes of the people. No law received sanction, no magistrate was elected save in the comitia. And since there was no citizen who was not inscribed in a curia, in a century, or in a tribe, it followed that no citizen was excluded from the right of suffrage, and that the Roman people was truly sovereign both de jure and de facto.

For the comitia to be legitimately assembled and for what took place to have the force of law, three conditions had to be met: first, the body or the magistrate who called these assemblies had to be invested with the necessary authority to do so; second, the assembly had to be held on one of the days permitted by law; third, the auguries had to be favorable.

The reason for the first regulation needs no explanation. The second is an administrative matter. Thus the comitia were not allowed to be held on holidays

---

[40] I say *Campus Martius* because it was here that the comitia centuriata gathered. In the two other forms of assembly, the people gathered in the *forum* or elsewhere, and then the

and market days, when people from the country, coming to Rome on business, did not have time to spend the day in the public forum. By means of the third rule, the senate held in check a proud and restless people, and appropriately tempered the ardor of seditious tribunes. But these latter found more than one way of getting around this constraint.

The laws and the election of leaders were not the only matters submitted to the judgment of the comitia. Since the Roman people had usurped the most important functions of government, it can be said that the fate of Europe was decided in its assemblies. This variety of objects gave rise to the various forms these assemblies took on according to the matters on which they had to pronounce.

In order to judge these various forms, it is enough to compare them. In instituting the curiae, Romulus had intended to contain the senate by means of the people and the people by means of the senate, while he dominated both equally. He therefore gave the people, by means of this form, all the authority of number to balance that of power and wealth which he left to the patricians. But in conformity with the spirit of the monarchy, he nevertheless left a greater advantage to the patricians through their clients' influence on the majority of the votes. This admirable institution of patrons and clients was a masterpiece of politics and humanity, without which the patriciate, so contrary to the spirit of the Republic, could not have subsisted. Only Rome had the honor of giving the world this fine example, which never led to any abuse, and which, for all that, has never been followed.

Since this same form of curiae had subsisted under the kings until Servius, and since the reign of the last Tarquin was not considered legitimate, royal laws were generally known by the name *leges curiatae*.

Under the Republic, the curiae, always limited to the four urban tribes and including no more than the populace of Rome, was unable to suit either the senate, which was at the head of the patricians, or

the tribunes, who, plebeians though they were, were at the head of the citizens who were in comfortable circumstances. The curiae therefore fell into discredit and their degradation was such that their thirty assembled lictors together did what the comitia curiata should have done.

The division by centuries was so favorable to the aristocracy, that at first difficult it is to see how the senate did not always prevail in the comitia which bears this name, and by which the consuls, the censors, and other crurale magistrates were elected. In fact, of the one hundred ninety-three centuries that formed the six classes of the entire Roman people, the first class contained ninety-eight, and, since the voting was counted by centuries only, this first class alone prevailed in the number of votes over all the rest. When all its centuries were in agreement, they did not even continue to gather the votes. Decisions made by the smallest number passed for a decision of the multitude; and it can be said that in the comitia centuriata business was regulated more by the majority of money than by one of votes.

But this extreme authority was tempered in two ways. First, since ordinarily the tribunes, and always a large number of plebeians, were in the class of the rich, they balanced the credit of the patricians in this first class.

The second way consisted in the following. Instead of at the outset making the centuries vote according to their order, which would have meant always beginning with the first, one century was chosen by lot, and that one[41] alone proceeded to the election. After this, all the centuries were called on another day according to their rank, repeated the same election and usually confirmed it. Thus the authority of example was removed from rank in order to give it to lot, in accordance with the principle of democracy.

There resulted from this custom still another advantage; namely that the citizens from the country had

---

capite censi had as much influence and authority as the first citizens.

[41] This century, having been chosen thus by lot, was called *prae rogativa*, on account of the fact that it was the first to be asked for its vote, and it is from this that the word *prerogative* is derived.

time between the two elections to inform themselves of the merit of the provisionally named candidate, so as to give their votes only on condition of their having knowledge of the issue. But on the pretext of speeding things up, this custom was finally abolished and the two elections were held on the same day.

Strictly speaking, the comitia tributa were the council of the Roman people. They were convened only by the tribunes. The tribunes were elected and passed their plebiscites there. Not only did the senate hold no rank in them, it did not even have the right to be present. And since the senators were forced to obey the laws upon which they could not vote, they were less free in this regard than the humblest citizens. This injustice was altogether ill-conceived, and was by itself enough to invalidate the decrees of a body to which all its members were not admitted. If all the patricians had been present at these comitia in virtue of the right they had as citizens, having then become simple private individuals, they would not have had a great deal of influence on a form of voting that was tallied by counting heads, and where the humblest proletarian had as much clout as the prince of the senate.

Thus it can be seen that besides the order that resulted from these various distributions for gathering the votes of so great a people, these distributions were not reducible to forms indifferent in themselves, but each one had effects relative to the viewpoints that caused it to be preferred.

Without going further into greater detail here, it is a consequence of the preceding clarifications that the comitia tributa were the most favorable to the popular government, and the comitia centuriata more favorable to the aristocracy. Regarding the comitia curiata, in which the populace of Rome alone formed the majority, since these were good only for favoring tyranny and evil designs, they fell of their own weight into disrepute, and even the seditious abstained from using a means that gave too much exposure to their projects. It is certain that all the majesty of the Roman people is found only in the curia centuriata, which alone were complete, for the comitia curiata excluded the rural tribes, and the comitia tributa the senate and the patricians.

As to the manner of counting the votes, among the early Romans it was as simple as their mores, though not so simple as in Sparta. Each gave his vote in a loud voice, and a clerk marked it down accordingly. The majority vote in each tribe determined the tribe's vote; the majority vote of the tribes determined the people's vote; and the same went for the curia and the centuries. This custom was good so long as honesty reigned among the citizens and each was ashamed to give his vote publicly in favor of an unjust proposal or an unworthy subject. But when the people became corrupt and votes were bought, it was fitting that they should give their votes in secret in order to restrain the buyers through distrust and to provide scoundrels the means of not being traitors.

I know that Cicero condemns this change and attributes the ruin of the Republic partly to it. But although I am aware of the weight that Cicero's authority should have here, I cannot agree with him. On the contrary, I think that, by having made not enough of these changes, the fall of the state was accelerated. Just as the regimen of healthy people is not suitable for the sick, one should not want to govern a corrupt people by means of the same laws that are suited to a good people. Nothing proves this maxim better than the long life of the Republic of Venice, whose shadow still exists, solely because its laws are suited only to wicked men.

Tablets were therefore distributed to the citizens by mean of which each man could vote without anyone knowing what his opinion was. New formalities were also established for collecting the tablets, counting the votes, comparing the numbers, and so on. None of this prevented the integrity of the officials in charge of these functions[42] from often being under suspicion. Finally, to prevent intrigue and vote trafficking, edicts were passed whose sheer multiplicity is proof of their uselessness.

Toward the end of the period of the Republic, it was often necessary to have recourse to extraordinary expedients in order to make up for the inadequacy of the law. Sometimes miracles were alleged. But this means, which could deceive the populace, did not

[42] Custodes, diribitores, rogatores suffragiorum.

deceive those who governed it. Sometimes an assembly was unexpectedly convened before the candidates had time to carry out their intrigues. Sometimes an entire session was spent on talk, when it was clear that the populace was won over and ready to take the wrong side on an issue. But finally ambition eluded everything; and what is unbelievable is that in the midst of so much abuse, this immense people, by virtue of its ancient regulations, did not cease to choose magistrates, pass laws, judge cases, or expedite private and public business, almost as easily as the senate itself could have done.

CHAPTER V: On the Tribunate

When it is not possible to establish an exact proportion between the constitutive parts of the state, or when indestructible causes continually alter the relationships between them, a special magistrature is then established that does not make up a larger body along with them. This magistrature restores each term to its true relationship to the others, and which creates a link or a middle term either between the prince and the people or between the prince and the sovereign, or on both sides at once, if necessary.

This body, which I will call the *tribunate*, is the preserver of the laws and the legislative power. It serves sometimes to protect the sovereign against the government, as the tribunes of the people did in Rome; sometimes to sustain the government against the people, as the Council of Ten now does in Venice; and sometimes to maintain equilibrium between the two, as the ephors did in Sparta.

The tribunate is not a constitutive part of the city and it should have no share in either the legislative or the executive power. But this is precisely what makes its own power the greater. For although it is unable to do anything, it can prevent everything. It is more sacred and more revered as a defender of the laws than the prince who executes them and the sovereign who gives them. This was very clearly apparent in Rome when the proud patricians, who always scorned the entire populace, were forced to bow before a humble official of the people, who had neither auspices nor jurisdiction.

A well tempered tribunate is the firmest support of a good constitution. But if it has the slightest bit too much force, it undermines everything. As to weakness, there is none in its nature; and provided it is something, it is never less than it ought to be.

It degenerates into tyranny when it usurps the executive power, of which it is merely the moderator, and when it wants to dispense the laws it ought only protect. The enormous power of the ephors, which was without danger so long as Sparta preserved its mores, hastened corruption once it had begun. The blood of Agis, who was slaughtered by these tyrants, was avenged by his successor. The crime and the punishment of the ephors equally hastened the fall of the republic; and after Cleomenes Sparta was no longer anything. Rome also perished in the same way, and the excessive power of the tribunes, which they had gradually usurped, finally served, with the help of the laws that were made to protect liberty, as a safeguard for the emperors who destroyed it. As for the Council of Ten in Venice, it is a tribunal of blood, equally horrible to the patricians and the people, and which, far from proudly protecting the laws, no longer serves any purpose, after their degradation, beyond that of delivering blows in the dark which no one dares notice.

Just like the government, the tribunate weakened as a result of the multiplication of its members. When the tribunes of the Roman people, who at first were two in number, then five, wanted to double this number, the senate let them do so, certain that one part would hold the others in check; and this did not fail to happen.

The best way to prevent usurpations by so formidable a body, one that no government has yet made use of, would be not to make this body permanent, but to regulate the intervals during which it would be suppressed. These intervals, which ought not be so long as to allow abuses time to grow in strength, can be fixed by law in such a way that it is easy to shorten them, as needed, by means of extraordinary commissions.

This way seems to me to have no disadvantage, for since, as I have said, the tribunate is not part of the constitution, it can be set aside without doing the constitution any harm, because a newly established magistrate begins not with the power his predecessor had, but with the power the law gives him.

CHAPTER VI: On Dictatorship

The inflexibility of the laws, which prevents them from adapting to circumstances, can in certain instances make them harmful and render them the instrument of the state's downfall in time of crisis. The order and the slowness of formal procedures require a space of time which circumstances sometimes do not permit. A thousand circumstances can present themselves which the legislator has not foreseen, and it is a very necessary bit of foresight to realize that not everything can be foreseen.

It is therefore necessary to avoid the desire to strengthen political institutions to the point of removing the power to suspend their effect. Sparta itself allowed its laws to lie dormant.

But only the greatest dangers can counterbalance the danger of altering the public order, and the sacred power of the laws should never be suspended except when it is a question of the safety of the homeland. In these rare and obvious cases, public safety can be provided for by a special act which confers the responsibility for it on someone who is most worthy. This commission can be carried out in two ways, according to the type of danger.

If increasing the activity of government is enough to remedy the situation, it is concentrated in one or two members. Thus it is not the authority of the laws that is altered, but merely the form of their administration. But if the peril is such that the apparatus of the laws is an obstacle to their being protected, then a supreme leader is named who silences all the laws and briefly suspends the sovereign authority. In such a case, the general will is not in doubt, and it is evident that the first intention of the people is that the state should not perish. In this manner, the suspension of legislative authority does not abolish it. The magistrate who silences it cannot make it speak; he dominates it without being able to represent it. He can do anything but make laws.

The first way was used by the Roman senate when, by a sacred formula, it entrusted the consuls with the responsibility for providing for the safety of the Republic. The second took place when one of the two consuls named a dictator,[43] a custom for which Alba had provided Rome the precedent.

In the beginning days of the Republic, there was frequent recourse to dictatorship, since the state did not yet have a sufficiently stable basis to be capable of sustaining itself by the force of its constitution. Since the mores at that time made many of the precautions superfluous that would have been necessary in other times, there was no fear either that a dictator would abuse his authority or that he would try to hold on to it beyond his term of office. On the contrary, it seemed that such a great power was a burden to the one in whom it was vested, so quickly did he hasten to rid himself of it, as if a position that took the place of the laws would have been too troublesome and dangerous!

Thus it is not so much the danger of its being abused as it is that of its being degraded which makes one criticize the injudicious use of this supreme magistrature in the early days of the Republic. For while it was being wasted on elections, dedications and purely formal proceedings, there was reason to fear that it would become less formidable in time of need, and that people would become accustomed to regard as empty a title that was used exclusively in empty ceremonies.

Toward the end of the Republic, the Romans, having become more circumspect, were as unreasonably sparing in their use of the dictatorship as they had formerly been lavish. It was easy to see that their fear was ill-founded; that the weakness of the capital then protected it against the magistrates who were in its midst; that a dictator could, under certain circumstances, defend the public liberty without ever being able to make an attack on it; and that Rome's chains would not be forged in Rome itself, but in its armies. The weak resistance that Marius offered Sulla and Pompey offered Caesar clearly demonstrated what

---

[43] This nomination was made at night and in secret, as if it were shameful to place a man beyond the laws.

could be expected of internal authority in the face of external force.

This error caused them to make huge mistakes; for example, failing to name a dictator in the Catalinian affair. For since this was a question merely of the interior of the town and, at most, of some province in Italy, with the unlimited authority that the laws give the dictator, he would have easily quelled the conspiracy, which was stifled only by a coming together of favor chance happenings, which human prudence has no right to expect.

Instead of that, the senate was content to entrust all its power to the consuls. Whence it happened that, in order to act effectively, Cicero was forced to exceed this power on a crucial point. And although the first transports of joy indicated approval of his conduct, eventually Cicero was justly called to account for the blood of citizens shed against the laws, a reproach that could not have been delivered against a dictator. But the eloquence of the consul carried the day. And since even he, Roman though he was, preferred his own glory to his homeland, he sought not so much the most legitimate and safest way of saving the state as he did the way that would get him all the honor for settling this affair.[44] Thus he was justly honored as the liberator of Rome and justly punished as a law-breaker. However brilliant his recall may have been, it undoubtedly was a pardon.

For the rest, whatever the manner in which this important commission was conferred, it is important to limit a dictatorship's duration to a very short period of time which cannot be prolonged. In the crises that call for its being established, the state is soon either destroyed or saved; and once the pressing need has passed, the dictatorship becomes tyrannical or needless. In Rome, where the dictators had terms of six months only, most of them abdicated before their terms had expired. If the term had been longer, perhaps they would have been tempted to prolong it further, as did the decemvirs with a one year term. The dictator only had time enough to see to the need

[44] He could not have been sure of this, had he proposed a dictator, since he did not dare name himself, and he could not be sure that his colleague would name him.

that got him elected. He did not have time to dream up other projects.

CHAPTER VII: On the Censorship

Just as the declaration of the general will takes place through the law, the declaration of the public judgment takes place through the censorship. Public opinion is the sort of law whose censor is the minister, and which he only applies to particular cases, after the example of the prince.

Thus the censorial tribunal, far from being the arbiter of the people's opinion, is merely its spokesman; and as soon as it deviates from this opinion, its decisions are vain and futile.

It is useless to distinguish the mores of a nation from the objects of its esteem, for all these things derive from the same principle and are necessarily intermixed. Among all the peoples of the world, it is not nature but opinion which decides the choice of their pleasures. Reform men's opinions, and their mores will soon become purified all by themselves. Men always love what is good or what they find to be so; but it is in this judgment that they make mistakes. Hence this is the judgment whose regulation is the point at issue. Whoever judges mores judges honor; and whoever judges honor derives his law from opinion.

The opinions of a people arise from its constitution. Although the law does not regulate mores, legislation is what gives rise to them. When legislation weakens, mores degenerate; but then the judgment of the censors will not do what the force of the laws has not done.

It follows from this that the censorship can be useful for preserving mores, but never for reestablishing them. Establish censors while the laws are vigorous. Once they have lost their vigor, everything is hopeless. Nothing legitimate has any force once the laws no longer have force.

The censorship maintains mores by preventing opinions from becoming corrupt, by preserving their rectitude through wise applications, and sometimes even by making a determination on them when they are still uncertain. The use of seconds in duels, which had been carried to the point of being a craze in the kingdom of France, was abolished by the following few words of the king's edict: *as for those who are cowardly enough to call upon seconds.* This judgment anticipated that of the public and suddenly made a determination. But when the same edicts tried to declare that it was also an act of cowardice to fight duels (which of course is quite true, but contrary to common opinion), the public mocked this decision; it concerned a matter about which its mind was already made up.

I have said elsewhere[45] that since public opinion is not subject to constraint, there should be no vestige of it in the tribunal established to represent it. It is impossible to show too much admiration for the skill with which this device, entirely lost among us moderns, was put into effect among the Romans and even better among the Lacedaemonians.

When a man of bad mores put forward a good proposal in the council of Sparta, the ephors ignored it and had the same proposal put forward by a virtuous citizen. What honor for the one, what shame for the other; and without having given praise or blame to either of the two! Certain drunkards of Samos[46] defiled the tribunals of the ephors. The next day, a public edict gave the Samians permission to be filthy. A true punishment would have been less severe than impunity such as this. When Sparta made a pronouncement on what was or was not decent, Greece did not appeal its judgments.

CHAPTER VIII: On Civil Religion

At first men had no other kings but the gods, and no other government than a theocratic one. They reasoned like Caligula, and then they reasoned correctly. A lengthy alteration of feelings and ideas is necessary before men can be resolved to accept a

fellow man as a master, in the hope that things will turn out well for having done so.

By the mere fact that a god was placed at the head of every political society, it followed that there were as many gods as there were peoples. Two peoples who were alien to one another and nearly always enemies, could not recognize the same master for very long. Two armies in combat with one another could not obey the same leader. Thus national divisions led to polytheism, and this in turn led to theological and civil intolerance which are by nature the same, as will be stated later.

The fanciful notion of the Greeks that they had rediscovered their gods among the beliefs of barbarian peoples arose from another notion they had of regarding themselves as the natural sovereigns of these peoples. But in our day it is a ridiculous bit of erudition which equates the gods of different nations: as if Moloch, Saturn, and Chronos could have been the same god; as if the Phoenicians' Baal, the Greeks' Zeus, and the Romans' Jupiter could have been the same; as if there could be anything in common among chimerical beings having different names!

But if it is asked how in pagan cultures, where each state has its own cult and its own gods, there are no wars of religion, I answer that it was for this very reason that each state, having its own cult as well as its own government, did not distinguish its gods from its laws. Political war was theological as well. The departments of the gods were, so to speak, fixed by national boundaries. The gods of one people had no rights over other peoples. The gods of the pagans were not jealous gods. They divided dominion over the world among themselves. Moses himself and the Hebrew people sometimes countenanced this idea in speaking of the god of Israel. It is true they regarded as nothing the gods of the Canaanites, a proscribed people destined for destruction, and whose land they were to occupy. But note how they spoke of the divinities of neighboring peoples whom they were forbidden to attack! *Is not the possession of what belongs to your god Chamos,* said Jephthah to the Ammonites, *lawfully yours? By the same right we possess the lands our victorious god has acquired*

---

[45] I merely call attention in this chapter to what I have treated at greater length in my *Letter to D'Alembert.*

[46] [Rousseau adds the following in the 1782 edition: "They are from another island which the delicacy of our language prohibits me from naming at this time."]

for himself.[47] It appears to me that here was a clear recognition of the parity between the rights of Chamos and those of the god of Israel.

But when the Jews, while in subjection to the kings of Babylon and later to the kings of Syria, wanted to remain steadfast in not giving recognition to any other god but their own, their refusal, seen as rebellion against the victor, brought them the persecutions we read of in their history, and of which there is no other precedent prior to Christianity.[48]

Since, therefore, each religion was uniquely tied to the laws of the state which prescribed it, there was no other way of converting a people except by enslaving it, nor any other missionaries than conquerors. And with the obligation to change cult being the law of the vanquished, it was necessary to begin by conquering before talking about it. Far from men fighting for the gods, it was, as it was in Homer, the gods who fought for men; each asked his own god for victory and paid for it with new altars. Before taking an area, the Romans summoned that area's gods to leave it. And when they allowed the Tarentines to keep their angry gods, it was because at that point they considered these gods to be in subjection to their own and forced to do them homage. They left the vanquished their gods, just as they left them their laws. A wreath to the Capitoline Jupiter was often the only tribute they imposed.

Finally, the Romans having spread this cult and their gods, along with their empire, and having themselves often adopted the gods of the vanquished by granting the right of the city to both alike, the peoples of this vast empire gradually found themselves to have multitudes of gods and cults, which were nearly the same everywhere. And that is how paganism finally became a single, identical religion in the known world.

Such were the circumstances under which Jesus came to establish a spiritual kingdom on earth. In separating the theological system from the political system, this made the state to cease being united and caused internal divisions that never ceased to agitate Christian peoples. But since this new idea of an otherworldly kingdom had never entered the heads of the pagans, they always regarded the Christians as true rebels who, underneath their hypocritical submission, were only waiting for the moment when they would become independent and the masters, and adroitly usurp the authority they pretended in their weakness to respect. This is the reason for the persecutions.

What the pagans feared happened. Then everything changed its appearance. The humble Christians changed their language, and soon this so-called otherworldly kingdom became, under a visible leader, the most violent despotism in this world.

However, since there has always been a prince and civil laws, this double power has given rise to a perpetual jurisdictional conflict that has made all good polity impossible in Christian states, and no one has ever been able to know whether it is the priest or the master whom one is obliged to obey.

Nevertheless, several peoples, even in Europe or nearby have wanted to preserve or reestablish the ancient system, but without success. The spirit of Christianity has won everything. The sacred cult has always remained or again become independent of the sovereign and without any necessary link to the state. Mohammed had very sound opinions. He tied his political system together very well, and so long as the form of his government subsisted under his successors, the caliphs, this government was utterly unified, and for that reason it was good. But as the Arabs became prosperous, lettered, polished, soft and cowardly, they were subjugated by barbarians. Then the division between the two powers began again. Although it is less apparent among the Mohammedans

[47] *Nonne ea quae possidet Chamos deus tuus, tibi jure debentur?* Such is the text of the Vulgate. Father de Carrières has translated it: *Do you not believe that you have the right to possess what belongs to your god Chamos?* I do not know the force of the Hebrew text; but I see that in the Vulgate Jephthah positively acknowledges the right of the god Chamos, and that the French translator weakened this recognition by adding an *according to you* which is not in the Latin.

[48] It is quite clear that the Phocian War, called the Holy War, was not a war of religion at all. It had for its object to punish sacrileges, and not to make unbelievers submit.

than among the Christians, it is there all the same, especially in the sect of Ali; and there are states, such as Persia, where it never ceases to be felt.

Among us, the kings of England have established themselves as heads of the Church, and the czars have done the same. But with this title, they became less its masters than its ministers. They have acquired not so much the right to change it as the power to maintain it. They are not its legislators; they are merely its princes. Wherever the clergy constitutes a body,[49] it is master and legislator in its own realm. Thus there are two powers, two sovereigns, in England and in Russia, just as there are everywhere else.

Of all the Christian writers, the philosopher Hobbes is the only one who clearly saw the evil and the remedy, who dared to propose the reunification of the two heads of the eagle and the complete restoration of political unity, without which no state or government will ever be well constituted. But he should have seen that the dominating spirit of Christianity was incompatible with his system, and that the interest of the priest would always be stronger than that of the state. It is not so much what is horrible and false in his political theory as what is just and true that has caused it to be hated.[50]

I believe that if the facts of history were developed from this point of view, it would be easy to refute the opposing sentiments of Bayle and Warburton, the one holding that no religion is useful to the body politic, while the other maintains, to the contrary, that Christianity is its firmest support. We could prove to the first that no state has ever been founded without religion serving as its base, and to the second that Christian law is at bottom more injurious than it is useful for the strong constitution of the state. To succeed in making myself understood, I need only give a bit more precision to the excessively vague ideas about religion that are pertinent to my subject.

When considered in relation to society, which is either general or particular, religion can also be divided into two kinds, namely the religion of the man and that of the citizen. The first—without temples, altars or rites, and limited to the purely internal cult of the supreme God and to the eternal duties of morality—is the pure and simple religion of the Gospel, the true theism, and what can be called natural divine law [droit]. The other, inscribed in a single country, gives it its gods, its own titulary patrons. It has its dogmas, its rites, its exterior cult prescribed by laws. Outside the nation that practices it, everything is infidel, alien and barbarous to it. It extends the duties and rights of man only as far as its altars. Such were all the religions of the early peoples, to which the name of civil or positive divine law [droit] can be given.

There is a third sort of religion which is more bizarre. In giving men two sets of legislation, two leaders, and two homelands, it subjects them to contradictory duties and prevents them from being simultaneously devout men and citizens. Such is the religion of the Lamas and of the Japanese, and such is Roman Christianity. It can be called the religion of the priest. It leads to a kind of mixed and unsociable law [droit] which has no name.

Considered from a political standpoint, these three types of religion all have their faults. The third is so bad that it is a waste of time to amuse oneself by proving it. Whatever breaks up social unity is worthless. All institutions that place man in contradiction with himself are of no value.

The second is good in that it unites the divine cult with love of the laws, and that, in making the homeland the object of its citizens' admiration, it teaches them that all service to the state is service to

---

[49] It should be carefully noted that it is not so much the formal assemblies, such as those of France, which bind the clergy together into a body, as it is the communion of the churches. Communion and excommunication are the social compact of the clergy, one with which it will always be the master of the peoples and the kings. All the priests who communicate together are citizens, even if they should be from the opposite ends of the world. This invention is a political masterpiece. There is nothing like this among the pagan priests; thus they never made up a body of clergy.

[50] Notice, among other things, in Grotius' letter to his brother, dated April 11, 1643, what this learned man approves of and what he criticizes in his book *De Cive*. It is true that, prone to being indulgent, he appears to forgive the author for his good points for the sake of his bad ones. But not everyone is so merciful.

its tutelary god. It is a kind of theocracy in which there ought to be no pontiff other than the prince and no priests other than the magistrates. To die for one's country is then to become a martyr; to violate its laws is to be impious. To subject a guilty man to public execration is to deliver him to the wrath of the gods: *sacer estod.*

On the other hand, it is bad in that, being based on error and lies, it deceives men, makes them credulous and superstitious, and drowns the true cult of the divinity in an empty ceremony. It is also bad when, on becoming exclusive and tyrannical, it makes a people bloodthirsty and intolerant, so that men breathe only murder and massacre, and believe they are performing a holy action in killing anyone who does not accept its gods. This places such a people in a natural state of war with all others, which is quite harmful to its own security.

Thus there remains the religion of man or Christianity (not that of today, but that of the Gospel, which is completely different). Through this holy, sublime, true religion, men, in being the children of the same God, all acknowledge one another as brothers, and the society that unites them is not dissolved even at death.

But since this religion has no particular relation to the body politic, it leaves laws with only the force the laws derive from themselves, without adding any other force to them. And thus one of the great bonds of a particular society remains ineffectual. Moreover, far from attaching the hearts of the citizens to the state, it detaches them from it as from all the other earthly things. I know of nothing more contrary to the social spirit.

We are told that a people of true Christians would form the most perfect society imaginable. I see but one major difficulty in this assumption, namely that a society of true Christians would no longer be a society of men.

I even say that this supposed society would not, for all its perfection, be the strongest or the most durable. By dint of being perfect, it would lack a bond of union; its destructive vice would be in its very perfection.

Each man would fulfill his duty; the people would be subject to the laws; the leaders would be just

and moderate, the magistrates would be upright and incorruptible; soldiers would scorn death; there would be neither vanity nor luxury. All of this is very fine, but let us look further.

Christianity is a completely spiritual religion, concerned exclusively with things heavenly. The homeland of the Christian is not of this world. He does his duty, it is true, but he does it with a profound indifference toward the success or failure of his efforts. So long as he has nothing to reproach himself for, it matters little to him whether anything is going well or poorly down here. If the state is flourishing, he hardly dares to enjoy the public felicity, for fear of becoming puffed up with his country's glory. If the state is in decline, he blesses the hand of God that weighs heavily on his people.

For the society to be peaceful and for harmony to be maintained, every citizen without exception would have to be an equally good Christian. But if, unhappily, there is a single ambitious man, a single hypocrite, a Cataline, for example, or a Cromwell, he would quite undoubtedly gain the upper hand on his pious compatriots. Christian charity does not readily allow one to think ill of his neighbors. Once he has discovered by some ruse the art of deceiving them and of laying hold of a part of the public authority, behold a man established in dignity! God wills that he be respected. Soon, behold a power! God wills that he be obeyed. Does the trustee of his power abuse it? He is the rod with which God punishes his children. It would be against one's conscience to expel the usurper. It would be necessary to disturb the public tranquillity, use violence and shed blood. All this accords ill with the meekness of a Christian. And after all, what difference does it make whether one is a free man or a serf in this vale of tears? The essential thing is getting to heaven, and resignation is but another means to that end.

What if a foreign war breaks out? The citizens march without reservation into combat; none among them dreams of deserting. They do their duty, but without passion for victory; they know how to die better than how to be victorious. What difference does it make whether they are the victors or the vanquished? Does not providence know better than they what they need? Just imagine the advantage a fierce, impetuous and passionate enemy could draw from their stoicism! Set them face to face with those generous peoples who were devoured by an ardent love of glory and homeland. Suppose your Christian republic is face to face with Sparta or Rome. The pious Christians will be beaten, crushed and destroyed before they realize where they are, or else they will owe their safety only to the scorn their enemies will conceive for them. To my way of thinking, the oath taken by Fabius' soldiers was a fine one. They did not swear to die or to win; they swore to return victorious. And they kept their promise. Christians would never have taken such an oath; they would have believed they were tempting God.

But I am deceiving myself in talking about a Christian republic; these terms are mutually exclusive. Christianity preaches only servitude and dependence. Its spirit is too favorable to tyranny for tyranny not to take advantage of it at all times. True Christians are made to be slaves. They know it and are hardly moved by this. This brief life has too little value in their eyes.

Christian troops, we are told, are excellent. I deny this. Is someone going to show me some? For my part, I do not know of any Christian troops. Someone will mention the crusades. Without disputing the valor of the crusaders, I will point out that quite far from being Christians, they were soldiers of the priest; they were citizens of the church; they were fighting for its spiritual country which the church, God knows how, had made temporal. Properly understood, this is a throwback to paganism. Since the Gospel does not establish a national religion, no holy war is possible among Christians.

Under the pagan emperors, Christian soldiers were brave. All the Christian authors affirm this, and I believe it. This was a competition for honor against the pagan troops. Once the emperors were Christians, this competition ceased. And when the cross expelled the eagle, all Roman valor disappeared.

But leaving aside political considerations, let us return to right and determine the principles that govern this important point. The right which the social compact gives the sovereign over the subjects does not, as I have said, go beyond the limits of public utility.[51] The subjects, therefore, do not have to account to the sovereign for their opinions, except to the extent that these opinions are of importance to the community. For it is of great importance to the state that each citizen have a religion that causes him to love his duties. But the dogmas of that religion are of no interest either to the state or its members, except to the extent that these dogmas relate to morality and to the duties which the one who professes them is bound to fulfill toward others. Each man can have in addition such opinions as he pleases, without it being any of the sovereign's business to know what they are. For since the other world is outside the province of the sovereign, whatever the fate of subjects in the life to come, it is none of its business, so long as they are good citizens in this life.

There is, therefore, a purely civil profession of faith, the articles of which it belongs to the sovereign to establish, not exactly as dogmas of religion, but as sentiments of sociability, without which it is impossible to be a good citizen or a faithful subject.[52] While not having the ability to obligate anyone to believe them, the sovereign can banish from the state anyone who does not believe them. It can banish him not for being impious but for being unsociable, for being incapable of sincerely loving the laws and justice, and of sacrificing his life, if necessary, for his duty. If, after having publicly acknowledged these same dogmas, a person acts as if he does not believe them,

---

[51] *In the Republic,* says the Marquis d'Argenson, *each man is perfectly free with respect to what does not harm others.* This is the invariable boundary. It cannot be expressed more precisely. I have been unable to deny myself the pleasure of occasionally citing this manuscript, even though it is unknown to the public, in order to pay homage to the memory of a famous and noteworthy man, who, even as a minister, retained the heart of a citizen, along with just and sound opinions on the government of his country.

[52] By pleading for Cataline, Caesar tried to establish the dogma of the mortality of the soul. To refute him, Cato and Cicero did not waste time philosophizing. They contented themselves with showing that Caesar spoke like a bad citizen and advanced a doctrine that was injurious to the state. In fact, this was what the Roman senate had to judge, and not a question of theology.

he should be put to death; he has committed the greatest of crimes: he has lied before the laws.

The dogmas of the civil religion ought to be simple, few in number, precisely worded, without explanations or commentaries. The existence of a powerful, intelligent, beneficent divinity that foresees and provides; the life to come; the happiness of the just; the punishment of the wicked; the sanctity of the social contract and of the laws. These are the positive dogmas. As for the negative dogmas, I am limiting them to just one, namely intolerance. It is part of the cults we have excluded.

Those who distinguish between civil and theological intolerance are mistaken, in my opinion. Those two types of intolerance are inseparable. It is impossible to live in peace with those one believes to be damned. To love them would be to hate God who punishes them. It is absolutely necessary either to reclaim them or torment them. Whenever theological intolerance is allowed, it is impossible for it not to have some civil effect;[53] and once it does, the sover-

eign no longer is sovereign, not even over temporal affairs. Thenceforward, priests are the true masters; kings are simply their officers.

Now that there no longer is and never again can be an exclusive national religion, tolerance should be shown to all those that tolerate others, so long as their dogmas contain nothing contrary to the duties of a citizen. But whoever dares to say *outside the church there is no salvation* ought to be expelled from the state, unless the state is the church and the prince is the pontiff. Such a dogma is good only in a theocratic government; in all other forms of government it is ruinous. The reason why Henry IV is said to have embraced the Roman religion should make every decent man, and above all any prince who knows how to reason, leave it.

CHAPTER IX: Conclusion

After laying down the true principles of political right and attempting to establish the state on this basis, it remains to support the state by means of its external relations, which would include the laws of nations, commerce, the right of war and conquest, public law, leagues, negotiations, treaties, and so on. But all that forms a new subject which is too vast for my nearsightedness. I should always set my sights on things that are nearer at hand to me.

END

---

[53] Marriage, for example, being a civil contract, has civil effects without which it is impossible for a society even to subsist. Suppose then that a clergy reaches the point where it ascribes to itself alone the right to permit this act (a right that must necessarily be usurped in every intolerant religion). In that case, is it not clear that in establishing the authority of the church in this matter, it will render ineffectual that of the prince, who will have no more subjects than those whom the clergy wishes to give him? Is it not also clear that the clergy—if master of whether to marry or not to marry people according to whether or not they accept this or that doctrine, according to whether they accept or reject this or that formula, according to whether they are more or less devout—in behaving prudently and holding firm, will alone dispose of inheritance, offices, the citizens, the state itself, which could not subsist, if composed solely of bastards? But, it will be said, abuses will be appealed; summonses and decrees will be issued; temporal holdings will be seized. What a pity! If it has a little—I will not say courage—but good sense, the clergy will serenely allow the appeals, the summonses, the decrees and the seizures, and it will end up master. It is not, it seems to me, a big sacrifice to abandon a part when one is sure of securing the whole.

SMITH
Theory of Moral Sentiments

PART I, SECTION III, CHAP. II

Of the origin of Ambition, and of the distinction of Ranks

It is because mankind are disposed to sympathize more entirely with our joy than with our sorrow, that we make parade of our riches, and conceal our poverty. Nothing is so mortifying as to be obliged to expose our distress to the view of the public, and to feel, that though our situation is open to the eyes of all mankind, no mortal conceives for us the half of what we suffer. Nay, it is chiefly from this regard to the sentiments of mankind, that we pursue riches and avoid poverty. For to what purpose is all the toil and bustle of this world? what is the end of avarice and ambition, of the pursuit of wealth, of power, and preheminence? Is it to supply the necessities of nature? The wages of the meanest labourer can supply them. We see that they afford him food and clothing, the comfort of a house, and of a family. If we examined his oeconomy with rigour, we should find that he spends a great part of them upon conveniences, which may be regarded as superfluities, and that, upon extraordinary occasions, he can give something even to vanity and distinction. What then is the cause of our aversion to his situation, and why should those who have been educated in the higher ranks of life, regard it as worse than death, to be reduced to live, even without labour, upon the same simple fare with him, to dwell under the same lowly roof, and to be clothed in the same humble attire? Do they imagine that their stomach is better, or their sleep sounder in a palace than in a cottage? The contrary has been so often observed, and, indeed, is so very obvious, though it had never been observed, that there is nobody ignorant of it. From whence, then, arises that emulation which runs through all the different ranks of men, and what are the advantages which we propose by that great purpose of human life which we call bettering our condition? To be observed, to be attended to, to be taken notice of with sympathy, complacency, and approbation, are all the advantages which we can propose to derive from it. It is the vanity, not the ease, or the pleasure, which interests us. But vanity is always founded upon the belief of our being the object of attention and approbation. The rich man glories in his riches, because he feels that they naturally draw upon him the attention of the world, and that mankind are disposed to go along with him in all those agreeable emotions with which the advantages of his situation so readily inspire him. At the thought of this, his heart seems to swell and dilate itself within him, and he is fonder of his wealth, upon this account, than for all the other advantages it procures him. The poor man, on the contrary, is ashamed of his poverty. He feels that it either places him out of the sight of mankind, or, that if they take any notice of him, they have, however, scarce any fellow-feeling with the misery and distress which he suffers. He is mortified upon both accounts; for though to be overlooked, and to be disapproved of, are things entirely different, yet as obscurity covers us from the daylight of honour and approbation, to feel that we are taken no notice of, necessarily damps the most agreeable hope, and disappoints the most ardent desire, of human nature. The poor man goes out and comes in unheeded, and when in the midst of a crowd is in the same obscurity as if shut up in his own hovel. Those humble cares and painful attentions which occupy those in his situation, afford no amusement to the dissipated and the gay. They turn away their eyes from him, or if the extremity of his distress forces them to look at him, it is only to spurn so disagreeable an object from among them. The fortunate and the proud wonder at the insolence of human wretchedness, that it should dare to present itself before them, and with the loathsome aspect of its misery presume to disturb the serenity of their happiness. The man of rank and distinction, on the contrary, is observed by all the world. Every body is eager to look at him, and to conceive, at least by sympathy, that joy and exultation with which his circumstances naturally inspire him. His actions are the objects of the public care. Scarce a word, scarce a gesture, can fall from him that is altogether neglected. In a great assembly he is the person upon whom all direct their eyes; it is upon him that their passions seem all to wait with expectation, in order to receive that movement and direction which he shall impress upon them; and if his behaviour is not altogether absurd, he has, every moment, an opportunity of interesting mankind, and of rendering himself the object of the observation and fellow-feeling of every body about him. It is this, which, notwithstanding the restraint it imposes, notwithstanding the loss of liberty with which it is attended, renders greatness the object of envy, and compensates, in the opinion of mankind, all that toil, all that anxiety, all those mortifications which must be undergone in the pursuit of it; and what is of yet more consequence, all that leisure, all that ease, all that careless security, which are forfeited for ever by the acquisition.

When we consider the condition of the great, in those delusive colours in which the imagination is apt to paint it, it seems to be almost the abstract idea of a perfect and happy state. It is the very state which, in all our waking dreams and idle reveries, we had sketched out to ourselves as the final object of all our desires. We feel, therefore, a peculiar sympathy with the satisfaction of those who are in it. We favour all their inclinations, and forward all their wishes. What pity, we think, that any thing should spoil and corrupt so agreeable a situation! We could even wish them immortal; and it seems hard to us, that death should at last put an end to such perfect enjoyment. It is cruel, we think, in Nature to compel them from their exalted stations to that humble, but hospitable home, which she has provided for all her children. Great King, live for ever! is the compliment, which, after the manner of eastern adulation, we should readily make them, if experience did not teach us its absurdity. Every calamity that befals them, every injury that is done them, excites in the breast of the spectator ten times more compassion and resentment than he would have felt, had the same things happened to other men. It is the misfortunes of Kings only which afford the proper subjects for tragedy. They resemble, in this respect, the misfortunes of lovers. Those two situations are the chief which interest us upon the theatre; because, in spite of all that reason and experience can tell us to the contrary, the prejudices of the imagination attach to these two states a happiness superior to any other. To disturb, or to put an end to such perfect enjoyment, seems to be the most atrocious of all injuries. The traitor who conspires against the life of his monarch, is thought a greater monster than any other murderer. All the innocent blood that was shed in the civil wars, provoked less indignation than the death of Charles I. A stranger to human nature, who saw the indifference of men about the misery of their inferiors, and the regret and indignation which they feel for the misfortunes and sufferings of those above them, would be apt to imagine, that pain must be more agonizing, and the convulsions of death more terrible to persons of higher rank, than to those of meaner stations.

Upon this disposition of mankind, to go along with all the passions of the rich and the powerful, is founded the distinction of ranks, and the order of society. Our obsequiousness to our superiors more frequently arises from our admiration for the advantages of their situation, than from any private expectations of benefit from their good will. Their benefits can extend but to a few; but their fortunes interest almost every body. We are eager to assist them in completing a system of happiness that approaches so near to perfection; and we desire to serve them for their own sake, without any other recompense but the vanity or the honour of obliging them. Neither is our deference to their inclinations founded chiefly, or altogether, upon a regard to the utility of such submission, and to the order of society, which is best supported by it. Even when the order of society seems to require that we should oppose them, we can hardly bring ourselves to do it. That kings are the servants of the people, to be obeyed, resisted, deposed, or punished, as the public conveniency may require, is the doctrine of reason and philosophy; but it is not the doctrine of Nature. Nature would teach us to submit to them for their own sake, to tremble and bow down before their exalted station, to regard their smile as a reward sufficient to compensate any services, and to dread their displeasure, though no other evil were to follow from it, as the severest of all mortifications. To treat them in any respect as men, to reason and dispute with them upon ordinary occasions, requires such resolution, that there are few men whose magnanimity can support them in it, unless they are likewise assisted by familiarity and acquaintance. The strongest motives, the most furious passions, fear, hatred, and resentment, are scarce sufficient to balance this natural disposition to respect them: and their conduct must, either justly or unjustly, have excited the highest degree of all those passions, before the bulk of the people can be brought to oppose them with violence, or to desire to see them either punished or deposed. Even when the people have been brought this length, they are apt to relent every moment, and easily relapse into their habitual state of deference to those whom they have been accustomed to look upon as their natural superiors. They cannot stand the mortification of their monarch. Compassion soon takes the place of resentment, they forget all past provocations, their old principles of loyalty revive, and they run to re-establish the ruined authority of their old masters, with the same violence with which they had opposed it. The death of Charles I. brought about the Restoration of the royal family. Compassion for James II. when he was seized by the populace in making his escape on ship-board, had almost prevented the Revolution, and made it go on more heavily than before.

Do the great seem insensible of the easy price at which they may acquire the public admiration; or do they seem to imagine that to them, as to other men, it must be the purchase either of sweat or of blood? By what important accomplishments is the young nobleman instructed to support the dignity of his rank, and to render himself worthy of that superiority over his fellow-citizens, to which the virtue of his ancestors had raised them? Is it by knowledge, by industry, by patience, by self-denial, or by virtue of any kind? As all his words, as all his motions are attended to, he learns an habitual regard to every circumstance of ordinary behaviour, and studies to perform all those small duties with the most exact propriety. As he is conscious how much he is observed, and how much mankind are disposed to favour all his inclinations, he acts, upon the most indifferent occasions, with that freedom and elevation which the thought of this naturally inspires. His air, his manner, his deportment, all mark that elegant and graceful sense of his own superiority, which those who are born to inferior stations can hardly ever arrive at. These are the arts by which he proposes to make mankind more easily submit to his authority, and to govern their inclinations according to his own pleasure: and in this he is seldom disappointed. These arts, supported by rank and preheminence, are, upon ordinary occasions, sufficient to govern the world. Lewis XIV. during the greater part of his reign, was regarded, not only in France, but over all Europe, as the most perfect model of a great prince. But what were the talents and virtues by which he acquired this great reputation? Was it by the scrupulous and inflexible justice of all his undertakings, by the immense dangers and difficulties with which they were attended, or by the unwearied and unrelenting application with which he pursued them? Was it by his extensive knowledge, by his exquisite judgement, or by his heroic valour? It was by none of these qualities. But he was, first of all, the most powerful prince in Europe, and consequently held the highest rank among kings; and then, says his historian, 'he surpassed all his courtiers in the gracefulness of his shape, and the majestic beauty of his features. The sound of his voice, noble and affecting, gained those hearts which his presence intimidated. He had a step and a deportment which could suit only him and his rank, and which would have been ridiculous in any other person. The embarrassment which he occasioned to those who spoke to him, flattered that secret satisfaction with which he felt his own superiority. The old officer, who was confounded and faultered in asking him a favour, and not being able to conclude his discourse, said to him: Sir, your majesty, I hope, will believe that I do not tremble thus before your enemies: had no difficulty to obtain what he demanded.' These frivolous accomplishments, supported by his rank, and, no doubt too, by a degree of other talents and virtues, which seems, however, not to have been much above mediocrity, established this prince in the esteem of his own age, and have drawn, even from posterity, a good deal of respect for his memory. Compared with these, in his own times, and in his own presence, no other virtue, it seems, appeared to have any merit. Knowledge, industry, valour, and beneficence, trembled, were abashed, and lost all dignity before them.

But it is not by accomplishments of this kind, that the man of inferior rank must hope to distinguish himself. Politeness is so much the virtue of the great, that it will do little honour to any body but themselves. The coxcomb, who imitates their manner, and affects to be eminent by the superior propriety of his ordinary behaviour, is rewarded with a double share of contempt for his folly and presumption. Why should the man, whom nobody thinks it worth while to look at, be very anxious about the manner in which he holds up his head, or disposes of his arms while he walks through a room? He is occupied surely with a very superfluous attention, and with an attention too that marks a sense of his own importance, which no other mortal can go along with. The most perfect modesty and plainness, joined to as much negligence as is consistent with the respect due to the company, ought to be the chief characteristics of the behaviour of a private man. If ever he hopes to distinguish himself, it must be by more important virtues. He must acquire dependants to balance the dependants of the great, and he has no other fund to pay them from, but the labour of his body, and the activity of his mind. He must cultivate these therefore: he must acquire superior knowledge in his profession, and superior industry in the exercise of it. He must be patient in labour, resolute in danger, and firm in distress. These talents he must bring into public view, by the difficulty, importance, and, at the same time, good judgment of his undertakings, and by the severe and unrelenting application with which he pursues them. Probity and

prudence, generosity and frankness, must characterize his behaviour upon all ordinary occasions; and he must, at the same time, be forward to engage in all those situations, in which it requires the greatest talents and virtues to act with propriety, but in which the greatest applause is to be acquired by those who can acquit themselves with honour. With what impatience does the man of spirit and ambition, who is depressed by his situation, look round for some great opportunity to distinguish himself? No circumstances, which can afford this, appear to him undesirable. He even looks forward with satisfaction to the prospect of foreign war, or civil dissension; and, with secret transport and delight, sees through all the confusion and bloodshed which attend them, the probability of those wished-for occasions presenting themselves, in which he may draw upon himself the attention and admiration of mankind. The man of rank and distinction, on the contrary, whose whole glory consists in the propriety of his ordinary behaviour, who is contented with the humble renown which this can afford him, and has no talents to acquire any other, is unwilling to embarrass himself with what can be attended either with difficulty or distress. To figure at a ball is his great triumph, and to succeed in an intrigue of gallantry, his highest exploit. He has an aversion to all public confusions, not from the love of mankind, for the great never look upon their inferiors as their fellow-creatures; nor yet from want of courage, for in that he is seldom defective; but from a consciousness that he possesses none of the virtues which are required in such situations, and that the public attention will certainly be drawn away from him by others. He may be willing to expose himself to some little danger, and to make a campaign when it happens to be the fashion. But he shudders with horror at the thought of any situation which demands the continual and long exertion of patience, industry, fortitude, and application of thought. These virtues are hardly ever to be met with in men who are born to those high stations. In all governments accordingly, even in monarchies, the highest offices are generally possessed, and the whole detail of the administration conducted, by men who were educated in the middle and inferior ranks of life, who have been carried forward by their own industry and abilities, though loaded with the jealousy, and opposed by the resentment, of all those who were born their superiors, and to whom the great, after having regarded them first with contempt, and afterwards with envy, are at last contented to truckle with the same abject meanness with which they desire that the rest of mankind should behave to themselves.

It is the loss of this easy empire over the affections of mankind which renders the fall from greatness so insupportable. When the family of the king of Macedon was led in triumph by Paulus Aemilius, their misfortunes, it is said, made them divide with their conqueror the attention of the Roman people. The sight of the royal children, whose tender age rendered them insensible of their situation, struck the spectators, amidst the public rejoicings and prosperity, with the tenderest sorrow and compassion. The king appeared next in the procession; and seemed like one confounded and astonished, and bereft of all sentiment, by the greatness of his calamities. His friends and ministers followed after him. As they moved along, they often cast their eyes upon their fallen sovereign, and always burst into tears at the sight; their whole behaviour demonstrating that they thought not of their own misfortunes, but were occupied entirely by the superior greatness of his. The generous Romans, on the contrary, beheld him with disdain and indignation, and regarded as unworthy of all compassion the man who could be so meanspirited as to bear to live under such calamities. Yet what did those calamities amount to? According to the greater part of historians, he was to spend the remainder of his days, under the protection of a powerful and humane people, in a state which in itself should seem worthy of envy, a state of plenty, ease, leisure, and security, from which it was impossible for him even by his own folly to fall. But he was no longer to be surrounded by that admiring mob of fools, flatterers, and dependants, who had formerly been accustomed to attend upon all his motions. He was no longer to be gazed upon by multitudes, nor to have it in his power to render himself the object of their respect, their gratitude, their love, their admiration. The passions of nations were no longer to

mould themselves upon his inclinations. This was that insupportable calamity which bereaved the king of all sentiment; which made his friends forget their own misfortunes; and which the Roman magnanimity could scarce conceive how any man could be so mean-spirited as to bear to survive.

'Love,' says my Lord Rochfaucault, 'is commonly succeeded by ambition; but ambition is hardly ever succeeded by love.' That passion, when once it has got entire possession of the breast, will admit neither a rival nor a successor. To those who have been accustomed to the possession, or even to the hope of public admiration, all other pleasures sicken and decay. Of all the discarded statesmen who for their own ease have studied to get the better of ambition, and to despise those honours which they could no longer arrive at, how few have been able to succeed? The greater part have spent their time in the most listless and insipid indolence, chagrined at the thoughts of their own insignificancy, incapable of being interested in the occupations of private life, without enjoyment, except when they talked of their former greatness, and without satisfaction, except when they were employed in some vain project to recover it. Are you in earnest resolved never to barter your liberty for the lordly servitude of a court, but to live free, fearless, and independent? There seems to be one way to continue in that virtuous resolution; and perhaps but one. Never enter the place from whence so few have been able to return; never come within the circle of ambition; nor ever bring yourself into comparison with those masters of the earth who have already engrossed the attention of half mankind before you.

Of such mighty importance does it appear to be, in the imaginations of men, to stand in that situation which sets them most in the view of general sympathy and attention. And thus, place, that great object which divides the wives of aldermen, is the end of half the labours of human life; and is the cause of all the tumult and bustle, all the rapine and injustice, which avarice and ambition have introduced into this world. People of sense, it is said, indeed despise place; that is, they despise sitting at the head of the table, and are indifferent who it is that is pointed out to the company by that frivolous circumstance, which the smallest advantage is capable of overbalancing. But rank, distinction pre-eminence, no man despises, unless he is either raised very much above, or sunk very much below, the ordinary standard of human nature; unless he is either so confirmed in wisdom and real philosophy, as to be satisfied that, while the propriety of his conduct renders him the just object of approbation, it is of little consequence though he be neither attended to, nor approved of; or so habituated to the idea of his own meanness, so sunk in slothful and sottish indifference, as entirely to have forgot the desire, and almost the very wish, for superiority.

As to become the natural object of the joyous congratulations and sympathetic attentions of mankind is, in this manner, the circumstance which gives to prosperity all its dazzling splendour; so nothing darkens so much the gloom of adversity as to feel that our misfortunes are the objects, not of the fellow-feeling, but of the contempt and aversion of our brethren. It is upon this account that the most dreadful calamities are not always those which it is most difficult to support. It is often more mortifying to appear in public under small disasters, than under great misfortunes. The first excite no sympathy; but the second, though they may excite none that approaches to the anguish of the sufferer, call forth, however, a very lively compassion. The sentiments of the spectators are, in this last case, less wide of those of the sufferer, and their imperfect fellow-feeling lends him some assistance in supporting his misery. Before a gay assembly, a gentleman would be more mortified to appear covered with filth and rags than with blood and wounds. This last situation would interest their pity; the other would provoke their laughter. The judge who orders a criminal to be set in the pillory, dishonours him more than if he had condemned him to the scaffold. The great prince, who, some years ago, caned a general officer at the head of his army, disgraced him irrecoverably. The punishment would have been much less had he shot him through the body. By the laws of honour, to strike with a cane dishonours, to strike with a sword does not, for an obvious reason. Those slighter punishments, when inflicted on a gentleman, to whom dishonour is the greatest of all evils, come to be regarded among a humane and generous people, as the most dreadful of any. With regard to persons of that rank, therefore, they are universally laid aside, and the law, while it takes their life upon many occasions, respects their honour upon almost all. To scourge a person of quality, or to set him in the pillory, upon account of any crime whatever, is a brutality of which no European government, except that of Russia, is capable.

A brave man is not rendered contemptible by being brought to the scaffold; he is, by being set in the pillory. His behaviour in the one situation may gain him universal esteem and admiration. No behaviour in the other can render him agreeable. The sympathy of the spectators supports him in the one case, and saves him from that shame, that consciousness that his misery is felt by himself only, which is of all sentiments the most unsupportable. There is no sympathy in the other; or, if there is any, it is not with his pain, which is a trifle, but with his consciousness of the want of sympathy with which this pain is attended. It is with his shame, not with his sorrow. Those who pity him, blush and hang down their heads for him. He droops in the same manner, and feels himself irrecoverably degraded by the punishment, though not by the crime. The man, on the contrary, who dies with resolution, as he is naturally regarded with the erect aspect of esteem and approbation, so he wears himself the same undaunted countenance; and, if the crime does not deprive him of the respect of others, the punishment never will. He has no suspicion that his situation is the object of contempt or derision to any body, and he can, with propriety, assume the air, not only of perfect serenity, but of triumph and exultation.

'Great dangers,' says the Cardinal de Retz, 'have their charms, because there is some glory to be got, even when we miscarry. But moderate dangers have nothing but what is horrible, because the loss of reputation always attends the want of success.' His maxim has the same foundation with what we have been just now observing with regard to punishments.

Human virtue is superior to pain, to poverty, to danger, and to death; nor does it even require its utmost efforts to despise them. But to have its misery exposed to insult and derision, to be led in triumph, to be set up for the hand of scorn to point at, is a situation in which its constancy is much more apt to fail. Compared with the contempt of mankind, all other external evils are easily supported.

CHAP. III

Of the corruption of our moral sentiments, which is occasioned by this disposition to admire the rich and the great, and to despise or neglect persons of poor and mean condition

This disposition to admire, and almost to worship, the rich and the powerful, and to despise, or, at least, to neglect persons of poor and mean condition, though necessary both to establish and to maintain the distinction of ranks and the order of society, is, at the same time, the great and most universal cause of the corruption of our moral sentiments. That wealth and greatness are often regarded with the respect and admiration which are due only to wisdom and virtue; and that the contempt, of which vice and folly are the only proper objects, is often most unjustly bestowed upon poverty and weakness, has been the complaint of moralists in all ages.

We desire both to be respectable and to be respected. We dread both to be contemptible and to be contemned. But, upon coming into the world, we soon find that wisdom and virtue are by no means the sole objects of respect; nor vice and folly, of contempt. We frequently see the respectful attentions of the world more strongly directed towards the rich and the great, than towards the wise and the virtuous. We see frequently the vices and follies of the powerful much less despised than the poverty and weakness of the innocent. To deserve, to acquire, and to enjoy the respect and admiration of mankind, are the great objects of ambition and emulation. Two different roads are presented to us, equally leading to the attainment of this so much desired object; the one, by the study of wisdom and the practice of virtue; the other,

by the acquisition of wealth and greatness. Two different characters are presented to our emulation; the one, of proud ambition and ostentatious avidity; the other, of humble modesty and equitable justice. Two different models, two different pictures, are held out to us, according to which we may fashion our own character and behaviour; the one more gaudy and glittering in its colouring; the other more correct and more exquisitely beautiful in its outline; the one forcing itself upon the notice of every wandering eye; the other, attracting the attention of scarce any body but the most studious and careful observer. They are the wise and the virtuous chiefly, a select, though, I am afraid, but a small party, who are the real and steady admirers of wisdom and virtue. The great mob of mankind are the admirers and worshippers, and, what may seem more extraordinary, most frequently the disinterested admirers and worshippers, of wealth and greatness.

The respect which we feel for wisdom and virtue is, no doubt, different from that which we conceive for wealth and greatness; and it requires no very nice discernment to distinguish the difference. But, notwithstanding this difference, those sentiments bear a very considerable resemblance to one another. In some particular features they are, no doubt, different, but, in the general air of the countenance, they seem to be so very nearly the same, that inattentive observers are very apt to mistake the one for the other.

In equal degrees of merit there is scarce any man who does not respect more the rich and the great, than the poor and the humble. With most men the presumption and vanity of the former are much more admired, than the real and solid merit of the latter. It is scarce agreeable to good morals, or even to good language, perhaps, to say, that mere wealth and greatness, abstracted from merit and virtue, deserve our respect. We must acknowledge, however, that they almost constantly obtain it; and that they may, therefore, be considered as, in some respects, the natural objects of it. Those exalted stations may, no doubt, be completely degraded by vice and folly. But the vice and folly must be very great, before they can operate this complete degradation. The profligacy of a man of fashion is looked upon with much less contempt and aversion, than that of a man of meaner condition. In the latter, a single transgression of the rules of temperance and propriety, is commonly more resented, than the constant and avowed contempt of them ever is in the former.

In the middling and inferior stations of life, the road to virtue and that to fortune, to such fortune, at least, as men in such stations can reasonably expect to acquire, are, happily in most cases, very nearly the same. In all the middling and inferior professions, real and solid professional abilities, joined to prudent, just, firm, and temperate conduct, can very seldom fail of success. Abilities will even sometimes prevail where the conduct is by no means correct. Either habitual imprudence, however, or injustice, or weakness, or profligacy, will always cloud, and sometimes depress altogether, the most splendid professional abilities. Men in the inferior and middling stations of life, besides, can never be great enough to be above the law, which must generally overawe them into some sort of respect for, at least, the more important rules of justice. The success of such people, too, almost always depends upon the favour and good opinion of their neighbours and equals; and without a tolerably regular conduct these can very seldom be obtained. The good old proverb, therefore, That honesty is the best policy, holds, in such situations, almost always perfectly true. In such situations, therefore, we may generally expect a considerable degree of virtue; and, fortunately for the good morals of society, these are the situations of by far the greater part of mankind.

In the superior stations of life the case is unhappily not always the same. In the courts of princes, in the drawing-rooms of the great, where success and preferment depend, not upon the esteem of intelligent and well-informed equals, but upon the fanciful and foolish favour of ignorant, presumptuous, and proud superiors; flattery and falsehood too often prevail over merit and abilities. In such societies the abilities to please, are more regarded than the abilities to serve. In quiet and peaceable times, when the storm is at a distance, the prince, or great man, wishes only to be amused, and is even apt to fancy that he has scarce any occasion for the service of any body,

or that those who amuse him are sufficiently able to serve him. The external graces, the frivolous accomplishments of that impertinent and foolish thing called a man of fashion, are commonly more admired than the solid and masculine virtues of a warrior, a statesman, a philosopher, or a legislator. All the great and awful virtues, all the virtues which can fit, either for the council, the senate, or the field, are, by the insolent and insignificant flatterers, who commonly figure the most in such corrupted societies, held in the utmost contempt and derision. When the duke of Sully was called upon by Lewis the Thirteenth, to give his advice in some great emergency, he observed the favourites and courtiers whispering to one another, and smiling at his unfashionable appearance. 'Whenever your majesty's father,' said the old warrior and statesman, 'did me the honour to consult me, he ordered the buffoons of the court to retire into the antechamber.'

It is from our disposition to admire, and consequently to imitate, the rich and the great, that they are enabled to set, or to lead what is called the fashion. Their dress is the fashionable dress; the language of their conversation, the fashionable style; their air and deportment, the fashionable behaviour. Even their vices and follies are fashionable; and the greater part of men are proud to imitate and resemble them in the very qualities which dishonour and degrade them. Vain men often give themselves airs of a fashionable profligacy, which, in their hearts, they do not approve of, and of which, perhaps, they are really not guilty. They desire to be praised for what they themselves do not think praise-worthy, and are ashamed of unfashionable virtues which they sometimes practise in secret, and for which they have secretly some degree of real veneration. There are hypocrites of wealth and greatness, as well as of religion and virtue; and a vain man is as apt to pretend to be what he is not, in the one way, as a cunning man is in the other. He assumes the equipage and splendid way of living of his superiors, without considering that whatever may be praise-worthy in any of these, derives its whole merit and propriety from its suitableness to that situation and fortune which both require and can easily support the expence. Many a poor man places his glory in being thought rich, without considering that the duties (if one may call such follies by so very venerable a name) which that reputation imposes upon him, must soon reduce him to beggary, and render his situation still more unlike that of those whom he admires and imitates, than it had been originally.

To attain to this envied situation, the candidates for fortune too frequently abandon the paths of virtue; for unhappily, the road which leads to the one, and that which leads to the other, lie sometimes in very opposite directions. But the ambitious man flatters himself that, in the splendid situation to which he advances, he will have so many means of commanding the respect and admiration of mankind, and will be enabled to act with such superior propriety and grace, that the lustre of his future conduct will entirely cover, or efface, the foulness of the steps by which he arrived at that elevation. In many governments the candidates for the highest stations are above the law; and, if they can attain the object of their ambition, they have no fear of being called to account for the means by which they acquired it. They often endeavour, therefore, not only by fraud and falsehood, the ordinary and vulgar acts of intrigue and cabal; but sometimes by the perpetration of the most enormous crimes, by murder and assassination, by rebellion and civil war, to supplant and destroy those who oppose or stand in the way of their greatness. They more frequently miscarry than succeed; and commonly gain nothing but the disgraceful punishment which is due to their crimes. But, though they should be so lucky as to attain that wished-for greatness, they are always most miserably disappointed in the happiness which they expect to enjoy in it. It is not ease or pleasure, but always honour, of one kind or another, though frequently an honour very ill understood, that the ambitious man really pursues. But the honour of his exalted station appears, both in his own eyes and in those of other people, polluted and defiled by the baseness of the means through which he rose to it. Though by the profusion of every liberal expence; though by excessive indulgence in every profligate pleasure, the wretched, but usual, resource of ruined characters; though by the hurry of public business, or by the prouder and more dazzling tumult of war,

he may endeavour to efface, both from his own memory and from that of other people, the remembrance of what he has done; that remembrance never fails to pursue him. He invokes in vain the dark and dismal powers of forgetfulness and oblivion. He remembers himself what he has done, and that remembrance tells him that other people must likewise remember it. Amidst all the gaudy pomp of the most ostentatious greatness; amidst the venal and vile adulation of the great and of the learned; amidst the more innocent, though more foolish, acclamations of the common people; amidst all the pride of conquest and the triumph of successful war, he is still secretly pursued by the avenging furies of shame and remorse; and, while glory seems to surround him on all sides, he himself, in his own imagination, sees black and foul infamy fast pursuing him, and every moment ready to overtake him from behind. Even the great Caesar, though he had the magnanimity to dismiss his guards, could not dismiss his suspicions. The remembrance of Pharsalia still haunted and pursued him. When, at the request of the senate, he had the generosity to pardon Marcellus, he told that assembly, that he was not unaware of the designs which were carrying on against his life; but that, as he had lived long enough both for nature and for glory, he was contented to die, and therefore despised all conspiracies. He had, perhaps, lived long enough for nature. But the man who felt himself the object of such deadly resentment, from those whose favour he wished to gain, and whom he still wished to consider as his friends, had certainly lived too long for real glory; or for all the happiness which he could ever hope to enjoy in the love and esteem of his equals.

PART VII, SECTION II, CHAP. IV

Of licentious Systems

All those systems, which I have hitherto given an account of, suppose that there is a real and essential distinction between vice and virtue, whatever these qualities may consist in. There is a real and essential difference between the propriety and impropriety of any affection, between benevolence and any other principle of action, between real prudence and short-sighted folly or precipitate rashness. In the main too all of them contribute to encourage the praise-worthy, and to discourage the blamable disposition.

It may be true, perhaps, of some of them, that they tend, in some measure, to break the balance of the affections, and to give the mind a particular bias to some principles of action, beyond the proportion that is due to them. The ancient systems, which place virtue in propriety, seem chiefly to recommend the great, the awful, and the respectable virtues, the virtues of self-government and self-command; fortitude, magnanimity, independency upon fortune, the contempt of all outward accidents, of pain, poverty, exile, and death. It is in these great exertions that the noblest propriety of conduct is displayed. The soft, the amiable, the gentle virtues, all the virtues of indulgent humanity are, in comparison, but little insisted upon, and seem, on the contrary, by the Stoics in particular, to have been often regarded as mere weaknesses which it behoved a wise man not to harbour in his breast.

The benevolent system, on the other hand, while it fosters and encourages all those milder virtues in the highest degree, seems entirely to neglect the more awful and respectable qualities of the mind. It even denies them the appellation of virtues. It calls them moral abilities, and treats them as qualities which do not deserve the same sort of esteem and approbation, that is due to what is properly denominated virtue. All those principles of action which aim only at our own interest, it treats, if that be possible, still worse. So far from having any merit of their own, they diminish, it pretends, the merit of benevolence, when they co-operate with it: and prudence, it is asserted, when employed only in promoting private interest, can never even be imagined a virtue.

That system, again, which makes virtue consist in prudence only, while it gives the highest encouragement to the habits of caution, vigilance, sobriety, and judicious moderation, seems to degrade equally both the amiable and respectable virtues, and to strip the former of all their beauty, and the latter of all their grandeur.

But notwithstanding these defects, the general tendency of each of those three systems is to encourage the best and most laudable habits of the human mind: and it were well for society, if, either mankind in general, or even those few who pretend to live according to any philosophical rule, were to regulate their conduct by the precepts of any one of them. We may learn from each of them something that is both valuable and peculiar. If it was possible, by precept and exhortation, to inspire the mind with fortitude and magnanimity, the ancient systems of propriety would seem sufficient to do this. Or if it was possible, by the same means, to soften it into humanity, and to awaken the affections of kindness and general love towards those we live with, some of the pictures with which the benevolent system presents us, might seem capable of producing this effect. We may learn from the system of Epicurus, though undoubtedly the most imperfect of all the three, how much the practice of both the amiable and respectable virtues is conducive to our own interest, to our own ease and safety and quiet even in this life. As Epicurus placed happiness in the attainment of ease and security, he exerted himself in a particular manner to show that virtue was, not merely the best and the surest, but the only means of acquiring those invaluable possessions. The good effects of virtue, upon our inward tranquillity and peace of mind, are what other philosophers have chiefly celebrated. Epicurus, without neglecting this topic, has chiefly insisted upon the influence of that amiable quality on our outward prosperity and safety. It was upon this account that his writings were so much studied in the ancient world by men of all different philosophical parties. It is from him that Cicero, the great enemy of the Epicurean system, borrows his most agreeable proofs that virtue alone is sufficient to secure happiness. Seneca, though a Stoic, the sect most opposite to that of Epicurus, yet quotes this philosopher more frequently than any other.

There are, however, some other systems which seem to take away altogether the distinction between vice and virtue, and of which the tendency is, upon that account, wholly pernicious: I mean the systems of the Duke of Rochefoucault and Dr. Mandeville. Tho' the notions of both these authors are in almost every respect erroneous, there are, however, some appearances in human nature, which, when viewed in a certain manner, seem at first sight to favour them. These, first slightly sketched out with the elegant and delicate precision of the Duke of Rochefoucault, and afterwards more fully represented with the lively and humorous, tho' coarse and rustic eloquence of Dr. Mandeville have thrown upon their doctrines an air of truth and probability which is very apt to impose upon the unskilful.

Dr. Mandeville, the most methodical of these two authors, considers whatever is done from a sense of propriety, from a regard to what is commendable and praise-worthy, as being done from a love of praise and commendation, or as he calls it from vanity. Man, he observes, is naturally much more interested in his own happiness than in that of others, and it is impossible that in his heart he can ever really prefer their prosperity to his own. Whenever he appears to do so, we may be assured that he imposes upon us, and that he is then acting from the same selfish motives as at all other times. Among his other selfish passions, vanity is one of the strongest, and he is always easily flattered and greatly delighted with the applauses of those about him. When he appears to sacrifice his own interest to that of his companions, he knows that his conduct will be highly agreeable to their self-love, and that they will not fail to express their satisfaction by bestowing upon him the most extravagant praises. The pleasure which he expects from this, over-balances, in his opinion, the interest which he abandons in order to procure it. His conduct, therefore, upon this occasion, is in reality just as selfish, and arises from just as mean a motive, as upon any other. He is flattered, however, and he flatters himself, with the belief that it is entirely disinterested; since, unless this was supposed, it would not seem to merit any commendation either in his own eyes or in those of others. All public spirit, therefore, all preference of public to private interest, is, according to him, a mere cheat and imposition upon mankind; and that human

virtue which is so much boasted of, and which is the occasion of so much emulation among men, is the mere offspring of flattery begot upon pride.

Whether the most generous and public-spirited actions may not, in some sense, be regarded as proceeding from self-love, I shall not at present examine. The decision of this question is not, I apprehend, of any importance towards establishing the reality of virtue, since self-love may frequently be a virtuous motive of action. I shall only endeavour to show that the desire of doing what is honourable and noble, of rendering ourselves the proper objects of esteem and approbation, cannot with any propriety be called vanity. Even the love of well-grounded fame and reputation, the desire of acquiring esteem by what is really estimable, does not deserve that name. The first is the love of virtue, the noblest and the best passion in human nature. The second is the love of true glory, a passion inferior no doubt to the former, but which in dignity appears to come immediately after it. He is guilty of vanity who desires praise for qualities which are either not praise-worthy in any degree, or not in that degree in which he expects to be praised for them; who sets his character upon the frivolous ornaments of dress and equipage, or upon the equally frivolous accomplishments of ordinary behaviour. He is guilty of vanity who desires praise for what indeed very well deserves it, but what he perfectly knows does not belong to him. The empty coxcomb who gives himself airs of importance which he has no title to, the silly liar who assumes the merit of adventures which never happened, the foolish plagiary who gives himself out for the author of what he has no pretensions to, are properly accused of this passion. He too is said to be guilty of vanity who is not contented with the silent sentiments of esteem and approbation, who seems to be fonder of their noisy expressions and acclamations than of the sentiments themselves, who is never satisfied but when his own praises are ringing in his ears, and who solicits with the most anxious importunity all external marks of respect, is fond of titles, of compliments, of being visited, of being attended, of being taken notice of in public places with the appearance of deference and attention. This frivolous passion is altogether different from either of the two former, and is the passion of the lowest and the least of mankind, as they are of the noblest and the greatest.

But though these three passions, the desire of rendering ourselves the proper objects of honour and esteem; or of becoming what is honourable and estimable; the desire of acquiring honour and esteem by really deserving those sentiments; and the frivolous desire of praise at any rate, are widely different; though the two former are always approved of, while the latter never fails to be despised; there is, however, a certain remote affinity among them, which, exaggerated by the humorous and diverting eloquence of this lively author, has enabled him to impose upon his readers. There is an affinity between vanity and the love of true glory, as both these passions aim at acquiring esteem and approbation. But they are different in this, that the one is a just, reasonable, and equitable passion, while the other is unjust, absurd, and ridiculous. The man who desires esteem for what is really estimable, desires nothing but what he is justly entitled to, and what cannot be refused him without some sort of injury. He, on the contrary, who desires it upon any other terms, demands what he has no just claim to. The first is easily satisfied, is not apt to be jealous or suspicious that we do not esteem him enough, and is seldom solicitous about receiving many external marks of our regard. The other, on the contrary, is never to be satisfied, is full of jealousy and suspicion that we do not esteem him so much as he desires, because he has some secret consciousness that he desires more than he deserves. The least neglect of ceremony, he considers as a mortal affront, and as an expression of the most determined contempt. He is restless and impatient, and perpetually afraid that we have lost all respect for him, and is upon this account always anxious to obtain new expressions of esteem, and cannot be kept in temper but by continual attention and adulation.

There is an affinity too between the desire of becoming what is honourable and estimable, and the desire of honour and esteem, between the love of virtue and the love of true glory. They resemble one another not only in this respect, that both aim at really being

what is honourable and noble, but even in that respect in which the love of true glory resembles what is properly called vanity, some reference to the sentiments of others. The man of the greatest magnanimity, who desires virtue for its own sake, and is most indifferent about what actually are the opinions of mankind with regard to him, is still, however, delighted with the thoughts of what they should be, with the consciousness that though he may neither be honoured nor applauded, he is still the proper object of honour and applause, and that if mankind were cool and candid and consistent with themselves, and properly informed of the motives and circumstances of his conduct, they would not fail to honour and applaud him. Though he despises the opinions which are actually entertained of him, he has the highest value for those which ought to be entertained of him. That he might think himself worthy of those honourable sentiments, and, whatever was the idea which other men might conceive of his character, that when he should put himself in their situation, and consider, not what was, but what ought to be their opinion, he should always have the highest idea of it himself, was the great and exalted motive of his conduct. As even in the love of virtue, therefore, there is still some reference, though not to what is, yet to what in reason and propriety ought to be, the opinion of others, there is even in this respect some affinity between it, and the love of true glory. There is, however, at the same time, a very great difference between them. The man who acts solely from a regard to what is right and fit to be done, from a regard to what is the proper object of esteem and approbation, though these sentiments should never be bestowed upon him, acts from the most sublime and godlike motive which human nature is even capable of conceiving. The man, on the other hand, who while he desires to merit approbation is at the same time anxious to obtain it, though he too is laudable in the main, yet his motives have a greater mixture of human infirmity. He is in danger of being mortified by the ignorance and injustice of mankind, and his happiness is exposed to the envy of his rivals and the folly of the public. The happiness of the other, on the contrary, is altogether secure and independent of fortune, and of the caprice of those he lives with. The contempt and hatred which may be thrown upon him by the ignorance of mankind, he considers as not belonging to him, and is not at all mortified by it. Mankind despise and hate him from a false notion of his character and conduct. If they knew him better, they would esteem and love him. It is not him whom, properly speaking, they hate and despise, but another person whom they mistake him to be. Our friend, whom we should meet at a masquerade in the garb of our enemy, would be more diverted than mortified, if under that disguise we should vent our indignation against him. Such are the sentiments of a man of real magnanimity, when exposed to unjust censure. It seldom happens, however, that human nature arrives at this degree of firmness. Though none but the weakest and most worthless of mankind are much delighted with false glory, yet, by a strange inconsistency, false ignominy is often capable of mortifying those who appear the most resolute and determined.

Dr. Mandeville is not satisfied with representing the frivolous motive of vanity, as the source of all those actions which are commonly accounted virtuous. He endeavours to point out the imperfection of human virtue in many other respects. In every case, he pretends, it falls short of that complete self-denial which it pretends to, and, instead of a conquest, is commonly no more than a concealed indulgence of our passions. Wherever our reserve with regard to pleasure falls short of the most ascetic abstinence, he treats it as gross luxury and sensuality. Every thing, according to him, is luxury which exceeds what is absolutely necessary for the support of human nature, so that there is vice even in the use of a clean shirt, or of a convenient habitation. The indulgence of the inclination to sex, in the most lawful union, he considers as the same sensuality with the most hurtful gratification of that passion, and derides that temperance and that chastity which can be practised at so cheap a rate. The ingenious sophistry of his reasoning, is here, as upon many other occasions, covered by the ambiguity of language. There are some of our passions which have no other names except those which mark the disagreeable and offensive degree. The spectator is more apt to take notice of them in this degree than in any other. When they shock his own sentiments, when they give him some sort of antipathy and uneasiness, he is necessarily obliged to attend to them, and is from thence naturally led to give them a name. When they fall in with the natural state of his own mind, he is very apt to overlook them altogether, and either gives them no name at all, or, if he give them any, it is one which marks rather the subjection and restraint of the passion, than the degree which it still is allowed to subsist in, after it is so subjected and restrained. Thus the common names of the love of pleasure, and of the love of sex, denote a vicious and offensive degree of those passions. The words temperance and chastity, on the other hand, seem to mark rather the restraint and subjection which they are kept under, than the degree which they are still allowed to subsist in. When he can show, therefore, that they still subsist in some degree, he imagines, he has entirely demolished the reality of the virtues of temperance and chastity, and shown them to be mere impositions upon the inattention and simplicity of mankind. Those virtues, however, do not require an entire insensibility to the objects of the passions which they mean to govern. They only aim at restraining the violence of those passions so far as not to hurt the individual, and neither disturb nor offend the society.

It is the great fallacy of Dr. Mandeville's book to represent every passion as wholly vicious, which is so in any degree and in any direction. It is thus that he treats every thing as vanity which has any reference, either to what are, or to what ought to be the sentiments of others: and it is by means of this sophistry, that he establishes his favourite conclusion, that private vices are public benefits. If the love of magnificence, a taste for the elegant arts and improvements of human life, for whatever is agreeable in dress, furniture, or equipage, for architecture, statuary, painting, and music, is to be regarded as luxury, sensuality, and ostentation, even in those whose situation allows, without any inconveniency, the indulgence of those passions, it is certain that luxury, sensuality, and ostentation are public benefits: since without the qualities upon which he thinks proper to bestow such opprobrious names, the arts of refinement could never find encouragement, and must languish for want of employment. Some popular ascetic doctrines which had been current before his time, and which placed virtue in the entire extirpation and annihilation of all our passions, were the real foundation of this licentious system. It was easy for Dr. Mandeville to prove, first, that this entire conquest never actually took place among men; and secondly, that, if it was to take place universally, it would be pernicious to society, by putting an end to all industry and commerce, and in a manner to the whole business of human life. By the first of these propositions he seemed to prove that there was no real virtue, and that what pretended to be such, was a mere cheat and imposition upon mankind; and by the second, that private vices were public benefits, since without them no society could prosper or flourish.

Such is the system of Dr. Mandeville, which once made so much noise in the world, and which, though, perhaps, it never gave occasion to more vice than what would have been without it, at least taught that vice, which arose from other causes, to appear with more effrontery, and to avow the corruption of its motives with a profligate audaciousness which had never been heard of before.

But how destructive soever this system may appear, it could never have imposed upon so great a number of persons, nor have occasioned so general an alarm among those who are the friends of better principles, had it not in some respects bordered upon the truth. A system of natural philosophy may appear very plausible, and be for a long time very generally received in the world, and yet have no foundation in nature, nor any sort of resemblance to the truth. The vortices of Des Cartes were regarded by a very ingenious nation, for near a century together, as a most satisfactory account of the revolutions of the heavenly bodies. Yet it has been demonstrated, to the conviction of all mankind, that these pretended causes of those wonderful effects, not only do not actually exist, but are utterly impossible, and if they did exist, could

produce no such effects as are ascribed to them. But it is otherwise with systems of moral philosophy, and an author who pretends to account for the origin of our moral sentiments, cannot deceive us so grossly, nor depart so very far from all resemblance to the truth. When a traveller gives an account of some distant country, he may impose upon our credulity the most groundless and absurd fictions as the most certain matters of fact. But when a person pretends to inform us of what passes in our neighbourhood, and of the affairs of the very parish which we live in, though here too, if we are so careless as not to examine things with our own eyes, he may deceive us in many respects, yet the greatest falsehoods which he imposes upon us must bear some resemblance to the truth, and must even have a considerable mixture of truth in them. An author who treats of natural philosophy, and pretends to assign the causes of the great phaenomena of the universe, pretends to give an account of the affairs of a very distant country, concerning which he may tell us what he pleases, and as long as his narration keeps within the bounds of seeming possibility, he need not despair of gaining our belief. But when he proposes to explain the origin of our desires and affections, of our sentiments of approbation and disapprobation, he pretends to give an account, not only of the affairs of the very parish that we live in, but of our own domestic concerns. Though here too, like indolent masters who put their trust in a steward who deceives them, we are very liable to be imposed upon, yet we are incapable of passing any account which does not preserve some little regard to the truth. Some of the articles, at least, must be just, and even those which are most overcharged must have had some foundation, otherwise the fraud would be detected even by that careless inspection which we are disposed to give. The author who should assign, as the cause of any natural sentiment, some principle which neither had any connexion with it, nor resembled any other principle which had some such connexion, would appear absurd and ridiculous to the most injudicious and unexperienced reader.

BURKE

Reflections on the Revolution in France

I flatter myself that I love a manly, moral, regulated liberty as well as any gentleman of that society,[1] be he who will; and perhaps I have given as good proofs of my attachment to that cause in the whole course of my public conduct. I think I envy liberty as little as they do to any other nation. But I cannot stand forward and give praise or blame to anything which relates to human actions, and human concerns, on a simple view of the object, as it stands stripped of every relation, in all the nakedness and solitude of metaphysical abstraction. Circumstances (which with some gentlemen pass for nothing) give in reality to every political principle its distinguishing color and discriminating effect. The circumstances are what render every civil and political scheme beneficial or noxious to mankind. Abstractedly speaking, government, as well as liberty, is good; yet could I, in common sense, ten years ago, have felicitated France on her enjoyment of a government (for she then had a government) without inquiry what the nature of that government was, or how it was administered? Can I now congratulate the same nation upon its freedom? Is it because liberty in the abstract may be classed amongst the blessings of mankind, that I am seriously to felicitate a madman, who has escaped from the protecting restraint and wholesome darkness of his cell, on his restoration to the enjoyment of light and liberty? Am I to congratulate a highwayman and murderer who has broke prison upon the recovery of his natural rights? This would be to act over again the scene of the criminals condemned to the galleys, and their heroic deliverer, the metaphysic Knight of the Sorrowful Countenance.

When I see the spirit of liberty in action, I see a strong principle at work; and this, for a while, is all I can possibly know of it. The wild *gas*, the fixed air, is plainly broke loose; but we ought to suspend our judgment until the first effervescence is a little subsided, till the liquor is cleared, and until we see something deeper than the agitation of a troubled and frothy surface. I must be tolerably sure, before I venture publicly to congratulate men upon a blessing, that they have really received one. Flattery corrupts both the receiver and the giver, and adulation is not of more service to the people than to kings. I should, therefore, suspend my congratulations on the new liberty of France until I was informed how it had been combined with government, with public force, with the discipline and obedience of armies, with the collection of an effective and well-distributed revenue, with morality and religion, with the solidity of property, with peace and order, with civil and social manners. All these (in their way) are good things, too, and without them liberty is not a benefit whilst it lasts, and is not likely to continue long. The effect of liberty to individuals is that they may do what they please; we ought to see what it will please them to do, before we risk congratulations which may be soon turned into complaints. Prudence would dictate this in the case of separate, insulated, private men, but liberty, when men act in bodies, is *power*. Considerate people, before they declare themselves, will observe the use which is made of *power*, and particularly of so trying a thing as *new* power in *new* persons of whose principles, tempers, and dispositions they have little or no experience, and in situations where those who appear the most stirring in the scene may possibly not be the real movers. . . .

You will observe that from Magna Charta to the Declaration of Right it has been the uniform policy of our constitution to claim and assert our liberties as an *entailed inheritance* derived to us from our forefathers, and to be transmitted to our posterity—as an estate

---

[1] The Society for Constitutional Information.

502

specially belonging to the people of this kingdom, without any reference whatever to any other more general or prior right. By this means our constitution preserves a unity in so great a diversity of its parts. We have an inheritable crown, an inheritable peerage, and a House of Commons and a people inheriting privileges, franchises, and liberties from a long line of ancestors.

This policy appears to me to be the result of profound reflection, or rather the happy effect of following nature, which is wisdom without reflection, and above it. A spirit of innovation is generally the result of a selfish temper and confined views. People will not look forward to posterity, who never look backward to their ancestors. Besides, the people of England well know that the idea of inheritance furnishes a sure principle of conservation and a sure principle of transmission, without at all excluding a principle of improvement. It leaves acquisition free, but it secures what it acquires. Whatever advantages are obtained by a state proceeding on these maxims are locked fast as in a sort of family settlement, grasped as in a kind of mortmain forever. By a constitutional policy, working after the pattern of nature, we receive, we hold, we transmit our government and our privileges in the same manner in which we enjoy and transmit our property and our lives. The institutions of policy, the goods of fortune, the gifts of providence are handed down to us, and from us, in the same course and order. Our political system is placed in a just correspondence and symmetry with the order of the world and with the mode of existence decreed to a permanent body composed of transitory parts, wherein, by the disposition of a stupendous wisdom, molding together the great mysterious incorporation of the human race, the whole, at one time, is never old or middle-aged or young, but, in a condition of unchangeable constancy, moves on through the varied tenor of perpetual decay, fall, renovation, and progression. Thus, by preserving the method of nature in the conduct of the state, in what we improve we are never wholly new; in what we retain we are never wholly obsolete. By adhering in this manner and on those principles to our forefathers, we are guided not by the superstition of antiquarians, but by the spirit

of philosophic analogy. In this choice of inheritance we have given to our frame of polity the image of a relation in blood, binding up the constitution of our country with our dearest domestic ties, adopting our fundamental laws into the bosom of our family affections, keeping inseparable and cherishing with the warmth of all their combined and mutually reflected charities our state, our hearths, our sepulchres, and our altars.

Through the same plan of a conformity to nature in our artificial institutions, and by calling in the aid of her unerring and powerful instincts to fortify the fallible and feeble contrivances of our reason, we have derived several other, and those no small, benefits from considering our liberties in the light of an inheritance. Always acting as if in the presence of canonized forefathers, the spirit of freedom, leading in itself to misrule and excess, is tempered with an awful gravity. This idea of a liberal descent inspires us with a sense of habitual native dignity which prevents that upstart insolence almost inevitably adhering to and disgracing those who are the first acquirers of any distinction. By this means our liberty becomes a noble freedom. It carries an imposing and majestic aspect. It has a pedigree and illustrating ancestors. It has its bearings and its ensigns armorial. It has its gallery of portraits, its monumental inscriptions, its records, evidences, and titles. We procure reverence to our civil institutions on the principle upon which nature teaches us to revere individual men: on account of their age and on account of those from whom they are descended. All your sophisters cannot produce anything better adapted to preserve a rational and manly freedom than the course that we have pursued, who have chosen our nature rather than our speculations, our breasts rather than our inventions, for the great conservatories and magazines of our rights and privileges.

You might, if you pleased, have profited of our example and have given to your recovered freedom a correspondent dignity. Your privileges, though discontinued, were not lost to memory. Your constitution, it is true, whilst you were out of possession, suffered waste and dilapidation; but you possessed in some parts the walls and in all the foundations of a noble and venerable castle. You might have repaired those walls; you might have built on those old foundations. Your constitution was suspended before it was perfected, but you had the elements of a constitution very nearly as good as could be wished. In your old states you possessed that variety of parts corresponding with the various descriptions of which your community was happily composed; you had all that combination and all that opposition of interests; you had that action and counteraction which, in the natural and in the political world, from the reciprocal struggle of discordant powers, draws out the harmony of the universe. These opposed and conflicting interests which you considered as so great a blemish in your old and in our present constitution interpose a salutary check to all precipitate resolutions. They render deliberation a matter, not of choice, but of necessity; they make all change a subject of *compromise,* which naturally begets moderation; they produce *temperaments* preventing the sore evil of harsh, crude, unqualified reformations, and rendering all the headlong exertions of arbitrary power, in the few or in the many, for ever impracticable. Through that diversity of members and interests, general liberty had as many securities as there were separate views in the several orders, whilst, by pressing down the whole by the weight of a real monarchy, the separate parts would have been prevented from warping and starting from their allotted places.

You had all these advantages in your ancient states, but you chose to act as if you had never been molded into civil society and had everything to begin anew. You begin ill, because you began by despising everything that belonged to you. You set up your trade without a capital. If the last generations of your country appeared without much luster in your eyes, you might have passed them by and derived your claims from a more early race of ancestors. Under a pious predilection for those ancestors, your imaginations would have realized in them a standard of virtue and wisdom beyond the vulgar practice of the hour; and you would have risen with the example to whose imitation you aspired. Respecting your forefathers, you would have been taught to respect yourselves. You would not have chosen to consider the French

as a people of yesterday, as a nation of lowborn servile wretches until the emancipating year of 1789. In order to furnish, at the expense of your honor, an excuse to your apologists here for several enormities of yours, you would not have been content to be represented as a gang of Maroon slaves suddenly broke loose from the house of bondage, and therefore to be pardoned for your abuse of the liberty to which you were not accustomed and ill fitted. Would it not, my worthy friend, have been wiser to have you thought, what I, for one, always thought you, a generous and gallant nation, long misled to your disadvantage by your high and romantic sentiments of fidelity, honor, and loyalty; that events had been unfavorable to you, but that you were not enslaved through any illiberal or servile disposition; that in your most devoted submission you were actuated by a principle of public spirit, and that it was your country you worshiped in the person of your king? Had you made it to be understood that in the delusion of this amiable error you had gone further than your wise ancestors, that you were resolved to resume your ancient privileges, whilst you preserved the spirit of your ancient and your recent loyalty and honor; or if, diffident of yourselves and not clearly discerning the almost obliterated constitution of your ancestors, you had looked to your neighbors in this land who had kept alive the ancient principles and models of the old common law of Europe meliorated and adapted to its present state — by following wise examples you would have given new examples of wisdom to the world. You would have rendered the cause of liberty venerable in the eyes of every worthy mind in every nation. You would have shamed despotism from the earth by showing that freedom was not only reconcilable, but, as when well disciplined it is, auxiliary to law. You would have had an unoppressive but a productive revenue. You would have had a flourishing commerce to feed it. You would have had a free constitution, a potent monarchy, a disciplined army, a reformed and venerated clergy, a mitigated but spirited nobility to lead your virtue, not to overlay it; you would have had a liberal order of commons to emulate and to recruit that nobility; you would have had a protected, satisfied, laborious, and obedient people, taught to seek and to recognize the happiness that is to be found by virtue in all conditions; in which consists the true moral equality of mankind, and not in that monstrous fiction which, by inspiring false ideas and vain expectations into men destined to travel in the obscure walk of laborious life, serves only to aggravate and embitter that real inequality which it never can remove, and which the order of civil life establishes as much for the benefit of those whom it must leave in a humble state as those whom it is able to exalt to a condition more splendid, but not more happy. You had a smooth and easy career of felicity and glory laid open to you, beyond anything recorded in the history of the world, but you have shown that difficulty is good for man.

Compute your gains: see what is got by those extravagant and presumptuous speculations which have taught your leaders to despise all their predecessors, and all their contemporaries, and even to despise themselves until the moment in which they become truly despicable. By following those false lights, France has bought undisguised calamities at a higher price than any nation has purchased the most unequivocal blessings! France has bought poverty by crime! France has not sacrificed her virtue to her interest, but she has abandoned her interest, that she might prostitute her virtue. All other nations have begun the fabric of a new government, or the reformation of an old, by establishing originally or by enforcing with greater exactness some rites or other of religion. All other people have laid the foundations of civil freedom in severer manners and a system of a more austere and masculine morality. France, when she let loose the reins of regal authority, doubled the license of a ferocious dissoluteness in manners and of an insolent irreligion in opinions and practice, and has extended through all ranks of life, as if she were communicating some privilege or laying open some secluded benefit, all the unhappy corruptions that usually were the disease of wealth and power. This is one of the new principles of equality in France.

France, by the perfidy of her leaders, has utterly disgraced the tone of lenient council in the cabinets of princes, and disarmed it of its most potent topics.

She has sanctified the dark, suspicious maxims of tyrannous distrust, and taught kings to tremble at (what will hereafter be called) the delusive plausibilities of moral politicians. Sovereigns will consider those who advise them to place an unlimited confidence in their people as subverters of their thrones, as traitors who aim at their destruction by leading their easy good-nature, under specious pretenses, to admit combinations of bold and faithless men into a participation of their power. This alone (if there were nothing else) is an irreparable calamity to you and to mankind. Remember that your parliament of Paris told your king that, in calling the states together, he had nothing to fear but the prodigal excess of their zeal in providing for the support of the throne. It is right that these men should hide their heads. It is right that they should bear their part in the ruin which their counsel has brought on their sovereign and their country. Such sanguine declarations tend to lull authority asleep; to encourage it rashly to engage in perilous adventures of untried policy; to neglect those provisions, preparations, and precautions which distinguish benevolence from imbecility, and without which no man can answer for the salutary effect of any abstract plan of government or of freedom. For want of these, they have seen the medicine of the state corrupted into its poison. They have seen the French rebel against a mild and lawful monarch with more fury, outrage, and insult than ever any people has been known to rise against the most illegal usurper or the most sanguinary tyrant. Their resistance was made to concession, their revolt was from protection, their blow was aimed at a hand holding out graces, favors, and immunities.

This was unnatural. The rest is in order. They have found their punishment in their success; laws overturned; tribunals subverted; industry without vigor; commerce expiring; the revenue unpaid, yet the people impoverished; a church pillaged, and a state not relieved; civil and military anarchy made the constitution of the kingdom; everything human and divine sacrificed to the idol of public credit, and national bankruptcy the consequence; and, to crown all, the paper securities of new, precarious, tottering power, the discredited paper securities of impoverished fraud and beggared rapine, held out as a currency for the support of an empire in lieu of the two great recognized species that represent the lasting, conventional credit of mankind, which disappeared and hid themselves in the earth from whence they came, when the principle of property, whose creatures and representatives they are, was systematically subverted.

Were all these dreadful things necessary? Were they the inevitable results of the desperate struggle of determined patriots, compelled to wade through blood and tumult to the quiet shore of a tranquil and prosperous liberty? No! nothing like it. The fresh ruins of France, which shock our feelings wherever we can turn our eyes, are not the devastation of civil war; they are the sad but instructive monuments of rash and ignorant counsel in time of profound peace. They are the display of inconsiderate and presumptuous, because unresisted and irresistible, authority. The persons who have thus squandered away the precious treasure of their crimes, the persons who have made this prodigal and wild waste of public evils (the last stake reserved for the ultimate ransom of the state) have met in their progress with little or rather with no opposition at all. Their whole march was more like a triumphal procession than the progress of a war. Their pioneers have gone before them and demolished and laid everything level at their feet. Not one drop of *their* blood have they shed in the cause of the country they have ruined. They have made no sacrifices to their projects of greater consequence than their shoebuckles, whilst they were imprisoning their king, murdering their fellow citizens, and bathing in tears and plunging in poverty and distress thousands of worthy men and worthy families. Their cruelty has not even been the base result of fear. It has been the effect of their sense of perfect safety, in authorizing treasons, robberies, rapes, assassinations, slaughters, and burnings throughout their harassed land. But the cause of all was plain from the beginning.

This unforced choice, this fond election of evil, would appear perfectly unaccountable if we did not consider the composition of the National Assembly. I do not mean its formal constitution, which, as it now stands, is exceptionable enough, but the materials of which, in a great measure, it is composed, which is of ten thousand times greater consequence than all the formalities in the world. If we were to know nothing of this assembly but by its title and function, no colors could paint to the imagination anything more venerable. In that light the mind of an inquirer, subdued by such an awful image as that of the virtue and wisdom of a whole people collected into a focus, would pause and hesitate in condemning things even of the very worst aspect. Instead of blamable, they would appear only mysterious. But no name, no power, no function, no artificial institution whatsoever can make the men of whom any system of authority is composed any other than God, and nature, and education, and their habits of life have made them. Capacities beyond these the people have not to give. Virtue and wisdom may be the objects of their choice, but their choice confers neither the one nor the other on those upon whom they lay their ordaining hands. They have not the engagement of nature, they have not the promise of revelation, for any such powers.

After I had read over the list of the persons and descriptions elected into the *Tiers Etat*, nothing which they afterwards did could appear astonishing. Among them, indeed, I saw some of known rank, some of shining talents; but of any practical experience in the state, not one man was to be found. The best were only men of theory. But whatever the distinguished few may have been, it is the substance and mass of the body which constitutes its character and must finally determine its direction. In all bodies, those who will lead must also, in a considerable degree, follow. They must conform their propositions to the taste, talent, and disposition of those whom they wish to conduct; therefore, if an assembly is viciously or feebly composed in a very great part of it, nothing but such a supreme degree of virtue as very rarely appears in the world, and for that reason cannot enter into calculation, will prevent the men of talent disseminated through it from becoming only the expert instruments of absurd projects! If, what is the more likely event, instead of that unusual degree of virtue, they should be actuated by sinister ambition and a lust of meretricious glory, then the feeble part of the assembly, to whom at first they conform, becomes in its turn the dupe and instrument of their designs. In this political traffic, the leaders will be obliged to bow to the ignorance of their followers, and the followers to become subservient to the worst designs of their leaders.

To secure any degree of sobriety in the propositions made by the leaders in any public assembly, they ought to respect, in some degree perhaps to fear, those whom they conduct. To be led any otherwise than blindly, the followers must be qualified, if not for actors, at least for judges; they must also be judges of natural weight and authority. Nothing can secure a steady and moderate conduct in such assemblies but that the body of them should be respectably composed, in point of condition in life or permanent property, of education, and of such habits as enlarge and liberalize the understanding.

In the calling of the States-General of France, the first thing that struck me was a great departure from the ancient course. I found the representation for the Third Estate composed of six hundred persons. They were equal in number to the representatives of both the other orders. If the orders were to act separately, the number would not, beyond the consideration of the expense, be of much moment. But when it became apparent that the three orders were to be melted down into one, the policy and necessary effect of this numerous representation became obvious. A very small desertion from either of the other two orders must throw the power of both into the hands of the third. In fact, the whole power of the state was soon resolved into that body. Its due composition became therefore of infinitely the greater importance.

Judge, Sir, of my surprise when I found that a very great proportion of the assembly (a majority, I believe, of the members who attended) was composed of practitioners in the law. It was composed, not of distinguished magistrates, who had given pledges to their country of their science, prudence, and integrity; not of leading advocates, the glory of the bar; not of renowned professors in universities;—but for the far greater part, as it must in such a number, of the inferior, unlearned, mechanical, merely instrumental members of the profession. There were distinguished exceptions, but the general composition was of obscure provincial advocates, of stewards of petty local jurisdictions, country attornies, notaries, and the whole train of the ministers of municipal litigation, the fomenters and conductors of the petty war of village vexation. From the moment I read the list, I saw distinctly, and very nearly as it has happened, all that was to follow.

The degree of estimation in which any profession is held becomes the standard of the estimation in which the professors hold themselves. Whatever the personal merits of many individual lawyers might have been, and in many it was undoubtedly very considerable, in that military kingdom no part of the profession had been much regarded except the highest of all, who often united to their professional offices great family splendor, and were invested with great power and authority. These certainly were highly respected, and even with no small degree of awe. The next rank was not much esteemed; the mechanical part was in a very low degree of repute.

Whenever the supreme authority is vested in a body so composed, it must evidently produce the consequences of supreme authority placed in the hands of men not taught habitually to respect themselves, who had no previous fortune in character at stake, who could not be expected to bear with moderation, or to conduct with discretion, a power which they themselves, more than any others, must be surprised to find in their hands. Who could flatter himself that these men, suddenly and, as it were, by enchantment snatched from the humblest rank of subordination, would not be intoxicated with their unprepared greatness? Who could conceive that men who are habitually meddling, daring, subtle, active, of litigious dispositions and unquiet minds would easily fall back into their old condition of obscure contention and laborious, low, unprofitable chicane? Who could doubt but that, at any expense to the state, of which they understood nothing, they must pursue their private interests, which they understand but too well? It was not an event depending on chance or contingency. It was inevitable; it was necessary; it was planted in the nature of things. They must *join* (if their capacity did not permit them to *lead*) in any project which could procure to them a *litigious constitution*; which could lay open to them those innumerable lucrative jobs which follow in the train of all great convulsions and revolutions in the state, and particularly in all great and violent permutations of property. Was it to be expected that they would attend to the stability of property, whose existence had always depended upon whatever rendered property questionable, ambiguous, and insecure? Their objects would be enlarged with their elevation, but their disposition and habits, and mode of accomplishing their designs, must remain the same.

Well! but these men were to be tempered and restrained by other descriptions, of more sober and more enlarged understandings. Were they then to be awed by the supereminent authority and awful dignity of a handful of country clowns who have seats in that assembly, some of whom are said not to be able to read and write, and by not a greater number of traders who, though somewhat more instructed and more conspicuous in the order of society, had never known anything beyond their counting house? No! Both these descriptions were more formed to be overborne and swayed by the intrigues and artifices of lawyers than to become their counterpoise. With such a dangerous disproportion, the whole must needs to be governed by them. To the faculty of law was joined a pretty considerable proportion of the faculty of medicine. This faculty had not, any more than that of the law, possessed in France its just estimation. Its professors, therefore, must have the qualities of men not habituated to sentiments of dignity. But supposing they had ranked as they ought to do, and as with us they do actually, the sides of sickbeds are not the academies for forming statesmen and legislators. Then came the dealers in stocks and funds, who must be eager, at any expense, to change their ideal paper wealth for the more solid substance of land. To these were joined men of other descriptions, from whom as little knowledge of, or attention to, the interests of a great state was to be expected, and as little regard to the stability of any institution; men formed to be instruments, not controls. Such in general was the composition of the *Tiers Etat* in the National Assembly, in which was scarcely to be perceived the slightest traces of what we call the natural landed interest of the country.

We know that the British House of Commons, without shutting its doors to any merit in any class, is, by the sure operation of adequate causes, filled with everything illustrious in rank, in descent, in hereditary and in acquired opulence, in cultivated talents, in military, civil, naval, and politic distinction that the country can afford. But supposing, what hardly can be supposed as a case, that the House of Commons should be composed in the same manner with the *Tiers Etat* in France, would this dominion of chicane be borne with patience or even conceived without horror? God forbid I should insinuate anything derogatory to that profession which is another priesthood, administering the rights of sacred justice. But whilst I revere men in the functions which belong to them, and would do as much as one man can do to prevent their exclusion from any, I cannot, to flatter them, give the lie to nature. They are good and useful in the composition; they must be mischievous if they preponderate so as virtually to become the whole. Their very excellence in their peculiar functions may be far from a qualification for others. It cannot escape observation that when men are too much confined to professional and faculty habits and, as it were, inveterate in the recurrent employment of that narrow circle, they are rather disabled than qualified for whatever depends on the knowledge of mankind, on experience in mixed affairs, on a comprehensive, connected view of the various, complicated, external and internal interests which go to the formation of that multifarious thing called a state.

After all, if the House of Commons were to have a wholly professional and faculty composition, what is the power of the House of Commons, circumscribed and shut in by the immovable barriers of laws, usages, positive rules of doctrine and practice, counterpoised by the House of Lords, and every moment of its existence at the discretion of the crown to continue, prorogue, or dissolve us? The power of the House of Commons, direct or indirect, is indeed great; and long may it be able to preserve its greatness and the spirit belonging to true greatness at the full; and it will do so as long as it can keep the breakers of law in India from becoming the makers of law for England. The power, however, of the House of Commons, when least diminished, is as a drop of water in the ocean, compared to that residing in a settled majority of your National Assembly. That assembly, since the destruction of the orders, has no fundamental law, no strict convention, no respected usage to restrain it. Instead of finding themselves obliged to conform to a fixed constitution, they have a power to make a constitution which shall conform to their designs. Nothing in heaven or upon earth can serve as a control on them. What ought to be the heads, the hearts, the dispositions that are qualified or that dare, not only to make laws under a fixed constitution, but at one heat to strike out a totally new constitution for a great kingdom, and in every part of it, from the monarch on the throne to the vestry of a parish? But—"fools rush in where angels fear to tread". In such a state of unbounded power for undefined and undefinable purposes, the evil of a moral and almost physical inaptitude of the man to the function must be the greatest we can conceive to happen in the management of human affairs.

Having considered the composition of the Third Estate as it stood in its original frame, I took a view of the representatives of the clergy. There, too, it appeared that full as little regard was had to the general security of property or to the aptitude of the deputies for the public purposes, in the principles of their election. That election was so contrived as to send a very large proportion of mere country curates to the great and arduous work of new-modeling a state: men who never had seen the state so much as in a picture — men who knew nothing of the world beyond the bounds of an obscure village; who, immersed in hopeless poverty, could regard all property, whether secular or ecclesiastical, with no other eye than that of envy; among whom must be many who, for the smallest hope of the meanest dividend in plunder, would

readily join in any attempts upon a body of wealth in which they could hardly look to have any share except in a general scramble. Instead of balancing the power of the active chicaners in the other assembly, these curates must necessarily become the active coadjutors, or at best the passive instruments, of those by whom they had been habitually guided in their petty village concerns. They, too, could hardly be the most conscientious of their kind who, presuming upon their incompetent understanding, could intrigue for a trust which led them from their natural relation to their flocks and their natural spheres of action to undertake the regeneration of kingdoms. This preponderating weight, being added to the force of the body of chicane in the *Tiers Etat*, completed that momentum of ignorance, rashness, presumption, and lust of plunder, which nothing has been able to resist.

To observing men it must have appeared from the beginning that the majority of the Third Estate, in conjunction with such a deputation from the clergy as I have described, whilst it pursued the destruction of the nobility, would inevitably become subservient to the worst designs of individuals in that class. In the spoil and humiliation of their own order these individuals would possess a sure fund for the pay of their new followers. To squander away the objects which made the happiness of their fellows would be to them no sacrifice at all. Turbulent, discontented men of quality, in proportion as they are puffed up with personal pride and arrogance, generally despise their own order. One of the first symptoms they discover of a selfish and mischievous ambition is a profligate disregard of a dignity which they partake with others. To be attached to the subdivision, to love the little platoon we belong to in society, is the first principle (the germ as it were) of public affections. It is the first link in the series by which we proceed toward a love to our country and to mankind. The interest of that portion of social arrangement is a trust in the hands of all those who compose it; and as none but bad men would justify it in abuse, none but traitors would barter it away for their own personal advantage.

There were in the time of our civil troubles in England (I do not know whether you have any such in your assembly in France) several persons, like the then Earl of Holland, who by themselves or their families had brought an odium on the throne by the prodigal dispensation of its bounties toward them, who afterwards joined in the rebellions arising from the discontents of which they were themselves the cause; men who helped to subvert that throne to which they owed, some of them, their existence, others all that power which they employed to ruin their benefactor. If any bounds are set to the rapacious demands of that sort of people, or that others are permitted to partake in the objects they would engross, revenge and envy soon fill up the craving void that is left in their avarice. Confounded by the complication of distempered passions, their reason is disturbed; their views become vast and perplexed; to others inexplicable, to themselves uncertain. They find, on all sides, bounds to their unprincipled ambition in any fixed order of things. Both in the fog and haze of confusion all is enlarged and appears without any limit.

When men of rank sacrifice all ideas of dignity to an ambition without a distinct object and work with low instruments and for low ends, the whole composition becomes low and base. Does not something like this now appear in France? Does it not produce something ignoble and inglorious — a kind of meanness in all the prevalent policy, a tendency in all that is done to lower along with individuals all the dignity and importance of the state? Other revolutions have been conducted by persons who, whilst they attempted or affected changes in the commonwealth, sanctified their ambition by advancing the dignity of the people whose peace they troubled. They had long views. They aimed at the rule, not at the destruction, of their country. They were men of great civil and great military talents, and if the terror, the ornament of their age. They were not like Jew brokers, contending with each other who could best remedy with fraudulent circulation and depreciated paper the wretchedness and ruin brought on their country by their degenerate councils. The compliment made to one of the great bad men of the old stamp (Cromwell) by his kinsman, a favorite poet of that time, shows what it was he proposed, and what indeed to a great degree he accomplished, in the success of his ambition:

> Still as *you* rise, the *state* exalted too,
> Finds no distemper whilst 'tis changed by
>   *you*;
> Changed like the world's great scene, when
>   without noise
> The rising sun night's *vulgar* lights destroys.

These disturbers were not so much like men usurping power as asserting their natural place in society. Their rising was to illuminate and beautify the world. Their conquest over their competitors was by outshining them. The hand that, like a destroying angel, smote the country communicated to it the force and energy under which it suffered. I do not say (God forbid), I do not say that the virtues of such men were to be taken as a balance to their crimes; but they were some corrective to their effects. Such was, as I said, our Cromwell. Such were your whole race of Guises, Condés, and Colignis. Such the Richelieus, who in more quiet times acted in the spirit of a civil war. Such, as better men, and in a less dubious cause, were your Henry the Fourth and your Sully, though nursed in civil confusions and not wholly without some of their taint. It is a thing to be wondered at, to see how very soon France, when she had a moment to respire, recovered and emerged from the longest and most dreadful civil war that ever was known in any nation. Why? Because among all their massacres they had not slain the *mind* in their country. A conscious dignity, a noble pride, a generous sense of glory and emulation was not extinguished. On the contrary, it was kindled and inflamed. The organs also of the state, however shattered, existed. All the prizes of honor and virtue, all the rewards, all the distinctions remained. But your present confusion, like a palsy, has attacked the fountain of life itself. Every person in your country, in a situation to be actuated by a principle of honor, is disgraced and degraded, and can entertain no sensation of life except in a mortified and humiliated indignation. But this generation will quickly pass away. The next generation of the nobility will resemble the artificers and clowns, and money-jobbers usurers, and Jews, who will be always their fellows, sometimes their masters.

Believe me, sir, those who attempt to level, never equalize. In all societies, consisting of various descriptions of citizens, some description must be uppermost. The levelers, therefore, only change and pervert the natural order of things; they load the edifice of society by setting up in the air what the solidity of the structure requires to be on the ground. The association of tailors and carpenters, of which the republic (of Paris, for instance) is composed, cannot be equal to the situation into which by the worst of usurpations—an usurpation on the prerogatives of nature—you attempt to force them.

The Chancellor of France, at the opening of the states, said, in a tone of oratorical flourish, that all occupations were honorable. If he meant only that no honest employment was disgraceful, he would not have gone beyond the truth. But in asserting that anything is honorable, we imply some distinction in its favor. The occupation of a hairdresser or of a working tallow-chandler cannot be a matter of honor to any person—to say nothing of a number of other more servile employments. Such descriptions of men ought not to suffer oppression from the state; but the state suffers oppression if such as they, either individually or collectively, are permitted to rule. In this you think you are combating prejudice, but you are at war with nature.[2]

[2] Ecclesiasticus, chap. xxxviii. verses 24, 25. "The wisdom of a learned man cometh by opportunity of leisure; and he that hath little business shall become wise".—"How can he get wisdom that holdeth the plough, and that glorieth in the goad; that driveth oxen; and is occupied in their labours; and whose talk is of bullocks"?
Ver. 27. "So every carpenter and work-master that laboureth night and day", etc.
Ver. 33. "They shall not be sought for in public counsel, nor sit high in the congregation: they shall not sit on the judge's seat, nor understand the sentence of judgment; they cannot declare justice and judgment, and they shall not be found where parables are spoken".
Ver. 34. "But they will maintain the state of the world".
I do not determine whether this book be canonical, as the Gallican church (till lately) has considered it, or apocryphal,

I do not, my dear Sir, conceive you to be of that sophistical, captious spirit, or of that uncandid dulness, as to require, for every general observation or sentiment, an explicit detail of the correctives and exceptions which reason will presume to be included in all the general propositions which come from reasonable men. You do not imagine that I wish to confine power, authority, and distinction to blood and names and titles. No, Sir. There is no qualification for government but virtue and wisdom, actual or presumptive. Wherever they are actually found, they have, in whatever state, condition, profession, or trade, the passport of Heaven to human place and honor. Woe to the country which would madly and impiously reject the service of the talents and virtues, civil, military, or religious, that are given to grace and to serve it, and would condemn to obscurity everything formed to diffuse luster and glory around a state. Woe to that country, too, that, passing into the opposite extreme, considers a low education, a mean contracted view of things, a sordid, mercenary occupation as a preferable title to command. Everything ought to be open, but not indifferently, to every man. No rotation; no appointment by lot; no mode of election operating in the spirit of sortition or rotation can be generally good in a government conversant in extensive objects. Because they have no tendency, direct or indirect, to select the man with a view to the duty or to accommodate the one to the other. I do not hesitate to say that the road to eminence and power, from obscure condition, ought not to be made too easy, nor a thing too much of course. If rare merit be the rarest of all rare things, it ought to pass through some sort of probation. The temple of honor ought to be seated on an eminence. If it be opened through virtue, let it be remembered, too, that virtue is never tried but by some difficulty and some struggle.

Nothing is a due and adequate representation of a state that does not represent its ability as well as its property. But as ability is a vigorous and active principle, and as property is sluggish, inert, and timid, it

as here it is taken. I am sure it contains a great deal of sense and truth.

never can be safe from the invasion of ability unless it be, out of all proportion, predominant in the representation. It must be represented, too, in great masses of accumulation, or it is not rightly protected. The characteristic essence of property, formed out of the combined principles of its acquisition and conservation, is to be *unequal*. The great masses, therefore, which excite envy and tempt rapacity must be put out of the possibility of danger. Then they form a natural rampart about the lesser properties in all their gradations. The same quantity of property, which is by the natural course of things divided among many, has not the same operation. Its defensive power is weakened as it is diffused. In this diffusion each man's portion is less than what, in the eagerness of his desires, he may flatter himself to obtain by dissipating the accumulations of others. The plunder of the few would indeed give but a share inconceivably small in the distribution to the many. But the many are not capable of making this calculation; and those who lead them to rapine never intend this distribution.

The power of perpetuating our property in our families is one of the most valuable and interesting circumstances belonging to it, and that which tends the most to the perpetuation of society itself. It makes our weakness subservient to our virtue, it grafts benevolence even upon avarice. The possessors of family wealth, and of the distinction which attends hereditary possession (as most concerned in it), are the natural *securities* for this transmission. With us the House of Peers is formed upon this principle. It is wholly composed of hereditary property and hereditary distinction, and made, therefore, the third of the legislature and, in the last event, the sole judge of all property in all its subdivisions. The House of Commons, too, though not necessarily, yet in fact, is always so composed, in the far greater part. Let those large proprietors be what they will—and they have their chance of being amongst the best—they are, at the very worst, the ballast in the vessel of the commonwealth. For though hereditary wealth and the rank which goes with it are too much idolized by creeping sycophants and the blind, abject admirers of power, they are too rashly slighted in shallow speculations of the petulant, assuming, short-sighted coxcombs of philosophy. Some decent, regulated preeminence, some preference (not exclusive appropriation) given to birth is neither unnatural, nor unjust, nor impolitic.

It is said that twenty-four millions ought to prevail over two hundred thousand. True; if the constitution of a kingdom be a problem of arithmetic. This sort of discourse does well enough with the lamppost for its second; to men who *may* reason calmly, it is ridiculous. The will of the many and their interest must very often differ, and great will be the difference when they make an evil choice. A government of five hundred country attornies and obscure curates is not good for twenty-four millions of men, though it were chosen by eight and forty millions, nor is it the better for being guided by a dozen of persons of quality who have betrayed their trust in order to obtain that power. At present, you seem in everything to have strayed out of the high road of nature. The property of France does not govern it. Of course, property is destroyed and rational liberty has no existence. All you have got for the present is a paper circulation and a stock-jobbing constitution; and as to the future, do you seriously think that the territory of France, upon the republican system of eighty-three independent municipalities (to say nothing of the parts that compose them), can ever be governed as one body or can ever be set in motion by the impulse of one mind? When the National Assembly has completed its work, it will have accomplished its ruin. These commonwealths will not long bear a state of subjection to the republic of Paris. They will not bear that this body should monopolize the captivity of the king and the dominion over the assembly calling itself national. Each will keep its own portion of the spoil of the church to itself; and it will not suffer either that spoil, or the more just fruits of their industry, or the natural produce of their soil to be sent to swell the insolence or pamper the luxury of the mechanics of Paris. In this they will see none of the equality, under the pretense of which they have been tempted to throw off their allegiance to their sovereign as well as the ancient constitution of their country. There can be no capital city in such a constitution as they have lately made. They have forgot that, when they framed democratic governments, they had virtually dismembered their country. The person whom they persevere in calling king has not power left to him by the hundredth part sufficient to hold together this collection of republics. The republic of Paris will endeavor, indeed, to complete the debauchery of the army, and illegally to perpetuate the assembly, without resort to its constituents, as the means of continuing its despotism. It will make efforts, by becoming the heart of a boundless paper circulation, to draw everything to itself; but in vain. All this policy in the end will appear as feeble as it is now violent. . . .

Far am I from denying in theory, full as far is my heart from withholding in practice (if I were of power to give or to withhold) the *real* rights of men. In denying their false claims of right, I do not mean to injure those which are real, and are such as their pretended rights would totally destroy. If civil society be made for the advantage of man, all the advantages for which it is made become his right. It is an institution of beneficence; and law itself is only beneficence acting by a rule. Men have a right to live by that rule; they have a right to do justice, as between their fellows, whether their fellows are in public function or in ordinary occupation. They have a right to the fruits of their industry and to the means of making their industry fruitful. They have a right to the acquisitions of their parents, to the nourishment and improvement of their offspring, to instruction in life, and to consolation in death. Whatever each man can separately do,without trespassing upon others, he has a right to do for himself; and he has a right to a fair portion of all which society, with all its combinations of skill and force, can do in his favor. In this partnership all men have equal rights, but not to equal things. He that has but five shillings in the partnership has a good a right to it as he that has five hundred pounds has to his larger proportion. But he has not a right to an equal dividend in the product of the joint stock; and as to the share of power, authority, and direction which each individual ought to have in the management of the state, that I must deny to be amongst the direct original rights of man in civil society; for I have

in my contemplation the civil social man, and no other. It is a thing to be settled by convention.

If civil society be the offspring of convention, that convention must be its law. That convention must limit and modify all the descriptions of constitution which are formed under it. Every sort of legislative, judicial, or executory power are its creatures. They can have no being in any other state of things; *and how can any man claim under the conventions of civil society rights which do not so much as suppose its existence—rights which are absolutely repugnant to it?* One of the first motives to civil society, and which becomes one of its fundamental rules, is *that no man should be judge in his own cause.* By this each person has at once divested himself of the first fundamental right of uncovenanted man, that is, to judge for himself and to assert his own cause. He abdicates all right to be his own governor. He inclusively, in a great measure, abandons the right of self-defense, the first law of nature. Men cannot enjoy the rights of an uncivil and of a civil state together. That he may obtain justice, he gives up his right of determining what it is in points the most essential to him. That he may secure some liberty, he makes a surrender in trust of the whole of it.

Government is not made in virtue of natural rights, which may and do exist in total independence of it, and exist in much greater clearness and in a much greater degree of abstract perfection; but their abstract perfection is their practical defect. By having a right to everything they want everything. Government is a contrivance of human wisdom to provide for human *wants.* Men have a right that these wants should be provided for by this wisdom. Among these wants is to be reckoned the want, out of civil society, of a sufficient restraint upon their passions. Society requires not only that the passions of individuals should be subjected, but that even in the mass and body, as well as in the individuals, the inclinations of men should frequently be thwarted, their will controlled, and their passions brought into subjection. This can only be done *by a power out of themselves,* and not, in the exercise of its function, subject to that will and to those passions which it is its office to bridle and subdue. In this sense the restraints on men, as well as their liberties, are to be reckoned among their rights. But as the liberties and the restrictions vary with times and circumstances and admit to infinite modifications, they cannot be settled upon any abstract rule; and nothing is so foolish as to discuss them upon that principle.

The moment your abate anything from the full rights of men, each to govern himself, and suffer any artificial, positive limitation upon those rights, from that moment the whole organization of government becomes a consideration of convenience. This it is which makes the constitution of a state and the due distribution of its powers a matter of the most delicate and complicated skill. It requires a deep knowledge of human nature and human necessities, and of the things which facilitate or obstruct the various ends which are to be pursued by the mechanism of civil institutions. The state is to have recruits to its strength, and remedies to its distempers. What is the use of discussing a man's abstract right to food or medicine? The question is upon the method of procuring and administering them. In that deliberation I shall always advise to call in the aid of the farmer and the physician rather than the professor of metaphysics.

The science of constructing a commonwealth, or renovating it, or reforming it, is, like every other experimental science, not to be taught *a priori*. Nor is it a short experience that can instruct us in that practical science, because the real effects of moral causes are not always immediate; but that which in the first instance is prejudicial may be excellent in its remoter operation, and its excellence may arise even from the ill effects it produces in the beginning. The reverse also happens: and very plausible schemes, with very pleasing commencements, have often shameful and lamentable conclusions. In states there are often some obscure and almost latent causes, things which appear at first view of little moment, on which a very great part of its prosperity or adversity may most essentially depend. The science of government being therefore so practical in itself and intended for such practical purposes—a matter which requires experience, and even more experience than any person can gain in his whole life, however sagacious and observing he

may be—it is with infinite caution that any man ought to venture upon pulling down an edifice which has answered in any tolerable degree for ages the common purposes of society, or on building it up again without having models and patterns of approved utility before his eyes.

These metaphysic rights entering into common life, like rays of light which pierce into a dense medium, are by the laws of nature refracted from their straight line. Indeed, in the gross and complicated mass of human passions and concerns the primitive rights of men undergo such a variety of refractions and reflections that it becomes absurd to talk of them as if they continued in the simplicity of their original direction. The nature of man is intricate; the objects of society are of the greatest possible complexity; and, therefore, no simple disposition or direction of power can be suitable either to man's nature or to the quality of his affairs. When I hear the simplicity of contrivance aimed at and boasted of in any new political constitutions, I am at no loss to decide that the artificers are grossly ignorant of their trade or totally negligent of their duty. The simple governments are fundamentally defective, to say no worse of them. If you were to contemplate society in but one point of view, all these simple modes of polity are infinitely captivating. In effect each would answer its single end much more perfectly than the more complex is able to attain all its complex purposes. But it is better that the whole should be imperfectly and anomalously answered than that, while some parts are provided for with great exactness, others might be totally neglected or perhaps materially injured by the over-care of a favorite member.

The pretended rights of these theorists are all extremes; and in proportion as they are metaphysically true, they are morally and politically false. The rights of men are in a sort of *middle*, incapable of definition, but not impossible to be discerned. The rights of men in governments are their advantages; and these are often in balances between differences of good, in compromises sometimes between good and evil, and sometimes between evil and evil. Political reason is a computing principle: adding, subtracting, multiplying, and dividing, morally and not metaphysically or mathematically, true moral denominations.

By these theorists the right of the people is almost always sophistically confounded with their power. The body of the community, whenever it can come to act, can meet with no effectual resistance; but till power and right are the same, the whole body of them has no right inconsistent with virtue, and the first of all virtues, prudence. Men have no right to what is not reasonable and to what is not for their benefit; for though a pleasant writer said, *liceat perire poetis,* when one of them, in cold blood, is said to have leaped into the flames of a volcanic revolution, *ardentem frigidus Aetnam insiluit,* I consider such a frolic rather as an unjustifiable poetic license than as one of the franchises of Parnassus; and whether he was a poet, or divine, or politician that chose to exercise this kind of right, I think that more wise, because more charitable, thoughts would urge me rather to save the man than to preserve his brazen slippers as the monuments of his folly.

The kind of anniversary sermons to which a great part of what I write refers, if men are not shamed out of their present course in commemorating the fact, will cheat many out of the principles, and deprive them of the benefits, of the revolution they commemorate. I confess to you, Sir, I never liked this continual talk of resistance and revolution, or the practice of making the extreme medicine of the constitution its daily bread. It renders the habit of society dangerously valetudinary; it is taking periodical doses of mercury sublimate and swallowing down repeated provocatives of cantharides to our love of liberty. . . .

History will record that on the morning of the 6th of October, 1789, the king and queen of France, after a day of confusion, alarm, dismay, and slaughter, lay down, under the pledged security of public faith, to indulge nature in a few hours of respite and troubled, melancholy repose. From this sleep the queen was first startled by the sentinel at her door, who cried out to her to save herself by flight—that this was the last proof of fidelity he could give—that they were upon him, and he was dead. Instantly he was cut down. A band of cruel ruffians and assassins, reeking

with his blood, rushed into the chamber of the queen and pierced with a hundred strokes of bayonets and poniards the bed, from whence this persecuted woman had but just time to fly almost naked, and, through ways unknown to the murderers, had escaped to seek refuge at the feet of a king and husband not secure of his own life for a moment.

This king, to say no more of him, and this queen, and their infant children (who once would have been the pride and hope of a great and generous people) were then forced to abandon the sanctuary of the most splendid palace in the world, which they left swimming in blood, polluted by massacre and strewed with scattered limbs and mutilated carcasses. Thence they were conducted into the capital of their kingdom. . . .

I hear, and I rejoice to hear, that the great lady, the other object of the triumph, has borne that day (one is interested that beings made for suffering should suffer well), and that she bears all the succeeding days, that she bears the imprisonment of her husband, and her own captivity, and the exile of her friends, and the insulting adulation of addresses, and the whole weight of her accumulated wrongs, with a serene patience, in a manner suited to her rank and race, and becoming the offspring of a sovereign distinguished for her piety and her courage; that, like her, she has lofty sentiments; that she feels with the dignity of a Roman matron; that in the last extremity she will save herself from the last disgrace; and that, if she must fall, she will fall by no ignoble hand.

It is now sixteen or seventeen years since I saw the queen of France, then the dauphiness, at Versailles, and surely never lighted on this orb, which she hardly seemed to touch, a more delightful vision. I saw her just above the horizon, decorating and cheering the elevated sphere she just began to move in—glittering like the morning star, full of life and splendor and joy. Oh! what a revolution! and what a heart must I have to contemplate without emotion that elevation and that fall! Little did I dream when she added titles of veneration to those of enthusiastic, distant, respectful love, that she should ever be obliged to carry the sharp antidote against disgrace concealed in that bosom; little did I dream that I should have lived to see such disasters fallen upon her in a nation of gallant men, in a nation of men of honor and of cavaliers. I thought ten thousand swords must have leaped from their scabbards to avenge even a look that threatened her with insult. But the age of chivalry is gone. That of sophisters, economists, and calculators has succeeded; and the glory of Europe is extinguished forever. Never, never more shall we behold that generous loyalty to rank and sex, that proud submission, that dignified obedience, that subordination of the heart which kept alive, even in servitude itself, the spirit of an exalted freedom. The unbought grace of life, the cheap defense of nations, the nurse of manly sentiment and heroic enterprise, is gone! It is gone, that sensibility of principle, that chastity of honor which felt a stain like a wound, which inspired courage whilst it mitigated ferocity, which ennobled whatever it touched, and under which vice itself lost half its evil by losing all its grossness.

This mixed system of opinion and sentiment had its origin in the ancient chivalry; and the principle, though varied in its appearance by the varying state of human affairs, subsisted and influenced through a long succession of generations even to the time we live in. If it should ever be totally extinguished, the loss I fear will be great. It is this which has given its character to modern Europe. It is this which has distinguished it under all its forms of government, and distinguished it to its advantage, from the states of Asia and possibly from those states which flourished in the most brilliant periods of the antique world. It was this which, without confounding ranks, had produced a noble equality and handed it down through all the gradations of social life. It was this opinion which mitigated kings into companions and raised private men to be fellows with kings. Without force or opposition, it subdued the fierceness of price and power, it obliged sovereigns to submit to the soft collar of social esteem, compelled stern authority to submit to elegance, and gave a domination, vanquisher of laws, to be subdued by manners.

But now all is to be changed. All the pleasing illusions which made power gentle and obedience liberal, which harmonized the different shades of life, and which, by a bland assimilation, incorporated into politics the sentiments which beautify and soften private society, are to be dissolved by this new conquering empire of light and reason. All the decent drapery of life is to be rudely torn off. All the super-added ideas, furnished from the wardrobe of a moral imagination, which the heart owns and the understanding ratifies as necessary to cover the defects of our naked, shivering nature, and to raise it to dignity in our own estimation, are to be exploded as a ridiculous, absurd, and antiquated fashion.

On this scheme of things, a king is but a man, a queen is but a woman; a woman is but an animal, and an animal not of the highest order. All homage paid to the sex in general as such, and without distinct views, is to be regarded as romance and folly. Regicide, and parricide, and sacrilege are but fictions of superstition, corrupting jurisprudence by destroying its simplicity. The murder of a king, or a queen, or a bishop, or a father are only common homicide; and if the people are by any chance or in any way gainers by it, a sort of homicide much the most pardonable, and into which we ought not to make too severe a scrutiny.

On the scheme of this barbarous philosophy, which is the offspring of cold hearts and muddy understandings, and which is as void of solid wisdom as it is destitute of all taste and elegance, laws are to be supported only by their own terrors and by the concern which each individual may find in them from his own private speculations or can spare to them from his own private interests. In the groves of *their* academy, at the end of every vista, you see nothing but the gallows. Nothing is left which engages the affections on the part of the commonwealth. On the principles of this mechanic philosophy, our institutions can never be embodied, if I may use the expression, in persons, so as to create in us love, veneration, admiration, or attachment. But that sort of reason which banishes the affections is incapable of filling their place. These public affections, combined with manners, are required sometimes as supplements, sometimes as correctives, always as aids to law. The precept given by a wise man, as well as a great critic, for the construction of poems is equally true as to states:—*Non satis est pulchra esse poemata, dulcia sunto.* There ought to be a system of manners in every nation which a well-informed mind would be disposed to relish. To make us love our country, our country ought to be lovely.

But power, of some kind or other, will survive the shock in which manners and opinions perish; and it will find other and worse means for its support. The usurpation which, in order to subvert ancient institutions, has destroyed ancient principles will hold power by arts similar to those by which it has acquired it. When the old feudal and chivalrous spirit of *fealty*, which, by freeing kings from fear, freed both kings and subjects from the precautions of tyranny, shall be extinct in the minds of men, plots and assassinations will be anticipated by preventive murder and preventive confiscation, and that long roll of grim and bloody maxims which form the political code of all power not standing on its own honor and the honor of those who are to obey it. Kings will be tyrants from policy when subjects are rebels from principle.

When ancient opinions and rules of life are taken away, the loss cannot possibly be estimated. From that moment we have no compass to govern us; nor can we know distinctly to what port we steer. Europe, undoubtedly, taken in a mass, was in a flourishing condition the day on which your revolution was completed. How much of that prosperous state was owing to the spirit of our old manners and opinions is not easy to say; but as such causes cannot be indifferent in their operation, we must presume that on the whole their operation was beneficial.

We are but too apt to consider things in the state in which we find them, without sufficiently adverting to the causes by which they have been produced and possibly may be upheld. Nothing is more certain than that our manners, our civilization, and all the good things which are connected with manners and with civilization have, in this European world of ours, depended for ages upon two principles and were, indeed, the result of both combined: I mean the spirit of a gentleman and the spirit of religion. The nobility and the clergy, the one by profession, the other by patronage, kept learning in existence, even in the midst of arms and confusions, and whilst governments were rather in their causes than formed. Learning paid back what it received to nobility and to priesthood, and paid it with usury, by enlarging their ideas and by furnishing their minds. Happy if they had all continued to know their indissoluble union and their proper place! Happy if learning, not debauched by ambition, had been satisfied to continue the instructor, and not aspired to be the master! Along with its natural protectors and guardians, learning will be cast into the mire and trodden down under the hoofs of a swinish multitude.

If, as I suspect, modern letters owe more than they are always willing to own to ancient manners, so do other interests which we value full as much as they are worth. Even commerce and trade and manufacture, the gods of our economical politicians, are themselves perhaps but creatures, are themselves but effects which, as first causes, we choose to worship. They certainly grew under the same shade in which learning flourished. They, too, may decay with their natural protecting principles. With you, for the present at least, they all threaten to disappear together. Where trade and manufactures are wanting to a people, and the spirit of nobility and religion remains, sentiment supplies, and not always ill supplies, their place; but if commerce and the arts should be lost in an experiment to try how well a state may stand without these old fundamental principles, what sort of a thing must be a nation of gross, stupid, ferocious, and, at the same time, poor and sordid barbarians, destitute of religion, honor, or manly pride, possessing nothing at present, and hoping for nothing hereafter? . . .

We know, and what is better, we feel inwardly, that religion is the basis of civil society and the source of all good and of all comfort. In England we are so convinced of this, that there is no rust of superstition with which the accumulated absurdity of the human mind might have crusted it over in the course of ages, that ninety-nine in a hundred of the people of England would not prefer to impiety. We shall never be such fools as to call in an enemy to the substance of any system to remove its corruptions, to supply its defects, or to perfect its construction. If our religious tenets should ever want a further elucidation, we shall not call on atheism to explain them. We shall not light up our temple from that unhallowed fire. It will be illuminated with other lights. It will be perfumed with other incense than the infectious stuff which is imported by the smugglers of adulterated metaphysics. If our ecclesiastical establishment should want a revision, it is not avarice or rapacity, public or private, that we shall employ for the audit, or receipt, or application of its consecrated revenue. Violently condemning neither the Greek nor the Armenian, nor, since heats are subsided, the Roman system of religion, we prefer the Protestant, not because we think it has less of the Christian religion in it, but because, in our judgment, it has more. We are Protestants, not from indifference, but from zeal.

We know, and it is our pride to know, that man is by his constitution a religious animal; that atheism is against, not only our reason, but our instincts; and that it cannot prevail long. But if, in the moment of riot and in a drunken delirium from the hot spirit drawn out of the alembic of hell, which in France is now so furiously boiling, we should uncover our nakedness by throwing off that Christian religion which has hitherto been our boast and comfort, and one great source of civilization amongst us and amongst many other nations, we are apprehensive (being well aware that the mind will not endure a void) that some uncouth, pernicious, and degrading superstition might take place of it.

For that reason, before we take from our establishment the natural, human means of estimation and give it up to contempt, as you have done, and in doing it have incurred the penalties you well deserve to suffer, we desire that some other may be presented to us in the place of it. We shall then form our judgment.

On these ideas, instead of quarrelling with establishments, as some do who have made a philosophy and a religion of their hostility to such institutions, we cleave closely to them. We are resolved to keep an established church, an established monarchy, an established aristocracy, and an established democracy, each in the degree it exists, and in no greater. I

shall show you presently how much of each of these we possess.

It has been the misfortune (not, as these gentlemen think it, the glory) of this age that everything is to be discussed as if the constitution of our country were to be always a subject rather of altercation than enjoyment. For this reason, as well as for the satisfaction of those among you (if any such you have among you) who may wish to profit of examples, I venture to trouble you with a few thoughts upon each of these establishments. I do not think they were unwise in ancient Rome who, when they wished to new-model their laws, set commissioners to examine the best constituted republics within their reach.

First, I beg leave to speak of our church establishment, which is the first of our prejudices, not a prejudice destitute of reason, but involving in it profound and extensive wisdom. I speak of it first. It is first and last and midst in our minds. For, taking ground on that religious system of which we are now in possession, we continue to act on the early received and uniformly continued sense of mankind. That sense not only, like a wise architect, hath built up the august fabric of states, but, like a provident proprietor, to preserve the structure from profanation and ruin, as a sacred temple purged from all the impurities of fraud and violence and injustice and tyranny, hath solemnly and forever consecrated the commonwealth and all that officiate in it. This consecration is made that all who administer the government of men, in which they stand in the person of God himself, should have high and worthy notions of their function and destination, that their hope should be full of immortality, that they should not look to the paltry pelf of the moment nor to the temporary and transient praise of the vulgar, but to a solid, permanent existence in the permanent part of their nature, and to a permanent fame and glory in the example they leave as a rich inheritance to the world.

Such sublime principles ought to be infused into persons of exalted situations, and religious establishments provided that may continually revive and enforce them. Every sort of moral, every sort of civil, every sort of politic institution, aiding the rational and natural ties that connect the human understanding and affections to the divine, are not more than necessary in order to build up that wonderful structure Man, whose prerogative it is to be in a great degree a creature of his own making, and who, when made as he ought to be made, is destined to hold no trivial place in the creation. But whenever man is put over men, as the better nature ought ever to preside, in that case more particularly, he should as nearly as possible be approximated to his perfection.

The consecration of the state by a state religious establishment is necessary, also, to operate with a wholesome awe upon free citizens, because, in order to secure their freedom, they must enjoy some determinate portion of power. To them, therefore, a religion connected with the state, and with their duty toward it, becomes even more necessary than in such societies where the people, by the terms of their subjection, are confined to private sentiments and the management of their own family concerns. All persons possessing any portion of power ought to be strongly and awfully impressed with an idea that they act in trust, and that they are to account for their conduct in that trust to the one great Master, Author, and Founder of society.

This principle ought even to be more strongly impressed upon the minds of those who compose the collective sovereignty than upon those of single princes. Without instruments, these princes can do nothing. Whoever uses instruments, in finding helps, finds also impediments. Their power is, therefore, by no means complete, nor are they safe in extreme abuse. Such persons, however elevated by flattery, arrogance, and self-opinion, must be sensible that, whether covered or not by positive law, in some way or other they are accountable even here for the abuse of their trust. If they are not cut off by a rebellion of their people, they may be strangled by the very janissaries kept for their security against all other rebellion. Thus we have seen the king of France sold by his soldiers for an increase of pay. But where popular authority is absolute and unrestrained, the people have an infinitely greater, because a far better founded, confidence in their own power. They are themselves, in

a great measure, their own instruments. They are nearer to their objects. Besides, they are less under responsibility to one of the greatest controlling powers on the earth, the sense of fame and estimation. The share of infamy that is likely to fall to the lot of each individual in public acts is small indeed, the operation of opinion being in the inverse ratio to the number of those who abuse power. Their own approbation of their own acts has to them the appearance of a public judgment in their favor. A perfect democracy is, therefore, the most shameless thing in the world. As it is the most shameless, it is also the most fearless. No man apprehends in his person that he can be made subject to punishment. Certainly the people at large never ought, for as all punishments are for example toward the conservation of the people at large, the people at large can never become the subject of punishment by any human hand. It is therefore of infinite importance that they should not be suffered to imagine that their will, any more than that of kings, is the standard of right and wrong. They ought to be persuaded that they are full as little entitled, and far less qualified with safety to themselves, to use any arbitrary power whatsoever; that therefore they are not, under a false show of liberty, but in truth to exercise an unnatural, inverted domination, tyrannically to exact from those who officiate in the state not an entire devotion to their interest, which is their right, but an abject submission to their occasional will, extinguishing thereby in all those who serve them all moral principle, all sense of dignity, all use of judgment, and all consistency of character; whilst by the very same process they give themselves up a proper, a suitable, but a most contemptible prey to the servile ambition of popular sycophants or courtly flatterers.

When the people have emptied themselves of all the lust of selfish will, which without religion it is utterly impossible they ever should, when they are conscious that they exercise, and exercise perhaps in a higher link of the order of delegation, the power, which to be legitimate must be according to that eternal, immutable law in which will and reason are the same, they will be more careful how they place power in base and incapable hands. In their nomination to office, they will not appoint to the exercise of authority as to a pitiful job, but as to a holy function, not according to their sordid, selfish interest, nor to their wanton caprice, nor to their arbitrary will, but they will confer that power (which any man may well tremble to give or to receive) on those only in whom they may discern that predominant proportion of active virtue and wisdom, taken together and fitted to the charge, such as in the great and inevitable mixed mass of human imperfections and infirmities is to be found.

When they are habitually convinced that no evil can be acceptable, either in the act or the permission, to him whose essence is good, they will be better able to extirpate out of the minds of all magistrates, civil, ecclesiastical, or military, anything that bears the least resemblance to a proud and lawless domination.

But one of the first and most leading principles on which the commonwealth and the laws are consecrated is, lest the temporary possessors and life-renters in it, unmindful of what they have received from their ancestors or of what is due to their posterity, should act as if they were the entire masters, that they should not think it among their rights to cut off the entail or commit waste on the inheritance by destroying at their pleasure the whole original fabric of their society, hazarding to leave to those who come after them a ruin instead of an habitation—and teaching these successors as little to respect their contrivances as they had themselves respected the institutions of their forefathers. By this unprincipled facility of changing the state as often, and as much, and in as many ways as there are floating fancies or fashions, the whole chain and continuity of the commonwealth would be broken. No one generation could link with the other. Men would become little better than the flies of a summer.

And first of all, the science of jurisprudence, the pride of the human intellect, which with all its defects, redundancies, and errors is the collected reason of ages, combining the principles of original justice with the infinite variety of human concerns, as a heap of old exploded errors, would be no longer studied. Personal self-sufficiency and arrogance (the certain attendants upon all those who have never experienced a wisdom greater than their own) would usurp the tribunal. Of course, no certain laws, establishing invariable grounds of hope and fear, would keep the actions of men in a certain course or direct them to a certain end. Nothing stable in the modes of holding property or exercising function could form a solid ground on which any parent could speculate in the education of his offspring or in a choice for their future establishment in the world. No principles would be early worked into the habits. As soon as the most able instructor had completed his laborious course of institution, instead of sending forth his pupil, accomplished in a virtuous discipline, fitted to procure him attention and respect in his place in society, he would find everything altered, and that he had turned out a poor creature to the contempt and derision of the world, ignorant of the true grounds of estimation. Who would insure a tender and delicate sense of honor to beat almost with the first pulses of the heart when no man could know what would be the test of honor in a nation continually varying the standard of its coin? No part of life would retain its acquisitions. Barbarism with regard to science and literature, unskilfulness with regard to arts and manufactures, would infallibly succeed to the want of a steady education and settled principle; and thus the commonwealth itself would, in a few generations, crumble away, be disconnected into the dust and powder of individuality, and at length dispersed to all the winds of heaven. To avoid, therefore, the evils of inconstancy and versatility, ten thousand times worse than those of obstinacy and the blindest prejudice, we have consecrated the state, that no man should approach to look into its defects or corruptions but with due caution, that he should never dream of beginning its reformation by its subversion, that he should approach to the faults of the state as to the wounds of a father, with pious awe and trembling solicitude. By this wise prejudice we are taught to look with horror on those children of their country who are prompt rashly to hack that aged parent in pieces and put him into the kettle of magicians, in hopes that by their poisonous weeds and wild incantations they may regenerate the paternal constitution and renovate their father's life.

Society is indeed a contract. Subordinate contracts for objects of mere occasional interest may be dissolved at pleasure—but the state ought not to be considered as nothing better than a partnership agreement in a trade of pepper and coffee, calico, or tobacco, or some other such low concern, to be taken up for a little temporary interest, and to be dissolved by the fancy of the parties. It is to be looked on with other reverence, because it is not a partnership in things subservient only to the gross animal existence of a temporary and perishable nature. It is a partnership in all science; a partnership in all art; a partnership in every virtue and in all perfection. As the ends of such a partnership cannot be obtained in many generations, it becomes a partnership not only between those who are living, but between those who are living, those who are dead, and those who are to be born. Each contract of each particular state is but a clause in the great primeval contract of eternal society, linking the lower with the higher natures, connecting the visible and invisible world, according to a fixed compact sanctioned by the inviolable oath which holds all physical and all moral natures, each in their appointed place. This law is not subject to the will of those who by an obligation above them, and infinitely superior, are bound to submit their will to that law. The municipal corporations of that universal kingdom are not morally at liberty at their pleasure, and on their speculations of a contingent improvement, wholly to separate and tear asunder the bands of their subordinate community and to dissolve it into an unsocial, uncivil, unconnected chaos of elementary principles. It is the first and supreme necessity only, a necessity that is not chosen but chooses, a necessity paramount to deliberation, that admits no discussion and demands no evidence, which alone can justify a resort to anarchy. This necessity is no exception to the rule, because this necessity itself is a part, too, of that moral and physical disposition of things to which man must be obedient by consent or force; but if that which is only submission to necessity should be made the object of choice, the law is broken, nature is disobeyed, and the rebellious are outlawed, cast forth, and exiled from this world of reason, and order, and peace, and virtue, and fruitful penitence, into the antagonist world of madness, discord, vice, confusion, and unavailing sorrow.

KANT

An Answer to the Question: What Is Enlightenment?

(1784)

Enlightenment is man's emergence from his self-imposed immaturity. Immaturity is the inability to use one's understanding without guidance from another. This immaturity is *self-imposed* when its cause lies not in lack of understanding, but in lack of resolve and courage to use it without guidance from another. *Sapere Aude!* "Have courage to use your own understanding!"—that is the motto of enlightenment.

Laziness and cowardice are the reasons why so great a proportion of men, long after nature has released them from alien guidance (*naturaliter maiorennes*), nonetheless gladly remain in lifelong immaturity, and why it is so easy for others to establish themselves as their guardians. It is so easy to be immature. If I have a book to serve as my understanding, a pastor to serve as my conscience, a physician to determine my diet for me, and so on, I need not exert myself at all. I need not think, if only I can pay: others will readily undertake the irksome work for me. The guardians who have so benevolently taken over the supervision of men have carefully seen to it that the far greatest part of them (including the entire fair sex) regard taking the step to maturity as very dangerous, not to mention difficult. Having first made their domestic livestock dumb, and having carefully made sure that these docile creatures will not take a single step without the go-cart to which they are harnessed, these guardians then show them the danger that threatens them, should they attempt to walk alone. Now this danger is not actually so great, for after falling a few

times they would in the end certainly learn to walk; but an example of this kind makes men timid and usually frightens them out of all further attempts.

Thus, it is difficult for any individual man to work himself out of the immaturity that has all but become his nature. He has even become fond of this state and for the time being is actually incapable of using his own understanding, for no one has ever allowed him to attempt it. Rules and formulas, those mechanical aids to the rational use, or rather misuse, of his natural gifts, are the shackles of a permanent immaturity. Whoever threw them off would still make only an uncertain leap over the smallest ditch, since he is unaccustomed to this kind of free movement. Consequently, only a few have succeeded, by cultivating their own minds, in freeing themselves from immaturity and pursuing a secure course.

But that the public should enlighten itself is more likely; indeed, if it is only allowed freedom, enlightenment is almost inevitable. For even among the entrenched guardians of the great masses a few will always think for themselves, a few who, after having themselves thrown off the yoke of immaturity, will spread the spirit of a rational appreciation for both their own worth and for each person's calling to think for himself. But it should be particularly noted that if a public that was first placed in this yoke by the guardians is suitably aroused by some of those who are altogether incapable of enlightenment, it may force the guardians themselves to remain under the yoke—so pernicious is it to instill prejudices, for they finally take revenge upon their originators, or on their descendants. Thus a public can only attain enlightenment slowly. Perhaps a revolution can overthrow auto-

[Reprinted from *Perpetual Peace and Other Essays*, translated by Ted Humphrey (Indianapolis: Hackett Publishing Company, 1983), by permission of the publisher.]

cratic despotism and profiteering or power-grabbing oppression, but it can never truly reform a manner of thinking; instead, new prejudices, just like the old ones they replace, will serve as a leash for the great unthinking mass.

Nothing is required for this enlightenment, however, except *freedom*; and the freedom in question is the least harmful of all, namely, the freedom to use reason *publicly* in all matters. But on all sides I hear: *"Do not argue!"* The officer says, "Do not argue, drill!" The taxman says, "Do not argue, pay!" The pastor says, "Do not argue, believe!" (Only one ruler in the world says, *"Argue* as much as you want and about what you want, *but obey!"*) In this we have [examples of] pervasive restrictions on freedom. But which restriction hinders enlightenment and which does not, but instead actually advances it? I reply: The *public* use of one's reason must always be free, and it alone can bring about enlightenment among mankind; the *private use* of reason may, however, often be very narrowly restricted, without otherwise hindering the progress of enlightenment. By the public use of one's own reason I understand the use that anyone as a *scholar* makes of reason before the entire *literate world.* I call the private use of reason that which a person may make in a *civic post* or office that has been entrusted to him. Now in many affairs conducted in the interests of a community, a certain mechanism is required by means of which some of its members must conduct themselves in an entirely passive manner so that through an artificial unanimity the government may guide them toward public ends, or at least prevent them from destroying such ends. Here one certainly must not argue, instead one must obey. However, insofar as this part of the machine also regards himself as a member of the community as a whole, or even of the world community, and as a consequence addresses the public in the role of a scholar, in the proper sense of that term, he can most certainly argue, without thereby harming the affairs for which as a passive member he is partly responsible. Thus it would be disastrous if an officer on duty who was given a command by his superior were to question the appropriateness or utility of the order. He must obey. But as a scholar he cannot be justly constrained

from making comments about errors in military service, or from placing them before the public for its judgment. The citizen cannot refuse to pay the taxes imposed on him; indeed, impertinent criticism of such levies, when they should be paid by him, can be punished as a scandal (since it can lead to widespread insubordination). But the same person does not act contrary to civic duty when, as a scholar, he publicly expresses his thoughts regarding the impropriety or even injustice of such taxes. Likewise a pastor is bound to instruct his catecumens and congregation in accordance with the symbol of the church he serves, for he was appointed on that condition. But as a scholar he has complete freedom, indeed even the calling, to impart to the public all of his carefully considered and well-intentioned thoughts concerning mistaken aspects of that symbol, as well as his suggestions for the better arrangement of religious and church matters. Nothing in this can weigh on his conscience. What he teaches in consequence of his office as a servant of the church he sets out as something with regard to which he has no discretion to teach in accord with his own lights; rather, he offers it under the direction and in the name of another. He will say, "Our church teaches this or that and these are the demonstrations it uses." He thereby extracts for his congregation all practical uses from precepts to which he would not himself subscribe with complete conviction, but whose presentation he can nonetheless undertake, since it is not entirely impossible that truth lies hidden in them, and, in any case, nothing contrary to the very nature of religion is to be found in them. If he believed he could find anything of the latter sort in them, he could not in good conscience serve in his position; he would have to resign. Thus an appointed teacher's use of his reason for the sake of his congregation is merely *private*, because, however large the congregation is, this use is always only domestic; in this regard, as a priest, he is not free and cannot be such because he is acting under instructions from someone else. By contrast, the cleric—as a scholar who speaks through his writings to the public as such, i.e., the world—enjoys in this *public use* of reason an unrestricted freedom to use his own rational capacities and to speak his own mind. For that the (spiritual) guardians of a people should themselves be immature is an absurdity that would insure the perpetuation of absurdities.

But would a society of pastors, perhaps a church assembly or venerable presbytery (as those among the Dutch call themselves), not be justified in binding itself by oath to a certain unalterable symbol in order to secure a constant guardianship over each of its members and through them over the people, and this for all time: I say that this is wholly impossible. Such a contract, whose intention is to preclude forever all further enlightenment of the human race, is absolutely null and void, even if it should be ratified by the supreme power, by parliaments, and by the most solemn peace treaties. One age cannot bind itself, and thus conspire, to place a succeeding one in a condition whereby it would be impossible for the later age to expand its knowledge (particularly where it is so very important), to rid itself of errors, and generally to increase its enlightenment. That would be a crime against human nature, whose essential destiny lies precisely in such progress; subsequent generations are thus completely justified in dismissing such agreements as unauthorized and criminal. The criterion of everything that can be agreed upon as a law by a people lies in this question: Can a people impose such a law on itself? Now it might be possible, in anticipation of a better state of affairs, to introduce a provisional order for a specific, short time, all the while giving all citizens, especially clergy, in their role as scholars, the freedom to comment publicly, i.e., in writing, on the present institution's shortcomings. The provisional order might last until insight into the nature of these matters had become so widespread and obvious that the combined (if not unanimous) voices of the populace could propose to the crown that it take under its protection those congregations that, in accord with their newly gained insight, had organized themselves under altered religious institutions, but without interfering with those wishing to allow matters to remain as before. However, it is absolutely forbidden that they unite into a religious organization that nobody may for the duration of a man's lifetime publicly question, for so doing would deny, render fruitless, and make detrimental to suc-

ceeding generations an era in man's progress toward improvement. A man may put off enlightenment with regard to what he ought to know, though only for a short time and for his own person; but to renounce it for himself, or, even more, for subsequent generations, is to violate and trample man's divine rights underfoot. And what a people may not decree for itself may still less be imposed on it by a monarch, for his lawgiving authority rests on his unification of the people's collective will in his own. If he only sees to it that all genuine or purported improvement is consonant with civil order, he can allow his subjects to do what they find necessary to their spiritual well-being, which is not his affair. However, he must prevent anyone from forcibly interfering with another's working as best he can to determine and promote his well-being. It detracts from his own majesty when he interferes in these matters, since the writings in which his subjects attempt to clarify their insights lend value to his conception of governance. This holds whether he acts from his own highest insight—whereby he calls upon himself the reproach, *"Caesar non est supra grammaticos.* [Caesar is not above the grammarians.]"—as well as, indeed even more, when he despoils his highest authority by supporting the spiritual despotism of some tyrants in his state over his other subjects.

If it is now asked, "Do we presently live in an *enlightened age?"* the answer is, "No, but we do live in an age of *enlightenment."* As matters now stand, a great deal is still lacking in order for men as a whole to be, or even to put themselves into a position to be able without external guidance to apply understanding confidently to religious issues. But we do have clear indications that the way is now being opened for men to proceed freely in this direction and that the obstacles to general enlightenment—to their release from their self-imposed immaturity—are gradually diminishing. In this regard, this age is the age of enlightenment, the century of Frederick.

A prince who does not find it beneath him to say that he takes it to be his *duty* to prescribe nothing, but rather to allow men complete freedom in religious matters—who thereby renounces the arrogant title of *tolerance*—is himself enlightened and deserves to be praised by a grateful present and by posterity as the first, at least where the government is concerned, to release the human race from immaturity and to leave everyone free to use his own reason in all matters of conscience. Under his rule, venerable pastors, in their role as scholars and without prejudice to their official duties, may freely and openly set out for the world's scrutiny their judgments and views, even where these occasionally differ from the accepted symbol. Still greater freedom is afforded to those who are not restricted by an official post. This spirit of freedom is expanding even where it must struggle against the external obstacles of governments that misunderstand their own function. Such governments are illuminated by the example that the existence of freedom need not give cause for the least concern regarding public order and harmony in the commonwealth. If only they refrain from inventing artifices to keep themselves in it, men will gradually raise themselves from barbarism.

I have focused on religious matters in setting out my main point concerning enlightenment, i.e., man's emergence from self-imposed immaturity, first because our rulers have no interest in assuming the role of their subjects' guardians with respect to the arts and sciences, and secondly because that form of immaturity is both the most pernicious and disgraceful of all. But the manner of thinking of a head of state who favors religious enlightenment goes even further, for he realizes that there is no danger to his *legislation* in allowing his subjects to use reason *publicly* and to set before the world their thoughts concerning better formulations of his laws, even if this involves frank criticism of legislation currently in effect. We have before us a shining example, with respect to which no monarch surpasses the one whom we honor.

But only a ruler who is himself enlightened and has no dread of shadows, yet who likewise has a well-disciplined, numerous army to guarantee public peace, can say what no republic may dare, namely: *"Argue as much as you want and about what you want, but obey!"* Here as elsewhere, when things are considered in broad perspective, a strange, unexpected pattern in human affairs reveals itself, one in which almost everything is paradoxical. A greater degree of civil freedom seems advantageous to a people's *spiritual* freedom; yet the former established impassable boundaries for the latter; conversely, a lesser degree of civil freedom provides enough room for all fully to expand their abilities. Thus, once nature has removed the hard shell from this kernel for which she has most fondly cared, namely, the inclination to and vocation for free *thinking*, the kernel gradually reacts on a people's mentality (whereby they become increasingly able to *act freely*), and it finally even influences the principles of *government*, which finds that it can profit by treating men, *who are now more than machines*, in accord with their dignity.*

Königsberg in Prussia, 30 September 1784
I. Kant

* Today I read in Büsching's *Wöchentliche Nachtrichten* for September 13th a notice concerning this month's *Berlinischen Monatsschift* that mentions *Mendelssohn's* answer to this same question. I have not yet seen this journal, otherwise I would have withheld the foregoing reflections, which I now set out in order to see to what extent two person's thoughts may coincidentally agree.

5

CONSTITUTIONALISM AND THE REDEFINITION OF LIBERTY

The idea of a constitution is so familiar that it is easy to think it is one of the few unproblematic ideas in political theory. Aristotle conducted a careful study of the constitutions of Greek city states, and the ancient Greeks and Romans established a typology of constitutions that we still use: monarchy and tyranny; aristocracy and oligarchy; and democracy. But both the purpose constitutions serve and the language and the concepts we use to think about them have changed over time. Modern constitutionalism, which is an achievement of the eighteenth century, relies on a new vocabulary and new concepts, and serves new purposes. The significance of the eighteenth-century construction of a new science of politics has often been missed because the novelty of the project of the construction of the two spheres of public and private life, which we take for granted, has not been understood. Before the eighteenth century there was no coherent project for limiting the powers of government, no ideal of liberty that made limited government seem necessary, and no conceptual tools for thinking about how government could be limited other than by dividing sovereignty (in England, dividing it between king, lords, and commons). Seventeenth-century governments did not hesitate to control the private lives of their subjects, whether requiring particular religious beliefs and practices, or deciding what clothes they should be allowed to wear. In England the limits on the power of the Crown were few and fragile until 1688. Toleration for Protestant dissenters was only securely established then. Habeas corpus was not adequately entrenched in law until 1679, and the principle of the independence of the judiciary was not securely established until 1701. The right to defense counsel in criminal trials was only established in the 1720s and 1730s, and the right of silence could scarcely exist without a right to counsel. With the exception of a few brief intermissions (particularly from 1642 until 1649), there was prepublication censorship of the press until the lapse of the Licensing Act in 1695. The rights embodied in the United States Bill of Rights (1791) are modern, not ancient or medieval.

Western societies all now share the conviction that the only legitimate governments are governments in which the people rule—a claim that underlies the American Revolution and is now unquestioned. It means that there can be no legitimacy without political liberty, a notion that would have seemed profoundly suspect in many European societies at least until 1918, when the idea of democracy began to be widely accepted (The key period for the expansion of woman suffrage, to take a crucial indicator, is 1913–28). The adoption of democratic values (leaving aside for present purposes the temporary triumphs of fascism and communism, both of which paid lip service to the idea of popular power) meant that wherever monarchies and aristocracies survived, they did so as puzzling anomalies. Monarchy was tolerable only insofar as it was ornamental not functional;

republicanism was everywhere, explicitly or tacitly, the new norm. The idea of popular rule and the language of republicanism are intimately associated, or rather have come to be associated. For the ancient Romans, at least in the days of what we call the Republic, a republic (*respublica*) was any form of good government: monarchies, aristocracies, and various sorts of popular constitution could all be *republics*. Right through into the eighteenth century, this usage remained commonplace. Late in the fourteenth century a new usage began to establish itself in Italy, by which any state that was not a monarchy was a republic; this more modern usage was taken for granted by Machiavelli and by Montesquieu, but it only became the norm throughout Europe and the Americas with the American and French revolutions. This new language initially involved a return to a classical ideal of liberty, but it went beyond the classics in claiming that the only good government was a state founded on the principle of political liberty. In an early modern world in which it was taken for granted that the term "democracy" described one of the worst forms of government, "republic" became the acceptable term for good government exercised by the people as a whole.

Of course, the opponents of republicanism were bound to reject the claims made on behalf of political liberty. Hobbes, for example, carefully defined liberty so that he could claim that the subject of an absolute monarch was just as free as the subject of a democratic republic: liberty, according to Hobbes, exists where there is no compulsion, whether physical or legal. Liberty consists in following one's own will: the idea of political liberty is therefore an oxymoron, a contradiction in terms, for politics constantly involves us in doing what others require us to do. In a democracy the minority are always being compelled by the majority. For a post-Machiavellian republican, as for an ancient Roman, liberty consisted in participating in the determination of policy: you are free only if you have a say when decisions are made. Others, seeking a compromise between Machiavelli and Hobbes, argued that you were free if you were subject only to the laws: if you could make your own choices within a reliable and predictable framework of law. By the late eighteenth century there were thus three competing ideas of liberty: political liberty (the right to collective self-government, or the freedom of the popular republic); civil liberty (the right to freedom under the law, or to protection from arbitrary action—a freedom one could have under an enlightened despotism); and Hobbesian liberty (the right to follow one's own will, or the freedom of the state of nature, which modern political theorists call "negative liberty").

The real driving force behind modern constitutionalism, however, lies in the recognition that there is something inadequate in all of these conceptions of liberty. In the city-state republics of ancient Greece and Rome or Renaissance Italy the ruling majority could ostracize, permanently exile, or execute their fellow citizens: individuals had rights as members of the state, but they had no rights that protected them from the state. It was easy for the opponents of republicanism to argue that the more democratic a republic, the more tumultuous and the less likely the republic would be to respect the rights of individuals. On the other hand, republicans argued that the claims of absolute monarchs to rule under the law could never be trusted; at any moment the façade of legality might be swept away, to be replaced by an arbitrary and naked power. In eighteenth-century France the rule of law was routinely accompanied by arbitrary arrest and imprisonment, the *lettre de cachet*; even in England, when there was considerable political liberty, law-abiding citizens could be press-ganged into the navy without due process or appeal. As for the Hobbesian conception of liberty, it implied that there was no real difference between government taxation and a highwayman demanding your money or your life. The weakness of all three conceptions of liberty was that they failed to establish proper limits on government power. In the second half of the seventeenth century a striking example of this was in the area of religious freedom. Most European governments imposed penalties, often harsh penalties, on those who failed to hold the religious views approved by the state. If there was to be such a thing as religious freedom, then there must be some effective way of limiting government power.

The ancients had recognized one form of limited government, mixed government, where there existed a balance of power between monarchy, aristocracy, and democracy. Thus Polybius had praised the Roman republic as a mixed government, and it was argued that mixed governments were slower to degenerate into tyranny, oligarchy, or anarchy. But the basis of mixed government was a balance of power between different groups in society—between, say, king, lords, and commons. In England, after the defeat of the king and the aristocracy in the first Civil War, or in the United States after the Revolution, it looked as if mixed government, as traditionally understood, was an impossibility, and yet the prospect of arbitrary and tyrannical government action seemed to many people greater, not less, than before.

How then to limit government power, when power was concentrated in the hands of a revolutionary army (as in Civil War England) or a democratic assembly (as in Paine's Philadelphia)? Cromwell and his supporters came up with two answers to this question that were to be of lasting importance. First, adopt a written constitution which would explicitly define the limits of government power (the Cromwellian Instrument of Government of 1653, the forerunner to the first great modern written constitution, the American constitution). Second, distinguish the powers of legislative, executive, and judiciary, and keep those powers separate and independent: what was to become, in Montesquieu's classic formulation, the doctrine of the separation of powers. It is easy to forget that there was something radically new in, for example, the idea of an independent judiciary not subject to executive interference, the essential precondition for any real separation of the powers.

These two principles, the written constitution and the separation of powers, in themselves could not protect a minority against a majority, though one could go further by entrenching certain fundamental rights in a bill of rights, as the English did in 1688 and the Americans did in 1791. Between the Revolution of 1688 and the American Revolution, a number of additional principles came to seem important. Let us call these "checks and balances," "the benefits of scale," "party conflict," and "freedom of the press." Those who advocated these new principles did so first by attacking the classical ideal of the city-state, and later by attacking the political theory of Rousseau, which was in part born of his experience of living in a city-state, that of Geneva.

The phrase "checks and balances" is often used carelessly as if it were a long-standing principle of constitutional analysis. Classical theorists talked of a balance within the mixed constitution: here, good decisions were made if the tendency of monarchy and aristocracy to degenerate into tyranny and oligarchy was counterbalanced by the power of the populace. And early modern theorists talked of checks or restraints on arbitrary power: principles such as no taxation without representation, habeas corpus, the impeachment of government ministers; the idea being that if the government was prevented from acting tyrannically or was punished when it did so, it would be forced to govern well. But the eighteenth-century idea of checks and balances is distinct from both of these earlier ideas, and from the idea of the separation of powers. The theory of the separation of powers implied that the legislature, executive, and judiciary should act separately and independently from one another. The theory of checks and balances held that, in order to ensure that no part of government became too strong, different parts of government should be allowed to interfere with, obstruct, and complicate the activities of each other. Thus the executive should be given a veto over legislation; the judiciary should be able to nullify laws; the legislature should be able to impeach the executive and should be able to veto executive appointments; the power of central government should be weakened by federalism; the power of the legislature should be weakened by bicameralism; and the power of the Supreme Court should be weakened by having the judges nominated by the executive and approved by the legislature.

Underlying the idea of setting government power against government power was a new type of political analysis, and a new set of political priorities. The new analysis was expressed in the belief that there could be a science of politics, i.e. a science predicting political developments. This is because individuals pursue their interests, and their interests are bound up in the offices they hold. In seeking to maximize their own power, politicians seek to enhance the power of their offices; thus their behavior becomes predictable, and can be modified by changing the institutional framework within which they operate. Consequently one can predict the conflicts and tensions that will arise within government by analyzing individual interests and the institutional conflicts that result from them. This view of government was well-established by the late seventeenth century, and was expressed by describing government as a machine or a system.

The new set of political principles resulted from a new fear of the legislature. In England until the early eighteenth century, the main threat to liberty was generally believed to come from the executive. But by the middle of the eighteenth century some commentators had reached the view that the growing power of the legislature meant that a government supported by a majority in the House of Commons would have excessive power. Arguing along these lines, David Hume praised the corruption of the legislators that enabled the executive, by buying their votes, to weaken the power of the legislature. It is reasonable to say that the concept of checks and balances was clearly defined in Hume's *Essays,* although the actual phrase was not used until later. The theory of checks and balances thus stood opposed to the simple democratic theory of, for example, Paine, who sought to establish a legislature which was responsive to the wishes of the people, and to concentrate power in its hands. Too simple a democracy would lead, it was argued, to what Tocqueville would later call the tyranny of the majority.

The next major innovation (after the written constitution, the separation of powers, a bill of rights, and the theory of checks and balances) lay in a new account of the consequences of conducting politics on a large scale. From Plato to Cicero, from Machiavelli to Montesquieu, the universal assumption was that republican government could function only in a city-state where the people could gather in the public square, debate, and vote. Republican government thus involved participatory democracy. Any state in which power was distributed across a large geographical expanse would have to be, it was assumed, some sort of monarchy. This assumption was first questioned by James Harrington during the English Civil War: he set out to reconstruct republicanism on the basis of representation rather than participation. Hume was to take up Harrington's ideas in his essay on "The Idea of a Perfect Commonwealth," and this was to provide a basis for Madison and Hamilton when they argued (against Montesquieu) that one could build a republic on the scale of a continent.

Government by representatives involves a number of gains and a number of losses. Chief among the losses is the fact that in an indirect democracy, the people no longer govern themselves. The gains are more complex. First, the people gain time—by handing over the task of ruling to others, they free themselves from the demands of constant political participation. Second, they place the government in the hands of an educated, experienced elite. In any representative system those who are elected are going to be, in general, more educated and more experienced than those who elect them. Representation is inherently elitist; indeed, the ancient Greeks argued that any system in which people were elected to office was either oligarchic or aristocratic (e.g., Aristotle, *Politics* 4.1294b). The larger the electoral districts and the longer the period between elections, the more elitist the system is likely to be. Third, the potential for creating a tyrannical majority is sharply reduced by the increase in scale: interests and opinions diverge much more widely across a large geographical territory than they do in the narrow confines of a few city streets. Fourth, representation brings with it complicated forms and elaborate procedures, and at the same time it reduces the size of the deliberating assembly. A crowd gathered in a public square is always in danger of turning into a mob, whereas a debating chamber in which legislation is subjected to careful scrutiny, in which there is ample opportunity for legislators to make amendments, in which there is time for consultation and reconsideration, is likely to remain calm and cautious even at moments of crisis. Relying on arguments such as these, Madison argued that a republic on a large scale would be infinitely preferable to an Athenian democracy.

As with the term "republic" and the phrase "checks and balances," it is tempting to take the idea of representation for granted. But "representation" is almost an unknown term in politics before the English Civil War when it enters the political arena from the religious disputes of the period, and thus becomes a significant conceptual issue for Hobbes in *Leviathan.* Church Councils had long claimed to "represent" the Church as a whole; for Anglicans the Synod represented the Church of England; the Presbyterians claimed similarly that the Elders represented the local church, and the General Assembly the national Church. It is natural for us to think that the House of Commons was always an assembly of representatives, but this idea came into prominence only in 1642, and the idea that a member of Parliament represents his constituency came even later. Before 1642, Parliament was a court and a way of giving the king counsel (a great council to stand alongside the king's Privy Council); its task was to identify the common good, not to represent the views of the nation. The language and to some extent the concept of representation is thus surprisingly novel, and also uniquely English. The French, it has been said, had no idea of representation before the French Revolution; delegates of the Third Estate, the commons (who with the clergy, the First Estate, and the nobility, the Second Estate, made up the Estates General) were instructed by their constituents on what to say and how to vote. They were agents, not representatives.

Checks and balances and representation are now part of the ordinary language of politics. We are all aware of party conflict, but it is often portrayed as something inherently regrettable, and people have little respect for partisan politics. Most eighteenth-century political theorists would have agreed, as they did not hesitate to condemn parties. Representatives ought to be independent, concerned only with the public welfare, not with the interests of party. Party conflict was likely to lead only to faction and tyranny. Madison considered one of the great advantages of a republic on a large scale to be the absence of scope within it for large and successful political parties. But some theorists thought that party conflict had its advantages, and that it played a crucial role in preserving freedom. Hume thought that the English constitution naturally gave rise to two parties, a party of order and a party of liberty, and that the balance between the two, if it could be sustained, was a healthy one. In 1743, Edward Spelman argued that "in all free governments there ever were and ever will be parties," and maintained that party conflict was not an effect of but a precondition for liberty. And in 1771, Jean Louis de Lolme, in his *Constitution of England,* provided what may be regarded as the first modern account of the formation of political parties.

Central to the arguments of Spelman and de Lolme is a new understanding of the activity of oppositions within a representative system. They aim to mobilize public opinion in an attempt to win seats in future elections and take over the government. Elected governments respond to opposition by trying to avoid provoking hostility: they seek to hold onto power by learning from their opponents. Thus, even if the opposition never takes power, it can shape policy. Opposition functions like the tail on a weather vane: when the government pursues unpopular policies, the opposition it encounters pushes it around and points it back toward popular policies. Party conflict, in the context of a public opinion that can be mobilized, is a feedback mechanism that makes governments responsive to the people.

Such arguments take for granted the existence of a free press: it comes as something of a shock to realize that, as late as 1771, the very year in which de Lolme's book was published, the British House of Commons was trying to prevent the publication of reports of its debates in newspapers. We should therefore extend our survey of new constitutional principles to include the idea of freedom of the press. Prepublication licensing of the press served a double function: on the one hand, it enabled the government to suppress seditious works; on the other, it provided a legal foundation for printer's copyright. With the striking exception of Milton's *Areopagitica* (1644), the seventeenth century saw few defenses of press freedom, and when prepublication licensing ended in 1695 it was not because there was widespread support for the principle of press freedom, but because there was no consensus on how best to administer censorship. It is only later that we find freedom of the press being turned into a principle of liberty, by Gordon in no. 15 of John Trenchard's and Thomas Gordon's *Cato's Letters* (1721), and rather more cautiously by Hume in the *Essays* (1741).

Between the English Revolution of 1642–60 and the American Constitution of 1789 the idea of liberty, and with it the theory of constitutional government, were transformed. The written constitution, the separation of powers, a bill of rights, checks and balances, representation, the benefits of party conflict, the case for freedom of the press: these were, to a much greater extent than is generally recognized, new ideas, ideas that made possible a new type of civil and political liberty, a new separation between private and public life. Many of these new ideas are to be found expressed, often in a preliminary and hesitant fashion, in the writings of David Hume. However, it is to Montesquieu, not Hume, that we owe the most widely influential account of the separation of powers. And the classic text that gave the fullest expression to a number of these new ideas (though not to all of them, for it had almost nothing to say in praise of party conflict) was Alexander Hamilton's and James Madison's *The Federalist.* But it is Benjamin Constant's lecture "On Ancient and Modern Liberty" that provides the best introduction to the new idea of liberty, for it brings out sharply the difference between ancient and modern conceptions of liberty, and it also brings out clearly the ambiguous place of Rousseau and of the French Revolution in any account of the progress of constitutionalism and of liberty.

Further Reading

On concepts of liberty: Isaiah Berlin, "Two Concepts of Liberty," in his *Liberty,* 2nd ed. (Oxford: Clarendon Press, 2002); Quentin Skinner, *Liberty Before Liberalism* (Cambridge: Cambridge University Press, 1997); and Philip Pettit, *Republicanism: A Theory of Freedom and Government* (Oxford: Oxford University Press, 1999). On the history of the idea of a republic: David Wootton, "The True Origins of Republicanism: the Disciples of Baron and the Counter-Example of Venturi," in *Il repubblicanesimo moderno: l'idea de Repubblica nella riflessione storica di Franco Venturi,* ed. M. Albertone

(Napoli: Bibliopolis, 2006), pp. 271–304. On the separation of powers: M.J.C. Vile, *Constitutionalism and the Separation of Powers* 2nd ed., (Indianapolis: Liberty Fund, 1998). On the right to counsel: J. M. Beattie, "Scales of Justice: Defense Counsel and the English Criminal Trial in the Eighteenth and Nineteenth Centuries," *Law and History Review* 9 (1991): 221–67. On checks and balances: David Wootton, "Liberty, Metaphor, and Mechanism: the Origins of Modern Constitutionalism," in *Liberty and American Experience in the Eighteenth Century,* ed. D. Womersley (Indianapolis: Liberty Fund, 2006), pp. 209–74. There is no good account of the history of the idea of representation, but see Brian Tierney, *Religion, Law and the Growth of Constitutional Thought, 1150–1650* (Cambridge: Cambridge University Press, 1982) as a corrective to Quentin Skinner, "Hobbes on Representation," *European Journal of Philosophy* 13 (2005), 155–84.

DAVID HUME
Of the Independency of Parliament

Political writers have established it as a maxim, that, in contriving any system of government, and fixing the several checks and controuls of the constitution, every man ought to be supposed a knave, and to have no other end, in all his actions, than private interest. By this interest we must govern him, and, by means of it, make him, notwithstanding his insatiable avarice and ambition, co-operate to public good. Without this, say they, we shall in vain boast of the advantages of any constitution, and shall find, in the end, that we have no security for our liberties or possessions, except the good will of our rulers; that is, we shall have no security at all.

It is, therefore, a just *political* maxim, that *every man must be supposed a knave:* Though at the same time, it appears somewhat strange, that a maxim should be true in *politics*, which is false in *fact*. But to satisfy us on this head, we may consider, that men are generally more honest in their private than in their public capacity, and will go greater lengths to serve a party, than when their own private interest is alone concerned. Honour is a great check upon mankind: But where a considerable body of men act together, this check is, in great measure, removed; since a man is sure to be approved of by his own party, for what promotes the common interest; and he soon learns to despise the clamours of adversaries. To which we may add, that every court or senate is determined by the greater number of voices; so that, if self-interest influences only the majority, (as it will always do) the whole senate follows the allurements of this separate interest, and acts as if it contained not one member, who had any regard to public interest and liberty.

When there offers, therefore, to our censure and examination, any plan of government, real or imaginary, where the power is distributed among several courts, and several orders of men, we should always consider the separate interest of each court, and each order; and, if we find that, by the skilful division of power, this interest must necessarily, in its operation, concur with

public, we may pronounce that government to be wise and happy. If, on the contrary, separate interest be not checked, and be not directed to the public, we ought to look for nothing but faction, disorder, and tyranny from such a government. In this opinion I am justified by experience, as well as by the authority of all philosophers and politicians, both antient and modern.

How much, therefore, would it have surprised such a genius as CICERO, or TACITUS, to have been told that, in a future age, there should arise a very regular system of *mixed* government, where the authority was so distributed, that one rank, whenever it pleased, might swallow up all the rest, and engross the whole power of the constitution. Such a government, they would say, will not be a mixed government. For so great is the natural ambition of men, that they are never satisfied with power; and if one order of men, by pursuing its own interest, can usurp upon every other order, it will certainly do so, and render itself, as far as possible, absolute and uncontroulable.

But, in this opinion, experience shews they would have been mistaken. For this is actually the case with the BRITISH constitution. The share of power, allotted by our constitution to the house of commons, is so great, that it absolutely commands all the other parts of the government. The king's legislative power is plainly no proper check to it. For though the king has a negative in framing laws; yet this, in fact, is esteemed of so little moment, that whatever is voted by the two houses, is always sure to pass into a law, the royal assent is little better than a form. The principal weight of the crown lies in the executive power. But besides that the executive power in every government is altogether subordinate to the legislative; besides this, I say, the exercise of this power requires an immense expence; and the commons have assumed to themselves the sole right of granting money. How easy, therefore, would it be for that house to wrest from the crown all these powers, one after another; by making every grant conditional, and choosing their time so well, that their refusal of supply should only distress the government, without giving foreign powers any advantage over us? Did the house of commons depend in the same manner on the king, and had none of the members any property but from his gift, would not he command all their resolutions, and be from that moment absolute? As to the house of lords, they are a very powerful support to the Crown, so long as they are, in their turn, supported by it; but both experience and reason shew, that they have no force or authority sufficient to maintain themselves alone, without such support.

How, therefore, shall we solve this paradox? And by what means is this member of our constitution confined within the proper limits; since, from our very constitution, it must necessarily have as much power as it demands, and can only be confined by itself? How is this consistent with our experience of human nature? I answer, that the interest of the body is here restrained by that of the individuals, and that the house of commons stretches not its power, because such an usurpation would be contrary to the interest of the majority of its members. The crown has so many offices at its disposal, that, when assisted by the honest and disinterested part of the house, it will always command the resolutions of the whole so far, at least, as to preserve the antient constitution from danger. We may, therefore, give to this influence what name we please; we may call it by the invidious appellations of *corruption* and *dependence*; but some degree and some kind of it are inseparable from the very nature of the constitution, and necessary to the preservation of our mixed government.

Instead then of asserting[1] absolutely, that the dependence of parliament, in every degree, is an infringement of British liberty, the country-party should have made some concessions to their adversaries, and have only examined what was the proper degree of this dependence, beyond which it became dangerous to liberty. But such a moderation is not to be expected in party-men of any kind. After a concession of this nature, all declamation must be abandoned; and a calm enquiry into the proper degree of court-influence and parliamentary dependence would have been expected

by the readers. And though the advantage, in such a controversy, might possibly remain to the *country-party*; yet the victory would not be so compleat as they wish for, nor would a true patriot have given an entire loose to his zeal, for fear of running matters into a contrary extreme, by diminishing too[2] far the influence of the crown. It was, therefore, thought best to deny, that this extreme could ever be dangerous to the constitution, or that the crown could ever have too little influence over members of parliament.

All questions concerning the proper medium between extremes are difficult to be decided; both because it is not easy to find *words* proper to fix this medium, and because the good and ill, in such cases, run so gradually into each other, as even to render our *sentiments* doubtful and uncertain. But there is a peculiar difficulty in the present case, which would embarrass the most knowing and most impartial examiner. The power of the crown is always lodged in a single person, either king or minister; and as this person may have either a greater or less degree of ambition, capacity, courage, popularity, or fortune, the power, which is too great in one hand, may become too little in another. In pure republics, where the authority is distributed among several assemblies or senates, the checks and controuls are more regular in their operation; because the members of such numerous assemblies may be presumed to be always nearly equal in capacity and virtue; and it is only their number, riches, or authority, which enter into consideration. But a limited monarchy admits not of any such stability; nor is it possible to assign to the crown such a determinate degree of power, as will, in every hand, form a proper counterbalance to the other parts of the constitution. This is an unavoidable disadvantage, among the many advantages, attending that species of government.

[1] See [Bolingbroke], *Dissertation on Parties* [1735] throughout.

[2] By that *influence of the crown*, which I would justify, I mean only that which arises from the offices and honours that are at the disposal of the crown. As to private *bribery*, it may be considered in the same light as the practice of employing spies, which is scarcely justifiable in a good minister, and is infamous in a bad one: But to be a spy, or to be corrupted, is always infamous under all ministers, and is to be regarded as a shameless prostitution. *Polybius* justly esteems the pecuniary influence of the senate and censors to be one of the regular and constitutional weights, which preserved the balance of the *Roman* government. Lib. vi. cap. 15.

Montesquieu

The Spirit of the Laws

Book XI: Laws that Comprise Political Liberty: Their Relation to the Constitution

Chapter I: General Conception

I distinguish those laws that comprise political liberty considered in relation to the constitution, from those laws that comprise liberty in relation to the individual citizen. The first type of laws will be the subject of this book; the second will be examined in the next book.

Chapter II: Different Meanings given to the Word Liberty

No word has been given more different meanings, no word has made such varied impressions upon the minds of men as that of liberty. Some have taken it to mean their capacity to depose at will a person to whom they have given tyrannical power; others to mean the capacity to elect someone they ought to obey; still others to mean the power to bear arms, and thus to be able to use violence; and finally, there are those who understand it as the privilege to be governed only by a man of their own nation, or by their own laws.[1] A certain people believed for a long time that liberty consisted of the privilege of wearing a long beard.[2] Some have reserved the term for one form of government and refused it to all others. Those who had relished republican government claimed that liberty belonged to it alone; the same was done by those who had enjoyed monarchical rule.[3] Finally, everyone has applied the term liberty to that form of government, which conforms to his own customs or inclinations. In a republic, the evils about which one complains are produced by means that are neither evident nor constant, and the laws seem to carry more weight than their executors. Thus liberty is usually considered a characteristic of republics, but not of monarchies. Finally, since in democracies, the people seems to be able to do almost everything it wishes, liberty has been considered a characteristic of that type of government as well. This is to confuse the power of the people with its liberty.

Chapter III: What Liberty Is

It is true that in democracies the people apparently does whatever it wishes. But doing what one wishes is not political liberty. In a state, that is, a society where laws exist, liberty can consist only in being able to do what one ought to will, and in not being constrained to do what one ought not to will.

We must distinguish independence from liberty. Liberty is the right to do everything the law permits. If a citizen could do what the law prohibits, he would no longer possess liberty because all others would have the same power.

Chapter IV: The Same Subject Continued

Neither democracy nor aristocracy is free by nature. Political liberty exists only in those governments where

[Reprinted from Montesquieu, *Selected Political Writings*, edited and translated by Melvin Richter (Indianapolis: Hackett Publishing Company, 1990), by permission of the publisher.]

[1] " 'I have,' says Cicero, 'copied the edict of Scaevola, which permits the Greeks to resolve their differences according to their own laws; with the result that they consider themselves to be a 'free people.' "

[2] "The Russians would not submit to Czar Peter's order that their beards be cut."

[3] "The Cappadocians refused the status of a republican state offered them by the Romans."

power is moderated (*les gouvernements modérés*). Even in them, liberty is not always found. Political liberty exists only when there is no abuse of power. But all experience proves that every man with power is led to abuse it; he will continue to apply his power until he discovers what are its limits. Indeed, even virtue itself must be kept within bounds. To prevent the abuse of power, things must be so ordered that power checks power. A constitution may be so framed that no one is compelled to do what is not made obligatory by law, nor forced to abstain from what the law permits.

Chapter V: The Objectives of States

Although all states share the same general objective, which is to preserve themselves, nevertheless, each of them has its own particular purpose. Aggrandizement was the objective of Rome; war, of Sparta; religion, of the laws of Israel; commerce, of Marseilles; public tranquillity, of Chinese laws;[4] navigation, of the laws of Rhodes; natural liberty, of savage regimes; in general, the pleasures of the ruler under despotism; the glory of the king and his state under monarchy; the independence of every individual is the objective of Polish legislation, and its consequence, the oppression of all.[5]

There is also a nation that has political liberty as the direct object of its constitution. We shall proceed to examine the principles upon which this nation bases its liberty. If they are sound, then liberty will be reflected there, as in a mirror.

To discover whether political liberty is established by a constitution, requires no great effort. If, once located, it can be recognized, why look further?

Chapter VI: The English Constitution

In every government, there are three sorts of powers: the legislative; the executive, in regard to those mat-

ters determined by the laws of nations; and the executive, in regard to those matters determined by the civil law.

By virtue of the first, the ruler or magistrate makes laws, either temporarily, or for all time, as well as correcting or abrogating those already in existence. By virtue of the second, he makes war or peace, sends or receives ambassadors, ensures security, and makes provision against invasion. By virtue of the third power, he punishes crimes, or passes judgment upon disputes arising among individuals. This is called the judicial power; the second, simply the executive power of the state.

For a citizen, political liberty is that tranquillity of mind which derives from his sense of security. Liberty of this kind presupposes a government so ordered that no citizen need fear another.

When both the legislative and executive powers are united in the same person or body of magistrates, there is no liberty. For then it may be feared that the same monarch or senate has made tyrannical laws in order to execute them in a tyrannical way.

Again, there is no liberty, if the power to judge is not separated from the legislative and executive powers. Were the judicial power joined to the legislative, the life and liberty of the citizens would be subject to arbitrary power. For the judge would then be the legislator. Were the judicial power joined to the executive, the judge could acquire enough strength to become an oppressor.

All would be lost if the same man, or the same body, whether composed of notables, nobles, or the people, were to exercise these three powers: that of making laws, that of executing public decisions, and that of judging crimes or disputes arising among individuals.

In most European kingdoms, the government is limited (*modéré*), because the ruler, who possesses the first two powers, leaves the exercise of the third to his subjects. But among the Turks, where all three powers are united in the sultan's person, a frightful despotism prevails.

In the Italian republics, where all three powers are combined, there is less liberty than in our monarchies. What is more, to maintain themselves, these republics require means just as violent as those used by the Turkish government. One proof of this is the state inquisi-

---

[4] "The natural aim of a state that has no foreign enemies or believes it has secured itself against them by barriers."

[5] "The peculiar disadvantage of the *liberum veto*." [The Polish Diet operated on the rule of unanimity. The *liberum veto* was the power on the part of any member to block legislation.]

tors;[6] another, the box into which any informer at any time may drop his letter of accusation.

Consider what can happen to a citizen of such republics: the same body of magistrates has, as executor of the laws, all the power it has given itself in its legislative capacity. It can plunder the state by what it decides in general (*ses volontés générales*); and, since it also has the judicial power, it can destroy any individual citizen by what it decides in his particular case (*ses volontés particulières*).

Here all power is united. Although there is none of the external pomp habitual to the despotic ruler, nevertheless, such power makes itself felt at every moment.

It is no less true that those rulers who have wished to become despots have always begun by uniting in their own persons all the magistracies (*toutes les magistratures*); and, in the case of many European kings, all the great offices of their state.

I concede that the pure hereditary aristocracy of the Italian republics does not correspond exactly to Asiatic despotism. The number of magistrates sometimes makes the magistracy less severe; not all nobles can always join in the same designs; and the variety of tribunals serve to limit one another. Thus in Venice, it is the Supreme Council that has the legislative power; the *pregardi*, the executive, the *quarantia*, the judicial. But what is most unfortunate derives from the fact that all these tribunals are formed from magistrates who belong to the same social estate (*corps*), which virtually turns them into one and the same power.

The judicial power ought not be given to a permanent senate, but should be exercised by persons drawn from the people as an estate (*corps*)[7] and this at certain times of the year, according to a procedure prescribed by law. The court formed in this way ought to last no longer than necessity requires.

In this way, the judicial power, so terrible to men, becomes, as it were, invisible and of no force (*invisible et nulle*) because it is attached neither to any estate (*état*) nor to any profession. There are no judges constantly in public view; it is the office that is feared, not the individuals who hold it.

Thus it is even necessary that in the indictments for grave crimes, the accused, in accordance with the law, should choose his judges, or, at least, be able to challenge enough of them that those remaining may be considered to have been chosen by him.

The other two powers might rather be assigned to magistrates or permanent bodies (*corps*), because their jurisdiction does not extend to any individual. One of these powers is nothing more than the general will (*la volonté générale*) of the state; the other, nothing more than the execution of that general will.

But although the makeup of tribunals ought not to be fixed, the same ought not to be true of their judgments, which should be determined only by the precise text of the law. If judgments came to nothing more than the individual opinion of the judge, men would live in society without knowing precisely what were the obligations they had contracted.

The accused ought not to be made to think that he has fallen into the hands of those inclined to do him violence. Thus it is not too much to require that his judges be either of the same rank (*condition*) as himself, or his peers (*pairs*).

If the legislative power allows the executive power the right to imprison those citizens who can provide security for their good behavior, then there is no longer any liberty. This would not be the case if such citizens were arrested in order to bring them to trial without delay under an indictment for a crime defined by law as subject to capital punishment. For then they would really be free, since they would be subject only to the power of the law.

But if the legislative power thinks itself endangered by a secret conspiracy against the state, or by communication with a foreign enemy, then it may for a short and limited time permit the executive power to arrest suspected citizens, who would be losing their liberty temporarily in order to preserve it for all time.

And this is the only reasonable means that may be substituted for the tyrannical magistracy of the ephors and the state inquisitors of Venice, who are also despotic.

In a free state, every man who is considered a free citizen ought to be governed by himself. Hence the people as an estate (*corps*) ought to have the legislative power. However, since that is impossible in large states

---

[6] "At Venice."
[7] "As at Athens."

and subject to many disadvantages in small ones, the people must do by its representatives everything it cannot itself do.

Everyone knows much better the needs of his city than those of other cities; he is a better judge of his neighbors' capacities than those possessed by their other compatriots. Members of the legislative body should not be drawn, therefore, from the nation in general. What is more appropriate is that the inhabitants of every place of importance elect a representative.

The great advantage of representatives is their capacity to discuss public business. For this the people [as a body] are quite unfitted, and this is among the greatest disadvantages of democracy.

It is not at all necessary that representatives, whose constituents have given them general directions, await as well specific directions on each issue, as is done in the diets of Germany. It is true that this way of proceeding would turn the words of deputies into something closer to the voice of the nation. But this would occasion infinite delays and turn every deputy into the master of every other. Thus, in the most urgent circumstances, all the nation's force might be arrested by the caprice of a single person.

Sidney has well observed that when the deputies represent a body or estate of the people (*un corps du peuple*), as in Holland, they ought to be accountable to their constituents. When the deputies represent boroughs (*bourgs*), as in England, the situation is not the same.

In the separate districts, all citizens ought to have the right to choose their representative by election. The only exception concerns those whose condition is so base that they are considered to have no will of their own.

Most ancient republics suffered from this great defect: the people had the right to take decisions involving action (*prendre des résolutions actives*) of a kind that required participating in the subsequent execution of such decisions. And of this they are quite incapable. They should enter into government only to the extent of choosing representatives, something which is very much within their reach. Although few men can assess precisely the qualifications of candidates for office, nevertheless everyone can know in general

whether or not the person he chooses is better informed (*éclairé*) than other candidates.

Nor ought the representative body be chosen to take some decision involving executive action by itself (*quelque résolution active*), for which it is not fit. Rather it ought to be chosen to make laws, or to see whether the laws it has already made have been well executed, both matters for which it is very well fitted, and indeed, can be done by no other body.

In every state there are always some people distinguished from the rest by their birth, wealth, or honors. If combined indiscriminately with the people, so that everyone counted equally, such common liberty would constitute slavery [for the distinguished]. Nor would they have any interest in defending this common liberty, because under it most decisions would go against them. Thus their share in legislation ought to be in proportion to the other advantages they enjoy in the state. And this can be assured only when they constitute on the one side, a body (*corps*) that has the right to check the people's actions, and, on the other, when the people have the right to check their actions.

In this way, the power to legislate will be entrusted both to the body of nobles and to the body chosen to represent the people. Each will assemble and deliberate separately; each will have its own views and interests.

As for the three powers mentioned above, the judicial, in a sense, has no force (*est en quelque façon nulle*). This leaves but two. They need a power so constituted that it can limit both of them. This can be done by that part of the legislative body which is composed of nobles, and is very well fitted to produce such an effect.

The body of nobles ought to be hereditary. In the first place, it is so by nature. What is more, it ought to be given a very considerable interest in maintaining its prerogatives, for these by their very existence are enough to provoke hatred and in a free state must always be in danger.

But a power based on hereditary principles may be led to attend to its own special interests and to forget those of the people. Hence in all matters where great profit can be extracted from corruption, as for example, when considering laws raising money, such a body of nobles should participate in legislation, not by its power to make laws, but only by its power to veto them.

What I call the power to make laws (*faculté de statuer*) is the right to ordain by itself (*le droit d'ordonner par soi-même*) and to amend what has been ordained by another. What I call the power to veto (*faculté d'empêcher*) is the right to void a decision taken elsewhere, the power held by Roman tribunes. And although the power to veto may be combined with the right to approve, yet such approval comes to nothing more than the declaration that no use will be made of the veto power. This is, therefore, the source of the other power [to approve].

The executive power ought to be in the hands of a monarch, because this part of government, which almost always requires rapid action, is better administered by one person than by many. On the other hand, whatever is determined by the legislative power is often better decided (*ordonné*) by many than by one.

If there were no monarch, if the executive power were entrusted to a number of persons taken from the legislative body, there would no longer be any liberty. For the two powers would be united, the same persons would sometimes in fact share, and always have the power to share, in both.

If the legislative power were to go without meeting for a considerable time, there would no longer be any liberty. For one of two things would occur: either there would no longer be any legislative decisions, and the state would fall into anarchy; or else decisions would be taken by the executive power, which would thus become absolute.

It would serve no purpose to have the legislative body always in session. Not only would this be inconvenient for the representatives, it would also preoccupy the executive power, which would think not of doing what it is meant to do, but rather of defending its prerogatives, and its right to execute [legislation].

Furthermore, were the legislative body continually in session, it might happen that new representatives would be chosen only to replace those who had died. In that case, if the legislative body were ever corrupted, there would be no remedy. When different legislative bodies succeed each other, the people, if it has a bad opinion of the one in power, may place its hopes upon the one that will succeed it. But if the legislative body always remained the same, then in the event that it were corrupted, the people with nothing further to hope from legislation, would either be overcome with fury, or fall into indolence.

The legislative body ought not to meet at its own initiative. For a body is not considered to possess a will until it is in session. If the decision to meet were not unanimous, then it would be impossible to determine which in fact is the legislative body, that part in session, or that part which is absent. Were it to have the power to adjourn itself, it might happen that it would never adjourn, and this would be dangerous in the event that it attempted to encroach upon the executive power. Besides, there are better and worse times for convening the legislative body. Thus it ought to be the executive power, which on the basis of what it knows about the circumstances, sets the time and duration of legislative meetings.

If the executive does not have the power to check the designs of the legislative, this body would become despotic. For if it could arrogate to itself all the power it wished, then it would annihilate all other powers.

But it does not follow that as a matter of reciprocity, the legislative ought to have the power to check the executive. For there are limits to what the executive power can do, and these derive from its very nature. It is unnecessary to set further bounds. Furthermore, the executive power is always exercised on short-term matters. The power of the Roman tribunes was defective because it could check not only the legislative, but the executive, and this caused great damage.

But if in a free state, the legislative power ought not to have the power to check the executive, it has the right and ought to have the means to investigate how the laws it has passed have been carried out. This is the advantage that such a government has over that of Crete and Sparta, where the *cosmoi* and ephors gave no account of their administration.[8]

---

8 [The ephors were the five Spartan magistrates, who, combining executive, judicial, and disciplinary powers, dominated the state, including two kings. The cosmoi were

Whatever the result of its investigation, the legislative body ought not to have the power to judge the personal acts or official conduct of the individual entrusted with the executive power. His person ought to be sacred because it is necessary to the state that the legislative body not become tyrannical. From the moment that this person [the executive] is accused or judged, liberty is no more.

In such a case, the state would be, not a monarchy but a republic that is not free. But whoever holds the executive power cannot abuse it without the aid of evil counselors, who, serving him as ministers, detest all laws, although these same laws may benefit them as men. These counselors may be investigated and punished, and this is an advantage of this government over that of Gnidus, under which the law did not permit calling the amimones[9] to account, even after their tenure of office was over.[10] Therefore the people could never obtain any satisfaction from these magistrates for the injustices they had committed.

In general, the judicial power ought not to be joined to any part of the legislative. However, this principle is subject to three exceptions, all deriving from the individual interest of the defendant.

The great are always subject to envy. Were they to be judged by the people, they would be in danger of being deprived of that privilege guaranteed to even the most humble citizen of a free state, that of judgment by their peers. Nobles, therefore, ought to be tried, not in the ordinary courts of their nation, but in that part of the legislative body which is made up of nobles.

It sometimes happens that the law, which is at the same time enlightened and blind, is too rigorous in some cases. But the judges of the nation are, as I have

already said, nothing more than the mouth which pronounces the words of the law. As such, they are inert and can moderate neither the force nor the rigor of the law. It is that part of the legislative body, which, as I have just elsewhere called indispensable, is equally so in this regard. One part of its supreme authority is to modify the law in the direction of the [intended purpose of] law itself by mitigating its severity. It might also happen that some citizen, acting in a public capacity, violates the rights of the people, and commits crimes that ordinary magistrates could not or would not punish. But in general, the legislative power is debarred from acting as a court and especially in such a case as this, when it represents the people, which is one of the interested parties. Thus the legislative power cannot do more than accuse. But before which body ought this to be done? Will the legislative power go and demean itself before the ordinary courts of law, which are inferior to it? Moreover, these courts are composed of men, who, like the legislative body itself, are drawn from the people. What is more likely than that the courts would be swayed by the authority of so great an accuser? No, in order to preserve both the dignity of the people and the security of the individual, that part of the legislature which represents the people must bring its charges before that part of the legislature which represents the nobles, a body with neither the same interests nor passions.

Here is an advantage that this type of government has over most ancient republics, which were defective in that the people was at the same time both judge and prosecutor.

As has been said, the executive power ought to take part in legislation through its power to veto, without which it would soon be stripped of its prerogatives. But if the legislative power participates in executing what it has enacted, then the executive power will be just as much undone.

If the monarch were to participate in legislation by his power to make laws, there would no longer be any liberty. Nevertheless, if he is to defend himself, he must take part in legislation, and this by his power to refuse consent.

This change of government at Rome was caused by the fact that the power to refuse consent was reserved

---

Cretan magistrates resembling the Spartan ephors. For discussions and criticisms, see Aristotle, *Politics*, II, 10; and Polybius, *History*, VI, 45–7.]

9 "These were magistrates elected annually by the people. See Stephen of Byzantium." [The amimones were magistrates elected for life in the republic of Cnidos.]

10 "The Roman magistrates could be held accountable after the expiration of their terms of office. See Dionysius of Halicarnasus, Book IX, the case of the tribune Genutius."

to the people rather than to the senate, which held one part of the executive power, or to the magistrates, which held the other.

Here, then, is the fundamental constitution of the government being discussed. Since the legislative body is made up of two parts, each is made dependent upon the other (*l'une enchainera l'autre*) by their mutual power to reject legislation. Both will be connected by the executive power, which itself will be connected to the legislative.

These three powers ought to produce repose, or inaction. But since the nature of things requires movement, all three powers are obliged to act, and to act together.

Since the executive power participates in the legislative only by its power to refuse its consent, it cannot be allowed to participate in debate. It is not even necessary that it have the power to propose legislation, since it [already] possesses the power to reject decisions. Thus it can veto those proposals made against its will.

In some ancient republics, public affairs were debated by an assembly of all the people. It was natural that in such a body the executive power could introduce proposals and participate in discussing them. Otherwise, decisions would have been extraordinarily confused.

If the executive power took any part in raising money other than by consenting [to decisions made elsewhere], there would no longer be any liberty. For in this way, the executive would be legislating on the single most important point taken up by a legislative body.

If the legislative power were to raise money, not annually, but for all time, it would run the risk of losing its liberty because the executive power would no longer depend upon it. When such a right is held in perpetuity, it makes no difference whether it derived from oneself or from someone else. There would be the same result if the legislative power were to provide, not annually, but in perpetuity for the land and sea forces, the command of which it ought to confide to the executive power.

To prevent the executive power from being able to oppress, the armies confided to it must be made up from the people, and have its spirit, as was the case at Rome until the time of Marius. There are but two means adequate to this end: either those serving in the army should have enough property to answer to their fellow-citizens for their conduct and be enrolled for one year only as was done at Rome. Or else, if there be a body of troops constituted as a standing army, and made up of the most despicable parts of the nation, the legislative power must be able to dismiss them at its pleasure. And the soldiers ought to live together with the people, and not have any separate camps, barracks or fortresses.

Once an army has been established, it ought to depend, not directly upon the legislative body, but upon the executive power. This follows from the very nature of the military enterprise, which consists more of action than of deliberation.

Men tend to place courage above timidity, action above prudence, force above discussion. An army will always despise a senate and respect its own officers. It will disregard orders emanating from a body whose members it believes to be timid, and therefore unworthy of commanding the army. Thus what happens is this: as soon as an army takes orders directly from a legislative body, the government will become dominated by the military. If the contrary of this has ever occurred, it has been due to extraordinary circumstances: the army has always been kept divided; or it has been composed of various units, each under the authority of a different province; or the principal cities occupy excellent positions, to which they owe their security, and thus there are no garrisons.

Holland is still more secure than Venice. If Holland's troops were to revolt, she could drown them, she could starve them out. For they are not quartered in cities that could furnish them with the supplies of food they need. Thus their means of subsistence is precarious.

If the army is under the authority of a legislative body, and special circumstances prevent the government from being dominated by the military, then two other undesirable things could happen rather than this one: either the army must destroy the government, or the government must greatly weaken the effectiveness of the army.

And to weaken the army in this way would be due to a cause certain to be fatal, and originating in the very weakness of the government.

The admirable work of Tacitus, *On the Manners and Customs of the Germans*, demonstrates that it is from them that the English have borrowed the idea of their political government.[11] This handsome system was discovered in the woods.

Since everything human must end, the state discussed here will lose its liberty and perish. Rome, Sparta, Carthage—all have perished. This state will perish when its legislative power becomes more corrupt than its executive.

It is not my concern to determine whether or not the English in fact enjoy such liberty. I need say no more than that it is established by their laws. Further than that I shall not look.

It is not my intent to depreciate other governments by this procedure, nor do I wish to assert that such extreme political liberty ought to be regretted by those who enjoy a moderate share of liberty. How could I say such a thing? For I have always believed that excess, even of reason, is not always desirable, and that men are almost always most comfortable with the mean, rather than the extreme.

Harrington, in his *Oceana*, has also sought to determine just how far the constitution of a state may carry liberty. But it may be said of him that he sought liberty without being able to recognize it when he saw it, that he built Chalcedon, although he had the shores of Byzantium before his eyes.[12]

---

[11] "*De minoribus rebus principes consultant, de majoribus omnes; ita tamen ut ea quoque quorum penes plebem arbitrium est apud principes pertractentur.*" ["On small matters the chiefs consult; on larger questions, the community; but with this limitation, that even the subjects, the decision of which rests with the people, are first handled by the chiefs." Tacitus, *Germania*, 11, trans. Maurice Hutton.]

[12] [Herodotus (IV, 144) reported that the Chaledonians could have built their city on the site of Byzantium but did not, despite the inherent superiority of the place. Thus Montesquieu reproaches Harrington for not appreciating the liberty existing in his own country and constructing instead the utopia of Oceana.]

THE FEDERALIST
[Nos. 9, 10, 14, 48, 51]

NO. 9 [HAMILTON]

The Utility of the Union as a Safeguard Against Domestic Faction and Insurrection

A Firm Union will be of the utmost moment to the peace and liberty of the States as a barrier against domestic faction and insurrection. It is impossible to read the history of the petty Republics of Greece and Italy, without feeling sensations of horror and disgust at the distractions with which they were continually agitated, and at the rapid succession of revolutions, by which they were kept in a state of perpetual vibration, between the extremes of tyranny and anarchy. If they exhibit occasional calms, these only serve as short-lived contrasts to the furious storms that are to succeed. If now and then intervals of felicity open themselves to view, we behold them with a mixture of regret arising from the reflection that the pleasing scenes before us are soon to be overwhelmed by the tempestuous waves of sedition and party rage. If momentary rays of glory break forth from the gloom, while they dazzle us with a transient and fleeting brilliancy, they at the same time admonish us to lament that the vices of government should pervert the direction and tarnish the luster of those bright talents and exalted endowments for which the favored soils, that produced them, have been so justly celebrated.

From the disorders that disfigure the annals of those republics, the advocates of despotism have drawn arguments, not only against the forms of republican government, but against the very principles of civil liberty. They have decried all free government, as inconsistent with the order of society, and have indulged themselves in malicious exultation over its friends and partisans. Happily for mankind, stupendous fabrics reared on the basis of liberty, which have flourished for ages, have in a few glorious instances refuted their gloomy sophisms. And, I trust, America will be the broad and solid foundation of other edifices not less magnificent, which will be equally permanent monuments of their errors.

But it is not to be denied that the portraits, they have sketched of republican government, were too just copies of the originals from which they were taken. If it had been found impracticable, to have devised models of a more perfect structure, the enlightened friends to liberty would have been obliged to abandon the cause of that species of government as indefensible. The science of politics, however, like most other sciences has received great improvement. The efficacy of various principles is now well understood, which were either not known at all, or imperfectly known to the ancients. The regular distribution of power into distinct departments—the introduction of legislature balances and checks—the institutions of courts composed of judges, holding their offices during good behavior—the representation of the people in the legislature by deputies of their own election—these are either wholly new discoveries or have made their principal progress toward perfection in modern times. They are means, and powerful means, by which the excellencies of republican government may be retained and its imperfections lessened or avoided. To this catalog of circumstances, that tend to the amelioration of popular systems of civil government, I shall venture, however novel it may appear to some, to add one more on a principle, which has been made the foundation of an objection to the New Constitution, I mean the ENLARGEMENT of the ORBIT within which such systems are to revolve either in respect to the dimensions of a single State, or to the consolidation of several smaller States into one great confederacy. The latter is that which immediately concerns the object under consideration. It will however be of use to examine the principle in its application to a single State which shall be attended to in another place.

The utility of a confederacy, as well to suppress faction and to guard the internal tranquillity of States, as to increase their external force and security, is in reality not a new idea. It has been practiced upon in different countries and ages, and has received the sanction of the most applauded writers, on the subjects of politics. The opponents of the PLAN proposed have with great assiduity cited and circulated the observations of Montesquieu on the necessity of a contracted territory for a republican government. But they seem not to have been apprised of the sentiments of that great man expressed in another part of his work, nor to have adverted to the consequences of the principle to which they subscribe, with such ready acquiescence.

When Montesquieu recommends a small extent for republics, the standards he had in view were of dimensions, far short of the limits of almost every one of these States. Neither Virginia, Massachusetts, Pennsylvania, New York, North Carolina, nor Georgia, can by any means be compared with the models, from which he reasoned and to which the terms of his description apply. If we therefore take his ideas on this point, as the criterion of truth, we shall be driven to the alternative, either of taking refuge at once in the arms of monarchy, or of splitting ourselves into an infinity of little jealous, clashing, tumultuous commonwealths, the wretched nurseries of unceasing discord and the miserable objects of universal pity or contempt. Some of the writers, who have come forward on the other side of the question, seem to have been aware of the dilemma; and have even been bold enough to hint at the division of the larger States, as a desirable thing. Such an infatuated policy, such a desperate expedient, might, by the multiplication of petty offices, answer the views of men, who possess not qualifications to extend their influence beyond the narrow circles of personal intrigue, but it could never promote the greatness or happiness of the people of America.

Referring the examination of the principle itself to another place, as has been already mentioned, it will be sufficient to remark here, that in the sense of the author who has been most emphatically quoted upon the occasion, it would only dictate a reduction of the SIZE of the more considerable MEMBERS of the Union; but would not militate against their being all comprehended in one Confederate Government. And this is the true question, in the discussion of which we are at present interested.

So far are the suggestions of Montesquieu from standing in opposition to a general Union of the States, that he explicitly treats of a CONFEDERATE REPUBLIC as the expedient for extending the sphere of popular government and reconciling the advantages of monarchy with those of republicanism.

"It is very probable (says he*) that mankind would have been obliged, at length, to live constantly under the government of a SINGLE PERSON, had they not contrived a kind of constitution, that has all the internal advantages of a republican, together with the external force of a monarchical government. I mean a CONFEDERATE REPUBLIC.

"This form of Government is a Convention, by which several smaller *States* agree to become members of a larger *one*, which they intend to form. It is a kind of assemblage of societies, that constitute a new one, capable of increasing by means of new associations, until they arrive to such a degree of power as to be able to provide for the security of the united body.

"A republic of this kind, able to withstand an external force, may support itself without any internal corruption. The form of this society prevents all manner of inconveniences.

"If a single member should attempt to usurp the supreme authority, he could not be supposed to have an equal authority and credit, in all the confederate states. Were he to have too great influence over one, this would alarm the rest. Were he to subdue a part, that which would still remain free might oppose him with forces, independent of those which he had usurped, and overpower him before he could be settled in his usurpation.

Spirit of Laws, Volume I. Book IX. Chapter I. [Publius]

"Should a popular insurrection happen, in one of the confederate States, the others are able to quell it. Should abuses creep into one part, they are reformed by those that remain sound. The State may be destroyed on one side, and not on the other; the confederacy may be dissolved, and the confederates preserve their sovereignty.

"As this government is composed of small republics it enjoys the internal happiness of each, and with respect to its external situation it is possessed, by means of the association of all the advantages of large monarchies."

I have thought it proper to quote at length these interesting passages, because they contain a luminous abridgment of the principal arguments in favor of the Union, and must effectually remove the false impressions, which a misapplication of other parts of the work was calculated to produce. They have at the same time an intimate connection with the more immediate design of this Paper; which is to illustrate the tendency of the Union to repress domestic faction and insurrection.

A distinction, more subtle than accurate has been raised between a *confederacy* and a *consolidation* of the States. The essential characteristic of the first is said to be, the restriction of its authority to the members in their collective capacities, without reaching to the individuals of whom they are composed. It is contended that the national council ought to have no concern with any object of internal administration. An exact equality of suffrage between the members has also been insisted upon as a leading feature of a Confederate Government. These positions are in the main arbitrary; they are supported neither by principle nor precedent. It has indeed happened that governments of this kind have generally operated in the manner, which the distinction, taken notice of, supposes to be inherent in their nature—but there have been in most of them extensive exceptions to the practice, which serve to prove as far as example will go, that there is no absolute rule on the subject. And it will be clearly shown, in the course of this investigation, that as far as the principle contended for has prevailed, it has been the cause of incurable disorder and imbecility in the government.

The definition of a *Confederate Republic* seems simply to be, "an assemblage of societies" or an association of two or more States into one State. The extent, modifications, and objects of the Federal authority are mere matters of discretion. So long as the separate organization of the members be not abolished, so long as it exists by a constitutional necessity for local purposes, though it should be in perfect subordination to the general authority of the Union, it would still be, in fact and in theory, an association of States, or a confederacy. The proposed Constitution, so far from implying an abolition of the State Governments, makes them constituent parts of the national sovereignty by allowing them a direct representation in the Senate, and leaves in their possession certain exclusive and very important portions of sovereign power. This fully corresponds, in every rational import of the terms, with the idea of a Federal Government.

In the Lycian confederacy, which consisted of twenty-three CITIES or republics, the largest were entitled to *three* votes in the COMMON COUNCIL, those of the middle class to *two* and the smallest to *one*. The COMMON COUNCIL had the appointment of all the judges and magistrates of the respective CITIES. This was certainly the most delicate species of interference in their internal administration; for if there be anything, that seems exclusively appropriated to the local jurisdictions, it is the appointment of their own officers. Yet Montesquieu, speaking of this association, says "Were I to give a model of an excellent confederate republic, it would be that of Lycia." Thus we perceive that the distinctions insisted upon were not within the contemplation of this enlightened civilian,* and we shall be led to conclude that they are the novel refinements of an erroneous theory.

[November 21, 1787]

---

*["Civilian" here has the technical sense of a student of the law.]

NO. 10   [MADISON]

The Same Subject Continued

Among the numerous advantages promised by a well-constructed Union, none deserves to be more accurately developed than its tendency to break and control the violence of faction. The friend of popular governments, never finds himself so much alarmed for their character and fate, as when he contemplates their propensity to this dangerous vice. He will not fail therefore to set a due value on any plan which, without violating the principles to which he is attached, provides a proper cure for it. The instability, injustice, and confusion introduced into the public councils, have in truth been the mortal diseases under which popular governments have everywhere perished; as they continue to be the favorite and fruitful topics from which the adversaries to liberty derive their most specious declamations. The valuable improvements made by the American Constitutions on the popular models, both ancient and modern, cannot certainly be too much admired; but it would be an unwarrantable partiality, to contend that they have as effectually obviated the danger on this side as was wished and expected. Complaints are everywhere heard from our most considerate and virtuous citizens, equally the friends of public and private faith, and of public and personal liberty; that our governments are too unstable; that the public good is disregarded in the conflicts of rival parties; and that measures are too often decided, not according to the rules of justice, and the rights of the minor party; but by the superior force of an interested and overbearing majority. However anxiously we may wish that these complaints had no foundation, the evidence of known facts will not permit us to deny that they are in some degree true. It will be found indeed, on a candid review of our situation, that some of the distresses under which we labor, have been erroneously charged on the operation of our governments; but it will be found, at the same time, that other causes will not alone account for many of our heaviest misfortunes; and particularly, for that prevailing and increasing distrust of public engagements, and alarm for private rights, which are echoed from one end of the continent to the other. These must be chiefly, if not wholly, effects of the unsteadiness and injustice, with which a factious spirit has tainted our public administration.

By a faction I understand a number of citizens, whether amounting to a majority or minority of the whole, who are united and actuated by some common impulse of passion, or of interest, adverse to the rights of other citizens, or to the permanent and aggregate interests of the community.

There are two methods of curing the mischiefs of faction: The one, by removing its causes; the other, by controlling its effects.

There are again two methods of removing the causes of faction: The one by destroying the liberty which is essential to its existence; the other, by giving to every citizen the same opinions, the same passions, and the same interests.

It could never be more truly said than of the first remedy, that it is worse than the disease. Liberty is to faction, what air is to fire, an aliment without which it instantly expires. But it could not be a less folly to abolish liberty, which is essential to political life, because it nourishes faction, than it would be to wish the annihilation of air, which is essential to animal life, because it imparts to fire its destructive agency.

The second expedient is as impracticable, as the first would be unwise. As long as the reason of man continues fallible, and he is at liberty to exercise it, different opinions will be formed. As long as the connection subsists between his reason and his self-love, his opinions and his passions will have a reciprocal influence on each other; and the former will be objects to which the latter will attach themselves. The diversity in the faculties of men from which the rights of property originate, is not less an insuperable obstacle to a uniformity of interests. The protection of these faculties is the first object of Government. From the protection of different and unequal faculties of acquiring property, the possession of different degrees and kinds of property immediately results: and from the influence of these on the sentiments and views of the respective proprietors, ensues a division of the society into different interests and parties.

The latent causes of faction are thus sown in the nature of man; and we see them everywhere brought into different degrees of activity, according to the different circumstances of civil society. A zeal for different opinions concerning religion, concerning Government and many other points, as well of speculation as of practice; an attachment to different leaders ambitiously contending for preeminence and power; or to persons of other descriptions whose fortunes have been interesting to the human passions, have in turn divided mankind into parties, inflamed them with mutual animosity, and rendered them much more disposed to vex and oppress each other, than to cooperate for their common good. So strong is this propensity of mankind to fall into mutual animosities, that where no substantial occasion presents itself, the most frivolous and fanciful distinctions have been sufficient to kindle their unfriendly passions, and excite their most violent conflicts. But the most common and durable source of factions, has been the various and unequal distribution of property. Those who hold, and those who are without property, have ever formed distinct interests in society. Those who are creditors, and those who are debtors, fall under a like discrimination. A landed interest, a manufacturing interest, a mercantile interest, a moneyed interest, with many lesser interests, grow up of necessity in civilized nations, and divide them into different classes, actuated by different sentiments and views. The regulation of these various and interfering interests forms the principal task of modern Legislation, and involves the spirit of party and faction in the necessary and ordinary operations of Government.

No man is allowed to be a judge in his own cause; because his interest would certainly bias his judgment, and, not improbably, corrupt his integrity. With equal, nay with greater reason, a body of men, are unfit to be both judges and parties, at the same time; yet, what are many of the most important acts of legislation, but so many judicial determinations, not indeed concerning the rights of single persons, but concerning the rights of large bodies of citizens; and what are the different classes of legislators, but advocates and parties to the causes which they determine? Is a law proposed concerning private debts? It is a question to which the creditors are parties on one side, and the debtors on the other. Justice ought to hold the balance between them. Yet the parties are and must be themselves the judges; and the most numerous party, or, in other words, the most powerful faction must be expected to prevail. Shall domestic manufactures be encouraged, and in what degree, by restrictions on foreign manufactures? are questions which would be differently decided by the landed and the manufacturing classes; and probably by neither, with a sole regard to justice and the public good. The apportionment of taxes on the various descriptions of property, is an act which seems to require the most exact impartiality; yet, there is perhaps no legislative act in which greater opportunity and temptation are given to a predominant party, to trample on the rules of justice. Every shilling with which they overburden the inferior number, is a shilling saved to their own pockets.

It is in vain to say, that enlightened statesmen will be able to adjust these clashing interests, and render them all subservient to the public good. Enlightened statesmen will not always be at the helm: Nor, in many cases, can such an adjustment be made at all, without taking into view indirect and remote considerations, which will rarely prevail over the immediate interest which one party may find in disregarding the rights of another, or the good of the whole.

The inference to which we are brought, is, that the *causes* of faction cannot be removed; and that relief is only to be sought in the means of controlling its *effects*.

If a faction consists of less than a majority, relief is supplied by the republican principle, which enables the majority to defeat its sinister views by regular vote: It may clog the administration, it may convulse the society; but it will be unable to execute and mask its violence under the forms of the Constitution. When a majority is included in a faction, the form of popular government on the other hand enables it to sacrifice to its ruling passion or interest, both the public good and the rights of other citizens. To secure the public good, and private rights, against the danger of such a faction, and at the same time to preserve the spirit and the form of popular government, is then the great object to which our inquiries are directed: Let me add that it is the great desideratum, by which alone this form of government can be rescued from the opprobrium under which it has so long labored, and be recommended to the esteem and adoption of mankind.

By what means is this object attainable? Evidently by one of two only. Either the existence of the same passion or interest in a majority at the same time, must be prevented; or the majority, having such coexistent passion or interest, must be rendered, by their number and local situation, unable to concert and carry into effect schemes of oppression. If the impulse and the opportunity be suffered to coincide, we well know that neither moral nor religious motives can be relied on as an adequate control. They are not found to be such on the injustice and violence of individuals, and lose their efficacy in proportion to the number combined together; that is, in proportion as their efficacy becomes needful.

From this view of the subject, it may be concluded that a pure Democracy, by which I mean, a Society, consisting of a small number of citizens, who assemble and administer the Government in person, can admit of no cure for the mischiefs of faction. A common passion or interest will, in almost every case, be felt by a majority of the whole; a communication and concert results from the form of Government itself; and there is nothing to check the inducements to sacrifice the weaker party, or an obnoxious individual. Hence it is, that such Democracies have ever been spectacles of turbulence and contention; have ever been found incompatible with personal security, or the rights of property; and have in general been as short in their lives, as they have been violent in their deaths. Theoretic politicians, who patronized this species of government, have erroneously supposed, that by reducing mankind to a perfect equality in their political rights, they would, at the same time, be perfectly equalized and assimilated in their possessions, their opinions, and their passions.

A Republic, by which I mean a Government in which the scheme of representation takes place, opens a different prospect, and promises the cure for which we are seeking. Let us examine the points in which it varies from pure Democracy, and we shall comprehend both the nature of the cure, and the efficacy which it must derive from the Union.

The two great points of difference between a Democracy and a Republic are, first, the delegation of the Government, in the latter, to a small number of citizens elected by the rest: secondly, the greater number of citizens, and greater sphere of country, over which the latter may be extended.

The effect of the first difference is, on the one hand, to refine and enlarge the public views, by passing them through the medium of a chosen body of citizens, whose wisdom may best discern the true interest of their country, and whose patriotism and love of justice, will be least likely to sacrifice it to temporary or partial considerations. Under such a regulation, it may well happen that the public voice pronounced by the representatives of the people, will be more consonant to the public good, than if pronounced by the people themselves convened for the purpose. On the other hand, the effect may be inverted. Men of factious tempers, of local prejudices, or of sinister designs, may by intrigue, by corruption, or by other means, first obtain the suffrages, and then betray the interests of the people. The question resulting is, whether small or extensive Republics are most favorable to the election of proper guardians of the public weal: and it is clearly decided in favor of the latter by two obvious considerations.

In the first place it is to be remarked, that however small the Republic may be, the Representatives must be raised to a certain number, in order to guard against the cabals of a few; and that however large it may be, they must be limited to a certain number, in order to guard against the confusion of a multitude. Hence the number of Representatives in the two cases, not being in proportion to that of the Constituents, and being proportionally greatest in the small Republic, it follows, that if the proportion of fit characters, be not less, in the large than in the small Republic, the former will present a greater option, and consequently a greater probability of a fit choice.

In the next place, as each Representative will be chosen by a greater number of citizens in the large than in the small Republic, it will be more difficult for unworthy candidates to practice with success the vicious arts, by which elections are too often carried; and the suffrages of the people being more free, will be more likely to center on men who possess the most attractive merit, and the most diffusive and established characters.

It must be confessed, that in this, as in most other cases, there is a mean, on both sides of which inconveniences will be found to lie. By enlarging too much the number of electors, you render the representative too little acquainted with all their local circumstances and lesser interests; as by reducing it too much, you render him unduly attached to these, and too little fit to comprehend and pursue great and national objects. The Federal Constitution forms a happy combination in this respect; the great and aggregate interests being referred to the national, and local and particular to the state legislatures.

The other point of difference is, the greater number of citizens and extent of territory which may be brought within the compass of Republican, than of Democratic Government; and it is this circumstance principally which renders factious combinations less to be dreaded in the former, than in the latter. The smaller the society, the fewer probably will be the distinct parties and interests composing it; the fewer the distinct parties and interests, the more frequently will a majority be found of the same party; and the smaller the number of individuals composing a majority, and the smaller the compass within which they are placed, the more easily will they concert and execute their plans of oppression. Extend the sphere, and you take in a greater variety of parties and interests; you make it less probable that a majority of the whole will have a common motive to invade the rights of other citizens; or if such a common motive exists, it will be more difficult for all who feel it to discover their own strength, and to act in unison with each other. Besides other impediments, it may be remarked, that where there is a consciousness of unjust or dishonorable purposes, communication is always checked by distrust, in proportion to the number whose concurrence is necessary.

Hence it clearly appears, that the same advantage, which a Republic has over a Democracy, in controlling the effects of faction, is enjoyed by a large over a small Republic—is enjoyed by the Union over the States composing it. Does this advantage consist in the substitution of Representatives, whose enlightened views and virtuous sentiments render them superior to local prejudices, and to schemes of injustice? It will not be denied, that the Representation of the Union will be most likely to possess these requisite endowments. Does it consist in the greater security afforded by a greater variety of parties, against the event of any one party being able to outnumber and oppress the rest? In an equal degree does the increased variety of parties, comprised within the Union, increase this security. Does it, in fine, consist in the greater obstacles opposed to the concert and accomplishment of the secret wishes of an unjust and interested majority? Here, again, the extent of the Union gives it the most palpable advantage.

The influence of factious leaders may kindle a flame within their particular States, but will be unable to spread a general conflagration through the other States: a religious sect, may degenerate into a political faction in a part of the Confederacy; but the variety of sects dispersed over the entire face of it, must secure the national Councils against any danger from that source: a rage for paper money, for an abolition of debts, for an equal division of property, or for any other improper or wicked project, will be less apt to pervade the whole body of the Union, than a particular member of it; in the same proportion as such a malady is more likely to taint a particular county or district, than an entire State.

In the extent and proper structure of the Union, therefore, we behold a Republican remedy for the diseases most incident to Republican Government. And according to the degree of pleasure and pride, we feel in being Republicans, ought to be our zeal in cherishing the spirit, and supporting the character of Federalists.

[November 22, 1787]

NO. 14   [MADISON]

An Objection Drawn From
the Extent of Country Answered

We have seen the necessity of the union as our bulwark against foreign danger, as the conservator of peace among ourselves, as the guardian of our commerce and other common interests, as the only substitute for those military establishments which have subverted the liberties of the old world; and as the proper antidote for the diseases of faction, which have proved fatal to other popular governments, and of which alarming symptoms have been betrayed by our own. All that remains, within this branch of our inquiries, is to take notice of an objection, that may be drawn from the great extent of country which the union embraces. A few observations on this subject will be the more proper, as it is perceived that the adversaries of the new constitution are availing themselves of a prevailing prejudice, with regard to the practicable sphere of republican administration, in order to supply by imaginary difficulties, the want of those solid objections, which they endeavor in vain to find.

The error which limits Republican Government to a narrow district, has been unfolded and refuted in preceding papers.* I remark here only, that it seems to owe its rise and prevalence chiefly to the confounding of a republic with a democracy: And applying to the former reasonings drawn from the nature of the latter. The true distinction between these forms was also adverted to on a former occasion. It is, that in a democracy, the people meet and exercise the government in person; in a republic they assemble and administer it by their representatives and agents. A democracy consequently must be confined to a small spot. A republic may be extended over a large region.

To this accidental source of the error may be added, the artifice of some celebrated authors, whose writings have had a great share in forming the modern standard of political opinions. Being subjects either of an absolute, or limited monarchy, they have endeavored to heighten the advantages or palliate the evils of those forms; by placing in comparison with them, the vices and defects of the republican, and by citing as specimens of the latter, the turbulent democracies of ancient Greece, and modern Italy. Under the confusion of names, it has been an easy task to transfer to a republic, observations applicable to a democracy only, and among others, the observation that it can never be established but among a small number of people, living within a small compass of territory.

Such a fallacy may have been the less perceived, as most of the popular governments of antiquity were of the democratic species; and even in modern Europe, to which we owe the great principle of representation, no example is seen of a government wholly popular, and founded at the same time wholly on that principle. If Europe has the merit of discovering this great mechanical power in government, by the simple agency of which, the will of the largest political body may be concentered, and its force directed to any object, which the public good requires; America can claim the merit of making the discovery the basis of unmixed and extensive republics. It is only to be lamented, that any of her citizens should wish to deprive her of the additional merit of displaying its full efficacy in the establishment of the comprehensive system now under her consideration.

As the natural limit of a democracy is that distance from the central point, which will just permit the most remote citizens to assemble as often as their public functions demand; and will include no greater number than can join in those functions; so the natural limit of a republic is that distance from the center, which will barely allow the representatives of the people to meet as often as may be necessary for the administration of public affairs. Can it be said, that the limits of the United States exceed this distance? It will not be said by those who recollect that the Atlantic coast is the longest side of the union; that during the term of thirteen years, the representatives of the States have been almost continually assembled; and that the members from the most distant states are not chargeable with greater intermissions of attendance, than those from the States in the neighborhood of Congress.

*[See Nos. 9 and 10 above.]

That we may form a juster estimate with regard to this interesting subject, let us resort to the actual dimensions of the union. The limits as fixed by the treaty of peace are on the east the Atlantic, on the south the latitude of thirty-one degrees, on the west the Mississippi, and on the north an irregular line running in some instances beyond the forty-fifth degree, in others falling as low as the forty-second. The southern shore of lake Erie lies below that latitude. Computing the distance between the thirty-first and forty-fifth degrees, it amounts to nine hundred and seventy-three common miles; computing it from thirty-one to forty-two degrees to seven hundred, sixty-four miles and an half. Taking the mean for the distance, the amount will be eight hundred, sixty-eight miles and three-fourths. The mean distance from the Atlantic to the Mississippi does not probably exceed seven hundred and fifty miles. On a comparison of this extent, with that of several countries in Europe, the practicability of rendering our system commensurate to it, appears to be demonstrable. It is not a great deal larger than Germany, where a Diet, representing the whole empire is continually assembled; or than Poland before the late dismemberment, where another national Diet was the depositary of the supreme power. Passing by France and Spain, we find that in Great Britain, inferior as it may be in size, the representatives of the northern extremity of the island, have as far to travel to the national Council, as will be required of those of the most remote parts of the union.

Favorable as this view of the subject may be, some observations remain which will place it in a light still more satisfactory.

In the first place it is to be remembered, that the general government is not to be charged with the whole power of making and administering laws. Its jurisdiction is limited to certain enumerated objects, which concern all the members of the republic, but which are not to be attained by the separate provisions of any. The subordinate governments which can extend their care to all those other objects, which can be separately provided for, will retain their due authority and activity. Were it proposed by the plan of the convention to abolish the governments of the particular States, its adversaries would have some ground for

their objection, though it would not be difficult to show that if they were abolished, the general government would be compelled by the principle of self preservation, to reinstate them in their proper jurisdiction.

A second observation to be made is, that the immediate object of the Federal Constitution is to secure the union of the Thirteen Primitive States, which we know to be practicable; and to add to them such other States, as may arise in their own bosoms, or in their neighborhoods, which we cannot doubt to be equally practicable. The arrangements that may be necessary for those angles and fractions of our territory, which lie on our northwestern frontier, must be left to those whom further discoveries and experience will render more equal to the task.

Let it be remarked in the third place, that the intercourse throughout the union will be daily facilitated by new improvements. Roads will everywhere be shortened, and kept in better order; accommodations for travelers will be multiplied and meliorated; an interior navigation on our eastern side will be opened throughout, or nearly throughout the whole extent of the Thirteen States. The communication between the western and Atlantic districts, and between different parts of each, will be rendered more and more easy by those numerous canals with which the beneficence of nature has intersected our country, and which art finds it so little difficult to connect and complete.

A fourth and still more important consideration is, that as almost every State will on one side or other, be a frontier, and will thus find in a regard to its safety, an inducement to make some sacrifices for the sake of the general protection; so the States which lie at the greatest distance from the heart of the union, and which of course may partake least of the ordinary circulation of its benefits, will be at the same time immediately contiguous to foreign nations, and will consequently stand on particular occasions, in greatest need of its strength and resources. It may be inconvenient for Georgia or the States forming our western or northeastern borders, to send their representatives to the seat of government, but they would find it more so to struggle alone against an invading enemy, or even to support alone the whole expense of those precautions, which may be dictated by the neighborhood of continual danger. If they should derive less benefit therefore from the union in some respects, than the less distant States, they will derive greater benefit from it in other respects, and thus the proper equilibrium will be maintained throughout.

I submit to you my fellow citizens, these considerations, in full confidence that the good sense which has so often marked your decisions, will allow them their due weight and effect; and that you will never suffer difficulties, however formidable in appearance or however fashionable the error on which they may be founded, to drive you into the gloomy and perilous scene into which the advocates for disunion would conduct you. Hearken not to the unnatural voice which tells you that the people of America, knit together as they are by so many cords of affection, can no longer live together as members of the same family; can no longer continue the mutual guardians of their mutual happiness; can no longer be fellow citizens of one great respectable and flourishing empire. Hearken not to the voice which petulantly tells you that the form of government recommended for your adoption is a novelty in the political world; that it has never yet had a place in the theories of the wildest projectors; that it rashly attempts what it is impossible to accomplish. No my countrymen, shut your ears against this unhallowed language. Shut your hearts against the poison which it conveys; the kindred blood which flows in the veins of American citizens, the mingled blood which they have shed in defense of their sacred rights, consecrate their union, and excite horror at the idea of their becoming aliens, rivals, enemies. And if novelties are to be shunned, believe me the most alarming of all novelties, the most wild of all projects, the most rash of all attempts, is that of rending us in pieces, in order to preserve our liberties and promote our happiness. But why is the experiment of an extended republic to be rejected merely because it may comprise what is new? Is it not the glory of the people of America, that whilst they have paid a decent regard to the opinions of former times and other nations, they have not suffered a blind veneration for antiquity, for custom, or for names, to overrule the suggestions of their own good sense, the knowledge of their own situation, and the lessons of their own experience? To this manly spirit, posterity will be indebted for the possession, and the world for the example of the numerous innovations displayed on the American theater, in favor of private rights and public happiness. Had no important step been taken by the leaders of the revolution for which a precedent could not be discovered, no government established of which an exact model did not present itself, the people of the United States might, at this moment, have been numbered among the melancholy victims of misguided councils, must at best have been laboring under the weight of some of those forms which have crushed the liberties of the rest of mankind. Happily for America, happily we trust for the whole human race, they pursued a new and more noble course. They accomplished a revolution which has no parallel in the annals of human society: They reared the fabrics of governments which have no model on the face of the globe. They formed the design of a great confederacy, which it is incumbent on their successors to improve and perpetuate. If their works betray imperfections, we wonder at the fewness of them. If they erred most in the structure of the union, this was the work most difficult to be executed; this is the work which had been new modeled by the act of your Convention, and it is that act on which you are now to deliberate and to decide.

[November 30, 1787]

NO. 48   [MADISON]

The Same Subject* Continued With a View to the Means of Giving Efficacy in Practice to That Maxim*

It was shown in the last paper, that the political apothegm there examined, does not require that the legislative, executive, and judiciary departments should

---

*[i.e., "The Meaning of the Maxim, which Requires a Separation of the Departments of Power" No. 47]

*[i.e., "that the legislative, executive, and judiciary departments ought to be separate and distinct." No. 47.]

be wholly unconnected with each other. I shall undertake in the next place, to show that unless these departments be so far connected and blended, as to give to each a constitutional control over the others, the degree of separation which the maxim requires as essential to a free government, can never in practice, be duly maintained.

It is agreed on all sides, that the powers properly belonging to one of the departments, ought not to be directly and completely administered by either of the other departments. It is equally evident, that neither of them ought to possess directly or indirectly, an overruling influence over the others in the administration of their respective powers. It will not be denied, that power is of an encroaching nature, and that it ought to be effectually restrained from passing the limits assigned to it. After discriminating therefore in theory, the several classes of power, as they may in their nature be legislative, executive, or judiciary, the next and most difficult task, is to provide some practical security for each against the invasion of the others. What this security ought to be, is the great problem to be solved. Will it be sufficient to mark with precision the boundaries of these departments in the Constitution of the government, and to trust to these parchment barriers against the encroaching spirit of power? This is the security which appears to have been principally relied on by the compilers of most of the American Constitutions. But experience assures us, that the efficacy of the provision has been greatly overrated; and that some more adequate defense is indispensably necessary for the more feeble, against the more powerful members of the government. The legislative department is everywhere extending the sphere of its activity, and drawing all power into its impetuous vortex.

The founders of our republics have so much merit for the wisdom which they have displayed, that no task can be less pleasing than that of pointing out the errors into which they have fallen. A respect for truth however obliges us to remark, that they seem never for a moment to have turned their eyes from the danger to liberty from the overgrown and all-grasping prerogative of an hereditary magistrate, supported and fortified by an hereditary branch of the legislative authority. They seem never to have recollected the danger from legislative usurpations; which by assembling all power in the same hands, must lead to the same tyranny as is threatened by executive usurpations.

In a government, where numerous and extensive prerogatives are placed in the hands of a hereditary monarch, the executive department is very justly regarded as the source of danger, and watched with all the jealousy which a zeal for liberty ought to inspire. In a democracy, where a multitude of people exercise in person the legislative functions, and are continually exposed by their incapacity for regular deliberation and concerted measures, to the ambitious intrigues of their executive magistrates, tyranny may well be apprehended on some favorable emergency, to start up in the same quarter. But in a representative republic, where the executive magistracy is carefully limited both in the extent and the duration of its power; and where the legislative power is exercised by an assembly, which is inspired by a supposed influence over the people with an intrepid confidence in its own strength; which is sufficiently numerous to feel all the passions which actuate a multitude; yet not so numerous as to be incapable of pursuing the objects of its passions, by means which reason prescribes; it is against the enterprising ambition of this department, that the people ought to indulge all their jealousy and exhaust all their precautions.

The legislative department derives a superiority in our governments from other circumstances. Its constitutional powers being at once more extensive and less susceptible of precise limits, it can with the greater facility, mask under complicated and indirect measures, the encroachments which it makes on the coordinate departments. It is not infrequently a question of real nicety in legislative bodies, whether the operation of a particular measure, will, or will not extend beyond the legislative sphere. On the other side, the executive power being restrained within a narrower compass, and being more simple in its nature; and the judiciary being described by landmarks, still less uncertain, projects of usurpation by either of these departments, would immediately betray and defeat themselves. Nor is this all: As the legislative department alone has access to the pockets of the people, and has in some Constitutions full discretion, and in all, a prevailing influence over the pecuniary rewards of those who fill the other departments, a dependence is thus created in the latter, which gives still greater facility to encroachments of the former.

I have appealed to our own experience for the truth of what I advance on this subject. Were it necessary to verify this experience by particular proofs, they might be multiplied without end. I might find a witness in every citizen who has shared in, or been attentive to, the course of public administrations. I might collect vouchers in abundance from the records and archives of every State in the Union. But as a more concise and at the same time, equally satisfactory evidence, I will refer to the example of two States, attested by two unexceptionable authorities.

The first example is that of Virginia, a State which, as we have seen, has expressly declared in its Constitution, that the three great departments ought not to be intermixed. The authority in support of it is Mr. Jefferson, who, besides his other advantages for remarking the operation of the government, was himself the chief magistrate of it. In order to convey fully the ideas with which his experience had impressed him on this subject, it will be necessary to quote a passage of some length from his very interesting "Notes on the State of Virginia" (p. 195), "All the powers of government, legislative, executive, and judiciary, result to the legislative body. The concentrating [of] these in the same hands is precisely the definition of despotic government. It will be no alleviation that these powers will be exercised by a plurality of hands, and not by a single one. One hundred seventy-three despots would surely be as oppressive as one. Let those who doubt it turn their eyes on the republic of Venice. As little will it avail us that they are chosen by ourselves. An *elective despotism*, was not the government we fought for; but one which should not only be founded on free principles, but in which the powers of government should be so divided and balanced among several bodies of magistracy, as that no one could transcend their legal limits, without being effectually checked and restrained by the others. For this reason that Convention which passed the ordinance of government, laid its foundation on this basis, that the legislative, executive, and judiciary departments should be separate and distinct, so that no person should exercise the powers of more than one of them at the same time. *But no barrier was provided between these several powers*. The ju-

diciary and executive members were left dependent on the legislative for their subsistence in office, and some of them for their continuance in it. If therefore the Legislature assumes executive and judiciary powers, no opposition is likely to be made; nor if made can it be effectual; because in that case, they may put their proceeding into the form of an act of Assembly, which will render them obligatory on the other branches. They have accordingly *in many* instances *decided rights* which should have been left to *judiciary controversy; and the direction of the executive during the whole time of their session, is becoming habitual and familiar.*"

The other State which I shall take for an example, is Pennsylvania; and the other authority the council of censors which assembled in the years 1783 and 1784. A part of the duty of this body, as marked out by the Constitution was, "to inquire whether the Constitution had been preserved inviolate in every part; and whether the legislative and executive branches of government had performed their duty as guardians of the people, or assumed to themselves, or exercised other or greater powers than they are entitled to by the Constitution." In the execution of this trust, the council were necessarily led to a comparison, of both the legislative and executive proceedings, with the constitutional powers of these departments; and from the facts enumerated, and to the truth of most of which, both sides in the council subscribed, it appears that the Constitution had been flagrantly violated by the Legislature in a variety of important instances.

A great number of laws had been passed violating without any apparent necessity, the rule requiring that all bills of public nature, shall be previously printed for the consideration of the people; although this is one of the precautions chiefly relied on by the Constitution, against improper acts of the Legislature.

The constitutional trial by jury had been violated; and powers assumed, which had not been delegated by the Constitution.

Executive powers had been usurped.

The salaries of the Judges, which the Constitution expressly requires to be fixed, had been occasionally varied; and cases belonging to the judiciary department, frequently drawn within legislative cognizance and determination.

Those who wish to see the several particulars falling under each of these heads, may consult the Journals of the council which are in print. Some of them, it will be found may be imputable to peculiar circumstances connected with the war: But the greater part of them may be considered as the spontaneous shoots of an ill-constituted government.

It appears also, that the executive department had not been innocent of frequent breaches of the Constitution. There are three observations however, which ought to be made on this head. *First.* A great proportion of the instances, were either immediately produced by the necessities of the war, or recommended by Congress or the Commander in Chief. *Secondly.* In most of the other instances, they conformed either to the declared or the known sentiments of the legislative department. *Thirdly.* The executive department of Pennsylvania is distinguished from that of the other States, by the number of members composing it. In this respect it has as much affinity to a legislative assembly, as to an executive council. And being at once exempt from the restraint of an individual responsibility for the acts of the body, and deriving confidence from mutual example and joint influence; unauthorized measures would of course be more freely hazarded, than where the executive department is administered by a single hand or by a few hands.

The conclusion which I am warranted in drawing from these observations is, that a mere demarcation on parchment of the constitutional limits of the several departments, is not a sufficient guard against those encroachments which lead to a tyrannical concentration of all the powers of government in the same hands.

[February 1, 1788]

NO. 51 [MADISON]

The Same Subject Continued With the Same View and Concluded

To what expedient then shall we finally resort for maintaining in practice the necessary partition of power among the several departments, as laid down in the constitution? The only answer that can be given is, that as all these exterior provisions are found to be inadequate, the defect must be supplied, by so contriving the interior structure of the government, as that its several constituent parts may, by their mutual relations, be the means of keeping each other in their proper places. Without presuming to undertake a full development of this important idea, I will hazard a few general observations, which may perhaps place it in a clearer light, and enable us to form a more correct judgment of the principles and structure of the government planned by the convention.

In order to lay a due foundation for that separate and distinct exercise of the different powers of government, which to a certain extent, is admitted on all hands to be essential to the preservation of liberty, it is evident that each department should have a will of its own; and consequently should be so constituted, that the members of each should have as little agency as possible in the appointment of the members of the others. Were this principle rigorously adhered to, it would require that all the appointments for the supreme executive, legislative, and judiciary magistracies, should be drawn from the same fountain of authority, the people, through channels, having no communication whatever with one another. Perhaps such a plan of constructing the several departments would be less difficult in practice than it may in contemplation appear. Some difficulties however, and some additional expense, would attend the execution of it. Some deviations therefore from the principle must be admitted. In the constitution of the judiciary department in particular, it might be inexpedient to insist rigorously on the principle; first, because peculiar qualifications being essential in the members, the primary consideration ought to be to select that mode of choice, which best secures these qualifications; secondly, because the permanent tenure by which the appointments are held in that department, must soon destroy all sense of dependence on the authority conferring them.

It is equally evident that the members of each department should be as little dependent as possible on those of the others, for the emoluments annexed to their offices. Were the executive magistrate, or the judges, not independent of the legislature in this particular, their independence in every other would be merely nominal.

But the great security against a gradual concentration of the several powers in the same department, consists in giving to those who administer each department, the necessary constitutional means, and personal motives, to resist encroachments of the others. The provision for defense must in this, as in all other cases, be made commensurate to the danger of attack. Ambition must be made to counteract ambition. The interest of the man must be connected with the constitutional rights of the place. It may be a reflection on human nature, that such devices should be necessary to control the abuses of government. But what is government itself but the greatest of all reflections on human nature? If men were angels, no government would be necessary. If angels were to govern men, neither external nor internal controls on government would be necessary. In framing a government which is to be administered by men over men, the great difficulty lies in this: You must first enable the government to control the governed; and in the next place, oblige it to control itself. A dependence on the people is no doubt the primary control on the government; but experience has taught mankind the necessity of auxiliary precautions.

This policy of supplying by opposite and rival interests, the defect of better motives, might be traced through the whole system of human affairs, private as well as public. We see it particularly displayed in all the subordinate distributions of power; where the constant aim is to divide and arrange the several offices in such a manner as that each may be a check on the other; that the private interest of every individual, may be a sentinel over the public rights. These inventions of prudence cannot be less requisite in the distribution of the supreme powers of the state.

But it is not possible to give to each department an equal power of self-defense. In republican government the legislative authority, necessarily, predominates. The remedy for this inconveniency is, to divide the legislature into different branches; and to render them by different modes of election, and different principles of action, as little connected with each other, as the nature of their common functions, and

their common dependence on the society, will admit. It may even be necessary to guard against dangerous encroachments by still further precautions. As the weight of the legislative authority requires that it should be thus divided, the weakness of the executive may require, on the other hand, that it should be fortified. An absolute negative, on the legislature, appears at first view to be the natural defense with which the executive magistrate should be armed. But perhaps it would be neither altogether safe, nor alone sufficient. On ordinary occasions, it might not be exerted with the requisite firmness; and on extraordinary occasions, it might be perfidiously abused. May not this defect of an absolute negative be supplied, by some qualified connection between this weaker department, and the weaker branch of the stronger department, by which the latter may be led to support the constitutional rights of the former, without being too much detached from the rights of its own department?

If the principles on which these observations are founded be just, as I persuade myself they are, and they be applied as a criterion, to the several state constitutions, and to the federal constitution, it will be found, that if the latter does not perfectly correspond with them, the former are infinitely less able to bear such a test.

There are moreover two considerations particularly applicable to the federal system of America, which place that system in a very interesting point of view.

First. In a single republic, all the power surrendered by the people, is submitted to the administration of a single government; and usurpations are guarded against by a division of the government into distinct and separate departments. In the compound republic of America, the power surrendered by the people, is first divided between two distinct governments, and then the portion allotted to each, subdivided among distinct and separate departments. Hence a double security arises to the rights of the people. The different governments will control each other; at the same time that each will be controlled by itself.

Second. It is of great importance in a republic, not only to guard the society against the oppression of its rulers; but to guard one part of the society against the injustice of the other part. Different interests necessarily exist in different classes of citizens. If a majority be united by a common interest, the rights of the minority will be insecure. There are but two methods of providing against this evil: The one by creating a will in the community independent of the majority, that is, of the society itself; the other by comprehending in the society so many separate descriptions of citizens, as will render an unjust combination of a majority of the whole, very improbable, if not impracticable. The first method prevails in all governments possessing an hereditary or self-appointed authority. This at best is but a precarious security; because a power independent of the society may as well espouse the unjust views of the major, as the rightful interests, of the minor party, and may possibly be turned against both parties. The second method will be exemplified in the federal republic of the United States. While all authority in it will be derived from and dependent on the society, the society itself will be broken into so many parts, interests, and classes of citizens, that the rights of individuals or of the minority, will be in little danger from interested combinations of the majority. In a free government, the security for civil rights must be the same as for religious rights. It consists in the one case in the multiplicity of interests, and in the other, in the multiplicity of sects. The degree of security in both cases will depend on the number of interests and sects; and this may be presumed to depend on the extent of country and number of people comprehended under the same government. This view of the subject must particularly recommend a proper federal system to all the sincere and considerate friends of republican government: Since it shows that in exact proportion as the territory of the union may be formed into more circumscribed confederacies or states, oppressive combinations of a majority will be facilitated, the best security under the republican form, for the rights of every class of citizens, will be diminished; and consequently, the stability and independence of some member of the government, the only other security, must be proportionally increased. Justice is the end of government. It is the end of civil society. It ever has been, and ever will be pursued, until it be obtained, or until liberty be lost in the pursuit. In a society under the forms of which the stronger faction can readily unite and oppress the weaker, anarchy may as truly be said to reign, as in a state of nature where the weaker individual is not secured against the violence of the stronger: And as in the latter state even the stronger individuals are prompted by the uncertainty of their condition, to submit to a government which may protect the weak as well as themselves: So in the former state, will the more powerful factions or parties be gradually induced by a like motive, to wish for a government which will protect all parties, the weaker as well as the more powerful. It can be little doubted, that if the state of Rhode Island was separated from the confederacy, and left to itself, the insecurity of rights under the popular form of government within such narrow limits, would be displayed by such reiterated oppressions of factious majorities, that some power altogether independent of the people would soon be called for by the voice of the very factions whose misrule had proved the necessity of it. In the extended republic of the United States, and among the great variety of interests, parties, and sects which it embraces, a coalition of a majority of the whole society could seldom take place on any other principles than those of justice and the general good; and there being thus less danger to a minor from the will of the major party, there must be less pretext also, to provide for the security of the former, by introducing into the government a will not dependent on the latter; or in other words, a will independent of the society itself. It is no less certain than it is important, notwithstanding the contrary opinions which have been entertained, that the larger the society, provided it lie within a practicable sphere, the more duly capable it will be of self government. And happily for the *republican cause*, the practicable sphere may be carried to a very great extent, by a judicious modification and mixture of the *federal principle*.

[February 6, 1788]

Benjamin Constant

On Ancient and Modern Liberty[1]

Gentlemen, I intend to present to you some distinctions, which are still quite novel, between two types of liberty. The differences between these two types of liberty have remained unrecognized until now, or at least they have been insufficiently recognized. One type is that liberty whose exercise was so dear to the ancient peoples; the other is that liberty which modern nations enjoy and value so highly.[2] If I am not mistaken, this inquiry will be interesting from two points of view.

First, the confusion between these two types of liberty has been the cause of many ills among us [the French] during some all-too-famous episodes of our revolution. France watched herself being tired out with hopeless efforts; her leaders, irritated by their inability to achieve their goals, sought to force her to enjoy a good for which she had no desire, and they resisted her when she sought to attain the good she did desire. Second, invited by our happy revolution (I call it happy, despite its excesses, because what interests me now is only its outcome) to enjoy the benefits of a representative government, it is both interesting and useful to inquire why this type of government, the only one at the present time which offers protection for a certain degree of liberty and for a certain degree of security, was almost totally unknown to the free peoples in antiquity. I know that there are people who have claimed to be able to identify some features of representative government among some of the ancient societies—in the republic of Sparta, for example, and among our ancestors the Gauls—but they are mistaken.

The government of Sparta was an austere aristocracy, and it was in no respect a representative government. The powers of the kings were limited, but they were limited by the ephors, and not by people invested with a mission comparable to that which, in our own time, election confers on the defenders of our liberties. The ephors, it is true, after having been established by the kings, were chosen by the people; but there were only five of them and their authority was as much religious as political. They shared in the actual performance of the tasks of government, that is to say in the executive power; and consequently their prerogative, just like that of almost all of the magistrates appointed by the people in the ancient republics, far from being simply a barrier against tyranny, itself became on occasion an intolerable tyranny.

The political system of the Gauls, which quite closely resembled the system to which one political party would like to return us, was simultaneously theocratic and militaristic. The priests enjoyed limitless power. The military class, or the nobility, had privileges that were certainly excessive and oppressive. The people were without rights and without guarantees. In Rome, the tribunes had, up to a certain point, a representative function. They acted on behalf of the plebeians for whom the nature of oligarchy is the same in every century; and whom it had forced to submit to so harsh an enslavement when the oligarchs had overthrown the kings. The people, however, exercised a large part of their political rights directly. They assembled to vote on laws and to judge patricians who had been accused of crimes. Thus there were only feeble traces of a representative system in Rome.

Representative government is thus a discovery of the modern world, and I will show you, gentlemen, that

---

[1] I am grateful to Christine Henderson for her comments on this translation.
[2] Constant repeatedly uses the word *jouissance*, translated here as "enjoy and value."

the circumstances of the human species in antiquity did not permit an institution of this sort to introduce itself or to sustain itself. The ancient peoples could not see the necessity of it, nor even recognize its advantages. Their form of social organization led them to desire a type of liberty quite different from that which representation ensures for us.

My purpose in tonight's lecture is to convince you of this truth. First ask yourselves, gentlemen, what an Englishman, a Frenchman, an inhabitant of the United States of America understands by the word "liberty." They would all agree that it consists in the right to be subjected only to the law; in the right not to be arrested, nor detained, nor put to death, nor maltreated in any manner on the arbitrary decision of any individual or group of individuals; in the right for each individual freely to speak his mind, to choose his occupation and to practice it, to dispose of his property, and even to destroy it; in the right to come and go without obtaining permission and without having to explain their motives and their activities. It is, for each individual, the right to assemble with other individuals, whether to discuss their welfare, or to participate in the religious worship they and their associates prefer, or simply to fill their days or their hours with whatever best accords with their inclinations and their fantasies. Finally, it is the right for each individual to influence the exercise of government, whether this is by the election of all or of some officers of the government, or by making appeals, petitions, or requests that the authorities are more or less obliged to take seriously. Now compare this liberty with that of the ancients.

The liberty of the ancients consisted in exercising collectively, but also directly, several of the rights, which taken together, make up a nation's sovereignty: deliberating in a public square on war and peace, and concluding treaties of alliance with other cities; voting on laws; determining guilt and innocence; and examining the accounts, the actions, and the conduct of the officials, making them appear before the whole people assembled, charging them with crimes, and finding them guilty or not guilty. But as this was the essence of what the ancients called liberty, they simultaneously accepted the complete subjection of the individual to the authority of the collective as being com-

patible with this collective liberty. You find among the ancients none or at least almost none of the privileges that we have just seen joining together to make up liberty as it is understood by the moderns. Among the ancients, all of the actions of private individuals were subjected to the strictest oversight. There was no scope for personal independence, not as far as the expression of opinions was concerned, nor as far as economic activity was concerned, nor, above all, as far as religious worship was concerned. The ability to choose one's form of worship, an ability that we regard as one of our most precious rights, would have seemed criminal and sacrilegious to the ancients. The authority of the collective was brought to bear in matters that seem to us to be purely technical, interfering with the choices of individuals. In Sparta, Terpander could not add a string to his lyre without the ephors taking exception.[3] The collective interfered yet again in the most intimate relationships: a young Spartan man could not freely meet with his new wife. In Rome the censors keep a close eye on domestic life. The laws regulated customs and habits, and since everything is a matter of custom and habit, there is nothing that the laws did not regulate.

Thus among the ancients, the individual, who was nearly always one of the rulers when it came to questions of state, was a slave in his private life. As a citizen, he chose war or peace; as a private individual, he was hedged in, surveilled, restricted in all his movements. As part of the collective, he interrogated, expropriated, punished, sacked, exiled, and condemned to death the officers of his government and those who commanded over him; as someone who was subject to the collective, he in his turn could be removed from his office, deprived of his rank, banished, or executed by the arbitrary decision of the whole of which he formed a part. Among the moderns the opposite is the case. The individual, who is his own master in his private life, is not, even in the freest of states, one of the rulers except in appearance. His sovereignty is restricted, and is almost all the time suspended. If, at

---

[3] Terpander, a poet and musician of the seventh century b.c., increased the number of strings in the lyre from four to seven.

fixed intervals, after lengthy intermissions, he exercises his sovereignty, even in its exercise he is hemmed in by limitations and restrictions, and all he is allowed to do is abdicate his authority.

Here, Gentlemen, I must pause for a moment to forestall an objection that you might want to make. There is to be found in antiquity one republic in which the enslavement of the life of the individual to the collective is not as complete as I have just described it. This republic is the most celebrated of all: you will already have guessed that I am referring to Athens. I will come back to Athens later, and I not only will concede that Athens is an exception, but will also explain how it comes to be one. We will see why, among all of the ancient states, Athens is the one that most closely resembles a modern state. Everywhere else social control had no limits. The ancients, as Condorcet says, had no notion of individual rights. Human beings were, one might say, thought of as nothing but machines whose springs were adjusted and whose cogwheels were powered by the law. This subjection characterized even the golden centuries of the Roman Republic: the individual was in some fashion lost in the nation, the citizen in the city. But now we must go back to the origin of this fundamental difference between the ancients and ourselves.

All the ancient republics were confined within narrow geographical limits. The most populous, the most powerful, the most extensive among them was not equal in size to the smallest of modern states. As an automatic consequence of their small size, the spirit of these republics was warlike, for each community was continually jostling against its neighbors or being jostled by them. Thus, under the impulse of necessity, this one came into conflict with that one, and when they were not actively fighting each other they were threatening each other. Those who did not want to be conquerors could not lay down their arms for fear of being conquered. All purchased their security, their independence, their very existence with their blood. Warfare was the constant preoccupation, and the almost routine activity, of the free states of the ancient world. Moreover, by another consequence that followed equally inevitably from this mode of life, all of these states were slave-owning. Small-scale produc-

tion, and, in some societies, even large-scale manufacturing, was entrusted to people who wore shackles.

Look at the modern world and what you see is completely different. The smallest contemporary states are much more extensive than Sparta, or than Rome during its first five centuries. Indeed, the very division of Europe into several states is, thanks to the progress of civilization, more apparent than real. While each society in the past was like a family living in isolation and born into enmity toward all the other families, now a single mass of human beings exists, which, although bearing different names and belonging to communities apparently organized on differing principles, is in fact homogeneous in its nature. This mass is strong enough to have nothing to fear from barbarian hordes. It is sufficiently advanced to regard war as a burden. Its uniform tendency is toward peace.

This difference of size results in another difference. War came first, then commerce; for war and commerce are simply two means of attaining the same end—that of possessing what one desires. Commerce is nothing but a form of homage paid to the strength of the possessor by the person who aspires to possession. It is an attempt to obtain by mutual agreement what you no longer hope to seize by violence. Someone who is always the stronger would never invent commerce. But experience demonstrates to them that war—that is to say, the pitting of their strength against someone else's—exposes them to a variety of frustrations and failures. And it is this that brings them to resort to commerce—that is to say, to a means (which is softer and more reliable) for getting someone else to acknowledge the coincidence of their interests. War overwhelms; commerce calculates. And for that very reason there must come a time when commerce substitutes for war. That time is now.

I do not intend to say that there were not, among the ancients, any commercial peoples. But these peoples were in one way or another an exception to the general rule. The limits of a lecture do not permit me to point out all of the obstacles which, in those days, stood in the way of the development of commerce; in any case you are just as familiar with them as I am. I will confine myself to mentioning just one. Ignorance of the compass forced sailors in antiquity to keep within sight of the coast whenever possible. To go beyond the Pillars of Hercules—that is to say, to pass through the straits of Gibraltar—was considered a foolhardy undertaking. It was only after many generations that the Phoenicians and the Carthaginians, the most skilled of the ancient navigators, summoned up enough courage for the undertaking, and it was a long time before anyone else was prepared to follow their example. In Athens—and I will say more about Athens shortly—money lent for investing in ships and cargo attracted an interest rate of sixty percent, while money for other investments was lent at twelve percent. These statistics give an indication of the extent to which long-distance voyages were thought to be dangerous.

Moreover, if I could permit myself a digression, which unfortunately would be too lengthy, I could show you, gentlemen, by a detailed account of the customs, the habits, and the manner with which they did business with other peoples, that the commercial peoples of the ancient world were even in their commercial activities imbued with the spirit of the age, with the atmosphere of war and of mutual hostility that surrounded them. In those days commerce was a happy accident; nowadays it is the normal state of affairs, the sole objective, the universal tendency, the true life of nations. Nations want peace and quiet, and with peace and quiet the comforts of life, and, as the means to the comforts of life, they want to engage in manufacturing. With every day that passes, war becomes more and more unsatisfactory as a means of getting what we want. The risks of war no longer offer, neither to individuals nor to nations, benefits that are comparable to the gains of peaceful labor and routine trade. Among the ancients, a victorious war increased the wealth of the nation and of individuals: wealth in slaves, in tribute money, in land available for distribution. Among the moderns, a victorious war invariably costs more than it brings in. Finally, thanks to commerce, to religion, to the intellectual and moral progress of the human species, there are no longer slaves in the European countries. Free men have to fill all of the occupations and see to all of the needs of society.

It is easy, gentlemen, to foresee the necessary consequence of these differences:

1. As the extent of a country increases, the political significance that falls to the share of each individual diminishes. The most insignificant citizen of Rome or of Sparta was of political importance. This is not true in the case of an ordinary citizen of Great Britain or the United States. His personal influence is an imperceptible component of the collective will that shapes the policy of the government.

2. The abolition of slavery has deprived the free population of all the leisure from which it benefited when most of the manual labor was performed by slaves. Without the slave population of Athens, twenty thousand Athenians could not have gathered each day on the main square to participate in political decision making.

3. Commerce does not leave, as war does, intervals of inactivity in the life of a man. The free peoples of antiquity were engaged in a perpetual exercise of their political rights, a daily discussion of the affairs of state, in dissensions, in secret meetings, in a constant process of forming and reconfiguring factions. These agitations were necessary, these time-wasting (if I may dare use the term) activities were essential, for without them these peoples would have languished under the burden of a painful inactivity. But for modern nations, the same activities would be a source of nothing but distress and tedium. There, every individual is fully occupied with his own investments and undertakings, with the rewards that he is getting or hopes to get, and he wants to be distracted from them only for a moment and as infrequently as possible. Finally, commerce inspires in men a keen love of individual independence. Commerce sees to their needs, satisfies their desires, without any intervention by the authorities. Their intervention is almost always—and I'm not sure why I say "almost"—destabilizing and destructive. Everytime the collectivity seeks to involve itself in the investments of individuals, it harms the investors. Everytime governments pretend to do our business for us, they do it less well and more expensively than we do.

I assured you, gentlemen, that I would return to the subject of Athens, which might be used as a counterexample to some of my claims, but which I will argue should be used as an example to confirm them all. Athens, as I have already acknowledged, was, of all the

Greek republics, the most commercial; and thus it allowed its citizens infinitely more personal liberty than did Rome or Sparta. If I had time to enter into a detailed history, I would show you that commerce eliminated among the Athenians many of the differences that distinguish ancient societies from modern societies. The outlook of the merchants of Athens was similar to that of the merchants of our own times. We learn from Xenophon that during the Peloponnesian War they moved their capital out of the mainland of Attica and transferred it to the islands of the archipelago. Commerce had created among them the movement of funds. We find in Isocrates evidence that they employed letters of exchange. Note too how closely their social behavior resembles our own. You will see (my source is Xenophon again) that husbands, in their relations with their wives, were satisfied when peace and a respectable friendship characterized their domestic lives, that they took into account the harsh ways of nature toward their all too fragile wives, that they closed their eyes to the irresistible power of the passions, pardoning the first failing and ignoring the second.[4] In relations between Athenians and foreigners, you will find Athenians handing the rights of citizenship to anyone who is prepared to come and live among them, to bring his family with him, and to establish a workshop or a trade. Finally, one cannot help but be struck by their excessive love of personal independence.

In Sparta, a philosopher[5] tells us, the citizens run over when an official calls them; but an Athenian would be horrified if people were to think him at the beck and call of an official. However, as several of the other circumstances which determined the character of ancient peoples also applied in Athens, as there was a slave population, and as the geographical extent of the state was very restricted, we find there vestiges of the form of liberty that was peculiar to the ancients. The people made the laws, examined the conduct of government officials, called on Pericles to hand over his accounts, and condemned to death the generals who had been in command at the battle of Arginusae.

At the same time they practiced ostracism, an arbitrary penalty approved by their laws and admired by legislators of the age: ostracism seems to us, as it ought, a shocking injustice. It proves that the individual was still more subordinate to the social collective in Athens than he is nowadays in any free state in Europe.

It follows from what I have said so far that we cannot enjoy any longer the liberty of the ancients, which was based upon constant and active participation in the collective authority. Our own sort of liberty must be based on the peaceable enjoyment of a personal independence. The role that everyone in antiquity played within the national sovereign identity was not, as it is in our own day, an abstract concept. The will of each individual had a real influence; the exercise of this will was a pleasure that was keen and frequently repeated. As a result, the ancients were prepared to make many sacrifices in order to preserve their political rights and their roles in the government of the state. Each individual took pride in the fact that his vote was of real significance, and his awareness of his personal importance more than compensated [for his loss]. This compensation no longer exists for us. Lost in the multitude, the individual almost never feels that he exercises any influence. His preferences never impose themselves on the collective, and as far as he can see it makes no difference whether he participates or not. The exercise of our political rights thus gives us only a fraction of the satisfaction that it gave the ancients, and at the same time the progress of civilization, the commercial tendencies of the age, and the growth in communication between the different nations have vastly increased the opportunities for pursuing individual happiness.

It follows that we are bound to be much more attached than the ancients were to our personal independence; for the ancients, when they sacrificed this independence in order to exercise their political rights, sacrificed less in order to obtain more, while in making the same sacrifice, we would be giving up more in order to obtain less. The goal of the ancients was the sharing of social power[6] among all of the citizens who

---

[4] Constant is discussing adultery, but confines himself to euphemisms.
[5] Montesquieu, following Xenophon: *Esprit des Lois*, bk. V.

[6] *Pouvoir social*, which I have generally translated in later occurrences as "power of the collective."

belonged to the same homeland. That was what they called liberty. The goal of the moderns is security of enjoyment of private pleasures; and they call liberty the guarantees institutions provide for these pleasures.

I said when I began that, because they failed to recognize these differences, men whose intentions were in other respects good caused infinite evils during our long and stormy Revolution. It would be wrong to criticize them too harshly; if they were wrong, it was with good reason. One cannot read the beautiful pages of the classical authors, one cannot follow the doings of antiquity's great men without feeling a nameless but quite distinct emotion, one that nothing modern can evoke. The old instincts of a human nature that, if I may so put it, predates our own, seem to return to life in us as we relive these memories. It is difficult not to regret those days, when the faculties of man developed in a direction that had been marked out in advance, when the scope for human ambition was so vast, when men were so forceful—with a strength that was their own, not borrowed—and when they had such a sense of their own energy and their own dignity. And when one allows oneself to be carried away by these regrets, it is impossible not to want to imitate that which we have lost. This response was a powerful one, particularly when we were living under governments that abused their power, governments that, without being strong, were persecutory, founded on absurd principles, and contemptible in practice. These governments drew strength from their contempt for due process, and sought only to belittle the human spirit. Some men still dare to sing us their praises today, as if we could ever forget that we were witness to and victims of their obstinacy, their feebleness, and their fall. The aims of our reformers were noble and generous. Who among us has not felt a lifting in his heart on entering the route that they seemed to have opened up? And shame on he who now feels no need to stress that acknowledging some faults committed by our first leaders is not the same as blackening their reputations, nor the same as disavowing the views that the friends of humanity have upheld throughout the ages.

But these men had drawn a number of their theories from the works of two philosophers who simply did not suspect that the passage of two thousand years might

have altered the predispositions of human beings. Perhaps on another occasion I will examine the intellectual system of the most illustrious of these philosophers, Jean-Jacques Rousseau, and then I will show that in transferring to our modern age an extensive communal authority or collective sovereignty, one that was appropriate in earlier centuries, this sublime genius, who was motivated by the purest love of liberty, unintentionally supplied disastrous excuses for more than one type of tyranny. Of course, in drawing attention to what I believe to be a mistake that it is important to expose, I will be restrained in my criticisms and respectful in my attribution of fault. I will certainly avoid making common cause with those who run down this great man. If by chance I seem to agree with them on a single issue, then I will be the first to suspect that I am in the wrong; and, in order to reassure myself for appearing for a single instant to be of the same opinion as them on any question, even one that is isolated and narrowly defined, I will have no choice but to disavow them and to condemn, as effectively as I can, these people who pretend to be my allies.

However, the truth must outweigh other factors. His prodigious talent and his extraordinary fame rightly ensure that Rousseau's writings have had an enormous influence and are treated with the greatest respect. In any case, it is not Rousseau, as we shall see, to whom we should principally attribute the error that I am attacking. Responsibility lies much more with one of those who came after him, someone less eloquent, but no less austere, and a thousand times more extreme in his opinions. I mean the abbot of Mably, who can be regarded as the leading representative of the intellectual system that, adopting the maxims of ancient liberty, wants every citizen to be completely subjugated so that the nation can be sovereign, and wants the individual to be enslaved so that the people can be free. The abbot of Mably, like Rousseau and like many others, followed the ancients in maintaining that, where the collective is supreme, the people are free; and all means seemed good to him to extend the power of the collective over those aspects of men's lives which seemed capable of resisting it, for he deplored the very possibility of independence. One regret he expresses over and over again in his writings is that the law can concern itself only with our actions. He would have liked it to concern itself with our most fleeting thoughts and feelings; he wanted it to pursue men relentlessly, and without leaving them any refuge where they could escape from its power. He only had to come across, in one society or another, no matter where or when, an oppressive decree, to convince himself at once that he had made a major discovery and to set about proposing it as a model to be imitated. He hated individual liberty in the way that one hates a personal enemy. If in the course of his historical inquiries he came across a nation where individuals had no freedom, even if the nation had no political liberty either, still he could not restrain himself from admiring it. He was absolutely thrilled by the Egyptians, because, he said, in ancient Egypt there was a law for everything, even for what one did in one's leisure time, or for how one relieved oneself. Everything was subjected to the legislator. Every moment of the day was occupied with some obligation. Even sexual intercourse was subject to this awesome authority, and it was the law that by turns granted and denied access to the marriage bed.

Sparta, which combined republican institutions with the same subjection of individuals, excited this philosopher to an even greater paroxysm of enthusiasm. Sparta looked to him like a vast monastery, and so it seemed to him to be the ideal image of a perfect republic. For Athens he had a profound contempt, and he would have been happy to say of that nation, the finest in Greece, what a member of the Académie française who was also a great nobleman said of that academy: "What a dreadful despotism! Everyone there does exactly what they want." I ought to add that this great nobleman was speaking of the Academy as it was thirty years ago.

Montesquieu, who was more observant because he was less hot-headed, did not quite make the same mistakes. He was struck by the differences I have described, but he did not discern their true cause. The Greek politicians who lived under a popular government did not recognize, he said, any authority but that of virtue. Modern politicians only talk to us about manufactures, about commerce, about investments,

about wealth, and even about luxury. He attributes this difference to the difference in character between republics and monarchies; he ought to have attributed it to the contrasting spirits of the ancient world and of the modern world. Citizens of republics and subjects of monarchies—they all want pleasure and profit,[7] and no one, in the present state of society, can avoid wanting them. In modern history, the people who have been the most firmly attached to their liberty, before the French won their freedom, have also been the people who have been the most firmly attached to all the pleasures of life; and they clung to their liberty above all because they believed it guaranteed the pleasures that they held so dear. In previous ages, where there was liberty, there was the capacity to bear privation; now, wherever there is privation, the people have to be enslaved if they are to resign themselves to it. It would be more feasible today to turn a nation of slaves into a nation of Spartans than to turn a free people into Spartans. The men who, swept away by the flood of events, found themselves to be the leaders of our revolution, were, as a necessary consequence of the education they had received, steeped in ancient opinions that had ceased to be valid, opinions that had been valorized by the philosophers of whom I have spoken. The metaphysics of Rousseau, in the middle of which appear suddenly, like flashes of lightning, sublime truths expressed in passages of rousing eloquence; the austerity of Mably, his intolerance, his hatred of all the human passions, his eagerness to enslave them all, his exaggerated views on the proper sphere of the laws, the difference between what he recommended and what had actually existed, his declamations against wealth and even against property itself— all these things were bound to bewitch men excited by a recent victory and who, having subordinated to themselves the authority of the laws, were quite happy to extend that authority over anything and everything. For them, the arguments of the two writers I have been discussing had a special status. Impartial in the matter, and pronouncing an anathema against the despotism of men, they had rewritten the text of the law as a series of axioms. So our leaders wanted to employ

---

[7] "Pleasure and profit" here translates *jouissances*.

the collective authority just as—or so their guides had taught them—it had been employed in the free states. They believed that everything ought still to give way before the will of the collective, and that all limitations on the rights of individuals would be more than compensated by their participating in the power of the collective.

You know, gentlemen, what the outcome was. Free institutions, grounded in an understanding of the spirit of this age, could have sustained themselves. But the attempt to rebuild the institutions of the ancients ended in their collapse, despite strenuous efforts and many heroic deeds that we ought to admire. This is because the power of the collective injured the independence of individuals in all sorts of ways without eliminating the need for that independence. The nation was far from convinced that a theoretical share of an abstract sovereignty was worth the sacrifices that were demanded of it. Its leaders echoed Rousseau in vain, telling it that the laws of liberty are a thousand times more restrictive than the yoke of tyranny. It wanted nothing to do with these restrictive laws and became so weary of them that at times it believed that the yoke of tyranny would be preferable. Well, now it has born the yoke of tyranny, and it knows better. It has discovered that the arbitrary will of a few individuals is even worse than the worst of laws. But the laws too ought to have their limits.

If I have succeeded, gentlemen, in getting you to share the convictions that in my opinion follow from these facts, then you will recognize with me the truth of the following principles. The independence of the individual is the first need of modern man; as a result, one should never ask him to sacrifice it in order to win political liberty. It follows that none of the numerous institutions that, in the ancient republics, restricted the liberty of the individual—institutions that have been too often praised—can be in any way acceptable in the modern world.

This truth, gentlemen, seems at first one that there is no need to establish. Many of our contemporary governments show no inclination to imitate the republics of antiquity. Nevertheless, no matter how little they are attracted to republican institutions, there are certain republican practices for which they feel a peculiar affection. It is unfortunate that they are precisely those that would allow them to banish, to exile, to confiscate. I remember that in 1802 the government slipped into a law on special tribunals an article that introduced Greek ostracism to France; and goodness knows how many eloquent speakers, in order to persuade us to approve this article—which was in the end withdrawn—spoke about the liberty of Athens and about all of the sacrifices that individuals should be prepared to make in order to preserve that liberty! Similarly, and much more recently, when the fearful authorities, were trying, rather halfheartedly, to control the outcome of elections, a newspaper that is not at all tainted with republicanism suggested we should revive the Roman censorship in order to exclude dangerous candidates.

So I think I won't be wasting time on a pointless digression if, in order to strengthen my case, I say a few words about these two widely praised institutions. Athenian ostracism depended on the presumption that the society has complete authority over its members. If one accepts this presumption, then it can be justified; and in a small state, where the influence of an individual who could appeal to his personal reputation, his prestige, and his clients, might often outweigh that of the masses, ostracism might seem to serve a purpose. But among us, individuals have rights that society ought to respect, and the influence of the individual is, as I have already remarked, so completely lost among a multitude of influences that equal or exceed it, that the harassment of an individual in order to reduce his influence is pointless and consequently unjust. No one has the right to send a citizen into exile if he has not been legally condemned—by a properly constituted court of law—under a law that establishes exile as the penalty for the action of which he is guilty. No one has the right to tear a citizen away from his homeland, a property owner from his property, a businessman from his business, a husband from his wife, a father from his children, a writer from his bookish thoughts, an old man from his routines. To exile someone for political reasons is really to assassinate them for political reasons. For an assembly to condemn someone to exile on grounds of public safety is really for that assembly to commit a crime against the safety of the public, for public safety always depends on respect for the law, on following proper procedures, and on the government standing by its commitments.

Roman censorship, like ostracism, relied on the exercise of a discretionary power. In a republic in which all of the citizens, thanks to their poverty, lived the simplest of lives,[8] in which they all lived in the same city, in which none of them earned his living by an activity that distracted him from affairs of state, and in which, as a consequence, they were all constantly observing and judging the exercise of the public authority, censorship could, on the one hand, have more influence; and on the other, less freedom of scope, as the arbitrary power of the censors was restrained by a species of moral surveillance exercised against them. But with the expansion of the republic, the complication of social relations, and the refinements of civilization, this institution was deprived of its preconditions, which also established its limits, and then censorship degenerated even in Rome. It was not censorship that had established good behavior; it was the simplicity of life that had made the censorship powerful and effective.

In France, an institution as arbitrary as censorship would be simultaneously ineffective and intolerable. In the present condition of society, good behavior is a matter of fine, slippery, indefinable nuances and would be distorted in a thousand different ways if one tried to define it more precisely. Only public opinion can get a grip on behavior; it alone can judge behavior because public opinion and popular behavior are similar in their nature. But public opinion would rise up against any constituted authority which sought to define more exactly what it should think. If the government of a modern society wanted, following the example of the Roman censors, to condemn a citizen by issuing an arbitrary injunction, then the whole society would appeal against this decree by refusing to approve the decisions of the tribunal.

What I have just said about the consequences of transplanting Roman censorship into a modern society applies to many other aspects of the organization of society, aspects in regard to which people appeal to

the example of antiquity even more frequently, and even more emphatically. Education is an example: we are always hearing just how necessary it is for the government to seize control of the newborn generations in order to shape them as it pleases, and these claims are supported by endless references to obscure texts. The Persians, the Egyptians, the Gauls, the ancient Greeks, the ancient Italians are cited one after another in this context. But, gentlemen, we are not Persians, ruled over by a despot, nor Egyptians, subjugated by priests, nor ancient Gauls, whom the druids could sacrifice on their altars, nor even Greeks or Romans, for whom a share in the power of the collective made up for their personal enslavement. We are moderns. Each of us wants to enjoy his rights and to develop his faculties in whatever way he chooses, providing we do no harm to others. Each of us wants to superintend the development of these faculties in the children whom nature has entrusted to our care, a care that will be all the more enlightened the stronger our affection for our offspring. We have no need of government, except insofar as it assembles and provides for us the general means of education; just as travelers accept the government's provision of the highways, without having government tell them which way to go. Religion too is a target for those who summon up memories from previous centuries. Bold defenders of the unity of the faith cite to us the laws of the ancients against foreign gods and prop up the rights of the Catholic church with the example of the Athenians who put Socrates to death for having undermined polytheism, and with that of Augustus, who wanted people to remain faithful to the religion of their fathers—a policy which meant that, a few years later, the Romans were feeding the first Christians to wild beasts.

Let us be wary, gentlemen, of this admiration for certain ancient practices that we choose to remember. Because we live in the modern day, I want a liberty which suits the modern age; and since we live in monarchies, I humbly beg our rulers not to borrow from the ancient republics techniques for oppressing us.

The liberty of the individual—that, I repeat, is the true form of modern liberty. Political liberty is the guarantee of individual liberty; and consequently political liberty is indispensable. But to ask people

---

[8] "Lives" here translates *moeurs*.

nowadays to sacrifice the whole of their individual liberty to their political liberty, as those of previous eras did, that's the surest way to deprive them of personal liberty, and, once that has been successfully done, political liberty will soon be taken from them as well. You will realize, gentlemen, that my observations in no way imply a devaluation of political liberty. I do not draw from the facts I have expounded to you the consequences that some would draw from them. From the fact that the ancients were free, and from the fact that we cannot be free in the way that they were free, some conclude that we are destined to be enslaved. They would like to construct the new political system on the basis of a small number of elements that they say are the only ones appropriate to the present state of the world. These elements are a set of prejudices with which to frighten men, egoism with which to corrupt them, frivolity with which to disorient them, coarse pleasures with which to degrade them, despotism with which to control them, and, of course, hard knowledge and exact sciences that despotism can use to improve its performance. It would be peculiar if this were the outcome of forty centuries during which the human species has extended its moral and physical capacities: I cannot believe it. I draw completely different conclusions from the differences that separate us from the ancient world. We must not weaken the guarantee, which is liberty; rather, we must extend the sphere of pleasure and profit. I do not want to renounce political liberty; I want to lay claim to civil liberty, along with other forms of political liberty. Governments now have no more right to lay claim to an illegitimate power than had governments then. But governments founded on a principle of legitimacy have less right than they had then to exercise an arbitrary authority over individuals. We still have now the rights that we have had since the beginning of time, the eternal rights to give our consent to laws, to deliberate regarding our interests, to be an integral part of the repeated social whole of which we are members. But governments have new duties. The progress of civilization, and the changes that have taken place over the centuries, require that authority show more respect for the habits, for the affections, and for the independence of individuals. In dealing with all of these

matters, it must employ greater prudence, and must display greater delicacy.

This restriction on authority, which conforms to its duties strictly interpreted, is also in line with its interests properly understood. For if the liberty that suits the moderns is different from that which suited the ancients, the despotism possible among the ancients is no longer possible among the moderns. Since we are often more distracted from political liberty than the ancients could have been, and, under ordinary conditions, less passionate about it, it is all too easy for us to pay insufficient attention to the guarantees that political liberty provides for us, and, if so, we always suffer for it; but at the same time, since we are much more attached to individual liberty than the ancients were, we will defend it, if it is attacked, with much more skill and persistence; moreover, we have means available to defend it that the ancients did not have.

Commerce makes the impact of arbitrary power on our lives more harmful than it has been in the past, because, since our investments are more varied, arbitrary power has to interfere more widely to reach them. But commerce also makes the action of arbitrary government easier to elude, because it changes the nature of property, which becomes, as a result of this change, almost impossible to seize. Commerce gives to property a new quality, that of movement and exchange. Without exchange, property is no more than a use value. Governments can always control use values, for they can simply prevent people from enjoying them, but exchange puts an invisible and insuperable obstacle in the path of the collective's exercise of its power. The effects of commerce extend further still: not only does it liberate the individual, but, in creating a system of credit, it makes government itself dependent on the market.

"Money," says a French author,[9] is the most dangerous weapon of despotism, but it is at the same time the most effective brake on its exercise of power. Credit is controlled by opinion; force is totally ineffectual where it is concerned; money hides itself or flees abroad; all activities of the state come to a halt. Credit did not have the same influence among the ancients as their

[9] Friedrich Melchoir von Grimm, in *Correspondence* (1813).

governments were stronger than individuals. Now individuals are stronger than our governments; wealth is a power more easily brought to bear at any instant, and more easily applied to a diversity of interests, and as a consequence, much more real and much more promptly obeyed. Power works by threat, wealth by rewards. One escapes power by deceiving it; in order to obtain the rewards of wealth, one has to serve it—thus wealth is bound to trump power.

The same causes ensure that the lives of individuals are less caught up in the political life of the collective. Individuals take their wealth far away; they carry with them all of the pleasures of their private lives. Commerce has brought the nations closer together and has given them customs and ways of life that are more or less alike. Their rulers may be hostile to each other, but their peoples are fellow citizens.

Let power, therefore, resign itself. We must have liberty, and we will have it; but since the liberty that we must have is different from that of the ancients, it follows that our liberty requires a different form of organization than the one that suited the liberty of the ancients. In the latter, the more time and the more effort a man gave over to the exercise of his political rights, the more he regarded himself as free; in the type of liberty which suits us, the more the exercise of our political rights leaves us time free to pursue our private interests, the more our liberty will be precious to us.

From this follows, gentlemen, the necessity of the representative system. The representative system is nothing but a system by which a nation transfers to a few individuals tasks that it cannot or does not want to perform itself. Poor men look after their own businesses; rich men hire managers to look after them. This sentence summarizes the history of the ancient and modern states. The representative system is a power of attorney given to a certain number of men by the populace, which wants its interests to be defended, but which nevertheless does not have the time to be always defending them itself. But, unless they have taken leave of their senses, the rich who hire managers check carefully and rigorously to see if their managers are doing their jobs, to ensure that they are not lazy, corrupt, or incompetent. And in order to judge how well their

agents are looking after their affairs, the principals, if they are prudent, ensure that they are well informed about the activities being managed. In the same way, a people who have had recourse to the representative system (in order to enjoy the form of liberty that suits them) ought to exercise a constant and active surveillance over their representatives, and to reserve the right, at times that are not far apart, to dismiss them if they have been unfaithful, and to revoke any powers that their representatives may have abused.

For, since modern liberty is different from ancient liberty, it follows that the former is vulnerable to a different sort of threat. The weakness of ancient liberty was that, preoccupied only with ensuring a share of the collective power, men might not sufficiently value individual rights and properties. The weakness of modern liberty is that, caught up in the enjoyment of our personal independence, and in the pursuit of our private interests, we may give up all too easily our right to a share in political power.

The holders of authority do not fail to exhort us to do exactly this. They are so eager to spare us every effort, except when it comes to obeying and paying! They say: "What, in the end, is the purpose of all your efforts; what motivates your labors; what is the goal to which you aspire? Is it not happiness? Well, this happiness; let us produce it, and we will give it to you." No, gentlemen, we must not let them produce it; no matter how touched we are by their tender interest in our welfare, let us ask authority to stay within its proper limits; let the state confine itself to administering justice. As for making ourselves happy, we will take care of that.

Could pleasure and profit make us happy if they had no guarantees to underwrite them? And where will we find such guarantees, if we give up our political liberty? To give up that liberty, gentlemen, would be an act of madness comparable to that of someone who, knowing his own apartment will be on the ground floor, builds a high-rise on sand, without laying any foundations. In any case, gentlemen, is it really entirely true that happiness, of whatever sort it may be, is the singular goal of the human species? If this were the case, our scope would be very limited and in the end we would not rise very high. There is not one of us who, if he wanted to reduce and restrict his moral capacities, to lower his aspirations, to give up being energetic, pursuing glory, and having profound and generous emotions, could not become both more bestial and more happy. No, gentlemen, I bear witness to this better part of our nature, this noble unease that pursues us and torments us, this burning desire to extend our understanding and develop our faculties. It is not to happiness alone; it is to self-improvement that destiny calls us, and political liberty is the most powerful, the most energetic means of improving human beings that heaven has given us.

Political liberty involves every citizen without exception in the examination and study of his most sacred interests. It aggrandizes the spirit, ennobles the mind, and establishes among all of them a sort of intellectual equality which makes for a people who are both glorious and powerful. Just see how a nation matures as soon as there is a mechanism to enable it regularly to exercise its political liberty. Watch our citizens of every social class, of every profession, stepping out of the sphere of their daily work and their private activities, and suddenly finding themselves exercising the important responsibilities that the constitution confers on them, choosing with discernment, resisting with energy, thwarting tricks, braving menaces, nobly resisting seductions. See a pure, profound, sincere patriotism triumphing in our cities and coming alive even in our villages, spreading through our factories, enlivening our countryside. See the solid and sound spirit of the practical farmer and the hardworking businessman become infused with a sense of our rights and of the necessity for institutions that guarantee them. Experts in the history of the abuses they have suffered,

and no less skilled in the remedies these abuses require, they keep the whole of France in their mind's eye, and, expressing the gratitude of the whole nation, they reward with their votes the most illustrious of all the defenders of liberty, who has remained faithful to his principles through the passage of thirty years.[10]

Far then, gentlemen, from renouncing either of the two species of liberty about which I have been speaking, it is essential, as I have shown, that we must learn to combine them. Institutions, as the celebrated author of *The History of the Medieval Republics* says, are the means through which the human species attains its destiny. They gain their highest purpose when they raise the greatest possible number of human beings to the highest level of moral awareness.

The work of the legislator is far from complete when he has simply made our lives peaceful. Even when the people are contented, there is still much to do. Our institutions must bring about the moral education of our citizens. They must respect their individual rights and show consideration for their independence by not interfering with their ways of earning a living, but they must also entrench their influence in public life, and invite the people to share, by their decisions and their votes, in the exercise of power. They must also guarantee the people a right of control and surveillance through the expression of their opinions. Educating them in this way by the practice of democracy for positions of responsibility, our institutions must develop in them both the desire and the capacity to live up to those responsibilities.

[10] A reference to the election of the Marquis de La Fayette as deputy for the Sarthe in 1818.

6

J. S. MILL: FEMINISM AND
THE PURSUIT OF HAPPINESS

J. S. Mill's *The Subjection of Women* (1869) deserves to be regarded as one of the most remarkable works of political theory ever written. Unfortunately, it was not only the least successful of Mill's books in his lifetime, but commentators on Mill make little effort to give a careful exposition of its argument. Moreover, feminist theorists have tended to criticize Mill for reformism, because they have failed to interpret *The Subjection* in the light of Mill's other works and in the context of his time.

It is difficult for us now to conceive of the pervasive tyranny to which women were subjected in mid-nineteenth-century England (as in other times, in other places), a tyranny which was customary, legal, and often brutal. Two examples at random: At the Anti-Slavery Convention of 1840, women delegates who had arrived from America were refused permission to take part, being allowed only to hear the proceedings from behind a curtain. As late as 1888 a case in which a man had beaten his wife with a poker, causing blood to flow from her ears, was dismissed from the courts, Mr. Justice Day observing that the prisoner had been merely exercising that control over his wife which was still sanctioned by the law of England, and the jury promptly acquitting, as directed.

To the age-old claim that women should be subject to men, Mill responded with a series of powerful arguments. Only two earlier works had had a scope and forcefulness remotely comparable to his: Mary Wollstonecraft's *Vindication of the Rights of Woman* (1792) and William Thompson's *Appeal of One Half the Human Race* (1825). Part of the strength of Mill's own work derives from its closeness to this earlier tradition, for Mill had been educated within the eighteenth-century view that the mind was shaped by experience and environment, and he self-consciously rejected the tendency of his contemporaries to resort to biological determinism when discussing race and gender. He read, admired, and understood Darwin's *Origin of Species* (1859), but he wrote before the great reactionary wave of social Darwinist writing, which sought to preserve the inferior status of women as natural and inevitable. Mill had the good fortune to be the last Enlightenment feminist.

Mill's argument is also infused with earlier traditions in a second respect. Early on in *The Subjection* he notes that a woman who kills her husband is guilty of a peculiar crime called petty treason. This implicit comparison between the sacrosanct authority of kings and of husbands intrigues Mill, because much of his argument consists of redirecting against the tyranny of husbands arguments which had long been made against the tyranny of monarchs. Thus, in the home, as in the kingdom, unchecked authority will frequently be abused; court life and patriarchal authority both encourage sycophancy and hypocrisy; and there can be no valid consent to slavery, whether imposed by conqueror or husband. In reapplying republican arguments to relations between the sexes, Mill was following the lead of Wollstonecraft, who had herself been much influenced by Rousseau and Thomas Paine.

Mill's argument needs to be read as dealing with only certain aspects of the subjection of women, those directly relating to their legal status. It was the law which insisted that the property of married women belonged to their husbands; that if they were beaten by their husbands they had not been assaulted; that if they were forcibly penetrated by their husbands they had not been raped; and it was the law which excluded women in general from the franchise, from public office, and from the respectable professions. The immediate beneficiaries of changes in the law would have been middle-class women, and it is their position with which he is mainly concerned. In Mill's day working-class men, as well as all women, were denied the vote. There was no provision of free universal education, so the children of the poor, whether boys or girls, were denied any prospect of upward mobility. Because working-class women were driven to work in the factories by economic desperation, they were forced to leave their babies in the care of others. This meant relying on bottle-feeding. But at a time when sterilization techniques were unknown (the word "pasteurize" entered English only in 1881), bottle-fed babies had extremely high mortality rates. It is hardly surprising, then, that Mill does not argue that nursing mothers should be free to go out to work, since like all his contemporaries he took it for granted that they would prefer to stay home. He had discussed the economic pressures on working-class families in his *Principles of Political Economy* (1848) and saw no need to return to the question in *The Subjection.*

Mill's assumption that housework is a full-time occupation now seems as strange as his conviction that mothers should normally stay with their infants. We need to remember just how arduous and time-consuming domestic labors were in a world without washing machines, vacuum cleaners, refrigerators, supermarkets, or automobiles. Nevertheless, Mill was not completely unaware of the evil consequences of the division of labor within the household. In his autobiography he wrote that during his childhood he had had "the great misfortune of having, in domestic matters, everything done for me." We should not assume, then, that he was uncritical of male reliance on unpaid female labor.

Mill may thus be cautiously defended against the late-twentieth-century protest that he approves of the division of labor within the middle-class household of his day. It was simply much harder for him to conceive of alternatives than it is for us. We can also defend him against the common charge that *The Subjection of Women* is marred by its failure to discuss sexuality and reproduction. On this question Mill's thinking, like that of many of his contemporaries, was shaped by the argument of Thomas Malthus's *Essay on the Principles of Population* (1798). Malthus had maintained that, unchecked, populations naturally grow more rapidly than supplies of food, leading inevitably to poverty and starvation. As a solution, Malthus advocated sexual abstinence. Mill himself certainly favored contraception as an alternative, but if he had expressed his private views on the subject in print he would immediately have been prosecuted. His silence on the question of sexuality and reproduction is thus involuntary.

Mill criticized his own father for marrying young and having nine children; Mill himself married late and had none. In *On Liberty* (1759) he argued that the state had the right to discourage procreation, since the whole of society suffers as a result of overpopulation, and the right also to interfere in the family by requiring that children of both sexes be adequately and equally educated. At the same time he argued that sexual acts between consenting adults were their own private affair (an argument which, as far as heterosexual sex is concerned, takes contraception for granted), and he also argued that there should be free discussion of ideas (including, naturally, ideas about sexuality and reproduction). One of the purposes of *On Liberty* was to establish the cultural and legal preconditions for women to claim control over their own bodies.

When placed back in this double context of Malthusianism and censorship, Mill's arguments in favor of careers for women who are unmarried or whose children have grown can be seen as referring not to a small and insignificant sector of the female population, but one that was believed to be growing and one that Mill must have hoped would grow rapidly. Mill's contemporaries were much preoccupied with what was called the surplus-woman problem, the growing number of women unable to find husbands who could afford to marry. Mill himself thought that people should marry late or not at all and that married people should reduce the number of their children through abstinence or contraception. Thus he foresaw a world in which child-rearing and housework would occupy fewer women and in which those it did occupy would be engaged in it for fewer years of their lives. Hence the urgent necessity of opening careers to women.

Read in the context of *On Liberty, The Subjection of Women* begins to appear as a more radical text than at first it seems. *On Liberty* itself represents Mill's attempt to resolve his disagreements with the greatest influence on his intellectual life, Jeremy Bentham (b. 1748). Bentham, the founder of utilitarianism, was a close friend of Mill's father, James Mill (b. 1773), himself one of the leading intellectuals of his day. Mill's education (famously, he learned Greek at the age of three) was little short of an indoctrination in the principles of Benthamism. We can briefly summarize these principles as follows. People naturally pursue happiness and flee pain (as Hobbes had argued), and morality consists simply in doing those things which are useful or pleasurable to oneself or others (as Hume had argued). Bentham believed one could calculate how much pleasure or pain a particular action would cause and therefore whether it was right or wrong. This *felicific calculus* was based on two assumptions. First, pleasures and pains are quantitative rather than qualitative (so that one can compare the amount of pleasure given me by a cold beer, allowing for both the duration and the intensity of the pleasure, with the amount of pleasure given me by a Shakespeare sonnet). Second, morality consists in maximizing the amount of pleasure in society, not in distributing it in any particular way. Nobody has a right to pleasure or to freedom from pain, and anyone's pleasures can be traded away if others will benefit. Thus if ten men were adrift in a lifeboat and faced with starvation, it would be perfectly proper for them to draw lots and eat one of their number, for the brief pain of the unlucky individual would be more than offset by the happiness of the nine survivors.

Bentham thus rejected all talk of rights as nonsense. There could be no right to life, nor to liberty. He favored representative government, but this was because he believed it was likely to be efficient and honest, and so to foster happiness. James Mill notoriously argued that no individual needed a right to vote, so long as the interests of all were represented. Thus it would be perfectly reasonable if only a random sample of the population was given the vote (everyone born on a certain day, for instance), and it was reasonable too to exclude women from the vote, as their interests were indistinguishable from their husbands'. It was this argument which provoked Thompson's *Appeal,* and J. S. Mill's own *Subjection* is, like his *Utilitarianism* (1863), a rejection of Benthamite theories.

Mill's first objection to Benthamism was deeply personal. He felt that he had been raised as a calculating machine, and at the age of twenty he entered into a deep depression because he felt incapable of enthusiasm or feeling. He found part of a solution in reading poetry. This led him to three important anti-Benthamite principles. First, some pleasures are qualitatively superior to others. Second, one does not achieve happiness by aiming at it, but achieves happiness as a side-effect of pursuing other projects. Third, it matters not only what you do, but what sort of person you are.

These three principles are foundational to *On Liberty*. Freedom of expression creates a marketplace for ideas, which makes possible intellectual progress, and intellectual progress makes possible higher pleasures and superior characters ("the improvement of mankind"). Moreover, integral to happiness is a sense that one is pursuing one's own projects and expressing one's own individuality. If people are told what to do and denied the freedom to learn from their own mistakes, they may be efficient, but they will not be happy. But if people are left free to choose how to live, different people will find happiness in so many different forms of life (this one a musician, that one an engineer) that only a society which offers a wide diversity of life choices can maximize happiness. Lastly, this variety is itself a precondition for progress, as it underpins intellectual diversity.

Mill was, after his crisis, still a utilitarian, in that he thought that morality consisted in furthering happiness, but he was now what has been termed an indirect utilitarian, since he believed happiness to be a side-effect of certain ways of life. Because these forms of life could only exist where there was liberty and because everyone had an interest in progress, people had (at least in countries advanced enough to provide some basic economic security) something that could properly be called a right to liberty, and liberty should not be regarded as something to be traded away in exchange for prosperity, stability, or harmony. This view of liberty is central to *The Subjection:* Women, like men, have a right to control their own lives, pursue their own ambitions, and differ from one another (Mill is strongly opposed to "stereotyping," even if he occasionally talks about women or the French in general). To deny women these rights is to deny them happiness. (This is true even if they themselves do not realize it. Mill favors diversity, but his arguments run counter to the sort of multiculturalism which would claim that a community is entitled to opt for patriarchalism.)

Benthamite utilitarianism was based on the assumption that people always recognized pleasure and pain and always knew which pleasures they preferred. Mill's indirect utilitarianism obliged him to claim that people were often short-sighted in their pursuit of happiness. They opted for a beer when they could have been studying Greek with a view to reading Homer. They opted for prosperity and security when they might have found more happiness in placing the welfare of others ahead of their own selfish interests (Mill advocated what he termed "the religion of humanity," a morality of putting other human beings first). Compulsory education and intellectual freedom were both essential if "improvement" was to be possible, but so too was propaganda and even legislation in favor of liberty and the higher pleasures. In Bentham's view reform consisted in changing laws and institutions so that people could obtain the pleasures they wanted to obtain; in Mill's view their pleasures and preferences needed to be reformed. How do you transform people as they are now into people as they might become, *without imposing improvement upon them?*

In *The Subjection* we can see Mill wrestling with this problem. He argues that women have a right to liberty and that, if men and women were treated equally, they might well prove to have identical abilities. He thus formulates a set of radical feminist arguments. But he wants both men and women as they are now to recognize the need for reform (and it is worth remembering that in Mill's day few women were feminists). He thus argues that even women brought up under conditions of inequality have valuable skills which should be put to public and not merely domestic use, and he argues that men would be happier living with wives who were companions and not merely servants. These reformist arguments can seem irritating today, particularly if Mill is misunderstood as saying that one should accept that women will never be first-rate philosophers or that women should be treated better in order to make men happier. But Mill has to show that one can move towards equality within an unequal world.

It may be helpful here to think back to the republican tradition. Machiavelli had argued that, once a people had been corrupted, it was incapable of accepting the responsibilities of freedom. Rousseau had agreed: It was necessary to force men to be free. Mill, to avoid either pessimism or compulsion, needs to show that one can make incremental progress towards true equality. His reformist arguments, in which he concedes that there are real differences between men (in general or on average) and women (in general or on average) in present society, are perfectly compatible with his radical arguments. It is worth noting too that Mill's recognition of difference points as often in a radical as in a reformist direction. He expects women to be great mathematicians, painters, and musicians as soon as they have the opportunity to be true professionals, not mere amateurs. He recognizes the need for women to have a literature of their own, different in character from men's, at least so long as inequality prevails—we can see him here groping towards the ideas of female solidarity and cultural criticism, which have become so important to the women's movement. And he expects women not only to be successful politicians, but to bring to political life "distinctively female" values, such as hostility to militarism.

Mill's *Subjection,* read in the context of his other work, is thus both more coherent and more radical than it is often said to be. Far from presenting radical and reformist arguments which are at odds with each other, it relies on a politics of progress which aspires to move from reform to cultural revolution. But no account of *The Subjection* would be complete without a discussion of the second great influence on Mill's intellectual life, Harriet Taylor, who was already married to John Taylor when she and Mill met in 1830. They at once fell in love and formed an intimate if Platonic relationship. John Taylor died in 1849, and Mill and Mrs. Taylor married two years later (after he had renounced the legal advantages the law gave husbands over their wives). She died in 1858, shortly before the publication of *On Liberty* and the compilation of *The Subjection.*

J. S. Mill never tired of claiming that he derived all his best ideas from Harriet Taylor and (after she died) her daughter Helen. He insisted that many of his works, especially *On Liberty,* were in effect joint productions. And he wrote his *Autobiography* primarily to acknowledge his debt to her. Mill himself testifies that Harriet encouraged in him more radical opinions—a sympathy with cooperative socialism, a commitment to democracy, an identification with feminism. Her own essay *The Enfranchisement of Women* is more radical and less reformist than Mill's *Subjection.* When, in *The Subjection,* Mill describes those intellectual aptitudes that seem to him (in contemporary society) distinctively female, it is Harriet's abilities he has in mind, just as his description of the perfect marriage is a description of their relationship.

Harriet's influence may pervade *The Subjection,* but it is also likely that their common experience was a key factor in shaping *On Liberty.* On the argument of *On Liberty* Mill acknowledges one supreme influence, Tocqueville's *Democracy in America* (1835–40). Tocqueville had argued that political freedom was likely to be accompanied by an increased uniformity of opinion and homogeneity of culture. Mill was to give considerable thought to devising voting systems designed to protect minorities from tyrannical majorities. But *On Liberty* is not just concerned with the dangers of illiberal legislation. Mill is also worried that informal public opinion may exercise its own "social tyranny" and penalize individuality and diversity.

Mill himself had some experience of such tyranny. In the eyes of his friends and acquaintances, his relationship with Harriet, another man's wife, was deeply anomalous and even downright offensive. His claim that she was his intellectual superior was held to be ridiculous, her radical influence on him, pernicious. The strength of purpose and independence of mind that Mill and Taylor showed in maintaining their relationship in face of the hostility of their families, friends, and associates is rarely comprehended. *On Liberty* is intended as a vindication of their conduct, for it insists that eccentrics are under no obligation to conform to popular prejudices and common standards of behavior. Read in this context, *On Liberty* is of a piece with *The Subjection,* for both attack those fetters of law and custom which had long denied to Harriet Taylor the right to take the lover of her choice, had firmly prevented her from freely expressing her views on divorce and contraception, and had always denied her recognition as one of the great intellects of her day. It is this direct experience of the intermingling of public issues and private lives which shaped Mill's liberal sentiments. Liberal political theory is deeply indebted to those long years when public opinion forced Harriet Taylor and J. S. Mill to offer at least an outward conformity to popular prejudice.

Further Reading

The classic study of Bentham, James Mill, and their associates is Elie Halévy, *The Growth of Philosophic Radicalism* (London: Faber and Faber, 1928). One of the best books on Bentham is Douglas Long, *Bentham on Liberty* (Toronto: University of Toronto Press, 1977). As a discussion of the philosophical issues associated with utilitarianism, J.J.C. Smart and Bernard Williams, *Utilitarianism For and Against* (Cambridge: Cambridge University Press, 1973) is admirable.

As an introduction to Mill's life and thought no book can improve on the *Autobiography,* ed. J. Stillinger (Oxford: Oxford University Press, 1971). Two valuable general surveys are John M. Robson, *The Improvement of Mankind* (London: Routledge and Kegan Paul, 1968) and Alan Ryan, *J. S. Mill* (London: Routlege and Kegan Paul, 1974). Much of the best recent work on *On Liberty* is collected in John Gray and G. W. Smith (eds.), *J. S. Mill: "On Liberty" In Focus* (London: Routledge, 1991).

Two influential discussions of *The Subjection of Women* are chapter 9 of Susan M. Okin, *Women in Western Political Thought* (Princeton: Princeton University Press, 1979) and Julia Annas, "Mill and the Subjection of Women," *Philosophy,* vol. 52 (1977), 179–94. For the wider context see Jane Rendall, *The Origins of Modern Feminism: Women in Britain, France and the United States, 1780–1860* (London: Macmillan, 1985). Mill's relationship with Harriet Taylor is studied in F. A. Hayek, *John Stuart Mill and Harriet Taylor* (London: Routledge and Kegan Paul, 1951). On Victorian discussions of birth control, see Angus McLaren, *Birth Control in Nineteenth-Century England* (London: Croom Helm, 1978), and on the impact of Darwin, see John Burrow, *Evolution and Society* (Cambridge: Cambridge University Press, 1966).

The standard survey of nineteenth-century English political thought is now John Burrow, Stefan Collini, and Donald Winch, *That Noble Science of Politics* (Cambridge: Cambridge University Press, 1983).

BENTHAM

An Introduction to the Principles of Morals and Legislation

CHAPTER I

Of the Principle of Utility

1.   Nature has placed mankind under the governance of two sovereign masters, *pain* and *pleasure*. It is for them alone to point out what we ought to do, as well as to determine what we shall do. On the one hand the standard of right and wrong, on the other the chain of causes and effects, are fastened to their throne. They govern us in all we do, in all we say, in all we think: every effort we can make to throw off our subjection, will serve but to demonstrate and confirm it. In words a man may pretend to abjure their empire: but in reality he will remain subject to it all the while. The *principle of utility*[1] recognizes this subjection, and assumes it for the foundation of that system, the object of which is to rear the fabric of felicity by the hands of reason and of law. Systems which attempt to question it, deal in sounds instead of senses, in caprice instead of reason, in darkness instead of light.

But enough of metaphor and declamation: it is not by such means that moral science is to be improved.

2.   The principle of utility is the foundation of the present work: it will be proper therefore at the outset to give an explicit and determinate account of what is meant by it. By the principle[2] of utility is meant that principle which approves or disapproves of every action whatsoever, according to the tendency which it appears to have to augment or diminish the happiness of the party whose interest is in question: or, what is the same thing in other words, to promote or to oppose that happiness. I say of every action whatsoever; and therefore not only of every action of a private individual, but of every measure of government.

3.   By utility is meant that property in any object, whereby it tends to produce benefit, advantage, pleasure, good, or happiness, (all this in the present case comes to the same thing) or (what comes again to the same thing) to prevent the happening of mischief, pain, evil, or unhappiness to the party whose interest

---

[1] Note by the Author, July 1822.

To this denomination has of late been added, or substituted, the *greatest happiness* or *greatest felicity* principle: this for shortness, instead of saying at length *that principle* which states the greatest happiness of all those whose interest is in question, as being the right and proper, and only right and proper and universally desirable, end of human action: of human action in every situation, and in particular in that of a functionary or set of functionaries exercising the powers of Government. The word *utility* does not so clearly point to the ideas of *pleasure* and *pain* as the words *happiness* and *felicity* do: nor does it lead us to the consideration of the *number*, of the interests affected; to the *number*, as being the circumstance, which contributes, in the largest proportion, to the formation of the standard here in question; the *standard of right and wrong*, by which alone the propriety of human conduct, in every situation, can with propriety be tried. This want of a sufficiently manifest connexion between the ideas of *happiness* and *pleasure* on the one hand, and the idea of *utility* on the other, I have every now and then found operating, and with but too much efficiency, as a bar to the acceptance, that might otherwise have been given, to this principle.

[2] The word principle is derived from the Latin *principium*: which seems to be compounded of the two words *primus*, first, or chief, and *cipium*, a termination which seems to be derived from *capio*, to take, as in *mancipium*, *municipium*; to which are analogous, *auceps*, *forceps*, and others. It is a term of very vague and very extensive signification: it is applied to any thing which is conceived to serve as a foundation or beginning to any series of operations: in some cases, of physical operations; but mental operations in the present case.

The principle here in question may be taken for an act of the mind; a sentiment; a sentiment of approbation; a sentiment which, when applied to an action, approves of its utility, as that quality of it by which the measure of approbation or disapprobation bestowed upon it ought to be governed.

is considered: if that party be the community in general, then the happiness of the community: if a particular individual, then the happiness of that individual.

4. The interest of the community is one of the most general expressions that can occur in the phraseology of morals: no wonder that the meaning of it is often lost. When it has a meaning, it is this. The community is a fictitious *body*, composed of the individual persons who are considered as constituting as it were its *members*. The interest of the community then is, what?—the sum of the interests of the several members who compose it.

5. It is in vain to talk of the interest of the community, without understanding what is the interest of the individual.[3] A thing is said to promote the interest, or to be *for* the interest, of an individual, when it tends to add to the sum total of his pleasures: or, what comes to the same thing, to diminish the sum total of his pains.

6. An action then may be said to be conformable to the principle of utility, or, for shortness sake, to utility, (meaning with respect to the community at large) when the tendency it has to augment the happiness of the community is greater than any it has to diminish it.

7. A measure of government (which is but a particular kind of action, performed by a particular person or persons) may be said to be conformable to or dictated by the principle of utility, when in like manner the tendency which it has to augment the happiness of the community is greater than any which it has to diminish it.

8. When an action, or in particular a measure of government, is supposed by a man to be conformable to the principle of utility, it may be convenient, for the purposes of discourse, to imagine a kind of law or dictate, called a law or dictate of utility; and to speak of the action in question, as being conformable to such law or dictate.

9. A man may be said to be a partizan of the principle of utility, when the approbation or disapprobation he annexes to any action, or to any measure, is determined by and proportioned to the tendency which he conceives it to have to augment or to di-

minish the happiness of the community: or in other words, to its conformity or unconformity to the laws or dictates of utility.

10. Of an action that is conformable to the principle of utility one may always say either that it is one that ought to be done, or at least that it is not one that ought not to be done. One may say also, that it is right it should be done; at least that it is not wrong it should be done: that it is a right action; at least that it is not a wrong action. When thus interpreted, the words *ought*, and *right* and *wrong*, and others of that stamp, have a meaning: when otherwise, they have none.

11. Has the rectitude of this principle been ever formally contested? It should seem that it had, by those who have not known what they have been meaning. Is it susceptible of any direct proof? it should seem not: for that which is used to prove every thing else, cannot itself be proved: a chain of proofs must have their commencement somewhere. To give such proof is as impossible as it is needless.

12. Not that there is or ever has been that human creature breathing, however stupid or perverse, who has not on many, perhaps on most occasions of his life, deferred to it. By the natural constitution of the human frame, on most occasions of their lives men in general embrace this principle, without thinking of it: if not for the ordering of their own actions, yet for the trying of their own actions, as well as of those of other men. There have been, at the same time, not many, perhaps, even of the most intelligent, who have been disposed to embrace it purely and without reserve. There are even few who have not taken some occasion or other to quarrel with it, either on account of their not understanding always how to apply it, or on account of some prejudice or other which they were afraid to examine into, or could not bear to part with. For such is the stuff that man is made of: in principle and in practice, in a right track and in a wrong one, the rarest of all human qualities is consistency.

13. When a man attempts to combat the principle of utility, it is with reasons drawn, without his being aware of it, from that very principle itself.[4] His

---

[3] Interest is one of those words, which not having any superior *genus*, cannot in the ordinary way be defined.

[4] 'The principle of utility,' (I have heard it said) 'is a dangerous principle: it is dangerous on certain occasions to consult

arguments, if they prove any thing, prove not that the principle is *wrong*, but that, according to the applications he supposes to be made of it, it is *misapplied.* Is it possible for a man to move the earth? Yes; but he must first find out another earth to stand upon.

14.   To disprove the propriety of it by arguments is impossible; but, from the causes that have been

---

it.' This is as much as to say, what? that it is not consonant to utility, to consult utility: in short, that it is *not* consulting it, to consult it.

Addition by the Author, July 1822.

Not long after the publication of the Fragment on Government, anno 1776, in which, in the character of an all-comprehensive and all-commanding principle, the principle of *utility* was brought to view, one person by whom observation to the above effect was made was *Alexander Wedderburn*, at that time Attorney or Solicitor General, afterwards successively Chief Justice of the Common Pleas, and Chancellor of England, under the successive titles of Lord Loughborough and Earl of Rosslyn. It was made—not indeed in my hearing, but in the hearing of a person by whom it was almost immediately communicated to me. So far from being self-contradictory, it was a shrewd and perfectly true one. By that distinguished functionary, the state of the Government was thoroughly understood: by the obscure individual, at that time not so much as supposed to be so: his disquisitions had not been as yet applied, with any thing like a comprehensive view, to the field of Constitutional Law, nor therefore to those features of the English Government, by which the greatest happiness of the ruling *one* with or without that of a favoured few, are now so plainly seen to be the only ends to which the course of it has at any time been directed. The *principle of utility* was an appellative, at that time employed—employed by me, as it had been by others, to designate that which in a more perspicuous and instructive manner, may, as above, be designated by the name of the *greatest happiness principle.* 'This principle' (said Wedderburn) 'is a dangerous one.' Saying so, he said that which, to a certain extent, is strictly true: a principle, which lays down, as the only *right* and justifiable end of Government, the greatest happiness of the greatest number—how can it be denied to be a dangerous one? dangerous it unquestionably is, to every government which has for its *actual* end or object, the greatest happiness of a certain *one*, with or without the addition of some comparatively small number of others, whom it is a matter of pleasure or accommodation to him to admit, each of them, to a share in the concern, on the footing of so many junior partners. *Dangerous* it therefore really was, to the interest—the sinister interest—of all those

---

mentioned, or from some confused or partial view of it, a man may happen to be disposed not to relish it. Where this is the case, if he thinks the settling of his opinions on such a subject worth the trouble, let him take the following steps and at length, perhaps, he may come to reconcile himself to it.

1. Let him settle with himself, whether he would wish to discard this principle altogether; if so, let him consider what it is that all his reasonings (in matters of politics especially) can amount to?

2. If he would, let him settle with himself, whether he would judge and act without any principle, or whether there is any other he would judge and act by?

3. If there be, let him examine and satisfy himself whether the principle he thinks he has found is really any separate intelligible principle; or whether it be not a mere principle in words, a kind of phrase, which at bottom expresses neither more nor less than the mere averment of his own unfounded sentiments; that is, what in another person he might be apt to call caprice?

4. If he is inclined to think that his own approbation or disapprobation, annexed to the idea of an act, without any regard to its consequences, is a sufficient foundation for him to judge and act upon, let him ask himself whether his sentiment is to be a standard of right and wrong, with respect to every other man, or whether every man's sentiment has the same privilege of being a standard to itself?

---

functionaries, himself included, whose interest it was, to maximize delay, vexation, and expense, in judicial and other modes of procedure, for the sake of the profit, extractible out of the expense. In a Government which had for its end in view the greatest happiness of the greatest number, Alexander Wedderburn might have been Attorney General and then Chancellor: but he would not have been Attorney General with £15,000 a year, nor Chancellor, with a peerage with a veto upon all justice, with £25,000 a year, and with 500 sinecures at his disposal, under the name of Ecclesiastical Benefices, besides *et cæteras.*

5. In the first case, let him ask himself whether his principle is not despotical, and hostile to all the rest of human race?

6. In the second case, whether it is not anarchical, and whether at this rate there are not as many different standards of right and wrong as there are men? and whether even to the same man, the same thing, which is right today, may not (without the least change in its nature) be wrong tomorrow? and whether the same thing is not right and wrong in the same place at the same time? and in either case, whether all argument is not at an end? and whether, when two men have said, 'I like this,' and 'I don't like it,' they can (upon such a principle) have any thing more to say?

7. If he should have said to himself, No: for that the sentiment which he proposes as a standard must be grounded on reflection, let him say on what particulars the reflection is to turn? if on particulars having relation to the utility of the act, then let him say whether this is not deserting his own principle, and borrowing assistance from that very one in opposition to which he sets it up: or if not on those particulars, on what other particulars?

8. If he should be for compounding the matter, and adopting his own principle in part, and the principle of utility in part, let him say how far he will adopt it?

9. When he has settled with himself where he will stop, then let him ask himself how he justifies to himself the adopting it so far? and why he will not adopt it any farther?

10. Admitting any other principle than the principle of utility to be a right principle, a principle that it is right for a man to pursue; admitting (what is not true) that the word *right* can have a meaning without reference to utility, let him say whether there is any such thing as a *motive* that a man can have to pursue the dictates of it: if there is, let him say what that motive is, and how it is to be distinguished from those which enforce the dictates of utility: if not, then lastly let him say what it is this other principle can be good for?

CHAPTER IV

Value of a Lot of Pleasure or Pain, How To Be Measured

1.   Pleasures then, and the avoidance of pains, are the *ends* which the legislator has in view: it behoves him therefore to understand their *value*. Pleasures and pains are the *instruments* he has to work with: it behoves him therefore to understand their force, which is again, in other words, their value.

2.   To a person considered by *himself*, the value of a pleasure or pain considered *by itself*, will be greater or less, according to the four following circumstances:[5]

  1. Its *intensity*.
  2. Its *duration*.
  3. Its *certainty* or *uncertainty*.
  4. Its *propinquity* or *remoteness*.

3.   These are the circumstances which are to be considered in estimating a pleasure or a pain considered each of them by itself. But when the value of any pleasure or pain is considered for the purpose of estimating the tendency of any *act* by which it is produced, there are two other circumstances to be taken into account; these are,

  5. Its *fecundity*, or the chance it has of being followed by sensations of the *same* kind: that is, pleasures, if it be a pleasure: pains, if it be a pain.

[5] These circumstances have since been nominated *elements* or *dimensions* of *value* in a pleasure or a pain.

Not long after the publication of the first edition, the following memoriter verses were framed, in the view of lodging more effectually, in the memory, these points, on which the whole fabric of morals and legislation may be seen to rest.

> Intense, long, certain, speedy, fruitful, pure—
> Such marks in *pleasures* and in *pains* endure.
> Such pleasures seek if *private* be thy end:
> If it be *public*, wide let them *extend*.
> Such *pains* avoid, whichever be thy view:
> If pains *must* come, let them *extend* to few.

6. Its *purity*, or the chance it has of *not* being followed by sensations of the *opposite* kind: that is, pains, if it be a pleasure: pleasures, if it be a pain.

These two last, however, are in strictness scarcely to be deemed properties of the pleasure or the pain itself; they are not, therefore, in strictness to be taken into the account of the value of that pleasure or that pain. They are in strictness to be deemed properties only of the act, or other event, by which such pleasure or pain has been produced; and accordingly are only to be taken into the account of the tendency of such act or such event.

4.　　To a *number* of persons, with reference to each of whom the value of a pleasure or a pain is considered, it will be greater or less, according to seven circumstances: to wit, the six preceding ones; *viz.*

1. Its *intensity*.
2. Its *duration*.
3. Its *certainty* or *uncertainty*.
4. Its *propinquity* or *remoteness*.
5. Its *fecundity*.
6. Its *purity*.

And one other; to wit;

7. Its *extent*; that is, the number of persons to whom it *extends*; or (in other words) who are affected by it.

5.　　To take an exact account then of the general tendency of any act, by which the interests of a community are affected, proceed as follows. Begin with any one person of those whose interests seem most immediately to be affected by it: and take an account,

1. Of the value of each distinguishable *pleasure* which appears to be produced by it in the *first* instance.
2. Of the value of each *pain* which appears to be produced by it in the *first* instance.
3. Of the value of each pleasure which appears to be produced by it *after* the first. This constitutes the *fecundity* of the first *pleasure* and the *impurity* of the first *pain*.
4. Of the value of each *pain* which appears to be produced by it after the first. This consti-

tutes the *fecundity* of the first *pain*, and the *impurity* of the first pleasure.

5. Sum up all the values of all the *pleasures* on the one side, and those of all the pains on the other. The balance, if it be on the side of pleasure, will give the *good* tendency of the act upon the whole, with respect to the interests of that *individual* person; if on the side of pain, the *bad* tendency of it upon the whole.
6. Take an account of the *number* of persons whose interests appear to be concerned; and repeat the above process with respect to each. *Sum up* the numbers expressive of the degrees of *good* tendency, which the act has, with respect to each individual, in regard to whom the tendency of it is *good* upon the whole: do this again with respect to each individual, in regard to whom the tendency of it is *good* upon the whole: do this again with respect to each individual, in regard to whom the tendency of it is *bad* upon the whole. Take the *balance*; which, if on the side of *pleasure*, will give the general *good tendency* of the act, with respect to the total number or community of individuals concerned; if on the side of pain, the general *evil tendency*, with respect to the same community.

6.　　It is not to be expected that this process should be strictly pursued previously to every moral judgment, or to every legislative or judicial operation. It may, however, be always kept in view: and as near as the process actually pursued on these occasions approaches to it, so near will such process approach to the character of an exact one.

7.　　The same process is alike applicable to pleasure and pain, in whatever shape they appear: and by whatever denomination they are distinguished: to pleasure, whether it be called *good* (which is properly the cause or instrument of pleasure) or *profit* (which is distant pleasure, or the cause or instrument of distant pleasure,) or *convenience*, or *advantage, benefit, emolument, happiness,* and so forth: to pain, whether it be called *evil,* (which corresponds to *good*) or *mischief*, or *inconvenience*, or *disadvantage*, or *loss*, or *unhappiness*, and so forth.

8. Nor is this a novel and unwarranted, any more than it is a useless theory. In all this there is nothing but what the practice of mankind, wheresoever they have a clear view of their own interest, is perfectly conformable to. An article of property, an estate in land, for instance, is valuable, on what account? On account of the pleasures of all kinds which it enables a man to produce, and what comes to the same thing the pains of all kinds which it enables him to avert. But the value of such an article of property is universally understood to rise or fall according to the length or shortness of the time which a man has in it: the certainty or uncertainty of its coming into possession: and the nearness or remoteness of the time at which, if at all, it is to come into possession. As to the *intensity* of the pleasures which a man may derive from it, this is never thought of, because it depends upon the use which each particular person may come to make of it; which cannot be estimated till the particular pleasures he may come to derive from it, or the particular pains he may come to exclude by means of it, are brought to view. For the same reason, neither does he think of the *fecundity* or *purity* of those pleasures.

Thus much for pleasure and pain, happiness and unhappiness, in *general*. We come now to consider the several particular kinds of pain and pleasure.

CHAPTER VII

Of Human Actions in General

1. The business of government is to promote the happiness of the society, by punishing and rewarding. That part of its business which consists in punishing, is more particularly the subject of penal law. In proportion as an act tends to disturb that happiness, in proportion as the tendency of it is pernicious, will be the demand it creates for punishment. What happiness consists of we have already seen: enjoyment of pleasures, security from pains.

2. The general tendency of an act is more or less pernicious, according to the sum total of its consequences: that is, according to the difference between the sum of such as are good, and the sum of such as are evil.

3. It is to be observed, that here, as well as henceforward, wherever consequences are spoken of, such only are meant as are *material*. Of the consequences of any act, the multitude and variety must needs be infinite: but such of them only as are material are worth regarding. Now among the consequences of an act, be they what they may, such only, by one who views them in the capacity of a legislator, can be said to be material,[6] as either consist of pain or pleasure, or have an influence in the production of pain or pleasure.[7]

4. It is also to be observed, that into the account of the consequences of the act, are to be taken not such only as might have ensued, were intention out of the question, but such also as depend upon the connexion there may be between these first-mentioned consequences and the intention. The connexion there is between the intention and certain consequences is, as we shall see hereafter,[8] a means of producing other consequences. In this lies the difference between rational agency and irrational.

5. Now the intention, with regard to the consequences of an act, will depend upon two things: 1. The state of the will or intention, with respect to the act itself. And, 2, The state of the understanding, or perceptive faculties, with regard to the circumstances which it is, or may appear to be, accompanied with. Now with respect to these circumstances, the perceptive faculty is susceptible of three states: consciousness, unconsciousness, and false consciousness. Consciousness, when the party believes precisely those circumstances, and no others, to subsist, which really do subsist: unconsciousness, when he fails of perceiving certain circumstances to subsist, which, however, do subsist: false consciousness, when he believes or imagines certain circumstances to subsist, which in truth do not subsist.

---

[6] Or of *importance*.

[7] In certain cases the consequences of an act may be material by serving as evidences indicating the existence of some other material fact, which is even *antecedent* to the act of which they are the consequences: but even here, they are material only because, in virtue of such their evidentiary quality, they have an influence, at a subsequent period of time, in the production of pain and pleasure: for example, by serving as grounds for conviction, and thence for punishment. See tit. [Simple Falsehoods], *verbo* [material].

[8] See B. I. tit. [Exemptions] and tit. [Extenuations].

6. In every transaction, therefore, which is examined with a view to punishment, there are four articles to be considered: 1. The *act* itself, which is done. 2. The *circumstances* in which it is done. 3. The *intentionality* that may have accompanied it. 4. The *consciousness,* unconsciousness, or false consciousness, that may have accompanied it.

What regards the act and the circumstances will be the subject of the present chapter: what regards intention and consciousness, that of the two succeeding.

7. There are also two other articles on which the general tendency of an act depends: and on that, as well as on other accounts, the demand which it creates for punishment. These are, 1. The particular *motive* or motives which gave birth to it. 2. The general *disposition* which it indicates. These articles will be the subject of two other chapters.

8. Acts may be distinguished in several ways, for several purposes.

They may be distinguished, in the first place, into *positive* and *negative*. By positive are meant such as consist in motion or exertion: by negative, such as consist in keeping at rest; that is, in forbearing to move or exert one's self in such and such circumstances. Thus, to strike is a positive act: not to strike on a certain occasion, a negative one. Positive acts are styled also acts of commission; negative, acts of omission or forbearance.[9]

9. Such acts, again, as are negative, may either be *absolutely* so, or *relatively*: absolutely, when they import the negation of all positive agency whatsoever; for instance, not to strike at all: relatively, when they import the negation of such or such a particular mode of agency; for instance, not to strike such a person or such a thing, or in such a direction.

10. It is to be observed, that the nature of the act, whether positive or negative, is not to be determined immediately by the form of the discourse made use of to express it. An act which is positive in its nature may be characterized by a negative expression: thus, not to be at rest, is as much as to say to move. So also an act, which is negative in its nature, may be characterized by a positive expression: thus, to forbear or omit to bring food to a person in certain circumstances, is signified by the single and positive term *to starve*.

11. In the second place, acts may be distinguished into *external* and *internal*. By external, are meant corporal acts; acts of the body: by internal, mental acts; acts of the mind. Thus, to strike is an external or exterior[10] act: to intend to strike, an internal or interior one.

12. Acts of *discourse* are a sort of mixture of the two: external acts, which are no ways material, nor attend with any consequences, any farther than as they serve to express the existence of internal ones. To speak to another to strike, to write to him to strike, to make signs to him to strike, are all so many acts of discourse.

13. Third, Acts that are external may be distinguished into *transitive* and *intransitive*. Acts may be called transitive, when the motion is communicated from the person of the agent to some foreign body: that is, to such a foreign body on which the effects of it are considered as being *material*; as where a man runs against you, or throws water in your face. Acts may be called intransitive, when the motion is communicated to no other body, on which the effects of it are regarded as material, than some part of the same person in whom it originated: as where a man runs, or washes himself.[11]

---

[9] The distinction between positive and negative acts runs through the whole system of offences, and sometimes makes a material difference with regard to their consequences. To reconcile us the better to the extensive, and, as it may appear on some occasions, the inconsistent signification here given to the word *act*, it may be considered, 1. That in many cases, where no exterior or overt act is exercised, the state which the mind is in at the time when the supposed act is said to happen, is as truly and directly the result of the will, as any exterior act, how plain and conspicuous soever. The not revealing a conspiracy, for instance, may be as perfectly the act of the will, as the joining in it. In the next place, that even though the mind should never have had the incident in question in contemplation (insomuch that the event of its not happening should not have been so much as obliquely intentional) still the state of the person's mind was in at the time when, if he *had* so willed, the incident might have happened, is in many cases productive of as material consequences; and not only as likely, but as fit to call for the interposition of other agents, as

the opposite one. Thus, when a tax is imposed, your not paying it is an act which at any rate must be punished in a certain manner, whether you happened to think of paying it or not.

[10] An exterior act is also called by lawyers *overt*.

[11] The distinction is well known to the latter grammarians:

14. An act of the transitive kind may be said to be in its *commencement*, or in the *first* stage of its progress, while the motion is confined to the person of the agent, and has not yet been communicated to any foreign body, on which the effects of it can be material. It may be said to be in its *termination*, or to be in the last stage of its progress, as soon as the motion or impulse has been communicated to some such foreign body. It may be said to be in the *middle* or intermediate stage or stages of its progress, while the motion, having passed from the person of the agent, has not yet been communicated to any such foreign body. Thus, as soon as a man has lifted up his hand to strike, the act he performs in striking you is in its commencement: as soon as his hand has reached you, it is in its termination. If the act be the motion of a body which is separated from the person of the agent before it reaches the object, it may be said, during that interval, to be in its intermediate progress,[12] or in *gradu mediativo*: as in the case where a man throws a stone or fires a bullet at you.

15. An act of the *in*transitive kind may be said to be in its commencement, when the motion or impulse is as yet confined to the member or organ in which it originated; and has not yet been communicated to any member or organ that is distinguishable from the former. It may be said to be in its termination, as soon as it has been applied to any other part of the same person. Thus, where a man poisons himself, while he is lifting up the poison to his mouth, the act is in its commencement: as soon as it has reached his lips, it is in its termination.[13]

16. In the third place, acts may be distinguished into *transient* and *continued*. Thus, to strike is a transient act: to lean, a continued one. To buy, a transient act: to keep in one's possession, a continued one.

17. In strictness of speech there is a difference between a *continued* act and a *repetition* of acts. It is a repetition of acts, when there are intervals filled up by acts of different natures: a continued act, when there are no such intervals. Thus, to lean, is one continued act: to keep striking, a repetition of acts.

18. There is a difference, again, between a *repetition* of acts, and a *habit* or *practice*. The term repetition of acts may be employed, let the acts in question be separated by ever such short intervals, and let the sum total of them occupy ever so short a space of time. The term habit is not employed but when the acts in question are supposed to be separated by long-continued intervals, and the sum total of them to occupy a considerable space of time. It is not (for instance) the drinking ever so many times, nor ever so much at a time, in the course of the same sitting, that will constitute a habit of drunkenness: it is necessary that such sittings themselves be frequently repeated. Every habit is a repetition of acts; or, to speak more strictly, when a man has frequently repeated such and such acts after considerable intervals, he is said to have persevered in or contracted a habit: but every repetition of acts is not a habit.[14]

19. Fourth, acts may be distinguished into *indivisible* and *divisible*. Indivisible acts are merely imaginary: they may be easily conceived, but can never be known to be exemplified. Such as are divisible may be so, with regard either to matter or to motion. An act indivisible with regard to matter, is the motion or rest of one single atom of matter. An act indivisible, with regard to motion, is the motion of any body, from one single atom of space to the next to it.

Fifth, acts may be distinguished into *simple* and *complex*: simple, such as the act of striking, the act of leaning, or the act of drinking, above instanced: complex, consisting each of a multitude of simple acts,

---

it is with them indeed that it took its rise: though by them it has been applied rather to the names than to the things themselves. To verbs, signifying transitive acts, as here described, they have given the name of transitive verbs: those significative of intransitive acts they have termed intransitive. These last are still more frequently called *neuter*; that is, *neither* active nor passive. The appellation seems improper: since, instead of their being *neither*, they are both in one.

To the class of acts that are here termed intransitive, belong those which constitute the 3rd class in the system of offences. See Chap. [Division] and B. I. tit. [Self regarding Offences].

[12] Or *in its migration*, or *in transitu*.

[13] These distinctions will be referred to in the next chapter: Chap. viii. [Intentionality]: and applied to practice in B. I. tit. [Extenuations].

[14] A habit, it should seem, can hardly in strictness be termed an aggregate of acts: acts being a sort of real archetypal entities, and habits a kind of fictitious entities or imaginary beings, supposed to be constituted by, or to result as it were out of, the former.

which, though numerous and heterogeneous, derive a sort of unity from the relation they bear to some common design or end; such as the act of giving a dinner, the act of maintaining a child, the act of exhibiting a triumph, the act of bearing arms, the act of holding a court, and so forth.

20.   It has been every now and then made a question, what it is in such a case that constitutes *one* act: where one act has ended, and another act has begun: whether what has happened has been one act or many.[15] These questions, it is now evident, may frequently be answered, with equal propriety, in opposite ways: and if there be any occasion on which they can be answered only in one way, the answer will depend upon the nature of the occasion, and the purpose for which the question is proposed. A man is wounded in two fingers at one stroke—Is it one wound or several? A man is beaten at 12 o'clock, and again at 8 minutes after 12—Is it one beating or several? You beat one man, and instantly in the same breath you beat another—Is this one beating or several? In any of these cases it may be *one*, perhaps, as to some purposes, and *several* as to others. These examples are given, that men may be aware of the ambiguity of language: and neither harass themselves with unsolvable doubts, nor one another with interminable disputes.

21.   So much with regard to acts considered in themselves: we come now to speak of the *circumstances* with which they may have been accompanied. These must necessarily be taken into the account before any thing can be determined relative to the consequences. What the consequences of an act may be upon the whole can never otherwise be ascertained: it can never be known whether it is beneficial, or indifferent, or mischievous. In some circumstances even to kill a man may be a beneficial act: in others, to set food before him may be a pernicious one.

22.   Now the circumstances of an act, are, what? Any objects[16] whatsoever. Take any act whatsoever, there is nothing in the nature of things that excludes any imaginable object from being a circumstance to

it. Any given object may be a circumstance to any other.[17]

23.   We have already had occasion to make mention for a moment of the *consequences* of an act: these were distinguished into material and immaterial. In like manner may the circumstances of it be distinguished. Now *materiality* is a relative term: applied to the consequences of an act, it bore relation to pain and pleasure: applied to the circumstances, it bears relation to the consequences. A circumstance may be said to be material, when it bears a visible relation in point of causality to the consequences: immaterial, when it bears no such visible relation.

24.   The consequences of an act are events.[18] A circumstance may be related to an event in point of causality in any one of four ways: 1. In the way of causation or production. 2. In the way of derivation. 3. In the way of collateral connexion. 4. In the way of conjunct influence. It may be said to be related to the event in the way of causation, when it is of the number of those that contribute to the production of such event: in the way of derivation, when it is of the number of the events to the production of which that in question has been contributory: in the way of collateral connexion, where the circumstances in question, and the event in question, without being either of them instrumental in the production of the other, are related, each of them, to some common object, which has been concerned in the production of them both: in the way of conjunct influence, when, whether related in any other way or not, they have both of them concurred in the production of some common consequence.

25.   An example may be of use. In the year 1628, Villiers, Duke of Buckingham, favourite and minister of

---

[15] Distinctions like these come frequently in question in the course of Procedure.

[16] Or entities. See B. II. tit. [Evidence], § [Facts].

[17] The etymology of the word circumstance is perfectly characteristic of its import: *circum stantia*, things standing round: objects standing round a given object. I forget what mathematician it was that defined God to be a circle, of which the centre is every where, but the circumference no where. In like manner the field of circumstances, belonging to any act, may be defined a circle, of which the circumference is no where, but of which the act in question is the centre. Now then, as any act may, for the purpose of discourse, be considered as a centre, any other act or object whatsoever may be considered as of the number of those that are standing round it.

[18] See B. II. tit. [Evidence], § [Facts].

Charles I. of England, received a wound and died. The man who gave it him was one Felton, who, exasperated at the mal-administration of which that minister was accused, went down from London to Portsmouth, where Buckingham happened then to be, made his way into his antechamber, and finding him busily engaged in conversation with a number of people round him, got close to him, drew a knife and stabbed him. In the effort, the assassin's hat fell off, which was found soon after, and, upon searching him, the bloody knife. In the crown of the hat were found scraps of papers, with sentences expressive of the purpose he was come upon. Here then, suppose the event in question is the wound received by Buckingham: Felton's drawing out his knife, his making his way into the chamber, his going down to Portsmouth, his conceiving an indignation at the idea of Buckingham's administration, that administration itself, Charles's appointing such a minister, and so on, higher and higher without end, are so many circumstances, related to the event of Buckingham's receiving the wound, in the way of causation or production: the bloodiness of the knife, a circumstance related to the same event in the way of derivation: the finding of the hat upon the ground, the finding the sentences in the hat, and the writing them, so many circumstances related to it in the way of collateral connexion: and the situation and conversations of the people about Buckingham, were circumstances related to the circumstances of Felton's making his way into the room, going down to Portsmouth, and so forth, in the way of conjunct influence; inasmuch as they contributed in common to the event of Buckingham's receiving the wound, by preventing him from putting himself upon his guard upon the first appearance of the intruder.[19]

[19] The division may be farther illustrated and confirmed by the more simple and particular case of animal generation. To production corresponds paternity: to derivation, filiation: to collateral connexion, collateral consanguinity: to conjunct influence, marriage and copulation.

If necessary, it might be again illustrated by the material image of a chain, such as that which, according to the ingenious fiction of the ancients, is attached to the throne of Jupiter. A section of this chain should then be exhibited by way of specimen, in the manner of the *diagram* of a pedigree. Such a figure I should accordingly have exhibited, had it not been for the apprehension that an exhibition of this sort,

26.   These several relations do not all of them attach upon an event with equal certainty. In the first place, it is plain, indeed, that every event must have some circumstance or other, and in truth, an indefinite multitude of circumstances, related to it in the way of production: it must of course have a still greater multitude of circumstances related to it in the way of collateral connexion. But it does not appear necessary that every event should have circumstances related to it in the way of derivation: nor therefore that it should have any related to it in the way of conjunct influence. But of the circumstances of all kinds which actually do attach upon an event, it is only a very small number that can be discovered by the utmost exertion of the human faculties: it is a still smaller number that ever actually do attract our notice: when occasion happens, more or fewer of them will be discovered by a man in proportion to the strength, partly of his intellectual powers, partly of his inclination.[20] It appears therefore that the multitude and description of such

while it made the subject a small matter clearer to one man out of a hundred, might, like the mathematical formularies we see sometimes employed for the like purpose, make it more obscure and formidable for the other ninety-nine.

[20] The more remote a connexion of this sort is, of course the more obscure. It will often happen that a connexion, the idea of which would at first sight appear extravagant and absurd, shall be rendered highly probable, and indeed indisputable, merely by the suggestion of a few intermediate circumstances.

At Rome, 390 years before the Christian æra, a goose sets up a cackling: two thousand years afterwards a king of France is murdered. To consider these two events, and nothing more, what can appear more extravagant than the notion that the former of them should have had any influence on the production of the latter? Fill up the gap, bring to mind a few intermediate circumstances, and nothing can appear more probable. It was the cackling of a parcel of geese, at the time the Gauls had surprised the Capitol, that saved the Roman commonwealth: had it not been for the ascendancy that commonwealth acquired afterwards over most of the nations of Europe, amongst others over France, the Christian religion, humanly speaking, could not have established itself in the manner it did in that country. Grant then, that such a man as Henry IV. would have existed, no man, however, would have had those motives, by which Ravaillac, misled by a mischievous notion concerning the dictates of that religion, was prompted to assassinate him.

of the circumstances belonging to an act, as may appear to be material, will be determined by two considerations: 1. By the nature of things themselves. 2. By the strength or weakness of the faculties of those who happen to consider them.

27. Thus much it seemed necessary to premise in general concerning acts, and their circumstances, previously to the consideration of the particular sorts of acts with their particular circumstances, with which we shall have to do in the body of the work. An act of some sort or other is necessarily included in the notion of every offence. Together with this act, under the notion of the same offence, are included certain circumstances: which circumstances enter into the essence of the offence, contribute by their conjunct influence to the production of its consequences, and in conjunction with the act are brought into view by the name by which it stands distinguished. These we shall have occasion to distinguish hereafter by the name of *criminative* circumstances.[21] Other circumstances again entering into combination with the act and the former set of circumstances, are productive of still farther consequences. These additional consequences, if they are of the beneficial kind, bestow, according to the value they bear in that capacity, upon the circumstances to which they owe their birth the appellation of *exculpative*[22] or *extenuative* circumstances:[23] if of the mischievous kind, they bestow on them the appellation of *aggravative* circumstances.[24] Of all these different sets of circumstances, the criminative are connected with the consequences of the original offence, in the way of production; with the act, and with one another, in the way of conjunct influence: the consequences of the original offence with them, and with the act respectively, in the way of derivation: the consequences of the modified offence, with the criminative, exculpative, and extenuative circumstances respectively, in the way also of derivation: these different sets of circumstances, with the consequences of the modified act or offence, in the way of production: and with one another (in respect of the consequences of the modified act or offence) in the way of conjunct influence. Lastly, whatever circumstances can be seen to be connected with the consequences of the offence, whether directly in the way of derivation, or obliquely in the way of collateral affinity (to wit, in virtue of its being connected, in the way of derivation, with some of the circumstances with which they stand connected in the same manner) bear a *material* relation to the offence in the way of evidence, they may accordingly be styled *evidentiary* circumstances, and may become of use, by being held forth upon occasion as so many proofs, indications, or evidences of its having been committed.[25]

CHAPTER XIV

Of the Proportion between Punishments and Offences

1. We have seen that the general object of all laws is to prevent mischief; that is to say, when it is worth while; but that, where there are no other means of doing this than punishment, there are four cases in which it is *not* worth while.

2. When it *is* worth while, there are four subordinate designs or objects, which, in the course of his endeavours to compass, as far as may be, that one general object, a legislator, whose views are governed by the principle of utility, comes naturally to propose to himself.

3. 1. His first, most extensive, and most eligible object, is to prevent, in as far as it is possible, and worth while, all sorts of offences whatsoever:[26] in other words, so to manage, that no offence whatsoever may be committed.

4. 2. But if a man must needs commit an offence of some kind or other, the next object is to induce him to commit an offence *less* mischievous, *rather* than

---

[21] See B. I. tit. [Crim. circumstances].
[22] See B. I. tit. [Extenuations].
[23] See B. I. tit. [Justifications].
[24] See B. I. tit. [Aggravations].

[25] See B. I. tit. [Accessory Offences] and B. II. tit. [Evidence].
It is evident that this analysis is equally applicable to incidents of a purely physical nature, as to those in which moral agency is concerned. If therefore it be just and useful here, it might be found not impossible, perhaps, to find some use for it in natural philosophy.
[26] By *offences* I mean, at present, acts which appear to him to have a tendency to produce mischief.

one *more* mischievous, of two offences that will either of them suit his purpose.

5.   3.   When a man has resolved upon a particular offence, the next object is to dispose him to do *no more* mischief than is *necessary* to his purpose: in other words, to do as little mischief as is consistent with the benefit he has in view.

6.   4.   The last object is, whatever the mischief be, which it is proposed to prevent, to prevent it at as *cheap* a rate as possible.

7.   Subservient to these four objects, or purposes, must be the rules or canons by which the proportion of punishments[27] to offences is to be governed.

8.   Rule 1. The first object, it has been seen, is to prevent, in as far as it is worth while, all sorts of offences; therefore,

The value of the punishment must not be less in any case than what is sufficient to outweigh that of the profit[28] *of the offence.*[29]

If it be, the offence (unless some other considerations, independent of the punishment, should intervene and operate efficaciously in the character of tutelary motives[30]) will be sure to be committed notwithstanding:[31] the whole lot of punishment will be thrown away: it will be altogether *inefficacious.*[32]

9.   The above rule has been often objected to, on account of its seeming harshness: but this can only have happened for want of its being properly understood. The strength of the temptation, *cæteris paribus*, is as the profit of the offence: the quantum of the punishment must rise with the profit of the offence: *cæteris paribus*, it must therefore rise with the strength of the temptation. This there is no disputing. True it is, that the stronger the temptation, the less conclusive is the indication which the act of delinquency affords of

---

[27] The same rules (it is to be observed) may be applied, with little variation, to rewards as well as punishment: in short, to motives in general, which, according as they are of the pleasurable or painful kind, are of the nature of *reward* or *punishment:* and, according as the act they are applied to produce is of the positive or negative kind, are styled impelling or restraining. See Chap. x. [Motives] 47.

[28] By the profit of an offence, is to be understood, not merely the pecuniary profit, but the pleasure or advantage, of whatever kind it be, which a man reaps, or expects to reap, from the gratification of the desire which prompted him to engage in the offence.[a]

It is the profit (that is, the expectation of the profit) of the offence that constitutes the *impelling* motive, or, where there are several, the sum of the impelling motives, by which a man is prompted to engage in the offence. It is the punishment, that is, the expectation of the punishment, that constitutes the *restraining* motive, which, either by itself, or in conjunction with others, is to act upon him in a *contrary* direction, so as to induce him to abstain from engaging in the offence. Accidental circumstances apart, the strength of the temptation is as the force of the seducing, that is, of the impelling motive or motives. To say then, as authors of great merit and great name have said, that the punishment ought not to increase with the strength of the temptation, is as much as to say in mechanics, that the moving force or *momentum* of the *power* need not increase in proportion to the momentum of the *burthen.*

[a] See Chap. x [Motives] §1.

[29] Beccaria, dei diletti, §6, id. trad. par. Morellet, §23.

[30] See Chap. xi. [Dispositions] 29.

[31] It is a well-known adage, though it is to be hoped not a true one, that every man has his price. It is commonly meant of a man's virtue. This saying, though in a very different sense, was strictly verified by some of the Anglo-Saxon laws: by which a fixed price was set, not upon a man's virtue indeed, but upon his life: that of the sovereign himself among the rest. For 200 shillings you might have killed a peasant: for six times as much, a nobleman: for six-and-thirty times as much you might have killed the king.[a] A king in those days was worthy exactly 7,200 shillings. If then the heir to the throne, for example, grew weary of waiting for it, he had a secure and legal way of gratifying his impatience: he had but to kill the king with one hand, and pay himself with the other, and all was right. An earl Godwin, or a duke Streon, could have bought the lives of a whole dynasty. It is plain, that if ever a king in those days died in his bed, he must have had something else, besides this law, to thank for it. This being the production of a remote and barbarous age, the absurdity of it is presently recognized: but, upon examination, it would be found, that the freshest laws of the most civilized nations are continually falling into the same error.[b] This, in short, is the case wheresoever the punishment is fixed while the profit of delinquency is indefinite: or, to speak more precisely, where the punishment is limited to such a mark, that the profit of delinquency may reach beyond it.

[a] Wilkins' Leg. Anglo-Sax. p. 71, 72. See Hume, Vol. I, App. I. p. 219.

[b] See in particular the *English Statute laws* throughout, *Bonaparte's* Penal Code, and the recently enacted or not enacted *Spanish* Penal Code.—*Note by the Author, July* 1822.

[32] See Chap. xiii. [Cases unmeet], §1.

the depravity of the offender's disposition.[33] So far then as the absence of any aggravation, arising from extraordinary depravity of disposition, may operate, or at the utmost, so far as the presence of a ground of extenuation, resulting from the innocence or beneficence of the offender's disposition, can operate, the strength of the temptation may operate in abatement of the demand for punishment. But it can never operate so far as to indicate the propriety of making the punishment ineffectual, which it is sure to be when brought below the level of the apparent profit of the offence.

The partial benevolence which should prevail for the reduction of it below this level, would counteract as well those purposes which such a motive would actually have in view, as those more extensive purposes which benevolence ought to have in view: it would be cruelty not only to the public, but to the very persons in whose behalf it pleads: in its effects, I mean, however opposite in its intention. Cruelty to the public, that is cruelty to the innocent, by suffering them, for want of an adequate protection, to lie exposed to the mischief of the offence: cruelty even to the offender himself, by punishing him to no purpose, and without the chance of compassing that beneficial end, by which alone the introduction of the evil of punishment is to be justified.

10.   Rule 2. But whether a given offence shall be prevented in a given degree by a given quantity of punishment, is never any thing better than a chance; for the purchasing of which, whatever punishment is employed, is so much expended in advance. However, for the sake of giving it the better chance of outweighing the profit of the offence,

The greater the mischief of the offence, the greater is the expense, which it may be worth while to be at, in the way of punishment.[34]

11.   Rule 3. The next object is, to induce a man to choose always the least mischievous of two offences; therefore

---

[33] See Chap. xi. [Dispositions], 42.

[34] For example, if it can ever be worth while to be at the expense of so horrible a punishment as that of burning alive, it will be more so in the view of preventing such a crime as that of murder or incendiarism, than in the view of preventing the uttering of a piece of bad money. See B. I. tit. [Defraudment touching the Coin] and [Incendiarism].

Where two offences come in competition, the punishment for the greater offence must be sufficient to induce a man to prefer the less.[35]

12. Rule 4. When a man has resolved upon a particular offence, the next object is, to induce him to do no more mischief than what is necessary for his purpose: therefore

The punishment should be adjusted in such manner to each particular offence, that for every part of the mischief there may be a motive to restrain the offender from giving birth to it.[36]

13.   Rule 5. The last object is, whatever mischief is guarded against, to guard against it at as cheap a rate as possible: therefore

The punishment ought in no case to be more than what is necessary to bring it into conformity with the rules here given.

14.   Rule 6. It is further to be observed, that owing to the different manners and degrees in which persons under different circumstances are affected by the same exciting cause, a punishment which is the same in name will not always either really produce, or even so much as appear to others to produce, in two different persons the same degree of pain: therefore

That the quantity actually inflicted on each individual offender may correspond to the quantity intended

---

[35] Espr. des Loix, L. vi. c. 16.

[36] If any one have any doubt of this, let him conceive the offence to be divided into as many separate offences as there are distinguishable parcels of mischief that result from it. Let it consist, for example, in a man's giving you ten blows, or stealing from you ten shillings. If then, for giving you ten blows, he is punished no more than for giving you five, the giving you five of these ten blows is an offence for which there is no punishment at all: which being understood, as often as a man gives you five blows, he will be sure to give you five more, since he may have the pleasure of giving you these five for nothing. In like manner, if for stealing from you ten shillings, he is punished no more than for stealing five, the stealing of the remaining five of those ten shillings is an offence for which there is no punishment at all. This rule is violated in almost every page of every body of laws I have ever seen.

The profit, it is to be observed, though frequently, is not constantly, proportioned to the mischief: for example, where a thief, along with the things he covets, steals others which are of no use to him. This may happen through wantonness, indolence, precipitation, &c. &c.

for similar offenders in general, the several circumstances influencing sensibility ought always to be taken into account.[37]

15.   Of the above rules of proportion, the four first, we may perceive, serve to mark out the limits on the side of diminution; the limits *below* which a punishment ought not to be *diminished:* the fifth, the limits on the side of increase; the limits *above* which it ought not to be *increased.* The five first are calculated to serve as guides to the legislator: the sixth is calculated, in some measure, indeed, for the same purpose; but principally for guiding the judge in his endeavours to conform, on both sides, to the intentions of the legislator.

16.   Let us look back a little. The first rule, in order to render it more conveniently applicable to practice, may need perhaps to be a little more particularly unfolded. It is to be observed, then, that for the sake of accuracy, it was necessary, instead of the word *quantity* to make use of the less perspicuous term *value.* For the word *quantity* will not properly include the circumstances either of certainty or proximity: circumstances which, in estimating the value of a lot of pain or pleasure, must always be taken into the account.[38] Now, on the one hand, a lot of punishment is a lot of pain; on the other hand, the profit of an offence is a lot of pleasure, or what is equivalent to it. But the profit of the offence is commonly more *certain* than the punishment, or, what comes to the same thing, *appears* so at least to the offender. It is at any rate commonly more *immediate.* It follows, therefore, that, in order to maintain its superiority over the profit of the offence, the punishment must have its value made up in some other way, in proportion to that whereby it falls short in the two points of *certainty* and *proximity.* Now there is no other way in which it can receive any addition to its *value,* but by receiving an addition in point of *magnitude.* Wherever then the value of the punishment falls short, either in point of *certainty,* or of *proximity,* of that of the profit of the offence, it must receive a proportionable addition in point of *magnitude.*[39]

17.   Yet farther. To make sure of giving the value of the punishment the superiority over that of the offence, it may be necessary, in some cases, to take into the account the profit not only of the *individual* offence to which the punishment is to be annexed, but also of such *other* offences of the *same sort* as the offender is likely to have already committed without detection. This random mode of calculation, severe as it is, it will be impossible to avoid having recourse to, in certain cases: in such, to wit, in which the profit is pecuniary, the chance of detection very small, and the obnoxious act of such a nature as indicates a habit: for example, in the case of frauds against the coin. If it be *not* recurred to, the practice of committing the offence will be sure to be, upon the balance of the account, a gainful practice. That being the case, the legislator will be absolutely sure of *not* being able to suppress it, and the whole punishment that is bestowed upon it will be thrown away. In a word (to keep to the same expressions we set out with) that whole quantity of punishment will be *inefficacious.*

18.   Rule 7. These things being considered, the three following rules may be laid down by way of supplement and explanation to Rule 1.

To enable the value of the punishment to outweigh that of the profit of the offence, it must be increased, in point of magnitude, in proportion as it falls short in point of certainty.

19.   Rule 8. *Punishment must be further increased in point of magnitude, in proportion as it falls short in point of proximity.*

20.   Rule 9. *Where the act is conclusively indicative of a habit, such an increase must be given to the punishment as may enable it to outweigh the profit not only of the individual offence, but of such other like offences as are likely to have been committed with impunity by the same offender.*

21.   There may be a few other circumstances or considerations which may influence, in some small degree, the demand for punishment: but as the propriety of these is either not so demonstrable, or not so constant, or the application of them not so determinate, as that of the foregoing, it may be doubted whether they be worth putting on a level with the others.

22.   Rule 10. *When a punishment, which in point of quality is particularly well calculated to answer its*

[37] See Chap. vi. [Sensibility].

[38] See Chap. iv. [Value].

[39] It is for this reason, for example, that simple compensation is never looked upon as sufficient punishment for theft or robbery.

intention, *cannot exist in less than a certain quantity,*
it may sometimes be of use, for the sake of employing it,
to stretch a little beyond that quantity which, on other
accounts, would be strictly necessary.

23.   Rule 11. *In particular, this may sometimes be*
the case, where the punishment proposed is of such a
nature as to be particularly well calculated to answer
the purpose of a moral lesson.[40]

24.   Rule 12. The tendency of the above considerations is to dictate an augmentation in the punishment: the following rule operates in the way of
diminution. There are certain cases (it has been seen[41])
in which, by the influence of accidental circumstances, punishment may be rendered unprofitable in
the whole: in the same cases it may chance to be rendered unprofitable as to a part only. Accordingly,

In adjusting the quantum of punishment, the cir-
cumstances, by which all punishment may be rendered
unprofitable, ought to be attended to.

25.   Rule 13. It is to be observed, that the more
various and minute any set of provisions are, the
greater the chance is that any article in them will not
be borne in mind: without which, no benefit can ensue from it. Distinctions, which are more complex
than what the conceptions of those whose conduct it
is designed to influence can take in, will even be worse
than useless. The whole system will present a confused appearance: and thus the effect, not only of the
proportions established by the articles in question, but
of whatever is connected with them, will be de-

stroyed.[42] To draw a precise line of direction in such
case seems impossible. However, by way of memento,
it may be of some use to subjoin the following rule.

Among provisions designed to perfect the proportion
between punishments and offences, if any occur, which,
by their own particular good effects, would not make up
for the harm they would do by adding to the intricacy
of the Code, they should be omitted.[43]

26.   It may be remembered, that the political
sanction, being that to which the sort of punishment
belongs, which in this chapter is all along in view, is
but one of four sanctions, which may all of them contribute their share towards producing the same effects.
It may be expected, therefore, that in adjusting the
quantity of political punishment, allowance should be
made for the assistance it may meet with from those
other controlling powers. True it is, that from each of
these several sources a very powerful assistance may
sometimes be derived. But the case is, that (setting
aside the moral sanction, in the case where the force
of it is expressly adopted into and modified by the political[44]) the force of those other powers is never determinate enough to be depended upon. It can never
be reduced, like political punishment, into exact lots,
nor meted out in number, quantity, and value. The
legislator is therefore obliged to provide the full complement of punishment, as if he were sure of not receiving any assistance whatever from any of those
quarters. If he does, so much the better: but lest he
should not, it is necessary he should, at all events,
make that provision which depends upon himself.

27.   It may be of use, in this place, to recapitulate
the several circumstances, which, in establishing the
proportion betwixt punishments and offences, are to
be attended to. These seem to be as follows:

---

[40] A punishment may be said to be calculated to answer the
purpose of a moral lesson, when, by reason of the ignominy
it stamps upon the offence, it is calculated to inspire the public with sentiments of aversion towards those pernicious
habits and dispositions with which the offence appears to be
connected; and thereby to inculcate the opposite beneficial
habits and dispositions.

It is this, for example, if any thing, that must justify the application of so severe a punishment as the infamy of a public exhibition, hereinafter proposed, for him who lifts up his
hand against a woman, or against his father. See B. I. tit.
[Simp. corporal injuries].

It is partly on this principle, I suppose, that military legislators have justified to themselves the inflicting death on the
soldier who lifts up his hand against his superior officer.

[41] See Chap. xiii. [Cases unmeet], §4.

[42] See B. II. tit. [Purposes], Append. tit. [Composition].

[43] Notwithstanding this rule, my fear is, that in the ensuing
model, I may be thought to have carried my endeavours at
proportionality too far. Hitherto scarce any attention has
been paid to it. Montesquieu seems to have been almost the
first who has had the least idea of any such thing. In such a
matter, therefore, excess seemed more eligible than defect.
The difficulty is to invent: that done, if any thing seems superfluous, it is easy to retrench.

[44] See B. I. tit. [Punishments].

1.   *On the part of the offence:*

1. The profit of the offence;
2. The mischief of the offence;
3. The profit and mischief of other greater or lesser offences, of different sorts, which the offender may have to choose out of;
4. The profit and mischief of other offences, of the same sort, which the same offender may probably have been guilty of already.

2.   *On the part of the punishment:*

5. The magnitude of the punishment: composed of its intensity and duration;
6. The deficiency of the punishment in point of certainty;
7. The deficiency of the punishment in point of proximity;
8. The quality of the punishment;
9. The accidental advantage in point of quality of a punishment, not strictly needed in point of quantity;
10. The use of a punishment of a particular quality, in the character of a moral lesson.

3.   *On the part of the offender:*

11. The responsibility of the class of persons in a way to offend;
12. The sensibility of each particular offender;
13. The particular merits or useful qualities of any particular offender, in case of a punishment which might deprive the community of the benefit of them;
14. The multitude of offenders on any particular occasion.

4.   *On the part of the public,* at any particular conjuncture:

15. The inclinations of the people, for or against any quantity or mode of punishment;

16. The inclinations of foreign powers.

5.   *On the part of the law;* that is, of the public for a continuance:

17. The necessity of making small sacrifices, in point of proportionality, for the sake of simplicity.

28.   There are some, perhaps, who, at first sight, may look upon the nicety employed in the adjustment of such rules, as so much labour lost: for gross ignorance, they will say, never troubles itself about laws, and passion does not calculate. But the evil of ignorance admits of cure:[45] and as to the proposition that passion does not calculate this, like most of these very general and oracular propositions, is not true. When matters of such importance as pain and pleasure are at stake, and these in the highest degree (the only matters, in short, that can be of importance) who is there that does not calculate? Men calculate, some with less exactness, indeed, some with more: but all men calculate. I would not say, that even a madman does not calculate.[46] Passion calculates, more or less, in every man: in different men, according to the warmth or coolness of their dispositions: according to the firmness or irritability of their minds: according to the nature of the motives by which they are acted upon. Happily, of all passions, that is the most given to calculation, from the excesses of which, by reason of its strength, constancy, and universality, society has most to apprend:[47] I mean that which corresponds to the motive of pecuniary interest: so that these niceties, if such they are to be called, have the best chance of being efficacious, where efficacy is of the most importance.

---

[45] See Append. tit. [Promulgation].

[46] There are few madmen but what are observed to be afraid of the strait waistcoat.

[47] See Chap. xii. [Consequences], 33.

MILL
On Liberty

*The grand, leading principle, towards which every
argument unfolded in these pages directly converges,
is the absolute and essential importance of human
development in its richest diversity.*

—Wilhelm von Humboldt:
Sphere and Duties of Government.

To the beloved and deplored memory of her who was
the inspirer, and in part the author, of all that is best in
my writings—the friend and wife whose exalted sense
of truth and right was my strongest incitement, and
whose approbation was my chief reward—I dedicate
this volume. Like all that I have written for many years,
it belongs as much to her as to me; but the work as it
stands has had, in a very insufficient degree, the inestimable advantage of her revision; some of the most
important portions having been reserved for a more
careful re-examination, which they are now never destined to receive. Were I but capable of interpreting to
the world one half the great thoughts and noble feelings which are buried in her grave, I should be the
medium of a greater benefit to it, than is ever likely to

This edition of *On Liberty* was drawn from the 1869 4th edition Longmans, Green, Reader, and Dyer.

arise from anything that I can write, unprompted and
unassisted by her all but unrivalled wisdom.

ON LIBERTY

Chapter I: Introductory

The subject of this Essay is not the so-called Liberty of
the Will, so unfortunately opposed to the misnamed
doctrine of Philosophical Necessity; but Civil, or Social Liberty: the nature and limits of the power which
can be legitimately exercised by society over the individual. A question seldom stated, and hardly ever discussed, in general terms, but which profoundly
influences the practical controversies of the age by its
latent presence, and is likely soon to make itself recognised as the vital question of the future. It is so far from
being new, that, in a certain sense, it has divided
mankind, almost from the remotest ages; but in the
stage of progress into which the more civilized portions of the species have now entered, it presents itself
under new conditions, and requires a different and
more fundamental treatment.

The struggle between Liberty and Authority is the
most conspicuous feature in the portions of history
with which we are earliest familiar, particularly in that
of Greece, Rome, and England. But in old times this
contest was between subjects, or some classes of subjects, and the Government. By liberty, was meant protection against the tyranny of the political rulers. The
rulers were conceived (except in some of the popular
governments of Greece) as in a necessarily antagonistic position to the people whom they ruled. They consisted of a governing One, or a governing tribe or caste,
who derived their authority from inheritance or conquest, who, at all events, did not hold it at the pleasure
of the governed, and whose supremacy men did not

venture, perhaps did not desire, to contest, whatever precautions might be taken against its oppressive exercise. Their power was regarded as necessary, but also as highly dangerous; as a weapon which they would attempt to use against their subjects, no less than against external enemies. To prevent the weaker members of the community from being preyed upon by innumerable vultures, it was needful that there should be an animal of prey stronger than the rest, commissioned to keep them down. But as the king of the vultures would be no less bent upon preying on the flock than any of the minor harpies, it was indispensable to be in a perpetual attitude of defence against his beak and claws. The aim, therefore, of patriots was to set limits to the power which the ruler should be suffered to exercise over the community; and this limitation was what they meant by liberty. It was attempted in two ways. First, by obtaining a recognition of certain immunities, called political liberties or rights, which it was to be regarded as a breach of duty in the ruler to infringe, and which if he did infringe, specific resistance, or general rebellion, was held to be justifiable. A second, and generally a later expedient, was the establishment of constitutional checks, by which the consent of the community, or of a body of some sort, supposed to represent its interests, was made a necessary condition to some of the more important acts of the governing power. To the first of these modes of limitation, the ruling power, in most European countries, was compelled, more or less, to submit. It was not so with the second; and, to attain this, or when already in some degree possessed, to attain it more completely, became everywhere the principal object of the lovers of liberty. And so long as mankind were content to combat one enemy by another, and to be ruled by a master, on condition of being guaranteed more or less efficaciously against his tyranny, they did not carry their aspirations beyond this point.

A time, however, came, in the progress of human affairs, when men ceased to think it a necessity of nature that their governors should be an independent power, opposed in interest to themselves. It appeared to them much better that the various magistrates of the State should be their tenants or delegates, revocable at their pleasure. In that way alone, it seemed, could they have complete security that the powers of government would never be abused to their disadvantage. By degrees this new demand for elective and temporary rulers became the prominent object of the exertions of the popular party, wherever any such party existed; and superseded, to a considerable extent, the previous efforts to limit the power of rulers. As the struggle proceeded for making the ruling power emanate from the periodical choice of the ruled, some persons began to think that too much importance had been attached to the limitation of the power itself. *That* (it might seem) was a resource against rulers whose interests were habitually opposed to those of the people. What was now wanted was, that the rulers should be identified with the people; that their interest and will should be the interest and will of the nation. The nation did not need to be protected against its own will. There was no fear of its tyrannizing over itself. Let the rulers be effectually responsible to it, promptly removable by it, and it could afford to trust them with power of which it could itself dictate the use to be made. Their power was but the nation's own power, concentrated, and in a form convenient for exercise. This mode of thought, or rather perhaps of feeling, was common among the last generation of European liberalism, in the Continental section of which it still apparently predominates. Those who admit any limit to what a government may do, except in the case of such governments as they think ought not to exist, stand out as brilliant exceptions among the political thinkers of the Continent. A similar tone of sentiment might by this time have been prevalent in our own country, if the circumstances which for a time encouraged it, had continued unaltered.

But, in political and philosophical theories, as well as in persons, success discloses faults and infirmities which failure might have concealed from observation. The notion, that the people have no need to limit their power over themselves, might seem axiomatic, when popular government was a thing only dreamed about, or read of as having existed at some distant period of the past. Neither was that notion necessarily disturbed by such temporary aberrations as those of the French Revolution, the worst of which were the work of an usurping few, and which, in any case, belonged, not to the permanent working of popular institutions, but to a sudden and convulsive outbreak against monarchical and aristocratic despotism. In time, however, a democratic republic came to occupy a large portion of the earth's surface, and made itself felt as one of the most powerful members of the community of nations; and elective and responsible government became subject to the observations and criticisms which wait upon a great existing fact. It was now perceived that such phrases as 'self-government,' and 'the power of the people over themselves,' do not express the true state of the case. The 'people' who exercise the power are not always the same people with those over whom it is exercised; and the 'self-government' spoken of is not the government of each by himself, but of each by all the rest. The will of the people, moreover, practically means the will of the most numerous or the most active *part* of the people; the majority, or those who succeed in making themselves accepted as the majority; the people, consequently, *may* desire to oppress a part of their number; and precautions are as much needed against this as against any other abuse of power. The limitation, therefore, of the power of government over individuals loses none of its importance when the holders of power are regularly accountable to the community, that is, to the strongest party therein. This view of things, recommending itself equally to the intelligence of thinkers and to the inclination of those important classes in European society to whose real or supposed interests democracy is adverse, has had no difficulty in establishing itself; and in political speculations 'the tyranny of the majority' is now generally included among the evils against which society requires to be on its guard.

Like other tyrannies, the tyranny of the majority was at first, and is still vulgarly, held in dread, chiefly as operating through the acts of the public authorities. But reflecting persons perceived that when society is itself the tyrant—society collectively, over the separate individuals who compose it—its means of tyrannizing are not restricted to the acts which it may do by the hands of its political functionaries. Society can and does execute its own mandates: and if it issues wrong mandates instead of right, or any mandates at all in things with which it ought not to meddle, it practises a social tyranny more formidable than many kinds of political oppression, since, though not usually upheld by such extreme penalties, it leaves fewer means of escape, penetrating much more deeply into the details of life, and enslaving the soul itself. Protection, therefore, against the tyranny of the magistrate is not enough: there needs protection also against the tyranny of the prevailing opinion and feeling; against the tendency of society to impose, by other means than civil penalties, its own ideas and practices as rules of conduct on those who dissent from them; to fetter the development, and, if possible, prevent the formation, of any individuality not in harmony with its ways, and compel all characters to fashion themselves upon the model of its own. There is a limit to the legitimate interference of collective opinion with individual independence: and to find that limit, and maintain it against encroachment, is as indispensable to a good condition of human affairs, as protection against political despotism.

But though this proposition is not likely to be contested in general terms, the practical question, where to place the limit—how to make the fitting adjustment between individual independence and social control—is a subject on which nearly everything remains to be done. All that makes existence valuable to any one, depends on the enforcement of restraints upon the actions of other people. Some rules of conduct, therefore, must be imposed, by law in the first place, and by opinion on many things which are not fit subjects for the operation of law. What these rules should be, is the principal question in human affairs; but if we except a few of the most obvious cases, it is one of those which least progress has been made in resolving. No two ages, and scarcely any two countries, have decided it alike; and the decision of one age or country is a wonder to another. Yet the people of any given age and country no more suspect any difficulty in it, than if it were a subject on which mankind had always been agreed. The rules which obtain among themselves appear to them self-evident and self-justifying. This all but universal illusion is one of the examples of the magical influence of custom, which is not only, as the proverb says, a second nature, but is continually mistaken for the first. The effect of custom, in preventing any misgiving respecting the rules of conduct which mankind impose on one another, is all the more complete because the subject is one on which it is not generally considered necessary that reasons should be given, either by one person to others, or by each to himself. People are accustomed to believe, and have been encouraged in the belief by some who aspire to the character of philosophers, that their feelings, on subjects of this nature, are better than reasons, and render reasons unnecessary. The practical principle which guides them to their opinions on the regulation of human conduct, is the feeling in each person's mind that everybody should be required to act as he, and those with whom he sympathizes, would like them to act. No one, indeed, acknowledges to himself that his standard of judgment is his own liking; but an opinion on a point of conduct, not supported by reasons, can only count as one person's preference; and if the reasons, when given, are a mere appeal to a similar preference felt by other people, it is still only many people's liking instead of one. To an ordinary man, however, his own preference, thus supported, is not only a perfectly satisfactory reason, but the only one he generally has for any of his notions of morality, taste, or propriety, which are not expressly written in his religious creed; and his chief guide in the interpretation even of that. Men's opinions, accordingly, on what is laudable or blameable, are affected by all the multifarious causes which influence their wishes in regard to the conduct of others, and which are as numerous as those which determine their wishes on any other subject. Sometimes their reason—at other times their prejudices or superstitions: often their social affections, not seldom their antisocial ones, their envy or jealousy, their arrogance or contemptuousness: but most commonly, their desires or fears for themselves—their legitimate or illegitimate self-interest. Wherever there is an ascendant class, a large portion of the morality of the country emanates from its class interests, and its feelings of class superiority. The morality between Spartans and Helots, between planters and negroes, between princes and subjects, between nobles and roturiers, between men and women, has been for the most part the creation of these class interests and feelings: and the sentiments thus generated, react in turn upon the moral feelings of the members of the ascendant class, in their relations among themselves. Where, on the other hand, a class, formerly ascendant, has lost its ascendancy, or where its ascendancy is unpopular, the prevailing moral sentiments frequently bear the impress of an impatient dislike of superiority. Another grand determining principle of the rules of conduct, both in act and forbearance, which have been enforced by law or opinion, has been the servility of mankind towards the supposed preferences or aversions of their temporal masters, or of their gods. This servility, though essentially selfish, is not hypocrisy; it gives rise to perfectly genuine sentiments of abhorrence; it made men burn magicians and heretics. Among so many baser influences, the general and obvious interests of society have of course had a share, and a large one, in the direction of the moral sentiments: less, however, as a matter of reason, and on their own account, than as a consequence of the sympathies and antipathies which grew out of them: and sympathies and antipathies which had little or nothing to do with the interests of society, have made themselves felt in the establishment of moralities with quite as great force.

The likings and dislikings of society, or of some powerful portion of it, are thus the main thing which has practically determined the rules laid down for general observance, under the penalties of law or opinion. And in general, those who have been in advance of society in thought and feeling, have left this condition of things unassailed in principle, however they may have come into conflict with it in some of its details. They have occupied themselves rather in inquiring what things society ought to like or dislike, than in questioning whether its likings or dislikings should be a law to individuals. They preferred endeavouring to alter the feelings of mankind on the particular points on which they were themselves heretical, rather than make common cause in defence of freedom, with heretics generally. The only case in which the higher ground has been taken on principle and maintained with consistency, by any but an individual here and there, is that of religious belief: a case instructive in many ways, and not least so as forming a most striking instance of the fallibility of what is called the moral sense: for the *odium theologicum*, in a sincere bigot, is one of the most unequivocal cases of moral feeling. Those who first broke the yoke of what called itself the Universal Church, were in general as little willing to permit difference of religious opinion as that church itself. But when the heat of the conflict was over, without giving a complete victory to any party, and each church or sect was reduced to limit its hopes to retaining possession of the ground it already occupied; minorities, seeing that they had no chance of becoming majorities, were under the necessity of pleading to those whom they could not convert, for permission to differ. It is accordingly on this battle field, almost solely, that the rights of the individual against society have been asserted on broad grounds of principle, and the claim of society to exercise authority over dissentients, openly controverted. The great writers to whom the world owes what religious liberty it possesses, have mostly asserted freedom of conscience as an indefeasible right, and denied absolutely that a human being is accountable to others for his religious belief. Yet so natural to mankind is intolerance in whatever they really care about, that religious freedom has hardly anywhere been practically realized, except where religious indifference, which dislikes to have its peace disturbed by theological quarrels, has added its weight to the scale. In the minds of almost all religious persons, even in the most tolerant countries, the duty of toleration is admitted with tacit reserves. One person will bear with dissent in matters of church government, but not of dogma; another can tolerate everybody, short of a Papist or an Unitarian; another, every one who believes in revealed religion; a few extend their charity a little further, but stop at the belief in a God and in a future state. Wherever the sentiment of the majority is still genuine and intense, it is found to have abated little of its claim to be obeyed.

In England, from the peculiar circumstances of our political history, though the yoke of opinion is perhaps heavier, that of law is lighter, than in most other countries of Europe; and there is considerable jealousy of direct interference, by the legislative or the executive power, with private conduct; not so much from any just regard for the independence of the individual, as from the still subsisting habit of looking on the government as representing an opposite interest to the public. The majority have not yet learnt to feel the power of the government their power, or its opinions their opinions. When they do so, individual liberty will probably be as much exposed to invasion from the government, as it already is from public opinion. But, as yet, there is a considerable amount of feeling ready to be called forth against any attempt of the law to control individuals in things in which they have not hitherto been accustomed to be controlled by it; and this with very little discrimination as to whether the matter is, or is not, within the legitimate sphere of legal control; insomuch that the feeling, highly salutary on the whole, is perhaps quite as often misplaced as well grounded in the particular instances of its application. There is, in fact, no recognised principle by which the propriety or impropriety of government interference is customarily tested. People decide according to their personal preferences. Some, whenever they see any good to be done, or evil to be remedied, would willingly instigate the government to undertake the business; while others prefer to bear almost any amount of social evil, rather than add one to the departments of human interests amenable to governmental control. And men range themselves on one or the other side in any particular case, according to this general direction of their sentiments; or according to the degree of interest which they feel in the particular thing which it is proposed that the government should do, or according to the belief they entertain that the government would, or would not, do it in the manner they prefer; but very rarely on account of any opinion to which they consistently adhere, as to what things are fit to be done by a government. And it seems to me that in consequence of this absence of rule or principle, one side is at present as often wrong as the other; the interference of government is, with about equal frequency, improperly invoked and improperly condemned.

The object of this Essay is to assert one very simple principle, as entitled to govern absolutely the dealings of society with the individual in the way of compulsion and control, whether the means used be physical force in the form of legal penalties, or the moral coercion of public opinion. That principle is, that the sole end for which mankind are warranted, individually or collectively, in interfering with the liberty of action of any of their number, is self-protection. That the only purpose for which power can be rightfully exercised over any member of a civilized community, against his will, is to prevent harm to others. His own good, either physical or moral, is not a sufficient warrant. He cannot rightfully be compelled to do or forbear because it will be better for him to do so, because it will make him happier, because, in the opinions of others, to do so would be wise, or even right. These are good reasons for remonstrating with him, or reasoning with him, or persuading him, or entreating him, but not for compelling him, or visiting him with any evil in case he do otherwise. To justify that, the conduct from which it is desired to deter him, must be calculated to produce evil to some one else. The only part of the conduct of any one, for which he is amenable to society, is that which concerns others. In the part which merely concerns himself, his independence is, of right, absolute. Over himself, over his own body and mind, the individual is sovereign.

It is, perhaps, hardly necessary to say that this doctrine is meant to apply only to human beings in the maturity of their faculties. We are not speaking of children, or of young persons below the age which the law may fix as that of manhood or womanhood. Those who are still in a state to require being taken care of by others, must be protected against their own actions as well as against external injury. For the same reason, we may leave out of consideration those backward states of society in which the race itself may be considered as in its nonage. The early difficulties in the way of spontaneous progress are so great, that there is seldom any choice of means for overcoming them; and a ruler full of the spirit of improvement is warranted in the use of any expedients that will attain an end, perhaps otherwise unattainable. Despotism is a legitimate mode of government in dealing with barbarians, provided the end be their improvement, and the means justified by actually effecting that end. Liberty, as a principle, has no application to any state of things anterior to the time when mankind have become capable of being improved by free and equal discussion. Until then, there is nothing for them but

implicit obedience to an Akbar or a Charlemagne, if they are so fortunate as to find one. But as soon as mankind have attained the capacity of being guided to their own improvement by conviction or persuasion (a period long since reached in all nations with whom we need here concern ourselves), compulsion, either in the direct form or in that of pains and penalties for non-compliance, is no longer admissible as a means to their own good, and justifiable only for the security of others.

It is proper to state that I forego any advantage which could be derived to my argument from the idea of abstract right, as a thing independent of utility. I regard utility as the ultimate appeal on all ethical questions; but it must be utility in the largest sense, grounded on the permanent interests of man as a progressive being. Those interests, I contend, authorize the subjection of individual spontaneity to external control, only in respect to those actions of each, which concern the interest of other people. If any one does an act hurtful to others, there is a *prima facie* case for punishing him, by law, or, where legal penalties are not safely applicable, by general disapprobation. There are also many positive acts for the benefit of others which he may rightfully be compelled to perform; such as, to give evidence in a court of justice; to bear his fair share in the common defence, or in any other joint work necessary to the interest of the society of which he enjoys the protection; and to perform certain acts of individual beneficence, such as saving a fellow-creature's life, or interposing to protect the defenceless against ill-usage, things which whenever it is obviously a man's duty to do, he may rightfully be made responsible to society for not doing. A person may cause evil to others not only by his actions but by his inaction, and in either case he is justly accountable to them for the injury. The latter case, it is true, requires a much more cautious exercise of compulsion than the former. To make any one answerable for doing evil to others, is the rule; to make him answerable for not preventing evil, is, comparatively speaking, the exception. Yet there are many cases clear enough and grave enough to justify that exception. In all things which regard the external relations of the individual, he is *de jure* amenable to those whose interests are concerned, and if need be, to society as their protector. There are often good reasons for not holding him to the responsibility; but these reasons must arise from the special expediencies of the case: either because it is a kind of case in which he is on the whole likely to act better, when left to his own discretion, than when controlled in any way in which society have it in their power to control him; or because the attempt to exercise control would produce other evils, greater than those which it would prevent. When such reasons as these preclude the enforcement of responsibility, the conscience of the agent himself should step into the vacant judgment seat, and protect those interests of others which have no external protection; judging himself all the more rigidly, because the case does not admit of his being made accountable to the judgment of his fellow-creatures.

But there is a sphere of action in which society, as distinguished from the individual, has, if any, only an indirect interest; comprehending all that portion of a person's life and conduct which affects only himself, or if it also affects others, only with their free, voluntary, and undeceived consent and participation. When I say only himself, I mean directly, and in the first instance: for whatever affects himself, may affect others through himself; and the objection which may be grounded on this contingency, will receive consideration in the sequel. This, then, is the appropriate region of human liberty. It comprises, first, the inward domain of consciousness; demanding liberty of conscience, in the most comprehensive sense; liberty of thought and feeling; absolute freedom of opinion and sentiment on all subjects, practical or speculative, scientific, moral, or theological. The liberty of expressing and publishing opinions may seem to fall under a different principle, since it belongs to that part of the conduct of an individual which concerns other people; but, being almost of as much importance as the liberty of thought itself, and resting in great part on the same reasons, is practically inseparable from it. Secondly, the principle requires liberty of tastes and pursuits; of framing the plan of our life to suit our own character; of doing as we like, subject to such consequences as may follow: without impediment from our fellow-creatures, so long as what we do does not harm them,

even though they should think our conduct foolish, perverse, or wrong. Thirdly, from this liberty of each individual, follows the liberty, within the same limits, of combination among individuals; freedom to unite, for any purpose not involving harm to others: the persons combining being supposed to be of full age, and not forced or deceived.

No society in which these liberties are not, on the whole, respected, is free, whatever may be its form of government; and none is completely free in which they do not exist absolute and unqualified. The only freedom which deserves the name, is that of pursuing our own good in our own way, so long as we do not attempt to deprive others of theirs, or impede their efforts to obtain it. Each is the proper guardian of his own health, whether bodily, or mental and spiritual. Mankind are greater gainers by suffering each other to live as seems good to themselves, than by compelling each to live as seems good to the rest.

Though this doctrine is anything but new, and, to some persons, may have the air of a truism, there is no doctrine which stands more directly opposed to the general tendency of existing opinion and practice. Society has expended fully as much effort in the attempt (according to its lights) to compel people to conform to its notions of personal, as of social excellence. The ancient commonwealths thought themselves entitled to practise, and the ancient philosophers countenanced, the regulation of every part of private conduct by public authority, on the ground that the State had a deep interest in the whole bodily and mental discipline of every one of its citizens; a mode of thinking which may have been admissible in small republics surrounded by powerful enemies, in constant peril of being subverted by foreign attack or internal commotion, and to which even a short interval of relaxed energy and self-command might so easily be fatal, that they could not afford to wait for the salutary permanent effects of freedom. In the modern world, the greater size of political communities, and above all, the separation between spiritual and temporal authority (which placed the direction of men's consciences in other hands than those which controlled their worldly affairs), prevented so great an interference by law in the details of private life; but the engines of moral repression have been wielded more strenuously against divergence from the reigning opinion in self-regarding, than even in social matters; religion, the most powerful of the elements which have entered into the formation of moral feeling, having almost always been governed either by the ambition of a hierarchy, seeking control over every department of human conduct, or by the spirit of Puritanism. And some of those modern reformers who have placed themselves in strongest opposition to the religions of the past, have been no way behind either churches or sects in their assertion of the right of spiritual domination: M. Comte, in particular, whose social system, as unfolded in his *Système de Politique Positive*, aims at establishing (though by moral more than by legal appliances) a despotism of society over the individual, surpassing anything contemplated in the political ideal of the most rigid disciplinarian among the ancient philosophers.

Apart from the peculiar tenets of individual thinkers, there is also in the world at large an increasing inclination to stretch unduly the powers of society over the individual, both by the force of opinion and even by that of legislation: and as the tendency of all the changes taking place in the world is to strengthen society, and diminish the power of the individual, this encroachment is not one of the evils which tend spontaneously to disappear, but, on the contrary, to grow more and more formidable. The disposition of mankind, whether as rulers or as fellow-citizens, to impose their own opinions and inclinations as a rule of conduct on others, is so energetically supported by some of the best and by some of the worst feelings incident to human nature, that it is hardly ever kept under restraint by anything but want of power; and as the power is not declining, but growing, unless a strong barrier of moral conviction can be raised against the mischief, we must expect, in the present circumstances of the world, to see it increase.

It will be convenient for the argument, if, instead of at once entering upon the general thesis, we confine ourselves in the first instance to a single branch of it, on which the principle here stated is, if not fully, yet to a certain point, recognised by the current opinions. This one branch is the Liberty of Thought: from

which it is impossible to separate the cognate liberty of speaking and of writing. Although these liberties, to some considerable amount, form part of the political morality of all countries which profess religious toleration and free institutions, the grounds, both philosophical and practical, on which they rest, are perhaps not so familiar to the general mind, nor so thoroughly appreciated by many even of the leaders of opinion, as might have been expected. Those grounds, when rightly understood, are of much wider application than to only one division of the subject, and a thorough consideration of this part of the question will be found the best introduction to the remainder. Those to whom nothing which I am about to say will be new, may therefore, I hope, excuse me, if on a subject which for now three centuries has been so often discussed, I venture on one discussion more.

Chapter II: Of the Liberty of Thought and Discussion

The time, it is to be hoped, is gone by, when any defence would be necessary of the 'liberty of the press' as one of the securities against corrupt or tyrannical government. No argument, we may suppose, can now be needed, against permitting a legislature or an executive, not identified in interest with the people, to prescribe opinions to them, and determine what doctrines or what arguments they shall be allowed to hear. This aspect of the question, besides, has been so often and so triumphantly enforced by preceding writers, that it needs not be specially insisted on in this place. Though the law of England, on the subject of the press, is as servile to this day as it was in the time of the Tudors, there is little danger of its being actually put in force against political discussion, except during some temporary panic, when fear of insurrection drives ministers and judges from their propriety;[1] and,

---

[1] These words had scarcely been written, when, as if to give them an emphatic contradiction, occurred the Government Press Prosecutions of 1858. That ill-judged interference with the liberty of public discussion has not, however, induced me to alter a single word in the text, nor has it at all weakened my conviction that, moments of panic excepted, the

speaking generally, it is not, in constitutional countries, to be apprehended, that the government, whether completely responsible to the people or not, will often attempt to control the expression of opinion, except when in doing so it makes itself the organ of the general intolerance of the public. Let us suppose, therefore, that the government is entirely at one with the people, and never thinks of exerting any power of coercion unless in agreement with what it conceives to be their voice. But I deny the right of the people to exercise such coercion, either by themselves or by their government. The power itself is illegitimate. The best government has no more title to it than the worst. It is as noxious, or more noxious, when exerted in accordance with public opinion, than when in opposition to it. If all mankind minus one, were of one opinion, and only one person were of the contrary opinion, mankind would be no more justified in silencing that one person, than he, if he had the power, would be

---

era of pains and penalties for political discussion has, in our own country, passed away. For, in the first place, the prosecutions were not persisted in; and, in the second, they were never, properly speaking, political prosecutions. The offence charged was not that of criticising institutions, or the acts or persons of rulers, but of circulating what was deemed an immoral doctrine, the lawfulness of Tyrannicide.

If the arguments of the present chapter are of any validity, there ought to exist the fullest liberty of professing and discussing, as a matter of ethical conviction, any doctrine, however immoral it may be considered. It would, therefore, be irrelevant and out of place to examine here, whether the doctrine of Tyrannicide deserves that title. I shall content myself with saying that the subject has been at all times one of the open questions of morals; that the act of a private citizen in striking down a criminal, who, by raising himself above the law, has placed himself beyond the reach of legal punishment or control, has been accounted by whole nations, and by some of the best and wisest of men, not a crime, but an act of exalted virtue; and that, right or wrong, it is not of the nature of assassination, but of civil war. As such, I hold that the instigation to it, in a specific case, may be a proper subject of punishment, but only if an overt act has followed, and at least a probable connexion can be established between the act and the instigation. Even then, it is not a foreign government, but the very government assailed, which alone, in the exercise of self-defence, can legitimately punish attacks directed against its own existence.

justified in silencing mankind. Were an opinion a personal possession of no value except to the owner; if to be obstructed in the enjoyment of it were simply a private injury, it would make some difference whether the injury was inflicted only on a few persons or on many. But the peculiar evil of silencing the expression of an opinion is, that it is robbing the human race; posterity as well as the existing generation; those who dissent from the opinion, still more than those who hold it. If the opinion is right, they are deprived of the opportunity of exchanging error for truth: if wrong, they lose, what is almost as great a benefit, the clearer perception and livelier impression of truth, produced by its collision with error.

It is necessary to consider separately these two hypotheses, each of which has a distinct branch of the argument corresponding to it. We can never be sure that the opinion we are endeavouring to stifle is a false opinion; and if we were sure, stifling it would be an evil still.

First: the opinion which it is attempted to suppress by authority may possibly be true. Those who desire to suppress it, of course deny its truth; but they are not infallible. They have no authority to decide the question for all mankind, and exclude every other person from the means of judging. To refuse a hearing to an opinion, because they are sure that it is false, is to assume that *their* certainty is the same thing as *absolute* certainty. All silencing of discussion is an assumption of infallibility. Its condemnation may be allowed to rest on this common argument, not the worse for being common.

Unfortunately for the good sense of mankind, the fact of their fallibility is far from carrying the weight in their practical judgment, which is always allowed to it in theory; for while every one well knows himself to be fallible, few think it necessary to take any precautions against their own fallibility, or admit the supposition that any opinion, of which they feel very certain, may be one of the examples of the error to which they acknowledge themselves to be liable. Absolute princes, or others who are accustomed to unlimited deference, usually feel this complete confidence in their own opinions on nearly all subjects. People more happily situated, who sometimes hear their opinions disputed, and are not wholly unused to be set right when they are wrong, place the same unbounded reliance only on such of their opinions as are shared by all who surround them, or to whom they habitually defer: for in proportion to a man's want of confidence in his own solitary judgment, does he usually repose, with implicit trust, on the infallibility of 'the world' in general. And the world, to each individual, means the part of it with which he comes in contact; his party, his sect, his church, his class of society: the man may be called, by comparison, almost liberal and large-minded to whom it means anything so comprehensive as his own country or his own age. Nor is his faith in this collective authority at all shaken by his being aware that other ages, countries, sects, churches, classes, and parties have thought, and even now think, the exact reverse. He devolves upon his own world the responsibility of being in the right against the dissentient worlds of other people; and it never troubles him that mere accident has decided which of these numerous worlds is the object of his reliance, and that the same causes which make him a Churchman in London, would have made him a Buddhist or a Confucian in Pekin. Yet it is as evident in itself, as any amount of argument can make it, that ages are no more infallible than individuals; every age having held many opinions which subsequent ages have deemed not only false but absurd; and it is as certain that many opinions, now general, will be rejected by future ages, as it is that many, once general, are rejected by the present.

The objection likely to be made to this argument, would probably take some such form as the following. There is no greater assumption of infallibility in forbidding the propagation of error, than in any other thing which is done by public authority on its own judgment and responsibility. Judgment is given to men that they may use it. Because it may be used erroneously, are men to be told that they ought not to use it at all? To prohibit what they think pernicious, is not claiming exemption from error, but fulfilling the duty incumbent on them, although fallible, of acting on their conscientious conviction. If we were never to act on our opinions, because those opinions may be wrong, we should leave all our interests uncared for, and all our duties unperformed. An objection which

applies to all conduct, can be no valid objection to any conduct in particular. It is the duty of governments, and of individuals, to form the truest opinions they can; to form them carefully, and never impose them upon others unless they are quite sure of being right. But when they are sure (such reasoners may say), it is not conscientiousness but cowardice to shrink from acting on their opinions, and allow doctrines which they honestly think dangerous to the welfare of mankind, either in this life or in another, to be scattered abroad without restraint, because other people, in less enlightened times, have persecuted opinions now believed to be true. Let us take care, it may be said, not to make the same mistake: but governments and nations have made mistakes in other things, which are not denied to be fit subjects for the exercise of authority: they have laid on bad taxes, made unjust wars. Ought we therefore to lay on no taxes, and, under whatever provocation, make no wars? Men, and governments, must act to the best of their ability. There is no such thing as absolute certainty, but there is assurance sufficient for the purposes of human life. We may, and must, assume our opinion to be true for the guidance of our own conduct: and it is assuming no more when we forbid bad men to pervert society by the propagation of opinions which we regard as false and pernicious.

I answer, that it is assuming very much more. There is the greatest difference between presuming an opinion to be true, because, with every opportunity for contesting it, it has not been refuted, and assuming its truth for the purpose of not permitting its refutation. Complete liberty of contradicting and disproving our opinion, is the very condition which justifies us in assuming its truth for purposes of action; and on no other terms can a being with human faculties have any rational assurance of being right.

When we consider either the history of opinion, or the ordinary conduct of human life, to what is it to be ascribed that the one and the other are no worse than they are? Not certainly to the inherent force of the human understanding; for, on any matter not self-evident, there are ninety-nine persons totally incapable of judging of it, for one who is capable; and the capacity of the hundredth person is only comparative; for the majority of the eminent men of every past generation held many opinions now known to be erroneous, and did or approved numerous things which no one will now justify. Why is it, then, that there is on the whole a preponderance among mankind of rational opinions and rational conduct? If there really is this preponderance—which there must be unless human affairs are, and have always been, in an almost desperate state—it is owing to a quality of the human mind, the source of everything respectable in man either as an intellectual or as a moral being, namely, that his errors are corrigible. He is capable of rectifying his mistakes, by discussion and experience. Not by experience alone. There must be discussion, to show how experience is to be interpreted. Wrong opinions and practices gradually yield to fact and argument: but facts and arguments, to produce any effect on the mind, must be brought before it. Very few facts are able to tell their own story, without comments to bring out their meaning. The whole strength and value, then, of human judgment, depending on the one property, that it can be set right when it is wrong, reliance can be placed on it only when the means of setting it right are kept constantly at hand. In the case of any person whose judgment is really deserving of confidence, how has it become so? Because he has kept his mind open to criticism of his opinions and conduct. Because it has been his practice to listen to all that could be said against him; to profit by as much of it as was just, and expound to himself, and upon occasion to others, the fallacy of what was fallacious. Because he has felt, that the only way in which a human being can make some approach to knowing the whole of a subject, is by hearing what can be said about it by persons of every variety of opinion, and studying all modes in which it can be looked at by every character of mind. No wise man ever acquired his wisdom in any mode but this; nor is it in the nature of human intellect to become wise in any other manner. The steady habit of correcting and completing his own opinion by collating it with those of others, so far from causing doubt and hesitation in carrying it into practice, is the only stable foundation for a just reliance on it: for, being cognisant of all that can, at least obviously, be said against him, and having taken up his position against all gainsayers—knowing that he has

sought for objections and difficulties, instead of avoiding them, and has shut out no light which can be thrown upon the subject from any quarter—he has a right to think his judgment better than that of any person, or any multitude, who have not gone through a similar process.

It is not too much to require that what the wisest of mankind, those who are best entitled to trust their own judgment, find necessary to warrant their relying on it, should be submitted to by that miscellaneous collection of a few wise and many foolish individuals, called the public. The most intolerant of churches, the Roman Catholic Church, even at the canonization of a saint, admits, and listens patiently to, a 'devil's advocate.' The holiest of men, it appears, cannot be admitted to posthumous honours, until all that the devil could say against him is known and weighed. If even the Newtonian philosophy were not permitted to be questioned, mankind could not feel as complete assurance of its truth as they now do. The beliefs which we have most warrant for, have no safeguard to rest on, but a standing invitation to the whole world to prove them unfounded. If the challenge is not accepted, or is accepted and the attempt fails, we are far enough from certainty still; but we have done the best that the existing state of human reason admits of; we have neglected nothing that could give the truth a chance of reaching us: if the lists are kept open, we may hope that if there be a better truth, it will be found when the human mind is capable of receiving it; and in the meantime we may rely on having attained such approach to truth, as is possible in our own day. This is the amount of certainty attainable by a fallible being, and this the sole way of attaining it.

Strange it is, that men should admit the validity of the arguments for free discussion, but object to their being 'pushed to an extreme;' not seeing that unless the reasons are good for an extreme case, they are not good for any case. Strange that they should imagine that they are not assuming infallibility, when they acknowledge that there should be free discussion on all subjects which can possibly be *doubtful*, but think that some particular principle or doctrine should be forbidden to be questioned because it is so *certain*, that is, because *they are certain* that it is certain. To call any proposition certain, while there is any one who would deny its certainty if permitted, but who is not permitted, is to assume that we ourselves, and those who agree with us, are the judges of certainty, and judges without hearing the other side.

In the present age—which has been described as 'destitute of faith, but terrified at scepticism'—in which people feel sure, not so much that their opinions are true, as that they should not know what to do without them—the claims of an opinion to be protected from public attack are rested not so much on its truth, as on its importance to society. There are, it is alleged, certain beliefs, so useful, not to say indispensable to well-being, that it is as much the duty of governments to uphold those beliefs, as to protect any other of the interests of society. In a case of such necessity, and so directly in the line of their duty, something less than infallibility may, it is maintained, warrant, and even bind, governments, to act on their own opinion, confirmed by the general opinion of mankind. It is also often argued, and still oftener thought, that none but bad men would desire to weaken these salutary beliefs; and there can be nothing wrong, it is thought, in restraining bad men, and prohibiting what only such men would wish to practise. This mode of thinking makes the justification of restraints on discussion not a question of the truth of doctrines, but of their usefulness; and flatters itself by that means to escape the responsibility of claiming to be an infallible judge of opinions. But those who thus satisfy themselves, do not perceive that the assumption of infallibility is merely shifted from one point to another. The usefulness of an opinion is itself matter of opinion: as disputable, as open to discussion, and requiring discussion as much, as the opinion itself. There is the same need of an infallible judge of opinions to decide an opinion to be noxious, as to decide it to be false, unless the opinion condemned has full opportunity of defending itself. And it will not do to say that the heretic may be allowed to maintain the utility or harmlessness of his opinion, though forbidden to maintain its truth. The truth of an opinion is part of its utility. If we would know whether or not it is desirable that a proposition should be believed, is it possible to exclude the consideration of whether or

not it is true? In the opinion, not of bad men, but of the best men, no belief which is contrary to truth can be really useful: and can you prevent such men from urging that plea, when they are charged with culpability for denying some doctrine which they are told is useful, but which they believe to be false? Those who are on the side of received opinions, never fail to take all possible advantage of this plea; you do not find *them* handling the question of utility as if it could be completely abstracted from that of truth: on the contrary, it is, above all, because their doctrine is the 'truth,' that the knowledge or the belief of it is held to be so indispensable. There can be no fair discussion of the question of usefulness, when an argument so vital may be employed on one side, but not on the other. And in point of fact, when law or public feeling do not permit the truth of an opinion to be disputed, they are just as little tolerant of a denial of its usefulness. The utmost they allow is an extenuation of its absolute necessity, or of the positive guilt of rejecting it.

In order more fully to illustrate the mischief of denying a hearing to opinions because we, in our own judgment, have condemned them, it will be desirable to fix down the discussion to a concrete case; and I choose, by preference, the cases which are least favourable to me—in which the argument against freedom of opinion, both on the score of truth and on that of utility, is considered the strongest. Let the opinions impugned be the belief in a God and in a future state, or any of the commonly received doctrines of morality. To fight the battle on such ground, gives a great advantage to an unfair antagonist; since he will be sure to say (and many who have no desire to be unfair will say it internally), Are these the doctrines which you do not deem sufficiently certain to be taken under the protection of law? Is the belief in a God one of the opinions, to feel sure of which, you hold to be assuming infallibility? But I must be permitted to observe, that it is not the feeling sure of a doctrine (be it what it may) which I call an assumption of infallibility. It is the undertaking to decide that question *for others*, without allowing them to hear what can be said on the contrary side. And I denounce and reprobate this pretension not the less, if put forth on the side of my most solemn convictions. However positive any one's persuasion may be, not only of the falsity but of the pernicious consequences—not only of the pernicious consequences, but (to adopt expressions which I altogether condemn) the immorality and impiety of an opinion; yet if, in pursuance of that private judgment, though backed by the public judgment of his country or his cotemporaries, he prevents the opinion from being heard in its defence, he assumes infallibility. And so far from the assumption being less objectionable or less dangerous because the opinion is called immoral or impious, this is the case of all others in which it is most fatal. These are exactly the occasions on which the men of one generation commit those dreadful mistakes, which excite the astonishment and horror of posterity. It is among such that we find the instances memorable in history, when the arm of the law has been employed to root out the best men and the noblest doctrines; with deplorable success as to the men, though some of the doctrines have survived to be (as if in mockery) invoked, in defence of similar conduct towards those who dissent from *them*, or from their received interpretation.

Mankind can hardly be too often reminded, that there was once a man named Socrates, between whom and the legal authorities and public opinion of his time, there took place a memorable collision. Born in an age and country abounding in individual greatness, this man has been handed down to us by those who best knew both him and the age, as the most virtuous man in it; while we know him as the head and prototype of all subsequent teachers of virtue, the source equally of the lofty inspiration of Plato and the judicious utilitarianism of Aristotle, '*i maestri di color che sanno,*' the two headsprings of ethical as of all other philosophy. This acknowledged master of all the eminent thinkers who have since lived—whose fame, still growing after more than two thousand years, all but outweighs the whole remainder of the names which make his native city illustrious—was put to death by his countrymen, after a judicial conviction, for impiety and immorality. Impiety, in denying the gods recognised by the State; indeed his accuser asserted (see the Apologia) that he believed in no gods at all. Immorality, in being, by his doctrines and instructions, a 'corruptor of youth.' Of these charges the

tribunal, there is every ground for believing, honestly found him guilty, and condemned the man who probably of all then born had deserved best of mankind, to be put to death as a criminal.

To pass from this to the only other instance of judicial iniquity, the mention of which, after the condemnation of Socrates, would not be an anti-climax: the event which took place on Calvary rather more than eighteen hundred years ago. The man who left on the memory of those who witnessed his life and conversation, such an impression of his moral grandeur, that eighteen subsequent centuries have done homage to him as the Almighty in person, was ignominiously put to death, as what? As a blasphemer. Men did not merely mistake their benefactor; they mistook him for the exact contrary of what he was, and treated him as that prodigy of impiety, which they themselves are now held to be, for their treatment of him. The feelings with which mankind now regard these lamentable transactions, especially the later of the two, render them extremely unjust in their judgment of the unhappy actors. These were, to all appearance, not bad men—not worse than men commonly are, but rather the contrary; men who possessed in a full, or somewhat more than a full measure, the religious, moral, and patriotic feelings of their time and people: the very kind of men who, in all times, our own included, have every chance of passing through life blameless and respected. The high-priest who rent his garments when the words were pronounced, which, according to all the ideas of his country, constituted the blackest guilt, was in all probability quite as sincere in his horror and indignation, as the generality of respectable and pious men now are in the religious and moral sentiments they profess; and most of those who now shudder at his conduct, if they had lived in his time, and been born Jews, would have acted precisely as he did. Orthodox Christians who are tempted to think that those who stoned to death the first martyrs must have been worse men than they themselves are, ought to remember that one of those persecutors was Saint Paul.

Let us add one more example, the most striking of all, if the impressiveness of an error is measured by the wisdom and virtue of him who falls into it. If ever any one, possessed of power, had grounds for thinking himself the best and most enlightened among his cotemporaries, it was the Emperor Marcus Aurelius. Absolute monarch of the whole civilized world, he preserved through life not only the most unblemished justice, but what was less to be expected from his Stoical breeding, the tenderest heart. The few failings which are attributed to him, were all on the side of indulgence: while his writings, the highest ethical product of the ancient mind, differ scarcely perceptibly, if they differ at all, from the most characteristic teachings of Christ. This man, a better Christian in all but the dogmatic sense of the word, than almost any of the ostensibly Christian sovereigns who have since reigned, persecuted Christianity. Placed at the summit of all the previous attainments of humanity, with an open, unfettered intellect, and a character which led him of himself to embody in his moral writings the Christian ideal, he yet failed to see that Christianity was to be a good and not an evil to the world, with his duties to which he was so deeply penetrated. Existing society he knew to be in a deplorable state. But such as it was, he saw, or thought he saw, that it was held together, and prevented from being worse, by belief and reverence of the received divinities. As a ruler of mankind, he deemed it his duty not to suffer society to fall in pieces; and saw not how, if its existing ties were removed, any others could be formed which could again knit it together. The new religion openly aimed at dissolving these ties: unless, therefore, it was his duty to adopt that religion, it seemed to be his duty to put it down. Inasmuch then as the theology of Christianity did not appear to him true or of divine origin; inasmuch as this strange history of a crucified God was not credible to him, and a system which purported to rest entirely upon a foundation to him so wholly unbelievable, could not be foreseen by him to be that renovating agency which, after all abatements, it has in fact proved to be; the gentlest and most amiable of philosophers and rulers, under a solemn sense of duty, authorized the persecution of Christianity. To my mind this is one of the most tragical facts in all history. It is a bitter thought, how different a thing the Christianity of the world might have been, if the Christian faith had been adopted as the religion of the empire under the auspices of Marcus Aurelius instead of those of Constantine. But it would be equally unjust to him and false to truth, to deny, that no one plea which can be urged for punishing anti-Christian teaching, was wanting to Marcus Aurelius for punishing, as he did, the propagation of Christianity. No Christian more firmly believes that Atheism is false, and tends to the dissolution of society, than Marcus Aurelius believed the same things of Christianity; he who, of all men then living, might have been thought the most capable of appreciating it. Unless any one who approves of punishment for the promulgation of opinions, flatters himself that he is a wiser and better man than Marcus Aurelius—more deeply versed in the wisdom of his time, more elevated in his intellect above it—more earnest in his search for truth, or more single-minded in his devotion to it when found;—let him abstain from that assumption of the joint infallibility of himself and the multitude, which the great Antoninus made with so unfortunate a result.

Aware of the impossibility of defending the use of punishment for restraining irreligious opinions, by any argument which will not justify Marcus Antoninus, the enemies of religious freedom, when hard pressed, occasionally accept this consequence, and say, with Dr. Johnson, that the persecutors of Christianity were in the right; that persecution is an ordeal through which truth ought to pass, and always passes successfully, legal penalties being, in the end, powerless against truth, though sometimes beneficially effective against mischievous errors. This is a form of the argument for religious intolerance, sufficiently remarkable not to be passed without notice.

A theory which maintains that truth may justifiably be persecuted because persecution cannot possibly do it any harm, cannot be charged with being intentionally hostile to the reception of new truths; but we cannot commend the generosity of its dealing with the persons to whom mankind are indebted for them. To discover to the world something which deeply concerns it, and of which it was previously ignorant; to prove to it that it had been mistaken on some vital point of temporal or spiritual interest, is as important a service as a human being can render to his fellow-creatures, and in certain cases, as in those of the early

Christians and of the Reformers, those who think with Dr. Johnson believe it to have been the most precious gift which could be bestowed on mankind. That the authors of such splendid benefits should be requited by martyrdom; that their reward should be to be dealt with as the vilest of criminals, is not, upon this theory, a deplorable error and misfortune, for which humanity should mourn in sackcloth and ashes, but the normal and justifiable state of things. The propounder of a new truth, according to this doctrine, should stand, as stood, in the legislation of the Locrians, the proposer of a new law, with a halter round his neck, to be instantly tightened if the public assembly did not, on hearing his reasons, then and there adopt his proposition. People who defend this mode of treating benefactors, cannot be supposed to set much value on the benefit; and I believe this view of the subject is mostly confined to the sort of persons who think that new truths may have been desirable once, but that we have had enough of them now.

But, indeed, the dictum that truth always triumphs over persecution, is one of those pleasant falsehoods which men repeat after one another till they pass into commonplaces, but which all experience refutes. History teems with instances of truth put down by persecution. If not suppressed for ever, it may be thrown back for centuries. To speak only of religious opinions: the Reformation broke out at least twenty times before Luther, and was put down. Arnold of Brescia was put down. Fra Dolcino was put down. Savonarola was put down. The Albigeois were put down. The Vaudois were put down. The Lollards were put down. The Hussites were put down. Even after the era of Luther, wherever persecution was persisted in, it was successful. In Spain, Italy, Flanders, the Austrian empire, Protestantism was rooted out; and, most likely, would have been so in England, had Queen Mary lived, or Queen Elizabeth died. Persecution has always succeeded, save where the heretics were too strong a party to be effectually persecuted. No reasonable person can doubt that Christianity might have been extirpated in the Roman Empire. It spread, and became predominant, because the persecutions were only occasional, lasting but a short time, and separated by

long intervals of almost undisturbed propagandism. It is a piece of idle sentimentality that truth, merely as truth, has any inherent power denied to error, of prevailing against the dungeon and the stake. Men are not more zealous for truth than they often are for error, and a sufficient application of legal or even of social penalties will generally succeed in stopping the propagation of either. The real advantage which truth has, consists in this, that when an opinion is true, it may be extinguished once, twice, or many times, but in the course of ages there will generally be found persons to rediscover it, until some one of its reappearances falls on a time when from favourable circumstances it escapes persecution until it has made such head as to withstand all subsequent attempts to suppress it.

It will be said, that we do not now put to death the introducers of new opinions: we are not like our fathers who slew the prophets, we even build sepulchres to them. It is true we no longer put heretics to death; and the amount of penal infliction which modern feeling would probably tolerate, even against the most obnoxious opinions, is not sufficient to extirpate them. But let us not flatter ourselves that we are yet free from the stain even of legal persecution. Penalties for opinion, or at least for its expression, still exist by law; and their enforcement is not, even in these times, so unexampled as to make it at all incredible that they may some day be revived in full force. In the year 1857, at the summer assizes of the county of Cornwall, an unfortunate man,[2] said to be of unexceptionable conduct in all relations of life, was sentenced to twenty-one months' imprisonment, for uttering, and writing on a gate, some offensive words concerning Christianity. Within a month of the same time, at the Old Bailey, two persons, on two separate occasions,[3] were rejected as jurymen, and one of them grossly insulted by the judge and by one of the counsel, because they honestly declared that they had no theological belief; and

[2] Thomas Pooley, Bodmin Assizes, July 31, 1857. In December following, he received a free pardon from the Crown.
[3] George Jacob Holyoake, August 17, 1857; Edward Truelove, July, 1857.

a third, a foreigner,[4] for the same reason, was denied justice against a thief. This refusal of redress took place in virtue of the legal doctrine, that no person can be allowed to give evidence in a court of justice, who does not profess belief in a God (any god is sufficient) and in a future state; which is equivalent to declaring such persons to be outlaws, excluded from the protection of the tribunals; who may not only be robbed or assaulted with impunity, if no one but themselves, or persons of similar opinions, be present, but any one else may be robbed or assaulted with impunity, if the proof of the fact depends on their evidence. The assumption on which this is grounded, is that the oath is worthless, of a person who does not believe in a future state; a proposition which betokens much ignorance of history in those who assent to it (since it is historically true that a large proportion of infidels in all ages have been persons of distinguished integrity and honour); and would be maintained by no one who had the smallest conception how many of the persons in greatest repute with the world, both for virtues and for attainments, are well known, at least to their intimates, to be unbelievers. The rule, besides, is suicidal, and cuts away its own foundation. Under pretence that atheists must be liars, it admits the testimony of all atheists who are willing to lie, and rejects only those who brave the obloquy of publicly confessing a detested creed rather than affirm a falsehood. A rule thus self-convicted of absurdity so far as regards its professed purpose, can be kept in force only as a badge of hatred, a relic of persecution; a persecution, too, having the peculiarity, that the qualification for undergoing it, is the being clearly proved not to deserve it. The rule, and the theory it implies, are hardly less insulting to believers than to infidels. For if he who does not believe in a future state, necessarily lies, it follows that they who do believe are only prevented from lying, if prevented they are, by the fear of hell. We will not do the authors and abettors of the rule the injury of supposing, that the conception which they have

formed of Christian virtue is drawn from their own consciousness.

These, indeed, are but rags and remnants of persecution, and may be thought to be not so much an indication of the wish to persecute, as an example of that very frequent infirmity of English minds, which makes them take a preposterous pleasure in the assertion of a bad principle, when they are no longer bad enough to desire to carry it really into practice. But unhappily there is no security in the state of the public mind, that the suspension of worse forms of legal persecution, which has lasted for about the space of a generation, will continue. In this age the quiet surface of routine is as often ruffled by attempts to resuscitate past evils, as to introduce new benefits. What is boasted of at the present time as the revival of religion, is always, in narrow and uncultivated minds, at least as much the revival of bigotry; and where there is the strong permanent leaven of intolerance in the feelings of a people, which at all times abides in the middle classes of this country, it needs but little to provoke them into actively persecuting those whom they have never ceased to think proper objects of persecution.[5] For it

---

[4] Baron de Gleichen, Marlborough-street Police Court, August 4, 1857.

[5] Ample warning may be drawn from the large infusion of the passions of a persecutor, which mingled with the general display of the worst parts of our national character on the occasion of the Sepoy insurrection. The ravings of fanatics or charlatans from the pulpit may be unworthy of notice; but the heads of the Evangelical party have announced as their principle for the government of Hindoos and Mahomedans, that no schools be supported by public money in which the Bible is not taught, and by necessary consequence that no public employment be given to any but real or pretended Christians. An Under-Secretary of State, in a speech delivered to his constituents on the 12th of November, 1857, is reported to have said: 'Toleration of their faith' (the faith of a hundred millions of British subjects), 'the superstition which they called religion, by the British Government, had had the effect of retarding the ascendancy of the British name, and preventing the salutary growth of Christianity. . . . Toleration was the great corner-stone of the religious liberties of this country; but do not let them abuse that precious word toleration.' As he understood it, it meant the complete liberty to all, freedom of worship, *among Christians, who worshipped upon the same foundation*. It meant toleration of

is this—it is the opinions men entertain, and the feelings they cherish, respecting those who disown the beliefs they deem important, which makes this country not a place of mental freedom. For a long time past, the chief mischief of the legal penalties is that they strengthen the social stigma. It is that stigma which is really effective, and so effective is it, that the profession of opinions which are under the ban of society is much less common in England, than is, in many other countries, the avowal of those which incur risk of judicial punishment. In respect to all persons but those whose pecuniary circumstances make them independent of the good will of other people, opinion, on this subject, is as efficacious as law; men might as well be imprisoned, as excluded from the means of earning their bread. Those whose bread is already secured, and who desire no favours from men in power, or from bodies of men, or from the public, have nothing to fear from the open avowal of any opinions, but to be ill-thought of and ill-spoken of, and this it ought not to require a very heroic mould to enable them to bear. There is no room for any appeal *ad misericordiam* in behalf of such persons. But though we do not now inflict so much evil on those who think differently from us, as it was formerly our custom to do, it may be that we do ourselves as much evil as ever by our treatment of them. Socrates was put to death, but the Socratic philosophy rose like the sun in heaven, and spread its illumination over the whole intellectual firmament. Christians were cast to the lions, but the Christian church grew up a stately and spreading tree, overtopping the older and less vigorous growths, and stifling them by its shade. Our merely social intolerance kills no one, roots out no opinions, but induces men to disguise them, or to abstain from any active effort for their diffusion. With us, heretical opinions do not per-

ceptibly gain, or even lose, ground in each decade or generation; they never blaze out far and wide, but continue to smoulder in the narrow circles of thinking and studious persons among whom they originate, without ever lighting up the general affairs of mankind with either a true or a deceptive light. And thus is kept up a state of things very satisfactory to some minds, because, without the unpleasant process of fining or imprisoning anybody, it maintains all prevailing opinions outwardly undisturbed, while it does not absolutely interdict the exercise of reason by dissentients afflicted with the malady of thought. A convenient plan for having peace in the intellectual world, and keeping all things going on therein very much as they do already. But the price paid for this sort of intellectual pacification, is the sacrifice of the entire moral courage of the human mind. A state of things in which a large portion of the most active and inquiring intellects find it advisable to keep the general principles and grounds of their convictions within their own breasts, and attempt, in what they address to the public, to fit as much as they can of their own conclusions to premises which they have internally renounced, cannot send forth the open, fearless characters, and logical, consistent intellects who once adorned the thinking world. The sort of men who can be looked for under it, are either mere conformers to commonplace, or time-servers for truth, whose arguments on all great subjects are meant for their hearers, and are not those which have convinced themselves. Those who avoid this alternative, do so by narrowing their thoughts and interest to things which can be spoken of without venturing within the region of principles, that is, to small practical matters, which would come right of themselves, if but the minds of mankind were strengthened and enlarged, and which will never be made effectually right until then: while that which would strengthen and enlarge men's minds, free and daring speculation on the highest subjects, is abandoned.

Those in whose eyes this reticence on the part of heretics is no evil, should consider in the first place, that in consequence of it there is never any fair and thorough discussion of heretical opinions; and that such of them as could not stand such a discussion, though they may be prevented from spreading, do not

---

all sects and denominations of *Christians who believed in the one mediation.*' I desire to call attention to the fact, that a man who has been deemed fit to fill a high office in the government of this country, under a liberal Ministry, maintains the doctrine that all who do not believe in the divinity of Christ are beyond the pale of toleration. Who, after this imbecile display, can indulge the illusion that religious persecution has passed away, never to return?

disappear. But it is not the minds of heretics that are deteriorated most, by the ban placed on all inquiry which does not end in the orthodox conclusions. The greatest harm done is to those who are not heretics, and whose whole mental development is cramped, and their reason cowed, by the fear of heresy. Who can compute what the world loses in the multitude of promising intellects combined with timid characters, who dare not follow out any bold, vigorous, independent train of thought, lest it should land them in something which would admit of being considered irreligious or immoral? Among them we may occasionally see some man of deep conscientiousness, and subtle and refined understanding, who spends a life in sophisticating with an intellect which he cannot silence, and exhausts the resources of ingenuity in attempting to reconcile the promptings of his conscience and reason with orthodoxy, which yet he does not, perhaps, to the end succeed in doing. No one can be a great thinker who does not recognise, that as a thinker it is his first duty to follow his intellect to whatever conclusions it may lead. Truth gains more even by the errors of one who, with due study and preparation, thinks for himself, than by the true opinions of those who only hold them because they do not suffer themselves to think. Not that it is solely, or chiefly, to form great thinkers, that freedom of thinking is required. On the contrary, it is as much and even more indispensable, to enable average human beings to attain the mental stature which they are capable of. There have been, and may again be, great individual thinkers, in a general atmosphere of mental slavery. But there never has been, nor ever will be, in that atmosphere, an intellectually active people. When any people has made a temporary approach to such a character, it has been because the dread of heterodox speculation was for a time suspended. Where there is a tacit convention that principles are not to be disputed; where the discussion of the greatest questions which can occupy humanity is considered to be closed, we cannot hope to find that generally high scale of mental activity which has made some periods of history so remarkable. Never when controversy avoided the subjects which are large and important enough to kindle enthusiasm, was the mind of a people

stirred up from its foundations, and the impulse given which raised even persons of the most ordinary intellect to something of the dignity of thinking beings. Of such we have had an example in the condition of Europe during the times immediately following the Reformation; another, though limited to the Continent and to a more cultivated class, in the speculative movement of the latter half of the eighteenth century; and a third, of still briefer duration, in the intellectual fermentation of Germany during the Goethian and Fichtean period. These periods differed widely in the particular opinions which they developed; but were alike in this, that during all three the yoke of authority was broken. In each, an old mental despotism had been thrown off, and no new one had yet taken its place. The impulse given at these three periods has made Europe what it now is. Every single improvement which has taken place either in the human mind or in institutions, may be traced distinctly to one or other of them. Appearances have for some time indicated that all three impulses are well nigh spent; and we can expect no fresh start, until we again assert our mental freedom.

Let us now pass to the second division of the argument, and dismissing the supposition that any of the received opinions may be false, let us assume them to be true, and examine into the worth of the manner in which they are likely to be held, when their truth is not freely and openly canvassed. However unwillingly a person who has a strong opinion may admit the possibility that his opinion may be false, he ought to be moved by the consideration that however true it may be, if it is not fully, frequently, and fearlessly discussed, it will be held as a dead dogma, not a living truth.

There is a class of persons (happily not quite so numerous as formerly) who think it enough if a person assents undoubtingly to what they think true, though he has no knowledge whatever of the grounds of the opinion, and could not make a tenable defence of it against the most superficial objections. Such persons, if they can once get their creed taught from authority, naturally think that no good, and some harm, comes of its being allowed to be questioned. Where their influence prevails, they make it nearly impossible for the received opinion to be rejected wisely and considerately, though it may still be rejected rashly and ignorantly; for to shut out discussion entirely is seldom possible, and when it once gets in, beliefs not grounded on conviction are apt to give way before the slightest semblance of an argument. Waiving, however, this possibility—assuming that the true opinion abides in the mind, but abides as a prejudice, a belief independent of, and proof against, argument—this is not the way in which truth ought to be held by a rational being. This is not knowing the truth. Truth, thus held, is but one superstition the more, accidentally clinging to the words which enunciate a truth.

If the intellect and judgment of mankind ought to be cultivated, a thing which Protestants at least do not deny, on what can these faculties be more appropriately exercised by any one, than on the things which concern him so much that it is considered necessary for him to hold opinions on them? If the cultivation of the understanding consists in one thing more than in another, it is surely in learning the grounds of one's own opinions. Whatever people believe, on subjects on which it is of the first importance to believe rightly, they ought to be able to defend against at least the common objections. But, some one may say, 'Let them be *taught* the grounds of their opinions. It does not follow that opinions must be merely parroted because they are never heard controverted. Persons who learn geometry do not simply commit the theorems to memory, but understand and learn likewise the demonstrations; and it would be absurd to say that they remain ignorant of the grounds of geometrical truths, because they never hear any one deny, and attempt to disprove them.' Undoubtedly: and such teaching suffices on a subject like mathematics, where there is nothing at all to be said on the wrong side of the question. The peculiarity of the evidence of mathematical truths is, that all the argument is on one side. There are no objections, and no answers to objections. But on every subject on which difference of opinion is possible, the truth depends on a balance to be struck between two sets of conflicting reasons. Even in natural philosophy, there is always some other explanation possible of the same facts; some geocentric theory instead of heliocentric, some phlogiston instead of oxygen; and it has to be shown why that other theory cannot be the true one: and until this is shown, and until we know how it is shown, we do not understand the grounds of our opinion. But when we turn to subjects infinitely more complicated, to morals, religion, politics, social relations, and the business of life, three-fourths of the arguments for every disputed opinion consist in dispelling the appearances which favour some opinion different from it. The greatest orator, save one, of antiquity, has left it on record that he always studied his adversary's case with as great, if not with still greater, intensity than even his own. What Cicero practised as the means of forensic success, requires to be imitated by all who study any subject in order to arrive at the truth. He who knows only his own side of the case, knows little of that. His reasons may be good, and no one may have been able to refute them. But if he is equally unable to refute the reasons on the opposite side; if he does not so much as know what they are, he has no ground for preferring either opinion. The rational position for him would be suspension of judgment, and unless he contents himself with that, he is either led by authority, or adopts, like the generality of the world, the side to which he feels most inclination. Nor is it enough that he should hear the arguments of adversaries from his own teachers, presented as they state them, and accompanied by what they offer as refutations. That is not the way to do justice to the arguments, or bring them into real contact with his own mind. He must be able to hear them from persons who actually believe them; who defend them in earnest, and do their very utmost for them. He must know them in their most plausible and persuasive form; he must feel the whole force of the difficulty which the true view of the subject has to encounter and dispose of; else he will never really possess himself of the portion of truth which meets and removes that difficulty. Ninety-nine in a hundred of what are called educated men are in this condition; even of those who can argue fluently for their opinions. Their conclusion may be true, but it might be false for anything they know: they have never thrown themselves into the mental position of those who think differently from them, and considered what such persons may have to say; and consequently they do not, in any proper sense of the word, know the doctrine which they themselves profess. They do not know those parts of it which explain and justify the remainder; the considerations which show that a fact which seemingly conflicts with another is reconcilable with it, or that, of two apparently strong reasons, one and not the other ought to be preferred. All that part of the truth which turns the scale, and decides the judgment of a completely informed mind, they are strangers to; nor is it ever really known, but to those who have attended equally and impartially to both sides, and endeavoured to see the reasons of both in the strongest light. So essential is this discipline to a real understanding of moral and human subjects, that if opponents of all important truths do not exist, it is indispensable to imagine them, and supply them with the strongest arguments which the most skilful devil's advocate can conjure up.

To abate the force of these considerations, an enemy of free discussion may be supposed to say, that there is no necessity for mankind in general to know and understand all that can be said against or for their opinions by philosophers and theologians. That it is not needful for common men to be able to expose all the misstatements or fallacies of an ingenious opponent. That it is enough if there is always somebody capable of answering them, so that nothing likely to mislead uninstructed persons remains unrefuted. That simple minds, having been taught the obvious grounds of the truths inculcated on them, may trust to authority for the rest, and being aware that they have neither knowledge nor talent to resolve every difficulty which can be raised, may repose in the assurance that all those which have been raised have been or can be answered, by those who are specially trained to the task.

Conceding to this view of the subject the utmost that can be claimed for it by those most easily satisfied with the amount of understanding of truth which ought to accompany the belief of it; even so, the argument for free discussion is no way weakened. For even this doctrine acknowledges that mankind ought to have a rational assurance that all objections have been satisfactorily answered; and how are they to be answered if that which requires to be answered is not spoken? or how can the answer be known to be satisfactory, if the objectors have no opportunity of show-

ing that it is unsatisfactory? If not the public, at least the philosophers and theologians who are to resolve the difficulties, must make themselves familiar with those difficulties in their most puzzling form; and this cannot be accomplished unless they are freely stated, and placed in the most advantageous light which they admit of. The Catholic Church has its own way of dealing with this embarrassing problem. It makes a broad separation between those who can be permitted to receive its doctrines on conviction, and those who must accept them on trust. Neither, indeed, are allowed any choice as to what they will accept; but the clergy, such at least as can be fully confided in, may admissibly and meritoriously make themselves acquainted with the arguments of opponents, in order to answer them, and may, therefore, read heretical books; the laity, not unless by special permission, hard to be obtained. This discipline recognises a knowledge of the enemy's case as beneficial to the teachers, but finds means, consistent with this, of denying it to the rest of the world: thus giving to the *élite* more mental culture, though not more mental freedom, than it allows to the mass. By this device it succeeds in obtaining the kind of mental superiority which its purposes require; for though culture without freedom never made a large and liberal mind, it can make a clever *nisi prius* advocate of a cause. But in countries professing Protestantism, this resource is denied; since Protestants hold, at least in theory, that the responsibility for the choice of a religion must be borne by each for himself, and cannot be thrown off upon teachers. Besides, in the present state of the world, it is practically impossible that writings which are read by the instructed can be kept from the uninstructed. If the teachers of mankind are to be cognisant of all that they ought to know, everything must be free to be written and published without restraint.

If, however, the mischievous operation of the absence of free discussion, when the received opinions are true, were confined to leaving men ignorant of the grounds of those opinions, it might be thought that this, if an intellectual, is no moral evil, and does not affect the worth of the opinions, regarded in their influence on the character. The fact, however, is, that not only the grounds of the opinion are forgotten in the absence of discussion, but too often the meaning of the opinion itself. The words which convey it, cease to suggest ideas, or suggest only a small portion of those they were originally employed to communicate. Instead of a vivid conception and a living belief, there remain only a few phrases retained by rote; or, if any part, the shell and husk only of the meaning is retained, the finer essence being lost. The great chapter in human history which this fact occupies and fills, cannot be too earnestly studied and meditated on.

It is illustrated in the experience of almost all ethical doctrines and religious creeds. They are all full of meaning and vitality to those who originate them, and to the direct disciples of the originators. Their meaning continues to be felt in undiminished strength, and is perhaps brought out into even fuller consciousness, so long as the struggle lasts to give the doctrine or creed an ascendancy over other creeds. At last it either prevails, and becomes the general opinion, or its progress stops; it keeps possession of the ground it has gained, but ceases to spread further. When either of these results has become apparent, controversy on the subject flags, and gradually dies away. The doctrine has taken its place, if not as a received opinion, as one of the admitted sects or divisions of opinion: those who hold it have generally inherited, not adopted it; and conversion from one of these doctrines to another, being now an exceptional fact, occupies little place in the thoughts of their professors. Instead of being, as at first, constantly on the alert either to defend themselves against the world, or to bring the world over to them, they have subsided into acquiescence, and neither listen, when they can help it, to arguments against their creed, nor trouble dissentients (if there be such) with arguments in its favour. From this time may usually be dated the decline in the living power of the doctrine. We often hear the teachers of all creeds lamenting the difficulty of keeping up in the minds of believers a lively apprehension of the truth which they nominally recognise, so that it may penetrate the feelings, and acquire a real mastery over the conduct. No such difficulty is complained of while the creed is still fighting for its existence: even the weaker combatants then know and feel what they are fighting for, and the difference between it and other doctrines; and in that

period of every creed's existence, not a few persons may be found, who have realized its fundamental principles in all the forms of thought, have weighed and considered them in all their important bearings, and have experienced the full effect on the character, which belief in that creed ought to produce in a mind thoroughly imbued with it. But when it has come to be an hereditary creed, and to be received passively, not actively—when the mind is no longer compelled, in the same degree as at first, to exercise its vital powers on the questions which its belief presents to it, there is a progressive tendency to forget all of the belief except the formularies, or to give it a dull and torpid assent, as if accepting it on trust dispensed with the necessity of realizing it in consciousness, or testing it by personal experience; until it almost ceases to connect itself at all with the inner life of the human being. Then are seen the cases, so frequent in this age of the world as almost to form the majority, in which the creed remains as it were outside the mind, incrusting and petrifying it against all other influences addressed to the higher parts of our nature; manifesting its power by not suffering any fresh and living conviction to get in, but itself doing nothing for the mind or heart, except standing sentinel over them to keep them vacant.

To what an extent doctrines intrinsically fitted to make the deepest impression upon the mind may remain in it as dead beliefs, without being ever realized in the imagination, the feelings, or the understanding, is exemplified by the manner in which the majority of believers hold the doctrines of Christianity. By Christianity I here mean what is accounted such by all churches and sects—the maxims and precepts contained in the New Testament. These are considered sacred, and accepted as laws, by all professing Christians. Yet it is scarcely too much to say that not one Christian in a thousand guides or tests his individual conduct by reference to those laws. The standard to which he does refer it, is the custom of his nation, his class, or his religious profession. He has thus, on the one hand, a collection of ethical maxims, which he believes to have been vouchsafed to him by infallible wisdom as rules for his government; and on the other, a set of every-day judgments and practices, which go a certain length with some of those maxims, not so great a length with others, stand in direct opposition to some, and are, on the whole, a compromise between the Christian creed and the interests and suggestions of worldly life. To the first of these standards he gives his homage; to the other his real allegiance. All Christians believe that the blessed are the poor and humble, and those who are ill-used by the world; that it is easier for a camel to pass through the eye of a needle than for a rich man to enter the kingdom of heaven; that they should judge not, lest they be judged; that they should swear not at all; that they should love their neighbour as themselves; that if one take their cloak, they should give him their coat also; that they should take no thought for the morrow; that if they would be perfect, they should sell all that they have and give it to the poor. They are not insincere when they say that they believe these things. They do believe them, as people believe what they have always heard lauded and never discussed. But in the sense of that living belief which regulates conduct, they believe these doctrines just up to the point to which it is usual to act upon them. The doctrines in their integrity are serviceable to pelt adversaries with; and it is understood that they are to be put forward (when possible) as the reasons for whatever people do that they think laudable. But any one who reminded them that the maxims require an infinity of things which they never even think of doing, would gain nothing but to be classed among those very unpopular characters who affect to be better than other people. The doctrines have no hold on ordinary believers—are not a power in their minds. They have an habitual respect for the sound of them, but no feeling which spreads from the words to the things signified, and forces the mind to take *them* in, and make them conform to the formula. Whenever conduct is concerned, they look round for Mr. A and B to direct them how far to go in obeying Christ.

Now we may be well assured that the case was not thus, but far otherwise, with the early Christians. Had it been thus, Christianity never would have expanded from an obscure sect of the despised Hebrews into the religion of the Roman empire. When their enemies said, 'See how these Christians love one another' (a remark not likely to be made by anybody now), they assuredly had a much livelier feeling of the meaning of their creed than they have ever had since. And to this cause, probably, it is chiefly owing that Christianity now makes so little progress in extending its domain, and after eighteen centuries, is still nearly confined to Europeans and the descendants of Europeans. Even with the strictly religious, who are much in earnest about their doctrines, and attach a greater amount of meaning to many of them than people in general, it commonly happens that the part which is thus comparatively active in their minds is that which was made by Calvin, or Knox, or some such person much nearer in character to themselves. The sayings of Christ coexist passively in their minds, producing hardly any effect beyond what is caused by mere listening to words so amiable and bland. There are many reasons, doubtless, why doctrines which are the badge of a sect retain more of their vitality than those common to all recognised sects, and why more pains are taken by teachers to keep their meaning alive; but one reason certainly is, that the peculiar doctrines are more questioned, and have to be oftener defended against open gainsayers. Both teachers and learners go to sleep at their post, as soon as there is no enemy in the field.

The same thing holds true, generally speaking, of all traditional doctrines—those of prudence and knowledge of life, as well as of morals or religion. All languages and literatures are full of general observations on life, both as to what it is, and how to conduct oneself in it; observations which everybody knows, which everybody repeats, or hears with acquiescence, which are received as truisms, yet of which most people first truly learn the meaning, when experience, generally of a painful kind, has made it a reality to them. How often, when smarting under some unforeseen misfortune or disappointment, does a person call to mind some proverb or common saying, familiar to him all his life, the meaning of which, if he had ever before felt it as he does now, would have saved him from the calamity. There are indeed reasons for this, other than the absence of discussion: there are many truths of which the full meaning *cannot* be realized, until personal experience has brought it home. But much more of the meaning even of these would have been understood, and what was understood would have been far more deeply impressed on the mind, if the man had been accustomed to hear it argued *pro* and *con* by people who did understand it. The fatal tendency of mankind to leave off thinking about a thing when it is no longer doubtful, is the cause of half their errors. A cotemporary author has well spoken of 'the deep slumber of a decided opinion.'

But what! (it may be asked) Is the absence of unanimity an indispensable condition of true knowledge? Is it necessary that some part of mankind should persist in error, to enable any to realize the truth? Does a belief cease to be real and vital as soon as it is generally received—and is a proposition never thoroughly understood and felt unless some doubt of it remains? As soon as mankind have unanimously accepted a truth, does the truth perish within them? The highest aim and best result of improved intelligence, it has hitherto been thought, is to unite mankind more and more in the acknowledgment of all important truths: and does the intelligence only last as long as it has not achieved its object? Do the fruits of conquest perish by the very completeness of the victory?

I affirm no such thing. As mankind improve, the number of doctrines which are no longer disputed or doubted will be constantly on the increase: and the well-being of mankind may almost be measured by the number and gravity of the truths which have reached the point of being uncontested. The cessation, on one question after another, of serious controversy, is one of the necessary incidents of the consolidation of opinion; a consolidation as salutary in the case of true opinions, as it is dangerous and noxious when the opinions are erroneous. But though this gradual narrowing of the bounds of diversity of opinion is necessary in both senses of the term, being at once inevitable and indispensable, we are not therefore obliged to conclude that all its consequences must be beneficial. The loss of so important an aid to the intelligent and living apprehension of a truth, as is afforded by the necessity of explaining it to, or defending it against, opponents, though not sufficient to outweigh, is no trifling drawback from, the benefit of its universal recognition. Where this advantage can no longer be had, I confess I should like to see the teachers of mankind endeavouring to provide a substitute for it; some contrivance for making the difficulties of the question as present to

the learner's consciousness, as if they were pressed upon him by a dissentient champion, eager for his conversion.

But instead of seeking contrivances for this purpose, they have lost those they formerly had. The Socratic dialectics, so magnificently exemplified in the dialogues of Plato, were a contrivance of this description. They were essentially a negative discussion of the great questions of philosophy and life, directed with consummate skill to the purpose of convincing any one who had merely adopted the commonplaces of received opinion, that he did not understand the subject—that he as yet attached no definite meaning to the doctrines he professed; in order that, becoming aware of his ignorance, he might be put in the way to attain a stable belief, resting on a clear apprehension both of the meaning of doctrines and of their evidence. The school disputations of the middle ages had a somewhat similar object. They were intended to make sure that the pupil understood his own opinion, and (by necessary correlation) the opinion opposed to it, and could enforce the grounds of the one and confute those of the other. These last-mentioned contests had indeed the incurable defect, that the premises appealed to were taken from authority, not from reason; and, as a discipline to the mind, they were in every respect inferior to the powerful dialectics which formed the intellects of the 'Socratici viri:' but the modern mind owes far more to both than it is generally willing to admit, and the present modes of education contain nothing which in the smallest degree supplies the place either of the one or of the other. A person who derives all his instruction from teachers or books, even if he escape the besetting temptation of contenting himself with cram, is under no compulsion to hear both sides; accordingly it is far from a frequent accomplishment, even among thinkers, to know both sides; and the weakest part of what everybody says in defence of his opinion, is what he intends as a reply to antagonists. It is the fashion of the present time to disparage negative logic—that which points out weaknesses in theory or errors in practice, without establishing positive truths. Such negative criticism would indeed be poor enough as an ultimate result; but as a means to attaining any positive knowledge or conviction worthy the name, it cannot be valued too highly; and until people are again systematically trained to it, there will be few great thinkers, and a low general average of intellect, in any but the mathematical and physical departments of speculation. On any other subject no one's opinions deserve the name of knowledge, except so far as he has either had forced upon him by others, or gone through of himself, the same mental process which would have been required of him in carrying on an active controversy with opponents. That, therefore, which when absent, it is so indispensable, but so difficult, to create, how worse than absurd it is to forego, when spontaneously offering itself! If there are any persons who contest a received opinion, or who will do so if law or opinion will let them, let us thank them for it, open our minds to listen to them, and rejoice that there is some one to do for us what we otherwise ought, if we have any regard for either the certainty or the vitality of our convictions, to do with much greater labour for ourselves.

It still remains to speak of one of the principal causes which make diversity of opinion advantageous, and will continue to do so until mankind shall have entered a stage of intellectual advancement which at present seems at an incalculable distance. We have hitherto considered only two possibilities: that the received opinion may be false, and some other opinion, consequently, true; or that, the received opinion being true, a conflict with the opposite error is essential to a clear apprehension and deep feeling of its truth. But there is a commoner case than either of these; when the conflicting doctrines, instead of being one true and the other false, share the truth between them; and the nonconforming opinion is needed to supply the remainder of the truth, of which the received doctrine embodies only a part. Popular opinions, on subjects not palpable to sense, are often true, but seldom or never the whole truth. They are a part of the truth; sometimes a greater, sometimes a smaller part, but exaggerated, distorted, and disjoined from the truths by which they ought to be accompanied and limited. Heretical opinions, on the other hand, are generally some of these suppressed and neglected truths, bursting the bonds which kept them down, and either seeking reconciliation with the truth contained in the common opinion, or fronting it as enemies, and setting themselves up, with similar exclusiveness, as the whole truth. The latter case is hitherto the most frequent, as, in the human mind, one-sidedness has always been the rule, and many-sidedness the exception. Hence, even in revolutions of opinion, one part of the truth usually sets while another rises. Even progress, which ought to superadd, for the most part only substitutes, one partial and incomplete truth for another; improvement consisting chiefly in this, that the new fragment of truth is more wanted, more adapted to the needs of the time, than that which it displaces. Such being the partial character of prevailing opinions, even when resting on a true foundation, every opinion which embodies somewhat of the portion of truth which the common opinion omits, ought to be considered precious, with whatever amount of error and confusion that truth may be blended. No sober judge of human affairs will feel bound to be indignant because those who force on our notice truths which we should otherwise have overlooked, overlook some of those which we see. Rather, he will think that so long as popular truth is one-sided, it is more desirable than otherwise that unpopular truth should have one-sided asserters too; such being usually the most energetic, and the most likely to compel reluctant attention to the fragment of wisdom which they proclaim as if it were the whole.

Thus, in the eighteenth century, when nearly all the instructed, and all those of the uninstructed who were led by them, were lost in admiration of what is called civilization, and of the marvels of modern science, literature, and philosophy, and while greatly overrating the amount of unlikeness between the men of modern and those of ancient times, indulged the belief that the whole of the difference was in their own favour; with what a salutary shock did the paradoxes of Rousseau explode like bombshells in the midst, dislocating the compact mass of one-sided opinion, and forcing its elements to recombine in a better form and with additional ingredients. Not that the current opinions were on the whole farther from the truth than Rousseau's were; on the contrary, they were nearer to it; they contained more of positive truth, and very much less of error. Nevertheless there lay in Rousseau's doctrine, and has floated down the stream of opinion along with it, a considerable amount of exactly those truths which the popular opinion wanted; and these are the deposit which was left behind when the flood subsided. The superior worth of simplicity of life, the enervating and demoralizing effect of the trammels and hypocrisies of artificial society, are ideas which have never been entirely absent from cultivated minds since Rousseau wrote; and they will in time produce their due effect, though at present needing to be asserted as much as ever, and to be asserted by deeds, for words, on this subject, have nearly exhausted their power.

In politics, again, it is almost a commonplace, that a party of order or stability, and a party of progress or reform, are both necessary elements of a healthy state of political life; until the one or the other shall have so enlarged its mental grasp as to be a party equally of order and of progress, knowing and distinguishing what is fit to be preserved from what ought to be swept away. Each of these modes of thinking derives its utility from the deficiencies of the other; but it is in a great measure the opposition of the other that keeps each within the limits of reason and sanity. Unless opinions favourable to democracy and to aristocracy, to property and to equality, to co-operation and to competition, to luxury and to abstinence, to sociality and individuality, to liberty and discipline, and all the other standing antagonisms of practical life, are expressed with equal freedom, and enforced and defended with equal talent and energy, there is no chance of both elements obtaining their due; one scale is sure to go up, and the other down. Truth, in the great practical concerns of life, is so much a question of the reconciling and combining of opposites, that very few have minds sufficiently capacious and impartial to make the adjustment with an approach to correctness, and it has to be made by the rough process of a struggle between combatants fighting under hostile banners. On any of the great open questions just enumerated, if either of the two opinions has a better claim than the other, not merely to be tolerated, but to be encouraged and countenanced, it is the one which happens at the particular time and place to be in a minority. That is the opinion which, for the time being, represents the neglected interests, the side of human well-being which is in danger of obtaining less than its share. I am aware that there is not, in this country, any intolerance of differences of opinion on most of these topics. They are adduced to show, by admitted and multiplied examples, the universality of the fact, that only through diversity of opinion is there, in the existing state of human intellect, a chance of fair play to all sides of the truth. When there are persons to be found, who form an exception to the apparent unanimity of the world on any subject, even if the world is in the right, it is always probable that dissentients have something worth hearing to say for themselves, and that truth would lose something by their silence.

It may be objected, 'But *some* received principles, especially on the highest and most vital subjects, are more than half-truths. The Christian morality, for instance, is the whole truth on that subject, and if any one teaches a morality which varies from it, he is wholly in error.' As this is of all cases the most important in practice, none can be fitter to test the general maxim. But before pronouncing what Christian morality is or is not, it would be desirable to decide what is meant by Christian morality. If it means the morality of the New Testament, I wonder that any one who derives his knowledge of this from the book itself, can suppose that it was announced, or intended, as a complete doctrine of morals. The Gospel always refers to a pre-existing morality, and confines its precepts to the particulars in which that morality was to be corrected, or superseded by a wider and higher; expressing itself, moreover, in terms most general, often impossible to be interpreted literally, and possessing rather the impressiveness of poetry or eloquence than the precision of legislation. To extract from it a body of ethical doctrine, has never been possible without eking it out from the Old Testament, that is, from a system elaborate indeed, but in many respects barbarous, and intended only for a barbarous people. St. Paul, a declared enemy to this Judaical mode of interpreting the doctrine and filling up the scheme of his Master, equally assumes a pre-existing morality, namely that of the Greeks and Romans; and his advice to Christians is in a great measure a system of accommodation to that; even to the extent of giving an apparent sanction to slavery. What is called Christian, but should rather be termed theological, morality, was not the work of Christ or the Apostles, but is of much later origin, having been gradually built up by the Catholic church of the first five centuries, and though not implicitly adopted by moderns and Protestants, has been much less modified by them than might have been expected. For the most part, indeed, they have contented themselves with cutting off the additions which had been made to it in the middle ages, each sect supplying the place by fresh additions, adapted to its own character and tendencies. That mankind owe a great debt to this morality, and to its early teachers, I should be the last person to deny; but I do not scruple to say of it, that it is, in many important points, incomplete and one-sided, and that unless ideas and feelings, not sanctioned by it, had contributed to the formation of European life and character, human affairs would have been in a worse condition than they now are. Christian morality (so called) has all the characters of a reaction; it is, in great part, a protest against Paganism. Its ideal is negative rather than positive; passive rather than active; Innocence rather than Nobleness; Abstinence from Evil, rather than energetic Pursuit of Good: in its precepts (as has been well said) 'thou shalt not' predominates unduly over 'thou shalt.' In its horror of sensuality, it made an idol of asceticism, which has been gradually compromised away into one of legality. It holds out the hope of heaven and the threat of hell, as the appointed and appropriate motives to a virtuous life: in this falling far below the best of the ancients, and doing what lies in it to give to human morality an essentially selfish character, by disconnecting each man's feelings of duty from the interests of his fellow-creatures, except so far as a self-interested inducement is offered to him for consulting them. It is essentially a doctrine of passive obedience; it inculcates submission to all authorities found established; who indeed are not to be actively obeyed when they command what religion forbids, but who are not to be resisted, far less rebelled against, for any amount of wrong to ourselves. And while, in the morality of the best Pagan nations, duty to the State holds even a disproportionate place, infringing on the just liberty of the individual; in purely Christian ethics, that grand department of duty is scarcely noticed or acknowledged. It is in the Koran, not the New Testament, that we read the maxim—'A ruler who appoints any man to an office, when there is in his dominions another man better qualified for it, sins against God and against the State.' What little recognition the idea of obligation to the public obtains in modern morality, is derived from Greek and Roman sources, not from Christian; as, even in the morality of private life, whatever exists of magnanimity, high-mindedness, personal dignity, even the sense of honour, is derived from the purely human, not the religious part of our education, and never could have grown out of a standard of ethics in which the only worth, professedly recognised, is that of obedience.

I am as far as any one from pretending that these defects are necessarily inherent in the Christian ethics, in every manner in which it can be conceived, or that the many requisites of a complete moral doctrine which it does not contain, do not admit of being reconciled with it. Far less would I insinuate this of the doctrines and precepts of Christ himself. I believe that the sayings of Christ are all, that I can see any evidence of their having been intended to be; that they are irreconcilable with nothing which a comprehensive morality requires; that everything which is excellent in ethics may be brought within them, with no greater violence to their language than has been done to it by all who have attempted to deduce from them any practical system of conduct whatever. But it is quite consistent with this, to believe that they contain, and were meant to contain, only a part of the truth; that many essential elements of the highest morality are among the things which are not provided for, nor intended to be provided for, in the recorded deliverances of the Founder of Christianity, and which have been entirely thrown aside in the system of ethics erected on the basis of those deliverances by the Christian Church. And this being so, I think it a great error to persist in attempting to find in the Christian doctrine that complete rule for our guidance, which its author intended it to sanction and enforce, but only partially to provide. I believe, too, that this narrow theory is becoming a grave practical evil, detracting greatly from the value of the moral training and instruction, which so many well-meaning persons are now at length exerting themselves to promote. I much fear that by attempting to form the mind and feelings on an exclusively religious type, and discarding those secular standards (as for want of a better name they may be called) which heretofore co-existed with and supplemented the Christian ethics, receiving some of its spirit, and infusing into it some of theirs, there will result, and is even now resulting, a low, abject, servile type of character, which, submit itself as it may to what it deems the Supreme Will, is incapable of rising to or sympathizing in the conception of Supreme Goodness. I believe that other ethics than any which can be evolved from exclusively Christian sources, must exist side by side with Christian ethics to produce the moral regeneration of mankind; and that the Christian system is no exception to the rule, that in an imperfect state of the human mind, the interests of truth require a diversity of opinions. It is not necessary that in ceasing to ignore the moral truths not contained in Christianity, men should ignore any of those which it does contain. Such prejudice, or oversight, when it occurs, is altogether an evil; but it is one from which we cannot hope to be always exempt, and must be regarded as the price paid for an inestimable good. The exclusive pretension made by a part of the truth to be the whole, must and ought to be protested against; and if a reactionary impulse should make the protestors unjust in their turn, this one-sidedness, like the other, may be lamented, but must be tolerated. If Christians would teach infidels to be just to Christianity, they should themselves be just to infidelity. It can do truth no service to blink the fact, known to all who have the most ordinary acquaintance with literary history, that a large portion of the noblest and most valuable moral teaching has been the work, not only of men who did not know, but of men who knew and rejected, the Christian faith.

I do not pretend that the most unlimited use of the freedom of enunciating all possible opinions would put an end to the evils of religious or philosophical sectarianism. Every truth which men of narrow capacity are in earnest about, is sure to be asserted, in-culcated, and in many ways even acted on, as if no other truth existed in the world, or at all events none that could limit or qualify the first. I acknowledge that the tendency of all opinions to become sectarian is not cured by the freest discussion, but is often heightened and exacerbated thereby; the truth which ought to have been, but was not, seen, being rejected all the more violently because proclaimed by persons regarded as opponents. But it is not on the impassioned partisan, it is on the calmer and more disinterested bystander, that this collision of opinions works its salutary effect. Not the violent conflict between parts of the truth, but the quiet suppression of half of it, is the formidable evil; there is always hope when people are forced to listen to both sides; it is when they attend only to one that errors harden into prejudices, and truth itself ceases to have the effect of truth, by being exaggerated into falsehood. And since there are few mental attributes more rare than that judicial faculty which can sit in intelligent judgment between two sides of a question, of which only one is represented by an advocate before it, truth has no chance but in proportion as every side of it, every opinion which embodies any fraction of the truth, not only finds advocates, but is so advocated as to be listened to.

We have now recognised the necessity to the mental well-being of mankind (on which all their other well-being depends) of freedom of opinion, and freedom of the expression of opinion, on four distinct grounds; which we will now briefly recapitulate.

First, if any opinion is compelled to silence, that opinion may, for aught we can certainly know, be true. To deny this is to assume our own infallibility.

Secondly, though the silenced opinion be an error, it may, and very commonly does, contain a portion of truth; and since the general or prevailing opinion on any subject is rarely or never the whole truth, it is only by the collision of adverse opinions that the remainder of the truth has any chance of being supplied.

Thirdly, even if the received opinion be not only true, but the whole truth; unless it is suffered to be, and actually is, vigorously and earnestly contested, it will, by most of those who receive it, be held in the manner of a prejudice, with little comprehension or feeling of its rational grounds. And not only this, but, fourthly, the meaning of the doctrine itself will be in danger of being lost, or enfeebled, and deprived of its vital effect on the character and conduct: the dogma becoming a mere formal profession, inefficacious for good, but cumbering the ground, and preventing the growth of any real and heartfelt conviction, from reason or personal experience.

Before quitting the subject of freedom of opinion, it is fit to take some notice of those who say, that the free expression of all opinions should be permitted, on condition that the manner be temperate, and do not pass the bounds of fair discussion. Much might be said on the impossibility of fixing where these supposed bounds are to be placed; for if the test be offence to those whose opinion is attacked, I think experience testifies that this offence is given whenever the attack is telling and powerful, and that every opponent who pushes them hard, and whom they find it difficult to answer, appears to them, if he shows any strong feeling on the subject, an intemperate opponent. But this, though an important consideration in a practical point of view, merges in a more fundamental objection. Undoubtedly the manner of asserting an opinion, even though it be a true one, may be very objectionable, and may justly incur severe censure. But the principal offences of the kind are such as it is mostly impossible, unless by accidental self-betrayal, to bring home to conviction. The gravest of them is, to argue sophistically, to suppress facts or arguments, to misstate the elements of the case, or misrepresent the opposite opinion. But all this, even to the most aggravated degree, is so continually done in perfect good faith, by persons who are not considered, and in many other respects may not deserve to be considered, ignorant or incompetent, that it is rarely possible on adequate grounds conscientiously to stamp the misrepresentation as morally culpable; and still less could law presume to interfere with this kind of controversial misconduct. With regard to what is commonly meant by intemperate discussion, namely invective, sarcasm, personality, and the like, the denunciation of these weapons would deserve more sympathy if it were ever proposed to interdict them equally to both sides; but it is only desired to restrain the employment of them against the prevailing opinion: against the un-

prevailing they may not only be used without general disapproval, but will be likely to obtain for him who uses them the praise of honest zeal and righteous indignation. Yet whatever mischief arises from their use, is greatest when they are employed against the comparatively defenceless; and whatever unfair advantage can be derived by any opinion from this mode of asserting it, accrues almost exclusively to received opinions. The worst offence of this kind which can be committed by a polemic, is to stigmatize those who hold the contrary opinion as bad and immoral men. To calumny of this sort, those who hold any unpopular opinion are peculiarly exposed, because they are in general few and uninfluential, and nobody but themselves feels much interested in seeing justice done them; but this weapon is, from the nature of the case, denied to those who attack a prevailing opinion: they can neither use it with safety to themselves, nor, if they could, would it do anything but recoil on their own cause. In general, opinions contrary to those commonly received can only obtain a hearing by studied moderation of language, and the most cautious avoidance of unnecessary offence, from which they hardly ever deviate even in a slight degree without losing ground: while unmeasured vituperation employed on the side of the prevailing opinion, really does deter people from professing contrary opinions, and from listening to those who profess them. For the interest, therefore, of truth and justice, it is far more important to restrain this employment of vituperative language than the other; and, for example, if it were necessary to choose, there would be much more need to discourage offensive attacks on infidelity, than on religion. It is, however, obvious that law and authority have no business with restraining either, while opinion ought, in every instance, to determine its verdict by the circumstances of the individual case; condemning every one, on whichever side of the argument he places himself, in whose mode of advocacy either want of candour, or malignity, bigotry, or intolerance of feeling manifest themselves; but not inferring these vices from the side which a person takes, though it be the contrary side of the question to our own: and giving merited honour to every one, whatever opinion he may hold, who has calmness to see and honesty to state what his opponents and their opinions really are, exaggerating nothing to their discredit, keeping nothing back which tells, or can be supposed to tell, in their favour. This is the real morality of public discussion: and if often violated, I am happy to think that there are many controversialists who to a great extent observe it, and a still greater number who conscientiously strive towards it.

Chapter III: Of Individuality, as One of the Elements of Well-Being

Such being the reasons which make it imperative that human beings should be free to form opinions, and to express their opinions without reserve; and such the baneful consequences to the intellectual, and through that to the moral nature of man, unless this liberty is either conceded, or asserted in spite of prohibition; let us next examine whether the same reasons do not require that men should be free to act upon their opinions—to carry these out in their lives, without hindrance, either physical or moral, from their fellowmen, so long as it is at their own risk and peril. This last proviso is of course indispensable. No one pretends that actions should be as free as opinions. On the contrary, even opinions lose their immunity, when the circumstances in which they are expressed are such as to constitute their expression a positive instigation to some mischievous act. An opinion that corn-dealers are starvers of the poor, or that private property is robbery, ought to be unmolested when simply circulated through the press, but may justly incur punishment when delivered orally to an excited mob assembled before the house of a corn-dealer, or when handed about among the same mob in the form of a placard. Acts, of whatever kind, which, without justifiable cause, do harm to others, may be, and in the more important cases absolutely require to be, controlled by the unfavourable sentiments, and, when needful, by the active interference of mankind. The liberty of the individual must be thus far limited; he must not make himself a nuisance to other people. But if he refrains from molesting others in what concerns them, and merely acts according to his own inclination and judgment in things which concern himself, the same rea-

sons which show that opinion should be free, prove also that he should be allowed, without molestation, to carry his opinions into practice at his own cost. That mankind are not infallible; that their truths, for the most part, are only half-truths; that unity of opinion, unless resulting from the fullest and freest comparison of opposite opinions, is not desirable, and diversity not an evil, but a good, until mankind are much more capable than at present of recognising all sides of the truth, are principles applicable to men's modes of action, not less than to their opinions. As it is useful that while mankind are imperfect there should be different opinions, so is it that there should be different experiments of living; that free scope should be given to varieties of character, short of injury to others; and that the worth of different modes of life should be proved practically, when any one thinks fit to try them. It is desirable, in short, that in things which do not primarily concern others, individuality should assert itself. Where, not the person's own character, but the traditions or customs of other people are the rule of conduct, there is wanting one of the principal ingredients of human happiness, and quite the chief ingredient of individual and social progress.

In maintaining this principle, the greatest difficulty to be encountered does not lie in the appreciation of means towards an acknowledged end, but in the indifference of persons in general to the end itself. If it were felt that the free development of individuality is one of the leading essentials of well-being; that it is not only a co-ordinate element with all that is designated by the terms civilization, instruction, education, culture, but is itself a necessary part and condition of all those things; there would be no danger that liberty should be undervalued, and the adjustment of the boundaries between it and social control would present no extraordinary difficulty. But the evil is, that individual spontaneity is hardly recognised by the common modes of thinking, as having any intrinsic worth, or deserving any regard on its own account. The majority, being satisfied with the ways of mankind as they now are (for it is they who make them what they are), cannot comprehend why those ways should not be good enough for everybody; and what is more, spontaneity forms no part of the ideal of the majority of moral and social reformers, but is rather looked on with jealousy, as a troublesome and perhaps rebellious obstruction to the general acceptance of what these reformers, in their own judgment, think would be best for mankind. Few persons, out of Germany, even comprehend the meaning of the doctrine which Wilhelm Von Humboldt, so eminent both as a *savant* and as a politician, made the text of a treatise—that 'the end of man, or that which is prescribed by the eternal or immutable dictates of reason, and not suggested by vague and transient desires, is the highest and most harmonious development of his powers to a complete and consistent whole'; that, therefore, the object 'towards which every human being must ceaselessly direct his efforts, and on which especially those who design to influence their fellow-men must ever keep their eyes, is the individuality of power and development'; that for this there are two requisites, 'freedom, and variety of situations'; and that from the union of these arise 'individual vigour and manifold diversity', which combine themselves in 'originality'.[6]

Little, however, as people are accustomed to a doctrine like that of Von Humboldt, and surprising as it may be to them to find so high a value attached to individuality, the question, one must nevertheless think, can only be one of degree. No one's idea of excellence in conduct is that people should do absolutely nothing but copy one another. No one would assert that people ought not to put into their mode of life, and into the conduct of their concerns, any impress whatever of their own judgment, or of their own individual character. On the other hand, it would be absurd to pretend that people ought to live as if nothing whatever had been known in the world before they came into it; as if experience had as yet done nothing towards showing that one mode of existence, or of conduct, is preferable to another. Nobody denies that people should be so taught and trained in youth, as to know and benefit by the ascertained results of human experience. But it is the privilege and proper condition of a human being, arrived at the maturity of his faculties, to use and interpret experience in his own

way. It is for him to find out what part of recorded experience is properly applicable to his own circumstances and character. The traditions and customs of other people are, to a certain extent, evidence of what their experience has taught *them*; presumptive evidence, and as such, have a claim to his deference: but, in the first place, their experience may be too narrow; or they may not have interpreted it rightly. Secondly, their interpretation of experience may be correct, but unsuitable to him. Customs are made for customary circumstances, and customary characters; and his circumstances or his character may be uncustomary. Thirdly, though the customs be both good as customs, and suitable to him, yet to conform to custom, merely as custom, does not educate or develop in him any of the qualities which are the distinctive endowment of a human being. The human faculties of perception, judgment, discriminative feeling, mental activity, and even moral preference, are exercised only in making a choice. He who does anything because it is the custom, makes no choice. He gains no practice either in discerning or in desiring what is best. The mental and moral, like the muscular powers, are improved only by being used. The faculties are called into no exercise by doing a thing merely because others do it, no more than by believing a thing only because others believe it. If the grounds of an opinion are not conclusive to the person's own reason, his reason cannot be strengthened, but is likely to be weakened, by his adopting it: and if the inducements to an act are not such as are consentaneous to his own feelings and character (where affection, or the rights of others, are not concerned) it is so much done towards rendering his feelings and character inert and torpid, instead of active and energetic.

He who lets the world, or his own portion of it, choose his plan of life for him, has no need of any other faculty than the ape-like one of imitation. He who chooses his plan for himself, employs all his faculties. He must use observation to see, reasoning and judgment to foresee, activity to gather materials for decision, discrimination to decide, and when he has decided, firmness and self-control to hold to his deliberate decision. And these qualities he requires and exercises exactly in proportion as the part of his con-

[6] *The Sphere and Duties of Government*, from the German of Baron Wilhelm von Humboldt, pp. 11–13.

duct which he determines according to his own judgment and feelings is a large one. It is possible that he might be guided in some good path, and kept out of harm's way, without any of these things. But what will be his comparative worth as a human being? It really is of importance, not only what men do, but also what manner of men they are that do it. Among the works of man, which human life is rightly employed in perfecting and beautifying, the first in importance surely is man himself. Supposing it were possible to get houses built, corn grown, battles fought, causes tried, and even churches erected and prayers said, by machinery—by automatons in human form—it would be a considerable loss to exchange for these automatons even the men and women who at present inhabit the more civilized parts of the world, and who assuredly are but starved specimens of what nature can and will produce. Human nature is not a machine to be built after a model, and set to do exactly the work prescribed for it, but a tree, which requires to grow and develop itself on all sides, according to the tendency of the inward forces which make it a living thing.

It will probably be conceded that it is desirable people should exercise their understandings, and that an intelligent following of custom, or even occasionally an intelligent deviation from custom, is better than a blind and simply mechanical adhesion to it. To a certain extent it is admitted, that our understanding should be our own: but there is not the same willingness to admit that our desires and impulses should be our own likewise; or that to possess impulses of our own, and of any strength, is anything but a peril and a snare. Yet desires and impulses are as much a part of a perfect human being, as beliefs and restraints: and strong impulses are only perilous when not properly balanced; when one set of aims and inclinations is developed into strength, while others, which ought to coexist with them, remain weak and inactive. It is not because men's desires are strong that they act ill; it is because their consciences are weak. There is no natural connexion between strong impulses and a weak conscience. The natural connexion is the other way. To say that one person's desires and feelings are stronger and more various than those of another, is merely to say that he has more of the raw material of human nature, and is therefore capable, perhaps of more evil, but certainly of more good. Strong impulses are but another name for energy. Energy may be turned to bad uses; but more good may always be made of an energetic nature, than of an indolent and impassive one. Those who have most natural feeling, are always those whose cultivated feelings may be made the strongest. The same strong susceptibilities which make the personal impulses vivid and powerful, are also the source from whence are generated the most passionate love of virtue, and the sternest self-control. It is through the cultivation of these, that society both does its duty and protects its interests: not by rejecting the stuff of which heroes are made, because it knows not how to make them. A person whose desires and impulses are his own—are the expression of his own nature, as it has been developed and modified by his own culture—is said to have a character. One whose desires and impulses are not his own, has no character, no more than a steam-engine has a character. If, in addition to being his own, his impulses are strong, and are under the government of a strong will, he has an energetic character. Whoever thinks that individuality of desires and impulses should not be encouraged to unfold itself, must maintain that society has no need of strong natures—is not the better for containing many persons who have much character—and that a high general average of energy is not desirable.

In some early states of society, these forces might be, and were, too much ahead of the power which society then possessed of disciplining and controlling them. There has been a time when the element of spontaneity and individuality was in excess, and the social principle had a hard struggle with it. The difficulty then was, to induce men of strong bodies or minds to pay obedience to any rules which required them to control their impulses. To overcome this difficulty, law and discipline, like the Popes struggling against the Emperors, asserted a power over the whole man, claiming to control all his life in order to control his character—which society had not found any other sufficient means of binding. But society has now fairly got the better of individuality; and the danger which threatens human nature is not the excess, but the deficiency, of personal impulses and preferences.

Things are vastly changed, since the passions of those who were strong by station or by personal endowment were in a state of habitual rebellion against laws and ordinances, and required to be rigorously chained up to enable the persons within their reach to enjoy any particle of security. In our times, from the highest class of society down to the lowest, every one lives as under the eye of a hostile and dreaded censorship. Not only in what concerns others, but in what concerns only themselves, the individual or the family do not ask themselves—what do I prefer? or, what would suit my character and disposition? or, what would allow the best and highest in me to have fair play, and enable it to grow and thrive? They ask themselves, what is suitable to my position? what is usually done by persons of my station and pecuniary circumstances? or (worse still) what is usually done by persons of a station and circumstances superior to mine? I do not mean that they choose what is customary, in preference to what suits their own inclination. It does not occur to them to have any inclination, except for what is customary. Thus the mind itself is bowed to the yoke: even in what people do for pleasure, conformity is the first thing thought of; they like in crowds; they exercise choice only among things commonly done: peculiarity of taste, eccentricity of conduct, are shunned equally with crimes: until by dint of not following their own nature, they have no nature to follow: their human capacities are withered and starved: they become incapable of any strong wishes or native pleasures, and are generally without either opinions or feelings of home growth, or properly their own. Now is this, or is it not, the desirable condition of human nature?

It is so, on the Calvinistic theory. According to that, the one great offence of man is self-will. All the good of which humanity is capable, is comprised in obedience. You have no choice; thus you must do, and no otherwise: 'whatever is not a duty, is a sin.' Human nature being radically corrupt, there is no redemption for any one until human nature is killed within him. To one holding this theory of life, crushing out any of the human faculties, capacities, and susceptibilities, is no evil: man needs no capacity, but that of surrendering himself to the will of God: and if he uses any of his faculties for any other purpose but to do that supposed will more effectually, he is better without them. This is the theory of Calvinism; and it is held, in a mitigated form, by many who do not consider themselves Calvinists; the mitigation consisting in giving a less ascetic interpretation to the alleged will of God; asserting it to be his will that mankind should gratify some of their inclinations; of course not in the manner they themselves prefer, but in the way of obedience, that is, in a way prescribed to them by authority; and, therefore, by the necessary conditions of the case, the same for all.

In some such insidious form there is at present a strong tendency to this narrow theory of life, and to the pinched and hidebound type of human character which it patronizes. Many persons, no doubt, sincerely think that human beings thus cramped and dwarfed, are as their Maker designed them to be; just as many have thought that trees are a much finer thing when clipped into pollards, or cut out into figures of animals, than as nature made them. But if it be any part of religion to believe that man was made by a good Being, it is more consistent with that faith to believe, that this Being gave all human faculties that they might be cultivated and unfolded, not rooted out and consumed, and that he takes delight in every nearer approach made by his creatures to the ideal conception embodied in them, every increase in any of their capabilities of comprehension, of action, or of enjoyment. There is a different type of human excellence from the Calvinistic; a conception of humanity as having its nature bestowed on it for other purposes than merely to be abnegated. 'Pagan self-assertion' is one of the elements of human worth, as well as 'Christian self-denial.'[7] There is a Greek ideal of self-development, which the Platonic and Christian ideal of self-government blends with, but does not supersede. It may be better to be a John Knox than an Alcibiades, but it is better to be a Pericles than either; nor would a Pericles, if we had one in these days, be without anything good which belonged to John Knox.

It is not by wearing down into uniformity all that is individual in themselves, but by cultivating it and calling it forth, within the limits imposed by the rights and

[7] Sterling's *Essays.*

interests of others, that human beings become a noble and beautiful object of contemplation; and as the works partake the character of those who do them, by the same process human life also becomes rich, diversified, and animating, furnishing more abundant aliment to high thoughts and elevating feelings, and strengthening the tie which binds every individual to the race, by making the race infinitely better worth belonging to. In proportion to the development of his individuality, each person becomes more valuable to himself, and is therefore capable of being more valuable to others. There is a greater fulness of life about his own existence, and when there is more life in the units there is more in the mass which is composed of them. As much compression as is necessary to prevent the stronger specimens of human nature from encroaching on the rights of others, cannot be dispensed with; but for this there is ample compensation even in the point of view of human development. The means of development which the individual loses by being prevented from gratifying his inclinations to the injury of others, are chiefly obtained at the expense of the development of other people. And even to himself there is a full equivalent in the better development of the social part of his nature, rendered possible by the restraint put upon the selfish part. To be held to rigid rules of justice for the sake of others, develops the feelings and capacities which have the good of others for their object. But to be restrained in things not affecting their good, by their mere displeasure, develops nothing valuable, except such force of character as may unfold itself in resisting the restraint. If acquiesced in, it dulls and blunts the whole nature. To give any fair play to the nature of each, it is essential that different persons should be allowed to lead different lives. In proportion as this latitude has been exercised in any age, has that age been noteworthy to posterity. Even despotism does not produce its worst effects, so long as individuality exists under it; and whatever crushes individuality is despotism, by whatever name it may be called, and whether it professes to be enforcing the will of God or the injunctions of men.

Having said that individuality is the same thing with development, and that it is only the cultivation of individuality which produces, or can produce, well-developed human beings, I might here close the argument: for what more or better can be said of any condition of human affairs, than that it brings human beings themselves nearer to the best thing they can be? or what worse can be said of any obstruction to good, than that it prevents this? Doubtless, however, these considerations will not suffice to convince those who most need convincing; and it is necessary further to show, that these developed human beings are of some use to the undeveloped—to point out to those who do not desire liberty, and would not avail themselves of it, that they may be in some intelligible manner rewarded for allowing other people to make use of it without hindrance.

In the first place, then, I would suggest that they might possibly learn something from them. It will not be denied by anybody, that originality is a valuable element in human affairs. There is always need of persons not only to discover new truths, and point out when what were once truths are true no longer, but also to commence new practices, and set the example of more enlightened conduct, and better taste and sense in human life. This cannot well be gainsaid by anybody who does not believe that the world has already attained perfection in all its ways and practices. It is true that this benefit is not capable of being rendered by everybody alike: there are but few persons, in comparison with the whole of mankind, whose experiments, if adopted by others, would be likely to be any improvement on established practice. But these few are the salt of the earth; without them, human life would become a stagnant pool. Not only is it they who introduce good things which did not before exist; it is they who keep the life in those which already existed. If there were nothing new to be done, would human intellect cease to be necessary? Would it be a reason why those who do the old things should forget why they are done, and do them like cattle, not like human beings? There is only too great a tendency in the best beliefs and practices to degenerate into the mechanical; and unless there were a succession of persons whose ever-recurring originality prevents the grounds of those beliefs and practices from becoming merely traditional, such dead matter would not resist the smallest shock from anything really alive, and there would be no reason why civilization should not die out, as in the Byzantine Empire. Persons of genius, it is true, are, and are always likely to be, a small minority; but in order to have them, it is necessary to preserve the soil in which they grow. Genius can only breathe freely in an *atmosphere* of freedom. Persons of genius are, *ex vi termini, more* individual than any other people—less capable, consequently, of fitting themselves, without hurtful compression, into any of the small number of moulds which society provides in order to save its members the trouble of forming their own character. If from timidity they consent to be forced into one of these moulds, and to let all that part of themselves which cannot expand under the pressure remain unexpanded, society will be little the better for their genius. If they are of a strong character, and break their fetters, they become a mark for the society which has not succeeded in reducing them to commonplace, to point at with solemn warning as 'wild,' 'erratic,' and the like; much as if one should complain of the Niagara river for not flowing smoothly between its banks like a Dutch canal.

I insist thus emphatically on the importance of genius, and the necessity of allowing it to unfold itself freely both in thought and in practice, being well aware that no one will deny the position in theory, but knowing also that almost every one, in reality, is totally indifferent to it. People think genius a fine thing if it enables a man to write an exciting poem, or paint a picture. But in its true sense, that of originality in thought and action, though no one says that it is not a thing to be admired, nearly all, at heart, think that they can do very well without it. Unhappily this is too natural to be wondered at. Originality is the one thing which unoriginal minds cannot feel the use of. They cannot see what it is to do for them: how should they? If they could see what it would do for them, it would not be originality. The first service which originality has to render them, is that of opening their eyes: which being once fully done, they would have a chance of being themselves original. Meanwhile, recollecting that nothing was ever yet done which some one was not the first to do, and that all good things which exist are the fruits of originality, let them be modest enough to believe that there is something still left for it to ac-

complish, and assure themselves that they are more in need of originality, the less they are conscious of the want.

In sober truth, whatever homage may be professed, or even paid, to real or supposed mental superiority, the general tendency of things throughout the world is to render mediocrity the ascendant power among mankind. In ancient history, in the middle ages, and in a diminishing degree through the long transition from feudality to the present time, the individual was a power in himself; and if he had either great talents or a high social position, he was a considerable power. At present individuals are lost in the crowd. In politics it is almost a triviality to say that public opinion now rules the world. The only power deserving the name is that of masses, and of governments while they make themselves the organ of the tendencies and instincts of masses. This is as true in the moral and social relations of private life as in public transactions. Those whose opinions go by the name of public opinion, are not always the same sort of public: in America they are the whole white population; in England, chiefly the middle class. But they are always a mass, that is to say, collective mediocrity. And what is a still greater novelty, the mass do not now take their opinions from dignitaries in Church or State, from ostensible leaders, or from books. Their thinking is done for them by men much like themselves, addressing them or speaking in their name, on the spur of the moment, through the newspapers. I am not complaining of all this. I do not assert that anything better is compatible, as a general rule, with the present low state of the human mind. But that does not hinder the government of mediocrity from being mediocre government. No government by a democracy or a numerous aristocracy, either in its political acts or in the opinions, qualities, and tone of mind which it fosters, ever did or could rise above mediocrity, except in so far as the sovereign. Many have let themselves be guided (which in their best times they always have done) by the counsels and influence of a more highly gifted and instructed One or Few. The initiation of all wise or noble things, comes and must come from individuals; generally at first from some one individual. The honour and glory of the average man is that he is capable of following that initiative; that he can respond internally to wise and noble things, and be led to them with his eyes open. I am not countenancing the sort of 'hero-worship' which applauds the strong man of genius for forcibly seizing on the government of the world and making it do his bidding in spite of itself. All he can claim is, freedom to point out the way. The power of compelling others into it, is not only inconsistent with the freedom and development of all the rest, but corrupting to the strong man himself. It does seem, however, that when the opinions of masses of merely average men are everywhere become or becoming the dominant power, the counterpoise and corrective to that tendency would be, the more and more pronounced individuality of those who stand on the higher eminences of thought. It is in these circumstances most especially, that exceptional individuals, instead of being deterred, should be encouraged in acting differently from the mass. In other times there was no advantage in their doing so, unless they acted not only differently, but better. In this age, the mere example of nonconformity, the mere refusal to bend the knee to custom, is itself a service. Precisely because the tyranny of opinion is such as to make eccentricity a reproach, it is desirable, in order to break through that tyranny, that people should be eccentric. Eccentricity has always abounded when and where strength of character has abounded; and the amount of eccentricity in a society has generally been proportional to the amount of genius, mental vigour, and moral courage which it contained. That so few now dare to be eccentric, marks the chief danger of the time.

I have said that it is important to give the freest scope possible to uncustomary things, in order that it may in time appear which of these are fit to be converted into customs. But independence of action, and disregard of custom, are not solely deserving of encouragement for the chance they afford that better modes of action, and customs more worthy of general adoption, may be struck out; nor is it only persons of decided mental superiority who have a just claim to carry on their lives in their own way. There is no reason that all human existence should be constructed on some one or some small number of patterns. If a person possesses any tolerable amount of common sense and experience, his own mode of laying out his existence is the best, not because it is the best in itself, but because it is his own mode. Human beings are not like sheep; and even sheep are not undistinguishably alike. A man cannot get a coat or a pair of boots to fit him, unless they are either made to his measure, or he has a whole warehouseful to choose from: and is it easier to fit him with a life than with a coat, or are human beings more like one another in their whole physical and spiritual conformation than in the shape of their feet? If it were only that people have diversities of taste, that is reason enough for not attempting to shape them all after one model. But different persons also require different conditions for their spiritual development; and can no more exist healthily in the same moral, than all the variety of plants can in the same physical, atmosphere and climate. The same things which are helps to one person towards the cultivation of his higher nature, are hindrances to another. The same mode of life is a healthy excitement to one, keeping all his faculties of action and enjoyment in their best order, while to another it is a distracting burthen, which suspends or crushes all internal life. Such are the differences among human beings in their sources of pleasure, their susceptibilities of pain, and the operation on them of different physical and moral agencies, that unless there is a corresponding diversity in their modes of life, they neither obtain their fair share of happiness, nor grow up to the mental, moral, and aesthetic stature of which their nature is capable. Why then should tolerance, as far as the public sentiment is concerned, extend only to tastes and modes of life which extort acquiescence by the multitude of their adherents? Nowhere (except in some monastic institutions) is diversity of taste entirely unrecognised; a person may, without blame, either like or dislike rowing, or smoking, or music, or athletic exercises, or chess, or cards, or study, because both those who like each of these things, and those who dislike them, are too numerous to be put down. But the man, and still more the woman, who can be accused either of doing 'what nobody does,' or of not doing 'what everybody does,' is the subject of as much depreciatory remark as if he or she had committed some grave moral delinquency. Persons require to possess a title, or some other badge of rank, or of the consideration of people of rank, to be able to indulge somewhat in the luxury of doing as they like without detriment to their estimation. To indulge somewhat, I repeat: for whoever allow themselves much of that indulgence, incur the risk of something worse than disparaging speeches—they are in peril of a commission *de lunatico,* and of having their property taken from them and given to their relations.[8]

There is one characteristic of the present direction of public opinion, peculiarly calculated to make it intolerant of any marked demonstration of individuality. The general average of mankind are not only moderate in intellect, but also moderate in inclinations: they have no tastes or wishes strong enough to incline them to do anything unusual, and they consequently do not understand those who have, and class all such with the wild and intemperate whom they are accustomed to look down upon. Now, in addition to this fact which is general, we have only to suppose that a strong movement has set in towards the improvement of morals, and it is evident what we have to expect. In these days such a movement has set in; much has actually been effected in the way of increased regularity of conduct, and discouragement of excesses; and there is a philanthropic spirit abroad, for the exercise of which there is no more inviting field than the moral and prudential improvement of our fellow-creatures. These tendencies of the times cause the public to be more disposed than at most former periods to prescribe general rules of conduct, and endeavour to make every one conform to the approved standard. And that standard, express or tacit, is to desire nothing strongly. Its ideal of character is to be without any marked character; to maim by compression, like a Chinese lady's foot, every part of human nature which stands out prominently, and tends to make the person markedly dissimilar in outline to commonplace humanity.

As is usually the case with ideals which exclude one-half of what is desirable, the present standard of approbation produces only an inferior imitation of the other half. Instead of great energies guided by vigorous reason, and strong feelings strongly controlled by a conscientious will, its result is weak feelings and weak energies, which therefore can be kept in outward conformity to rule without any strength either of will or of reason. Already energetic characters on any large scale are becoming merely traditional. There is now scarcely any outlet for energy in this country except business. The energy expended in this may still be regarded as considerable. What little is left from that employment, is expended on some hobby; which may be a useful, even a philanthropic hobby, but is always some one thing, and generally a thing of small dimensions. The greatness of England is now all collective: individually small, we only appear capable of anything great by our habit of combining; and with this our moral and religious philanthropists are perfectly contented. But it was men of another stamp than this that made England what it has been; and men of another stamp will be needed to prevent its decline.

The despotism of custom is everywhere the standing hindrance to human advancement, being in un-

---

[8] There is something both contemptible and frightful in the sort of evidence on which, of late years, any person can be judicially declared unfit for the management of his affairs; and after his death, his disposal of his property can be set aside, if there is enough of it to pay the expenses of litigation—which are charged on the property itself. All the minute details of his daily life are pried into, and whatever is found which, seen through the medium of the perceiving and describing faculties of the lowest of the low, bears an appearance unlike absolute commonplace, is laid before the jury as evidence of insanity, and often with success; the jurors being little, if at all, less vulgar and ignorant than the witnesses; while the judges, with that extraordinary want of knowledge of human nature and life which continually astonishes us in English lawyers, often help to mislead them. These trials speak volumes as to the state of feeling and opinion among the vulgar with regard to human liberty. So far from setting any value on individuality—so far from respecting the right of each individual to act, in things indifferent, as seems good to his own judgment and inclinations, judges and juries cannot even conceive that a person in a state of sanity can desire such freedom. In former days, when it was proposed to burn atheists, charitable people used to suggest putting them in a madhouse instead: it would be nothing surprising now-a-days were we to see this done, and the doers applauding themselves, because, instead of persecuting for religion, they had adopted so humane and Christian a mode of treating these unfortunates, not without a silent satisfaction at their having thereby obtained their deserts.

ceasing antagonism to that disposition to aim at something better than customary, which is called, according to circumstances, the spirit of liberty, or that of progress or improvement. The spirit of improvement is not always a spirit of liberty, for it may aim at forcing improvements on an unwilling people; and the spirit of liberty, in so far as it resists such attempts, may ally itself locally and temporarily with the opponents of improvement; but the only unfailing and permanent source of improvement is liberty, since by it there are as many possible independent centres of improvement as there are individuals. The progressive principle, however, in either shape, whether as the love of liberty or of improvement, is antagonistic to the sway of Custom, involving at least emancipation from that yoke; and the contest between the two constitutes the chief interest of the history of mankind. The greater part of the world has, properly speaking, no history, because the despotism of Custom is complete. This is the case over the whole East. Custom is there, in all things, the final appeal; justice and right mean conformity to custom; the argument of custom no one, unless some tyrant intoxicated with power, thinks of resisting. And we see the result. Those nations must once have had originality; they did not start out of the ground populous, lettered, and versed in many of the arts of life; they made themselves all this, and were then the greatest and most powerful nations of the world. What are they now? The subjects or dependents of tribes whose forefathers wandered in the forests when theirs had magnificent palaces and gorgeous temples, but over whom custom exercised only a divided rule with liberty and progress. A people, it appears, may be progressive for a certain length of time, and then stop: when does it stop? When it ceases to possess individuality. If a similar change should befall the nations of Europe, it will not be in exactly the same shape: the despotism of custom with which these nations are threatened is not precisely stationariness. It proscribes singularity, but it does not preclude change, provided all change together. We have discarded the fixed costumes of our forefathers; every one must still dress like other people, but the fashion may change once or twice a year. We thus take care that when there is change it shall be for change's sake, and

not from any idea of beauty or convenience; for the same idea of beauty or convenience would not strike all the world at the same moment, and be simultaneously thrown aside by all at another moment. But we are progressive as well as changeable: we continually make new inventions in mechanical things, and keep them until they are again superseded by better; we are eager for improvement in politics, in education, even in morals, though in this last our idea of improvement chiefly consists in persuading or forcing other people to be as good as ourselves. It is not progress that we object to; on the contrary, we flatter ourselves that we are the most progressive people who ever lived. It is individuality that we war against: we should think we had done wonders if we had made ourselves all alike; forgetting that the unlikeness of one person to another is generally the first thing which draws the attention of either to the imperfection of his own type, and the superiority of another, or the possibility, by combining the advantages of both, of producing something better than either. We have a warning example in China—a nation of much talent, and, in some respects, even wisdom, owing to the rare good fortune of having been provided at an early period with a particularly good set of customs, the work, in some measure, of men to whom even the most enlightened European must accord, under certain limitations, the title of sages and philosophers. They are remarkable, too, in the excellence of their apparatus for impressing, as far as possible, the best wisdom they possess upon every mind in the community, and securing that those who have appropriated most of it shall occupy the posts of honour and power. Surely the people who did this have discovered the secret of human progressiveness, and must have kept themselves steadily at the head of the movement of the world. On the contrary, they have become stationary—have remained so for thousands of years; and if they are ever to be farther improved, it must be by foreigners. They have succeeded beyond all hope in what English philanthropists are so industriously working at—in making a people all alike, all governing their thoughts and conduct by the same maxims and rules; and these are the fruits. The modern *régime* of public opinion is, in an unorganized form, what the Chinese educational and political systems are in an organized; and unless individuality shall be able successfully to assert itself against this yoke, Europe, notwithstanding its noble antecedents and its professed Christianity, will tend to become another China.

What is it that has hitherto preserved Europe from this lot? What has made the European family of nations an improving, instead of a stationary portion of mankind? Not any superior excellence in them, which, when it exists, exists as the effect, not as the cause; but their remarkable diversity of character and culture. Individuals, classes, nations, have been extremely unlike one another: they have struck out a great variety of paths, each leading to something valuable; and although at every period those who travelled in different paths have been intolerant of one another, and each would have thought it an excellent thing if all the rest could have been compelled to travel his road, their attempts to thwart each other's development have rarely had any permanent success, and each has in time endured to receive the good which the others have offered. Europe is, in my judgment, wholly indebted to this plurality of paths for its progressive and many-sided development. But it already begins to possess this benefit in a considerably less degree. It is decidedly advancing towards the Chinese ideal of making all people alike. M. de Tocqueville, in his last important work, remarks how much more the Frenchmen of the present day resemble one another, than did those even of the last generation. The same remark might be made of Englishmen in a far greater degree. In a passage already quoted from Wilhelm von Humboldt, he points out two things as necessary conditions of human development, because necessary to render people unlike one another; namely, freedom, and variety of situations. The second of these two conditions is in this country every day diminishing. The circumstances which surround different classes and individuals, and shape their characters, are daily becoming more assimilated. Formerly, different ranks, different neighbourhoods, different trades and professions, lived in what might be called different worlds; at present, to a great degree in the same. Comparatively speaking, they now read the same things, listen to the same things, see the same things, go to the same

places, have their hopes and fears directed to the same objects, have the same rights and liberties, and the same means of asserting them. Great as are the differences of position which remain, they are nothing to those which have ceased. And the assimilation is still proceeding. All the political changes of the age promote it, since they all tend to raise the low and to lower the high. Every extension of education promotes it, because education brings people under common influences, and gives them access to the general stock of facts and sentiments. Improvements in the means of communication promote it, by bringing the inhabitants of distant places into personal contact, and keeping up a rapid flow of changes of residence between one place and another. The increase of commerce and manufactures promotes it, by diffusing more widely the advantages of easy circumstances, and opening all objects of ambition, even the highest, to general competition, whereby the desire of rising becomes no longer the character of a particular class, but of all classes. A more powerful agency than even all these, in bringing about a general similarity among mankind, is the complete establishment, in this and other free countries, of the ascendancy of public opinion in the State. As the various social eminences which enabled persons entrenched on them to disregard the opinion of the multitude, gradually become levelled; as the very idea of resisting the will of the public, when it is positively known that they have a will, disappears more and more from the minds of practical politicians; there ceases to be any social support for nonconformity—any substantive power in society, which, itself opposed to the ascendancy of numbers, is interested in taking under its protection opinions and tendencies at variance with those of the public.

The combination of all these causes forms so great a mass of influences hostile to Individuality, that it is not easy to see how it can stand its ground. It will do so with increasing difficulty, unless the intelligent part of the public can be made to feel its value—to see that it is good there should be differences, even though not for the better, even though, as it may appear to them, some should be for the worse. If the claims of Individuality are ever to be asserted, the time is now, while much is still wanting to complete the enforced assimilation. It is only in the earlier stages that any stand can be successfully made against the encroachment. The demand that all other people shall resemble ourselves, grows by what it feeds on. If resistance waits till life is reduced *nearly* to one uniform type, all deviations from that type will come to be considered impious, immoral, even monstrous and contrary to nature. Mankind speedily become unable to conceive diversity, when they have been for some time unaccustomed to see it.

Chapter IV: Of the Limits to the Authority of Society over the Individual

What, then, is the rightful limit to the sovereignty of the individual over himself? Where does the authority of society begin? How much of human life should be assigned to individuality, and how much to society?

Each will receive its proper share, if each has that which more particularly concerns it. To individuality should belong the part of life in which it is chiefly the individual that is interested; to society, the part which chiefly interests society.

Though society is not founded on a contract, and though no good purpose is answered by inventing a contract in order to deduce social obligations from it, every one who receives the protection of society owes a return for the benefit, and the fact of living in society renders it indispensable that each should be bound to observe a certain line of conduct towards the rest. This conduct consists first, in not injuring the interests of one another; or rather certain interests, which, either by express legal provision or by tacit understanding, ought to be considered as rights; and secondly, in each person's bearing his share (to be fixed on some equitable principle) of the labours and sacrifices incurred for defending the society or its members from injury and molestation. These conditions society is justified in enforcing at all costs to those who endeavour to withhold fulfilment. Nor is this all that society may do. The acts of an individual may be hurtful to others, or wanting in due consideration for their welfare, without going the length of violating any of their constituted rights. The offender may then be justly punished by opinion, though not by law. As soon as any part of a person's conduct affects prejudicially the interests of others, society has jurisdiction over it, and the question whether the general welfare will or will not be promoted by interfering with it, becomes open to discussion. But there is no room for entertaining any such question when a person's conduct affects the interests of no persons besides himself, or needs not affect them unless they like (all the persons concerned being of full age, and the ordinary amount of understanding). In all such cases there should be perfect freedom, legal and social, to do the action and stand the consequences.

It would be a great misunderstanding of this doctrine to suppose that it is one of selfish indifference, which pretends that human beings have no business with each other's conduct in life, and that they should not concern themselves about the well-doing or well-being of one another, unless their own interest is involved. Instead of any diminution, there is need of a great increase of disinterested exertion to promote the good of others. But disinterested benevolence can find other instruments to persuade people to their good, than whips and scourges, either of the literal or the metaphorical sort. I am the last person to undervalue the self-regarding virtues; they are only second in importance, if even second, to the social. It is equally the business of education to cultivate both. But even education works by conviction and persuasion as well as by compulsion, and it is by the former only that, when the period of education is past, the self-regarding virtues should be inculcated. Human beings owe to each other help to distinguish the better from the worse, and encouragement to choose the former and avoid the latter. They should be for ever stimulating each other to increased exercise of their higher faculties, and increased direction of their feelings and aims towards wise instead of foolish, elevating instead of degrading, objects and contemplations. But neither one person, nor any number of persons, is warranted in saying to another human creature of ripe years, that he shall not do with his life for his own benefit what he chooses to do with it. He is the person most interested in his own well-being: the interest which any other person, except in cases of strong personal attachment, can have in it, is trifling, compared with that which he himself has; the interest which society has in him individually (except as to his conduct to others) is fractional, and altogether indirect: while, with respect to his own feelings and circumstances, the most ordinary man or woman has means of knowledge immeasurably surpassing those that can be possessed by any one else. The interference of society to overrule his judgment and purposes in what only regards himself, must be grounded on general presumptions; which may be altogether wrong, and even if right, are as likely as not to be misapplied to individual cases, by persons no better acquainted with the circumstances of such cases than those are who look at them merely from without. In this department, therefore, of human affairs, Individuality has its proper field of action. In the conduct of human beings towards one another, it is necessary that general rules should for the most part be observed, in order that people may know what they have to expect; but in each person's own concerns, his individual spontaneity is entitled to free exercise. Considerations to aid his judgment, exhortations to strengthen his will, may be offered to him, even obtruded on him, by others; but he himself is the final judge. All errors which he is likely to commit against advice and warning, are far outweighed by the evil of allowing others to constrain him to what they deem his good.

I do not mean that the feelings with which a person is regarded by others, ought not to be in any way affected by his self-regarding qualities or deficiencies. This is neither possible nor desirable. If he is eminent in any of the qualities which conduce to his own good, he is, so far, a proper object of admiration. He is so much the nearer to the ideal perfection of human nature. If he is grossly deficient in those qualities, a sentiment the opposite of admiration will follow. There is a degree of folly, and a degree of what may be called (though the phrase is not unobjectionable) lowness or depravation of taste, which, though it cannot justify doing harm to the person who manifests it, renders him necessarily and properly a subject of distaste, or, in extreme cases, even of contempt: a person could not have the opposite qualities in due strength without entertaining these feelings. Though doing no wrong to any one, a person may so act as to compel us to judge him, and feel to him, as a fool, or as a being of an inferior order: and since this judgment and feeling are a fact which he would prefer to avoid, it is doing him a service to warn him of it beforehand, as of any other disagreeable consequence to which he exposes himself. It would be well, indeed, if this good office were much more freely rendered than the common notions of politeness at present permit, and if one person could honestly point out to another that he thinks him in fault, without being considered unmannerly or presuming. We have a right, also, in various ways, to act upon our unfavourable opinion of any one, not to the oppression of his individuality, but in the exercise of ours. We are not bound, for example, to seek his society; we have a right to avoid it (though not to parade the avoidance), for we have a right to choose the society most acceptable to us. We have a right, and it may be our duty, to caution others against him, if we think his example or conversation likely to have a pernicious effect on those with whom he associates. We may give others a preference over him in optional good offices, except those which tend to his improvement. In these various modes a person may suffer very severe penalties at the hands of others, for faults which directly concern only himself; but he suffers these penalties only in so far as they are the natural, and, as it were, the spontaneous consequences of the faults themselves, not because they are purposely inflicted on him for the sake of punishment. A person who shows rashness, obstinacy, self-conceit—who cannot live within moderate means—who cannot restrain himself from hurtful indulgences—who pursues animal pleasures at the expense of those of feeling and intellect—must expect to be lowered in the opinion of others, and to have a less share of their favourable sentiments; but of this he has no right to complain, unless he has merited their favour by special excellence in his social relations, and has thus established a title to their good offices, which is not affected by his demerits towards himself.

What I contend for is, that the inconveniences which are strictly inseparable from the unfavourable judgment of others, are the only ones to which a person should ever be subjected for that portion of his conduct and character which concerns his own good, but which does not affect the interests of others in their relations with him. Acts injurious to others require a totally different treatment. Encroachment on their rights; infliction on them of any loss or damage not justified by his own rights; falsehood or duplicity in dealing with them; unfair or ungenerous use of advantages over them; even selfish abstinence from defending them against injury—these are fit objects of moral reprobation, and, in grave cases, of moral retribution and punishment. And not only these acts, but the dispositions which lead to them, are properly immoral, and fit subjects of disapprobation which may rise to abhorrence. Cruelty of disposition; malice and ill-nature; that most anti-social and odious of all passions, envy; dissimulation and insincerity; irascibility on insufficient cause, and resentment disproportioned to the provocation; the love of domineering over others; the desire to engross more than one's share of advantages (the *pleonexia* of the Greeks); the pride which derives gratification from the abasement of others; the egotism which thinks self and its concerns more important than everything else, and decides all doubtful questions in its own favour;—these are moral vices, and constitute a bad and odious moral character: unlike the self-regarding faults previously mentioned, which are not properly immoralities, and to whatever pitch they may be carried, do not constitute wickedness. They may be proofs of any amount of folly, or want of personal dignity and self-respect; but they are only a subject of moral reprobation when they involve a breach of duty to others, for whose sake the individual is bound to have care for himself. What are called duties to ourselves are not socially obligatory, unless circumstances render them at the same time duties to others. The term duty to oneself, when it means anything more than prudence, means self-respect or self-development; and for none of these is any one accountable to his fellow creatures, because for none of them is it for the good of mankind that he be held accountable to them.

The distinction between the loss of consideration which a person may rightly incur by defect of prudence or of personal dignity, and the reprobation which is due to him for an offence against the rights of others, is not a merely nominal distinction. It makes a vast difference both in our feelings and in our conduct towards him, whether he displeases us in things in which we think we have a right to control him, or in things in which we know that we have not. If he displeases us, we may express our distaste, and we may stand aloof from a person as well as from a thing that displeases us; but we shall not therefore feel called on to make his life uncomfortable. We shall reflect that he already bears, or will bear, the whole penalty of his error; if he spoils his life by mismanagement, we shall not, for that reason, desire to spoil it still further: instead of wishing to punish him, we shall rather endeavour to alleviate his punishment, by showing him how he may avoid or cure the evils his conduct tends to bring upon him. He may be to us an object of pity, perhaps of dislike, but not of anger or resentment; we shall not treat him like an enemy of society: the worst we shall think ourselves justified in doing is leaving him to himself, if we do not interfere benevolently by showing interest or concern for him. It is far otherwise if he has infringed the rules necessary for the protection of his fellow-creatures, individually or collectively. The evil consequences of his acts do not then fall on himself, but on others; and society, as the protector of all its members, must retaliate on him; must inflict pain on him for the express purpose of punishment, and must take care that it be sufficiently severe. In the one case, he is an offender at our bar, and we are called on not only to sit in judgment on him, but, in one shape or another, to execute our own sentence: in the other case, it is not our part to inflict any suffering on him, except what may incidentally follow from our using the same liberty in the regulation of our own affairs, which we allow to him in his.

The distinction here pointed out between the part of a person's life which concerns only himself, and that which concerns others, many persons will refuse to admit. How (it may be asked) can any part of the conduct of a member of society be a matter of indifference to the other members? No person is an entirely isolated being; it is impossible for a person to do anything seriously or permanently hurtful to himself, without mischief reaching at least to his near connexions, and often far beyond them. If he injures his property, he does harm to those who directly or indirectly derived support from it, and usually diminishes, by a greater or less amount, the general resources of the community. If he deteriorates his bodily or mental faculties, he not only brings evil upon all who depended on him for any portion of their happiness, but disqualifies himself for rendering the services which he owes to his fellow creatures generally; perhaps becomes a burthen on their affection or benevolence; and if such conduct were very frequent, hardly any offence that is committed would detract more from the general sum of good. Finally, if by his vices or follies a person does no direct harm to others, he is nevertheless (it may be said) injurious by his example; and ought to be compelled to control himself, for the sake of those whom the sight or knowledge of his conduct might corrupt or mislead.

And even (it will be added) if the consequences of misconduct could be confined to the vicious or thoughtless individual, ought society to abandon to their own guidance those who are manifestly unfit for it? If protection against themselves is confessedly due to children and persons under age, is not society equally bound to afford it to persons of mature years who are equally incapable of self-government? If gambling, or drunkenness, or incontinence, or idleness, or uncleanliness, are as injurious to happiness, and as great a hindrance to improvement, as many or most of the acts prohibited by law, why (it may be asked) should not law, so far as is consistent with practicability and social convenience, endeavour to repress these also? And as a supplement to the unavoidable imperfections of law, ought not opinion at least to organize a powerful police against these vices, and visit rigidly with social penalties those who are known to practise them? There is no question here (it may be said) about restricting individuality, or impeding the trial of new and original experiments in living. The only things it is sought to prevent are things which have been tried and condemned from the beginning of the world until now; things which experience has shown not to be useful or suitable to any person's individuality. There must be some length of time and amount of experience, after which a moral or prudential truth may be regarded as established: and it is merely desired to prevent generation after generation from

falling over the same precipice which has been fatal to their predecessors.

I fully admit that the mischief which a person does to himself may seriously affect, both through their sympathies and their interests, those nearly connected with him, and in a minor degree, society at large. When, by conduct of this sort, a person is led to violate a distinct and assignable obligation to any other person or persons, the case is taken out of the self-regarding class, and becomes amenable to moral disapprobation in the proper sense of the term. If, for example, a man, through intemperance or extravagance, becomes unable to pay his debts, or, having undertaken the moral responsibility of a family, becomes from the same cause incapable of supporting or educating them, he is deservedly reprobated, and might be justly punished; but it is for the breach of duty to his family or creditors, not for the extravagance. If the resources which ought to have been devoted to them, had been diverted from them for the most prudent investment, the moral culpability would have been the same. George Barnwell murdered his uncle to get money for his mistress, but if he had done it to set himself up in business, he would equally have been hanged. Again, in the frequent case of a man who causes grief to his family by addiction to bad habits, he deserves reproach for his unkindness or ingratitude; but so he may for cultivating habits not in themselves vicious, if they are painful to those with whom he passes his life, or who from personal ties are dependent on him for their comfort. Whoever fails in the consideration generally due to the interests and feelings of others, not being compelled by some more imperative duty, or justified by allowable self-preference, is a subject of moral disapprobation for that failure, but not for the cause of it, nor for the errors, merely personal to himself, which may have remotely led to it. In like manner, when a person disables himself, by conduct purely self-regarding, from the performance of some definite duty incumbent on him to the public, he is guilty of a social offence. No person ought to be punished simply for being drunk; but a soldier or a policeman should be punished for being drunk on duty. Whenever, in short, there is a definite damage, or a definite risk of damage, either to an individual or to the public, the case is taken out of the province of liberty, and placed in that of morality or law.

But with regard to the merely contingent, or, as it may be called, constructive injury which a person causes to society, by conduct which neither violates any specific duty to the public, nor occasions perceptible hurt to any assignable individual except himself; the inconvenience is one which society can afford to bear, for the sake of the greater good of human freedom. If grown persons are to be punished for not taking proper care of themselves, I would rather it were for their own sake, than under pretence of preventing them from impairing their capacity of rendering to society benefits which society does not pretend it has a right to exact. But I cannot consent to argue the point as if society had no means of bringing its weaker members up to its ordinary standard of rational conduct, except waiting till they do something irrational, and then punishing them, legally or morally, for it. Society has had absolute power over them during all the early portion of their existence: it has had the whole period of childhood and nonage in which to try whether it could make them capable of rational conduct in life. The existing generation is master both of the training and the entire circumstances of the generation to come; it cannot indeed make them perfectly wise and good, because it is itself so lamentably deficient in goodness and wisdom; and its best efforts are not always, in individual cases, its most successful ones; but it is perfectly well able to make the rising generation, as a whole, as good as, and a little better than, itself. If society lets any considerable number of its members grow up mere children, incapable of being acted on by rational consideration of distant motives, society has itself to blame for the consequences. Armed not only with all the powers of education, but with the ascendancy which the authority of a received opinion always exercises over the minds who are least fitted to judge for themselves; and aided by the natural penalties which cannot be prevented from falling on those who incur the distaste or the contempt of those who know them; let not society pretend that it needs, besides all this, the power to issue commands and enforce obedience in the personal concerns of individuals, in which, on all principles of justice and policy, the decision ought to rest with those who are to abide

the consequences. Nor is there anything which tends more to discredit and frustrate the better means of influencing conduct, than a resort to the worse. If there be among those whom it is attempted to coerce into prudence or temperance, any of the material of which vigorous and independent characters are made, they will infallibly rebel against the yoke. No such person will ever feel that others have a right to control him in his concerns, such as they have to prevent him from injuring them in theirs; and it easily comes to be considered a mark of spirit and courage to fly in the face of such usurped authority, and do with ostentation the exact opposite of what it enjoins; as in the fashion of grossness which succeeded, in the time of Charles II., to the fanatical moral intolerance of the Puritans. With respect to what is said of the necessity of protecting society from the bad example set to others by the vicious or the self-indulgent; it is true that bad example may have a pernicious effect, especially the example of doing wrong to others with impunity to the wrong-doer. But we are now speaking of conduct which, while it does no wrong to others, is supposed to do great harm to the agent himself: and I do not see how those who believe this, can think otherwise than that the example, on the whole, must be more salutary than hurtful, since, if it displays the misconduct, it displays also the painful or degrading consequences which, if the conduct is justly censured, must be supposed to be in all or most cases attendant on it.

But the strongest of all the arguments against the interference of the public with purely personal conduct, is that when it does interfere, the odds are that it interferes wrongly, and in the wrong place. On questions of social morality, of duty to others, the opinion of the public, that is, of an overruling majority, though often wrong, is likely to be still oftener right; because on such questions they are only required to judge of their own interests; of the manner in which some mode of conduct, if allowed to be practised, would affect themselves. But the opinion of a similar majority, imposed as a law on the minority, on questions of self-regarding conduct, is quite as likely to be wrong as right; for in these cases public opinion means, at the best, some people's opinion of what is good or bad for other people; while very often it does not even mean that; the public, with the most perfect indifference, passing over the pleasure or convenience of those whose conduct they censure, and considering only their own preference. There are many who consider as an injury to themselves any conduct which they have a distaste for, and resent it as an outrage to their feelings; as a religious bigot, when charged with disregarding the religious feelings of others, has been known to retort that they disregard his feelings, by persisting in their abominable worship or creed. But there is no parity between the feeling of a person for his own opinion, and the feeling of another who is offended at his holding it; no more than between the desire of a thief to take a purse, and the desire of the right owner to keep it. And a person's taste is as much his own peculiar concern as his opinion or his purse. It is easy for any one to imagine an ideal public, which leaves the freedom and choice of individuals in all uncertain matters undisturbed, and only requires them to abstain from modes of conduct which universal experience has condemned. But where has there been seen a public which set any such limit to its censorship? or when does the public trouble itself about universal experience? In its interferences with personal conduct it is seldom thinking of anything but the enormity of acting or feeling differently from itself; and this standard of judgment, thinly disguised, is held up to mankind as the dictate of religion and philosophy, by nine-tenths of all moralists and speculative writers. These teach that things are right because they are right; because we feel them to be so. They tell us to search in our own minds and hearts for laws of conduct binding on ourselves and on all others. What can the poor public do but apply these instructions, and make their own personal feelings of good and evil, if they are tolerably unanimous in them, obligatory on all the world?

The evil here pointed out is not one which exists only in theory; and it may perhaps be expected that I should specify the instances in which the public of this age and country improperly invests its own preferences with the character of moral laws. I am not writing an essay on the aberrations of existing moral feeling. That is too weighty a subject to be discussed parenthetically, and by way of illustration. Yet examples are necessary, to show that the principle I maintain is of serious and practical moment, and that I am not endeavouring to erect a barrier against imaginary evils. And it is not difficult to show, by abundant in-

stances, that to extend the bounds of what may be called moral police, until it encroaches on the most unquestionably legitimate liberty of the individual, is one of the most universal of all human propensities.

As a first instance, consider the antipathies which men cherish on no better grounds than that persons whose religious opinions are different from theirs, do not practise their religious observances, especially their religious abstinences. To cite a rather trivial example, nothing in the creed or practice of Christians does more to envenom the hatred of Mahomedans against them, than the fact of their eating pork. There are few acts which Christians and Europeans regard with more unaffected disgust, than Mussulmans regard this particular mode of satisfying hunger. It is, in the first place, an offence against their religion; but this circumstance by no means explains either the degree or the kind of their repugnance; for wine also is forbidden by their religion, and to partake of it is by all Mussulmans accounted wrong, but not disgusting. Their aversion to the flesh of the 'unclean beast' is, on the contrary, of that peculiar character, resembling an instinctive antipathy, which the idea of uncleanness, when once it thoroughly sinks into the feelings, seems always to excite even in those whose personal habits are anything but scrupulously cleanly, and of which the sentiment of religious impurity, so intense in the Hindoos, is a remarkable example. Suppose now that in a people, of whom the majority were Mussulmans, that majority should insist upon not permitting pork to be eaten within the limits of the country. This would be nothing new in Mahomedan countries.[9] Would it be a legitimate exercise of the moral authority of pub-

[9] The case of the Bombay Parsees is a curious instance in point. When this industrious and enterprising tribe, the descendants of the Persian fire-worshippers, flying from their native country before the Caliphs, arrived in Western India, they were admitted to toleration by the Hindoo sovereigns, on condition of not eating beef. When those regions afterwards fell under the dominion of Mahomedan conquerors, the Parsees obtained from them a continuance of indulgence, on condition of refraining from pork. What was at first obedience to authority became a second nature, and the Parsees to this day abstain both from beef and pork. Though not required by their religion, the double abstinence has had time to grow into a custom of their tribe; and custom, in the East, is a religion.

lic opinion? and if not, why not? The practice is really revolting to such a public. They also sincerely think that it is forbidden and abhorred by the Deity. Neither could the prohibition be censured as religious persecution. It might be religious in its origin, but it would not be persecution for religion, since nobody's religion makes it a duty to eat pork. The only tenable ground of condemnation would be, that with the personal tastes and self-regarding concerns of individuals the public has no business to interfere.

To come somewhat nearer home: the majority of Spaniards consider it a gross impiety, offensive in the highest degree to the Supreme Being, to worship him in any other manner than the Roman Catholic; and no other public worship is lawful on Spanish soil. The people of all Southern Europe look upon a married clergy as not only irreligious, but unchaste, indecent, gross, disgusting. What do Protestants think of these perfectly sincere feelings, and of the attempt to enforce them against non-Catholics? Yet, if mankind are justified in interfering with each other's liberty in things which do not concern the interests of others, on what principle is it possible consistently to exclude these cases? or who can blame people for desiring to suppress what they regard as a scandal in the sight of God and man? No stronger case can be shown for prohibiting anything which is regarded as a personal immorality, than is made out for suppressing these practices in the eyes of those who regard them as impieties; and unless we are willing to adopt the logic of persecutors, and to say that we may persecute others because we are right, and that they must not persecute us because they are wrong, we must beware of admitting a principle of which we should resent as a gross injustice the application to ourselves.

The preceding instances may be objected to, although unreasonably, as drawn from contingencies impossible among us: opinion, in this country, not being likely to enforce abstinence from meats, or to interfere with people for worshipping, and for either marrying or not marrying, according to their creed or inclination. The next example, however, shall be taken from an interference with liberty which we have by no means passed all danger of. Wherever the Puritans have been sufficiently powerful, as in New En-

gland, and in Great Britain at the time of the Commonwealth, they have endeavoured, with considerable success, to put down all public, and nearly all private, amusements: especially music, dancing, public games, or other assemblages for purposes of diversion, and the theatre. There are still in this country large bodies of persons by whose notions of morality and religion these recreations are condemned; and those persons belonging chiefly to the middle class, who are the ascendant power in the present social and political condition of the kingdom, it is by no means impossible that persons of these sentiments may at some time or other command a majority in Parliament. How will the remaining portion of the community like to have the amusements that shall be permitted to them regulated by the religious and moral sentiments of the stricter Calvinists and Methodists? Would they not, with considerable peremptoriness, desire these intrusively pious members of society to mind their own business? This is precisely what should be said to every government and every public, who have the pretension that no person shall enjoy any pleasure which they think wrong. But if the principle of the pretension be admitted, no one can reasonably object to its being acted on in the sense of the majority, or other preponderating power in the country; and all persons must be ready to conform to the idea of a Christian commonwealth, as understood by the early settlers in New England, if a religious profession similar to theirs should ever succeed in regaining its lost ground, as religions supposed to be declining have so often been known to do.

To imagine another contingency, perhaps more likely to be realized than the one last mentioned. There is confessedly a strong tendency in the modern world towards a democratic constitution of society, accompanied or not by popular political institutions. It is affirmed that in the country where this tendency is most completely realized—where both society and the government are most democratic—the United States—the feeling of the majority, to whom any appearance of a more showy or costly style of living than they can hope to rival is disagreeable, operates as a tolerably effectual sumptuary law, and that in many parts of the Union it is really difficult for a person possessing a very large income, to find any mode of spending it, which will not incur popular disapprobation. Though such statements as these are doubtless much exaggerated as a representation of existing facts, the state of things they describe is not only a conceivable and possible, but a probable result of democratic feeling, combined with the notion that the public has a right to a veto on the manner in which individuals shall spend their incomes. We have only further to suppose a considerable diffusion of Socialist opinions, and it may become infamous in the eyes of the majority to possess more property than some very small amount, or any income not earned by manual labour. Opinions similar in principle to these, already prevail widely among the artizan class, and weigh oppressively on those who are amenable to the opinion chiefly of that class, namely, its own members. It is known that the bad workmen who form the majority of the operatives in many branches of industry, are decidedly of opinion that bad workmen ought to receive the same wages as good, and that no one ought to be allowed, through piecework or otherwise, to earn by superior skill or industry more than others can without it. And they employ a moral police, which occasionally becomes a physical one, to deter skilful workmen from receiving, and employers from giving, a larger remuneration for a more useful service. If the public have any jurisdiction over private concerns, I cannot see that these people are in fault, or that any individual's particular public can be blamed for asserting the same authority over his individual conduct, which the general public asserts over people in general.

But, without dwelling upon supposititious cases, there are, in our own day, gross usurpations upon the liberty of private life actually practised, and still greater ones threatened with some expectation of success, and opinions propounded which assert an unlimited right in the public not only to prohibit by law everything which it thinks wrong, but in order to get at what it thinks wrong, to prohibit any number of things which it admits to be innocent.

Under the name of preventing intemperance, the people of one English colony, and of nearly half the United States, have been interdicted by law from making any use whatever of fermented drinks, except for medical purposes: for prohibition of their sale is in fact, as it is intended to be, prohibition of their use.

And though the impracticability of executing the law has caused its repeal in several of the States which had adopted it, including the one from which it derives its name, an attempt has notwithstanding been commenced, and is prosecuted with considerable zeal by many of the professed philanthropists, to agitate for a similar law in this country. The association, or 'Alliance' as it terms itself, which has been formed for this purpose, has acquired some notoriety through the publicity given to a correspondence between its Secretary and one of the very few English public men who hold that a politician's opinions ought to be founded on principles. Lord Stanley's share in this correspondence is calculated to strengthen the hopes already built on him, by those who know how rare such qualities as are manifested in some of his public appearances, unhappily are among those who figure in political life. The organ of the Alliance, who would 'deeply deplore the recognition of any principle which could be wrested to justify bigotry and persecution,' undertakes to point out the 'broad and impassable barrier' which divides such principles from those of the association. 'All matters relating to thought, opinion, conscience, appear to me,' he says, 'to be without the sphere of legislation; all pertaining to social act, habit, relation, subject only to a discretionary power vested in the State itself, and not in the individual, to be within it.' No mention is made of a third class, different from either of these, viz. acts and habits which are not social, but individual; although it is to this class, surely, that the act of drinking fermented liquors belongs. Selling fermented liquors, however, is trading, and trading is a social act. But the infringement complained of is not on the liberty of the seller, but on that of the buyer and consumer; since the State might just as well forbid him to drink wine, as purposely make it impossible for him to obtain it. The Secretary, however, says, 'I claim, as a citizen, a right to legislate whenever my social rights are invaded by the social act of another.' And now for the definition of these 'social rights.' 'If anything invades my social rights, certainly the traffic in strong drink does. It destroys my primary right of security, by constantly creating and stimulating social disorder. It invades my right of equality, by deriving a profit from the creation of a misery I am taxed to support. It impedes my right to free moral and intellectual development, by surrounding my path with dangers, and by weakening and demoralizing society, from which I have a right to claim mutual aid and intercourse.' A theory of 'social rights,' the like of which probably never before found its way into distinct language: being nothing short of this—that it is the absolute social right of every individual, that every other individual shall act in every respect exactly as he ought; that whosoever fails thereof in the smallest particular, violates my social right, and entitles me to demand from the legislature the removal of the grievance. So monstrous a principle is far more dangerous than any single interference with liberty; there is no violation of liberty which it would not justify; it acknowledges no right to any freedom whatever, except perhaps to that of holding opinions in secret, without ever disclosing them: for, the moment an opinion which I consider noxious passes any one's lips, it invades all the 'social rights' attributed to me by the Alliance. The doctrine ascribes to all mankind a vested interest in each other's moral, intellectual, and even physical perfection, to be defined by each claimant according to his own standard.

Another important example of illegitimate interference with the rightful liberty of the individual, not simply threatened, but long since carried into triumphant effect, is Sabbatarian legislation. Without doubt, abstinence on one day in the week, so far as the exigencies of life permit, from the usual daily occupation, though in no respect religiously binding on any except Jews, is a highly beneficial custom. And inasmuch as this custom cannot be observed without a general consent to that effect among the industrious classes, therefore, in so far as some persons by working may impose the same necessity on others, it may be allowable and right that the law should guarantee to each the observance by others of the custom, by suspending the greater operations of industry on a particular day. But this justification, grounded on the direct interest which others have in each individual's observance of the practice, does not apply to the self-chosen occupations in which a person may think fit to employ his leisure; nor does it hold good, in the smallest degree, for legal restrictions on amusements. It is

true that the amusement of some is the day's work of others; but the pleasure, not to say the useful recreation, of many, is worth the labour of a few, provided the occupation is freely chosen, and can be freely resigned. The operatives are perfectly right in thinking that if all worked on Sunday, seven days' work would have to be given for six days' wages: but so long as the great mass of employments are suspended, the small number who for the enjoyment of others must still work, obtain a proportional increase of earnings; and they are not obliged to follow those occupations, if they prefer leisure to emolument. If a further remedy is sought, it might be found in the establishment by custom of a holiday on some other day of the week for those particular classes of persons. The only ground, therefore, on which restrictions on Sunday amusements can be defended, must be that they are religiously wrong; a motive of legislation which never can be too earnestly protested against. 'Deorum injuriae Diis curae.' It remains to be proved that society or any of its officers holds a commission from on high to avenge any supposed offence to Omnipotence, which is not also a wrong to our fellow creatures. The notion that it is one man's duty that another should be religious, was the foundation of all the religious persecutions ever perpetrated, and if admitted, would fully justify them. Though the feeling which breaks out in the repeated attempts to stop railway travelling on Sunday, in the resistance to the opening of Museums, and the like, has not the cruelty of the old persecutors, the state of mind indicated by it is fundamentally the same. It is a determination not to tolerate others in doing what is permitted by their religion, because it is not permitted by the persecutor's religion. It is a belief that God not only abominates the act of the misbeliever, but will not hold us guiltless if we leave him unmolested.

I cannot refrain from adding to these examples of the little account commonly made of human liberty, the language of downright persecution which breaks out from the press of this country, whenever it feels called on to notice the remarkable phenomenon of Mormonism. Much might be said on the unexpected and instructive fact, that an alleged new revelation, and a religion founded on it, the product of palpable

imposture, not even supported by the *prestige* of extraordinary qualities in its founder, is believed by hundreds of thousands, and has been made the foundation
of a society, in the age of newspapers, railways, and the
electric telegraph. What here concerns us is, that this
religion, like other and better religions, has its martyrs;
that its prophet and founder was, for his teaching, put
to death by a mob; that others of its adherents lost their
lives by the same lawless violence; that they were
forcibly expelled, in a body, from the country in which
they first grew up; while, now that they have been
chased into a solitary recess in the midst of a desert,
many in this country openly declare that it would be
right (only that it is not convenient) to send an expedition against them, and compel them by force to conform to the opinions of other people. The article of
the Mormonite doctrine which is the chief provoca-
tive to the antipathy which thus breaks through the ordinary restraints of religious tolerance, is its sanction
of polygamy; which, though permitted to Mahomedans, and Hindoos, and Chinese, seems to excite unquenchable animosity when practised by persons who
speak English, and profess to be a kind of Christians.
No one has a deeper disapprobation than I have of this
Mormon institution; both for other reasons, and because, far from being in any way countenanced by the
principle of liberty, it is a direct infraction of that principle, being a mere rivetting of the chains of one half
of the community, and an emancipation of the other
from reciprocity of obligation towards them. Still, it
must be remembered that this relation is as much voluntary on the part of the women concerned in it, and
who may be deemed the sufferers by it, as is the case
with any other form of the marriage institution; and
however surprising this fact may appear, it has its explanation in the common ideas and customs of the
world, which teaching women to think marriage the
one thing needful, make it intelligible that many a
woman should prefer being one of several wives, to not
being a wife at all. Other countries are not asked to
recognise such unions, or release any portion of their
inhabitants from their own laws on the score of Mormonite opinions. But when the dissentients have conceded to the hostile sentiments of others, far more
than could justly be demanded; when they have left

the countries to which their doctrines were unacceptable, and established themselves in a remote corner of
the earth, which they have been the first to render hab-
itable to human beings; it is difficult to see on what
principles but those of tyranny they can be prevented
from living there under what laws they please, provided they commit no aggression on other nations,
and allow perfect freedom of departure to those who
are dissatisfied with their ways. A recent writer, in
some respects of considerable merit, proposes (to use
his own words) not a crusade, but a *civilizade*, against
this polygamous community, to put an end to what
seems to him a retrograde step in civilization. It also
appears so to me, but I am not aware that any community has a right to force another to be civilized. So
long as the sufferers by the bad law do not invoke assistance from other communities, I cannot admit that
persons entirely unconnected with them ought to step
in and require that a condition of things with which
all who are directly interested appear to be satisfied,
should be put an end to because it is a scandal to persons some thousands of miles distant, who have no
part or concern in it. Let them send missionaries, if
they please, to preach against it; and let them, by any
fair means (of which silencing the teachers is not one),
oppose the progress of similar doctrines among their
own people. If civilization has got the better of barbarism when barbarism had the world to itself, it is too
much to profess to be afraid lest barbarism, after having been fairly got under, should revive and conquer
civilization. A civilization that can thus succumb to its
vanquished enemy, must first have become so degenerate, that neither its appointed priests and teachers,
nor anybody else, has the capacity, or will take the
trouble, to stand up for it. If this be so, the sooner
such a civilization receives notice to quit, the better. It
can only go on from bad to worse, until destroyed and
regenerated (like the Western Empire) by energetic
barbarians.

Chapter V: Applications

The principles asserted in these pages must be more
generally admitted as the basis for discussion of details, before a consistent application of them to all the

various departments of government and morals can be attempted with any prospect of advantage. The few observations I propose to make on questions of detail, are designed to illustrate the principles, rather than to follow them out to their consequences. I offer, not so much applications, as specimens of application; which may serve to bring into greater clearness the meaning and limits of the two maxims which together form the entire doctrine of this Essay, and to assist the judgment in holding the balance between them, in the cases where it appears doubtful which of them is applicable to the case.

The maxims are, first, that the individual is not accountable to society for his actions, in so far as these concern the interests of no person but himself. Advice, instruction, persuasion, and avoidance by other people if thought necessary by them for their own good, are the only measures by which society can justifiably express its dislike or disapprobation of his conduct. Secondly, that for such actions as are prejudicial to the interests of others, the individual is accountable, and may be subjected either to social or to legal punishment, if society is of opinion that the one or the other is requisite for its protection.

In the first place, it must by no means be supposed, because damage, or probability of damage, to the interests of others, can alone justify the interference of society, that therefore it always does justify such interference. In many cases, an individual, in pursuing a legitimate object, necessarily and therefore legitimately causes pain or loss to others, or intercepts a good which they had a reasonable hope of obtaining. Such oppositions of interest between individuals often arise from bad social institutions, but are unavoidable while those institutions last; and some would be unavoidable under any institutions. Whoever succeeds in an overcrowded profession, or in a competitive examination; whoever is preferred to another in any contest for an object which both desire, reaps benefit from the loss of others, from their wasted exertion and their disappointment. But it is, by common admission, better for the general interest of mankind, that persons should pursue their objects undeterred by this sort of consequences. In other words, society admits no right, either legal or moral, in the disappointed competitors,

to immunity from this kind of suffering; and feels called on to interfere, only when means of success have been employed which it is contrary to the general interest to permit—namely, fraud or treachery, and force.

Again, trade is a social act. Whoever undertakes to sell any description of goods to the public, does what affects the interest of other persons, and of society in general; and thus his conduct, in principle, comes within the jurisdiction of society: accordingly, it was once held to be the duty of governments, in all cases which were considered of importance, to fix prices, and regulate the processes of manufacture. But it is now recognised, though not till after a long struggle, that both the cheapness and the good quality of commodities are most effectually provided for by leaving the producers and sellers perfectly free, under the sole check of equal freedom to the buyers for supplying themselves elsewhere. This is the so-called doctrine of Free Trade, which rests on grounds different from, though equally solid with, the principle of individual liberty asserted in this Essay. Restrictions on trade, or on production for purposes of trade, are indeed restraints; and all restraint, *qua* restraint, is an evil: but the restraints in question affect only that part of conduct which society is competent to restrain, and are wrong solely because they do not really produce the results which it is desired to produce by them. As the principle of individual liberty is not involved in the doctrine of Free Trade, so neither is it in most of the questions which arise respecting the limits of that doctrine; as for example, what amount of public control is admissible for the prevention of fraud by adulteration; how far sanitary precautions, or arrangements to protect workpeople employed in dangerous occupations, should be enforced on employers. Such questions involve considerations of liberty, only in so far as leaving people to themselves is always better, *caeteris paribus*, than controlling them: but that they may be legitimately controlled for these ends, is in principle undeniable. On the other hand, there are questions relating to interference with trade, which are essentially questions of liberty; such as the Maine Law, already touched upon; the prohibition of the importation of opium into China; the restriction of the sale of poisons; all cases, in short, where the object of the interference is to make it impossible or difficult to obtain a particular commodity. These interferences are objectionable, not as infringements on the liberty of the producer or seller, but on that of the buyer.

One of these examples, that of the sale of poisons, opens a new question; the proper limits of what may be called the functions of police; how far liberty may legitimately be invaded for the prevention of crime, or of accident. It is one of the undisputed functions of government to take precautions against crime before it has been committed, as well as to detect and punish it afterwards. The preventive function of government, however, is far more liable to be abused, to the prejudice of liberty, than the punitory function; for there is hardly any part of the legitimate freedom of action of a human being which would not admit of being represented, and fairly too, as increasing the facilities for some form or other of delinquency. Nevertheless, if a public authority, or even a private person, sees any one evidently preparing to commit a crime, they are not bound to look on inactive until the crime is committed, but may interfere to prevent it. If poisons were never bought or used for any purpose except the commission of murder, it would be right to prohibit their manufacture and sale. They may, however, be wanted not only for innocent but for useful purposes, and restrictions cannot be imposed in the one case without operating in the other. Again, it is a proper office of public authority to guard against accidents. If either a public officer or any one else saw a person attempting to cross a bridge which had been ascertained to be unsafe, and there were no time to warn him of his danger, they might seize him and turn him back, without any real infringement of his liberty; for liberty consists in doing what one desires, and he does not desire to fall into the river. Nevertheless, when there is not a certainty, but only a danger of mischief, no one but the person himself can judge of the sufficiency of the motive which may prompt him to incur the risk: in this case, therefore, (unless he is a child, or delirious, or in some state of excitement or absorption incompatible with the full use of the reflecting faculty) he ought, I conceive, to be only warned of the danger; not forcibly prevented from exposing himself to it. Simi-lar considerations, applied to such a question as the sale of poisons, may enable us to decide which among the possible modes of regulation are or are not contrary to principle. Such a precaution, for example, as that of labelling the drug with some word expressive of its dangerous character, may be enforced without violation of liberty: the buyer cannot wish not to know that the thing he possesses has poisonous qualities. But to require in all cases the certificate of a medical practitioner, would make it sometimes impossible, always expensive, to obtain the article for legitimate uses. The only mode apparent to me, in which difficulties may be thrown in the way of crime committed through this means, without any infringement, worth taking into account, upon the liberty of those who desire the poisonous substance for other purposes, consists in providing what, in the apt language of Bentham, is called 'preappointed evidence.' This provision is familiar to every one in the case of contracts. It is usual and right that the law, when a contract is entered into, should require as the condition of its enforcing performance, that certain formalities should be observed, such as signatures, attestation of witnesses, and the like, in order that in case of subsequent dispute, there may be evidence to prove that the contract was really entered into, and that there was nothing in the circumstances to render it legally invalid: the effect being, to throw great obstacles in the way of fictitious contracts, or contracts made in circumstances which, if known, would destroy their validity. Precautions of a similar nature might be enforced in the sale of articles adapted to be instruments of crime. The seller, for example, might be required to enter in a register the exact time of the transaction, the name and address of the buyer, the precise quality and quantity sold; to ask the purpose for which it was wanted, and record the answer he received. When there was no medical prescription, the presence of some third person might be required, to bring home the fact to the purchaser, in case there should afterwards be reason to believe that the article had been applied to criminal purposes. Such regulations would in general be no material impediment to obtaining the article, but a very considerable one to making an improper use of it without detection.

The right inherent in society, to ward off crimes against itself by antecedent precautions, suggests the obvious limitations to the maxim, that purely self-regarding misconduct cannot properly be meddled with in the way of prevention or punishment. Drunkenness, for example, in ordinary cases, is not a fit subject for legislative interference; but I should deem it perfectly legitimate that a person, who had once been convicted of any act of violence to others under the influence of drink, should be placed under a special legal restriction, personal to himself; that if he were afterwards found drunk, he should be liable to a penalty, and that if when in that state he committed another offence, the punishment to which he would be liable for that other offence should be increased in severity. The making himself drunk, in a person whom drunkenness excites to do harm to others, is a crime against others. So, again, idleness, except in a person receiving support from the public, or except when it constitutes a breach of contract, cannot without tyranny be made a subject of legal punishment; but if, either from idleness or from any other avoidable cause, a man fails to perform his legal duties to others, as for instance to support his children, it is no tyranny to force him to fulfil that obligation, by compulsory labour, if no other means are available.

Again, there are many acts which, being directly injurious only to the agents themselves, ought not to be legally interdicted, but which, if done publicly, are a violation of good manners, and coming thus within the category of offences against others, may rightfully be prohibited. Of this kind are offences against decency; on which it is unnecessary to dwell, the rather as they are only connected indirectly with our subject, the objection to publicity being equally strong in the case of many actions not in themselves condemnable, nor supposed to be so.

There is another question to which an answer must be found, consistent with the principles which have been laid down. In cases of personal conduct supposed to be blameable, but which respect for liberty precludes society from preventing or punishing, because the evil directly resulting falls wholly on the agent; what the agent is free to do, ought other persons to be equally free to counsel or instigate? This ques-

tion is not free from difficulty. The case of a person who solicits another to do an act, is not strictly a case of self-regarding conduct. To give advice or offer inducements to any one, is a social act, and may, therefore, like actions in general which affect others, be supposed amenable to social control. But a little reflection corrects the first impression, by showing that if the case is not strictly within the definition of individual liberty, yet the reasons on which the principle of individual liberty is grounded, are applicable to it. If people must be allowed, in whatever concerns only themselves, to act as seems best to themselves at their own peril, they must equally be free to consult with one another about what is fit to be so done; to exchange opinions, and give and receive suggestions. Whatever it is permitted to do, it must be permitted to advise to do. The question is doubtful, only when the instigator derives a personal benefit from his advice; when he makes it his occupation, for subsistence or pecuniary gain, to promote what society and the State consider to be an evil. Then, indeed, a new element of complication is introduced; namely, the existence of classes of persons with an interest opposed to what is considered as the public weal, and whose mode of living is grounded on the counteraction of it. Ought this to be interfered with, or not? Fornication, for example, must be tolerated, and so must gambling; but should a person be free to be a pimp, or to keep a gambling-house? The case is one of those which lie on the exact boundary line between two principles, and it is not at once apparent to which of the two it properly belongs. There are arguments on both sides. On the side of toleration it may be said, that the fact of following anything as an occupation, and living or profiting by the practice of it, cannot make that criminal which would otherwise be admissible; that the act should either be consistently permitted or consistently prohibited; that if the principles which we have hitherto defended are true, society has no business, as society, to decide anything to be wrong which concerns only the individual; that it cannot go beyond dissuasion, and that one person should be as free to persuade, as another to dissuade. In opposition to this it may be contended, that although the public, or the State, are not warranted in authoritatively deciding, for purposes of repression or punishment, that such or such conduct affecting only the interests of the individual is good or bad, they are fully justified in assuming, if they regard it as bad, that its being so or not is at least a disputable question: That, this being supposed, they cannot be acting wrongly in endeavouring to exclude the influence of solicitations which are not disinterested, of instigators who cannot possibly be impartial—who have a direct personal interest on one side, and that side the one which the State believes to be wrong, and who confessedly promote it for personal objects only. There can surely, it may be urged, be nothing lost, no sacrifice of good, by so ordering matters that persons shall make their election, either wisely or foolishly, on their own prompting, as free as possible from the arts of persons who stimulate their inclinations for interested purposes of their own. Thus (it may be said) though the statutes respecting unlawful games are utterly indefensible—though all persons should be free to gamble in their own or each other's houses, or in any place of meeting established by their own subscriptions, and open only to the members and their visitors—yet public gambling-houses should not be permitted. It is true that the prohibition is never effectual, and that, whatever amount of tyrannical power may be given to the police, gambling-houses can always be maintained under other pretences; but they may be compelled to conduct their operations with a certain degree of secrecy and mystery, so that nobody knows anything about them but those who seek them; and more than this, society ought not to aim at. There is considerable force in these arguments. I will not venture to decide whether they are sufficient to justify the moral anomaly of punishing the accessary, when the principal is (and must be) allowed to go free; of fining or imprisoning the procurer, but not the fornicator, the gambling-house keeper, but not the gambler. Still less ought the common operations of buying and selling to be interfered with on analogous grounds. Almost every article which is bought and sold may be used in excess, and the sellers have a pecuniary interest in encouraging that excess; but no argument can be founded on this, in favour, for instance, of the Maine Law; because the class of dealers in strong drinks, though interested in

their abuse, are indispensably required for the sake of their legitimate use. The interest, however, of these dealers in promoting intemperance is a real evil, and justifies the State in imposing restrictions and requiring guarantees which, but for that justification, would be infringements of legitimate liberty.

A further question is, whether the State, while it permits, should nevertheless indirectly discourage conduct which it deems contrary to the best interests of the agent; whether, for example, it should take measures to render the means of drunkenness more costly, or add to the difficulty of procuring them by limiting the number of the places of sale. On this as on most other practical questions, many distinctions require to be made. To tax stimulants for the sole purpose of making them more difficult to be obtained, is a measure differing only in degree from their entire prohibition; and would be justifiable only if that were justifiable. Every increase of cost is a prohibition, to those whose means do not come up to the augmented price; and to those who do, it is a penalty laid on them for gratifying a particular taste. Their choice of pleasures, and their mode of expending their income, after satisfying their legal and moral obligations to the State and to individuals, are their own concern, and must rest with their own judgment. These considerations may seem at first sight to condemn the selection of stimulants as special subjects of taxation for purposes of revenue. But it must be remembered that taxation for fiscal purposes is absolutely inevitable; that in most countries it is necessary that a considerable part of that taxation should be indirect; that the State, therefore, cannot help imposing penalties, which to some persons may be prohibitory, on the use of some articles of consumption. It is hence the duty of the State to consider, in the imposition of taxes, what commodities the consumers can best spare; and *a fortiori*, to select in preference those of which it deems the use, beyond a very moderate quantity, to be positively injurious. Taxation, therefore, of stimulants, up to the point which produces the largest amount of revenue (supposing that the State needs all the revenue which it yields) is not only admissible, but to be approved of.

The question of making the sale of these commodities a more or less exclusive privilege, must be answered differently, according to the purposes to which the restriction is intended to be subservient. All places of public resort require the restraint of a police, and places of this kind peculiarly, because offences against society are especially apt to originate there. It is, therefore, fit to confine the power of selling these commodities (at least for consumption on the spot) to persons of known or vouched-for respectability of conduct; to make such regulations respecting hours of opening and closing as may be requisite for public surveillance, and to withdraw the licence if breaches of the peace repeatedly take place through the connivance or incapacity of the keeper of the house, or if it becomes a rendezvous for concocting and preparing offences against the law. Any further restriction I do not conceive to be, in principle, justifiable. The limitation in number, for instance, of beer and spirit houses, for the express purpose of rendering them more difficult of access, and diminishing the occasions of temptation, not only exposes all to an inconvenience because there are some by whom the facility would be abused, but is suited only to a state of society in which the labouring classes are avowedly treated as children or savages, and placed under an education of restraint, to fit them for future admission to the privileges of freedom. This is not the principle on which the labouring classes are professedly governed in any free country; and no person who sets due value on freedom will give his adhesion to their being so governed, unless after all efforts have been exhausted to educate them for freedom and govern them as freemen, and it has been definitively proved that they can only be governed as children. The bare statement of the alternative shows the absurdity of supposing that such efforts have been made in any case which needs be considered here. It is only because the institutions of this country are a mass of inconsistencies, that things find admittance into our practice which belong to the system of despotic, or what is called paternal, government, while the general freedom of our institutions precludes the exercise of the amount of control necessary to render the restraint of any real efficacy as a moral education.

It was pointed out in an early part of this Essay, that the liberty of the individual, in things wherein the individual is alone concerned, implies a corresponding liberty in any number of individuals to regulate by mutual agreement such things as regard them jointly, and regard no persons but themselves. This question presents no difficulty, so long as the will of all the persons implicated remains unaltered; but since that will may change, it is often necessary, even in things in which they alone are concerned, that they should enter into engagements with one another; and when they do, it is fit, as a general rule, that those engagements should be kept. Yet, in the laws, probably, of every country, this general rule has some exceptions. Not only persons are not held to engagements which violate the rights of third parties, but it is sometimes considered a sufficient reason for releasing them from an engagement, that it is injurious to themselves. In this and most other civilized countries, for example, an engagement by which a person should sell himself, or allow himself to be sold, as a slave, would be null and void; neither enforced by law nor by opinion. The ground for thus limiting his power of voluntarily disposing of his own lot in life, is apparent, and is very clearly seen in this extreme case. The reason for not interfering, unless for the sake of others, with a person's voluntary acts, is consideration for his liberty. His voluntary choice is evidence that what he so chooses is desirable, or at the least endurable, to him, and his good is on the whole best provided for by allowing him to take his own means of pursuing it. But by selling himself for a slave, he abdicates his liberty; he foregoes any future use of it beyond that single act. He therefore defeats, in his own case, the very purpose which is the justification of allowing him to dispose of himself. He is no longer free; but is thenceforth in a position which has no longer the presumption in its favour, that would be afforded by his voluntarily remaining in it. The principle of freedom cannot require that he should be free not to be free. It is not freedom, to be allowed to alienate his freedom. These reasons, the force of which is so conspicuous in this peculiar case, are evidently of far wider application; yet a limit is everywhere set to them by the necessities of life, which continually require, not indeed that we should resign our freedom, but that we should consent to this and the other limitation of it. The principle, however, which demands uncontrolled freedom of action in all that concerns only the agents themselves, requires that those who have become bound to one another, in things which concern no third party, should be able to release one another from the engagement: and even without such voluntary release, there are perhaps no contracts or engagements, except those that relate to money or money's worth, of which one can venture to say that there ought to be no liberty whatever of retractation. Baron Wilhelm von Humboldt, in the excellent essay from which I have already quoted, states it as his conviction, that engagements which involve personal relations or services, should never be legally binding beyond a limited duration of time; and that the most important of these engagements, marriage, having the peculiarity that its objects are frustrated unless the feelings of both the parties are in harmony with it, should require nothing more than the declared will of either party to dissolve it. This subject is too important, and too complicated, to be discussed in a parenthesis, and I touch on it only so far as is necessary for purposes of illustration. If the conciseness and generality of Baron Humboldt's dissertation had not obliged him in this instance to content himself with enunciating his conclusion without discussing the premises, he would doubtless have recognised that the question cannot be decided on grounds so simple as those to which he confines himself. When a person, either by express promise or by conduct, has encouraged another to rely upon his continuing to act in a certain way—to build expectations and calculations, and stake any part of his plan of life upon that supposition—a new series of moral obligations arises on his part towards that person, which may possibly be overruled, but cannot be ignored. And again, if the relation between two contracting parties has been followed by consequences to others; if it has placed third parties in any peculiar position, or, as in the case of marriage, has even called third parties into existence, obligations arise on the part of both the contracting parties towards those third persons, the fulfilment of which, or at all events the mode of fulfilment, must be greatly affected by the continuance or disruption of the relation between the original parties to the contract. It does not follow, nor

can I admit, that these obligations extend to requiring the fulfilment of the contract at all costs to the happiness of the reluctant party; but they are a necessary element in the question; and even if, as Von Humboldt maintains, they ought to make no difference in the *legal* freedom of the parties to release themselves from the engagement (and I also hold that they ought not to make *much* difference), they necessarily make a great difference in the *moral* freedom. A person is bound to take all these circumstances into account, before resolving on a step which may affect such important interests of others; and if he does not allow proper weight to those interests, he is morally responsible for the wrong. I have made these obvious remarks for the better illustration of the general principle of liberty, and not because they are at all needed on the particular question, which, on the contrary, is usually discussed as if the interest of children was everything, and that of grown persons nothing.

I have already observed that, owing to the absence of any recognised general principles, liberty is often granted where it should be withheld, as well as withheld where it should be granted; and one of the cases in which, in the modern European world, the sentiment of liberty is the strongest, is a case where, in my view, it is altogether misplaced. A person should be free to do as he likes in his own concerns; but he ought not to be free to do as he likes in acting for another, under the pretext that the affairs of the other are his own affairs. The State, while it respects the liberty of each in what specially regards himself, is bound to maintain a vigilant control over his exercise of any power which it allows him to possess over others. This obligation is almost entirely disregarded in the case of the family relations, a case, in its direct influence on human happiness, more important than all others taken together. The almost despotic power of husbands over wives needs not be enlarged upon here, because nothing more is needed for the complete removal of the evil, than that wives should have the same rights, and should receive the protection of law in the same manner, as all other persons; and because, on this subject, the defenders of established injustice do not avail themselves of the plea of liberty, but stand forth openly as the champions of power. It is in the case of children, that misapplied notions of liberty are a real obstacle to the fulfilment by the State of its duties. One would almost think that a man's children were supposed to be literally, and not metaphorically, a part of himself, so jealous is opinion of the smallest interference of law with his absolute and exclusive control over them; more jealous than of almost any interference with his own freedom of action: so much less do the generality of mankind value liberty than power. Consider, for example, the case of education. Is it not almost a self-evident axiom, that the State should require and compel the education, up to a certain standard, of every human being who is born its citizen? Yet who is there that is not afraid to recognise and assert this truth? Hardly any one indeed will deny that it is one of the most sacred duties of the parents (or, as law and usage now stand, the father), after summoning a human being into the world, to give to that being an education fitting him to perform his part well in life towards others and towards himself. But while this is unanimously declared to be the father's duty, scarcely anybody, in this country, will bear to hear of obliging him to perform it. Instead of his being required to make any exertion or sacrifice for securing education to the child, it is left to his choice to accept it or not when it is provided gratis! It still remains unrecognised, that to bring a child into existence without a fair prospect of being able, not only to provide food for its body, but instruction and training for its mind, is a moral crime, both against the unfortunate offspring and against society; and that if the parent does not fulfil this obligation, the State ought to see it fulfilled, at the charge, as far as possible, of the parent.

Were the duty of enforcing universal education once admitted, there would be an end to the difficulties about what the State should teach, and how it should teach, which now convert the subject into a mere battle-field for sects and parties, causing the time and labour which should have been spent in educating, to be wasted in quarrelling about education. If the government would make up its mind to *require* for every child a good education, it might save itself the trouble of *providing* one. It might leave to parents to obtain the education where and how they pleased, and content itself with helping to pay the school fees of the poorer classes of children, and defraying the entire school expenses of those who have no one else to pay for them. The objections which are urged with reason against State education, do not apply to the enforcement of education by the State, but to the State's taking upon itself to direct that education: which is a totally different thing. That the whole or any large part of the education of the people should be in State hands, I go as far as any one in deprecating. All that has been said of the importance of individuality of character, and diversity in opinions and modes of conduct, involves, as of the same unspeakable importance, diversity of education. A general State education is a mere contrivance for moulding people to be exactly like one another: and as the mould in which it casts them is that which pleases the predominant power in the government, whether this be a monarch, a priesthood, an aristocracy, or the majority of the existing generation in proportion as it is efficient and successful, it establishes a despotism over the mind, leading by natural tendency to one over the body. An education established and controlled by the State should only exist, if it exist at all, as one among many competing experiments, carried on for the purpose of example and stimulus, to keep the others up to a certain standard of excellence. Unless, indeed, when society in general is in so backward a state that it could not or would not provide for itself any proper institutions of education, unless the government undertook the task: then, indeed, the government may, as the less of two great evils, take upon itself the business of schools and universities, as it may that of joint stock companies, when private enterprise, in a shape fitted for undertaking great works of industry, does not exist in the country. But in general, if the country contains a sufficient number of persons qualified to provide education under government auspices, the same persons would be able and willing to give an equally good education on the voluntary principle, under the assurance of remuneration afforded by a law rendering education compulsory, combined with State aid to those unable to defray the expense.

The instrument for enforcing the law could be no other than public examinations, extending to all children, and beginning at an early age. An age might be fixed at which every child must be examined, to ascertain if he (or she) is able to read. If a child proves unable, the father, unless he has some sufficient ground of excuse, might be subjected to a moderate fine, to be worked out, if necessary, by his labour, and the child might be put to school at his expense. Once in every year the examination should be renewed, with a gradually extending range of subjects, so as to make the universal acquisition, and what is more, retention, of a certain minimum of general knowledge, virtually compulsory. Beyond that minimum, there should be voluntary examinations on all subjects, at which all who come up to a certain standard of proficiency might claim a certificate. To prevent the State from exercising, through these arrangements, an improper influence over opinion, the knowledge required for passing an examination (beyond the merely instrumental parts of knowledge, such as languages and their use) should, even in the higher classes of examinations, be confined to facts and positive science exclusively. The examinations on religion, politics, or other disputed topics, should not turn on the truth or falsehood of opinions, but on the matter of fact that such and such an opinion is held, on such grounds, by such authors, or schools, or churches. Under this system, the rising generation would be no worse off in regard to all disputed truths, than they are at present; they would be brought up either churchmen or dissenters as they now are, the State merely taking care that they should be instructed churchmen, or instructed dissenters. There would be nothing to hinder them from being taught religion, if their parents chose, at the same schools where they were taught other things. All attempts by the State to bias the conclusions of its citizens on disputed subjects, are evil; but it may very properly offer to ascertain and certify that a person possesses the knowledge, requisite to make his conclusions, on any given subject, worth attending to. A student of philosophy would be the better for being able to stand an examination both in Locke and in Kant, whichever of the two he takes up with, or even if with neither: and there is no reasonable objection to examining an atheist in the evidences of Christianity, provided he is not required to profess a belief in them. The examinations, however,

in the higher branches of knowledge should, I conceive, be entirely voluntary. It would be giving too dangerous a power to governments, were they allowed to exclude any one from professions, even from the profession of teacher, for alleged deficiency of qualifications: and I think, with Wilhelm von Humboldt, that degrees, or other public certificates of scientific or professional acquirements, should be given to all who present themselves for examination, and stand the test; but that such certificates should confer no advantage over competitors, other than the weight which may be attached to their testimony by public opinion.

It is not in the matter of education only, that misplaced notions of liberty prevent moral obligations on the part of parents from being recognised, and legal obligations from being imposed, where there are the strongest grounds for the former always, and in many cases for the latter also. The fact itself, of causing the existence of a human being, is one of the most responsible actions in the range of human life. To undertake this responsibility—to bestow a life which may be either a curse or a blessing—unless the being on whom it is to be bestowed will have at least the ordinary chances of a desirable existence, is a crime against that being. And in a country either over-peopled or threatened with being so, to produce children, beyond a very small number, with the effect of reducing the reward of labour by their competition, is a serious offence against all who live by the remuneration of their labour. The laws which, in many countries on the Continent, forbid marriage unless the parties can show that they have the means of supporting a family, do not exceed the legitimate powers of the State: and whether such laws be expedient or not (a question mainly dependent on local circumstances and feelings), they are not objectionable as violations of liberty. Such laws are interferences of the State to prohibit a mischievous act—an act injurious to others, which ought to be a subject of reprobation, and social stigma, even when it is not deemed expedient to superadd legal punishment. Yet the current ideas of liberty, which bend so easily to real infringements of the freedom of the individual in things which concern only himself, would repel the attempt to put any restraint upon his inclinations when the consequence of their indulgence is a life or lives of wretchedness and depravity to the offspring, with manifold evils to those sufficiently within reach to be in any way affected by their actions. When we compare the strange respect of mankind for liberty, with their strange want of respect for it, we might imagine that a man had an indispensable right to do harm to others, and no right at all to please himself without giving pain to any one.

I have reserved for the last place a large class of questions respecting the limits of government interference, which, though closely connected with the subject of this Essay, do not, in strictness, belong to it. These are cases in which the reasons against interference do not turn upon the principle of liberty: the question is not about restraining the actions of individuals, but about helping them: it is asked whether the government should do, or cause to be done, something for their benefit, instead of leaving it to be done by themselves, individually, or in voluntary combination.

The objections to government interference, when it is not such as to involve infringement of liberty, may be of three kinds.

The first is, when the thing to be done is likely to be better done by individuals than by the government. Speaking generally, there is no one so fit to conduct any business, or to determine how or by whom it shall be conducted, as those who are personally interested in it. This principle condemns the interferences, once so common, of the legislature, or the officers of government, with the ordinary processes of industry. But this part of the subject has been sufficiently enlarged upon by political economists, and is not particularly related to the principles of this Essay.

The second objection is more nearly allied to our subject. In many cases, though individuals may not do the particular thing so well, on the average, as the officers of government, it is nevertheless desirable that it should be done by them, rather than by the government, as a means to their own mental education—a mode of strengthening their active faculties, exercising their judgment, and giving them a familiar knowledge of the subjects with which they are thus left to deal. This is a principal, though not the sole, recommendation of jury trial (in cases not political); of free

and popular local and municipal institutions; of the conduct of industrial and philanthropic enterprises by voluntary associations. These are not questions of liberty, and are connected with that subject only by remote tendencies; but they are questions of development. It belongs to a different occasion from the present to dwell on these things as parts of national education; as being, in truth, the peculiar training of a citizen, the practical part of the political education of a free people, taking them out of the narrow circle of personal and family selfishness, and accustoming them to the comprehension of joint interests, the management of joint concerns—habituating them to act from public or semi-public motives, and guide their conduct by aims which unite instead of isolating them from one another. Without these habits and powers, a free constitution can neither be worked nor preserved; as is exemplified by the too-often transitory nature of political freedom in countries where it does not rest upon a sufficient basis of local liberties. The management of purely local business by the localities, and of the great enterprises of industry by the union of those who voluntarily supply the pecuniary means, is further recommended by all the advantages which have been set forth in this Essay as belonging to individuality of development, and diversity of modes of action. Government operations tend to be everywhere alike. With individuals and voluntary associations, on the contrary, there are varied experiments, and endless diversity of experience. What the State can usefully do, is to make itself a central depository, and active circulator and diffuser, of the experience resulting from many trials. Its business is to enable each experimentalist to benefit by the experiments of others; instead of tolerating no experiments but its own.

The third, and most cogent reason for restricting the interference of government, is the great evil of adding unnecessarily to its power. Every function superadded to those already exercised by the government, causes its influence over hopes and fears to be more widely diffused, and converts, more and more, the active and ambitious part of the public into hangers-on of the government, or of some party which aims at becoming the government. If the roads, the railways, the banks, the insurance offices, the great joint-stock companies, the universities, and the public charities, were all of them branches of the government; if, in addition, the municipal corporations and local boards, with all that now devolves on them, became departments of the central administration; if the employees of all these different enterprises were appointed and paid by the government, and looked to the government for every rise in life; not all the freedom of the press and popular constitution of the legislature would make this or any other country free otherwise than in name. And the evil would be greater, the more efficiently and scientifically the administrative machinery was constructed—the more skilful the arrangements for obtaining the best qualified hands and heads with which to work it. In England it has of late been proposed that all the members of the civil service of government should be selected by competitive examination, to obtain for those employments the most intelligent and instructed persons procurable; and much has been said and written for and against this proposal. One of the arguments most insisted on by its opponents, is that the occupation of a permanent official servant of the State does not hold out sufficient prospects of emolument and importance to attract the highest talents, which will always be able to find a more inviting career in the professions, or in the service of companies and other public bodies. One would not have been surprised if this argument had been used by the friends of the proposition, as an answer to its principal difficulty. Coming from the opponents it is strange enough. What is urged as an objection is the safety-valve of the proposed system. If indeed all the high talent of the country *could* be drawn into the service of the government, a proposal tending to bring about that result might well inspire uneasiness. If every part of the business of society which required organized concert, or large and comprehensive views, were in the hands of the government, and if government offices were universally filled by the ablest men, all the enlarged culture and practised intelligence in the country, except the purely speculative, would be concentrated in a numerous bureaucracy, to whom alone the rest of the community would look for all things: the multitude for direction and dictation in all they had to do; the able and aspir-

ing for personal advancement. To be admitted into the ranks of this bureaucracy, and when admitted, to rise therein, would be the sole objects of ambition. Under this regime, not only is the outside public ill-qualified, for want of practical experience, to criticize or check the mode of operation of the bureaucracy, but even if the accidents of despotic or the natural working of popular institutions occasionally raise to the summit a ruler or rulers of reforming inclinations, no reform can be effected which is contrary to the interest of the bureaucracy. Such is the melancholy condition of the Russian empire, as shown in the accounts of those who have had sufficient opportunity of observation. The Czar himself is powerless against the bureaucratic body; he can send any one of them to Siberia, but he cannot govern without them, or against their will. On every decree of his they have a tacit veto, by merely refraining from carrying it into effect. In countries of more advanced civilization and of a more insurrectionary spirit, the public, accustomed to expect everything to be done for them by the State, or at least to do nothing for themselves without asking from the State not only leave to do it, but even how it is to be done, naturally hold the State responsible for all evil which befals them, and when the evil exceeds their amount of patience, they rise against the government and make what is called a revolution; whereupon somebody else, with or without legitimate authority from the nation, vaults into the seat, issues his orders to the bureaucracy, and everything goes on much as it did before; the bureaucracy being unchanged, and nobody else being capable of taking their place.

A very different spectacle is exhibited among a people accustomed to transact their own business. In France, a large part of the people having been engaged in military service, many of whom have held at least the rank of non-commissioned officers, there are in every popular insurrection several persons competent to take the lead, and improvise some tolerable plan of action. What the French are in military affairs, the Americans are in every kind of civil business; let them be left without a government, every body of Americans is able to improvise one, and to carry on that or any other public business with a sufficient amount of intelligence, order, and decision. This is what every free people ought to be: and a people capable of this is certain to be free; it will never let itself be enslaved by any man or body of men because these are able to seize and pull the reins of the central administration. No bureaucracy can hope to make such a people as this do or undergo anything that they do not like. But where everything is done through the bureaucracy, nothing to which the bureaucracy is really adverse can be done at all. The constitution of such countries is an organization of the experience and practical ability of the nation, into a disciplined body for the purpose of governing the rest; and the more perfect that organization is in itself, the more successful in drawing to itself and educating for itself the persons of greatest capacity from all ranks of the community, the more complete is the bondage of all, the members of the bureaucracy included. For the governors are as much the slaves of their organization and discipline, as the governed are of the governors. A Chinese mandarin is as much the tool and creature of a despotism as the humblest cultivator. An individual Jesuit is to the utmost degree of abasement the slave of his order, though the order itself exists for the collective power and importance of its members.

It is not, also, to be forgotten, that the absorption of all the principal ability of the country into the governing body is fatal, sooner or later, to the mental activity and progressiveness of the body itself. Banded together as they are—working a system which, like all systems, necessarily proceeds in a great measure by fixed rules—the official body are under the constant temptation of sinking into indolent routine, or, if they now and then desert that mill-horse round, of rushing into some half-examined crudity which has struck the fancy of some leading member of the corps: and the sole check to these closely allied, though seemingly opposite, tendencies, the only stimulus which can keep the ability of the body itself up to a high standard, is liability to the watchful criticism of equal ability outside the body. It is indispensable, therefore, that the means should exist, independently of the government, of forming such ability, and furnishing it with the opportunities and experience necessary for a correct judgment of great practical affairs. If we would possess permanently a skilful and efficient body of functionaries—above all a body able to

originate and willing to adopt improvements; if we would not have our bureaucracy degenerate into a pedantocracy, this body must not engross all the occupations which form and cultivate the faculties required for the government of mankind.

To determine the point at which evils, so formidable to human freedom and advancement, begin, or rather at which they begin to predominate over the benefits attending the collective application of the force of society, under its recognised chiefs, for the removal of the obstacles which stand in the way of its well-being; to secure as much of the advantages of centralized power and intelligence, as can be had without turning into governmental channels too great a proportion of the general activity—is one of the most difficult and complicated questions in the art of government. It is, in a great measure, a question of detail, in which many and various considerations must be kept in view, and no absolute rule can be laid down. But I believe that the practical principle in which safety resides, the ideal to be kept in view, the standard by which to test all arrangements intended for overcoming the difficulty, may be conveyed in these words: the greatest dissemination of power consistent with efficiency; but the greatest possible centralization of information, and diffusion of it from the centre. Thus, in municipal administration, there would be, as in the New England States, a very minute division among separate officers, chosen by the localities, of all business which is not better left to the persons directly interested; but besides this, there would be, in each department of local affairs, a central superintendence, forming a branch of the general government. The organ of this superintendence would concentrate, as in a focus, the variety of information and experience derived from the conduct of that branch of public business in all the localities, from everything analogous which is done in foreign countries, and from the general principles of political science. This central organ should have a right to know all that is done, and its special duty should be that of making the knowledge acquired in one place available for others. Emancipated from the petty prejudices and narrow views of a locality by its elevated position and comprehensive sphere of observation, its advice would naturally carry much authority;

but its actual power, as a permanent institution, should, I conceive, be limited to compelling the local officers to obey the laws laid down for their guidance. In all things not provided for by general rules, those officers should be left to their own judgment, under responsibility to their constituents. For the violation of rules, they should be responsible to law, and the rules themselves should be laid down by the legislature; the central administrative authority only watching over their execution, and if they were not properly carried into effect, appealing, according to the nature of the case, to the tribunals to enforce the law, or to the constituencies to dismiss the functionaries who had not executed it according to its spirit. Such, in its general conception, is the central superintendence which the Poor Law Board is intended to exercise over the administrators of the Poor Rate throughout the country. Whatever powers the Board exercises beyond this limit, were right and necessary in that peculiar case, for the cure of rooted habits of maladministration in matters deeply affecting not the localities merely, but the whole community; since no locality has a moral right to make itself by mismanagement a nest of pauperism, necessarily overflowing into other localities, and impairing the moral and physical condition of the whole labouring community. The powers of administrative coercion and subordinate legislation possessed by the Poor Law Board (but which, owing to the state of opinion on the subject, are very scantily exercised by them), though perfectly justifiable in a case of first-rate national interest, would be wholly out of place in the superintendence of interests purely local. But a central organ of information and instruction for all the localities, would be equally valuable in all departments of administration. A government cannot have too much of the kind of activity which does not impede, but aids and stimulates, individual exertion and development. The mischief begins when, instead of calling forth the activity and powers of individuals and bodies, it substitutes its own activity for theirs; when, instead of informing, advising, and, upon occasion, denouncing, it makes them work in fetters, or bids them stand aside and does their work instead of them. The worth of a State, in the long run, is the worth of the individuals composing it; and a State which postpones the interests of *their* mental expansion and elevation, to a little more of administrative skill, or of that semblance of it which practice gives, in the details of business; a State which dwarfs its men, in order that they may be more docile instruments in its hands even for beneficial purposes—will find that with small men no great thing can really be accomplished; and that the perfection of machinery to which it has sacrificed everything, will in the end avail it nothing, for want of the vital power which, in order that the machine might work more smoothly, it has preferred to banish.

MILL

The Subjection of Women

CHAPTER I

The object of this Essay is to explain as clearly as I am able, the grounds of an opinion which I have held from the very earliest period when I had formed any opinions at all on social or political matters, and which, instead of being weakened or modified, has been constantly growing stronger by the progress of reflection and the experience of life: That the principle which regulates the existing social relations between the two sexes—the legal subordination of one sex to the other—is wrong in itself, and now one of the chief hindrances to human improvement; and that it ought to be replaced by a principle of perfect equality, admitting no power or privilege on the one side, nor disability on the other.

The very words necessary to express the task I have undertaken, show how arduous it is. But it would be a mistake to suppose that the difficulty of the case must lie in the insufficiency or obscurity of the grounds of reason on which my conviction rests. The difficulty is that which exists in all cases in which there is a mass of feeling to be contended against. So long as an opinion is strongly rooted in the feelings, it gains rather than loses in stability by having a preponderating weight of argument against it. For if it were accepted as a result of argument, the refutation of the argument might shake the solidity of the conviction; but when it rests solely on feeling, the worse it fares in argumentative contest, the more persuaded its adherents are that their feeling must have some deeper ground, which the arguments do not reach; and while the feeling remains, it is always throwing up fresh intrenchments of argument to repair any breach made in the old. And there are so many causes tending to make the feelings connected with this subject the most intense and most deeply-rooted of all those which gather round and protect old institutions and customs, that

we need not wonder to find them as yet less undermined and loosened than any of the rest by the progress of the great modern spiritual and social transition; nor suppose that the barbarisms to which men cling longest must be less barbarisms than those which they earlier shake off.

In every respect the burthen is hard on those who attack an almost universal opinion. They must be very fortunate as well as unusually capable if they obtain a hearing at all. They have more difficulty in obtaining a trial, than any other litigants have in getting a verdict. If they do extort a hearing, they are subjected to a set of logical requirements totally different from those extracted from other people. In all other cases, the burthen of proof is supposed to lie with the affirmative. If a person is charged with a murder, it rests with those who accuse him to give proof of his guilt, not with himself to prove his innocence. If there is a difference of opinion about the reality of any alleged historical event, in which the feelings of men in general are not much interested, as the Siege of Troy for example, those who maintain that the event took place are expected to produce their proofs, before those who take the other side can be required to say anything; and at no time are these required to do more than show that the evidence produced by the others is of no value. Again, in practical matters, the burthen of proof is supposed to be with those who are against liberty; who contend for any restriction or prohibition; either any limitation of the general freedom of human action, or any disqualification or disparity of privilege affecting one person or kind of persons, as compared with others. The *a priori* presumption is in favour of freedom and impartiality. It is held that there should be no restraint not required by the general good, and that the law should be no respecter of persons, but should treat all alike, save where dissimilarity of treatment is required by positive reasons, either of justice or of policy. But of none of these rules of evidence will the benefit be allowed to those who maintain the opinion I profess. It is useless for me to say that those who maintain the doctrine that men have a right to command and women are under an obligation to obey, or that men are fit for government and women unfit, are on the affirmative side of the question, and that they are bound to show positive evidence for the assertions, or submit to their rejection. It is equally unavailing for me to say that those who deny to women any freedom or privilege rightly allowed to men, having the double presumption against them that they are opposing freedom and recommending partiality, must be held to the strictest proof of their case, and unless their success be such as to exclude all doubt, the judgment ought to go against them. These would be thought good pleas in any common case; but they will not be thought so in this instance. Before I could hope to make any impression, I should be expected not only to answer all that has ever been said by those who take the other side of the question, but to imagine all that could be said by them—to find them in reasons, as well as answer all I find: and besides refuting all arguments for the affirmative, I shall be called upon for invincible positive arguments to prove a negative. And even if I could do all this, and leave the opposite party with a host of unanswered arguments against them, and not a single unrefuted one on their side, I should be thought to have done little; for a cause supported on the one hand by universal usage, and on the other by so great a preponderance of popular sentiment, is supposed to have a presumption in its favour, superior to any conviction which an appeal to reason has power to produce in any intellects but those of a high class.

I do not mention these difficulties to complain of them; first, because it would be useless; they are inseparable from having to contend through people's understandings against the hostility of their feelings and practical tendencies: and truly the understandings of the majority of mankind would need to be much better cultivated than has ever yet been the case, before they can be asked to place such reliance in their own power of estimating arguments, as to give up practical principles in which they have been born and bred and which are the basis of much of the existing order

of the world, at the first argumentative attack which they are not capable of logically resisting. I do not therefore quarrel with them for having too little faith in argument, but for having too much faith in custom and the general feeling. It is one of the characteristic prejudices of the reaction of the nineteenth century against the eighteenth, to accord to the unreasoning elements in human nature the infallibility which the eighteenth century is supposed to have ascribed to the reasoning elements. For the apotheosis of Reason we have substituted that of Instinct; and we call everything instinct which we find in ourselves and for which we cannot trace any rational foundation. This idolatry, infinitely more degrading than the other, and the most pernicious of the false worships of the present day, of all of which it is now the main support, will probably hold its ground until it gives way before a sound psychology, laying bare the real root of much that is bowed down to as the intention of Nature and the ordinance of God. As regards the present question, I am willing to accept the unfavourable conditions which the prejudice assigns to me. I consent that established custom, and the general feeling, should be deemed conclusive against me, unless that custom and feeling from age to age can be shown to have owed their existence to other causes than their soundness, and to have derived their power from the worse rather than the better parts of human nature. I am willing that judgment should go against me, unless I can show that my judge has been tampered with. The concession is not so great as it might appear; for to prove this, is by far the easiest portion of my task.

The generality of a practice is in some cases a strong presumption that it is, or at all events once was, conducive to laudable ends. This is the case, when the practice was first adopted, or afterwards kept up, as a means to such ends, and was grounded on experience of the mode in which they could be most effectually attained. If the authority of men over women, when first established, had been the result of a conscientious comparison between different modes of constituting the government of society; if, after trying various other modes of social organization—the government of women over men, equality between the two, and such mixed and divided modes of government as might be invented—it had been decided, on the testimony of experience, that the mode in which women are wholly under the rule of men, having no share at all in public concerns, and each in private being under the legal obligation of obedience to the man with whom she has associated her destiny, was the arrangement most conducive to the happiness and well being of both; its general adoption might then be fairly thought to be some evidence that, at the time when it was adopted, it was the best: though even then the considerations which recommended it may, like so many other primeval social facts of the greatest importance, have subsequently, in the course of ages, ceased to exist. But the state of the case is in every respect the reverse of this. In the first place, the opinion in favour of the present system, which entirely subordinates the weaker sex to the stronger, rests upon theory only; for there never has been trial made of any other: so that experience, in the sense in which it is vulgarly opposed to theory, cannot be pretended to have pronounced any verdict. And in the second place, the adoption of this system of inequality never was the result of deliberation, or forethought, or any social ideas, or any notion whatever of what conduced to the benefit of humanity or the good order of society. It arose simply from the fact that from the very earliest twilight of human society, every woman (owing to the value attached to her by men, combined with her inferiority in muscular strength) was found in a state of bondage to some man. Laws and systems of polity always begin by recognising the relations they find already existing between individuals. They convert what was a mere physical fact into a legal right, give it the sanction of society, and principally aim at the substitution of public and organized means of asserting and protecting these rights, instead of the irregular and lawless conflict of physical strength. Those who had already been compelled to obedience became in this manner legally bound to it. Slavery, from being a mere affair of force between the master and the slave, became regularized and a matter of compact among the masters, who, binding themselves to one another for common protection, guaranteed by their collective strength the private possessions of each, including his slaves. In early times, the great majority of the male

sex were slaves, as well as the whole of the female. And many ages elapsed, some of them ages of high cultivation, before any thinker was bold enough to question the rightfulness, and the absolute social necessity, either of the one slavery or of the other. By degrees such thinkers did arise: and (the general progress of society assisting) the slavery of the male sex has, in all the countries of Christian Europe at least (though, in one of them, only within the last few years) been at length abolished, and that of the female sex has been gradually changed into a milder form of dependence. But this dependence, as it exists at present, is not an original institution, taking a fresh start from considerations of justice and social expediency—it is the primitive state of slavery lasting on, through successive mitigations and modifications occasioned by the same causes which have softened the general manners, and brought all human relations more under the control of justice and the influence of humanity. It has not lost the taint of its brutal origin. No presumption in its favour, therefore, can be drawn from the fact of its existence. The only such presumption which it could be supposed to have, must be grounded on its having lasted till now, when so many other things which came down from the same odious source have been done away with. And this, indeed, is what makes it strange to ordinary ears, to hear it asserted that the inequality of rights between men and women has no other source than the law of the strongest.

That this statement should have the effect of a paradox, is in some respects creditable to the progress of civilization, and the improvement of the moral sentiments of mankind. We now live—that is to say, one or two of the most advanced nations of the world now live—in a state in which the law of the strongest seems to be entirely abandoned as the regulating principle of the world's affairs: nobody professes it, and, as regards most of the relations between human beings, nobody is permitted to practise it. When any one succeeds in doing so, it is under cover of some pretext which gives him the semblance of having some general social interest on his side. This being the ostensible state of things, people flatter themselves that the rule of mere force is ended; that the law of the strongest cannot be the reason of existence of anything which has remained in full operation down to the present time. However any of our present institutions may have begun, it can only, they think, have been preserved to this period of advanced civilization by a well-grounded feeling of its adaptation to human nature, and conduciveness to the general good. They do not understand the great vitality and durability of institutions which place right on the side of might; how intensely they are clung to; how the good as well as the bad propensities and sentiments of those who have power in their hands, become identified with retaining it; how slowly these bad institutions give way, one at a time, the weakest first, beginning with those which are least interwoven with the daily habits of life; and how very rarely those who have obtained legal power because they first had physical, have ever lost their hold of it until the physical power had passed over to the other side. Such shifting of the physical force not having taken place in the case of women; this fact, combined with all the peculiar and characteristic features of the particular case, made it certain from the first that this branch of the system of right founded on might, though softened in its most atrocious features at an earlier period than several of the others, would be the very last to disappear. It was inevitable that this one case of a social relation grounded on force, would survive through generations of institutions grounded on equal justice, an almost solitary exception to the general character of their laws and customs; but which, so long as it does not proclaim its own origin, and as discussion has not brought out its true character, is not felt to jar with modern civilization, any more than domestic slavery among the Greeks jarred with their notion of themselves as a free people.

The truth is, that people of the present and the last two or three generations have lost all practical sense of the primitive condition of humanity; and only the few who have studied history accurately, or have much frequented the parts of the world occupied by the living representatives of ages long past, are able to form any mental picture of what society then was. People are not aware how entirely, in former ages, the law of superior strength was the rule of life; how publicly and openly it was avowed, I do not say cynically or shamelessly— for these words imply a feeling that there was some-

thing in it to be ashamed of, and no such notion could find a place in the faculties of any person in those ages, except a philosopher or a saint. History gives a cruel experience of human nature, in shewing how exactly the regard due to the life, possessions, and entire earthly happiness of any class of persons, was measured by what they had the power of enforcing; how all who made any resistance to authorities that had arms in their hands, however dreadful might be the provocation, had not only the law of force but all other laws, and all the notions of social obligation against them; and in the eyes of those whom they resisted, were not only guilty of crime, but of the worst of all crimes, deserving the most cruel chastisement which human beings could inflict. The first small vestige of a feeling of obligation in a superior to acknowledge any right in inferiors, began when he had been induced, for convenience, to make some promise to them. Though these promises, even when sanctioned by the most solemn oaths, were for many ages revoked or violated on the most trifling provocation or temptation, it is probable that this, except by persons of still worse than the average morality, was seldom done without some twinges of conscience. The ancient republics, being mostly grounded from the first upon some kind of mutual compact, or at any rate formed by an union of persons not very unequal in strength, afforded, in consequence, the first instance of a portion of human relations fenced round, and placed under the dominion of another law than that of force. And though the original law of force remained in full operation between them and their slaves, and also (except so far as limited by express compact) between a commonwealth and its subjects, or other independent commonwealths; the banishment of that primitive law even from so narrow a field, commenced the regeneration of human nature, by giving birth to sentiments of which experience soon demonstrated the immense value even for material interests, and which thenceforward only required to be enlarged, not created. Though slaves were no part of the commonwealth, it was in the free states that slaves were first felt to have rights as human beings. The Stoics were, I believe, the first (except so far as the Jewish law constitutes an exception) who taught as a part of morality that men were bound by moral obligations to their slaves. No one, after Christianity became ascendant, could ever again have been a stranger to this belief, in theory; nor, after the rise of the Catholic Church, was it ever without persons to stand up for it. Yet to enforce it was the most arduous task which Christianity ever had to perform. For more than a thousand years the Church kept up the contest, with hardly any perceptible success. It was not for want of power over men's minds. Its power was prodigious. It could make kings and nobles resign their most valued possessions to enrich the Church. It could make thousands, in the prime of life and the height of worldly advantages, shut themselves up in convents to work out their salvation by poverty, fasting, and prayer. It could send hundreds of thousands across land and sea, Europe and Asia, to give their lives for the deliverance of the Holy Sepulchre. It could make kings relinquish wives who were the object of their passionate attachment, because the Church declared that they were within the seventh (by our calculation the fourteenth) degree of relationship. All this it did; but it could not make men fight less with one another, nor tyrannize less cruelly over the serfs, and when they were able, over burgesses. It could not make them renounce either of the applications of force; force militant, or force triumphant. This they could never be induced to do until they were themselves in their turn compelled by superior force. Only by the growing power of kings was an end put to fighting except between kings, or competitors for kingship; only by the growth of a wealthy and warlike bourgeoisie in the fortified towns, and of a plebeian infantry which proved more powerful in the field than the in disciplined chivalry, was the insolent tyranny of the nobles over the bourgeoisie and peasantry brought within some bounds. It was persisted in not only until, but long after, the oppressed had obtained a power enabling them often to take conspicuous vengeance; and on the Continent much of it continued to the time of the French Revolution, though in England the earlier and better organization of the democratic classes put an end to it sooner, by establishing equal laws and free national institutions.

If people are mostly so little aware how completely, during the greater part of the duration of our species, the law of force was the avowed rule of general conduct, any other being only a special and exceptional consequence of peculiar ties—and from how very recent a date it is that the affairs of society in general have been even pretended to be regulated according to any moral law; as little do people remember or consider, how institutions and customs which never had any ground but the law of force, last on into ages and states of general opinion which never would have permitted their first establishment. Less than forty years ago, Englishmen might still by law hold human beings in bondage as saleable property: within the present century they might kidnap them and carry them off, and work them literally to death. This absolutely extreme case of the law of force, condemned by those who can tolerate almost every other form of arbitrary power, and which, of all others, presents features the most revolting to the feelings of all who look at it from an impartial position, was the law of civilized and Christian England within the memory of persons now living: and in one half of Anglo-Saxon America three or four years ago, not only did slavery exist, but the slave trade, and the breeding of slaves expressly for it, was a general practice between slave states. Yet not only was there a greater strength of sentiment against it, but, in England at least, a less amount either of feeling or of interest in favour of it, than of any other of the customary abuses of force: for its motive was the love of gain, unmixed and undisguised; and those who profited by it were a very small numerical fraction of the country, while the natural feeling of all who were not personally interested in it, was unmitigated abhorrence. So extreme an instance makes it almost superfluous to refer to any other: but consider the long duration of absolute monarchy. In England at present it is the almost universal conviction that military despotism is a case of the law of force, having no other origin or justification. Yet in all the great nations of Europe except England it either still exists, or has only just ceased to exist, and has even now a strong party favourable to it in all ranks of the people, especially among persons of station and consequence. Such is the power of an established system, even when far from universal; when not only in almost every period of history there have been great and well-known examples of the contrary system, but these have almost invariably been afforded by the most illustrious and most prosperous communities. In this case, too, the possessor of the undue power, the person directly interested in it, is only one person, while those who are subject to it and suffer from it are literally all the rest. The yoke is naturally and necessarily humiliating to all persons, except the one who is on the throne, together with, at most, the one who expects to succeed to it. How different are these cases from that of the power of men over women! I am not now prejudging the question of its justifiableness. I am showing how vastly more permanent it could not but be, even if not justifiable, than these other dominations which have nevertheless lasted down to our own time. Whatever gratification of pride there is in the possession of power, and whatever personal interest in its exercise, is in this case not confined to a limited class, but common to the whole male sex. Instead of being, to most of its supporters, a thing desirable chiefly in the abstract, or, like the political ends usually contended for by factions, of little private importance to any but the leaders; it comes home to the person and hearth of every male head of a family, and of every one who looks forward to being so. The clodhopper exercises, or is to exercise, his share of the power equally with the highest nobleman. And the case is that in which the desire of power is the strongest: for every one who desires power, desires it most over those who are nearest to him, with whom his life is passed, with whom he has most concerns in common, and in whom any independence of his authority is oftenest likely to interfere with his individual preferences. If, in the other cases specified, powers manifestly grounded only on force, and having so much less to support them, are so slowly and with so much difficulty got rid of, much more must it be so with this, even if it rests on no better foundation than those. We must consider, too, that the possessors of the power have facilities in this case, greater than in any other, to prevent any uprising against it. Every one of the subjects lives under the very eye, and almost, it may be said, in the hands, of one of the masters—in closer intimacy with him than with any of her fellow-subjects; with no means of combining against him, no power of even locally overmastering him, and,

on the other hand, with the strongest motives for seeking his favour and avoiding to give him offence. In struggles for political emancipation, everybody knows how often its champions are bought off by bribes, or daunted by terrors. In the case of women, each individual of the subject-class is in a chronic state of bribery and intimidation combined. In setting up the standard of resistance, a large number of the leaders, and still more of the followers, must make an almost complete sacrifice of the pleasures or the alleviations of their own individual lot. If ever any system of privilege and enforced subjection had its yoke tightly riveted on the necks of those who are kept down by it, this has. I have not yet shown that it is a wrong system: but every one who is capable of thinking on the subject must see that even if it is, it was certain to outlast all other forms of unjust authority. And when some of the grossest of the other forms still exist in many civilized countries, and have only recently been got rid of in others, it would be strange if that which is so much the deepest-rooted had yet been perceptibly shaken anywhere. There is more reason to wonder that the protests and testimonies against it should have been so numerous and so weighty as they are.

Some will object, that a comparison cannot fairly be made between the government of the male sex and the forms of unjust power which I have adduced in illustration of it, since these are arbitrary, and the effect of mere usurpation, while it on the contrary is natural. But was there ever any domination which did not appear natural to those who possessed it? There was a time when the division of mankind into two classes, a small one of masters and a numerous one of slaves, appeared, even to the most cultivated minds, to be a natural, and the only natural, condition of the human race. No less an intellect, and one which contributed no less to the progress of human thought, than Aristotle, held this opinion without doubt or misgiving; and rested it on the same premises on which the same assertion in regard to the dominion of men over women is usually based, namely that there are different natures among mankind, free natures, and slave natures; that the Greeks were of a free nature, the barbarian races of Thracians and Asiatics of a slave nature. But why need I go back to Aristotle? Did not the slaveowners of the Southern United States maintain the same doctrine, with all the fanaticism with which men cling to the theories that justify their passions and legitimate their personal interests? Did they not call heaven and earth to witness that the dominion of the white man over the black is natural, that the black race is by nature incapable of freedom, and marked out for slavery? some even going so far as to say that the freedom of manual labourers is an unnatural order of things anywhere. Again, the theorists of absolute monarchy have always affirmed it to be the only natural form of government; issuing from the patriarchal, which was the primitive and spontaneous form of society, framed on the model of the paternal, which is anterior to society itself, and, as they contend, the most natural authority of all. Nay, for that matter, the law of force itself, to those who could not plead any other, has always seemed the most natural of all grounds for the exercise of authority. Conquering races hold it to be Nature's own dictate that the conquered should obey the conquerors, or, as they euphoniously paraphrase it, that the feebler and more unwarlike races should submit to the braver and manlier. The smallest acquaintance with human life in the middle ages, shows how supremely natural the dominion of the feudal nobility over men of low condition appeared to the nobility themselves, and how unnatural the conception seemed, of a person of the inferior class claiming equality with them, or exercising authority over them. It hardly seemed less so to the class held in subjection. The emancipated serfs and burgesses, even in their most vigorous struggles, never made any pretension to a share of authority; they only demanded more or less of limitation to the power of tyrannizing over them. So true is it that unnatural generally means only uncustomary, and that everything which is usual appears natural. The subjection of women to men being a universal custom, any departure from it quite naturally appears unnatural. But how entirely, even in this case, the feeling is dependent on custom, appears by ample experience. Nothing so much astonishes the people of distant parts of the world, when they first learn anything about England, as to be told that it is under a queen: the thing seems to them so unnatural as to be almost incredible. To Englishmen this does not seem in the least degree unnatural, because they are used to it; but they do feel it unnatural that women should be soldiers or members of parliament. In the feudal ages, on the contrary, war and politics were not thought unnatural to women, because not unusual; it seemed natural that women of the privileged classes should be of manly character, inferior in nothing but bodily strength to their husbands and fathers. The independence of women seemed rather less unnatural to the Greeks than to other ancients, on account of the fabulous Amazons (whom they believed to be historical), and the partial example afforded by the Spartan women; who, though no less subordinate by law than in other Greek states, were more free in fact, and being trained to bodily exercises in the same manner with men, gave ample proof that they were not naturally disqualified for them. There can be little doubt that Spartan experience suggested to Plato, among many other of his doctrines, that of the social and political equality of the two sexes.

But, it will be said, the rule of men over women differs from all these others in not being a rule of force: it is accepted voluntarily; women make no complaint, and are consenting parties to it. In the first place, a great number of women do not accept it. Ever since there have been women able to make their sentiments known by their writings (the only mode of publicity which society permits to them), an increasing number of them have recorded protests against their present social condition: and recently many thousands of them, headed by the most eminent women known to the public, have petitioned Parliament for their admission to the Parliamentary Suffrage. The claim of women to be educated as solidly, and in the same branches of knowledge, as men, is urged with growing intensity, and with a great prospect of success; while the demand for their admission into professions and occupations hitherto closed against them, becomes every year more urgent. Though there are not in this country, as there are in the United States, periodical Conventions and an organized party to agitate for the Rights of Women, there is a numerous and active Society organized and managed by women, for the more limited object of obtaining the political franchise. Nor is it only in our own country and in America that women are beginning to protest, more or less collectively, against the disabilities under which they labour. France, and Italy, and Switzerland, and Russia now afford examples of the same thing. How many more women there are who silently cherish similar aspirations, no one can possibly know; but there are abundant tokens how many *would* cherish them, were they not so strenuously taught to repress them as contrary to the proprieties of their sex. It must be remembered, also, that no enslaved class ever asked for complete liberty at once. When Simon de Montfort called the deputies of the commons to sit for the first time in Parliament, did any of them dream of demanding that an assembly, elected by their constituents, should make and destroy ministries, and dictate to the king in affairs of state? No such thought entered into the imagination of the most ambitious of them. The nobility had already these pretensions; the commons pretended to nothing but to be exempt from arbitrary taxation, and from the gross individual oppression of the king's officers. It is a political law of nature that these who are under any power of ancient origin, never begin by complaining of the power itself, but only of its oppressive exercise. There is never any want of women who complain of ill usage by their husbands. There would be infinitely more, if complaint were not the greatest of all provocatives to a repetition and increase of the ill usage. It is this which frustrates all attempts to maintain the power but protect the woman against its abuses. In no other case (except that of a child) is the person who has been proved judicially to have suffered an injury, replaced under the physical power of the culprit who inflicted it. Accordingly wives, even in the most extreme and protracted cases of bodily ill usage, hardly ever dare avail themselves of the laws made for their protection: and if, in a moment of irrepressible indignation, or by the interference of neighbours, they are induced to do so, their whole effort afterwards is to disclose as little as they can, and to beg off their tyrant from his merited chastisement.

All causes, social and natural, combine to make it unlikely that women should be collectively rebellious to the power of men. They are so far in a position different from all other subject classes, that their masters require something more from them than actual service. Men do not want solely the obedience of women, they want their sentiments. All men, except the most brutish, desire to have, in the woman most nearly connected with them, not a forced slave but a willing one, not a slave merely, but a favourite. They have therefore put everything in practice to enslave their minds. The masters of all other slaves rely, for maintaining obedience, on fear; either fear of themselves, or religious fears. The masters of women wanted more than simple obedience, and they turned the whole force of education to effect their purpose. All women are brought up from the very earliest years in the belief that their idéal of character is the very opposite to that of men; not self-will, and government by self-control, but submission, and yielding to the control of others. All the moralities tell them that it is the duty of women, and all the current sentimentalities that it is their nature, to live for others; to make complete abnegation of themselves, and to have no life but in their affections. And by their affections are meant the only ones they are allowed to have—those to the men with whom they are connected, or to the children who constitute an additional and indefeasible tie between them and a man. When we put together three things —first, the natural attraction between opposite sexes; secondly, the wife's entire dependence on the husband, every privilege or pleasure she has being either his gift, or depending entirely on his will; and lastly, that the principal object of human pursuit, consideration, and all objects of social ambition, can in general be sought or obtained by her only through him, it would be a miracle if the object of being attractive to men had not become the polar star of feminine education and formation of character. And, this great means of influence over the minds of women having been acquired, an instinct of selfishness made men avail themselves of it to the utmost as a means of holding women in subjection, by representing to them meekness, submissiveness, and resignation of all individual will into the hands of a man, as an essential part of sexual attractiveness. Can it be doubted that any of the other yokes which mankind have succeeded in breaking, would have subsisted till now if the same means had existed, and had been as sedulously used, to bow down their minds to it? If it had been made the object of the life of every young plebeian to find personal favour in the eyes of some patrician, of every young serf with some seigneur; if domestication with him, and a share of his personal affections, had been held out as the prize which they all should look out for, the most gifted and aspiring being able to reckon on the most desirable prizes; and if, when this prize had been obtained, they had been shut out by a wall of brass from all interests not centering in him, all feelings and desires but those which he shared or inculcated; would not serfs and seigneurs, plebeians and patricians, have been as broadly distinguished at this day as men and women are? and would not all but a thinker here and there, have believed the distinction to be a fundamental and unalterable fact in human nature?

The preceding considerations are amply sufficient to show that custom, however universal it may be, affords in this case no presumption, and ought not to create any prejudice, in favour of the arrangements which place women in social and political subjection to men. But I may go farther, and maintain that the course of history, and the tendencies of progressive human society, afford not only no presumption in favour of this system of inequality of rights, but a strong one against it; and that, so far as the whole course of human improvement up to this time, the whole stream of modern tendencies, warrants any inference on the subject, it is, that this relic of the past is discordant with the future, and must necessarily disappear.

For, what is the peculiar character of the modern world—the difference which chiefly distinguishes modern institutions, modern social ideas, modern life itself, from those of times long past? It is, that human beings are no longer born in their place in life, and chained down by an inexorable bond to the place they are born to, but are free to employ their faculties, and such favourable chances as offer, to achieve the lot which may appear to them most desirable. Human society of old was constituted on a very different principle. All were born to a fixed social position, and were mostly kept in it by law, or interdicted from any means by which they could emerge from it. As some men are born white and others black, so some were born slaves and others freemen and citizens; some were born patricians, others plebeians; some were born feudal nobles, others commoners and *roturiers*. A slave or serf could never make himself free, nor, except by the will of his master, become so. In most European countries it was not till towards the close of the middle ages, and as a consequence of the growth of regal power, that commoners could be ennobled. Even among nobles, the eldest son was born the exclusive heir to the paternal possessions, and a long time elapsed before it was fully established that the father could disinherit him. Among the industrious classes, only those who were born members of a guild, or were admitted into it by its members, could lawfully practise their calling within its local limits; and nobody could practise any calling deemed important, in any but the legal manner—by processes authoritatively prescribed. Manufacturers have stood in the pillory for presuming to carry on their business by new and improved methods. In modern Europe, and most in those parts of it which have participated most largely in all other modern improvements, diametrically opposite doctrines now prevail. Law and government do not undertake to prescribe by whom any social or industrial operation shall or shall not be conducted, or what modes of conducting them shall be lawful. These things are left to the unfettered choice of individuals. Even the laws which required that workmen should serve an apprenticeship, have in this country been repealed: there being ample assurance that in all cases in which an apprenticeship is necessary, its necessity will suffice to enforce it. The old theory was, that the least possible should be left to the choice of the individual agent; that all he had to do should, as far as practicable, be laid down for him by superior wisdom. Left to himself he was sure to go wrong. The modern conviction, the fruit of a thousand years of experience, is, that things in which the individual is the person directly interested, never go right but as they are left to his own discretion; and that any regulation of them by authority, except to protect the rights of others, is sure to be mischievous. This conclusion, slowly arrived at, and not adopted until almost every possible application of the contrary theory had been made with disastrous result, now (in the industrial department) prevails universally in the most advanced countries, almost universally in all that have pretensions to any sort of advancement. It is not that all processes are supposed to be equally good, or all persons to be equally qualified for everything; but that freedom of individual choice is now known to be the only thing which procures the adoption of the best processes, and throws each operation into the hands of those who are best qualified for it. Nobody thinks it necessary to make a law that only a strong-armed man shall be a blacksmith. Freedom and competition suffice to make blacksmiths strong-armed men, because the weak-armed can earn more by engaging in occupations for which they are more fit. In consonance with this doctrine, it is felt to be an overstepping of the proper bounds of authority to fix beforehand, on some general presumption, that certain persons are not fit to do certain things. It is now thoroughly known and admitted that if some such presumptions exist, no such presumption is infallible. Even if it be well grounded in a majority of cases, which it is very likely not to be, there will be a minority of exceptional cases in which it does not hold: and in those it is both an injustice to the individuals, and a detriment to society, to place barriers in the way of their using their faculties for their own benefit and for that of others. In the cases, on the other hand, in which the unfitness is real, the ordinary motives of human conduct will on the whole suffice to prevent the incompetent person from making, or from persisting in, the attempt.

If this general principle of social and economical science is not true; if individuals, with such help as they can derive from the opinion of those who know them, are not better judges than the law and the government, of their own capacities and vocation; the world cannot too soon abandon this principle, and return to the old system of regulations and disabilities. But if the principle is true, we ought to act as if we believed it, and not to ordain that to be born a girl instead of a boy, any more than to be born black instead of white, or a commoner instead of a nobleman, shall decide the person's position through all life—shall interdict people from all the more elevated social positions, and from all, except a few, respectable occupations. Even were we to admit the utmost that is ever pretended as to the superior fitness of men for all the functions now reserved to them, the same argument applies which forbids a legal qualification for members of Parliament. If only once in a dozen years the conditions of eligibility exclude a fit person, there is a real loss, while the exclusion of thousands of unfit persons is no gain; for if the constitution of the electoral body disposes them to choose unfit persons, there are always plenty of such persons to choose from. In all things of any difficulty and importance, those who can do them well are fewer than the need, even with the most unrestricted latitude of choice: and any limitation of the field of selection deprives society of some chances of being served by the competent, without ever saving it from the incompetent.

At present, in the more improved countries, the disabilities of women are the only case, save one, in which laws and institutions take persons at their birth, and ordain that they shall never in all their lives be allowed to compete for certain things. The one exception is that of royalty. Persons still are born to the throne; no one, not of the reigning family, can ever occupy it, and no one even of that family can, by any means but the course of hereditary succession, attain it. All other dignities and social advantages are open to the whole male sex: many indeed are only attainable by wealth, but wealth may be striven for by any one, and is actually obtained by many men of the very humblest origin. The difficulties, to the majority, are indeed insuperable without the aid of fortunate accidents; but no male human being is under any legal ban: neither law nor opinion superadd artificial obstacles to the natural ones. Royalty, as I have said, is excepted: but in this case every one feels it to be an exception—an anomaly in the modern world, in marked opposition to its customs and principles, and to be justified only by extraordinary special expediencies, which, though individuals and nations differ in estimating their weight, unquestionably do in fact exist. But in this exceptional case, in which a high social function is, for important reasons, bestowed on birth instead of being put up to competition, all free nations contrive to adhere in substance to the principle from which they nominally derogate; for they circumscribe this high function by conditions avowedly intended to prevent the person to whom it ostensibly belongs from really performing it; while the person by whom it is performed, the responsible minister, does obtain the post by a competition from which no full-grown citizen of the male sex is legally excluded. The disabilities, therefore, to which women are subject from the mere fact of their birth, are the solitary examples of the kind in modern legislation. In no instance except this, which comprehends half the human race, are the higher social functions closed against any one by a fatality of birth which no exertions, and no change of circumstances, can overcome; for even religious disabilities (besides that in England and in Europe they have practically almost ceased to exist) do not close any career to the disqualified person in case of conversion.

The social subordination of women thus stands out an isolated fact in modern social institutions; a solitary breach of what has become their fundamental law; a single relic of an old world of thought and practice exploded in everything else, but retained in the one thing of most universal interest; as if a gigantic dolmen, or a vast temple of Jupiter Olympius, occupied the site of St. Paul's and received daily worship, while the surrounding Christian churches were only resorted to on fasts and festivals. This entire discrepancy between one social fact and all those which accompany it, and the radical opposition between its nature and the progressive movement which is the boast of the modern world, and which has successively swept away everything else of an analogous character, surely affords, to a conscientious observer of human tendencies, serious matter for reflection. It raises a prima facie presumption on the unfavourable side, far outweighing any which custom and usage could in such circumstances create on the favourable; and should at least suffice to make this, like the choice between republicanism and royalty, a balanced question.

The least that can be demanded is, that the question should not be considered as prejudged by existing fact and existing opinion, but open to discussion on its merits, as a question of justice and expediency: the decision on this, as on any of the other social arrangements of mankind, depending on what an enlightened estimate of tendencies and consequences may

show to be most advantageous to humanity in general, without distinction of sex. And the discussion must be a real discussion, descending to foundations, and not resting satisfied with vague and general assertions. It will not do, for instance, to assert in general terms, that the experience of mankind has pronounced in favour of the existing system. Experience cannot possibly have decided between two courses, so long as there has only been experience of one. If it be said that the doctrine of the equality of the sexes rests only on theory, it must be remembered that the contrary doctrine also has only theory to rest upon. All that is proved in its favour by direct experience, is that mankind have been able to exist under it, and to attain the degree of improvement and prosperity which we now see; but whether that prosperity has been attained sooner, or is now greater, than it would have been under the other system, experience does not say. On the other hand, experience does say, that every step in improvement has been so invariably accompanied by a step made in raising the social position of women, that historians and philosophers have been led to adopt their elevation or debasement as on the whole the surest test and most correct measure of the civilization of a people or an age. Through all the progressive period of human history, the condition of women has been approaching nearer to equality with men. This does not of itself prove that the assimilation must go on to complete equality; but it assuredly affords some presumption that such is the case.

Neither does it avail anything to say that the *nature* of the two sexes adapts them to their present functions and position, and renders these appropriate to them. Standing on the ground of common sense and the constitution of the human mind, I deny that any one knows, or can know, the nature of the two sexes, as long as they have only been seen in their present relation to one another. If men had ever been found in society without women, or women without men, or if there had been a society of men and women in which the women were not under the control of the men, something might have been positively known about the mental and moral differences which may be inherent in the nature of each. What is now called the nature of women is an eminently artificial thing—the result of forced repression in some directions, unnatural stimulation in others. It may be asserted without scruple, that no other class of dependents have had their character so entirely distorted from its natural proportions by their relation with their masters; for, if conquered and slave races have been, in some respects, more forcibly repressed, whatever in them has not been crushed down by an iron heel has generally been let alone, and if left with any liberty of development, it has developed itself according to its own laws; but in the case of women, a hot-house and stove cultivation has always been carried on of some of the capabilities of their nature, for the benefit and pleasure of their masters. Then, because certain products of the general vital force sprout luxuriantly and reach a great development in this heated atmosphere and under this active nurture and watering, while other shoots from the same root, which are left outside in the wintry air, with ice purposely heaped all round them, have a stunted growth, and some are burnt off with fire and disappear; men, with that inability to recognise their own work which distinguishes the unanalytic mind, indolently believe that the tree grows of itself in the way they have made it grow, and that it would die if one half of it were not kept in a vapour bath and the other half in the snow.

Of all difficulties which impede the progress of thought, and the formation of well-grounded opinions on life and social arrangements, the greatest is now the unspeakable ignorance and inattention of mankind in respect to the influences which form human character. Whatever any portion of the human species now are, or seem to be, such, it is supposed, they have a natural tendency to be: even when the most elementary knowledge of the circumstances in which they have been placed, clearly points out the causes that made them what they are. Because a cottier deeply in arrears to his landlord is not industrious, there are people who think that the Irish are naturally idle. Because constitutions can be overthrown when the authorities appointed to execute them turn their arms against them, there are people who think the French incapable of free government. Because the Greeks cheated the Turks, and the Turks only plundered the Greeks, there are persons who think that the Turks are naturally

more sincere: and because women, as is often said, care nothing about politics except their personalities, it is supposed that the general good is naturally less interesting to women than to men. History, which is now so much better understood than formerly, teaches another lesson: if only by showing the extraordinary susceptibility of human nature to external influences, and the extreme variableness of those of its manifestations which are supposed to be most universal and uniform. But in history, as in travelling, men usually see only what they already had in their own minds; and few learn much from history, who do not bring much with them to its study.

Hence, in regard to that most difficult question, what are the natural differences between the two sexes—a subject on which it is impossible in the present state of society to obtain complete and correct knowledge—while almost everybody dogmatizes upon it, almost all neglect and make light of the only means by which any partial insight can be obtained into it. This is, an analytic study of the most important department of psychology, the laws of the influence of circumstances on character. For, however great and apparently ineradicable the moral and intellectual differences between men and women might be, the evidence of their being natural differences could only be negative. Those only could be inferred to be natural which could not possibly be artificial—the residuum, after deducting every characteristic of either sex which can admit of being explained from education or external circumstances. The profoundest knowledge of the laws of the formation of character is indispensable to entitle any one to affirm even that there is any difference, much more what the difference is, between the two sexes considered as moral and rational beings; and since no one, as yet, has that knowledge, (for there is hardly any subject which, in proportion to its importance, has been so little studied), no one is thus far entitled to any positive opinion on the subject. Conjectures are all that can at present be made; conjectures more or less probable, according as more or less authorized by such knowledge as we yet have of the laws of psychology, as applied to the formation of character.

Even the preliminary knowledge, what the differences between the sexes now are, apart from all question as to how they are made what they are, is still in the crudest and most incomplete state. Medical practitioners and physiologists have ascertained, to some extent, the differences in bodily constitution; and this is an important element to the psychologist: but hardly any medical practitioner is a psychologist. Respecting the mental characteristics of women; their observations are of no more worth than those of common men. It is a subject on which nothing final can be known, so long as those who alone can really know it, women themselves, have given but little testimony, and that little, mostly suborned. It is easy to know stupid women. Stupidity is much the same all the world over. A stupid person's notions and feelings may confidently be inferred from those which prevail in the circle by which the person is surrounded. Not so with those whose opinions and feelings are an emanation from their own nature and faculties. It is only a man here and there who has any tolerable knowledge of the character even of the women of his own family. I do not mean, of their capabilities; these nobody knows, not even themselves, because most of them have never been called out. I mean their actually existing thoughts and feelings. Many a man thinks he perfectly understands women, because he has had amatory relations with several, perhaps with many of them. If he is a good observer, and his experience extends to quality as well as quantity, he may have learnt something of one narrow department of their nature—an important department, no doubt. But of all the rest of it, few persons are generally more ignorant, because there are few from whom it is so carefully hidden. The most favourable case which a man can generally have for studying the character of a woman, is that of his own wife: for the opportunities are greater, and the cases of complete sympathy not so unspeakably rare. And in fact, this is the source from which any knowledge worth having on the subject has, I believe, generally come. But most men have not had the opportunity of studying in this way more than a single case: accordingly one can, to an almost laughable degree, infer what a man's wife is like, from his opinions about women in general. To make even this one case yield any result, the woman must be worth knowing, and the man not only a competent judge, but of a charac-

ter so sympathetic in itself, and so well adapted to hers, that he can either read her mind by sympathetic intuition, or has nothing in himself which makes her shy of disclosing it. Hardly anything, I believe, can be more rare than this conjunction. It often happens that there is the most complete unity of feeling and community of interests as to all external things, yet the one has as little admission into the internal life of the other as if they were common acquaintance. Even with true affection, authority on the one side and subordination on the other prevent perfect confidence. Though nothing may be intentionally withheld, much is not shown. In the analogous relation of parent and child, the corresponding phenomenon must have been in the observation of every one. As between father and son, how many are the cases in which the father, in spite of real affection on both sides, obviously to all the world does not know, nor suspect, parts of the son's character familiar to his companions and equals. The truth is, that the position of looking up to another is extremely unpropitious to complete sincerity and openness with him. The fear of losing ground in his opinion or in his feelings is so strong, that even in an upright character, there is an unconscious tendency to show only the best side, or the side which, though not the best, is that which he most likes to see: and it may be confidently said that thorough knowledge of one another hardly ever exists, but between persons who, besides being intimates, are equals. How much more true, then, must all this be, when the one is not only under the authority of the other, but has it inculcated on her as a duty to reckon everything else subordinate to his comfort and pleasure, and to let him neither see nor feel anything coming from her, except what is agreeable to him. All these difficulties stand in the way of a man's obtaining any thorough knowledge even of the one woman whom alone, in general, he has sufficient opportunity of studying. When we further consider that to understand one woman is not necessarily to understand any other woman; that even if he could study many women of one rank, or of one country, he would not thereby understand women of other ranks or countries; and even if he did, they are still only the women of a single period of history; we may safely assert that the knowledge which men can acquire of women, even as they have been and are, without reference to what they might be, is wretchedly imperfect and superficial, and always will be so, until women themselves have told all that they have to tell.

And this time has not come; nor will it come otherwise than gradually. It is but of yesterday that women have either been qualified by literary accomplishments, or permitted by society, to tell anything to the general public. As yet very few of them dare tell anything, which men, on whom their literary success depends, are unwilling to hear. Let us remember in what manner, up to a very recent time, the expression, even by a male author, of uncustomary opinions, or what are deemed eccentric feelings, usually was, and in some degree still is, received; and we may form some faint conception under what impediments a woman, who is brought up to think custom and opinion her sovereign rule, attempts to express in books anything drawn from the depths of her own nature. The greatest woman who has left writings behind her sufficient to give her an eminent rank in the literature of her country, thought it necessary to prefix as a motto to her boldest work, "Un homme peut braver l'opinion; une femme doit s'y soumettre."* The greater part of what women write about women is mere sycophancy to men. In the case of unmarried women, much of it seems only intended to increase their chance of a husband. Many, both married and unmarried, overstep the mark, and inculcate a servility beyond what is desired or relished by any man, except the very vulgarest. But this is not so often the case as, even at a quite late period, it still was. Literary women are becoming more freespoken, and more willing to express their real sentiments. Unfortunately, in this country especially, they are themselves such artificial products, that their sentiments are compounded of a small element of individual observation and consciousness, and a very large one of acquired associations. This will be less and less the case, but it will remain true to a great extent, as long as social institutions do not admit the same free development of originality in women which is possible to men. When that time comes, and not before, we shall see, and not merely hear, as much as it

is necessary to know of the nature of women, and the adaptation of other things to it.

I have dwelt so much on the difficulties which at present obstruct any real knowledge by men of the true nature of women, because in this as in so many other things "opinio copiæ inter maximas causas inopæ est;" and there is little chance of reasonable thinking on the matter, while people flatter themselves that they perfectly understand a subject of which most men know absolutely nothing, and of which it is at present impossible that any man, or all men taken together, should have knowledge which can qualify them to lay down the law to women as to what is, or is not, their vocation. Happily, no such knowledge is necessary for any practical purpose connected with the position of women in relation to society and life. For, according to all the principles involved in modern society, the question rests with women themselves—to be decided by their own experience, and by the use of their own faculties. There are no means of finding what either one person or many can do, but by trying—and no means by which any one else can discover for them what it is for their happiness to do or leave undone.

One thing we may be certain of—that what is contrary to women's nature to do, they never will be made to do by simply giving their nature free play. The anxiety of mankind to interfere in behalf of nature, for fear lest nature should not succeed in effecting its purpose, is an altogether unnecessary solicitude. What women by nature cannot do, it is quite superfluous to forbid them from doing. What they can do, but not so well as the men who are their competitors, competition suffices to exclude them from; since nobody asks for protective duties and bounties in favour of women; it is only asked that the present bounties and protective duties in favour of men should be recalled. If women have a greater natural inclination for some things than for others, there is no need of laws or social inculcation to make the majority of them do the former in preference to the latter. Whatever women's services are most wanted for, the free play of competition will hold out the strongest inducements to them to undertake. And, as the words imply, they are most wanted for the things for which they are most fit; by

* Title-page of Mme. de Stael's "Delphine."

the apportionment of which to them, the collective faculties of the two sexes can be applied on the whole with the greatest sum of valuable result.

The general opinion of men is supposed to be, that the natural vocation of a woman is that of a wife and mother. I say, is supposed to be, because, judging from acts—from the whole of the present constitution of society—one might infer that their opinion was the direct contrary. They might be supposed to think that the alleged natural vocation of women was of all things the most repugnant to their nature; insomuch that if they are free to do anything else—if any other means of living, or occupation of their time and faculties, is open, which has any chance of appearing desirable to them—there will not be enough of them who will be willing to accept the condition said to be natural to them. If this is the real opinion of men in general, it would be well that it should be spoken out. I should like to hear somebody openly enunciating the doctrine (it is already implied in much that is written on the subject)—"It is necessary to society that women should marry and produce children. They will not do so unless they are compelled. Therefore it is necessary to compel them." The merits of the case would then be clearly defined. It would be exactly that of the slave-holders of South Carolina and Louisiana. "It is necessary that cotton and sugar should be grown. White men cannot produce them. Negroes will not, for any wages which we choose to give. *Ergo* they must be compelled." An illustration still closer to the point is that of impressment. Sailors must absolutely be had to defend the country. It often happens that they will not voluntarily enlist. Therefore there must be the power of forcing them. How often has this logic been used! and, but for one flaw in it, without doubt it would have been successful up to this day. But it is open to the retort—First pay the sailors the honest value of their labour. When you have made it as well worth their while to serve you, as to work for other employers, you will have no more difficulty than others have in obtaining their services. To this there is no logical answer except "I will not:" and as people are now not only ashamed, but are not desirous, to rob the labourer of his hire, impressment is no longer advocated. Those who attempt to force women into marriage by closing

all other doors against them, lay themselves open to a similar retort. If they mean what they say, their opinion must evidently be, that men do not render the married condition so desirable to women, as to induce them to accept it for its own recommendations. It is not a sign of one's thinking the boon one offers very attractive, when one allows only Hobson's choice, "that or none." And here, I believe, is the clue to the feelings of those men, who have a real antipathy to the equal freedom of women. I believe they are afraid, not lest women should be unwilling to marry, for I do not think that any one in reality has that apprehension; but lest they should insist that marriage should be on equal conditions; lest all women of spirit and capacity should prefer doing almost anything else, not in their own eyes degrading, rather than marry, when marrying is giving themselves a master, and a master too of all their earthly possessions. And truly, if this consequence were necessarily incident to marriage, I think that the apprehension would be very well founded. I agree in thinking it probable that few women, capable of anything else, would, unless under an irresistible *entrainement*, rendering them for the time insensible to anything but itself, choose such a lot, when any other means were open to them of filling a conventionally honourable place in life: and if men are determined that the law of marriage shall be a law of despotism, they are quite right, in point of mere policy, in leaving to women only Hobson's choice. But, in that case, all that has been done in the modern world to relax the chain on the minds of women, has been a mistake. They never should have been allowed to receive a literary education. Women who read, much more women who write, are, in the existing constitution of things, a contradiction and a disturbing element: and it was wrong to bring women up with any acquirements but those of an odalisque, or of a domestic servant.

CHAPTER II

It will be well to commence the detailed discussion of the subject by the particular branch of it to which the course of our observations has led us: the conditions which the laws of this and all other countries annex to the marriage contract. Marriage being the destination appointed by society for women, the prospect they are brought up to, and the object which it is intended should be sought by all of them, except those who are too little attractive to be chosen by any man as his companion; one might have supposed that everything would have been done to make this condition as eligible to them as possible, that they might have no cause to regret being denied the option of any other. Society, however, both in this, and, at first, in all other cases, has preferred to attain its object by foul rather than fair means: but this is the only case in which it has substantially persisted in them even to the present day. Originally women were taken by force, or regularly sold by their father to the husband. Until a late period in European history, the father had the power to dispose of his daughter in marriage at his own will and pleasure, without any regard to hers. The Church, indeed, was so far faithful to a better morality as to require a formal "yes" from the woman at the marriage ceremony; but there was nothing to shew that the consent was other than compulsory; and it was practically impossible for the girl to refuse compliance if the father persevered, except perhaps when she might obtain the protection of religion by a determined resolution to take monastic vows. After marriage, the man had anciently (but this was anterior to Christianity) the power of life and death over his wife. She could invoke no law against him; he was her sole tribunal and law. For a long time he could repudiate her, but she had no corresponding power in regard to him. By the old laws of England, the husband was called the *lord* of the wife; he was literally regarded as her sovereign, inasmuch that the murder of a man by his wife was called treason (*petty* as distinguished from *high* treason), and was more cruelly avenged than was usually the case with high treason, for the penalty was burning to death. Because these various enormities have fallen into disuse (for most of them were never formally abolished, or not until they had long ceased to be practised) men suppose that all is now as it should be in regard to the marriage contract; and we are continually told that civilization and Christianity have restored to the woman her just rights. Meanwhile the

wife is the actual bond-servant of her husband: no less so, as far as legal obligation goes, than slaves commonly so called. She vows a lifelong obedience to him at the altar, and is held to it all through her life by law. Casuists may say that the obligation of obedience stops short of participation in crime, but it certainly extends to everything else. She can do no act whatever but by his permission, at least tacit. She can acquire no property but for him; the instant it becomes hers, even if by inheritance, it becomes *ipso facto* his. In this respect the wife's position under the common law of England is worse than that of slaves in the laws of many countries: by the Roman law, for example, a slave might have his peculium, which to a certain extent the law guaranteed to him for his exclusive use. The higher classes in this country have given an analogous advantage to their women, through special contracts setting aside the law, by conditions of pin-money, &c.: since parental feeling being stronger with fathers than the class feeling of their own sex, a father generally prefers his own daughter to a son-in-law who is a stranger to him. By means of settlements, the rich usually contrive to withdraw the whole or part of the inherited property of the wife from the absolute control of the husband: but they do not succeed in keeping it under her own control; the utmost they can do only prevents the husband from squandering it, at the same time debarring the rightful owner from its use. The property itself is out of the reach of both; and as to the income derived from it, the form of settlement most favourable to the wife (that called "to her separate use") only precludes the husband from receiving it instead of her: it must pass through her hands, but if he takes it from her by personal violence as soon as she receives it, he can neither be punished, nor compelled to restitution. This is the amount of the protection which, under the laws of this country, the most powerful nobleman can give to his own daughter as respects her husband. In the immense majority of cases there is no settlement: and the absorption of all rights, all property, as well as all freedom of action, is complete. The two are called "one person in law," for the purpose of inferring that whatever is hers is his, but the parallel inference is never drawn that whatever is his is hers; the maxim is not applied against the man, except to make him responsible to third parties for her acts, as a master is for the acts of his slaves or of his cattle. I am far from pretending that wives are in general no better treated than slaves; but no slave is a slave to the same lengths, and in so full a sense of the word, as a wife is. Hardly any slave, except one immediately attached to the master's person, is a slave at all hours and all minutes; in general he has, like a soldier, his fixed task, and when it is done, or when he is off duty, he disposes, within certain limits, of his own time, and has a family life into which the master rarely intrudes. "Uncle Tom" under his first master had his own life in his "cabin," almost as much as any man whose work takes him away from home, is able to have in his own family. But it cannot be so with the wife. Above all, a female slave has (in Christian countries) an admitted right, and is considered under a moral obligation, to refuse to her master the last familiarity. Not so the wife: however brutal a tyrant she may unfortunately be chained to—though she may know that he hates her, though it may be his daily pleasure to torture her, and though she may feel it impossible not to loathe him— he can claim from her and enforce the lowest degradation of a human being, that of being made the instrument of an animal function contrary to her inclinations. While she is held in this worst description of slavery as to her own person, what is her position in regard to the children in whom she and her master have a joint interest? They are by law *his* children. He alone has any legal rights over them. Not one act can she do towards or in relation to them, except by delegation from him. Even after he is dead she is not their legal guardian, unless he by will has made her so. He could even send them away from her, and deprive her of the means of seeing or corresponding with them, until this power was in some degree restricted by Serjeant Talfourd's Act. This is her legal state. And from this state she has no means of withdrawing herself. If she leaves her husband, she can take nothing with her, neither her children nor anything which is rightfully her own. If he chooses, he can compel her to return, by law, or by physical force; or he may content himself with seizing for his own use anything which she may earn, or which may be given to her by her relations. It is only legal separation by a decree of a court

of justice, which entitles her to live apart, without being forced back into the custody of an exasperated jailer—or which empowers her to apply any earnings to her own use, without fear that a man whom perhaps she has not seen for twenty years will pounce upon her some day and carry all off. This legal separation, until lately, the courts of justice would only give at an expense which made it inaccessible to any one out of the higher ranks. Even now it is only given in cases of desertion, or of the extreme of cruelty; and yet complaints are made every day that it is granted too easily. Surely, if a woman is denied any lot in life but that of being the personal body-servant of a despot, and is dependent for everything upon the chance of finding one who may be disposed to make a favourite of her instead of merely a drudge, it is a very cruel aggravation of her fate that she should be allowed to try this chance only once. The natural sequel and corollary from this state of things would be, that since her all in life depends upon obtaining a good master, she should be allowed to change again and again until she finds one. I am not saying that she ought to be allowed this privilege. That is a totally different consideration. The question of divorce, in the sense involving liberty of remarriage, is one into which it is foreign to my purpose to enter. All I now say is, that to those to whom nothing but servitude is allowed, the free choice of servitude is the only, though a most insufficient, alleviation. Its refusal completes the assimilation of the wife to the slave—and the slave under not the mildest form of slavery: for in some slave codes the slave could, under certain circumstances of ill usage, legally compel the master to sell him. But no amount of ill usage, without adultery superadded, will in England free a wife from her tormentor.

I have no desire to exaggerate, nor does the case stand in any need of exaggeration. I have described the wife's legal position, not her actual treatment. The laws of most countries are far worse than the people who execute them, and many of them are only able to remain laws by being seldom or never carried into effect. If married life were all that it might be expected to be, looking to the laws alone, society would be a hell upon earth. Happily there are both feelings and interests which in many men exclude, and in most, greatly temper, the impulses and propensities which lead to tyranny: and of those feelings, the tie which connects a man with his wife affords, in a normal state of things, incomparably the strongest example. The only tie which at all approaches to it, that between him and his children, tends, in all save exceptional cases, to strengthen, instead of conflicting with, the first. Because this is true; because men in general do not inflict, nor women suffer, all the misery which could be inflicted and suffered if the full power of tyranny with which the man is legally invested were acted on; the defenders of the existing form of the institution think that all its iniquity is justified, and that any complaint is merely quarrelling with the evil which is the price paid for every great good. But the mitigations in practice, which are compatible with maintaining in full legal force this or any other kind of tyranny, instead of being any apology for despotism, only serve to prove what power human nature possesses of reacting against the vilest institutions, and with what vitality the seeds of good as well as those of evil in human character diffuse and propagate themselves. Not a word can be said for despotism in the family which cannot be said for political despotism. Every absolute king does not sit at his window to enjoy the groans of his tortured subjects, nor strips them of their last rag and turns them out to shiver in the road. The despotism of Louis XVI. was not the despotism of Philippe le Bel, or of Nadir Shah, or of Caligula; but it was bad enough to justify the French Revolution, and to palliate even its horrors. If an appeal be made to the intense attachments which exist between wives and their husbands, exactly as much may be said of domestic slavery. It was quite an ordinary fact in Greece and Rome for slaves to submit to death by torture rather than betray their masters. In the proscriptions of the Roman civil wars it was remarked that wives and slaves were heroically faithful, sons very commonly treacherous. Yet we know how cruelly many Romans treated their slaves. But in truth these intense individual feelings nowhere rise to such a luxuriant height as under the most atrocious institutions. It is part of the irony of life, that the strongest feelings of devoted gratitude of which human nature seems to be susceptible, are called forth in human beings towards those who, having the power entirely to crush their earthly existence, voluntarily refrain from using that power. How great a place in most men this sentiment fills, even in religious devotion, it would be cruel to inquire. We daily see how much their gratitude to Heaven appears to be stimulated by the contemplation of fellow-creatures to whom God has not been so merciful as he has to themselves.

Whether the institution to be defended is slavery, political absolutism, or the absolutism of the head of a family, we are always expected to judge of it from its best instances; and we are presented with pictures of loving exercise of authority on one side, loving submission to it on the other—superior wisdom ordering all things for the greatest good of the dependents, and surrounded by their smiles and benedictions. All this would be very much to the purpose if any one pretended that there are no such things as good men. Who doubts that there may be great goodness, and great happiness, and great affection, under the absolute government of a good man? Meanwhile, laws and institutions require to be adapted, not to good men, but to bad. Marriage is not an institution designed for a select few. Men are not required, as a preliminary to the marriage ceremony, to prove by testimonials that they are fit to be trusted with the exercise of absolute power. The tie of affection and obligation to a wife and children is very strong with those whose general social feelings are strong, and with many who are little sensible to any other social ties; but there are all degrees of sensibility and insensibility to it, as there are all grades of goodness and wickedness in men, down to those whom no ties will bind, and on whom society has no action but through its *ultima ratio*, the penalties of the law. In every grade of this descending scale are men to whom are committed all the legal powers of a husband. The vilest malefactor has some wretched woman tied to him, against whom he can commit any atrocity except killing her, and, if tolerably cautious, can do that without much danger of the legal penalty. And how many thousands are there among the lowest classes in every country, who, without being in a legal sense malefactors in any other respect, because in every other quarter their aggressions meet with resistance, indulge the utmost habitual excesses of bodily violence towards the unhappy wife, who alone, at least of grown persons, can neither repel nor escape from their brutality; and towards whom the excess of dependence inspires their mean and savage natures, not with a generous forbearance, and a point of honour to behave well to one whose lot in life is trusted entirely to their kindness, but on the contrary with a notion that the law has delivered her to them as their thing, to be used at their pleasure, and that they are not expected to practise the consideration towards her which is required from them towards everybody else. The law, which till lately left even these atrocious extremes of domestic oppression practically unpunished, has within these few years made some feeble attempts to repress them. But its attempts have done little, and cannot be expected to do much, because it is contrary to reason and experience to suppose that there can be any real check to brutality, consistent with leaving the victim still in the power of the executioner. Until a conviction for personal violence, or at all events a repetition of it after a first conviction, entitles the woman *ipso facto* to a divorce, or at least to a judicial separation, the attempt to repress these "aggravated assaults" by legal penalties will break down for want of a prosecutor, or for want of a witness.

When we consider how vast is the number of men, in any great country, who are little higher than brutes, and that this never prevents them from being able, through the law of marriage, to obtain a victim, the breadth and depth of human misery caused in this shape alone by the abuse of the institution swells to something appalling. Yet these are only the extreme cases. They are the lowest abysses, but there is a sad succession of depth after depth before reaching them. In domestic as in political tyranny, the case of absolute monsters chiefly illustrates the institution by showing that there is scarcely any horror which may not occur under it if the despot pleases, and thus setting in a strong light what must be the terrible frequency of things only a little less atrocious. Absolute fiends are as rare as angels, perhaps rarer: ferocious savages, with occasional touches of humanity, are however very frequent: and in the wide interval which separates these from any worthy representatives of the human species, how many are the forms and gradations of animalism and selfishness, often under an outward varnish of civ-ilization and even cultivation, living at peace with the law, maintaining a creditable appearance to all who are not under their power, yet sufficient often to make the lives of all who are so, a torment and a burthen to them! It would be tiresome to repeat the commonplaces about the unfitness of men in general for power, which, after the political discussions of centuries, every one knows by heart, were it not that hardly any one thinks of applying these maxims to the case in which above all others they are applicable, that of power, not placed in the hands of a man here and there, but offered to every adult male, down to the basest and most ferocious. It is not because a man is not known to have broken any of the Ten Commandments, or because he maintains a respectable character in his dealings with those whom he cannot compel to have intercourse with him, or because he does not fly out into violent bursts of ill-temper against those who are not obliged to bear with him, that it is possible to surmise of what sort his conduct will be in the unrestraint of home. Even the commonest men reserve the violent, the sulky, the undisguisedly selfish side of their character for those who have no power to withstand it. The relation of superiors to dependents is the nursery of these vices of character, which, wherever else they exist, are an overflowing from that source. A man who is morose or violent to his equals, is sure to be one who has lived among inferiors, whom he could frighten or worry into submission. If the family in its best forms is, as it is often said to be, a school of sympathy, tenderness, and loving forgetfulness of self, it is still oftener, as respects its chief, a school of wilfulness, overbearingness, unbounded self-indulgence, and a double-dyed and idealized selfishness, of which sacrifice itself is only a particular form: the care for the wife and children being only care for them as parts of the man's own interests and belongings, and their individual happiness being immolated in every shape to his smallest preferences. What better is to be looked for under the existing form of the institution? We know that the bad propensities of human nature are only kept within bounds when they are allowed no scope for their indulgence. We know that from impulse and habit, when not from deliberate purpose, almost every one to whom others yield, goes on encroaching upon them, until a point is reached at which they are compelled to resist. Such being the common tendency of human nature; the almost un-limited power which present social institutions give to the man over at least one human being—the one with whom he resides, and whom he has always present—this power seeks out and evokes the latent germs of selfishness in the remotest corners of his nature—fans its faintest sparks and smoldering embers—offers to him a license for the indulgence of those points of his original character which in all other relations he would have found it necessary to repress and conceal, and the repression of which would in time have be-come a second nature. I know that there is another side to the question. I grant that the wife, if she cannot effectually resist, can at least retaliate; she, too, can make the man's life extremely uncomfortable, and by that power is able to carry many points which she ought, and many which she ought not, to prevail in. But this instrument of self-protection—which may be called the power of the scold, or the shrewish sanc-tion—has the fatal defect, that it avails most against the least tyrannical superiors, and in favour of the least deserving dependents. It is the weapon of irritable and self-willed women; of those who would make the worst use of power if they themselves had it, and who gen-erally turn this power to a bad use. The amiable can-not use such an instrument, the highminded disdain it. And on the other hand, the husbands against whom it is used most effectively are the gentler and more in-offensive; those who cannot be induced, even by provocation, to resort to any very harsh exercise of au-thority. The wife's power of being disagreeable gener-ally only establishes a counter-tyranny, and makes victims in their turn chiefly of those husbands who are least inclined to be tyrants.

What is it, then, which really tempers the corrupt-ing effects of the power, and makes it compatible with such amount of good as we actually see? Mere femi-nine blandishments, though of great effect in individ-ual instances, have very little effect in modifying the general tendencies of the situation; for their power only lasts while the woman is young and attractive, of-ten only while her charm is new, and not dimmed by familiarity; and on many men they have not much in-fluence at any time. The real mitigating causes are, the personal affection which is the growth of time, in so far as the man's nature is susceptible of it, and the woman's character sufficiently congenial with his to excite it; their common interests as regards the chil-dren, and their general community of interest as con-cerns third persons (to which however there are very great limitations); the real importance of the wife to his daily comforts and enjoyments, and the value he consequently attaches to her on his personal account, which, in a man capable of feeling for others, lays the foundation of caring for her on her own; and lastly, the influence naturally acquired over almost all human beings by those near to their persons (if not actually disagreeable to them): who, both by their direct entreaties, and by the insensible contagion of their feelings and dispositions, are often able, unless coun-teracted by some equally strong personal influence, to obtain a degree of command over the conduct of the superior, altogether excessive and unreasonable. Through these various means, the wife frequently ex-ercises even too much power over the man; she is able to affect his conduct in things in which she may not be qualified to influence it for good—in which her influence may be not only unenlightened, but em-ployed on the morally wrong side; and in which he would act better if left to his own prompting. But nei-ther in the affairs of families nor in those of states is power a compensation for the loss of freedom. Her power often gives her what she has no right to, but does not enable her to assert her own rights. A Sultan's favourite slave has slaves under her, over whom she tyrannizes; but the desirable thing would be that she should neither have slaves nor be a slave. By entirely sinking her own existence in her husband; by having no will (or persuading him that she has no will) but his, in anything which regards their joint relation, and by making it the business of her life to work upon his sentiments, a wife may gratify herself by influencing, and very probably perverting, his conduct, in those of his external relations which she has never qualified herself to judge of, or in which she is herself wholly influenced by some personal or other partiality or prej-udice. Accordingly, as things now are, those who act most kindly to their wives, are quite as often made worse, as better, by the wife's influence, in respect to all interests extending beyond the family. She is taught that she has no business with things out of that sphere; and accordingly she seldom has any honest and conscientious opinion on them; and therefore hardly ever meddles with them for any legitimate purpose, but generally for an interested one. She neither knows nor cares which is the right side in politics, but she knows what will bring in money or invitations, give her husband a title, her son a place, or her daughter a good marriage.

But how, it will be asked, can any society exist without government? In a family, as in a state, some one person must be the ultimate ruler. Who shall decide when married people differ in opinion? Both cannot have their way, yet a decision one way or the other must be come to.

It is not true that in all voluntary association between two people, one of them must be absolute master: still less that the law must determine which of them it shall be. The most frequent case of voluntary association, next to marriage, is partnership in business: and it is not found or thought necessary to enact that in every partnership, one partner shall have entire control over the concern, and the others shall be bound to obey his orders. No one would enter into partnership on terms which would subject him to the responsibilities of a principal, with only the powers and privileges of a clerk or agent. If the law dealt with other contracts as it does with marriage, it would ordain that one partner should administer the common business as if it was his private concern; that the others should have only delegated powers; and that this one should be designated by some general presumption of law, for example as being the eldest. The law never does this: nor does experience show it to be necessary that any theoretical inequality of power should exist between the partners, or that the partnership should have any other conditions than what they may themselves appoint by their articles of agreement. Yet it might seem that the exclusive power might be conceded with less danger to the rights and interests of the inferior, in the case of partnership than in that of marriage, since he is free to cancel the power by withdrawing from the connexion. The wife has no such power, and even if she had, it is

almost always desirable that she should try all measures before resorting to it.

It is quite true that things which have to be decided every day, and cannot adjust themselves gradually, or wait for a compromise, ought to depend on one will: one person must have their sole control. But it does not follow that this should always be the same person. The natural arrangement is a division of powers between the two; each being absolute in the executive branch of their own department, and any change of system and principle requiring the consent of both. The division neither can nor should be preestablished by the law, since it must depend on individual capacities and suitabilities. If the two persons chose, they might pre-appoint it by the marriage contract, as pecuniary arrangements are now often pre-appointed. There would seldom be any difficulty in deciding such things by mutual consent, unless the marriage was one of those unhappy ones in which all other things, as well as this, become subjects of bickering and dispute. The division of rights would naturally follow the division of duties and functions; and that is already made by consent, or at all events not by law, but by general custom, modified and modifiable at the pleasure of the persons concerned.

The real practical decision of affairs, to whichever may be given the legal authority, will greatly depend, as it even now does, upon comparative qualifications. The mere fact that he is usually the eldest, will in most cases give the preponderance to the man; at least until they both attain a time of life at which the difference in their years is of no importance. There will naturally also be a more potential voice on the side, whichever it is, that brings the means of support. Inequality from this source does not depend on the law of marriage, but on the general conditions of human society, as now constituted. The influence of mental superiority, either general or special, and of superior decision of character, will necessarily tell for much. It always does so at present. And this fact shows how little foundation there is for the apprehension that the powers and responsibilities of partners in life (as of partners in business), cannot be satisfactorily apportioned by agreement between themselves. They always are so apportioned, except in cases in which the marriage institution is a failure. Things never come to an issue of downright power on one side, and obedience on the other, except where the connexion altogether has been a mistake, and it would be a blessing to both parties to be relieved from it. Some may say that the very thing by which an amicable settlement of differences becomes possible, is the power of legal compulsion known to be in reserve; as people submit to an arbitration because there is a court of law in the background, which they know that they can be forced to obey. But to make the cases parallel, we must suppose that the rule of the court of law was, not to try the cause, but to give judgment always for the same side, suppose the defendant. If so, the amenability to it would be a motive with the plaintiff to agree to almost any arbitration, but it would be just the reverse with the defendant. The despotic power which the law gives to the husband may be a reason to make the wife assent to any compromise by which power is practically shared between the two, but it cannot be the reason why the husband does. That there is always among decently conducted people a practical compromise, though one of them at least is under no physical or moral necessity of making it, shows that the natural motives which lead to a voluntary adjustment of the united life of two persons in a manner acceptable to both, do on the whole, except in unfavourable cases, prevail. The matter is certainly not improved by laying down as an ordinance of law, that the superstructure of free government shall be raised upon a legal basis of despotism on one side and subjection on the other, and that every concession which the despot makes may, at his mere pleasure, and without any warning, be recalled. Besides that no freedom is worth much when held on so precarious a tenure, its conditions are not likely to be the most equitable when the law throws so prodigious a weight into one scale; when the adjustment rests between two persons one of whom is declared to be entitled to everything, the other not only entitled to nothing except during the good pleasure of the first, but under the strongest moral and religious obligation not to rebel under any excess of oppression.

A pertinacious adversary, pushed to extremities, may say, that husbands indeed are willing to be reasonable, and to make fair concessions to their partners without being compelled to it, but that wives are not: that if allowed any rights of their own, they will acknowledge no rights at all in any one else, and never will yield in anything, unless they can be compelled, by the man's mere authority, to yield in everything. This would have been said by many persons some generations ago, when satires on women were in vogue, and men thought it a clever thing to insult women for being what men made them. But it will be said by no one now who is worth replying to. It is not the doctrine of the present day that women are less susceptible of good feeling, and consideration for those with whom they are united by the strongest ties, than men are. On the contrary, we are perpetually told that women are better than men, by those who are totally opposed to treating them as if they were as good; so that the saying has passed into a piece of tiresome cant, intended to put a complimentary face upon an injury, and resembling those celebrations of royal clemency which, according to Gulliver, the king of Lilliput always prefixed to his most sanguinary decrees. If women are better than men in anything, it surely is in individual self-sacrifice for those of their own family. But I lay little stress on this, so long as they are universally taught that they are born and created for self-sacrifice. I believe that equality of rights would abate the exaggerated self-abnegation which is the present artificial ideal of feminine character, and that a good woman would not be more self-sacrificing than the best man: but on the other hand, men would be much more unselfish and self-sacrificing than at present, because they would no longer be taught to worship their own will as such a grand thing that it is actually the law for another rational being. There is nothing which men so easily learn as this self-worship: all privileged persons, and all privileged classes, have had it. The more we descend in the scale of humanity, the intenser it is; and most of all in those who are not, and can never expect to be, raised above any one except an unfortunate wife and children. The honourable exceptions are proportionally fewer than in the case of almost any other human infirmity. Philosophy and religion, instead of keeping it in check, are generally suborned to defend it; and nothing controls it but that practical feeling of the equality of human beings, which is the theory of Christianity, but which Christianity will never practically teach, while it sanctions institutions grounded on an arbitrary preference of one human being over another.

There are, no doubt, women, as there are men, whom equality of consideration will not satisfy; with whom there is no peace while any will or wish is regarded but their own. Such persons are a proper subject for the law of divorce. They are only fit to live alone, and no human beings ought to be compelled to associate their lives with them. But the legal subordination tends to make such characters among women more, rather than less, frequent. If the man exerts his whole power, the woman is of course crushed: but if she is treated with indulgence, and permitted to assume power, there is no rule to set limits to her encroachments. The law, not determining her rights, but theoretically allowing her none at all, practically declares that the measure of what she has a right to, is what she can contrive to get.

The equality of married persons before the law, is not only the sole mode in which that particular relation can be made consistent with justice to both sides, and conducive to the happiness of both, but it is the only means of rendering the daily life of mankind, in any high sense, a school of moral cultivation. Though the truth may not be felt or generally acknowledged for generations to come, the only school of genuine moral sentiment is society between equals. The moral education of mankind has hitherto emanated chiefly from the law of force, and is adapted almost solely to the relations which force creates. In the less advanced states of society, people hardly recognise any relation with their equals. To be an equal is to be an enemy. Society, from its highest place to its lowest, is one long chain, or rather ladder, where every individual is either above or below his nearest neighbour, and wherever he does not command he must obey. Existing moralities, accordingly, are mainly fitted to a relation of command and obedience. Yet command and obedience are but unfortunate necessities of human life: society in equality is its normal state. Already in modern life, and more and more as it progressively improves, command and obedience become exceptional facts in life, equal association its general rule. The morality of the first ages rested on the obligation to submit to power; that of the ages next following, on the right of the weak to the forbearance and protection of the strong. How much longer is one form of society and life to content itself with the morality made for another? We have had the morality of submission, and the morality of chivalry and generosity; the time is now come for the morality of justice. Whenever, in former ages, any approach has been made to society in equality, Justice has asserted its claims as the foundation of virtue. It was thus in the free republics of antiquity. But even in the best of these, the equals were limited to the free male citizens; slaves, women, and the unenfranchised residents were under the law of force. The joint influence of Roman civilization and of Christianity obliterated these distinctions, and in theory (if only partially in practice) declared the claims of the human being, as such, to be paramount to those of sex, class, or social position. The barriers which had begun to be levelled were raised again by the northern conquests; and the whole of modern history consists of the slow process by which they have since been wearing away. We are entering into an order of things in which justice will again be the primary virtue; grounded as before on equal, but now also on sympathetic association; having its root no longer in the instinct of equals for self-protection, but in a cultivated sympathy between them; and no one being now left out, but an equal measure being extended to all. It is no novelty that mankind do not distinctly foresee their own changes, and that their sentiments are adapted to past, not to coming ages. To see the futurity of the species has always been the privilege of the intellectual élite, or of those who have learnt from them; to have the feelings of that futurity has been the distinction, and usually the martyrdom, of a still rarer élite. Institutions, books, education, society, all go on training human beings for the old, long after the new has come; much more when it is only coming. But the true virtue of human beings is fitness to live together as equals; claiming nothing for themselves but what they as freely concede to every one else; regarding command of any kind as an exceptional necessity, and in all cases a temporary one; and preferring, whenever possible, the society of those with whom leading and following can be alternate and reciprocal. To these virtues, nothing in life as at present constituted gives cultivation by exercise. The family is a school of despotism, in which the virtues of despotism, but also its vices, are largely nourished. Citizenship, in free countries, is partly a school of society in equality; but citizenship fills only a small place in modern life, and does not come near the daily habits or inmost sentiments. The family, justly constituted, would be the real school of the virtues of freedom. It is sure to be a sufficient one of everything else. It will always be a school of obedience for the children, of command for the parents. What is needed is, that it should be a school of sympathy in equality, of living together in love, without power on one side or obedience on the other. This it ought to be between the parents. It would then be an exercise of those virtues which each requires to fit them for all other association, and a model to the children of the feelings and conduct which their temporary training by means of obedience is designed to render habitual, and therefore natural, to them. The moral training of mankind will never be adapted to the conditions of the life for which all other human progress is a preparation, until they practise in the family the same moral rule which is adapted to the normal constitution of human society. Any sentiment of freedom which can exist in a man whose nearest and dearest intimacies are with those of whom he is absolute master, is not the genuine or Christian love of freedom, but, what the love of freedom generally was in the ancients and in the middle ages—an intense feeling of the dignity and importance of his own personality; making him disdain a yoke for himself, of which he has no abhorrence whatever in the abstract, but which he is abundantly ready to impose on others for his own interest or glorification.

I readily admit (and it is the very foundation of my hopes) that numbers of married people even under the present law, (in the higher classes of England probably a great majority), live in the spirit of a just law of equality. Laws never would be improved, if there were not numerous persons whose moral sentiments are better than the existing laws. Such persons ought to support the principles here advocated; of which the only object is to make all other married couples similar to what these are now. But persons even of considerable moral worth, unless they are also thinkers, are very ready to believe that laws or practices, the evils of which they have not personally experienced, do not produce any evils, but (if seeming to be generally approved of) probably do good, and that it is wrong to object to them. It would, however, be a great mistake in such married people to suppose, because the legal conditions of the tie which unites them do not occur to their thoughts once in a twelvemonth, and because they live and feel in all respects as if they were legally equals, that the same is the case with all other married couples, wherever the husband is not a notorious ruffian. To suppose this, would be to show equal ignorance of human nature and of fact. The less fit a man is for the possession of power—the less likely to be allowed to exercise it over any person with that person's voluntary consent—the more does he hug himself in the consciousness of the power the law gives him, exact its legal rights to the utmost point which custom (the custom of men like himself) will tolerate, and take pleasure in using the power, merely to enliven the agreeable sense of possessing it. What is more; in the most naturally brutal and morally uneducated part of the lower classes, the legal slavery of the woman, and something in the merely physical subjection to their will as an instrument, causes them to feel a sort of disrespect and contempt towards their own wife which they do not feel towards any other woman, or any other human being, with whom they come in contact; and which makes her seem to them an appropriate subject for any kind of indignity. Let an acute observer of the signs of feeling, who has the requisite opportunities, judge for himself whether this is not the case: and if he finds that it is, let him not wonder at any amount of disgust and indignation that can be felt against institutions which lead naturally to this depraved state of the human mind.

We shall be told, perhaps, that religion imposes the duty of obedience; as every established fact which is too bad to admit of any other defence, is always presented to us as an injunction of religion. The Church, it is very true, enjoins it in her formularies, but it would be difficult to derive any such injunction from

Christianity. We are told that St. Paul said, "Wives, obey your husbands:" but he also said, "Slaves, obey your masters." It was not St. Paul's business, nor was it consistent with his object, the propagation of Christianity, to incite any one to rebellion against existing laws. The apostle's acceptance of all social institutions as he found them, is no more to be construed as a disapproval of attempts to improve them at the proper time, than his declaration, "The powers that be are ordained of God," gives his sanction to military despotism, and to that alone, as the Christian form of political government, or commands passive obedience to it. To pretend that Christianity was intended to stereotype existing forms of government and society, and protect them against change, is to reduce it to the level of Islamism or of Brahminism. It is precisely because Christianity has not done this, that it has been the religion of the progressive portion of mankind, and Islamism, Brahminism, &c., have been those of the stationary portions; or rather (for there is no such thing as a really stationary society) of the declining portions. There have been abundance of people, in all ages of Christianity, who tried to make it something of the same kind; to convert us into a sort of Christian Mussulmans, with the Bible for a Koran, prohibiting all improvement: and great has been their power, and many have had to sacrifice their lives in resisting them. But they have been resisted, and the resistance has made us what we are, and will yet make us what we are to be.

After what has been said respecting the obligation of obedience, it is almost superfluous to say anything concerning the more special point included in the general one—a woman's right to her own property; for I need not hope that this treatise can make any impression upon those who need anything to convince them that a woman's inheritance or gains ought to be as much her own after marriage as before. The rule is simple: whatever would be the husband's or wife's if they were not married, should be under their exclusive control during marriage; which need not interfere with the power to tie up property by settlement, in order to preserve it for children. Some people are sentimentally shocked at the idea of a separate interest in money matters, as inconsistent with the ideal fusion of two lives into one. For my own part, I am one of the strongest supporters of community of goods, when resulting from an entire unity of feeling in the owners, which makes all things common between them. But I have no relish for a community of goods resting on the doctrine, that what is mine is yours but what is yours is not mine; and I should prefer to decline entering into such a compact with any one, though I were myself the person to profit by it.

This particular injustice and oppression to women, which is, to common apprehensions, more obvious than all the rest, admits of remedy without interfering with any other mischiefs: and there can be little doubt that it will be one of the earliest remedied. Already, in many of the new and several of the old States of the American Confederation, provisions have been inserted even in the written Constitutions, securing to women equality of rights in this respect: and thereby improving materially the position, in the marriage relation, of those women at least who have property, by leaving them one instrument of power which they have not signed away; and preventing also the scandalous abuse of the marriage institution, which is perpetrated when a man entraps a girl into marrying him without a settlement, for the sole purpose of getting possession of her money. When the support of the family depends, not on property, but on earnings, the common arrangement, by which the man earns the income and the wife superintends the domestic expenditure, seems to me in general the most suitable division of labour between the two persons. If, in addition to the physical suffering of bearing children, and the whole responsibility of their care and education in early years, the wife undertakes the careful and economical application of the husband's earnings to the general comfort of the family; she takes not only her fair share, but usually the larger share, of the bodily and mental exertion required by their joint existence. If she undertakes any additional portion, it seldom relieves her from this, but only prevents her from performing it properly. The care which she is herself disabled from taking of the children and the household, nobody else takes; those of the children who do not die, grow up as they best can, and the management of the household is likely to be so bad, as even in point of economy to be a great drawback from the value of the wife's earnings. In an otherwise just state of things, it is not, therefore, I think, a desirable custom, that the wife should contribute by her labour to the income of the family. In an unjust state of things, her doing so may be useful to her, by making her of more value in the eyes of the man who is legally her master; but, on the other hand, it enables him still farther to abuse his power, by forcing her to work, and leaving the support of the family to her exertions, while he spends most of his time in drinking and idleness. The *power* of earning is essential to the dignity of a woman, if she has not independent property. But if marriage were an equal contract, not implying the obligation of obedience; if the connexion were no longer enforced to the oppression of those to whom it is purely a mischief, but a separation, on just terms (I do not now speak of a divorce), could be obtained by any woman who was morally entitled to it; and if she would then find all honourable employments as freely open to her as to men; it would not be necessary for her protection, that during marriage she should make this particular use of her faculties. Like a man when he chooses a profession, so, when a woman marries, it may in general be understood that she makes choice of the management of a household, and the bringing up of a family, as the first call upon her exertions, during as many years of her life as may be required for the purpose; and that she renounces, not all other objects and occupations, but all which are not consistent with the requirements of this. The actual exercise, in a habitual or systematic manner, of outdoor occupations, or such as cannot be carried on at home, would by this principle be practically interdicted to the greater number of married women. But the utmost latitude ought to exist for the adaptation of general rules to individual suitabilities; and there ought to be nothing to prevent faculties exceptionally adapted to any other pursuit, from obeying their vocation notwithstanding marriage: due provision being made for supplying otherwise any falling-short which might become inevitable, in her full performance of the ordinary functions of mistress of a family. These things, if once opinion were rightly directed on the subject, might with perfect safety be left to be regulated by opinion, without any interference of law.

CHAPTER III

On the other point which is involved in the just equality of women, their admissibility to all the functions and occupations hitherto retained as the monopoly of the stronger sex, I should anticipate no difficulty in convincing any one who has gone with me on the subject of the equality of women in the family. I believe that their disabilities elsewhere are only clung to in order to maintain their subordination in domestic life; because the generality of the male sex cannot yet tolerate the idea of living with an equal. Were it not for that, I think that almost every one, in the existing state of opinion in politics and political economy, would admit the injustice of excluding half the human race from the greater number of lucrative occupations, and from almost all high social functions; ordaining from their birth either that they are not, and cannot by any possibility become, fit for employments which are legally open to the stupidest and basest of the other sex, or else that however fit they may be, those employments shall be interdicted to them, in order to be preserved for the exclusive benefit of males. In the last two centuries, when (which was seldom the case) any reason beyond the mere existence of the fact was thought to be required to justify the disabilities of women, people seldom assigned as a reason their inferior mental capacity; which, in times when there was a real trial of personal faculties (from which all women were not excluded) in the struggles of public life, no one really believed in. The reason given in those days was not women's unfitness, but the interest of society, by which was meant the interest of men; just as the *raison d'état*, meaning the convenience of the government, and the support of existing authority, was deemed a sufficient explanation and excuse for the most flagitious crimes. In the present day, power holds a smoother language, and whomsoever it oppresses, always pretends to do so for their own good: accordingly, when anything is forbidden to women, it is thought necessary to say, and desirable to believe, that they are incapable of doing it, and that they depart from their real path of success and happiness when they aspire to it. But to make this reason plausible (I do not say valid), those by whom it is urged must be prepared to carry it to a much greater length than any one ventures to do in the face of present experience. It is not sufficient to maintain that women on the average are less gifted than men on the average, with certain of the higher mental faculties, or that a smaller number of women than of men are fit for occupations and functions of the highest intellectual character. It is necessary to maintain that no women at all are fit for them, and that the most eminent women are inferior in mental faculties to the most mediocre of the men on whom those functions at present devolve. For if the performance of the function is decided either by competition, or by any mode of choice which secures regard to the public interest, there needs be no apprehension that any important employments will fall into the hands of women inferior to average men, or to the average of their male competitors. The only result would be that there would be fewer women than men in such employments; a result certain to happen in any case, if only from the preference always likely to be felt by the majority of women for the one vocation in which there is nobody to compete with them. Now, the most determined depreciator of women will not venture to deny, that when we add the experience of recent times to that of ages past, women, and not a few merely, but many women, have proved themselves capable of everything, perhaps without a single exception, which is done by men, and of doing it successfully and creditably. The utmost that can be said is, that there are many things which none of them have succeeded in doing as well as they have been done by some men—many in which they have not reached the very highest rank. But there are extremely few, dependent only on mental faculties, in which they have not attained the rank next to the highest. Is not this enough, and much more than enough, to make it a tyranny to them, and a detriment to society, that they should not be allowed to compete with men for the exercise of these functions? Is it not a mere truism to say, that such functions are often filled by men far less fit for them than numbers of women, and who would be beaten by women in any fair field of competition? What difference does it make that there may be men somewhere, fully employed about other things, who may be still better qualified for the things

in question than these women? Does not this take place in all competitions? Is there so great a superfluity of men fit for high duties, that society can afford to reject the service of any competent person? Are we so certain of always finding a man made to our hands for any duty or function of social importance which falls vacant, that we lose nothing by putting a ban upon one-half of mankind, and refusing beforehand to make their faculties available, however distinguished they may be? And even if we could do without them, would it be consistent with justice to refuse to them their fair share of honour and distinction, or to deny to them the equal moral right of all human beings to choose their occupation (short of injury to others) according to their own preferences, at their own risk? Nor is the injustice confined to them: it is shared by those who are in a position to benefit by their services. To ordain that any kind of persons shall not be physicians, or shall not be advocates, or shall not be members of parliament, is to injure not them only, but all who employ physicians or advocates, or elect members of parliament, and who are deprived of the stimulating effect of greater competition on the exertions of the competitors, as well as restricted to a narrower range of individual choice.

It will perhaps be sufficient if I confine myself, in the details of my argument, to functions of a public nature: since, if I am successful as to those, it probably will be readily granted that women should be admissible to all other occupations to which it is at all material whether they are admitted or not. And here let me begin by marking out one function, broadly distinguished from all others, their right to which is entirely independent of any question which can be raised concerning their faculties. I mean the suffrage, both parliamentary and municipal. The right to share in the choice of those who are to exercise a public trust, is altogether a distinct thing from that of competing for the trust itself. If no one could vote for a member of parliament who was not fit to be a candidate, the government would be a narrow oligarchy indeed. To have a voice in choosing those by whom one is to be governed, is a means of self-protection due to every one, though he were to remain for ever excluded from the function of governing: and that women are considered fit to have such a choice, may be presumed from the fact, that the law already gives it to women in the most important of all cases to themselves: for the choice of the man who is to govern a woman to the end of life, is always supposed to be voluntarily made by herself. In the case of election to public trusts, it is the business of constitutional law to surround the right of suffrage with all needful securities and limitations; but whatever securities are sufficient in the case of the male sex, no others need be required in the case of women. Under whatever conditions, and within whatever limits, men are admitted to the suffrage, there is not a shadow of justification for not admitting women under the same. The majority of the women of any class are not likely to differ in political opinion from the majority of the men of the same class, unless the question be one in which the interests of women, as such, are in some way involved; and if they are so, women require the suffrage, as their guarantee of just and equal consideration. This ought to be obvious even to those who coincide in no other of the doctrines for which I contend. Even if every woman were a wife, and if every wife ought to be a slave, all the more would these slaves stand in need of legal protection: and we know what legal protection the slaves have, where the laws are made by their masters.

With regard to the fitness of women, not only to participate in elections, but themselves to hold offices or practise professions involving important public responsibilities; I have already observed that this consideration is not essential to the practical question in dispute: since any woman, who succeeds in an open profession, proves by that very fact that she is qualified for it. And in the case of public offices, if the political system of the country is such as to exclude unfit men, it will equally exclude unfit women: while if it is not, there is no additional evil in the fact that the unfit persons whom it admits may be either women or men. As long therefore as it is acknowledged that even a few women may be fit for these duties, the laws which shut the door on those exceptions cannot be justified by any opinion which can be held respecting the capacities of women in general. But, though this last consideration is not essential, it is far from being irrelevant. An unprejudiced view of it gives additional strength to the arguments against the disabilities of women, and reinforces them by high considerations of practical utility.

Let us at first make entire abstraction of all psychological considerations tending to show, that any of the mental differences supposed to exist between women and men are but the natural effect of the differences in their education and circumstances, and indicate no radical difference, far less radical inferiority, of nature. Let us consider women only as they already are, or as they are known to have been; and the capacities which they have already practically shown. What they have done, that at least, if nothing else, it is proved that they can do. When we consider how sedulously they are all trained away from, instead of being trained towards, any of the occupations or objects reserved for men, it is evident that I am taking a very humble ground for them, when I rest their case on what they have actually achieved. For, in this case, negative evidence is worth little, while any positive evidence is conclusive. It cannot be inferred to be impossible that a woman should be a Homer, or an Aristotle, or a Michael Angelo, or a Beethoven, because no woman has yet actually produced works comparable to theirs in any of those lines of excellence. This negative fact at most leaves the question uncertain, and open to psychological discussion. But it is quite certain that a woman can be a Queen Elizabeth, or a Deborah, or a Joan of Arc, since this is not inference, but fact. Now it is a curious consideration, that the only things which the existing law excludes women from doing, are the things which they have proved that they are able to do. There is no law to prevent a woman from having written all the plays of Shakespeare, or composed all the operas of Mozart. But Queen Elizabeth or Queen Victoria, had they not inherited the throne, could not have been intrusted with the smallest of the political duties, of which the former showed herself equal to the greatest.

If anything conclusive could be inferred from experience, without psychological analysis, it would be that the things which women are not allowed to do are the very ones for which they are peculiarly qualified; since their vocation for government has made its way, and become conspicuous, through the very few opportunities which have been given; while in the lines of distinction which apparently were freely open to them, they have by no means so eminently distinguished themselves. We know how small a number of reigning queens history presents, in comparison with that of kings. Of this smaller number a far larger proportion have shown talents for rule; though many of them have occupied the throne in different periods. It is remarkable, too, that they have, in a great number of instances, been distinguished by merits the most opposite to the imaginary and conventional character of women: they have been as much remarked for the firmness and vigour of their rule, as for its intelligence. When, to queens and empresses, we add regents, and viceroys of provinces, the list of women who have been eminent rulers of mankind swells to a great length.* This fact is so undeniable, that some one, long ago, tried to retort the argument, and turned the admitted truth into an additional insult, by saying that queens are better than kings, because under kings women govern, but under queens, men.

It may seem a waste of reasoning to argue against a bad joke; but such things do affect people's minds; and I have heard men quote this saying, with an air as if they thought that there was something in it. At any rate, it will serve as well as anything else for a starting point in discussion. I say, then, that it is not true that under kings, women govern. Such cases are entirely

---

* Especially is this true if we take into consideration Asia as well as Europe. If a Hindoo principality is strongly, vigilantly, and economically governed; if order is preserved without oppression; if cultivation is extending, and the people prosperous, in three cases out of four that principality is under a woman's rule. This fact, to me an entirely unexpected one, I have collected from a long official knowledge of Hindoo governments. There are many such instances: for though, by Hindoo institutions, a woman cannot reign, she is the legal regent of a kingdom during the minority of the heir; and minorities are frequent, the lives of the male rulers being so often prematurely terminated through the effect of inactivity and sensual excesses. When we consider that these princesses have never been seen in public, have never conversed with any man not of their own family except from behind a curtain, that they do not read, and if they did, there is no book in their languages which can give them the smallest instruction on political affairs; the example they afford of the natural capacity of women for government is very striking.

exceptional: and weak kings have quite as often governed ill through the influence of male favourites, as of female. When a king is governed by a woman merely through his amatory propensities, good government is not probable, though even then there are exceptions. But French history counts two kings who have voluntarily given the direction of affairs during many years, the one to his mother, the other to his sister: one of them, Charles VIII., was a mere boy, but in doing so he followed the intentions of his father Louis XI, the ablest monarch of his age. The other, Saint Louis, was the best, and one of the most vigorous rulers, since the time of Charlemagne. Both these princesses ruled in a manner hardly equalled by any prince among their contemporaries. The emperor Charles the Fifth, the most politic prince of his time, who had as great a number of able men in his service as a ruler ever had, and was one of the least likely of all sovereigns to sacrifice his interest to personal feelings, made two princesses of his family successively Governors of the Netherlands, and kept one or other of them in that post during his whole life, (they were afterwards succeeded by a third). Both ruled very successfully, and one of them, Margaret of Austria, was one of the ablest politicians of the age. So much for one side of the question. Now as to the other. When it is said that under queens men govern, is the same meaning to be understood as when kings are said to be governed by women? Is it meant that queens choose as their instruments of government, the associates of their personal pleasures? The case is rare even with those who are as unscrupulous on the latter point as Catherine II.: and it is not in these cases that the good government, alleged to arise from male influence, is to be found. If it be true, then, that the administration is in the hands of better men under a queen than under an average king, it must be that queens have a superior capacity for choosing them; and women must be better qualified than men both for the position of sovereign, and for that of chief minister; for the principal business of a prime minister is not to govern in person, but to find the fittest persons to conduct every department of public affairs. The more rapid insight into character, which is one of the admitted points of superiority in women over men, must certainly make them, with anything like parity of qualifications in other respects, more apt than men in that choice of instruments, which is nearly the most important business of every one who has to do with governing mankind. Even the unprincipled Catherine de' Medici could feel the value of a Chancellor de l'Hôpital. But it is also true that most great queens have been great by their own talents for government, and have been well served precisely for that reason. They retained the supreme direction of affairs in their own hands: and if they listened to good advisers, they gave by that fact the strongest proof that their judgment fitted them for dealing with the great questions of government.

Is it reasonable to think that those who are fit for the greater functions of politics, are incapable of qualifying themselves for the less? Is there any reason in the nature of things, that the wives and sisters of princes should, whenever called on, be found as competent as the princes themselves to *their* business, but that the wives and sisters of statesmen, and administrators, and directors of companies, and managers of public institutions, should be unable to do what is done by their brothers and husbands? The real reason is plain enough; it is that princesses, being more raised above the generality of men by their rank than placed below them by their sex, have never been taught that it was improper for them to concern themselves with politics; but have been allowed to feel the liberal interest natural to any cultivated human being, in the great transactions which took place around them, and in which they might be called on to take a part. The ladies of reigning families are the only women who are allowed the same range of interests and freedom of development as men; and it is precisely in their case that there is not found to be any inferiority. Exactly where and in proportion as women's capacities for government have been tried, in that proportion have they been found adequate.

This fact is in accordance with the best general conclusions which the world's imperfect experience seems as yet to suggest, concerning the peculiar tendencies and aptitudes characteristic of women, as women have hitherto been. I do not say, as they will continue to be; for, as I have already said more than once, I consider it presumption in any one to pretend to decide what women are or are not, can or cannot be, by natural constitution. They have always hitherto been kept, as far as regards spontaneous development, in so unnatural a state, that their nature cannot but have been greatly distorted and disguised; and no one can safely pronounce that if women's nature were left to choose its direction as freely as men's, and if no artificial bent were attempted to be given to it except that required by the conditions of human society, and given to both sexes alike, there would be any material difference, or perhaps any difference at all, in the character and capacities which would unfold themselves. I shall presently show, that even the least contestable of the differences which now exist, are such as may very well have been produced merely by circumstances, without any difference of natural capacity. But, looking at women as they are known in experience, it may be said of them, with more truth than belongs to most other generalizations on the subject, that the general bent of their talents is towards the practical. This statement is conformable to all the public history of women, in the present and the past. It is no less borne out by common and daily experience. Let us consider the special nature of the mental capacities most characteristic of a woman of talent. They are all of a kind which fits them for practice, and makes them tend towards it. What is meant by a woman's capacity of intuitive perception? It means, a rapid and correct insight into present fact. It has nothing to do with general principles. Nobody ever perceived a scientific law of nature by intuition, nor arrived at a general rule of duty or prudence by it. These are results of slow and careful collection and comparison of experience; and neither the men nor the women of intuition usually shine in this department, unless, indeed, the experience necessary is such as they can acquire by themselves. For what is called their intuitive sagacity makes them peculiarly apt in gathering such general truths as can be collected from their individual means of observation. When, consequently, they chance to be as well provided as men are with the results of other people's experience, by reading and education, (I use the word chance advisedly, for, in respect to the knowledge that tends to fit them for the greater concerns of life, the only educated women are the self-educated) they are better furnished than men in general with the essential requisites of skilful and successful practice. Men who have been much taught, are apt to be deficient in the sense of present fact; they do not see, in the facts which they are called upon to deal with, what is really there, but what they have been taught to expect. This is seldom the case with women of any ability. Their capacity of "intuition" preserves them from it. With equality of experience and of general faculties, a woman usually sees much more than a man of what is immediately before her. Now this sensibility to the present, is the main quality on which the capacity for practice, as distinguished from theory, depends. To discover general principles, belongs to the speculative faculty: to discern and discriminate the particular cases in which they are and are not applicable, constitutes practical talent: and for this, women as they now are have a peculiar aptitude. I admit that there can be no good practice without principles, and that the predominant place which quickness of observation holds among a woman's faculties, makes her particularly apt to build over-hasty generalizations upon her own observation; though at the same time no less ready in rectifying those generalizations, as her observation takes a wider range. But the corrective to this defect, is access to the experience of the human race; general knowledge—exactly the thing which education can best supply. A woman's mistakes are specifically those of a clever self-educated man, who often sees what men trained in routine do not see, but falls into errors for wanting of knowing things which have long been known. Of course he has acquired much of the pre-existing knowledge, or he could not have got on at all; but what he knows of it he has picked up in fragments and at random, as women do.

But this gravitation of women's minds to the present, to the real, to actual fact, while in its exclusiveness it is a source of errors, is also a most useful counteractive of the contrary error. The principal and most characteristic aberration of speculative minds as such, consists precisely in the deficiency of this lively perception and ever-present sense of objective fact. For want of this, they often not only overlook the contradiction which outward facts oppose to their theories, but lose sight of the legitimate purpose of speculation altogether, and let their speculative faculties go astray into regions not peopled with real beings, animate or inanimate, even idealized, but with personified shadows created by the illusions of metaphysics or by the mere entanglement of words, and think these shadows the proper objects of the highest, the most transcendant, philosophy. Hardly anything can be of greater value to a man of theory and speculation who employs himself not in collecting materials of knowledge by observation, but in working them up by processes of thought into comprehensive truths of science and laws of conduct, than to carry on his speculations in the companionship, and under the criticism, of a really superior woman. There is nothing comparable to it for keeping his thoughts within the limits of real things, and the actual facts of nature. A woman seldom runs wild after an abstraction. The habitual direction of her mind to dealing with things as individuals rather than in groups, and (what is closely connected with it) her more lively interest in the present feelings of persons, which makes her consider first of all, in anything which claims to be applied to practice, in what manner persons will be affected by it—these two things make her extremely unlikely to put faith in any speculation which loses sight of individuals, and deals with things as if they existed for the benefit of some imaginary entity, some mere creation of the mind, not resolvable into the feelings of living beings. Women's thoughts are thus as useful in giving reality to those of thinking men, as men's thoughts in giving width and largeness to those of women. In depth, as distinguished from breadth, I greatly doubt if even now, women, compared with men, are at any disadvantage.

If the existing mental characteristics of women are thus valuable even in aid of speculation, they are still more important, when speculation has done its work, for carrying out the results of speculation into practice. For the reasons already given, women are comparatively unlikely to fall into the common error of men, that of sticking to their rules in a case whose specialities either take it out of the class to which the rules are applicable, or require a special adaptation of them. Let us now consider another of the admitted superiorities of clever women, greater quickness of apprehension. Is not this preeminently a quality which fits a person for practice? In action, everything continually depends upon deciding promptly. In speculation, nothing does. A mere thinker can wait, can take time to consider, can collect additional evidence; he is not obliged to complete his philosophy at once, lest the opportunity should go by. The power of drawing the best conclusion possible from insufficient data is not indeed useless in philosophy; the construction of a provisional hypothesis consistent with all known facts is often the needful basis for further inquiry. But this faculty is rather serviceable in philosophy, than the main qualification for it: and, for the auxiliary as well as for the main operation, the philosopher can allow himself any time he pleases. He is in no need of the capacity of doing rapidly what he does; what he rather needs is patience, to work on slowly until imperfect lights have become perfect, and a conjecture has ripened into a theorem. For those, on the contrary, whose business is with the fugitive and perishable—with individual facts, not kinds of facts—rapidity of thought is a qualification next only in importance to the power of thought itself. He who has not his faculties under immediate command, in the contingencies of action, might as well not have them at all. He may be fit to criticize, but he is not fit to act. Now it is in this that women, and the men who are most like women, confessedly excel. The other sort of man, however pre-eminent may be his faculties, arrives slowly at complete command of them: rapidity of judgment and promptitude of judicious action, even in the things he knows best, are the gradual and late result of strenuous effort grown into habit.

It will be said, perhaps, that the greater nervous susceptibility of women is a disqualification for practice, in anything but domestic life, by rendering them mobile, changeable, too vehemently under the influence of the moment, incapable of dogged perseverance, unequal and uncertain in the power of using their faculties. I think that these phrases sum up the greater part of the objections commonly made to the fitness of women for the higher class of serious business. Much of all this is the mere overflow of nervous energy run to waste, and would cease when the energy was directed to a definite end. Much is also the result of conscious or unconscious cultivation; as we see by the almost total disappearance of "hysterics" and fainting fits, since they have gone out of fashion. Moreover, when people are brought up, like many women of the higher classes (though less so in our own country than in any other) a kind of hothouse plants, shielded from the wholesome vicissitudes of air and temperature, and untrained in any of the occupations and exercises which give stimulus and development to the circulatory and muscular system, while their nervous system, especially in its emotional department, is kept in unnaturally active play; it is no wonder if those of them who do not die of consumption, grow up with constitutions liable to derangement from slight causes, both internal and external, and without stamina to support any task, physical or mental, requiring continuity of effort. But women brought up to work for their livelihood show none of these morbid characteristics, unless indeed they are chained to an excess of sedentary work in confined and unhealthy rooms. Women who in their early years have shared in the healthful physical education and bodily freedom of their brothers, and who obtain a sufficiency of pure air and exercise in after-life, very rarely have any excessive susceptibility of nerves which can disqualify them for active pursuits. There is indeed a certain proportion of persons, in both sexes, in whom an unusual degree of nervous sensibility is constitutional, and of so marked a character as to be the feature of their organization which exercises the greatest influence over the whole character of the vital phenomena. This constitution, like other physical conformations, is hereditary, and is transmitted to sons as well as daughters; but it is possible, and probable, that the nervous temperament (as it is called) is inherited by a greater number of women than of men. We will assume this as a fact: and let me then ask, are men of nervous temperament found to be unfit for the duties and pursuits usually followed by men? If not, why should women of the same temperament be unfit for them? The peculiarities of the temperament are, no doubt, within certain limits, an obstacle to success in some employments, though an aid to it in others. But when the occupation is suitable to the temperament, and sometimes even when it is unsuitable, the most brilliant examples of success are continually given by the men of high nervous sensibility. They are distinguished in their practical manifestations chiefly by this, that being susceptible of a higher degree of excitement than those of another physical constitution, their powers when excited differ more than in the case of other people, from those shown in their ordinary state: they are raised, as it were, above themselves, and do things with ease which they are wholly incapable of at other times. But this lofty excitement is not, except in weak bodily constitutions, a mere flash, which passes away immediately, leaving no permanent traces, and incompatible with persistent and steady pursuit of an object. It is the character of the nervous temperament to be capable of *sustained* excitement, holding out through long continued efforts. It is what is meant by *spirit*. It is what makes the highbred racehorse run without slackening speed till he drops down dead. It is what has enabled so many delicate women to maintain the most sublime constancy not only at the stake, but through a long preliminary succession of mental and bodily tortures. It is evident that people of this temperament are particularly apt for what may be called the executive department of the leadership of mankind. They are the material of great orators, great preachers, impressive diffusers of moral influences. Their constitution might be deemed less favourable to the qualities required from a statesman in the cabinet, or from a judge. It would be so, if the consequence necessarily followed that because people are excitable they must always be in a state of excitement. But this is wholly a question of training. Strong feeling is the instrument and element of strong self-control: but it requires to be cultivated in that direction. When it is, it forms not the heroes of impulse only, but those also of self-conquest. History and experience prove that the most passionate characters are the most fanatically rigid in their feelings of duty, when their passion has been trained to act in that direction. The judge who gives a just decision in a case where his feelings are intensely interested on the other side, derives from that same strength of feeling the determined sense of the obligation of justice, which enables him to achieve this victory over himself. The capability of that lofty enthusiasm which takes the human being out of his every-day character, reacts upon the daily character itself. His aspirations and powers when he is in this exceptional state, become the type with which he compares, and by which he estimates, his sentiments and proceedings at other times: and his habitual purposes assume a character moulded by and assimilated to the moments of lofty excitement, although those, from the physical nature of a human being, can only be transient. Experience of races, as well as of individuals, does not show those of excitable temperament to be less fit, on the average, either for speculation or practice, than the more unexcitable. The French, and the Italians, are undoubtedly by nature more nervously excitable than the Teutonic races, and, compared at least with the English, they have a much greater habitual and daily emotional life: but have they been less great in science, in public business, in legal and judicial eminence, or in war? There is abundant evidence that the Greeks were of old, as their descendants and successors still are, one of the most excitable of the races of mankind. It is superfluous to ask, what among the achievements of men they did not excel in. The Romans, probably, as an equally southern people, had the same original temperament: but the stern character of their national discipline, like that of the Spartans, made them an example of the opposite type of national character; the greater strength of their natural feelings being chiefly apparent in the intensity which the same original temperament made it possible to give to the artificial. If these cases exemplify what a naturally excitable people may be made, the Irish Celts afford one of the aptest examples of what they are when left to themselves; (if those can be said to be left to themselves who have been for centuries under the indirect influence of bad government, and the direct training of a Catholic hierarchy and of a sincere belief in the Catholic religion). The Irish character must be considered, therefore, as an unfavourable case: yet, whenever the circumstances of the individual have been at all favourable, what people have shown greater capacity for the most varied and multifarious individual eminence? Like the French compared with the English, the Irish with the Swiss, the Greeks or Italians compared with the German races, so women compared with men may be found, on the average, to do the same things with some variety in the particular kind of excellence. But, that they would do them fully as well on the whole, if their education and cultivation were adapted to correcting instead of aggravating the infirmities incident to their temperament, I see not the smallest reason to doubt.

Supposing it, however, to be true that women's minds are by nature more mobile than those of men, less capable of persisting long in the same continuous effort, more fitted for dividing their faculties among many things than for travelling in any one path to the highest point which can be reached by it: this may be true of women as they now are (though not without great and numerous exceptions), and may account for their having remained behind the highest order of men in precisely the things in which this absorption of the whole mind in one set of ideas and occupations may seem to be most requisite. Still, this difference is one which can only affect the kind of excellence, not the excellence itself, or its practical worth: and it remains to be shown whether this exclusive working of a part of the mind, this absorption of the whole thinking faculty in a single subject, and concentration of it on a single work, is the normal and healthful condition of the human faculties, even for speculative uses. I believe that what is gained in special development by this concentration, is lost in the capacity of the mind for the other purposes of life; and even in abstract thought, it is my decided opinion that the mind does more by frequently returning to a difficult problem, than by sticking to it without interruption. For the purposes, at all events, of practice, from its highest to its humblest departments, the capacity of passing promptly from one subject of consideration to another, without letting the active spring of the intellect run down between the two, is a power far more valuable; and this power women pre-eminently possess, by virtue of the very mobility of which they are accused. They perhaps have it from nature, but they certainly have it by training and education; for nearly the whole of the occupations of women consist in the management of small but multitudinous details, on each of which the mind cannot dwell even for a minute, but must pass on to other things, and if anything requires longer thought, must steal time at odd moments for thinking of it. The capacity indeed which women

show for doing their thinking in circumstances and at times which almost any man would make an excuse to himself for not attempting it, has often been noticed: and a woman's mind, though it may be occupied only with small things, can hardly ever permit itself to be vacant, as a man's so often is when not engaged in what he chooses to consider the business of his life. The business of a woman's ordinary life is things in general, and can as little cease to go on as the world to go round.

But (it is said) there is anatomical evidence of the superior mental capacity of men compared with women: they have a larger brain. I reply, that in the first place the fact itself is doubtful. It is by no means established that the brain of a woman is smaller than that of a man. If it is inferred merely because a woman's bodily frame generally is of less dimensions than a man's, this criterion would lead to strange consequences. A tall and large-boned man must on this showing be wonderfully superior in intelligence to a small man, and an elephant or a whale must prodigiously excel mankind. The size of the brain in human beings, anatomists say, varies much less than the size of the body, or even of the head, and the one cannot be at all inferred from the other. It is certain that some women have as large a brain as any man. It is within my knowledge that a man who had weighed many human brains, said that the heaviest he knew of, heavier even than Cuvier's (the heaviest previously recorded,) was that of a woman. Next, I must observe that the precise relation which exists between the brain and the intellectual powers is not yet well understood, but is a subject of great dispute. That there is a very close relation we cannot doubt. The brain is certainly the material organ of thought and feeling: and (making abstraction of the great unsettled controversy respecting the appropriation of different parts of the brain to different mental faculties) I admit that it would be an anomaly, and an exception to all we know of the general laws of life and organization, if the size of the organ were wholly indifferent to the function; if no accession of power were derived from the greater magnitude of the instrument. But the exception and the anomaly would be fully as great if the organ exercised influence by its magnitude *only*. In all the more delicate operations of nature—of which those of the animated creation are the most delicate, and those of the nervous system by far the most delicate of these— differences in the effect depend as much on differences of quality in the physical agents, as on their quantity: and if the quality of an instrument is to be tested by the nicety and delicacy of the work it can do, the indications point to a greater average fineness of quality in the brain and nervous system of women than of men. Dismissing abstract difference of quality, a thing difficult to verify, the efficiency of an organ is known to depend not solely on its size but on its activity: and of this we have an approximate measure in the energy with which the blood circulates through it, both the stimulus and the reparative force being mainly dependent on the circulation. It would not be surprising—it is indeed an hypothesis which accords well with the differences actually observed between the mental operations of the two sexes—if men on the average should have the advantage in the size of the brain, and women in activity of cerebral circulation. The results which conjecture, founded on analogy, would lead us to expect from this difference of organization, would correspond to some of those which we most commonly see. In the first place, the mental operations of men might be expected to be slower. They would neither be so prompt as women in thinking, nor so quick to feel. Large bodies take more time to get into full action. On the other hand, when once got thoroughly into play, men's brain would bear more work. It would be more persistent in the line first taken; it would have more difficulty in changing from one mode of action to another, but, in the one thing it was doing, it could go on longer without loss of power or sense of fatigue. And do we not find that the things in which men most excel women are those which require most plodding and long hammering at a single thought, while women do best what must be done rapidly? A woman's brain is sooner fatigued, sooner exhausted; but given the degree of exhaustion, we should expect to find that it would recover itself sooner. I repeat that this speculation is entirely hypothetical; it pretends to no more than to suggest a line of enquiry. I have before repudiated the notion of its being yet certainly known that there is any natural dif-

ference at all in the average strength or direction of the mental capacities of the two sexes, much less what that difference is. Nor is it possible that this should be known, so long as the psychological laws of the formation of character have been so little studied, even in a general way, and in the particular case never scientifically applied at all; so long as the most obvious external causes of difference of character are habitually disregarded—left unnoticed by the observer, and looked down upon with a kind of supercilious contempt by the prevalent schools both of natural history and of mental philosophy: who, whether they look for the source of what mainly distinguishes human beings from one another, in the world of matter or in that of spirit, agree in running down those who prefer to explain these differences by the different relations of human beings to society and life.

To so ridiculous an extent are the notions formed of the nature of women, mere empirical generalizations, framed, without philosophy or analysis, upon the first instances which present themselves, that the popular idea of it is different in different countries, according as the opinions and social circumstances of the country have given to the women living in it any speciality of development or non-development. An Oriental thinks that women are by nature peculiarly voluptuous; see the violent abuse of them on this ground in Hindoo writings. An Englishman usually thinks that they are by nature cold. The sayings about women's fickleness are mostly of French origin; from the famous distich of Francis the First, upward and downward. In England it is a common remark, how much more constant women are than men. Inconstancy has been longer reckoned discreditable to a woman, in England than in France; and Englishwomen are besides, in their inmost nature, much more subdued to opinion. It may be remarked by the way, that Englishmen are in peculiarly unfavourable circumstances for attempting to judge what is or is not natural, not merely to women, but to men, or to human beings altogether, at least if they have only English experience to go upon: because there is no place where human nature shows so little of its original lineaments. Both in a good and a bad sense, the English are farther from a state of nature than any other modern people. They are, more than any other people, a product of civilization and discipline. England is the country in which social discipline has most succeeded, not so much in conquering, as in suppressing, whatever is liable to conflict with it. The English, more than any other people, not only act but feel according to rule. In other countries, the taught opinion, or the requirement of society, may be the stronger power, but the promptings of the individual nature are always visible under it, and often resisting it: rule may be stronger than nature, but nature is still there. In England, rule has to a great degree substituted itself for nature. The greater part of life is carried on, not by following inclination under the control of rule, but by having no inclination but that of following a rule. Now this has its good side doubtless, though it has also a wretchedly bad one; but it must render an Englishman peculiarly ill-qualified to pass a judgment on the original tendencies of human nature from his own experience. The errors to which observers elsewhere are liable on the subject, are of a different character. An Englishman is ignorant respecting human nature, a Frenchman is prejudiced. An Englishman's errors are negative, a Frenchman's positive. An Englishman fancies that things do not exist, because he never sees them; a Frenchman thinks they must always and necessarily exist, because he does see them. An Englishman does not know nature, because he has had no opportunity of observing it; a Frenchman generally knows a great deal of it, but often mistakes it, because he has only seen it sophisticated and distorted. For the artificial state superinduced by society disguises the natural tendencies of the thing which is the subject of observation, in two different ways: by extinguishing the nature, or by transforming it. In the one case there is but a starved residuum of nature remaining to be studied; in the other case there is much, but it may have expanded in any direction rather than that in which it would spontaneously grow.

I have said that it cannot now be known how much of the existing mental differences between men and women is natural, and how much artificial; whether there are any natural differences at all; or, supposing all artificial causes of difference to be withdrawn, what natural character would be revealed. I am not about

to attempt what I have pronounced impossible: but doubt does not forbid conjecture, and where certainty is unattainable, there may yet be the means of arriving at some degree of probability. The first point, the origin of the differences actually observed, is the one most accessible to speculation; and I shall attempt to approach it, by the only path by which it can be reached; by tracing the mental consequences of external influences. We cannot isolate a human being from the circumstances of his condition, so as to ascertain experimentally what he would have been by nature; but we can consider what he is, and what his circumstances have been, and whether the one would have been capable of producing the other.

Let us take, then, the only marked case which observation affords, of apparent inferiority of women to men, if we except the merely physical one of bodily strength. No production in philosophy, science, or art, entitled to the first rank, has been the work of a woman. Is there any mode of accounting for this, without supposing that women are naturally incapable of producing them?

In the first place, we may fairly question whether experience has afforded sufficient grounds for an induction. It is scarcely three generations since women, saving very rare exceptions, have begun to try their capacity in philosophy, science, or art. It is only in the present generation that their attempts have been at all numerous; and they are even now extremely few, everywhere but in England and France. It is a relevant question, whether a mind possessing the requisites of first-rate eminence in speculation or creative art could have been expected, on the mere calculation of chances, to turn up during that lapse of time, among the women whose tastes and personal position admitted of their devoting themselves to these pursuits. In all things which there has yet been time for—in all but the very highest grades in the scale of excellence, especially in the department in which they have been longest engaged, literature (both prose and poetry)— women have done quite as much, have obtained fully as high prizes and as many of them, as could be expected from the length of time and the number of competitors. If we go back to the earlier period when very few women made the attempt, yet some of those few made it with distinguished success. The Greeks always accounted Sappho among their great poets; and we may well suppose that Myrtis, said to have been the teacher of Pindar, and Corinna, who five times bore away from him the prize of poetry, must at least have had sufficient merit to admit of being compared with that great name. Aspasia did not leave any philosophical writings; but it is an admitted fact that Socrates resorted to her for instruction, and avowed himself to have obtained it.

If we consider the works of women in modern times, and contrast them with those of men, either in the literary or the artistic department, such inferiority as may be observed resolves itself essentially into one thing: but that is a most material one; deficiency of originality. Not total deficiency; for every production of mind which is of any substantive value, has an originality of its own — is a conception of the mind itself, not a copy of something else. Thoughts original, in the sense of being unborrowed — of being derived from the thinker's own observations or intellectual processes — are abundant in the writings of women. But they have not yet produced any of those great and luminous new ideas which form an era in thought, nor those fundamentally new conceptions in art, which open a vista of possible effects not before thought of, and found a new school. Their compositions are mostly grounded on the existing fund of thought, and their creations do not deviate widely from existing types. This is the sort of inferiority which their works manifest: for in point of execution, in the detailed application of thought, and the perfection of style, there is no inferiority. Our best novelists in point of composition, and of the management of denial, have mostly been women; and there is not in all modern literature a more eloquent vehicle of thought than the style of Madame de Stael, nor, as a specimen of purely artistic excellence, anything superior to the prose of Madame Sand, whose style acts upon the nervous system like a symphony of Haydn or Mozart. High originality of conception is, as I have said, what is chiefly wanting. And now to examine if there is any manner in which this deficiency can be accounted for.

Let us remember, then, so far as regards mere thought, that during all that period in the world's existence, and in the progress of cultivation, in which great and fruitful new truths could be arrived at by mere force of genius, with little previous study and accumulation of knowledge — during all that time women did not concern themselves with speculation at all. From the days of Hypatia to those of the Reformation, the illustrious Heloisa is almost the only woman to whom any such achievement might have been possible; and we know not how great a capacity of speculation in her may have been lost to mankind by the misfortunes of her life. Never since any considerable number of women have began to cultivate serious thought, has originality been possible on easy terms. Nearly all the thoughts which can be reached by mere strength of original faculties, have long since been arrived at; and originality, in any high sense of the word, is now scarcely ever attained but by minds which have undergone elaborate discipline, and are deeply versed in the results of previous thinking. It is Mr. Maurice, I think, who has remarked on the present age, that its most original thinkers are those who have known most thoroughly what had been thought by their predecessors: and this will always henceforth be the case. Every fresh stone in the edifice has now to be placed on the top of so many others, that a long process of climbing, and of carrying up materials, has to be gone through by whoever aspires to take a share in the present stage of the work. How many women are there who have gone through any such process? Mrs. Somerville, alone perhaps of women, knows as much of mathematics as is now needful for making any considerable mathematical discovery: is it any proof of inferiority in women, that she has not happened to be one of the two or three persons who in her lifetime have associated their names with some striking advancement of the science? Two women, since political economy has been made a science, have known enough of it to write usefully on the subject: of how many of the innumerable men who have written on it during the same time, is it possible with truth to say more? If no woman has hitherto been a great historian, what woman has had the necessary erudition? If no woman is a great philologist, what woman has studied Sanscrit and Slavonic, the Gothic of Ulphila and the Persic of the Zendavesta? Even in practical matters we all know what is the value of the originality of untaught geniuses. It means, inventing over again in its rudimentary form something already invented and improved upon by many successive inventors. When women have had the preparation which all men now require to be eminently original, it will be time enough to begin judging by experience of their capacity for originality.

It no doubt often happens that a person, who has not widely and accurately studied the thoughts of others on a subject, has by natural sagacity a happy intuition, which he can suggest, but cannot prove, which yet when matured may be an important addition to knowledge: but even then, no justice can be done to it until some other person, who does possess the previous acquirements, takes it in hand, tests it, gives it a scientific or practical form, and fits it into its place among the existing truths of philosophy or science. Is it supposed that such felicitous thoughts do not occur to women? They occur by hundreds to every woman of intellect. But they are mostly lost, for want of a husband or friend who has the other knowledge which can enable him to estimate them properly and bring them before the world: and even when they are brought before it, they generally appear as his ideas, not their real author's. Who can tell how many of the most original thoughts put forth by male writers, belong to a woman by suggestion, to themselves only by verifying and working out? If I may judge by my own case, a very large proportion indeed.

If we turn from pure speculation to literature in the narrow sense of the term, and the fine arts, there is a very obvious reason why women's literature is, in its general conception and in its main features, an imitation of men's. Why is the Roman literature, as critics proclaim to satiety, not original, but an imitation of the Greek? Simply because the Greeks came first. If women lived in a different country from men, and had never read any of their writings, they would have had a literature of their own. As it is, they have not created one, because they found a highly advanced literature already created. If there had been no suspension of the knowledge of antiquity, or if the Renaissance had occurred before the Gothic cathedrals were built, they never would have been built. We see that, in France and Italy, imitation of the ancient literature stopped the original development even after it had commenced. All women who write are pupils of the great male writers. A painter's early pictures, even if he be a Raffaelle, are undistinguishable in style from those of his master. Even a Mozart does not display his powerful originality in his earliest pieces. What years are to a gifted individual, generations are to a mass. If women's literature is destined to have a different collective character from that of men, depending on any difference of natural tendencies, much longer time is necessary than has yet elapsed, before it can emancipate itself from the influence of accepted models, and guide itself by its own impulses. But if, as I believe, there will not prove to be any natural tendencies common to women, and distinguishing their genius from that of men, yet every individual writer among them has her individual tendencies, which at present are still subdued by the influence of precedent and example: and it will require generations more, before their individuality is sufficiently developed to make head against that influence.

It is in the fine arts, properly so called, that the *prima facie* evidence of inferior original powers in women at first sight appears the strongest: since opinion (it may be said) does not exclude them from these, but rather encourages them, and their education, instead of passing over this department, is in the affluent classes mainly composed of it. Yet in this line of exertion they have fallen still more short than in many others, of the highest eminence attained by men. This shortcoming, however, needs no other explanation than the familiar fact, more universally true in the fine arts than in anything else; the vast superiority of professional persons over amateurs. Women in the educated classes are almost universally taught more or less of some branch or other of the fine arts, but not that they may gain their living or their social consequence by it. Women artists are all amateurs. The exceptions are only of the kind which confirm the general truth. Women are taught music, but not for the purpose of composing, only of executing it: and accordingly it is only as composers, that men, in music, are superior to women. The only one of the fine arts which women do follow, to any extent, as a profession, and an occupation for life, is the histrionic; and in that they are confessedly equal, if not superior, to men. To make the comparison fair, it should be made between the productions of women in any branch of art, and those of men not following it as a profession. In musical composition, for example, women surely have produced fully as good things as have ever been produced by male amateurs. There are now a few women, a very few, who practise painting as a profession, and these are already beginning to show quite as much talent as could be expected. Even male painters (*pace* Mr. Ruskin) have not made any very remarkable figure these last centuries, and it will be long before they do so. The reason why the old painters were so greatly superior to the modern, is that a greatly superior class of men applied themselves to the art. In the fourteenth and fifteenth centuries the Italian painters were the most accomplished men of their age. The greatest of them were men of encyclopædical acquirements and powers, like the great men of Greece. But in their times fine art was, to men's feelings and conceptions, among the grandest things in which a human being could excel; and by it men were made, what only political or military distinction now makes them, the companions of sovereigns, and the equals of the highest nobility. In the present age, men of anything like similar calibre find something more important to do, for their own fame and the uses of the modern world, than painting: and it is only now and then that a Reynolds or a Turner (of whose relative rank among eminent men I do not pretend to an opinion) applies himself to that art. Music belongs to a different order of things; it does not require the same general powers of mind, but seems more dependant on a natural gift: and it may be thought surprising that no one of the great musical composers has been a woman. But even this natural gift, to be made available for great creations, requires study, and professional devotion to the pursuit. The only countries which have produced first-rate composers, even of the male sex, are Germany and Italy—countries in which, both in point of special and of general cultivation, women have remained far behind France and England, being generally (it may be said without exaggeration) very little educated, and having scarcely cultivated at all any of the higher faculties of mind. And in those countries the men who are acquainted with the principles of musical composition must be counted by hundreds, or more probably by thousands, the women barely by scores: so that here again, on the doctrine of averages, we cannot reasonably expect to see more than one eminent woman to fifty eminent men; and the last three centuries have not produced fifty eminent male composers either in Germany or in Italy.

There are other reasons, besides those which we have now given, that help to explain why women remain behind men, even in the pursuits which are open to both. For one thing, very few women have time for them. This may seem a paradox; it is an undoubted social fact. The time and thoughts of every woman have to satisfy great previous demands on them for things practical. There is, first, the superintendence of the family and the domestic expenditure, which occupies at least one woman in every family, generally the one of mature years and acquired experience; unless the family is so rich as to admit of delegating that task to hired agency, and submitting to all the waste and malversation inseparable from that mode of conducting it. The superintendence of a household, even when not in other respects laborious, is extremely onerous to the thoughts; it requires incessant vigilance, an eye which no detail escapes, and presents questions for consideration and solution, foreseen and unforeseen, at every hour of the day, from which the person responsible for them can hardly ever shake herself free. If a woman is of a rank and circumstances which relieve her in a measure from these cares, she has still devolving on her the management for the whole family of its intercourse with others—of what is called society, and the less the call made on her by the former duty, the greater is always the development of the latter: the dinner parties, concerts, evening parties, morning visits, letter writing, and all that goes with them. All this is over and above the engrossing duty which society imposes exclusively on women, of making themselves charming. A clever woman of the higher ranks finds nearly a sufficient employment of her talents in cultivating the graces of manner and the arts of conversation. To look only at the outward side of the subject: the great and continual exercise of thought which all women who attach any value to dressing well (I do not mean expensively, but with taste, and perception of natural and of artificial *convenance*) must bestow upon their own dress, perhaps also upon that of their daughters, would alone go a great way towards achieving respectable results in art, or science, or literature, and does actually exhaust much of the time and mental power they might have to spare for either.* If it were possible that all this number of little practical interests (which are made great to them) should leave them either much leisure, or much energy and freedom of mind, to be devoted to art or speculation, they must have a much greater original supply of active faculty than the vast majority of men. But this is not all. Independently of the regular offices of life which devolve upon a woman, she is expected to have her time and faculties always at the disposal of everybody. If a man has not a profession to exempt him from such demands, still, if he has a pursuit, he offends nobody by devoting his time to it; occupation is received as a valid excuse for his not answering to every casual demand which may be made on him. Are a woman's occupations, especially her chosen and voluntary ones, ever regarded as excusing her from any of what are termed the calls of society? Scarcely are her most necessary and recognised duties allowed as an exemption. It requires an illness in the family, or something else out of the common way, to entitle her to give her own business the precedence over other people's amusement. She must always be at the beck and call of somebody, generally of everybody.

* "It appears to be the same right turn of mind which enables a man to acquire the *truth*, or the just idea of what is right, in the ornaments, as in the more stable principles of art. It has still the same centre of perfection, though it is the centre of a smaller circle.—To illustrate this by the fashion of dress, in which there is allowed to be a good or bad taste. The component parts of dress are continually changing from great to little, from short to long; but the general form still remains: it is still the same general dress which is comparatively fixed, though on a very slender foundation; but it is on this which fashion must rest. He who invents with the most success, or dresses in the best taste, would probably, from the same sagacity employed to greater purposes, have discovered equal skill, or have formed the same correct taste, in the highest labours of art."—*Sir Joshua Reynolds' Discourses*, Disc. vii.

If she has a study or a pursuit, she must snatch any short interval which accidentally occurs to be employed in it. A celebrated woman, in a work which I hope will some day be published, remarks truly that everything a woman does is done at odd times. Is it wonderful, then, if she does not attain the highest eminence in things which require consecutive attention, and the concentration on them of the chief interest of life? Such is philosophy, and such, above all, is art, in which, besides the devotion of the thoughts and feelings, the hand also must be kept in constant exercise to attain high skill.

There is another consideration to be added to all these. In the various arts and intellectual occupations, there is a degree of proficiency sufficient for living by it, and there is a higher degree on which depend the great productions which immortalize a name. To the attainment of the former, there are adequate motives in the case of all who follow the pursuit professionally: the other is hardly ever attained where there is not, or where there has not been at some period of life, an ardent desire of celebrity. Nothing less is commonly a sufficient stimulus to undergo the long and patient drudgery, which, in the case even of the greatest natural gifts, is absolutely required for great eminence in pursuits in which we already possess so many splendid memorials of the highest genius. Now, whether the cause be natural or artificial, women seldom have this eagerness for fame. Their ambition is generally confined within narrower bounds. The influence they seek is over those who immediately surround them. Their desire is to be liked, loved, or admired, by those whom they see with their eyes: and the proficiency in knowledge, arts, and accomplishments, which is sufficient for that, almost always contents them. This is a trait of character which cannot be left out of the account in judging of women as they are. I do not at all believe that it is inherent in women. It is only the natural result of their circumstances. The love of fame in men is encouraged by education and opinion: to "scorn delights and live laborious days" for its sake, is accounted the part of "noble minds," even if spoken of as their "last infirmity," and is stimulated by the access which fame gives to all objects of ambition, including even the favour of women; while to women themselves all these objects are closed, and the desire of fame itself considered daring and unfeminine. Besides, how could it be that a woman's interests should not be all concentrated upon the impressions made on those who come into her daily life, when society has ordained that all her duties should be to them, and has contrived that all her comforts should depend on them? The natural desire of consideration from our fellow creatures is as strong in a woman as in a man; but society has so ordered things that public consideration is, in all ordinary cases, only attainable by her through the consideration of her husband or of her male relations, while her private consideration is forfeited by making herself individually prominent, or appearing in any other character than that of an appendage to men. Whoever is in the least capable of estimating the influence on the mind of the entire domestic and social position and the whole habit of a life, must easily recognise in that influence a complete explanation of nearly all the apparent differences between women and men, including the whole of those which imply any inferiority.

As for moral differences, considered as distinguished from intellectual, the distinction commonly drawn is to the advantage of women. They are declared to be better than men; an empty compliment, which must provoke a bitter smile from every woman of spirit, since there is no other situation in life in which it is the established order, and considered quite natural and suitable, that the better should obey the worse. If this piece of idle talk is good for anything, it is only as an admission by men, of the corrupting influence of power; for that is certainly the only truth which the fact, if it be a fact, either proves or illustrates. And it *is* true that servitude, except when it actually brutalizes, though corrupting to both, is less so to the slaves than to the slave-masters. It is wholesomer for the moral nature to be restrained, even by arbitrary power, than to be allowed to exercise arbitrary power without restraint. Women, it is said, seldomer fall under the penal law—contribute a much smaller number of offenders to the criminal calendar, than men. I doubt not that the same thing may be said, with the same truth, of negro slaves. Those who are under the control of others cannot often commit crimes, unless at the command and for the purposes of their masters. I do not know a more signal instance of the blindness with which the world, including the herd of studious men, ignore and pass over all the influences of social circumstances, than their silly depreciation of the intellectual, and silly panegyrics on the moral, nature of women.

The complimentary dictum about women's superior moral goodness may be allowed to pair off with the disparaging one respecting their greater liability to moral bias. Women, we are told, are not capable of resisting their personal partialities: their judgment in grave affairs is warped by their sympathies and antipathies. Assuming it to be so, it is still to be proved that women are oftener misled by their personal feelings than men by their personal interests. The chief difference would seem in that case to be, that men are led from the course of duty and the public interest by their regard for themselves, women (not being allowed to have private interests of their own) by their regard for somebody else. It is also to be considered, that all the education which women receive from society inculcates on them the feeling that the individuals connected with them are the only ones to whom they owe any duty—the only ones whose interest they are called upon to care for; while, as far as education is concerned, they are left strangers even to the elementary ideas which are presupposed in any intelligent regard for larger interests or higher moral objects. The complaint against them resolves itself merely into this, that they fulfil only too faithfully the sole duty which they are taught, and almost the only one which they are permitted to practise.

The concessions of the privileged to the unprivileged are so seldom brought about by any better motive than the power of the unprivileged to extort them, that any arguments against the prerogative of sex are likely to be little attended to by the generality, as long as they are able to say to themselves that women do not complain of it. That fact certainly enables men to retain the unjust privilege some time longer; but does not render it less unjust. Exactly the same thing may be said of the women in the harem of an Oriental: they do not complain of not being allowed the freedom of European women. They think our women insufferably bold and unfeminine. How rarely it is that even men complain of the general order of society; and how much rarer still would such complaint be, if they did not know of any different order existing anywhere else. Women do not complain of the general lot of women; or rather they do, for plaintive elegies on it are very common in the writings of women, and were still more so as long as the lamentations could not be suspected of having any practical object. Their complaints are like the complaints which men make of the general unsatisfactoriness of human life; they are not meant to imply blame, or to plead for any change. But though women do not complain of the power of husbands, each complains of her own husband, or of the husbands of her friends. It is the same in all other cases of servitude, at least in the commencement of the emancipatory movement. The serfs did not at first complain of the power of their lords, but only of their tyranny. The Commons began by claiming a few municipal privileges; they next asked an exemption for themselves from being taxed without their own consent; but they would at that time have thought it a great presumption to claim any share in the king's sovereign authority. The case of women is now the only case in which to rebel against established rules is still looked upon with the same eyes as was formerly a subject's claim to the right of rebelling against his king. A woman who joins in any movement which her husband disapproves, makes herself a martyr, without even being able to be an apostle, for the husband can legally put a stop to her apostleship. Women cannot be expected to devote themselves to the emancipation of women, until men in considerable number are prepared to join with them in the undertaking.

CHAPTER IV

There remains a question, not of less importance than those already discussed, and which will be asked the most importunately by those opponents whose conviction is somewhat shaken on the main point. What good are we to expect from the changes proposed in our customs and institutions? Would mankind be at all better off if women were free? If not, why disturb their minds, and attempt to make a social revolution in the name of an abstract right?

It is hardly to be expected that this question will be asked in respect to the change proposed in the condition of women in marriage. The sufferings, immoralities, evils of all sorts, produced in innumerable cases by the subjection of individual women to individual men, are far too terrible to be overlooked. Unthinking or uncandid persons, counting those cases alone which are extreme, or which attain publicity, may say that the evils are exceptional; but no one can be blind to their existence, nor, in many cases, to their intensity. And it is perfectly obvious that the abuse of the power cannot be very much checked while the power remains. It is a power given, or offered, not to good men, or to decently respectable men, but to all men; the most brutal, and the most criminal. There is no check but that of opinion, and such men are in general within the reach of no opinion but that of men like themselves. If such men did not brutally tyrannize over the one human being whom the law compels to bear everything from them, society must already have reached a paradisiacal state. There could be no need any longer of laws to curb men's vicious propensities. Astræ must not only have returned to earth, but the heart of the worst man must have become her temple. The law of servitude in marriage is a monstrous contradiction to all the principles of the modern world, and to all the experience through which those principles have been slowly and painfully worked out. It is the sole case, now that negro slavery has been abolished, in which a human being in the plenitude of every faculty is delivered up to the tender mercies of another human being, in the hope forsooth that this other will use the power solely for the good of the person subjected to it. Marriage is the only actual bondage known to our law. There remain no legal slaves, except the mistress of every house.

It is not, therefore, on this part of the subject, that the question is likely to be asked, *Cui bono?* We may be told that the evil would outweigh the good, but the reality of the good admits of no dispute. In regard, however, to the larger question, the removal of women's disabilities—their recognition as the equals of men in all that belongs to citizenship—the opening to them of all honourable employments, and of the training and education which qualifies for those employments —there are many persons for whom it is not enough that the inequality has no just or legitimate defence; they require to be told what express advantage would be obtained by abolishing it.

To which let me first answer, the advantage of having the most universal and pervading of all human relations regulated by justice instead of injustice. The vast amount of this gain to human nature, it is hardly possible, by any explanation or illustration, to place in a stronger light than it is placed by the bare statement, to any one who attaches a moral meaning to words. All the selfish propensities, the self-worship, the unjust self-preference, which exist among mankind, have their source and root in, and derive their principal nourishment from, the present constitution of the relation between men and women. Think what it is to a boy, to grow up to manhood in the belief that without any merit or any exertion of his own, though he may be the most frivolous and empty or the most ignorant and stolid of mankind, by the mere fact of being born a male he is by right the superior of all and every one of an entire half of the human race: including probably some whose real superiority to himself he has daily or hourly occasion to feel; but even if in his whole conduct he habitually follows a woman's guidance, still, if he is a fool, he thinks that of course she is not, and cannot be, equal in ability and judgment to himself; and if he is not a fool, he does worse—he sees that she is superior to him, and believes that, notwithstanding her superiority, he is entitled to command and she is bound to obey. What must be the effect on his character, of this lesson? And men of the cultivated classes are often not aware how deeply it sinks into the immense majority of male minds. For, among right-feeling and well-bred people, the inequality is kept as much as possible out of sight; above all, out of sight of the children. As much obedience is required from boys to their mother as to their father: they are not permitted to domineer over their sisters, nor are they accustomed to see these postponed to them, but the contrary; the compensations of the chivalrous feeling being made prominent, while the servitude which requires them is kept in the background. Well brought-

up youths in the higher classes thus often escape the bad influences of the situation in their early years, and only experience them when, arrived at manhood, they fall under the dominion of facts as they really exist. Such people are little aware, when a boy is differently brought up, how early the notion of his inherent superiority to a girl arises in his mind; how it grows with his growth and strengthens with his strength: how it is inoculated by one schoolboy upon another; how early the youth thinks himself superior to his mother, owing her perhaps forbearance, but no real respect; and how sublime and sultan-like a sense of superiority he feels, above all, over the woman whom he honours by admitting her to a partnership of his life. Is it imagined that all this does not pervert the whole manner of existence of the man, both as an individual and as a social being? It is an exact parallel to the feeling of a hereditary king that he is excellent above others by being born a king, or a noble by being born a noble. The relation between husband and wife is very like that between lord and vassal, except that the wife is held to more unlimited obedience than the vassal was. However the vassal's character may have been affected, for better and for worse, by his subordination, who can help seeing that the lord's was affected greatly for the worse? whether he was led to believe that his vassals were really superior to himself, or to feel that he was placed in command over people as good as himself, for no merits or labours of his own, but merely for having, as Figaro says, taken the trouble to be born. The self-worship of the monarch, or of the feudal superior, is matched by the self-worship of the male. Human beings do not grow up from childhood in the possession of unearned distinctions, without pluming themselves upon them. Those whom privileges not acquired by their merit, and which they feel to be disproportioned to it, inspire with additional humility, are always the few, and the best few. The rest are only inspired with pride, and the worst sort of pride, that which values itself upon accidental advantages, not of its own achieving. Above all, when the feeling of being raised above the whole of the other sex is combined with personal authority over one individual among them; the situation, if a school of conscientious and affectionate forbearance to those whose strongest points of character are conscience and affection, is to men of another quality a regularly constituted Academy or Gymnasium for training them in arrogance and overbearingness; which vices, if curbed by the certainty of resistance in their intercourse with other men, their equals, break out towards all who are in a position to be obliged to tolerate them, and often revenge themselves upon the unfortunate wife for the involuntary restraint which they are obliged to submit to elsewhere.

The example afforded, and the education given to the sentiments, by laying the foundation of domestic existence upon a relation contradictory to the first principles of social justice, must, from the very nature of man, have a perverting influence of such magnitude, that it is hardly possible with our present experience to raise our imaginations to the conception of so great a change for the better as would be made by its removal. All that education and civilization are doing to efface the influences on character of the law of force, and replace them by those of justice, remains merely on the surface, as long as the citadel of the enemy is not attacked. The principle of the modern movement in morals and politics, is that conduct, and conduct alone, entitles to respect: that not what men are, but what they do, constitutes their claim to deference; that, above all, merit, and not birth, is the only rightful claim to power and authority. If no authority, not in its nature temporary, were allowed to one human being over another, society would not be employed in building up propensities with one hand which it has to curb with the other. The child would really, for the first time in man's existence on earth, be trained in the way he should go, and when he was old there would be a chance that he would not depart from it. But so long as the right of the strong to power over the weak rules in the very heart of society, the attempt to make the equal right of the weak the principle of its outward actions will always be an uphill struggle; for the law of justice, which is also that of Christianity, will never get possession of men's inmost sentiments; they will be working against it, even when bending to it.

The second benefit to be expected from giving to women the free use of their faculties, by leaving them the free choice of their employments, and opening to them the same field of occupation and the same prizes and encouragements as to other human beings, would be that of doubling the mass of mental faculties available for the higher service of humanity. Where there is now one person qualified to benefit mankind and promote the general improvement, as a public teacher, or an administrator of some branch of public or social affairs, there would then be a chance of two. Mental superiority of any kind is at present everywhere so much below the demand; there is such a deficiency of persons competent to do excellently anything which it requires any considerable amount of ability to do; that the loss to the world, by refusing to make use of one-half of the whole quantity of talent it possesses, is extremely serious. It is true that this amount of mental power is not totally lost. Much of it is employed, and would in any case be employed, in domestic management, and in the few other occupations open to women; and from the remainder indirect benefit is in many individual cases obtained, through the personal influence of individual women over individual men. But these benefits are partial; their range is extremely circumscribed; and if they must be admitted, on the one hand, as a deduction from the amount of fresh social power that would be acquired by giving freedom to one-half of the whole sum of human intellect, there must be added, on the other, the benefit of the stimulus that would be given to the intellect of men by the competition; or (to use a more true expression) by the necessity that would be imposed on them of deserving precedency before they could expect to obtain it.

This great accession to the intellectual power of the species, and to the amount of intellect available for the good management of its affairs, would be obtained, partly, through the better and more complete intellectual education of women, which would then improve *pari passu* with that of men. Women in general would be brought up equally capable of understanding business, public affairs, and the higher matters of speculation, with men in the same class of society; and the select few of the one as well as of the other sex, who were qualified not only to comprehend what is done or thought by others, but to think or do something considerable themselves, would meet with the same facilities for improving and training their capacities in the one sex as in the other. In this way, the widening of the sphere of action for women would operate for good, by raising their education to the level of that of men, and making the one participate in all improvements made in the other. But independently of this, the mere breaking down of the barrier would of itself have an educational virtue of the highest worth. The mere getting rid of the idea that all the wider subjects of thought and action, all the things which are of general and not solely of private interest, are men's business, from which women are to be warned off— positively interdicted from most of it, coldly tolerated in the little which is allowed them—the mere consciousness a woman would then have of being a human being like any other, entitled to choose her pursuits, urged or invited by the same inducements as any one else to interest herself in whatever is interesting to human beings, entitled to exert the share of influence on all human concerns which belongs to an individual opinion, whether she attempted actual participation in them or not—this alone would effect an immense expansion of the faculties of women, as well as enlargement of the range of their moral sentiments.

Besides the addition to the amount of individual talent available for the conduct of human affairs, which certainly are not at present so abundantly provided in that respect that they can afford to dispense with one-half of what nature proffers; the opinion of women would then possess a more beneficial, rather than a greater, influence upon the general mass of human belief and sentiment. I say a more beneficial, rather than a greater influence; for the influence of women over the general tone of opinion has always, or at least from the earliest known period, been very considerable. The influence of mothers on the early character of their sons, and the desire of young men to recommend themselves to young women, have in all recorded times been important agencies in the formation of character, and have determined some of the chief steps in the progress of civilization. Even in the Homeric age, αἰδώς towards the Τρωάδας ἑλκεσιπέπλους is an acknowledged and powerful motive of action in the great Hector. The moral influence of women has had two modes of operation. First, it has been a softening influence. Those who were most liable to be the victims of violence, have naturally tended as much

as they could towards limiting its sphere and mitigating its excesses. Those who were not taught to fight, have naturally inclined in favour of any other mode of settling differences rather than that of fighting. In general, those who have been the greatest sufferers by the indulgence of selfish passion, have been the most earnest supporters of any moral law which offered a means of bridling passion. Women were powerfully instrumental in inducing the northern conquerors to adopt the creed of Christianity, a creed so much more favourable to women than any that preceded it. The conversion of the Anglo-Saxons and of the Franks may be said to have been begun by the wives of Ethelbert and Clovis. The other mode in which the effect of women's opinion has been conspicuous, is by giving a powerful stimulus to those qualities in men, which, not being themselves trained in, it was necessary for them that they should find in their protectors. Courage, and the military virtues generally, have at all times been greatly indebted to the desire which men felt of being admired by women: and the stimulus reaches far beyond this one class of eminent qualities, since, by a very natural effect of their position, the best passport to the admiration and favour of women has always been to be thought highly of by men. From the combination of the two kinds of moral influence thus exercised by women, arose the spirit of chivalry: the peculiarity of which is, to aim at combining the highest standard of the warlike qualities with the cultivation of a totally different class of virtues—those of gentleness, generosity, and self-abnegation, towards the non-military and defenceless classes generally, and a special submission and worship directed towards women; who were distinguished from the other defenceless classes by the high rewards which they had it in their power voluntarily to bestow on those who endeavoured to earn their favour, instead of extorting their subjection. Though the practice of chivalry fell even more sadly short of its theoretic standard than practice generally falls below theory, it remains one of the most precious monuments of the moral history of our race; as a remarkable instance of a concerted and organized attempt by a most disorganized and distracted society, to raise up and carry into practice a moral ideal greatly in advance of its social condition and institutions; so much so as to have been completely frustrated in the main object, yet never entirely inefficacious, and which has left a most sensible, and for the most part a highly valuable impress on the ideas and feelings of all subsequent times.

The chivalrous ideal is the acme of the influence of women's sentiments on the moral cultivation of mankind: and if women are to remain in their subordinate situation, it were greatly to be lamented that the chivalrous standard should have passed away, for it is the only one at all capable of mitigating the demoralizing influences of that position. But the changes in the general state of the species rendered inevitable the substitution of a totally different ideal of morality for the chivalrous one. Chivalry was the attempt to infuse moral elements into a state of society in which everything depended for good or evil on individual prowess, under the softening influences of individual delicacy and generosity. In modern societies, all things, even in the military department of affairs, are decided, not by individual effort, but by the combined operations of numbers; while the main occupation of society has changed from fighting to business, from military to industrial life. The exigencies of the new life are no more exclusive of the virtues of generosity than those of the old, but it no longer entirely depends on them. The main foundations of the moral life of modern times must be justice and prudence; the respect of each for the rights of every other, and the ability of each to take care of himself. Chivalry left without legal check all forms of wrong which reigned unpunished throughout society; it only encouraged a few to do right in preference to wrong, by the direction it gave to the instruments of praise and admiration. But the real dependence of morality must always be upon its penal sanctions—its power to deter from evil. The security of society cannot rest on merely rendering honour to right, a motive so comparatively weak in all but a few, and which on very many does not operate at all. Modern society is able to repress wrong through all departments of life, by a fit exertion of the superior strength which civilization has given it, and thus to render the existence of the weaker members of society (no longer defenceless but protected by law) tolerable to them, without reliance on the chivalrous feelings of those who are in a position to tyranize. The beauties and graces of the chivalrous character are still what they were, but the rights of the weak, and the general comfort of human life, now rest on a far surer and steadier support; or rather, they do so in every relation of life except the conjugal.

At present the moral influence of women is no less real, but it is no longer of so marked and definite a character: it has more nearly merged in the general influence of public opinion. Both through the contagion of sympathy, and through the desire of men to shine in the eyes of women, their feelings have great effect in keeping alive what remains of the chivalrous ideal—in fostering the sentiments and continuing the traditions of spirit and generosity. In these points of character, their standard is higher than that of men; in the quality of justice, somewhat lower. As regards the relations of private life it may be said generally, that their influence is, on the whole, encouraging to the softer virtues, discouraging to the sterner: though the statement must be taken with all the modifications dependent on individual character. In the chief of the greater trials to which virtue is subject in the concerns of life—the conflict between interest and principle—the tendency of women's influence is of a very mixed character. When the principle involved happens to be one of the very few which the course of their religious or moral education has strongly impressed upon themselves, they are potent auxiliaries to virtue: and their husbands and sons are often prompted by them to acts of abnegation which they never would have been capable of without that stimulus. But, with the present education and position of women, the moral principles which have been impressed on them cover but a comparatively small part of the field of virtue, and are, moreover, principally negative; forbidding particular acts, but having little to do with the general direction of the thoughts and purposes. I am afraid it must be said, that disinterestedness in the general conduct of life—the devotion of the energies to purposes which hold out no promise of private advantages to the family—is very seldom encouraged or supported by women's influence. It is small blame to them that they discourage objects of which they have not learnt to see the advantage, and which withdraw their men from them, and from the interests of the family. But the consequence is that women's influence is often anything but favourable to public virtue.

Women have, however, some share of influence in giving the tone to public moralities since their sphere of action has been a little widened, and since a considerable number of them have occupied themselves practically in the promotion of objects reaching beyond their own family and household. The influence of women counts for a great deal in two of the most marked features of modern European life—its aversion to war, and its addiction to philanthropy. Excellent characteristics both; but unhappily, if the influence of women is valuable in the encouragement it gives to these feelings in general, in the particular applications the direction it gives to them is at least as often mischievous as useful. In the philanthropic department more particularly, the two provinces chiefly cultivated by women are religious proselytism and charity. Religious proselytism at home, is but another word for embittering of religious animosities: abroad, it is usually a blind running at an object, without either knowing or heeding the fatal mischiefs—fatal to the religious object itself as well as to all other desirable objects—which may be produced by the means employed. As for charity, it is a matter in which the immediate effect on the persons directly concerned, and the ultimate consequence to the general good, are apt to be at complete war with one another: while the education given to women—an education of the sentiments rather than of the understanding—and the habit inculcated by their whole life, of looking to immediate effects on persons, and not to remote effects on classes of persons—make them both unable to see, and unwilling to admit, the ultimate evil tendency of any form of charity or philanthropy which commends itself to their sympathetic feelings. The great and continually increasing mass of unenlightened and shortsighted benevolence, which, taking the care of people's lives out of their own hands, and relieving them from the disagreeable consequences of their own acts, saps the very foundations of the self-respect, self-help, and self-control which are the essential conditions both of individual prosperity and of social virtue—this waste of resources and of benevolent feelings in doing harm

instead of good, is immensely swelled by women's contributions, and stimulated by their influence. Not that this is a mistake likely to be made by women, where they have actually the practical management of schemes of beneficence. It sometimes happens that women who administer public charities—with that insight into present fact, and especially into the minds and feelings of those with whom they are in immediate contact, in which women generally excel men—recognise in the clearest manner the demoralizing influence of the alms given or the help afforded, and could give lessons on the subject to many a male political economist. But women who only give their money, and are not brought face to face with the effects it produces, how can they be expected to foresee them? A woman born to the present lot of women, and content with it, how should she appreciate the value of self-dependence? She is not self-dependent; she is not taught self-dependence; her destiny is to receive everything from others, and why should what is good enough for her be bad for the poor? Her familiar notions of good are of blessings descending from a superior. She forgets that she is not free, and that the poor are; that if what they need is given to them unearned, they cannot be compelled to earn it: that everybody cannot be taken care of by everybody, but there must be some motive to induce people to take care of themselves; and that to be helped to help themselves, if they are physically capable of it, is the only charity which proves to be charity in the end.

These considerations shew how usefully the part which women take in the formation of general opinion, would be modified for the better by that more enlarged instruction, and practical conversancy with the things which their opinions influence, that would necessarily arise from their social and political emancipation. But the improvement it would work through the influence they exercise, each in her own family, would be still more remarkable.

It is often said that in the classes most exposed to temptation, a man's wife and children tend to keep him honest and respectable, both by the wife's direct influence, and by the concern he feels for their future welfare. This may be so, and no doubt often is so, with those who are more weak than wicked; and this beneficial influence would be preserved and strengthened under equal laws; it does not depend on the woman's servitude, but is, on the contrary, diminished by the disrespect which the inferior class of men always at heart feel towards those who are subject to their power. But when we ascend higher in the scale, we come among a totally different set of moving forces. The wife's influence tends, as far as it goes, to prevent the husband from falling below the common standard of approbation of the country. It tends quite as strongly to hinder him from rising above it. The wife is the auxiliary of the common public opinion. A man who is married to a woman his inferior in intelligence, finds her a perpetual dead weight, or, worse than a dead weight, a drag, upon every aspiration of his to be better than public opinion requires him to be. It is hardly possible for one who is in these bonds, to attain exalted virtue. If he differs in his opinion from the mass—if he sees truth which have not yet dawned upon them, or if, feeling in his heart truths which they nominally recognise, he would like to act up to those truths more conscientiously than the generality of mankind—to all such thoughts and desires, marriage is the heaviest of drawbacks, unless he be so fortunate as to have a wife as much above the common level as he himself is.

For, in the first place, there is always some sacrifice of personal interest required; either of social consequence, or of pecuniary means; perhaps the risk of even the means of subsistence. These sacrifices and risks he may be willing to encounter for himself; but he will pause before he imposes them on his family. And his family in this case means his wife and daughters; for he always hopes that his sons will feel as he feels himself, and that what he can do without, they will do without, willingly, in the same cause. But his daughters—their marriage may depend upon it: and his wife, who is unable to enter into or understand the objects for which these sacrifices are made—who, if she thought them worth any sacrifice, would think so on trust, and solely for his sake—who can participate in none of the enthusiasm or the self-approbation he himself may feel, while the things which he is disposed to sacrifice are all in all to her; will not the best and most unselfish man hesitate the longest before bringing on her this consequence? If it be not the

comforts of life, but only social consideration, that is at stake, the burthen upon his conscience and feelings is still very severe. Whoever has a wife and children has given hostages to Mrs. Grundy. The approbation of that potentate may be a matter of indifference to him, but it is of great importance to his wife. The man himself may be above opinion, or may find sufficient compensation in the opinion of those of his own way of thinking. But to the women connected with him, he can offer no compensation. The almost invariable tendency of the wife to place her influence in the same scale with social consideration, is sometimes made a reproach to women, and represented as a peculiar trait of feebleness and childishness of character in them: surely with great injustice. Society makes the whole life of a woman, in the easy classes, a continued self-sacrifice; it exacts from her an unremitting restraint of the whole of her natural inclinations, and the sole return it makes to her for what often deserves the name of a martyrdom, is consideration. Her consideration is inseparably connected with that of her husband, and after paying the full price for it, she finds that she is to lose it, for no reason of which she can feel the cogency. She has sacrificed her whole life to it, and her husband will not sacrifice to it a whim, a freak, an eccentricity; something not recognised or allowed for by the world, and which the world will agree with her in thinking a folly, if it thinks no worse! The dilemma is hardest upon that very meritorious class of men, who, without possessing talents which qualify them to make a figure among those with whom they agree in opinion, hold their opinion from conviction, and feel bound in honour and conscience to serve it, by making profession of their belief, and giving their time, labour, and means, to anything undertaken in its behalf. The worst case of all is when such men happen to be of a rank and position which of itself neither gives them, nor excludes them from, what is considered the best society; when their admission to it depends mainly on what is thought of them personally—and however unexceptionable their breeding and habits, their being identified with opinions and public conduct unacceptable to those who give the tone to society would operate as an effectual exclusion. Many a woman flatters herself (nine times out of ten quite erroneously) that nothing prevents her and her husband from moving in the highest society of her neighbourhood—society in which others well known to her, and in the same class of life, mix freely—except that her husband is unfortunately a Dissenter, or has the reputation of mingling in low radical politics. That it is, she thinks, which hinders George from getting a commission or a place, Caroline from making an advantageous match, and prevents her and her husband from obtaining invitations, perhaps honours, which, for aught she sees, they are as well entitled to as some folks. With such an influence in every house, either exerted actively, or operating all the more powerfully for not being asserted, is it any wonder that people in general are kept down in that mediocrity of respectability which is becoming a marked characteristic of modern times?

There is another very injurious aspect in which the effect, not of women's disabilities directly, but of the broad line of difference which those disabilities create between the education and character of a woman and that of a man, requires to be considered. Nothing can be more unfavourable to that union of thoughts and inclinations which is the ideal of married life. Intimate society between people radically dissimilar to one another, is an idle dream. Unlikeness may attract, but it is likeness which retains; and in proportion to the likeness is the suitability of the individuals to give each other a happy life. While women are so unlike men, it is not wonderful that selfish men should feel the need of arbitrary power in their own hands, to arrest *in limine* the life-long conflict of inclinations, by deciding every question on the side of their own preference. When people are extremely unlike, there can be no real identity of interest. Very often there is conscientious difference of opinion between married people, on the highest points of duty. Is there any reality in the marriage union where this takes place? Yet it is not uncommon anywhere, when the woman has any earnestness of character; and it is a very general case indeed in Catholic countries, when she is supported in her dissent by the only other authority to which she is taught to bow, the priest. With the usual barefacedness of power not accustomed to find itself disputed, the influence of priests over women is at-

tacked by Protestant and Liberal writers, less for being bad in itself, than because it is a rival authority to the husband, and raises up a revolt against his infallibility. In England, similar differences occasionally exist when an Evangelical wife has allied herself with a husband of a different quality; but in general this source at least of dissension is got rid of, by reducing the minds of women to such a nullity, that they have no opinions but those of Mrs. Grundy, or those which the husband tells them to have. When there is no difference of opinion, differences merely of taste may be sufficient to detract greatly from the happiness of married life. And though it may stimulate the amatory propensities of men, it does not conduce to married happiness, to exaggerate by differences of education whatever may be the native differences of the sexes. If the married pair are well-bred and well-behaved people, they tolerate each other's tastes; but is mutual toleration what people look forward to, when they enter into marriage? These differences of inclination will naturally make their wishes different, if not restrained by affection or duty, as to almost all domestic questions which arise. What a difference there must be in the society which the two persons will wish to frequent, or be frequented by! Each will desire associates who share their own tastes: the persons agreeable to one, will be indifferent or positively disagreeable to the other; yet there can be none who are not common to both, for married people do not now live in different parts of the house and have totally different visiting lists, as in the reign of Louis XV. They cannot help having different wishes as to the bringing up of the children: each will wish to see reproduced in them their own tastes and sentiments: and there is either a compromise, and only a half-satisfaction to either, or the wife has to yield—often with bitter suffering; and, with or without intention, her occult influence continues to counterwork the husband's purposes.

It would of course be extreme folly to suppose that these differences of feeling and inclination only exist because women are brought up differently from men, and that there would not be differences of taste under any imaginable circumstances. But there is nothing beyond the mark in saying that the distinction in bringing-up immensely aggravates those differences, and renders them wholly inevitable. While women are brought up as they are, a man and a woman will but rarely find in one another real agreement of tastes and wishes as to daily life. They will generally have to give it up as hopeless, and renounce the attempt to have, in the intimate associate of their daily life, that *idem velle, idem nolle*, which is the recognised bond of any society that is really such: or if the man succeeds in obtaining it, he does so by choosing a woman who is so complete a nullity that she has no *velle* or *nolle* at all, and is as ready to comply with one thing as another if anybody tells her to do so. Even this calculation is apt to fail; dulness and want of spirit are not always a guarantee of the submission which is so confidently expected from them. But if they were, is this the ideal of marriage? What, in this case, does the man obtain by it, except an upper servant, a nurse, or a mistress? On the contrary, when each of two persons, instead of being a nothing, is a something; when they are attached to one another, and are not too much unlike to begin with; the constant partaking in the same things, assisted by their sympathy, draws out the latent capacities of each for being interested in the things which were at first interesting only to the other; and works a gradual assimilation of the tastes and characters to one another, partly by the insensible modification of each, but more by a real enriching of the two natures, each acquiring the tastes and capacities of the other in addition to its own. This often happens between two friends of the same sex, who are much associated in their daily life: and it would be a common, if not the commonest, case in marriage, did not the totally different bringing-up of the two sexes make it next to an impossibility to form a really well-assorted union. Were this remedied, whatever differences there might still be in individual tastes, there would at least be, as a general rule, complete unity and unanimity as to the great objects of life. When the two persons both care for great objects, and are a help and encouragement to each other in whatever regards these, the minor matters on which their tastes may differ are not all-important to them; and there is a foundation for solid friendship, of an enduring character, more likely than anything else to make it, through the whole of life, a greater pleasure to each to give pleasure to the other, than to receive it.

I have considered, thus far, the effects on the pleasures and benefits of the marriage union which depend on the mere unlikeness between the wife and the husband: but the evil tendency is prodigiously aggravated when the unlikeness is inferiority. Mere unlikeness, when it only means difference of good qualities, may be more a benefit in the way of mutual improvement, than a drawback from comfort. When each emulates, and desires and endeavours to acquire, the other's peculiar qualities, the difference does not produce diversity of interest, but increased identity of it, and makes each still more valuable to the other. But when one is much the inferior of the two in mental ability and cultivation, and is not actively attempting by the other's aid to rise to the other's level, the whole influence of the connexion upon the development of the superior of the two is deteriorating: and still more so in a tolerably happy marriage than in an unhappy one. It is not with impunity that the superior in intellect shuts himself up with an inferior, and elects that inferior for his chosen, and sole completely intimate, associate. Any society which is not improving, is deteriorating: and the more so, the closer and more familiar it is. Even a really superior man almost always begins to deteriorate when he is habitually (as the phrase is) king of his company: and in his most habitual company the husband who has a wife inferior to him is always so. While his self-satisfaction is incessantly ministered to on the one hand, on the other he insensibly imbibes the modes of feeling, and of looking at things, which belong to a more vulgar or a more limited mind than his own. This evil differs from many of those which have hitherto been dwelt on, by being an increasing one. The association of men with women in daily life is much closer and more complete than it ever was before. Men's life is more domestic. Formerly, their pleasures and chosen occupations were among men, and in men's company: their wives had but a fragment of their lives. At the present time, the progress of civilization, and the turn of opinion against the rough amusements and convivial excesses which formerly occupied most men in their hours of relaxation—together with (it must be said) the improved tone of modern feeling as to the reciprocity of duty which binds the husband towards the wife—have thrown the man very much more upon home and its inmates, for his personal and social pleasures: while the kind and degree of improvement which has been made in women's education, has made them in some degree capable of being his companions in ideas and mental tastes, while leaving them, in most cases, still hopelessly inferior to him. His desire of mental communion is thus in general satisfied by a communion from which he learns nothing. An unimproving and unstimulating companionship is substituted for (what he might otherwise have been obliged to seek) the society of his equals in powers and his fellows in the higher pursuits. We see, accordingly, that young men of the greatest promise generally cease to improve as soon as they marry, and, not improving, inevitably degenerate. If the wife does not push the husband forward, she always holds him back. He ceases to care for what she does not care for; he no longer desires, and ends by disliking and shunning, society congenial to his former aspirations, and which would now shame his falling-off from them; his higher faculties both of mind and heart cease to be called into activity. And this change coinciding with the new and selfish interests which are created by the family, after a few years he differs in no material respect from those who have never had wishes for anything but the common vanities and the common pecuniary objects.

What marriage may be in the case of two persons of cultivated faculties, identical in opinions and purposes, between whom there exists that best kind of equality, similarity of powers and capacities with reciprocal superiority in them—so that each can enjoy the luxury of looking up to the other, and can have alternately the pleasure of leading and of being led in the path of development—I will not attempt to describe. To those who can conceive it, there is no need; to those who cannot, it would appear the dream of an enthusiast. But I maintain, with the profoundest conviction, that this, and this only, is the ideal of marriage; and that all opinions, customs, and institutions which favour any other notion of it, or turn the conceptions and aspirations connected with it into any other direction, by whatever pretences they may be coloured,

are relics of primitive barbarism. The moral regeneration of mankind will only really commence, when the most fundamental of the social relations is placed under the rule of equal justice, and when human beings learn to cultivate their strongest sympathy with an equal in rights and in cultivation.

Thus far, the benefits which it has appeared that the world would gain by ceasing to make sex a disqualification for privileges and a badge of subjection, are social rather than individual; consisting in an increase of the general fund of thinking and acting power, and an improvement in the general conditions of the association of men with women. But it would be a grievous understatement of the case to omit the most direct benefit of all, the unspeakable gain in private happiness to the liberated half of the species; the difference to them between a life of subjection to the will of others, and a life of rational freedom. After the primary necessities of food and raiment, freedom is the first and strongest want of human nature. While mankind are lawless, their desire is for lawless freedom. When they have learnt to understand the meaning of duty and the value of reason, they incline more and more to be guided and restrained by these in the exercise of their freedom; but they do not therefore desire freedom less; they do not become disposed to accept the will of other people as the representative and interpreter of those guiding principles. On the contrary, the communities in which the reason has been most cultivated, and in which the idea of social duty has been most powerful, are those which have most strongly asserted the freedom of action of the individual—the liberty of each to govern his conduct by his own feelings of duty, and by such laws and social restraints as his own conscience can subscribe to.

He who would rightly appreciate the worth of personal independence as an element of happiness, should consider the value he himself puts upon it as an ingredient of his own. There is no subject on which there is a greater habitual difference of judgment between a man judging for himself, and the same man judging for other people. When he hears others complaining that they are not allowed freedom of action—that their own will has not sufficient influence in the regulation of their affairs—his inclination is, to ask, what are their grievances? what positive damage they sustain? and in what respect they consider their affairs to be mismanaged? and if they fail to make out, in answer to these questions, what appears to him a sufficient case, he turns a deaf ear, and regards their complaint as the fanciful querulousness of people whom nothing reasonable will satisfy. But he has a quite different standard of judgment when he is deciding for himself. Then, the most unexceptionable administration of his interests by a tutor set over him, does not satisfy his feelings: his personal exclusion from the deciding authority appears itself the greatest grievance of all, rendering it superfluous even to enter into the question of mismanagement. It is the same with nations. What citizen of a free country would listen to any offers of good and skilful administration, in return for the abdication of freedom? Even if he could believe that good and skilful administration can exist among a people ruled by a will not their own, would not the consciousness of working out their own destiny under their own moral responsibility be a compensation to his feelings for great rudeness and imperfection in the details of public affairs? Let him rest assured that whatever he feels on this point, women feel in a fully equal degree. Whatever has been said or written, from the time of Herodotus to the present, of the ennobling influence of free government—the nerve and spring which it gives to all the faculties, the larger and higher objects which it presents to the intellect and feelings, the more unselfish public spirit, and calmer and broader views of duty, that it engenders, and the generally loftier platform on which it elevates the individual as a moral, spiritual, and social being— is every particle as true of women as of men. Are these things no important part of individual happiness? Let any man call to mind what he himself felt on emerging from boyhood—from the tutelage and control of even loved and affectionate elders—and entering upon the responsibilities of manhood. Was it not like the physical effect of taking off a heavy weight, or releasing him from obstructive, even if not otherwise painful, bonds? Did he not feel twice as much alive, twice as much a human being, as before? And does he imagine that women have none of these feelings? But it is a striking fact, that the satisfactions and mortifica-

tions of personal pride, though all in all to most men when the case is their own, have less allowance made for them in the case of other people, and are less listened to as a ground or a justification of conduct, than any other natural human feelings; perhaps because men compliment them in their own case with the names of so many other qualities, that they are seldom conscious how mighty an influence these feelings exercise in their own lives. No less large and powerful is their part, we may assure ourselves, in the lives and feelings of women. Women are schooled into suppressing them in their most natural and most healthy direction, but the internal principle remains, in a different outward form. An active and energetic mind, if denied liberty, will seek for power: refused the command of itself, it will assert its personality by attempting to control others. To allow to any human beings no existence of their own but what depends on others, is giving far too high a premium on bending others to their purposes. Where liberty cannot be hoped for, and power can, power becomes the grand object of human desire; those to whom others will not leave the undisturbed management of their own affairs, will compensate themselves, if they can, by meddling for their own purposes with the affairs of others. Hence also women's passion for personal beauty, and dress and display; and all the evils that flow from it, in the way of mischievous luxury and social immorality. The love of power and the love of liberty are in eternal antagonism. Where there is least liberty, the passion for power is the most ardent and unscrupulous. The desire of power over others can only cease to be a depraving agency among mankind, when each of them individually is able to do without it: which can only be where respect for liberty in the personal concerns of each is an established principle.

But it is not only through the sentiment of personal dignity, that the free direction and disposal of their own faculties is a source of individual happiness, and to be fettered and restricted in it, a source of unhappiness, to human beings, and not least to women. There is nothing, after disease, indigence, and guilt, so fatal to the pleasurable enjoyment of life as the want of a worthy outlet for the active faculties. Women who have the cares of a family, and while they have the cares of a family, have this outlet, and it generally suffices for them: but what of the greatly increasing number of women, who have had no opportunity of exercising the vocation which they are mocked by telling them is their proper one? What of the women whose children have been lost to them by death or distance, or have grown up, married, and formed homes of their own? There are abundant examples of men who, after a life engrossed by business, retire with a competency to the enjoyment, as they hope, of rest, but to whom, as they are unable to acquire new interests and excitements that can replace the old, the change to a life of inactivity brings ennui, melancholy, and premature death. Yet no one thinks of the parallel case of so many worthy and devoted women, who, having paid what they are told is their debt to society—having brought up a family blamelessly to manhood and womanhood—having kept a house as long as they had a house needing to be kept—are deserted by the sole occupation for which they have fitted themselves; and remain with undiminished activity but with no employment for it, unless perhaps a daughter or daughter-in-law is willing to abdicate in their favour the discharge of the same functions in her younger household. Surely a hard lot for the old age of those who have worthily discharged, as long as it was given to them to discharge, what the world accounts their only social duty. Of such women, and of those others to whom this duty has not been committed at all—many of whom pine through life with the consciousness of thwarted vocations, and activities which are not suffered to expand—the only resources, speaking generally, are religion and charity. But their religion, though it may be one of feeling, and of ceremonial observance, cannot be a religion of action, unless in the form of charity. For charity many of them are by nature admirably fitted; but to practise it usefully, or even without doing mischief, requires the education, the manifold preparation, the knowledge and the thinking powers, of a skilful administrator. There are few of the administrative functions of government for which a person would not be fit, who is fit to bestow charity usefully. In this as in other cases (pre-eminently in that of the education of children), the duties permitted to women cannot be performed properly, without their

being trained for duties which, to the great loss of society, are not permitted to them. And here let me notice the singular way in which the question of women's disabilities is frequently presented to view, by those who find it easier to draw a ludicrous picture of what they do not like, than to answer the arguments for it. When it is suggested that women's executive capacities and prudent counsels might sometimes be found valuable in affairs of state, these lovers of fun hold up to the ridicule of the world, as sitting in parliament or in the cabinet, girls in their teens, or young wives of two or three and twenty, transported bodily, exactly as they are, from the drawing-room to the House of Commons. They forget that males are not usually selected at this early age for a seat in Parliament, or for responsible political functions. Common sense would tell them that if such trusts were confided to women, it would be to such as having no special vocation for married life, or preferring another employment of their faculties (as many women even now prefer to marriage some of the few honourable occupations within their reach), have spent the best years of their youth in attempting to qualify themselves for the pursuits in which they desire to engage; or still more frequently perhaps, widows or wives of forty or fifty, by whom the knowledge of life and faculty of government which they have acquired in their families, could by the aid of appropriate studies be made available on a less contracted scale. There is no country of Europe in which the ablest men have not frequently experienced, and keenly appreciated, the value of the advice and help of clever and experienced women of the world, in the attainment both of private and of public objects; and there are important matters of public administration to which few men are equally competent with such women; among others, the detailed control of expenditure. But what we are now discussing is not the need which society has of the services of women in public business, but the dull and hopeless life to which it so often condemns them, by forbidding them to exercise the practical abilities which many of them are conscious of, in any wider field than one which to some of them never was, and to others is no longer, open. If there is anything vitally important to the happiness of human beings, it is that they should relish their habitual pursuit. This requisite of an enjoyable life is very imperfectly granted, or altogether denied, to a large part of mankind; and by its absence many a life is a failure, which is provided, in appearance, with every requisite of success. But if circumstances which society is not yet skilful enough to overcome, render such failures often for the present inevitable, society need not itself inflict them. The injudiciousness of parents, a youth's own inexperience, or the absence of external opportunities for the congenial vocation, and their presence for an uncongenial, condemn numbers of men to pass their lives in doing one thing reluctantly and ill, when there are other things which they could have done well and happily. But on women this sentence is imposed by actual law, and by customs equivalent to law. What, in unenlightened societies, colour, race, religion, or in the case of a conquered country, nationality, are to some men, sex is to all women; a peremptory exclusion from almost all honourable occupations, but either such as cannot be fulfilled by others, or such as those others do not think worthy of their acceptance. Sufferings arising from causes of this nature usually meet with so little sympathy, that few persons are aware of the great amount of unhappiness even now produced by the feeling of a wasted life. The case will be even more frequent, as increased cultivation creates a greater and greater disproportion between the ideas and faculties of women, and the scope which society allows to their activity.

When we consider the positive evil caused to the disqualified half of the human race by their disqualification—first in the loss of the most inspiriting and elevating kind of personal enjoyment, and next in the weariness, disappointment, and profound dissatisfaction with life, which are so often the substitute for it; one feels that among all the lessons which men require for carrying on the struggle against the inevitable imperfections of their lot on earth, there is no lesson which they more need, than not to add to the evils which nature inflicts, by their jealous and prejudiced restrictions on one another. Their vain fears only substitute other and worse evils for those which they are idly apprehensive of: while every restraint on the freedom of conduct of any of their human fellow creatures, (otherwise than by making them responsible for any evil actually caused by it), dries up *pro tanto* the principal fountain of human happiness, and leaves the species less rich, to an inappreciable degree, in all that makes life valuable to the individual human being.

7

MARX AND MARXISM

"And now as to myself, no credit is due to me for discovering the existence of classes in modern society, nor yet the struggle between them. Long before me bourgeois historians had described the historical development of this class struggle, and bourgeois economists the economic anatomy of the classes" (Letter to Weydemeyer, 1852).

Long years of debate between Marxists and their opponents have resulted in considerable confusion about which arguments are characteristically 'Marxist' and which are not. As an economic theorist, Karl Marx (1818–83) was the heir of Adam Smith (1723–90) and David Ricardo (1772–1823), and many views that are now attacked as Marxist were once the respectable opinions of liberal political economists. Thus Marx writes, "Assume a particular state of development in the productive forces of man and you will get a particular form of commerce and consumption. Assume particular stages of development in production, commerce, and consumption and you will have a corresponding social order, a corresponding organization of the family and of the ranks and classes, in a word a corresponding civil society. Presuppose a particular civil society and you will get particular political conditions which are only the official expression of civil society" (Letter to Anenkov, 1846). Much of what we think of as Marxism is summed up in these few sentences, and yet there is nothing in them that would have surprised a philosopher of the Scottish Enlightenment, and nothing with which Smith would have disagreed. On this theory human history has primarily been shaped by the development of technology and falls naturally into four major epochs: hunting and gathering; pastoral agriculture, resulting from the domestication of animals; the cultivation of food plants; and increased commercialization, with the development of metallurgy. Each has been associated with different types of property, social inequality, and political power. Marx simply extended this line of argument into the modern day: "The hand-mill gives you society with the feudal lord; the steam-mill society with the industrial capitalist" (*The Poverty of Philosophy*).

Clearly technology does constrain the types of social organization, property, and power that are possible within a society, although perhaps not as straightforwardly as Marx thought. Thus a slave-owning society is incompatible with a complex technology, as slaves cannot be trusted to work with a will or make every effort to improve their skills. Marx is often called a "materialist," but it is worth noting that technological determinism is scarcely materialism. Marx is committed to the view that the capacities and powers a society has in manipulating nature influence the practices and beliefs of that society; but capacities and powers are skills, theories, and habits: They are not in themselves material entities.

Marx was not merely a technological determinist. He believed that human beings constantly seek to improve their control over nature and that this builds a principle of progress into history: "The economic forms in which men produce, consume, exchange, are *transitory and historical*. When

new productive forces are won, men change their mode of production and with the mode of production all the economic relations which are merely the necessary conditions of this particular mode
of production." Clearly, since the beginning of history, there has been immense technological
progress, and this progress has transformed society. But progress has been extremely erratic, and in
some societies there have been long periods during which technology appears to have remained effectively static. Under capitalism, competition forces constant technological progress, but in pre-
capitalist societies there may be real obstacles to the investment of resources and to the change of
methods that progress requires. Marx himself recognized this problem, for he argued that in some
societies (which he described as Asiatic despotisms) the state imposes such heavy taxes that innovation is permanently stifled; but, though he was aware of the problem, the general theory of
historical materialism takes progress for granted. In this respect Marx was very much a typical nineteenth-century thinker.

Technological determinism and the presumption of progress are the two founding principles of historical materialism, a theory which Marx first formulated in 1845. In addition, the theory depends on
three technical concepts:

(1) the *forces* of production (the technology, both in the broad sense of powers and skills and in the
    more narrow sense of ways of organizing production—the assembly line, for example) which
    make it possible to put the *means* of production (raw materials, tools, machines, human beings)
    to work;

(2) the *relations* of production (not in the peculiar sense of the relations between workers on an as-
    sembly line, but in the sense of types of *control* over the means of production, such as slavery
    and wage-labor); and

(3) the *superstructure* (the law courts, policemen, armies, bureaucracies, and the political, educa-
    tional, and religious institutions required to preserve a system of property relations).

Improvements in the forces of production lead to new relations of production; further improvements
take place until the old relations of production become an obstacle, which is finally swept away by
economic, political, and cultural revolution, i.e. by the transformation of both the relations of production and the superstructure.

This theory is based on the claim that opponents of change will never be able to effectively block
progress (which benefits humankind as a whole) for very long. One can easily imagine circumstances,
however, where the ruling groups have a monopoly of military force, or where change seems more
likely to benefit an unpopular minority than the vast majority; under such circumstances it is hard to
see why technical progress might not be halted indefinitely. A striking example is Japan in the late
seventeenth and early eighteenth century, which abandoned guns and artillery, despite the fact that
they had proved effective in warfare, because they were a threat to the culture of the Samurai; in Europe, on the other hand, developments in military technology led the way in encouraging both scientific enquiry and new manufacturing methods.

There are more specific problems with the theory of historical materialism. Why, for example, did
the development of markets within the slave societies of ancient Greece and Rome not lead directly
to capitalism? Why did the "Dark Ages" intervene, followed by feudalism? It is hard to see why this
detour should have been necessary; yet if it was a merely accidental product of circumstances, then
it is clear that the development of the forces of production is not the crucial causal agent at work

throughout history. In Marx's defense it may be noted that this was a problem not only for his theory, but also for the account of historical change offered by Adam Smith in *The Wealth of Nations.* But Smith was very conscious that the actual history of Europe accorded very imperfectly with his theoretical model and that he needed to explain the discrepancy. Marx was less worried by the problem than he should have been.

Marx did not formulate historical materialism simply because he and Friedrich Engels (1820–1895), his close associate, had been reading English political economists. He was also attracted to it because it offered an account of historical change which was similar in structure to the theory of the greatest German philosopher of the previous generation, Friedrich Hegel (1770–1831). Hegel had argued that history embodied the cumulative progress of the human intellect, despite the fact that individuals themselves had not known where history was going or what was driving it. History was thus a process without a subject, but it was not a merely natural process, as it was the result of will and intention. What drove history was conflict between and within cultures. The result was not a linear but a 'dialectical' progress. Thus in the Middle Ages an otherworldly Church had been in bitter conflict with a this-worldly State. But the Church had had to adopt worldly methods, while the State had had to come to respect abstract principles of right and law. Out of this conflict had emerged the modern State, "the image and the actuality of reason," in which the antithesis between the worldly and the spiritual had been overcome. Until the present, cultural progress had always involved negative as well as positive developments. Since cultures are embodied by nations, the progress of history can be traced by following the advance of culture, first in one nation, and then in another, and the history of cultural change can be used to explain the rise of great powers and the outcomes of battles. For Hegel, in G. A. Cohen's summary, "History is the history of the world spirit (and, derivatively, human consciousness) which undergoes growth in self-knowledge, the stimulus and vehicle of which is a culture, which perishes when it has stimulated more growth than it can contain." For Marx, "History is the history of human industry, which undergoes growth in productive power, the stimulus and vehicle of which is an economic structure, which perishes when it has stimulated more growth than it can contain."

Both Hegel and Marx believed that they lived at an exceptional moment in history, the moment when individuals, because they understood the principles governing historical change, could intervene consciously to shape change and could become the knowing subjects, not merely the unwitting victims, of the historical process. But for Hegel history had reached its endpoint in the Prussian state, Protestantism, and his own philosophy. Marx believed that a fundamental transformation was necessary before history could be said to have culminated. Up to now the historical process had been outside anyone's control, not simply because the fundamental role of technology had been misunderstood, but also because all previous developed societies had been able to support only a small, wealthy, educated elite who controlled the process of production. As a result, these societies were riven by class conflict, and no one group could control the outcome of events or shape social change, for change was the unforeseeable outcome of conflicting forces clashing in highly particular circumstances. Modern technology, however, offered for the first time the possibility of a universal prosperity. In a classless society, social change would not be opaque and unpredictable; it could for the first time be understood, planned, and controlled. The end of class conflict would therefore be the end of history as we know it. To this claim there is a simple objection: Class divisions may be the most important divisions in contemporary society (although this rather depends on its being possible to show that race and gender divisions are merely an expression of class divisions), but their elimination would leave real conflicts of interests, conflicts which would continue to make the outcome of social change unpredictable. Divisions between consumers and producers, between regions, between those favoring economic expansion and those concerned to protect the environment, to give just a few examples, would leave considerable scope for conflict within a classless society.

Marx's belief that a classless society would understand what it was about (and would therefore be free of 'ideology', or misconceptions resulting from observing society from the point of view of a particular interest group) is merely one aspect of his general claim that communism would put an end to alienation, or estrangement. The term *alienation* refers to a range of possible frustrations. If I set out to bake a cake and manage to follow the recipe successfully, then I am proud of the result; but if the cake burns, then I take no satisfaction in what I have produced. Frustration results from the fact that I do not identify with what I have produced, do not recognize it as my own achievement. If I bake a beautiful birthday cake, but do so, not in order to celebrate my son's birthday but to make some money, then the cake is no longer an expression of affection but merely embodies my response to economic incentives. If I have to work long hours in a cake factory, where I merely tend a machine which mixes the dough, then I feel no pride in the final product, and I resent my hours of labor because they take me away from other activities through which I can still express my creativity, perhaps gardening, or playing the violin, or telling jokes to my friends. If the cake factory in which I work lays me off because of a downturn in the market, then I am part of a society in which human effort is squandered and apparently impersonal forces (which result, however, from individual decisions) shape people's lives.

Under communism, Marx believed, most of these different types of alienation would be overcome. Klutzes would still burn cakes, of course, but people would not be forced into unemployment or denied the leisure and facilities required for creative self-expression. There would still be chores to be done, but in a society in which there was a strong sense of community, people would put in time on an assembly line in the same reasonably cheerful way that people now give over time to vacuuming the house or cutting the lawn, for they would be clear that they and their loved ones would benefit. The social causes of alienation would be eliminated. (Of course, there would still be plenty of frustrations: Despite years of practice, I might never prove to be anything but a mediocre cook.)

Communism is thus for Marx an ethical, psychological, and social ideal. It is the proper culmination of a history in which alienation has been progressively intensified as individuals have become subject to market forces outside their control and forced to work (when they can find work), not for themselves and their loved ones, but for strangers. Class struggle and alienation were the negative aspects of progress under capitalism, but they would disappear when private ownership of the means of production was replaced by collective control. Marx became a communist in 1843 and remained one for the rest of his life. Before 1848 communist political movements were primarily to be found in France, and it was in exile there (Marx had had to flee Germany after his radical newspaper, the *Rheinische Zeitung,* was suppressed in 1843) that Marx encountered communism. He was to spend the rest of his life trying to develop communism as an international movement, publishing the *Communist Manifesto* during the revolutions of 1848 and founding the International Working Men's Association in 1864.

Political economists before Marx had stressed the reality of class struggle. Ricardo, for example, had argued that there were three sources of income: rent, profit, and labor. But rents were largely the result of monopoly interests controlling the market; landlords and bankers were parasitic on workers and industrialists. What was even more disturbing was that Ricardo was unable to provide a satisfactory explanation for profits. Prices, he argued, were ultimately determined by the amounts of labor embodied in objects sold: It was easy for successors to argue that if values were entirely the product of labor, then there ought to be no profits, only wages. Finally, Ricardo argued that as economies expanded there was a natural tendency for profits to fall (the most fertile fields were the first cultivated, and the shallowest mines the first dug; later expansion involved more effort for less return) and that consequently wages must be pushed downwards until they reached the barest subsistence level. Ricardo's Iron Law of Wages and Malthus's Principle of Population combined to suggest that the working class must find itself worse and worse off, even as the economy grew and technology progressed. Moreover, Ricardo argued as the scale of production increased, the economic cycles intensified, bust following rapidly on boom, while technological progress reduced the demand for labor, which in turn reduced the market for goods. Capitalism thus manufactured poverty and intensified class conflict. This analysis seemed to be confirmed, not falsified, by the initial stages of the industrial revolution. Engels had lived in Manchester, the greatest center of manufacturing industry in the world, and had first-hand experience of the social consequences of the new technology.

Marx believed that he was the first to see the logical outcome of this process. "What I did that was new was to prove: 1) that the existence of classes is only bound up with particular, historic phases in the development of production; 2) that the class struggle necessarily leads to the dictatorship of the proletariat; 3) that this dictatorship itself only constitutes the transition to the abolition of all classes and to a classless society" (Letter to Weydemeyer). Marx thus believed his own claim to originality lay in his having shown that communist revolution was the natural outcome of contemporary social change. Why? Because the factory assembled the working class and trained it in cooperation. In previous social orders, the oppressed classes had been relatively weak. But capitalism constantly expanded the size of the working class, as small farmers, shopkeepers, and craftsmen were driven out of business and into wage labor. It brought the new workers together into large factories, where they worked in close cooperation and were acutely aware of their common interest in demanding higher wages. And it rendered the employer obsolete: Factories were run by technical experts, who were themselves mere wage workers. It was inevitable that workers would try to seize factories in order to run them for their own benefit and that they would call for a planned economy in order to make possible full and stable employment. This coming revolution would mark the emergence, not of a new system of exploitation (as all previous revolutions had done), but of a classless society.

Marx remained confident of this prediction, even though the years between 1851 and 1870 saw relatively stable trading conditions and no important revolutionary upheavals. He retreated to the British Museum, where he worked on an analysis of capitalist economies designed to demonstrate the inevitability of their collapse, an analysis published in *Capital* vol. 1 (1867). There he argued, first, that profits resulted from the fact that labor was unlike any other commodity one could purchase in the market: Laborers could produce more than it cost to reproduce them (i.e. feed, clothe, educate them), and so produced a *surplus value*. Wages appeared to be a fair payment for the value of what workers produced; they were in fact something quite different: a fair payment for the cost of producing laborers. Second, he argued that there was a natural tendency for profits to fall, not because of the Ricardian "law of diminishing returns," but because technological progress meant that there was a constantly growing proportion of investment in machines and raw materials, not in labor. But since profit came only from surplus value, which was produced only by laborers, profits on investment must fall unless exploitation was constantly increased. Third, Marx stressed that capitalist relations of production tended to be opaque to those caught up in them. Not only did wages appear fair, but economic change seemed to be the result of "natural," or at least impersonal, forces. It was all too easy to lose sight of the fact that the existing economy was not natural but the product of an historical process (where small producers had been forced to become wage workers), that it was dependent on social institutions (particular laws governing property relations, for example), and that it might one day be replaced by a quite different social order. It was easy to "fetishize" existing social relations by assuming that contemporary social relations were the only possible social relations.

The argument of *Capital* thus cuts two ways. On the one hand, Marx holds firm to his claim that, as capitalism progresses, it digs its own grave. On the other hand, he stresses the obstacles which prevent the working class from recognizing its opportunity to reshape history: The fetishism of commodities and the invisibility of surplus value make socialism appear utopian, not practical.

Since Marx's death in 1883, one can identify three main currents of socialism that have claimed to be his true heirs. First, the great Social Democratic parties of the late nineteenth and early twentieth centuries, under the influence of Karl Kautsky (1854–1938) argued in favor of a slow, peaceful transition from a competitive to a planned economy via the development of the welfare state and nationalization. Second, left-communists, such as Rosa Luxemburg (1871–1919), argued that revolution would be the result of a largely spontaneous escalation of the demands made by militant workers and factory councils and the new regime would thus be rooted in popular participation and democratic representative institutions. Third, the followers of Lenin (1870–1923) argued that the workers, left to themselves, would always be seduced by reformist proposals unless they were educated and led by a professionalized revolutionary party (although Lenin's own views during the excitement of the Russian revolution of 1917, as expressed in *State and Revolution,* were indistinguishable from those of the left-communists). Leninists insisted that the dictatorship of the proletariat must involve a period when civil rights were restricted, not expanded, and that political freedom must be sacrificed in the short term in order to establish the social and economic preconditions for a classless society at some future date.

The emergence of communist states organized on Leninist principles and seeking to establish socialism in relatively backward societies resulted in three main schools in the interpretation of Marx. One, whose greatest representative was the Hungarian philosopher Georg Lukacs (1885–1971), argued that Leninism was compatible with Marxism, which was itself the result of a materialist rethinking of Hegel. Another, inspired by Erich Fromm (b. 1900), turned its back on the Marx of *Capital,* who was rejected as an economic determinist, but praised Marx's youthful writings, particularly "The 1844 Manuscripts," unpublished in Marx's own lifetime, and written before Marx became an historical materialist, for their preoccupation with alienation as the pervasive evil of modern society. A third, whose most distinguished representative was Karl Popper (b. 1902), argued that totalitarianism was the natural consequence of Marxism and defended individualism, liberalism, and empiricism against collectivism, determinism, and dogmatism.

A new phase in the study of Marx began with the publication in 1978 of G. A. Cohen's *Karl Marx's Theory of History: A Defence.* Cohen was the first to try to give a rigorous philosophical analysis of Marx's theories. He rejected Marx's arguments for surplus value and the declining rate of profit as spurious and self-contradictory, but he insisted that historical materialism was a coherent and defensible theory. Cohen argued that, in order to defend Marx, one had to recognize him as offering functional explanations: Superstructures and social relations change in order to ensure the continuing development of the forces of production.

In reply, Jon Elster has insisted that, insofar as Marxism depends on functional explanations, it fails, because functional relationships depend either on deliberate planning or on feedback mechanisms which eliminate errors. Marx insists that history is not the result of a planned process. But neither is it a process, like economic growth or Darwinian evolution, where change obeys a logic because there is a mechanism (the market or natural selection) for eliminating nonfunctional developments and reinforcing functional ones. What is the mechanism in contemporary society which eliminates policies which are dysfunctional as far as the forces of production are concerned? Marx argued that in modern societies governments pursue policies that favor capitalists, but what is to prevent them pursuing policies which are in the interests, not of capital, but of government itself, or even of working-class voters? Obviously stock exchanges, currency markets, and political donations have a considerable influence on policy, but keeping capitalists happy is not the government's only or always its primary objective, and the actual policies pursued by governments may be very different from those which would result in the biggest profits or the most rapid technological progress. Social change depends on the actions of individuals, and any explanation (Elster argues) must respect the principle of methodological individualism: It must be possible to express it in terms of the beliefs and motives of individual agents. Cohen's defense of Marx fails because it cannot identify a mechanism which ensures that the actions of individuals serve the required functions, nor does it offer a test to distinguish those aspects of social relations which are "functional" from those which are "dysfunctional" in order to show that such a mechanism (even if unidentified) must exist. Elster's arguments leave little scope for a defense of Marxism as Marx himself understood it, although many "Marxist" arguments may still be true.

Further Reading

Two books on Hegel provide useful introductions: Allen Wood, *Hegel's Ethical Thought* (Cambridge: Cambridge University Press, 1990) and Steven B. Smith, *Hegel's Critique of Liberalism* (Chicago: Chicago University Press, 1989).

No brief list can do justice to the range and variety of books on Marx and Marxism. The best introduction which is both short and sophisticated is Jon Elster, *An Introduction to Karl Marx* (Cambridge: Cambridge University Press, 1986). Fundamental is G. A. Cohen, *Karl Marx's Theory of History: A Defence* (Oxford: Oxford University Press, 1978). For a vivid picture of Marx's life in England, there is Yvonne Kapp, *Eleanor Marx,* vol. 1 (2 vols., London: Lawrence and Wishart, 1972–76). On Engels, see Gareth Stedman Jones, "Engels and the History of Marxism," in Eric Hobsbawm (ed.), *The History of Marxism,* vol. 1 (Brighton: Harvester Press, 1982), pp. 290–326, and Stephen Marcus, *Engels, Manchester and the Working Class* (New York: Random House, 1974).

The best general survey of Marxism is Leszek Kolakowski, *Main Currents of Marxism* (3 vols., Oxford: Oxford University Press, 1978). But for an outstanding introductory survey see Perry Anderson, *Considerations on Western Marxism* (London: NLB, 1976). The best short account of Lenin is Marcel Liebman, *Leninism under Lenin* (London: Merlin Press, 1975).

Nobody should read Marx without having some sense of his place within the history of economic theory. A sound elementary introduction is Robert Heilbroner, *The Worldly Philosophers* (New York: Simon and Schuster, 1953). A good starting point for anyone wanting to compare Marx's theory of history with Adam Smith's is A. S. Skinner's essay in A. S. Skinner and T. Wilson (eds.), *Essays on Adam Smith* (Oxford: Clarendon Press, 1975).

Hegel
Introduction to the Philosophy of History

TWO

Reason in History

The only thought which philosophy brings with it, in regard to history, is the simple thought of Reason—the thought that Reason rules the world, and that world history has therefore been rational in its course. This conviction and insight is a *presupposition* in regard to history as such, although it is not a presupposition in philosophy itself.

In philosophy, speculative reflection has shown that Reason is the *substance* as well as the *infinite power*; that Reason is for itself the *infinite material* of all natural and spiritual life, as well as the *infinite form*, and that its actualization of itself is its content. (And we can stand by the term "Reason" here, without examining its relation and connection with "God" more closely.)

Thus Reason is the *substance* [of our historic world] in the sense that it is that whereby and wherein all reality has its being and subsistence. It is the *infinite power*, since Reason is not so powerless as to arrive at nothing more than the ideal, the ought, and to remain outside reality—who knows where—as something peculiar in the heads of a few people. Reason is the *infinite content*, the very stuff of all essence and truth, which it gives to its own *activity* to be worked up. For, unlike finite activity, it does not need such conditions as an external material, or given means from which to get its nourishment and the objects of its activity. It lives on itself, and it is itself the material upon which it works. Just as Reason is its own presupposition and the absolute goal, so it is the activation of that goal in

[Reprinted from Hegel, *Introduction to the Philosophy of History*, translated by Leo Rauch. (Indianapolis: Hackett Publishing Company, 1988), by permission of the publisher.]

world history—bringing it forth from the inner source to external manifestation, not only in the natural universe but also in the spiritual. That this Idea is the True, the Eternal, simply the Power—that it reveals itself in the world, and that nothing else is revealed in the world but that Idea itself, its glory and majesty—this, as we said, is what has been shown in philosophy, and it is here presupposed as already proven.

Those of you who are not yet acquainted with philosophy can at least be expected to come to these lectures on world history with the belief in Reason, with the desire, the thirst to know it. And indeed what must be presupposed as a subjective need in the study of the sciences is the desire for rational insight, for knowledge, not merely for a collection of facts. Thus, even if you do not bring to world history the thought and the knowledge of Reason, you ought at least to have the firm and unconquerable belief that there is Reason in history, together with the belief that the world of intelligence and self-conscious will is not subject to chance, but rather that it must demonstrate itself in the light of the self-conscious Idea.

But in fact I need not require this belief on your part in advance. What I have said so far, and will say again, is not just to be taken as a presupposition of our science, but as a summary of the totality—as the *result* of the discussion upon which we are embarking, a result that is known to *me* because I already know that totality. Thus it is the consideration of world history itself that must reveal its rational process—namely, that it has been the rational, necessary course of the World Spirit, the Spirit whose nature is indeed always one and the same, but which reveals this one nature in the world's reality. As I said, this must be the outcome of the study of history.

Yet we must take history as it is, and proceed historically, i.e., empirically. Among other things, we must not be misled by the professional historians, particularly the Germans, who possess great authority, and do precisely what they accuse philosophers of doing, namely creating *a priori* fabrications in history. For example, there is a widespread fabrication that there existed an original, primeval people, taught directly by God and having complete insight and wisdom, with a penetrating knowledge of all the laws of nature and spiritual truth; or that there were such or such priestly peoples; or, to speak of something more specific, that there was a Roman epic from which the Roman historians drew their earliest history, and so on. Let us leave all such *a priori* constructions to the clever professionals for whom (in Germany) such constructions are not uncommon.

As the first condition to be observed, we could therefore declare that we must apprehend the historical faithfully. But with such general terms as "apprehend" and "faithfully" there lies an ambiguity. Even the ordinary, average historian, who believes and says that he is merely receptive to his data, is not passive in his thinking; he brings his categories along with him, and sees his data through them. In every treatise that is to be scientific, Reason must not slumber, and reflection must be actively applied. To him who looks at the world rationally, the world looks rational in return. The relation is mutual. But the various kinds of reflection, of possible viewpoints, of judgment even in regard to the mere importance and unimportance of facts (the most basic category in historical judgment) —all this does not concern us here.

In regard to the general conviction that Reason rules and has ruled in the world and likewise in world history, I would like to draw your attention to just two versions of that conviction. These will enable us to get closer to that main point which is so difficult, and at the same time to point ahead to our further discussion.

A.   *To begin with, there is the historical fact* that the Greek, Anaxagoras, was the first to say that *nous*— understanding in general, or Reason—rules the world. By this he did not mean an intelligence as self-conscious reason or a mind as such. We must take care to differentiate *nous* and "mind" from one another. The movement of the solar system follows immutable laws. These laws are its Reason. But neither the sun, nor the planets that revolve around it according to these laws, have any consciousness of them.

Such a thought—that there is Reason in nature, that nature is governed unchangeably by general laws— does not surprise us. We are accustomed to thinking in this way, and we do not make much of it. I have merely mentioned this historical fact to make you aware of what history shows: namely, that a thought which seems trivial to us was not always commonplace in the world, but rather was epoch-making in the history of the human spirit. Aristotle says of Anaxagoras, as the originator of this thought, that he appeared like a sober man among the drunken ones. From Anaxagoras, Socrates took it up, and it immediately became the dominant thought in philosophy (except for the philosophy of Epicurus, which ascribed all events to chance).

Plato has Socrates say: "I was delighted with this thought, and I was hoping to have found a teacher who would explain nature according to Reason, and show in each particular thing its particular purpose, as well as the universal purpose in the totality. Not for a great fortune would I have given up this hope. But how disappointed I was when I so eagerly took up the writings of Anaxagoras himself, and I found that he brought in to his explanation merely external causes such as Air, the Ether, Water and the like—instead of Reason." [*Phaedo*, 97c–98c]

We can see that what Socrates found so unsatisfying in the principle of Anaxagoras was not the principle itself, but rather Anaxagoras' failure to apply it to concrete nature: that this nature was not understood or conceived on the basis of that principle, but that the principle was held to as something abstract. Nature was not grasped as a development of Reason, not as an organic whole brought forth by Reason. At the very outset, therefore, I want to call your attention to the difference between maintaining a conception, a principle, a truth in a merely abstract way, and carrying it through to a fuller determination and a concrete development. This difference—i.e., between the abstract and the concrete—is basic to all philosophy as well. Thus at the end of our discussion of world history, we shall be returning to this point especially, in dealing with the most recent political situation.

B.   *The second version of the thought* that Reason rules the world is related to a further application of it, with which we are well acquainted in the form of the religious truth that the world is not subject to chance and to the external contingencies, but that it is ruled by a *Providence*. I explained earlier that I do not wish to make any demands on your belief in this principle of Providence. Yet I might appeal to your belief in it in this *religious form*—if, that is, the distinctive character of the science of philosophy allowed presuppositions to count at all. To put it another way, the appeal to your belief is not necessary because the science we wish to discuss will itself provide the proof of the correctness of that principle, if not the proof of its truth. The truth, then, that there is a divine providence presiding over the events of the world, corresponds to the stated principle: for divine providence is wisdom with infinite power, realizing its own ends, i.e., the absolute, rational end-goal of the world, while Reason is Thought, quite freely determining itself.

But now we also see a difference emerging. There is, indeed, a contradiction between this belief in providence and our principle—rather like the difference between the dictum of Anaxagoras and the expectations of Socrates in regard to it. That belief in a providence is indefinite in the same way: it does not advance to any definite conclusion, as applied to the totality of things and to the all-encompassing course of world history. To explain history, however, means to reveal the passions of human beings, their talents, their active powers. This definiteness of providence is what is usually taken for its *plan*. Yet it is this very plan that is supposed to be hidden from our view, so that we would be presumptuous to want to understand it.

The ignorance of Anaxagoras, as to how Reason manifests itself in reality, was sincere. The awareness of that thought—whether in him or in Greece in general—had not yet gone any further. He could not yet apply his principle to the concrete events, and understand concrete reality in terms of that principle. It was Socrates who took the first step towards grasping the union of the concrete with the universal. Anaxagoras, therefore, was not explicitly opposed to such an application of the universal to the concrete. But the belief in providence *is* opposed at least to the large-scale application of the principle, and to our comprehending the plan of providence. Here and there, in particular

cases, the application is allowed: pious souls see in certain individual events not merely the workings of chance, but of God's hand—for example, when an individual in great distress and need receives help unexpectedly. But these purposes themselves are of a restricted sort, for they are only the particular purposes of this individual.

In world history, however, we are concerned with "individuals" that are nations, with wholes that are states. Accordingly, we cannot stop at the (so to speak) "retail" version of the belief in providence—still less we can be content with the merely abstract, indefinite belief which goes only so far as the general view that there is a providence, and says nothing more of its more definite acts. On the contrary, we must seriously try to recognize the ways of providence, and to connect its means and manifestations in history—relating these to that universal principle.

But in mentioning the possibility of our knowing the plan of divine providence in general, I have touched on a question that has become prominent in our own time: the question about the possibility of our knowing God—or, inasmuch as it has ceased to be a question, there is the doctrine (which has now become a prejudice) that it is impossible to know God. Holy Scripture commands it as our highest duty not only to love God but also to know God. But in direct opposition to this, there now prevails the denial of what is there written: that it is the Spirit that leads us to truth, that the Spirit knows all things and penetrates even to the depths of the Godhead.*

When the Divine Being is placed beyond the reach of our knowing and beyond human affairs altogether, we gain the convenience of indulging in our own imaginings. We are thereby excused from having to give our knowledge some relation to the Divine and the True. On the contrary, the vanity of human knowledge and subjective feeling receives a complete justification for itself. And when pious humility places the knowing of God at a distance, it knows full well what it has thereby gained for its arbitrariness and vain efforts.

---

*See I Corinthians 2:10. "God has revealed these things to us through the Spirit. For the Spirit searches all things, even the depths of God." [Translator's note.]

I could not avoid mentioning the connection between our thesis (that Reason rules the world and has ruled it) and the question about the possibility of our knowing God, since I did not want to dodge the accusation that philosophy shuns (or must shun) all discussion of religious truths due to a bad conscience about them. On the contrary, in modern times we have come to the point where philosophy has to take up the defense of religious truths against many types of theological doctrine. In the Christian religion God has revealed Himself: that is to say, He has allowed human beings to understand what He is, so that He is no longer hidden and secret. With this possibility of our knowing God, the obligation to know Him is placed upon us. God wants no narrow-minded souls and empty heads for His children. Rather, He wants those who (however poor in spirit) are rich in the knowledge of Him, and who place the highest value in this knowledge of Him. The development of the thinking spirit, which began from this basis in the revelation of the Divine Being, must finally come to the point where what was originally present only to feeling and to the imagining spirit, can now be grasped by thought. And the time must finally come when we comprehend the rich product of creative Reason that is world history.

For some time, it was customary to admire God's wisdom at work in animals, in plants, and in the destinies of individuals. If we grant that providence reveals itself in such objects and materials, then why not also in world history? Here, the material seems too great. Yet the divine wisdom, i.e., Reason, is one and the same on the large scale and on the small, and we must not consider God to be too weak to apply His wisdom on a large scale. In our knowledge, we aim for the insight that whatever was intended by the Eternal Wisdom has come to fulfillment—as in the realm of nature, so in the realm of spirit that is active and actual in the world. To that extent our approach is a theodicy, a justification of the ways of God. Leibniz attempted a theodicy in metaphysical terms, using indefinite abstract categories—so that when once the evil in the world was comprehended in this way, the thinking mind was supposed to be reconciled to it. Nowhere, in fact, is there a greater challenge to such intellectual reconciliation than in world history. This reconciliation can be achieved only through the recognition of that positive aspect, in which the negative disappears as something subordinate and overcome. It is attained (on the one hand) through the awareness of the true end-goal of the world, and (on the other) through the awareness that this end has been actualized in the world and that the evil has not prevailed in it in any ultimate sense.

For this purpose, however, the mere belief in *nous* and providence is still quite inadequate. "Reason"— which is said to rule the world—is just as indefinite a term as "Providence." We hear Reason spoken of, without anyone being able to say just what its definition is, or its content (according to which we could judge whether something is rational or irrational). To grasp Reason in its definition—that is of primary importance. If we merely stick to the bare term, "Reason," throughout the rest of what we say is just words. With these declarations behind us, we can go on to the second viewpoint we wish to consider in this Introduction.

THREE

Freedom, the Individual, and the State

If we think of Reason in its relation to the world, then the question of the *definition* of Reason in itself coincides with the question about the *final goal* of the world. Implicit in that latter term is the suggestion that the goal is to be realized, made actual. There are two things to be considered here: the content of that goal (i.e., the definition itself, as such), and its actualization.

At the outset we must note that our object—*world history*—takes place in the realm of the Spirit. The term "world" includes both physical and mental nature. Physical nature impinges on world history as well, and from the very beginning we shall have to draw attention to the fundamental relations [between the two natures] in the definition. But it is Spirit, and the process of its development, that is the substance of history. Nature in itself, which is likewise a rational system in its particular and characteristic element, is not our concern here, except as related to Spirit.

Spirit is to be observed in the theater of world history, where it has its most concrete reality. In spite of this, however (or rather in order for us to grasp the universal aspect in this mode of Spirit's concrete reality), we must set forth, before all else, some abstract definitions of the *nature of Spirit*. These can, of course, be no more than mere assertions here. This is not the place to go into the Idea of Spirit in a speculative fashion, for what can be said in an introduction is simply to be taken historically—as a presupposition which (as we said) has either been worked out and proven elsewhere, or else is to receive its verification only as the outcome of the science of history itself.

We have therefore to address the following topics:

I.   The abstract characteristics of the nature of Spirit
II.   The means Spirit uses in order to realize its Idea
III. The shape taken on by Spirit in its complete realization in the world—the State.

I.   THE NATURE OF SPIRIT. This can be seen by looking at its complete antithesis—matter. Just as the essence of matter is gravity [that is, in being determined by a force outside it], so the essence of Spirit is its freedom [that is, in its self-determination]. Everyone will immediately agree that Spirit is endowed with freedom, among other characteristics. Philosophy, however, teaches us that all the characteristics of Spirit subsist only by means of freedom; that all of them are only the means to freedom, and that they seek and produce only freedom. This is one of the truths of speculative philosophy: that freedom is the only truth of Spirit.

Matter has weight insofar as it strives toward a central point outside itself. It is essentially composed of parts which are separable. It seeks its unity, which would be its own negation, its opposite. If it were to achieve this, it would no longer be matter but would have perished. It strives toward the ideal, for in unity [i.e., in being self-determining, self-moving], matter is idealized.

Spirit, on the other hand, is that which has a center in itself. Its unity is not outside itself; rather, it has found it within its own self. It is in its own self and

alone unto itself. While matter has its "substance" [i.e., its source of support] outside itself, Spirit is autonomous and self-sufficient, a Being-by-itself (*Bei-sich-selbst-sein*). But this, precisely, is freedom—for when I am dependent, I relate myself to something else, something which I am not; as dependent, I cannot be without something which is external. I am free when I exist independently, all by myself. This self-sufficient being is self-consciousness, the consciousness of the self.

Two things must be distinguished in the consciousness: first, the fact *that* I know; and second, *what* I know. In self-consciousness, the two—subject and object—coincide. Spirit knows itself: it is the judging of its own nature, and at the same time it is the activity of coming to itself, of producing itself, making itself actually what it is in itself potentially.

According to this abstract definition, we can say of world history that it is the exhibition of the Spirit, the working out of the explicit knowledge of what it is potentially. Just as the germ of the plant carries within itself the entire nature of the tree, even the taste and shape of its fruit, so the first traces of Spirit virtually contain all history.

In the world of the ancient Orient, people do not yet know that the Spirit—the human as such—is free. Because they do not know this, they are not free. They know only that *one* person is free; but for this very reason such freedom is mere abitrariness, savagery, stupified passion; or even a softness or tameness of passion, which is itself a mere accident of nature and therefore quite arbitrary. This *one* person is therefore only a despot, not a free man.

It was among the Greeks that the consciousness of freedom first arose, and thanks to that consciousness they were free. But they, and the Romans as well, knew only that *some* persons are free, not the human as such. Even Plato and Aristotle did not know this. Not only did the Greeks have slaves, therefore—and Greek life and their splendid freedom were bound up with this—but their freedom itself was partly a matter of mere chance, a transient and limited flowering, and partly a hard servitude of the human and the humane.

It was first the Germanic peoples, through Christianity, who came to the awareness that *every* human is free by virtue of being human, and that the freedom of spirit comprises our most human nature. This awareness arose first in religion, in the innermost region of Spirit. But to introduce this principle into worldly reality as well: that was a further task, requiring long effort and civilization to bring it into being. For example, slavery did not end immediately with the acceptance of the Christian religion; freedom did not suddenly prevail in Christian states; nor were governments and constitutions organized on a rational basis, or indeed upon the principle of freedom.

This application of the principle of freedom to worldly reality—the dissemination of this principle so that it permeates the worldly situation—this is the long process that makes up history itself. I have already drawn attention to the distinction between a principle as such and its application, its introduction and implementation in the actuality of spirit and life. This distinction is fundamental to our science, and it must be kept in mind. Just as this distinction was noted in a preliminary way with regard to the Christian principle of self-consciousness and freedom, so has its essential place in regard to the principle of freedom in general. World history is the progress in the consciousness of freedom—a progress that we must come to know in its necessity.

Above, I made a general statement regarding the different levels in the awareness of freedom—namely, that the Orientals knew only that *one* person is free; the Greeks and Romans that *some* are free; while *we* know that *all* humans are implicitly free, *qua* human. At the same time, this statement gives us the division of world history and the basis for our consideration of it. But this is noted merely provisionally and in passing. We must first explain some other concepts.

The *final goal of the world*, we said, is Spirit's consciousness of its freedom, and hence also the actualization of that very freedom. This, then, is what characterizes the spiritual world—and this therefore is the substantially real world, to which the physical world is subordinate (or, to say this in speculative terms, the physical world has no truth as against the spiritual). But this "freedom," as so far described, is itself indefinite and infinitely ambiguous. As the highest of concepts it carries with it infinitely many misunderstandings, confusions and errors, and comprises all possible excesses within it. Never has all this been better known and felt than at the present time. For the time being, however, we must content ourselves with using it in that general sense.

We have also drawn attention to the importance of the infinite difference between the principle, which is as yet merely implicit, and that which is real. But at the same time it is freedom in itself that contains the infinite necessity of bringing itself to consciousness (for in its very concept it is knowledge of itself) and thereby to reality. Freedom is for itself the goal to be achieved, and the only goal of Spirit.

It is this final goal—freedom—toward which all the world's history has been working. It is this goal to which all the sacrifices have been brought upon the broad altar of the earth in the long flow of time. This is the one and only goal that accomplishes itself and fulfills itself—the only constant in the change of events and conditions, and the truly effective thing in them all. It is this goal that is God's will for the world. But God is the absolutely perfect Being, and He can therefore will nothing but Himself, His own will. The nature of His will, however—i.e., His own nature, that is what we are here calling the Idea of freedom (since we are translating the religious image into philosophic thought). The question that now follows immediately, then, can be this: What means does this Idea of freedom use for its realization? This is the second point to be considered.

II. THE MEANS OF THE SPIRIT. This question—as to the *means* whereby freedom develops itself into a world—leads us into the phenomenon of history itself. While freedom as such is primarily an internal concept, its means are external: namely, the phenomena which present themselves directly before our eyes in history. Our first look at history convinces us that the actions of human beings stem from their needs, their passions, their interests, their characters and talents. And it appears that the only springs of action in this theater of activity, and the mainsprings, are these needs, passions, and interests. Of course, the play also involves universal aims, benevolence, noble patriotism, and so on. But these virtues and their universality are insignificant in their relation to the world and its doings.

We might well see the ideal of Reason realized in these subjective individuals themselves and in their sphere of influence, but individuals are of slight importance compared to the mass of the human race; likewise, the scope of their virtues is relatively restricted in its range. Instead, it is the passions, the aims of particular interests, the satisfaction of selfish desire that are the most forceful things. They get their power from the fact that they observe none of the limits which the law and morality would seek to impose upon them—and from the fact that these forces of nature are closer and more immediate to human beings than the artificial and tedious discipline toward order and moderation, toward law and morality.

When we look at this drama of human passions, and observe the consequences of their violence and of the unreason that is linked not only to them but also (and especially) to good intentions and rightful aims; when we see arising from them all the evil, the wickedness, the decline of the most flourishing nations mankind has produced, we can only be filled with grief for all that has come to nothing. And since this decline and fall is not merely the work of nature but the will of men, we might well end with moral outrage over such a drama, and with a revolt of our good spirit (if there is a spirit of goodness in us). Without rhetorical exaggeration, we could paint the most fearful picture of the misfortunes suffered by the noblest of nations and states as well as by private virtues—and with that picture we could arouse feelings of the deepest and most helpless sadness, not to be outweighed by any consoling outcome. We can strengthen ourselves against this, or escape it, only by thinking that, well, so it was at one time; it is fate; there is nothing to be done about it now. And finally—in order to cast off the tediousness that this reflection of sadness could produce in us and to return to involvement in our own life, to the present of our own aims and interests—we return to the selfishness of standing on a quiet shore where we can be secure in enjoying the distant sight of confusion and wreckage.

But as we contemplate history as this slaughter-bench, upon which the happiness of nations, the wis-

dom of states, and the virtues of individuals were sacrificed, the question necessarily comes to mind: What was the ultimate goal for which these monstrous sacrifices were made? And from this there usually follows the question which we made the starting-point of our consideration. And in this perspective the events that present such a grim picture for our troubled feeling and thoughtful reflection have to be seen as the *means* for what we claim is the substantial definition, the absolute end-goal or, equally, the true *result* of world history.

From the outset we have altogether avoided taking the path that goes from that picture of the particular events to the universal meaning. In any case, it is no service to those emotional reflections to rise above those feelings and in that way to solve the riddles of providence which the mournful view has given up on. It is far more characteristic of such reflections to enjoy the misery of the empty and fruitless sublimities of that negative outcome. We must return, therefore, to our original standpoint; and the elements that we wish to adduce will also contain the essential determinations through which the questions arising from that picture of human suffering can be answered.

The *first* thing we note is what we have already remarked upon, but which cannot be repeated too often, since it concerns the matter at hand: namely, that what we have called the principle, the final goal, the determination, or the nature and concept of Spirit, is only something general and abstract. A principle, or rule, or law is something internal which, whatever truth it has within it, is not completely actual. Aims, principles, and the like are, to begin with, in our thoughts—only in our inner intentions but not yet to be found in reality. What is implicit in itself is a possibility, a potentiality, but it has not yet emerged from its own inwardness into outer existence.

For actuality, there must be a *second* element added —and that is activity or actualization. The principle of this is the will, i.e., human activity in general. Only through this activity is the concept (along with its implicit determinations) realized, actualized—for these aims and principles are not immediately valid in and of themselves. The activity which puts them into operation and into existence is that which stems from human need, drive, inclination, and passion. I bring something into act and being because it suits me to do so: I must be involved in it; in acting on my desires I must be satisfied. A purpose for which I am to be active must in some way be my purpose as well. My own purpose must in some way be satisfied in it, even if the purpose for which I am active also has many other aspects that do not concern me. This is the infinite right of the subjective individual, to satisfy himself in his activity and work. If people are expected to have an interest in something, they themselves must be involved in it, and they must find their own sense of self satisfied in it.

There is a misunderstanding to be avoided here. It may be said of an individual, reproachfully, that he is an "interested party"—namely, that he is out for his private advantage, without regard for the common interest; he cloaks his own advantage in it, and even sacrifices the common interest in favor of his own. Yet one who is active in behalf of something is not merely "interested" but is interested *in it*. Language expresses this difference correctly. Nothing happens therefore, nothing is accomplished, unless the individuals involved are satisfied as well. They are particular persons, and this means that they have their own particular needs, drives, and interests. Among these needs there is not only one's own need and will, but also one's individual insight, conviction, or at least one's own viewpoint (if the need for argument, for understanding, and for reasoning is at all aroused). Hence people demand, as well, that if they are expected to be active in behalf of something, then it should be in accord with their views—so that their opinions can be in sympathy with it, whether in regard to the utility of it, or their own rights or advantage. This is especially an essential aspect of our time, in which people are less drawn to something by their trust in authority, and would prefer to devote their activity to a cause on the basis of their own understanding of it, their independent conviction and opinions.

We say, therefore, that nothing at all has come to pass without the interest of those whose activity is involved in it. And since we call an interest a "passion" —when all of one's individuality, to the neglect of all other interests and purposes one might have, is placed

in the service of some cause; and every fiber of one's being, every last ounce of will-power is committed to it, so that all of one's needs and forces are concentrated upon it—we must assert as a general proposition that *nothing great* has been accomplished in the world *without passion*.

There are two elements that enter into our topic: the first is the Idea, the other is human passion; the first is the warp, the other the woof in the great tapestry of world history that is spread out before us. The concrete meeting point and union of the two is in ethical freedom in the state. We have already spoken of the Idea of freedom, as the essential nature of Spirit and the final goal of history. Passion is often seen as something that is not quite right, something more or less evil: the human being ought to have no passions; and the term "passion" is not quite the right word for what I want to express. What I generally understand by this word is human activity stemming from individual interests, from special goals or from self-seeking purposes if you like; but "passion" occurs when people place the entire energy of their will and character in these goals, sacrificing something else that might well be a goal, or even everything else.

This particular "passionate" content is so bound up with a person's will, that it is inseparable from it and comprises all that determines it; through it, the person is what he is. What is *there* is the individual, not Man in general. It is not Man that exists, but the specific individual. The term "character" expresses this uniqueness of will and intelligence as well; but "character" embraces all the particularities of the person, the modes of behavior in private relationships, etc., and this very uniqueness is asserted in nothing other than a person's effectiveness and activity.

I shall therefore use the term "passion" to signify the particular uniqueness of a person's character—to the extent that the uniqueness of will does not have a merely private content, but is also what drives and motivates actions of a universal scope. "Passion" is primarily the subjective and thus the formal aspect of energy, of will and activity, so that the content or goal remains as yet undetermined. At the same time it is there in one's own conviction, one's own insight and conscience. What matters is always the content of my conviction, the aim of my passion, and whether the one or the other is more genuine. But conversely, whichever is more genuine will enter into existence and become actual.

From this comment about the second essential element in the realization of a historical aim, it follows (if, for a moment, we look at the state) that the state is well constituted and internally strong if the private interest of the citizens is united with the universal goal of the state, so that each finds its fulfillment and realization in the other. This is a proposition of the highest intrinsic importance. But before this unity is brought into being, the state must undergo much struggle with private interests and passions, in a long and hard discipline of them. And the state needs many institutions, devices and practical arrangements, together with long struggles of the understanding, before it arrives at an awareness of what is appropriate to its goal. The era of such a unity constitutes the period of a state's flowering, the time of its excellence, power, and prosperity.

But world history does not begin with any conscious goal, such as we find in the particular spheres of human life. The simple social instinct of human beings already involves the conscious goal of securing life and property; and insofar as this life in common has already come into being, that goal is extended further. World history begins with its universal goal: the fulfillment of the concept of Spirit—still only *implicit* (*an sich*), i.e., as its nature. That goal is the inner, indeed the innermost, unconscious drive; and the entire business of world history is (as we said) the work of bringing it to consciousness.

Thus, what we called the subjective aspect—needs, drives, passions, particular interests, as well as opinions and subjective views—all this is immediately apparent to consciousness (*für sich*). It makes its entrance in the guise of a natural being, or of a natural will. This imponderable mass of wills, interests, and activities—these are the tools and means of the World Spirit for achieving its goal, to elevate it to consciousness and to actualize it. And this goal is none other than to find itself, to come to itself, and to behold itself as actuality. But since those very life-forms of individuals and nations, in seeking to satisfy their own interests, are at the same time the tools and means of something higher and greater (of which they know nothing and which they fulfill unconsciously), all this could well be questioned, and it has been questioned. It has been denied, decried, and scorned in many ways as mere dreaming, mere "philosophy."

But on this question I have made my position clear from the very beginning. I laid down our presupposition (which is to appear only at the end, as the result of our investigation) and our belief, that Reason rules the world, which means that it has ruled history as well. Everything else is subordinate in relation to this universal and substantial Reason, in and for itself; it serves that Reason as its means. Moreover, this Reason is immanent in historical existence, and fulfills itself in and through it. The union of the universal, existing in and for itself, with the individual subjective aspect, so that this union alone is the truth—all this is speculative, and it is handled in this general form in metaphysical logic. But in the course of the world history itself, conceived as being still on the march, the pure end-goal of history is still not the content of need and interest; and although need and interest are unaware of the end-goal, the universal is still implicit in particular goals and fulfills itself in them.

The question [as to the union of the universal and the subjective] also takes the form of the union of *freedom* and *necessity*. For we regard the immanent development of Spirit as necessary because it is in and for itself, while we ascribe to freedom whatever appears in the conscious will of human beings as their interest. Since the speculative metaphysical aspect of this connection belongs to the sphere of logic, we cannot analyze it here. We can only mention the main points relevant to it.

It is demonstrated in philosophy that the Idea proceeds to its infinite antithesis: on the one hand there is the Idea in its freely universal mode wherein it remains self-sufficient (*bei sich*); and on the other hand there is the Idea as pure abstract reflection into itself (*in sich*), which is formal being for itself (*für sich*)—the ego or the formal freedom which belongs only to Spirit. Thus, on the one side, the universal Idea subsists as the substantial totality of things; and on the other side as the abstractness of arbitrary free will. This reflection into itself is the individual self-consciousness; it is the Other to the Idea in general, and thus it subsists in absolute finitude. For this very reason this Other is the finitude, the determinate element for the universal absolute: it is the side of the Absolute's existence, the ground of its formal reality, and the ground for the reverence due to God.

To grasp the absolute bonding of this antithesis—that is the profound task of metaphysics. Moreover, with the general positing of this finitude, all particularity is posited. In a formal sense, the Will wills itself, asserting the [singular] ego in everything that it intends and does. Even the pious individual wants to be saved, to be blessed [thus asserting his selfhood]. This pole of the antithesis, the individual existing for himself, is a particular entity—in contrast to the absolute universal essence—and it is as such that he knows this particularity of his and wills it. He is altogether at the standpoint of appearance. This is the sphere of particular aims, where the individuals assert themselves in their particularity, fulfilling it and actualizing it.

This standpoint, then, is also the standpoint of happiness or unhappiness. That individual is happy who has accommodated his existence to his particular character, will, and arbitrariness, so that he enjoys himself in his existence. But world history is not the place for happiness. Periods of happiness are empty pages in history, for they are the periods of harmony, times when the antithesis is missing. As reflection into self, this freedom is altogether abstract, it is the formal element of the activity of the absolute Idea. Activity is the unifying middle term of the syllogism: one pole is the universal, the Idea that rests in the inner pit of Spirit; the other pole is externality as such, objective matter. Activity is the middle term which translates the universal and internal into external objectivity.

I will try to make what I have said more evident and clear by giving some examples.

Building a house is, to begin with, an inner goal and purpose. As the means to that end, there are particular materials—iron, wood, stone. The elements are applied, in order to work up these materials: fire to melt the iron; air to blow up the fire; water to turn the wheels for cutting the wood, etc. The result is that the air, which helped in building the house, is now shut out by the house, since it excludes the wind; similarly the house keeps out streams of water because it excludes the rain; and insofar as the house is made fireproof it excludes the destructiveness of fire. The stones and beams are obedient to earth's gravity, and because they press downward high walls are set up. Thus the elements are utilized according to their nature, and yet they cooperate toward a product by which they themselves are being limited. In a similar way the human passions satisfy themselves; they fulfill their goals according to their natural determination and they bring forth the edifice of human society, in which they have provided for law and order as forces *against* themselves (i.e., restraining those passions).

The above-mentioned connection further entails the following: namely, that in world history the outcome of human actions is something other than what the agents aim at and actually achieve, something other than what they immediately know and will. They fulfill their own interests, but something further is thereby brought into being, something which is inwardly involved in what they do but which was not in their consciousness or part of their intention.

As an analogous example, let us consider the case of a man who, for revenge (and perhaps "justly," i.e., in return for an unjust injury) sets fire to another man's house. The immediate act is thus linked to further effects [on neighboring properties], i.e., effects which are in themselves external to the act and do not intrinsically belong to it. As such, the act involves merely the holding of a small flame to a small part of a roof beam. As yet, nothing more than this has been done—but further effects will follow of themselves. The ignited portion of the beam is connected to its other parts, and these to the woodwork of the entire house, this house to other houses nearby—and so a widespread conflagration ensues, which affects many more people than the one against whom the act of vengeance was directed, consuming their goods and property, and even costing many of them their lives. This result lay neither in the act as such, nor in the intention of the man who started it all.

But the action has yet another general aspect: the aim of the man who perpetrated the act of arson was to be revenged upon one individual through the destruction of his property; but arson is also a crime, and entails punishment. This may not have been in the consciousness of the perpetrator, still less in his intention. But this is [entailed in] his act in itself—and these are the universal, substantial aspects of it that are brought about by it. It is precisely this that should be kept in mind in this example: that there can be something more involved in the immediate action than what is in the intention or the consciousness of the agent. The example has a further implication, however: the substance of an action, and thus the action itself, can turn against the agent, recoiling against him, to destroy him.

This union of the two poles—the realization of the universal Idea in immediate actuality, and the elevation of the singular [agency] into universal truth— occurs, first of all, under the presupposition of the distinctness of the two sides and their indifference toward one another. In their actions, the agents have finite aims and particular interests, but they also know and think. The content of their aims is permeated by the universal and essential determinations of what is right, good, duty, etc. (Bare desire, volition in its crude and savage form, falls outside the theater and sphere of world history.) And these universal determinations, which are also the guidelines for aims and actions, have a specific content; for something as empty of content as the Good or the Good Will has no place at all in living actuality. If men are to act, they must not only will the good, but they must also know whether this or that is good.

But as for the question of just what is good or not good, right or not right—in the ordinary situations of private life, that question is answered by the laws and customs of a state. There is no great difficulty in knowing what these are. Every individual has his station in life, and he knows, on the whole, what the right and honorable course of action is. To declare, in ordinary private relations, that it is so difficult to choose what is right and good; to see a superior morality in finding difficulties and raising scruples—all this rather indicates an evil and perverse will. This is a will that seeks to evade its duties, which are not hard to know; or at best we may ascribe this to an idleness of thought, a small-minded will that gives itself not much to do, and thus falls into self-indulgence and moral smugness.

The situation is quite different in regard to the great historical relations. It is here that we find the great collisions between, on one hand, the system of established and recognized duties, laws, and rights, and, on the other, the possibilities which stand opposed to that system. These are possibilities that are injurious to the established order, destroying its foundations and its very existence—yet they have a content that can appear to be good, advantageous on the whole, even essential and necessary. These possiblities now become historical. They involve a universal concept, but one of a different sort from that which serves as the basis for the continued existence of a people or a state. This universal concept is a moving force of the productive Idea, an element of the truth that is forever striving toward itself, pressing on toward itself. The historical men —the *world-historical individuals*—are those whose aims embody a universal concept of this kind.

Caesar was such a man. At one point he was in danger of losing the position to which he had raised himself—a position, if not of predominance, at least of equality with the others who stood at the head of the state. Indeed, he was in danger of falling into the power of those who were about to become his enemies. These enemies, though they were pursuing their personal aims, had the formal state-structure on their side, with all the might of apparent legality. Caesar fought to retain his position, honor, and security—and since his opponents held power over the provinces, Caesar's victory over these men amounted to the conquest of the entire Roman empire. Thus, although he left the form of the state-structure unchanged, Caesar became the sole ruler of the state. The accomplishing of his originally negative aim—i.e., the autocratic control of Rome—was at the same time an essential determination in the history of Rome and of the world. It was not only the achievement of his personal victory; it was also an instinct that fulfilled what the time intrinsically demanded.

The great men in history are those whose own particular aims contain the substantial will that is the will of the World Spirit. They can be called *heroes*, because they have drawn their aim and their vocation not merely from the calm and orderly system that is the sanctified course of things, but rather from a source whose content is hidden and has not yet matured into present existence. This source is the inner Spirit that is as yet hidden beneath the surface; it knocks at the outer world as though that were a shell, and shatters it because that inner Spirit is a kernel that is different from the kernel in the outer world's shell. Thus, these men seem to create from within themselves, and their actions have produced a set of conditions and worldly relations which seem to be only *their* interest, and *their* work.

These heroic individuals, in fulfilling these aims of theirs, had no consciousness of the Idea at all. On the contrary, they were practical and political men. Yet at the same time they were thoughtful men, with insight into what was needed and what was timely: their insight was the very truth of their time and their world—the next species, so to speak, which was already there in the inner source. It was theirs to know it, this universal concept, the necessary next stage of their world—to make this their aim and to put their energy into it. The world-historical men, the heroes of an era, are therefore to be recognized as the insightful ones; their deeds and their words are the best of their time. Great men have worked to satisfy themselves, not others. Whatever they might have learned from others in the way of well-intentioned advice—all this would have been narrow-minded and distorted under the circumstances. For they were the ones who best understood what was right, and from them all the others learned it, and approved their actions, or at least accommodated themselves to them. The advanced Spirit is thus the inner soul of all individuals; but this is an unconscious inwardness which the great men bring to consciousness for them. This is why the others follow these soul-leaders; for they feel the irresistible force of their own spirit coming out in the heroes.

If we take another look at the final destiny of these world-historical individuals who had the calling to manage the affairs of the World Spirit, we find that their destiny was by no means happy. They attained no calm enjoyment, their entire life was toil and trou-

ble; their entire nature was nothing but their master-passion. Once their goal is achieved they fall away like empty shells from the kernel. They die young, like Alexander; they are murdered, like Caesar; they are exiled, like Napoleon to St. Helena. There is a horrible consolation in the fact that these historical men did not achieve what is called happiness—a happiness found only in private life, and under very different external circumstances—and this is a comfort that can be drawn from history by those who need it. But those who need that consolation are also the envious, who resent greatness and eminence, who seek to belittle greatness and to find fault with it. Thus, in modern times it has been demonstrated all too often that princes are not at all happy on their thrones—so that we are not to begrudge them their position, and are to be glad that it is they who are there, not we. The free man, however, is not envious, but gladly recognizes what is great and exalted, and rejoices in it.

It is in the light of these general elements, therefore—elements that constitute the interest and thus the passions of individuals—that these historical men are to be regarded. Men are great for having willed and accomplished something great—not something based on conceit or presumptuousness, but rather something right and necessary. This standpoint excludes the so-called psychological view which best serves the interests of envy, for it explains all actions as coming from some subjective source, great or small, in the individual—some pathological craving for the sake of which all his actions are done, as though there never had been anyone who acted from moral motives.

Alexander of Macedon conquered part of Greece, and then Asia—*therefore* he must have had a *craving* for conquest. Or he acted from a craving for fame, and the supposed proof that this is what drove him is that his actions did bring him fame. What schoolmaster has not demonstrated that Alexander the Great and Julius Caesar were driven by such passions, and that they were therefore immoral? And from this it immediately follows that he, the schoolmaster, is more admirable than they, since he has no such passions—the proof being that *he* has not conquered Asia nor defeated Darius and Porus, but that *he* is willing to live and let live.

These psychologists are particularly fond of latching on to the peculiarities of great historical figures as private persons. A man must eat and drink, he enters into relations with friends and acquaintances, he has feelings and moments of anger. As a familiar saying has it, "No man is a hero to his valet." To this I added—and Goethe repeated it ten years later—"but not because the former is no hero, but because the latter is a valet." He takes off the hero's boots, helps him into bed, knows that he likes his champagne, etc. Served by such psychological valets in historical writing, the historical personage comes off badly; he is degraded, brought down to the valet level, or even a few degrees below the morality of these fine connoisseurs of humanity. Homer's Thersites, who reproaches the kings, is a typical figure for all times. True, Thersites does not always get thumped with a stout stick, as he does in the Homeric era. But envy and egotism—these are the thorns in his flesh; and the undying worm that gnaws at him is the torturing thought that his admirable intentions and criticisms remain altogether ineffectual in the world. One may even take a certain malicious pleasure at the ultimate fate of Thersites.

A world-historical individual is not so circumspect as to want this, that, and the other, and to take account of everything; rather, he commits himself unreservedly to one purpose alone. So it happens that such individuals treat other interests, even sacred ones, in a casual way—a mode of conduct certainly open to moral censure. But so great a figure must necessarily trample on many an innocent flower, crushing much that gets in his way.

The particular interest linked to passion is thus inseparable from the actualization of the universal principle; for the universal is the outcome of the particular and determinate, and from its negation. It is the particular that is involved in the struggle with others, and of which one part is doomed to perish. It is not the universal Idea which involves itself in antithesis and struggle, exposing itself to danger; it remains in the background, and is preserved against attack or injury.

This may be called the *Cunning of Reason*, that it allows the passions to work for it, while what it brings into existence suffers loss and injury. This is the phenomenal world, part of which is negative, part posi-

tive. Compared to the universal, the particular is for the most part too slight in importance: individuals are surrendered and sacrificed. The Idea pays the ransom of existence and transience—not out of its own pocket, but with the passions of individuals.

Some might find it acceptable to see individuals sacrificed, along with their aims and fulfillments, consigning their happiness to the realm of chance (to which it belongs), and even to regard individuals altogether under the category of means to an end. Yet there is that aspect of theirs which we must refuse to see in this light, even for the sake of the highest goal, simply because there is that in individuals which is not to be made subordinate, but is something intrinsically eternal and divine. This is *morality, ethics, religious commitment*. Already when we spoke of the role of individuals in the actualization of the rational goal, we touched upon the subjective aspect, the interests of individuals, their needs and drives, their views and insights—and although we said that this was the formal aspect in them, it has an infinite right to be satisfied. In speaking of a "means", we at first imagine something merely external to the "end" and having no part in it. But in actuality even natural things in general, even the most common lifeless objects used as means must already be such as to be appropriate to their end and must have something in common with it. Humans do not see themselves as the "means" for the goals of Reason in that entirely external sense at all. On the contrary, not only do they use the occasion to satisfy their particular interests whose content is different from that goal, but they also have a part in that rational goal itself; for that very reason they are to be regarded as ends in themselves.

They are not ends in themselves in the merely formal sense, like the world of living things in general—so that the individual life could be subordinated to human life in general, and might justifiably be used as a means to it. On the contrary, humans are ends in themselves with respect to the content of the goal [of Reason]. This determines what we want to exclude from the category of means—morality, ethics, religion. In other words, the human being is an end in himself only by virtue of the divine in him—by virtue of what, from the very outset, was called "Reason", and called "freedom" too, because Reason is self-activating and self-determining. And although we cannot go into the further development of it here, we assert that morality, ethics and religion have their basis and their source in Reason and freedom, so that they are intrinsically exalted above necessity and chance.

But it must be said here that individuals—to the extent that they are aware of their freedom—are responsible for any ethical and religious deterioration, and for the weakening of ethics and religion. This is the seal of the absolutely high vocation of Man, that he or she knows what is good and what is evil, and that it is for him or her to will either the good or the evil. It is the mark of the human, in other words, to be capable of bearing such responsibility, not only for the evil but also for the good; and responsibility not only for this, that, or another thing, but responsibility for the good and evil stemming from his or her individual freedom. Animals alone are truly innocent. (It would, however, take an extensive analysis—as extensive as that needed for the analysis of freedom itself—in order to rule out or avoid all the usual misunderstandings involved in saying that what is called "innocence" means ignorance of evil itself.)

When we contemplate the fate that virtue, the ethical, even religion have suffered in history, we must not fall into the litany of lamentation, about how the good and pious often (or even for the most part) fare ill in the world, while the evil and wicked prosper. By the term "prosperity" one may understand a wide variety of things, including wealth, external honors, and the like. But when we speak of such things as though they were intrinsic goals, we still cannot make the so-called prosperity or misfortune of this or that single individual into an element of the rational world-order. To this world-goal there often goes the demand—with more of a justification than any demand for the happiness or the good fortune of individuals—that good, ethical, and righteous goals should find their realization and security in that world-goal, and under its auspices. What makes people morally dissatisfied (and this is a dissatisfaction upon which they pride themselves) is that they do not see the present as measuring up to the goals they hold as right and good. This applies especially to contemporary ideal models of political institutions—thus contrasting the way things *are* with the way they *ought* to be.

Here it is not the particular interest, not the passion, that demands to be satisfied, but rather the demands of Reason, Justice, and Freedom. And once it is furnished with this title, the demand becomes haughty, and it is not only dissatisfied (all too easily) with world conditions, but even rebels against them. To appreciate such feeling and such purposes, one must examine the demands raised, the dogmatic opinions asserted. At no time so much as in our own have general principles and ideas been raised up with greater pretentiousness. History usually presents itself as a struggle of passions. In our time, although there is no lack of passion, history shows itself (to some) to be predominantly the struggle between justifiable ideas and (to others) to be essentially the struggle of passions and subjective interests that merely pretend to have a higher justification of this kind. In the name of the final destiny of Reason, these pretended demands for justification are taken as absolute goals—in the same way as religion, ethics, morality.

As was said, nothing is more common today than the complaint that the *ideals* raised by fantasy are not being realized, that these glorious dreams are being destroyed by cold actuality. On their life-voyage, these ideals smash up on the rock of hard reality. They can only be subjective, after all; they belong to that individuality of the solitary subject (*Individualität des Einzelnen*) which takes itself for the highest and wisest. Ideals of that sort do not belong here—for, what the individual (*Individuum*) spins out for himself in his isolation (*Einzelheit*) cannot serve as law for the universal reality, just as the world's law is not for the single individual (*einzelnen Individuen*) alone (who may come off much worse for it).

But by the term "ideal" we also understand the ideal of Reason, of the good, the true. Poets such as Schiller have presented these ideals in very moving and emotional ways, with the feeling of deep sorrow at the fact that they may never be realized. If, on the contrary, we say that universal Reason does manifest itself in the world, then this certainly has nothing to do with any empirical detail—for that can be better or worse, since the elements of contingency, of particularity, receive from the Idea the power to exercise their tremendous authority in that sphere.

There is much to find fault with, therefore, in the details of the world of appearances. This subjective fault-finding—which is concerned only with the detail and its shortcomings, and does not recognize the universal Reason in it—is all too easy. Having the assurance of its good intentions for the well-being of the totality, together with the appearance of good-heartedness, it can give itself airs and make much of itself. It is easier to discern the shortcomings in individuals, in states, in providence, than to see their true significance. For in negative fault-finding one stands above the thing, notably and with a superior air, without being drawn into it, i.e., without having grasped the thing itself in its positive aspect. Generally, the critic mellows with age; youth is always dissatisfied. That mellowness of age is a ripeness of judgment—which not only accepts the bad, through disinterestedness, but is also led to what is substantial and solid in the matter in question by having been instructed more deeply by the seriousness of life.

The insight to which philosophy ought to lead, therefore (in contrast to what happens to those ideals), is that the real world is as it ought to be, that the truly good, the universal divine Reason, is also the power capable of actualizing itself. This good, this Reason—in its most concrete representation—is God. God governs the world: the content of His governance, the fulfillment of His plan, is world history. Philosophy seeks to understand this plan: for only what is fulfilled according to that plan has reality; what is not in accord with it, is but a worthless existence. In the pure light of this divine Idea (which is no mere ideal) the illusion that the world is a mad or foolish happening disappears. Philosophy seeks to know the content, the actuality of the divine Idea, and to justify the despised reality—for Reason is the perception of God's work.

As for the deterioration, the damage, and decline of religious, ethical, and moral aims and conditions in general, we must say this: Although these values are infinite and eternal in their inner essence, their external expressions can take on limited forms, which in their natural interrelatedness subsist under the command of contingency. This is why they are transitory,

and exposed to deterioration and damage. Religion and the ethical—like any other inherently universal essences—have the characteristic of being present in the individual soul (according to their concept, and therefore truly), even if they do not have in that soul the advantage of the full extent of culture or of application to fully developed circumstances. The religiosity or the ethics in a limited mode of life—of a shepherd, say, or of a peasant, limited in their concentrated inwardness to a few and altogether simple circumstances of life—has infinite value, the same value as the religiosity and ethics of a cultivated intellect, and of an existence that is rich in the scope of its relations and activities.

This inner center, this simple region of the rights of subjective freedom; the seat of volition, resolution, and action, and of the abstract content of conscience, embracing the responsibility and worth of the individual—all this remains untouched, entirely removed from the loud noise of world history, removed not only from the external and temporal changes, but also from those changes that are entailed by the absolute necessity of the concept of freedom itself. In general, however, there is this point to be noted: that whatever can claim to be noble and grand in the world still has something higher above it. The claim of the World Spirit supersedes all particular claims.

This may suffice in regard to the means used by the World Spirit for the realization of its concept. Simply and abstractly, the "means" is the activity of those in whom Reason is present as their intrinsically substantial essence—though primarily as a still obscure ground, one that is hidden from them. The matter becomes more complex and more difficult, however, when we regard individuals not merely as active, but more concretely, with the more definite content of their religion and ethics—for these factors have a part in Reason, and hence in its absolute rights. Here the bare relation of means-to-end falls away, and the principal points of view that have arisen regarding the bearing of the absolute goal of Spirit upon this aspect of life have been briefly considered.

III.   THE STATE AS REALIZATION OF SPIRIT. The third point to be considered is the goal to be achieved by these means, i.e., the form it takes in actuality. We have spoken of "means"; but in the fulfillment of a finite subjective goal there is also a *material* element, which is already there or must be provided for the actualization. On this analogy the question would be: What is the material in which the rational end-goal is to be realized? Again, it is primarily the human subject, human needs, subjectivity in general. The rational comes to existence in human knowing and willing, as its material.

We have considered the subjective will—how it has an aim which is made the truth of a reality, and especially insofar as this is a great world-historical passion. As a subjective will, with limited passions, the human will is dependent; and it can only satisfy its particular aims within the limits of this dependency. Yet the subjective will also has a substantial life of its own, an acutality within which it moves among essences, and has the essential itself as the goal of its existence.

This essential being is itself the union of two wills: the subjective will and the rational will. This is an ethical totality, the *state*. It is the reality wherein the individual has and enjoys his freedom—but only insofar as he knows, believes, and wills the universal. Yet we ought not to understand this as though the subjective will of the individual came to its fulfillment and enjoyment by way of the common or universal will, with the common will serving as a mere means for the individual—as if the individual were to limit his freedom among other individuals, so that this mutual limitation and inconvenience would provide for each some small space for movement. As against this negative concept of freedom, it is rather law, ethical life, the state (and they alone) that comprise the positive reality and satisfaction of freedom. The freedom which is limited in the state is that of caprice, the freedom that relates to the particularity of individual needs.

The subjective will—passion—is the actuating element, the realizing force [of Reason]. The Idea is the inner source. The State is the externally existing, genuinely ethical life. It is the union of the universal essential will with the subjective will—and this is ethics. The individual, living in this union, has his own ethical life, he has a value consisting in this substantiality alone. Sophocles' Antigone says: "The divine commands are not of yesterday, nor of today—no, they live forever, and no one can say whence they came." The laws of ethics are not accidental, but are the rational itself. The proper goal of the State is to make this substantiality count in the actual doings of human beings and in their convictions, making it present and self-sustaining there.

It is the absolute interest of Reason that this ethical whole should be present. And herein lies the justification and the merit of the heroes who founded states, no matter how crude. In world history we are concerned only with those peoples that have formed states. For we must understand that the State is the realization of freedom, i.e., of the absolute end-goal, and that it exists for its own sake. We must understand, further, that all the value that human beings possess, all of their spiritual reality, they have through the State alone. Their spiritual reality consists in the fact that their essence—rationality—is objectively there for them as knowers, and that the rationality has an immediate objective existence for them. Only in that way is a man a consciousness, with an ethical way of life, the legal and ethical life of the State. For the True, is as we said, the union of the universal (or general) will and subjective will; and the universal dimension is in the State's laws, in the universal and rational arrangements.

The State is the divine Idea, as it exists on earth. In this perspective, the State is the precise object of world history in general. It is in the State that freedom attains its objectivity, and lives in the enjoyment of this objectivity. For the law of the State is the objectification of Spirit; it is will in its true form. Only the will that is obedient to the law is free, for it obeys itself and, being self-sufficient, it is free. Insofar as the State, our country, constitutes a community of existence, and insofar as the subjective will of human beings submits to laws, the antithesis between freedom and necessity disappears. The rational is the necessary, the substantiality of a shared existence; and we are free to the extent that we acknowledge it as law, and follow it as the very substance of our being. The objective and the subjective will are then reconciled, as one and the same serene whole.

The ethical life of the State is not of the moral or reflective kind, wherein one's individual conviction rules supreme. This latter is more appropriate to the modern world; the true ethics of antiquity is rooted in the principle of abiding by one's duty. An Athenian citizen did what was required of him as if by instinct. But if I reflect upon the object of my activity, I must have the consciousness that my will has been called upon. Ethical life, however, is the sense of duty (unquestioned, unconscious), the substantial law—a "second nature," as it has rightly been called (since the "first nature" of human beings is our immediate animal being).

The detailed development of the concept of the State is for the philosophy of right to provide—although we must point out that in the legal theories of our time, various errors are current which are taken for established truths and have become prejudices. We will mention just a few, principally those related to the goal of our [philosophical study of] history.

A. *The theory that confronts us first* is the direct contrary to our concept of the State as the actualization of freedom: namely, the view that the human being is free by nature, but that in society and in the state (of which he is necessarily a part) he must limit this natural freedom of his. That the human being is free by nature is entirely correct, in the sense that he is free according to the concept of humanity; but for that very reason man is free only in terms of his implicit destiny (which is there to be fulfilled). The "nature" of a thing always amounts to the same thing as its "concept"; but it is true that the concept of humanity does include the way the human being exists in his merely natural immediate existence.

The theory before us assumes, generally, a "state of nature." Man is represented as possessing natural rights and enjoying the unlimited exercise of his freedom. This assumption is not directly taken for historical fact. There would also be some difficulty, if it were taken seriously, in providing a proof that any such a natural condition existed in the present or anywhere in the past. One can certainly point to the existence of savage conditions, but these are shown to be linked to the passions, to barbarism and acts of violence—and yet these are linked, however primitive they are, to social institutions involving so-called limitations of freedom. The assumption is one of those nebulous images

necessarily produced by the theory (i.e., the image of the noble savage) to which it ascribes existence, without historical justification.

What we find such a "state of nature" to be, in its empirical existence, corresponds equally well to the concept of it. Freedom, as the ideal dimension of original nature, does not exist as an original and natural state. On the contrary, it must first be achieved and won, and indeed won through an endless process involving the discipline of knowledge and will. So, the "state of nature" is not an ideal condition, but a condition of injustice, of violence, of untamed natural drives, inhuman acts, and emotions. There is, to be sure, a limitation imposed upon this state of nature by society and the civil state, but it is no more than a limiting of blunt emotions and crude impulses, as well as the limiting of the reflective arbitrariness of caprice and passion. This limitation is part of the process through which the eventual consciousness of freedom and will to be truly free (according to the concept of freedom, i.e., as rational) is first brought forth. According to that concept, freedom involves law and morality, and these are—in and for themselves—universal essences, objects and aims. These must first be found through the activity of self-developing thought, in opposition to sense experience. Then they must be absorbed and incorporated into the primarily sensuous will, even against its natural inclination.

Freedom is forever misunderstood in this way, being known in only a formal, subjective sense, abstracted from its essential objects and aims. This is why the limiting of the impulses, desires, passions that are proper to the particular individual, as such—the limiting of arbitrary caprice—is taken to be a limiting of freedom. On the contrary, such limitation is simply the condition from which emancipation proceeds; and society and the State are the conditions wherein freedom is actualized.

B. *There is a second theory to be mentioned*, and this denies the general development of [abstract] Right into the form of Law. The *patriarchal* condition (prevailing either in the entire human race, or at least in some single branches of it) is regarded as the situation in which the ethical and emotional element finds its fulfillment, along with the element of [abstract] Right. Only in connection with these ethical and emotional elements [says this theory] can justice be truly exercised in accord with its content. The patriarchal condition is based upon the family relation, in which the absolutely primitive form of ethical life is consciously developed, followed by the higher form in the state. The patriarchal relation is a transitional condition: the family having grown into a tribe or a people, the unifying bond has ceased to be the bond of love and trust, and has become one of service.

Here we must speak primarily of the ethics of family life. The family may be seen as a single person: in that case, its members have either surrendered their personal claims against one another, along with their legal claims, their extended personal interests, and their selfishness (as in the case of parents); or else they have not yet arrived at the point of asserting such claims against one another (as in the case of children, who are initially in that state of nature discussed above). They are therefore immersed in a unity of feeling, of love, of trust and faith in one another. In this union of love, the individual has the consciousness of self in the consciousness of the other; the individual self is externalized, and in this mutual externalization the individual has won self-hood—and each has gained the other's self with his or her own, since each is at one with the other.

The further interests involved in the needs and external concerns of life (along with the internal development of those interests in regard to the children) constitute a common purpose for the family. The spirit of the family (e.g., in the Roman Penates) is as much *one* substantial entity as is the Spirit of a people in their state. In both, ethical life consists in the feeling, the consciousness, and the will—not of the individual personality and its interests, but of the common personality and interests of all the members in general. But in the family this unity is one of feeling, remaining within the limits of the natural order of things. This piety of family-feeling has to be respected to the highest degree by the state. As a result of this family-feeling, the state has, as its members, individuals who are already ethical in themselves (which they would not be as self-interested persons); and as its members they

bring to the state its solid foundation, because each one feels himself to be united with the totality. But the extension of the family to a patriarchal whole goes beyond blood-ties (the natural aspect); and outside these ties, individuals must assume the status of [distinct] persons.

If we were to consider the patriarchal relation in its wider scope, we would be led to a discussion of theocracy: the head of the patriarchal tribe is also its priest. Where the family has not yet been distinguished from civil society and the state, the separation of religion from the family has not yet happened either—and insofar as the piety of family-feeling itself remains an inwardness of feeling, it is not likely to happen.

We have considered two aspects of freedom—the objective and the subjective. Now if freedom means that the individuals give their consent, then it is easy to see that only the subjective element is meant. What follows naturally from this principle is that no law can be valid unless everyone agrees to it. And immediately we come to the implication that the minority view must yield to the majority—the greater number decides. But then, as Jean-Jacques Rousseau noted, there is no longer any freedom, since the will of the minority is no longer taken into account. In the Polish parliament, each individual member had to consent before a law was passed—and for the sake of that freedom the state collapsed. Moreover, it is a false and dangerous assumption that *only* the people possess reason and insight, and know what is right. Any faction of the people can put itself forward as standing for the People. But what really constitutes a state is a matter of trained intelligence, not a matter of "the people."

If the only criterion of political liberty is the principle of the will of the individual—namely, that each individual is to give his or her consent to everything done by or for the state, and that without such unanimous consent no decision can be taken—then there is actually no such thing as an independent *form of government* operating autonomously. Presumably, the only arrangement that would then be needed would be, first, a neutral center (without any will) that would note what seemed (to it) to be the needs of the state, and would communicate its views; and, second, a mechanism for assembling all individuals and tabulating their votes for the various propositions before them; in that way the decision would be already made.

The state is an abstraction, having its merely general reality in its citizens; but it is actual, and its merely general existence must define itself as an individual will and activity. This creates the need for government and administration in general, involving the selection of individuals to take the helm in political affairs: they must take decisions about these matters, determine how those decisions are to be carried out, and direct the citizens in the implementation of them. Thus, even in a democracy, if the people decide to embark on a war, there must be a general to lead the army.

Only by means of the state-structure does the abstraction that is the state acquire life and actuality—and in any such structure there is a difference between those who command and those who obey. Obedience, however, seems to be inconsistent with freedom—and those who are in command seem to be doing precisely what contradicts the concept of freedom, which is the very basis of the state. If, then, the difference between commanding and obeying is a necessary one, because otherwise nothing would get done (though indeed this seems only a matter of necessity, something external and contrary to freedom abstractly understood), then the institutions of government must at least be such that as few as possible of the citizens have merely to obey, and the authorities have as little arbitrary power as possible. The range within which commanding authority is necessary should be for the people to decide; in its main outline it should be determined by the will of the many or of every individual citizen, for in that way the state, as an actuality and as an individuated unity, will gain its force and strength.

The primary consideration, above all, is the difference between those who govern and those who are governed. The forms of governance have been correctly classified into monarchy, aristocracy, and democracy. Here we must note, however, that monarchy itself can be divided again into despotism and monarchy proper. In all these merely conceptual classifications, it is only the fundamental differences that are emphasized. These are therefore not to be taken as exhausting the concrete possibilities of forms, types, or modes of government. It is significant that the types of government admit of many variations, not only as subtypes of the above, but also as mixtures of these essential types of order, mixtures which are formless, untenable and inconsistent distortions of those forms. In this clash of forms, therefore, the question is: Which is the *best* form of government? That is, through what arrangements, organization, or mechanism of state power is the intrinsic purpose of the state fulfilled most effectively?

Of course, this purpose can be seen in a variety of ways—e.g., as the calm enjoyment of civil life, or as universal happiness. Goals of this kind have resulted in the formulation of so-called ideals of government, including ideals involving the education of princes (Fenelon) or of the rulers, as the aristocracy in general (Plato). The main emphasis was on the nature of those who stand at the head of the state—and in ideal accounts of this kind, no thought was given to the content of the state's organic institutions. The question as to the best form of government is often stated not only as though the theory about it is a matter of free subjective conviction, but also as though the actual introduction of one form (as the one recognized to be best or as a better one) were the consequence of an entirely theoretical decision—as though the type of government were nothing more than a matter of free choice determined by reflection. In this altogether naive sense, the Persian leaders (though not the Persian people) deliberated about what form of government they wished to introduce into Persia. They had conspired to overthrow the false Smerdis and the Magi; and after the success of the conspiracy they deliberated on the form of government because there was no heir to the throne, and Herodotus tells the story of that deliberation with the same naiveté.*

Nowadays, the form of government of a land or a people is not represented as being so entirely dependent on their free choice. The underlying conception of freedom, regarded abstractly, has led to the widespread acceptance of the theory that the *republic* counts as the only just and genuine form of government. And there are many men who—despite the fact

*Herodotus, The Persian Wars, Book III, Ch. 80–83. [Translator's note.]

that they occupy high posts in monarchical systems of government—are not opposed to the idea of a republic and even support it. Yet they realize that although the republic may be the best of systems, it cannot be instituted everywhere. And so they realize that—people being what they are—we must be content with less freedom; and that under existing circumstances, given that moral condition of the people, the most useful form of government may be monarchy. Even in this view, although the necessity of a certain form of government is seen to be dependent on the condition of a people, that condition itself is regarded only as the result of external contingency. Such a view is based on the intellectually reflective division between the concept and its reality: either the intellect holds to a merely abstract (and hence untrue) concept; or it does not grasp the idea itself; or (what amounts to the same thing in terms of content, though not in formal terms) the intellect lacks a concrete awareness of what a people or state is.

Further on we shall show that a people's form of government comprises one substance—one spirit—with its religion, its art, and philosophy, or at least with its thoughts and imaginings, its culture in general (not to mention other influences of an external sort, such as the climate, its neighbors, its place in the world). A state is an individual totality, from which it is impossible to isolate all by itself a particular aspect such as its form of government (although that aspect is of the highest importance); no one aspect is to be deliberated upon and voted upon in that isolated form. Not only is the form of government intimately connected with those other spiritual forces and dependent upon them, but the characterization of the entire spiritual individuality, including all its powers, is only one element in the history of the totality: it has been predetermined in the course of that history, and its history comprises the highest sanction of the constitution, as well as its highest necessity.

The first formation of a state is authoritarian and instinctive. Yet even force, obedience, and fear of a despotic ruler already involve some connection of wills. In the primitive state, it is already the case that the particular will of the individuals (*Individuen*) does not count; one's own particularity (*Particularität*) is set aside, and the universal will (*allgemeine Wille*) is what is essential. This unity of the universal and the individual (*Einzelne*) is the Idea itself, which is now present as the state and which goes on to develop itself further. The abstract (although necessary) course in the development of truly independent states, therefore, is that they begin with monarchy (whether it be patriarchal and pastoral or warlike). Then particularity (*Besonderheit*) and individuality (*Einzelnheit*) assert themselves—in aristocracy or democracy. The conclusion of the process is that this particularity is subjected to *one* power, which can be no other than [constitutional] monarchy—such that the particular spheres have their independence apart from it. Thus we must distinguish between a first and a second form of monarchy. This progression is a necessary one, such that each form of government in the sequence is not a matter of choice, but rather is such as to conform to the Spirit of the people.

What is important in deciding the form of a state, its constitution, is the development of the rational condition, i.e., the political condition as such, the liberation of the conceptual elements—so that the particular powers are separated from one another and become complete in themselves, yet in their very freedom cooperating toward one purpose and being sustained by it; in short, forming an organic whole. Thus the state is freedom subsisting on its own account, rationally self-conscious, and objectively knowing itself to be such. Its objectivity is in the very fact that its elements are not merely present in a set of ideals, but are rather to be found in a characteristic reality. And in their effective self-relation, these elements pass over into that activity whereby the totality, the soul, the individual unity is produced as their result.

The state is the Idea of Spirit in the externalized form of human will and its freedom. It is in the state, therefore, that historical change occurs essentially, and the elements of the Idea are reflected in the state as various political *principles*. The forms of government, in which the world-historical peoples have blossomed, are characteristic of those peoples. Thus the various forms do not present one universal basis of government—as though the differences consisted only in determinate modes of expression and development [of this universal basis]. Rather, there is a difference, here, in the underlying principles themselves.

Accordingly, when we compare the forms of government of ancient world-historical peoples, there is nothing they can tell us regarding the ultimate principle of the state, as a principle that would be applicable to our own time. In the fields of science and art, the matter is quite different: ancient philosophy provides the basis for modern philosophy to such a degree that the ancient is contained in the modern. The relationship that appears, here, is that of an unbroken development of one edifice, whose foundation, walls, and roof have remained the same. And in art, that of the Greeks sets the highest standard just as it is. But in regard to the types of government the situation is quite different: the ancient and the modern have no essential principle in common. To be sure, there are abstract definitions and doctrines concerning lawful government, to the effect that intelligence and virtue should rule—these ideas are certainly shared. Yet nothing is more misguided than to look for models among the Greeks, the Romans, or Orientals for the constitutional structures of our own time. From Oriental culture we have fine pictures of patriarchal conditions, paternalistic government, and devotion on the part of the peoples; from the Greeks and Romans we have descriptions of popular freedom, where the constitution admitted all citizens to participation in the deliberations and decisions concerning general affairs and laws.

This is the general opinion in our time as well—but with the modification that since our states are so large and the population so multitudinous, the people must express its will, not directly but indirectly, through its representatives, who contribute to decisions concerning public affairs and laws. The so-called representative system of government is the logical form to which we link our image of a free system, and this link has become a firm prejudice. In it, the people are separated from the government. But there is something malicious in this antithesis: it is a trick of bad will, suggesting that the people are the totality of the state after all. Underlying this idea, moreover, is the principle of individuality, the absoluteness of subjective will (which we discussed above).

The main point [against this mistake] is that this freedom, as defined by its concept, is not based on subjective will and caprice, as its principle, but on the insight into the universal will; and that the system of freedom is the free development of its elements. Subjective will is an entirely formal concept, which does not in any way entail *what* it is that is willed. Only the rational will is this universal will, which determines and develops itself in itself, and unfolds its elements as its organic parts. The ancients knew nothing of this "gothic" intellectual architecture of Reason.

Earlier we set up two elements for consideration: the first was the Idea of freedom as the absolute end-goal; the second was the means to that end, the subjective aspect in knowing and willing, with all their vitality, movement, and activity. Then we went on to see the state as the ethical whole and the reality of freedom, and hence as the objective unity of both those preceding elements. For although we have distinguished the two sides for the purpose of our discussion, it must be carefully noted that they cohere together exactly, and that this mutual entailment is to be found in each of the two elements when we examine each separately.

On one hand we have recognized the Idea, in its determinacy, as the freedom that knows and wills itself, and has only itself as its goal. This is the simple concept of Reason—and at the same time it is what we called the subject, self-consciousness, the Spirit as it exists in the world. If, on the other hand, we consider subjectivity itself, we find that the process of subjective knowing and willing is [nothing other than] thinking. But insofar as I thoughtfully know and will, I will the universal object, the substance of what is in and for itself rational.

Thus we see an intrinsic unification of the objective aspect, the concept, with the subjective aspect. The objective existence of this unification is the state, which is therefore the basis and the center of the other concrete aspects of the life of a people—its art, its laws, its ethics, its religion, its science. All spiritual activity has this goal alone, to make itself aware of this unification, i.e., of its freedom.

Among the different forms of this conscious unification [combining the objective and the subjective], *religion* stands at the pinnacle. Here the existing worldly Spirit becomes aware of the absolute Spirit—and in this consciousness of the essence in and for itself, the human will renounces its particular interest. In devotion all this is set aside, and there is no longer any concern with particulars. Through [acts of] sacrifice we express our renunciation of our property, of our will, and of our particular perceptions. The religious concentration of mind appears as feeling, yet it also goes over into meditation: [active] worship is meditation externalized.

In *art* we have the second form of the unification of the objective and the subjective in Spirit. Art enters more into actuality and sense experience than religion does: in its noblest posture, it is there to present not the mind of God, of course, but the outer form of God, and thus the divine and the spiritual as such. Through art, the divine becomes visible: to fantasy and to sight.

The True, however, does not just achieve representation and feeling (as in religion), and the visual (as in art); it also comes to the thinking Spirit—and we thereby arrive at the third form of the unification: *philosophy*, the highest, the freest, and the wisest configuration of Spirit. We can not propose to consider these three configurations here; all we can do is mention them, since they occupy the same ground as does the object of our study, the *state*.

The universal [dimension] that manifests itself in the state and is known in it—the form which is to include all that is—comprises the *culture* of a nation, taken altogether. The specific content, however, which takes on the form of universality and which inheres in the concrete actuality that is the state, is the Spirit of the people itself. The actual state is animated by this Spirit in all its particular affairs, wars, institutions, etc. But man must also know of this Spirit of his, as his own essence, and create for himself the consciousness of his own unity with it, a unity that is fundamental. For we said that the ethical is the union of the subjective and the universal will. Spirit, however, must come to an explicit consciousness of this union, and the center-point of such knowing is *religion*. Art and philosophy are only the different aspects and forms of this same content.

In considering religion, the question is whether it knows the True, the Idea, in its division or in its true unity. As the Idea in its division, [religion knows] God as the abstractly supreme being, the Lord of heaven and earth, above and beyond all else, and excluded from human actuality. As the Idea in its unity, [religion knows] God as the unity of universal and individual (*Einzelne*), since in Him the individual is seen positively as well, in the idea of the Incarnation. Religion is the place wherein a people gives itself the definition of what it holds to be true. The definition comprises everything belonging to the essentiality of the object, and in it the nature of the object is reduced to a simple basic determination, as the mirror of all determinacy—the universal soul of all particular things. Thus the representation of God constitutes the general foundation of a people [i.e., of its conscious unity].

In this aspect, religion stands in the closest connection to the principle of the state. There can be freedom only where individuality (*Individualität*) is recognized as a positive [aspect] of the divine being. But there is a further connection between religion and the state: on the negative side, secular reality is seen as merely temporal, as motivating itself in individual interests (*in einzelnen Interessen*), and therefore as relative and having no justification. Secular reality is justified only insofar as its absolute soul, its principle, is justified absolutely; and it receives this justification only by being recognized as the manifestation of the essence of God. It is for this reason that the state rests upon religion.

In our time we hear this repeated often—that the state rests on religion—and most of the time nothing more is meant than that God-fearing individuals are the more inclined and ready to do their duty because obedience to the sovereign and the law is so easily linked to the fear of God. Certainly, the fear of God, by placing the universal aim above the particular individual, can also turn against the latter,* can become fanatical and act against the state, burning its build-

---

*This is unclear unless we take "the latter" as a mistaken transcription of Hegel's lecture. Obviously, it should read "the former", since it is against the state (the universal) that the said actions are taken. [Translator's note.]

ings and destroying its institutions. So the received opinion is that the fear of God should be moderated and should be held with a certain coolness, lest it turn against what is supposed to be protected and maintained by it, and overwhelm it in a storm. Religion has within it at least the possibility of doing just that.

Having arrived at the correct conviction that the state rests on religion, religion can take the position that the state is already there, and that in order to maintain the state, religion must be brought in—in buckets and bushels—to be impressed on people's minds. It is entirely correct that people should be trained in religion, but not in something that is not yet there. For when we say that the state is founded on religion, that the state has its roots in religion, then we mean essentially that religion is prior, and that the state has arisen from it and continues to do so. Or, in other words, the state's principles must be regarded as valid in and for themselves; and they can only be so regarded inasmuch as they are acknowledged to be determinations of the divine nature itself. Thus whatever the nature of the shared religion may be, the nature of the state and its structure must agree with it. The state has truly arisen from religion in the sense that the Athenian or the Roman state, for example, was possible only in the context of the specific paganism of these peoples; similarly, a Catholic state will have a spirit and structure that are different from those of a Protestant state.

That call—that urge and drive—to implant religion in the state, could be taken as a cry of fear and distress (as it so often seems to be), expressing the danger that religion is about to disappear from the state or has already done so. But in that case, the situation would be serious, even more serious than the call intends: for in it there is the belief that religion can be implanted and inculcated as a defense against evil. But religion is not at all such an instrument. As an instrument in the production of itself, the self-productive process goes far deeper.

Another and quite opposite foolishness we meet within our own time is that of trying to invent and institute types of government without taking account of religion. The Catholic religion (although, like Protestantism, a form of Christianity) does not ascribe to the state the inherent justice and ethical status that lie in the inwardness of the Protestant principle. That sundering of constitutional law from the ethical arises necessarily from the very nature of Catholicism, which does not recognize law and the ethical as independent, as substantial. But these constitutional principles and institutions—once they are torn away from inwardness, from the last sanctuary of conscience, the quiet place where religion resides—do not have an actual [conscious] center, because they remain abstract and indefinite.

Let us now sum up what we have said about the State: The vitality of the State in the individual citizens is what we have called its ethical life. The laws and institutions of the State are the rights of its citizens. Its nature, its soil, its mountains, air, and waters —these are *their* land, their country, their outward property. The history of the state is in their acts, and what their ancestors have achieved belongs to the citizens of today and lives in their memory. All of this is their possession, just as they are possessed by it, for it constitutes their substance, their being.

Their imagination is filled with all this, and their will is the willing of these laws and this country. It is the temporal whole that constitutes one being, the Spirit of one people. To it belong the individual citizens: each individual is the child of his people, and likewise the child of his time (insofar as the state is seen to be in the process of developing). No one is left behind by his time, nor can he overstep. This spiritual entity is his very own, and he is its representative. It is that context in which he stands, and from which he goes forth. Among the Athenians, Athens had a double meaning: first, it meant the totality of its institutions; but then also the goddess, who displayed the Spirit of the people, its unity.

This Spirit of a people is a *determinate* spirit, and it is also determined by the historic stage of its development, as we have just said. This spirit therefore constitutes the basis and the content of its self-consciousness in the various forms of which we have spoken [i.e., art, religion, and philosophy]. For in its consciousness of itself, Spirit must be objective to itself; and objectivity immediately involves the emergence of differences which subsist as the totality of all the differentiated spheres of objective spirit. In the same way, the soul exists only insofar as it is an organization of its members, which—by taking themselves together in its simple unity—produce the soul. Thus the people is *one* individuality in its essence: in religion it is pictured, worshipped and enjoyed as God in His essence; in art it is displayed in imagery and vision; in philosophy it is recognized and comprehended as thought. Because of the fundamental identity of their substance, their content and object, these configurations stand in an indissoluble unity with the Spirit of the state. The form of the state as we know it can exist only in the context of a definite religion—just as only *this* philosophy and only *this* art can exist in *this* state.

Moreover, the determinate National Spirit is only *one* individual in the course of world history—for world history is the displaying of the divine, the absolute development of Spirit in its highest forms. In this sequence of stages, it attains self-consciousness, which is its truth. The configurations of these stages are the world-historical National Spirits—the determinate shapes of their ethical life, their form of government, their art, religion, and philosophy. The boundless drive of the World Spirit, its irresistible thrust, is toward the realization of these stages—for this articulation of stages, together with their realization, comprise the concept of Spirit.

World history only shows us how the World Spirit comes gradually to the consciousness of truth and the willing of it. This consciousness and will dawns in the Spirit; Spirit finds its main points, and in the end it arrives at full consciousness.

HEGEL
Philosophy of Right

WORLD HISTORY

341. *Universal Spirit* comes into existence through a variety of elements: in art it is through the element of vision and image; in religion it is through feeling and representational thinking; in philosophy it is through thought pure and free. In world history it is through the element of spiritual actuality in its entire scope of internal and external expression. World history is a court of judgment—because in its implicit and explicit *universality*, the *particular* is present only as *ideal* (whether it be the Roman Penates, civil society, or the different national spirits in all their diversity). And the activity of Spirit in this element has to make this plain.

342. Moreover, world history does not just render a verdict of might—i.e., it is not the abstract and non-rational necessity of a blind fate. On the contrary —since Spirit is implicitly and explicitly Reason, and becomes explicit to itself only in knowledge—world history is the necessary development of the elements of Reason out of the concept of Spirit's freedom alone, along with the self-consciousness and freedom of Spirit. It is the display and *actualization* of the universal Spirit.

343. Spirit's history is its *act*. Spirit is only what it does, and its act is to make itself the object of its own consciousness, to apprehend itself as Spirit, explaining itself to itself. This self-apprehension is Spirit's very being; and the *fulfillment* of this apprehension is at one and the same time the externalization of Spirit and the transition beyond it. To say it in formal terms, we can speak of our apprehending that apprehension anew; and then the return of Spirit into itself after its externalization is Spirit at a higher stage than the initial apprehension.

[Reprinted from Hegel, *Introduction to the Philosophy of History*, translated by Leo Rauch. (Indianapolis: Hackett Publishing Company, 1988), by permission of the publisher.]

[*Remark:*] The question that arises here is that of *perfectibility* of mankind—as discussed, for example, in Lessing's *Education of the Human Race* (1780). Those who have argued for such perfectibility have a notion of the human spirit: that it is in man's nature to have "Know Thyself" as a law of his *being;* and that to the extent that he grasps what *he is*, he has risen to a higher form than that which constituted his mere being, earlier. But to those who reject this thought, "Spirit" has remained an empty word—just as history has remained, for them, a superficial play of *accidental,* "merely human" strivings and passions (as they are called). Even if these critics speak of history in terms of *Providence* and its *Plan*, and thus express a faith in a higher power, the plan of Providence remains an empty idea for them, since they expressly declare that it is unknowable and incomprehensible.

344. In this activity of the World Spirit, states, nations, and individuals arise with their *particular determinate principle*. This principle is displayed and actualized in their form of government and in the entire range of their conditions. These states, nations, and individuals are aware of all this, and are deeply committed to the interests involved. Yet at the same time they are the unconscious tools and organs of the World Spirit in its deep activity, wherein these forms pass away, while the Spirit implicitly and explicitly prepares and works out its own transition to its next higher stage.

345. The concepts of justice and virtue; wrongdoing, force, and vice; talents and their achievements; passions, great and small; guilt and innocence; grandeur in individual and national life; independence, happiness and unhappiness for states and single individuals—all these have their distinct meaning and value in the sphere of conscious actuality. In that sphere they are judged and find their justification (however incomplete it may be). World history falls outside these viewpoints. In it, the necessary element of the Idea of

738

the World Spirit is its present stage; and this receives its *absolute* legitimation in history. And the nation which expresses that Idea in its own achievements receives fulfillment, happiness, and fame.

346. History is the configuration of Spirit in the form of what happens, i.e., in the form of immediate natural actuality. For this reason, the stages of its development are out there as *immediate natural principles*. And these principles, because they are natural, are a multitude of independent units, so that only *one* of them pertains to any *one* nation. This is its *geographic* and *anthropological* existence.

347. The nation—to which such an instance of the Idea pertains as a *natural* principle—is entrusted with implementing it as the World Spirit progresses in developing its self-consciousness. This nation is predominant in world history for this epoch—*and only once can it be predominant* and *epoch-making in history*. (See paragraph 346.) This nation has an absolute right as the vehicle of the World Spirit in the present stage of its development. Against it, the spirits of other nations have no rights—and they, along with those whose epoch has passed, do not count at that time in world history.

[*Remark:*] The specific history of a world-historical nation comprises, on the one hand, the development of its principle from its infantile condition in the husk, to the time when it blossoms into its free ethical self-consciousness, and it forces its way into universal history. But on the other hand it also comprises the period of that nation's decline and fall—for that is how the emergence of a higher principle is marked upon it as the negating of its own. This signifies the transition of Spirit into that higher principle, and therefore the passing of world history to *another* nation. The declining nation has by then lost its absolute interest; and even if it adopts the higher principle for itself as something positive, this is not something immanently vital for it. It may lose its independence; or it may drag on as a particular state or part of a group of states, involving itself, according to circumstances, in various enterprises at home or wars abroad.

348. At the actual point of all actions, including world-historical ones, *individuals* are the agents that give subjectivity to what is substantial. They are the vi-

talizing force behind the substantial deed of the World Spirit, and are thus directly identical with it, although its aim and object is hidden from them. (See paragraph 344.) For this they receive no honor or gratitude from their contemporary world, nor from the public opinon of the later world—but their share at the hands of that public opinion is *undying fame* as the formal subjective agents of those deeds.

349. At its beginning, a nation is not yet a state. The transition from a family, a horde, a tribe, a multitude, etc., to the condition of being a state—this constitutes the *formal* realization of the Idea in general, in that nation. A nation is, *implicitly*, an ethical substance. But without the formal condition of statehood it lacks a universal and universally valid objectification in laws as its conscious characteristics—and therefore it is not recognized, either by itself or by others. Without objective legality and rationality explicitly established (by means of government), a nation's independence is merely formal, and is not yet sovereignty.

[*Remark:*] Even in the ordinary view of things, no one calls a patriarchal condition a government, or a nation in this condition a state, or its independence sovereignty. Prior to actual history, therefore, we have either a condition of dull innocence, without all interest, or the bravery of formal struggle for recognition and revenge.

350. It is the absolute right of the Idea to manifest itself in legal determinations and objective institutions, beginning with laws of marriage and agriculture. Whether that actualization takes the form of divine legislation and favor, or force and wrongdoing—this right is the *right of heroes* to establish states.

351. In the same light, it happens that civilized nations regard and treat other nations as barbarian when these others lag behind and so lack the substantial elements of statehood. (Thus cattle-raising people might regard a nation of huntsmen as barbarians, while an agricultural people might regard both as barbarian, etc.) The civilized nation is aware of the disparity in rights, between its own and those of barbarian peoples, whose independence they regard and treat as something merely formal and lacking all foundation.

[*Remark:*] In the wars and quarrels that arise in these circumstances, what makes them significant for world history is that they are struggles for recognition related to a specific cultural value. [Thus nomadic herdsmen have a different concept of the land from that held by crop-growers, etc.]

352.   The different concrete ideas, which are the spirits of various peoples, have their truth and determinacy in the concrete Idea which is *absolute universality*: the World Spirit. Around its throne they stand as executives of its acutalization, and as witnesses and ornaments to its grandeur. As Spirit, its only activity is to know itself in absolute terms—and in that way to free its consciousness from the form of natural immediacy, and to come to itself. Hence the *principles* of the various configurations of this self-consciousness, in the course of its liberation, are the world-historical realms, of which there are four:

353.   In the *first*, or as an *immediate revelation*, the World Spirit has the form of *substantial* Spirit as its principle: the identity wherein individuality remains sunk in its essence, and unjustified on its own account (*für sich*).

The *second* principle is this substantial Spirit in its knowing, so that this substance is its positive content, but it is also conscious of itself. This *being-for-self* is the living form of Spirit—the beautiful ethical individuality. [This is an individuality combining the Beautiful and the Good as primary values (in Greek: *kalokagathia*).]

The *third* principle is the inward deepening of this knowing self-consciousness, to the point of *abstract universality*, and thus to the point of Spirit's infinite opposition to the objective world which has abandoned spirituality in the process.

The principle of the *fourth* configuration is the reversal of this opposition by Spirit: by going into its own inwardness for its truth as well as its own concrete essence, it finally comes to be at home in objectivity and reconciled to it. In thus returning to the earlier substantiality, Spirit has *returned from its infinite opposition*. Spirit now creates and knows its truth as its own thought, and as a world of lawlike actuality.

354.   In accordance with these four principles, there are *four* world-historical realms: the Oriental, the Greek, the Roman, and the Germanic.

355.   A. *The Oriental World.* This first realm is the substantial world which is emerging from a natural patriarchal totality. In the perspective of this world, which is inwardly undivided, the worldly government is a theocracy; the ruler is a high priest or is even God himself; the state structure and legislation are at the same time religion—just as the religious and moral commandments, or rather customs, are state decrees. In the splendor of this totality, the individual personality has no rights and is suppressed. External nature is directly divine or is God's ornament. The history of the actual world is poetry. Various distinctions develop between classes of people, according to the different aspects of custom, government and state; and these distinctions, operating by simple custom in place of laws, become ponderous, elaborate and superstitious ceremonies. The contingencies of personal power, of arbitrary rule, and of class differences, take on the natural rigidity of castes. The Oriental state, therefore, is alive only in the outward movement of conquest, or in elemental frenzy and devastation. Inner calm occurs only in private life, sunk into weakness and exhaustion.

[*Remark* omitted here.]

356.   B. *The Greek World.* Here we have cultural life which still possesses the substantial unity of the finite and the infinite—but only as a mysterious foundation, repressed into an obscured memory, in cult practices carried on in caves, and in images retained by tradition. This background—gradually emerging out of self-differentiating Spirit into individual spirituality, and rebirth in the full daylight of knowing—is moderated and transfigured into beauty and the ethical life of freedom and happiness. It is therefore in this sort of world that we see the principle of personal individuality arising, although it is still not fully autonomous but is kept within its own ideal unity instead [e.g., the individual identifies with the city.] As a result of this inadequate individuation, the [Greek] totality falls apart into a group of individual national spirits on the one hand [e.g., Athens, Sparta, Corinth, etc.]; and, on the other hand, the ultimate resolution of the will is not yet placed in the subjectivity of independent self-consciousness but in a higher external power [e.g., Alexander]; the satisfaction of particular needs, more-

over, is not yet a task accepted by free men but is rather relegated to a class of slaves.

357.   C. *The Roman World.* Here the process of social differentiation is carried to the point where ethical life is absolutely torn asunder into its extremes: [private life versus public life], *personal* self-consciousness against *abstract universality.* This opposition begins with the antithesis between the substantive outlook of an aristocratic class and the principle of free personality in its democratic form. On the aristocratic side it deteriorates into superstition and the assertion of cold, greedy force; the democratic side sinks into the depravity of a rabble. The dissolution of the social totality ends with universal misfortune and the death of ethical life. National individualities die off and fade into the unity of a Pantheon [i.e., with the deification of emperors]. All individuals are degraded to the status of private persons, as equals having formal rights, and are held together by nothing more than abstract self-will driven to monstrous extremes.

358.   D. *The Germanic World.* Spirit has thus inflicted injury on itself and its world—followed by the infinite grief for the Crucified God, for which the Jewish people was held in readiness. Out of all this, the Spirit driven back into itself, grasps the absolute *turning point* in the extremity of its absolute *negativity:* the *infinite positivity* of its own inwardness, the principle which asserts the unity of the divine and the human natures. This reconciliation (of divine and human) as the objective truth and freedom—that appears within self-consciousness and subjectivity—is a reconciliation entrusted to the northern principle of the Germanic peoples to fulfill.

359.   In its inwardness, the principle is still abstract. Existing in the inner sense as faith, hope and love, it reconciles and resolves all antitheses. The principle unfolds its content, elevating it to actuality and self-conscious rationality—to a secular realm that proceeds from the heart, from loyalty and the fellowship of free men. In the subjectivity of its source, that *secular* realm is also a realm of crude arbitrariness and barbarous custom. It stands opposed to the world beyond, an *intellectual* realm—whose content is certainly that truth of its Spirit; but since this Spirit still does not *think,* that intellectual realm remains veiled in barbarous imagery. And as spiritual power over the actual heart and mind, this other-worldly realm acts against it as an unfree [i.e., authoritative] and frightful force.

360.   Despite the hard struggle between these absolutely opposed realms—i.e., the other-worldly vs. the this-worldly; or Church vs. Empire—they nevertheless are rooted in a single unity and Idea. Thus the spiritual realm degrades its heaven to the earthly here-and-now, and to a common worldliness, both in actuality and in representation. The worldly realm, on the other hand, raises its abstract independence to the level of thought and to the principle of rational being and knowing, i.e., to the rationality of right and law. Thus the antithesis between them withers away to nothing. The present world has stripped off its barbarism and unjust arbitrariness, and truth has put aside its world of beyond and its casual power. Thus the genuine reconciliation has become objective fact, revealing the *State* to be the image and the actuality of Reason. The State is where self-consciousness finds the actuality of its substantive knowing and willing, as an organic development; in *religion,* similarly, self-consciousness finds the feeling and image of its own truth as an ideal essence; but in *philosophy* it finds the freely grasped cognition of this truth to be one and the same in its complementary manifestations—in the *state,* in nature, and in the *ideal world.*

MARX

On the Jewish Question

BRUNO BAUER,
THE JEWISH QUESTION,
BRAUNSCHWEIG, 1843

The German Jews want emancipation. What kind of emancipation? *Civil, political* emancipation.

Bruno Bauer answers them: No one in Germany is politically emancipated. We are not free ourselves. How shall we liberate you? You Jews are *egoists* when you claim a special emancipation for yourselves as Jews. As Germans, you should work for the political emancipation of Germany, as men, for the emancipation of mankind; and you should feel the particular form of your oppression and shame not as an exception to the rule but rather as its confirmation.

Or do Jews desire to be put on an equal footing with *Christian subjects?* If so, they recognize the *Christian state* as legitimate, as the regime of general subjugation. Why should they be displeased at their particular yoke if the general yoke pleases them? Why should Germans be interested in the liberation of Jews if Jews are not interested in the liberation of Germans?

The *Christian* state takes cognizance only of *privileges.* In it the Jew has the privilege of being a Jew. As a Jew he has rights that Christians do not have. Why does he want rights he does not have and that Christians enjoy?

If the Jew wants to be emancipated from the Christian state, he is demanding that the Christian state abandon its *religious* prejudice. But does the Jew abandon *his* religious prejudice? Has he, then, the right to demand of another this abdication of religion?

Translated from the German by Loyd D. Easton and Kurt H. Guddat. Reprinted by permission of Loyd D. Easton and Mrs. Kurt H. Guddat.

By *its very nature* the Christian state cannot emancipate the Jew; but, Bauer adds, the Jew by his very nature cannot be emancipated. So long as the state remains Christian and the Jew remains Jewish, both are equally incapable of giving as well as receiving emancipation.

The Christian state can only behave toward the Jew in the manner of the Christian state—that is, permitting the separation of the Jew from other subjects as a privilege but making him feel the pressure of the other separate spheres of society, and feel them all the more heavily, since he stands in *religious* opposition to the predominant religion. But the Jew in turn can behave toward the state only in a Jewish manner, that is as a foreigner, since he opposes his chimerical nationality to actual nationality, his illusory law to actual law. He imagines that his separation from humanity is justified, abstains on principle from participation in the historical movement, looks to a future that has nothing in common with the future of mankind as a whole, and regards himself as a part of the Jewish people, the chosen people.

On what basis, then, do you Jews want emancipation? On the basis of your religion? It is the mortal enemy of the religion of the state. As citizens? There are no citizens in Germany. As men? You are not men, just as those to whom you appeal are not men.

After criticizing previous positions and solutions, Bauer formulates the question of Jewish emancipation in a new way. What is the *nature*, he asks, of the Jew who is to be emancipated and the Christian state that is to emancipate him? He answers with a critique of the Jewish religion, analyzes the *religious* antagonism between Judaism and Christianity, and explains the essence of the Christian state—all this with dash, acuteness, wit, and thoroughness in a style as precise as it is pregnant and energetic.

How then does Bauer settle the Jewish question? What is the result? The formulation of a question is its solution. Criticism of the Jewish question provides the answer to the Jewish question. The résumé thus follows:

We must emancipate ourselves before we can emancipate others.

The most persistent form of the antagonism between the Jew and the Christian is the *religious* antagonism. How is an antagonism to be resolved? By making it impossible. And how is a *religious* antagonism made impossible? By *abolishing religion*. Once Jew and Christian recognize their respective religions as nothing more than *different stages in the evolution of the human spirit*, as different snake skins shed by *history*, and recognize *man* as the snake that wore them, they will no longer find themselves in religious antagonism but only in a critical, *scientific*, and human relationship. *Science*, then, constitutes their unity. Contradictions in science, however, are resolved by science itself.

The *German* Jew is particularly affected by the general lack of political emancipation and the pronounced Christianity of the state. With Bauer, however, the Jewish question has a universal significance independent of specific German conditions. It is the question of the relation of religion to the state, of the *contradiction between religious prejudice and political emancipation*. Emancipation from religion is presented as a condition both for the Jew who seeks political emancipation and for the state which is to emancipate him and is to be emancipated itself as well.

"Very well, you say—and the Jew himself says it—the Jew should not be emancipated because he is Jew or because he has such excellent and universal ethical principles but rather because he takes second place to the *citizen* and becomes one in spite of being and wanting to remain a Jew. That is, he is and remains a Jew in spite of the fact that he is a *citizen* living in universally human relationships; his Jewish and restricted nature always triumphs in the end over his human and political obligations. The *prejudice* remains even though it has been overtaken by *universal* principles. But if it remains, it rather overtakes everything else." "The Jew could remain a Jew in political life only in a so-

phistical sense, only in appearance; thus if he wanted to remain a Jew, this mere appearance would become the essential thing and would triumph. In other words, his *life in the state* would be only a semblance or a momentary exception to the real nature of things, an exception to the rule." ("The Capacity of Present-day Jews and Christians to Become Free," *Twenty-one Sheets from Switzerland* [*Einundzwanzig Bogen aus der Schweiz*], p. 57.)

Let us see, on the other hand, how Bauer describes the role of the state:

"France," he says, "recently (Proceedings of the Chamber of Deputies, 26 December 1840) gave us, in connection with the Jewish question and all other *political* questions (since the July Revolution), a glimpse of a life which is free but which revokes its freedom by law, thus revealing it to be a sham, and on the other hand, denies its free law by its acts." (*The Jewish Question*, p. 64.)

"Universal freedom is not yet established as law in France, and the *Jewish question is not yet settled* because legal freedom—that all citizens are equal—is limited in actual life which is still dominated and fragmented by religious privileges, and because the lack of freedom in actual life reacts on the law, compelling it to sanction the division of inherently free citizens into the oppressed and the oppressors" (p. 65).

When, therefore, would the Jewish question be settled in France?

"The Jew, for instance, would really have ceased being a Jew if he did not let himself be hindered by his code from fulfilling his duties toward the state and his fellow citizens—if he went, for example, to the Chamber of Deputies and took part in public affairs on the Sabbath. Every *religious privilege*, including the monopoly of a privileged church, would have to be abolished, and if a few or many or *even the overwhelming majority still felt obliged to fulfill their religious duties*, such a practice should be left to them *as a purely private matter*" (p. 65). "There is no

longer any religion if there is no privileged religion. Take from religion its power of excommunication and it ceases to exist" (p. 66). "Just as M.
Martin du Nord saw the proposal to omit any
mention of Sunday in the law as a declaration
that Christianity had ceased to exist, with equal
right (and one well-founded) a declaration that
the Sabbath-law is no longer binding for the Jew
would proclaim the end of Judaism" (p. 71).

Bauer thus demands, on the one hand, that the Jew
give up Judaism and man give up religion in order to
be emancipated *as a citizen*. On the other hand, he
holds that from the *political* abolition of religion there
logically follows the abolition of religion altogether.
The state which presupposes religion is as yet no true,
no actual state. "To be sure, the religious view reinforces the state. But what state? *What kind of state?*"
(p. 97).

At this point Bauer's *one-sided* approach to the Jewish question becomes apparent.

It is by no means sufficient to ask: Who should
emancipate and who should be emancipated? Criticism has to be concerned with a third question. It must
ask: *What kind of emancipation* is involved and what
are its underlying conditions? Criticism of *political
emancipation* itself is primarily the final critique of the
Jewish question and its true resolution into the *"universal question of the age."*

Since Bauer does not raise the question to this level,
he falls into contradictions. He presents conditions that
are not based on the essence of *political* emancipation. He raises questions that are irrelevant to his
problem and solves problems that leave his question
untouched. Bauer says of the opponents of Jewish
emancipation, "Their mistake simply lay in assuming
the Christian state to be the only true state without
subjecting it to the same criticism they applied to
Judaism" (p. 3). Here we find Bauer's mistake in
subjecting *only* the "Christian state," not the "state as
such," to criticism, in failing to examine the *relation
between political emancipation and human emancipation*, and hence presenting conditions that are only
explicable from his uncritical confusion of political
emancipation with universal human emancipation.

Bauer asks the Jews: Have you the right to demand *political emancipation* from your standpoint? We ask, on
the contrary: Has the standpoint of *political* emancipation the right to demand from the Jews the abolition
of Judaism and from man the abolition of religion?

The Jewish question has a different aspect according to the state in which the Jew finds himself. In Germany, where there is no political state and no state as
such exists, the Jewish question is purely *theological*.
The Jew finds himself in *religious* opposition to a state
acknowledging Christianity as its foundation. This state
is a theologian *ex professo*. Criticism is here criticism
of theology, double-edged criticism of Christian and
of Jewish theology. But however *critical* we might be,
we are still moving in theology.

In France, a *constitutional* state, the Jewish question
is a question of constitutionalism, a question of the *incompleteness of political emancipation*. As the *semblance* of a state religion is preserved there, if only by
the meaningless and self-contradictory formula of a *religion of the majority*, the relation of the Jew to the
state also retains the *semblance* of a religious or theological opposition.

Only in the free states of North America—or at least
in some of them—does the Jewish question lose its
theological significance and become a truly *secular*
question. Only where the political state exists in its
complete development can the relation of the Jew,
and generally speaking the religious man, to the political state, that is, the relation of religion to state, appear in its characteristic and pure form. Criticism of
this relation ceases to be theological once the state
abandons a *theological* posture toward religion, once
it relates itself to religion as a state, that is, *politically*.
Criticism then becomes *criticism of the political state*.
Where the question here ceases to be *theological*,
Bauer's criticism ceases to be critical. "*In the United
States there is neither a state religion, nor a religion declared to be that of the majority, nor a pre-eminence of
one faith over another. The state is foreign to all faiths.*"
(Gustave de Beaumont, *Marie ou l'esclavage aux Etats-
Unis* . . . [Brussels, 1835], p. 214.) There are even
some states in North America where "*the constitution
imposes no religious beliefs or sectarian practice as the
condition of political rights*" (loc. cit., p. 225). Yet "*no

one in the United States believes that a man without re-ligion can be an honest man" (loc. cit., p. 224). And North America is pre-eminently the land of religiosity as Beaumont, Tocqueville, and the Englishman Hamilton assure us unanimously. The North American states, however, serve only as an example. The question is: What is the relation of *complete* political emancipation to religion? If we find even in a country with full political emancipation that religion not only *exists* but is *fresh* and *vital*, we have proof that the existence of religion is not incompatible with the full development of the state. But since the existence of religion implies a defect, the source of this defect must be sought in the *nature* of the state itself. We no longer take religion to be the *basis* but only the *manifestation* of secular narrowness. Hence we explain religious restriction of free citizens on the basis of their secular restriction. We do not claim that they must transcend their religious restriction in order to transcend their secular limitations. We do claim that they will transcend their religious restriction once they have transcended their secular limitations. We do not convert secular questions into theological ones. We convert theological questions into secular questions. History has long enough been resolved into superstition, but now we can resolve superstition into history. The question of the *relation of political emancipation to religion* becomes for us a question of the *relation of political emancipation to human emancipation*. We criticize the religious weaknesses of the political state by criticizing the political state in its *secular* constitution *apart from* the religious defects. In human terms we resolve the contradiction between the state and a *particular religion* such as *Judaism* into the contradiction between the state and *particular secular* elements, the contradiction between the state and *religion generally* into the contradiction between the state and its *presuppositions*.

The *political* emancipation of the Jew, the Christian, or the *religious* man generally is the *emancipation of the state* from Judaism, from Christianity, from *religion* in general. In a form and manner corresponding to its nature, the *state* as such emancipates itself from religion by emancipating itself from the *state religion*, that is, by recognizing no religion and recog-

nizing itself simply as the state. *Political* emancipation from religion is not complete and consistent emancipation from religion because political emancipation is not the complete and consistent form of *human* emancipation.

The limits of political emancipation are seen at once in the fact that the *state* can free itself from a limitation without man *actually* being free from it, in the fact that a state can be a *free state* without men becoming *free men*. Bauer himself tacitly admits this in setting the following condition of political emancipation: "Every religious privilege, including the monopoly of a privileged church, would have to be abolished. If a few or many or even the *overwhelming majority still felt obliged to fulfill their religious duties*, such a practice should be left to them as a *purely private matter*." The *state* can thus emancipate itself from religion even though the *overwhelming majority* is still religious. And the overwhelming majority does not cease being religious by being religious *in private*.

But the attitude of the state, particularly the *free state*, toward religion is still only the attitude of the *men* who make up the state. Hence it follows that man frees himself from a limitation *politically, through the state*, by overcoming the limitation in an *abstract, limited*, and partial manner, in contradiction with himself. Further, when man frees himself *politically*, he does so *indirectly*, through an *intermediary*, even if the *intermediary* is *necessary*. Finally, even when man proclaims himself an atheist through the medium of the state — that is, when he declares the state to be atheistic — he is still captive to religion since he only recognizes his atheism indirectly through an intermediary. Religion is merely the indirect recognition of man through a *mediator*. The state is the mediator between man and the freedom of man. As Christ is the mediator on whom man unburdens all his own divinity and all his *religious ties*, so is the state the mediator to which man transfers all his unholiness and all his *human freedom*.

The *political* elevation of man above religion shares all the defects and all the advantages of any political elevation. If the state as state, for example, abolishes *private property*, man proclaims private property is *overcome politically* once he abolishes the *property* *qualification* for active and passive voting as has been done in many North American states. *Hamilton* interprets this fact quite correctly in political terms: *"The great majority of the people have gained a victory over property owners and financial wealth."*[*] Is not private property ideally abolished when the have-nots come to legislate for the haves? The *property qualification* is the last *political* form for recognizing private property.

Yet the political annulment of private property not only does not abolish it but even presupposes it. The state abolishes distinctions of *birth, rank, education,* and *occupation* in its fashion when it declares them to be *non-political* distinctions, when it proclaims that every member of the community *equally* participates in popular sovereignty without regard to these distinctions, and when it deals with all elements of the actual life of the nation from the standpoint of the state. Nevertheless the state permits private property, education, and occupation to *act* and manifest their *particular* nature as private property, education, and occupation in their *own* ways. Far from overcoming these *factual* distinctions, the state exists only by presupposing them; it is aware of itself as a *political state* and makes its *universality* effective only in opposition to these elements. *Hegel,* therefore, defines the relation of the *political state* to religion quite correctly in saying: "If the state is to have specific existence as the *self-knowing ethical actuality* of Spirit, it must be *distinct* from the form of authority and faith; this distinction emerges only as the ecclesiastical sphere is *divided* within itself; *only* thus has the state attained *universality* of thought, the principle of its form, *above particular* churches and only thus does it bring that universality into existence." (Hegel's *Philosophy of Law,* 1st ed., p. 346 [§270].) Exactly! Only thus *above* the *particular* elements is the state a universality.

By its nature the perfected political state is man's *species-life* in *opposition* to his material life. All the presuppositions of this egoistic life remain in *civil so-*

[* Thomas Hamilton, *Men and Manners in America* (2 vols.; Edinburgh: William Blackwood, 1833). Marx quotes from the German translation, *Die Menschen und die Sitten in den Vereinigten Staaten von Nordamerika* (Mannheim: Hoff, 1834), Vol I, p. 146.]

ciety outside the state, but as qualities of civil society. Where the political state has achieved its full development, man leads a double life, a heavenly and an earthly life, not only in thought or consciousness but in *actuality*. In the *political community* he regards himself as a *communal being*; but in *civil society* he is active as a *private individual*, treats other men as means, reduces himself to a means, and becomes the plaything of alien powers. The political state is as spiritual in relation to civil society as heaven is in relation to earth. It stands in the same opposition to civil society and goes beyond it in the same way as religion goes beyond the limitation of the profane world, that is, by recognizing, reestablishing, and necessarily allowing itself to be dominated by it. In his *innermost* actuality, in civil society, man is a profane being. Here, where he counts as an actual individual to himself and others, he is an *illusory* phenomenon. In the state where he counts as a species-being, on the other hand, he is an imaginary member of an imagined sovereignty, divested of his actual individual life and endowed with an unactual universality.

The conflict in which man as believer in a *particular* religion finds himself—a conflict with his own citizenship and other men as members of the community—is reduced to the *secular* split between the *political* state and *civil society*. For man as *bourgeois* [or part of civil society], "life in the state is only a semblance or a momentary exception to the real nature of things, an exception to the rule." Certainly the *bourgeois*, like the Jew, participates in the life of the state only in a sophistical way just as the *citoyen* is only sophistically a Jew or *bourgeois*; but this sophistry is not personal. It is the *sophistry of the political state* itself. The difference between the religious man and the citizen is the difference between the shopkeeper and the citizen, between the day laborer and the citizen, between the landowner and the citizen, between the *living individual* and the *citizen*. The contradiction between the religious and political man is the same as that between *bourgeois* and *citoyen*, between the member of civil society and his *political lion skin*.

This secular conflict to which the Jewish question ultimately is reduced—the relation between the political state and its presuppositions, whether the presuppositions be material elements such as private property or spiritual elements such as education and religion, the conflict between *general* and *private interest*, the split between the *political state* and *civil society* — these secular contradictions Bauer leaves untouched while attacking their *religious* expression. "It is precisely its foundation, need, which assures the maintenance of *civil society* and *guarantees its necessity* but exposes its maintenance to constant danger, sustains an element of uncertainty in civil society, and produces that constantly alternating mixture of poverty and wealth, of adversity and prosperity, and change in general" (p. 8).

Consider his entire section, "Civil Society" (pp. 8–9), which closely follows the main features of Hegel's philosophy of law. Civil society in opposition to the political state is recognized as necessary since the political state is recognized as necessary.

Political emancipation is indeed a great step forward. It is not, to be sure, the final form of universal human emancipation, but it is the final form *within* the prevailing order of things. It is obvious that we are here talking about actual, practical emancipation.

Man emancipates himself *politically* from religion by banishing it from the sphere of public law into private right. It is no longer the spirit of the *state* where man — although in a limited way, under a particular form, and in a particular sphere — associates in community with other men as a species-being. It has become the spirit of *civil society*, of the sphere of egoism, of the *bellum omnium contra omnes*. It is no longer the essence of *community* but the essence of *division*. It has become what it was *originally*, an expression of the *separation* of man from his *community*, from himself and from other men. It is now only the abstract confession of particular peculiarity, of *private whim*, of caprice. The infinite splits of religion in North America, for example, already give it the *external* form of a purely individual matter. It has been tossed among numerous private interests and exiled from the community as a community. But one must not be deceived about the scope of political emancipation. The splitting of man into *public* and *private*, the *displacement* of religion from the state to civil society, is not just a step in political emancipation but its *completion*. It as

little abolishes man's *actual* religiosity as it seeks to abolish it.

The *disintegration* of man into Jew and citizen, Protestant and citizen, religious man and citizen does not belie citizenship or circumvent political emancipation. It is *political emancipation itself*, the *political* mode of emancipation from religion. To be sure, in periods when the political state as such is forcibly born from civil society, when men strive to liberate themselves under the form of political self-liberation, the state can and must go as far as to *abolish* and *destroy* religion, but only in the way it abolishes private property by setting a maximum, confiscation, and progressive taxation or only in the way it abolishes life by the *guillotine*. In moments of special concern for itself political life seeks to repress its presupposition, civil society and its elements, and to constitute itself the actual, harmonious species-life of man. But it can do this only in *violent* contradiction with its own conditions of existence by declaring the revolution to be *permanent*, and thus the political drama is bound to end with the restoration of religion, private property, and all the elements of civil society just as war ends with peace.

Indeed, the perfected Christian state is not the so-called *Christian* state acknowledging Christianity as its foundation in the state religion and excluding all others. It is, rather, the *atheistic* state, the *democratic* state, the state that relegates religion to the level of other elements of civil society. The state that is still theological and still officially prescribes belief in Christianity has not yet dared to declare itself to be *a state* and has not yet succeeded in expressing in *secular* and *human* form, in its *actuality* as a state, those *human* foundations of which Christianity is the sublime expression. The so-called Christian state is simply a *non-state*, for it is only the *human foundation* of Christianity, not Christianity as a religion, which can realize itself in actual human creations.

The so-called Christian state is a Christian denial of the state, not in any way the political actualization of Christianity. The state that still professes Christianity in the form of religion does not profess it in political form because it still behaves religiously toward religion — that is, it is not the *actual expression* of the human basis of religion since it still deals with the *unreality* and *imaginary* form of this human core. The so-called Christian state is an *imperfect* one, which treats Christianity as the *supplement* and *sanctification* of its imperfection. Hence religion necessarily becomes a *means* to an end, and the state is a *hypocrite*. There is a great difference between a *perfected* state that counts religion as one of its *prerequisites* because of a lack in the general *nature* of the state and an *imperfect* state that proclaims religion as its *foundation* because of a lack in its *particular existence* as an imperfect state. In the latter, religion becomes *imperfect politics*. In the former, the inadequacy of even perfected *politics* is apparent in religion. The so-called Christian state needs the Christian religion to complete itself *as a state*. The democratic state, the real state, needs no religion for its political fulfillment. It can, rather, do without religion because it fulfills the human basis of religion in a secular way. The so-called Christian state, on the other hand, behaves toward religion in a political way and toward politics in a religious way. As it reduces political forms to mere appearance, it equally reduces religion to a mere appearance.

To express this contradiction clearly let us consider Bauer's construct of the Christian state, a construct derived from this perception of the Christian-Germanic state.

"To prove the *impossibility* or *non-existence* of a Christian state," says Bauer, "we have recently and more frequently been referred to those passages in the Gospel which the [present] state *not only* does *not* follow but *also cannot unless it wants to dissolve itself completely.*" "But the matter is not so easily settled. What do those Gospel passages demand? Supernatural self-renunciation and submission to the authority of revelation, turning away from the state, the abolition of secular relationships. But the Christian state demands and achieves all these things. It has made the *spirit of the Gospel* its own, and if it does not reproduce it in exactly the same words as the Gospel, that is because it expresses that spirit in political forms borrowed from the political system of this world but reduced to mere

appearance by the religious rebirth they must undergo. This withdrawal from the state is realized through the forms of the state" (p. 55).

Bauer goes on to show how the people of a Christian state do not constitute a nation with a will of its own but have their true existence in the ruler to whom they are subject but who is alien to them by origin and nature since he was given to them by God without their consent. Further, the laws of this nation are not its own doing but are positive revelations. The supreme ruler requires privileged intermediaries in his relations with his own people, the masses, themselves split into a multitude of distinct spheres formed and determined by chance and differentiated from each other by their interests and particular passions and prejudices but permitted as a privilege to isolate themselves from each other, etc. (p. 56).

But Bauer himself says: "If politics is to be nothing more than religion, it cannot be politics any more than cleaning cooking pans can be regarded as an economic matter if it is to be treated religiously" (p. 108). But in the Christian-Germanic state, religion is an "economic matter" just as "economic matters" are religion. In the Christian-Germanic state, the dominance of religion is the religion of domination.

The separation of the "spirit of the Gospel" from the "letter of the Gospel" is an *irreligious* act. The state that permits the Gospel to speak in the letter of politics or in any other letter than that of the Holy Spirit commits a sacrilege if not in the eyes of men at least in the eyes of its own religion. The state that acknowledges Christianity as its highest rule and the *Bible* as its *charter* must be confronted with the *words* of Holy Writ, for the Writ is holy in every word. This state as well as the *human rubbish* on which it is based finds itself involved in a painful contradiction, a contradiction insoluble from the standpoint of religious consciousness based on the teaching of the Gospel, which it "not only does not follow but *also cannot unless it wants to dissolve itself completely as a state.*" And why does it not want to dissolve itself completely? It cannot answer this question either for itself or others. In its *own consciousness* the official Christian state is an *ought* whose realization is impossible. It knows it can affirm the *actuality* of its own existence only by lying to itself and hence remains dubious, unreliable, and problematic. Criticism is thus completely right in forcing the state that appeals to the Bible into a mental derangement in which it no longer knows whether it is an *illusion* or a *reality*, in which the infamy of its *secular* purposes cloaked by religion irreconcilably conflicts with the integrity of its *religious* consciousness viewing religion as the world's purpose. Such a state can only free itself of inner torment by becoming the *constable* of the Catholic Church. In relation to that church, which claims secular power as its servant, the state, the *secular* power claiming to dominate the religious spirit, is impotent.

In the so-called Christian state what counts is indeed *alienation* but not *man*. The only man who does count, the *king*, is still religious, specifically distinguished from others and directly connected with heaven, with God. The relations prevailing here are still relations of *faith*. The religious spirit is still not actually secularized.

But the religious spirit cannot *actually* be secularized, for what is it, in fact, but the *unsecular* form of a stage in the development of the human spirit? The religious spirit can only be actualized if the stage of development of the human spirit it expresses religiously emerges into and assumes its *secular* form. This is what happens in the *democratic* state. The basis of the democratic state is not Christianity but the *human ground* of Christianity. Religion remains the ideal, unsecular consciousness of its members because it is the ideal form of the *stage of human development* attained in the democratic state.

The members of the political state are religious by virtue of the dualism between individual life and species-life, between the life of civil society and political life. They are religious inasmuch as man regards as his true life the political life remote from his actual individuality, inasmuch as religion is here the spirit of civil society expressing the generation and withdrawal of man from man. Political democracy is Christian in that it regards man—not merely one but every man—as *sovereign* and supreme. But this means man in his uncivilized and unsocial aspect, in his fortuitous existence and just as he is, corrupted by the entire organization of our society, lost and alienated from himself, oppressed by inhuman relations and elements—in a word, man who is not yet an *actual* species-being. The sovereignty of man—though as alien and distinct from actual men—which is the chimera, dream, and postulate of Christianity, is a tangible and present actuality, a secular maxim, in democracy.

In the perfected democracy the religious and theological consciousness appears to itself all the more religious and theological for being apparently without political significance or mundane purposes—for being a spiritual affair eschewing the world, an expression of reason's limitation, a product of whim and fantasy, an actual life in the beyond. Christianity here achieves the *practical* expression of its universal religious meaning in that the most varied views are grouped together in the form of Christianity and, what is more, others are not asked to profess Christianity but only religion in general, any kind of religion (cf. Beaumont, *op. cit.*). The religious consciousness revels in the wealth of religious contradictions and multiplicity.

We have thus shown: Political emancipation from religion permits religion, though not privileged religion, to continue. The contradiction in which the adherent of a specific religion finds himself in relation to his citizenship is only *one aspect* of the universal *secular contradiction between the political state and civil society*. The fulfillment of the Christian state is a state that acknowledges itself as a state and ignores the religion of its members. The emancipation of the state from religion is not the emancipation of actual man from religion.

We thus do not say with Bauer to the Jews: You cannot be politically emancipated without radically emancipating yourselves from Judaism. Rather we tell them: Because you can be emancipated politically without completely and fully renouncing Judaism, *political emancipation* by itself is not *human* emancipation. If you Jews want to be politically emancipated without emancipating yourselves humanly, the incompleteness and contradiction lies not only in you but in the *essence* and *category* of political emancipation. If you are engrossed in this category, you share a general bias. Just as the state *evangelizes* when, in spite of being a state, it behaves toward the Jew in a Christian way, the Jew *acts politically* when, in spite of being a Jew, he demands civil rights.

But if man can be emancipated politically and acquire civil rights even though he is a Jew, can he claim and acquire the so-called *rights of man?* Bauer *denies* it.

"The question is whether the Jew as such—i.e. the Jew who avows that his true nature compels him to live in eternal separation from others— is able to acquire the *universal rights of man* and grant them to others."

"The idea of the rights of man was discovered in the Christian world only in the last century. It is not an innate idea but rather is acquired in struggle against historical traditions in which man has hitherto been educated. Thus the rights of man are neither a gift of nature nor a legacy from past history but the reward of struggle against the accident of birth and privileges transmitted by history from generation to generation up to the present. They are the result of culture, and only he can possess them who has earned and deserved them."

"But can the Jew actually take possession of them? As long as he remains a Jew the limited nature which makes him a Jew must triumph over the human nature which should link him as a man with others and must separate him from non-Jews. By this separation he proclaims that the special nature which makes him a Jew is his true and highest nature to which his human nature must yield."

"In the same way, the Christian as Christian cannot grant the rights of man." (Pp. 19, 20.)

According to Bauer man must sacrifice the *"privilege of faith"* to be able to acquire the universal rights of man. Let us consider for a moment these so-called rights and indeed in their most authentic form, the form they have among their *discoverers*, the North Americans and the French. In part these rights are *political* rights that can be exercised only in community with others. *Participation* in the *community*, indeed the *political* community or *state*, constitutes their substance. They belong in the category of *political freedom*, of *civil rights*, which by no means presupposes

the consistent and positive transcendence of religion and thus of Judaism, as we have seen. There is left for consideration the other part, the *rights of man* as distinct from the *rights of the citizen*.

Among these is freedom of conscience, the right to practice one's chosen religion. The *privilege of faith* is expressly recognized either as a *right of man* or as a consequence of a right of man, freedom.

Declaration of the Rights of Man and of the Citizen, 1791, Art. 10: "No one is to be disturbed on account of his beliefs, even religious beliefs." In Title I of the Constitution of 1791 there is guaranteed as a human right: "The liberty of every man to practice the *religious worship* to which he is attached."

The *Declaration of the Rights of Man*, etc., 1793, includes among human rights, Art. 7: "Freedom of worship." Moreover, it even maintains in regard to the right to express views and opinions, to assemble, and to worship: "The need to proclaim these *rights* assumes either the presence or recent memory of despotism." Compare the Constitution of 1795, Title XIV, Art. 354.

Constitution of Pennsylvania, Art. 9, §3: "All men have a natural and indefeasible *right* to worship Almighty God according to the dictates of their own consciences; no man can of right be compelled to attend, erect, or support any place of worship, or to maintain any ministry against his consent; no human authority can, in any case whatever, interfere with the rights of conscience and control the prerogatives of the soul."

Constitution of New Hampshire, Arts. 5 and 6: "Among the natural rights, some are in their very nature unalienable, because no equivalent can be conceived for them. Of this kind are the *rights* of conscience." (Beaumont, *loc. cit.*, pp. 213, 214.)

The incompatibility between a religion and the rights of man is so little implied in the concept of the rights of man that the *right to be religious* according to one's liking and to practice a particular religion is explicitly included among the rights of man. The *privilege of faith* is a *universal human right*.

The *rights of man as such* are distinguished from the *rights of the citizen*. Who is this *man* distinguished from the *citizen*? None other than the *member of civil society*. Why is the member of the civil society called "man," man without qualification, and why are his rights called the *rights of man*? How can we explain this? By the relation of the political state to civil society and by the nature of political emancipation.

Let us note first of all that the so-called *rights of man* as distinguished from the *rights of the citizen* are only the rights of the *member of civil society*, that is, of egoistic man, man separated from other men and from the community. The most radical constitution, the Constitution of 1793, may be quoted:

> *Declaration of the Rights of Man and of the Citizen.*
> *Art. 2.* "These rights (the natural and imprescriptible rights) are: *equality, liberty, security, property.*"

What is this *liberty*?

> *Art. 6.* "Liberty is the power belonging to each man to do anything which does not impair the rights of others," or according to the Declaration of the Rights of Man of 1791: "Liberty is the power to do anything which does not harm others."

Liberty is thus the right to do and perform anything that does not harm others. The limits within which each can act *without harming* others is determined by law just as the boundary between two fields is marked by a stake. This is the liberty of man viewed as an isolated monad, withdrawn into himself. Why, according to Bauer, is the Jew not capable of acquiring human rights? "As long as he remains a Jew the limited nature which makes him a Jew must triumph over the human nature which should link him as a man with others and must separate him from non-Jews." But liberty as a right of man is not based on the association of man with man but rather on the separation of man from

man. It is the *right* of this separation, the right of the *limited* individual limited to himself.

The practical application of the right of liberty is the right of *private property*.

What is property as one of the rights of man?

> *Art. 16* (Constitution of 1793): "The right of *property* is that belonging to every citizen to enjoy and dispose of his goods, his revenues, the fruits of his labor and of his industry *as he wills.*"

The right of property is thus the right to enjoy and dispose of one's possessions as one wills, without regard for other men and independently of society. It is the right of self-interest. This individual freedom and its application as well constitutes the basis of civil society. It lets every man find in other men not the *realization* but rather the *limitation* of his own freedom. It proclaims above all the right of man "to enjoy and dispose of his goods, his revenues, the fruits of his labor and of his industry *as he wills.*"

There still remain the other rights of man, equality and security.

"Equality"—here used in its non-political sense—is only the equal right to *liberty* as described above, viz., that every man is equally viewed as a self-sufficient monad. The Constitution of 1705 defines the concept of equality with this significance:

> *Art. 3* (Constitution of 1795): "Equality consists in the fact that the law is the same for all, whether it protects or whether it punishes."

And security?

> *Art. 8* (Constitution of 1793): "Security consists in the protection accorded by society to each of its members for the preservation of his person, his rights and his property."

Security is the supreme social concept of civil society, the concept of the *police*, the concept that the whole society exists only to guarantee to each of its members the preservation of his person, his rights, and his property. In this sense Hegel calls civil society "the state as necessity and rationality."

Civil society does not raise itself above its egoism through the concept of security. Rather, security is the *guarantee* of the egoism.

Thus none of the so-called rights of men goes beyond the egoistic man, the man withdrawn into himself, his private interest and his private choice, and separated from the community as a member of civil society. Far from viewing man here in his species-being, his species-life itself—society—rather appears to be an external framework for the individual, limiting his original independence. The only bond between men is natural necessity, need and private interest, the maintenance of their property and egoistic persons.

It is somewhat curious that a nation just beginning to free itself, tearing down all the barriers between different sections of the people and founding a political community, should solemnly proclaim (Declaration of 1791) the justification of the egoistic man, man separated from his fellow men and from the community, and should even repeat this proclamation at a moment when only the most heroic sacrifice can save the nation and hence is urgently required, when the sacrifice of all the interests of civil society is highly imperative and egoism must be punished as crime (Declaration of the Rights of Man of 1793). This becomes even more curious when we observe that the political liberators reduce citizenship, the *political community*, to a mere *means* for preserving these so-called rights of man and that the citizen thus is proclaimed to be the servant of the egoistic man, the sphere in which man acts as a member of the community is degraded below that in which he acts as a fractional being, and finally man as bourgeois rather than man as citizen is considered to be the *proper* and *authentic* man.

"The *goal* of all *political association* is the *preservation* of the natural and imprescriptible rights of man." (Declaration of the Rights of Man, etc., of 1791, Art. 2.) "*Government* is instituted to guarantee man's enjoyment of his natural and imprescriptible rights." (Declaration, etc., of 1793, Art. 1.) Thus even at the time of its youthful enthusiasm fired by the urgency of circumstances political life is proclaimed to be a mere *means* whose end is life in civil society. To be sure, revolutionary practice flagrantly contradicts its theory.

While security, for example, is proclaimed to be one of the rights of man, the violation of the privacy of correspondence is publicly established as the order of the day. While the "*unlimited* freedom of the press" (Constitution of 1793, Art. 122) as a consequence of the rights of man and individual freedom is guaranteed, freedom of the press is completely abolished because "freedom of the press should not be permitted to compromise public liberty." ("Robespierre jeune," *Parliamentary History of the French Revolution*, by Buchez and Roux, Vol. 28, p. 159.) This means that the human right of liberty ceases to be a right when it comes into conflict with *political* life while theoretically political life is only the guarantee of the rights of man, the rights of individual man, and should be abandoned once it contradicts its *end*, these rights of man. But the practice is only the exception, the theory is the rule. Even if we choose to regard revolutionary practice as the correct expression of this relationship, the problem still remains unsettled as to why the relationship is inverted in the consciousness of the political liberators so that the end appears as means and the means as the end. This optical illusion of their consciousness would always be the same problem, though a psychological, a theoretical problem.

The problem is easily settled.

Political emancipation is also the *dissolution* of the old society on which rests the sovereign power, the character of the state as alienated from the people. The political revolution is the revolution of civil society. What was the character of the old society? It can be described in one word. *Feudalism.* The old civil society had a *directly political* character, that is, the elements of civil life such as property, the family, the mode and manner of work, for example, were raised into elements of political life in the form of landlordism, estates, and corporations. In this form they determined the relation of the particular individual to the *state as a whole*, that is, his *political* relation, his separation and exclusion from other parts of society. For the feudal organization of national life did not elevate property or labor to the level of social elements but rather completed their *separation* from the state as a whole and established them as *separate* societies within society. Thus the vital functions and conditions of civil society always remained political, but political in the feudal sense. That is, they excluded the individual from the state as a whole and transformed the *special* relation between his corporation and the state into his own general relation to national life, just as they transformed his specific civil activity and situation into a general activity and situation. As a consequence of this organization, there necessarily appears the unity of the state as well as its consciousness, will, and activity—the general political power—likewise the *special* business of the ruler and his servants, separated from the people.

The political revolution, which overthrew this domination, turned the business of the state into the people's business, and made the political state the business of *all,* that is, an actual state—this revolution inevitably destroyed all estates, corporations, guilds, and privileges variously expressing the separation of the people from their community. The political revolution thereby *abolished* the *political character of civil society.* It shattered civil society into its constituent elements—on the one hand *individuals* and on the other the *material* and *spiritual elements* constituting the vital content and civil situation of these individuals. It released the political spirit, which had been broken, fragmented, and lost, as it were, in the various cul-de-sacs of feudal society. It gathered up this scattered spirit, liberated it from its entanglement with civil life, and turned it into the sphere of the community, the *general* concern of the people ideally independent of these *particular* elements of civil life. A *particular* activity and situation in life sank into a merely individual significance, no longer forming the general relation of the individual to the state as a whole. Public business as such rather became the general business of every individual and the political function became his general function.

But the fulfillment of the idealism of the state was at the same time the fulfillment of the materialism of civil society. The throwing off of the political yoke was at the same time the throwing off of the bond that had fettered the egoistic spirit of civil society. Political emancipation was at the same time the emancipation of civil society from politics, from the *appearance* of a general content.

Feudal society was dissolved into its foundation, into *man.* But into man as he actually was the foundation of that society, into *egoistical* man.

This *man,* the member of civil society, is now the basis and presupposition of the *political* state. He is recognized as such by the state in the rights of man.

But the freedom of egoistic man and the recognition of this freedom is rather the recognition of the *unbridled* movement of the spiritual and material elements forming the content of his life.

Thus man was not freed from religion; he received religious freedom. He was not freed from property. He received freedom of property. He was not freed from the egoism of trade but received freedom to trade.

The *constitution* of the *political state* and the dissolution of civil society into independent *individuals*— whose relation is *law* just as the relation of estates and guilds was *privilege*—is accomplished in *one and the same act.* As a member of civil society man is the *nonpolitical* man but necessarily appears to be *natural* man. The *rights of man* appear to be *natural rights* because *self-conscious activity* is concentrated on the *political act.* The egoistic man is the *passive* and *given* result of the dissolved society, an object of *immediate certainty* and thus a *natural* object. The *political revolution* dissolves civil life into its constituent elements without *revolutionizing* these elements themselves and subjecting them to criticism. It regards civil society—the realm of needs, labor, private interests, and private right—as the *basis of its existence,* as a *presupposition* needing no ground, and thus as its *natural basis.* Finally, man as a member of civil society is regarded as *authentic* man, *man* as distinct from *citizen,* since he is man in his sensuous, individual, and *most intimate* existence while *political* man is only the abstract and artificial man, man as an *allegorical, moral* person. Actual man is recognized only in the form of an *egoistic* individual, *authentic* man, only in the form of *abstract citizen.*

The abstraction of the political man was correctly depicted by Rousseau:

"Whoever dares to undertake the founding of a nation must feel himself capable of **changing,**[*]

[* Boldface type identified Marx's emphasis in the quotation.]

so to speak, **human nature** and **transforming** each individual who is in himself a complete but isolated whole, into a **part** of something greater than himself from which he somehow derives his life and existence, substituting a **limited** and **moral existence** for physical and independent existence. **Man** must be deprived of **his own powers** and given alien powers which he cannot use without the aid of others." (*Social Contract*, Bk. II, London, 1782, p. 67.)

All emancipation is *restoration* of the human world and the relationships of *men themselves*.

Political emancipation is a reduction of man to a member of civil society, to an *egoistic independent* individual on the one hand and to a *citizen*, a moral person, on the other.

Only when the actual, individual man has taken back into himself the abstract citizen and in his everyday life, his individual work, and his individual relationships has become a *species-being*, only when he has recognized and organized his own powers as *social* powers so that social force is no longer separated from him as *political* power, only then is human emancipation complete.

BRUNO BAUER, "*THE CAPACITY OF PRESENT-DAY JEWS AND CHRISTIANS TO BECOME FREE*," TWENTY-ONE SHEETS [FROM SWITZERLAND (*ED. GEORG HERWEGH*), ZURICH AND WINTERTHUR, 1843], PP. 56–71.

Here Bauer deals with the relation between the *Jewish and Christian religion* and their relation to criticism. Their relation to criticism is their bearing "on the capacity to become free."

Accordingly: "The Christian has only one stage to surpass—namely, his religion—in order to abandon religion in general" and thus become free. "The Jew, on the other hand, has to break not only with his Jewish nature but also with the development, the completion, of his religion, a development which has remained alien to him" (p. 71).

Thus Bauer here transforms the question of Jewish emancipation into a purely religious one. The theological difficulty as to whether the Jew or the Christian has the better prospect of salvation is here reproduced in the enlightened form: Which of the two is *more capable of emancipation?* It is thus no longer the question: Does Judaism or Christianity emancipate? but rather, on the contrary: Which emancipates more, the negation of Judaism or the negation of Christianity?

"If they want to be free, the Jews should not embrace Christianity but Christianity in dissolution, religion generally in dissolution—enlightenment, criticism and its results, free humanity" (p. 70).

For the Jew it is still a matter of *professing faith*, not Christianity but rather Christianity in dissolution.

Bauer requires the Jew to break with the essence of the Christian religion, a requirement which does not follow, as he says himself, from the development of the Jewish nature.

When Bauer, at the end of his *Jewish Question*, interpreted Judaism merely as a crude religious criticism of Christianity and hence gave it "only" a religious significance, it was to be expected that he would also transform the emancipation of the Jews into a philosophico-theological act.

Bauer views the *ideal* and abstract essence of the Jew, his *religion*, as his *whole* nature. Hence he correctly infers: "The Jew contributes nothing to mankind if he disregards his narrow law," if he cancels all his Judaism (p. 65).

The relation of Jews to Christian thus becomes the following: the sole interest of the Christian in the emancipation of the Jew is a general human interest, a *theoretical* interest. Judaism is an offensive fact to the religious eye of the Christian. As soon as the Christian's eye ceases to be religious, this fact ceases to offend it. In and for itself the emancipation of the Jew is not a task for the Christian.

The Jew, on the other hand, not only has to finish his own task but also the task of the Christian—[Bruno Bauer's] *Critique of the* [*Gospel History of the*] *Synop-*

tics and [Strauss'] *Life of Jesus*, etc.—if he wants to emancipate himself.

"They can look after themselves: they will determine their own destiny; but history does not allow itself to be mocked" (p. 71).

We will try to break with the theological formulation of the issue. The question concerning the Jew's capacity for emancipation becomes for us the question: What specific *social* element is to be overcome in order to abolish Judaism? For the modern Jew's capacity for emancipation is the relation of Judaism to the emancipation of the modern world. This relation follows necessarily from the particular position of Judaism in the modern subjugated world.

Let us consider the actual, secular Jew—not the *sabbath Jew*, as Bauer does, but the *everyday Jew*.

Let us look for the secret of the Jew not in his religion but rather for the secret of the religion in the actual Jew.

What is the secular basis of Judaism? *Practical* need, *self-interest*.

What is the worldly cult of the Jew? *Bargaining*. What is his worldly god? *Money*.

Very well! Emancipation from *bargaining* and *money*, and thus from practical and real Judaism would be the self-emancipation of our era.

An organization of society that would abolish the pre-conditions of bargaining and thus its possibility would render the Jew impossible. His religious consciousness would dissolve like a dull mist in the actual life-giving air of society. On the other hand, when the Jew recognizes this *practical* nature of his as futile and strives to eliminate it, he works away from his previous development toward general *human emancipation* and opposes the *supreme practical* expression of human self-alienation.

Thus we perceive in Judaism a general and *contemporary anti-social* element, which has been carried to its present high point by a historical development in which the Jews have contributed to this element, a point at which it must necessarily dissolve itself.

The *emancipation of the Jews*, in the final analysis, is the emancipation of mankind from *Judaism*.

The Jew has already emancipated himself in a Jewish way. "The Jew who is only tolerated in Vienna, for example, determines the fate of the whole empire through his financial power. The Jew who may be without rights in the smallest German state decides the destiny of Europe. While corporations and guilds exclude the Jew or are unfavorable to him, audacity in industry mocks the obstinacy of the medieval institutions." (B. Bauer, *The Jewish Question*, p. 114.)

This is no isolated fact. The Jew has emancipated himself in a Jewish way not only by acquiring financial power but also because, with and without him, *money* has become a world power, and the practical Jewish spirit has become the practical spirit of Christian nations. The Jews have emancipated themselves insofar as the Christian have become Jews.

For example, the pious and politically free inhabitant of New England, Captain Hamilton reports, is a kind of *Laocoön* who does not make the slightest effort to free himself from the serpents strangling him. *Mammon* is his idol to whom he prays not only with his lips but with all the power of his body and soul. In his eyes the world is nothing but a stock exchange, and he is convinced that here below he has no other destiny than to become richer than his neighbor. Bargaining dominates his every thought, exchange in things constitutes his only recreation. When he travels, he carries his shop or office on his back, as it were, and talks of nothing but interest and profit. If he loses sight of his own business for a moment, it is only in order to poke his nose into that of others.

Indeed, the practical domination of Judaism over the Christian world in North America has achieved such clear and common expression that the *very preaching of the Gospel*, the Christian ministry, has become an article of commerce and the bankrupt merchant takes to the Gospel while the minister who has become rich goes into business. "*That man whom you see at the head of a respectable congregation began as a merchant; his business having failed, he became a minister; the other started with the ministry, but as soon as he had acquired a sum of money, he left the pulpit for business. In the eyes of many, the religious ministry is a veritable commercial career.*" (Beaumont, *loc. cit.*, pp. 185, 186.)

According to Bauer it is a hypocritical situation when the Jew is deprived of political rights in theory while he wields enormous power in practice, when he exercises the political influence *wholesale* denied to him in retail (*The Jewish Question*, p. 114).

The contradiction existing between the practical political power of the Jew and his political rights is the contradiction between politics and financial power in general. While politics ideally is superior to financial power, in actual fact it has become its serf.

Judaism has persisted *alongside* Christianity not only as the religious critique of Christianity, not only as the concrete doubt concerning the religious descent of Christianity, but equally because the practical Jewish spirit, Judaism, has perpetuated itself in Christian society and there even attained its highest development. The Jew, who exists as a special member of civil society, is only the special manifestation of civil society's Judaism.

Judaism has survived not in spite of but by means of history.

Out of its own entrails, civil society ceaselessly produces the Jew.

What actually was the foundation of the Jewish religion? Practical need, egoism.

Hence, the Jew's monotheism is actually the polytheism of many needs, a polytheism that makes even the toilet an object of divine law. *Practical need, egoism* is the principle of *civil society* and appears purely as such as soon as civil society has fully delivered itself to the political state. The god of *practical need and self-interest* is *money*.

Money is the jealous god of Israel before whom no other god may exist. Money degrades all the gods of mankind—and converts them into commodities. Money is the general, self-sufficient *value* of everything. Hence it has robbed the whole world, the human world as well as nature, of its proper worth. Money is the alienated essence of man's labor and life, and this alien essence dominates him as he worships it.

The god of the Jews has been secularized and has become the god of the world. The bill of exchange is the Jew's actual god. His god is only an illusory bill of exchange.

The view of nature achieved under the rule of private property and money is an actual contempt for and practical degradation of nature which does, to be sure, exist in the Jewish religion, but only in imagination.

In this sense Thomas Münzer declared it to be intolerable "that every creature should be turned into property, the fish in the water, the birds in the air, the plants of the earth—the creature must also become free."

That which is contained abstractly in the Jewish religion—contempt for theory, for art, for history, for man as an end in himself—is the *actual conscious* standpoint and virtue of the monied man. The species-relation itself, the relation between man and woman, etc., becomes an object of commerce! The woman is bought and sold.

The *chimerical* nationality of the Jew is the nationality of the merchant, particularly of the monied man.

The Jew's unfounded, superficial law is only the religious caricature of unfounded, superficial morality and law in general, the caricature of merely *formal* ceremonies encompassing the world of self-interest.

Here also the highest relation of man is the *legal* relation, the relation to laws which apply to him not because they are laws of his own will and nature but because they *dominate* him and because defection from them will be *avenged*.

Jewish Jesuitism, the same practical Jesuitism Bauer finds in the Talmud, is the relationship of the world of self-interest to the laws governing it, and the cunning circumvention of these laws is that world's main art.

Indeed, the movement of that world within its law is necessarily a continuous abrogation of the law.

Judaism could not develop further as *religion*, could not develop further theoretically, because the perspective of practical need is limited by its very nature and soon exhausted.

By its very nature, the religion of practical need could not find fulfillment in theory but only in *practice* [*Praxis*], simply because practice is its truth.

Judaism could create no new world; it could only draw the new creations and conditions of the world into the compass of its own activity because practical need, whose rationale is self-interest, remains passive, never willfully extending itself but only *finding* itself extended with the continuous development of social conditions.

Judaism reaches its height with the perfection of civil society, but civil society achieves perfection only in the *Christian* world. Only under the reign of Christianity, which makes *all* national, natural, moral, and theoretical relationships *external* to man, was civil society able to separate itself completely from political life, sever all man's species-ties, substitute egoism and selfish need for those ties, and dissolve the human world into a world of atomistic, mutually hostile individuals.

Christianity arose out of Judaism. It has again dissolved itself into Judaism.

From the outset the Christian was the theorizing Jew. Hence, the Jew is the practical Christian, and the practical Christian has again become a Jew.

Christianity overcame real Judaism only in appearance. It was too *noble,* too spiritual, to eliminate the crudeness of practical need except by elevating it into the blue.

Christianity is the sublime thought of Judaism, and Judaism is the common practical application of Christianity. But this application could only become universal after Christianity as religion par excellence had *theoretically* completed the alienation of man from himself and from nature.

Only then could Judaism attain universal dominion and convert externalized man and nature into *alienable* and saleable objects subservient to egoistic need, dependent on bargaining.

Selling is the practice of externalization. As long as man is captivated in religion, knows his nature only as objectified, and thereby converts his nature into an *alien* illusory being, so under the dominion of egoistic need he can only act practically, only practically produce objects, by subordinating both his products and this activity to the domination of an alien being, bestowing upon them the significance of an alien entity —of money.

The Christian egoism of eternal bliss in its practical fulfillment necessarily becomes the material egoism of the Jew, heavenly need is converted into earthly need, and subjectivism becomes selfishness. We do not explain the Jew's tenacity from his religion but rather from the human basis of his religion, from practical need, from egoism.

Since the Jew's real nature has been generally actualized and secularized in civil society, civil society could not convince the Jew of the *unreality* of his *religious* nature which is precisely the ideal representation of practical need. Thus not only in the Pentateuch or Talmud but also in present society we find the nature of the contemporary Jew, not as an abstract nature but a supremely empirical nature, not only as the Jew's narrowness but as the Jewish narrowness of society.

When society succeeds in transcending the *empirical* essence of Judaism—bargaining and all its conditions—the Jew becomes *impossible* because his consciousness no longer has an object, the subjective basis of Judaism—practical need—is humanized, and the conflict between the individual sensuous existence of man and his species-existence is transcended.

The *social* emancipation of the Jew is the *emancipation of society from Judaism.*

MARX

Toward a Critique of Hegel's *Philosophy of Right*: Introduction

For Germany the *criticism of religion* has been essentially completed, and criticism of religion is the premise of all criticism.

The *profane* existence of error is compromised when its *heavenly oratio pro aris et focis* [defense of altar and hearth] has been refuted. Man, who has found only the *reflection* of himself in the fantastic reality of heaven where he sought a supernatural being, will no longer be inclined to find the *semblance* of himself, only the non-human being, where he seeks and must seek his true reality.

The basis of irreligious criticism is: *Man makes religion*, religion does not make man. And indeed religion is the self-consciousness and self-regard of man who has either not yet found or has already lost himself. But *man* is not an abstract being squatting outside the world. Man is *the world of men*, the state, society. This state and this society produce religion, which is an *inverted consciousness of the world* because they are an *inverted world*. Religion is the generalized theory of this world, its encyclopaedic compendium, its logic in popular form, its spiritualistic point d'honneur, its enthusiasm, its moral sanction, its solemn complement, its general ground of consolation and justification. It is the *fantastic realization* of the human essence inasmuch as the *human essence* possesses no true reality. The struggle against religion is therefore indirectly the struggle against *that world* whose spiritual *aroma* is religion.

Religious suffering is the *expression* of real suffering and at the same time the *protest* against real suffering. Religion is the sigh of the oppressed creature, the heart of a heartless world, as it is the spirit of spiritless conditions. It is the *opium* of the people.

The abolition of religion as people's *illusory* happiness is the demand for their *real* happiness. The demand to abandon illusions about their condition is a *demand to abandon a condition which requires illusions*. The criticism of religion is thus in *embryo* a *criticism of the vale of tears* whose *halo* is religion.

Criticism has plucked imaginary flowers from the chain, not so that man will wear the chain that is without fantasy or consolation but so that he will throw it off and pluck the living flower. The criticism of religion disillusions man so that he thinks, acts, and shapes his reality like a disillusioned man who has come to his senses, so that he revolves around himself and thus around his true sun. Religion is only the illusory sun that revolves around man so long as he does not revolve about himself.

Thus it is the *task of history*, once the *otherworldly truth* has disappeared, to establish the *truth of this world*. The immediate *task of philosophy* which is in the service of history is to unmask human self-alienation in its *unholy forms* now that it has been unmasked in its *holy form*. Thus the criticism of heaven turns into the criticism of the earth, the *criticism of religion* into the *criticism of law*, and the *criticism of theology* into the *criticism of politics*.

The following exposition—a contribution to this undertaking [developed from the unpublished "Critique of Hegel's Philosophy of the State" written in Kreuznach]—does not directly pertain to the original but to a copy, the German *philosophy* of the state and law, for the simple reason that it deals with *Germany*.

If one were to proceed from the *status quo* itself in Germany, even in the only appropriate way, *that is*, negatively, the result would still be an *anachronism*. Even the negation of our political present is already a dusty fact in the historical lumber room of modern nations. If I negate powdered wigs, I am still left with unpowdered wigs. If I negate German conditions of

Translated from the German by Loyd D. Easton and Kurt H. Guddat. Reprinted by permission of Loyd D. Easton and Mrs. Kurt H. Guddat.

1843, I am hardly, according to French chronology, in the year 1789 and still less in the focus of the present.

Indeed, German history plumes itself on a development no nation in the historical firmament previously exhibited or will ever copy. We have in point of fact shared in the restorations of the modern nations without sharing in their revolutions—on the one hand because our masters were afraid, and on the other because they were not afraid. Led by our shepherds, we found ourselves in the company of freedom only once, on the *day of its burial*.

A school of thought that legitimizes today's infamy by yesterday's, a school of thought that explains every cry of the serf against the knout as rebellion once the knout is time-honored, ancestral, and historical, a school to which history shows only its *a posteriori*, as the God of Israel did to his servant Moses—the *Historical School of Law*—might have invented German history if it were not an invention of German history. A Shylock, but a servile Shylock, that school swears on its bond, on its historical bond, its Christian-Germanic bond, for every pound of flesh cut from the heart of the people.

Good-natured enthusiasts, German chauvinists by extraction and liberals by reflection, on the other hand, seek our history of freedom beyond our history in the primeval Teutonic forests. But how does the history of our freedom differ from the history of the wild boar's freedom if it is only to be found in the forests? As the proverb says, what is shouted into the forest, the forest echoes back. So peace to the primeval Teutonic forests!

War on German conditions! By all means! They are *below the level of history, beneath all criticism*, but they are still an object of criticism just as the criminal below the level of humanity is still an object of the *executioner*. In its struggle against these conditions criticism is not a passion of the head but the head of passion. It is not a lancet, it is a weapon. Its object is an *enemy* it wants not to refute but to *destroy*. For the spirit of these conditions has already been refuted. In and for themselves they are objects not *worthy of thought* but *existences* as despicable as they are despised. Criticism itself does not even need to be concerned with this matter, for it is already clear about it.

Criticism is no longer an *end in itself* but simply a *means*. Its essential pathos is *indignation*, its essential task, *denunciation*.

It is a matter of describing the pervasive, suffocating pressure of all social spheres on one another, the general but passive dejection, the narrowness that recognized but misunderstands itself—this framed in a system of government that lives on the conservation of all meanness and is nothing but *meanness* in government.

What a sight! Society is forever splitting into the most varied races opposing one another with petty antipathies, bad consciences, and brutal mediocrity, and precisely because of their mutually ambiguous and distrustful situation they are all treated by their *rulers* as merely *tolerated existences*, without exception, though with varying formalities. And they are forced to recognize and acknowledge their being *dominated*, *ruled*, and *possessed* as a *concession from heaven!* On the other side are the rulers themselves whose greatness is inversely proportional to their number!

The criticism dealing with this matter is criticism in *hand-to-hand* combat, and in such a combat the point is not whether the opponent is noble, equal, or *interesting*, the point is to *strike* him. The point is to permit the Germans not even a moment of self-deception and resignation. We must make the actual pressure more pressing by adding to it the consciousness of pressure and make the shame more shameful by publicizing it. Every sphere of German society must be shown as the *partie honteuse* of German society, and we have to make these petrified social relations dance by singing their own tune! The people must be taught to be *terrified* of themselves to give them *courage*. This will fulfill an imperative need of the German nation, and the needs of nations are themselves the ultimate grounds of their satisfaction.

And even for *modern* nations this struggle against the restricted content of the German *status quo* cannot be without interest, for the German *status quo* is the *open fulfillment of the Ancien Régime*, and the *Ancien Régime* is the *hidden deficiency of the modern state*. The struggle against the German political present is the struggle against the past of modern nations, and they are still burdened with reminders of that past.

It is instructive for them to see the *Ancien Régime*, which lived through its *tragedy* with them, play its *comedy* as a German ghost. The history of the *Ancien Régime* was *tragic* so long as it was the established power in the world, while freedom on the other hand was a personal notion—in short, as long as it believed and had to believe in its own validity. As long as the *Ancien Régime* as an existing world order struggled against a world that was just coming into being, there was on its side a historical but not a personal error. Its downfall was therefore tragic.

On the other hand, the present German regime—an anachronism, a flagrant contradiction of generally accepted axioms, the nullity of the *Ancien Régime* exhibited to the whole world—only imagines that it believes in itself and demands that the world imagine the same thing. If it is believed in its own *nature*, would it try to hide that nature under the *semblance* of an alien nature and seek its salvation in hypocrisy and sophism? The modern *Ancien Régime* is merely the *comedian* in a world whose *real heroes* are dead. History is thorough and goes through many phases as it conducts an old form to the grave. The final phase of a world-historical form is *comedy*. The Greek gods, already tragically and mortally wounded in Aeschylus' *Prometheus Bound*, had to die again comically in Lucian's dialogues. Why this course of history? So that mankind may part from its past *happily*. This *happy* historical destiny we vindicate for the political authorities of Germany.

But once *modern* political and social reality itself is subjected to criticism, once criticism arrives at truly human problems, it either finds itself outside the German *status quo* or it would deal with its object at *a level below* its objects. For example! The relation of industry and the world of wealth in general to the political world is a major problem of modern times. In what form is this problem beginning to preoccupy the Germans? In the form of *protective tariffs*, the *system of prohibition*, and *political economy*. German chauvinism has gone from man to matter and thus one fine day our barons of cotton and heroes of iron saw themselves transformed into patriots. Thus in Germany we are beginning to recognize the sovereignty of monopoly at home by investing it with *sovereignty abroad*. We

are about to begin in Germany where France and England are about to end. The old rotten condition against which these countries are revolting in theory and which they bear as chains is greeted in Germany as the dawn of a glorious future which as yet hardly dares to pass from *crafty* [*listigen*: Friedrich List] theory to the most ruthless practice. Whereas the problem in France and England reads: *political economy* or the *rule of society over wealth*, in Germany it reads: *political economy* or the *rule of private property over nationality*. Thus in France and England it is a question of abolishing monopoly that has developed to its final consequences; in Germany it is a question of proceeding to the final consequences of monopoly. There it is a question of solution; here, still a question of collision. This is an adequate example of the *German* form of modern problems, an example of how our history, like a raw recruit, still has had to do extra drill on matters threshed over in history.

If the *total* German development were not in advance of its *political* development, a German could at the most have a share in the problems of the present like that of a *Russian*. But if the single individual is not bound by the limitations of his nation, still less is the nation as a whole liberated by the liberation of one individual. The Scythians made no progress toward Greek culture even though Greece had a Scythian among her philosophers.

Fortunately we are Germans and not Scythians.

As the ancient countries lived their pre-history in imagination, in *mythology*, so we Germans have lived our post-history in thought, in *philosophy*. We are *philosophical* contemporaries of the present without being its *historical* contemporaries. German philosophy is the *ideal extension* of German history. If, therefore, we criticize the *oeuvres posthumes* of our ideal history—philosophy—instead of the *oeuvres incomplètes* of our real history, our criticism is in the center of questions of which the present says: *That is the question*. That which in progressive nations is a *practical* break with modern political conditions is in Germany, where these conditions do not yet exist, just a *critical* break with the philosophical reflection of those conditions.

The *German philosophy of law and of the state* is the only *German history* which stands *al pari* with the *official* modern present. The German nation must therefore join its dream-history to its present conditions and criticize not only these present conditions but also their abstract continuation. Its future can be *limited* neither to the direct negation of its real political and legal conditions nor to their direct fulfillment, for it has the direct negation of its real conditions in its ideal conditions and has almost *outlived* the direct fulfillment of its ideal conditions in the view of neighboring countries. Hence, the *practical* political party in Germany rightly demands the *negation of philosophy*. It is wrong not in its demand but in stopping at the demand it neither seriously fulfills nor can fulfill. It supposes that it accomplishes that negation by turning its back on philosophy, looking aside, and muttering a few petulant and trite phrases about it. Because its outlook is so limited it does not even count philosophy as part of *German* actuality or even imagines it is *beneath* German practice and its theories. You demand starting from *actual germs of life* but forget that the actual lifegerm of the German nation has so far sprouted only inside its *cranium*. In short: *you cannot transcend* [aufheben] *philosophy without actualizing it.*

The same error, but with the factors *reversed*, was committed by the *theoretical* party which originated in philosophy.

In the present struggle the theoretical party saw *only* the *critical struggle of philosophy against the German world*. It did not consider that *previous philosophy* itself belongs to this world and is its *complement*, although an ideal one. Critical toward its counterpart, it was not critical of itself. Starting from the *presuppositions* of philosophy, it either stopped at philosophy's given results or passed off demands and results from somewhere else as direct demands and results from philosophy. But these latter—their legitimacy assumed—can only be obtained by the *negation of previous philosophy*, by the negation of philosophy as philosophy. We shall later give a closer account of this party. Its main defect may be summarized as follows: *It believed that it could actualize philosophy without transcending it.*

The criticism of the *German philosophy of the state and law*, which attained its most consistent, profound, and final formulation with *Hegel*, is at once a critical

analysis of the modern state and the actuality connected with it and also the decisive negation of all previous *forms* of *German political and legal consciousness* whose most prominent and general expression at the level of *science* is precisely the *speculative philosophy of law*. If the speculative philosophy of law—that abstract and extravagant *thinking* about the modern state whose reality remains in the beyond, if only beyond the Rhine—was possible only in Germany, conversely the *German* conception of the modern state in abstraction from *actual man* was possible only because and insofar as the modern state abstracts itself from *actual man* or satisfies the *whole* man only in an illusory way. In politics the Germans have *thought* what other nations have *done*. Germany has been their *theoretical conscience*. The abstraction and presumption of its thought always kept pace with the one-sided and stunted character of their actuality. If the *status quo* of the *German political system* [Staatswesen] expresses *the completion of the Ancien Régime*, the thorn in the flesh of the modern state, the *status quo* of *German political science* [Staatswissen] expresses the *incompletion of the modern state*, the damage to the flesh itself.

As the resolute opponent of the previous mode of *German* political consciousness, the criticism of speculative philosophy of law does not proceed in its own sphere but proceeds to *tasks* that can be solved by only one means—*practice* [Praxis].

The question arises: Can Germany reach a practice *à la hauteur des principes, that is,* a *revolution*, which will raise it not only to the *official level* of modern nations but to the *human level* which will be their immediate future?

The weapon of criticism obviously cannot replace the criticism of weapons. Material force must be overthrown by material force. But theory also becomes a material force once it has gripped the masses. Theory is capable of gripping the masses when it demonstrates *ad hominem*, and it demonstrates *ad hominem* when it becomes radical. To be radical is to grasp things by the root. But for man the root is man himself. The clear proof of the radicalism of German theory and hence of its political energy is that it proceeds from the decisive *positive* transcendence of religion. The criticism of religion ends with the doctrine that *man is the highest being for man*, hence with the *categorical imperative to overthrow all conditions* in which man is a degraded, enslaved, neglected, contemptible being—conditions that cannot better be described than by the exclamation of a Frenchman on the occasion of a proposed dog tax: Poor dogs! They want to treat you like human beings!

Even historically, theoretical emancipation has a specific practical significance for Germany. For Germany's *revolutionary* past is theoretical—it is the *Reformation*. As the revolution then began in the brain of the *monk*, now it begins in the brain of the *philosopher*.

Luther, to be sure, overcame bondage based on *devotion* by replacing it with bondage based on *conviction*. He shattered faith in authority by restoring the authority of faith. He turned priests into laymen by turning laymen into priests. He freed man from outward religiosity by making religiosity the inwardness of man. He emancipated the body from its chains by putting chains on the heart.

But if Protestantism was not the true solution, it was the true formulation of the problem. The question was no longer the struggle of the layman against the *priest external to him* but of his struggle against *his own inner priest*, his *priestly nature*. And if the Protestant transformation of German laymen into priests emancipated the lay popes—the *princes* with their clerical set, the privileged, and the Philistines—the philosophical transformation of priestly Germans into men will emancipate the *people*. But little as emancipation stops with princes, just as little will *secularization* of property stop with the *confiscation of church property* set in motion chiefly by hypocritical Prussia. At that time the Peasants' War, the most radical fact of German history, came to grief because of theology. Today, when theology itself has come to grief, the most unfree fact of German history—our *status quo*—will be shattered by philosophy. On the eve of the Reformation official Germany was the most abject vassal of Rome. On the eve of its revolution Germany is the abject vassal of something less than Rome—of Prussia and Austria, of ignorant country squires and Philistines.

But a major difficulty seems to stand in the way of a *radical* German revolution.

Revolutions require a *passive* element, a *material* basis. Theory is actualized in a people only insofar as it actualizes their needs. But will the enormous discrepancy between the demands of German thought and the answers of German actuality correspond to a similar discrepancy between civil society and the state, and within civil society itself? Will theoretical needs be immediate practical needs? It is not enough that thought should seek its actualization; actuality must itself strive toward thought.

But Germany has not risen to the intermediate stages of political emancipation at the same time as the modern nations. It has not yet reached in practice even the stages it has surpassed in theory. How can it clear with a *salto mortale* not only its own limitations but also those of modern nations—limitations which in actuality it must experience and strive for as an emancipation from its actual limitations? A radical revolution can only be a revolution of radical needs whose preconditions and birthplaces appear to be lacking.

But if Germany has attended the development of modern nations only through the abstract activity of thought without taking an active part in the real struggles of this development, it has also shared the *sufferings* of this development without sharing its enjoyments or partial satisfaction. Abstract activity on one side corresponds to abstract suffering on the other. One fine day Germany will find itself at the level of European decadence before ever having reached the level of European emancipation. It will be comparable to a *fetishist* wasting away from the diseases of Christianity.

Considering *German governments*, we find that owing to the circumstances of the time, the situation of Germany, the outlook of German culture, and finally their own fortunate instinct they are driven to combine the *civilized deficiencies* of the *modern political order* (whose advantages we do not enjoy) with the *barbarous deficiencies* of the *Ancien Régime* (which we enjoy in full). Hence Germany must participate more and more if not in the sense [*Verstand*] at least in the nonsense [*Unverstand*] of those political forms transcending its *status quo*. Is there, for example, another country in the whole world which as naïvely as so-called constitutional Germany shares all the illusions of constitutional statehood without sharing its realities? And was it not, necessarily, a German government's bright idea to combine the tortures of censorship with the tortures of the French September laws [of 1835] presupposing freedom of the press? As the *gods* of all nations were found in the Roman Pantheon, the *sins* of all forms of the state will be found in the Holy German Empire. That this eclecticism will reach an unprecedented height is particularly guaranteed by the *politico-aesthetic gourmanderie* of a German king [Friedrich Wilhelm IV] who plans to play all the roles of monarchy—feudal or bureaucratic, absolute or constitutional, autocratic or democratic—if not in the person of the people at least in his *own*, and if not for the people at least for *himself. As the deficiency of the political present erected into a system, Germany* will not be able to shed the specifically German limitations without shedding the general limitations of the political present.

Radical revolution, *universal human* emancipation, is not a utopian dream for Germany. What is utopian is the partial, the *merely* political revolution, the revolution which would leave the pillars of the house standing. What is the basis of a partial and merely political revolution? It is *part of the civil society* emancipating itself and attaining *universal* supremacy, a particular class by virtue of its *special situation* undertaking the general emancipation of society. This class emancipates the whole of society but only on the condition that the whole of society is in the same position as this class, *for example*, that it has or can easily acquire money and education.

No class in civil society can take this role without arousing an impulse of enthusiasm in itself and in the masses, an impulse in which it fraternizes and merges with society at large, identifies itself with it, and is experienced and recognized as its *general representative* —an impulse in which its claims and rights are truly the rights and claims of society itself and in which it is actually the social head and the social heart. Only in the name of the general rights of society can a particular class claim general supremacy. Revolutionary energy and intellectual self-confidence are not by themselves sufficient to seize this emancipatory position and hence the political control of all spheres of society in the interest of its own. If a *popular revolution* is to coincide with the *emancipation of a particular* class of civil society, if *one* class is to stand for the whole society, all the defects of society must conversely be concentrated in another class. A particular class must be the class of general offense and the incorporation of general limitation. A particular social sphere must stand for the *notorious crime* of society as a whole so that emancipation from this sphere appears as general self-emancipation. For *one* class to be the class of emancipation *par excellence*, conversely another must be the obvious class of oppression. The negative, general significance of the French nobility and clergy determined the positive, general significance of the *bourgeoisie* standing next to and opposing them.

But in Germany every class lacks not only the consistency, penetration, courage, and ruthlessness which could stamp it as the negative representative of society. There is equally lacking in every class that breadth of soul which identified itself, if only momentarily, with the soul of the people—that genius for inspiring material force toward political power, that revolutionary boldness which flings at its adversary the defiant words, *I am nothing and I should be everything*. The main feature of German morality and honor in classes as well as individuals is rather a *modest egoism* displaying its narrowness and allowing it to be displayed against itself. The relationship of the different spheres of German society is therefore not dramatic but epic. Each of them begins to be aware of itself and place itself beside the others, not as soon as it is oppressed but as soon as circumstances, without its initiative, create a social layer on which it can exert pressure in turn. Even the *moral self-esteem of the German middle class* rests only on its awareness of being the general representative of the philistine mediocrity of all the other classes. Hence, not only do German kings ascend their thrones *mal à propos*, but every section of civil society goes through a defeat before it celebrates victory, develops its own obstacles before it overcomes those facing it, asserts its narrow-minded nature before it can assert its generosity so that even the opportunity of playing a great role has always passed before it actually existed and each class is involved in a struggle against the class beneath as soon as it begins to struggle with the class above it. Hence princes struggle against kings, the bureaucrat against the nobility, and the bourgeoisie against them all, while the proletariat is already beginning to struggle against the bourgeoisie. The middle class hardly dares to conceive the idea of emancipation from its own perspective. The development of social conditions and the progress of political theory show that perspective to be already antiquated or at least problematic.

In France it is enough to be something for one to want to be everything. In Germany no one can be anything unless he is prepared to renounce everything. In France partial emancipation is the basis of universal emancipation. In Germany universal emancipation is the *conditio sine qua non* of any partial emancipation. In France it is the actuality, in Germany the impossibility, of gradual emancipation which must give birth to complete freedom. In France every class of the nation is *politically idealistic* and experiences itself first of all not as a particular class but as representing the general needs of society. The role of *emancipator* thus passes successively and dramatically to different classes of people until it finally reaches the class which actualizes social freedom, no longer assuming certain conditions external to man and yet created by human society but rather organizing all the conditions of human existence on the basis of social freedom. In Germany, by contrast, where practical life is as mindless as mental life is impractical, no class in civil society has any need or capacity for general emancipation until it is forced to it by its *immediate* condition, by *material* necessity, by its *very chains*.

Where then, is the *positive* possibility of German emancipation?

Answer: In the formation of a class with *radical chains,* a class in civil society that is not of civil society, a class that is the dissolution of all classes, a sphere of society having a universal character because of its universal suffering and claiming no *particular* right because no *particular wrong* but *unqualified wrong* is perpetrated on it; a sphere that can invoke no *traditional* title but only a *human* title, which does not partially oppose the consequences but totally opposes

the premises of the German political system; a sphere, finally, that cannot emancipate itself without emancipating itself from all the other spheres of society, thereby emancipating them; a sphere, in short, that is the *complete loss* of humanity and can only redeem itself through the *total redemption of humanity*. This dissolution of society as a particular class is the *proletariat*.

The proletariat is only beginning to appear in Germany as a result of the rising *industrial* movement. For it is not poverty from *natural circumstances* but *artificially produced* poverty, not the human masses mechanically oppressed by the weight of society but the masses resulting from the *acute disintegration* of society, and particularly of the middle class, which gives rise to the proletariat—though also, needless to say, poverty from natural circumstances and Christian-Germanic serfdom gradually join the proletariat.

Heralding the *dissolution of the existing order of things,* the proletariat merely announces the *secret of its own existence* because it *is* the *real* dissolution of this order. Demanding the *negation of private property*, the proletariat merely raises to the *principle of society* what society has raised to the principle *of the proletariat,* what the proletariat already embodies as the negative result of society without its action. The proletarian thus has the same right in the emerging order of things as the *German king* has in the existing order when he calls the people *his* people or a horse *his* horse. Declaring the people to be his private property, the king merely proclaims that the private owner is king.

As philosophy finds its *material* weapons in the proletariat, the proletariat finds its *intellectual* weapons in philosophy. And once the lightning of thought has deeply struck this unsophisticated soil of the people, the *Germans* will emancipate themselves to become *men.*

Let us summarize the result:

The only emancipation of Germany possible *in practice* is emancipation based on *the* theory proclaiming that man is the highest essence of man. In Germany emancipation from the *Middle Ages* is possible only as emancipation at the same time from *partial* victories over the Middle Ages. In Germany *no* brand of bondage can be broken without *every* brand of bondage being broken. Always seeking *fundamentals,* Germany can only make a *fundamental* revolution. The *emancipation of the German* is the *emancipation of mankind.* The *head* of this emancipation is *philosophy,* its *heart* is the *proletariat.* Philosophy cannot be actualized without the transcendence [*Aufhebung*] of the proletariat, the proletariat cannot be transcended without the actualization of philosophy.

When all the inner conditions are fulfilled, the *day of German resurrection* will be announced by the *crowing of the French rooster.*

Marx

Alienated Labor

We have proceeded from the presuppositions of political economy. We have accepted its language and its laws. We presupposed private property, the separation of labor, capital and land, hence of wages, profit of capital and rent, likewise the division of labor, competition, the concept of exchange value, etc. From political economy itself, in its own words, we have shown that the worker sinks to the level of a commodity, the most miserable commodity; that the misery of the worker is inversely proportional to the power and volume of his production; that the necessary result of competition is the accumulation of capital in a few hands and thus the revival of monopoly in a more frightful form; and finally that the distinction between capitalist and landowner, between agricultural laborer and industrial worker, disappears and the whole society must divide into the two classes of *proprietors* and propertyless *workers*.

Political economy proceeds from the fact of private property. It does not explain private property. It grasps the actual, *material* process of private property in abstract and general formulae which it then takes as *laws*. It does not *comprehend* these laws, that is, does not prove them as proceeding from the nature of private property. Political economy does not disclose the reason for the division between capital and labor, between capital and land. When, for example, the relation of wages to profits is determined, the ultimate basis is taken to be the interest of the capitalists; that is, political economy assumes what it should develop. Similarly, competition is referred to at every point and explained from external circumstances. Political economy teaches us nothing about the extent to which these external, apparently accidental circumstances are simply the expression of a necessary development. We have seen how political economy regards exchange itself as an accidental fact. The only wheels which political economy puts in motion are *greed* and the *war among the greedy, competition.*

Just because political economy does not grasp the interconnections within the movement, the doctrine of competition could stand opposed to the doctrine of monopoly, the doctrine of freedom of craft to that of the guild, the doctrine of the division of landed property to that of the great estate. Competition, freedom of craft, and division of landed property were developed and conceived only as accidental, deliberate, forced consequences of monopoly, the guild, and feudal property, rather than necessary, inevitable, natural consequences.

We now have to grasp the essential connection among private property, greed, division of labor, capital and landownership, and the connection of exchange with competition, of value with the devaluation of men, of monopoly with competition, etc., and of this whole alienation with the *money*-system.

Let us not put ourselves in a fictitious primordial state like a political economist trying to clarify things. Such a primordial state clarifies nothing. It merely pushes the issue into a gray, misty distance. It acknowledges as a fact or event what it should deduce, namely, the necessary relation between two things: for example, between division of labor and exchange. In such a manner theology explains the origin of evil by the fall of man. That is, it asserts as a fact in the form of history what it should explain.

We proceed from a *present* fact of political economy.

The worker becomes poorer the more wealth he produces, the more his production increases in power and extent. The worker becomes a cheaper commodity the more commodities he produces. The *increase*

Translated from the German by Loyd D. Easton and Kurt H. Guddat. Reprinted by permission of Loyd D. Easton and Mrs. Kurt H. Guddat.

in value of the world of things is directly proportional to the *decrease in value* of the human world. Labor not only produces commodities. It also produces itself and the worker as a *commodity*, and indeed in the same proportion as it produces commodities in general.

This fact simply indicates that the object which labor produces, its product, stands opposed to it as an *alien thing*, as a *power independent* of the producer. The product of labor is labor embodied and made objective in a thing. It is the *objectification* of labor. The realization of labor is its objectification. In the viewpoint of political economy this realization of labor appears as the *diminution* of the worker, the objectification as the *loss of and subservience to the object*, and the appropriation as *alienation* [*Entfremdung*], as externalization [*Entäusserung*].

So much does the realization of labor appear as diminution that the worker is diminished to the point of starvation. So much does objectification appear as loss of the object that the worker is robbed of the most essential objects not only of life but also of work. Indeed, work itself becomes a thing of which he can take possession only with the greatest effort and with the most unpredictable interruptions. So much does the appropriation of the object appear as alienation that the more objects the worker produces, the fewer he can own and the more he falls under the domination of his product, of capital.

All these consequences follow from the fact that the worker is related to the *product of his labor* as to an *alien* object. For it is clear according to this premise: The more the worker exerts himself, the more powerful becomes the alien objective world which he fashions against himself, the poorer he and his inner world become, the less there is that belongs to him. It is the same in religion. The more man attributes to God, the less he retains in himself. The worker puts his life into the object; then it no longer belongs to him but to the object. The greater his activity, the poorer is the worker. What the product of his work is, he is not. The greater this product is, the smaller he is himself. The *externalization* of the worker in his product means not only that his work becomes an object, an *external* existence, but also that it exists *outside him* independently, alien, an autonomous power, opposed to him.

The life he has given to the object confronts him as hostile and alien.

Let us now consider more closely the *objectification*, the worker's production and with it the *alienation* and *loss* of the object, his product.

The worker can make nothing without *nature*, without the *sensuous external world*. It is the material wherein his labor realizes itself, wherein it is active, out of which and by means of which it produces.

But as nature furnishes to labor the *means of life* in the sense that labor cannot *live* without objects upon which labor is exercised, nature also furnishes the *means of life* in the narrower sense, namely, the means of physical subsistence of the *worker* himself.

The more the worker *appropriates* the external world and sensuous nature through his labor, the more he deprives himself of the *means of life* in two respects: first, that the sensuous external world gradually ceases to be an object belonging to his labor, a *means of life* of his work; secondly, that it gradually ceases to be a *means of life* in the immediate sense, a means of physical subsistence of the worker.

In these two respects, therefore, the worker becomes a slave to his objects; first, in that he receives an *object of labor*, that is, he receives *labor*, and secondly that he receives the *means of subsistence*. The first enables him to exist as a *worker* and the second as a *physical subject*. The terminus of this slavery is that he can only maintain himself as a *physical subject* so far as he is a *worker*, and only as a *physical subject* is he a worker.

(The alienation of the worker in his object is expressed according to the laws of political economy as follows: the more the worker produces, the less he has to consume; the more values he creates the more worthless and unworthy he becomes; the better shaped his product, the more misshapen is he; the more civilized his product, the more barbaric is the worker; the more powerful the work, the more powerless becomes the worker; the more intelligence the work has, the more witless is the worker and the more he becomes a slave of nature.)

Political economy conceals the alienation in the nature of labor by ignoring the direct relationship between the worker (labor) *and production*. To be sure, labor produces marvels for the wealthy but it produces deprivation for the worker. It produces palaces, but hovels for the worker. It produces beauty, but mutilation for the worker. It displaces labor through machines, but it throws some workers back into barbarous labor and turns others into machines. It produces intelligence, but for the worker it produces imbecility and cretinism.

The direct relationship of labor to its products is the relationship of the worker to the objects of his production. The relationship of the rich to the objects of production and to production itself is only a *consequence* of this first relationship and confirms it. Later we shall observe the latter aspect.

Thus, when we ask, What is the essential relationship of labor? we ask about the relationship of the *worker* to production.

Up to now we have considered the alienation, the externalization of the worker only from one side: his *relationship to the products of his labor*. But alienation is shown not only in the result but also in the *process of production*, in the *producing activity* itself. How could the worker stand in an alien relationship to the product of his activity if he did not alienate himself from himself in the very act of production? After all, the product is only the résumé of activity, of production. If the product of work is externalization, production itself must be active externalization, externalization of activity, activity of externalization. Only alienation—and externalization in the activity of labor itself—is summarized in the alienation of the object of labor.

What constitutes the externalization of labor?

First is the fact that labor is *external* to the laborer—that is, it is not part of his nature—and that the worker does not affirm himself in his work but denies himself, feels miserable and unhappy, develops no free physical and mental energy but mortifies his flesh and ruins his mind. The worker, therefore feels at ease only outside work, and during work he is outside himself. He is at home when he is not working and when he is working he is not at home. His work, therefore, is not voluntary, but coerced, *forced labor.* It is not the satisfaction of a need but only a *means* to satisfy other needs. Its alien character is obvious from the fact that as soon as no physical or other pressure exists, labor is avoided like the plague. External labor, labor in which

man is externalized, is labor of self-sacrifice, of penance. Finally, the external nature of work for the worker appears in the fact that it is not his own but another person's, that in work he does not belong to himself but to someone else. In religion the spontaneity of human imagination, the spontaneity of the human brain and heart, acts independently of the individual as an alien, divine or devilish activity. Similarly, the activity of the worker is not his own spontaneous activity. It belongs to another. It is the loss of his own self.

The result, therefore, is that man (the worker) feels that he is acting freely only in his animal functions—eating, drinking, and procreating, or at most in his shelter and finery—while in his human functions he feels only like an animal. The animalistic becomes the human and the human the animalistic.

To be sure, eating, drinking, and procreation are genuine human functions. In abstraction, however, and separated from the remaining sphere of human activities and turned into final and sole ends, they are animal functions.

We have considered labor, the act of alienation of practical human activity, in two aspects: (1) the relationship of the worker to the *product of labor* as an alien object dominating him. This relationship is at the same time the relationship to the sensuous external world, to natural objects as an alien world hostile to him; (2) the relationship of labor to the *act of production* in *labor*. This relationship is that of the worker to his own activity as alien and not belonging to him, activity as passivity, power as weakness, procreation as emasculation, the worker's *own* physical and spiritual energy, his personal life—for what else is life but activity—as an activity turned against him, independent of him, and not belonging to him. *Self-alienation*, as against the alienation of the *object*, stated above.

We have now to derive a third aspect of *alienated labor* from the two previous ones.

Man is a species-being [*Gattungswesen*] not only in that he practically and theoretically makes his own species as well as that of other things his object, but also—and this is only another expression for the same thing—in that as present and living species he considers himself to be a *universal* and consequently free being.

The life of the species in man as in animals is physical in that man, (like the animal) lives by inorganic nature. And as man is more universal than the animal, the realm of inorganic nature by which he lives is more universal. As plants, animals, minerals, air, light, etc., in theory form a part of human consciousness, partly as objects of natural science, partly as objects of art—his spiritual inorganic nature of spiritual means of life which he first must prepare for enjoyment and assimilation—so they also form in practice a part of human life and human activity. Man lives physically only by these products of nature; they may appear in the form of food, heat, clothing, housing, etc. The universality of man appears in practice in the universality which makes the whole of nature his *inorganic* body: (1) as a direct means of life, and (2) as the matter, object, and instrument of his life activity. Nature is the *inorganic body* of man, that is, nature insofar as it is not the human body. Man *lives* by nature. This means that nature is his *body* with which he must remain in perpetual process in order not to die. That the physical and spiritual life of man is tied up with nature is another way of saying that nature is linked to itself, for man is a part of nature.

In alienating (1) nature from man, and (2) man from himself, his own active function, his life activity, alienated labor also alienates the *species* from him; it makes *species-life* the means of individual life. In the first place it alienates species-life and the individual life, and secondly it turns the latter in its abstraction into the purpose of the former, also in its abstract and alienated form.

For labor, *life activity*, and *productive life* appear to man at first only as a *means* to satisfy a need, the need to maintain physical existence. Productive life, however, is species-life. It is life begetting life. In the mode of life activity lies the entire character of a species, its species-character; and free conscious activity is the species-character of man. Life itself appears only as a *means of life*.

The animal is immediately one with its life activity, not distinct from it. The animal is *its life activity*. Man makes his life activity itself into an object of will and consciousness. He has conscious life activity. It is not a determination with which he immediately identifies.

Conscious life activity distinguishes man immediately from the life activity of the animal. Only thereby is he a species-being. Or rather, he is only, a conscious being—that is, his own life is an object for him—since he is a species-being. Only on that account is his activity free activity. Alienated labor reverses the relationship in that man, since he is a conscious being, makes his life activity, his *essence*, only a means for his *existence*.

The practical creation of an *objective world*, the *treatment* of inorganic nature, is proof that man is a conscious species-being, that is, a being which is related to its species as to its own essence or is related to itself as a species-being. To be sure animals also produce. They build themselves nests, dwelling places, like the bees, beavers, ants, etc. But the animal produces only what is immediately necessary for itself or its young. It produces in a one-sided way while man produces universally. The animal produces under the domination of immediate physical need while man produces free of physical need and only genuinely so in freedom from such need. The animal only produces itself while man reproduces the whole of nature. The animal's product belongs immediately to its physical body while man is free when he confronts his product. The animal builds only according to the standard and need of the species to which it belongs while man knows how to produce according to the standard of any species and at all times knows how to apply an intrinsic standard to the object. Thus man creates also according to the laws of beauty.

In the treatment of the objective world, therefore, man proves himself to be genuinely a *species-being*. This production is his active species-life. Through it nature appears as *his* work and his actuality. The object of labor is thus the *objectification of man's species-life*: he produces himself not only intellectually, as in consciousness, but also actively in a real sense and sees himself in a world he made. In taking from man the object of his production, alienated labor takes from his *species-life*, his actual and objective existence as a species. It changes his superiority to the animal to inferiority, since he is deprived of nature, his inorganic body.

By degrading free spontaneous activity to the level of a means, alienated labor makes the species-life of man a means of his physical existence.

The consciousness which man has from his species is altered through alienation, so that species-life becomes a means for him.

(3) Alienated labor hence turns the *species-existence of man*, and also nature as his mental species-capacity, into an existence *alien* to him, into the *means* of his *individual existence*. It alienates his spiritual nature, his *human essence*, from his own body and likewise from nature outside him.

(4) A direct consequence of man's alienation from the product of his work, from his life activity, and from his species-existence, is the *alienation of man* from *man*. When man confronts himself, he confronts *other* men. What holds true of man's relationship to his work, to the product of his work, and to himself, also holds true of man's relationship to other men, to their labor, and the object of their labor.

In general, the statement that man is alienated from his species-existence means that one man is alienated from another just as each man is alienated from human nature.

The alienation of man, the relation of man to himself, is realized and expressed in the relation between man and other men.

Thus in the relation of alienated labor every man sees the others according to the standard and the relation in which he finds himself as a worker.

We began with an economic fact, the alienation of the worker and his product. We have given expression to the concept of this fact: *alienated, externalized* labor. We have analyzed this concept and have thus analyzed merely a fact of political economy.

Let us now see further how the concept of alienated, externalized labor must express and respect itself in actuality.

If the product of labor is alien to me, confronts me as an alien power, to whom then does it belong?

If my own activity does not belong to me, if it is an alien and forced activity, to whom then does it belong?

To a being *other* than myself.

Who is this being?

Gods? To be sure, in early times the main production, for example, the building of temples in Egypt, India, and Mexico, appears to be in the service of the gods, just as the product belongs to the gods. But gods alone were never workmasters. The same is true of *nature*. And what a contradiction it would be if the more man subjugates nature through his work and the more the miracles of gods are rendered superfluous by the marvels of industry, man should renounce his joy in producing and the enjoyment of his product for love of these powers.

The *alien* being who owns labor and the product of labor, whom labor serves and whom the product of labor satisfies can only be *man* himself.

That the product of labor does not belong to the worker and an alien power confronts him is possible only because this product belongs to *a man other than the worker*. If his activity is torment for him, it must be the *pleasure* and the life-enjoyment for another. Not gods, not nature, but only man himself can be this alien power over man.

Let us consider the statement previously made, that the relationship of man to himself is *objective* and *actual* to him only through his relationships to other men. If man is related to the product of his labor, to his objectified labor, as to an *alien*, hostile, powerful object independent of him, he is so related that another alien, hostile, powerful man independent of him is the lord of this object. If he is unfree in relation to his own activity, he is related to it as bonded activity, activity under the domination, coercion, and yoke of another man.

Every self-alienation of man, from himself and from nature, appears in the relationship which he postulates between other men and himself and nature. Thus religious self-alienation appears necessarily in the relation of laity to priest, or also to a mediator, since we are here now concerned with the spiritual world. In the practical real world self-alienation can appear only in the practical real relationships to other men. The means whereby the alienation proceeds is a *practical* means. Through alienated labor man thus not only produces his relationship to the object and to the act of production as an alien man at enmity with him. He also creates the relation in which other men stand to his production and product, and the relation in which he stands to these other men. Just as he begets his own production as loss of his reality, as his punishment; just as he begets his own product as a loss, a product not belonging to him, so he begets the domination of the non-producer over production and over product. As he alienates his own activity from himself, he confers upon the stranger an activity which is not his own.

Up to this point, we have investigated the relationship only from the side of the worker and will later investigate it also from the side of the non-worker.

Thus through *alienated externalized labor* does the worker create the relation to this work of man alienated to labor and standing outside it. The relation of the worker to labor produces the relation of the capitalist to labor, or whatever one wishes to call the lord of labor. *Private property* is thus product, result, and necessary consequence of *externalized labor,* of the external relation of the worker to nature and to himself.

Private property thus is derived, through analysis, from the concept of *externalized labor,* that is, *externalized man,* alienated labor, alienated life, and *alienated* man.

We have obtained the concept of *externalized labor (externalized life)* from political economy as a result of the *movement of private property.* But the analysis of this idea shows that though private property appears to be the ground and cause of externalized labor, it is rather a consequence of externalized labor, just as gods are *originally* not the cause but the effect of an aberration of the human mind. Later this relationship reverses.

Only at the final culmination of the development of private property does this, its secret, reappear—namely, that on the one hand it is the *product* of externalized labor and that secondly it is the *means* through which labor externalizes itself, the *realization of this externalization.*

This development throws light on several conflicts hitherto unresolved.

(1) Political economy proceeds from labor as the very soul of production and yet gives labor nothing, private property everything. From this contradiction Proudhon decided in favor of labor and against private property. We perceive, however, that this apparent contradiction is the contradiction of *alienated labor* with itself and that political economy has only formulated the laws of alienated labor.

Therefore we also perceive that *wages* and *private property* are identical: for when the product, the object of labor, pays for the labor itself, wages are only a necessary consequence of the alienation of labor. In wages labor appears not as an end in itself but as the servant of wages. We shall develop this later and now only draw some conclusions.

An enforced *raising of wages* (disregarding all other difficulties, including that this anomaly could only be maintained forcibly) would therefore be nothing but a *better slave-salary* and would not achieve either for the worker or for labor human significance and dignity.

Even the *equality of wages,* as advanced by Proudhon, would only convert the relation of the contemporary worker to his work into the relation of all men to labor. Society would then be conceived as an abstract capitalist.

Wages are a direct result of alienated labor, and alienated labor is the direct cause of private property. The downfall of one is necessarily the downfall of the other.

(2) From the relation of alienated labor to private property it follows further that the emancipation of society from private property, etc., from servitude, is expressed in its *political* form as the *emancipation of workers,* not as though it is only a question of their emancipation but because in their emancipation is contained universal human emancipation. It is contained in their emancipation because the whole of human servitude is involved in the relation of worker to production, and all relations of servitude are only modifications and consequences of the worker's relation to production.

As we have found the concept of *private property* through *analysis* from the concept of *alienated, externalized labor,* so we can develop all the *categories* of political economy with the aid of these two factors, and we shall again find in each category—for example, barter, competition, capital, money—only a *particular* and *developed expression* of these primary foundations.

Before considering this configuration, however, let us try to solve two problems.

(1) To determine the general *nature of private property* as a result of alienated labor in its relation to *truly human* and *social property.*

(2) We have taken the *alienation of labor* and its *externalization* as a fact and analyzed this fact. How, we ask now, does it happen that *man externalizes* his *labor*, alienates it? How is this alienation rooted in the nature of human development? We have already achieved much in resolving the problem by *transforming* the question concerning the *origin of private property* into the question concerning the relationship of *externalized labor* to evolution of humanity. In talking about *private property* one believes he is dealing with something external to man. Talking of labor, one is immediately dealing with man himself. This new formulation of the problem already contains its solution.

On (1) *The general nature of private property and its relation to truly human property.*

We have resolved alienated labor into two parts which mutually determine each other or rather are only different expressions of one and the same relationship. *Appropriation* appears as *alienation*, as *externalization*; *externalization* as *appropriation*; *alienation* as the true *naturalization*.

We considered the one side, *externalized* labor, in relation to the *worker* himself, that is, the relation of *externalized labor to itself*. We have found the *property relation of the non-worker* to the *worker* and *labor* to be the product, the necessary result, of this relationship. *Private property* as the material, summarized expression of externalized labor embraces both relationships—the *relationship of worker to labor, the product of his work, and the non-worker*; and the relationship of the *non-worker to the worker* and *the product of his labor.*

As we have seen that in relation to the worker who *appropriates* nature through his labor the appropriation appears as alienation—self-activity as activity for another and of another, living as the sacrifice of life, production of the object as loss of it to an alien power, an *alien* man—we now consider the relationship of this *alien* man to the worker, to labor and its object.

It should be noted first that everything which appears with the worker as an *activity of externalization* and an *activity of alienation* appears with the non-worker as a *condition of externalization*, a *condition of alienation.*

Secondly, that the *actual, practical attitude* of the worker in production and to his product (as a condition of mind) appears as a *theoretical* attitude in the non-worker confronting him.

Thirdly, the non-worker does everything against the worker which the worker does against himself, but he does not do against his own self what he does against the worker.

Let us consider more closely these three relationships. [Here the manuscript breaks off, unfinished.]

MARX
Theses on Feuerbach

(1)

The chief defect of all previous materialism (including Feuerbach's) is that the object, actuality, sensuousness is conceived only in the form of the *object or perception* [*Anschauung*], but not as *sensuous human activity, practice* [*Praxis*], not subjectively. Hence in opposition to materialism the *active* side was developed by idealism—but only abstractly since idealism naturally does not know actual, sensuous activity as such. Feuerbach wants sensuous objects actually different from thought objects: but he does not comprehend human activity itself as *objective*. Hence in *The Essence of Christianity* he regards only the theoretical attitude as the truly human attitude, while practice is understood and fixed only in its dirtily Jewish form of appearance. Consequently he does not comprehend the significance of "revolutionary," of "practical-critical" activity.

(2)

The question whether human thinking can reach objective truth—is not a question of theory but a *practical* question. In practice man must prove the truth, that is, actuality and power, this-sidedness of his thinking. The dispute about the actuality or non-actuality of thinking—thinking isolated from practice—is a purely *scholastic* question.

(3)

The materialistic doctrine concerning the change of circumstances and education forgets that circum-

Translated from the German by Loyd D. Easton and Kurt H. Guddat. Reprinted by permission of Loyd D. Easton and Mrs. Kurt H. Guddat.

stances are changed by men and that the educator must himself be educated. Hence this doctrine must divide society into two parts—one of which towers above [as in Robert Owen, Engels added].

The coincidence of the change of circumstances and of human activity or self-change can be comprehended and rationally understood only as *revolutionary practice.*

(4)

Feuerbach starts out from the fact of religious self-alienation, the duplication of the world into a religious and secular world. His work consists in resolving the religious world into its secular basis. But the fact that the secular basis becomes separate from itself and establishes an independent realm in the clouds can only be explained by the cleavage and self-contradictoriness of the secular basis. Thus the latter must itself be both understood in its contradiction and revolutionized in practice. For instance, after the earthly family is found to be the secret of the holy family, the former must then be theoretically and practically nullified.

(5)

Feuerbach, not satisfied with *abstract thinking*, wants *perception*; but he does not comprehend sensuousness as *practical*, human-sensuous activity.

(6)

Feuerbach resolves the religious essence into the *human* essence. But the essence of man is no abstraction inhering in each single individual. In its actuality it is the ensemble of social relationships.

Feuerbach, who does not go into the criticism of this actual essence, is hence compelled

1. to abstract from the historical process and to establish religious feeling as something self-contained, and to presuppose an abstract—*isolated*—human individual;

2. to view the essence of man merely as "species," as the inner, dumb generality which unites the many individuals *naturally*.

(7)

Feuerbach does not see, consequently, that "religious feeling" is itself a social product and that the abstract individual he analyzes belongs to a particular form of society.

(8)

All social life is essentially *practical*. All mysteries which lead theory to mysticism find their rational solution in human practice and the comprehension of this practice.

(9)

The highest point attained by perceptual materialism, that is, materialism that does not comprehend sensuousness as practical activity, is the view of separate individuals and civil society.

(10)

The standpoint of the old materialism is civil society; the standpoint of the new is human society or socialized humanity.

(11)

The philosophers have only *interpreted* the world in various ways; the point is, to *change* it.

Marx and Engels
The German Ideology

Preface

Until now men have constantly had false conceptions of themselves, about what they are or what they ought to be. They have related themselves to one another in conformity with their ideas of God, of normal man, etc. The phantoms of their imagination have gotten too big for them. They, the creators, have been bowing to their creations. Let us liberate them from their chimeras, from their ideas, dogmas, imaginary beings, under whose yoke they are languishing. Let us rebel against the rule of thoughts. Let us teach man, says one person, to exchange these imaginings for thoughts that correspond to man's essence; let us teach man to be critical toward them, says another; let us teach man to get rid of them altogether, says a third. Then—existing reality will collapse.

Such innocent and childlike fantasies make up the core of recent Young-Hegelian philosophy which not only is received with horror and awe by the German public, but is also propounded by the *philosophic heroes* themselves with a ceremonious consciousness of its cataclysmic dangerousness and criminal disregard. The first volume of the present publication attempts to unmask these sheep who consider themselves and are taken to be wolves, to show how their bleating only follows in philosophy the conceptions of the average German citizen, to indicate how the boasting of these philosophic exegetes simply mirrors the wretchedness of actual conditions in Germany. This publication aims to debunk and discredit that philosophic struggle with shadows of reality which so appeals to the dreamy, drowsy German people.

Translated from the German by Loyd D. Easton and Kurt H. Guddat. Reprinted by permission of Loyd D. Easton and Mrs. Kurt H. Guddat.

A clever fellow once got the idea that people drown because they are possessed by the *idea of gravity*. If they would get this notion out of their heads by seeing it as religious superstition, they would be completely safe from all danger of water. For his entire life he fought against the illusion of gravity while all statistics gave him new and abundant evidence of its harmful effects. That kind of fellow is typical of the new revolutionary philosophers in Germany.

* * *

1. Ideology in General, Especially German Philosophy.[*] ((We know only one science, the science of history. History can be viewed from two sides: it can be divided into the history of nature and that of man. The two sides, however, are not to be seen as independent entities. As long as man has existed, nature and man have affected each other. The history of nature, so-called natural history, does not concern us here at all. But we will have to discuss the history of man, since almost all ideology amounts to either a distorted interpretation of this history or a complete abstraction from it. Ideology itself is only one of the sides of this history.))

The premises from which we start are not arbitrary; they are no dogmas but rather actual premises from which abstraction can be made only in imagination. They are the real individuals, their actions, and their material conditions of life, those which they find existing as well as those which they produce through their actions. These premises can be substantiated in a purely empirical way.

The first premise of all human history, of course, is the existence of living human individuals. ((The first

[*This heading and subsequent material within double parentheses were crossed out in the original manuscript.]

historical act of these individuals, the act by which they distinguish themselves from animals, is not the fact that they think but the fact that they begin to *produce their means of subsistence*.)) The first fact to be established, then, is the physical organization of these individuals and their consequent relationship to the rest of nature. Of course, we cannot discuss here the physical nature of man or the natural conditions in which man finds himself—geological, orohydrographical, climatic, and others. ((These relationships affect not only the original and natural organization of men, especially as to race, but also his entire further development or non-development up to the present.)) All historiography must proceed from these natural bases and their modification in the course of history through the actions of men.

Man can be distinguished from the animal by consciousness, religion, or anything else you please. He begins to distinguish himself from the animal the moment he begins to *produce* his means of subsistence, a step required by his physical organization. By producing food, man indirectly produces his material life itself.

The way in which man produces his food depends first of all on the nature of the means of subsistence that he finds and has to reproduce. This mode of production must not be viewed simply as reproduction of the physical existence of individuals. Rather it is a definite form of their activity, a definite way of expressing their life, a definite *mode of life*. As individuals express their life, so they are. What they are, therefore, coincides with what they produce, with *what* they produce and *how* they produce. The nature of individuals thus depends on the material conditions which determine their production.

This production begins with *population growth* which in turn presupposes *interaction* [*Verkehr*] among individuals. The form of such interaction is again determined by production.[*]

[*Break in manuscript text indicated by triple indentation of first line of the following paragraph. In all the text to follow some long paragraphs have been divided to facilitate reading, but in such cases the first lines of the new paragraphs have ordinary indentations.]

The relations of various nations with one another depend upon the extent to which each of them has developed its productive forces, the division of labor, and domestic commerce. This proposition is generally accepted. But not only the relation of one nation to others, but also the entire internal structure of the nation itself depends on the stage of development achieved by its production and its domestic and international commerce. How far the productive forces of a nation are developed is shown most evidently by the degree to which the division of labor has been developed. Each new productive force, insofar as it is not only a quantitative extension of productive forces already known (e.g. cultivation of land) will bring about a further development of the division of labor.

The division of labor in a nation leads first of all to the separation of industrial-commercial labor from agricultural labor and consequently to the separation of *town* and *country* and to a clash of their interests. Its further development leads to the separation of commercial from industrial labor. At the same time, within these various branches, there develop through the division of labor further various divisions among the individuals cooperating in specific kinds of labor. The relative position of these individual groups is determined by the methods employed in agricultural, industrial, and commercial labor (patriarchalism, slavery, estates, classes). The same conditions can be observed in the relations of various nations if commerce has been further developed.

The different stages of development in the division of labor are just so many different forms of ownership; that is, the stage in the division of labor also determines the relations of individuals to one another so far as the material, instrument, and product of labor are concerned.

The first form of ownership is tribal ownership. It corresponds to the undeveloped stage of production where people live by hunting and fishing, by breeding animals or, in the highest stage, by agriculture. Great areas of uncultivated land are equipped in the latter case. The division of labor at this stage is still very undeveloped and confined to extending the natural division of labor in the family. The social structure thus is limited to an extension of the family: patriarchal family chieftains, below them the members of the tribe, finally the slaves. The slavery latent in the family develops only gradually with the increase in population, the increase of wants, and the extension of external relations in war as well as in barter.

The second form is the ancient communal and state ownership which proceeds especially from the union of several tribes into a *city* by agreement or by conquest; this form is still accompanied by slavery. Alongside communal ownership there already develops movable, and later even immovable, private property, but as an abnormal form subordinate to communal ownership. The citizens hold power over their laboring slaves only in community and are therefore bound to the form of communal ownership. The communal private property of the active citizens compels them to remain in this natural form of association over against their slaves. Hence the whole social structure based on communal ownership and with it the power of the people decline as immovable private property develops. The division of labor is developed to a larger extent. We already find antagonism between town and country and later antagonism between states representing urban interests and those representing rural interests. Within the cities themselves we find the antagonism between industry and maritime commerce. The class relation between citizens and slaves is then fully developed.

With the development of private property we encounter for the first time those conditions which we shall find again with modern private property, only on a larger scale. On the one hand, there is the concentration of private property which began very early in Rome (as proved by the Licinian agrarian law) and proceeded very rapidly from the time of the civil wars and particularly under the emperors. On the other hand, there is linked to this the transformation of the plebeian small peasantry into a proletariat that never achieved an independent development because of its intermediate position between propertied citizens and slaves.

The third form is feudal or estate ownership. Antiquity started out from the *town* and the small territory around it; the Middle Ages started out from the *country*. This different starting-point was caused by the sparse population at that time, scattered over a large area and receiving no large population increase from the conquerors. In contrast to Greece and Rome, the feudal development began in a much larger area, prepared by the Roman conquests and the spreading of agriculture initially connected with these conquests. The last centuries of the declining Roman Empire and its conquest by the barbarians destroyed many productive forces. Agriculture had declined, trade had come to a standstill or had been interrupted by force, and the rural and urban population had decreased. These conditions and the mode of organization of the conquest determined by them developed feudal property under the influence of the Germanic military constitution. Like tribal and communal ownership, it is based again on a community. While the slaves stood in opposition to the ancient community, here the serfs as the direct producing class stand in opposition. As soon as feudalism is fully developed, there also emerges antagonism to the towns. The hierarchical system of land ownership and the armed bodies of retainers gave the nobility power over the serfs. Like the ancient communal ownership this feudal organization was an association directed against a subjected producing class. But the form of association and the relation to the direct producers were different because of the different conditions of production.

This feudal organization of land ownership had its counterpart in the *towns* in the form of corporate property, the feudal organization of the trades. Property consisted mainly in the labor of each individual. The necessity for association against the organized robber nobility, the need for communal markets in an age when the industrialist was at the same time a merchant, the growing competition of escaped serfs pouring into the rising cities, and the feudal structure of the whole country gave rise to *guilds*. The gradually accumulated capital of individual craftsmen and their stable number in comparison to the growing population produced the relationship of journeyman and apprentice. In the towns, this led to a hierarchy similar to that in the country.

The main form of property during the feudal times consisted on the one hand of landed property with serf labor and on the other hand, individual labor with small capital controlling the labor of journeymen. The organization of both was determined by the limited conditions of production: small-scale, primitive cultivation of land and industry based on crafts. There was little division of labor when feudalism was at its peak. Every district carried in itself the antagonism of town and country. Though division into estates was strongly marked, there was no division of importance apart from the differentiation of princes, nobility, clergy, and peasants in the country, and masters, journeymen, apprentices, and soon the mob of day laborers in the cities. The strip-system hindered such a division in agriculture; cottage industry of the peasants themselves emerged; and in industry there was no division of labor at all within particular trades, and very little among them. The separation of industry and commerce occurred in older towns, and in newer towns it developed later when they entered into mutual relations.

The merger of larger territories into feudal kingdoms was a necessity for the landed nobility as well as for the cities. The organization of the ruling class, the nobility, had a monarch at its head in all instances.

The fact is, then, that definite individuals who are productively active in a specific way enter into these definite social and political relations. In each particular instance, empirical observation must show empirically, without any mystification or speculation, the connection of the social and political structure with production. The social structure and the state continually evolve out of the life-process of definite individuals, but individuals not as they may appear in their own or other people's imagination but rather as they *really* are, that is, as they work, produce materially, and act under definite material limitations, presuppositions, and conditions independent of their will.

((The ideas which these individuals form are ideas either about their relation to nature, their mutual relations, or their own nature. It is evident that in all these cases these ideas are the conscious expression—real or illusory—of their actual relationships and activities, of their production and commerce, and of their social and political behavior. The opposite assumption is possible only if, in addition to the spirit of the actual and materially evolved individuals, a separate spirit is presupposed. If the conscious expression of the actual relations of these individuals is illusory, if in their imagination they turn reality upside down, this in turn is a result of their limited mode of activity and their limited social relations arising from it.))

The production of ideas, of conceptions, of consciousness is directly interwoven with the material activity and the material relationships of men; it is the language of actual life. Conceiving, thinking, and the intellectual relationships of men appear here as the direct result of their material behavior. The same applies to intellectual production as manifested in a people's language of politics, law, morality, religion, metaphysics, etc. Men are the producers of their conceptions, ideas, etc., but these are real, active men, as they are conditioned by a definite development of their productive forces and of the relationships corresponding to these up to their highest forms. Consciousness can never be anything else except conscious existence, and the existence of men is their actual life-process. If men and their circumstances appear upside down in all ideology as in a camera obscura, this phenomenon is caused by their historical life-process, just as the inversion of objects on the retina is caused by their immediate physical life.

In direct contrast to German philosophy, which descends from heaven to earth, here one ascends from earth to heaven. In other words, to arrive at man in the flesh, one does not set out from what men say, imagine, or conceive, nor from man as he is described, thought about, imagined, or conceived. Rather one sets out from real, active men and their actual life-process and demonstrates the development of ideological reflexes and echoes of that process. The phantoms formed in the human brain, too, are necessary sublimations of man's material life-process which is empirically verifiable and connected with material premises. Morality, religion, metaphysics, and all the rest of ideology and their corresponding forms of consciousness no longer seem to be independent. They have no history or development. Rather, men who develop their material production and their material relationships alter their thinking and the products of their thinking along with their real existence. Consciousness does not determine life, but life determines consciousness. In the first view the starting point is consciousness taken as a living individual; in the second it is the real living individuals themselves as they exist in real life, and consciousness is considered only as *their* consciousness.

This view is not devoid of premises. It proceeds from real premises and does not abandon them for a moment. These premises are men, not in any fantastic isolation and fixation, but in their real, empirically perceptible process of development under certain conditions. When this active life-process is presented, history ceases to be a collection of dead facts as it is with the empiricists who are themselves still abstract, or an imagined activity of imagined subjects, as with the idealists.

Where speculation ends, namely in actual life, there real, positive science begins as the representation of the practical activity and practical process of the development of men. Phrases about consciousness cease and real knowledge takes their place. With the description of reality, independent philosophy loses its medium of existence. At best, a summary of the most general results, abstractions derived from observation of the historical development of men, can take its place. Apart from actual history, these abstractions have in themselves no value whatsoever. They can only serve to facilitate the arrangement of historical material and to indicate the sequence of its particular strata. By no means do they give us a recipe or schema, as philosophy does, for trimming the epochs of history. On the contrary, the difficulties begin only when we start the observation and arrangement of the material, the real description, whether of a past epoch or of the present. The removal of these difficulties is governed by premises we cannot state here. Only the study of the real-life process and the activity of the individuals of any given epoch will yield them. We shall select here some of these abstractions which we use in opposing ideology, and we shall illustrate them by historical examples.

⟨⟨*Feuerbach*⟩⟩[*] [. . . (at least two manuscript pages missing)] in reality and for the *practical* materi-

alist, that is, the *communist*, it is a question of revolutionizing the world as it is, of practically tackling and changing existing things. Though we sometimes find such views with Feuerbach, they never go beyond isolated surmises and have much too little influence on his general outlook to be considered here as anything but embryos capable of development. Feuerbach's "conception" of the sensuous world is confined to mere perception [*Anschauung*] of it on the one hand and to mere sensation [*Empfindung*] on the other. He speaks of "Man" instead of "real historical men." "Man" is actually "the German." In the first case, in the *perception* of the sensuous world, he necessarily encounters things which contradict his consciousness and feeling and disturb the harmony he presupposes of all parts of the sensuous world and especially of man with nature. ⟨Feuerbach's mistake is not that he subordinates the flatly obvious, the sensuous *appearance*, to the sensuous reality established by closer examination of the sensuous facts, but that he cannot, after all, cope with sensuousness except by looking at it with the "eyes," that is, through the "eyeglasses" of the *philosopher*⟩[†] To remove this disturbance, he must take refuge in a dual perception: a profane one which apprehends only the "flatly obvious" and a higher, philosophical one which gets at the "true essence" of things. He does not see that the world surrounding him is not something directly given and the same from all eternity but the product of industry and of the state of society in the sense that it is a historical product, the result of the activity of a whole succession of generations, each standing on the shoulders of the preceding one, developing further its industry and commerce, and modifying its social order according to changed needs. Even the objects of the simplest "sensuous certainty" are given to him only through social development, industry, and commercial relationships. The cherry tree, like almost all fruit trees, was transplanted into our zone by *commerce* only a few centuries ago, as we

---

Each manuscript page is halved lengthwise into two columns, the left filled with most of the text in Engels's script—he wrote more smoothly and quickly than Marx—from joint dictation.]
[†Single pointed brackets for adjacent addenda in Engels's writing in the right column of the manuscript page.]

[*Double pointed brackets for adjacent addenda in Marx's handwriting in the right column of the manuscript page.

know, and only *by* this action of a particular society in a particular time has it become "sensuous certainty" for Feuerbach.

Incidentally, when we conceive things as they really are and happened, any profound philosophical problem is resolved quite simply into an empirical fact, as will be seen even more clearly below. For example, the important question of the relation of man to nature (Bruno [Bauer] even goes so far as to speak of the "antitheses in nature and history" as if these were two separate "things" and man did not always have before him a historical nature and a natural history) from which all the "unfathomably lofty works" on "Substance" and "Self-consciousness" were born, collapses when we understand that the celebrated "unity of man with nature" has always existed in industry in varying forms in every epoch according to the lesser or greater development of industry, just like the "struggle" of man with nature, right up to the development of his productive forces on a corresponding basis. Industry and commerce, production and the exchange of the necessities of life, determine distribution and the structure of the various social classes, and are in turn determined as to the mode in which they are carried on. And so it happens that in Manchester, for instance, Feuerbach sees only factories and machines, where a hundred years ago only spinning wheels and weaving looms could be seen, or in the Campagna di Roma he discovers only pasture and swamps, where in the time of Augustus he would have found nothing but the vineyards and villas of Romas capitalists.

Feuerbach speaks in particular of the viewpoint of natural science. He mentions secrets disclosed only to the eye of the physicist and chemist. But where would natural science be without industry and commerce? Even this "pure" natural science receives its aim, like its material, only through commerce and industry, through the sensuous activity of men. So much is this activity, this continuous sensuous working and creating, this production, the basis of the whole sensuous world as it now exists, that, were it interrupted for only a year, Feuerbach would find not only a tremendous change in the natural world but also would soon find missing the entire world of men and his own perceptual faculty, even his own existence. Of course, the pri-

ority of external nature remains, and all this has no application to the original men produced by generatio aequivoca [spontaneous generation]. But this differentiation has meaning only insofar as man is considered distinct from nature. And after all, the kind of nature that preceded human history is by no means the nature in which Feuerbach lives, the nature which no longer exists anywhere, except perhaps on a few Australian coral islands of recent origin, and which does not exist for Feuerbach either.

Feuerbach admittedly has a great advantage over the "pure" materialists because he realizes that man too is "sensuous object"; but he sees man only as "sensuous object," not as "sensuous activity," because he remains in the realm of theory and does not view men in their given social connection, not under their existing conditions of life which have made them what they are. He never arrives at the really existing active men, but stops at the abstraction "Man" and gets only to the point of recognizing the "true, individual, corporeal man" emotionally, that is, he knows no other "human relationships" of man to man than love and friendship, and these idealized. He gives no criticism of the present conditions of life. He never manages to view the sensuous world as the total living sensuous *activity* of the individuals composing it. When he sees, for example, a crowd of scrofulous, over-worked, and consumptive wretches instead of healthy men, he is compelled to take refuge in the "higher perception" and "ideal compensation in the species." Thus he relapses into idealism at the very point where the communistic materialist sees the necessity and at the same time the condition of transforming industry as well as the social structure.

As far as Feuerbach is a materialist he does not deal with history, and as far as he deals with history he is not a materialist. Materialism and history completely diverge with him, a fact which should already be obvious from what has been said.

⟨⟨*History*⟩⟩ In dealing with Germans devoid of premises, we must begin by stating the first premise of all human existence, and hence of all history, the premise, namely, that men must be able to live in order to be able "to make history." ⟨⟨*Hegel*, Geological, hydrographical, etc., conditions. Human bodies. Needs, labor.⟩⟩ But life involves above all eating and drinking, shelter, clothing, and many other things. The first historical act is thus the production of the means to satisfy these needs, the production of material life itself. This is a historical act, a fundamental condition of all history which must be fulfilled in order to sustain human life every day and every hour, today as well as thousands of years ago. Even when sensuousness is reduced to a minimum, to a stick as with Saint Bruno [Bauer], it presupposes the activity of producing the stick. The first principle therefore in any theory of history is to observe this fundamental fact in its entire significance and all its implications and to attribute to this fact its due importance. The Germans have never done this, as we all know, so they have never had an *earthly* basis for history and consequently have never had a historian. Though the French and the English grasped the connection of this fact with so-called history only in an extremely one-sided way, particularly so long as they were involved in political ideology, they nevertheless made the first attempts to give historiography a materialistic basis by writing histories of civil society, commerce, and industry.

The second point is that once a need is satisfied, which requires the action of satisfying and the acquisition of the instrument for this purpose, new needs arise. The production of new needs is the first historical act. Here we see immediately where the great historical wisdom of the Germans comes from. When they run out of positive material and are not dealing with theological, political, or literary nonsense, they do not think of history at all but of "prehistoric times," without explaining how we can get from the nonsense of "prehistory" to history proper. With their historical speculation, on the other hand, they seize upon "prehistory" because they believe that there they are safe from interference by "crude facts" and can give full rein to their speculative impulses to establish and tear down hypotheses by the thousand.

The third circumstance entering into historical development from the very beginning is the fact that men who daily remake their own lives begin to make other men, begin to propagate: the relation between husband and wife, parents and children, the *family*.

The family, initially the only social relationship, becomes later a subordinate relationship (except in Germany) when increased needs produce new social relations and an increased population creates new needs. It must then be treated and developed in accordance with the existing empirical data and not according to the "concept of the family" as is customary in Germany. These three aspects of social activity are not to be taken as three different stages, but just for what they are, three aspects. To make it clear for the Germans we might call them three "moments" which have existed simultaneously ever since the dawn of history and the first men and still exist today.

The production of life, of one's own life in labor and of another in procreation, now appears as a double relationship: on the one hand as a natural relationship, on the other as a social one. The latter is social in the sense that individuals cooperate, no matter under what conditions, in what manner, and for what purpose. Consequently a certain mode of production or industrial stage is always combined with a certain mode of cooperation or social stage, and this mode of cooperation is itself a "productive force." We observe in addition that the multitude of productive forces accessible to men determines the nature of society and that the "history of mankind" must always be studied and treated in relation to the history of industry and exchange. It is also clear, however, why it is impossible in Germany to write such a history. The Germans lack not only the power of comprehension required and the material but also "sensuous certainty." On the other side of the Rhine people cannot have any experience of these matters because history has come to a standstill there. It is obvious at the outset that there is a materialistic connection among men determined by their needs and their modes of production and as old as men themselves. This connection is forever assuming new forms and thus presents a "history" even in absence of any political or religious nonsense which might hold men together in addition.

Having considered four moments, four aspects of the primary historical relationship, we now find that man also possesses "consciousness." ⟨⟨Men have history because they must *produce* their life, and [. . .?] in a *certain* way: this is determined by their physical organization; their consciousness is determined in the same way.⟩⟩ But this consciousness is not inherent, not "pure." From the start the "spirit" bears the curse of being "burdened" with matter which makes its appearance in the form of agitated layers of air, sounds, in short, in the form of language. Language is as old as consciousness. It *is* practical consciousness which exists also for other men and hence exists for me personally as well. Language, like consciousness, only arises from the need and necessity of relationships with other men. ⟨⟨My relationship to my surroundings is my consciousness.⟩⟩ Where a relationship exists, it exists for me. The animal has no "*relations*" with anything, no relations at all. Its relation to others does not exist as a relation. Consciousness is thus from the very beginning a social product and will remain so as long as men exist. At first consciousness is concerned only with the *immediate* sensuous environment and a limited relationship with other persons and things outside the individual who is becoming conscious of himself. At the same time it is consciousness of nature which first appears to man as an entirely alien, omnipotent, and unassailable force. Men's relations with this consciousness are purely animal, and they are overawed by it like beasts. Hence it is a purely animal consciousness of nature (natural religion)—for the very reason that nature is not yet modified historically. On the other hand it is consciousness of the necessity to come in contact with other individuals; it is the beginning of man's consciousness of the fact that he lives in a society. This beginning is as animalistic as social life itself at this stage. It is the mere consciousness of being a member of a flock, and the only difference between sheep and man is that man possesses consciousness instead of instinct, or in other words his instinct is more conscious.

⟨⟨We here see immediately that this natural religion or particular relation to nature is determined by the form of society and vice versa. As it is the case everywhere, the identity of nature and man appears in such a way that the restricted behavior of men toward nature determines their restricted behavior to one another, and their restricted behavior to one another determines their restricted behavior to nature.⟩⟩ This sheeplike or tribal consciousness receives further de-

velopment and formation through increased productivity, the increase of needs, and what is fundamental to both, the increase of population. Along with these, division of labor develops which originally was nothing but the division of labor in the sexual act, then that type of division of labor which comes about spontaneously or "naturally" because of natural predisposition (e.g. physical strength), needs, accidents, etc., etc. The division of labor is a true division only from the moment a division of material and mental labor appears. ⟨⟨This first form of ideologists, *priests*, is concurrent.⟩⟩ From this moment on consciousness can really boast of being something other than consciousness of existing practice, of *really* representing something without representing something real. From this moment on consciousness can emancipate itself from the world and proceed to the formation of "pure" theory, theology, philosophy, ethics, etc. But even if this theory, theology, philosophy, ethics, comes into conflict with existing relations, this can only occur because existing social relations have come into conflict with the existing force of production. Incidentally this can also occur in national relationships through a conflict not within the nation but between a particular national consciousness and the practice of other nations, that is, between the national and the general consciousness of a nation (as we observe now in Germany). ⟨⟨*Religion*. The Germans and *ideology* as such.⟩⟩ Since this contradiction appears only as a contradiction within national consciousness, and since the struggle seems to be limited to this na⟨⟨tional crap just because this nation is crap in and for itself.⟩⟩

Moreover it does not make any difference what consciousness starts to do on its own. The only result we obtain from all such muck is that these three moments —the force of production, the state of society, and consciousness—can and must come into conflict with one another because the *division of labor* implies the possibility, indeed the necessity, that intellectual and material activity ⟨⟨activity and thinking, that is, thoughtless activity and inactive thought [later deleted]⟩⟩—enjoyment and labor, production and consumption—are given to different individuals, and the only possibility of their not coming into conflict lies in again transcending the division of labor. It is self-evident that words such as "specters," "bonds," "higher being," "concept," "scruple," are only the idealistic, spiritual expression, the apparent conception of the isolated individual, the image of very empirical fetters and restrictions within which the mode of production of life and the related form of interaction move. ⟨⟨This idealistic expression of existing economic restrictions is present not only in pure theory but also in practical consciousness; that is to say, having emancipated itself and having entered into conflict with the existing mode of production, consciousness shapes not only religions and philosophies but also states.⟩⟩

With the division [*Teilung*] of labor, in which all these conflicts are implicit and which is based on the natural division of labor in the family and the partition of society into individual families opposing one another, there is at the same time distribution [*Verteilung*], indeed *unequal* distribution, both quantitative and qualitative, of labor and its products, hence property which has its first form, its nucleus, in the family where wife and children are the slaves of the man. The latent slavery in the family, though still very crude, is the first property. Even at this initial stage, however, it corresponds perfectly to the definition of modern economists who call it the power of controlling the labor of others. ⟨Division of labor and private property are identical expressions. What is said in the former in regard to activity is expressed in the latter in regard to the product of the activity.⟩

Furthermore, the division of labor implies the conflict between the interest of the individual or the individual family and the communal interest of all individuals having contact with one another. The communal interest does not exist only in the imagination, as something "general," but first of all in reality, as a mutual interdependence of those individuals among whom the labor is divided. And finally, the division of labor offers us the first example for the fact that man's own act becomes an alien power opposed to him and enslaving him instead of being controlled by him—as long as man remains in natural society, as long as a split exists between the particular and the common interest, and as long as the activity is not voluntarily but naturally divided. For as soon as labor is distributed, each person has a particular, exclusive area of activity which is imposed on him and from which he cannot escape. He is a hunter, a fisherman, a herdsman, or a critical critic, and he must remain so if he does not want to lose his means of livelihood. In communist society, however, where nobody has an exclusive area of activity and each can train himself in any branch he wishes, society regulates the general production, making it possible for me to do one thing today and another tomorrow, to hunt in the morning, fish in the afternoon, breed cattle in the evening, criticize after dinner, just as I like, without ever becoming a hunter, a fisherman, a herdsman, or a critic. This fixation of social activity, this consolidation of our own products into an objective power above us, growing out of our control, thwarting our expectations, and nullifying our calculations, is one of the chief factors in historical development so far, [. . . (nine lines deleted and illegible)]

⟨[beside previous paragraph] Out of this very contradiction between the interest of the individual and that of the community the latter takes an independent form as the *State*, separated from the real interests of individual and community, and at the same time as an illusory communal life, but always based on the real bonds present in every family and every tribal conglomeration, such as flesh and blood, language, division of labor on a larger scale, and other interests, and particularly based, as we intend to show later, on the classes already determined by the division of labor, classes which form in any such mass of people and of which one dominates all the others. It follows from this that all struggles within the State, the struggle between democracy, aristocracy and monarchy, the struggle for franchise, etc., etc., are nothing but the illusory forms in which the real struggles of different classes are carried out among one another (the German theoreticians do not have the faintest inkling of this fact, although they have had sufficient information in the *Deutsch-Französische Jahrbücher* and *The Holy Family*). Furthermore, it follows that every class striving to gain control—even when such control means the transcendence of the entire old form of society and of control itself, as is the case with the proletariat—must first win political power in order to represent its interest in turn as the universal interest, something which the class is forced to do immediately.) 《Just because individuals seek *only* their particular interest, which for them does not coincide with their communal interest, the latter will be imposed on them as something "alien" and "independent," as a "universal" interest of a particular and peculiar nature in its turn. Otherwise they themselves must remain within this discord, as in democracy. On the other hand, the *practical* struggle of these particular interests, which constantly *really* run counter to the communal and illusory communal interests, necessitates *practical* intervention and control through the illusory "universal" interest in the form of the State.

Communism is for us not a *state of affairs* still to be established, not an *ideal* to which reality [will] have to adjust. We call communism the *real* movement which abolishes the present state of affairs. The conditions of this movement result from premises now in existence.》 The social power, that is, the multiplied productive force from the cooperation of different individuals determined by the division of labor, appears to these individuals not as their own united power but as a force alien and outside them because their cooperation is not voluntary but has come about naturally. They do not know the origin and the goal of this alien force, and they cannot control it. On the contrary, it passes through a peculiar series of phases and stages independent of the will and the action of men, even directing their will. X [Insertion mark for paragraph to follow] How else could property, for example, have a history at all and assume various forms? How else could landed property, according to different premises, have changed in France from parcellation to centralization in the hands of a few, and in England from centralization in the hands of a few to parcellation, as is actually the case today? Or how does it happen that trade, which after all is nothing more than the exchange of products of various individuals and countries, rules the entire world through supply and demand —a relation, as an English economist says, which hovers over the earth like the fate of antiquity, distributing fortune and misfortune with invisible hand, establishing and overthrowing empires, causing nations to rise and to disappear? How could this go on, while with the abolition of the basis of private property, with com-

munistic regulation of production and hence with abolition of the alienation between men and their own products, the power of supply and demand is completely dissolved and men regain control of exchange, production, and the mode of their mutual relationships?

《《X This "*alienation*," to use a term which the philosophers will understand, can be abolished only on the basis of two *practical* premises. To become an "intolerable" power, that is, a power against which men make a revolution, it must have made the great mass of humanity "propertyless" and this at the same time in contradiction to an existing world of wealth and culture, both of which presuppose a great increase in productive power and a high degree of its development. On the other hand, this development of productive forces (which already implies the actual empirical existence of men on a *world-historical* rather than local scale) is an absolutely necessary practical premise because, without it, *want* is merely made general, and with *destitution* the struggle for necessities and all the old muck would necessarily be reproduced; and furthermore, because only with this universal development of productive forces is a *universal* commerce among men established which produces in all nations simultaneously the phenomenon of a "propertyless" mass (universal competition), makes each nation dependent on the revolutions of the others, and finally replaces local individuals with *world-historical*, empirically universal individuals. Without this, (1) communism could only exist locally; (2) the *forces* of interaction themselves could not have developed as *universal* and thus intolerable powers, but would have remained homebred, superstitious "conditions"; (3) any extension of interaction would abolish local communism. Empirically, communism is only possible as the act of dominant peoples "all at once" and simultaneously, which presuppose the universal development of productive power and worldwide interaction linked with communism. Besides, the mass of *propertyless* workers—labor power on a mass scale cut off from capital or even limited satisfaction, and hence no longer just temporarily deprived of work as a secure source of life—presupposes a *world market* through competition. The proletariat can thus only exist *world-*

historically, just as communism, its activity, can only have a "world-historical" existence. World-historical existence of individuals means existence of individuals which is directly bound up with world history.⟩⟩

The form of interaction determined by and in turn determining the existing productive forces at all previous historical stages is *civil society.* It is clear from what has been said above, that civil society has as its premise and basis the simple family and the multiple family, the so-called tribe. More detailed definitions are contained in our remarks above. Already we see here how civil society is the true focus and scene of all history. We see how nonsensical is the old conception of history which neglects real relationships and restricts itself to high-sounding dramas of princes and states.

So far we have concerned ourselves mainly with one aspect of human activity, how man *affects nature.* ⟨⟨Interaction and productive power.⟩⟩ The other aspect, how *man affects man* — origin of the state and the relation of the state to civil society [. . .]

History is nothing but the succession of separate generations, each of which exploits the materials, capital, and productive forces handed down to it by all preceding generations. On the one hand, it thus continues the traditional activity in completely changed circumstances and, on the other, modifies the old circumstances with a completely changed activity. This can be speculatively distorted so that later history is made the goal of earlier history, for example, the goal ascribed to the discovery of America is to assure the outbreak of the French Revolution. History then obtains its own aims and becomes a "person ranking with other persons" (to wit: "Self-consciousness, Criticism, the Unique," etc.), while what is designated with the words "destiny," "goal," "germ," or "idea" of earlier history is nothing more than an abstraction formed from later history, an abstraction from the active influence which earlier history exercises on later history.

The further the separate spheres that interact on one another extend in the course of this development, the more the original isolation of separate nationalities is destroyed by the developed mode of production, commerce, and division of labor between various nations naturally brought forth by these and the more does history become world history. For instance, when a

machine is invented in England to deprive countless workers of bread in India and China and revolutionize the entire life of these empires, it becomes a world-historical fact. Sugar and coffee proved their world-historical importance in the nineteenth century when the lack of these products, occasioned by the Napoleonic Continental System, caused the Germans to rise against Napoleon. Lack of sugar and coffee thus became the real basis of the glorious Wars of Liberation of 1813. Hence the transformation of history into world history is not a mere abstract act of the "Self-consciousness," the world spirit, or of any other metaphysical specter, but a completely material, empirically verifiable act, an act for which every individual furnishes proof as he comes and goes, eats, drinks, and clothes himself.

⟨⟨*On the Production of Consciousness*⟩⟩ In history up to the present it is certainly an empirical fact that separate individuals, with the broadening of their activity into world-historical activity, have become more and more enslaved to a power alien to them (a hardship they conceive as chicanery on the part of the so-called World Spirit, etc.), a power which has become increasingly great and finally turns out to be the *world market.* But it is just as empirically established that by the overthrow of the existing state of society by the communist revolution (more about this below) and the abolition of private property which is identical with it, this alien power so baffling to German theoreticians will be dissolved. Then the liberation of each single individual will be accomplished to the extent that history becomes world history. Hence it is clear that the real intellectual wealth of the individual depends entirely on the wealth of his real connections. Only in this way will separate individuals be liberated from the various national and local barriers, be brought into practical connection with the material and intellectual production of the whole world, and be able to enjoy this all-sided production of the whole earth (the creations of man). *All-around* dependence, that natural form of the *world-historical* cooperation of individuals, will be transformed by the communist revolution into the control and conscious governance of these powers, which, born of the interaction of men, have until now overawed and governed men as powers completely alien to them. Now this view can be expressed again speculatively and idealistically, that is, fantastically, as "self-generation of the species" ("society as the subject"), and thereby the consecutive series of interrelated individuals can be conceived as a single individual which accomplishes the mystery of generating itself. It is clear here that individuals certainly generate *one another*, physically and mentally, but do not generate themselves either in the nonsense of Saint Bruno [Bauer] ⟨⟨or in the sense of the "Unique," of "made" Man⟩⟩ .

Finally, from the conception of history as developed above we obtain these further conclusions: (1) In the development of productive forces there comes a stage when productive forces and means of interaction are achieved which under the existing relationships cause nothing but mischief and are no longer productive forces but rather destructive ones (machinery and money). Connected with this is a class which has to bear all the burdens of society without enjoying its advantages. It is excluded from society and forced into extreme opposition to all other classes. It constitutes the majority of all members of society, and from it arises a consciousness of the necessity of fundamental revolution, communist consciousness, which may of course arise also in the other classes perceiving the situation of this class. (2) The conditions under which definite productive forces can be applied are the conditions of the rule of a definite class of society whose social power, deriving from its property, has its *practical*-idealistic expression in the form of the state as it happens to exist then. Therefore, every revolutionary struggle is directed against a class which until then has been in power. ⟨⟨The people are interested in maintaining the present state of production.⟩⟩ (3) In all revolutions up till now the mode of activity remained unchanged, and it was only a question of a different distribution of this activity, a new distribution of labor to other persons. But the communist revolution is directed against the preceding *mode* of activity, does away with *labor*, and abolishes the rule of all classes along with the classes themselves, because it is accomplished by the class which society no longer recognizes as a class and is itself the expression of the dissolution of all classes, nationalities, etc. (4) For the

production of this communist consciousness on a mass scale and for the success of the cause itself, the alteration of men on a mass scale is required. This can only take place in a practical movement, in a *revolution*. A revolution is necessary, therefore, not only because the *ruling* class cannot be overthrown in any other way but also because the class *overthrowing* it can succeed only by revolution in getting rid of all the traditional muck and become capable of establishing society anew.

This conception of history depends on our ability to set forth the real process of production, starting out from the material production of life itself, and to comprehend the form of interaction connected with this and created by this mode of production, that is, by civil society in its various stages, as the basis of all history. We have to show civil society in action as State and also explain all the different theoretical products and forms of consciousness, religion, philosophy, ethics, etc., and trace their genesis from that basis. The whole thing can be depicted in its totality (and thus the reciprocal action of these various sides too). Unlike the idealistic view of history this conception does not look for a category in every historical period; rather it remains constantly on the real *ground* of history. It does not explain practice from the idea but explains the formation of ideas from material practice. Consequently it arrives at the conclusion that all forms and products of consciousness cannot be dissolved by mental criticism, by resolution into "Self-consciousness" or transformation into "apparitions," "specters," "fancies," etc., but only by the practical overthrow of the actual social relations which gave rise to this idealistic trickery. Not criticism but revolution is the driving force of history and also of religion, philosophy, and all other types of theory. It shows that history does not end by being resolved into "Self-consciousness" as "spirit of the Spirit," but that there is a material result at each historical stage, a sum of productive forces, a historically created relation of individuals to nature and to one another which is handed down to each generation from its predecessor—a mass of productive forces, capital funds, and conditions which on the one hand is modified by the new generation but on the other hand also prescribes its conditions of life, giving it a definite development and a special character. It shows, therefore, that circumstances make men just as much as men make circumstances.

The sum of productive forces, capital funds, and social forms of interaction which every individual and every generation finds existing is the real basis of what the philosophers have conceived as "Substance" and "essence of Man," what they have apotheosized and attacked, that is, a real basis which is not in the least disturbed in its effect and influence on the development of men by the fact that these philosophers revolt against it as "Self-consciousness" and the "Unique." These conditions of life which the various generations find in existence also decide whether periodical and recurring revolutionary tremors will be strong enough to overthrow the basis of the entire existing system. If these material elements of total revolution are not present (namely, the existing productive forces on the one hand and the formation of a revolutionary mass on the other, a mass which revolts not only against particular conditions of the prevailing society but against the prevailing "production of life" itself, the "total activity" on which it was based) then it is absolutely immaterial, so far as practical development is concerned, whether the *idea* of this revolution has already been expressed a hundred times, as the history of communism proves.

* * *

In every epoch the ideas of the ruling class are the ruling ideas, that is, the class that is the ruling *material* power of society is at the same time its ruling *intellectual* power. The class having the means of material production has also control over the means of intellectual production, so that it also controls, generally speaking, the ideas of those who lack the means of intellectual production. The ruling ideas are nothing more than the ideal expression of the dominant material relationships grasped as ideas, hence of the relationships which make the one class the ruling one and therefore the ideas of its domination. The individuals who comprise the ruling class possess among other things consciousness and thought. Insofar as they rule

as a class and determine the extent of a historical epoch, it is self-evident that they do it in its entire range. Among other things they rule also as thinkers and producers of ideas and regulate the production and distribution of the ideas of their age. Their ideas are the ruling ideas of the epoch. For example, in an age and in a country where royal power, aristocracy, and bourgeoisie are contending for domination and where control is shared, the doctrine of the separation of powers proves to be the dominant idea and is expressed as an "eternal law."

The division of labor, which we saw above (pp. [424–25]) as one of the chief forces of history up till now, is expressed also in the ruling class as the division of mental and material labor, so that within this class one part appears as the thinkers of the class (its active, conceptive ideologists who make perfecting the illusion of this class about itself their main source of livelihood), while the others' attitude toward these ideas and illusions is more passive and receptive because they are really the active members of this class and have less time to make up illusions and ideas about themselves. Within this class this split can even develop into opposition and hostility between the two parts, which disappears, however, in the case of a practical collision where the class itself is in danger. In this case the appearance that the ruling ideas were not ideas of the ruling class with a power distinct from the power of this class also vanishes. The existence of revolutionary ideas in a particular epoch presupposes the existence of a revolutionary class. About the premises for the latter we have made sufficient comment above (pp. [427–28]).

If in considering the course of history we detach the ideas of the ruling class from the ruling class itself and attribute to them an independent existence, if we confine ourselves to saying that these or those ideas prevailed in a certain epoch without bothering ourselves about their conditions of production or producers, if we ignore the individuals and world conditions which are the source of the ideas, we can say, for example, that during the time when aristocracy was dominant the concepts of honor, loyalty, etc., prevailed; during the dominion of the bourgeoisie, the concepts of freedom, equality, etc. The ruling class itself generally imagines this to be the case. This conception of history, common to all historians particularly since the eighteenth century, will necessarily come up against the phenomenon that increasingly the abstract ideas prevail, that is, ideas that increasingly take on the form of universality. Each new class which displaces the one previously dominant is forced, simply to be able to carry out its aim, to represent its interest as the common interest of all members of society, that is, ideally expressed. It has to give its ideas the form of universality and represent them as the only rational, universally valid ones. The class making revolution emerges at the outset simply because it is opposed to a *class* not as a class but as a representative of the whole of society. It appears as the whole mass of society confronting one ruling class. ⟨⟨Universality corresponds to (1) class versus estate, (2) competition, world trade, etc., (3) the great numerical strength of the ruling class, (4) the illusion of *common* interests (in the beginning this illusion is true), (5) the delusion of ideologists and the division of labor.⟩⟩ It can do this because in the beginning its interest really is more attached to the common interest of all other non-ruling classes and because under the pressure of prevailing conditions its interest has not yet been able to develop as the particular interest of a particular class. Its victory, therefore, benefits also many individuals of other classes which do not win power but only insofar as it now puts these individuals in a position to raise themselves into the ruling class. When the French bourgeoisie overthrew the power of the aristocracy, it permitted many proletarians to raise themselves above the proletariat, but only insofar as they became bourgeois. Every new class, therefore, achieves dominance only on a broader basis than that of the previous class ruling, whereas the opposition of the non-ruling class against the new ruling class later develops all the more sharply and deeply. Both these factors mean that the struggle to be waged against this new ruling class aims at a more decided and more radical negation of the previous conditions of society than could all previous classes striving for dominance.

This entire appearance, that the rule of a certain class is only the rule of certain ideas, comes to a natural end as soon as class rule in general ceases to be the form in which society is organized, as soon as it is no longer necessary to represent a particular interest as general or "the general interest" as dominant.

When ruling ideas are separated from ruling individuals and above all from relationships resulting from a given level of the mode of production and the conclusion has been reached that ideas are always ruling history, it is very easy to *abstract* from these various ideas "*the* ideas," the Idea, etc., as the dominant force in history and thus understand all these separate ideas and concepts as "Self-determinations" of *the* Concept developing in history. It follows, of course, that all the relationships of men can be derived from the concept of man, man as conceived, the essence of man, *Man*. This has been done in speculative philosophy. ⟨⟨Hegel himself admits at the end of the *Philosophy of History* that he "has considered the progress of the *Concept* only" and has presented the "true *theodicy*" in history (p. 446).⟩⟩ Now one can go back again to the producers of "the Concept," to the theorists, ideologists, and philosophers, and one comes to the conclusion that the philosophers, the thinkers as such, have always been dominant in history—a conclusion, as we see, already advanced by Hegel. Thus the whole trick of proving the hegemony (Stirner calls it hierarchy) of Spirit in history is confined to the following three efforts.

No. 1. One must separate the ideas of those ruling for empirical reasons, under empirical conditions, and as material individuals from the actual rulers; one must recognize the rule of ideas or illusions in history.

No. 2. One must put order into this rule of ideas, prove a mystical connection among the successive ruling ideas, which is managed by seeing them as "self-determinations" of "the Concept" (this is possible because these ideas are actually connected with one another by virtue of their empirical basis and because as *mere* ideas they become self-distinctions, distinctions made by thought).

No. 3. To remove the mystical appearance of this "self-determining Concept" one changes it into a person—"Self-Consciousness"—or, to make it appear thoroughly materialistic, into a series of persons who represent "the Concept" in history, into "the thinkers," "philosophers," ideologists who again are understood as the manufacturers of history, "the council of guardians," the rulers. ⟨⟨Man = the "rational human spirit."⟩⟩ Thus all materialistic elements have been removed from history and full rein can be given to one's speculative steed.

This historical method which prevailed in Germany and particularly the reason why it prevailed must be explained from its connection with the illusion of ideologists in general, for example, the illusions of jurists, politicians (even of the practical statesmen among them), and from the dogmatic dreamings and distortions of these fellows. It is very simply explained from their practical position in life, their employment, and the division of labor.

While in ordinary life every shopkeeper is very well able to distinguish between what somebody professes to be and what he really is, our historians have not yet achieved this trivial insight. They take every epoch at its word and believe everything it says and imagines about itself. [Pages 36 through 39 in Marx's pagination missing here.]

[*Division of Labor*][. . .] are found. From the first, there follows the premise of a highly developed division of labor and extensive commerce; from the second, the locality. In the first case, individuals must be brought together; in the second, they find themselves alongside the given instrument of production as instruments of production themselves. Here arises the difference between natural instruments of production and those created by civilization. The *land* (water, etc.) can be regarded as a natural instrument of production. In the first case, with the natural instrument of production, individuals are subservient to nature; in the second, to a product of labor. In the first case, property (landed property) appears as direct natural domination; in the second, as domination of labor, particularly of accumulated labor, capital. The first case presupposes that the individuals are united by some bond: family, tribe, the land itself, etc. The second case presupposes that they are independent of one another and are only held together by exchange. In the first case, the exchange is mainly an exchange between men and nature in which the labor of men is exchanged for the products of nature; in the second, it is predominantly an exchange of men among themselves. In the first case, average human common sense suffices; physical activity is not as yet separated from mental activity. In the second, the division between physical and mental labor already must be practically completed. In the first case, the domination of the proprietor over non-proprietors may be based on a personal relationship or kind of community; in the second, it must have taken on physical shape in a third party: money. In the first case, small industry exists, but determined by the utilization of the natural instrument of production and hence without distribution of labor among various individuals; in the second, industry exists only in and through division of labor.

We started from instruments of production and showed that private property was a necessity for certain industrial stages. In *industrie extractive* private property still coincides with labor. In small industry and agriculture up till now property is the necessary consequence of the existing instruments of production. Only with big industry does the contradiction between the instrument of production and private property appear; it is the product of big industry. In addition, big industry must be highly developed to produce it. Only with big industry is the abolition of private property possible.

The greatest division of material and intellectual labor is the separation of town and country. The opposition between the two begins with the transition from barbarism to civilization, from the tribe to the state, from locality to nation, and runs through the whole history of civilization to the present day (the Anti-Corn-Law League). With the existence of towns there is the necessity of administration, police, taxes, etc., in short of municipal life and thus politics in general. Here first became apparent the division of the population into two great classes directly based on the division of labor and the instruments of production. The town already shows in actual fact a concentration of population, of instruments of production, of capital, satisfactions, and needs, while the country demonstrates the opposite, isolation and separation. The antagonism between town and country can exist only with private property. It is the crassest expression of the subsumption of the individual under the division of labor, under a definite activity forced upon him, a subsumption making one man into a narrow town animal, the other into a narrow country animal, and every day creates anew the conflict between their interests. Labor is again the main thing here, power *over* individuals, and as long as this power exists, private property must exist. The overcoming of the antagonism between town and country is one of the first conditions of communal life, a condition depending on a mass of material premises. Mere will, as anyone can see at first glance, cannot fulfill this condition. (We will have to discuss these conditions.) Separation of town and country can also be understood as the separation of capital and landed property, as the beginning of capital's existence and development independent of landed property, the beginning of property based only on labor and exchange.

In towns that had not existed before but were newly built by freed serfs in the Middle Ages, each man's particular labor was his only property except for the small capital he brought with him consisting only of the most necessary tools of his craft. The competition of serfs constantly taking refuge in the towns, the constant war of the country against the town, and thus the necessity of an organized municipal military force, the bond of common ownership in a particular kind of labor, the necessity of sharing buildings for the sale of their wares when craftsmen were also traders, and consequently the exclusion of unauthorized persons from these buildings, the conflict of interests among various crafts, the necessity of protecting their laboriously acquired skill, and the feudal organization of the entire country—all these were causes of the union of workers of each craft into guilds. At this point we need not go further into the numerous modifications of the guild system with later historical developments. The flight of serfs into the towns continued without interruption through the entire Middle Ages. These serfs, persecuted by their lords in the country, came separately into the towns where they found an organized community against which they were powerless and in which they had to adjust to the station which their organized urban competitors assigned to them according to their need of labor and their interest. Arriving separately, these workers were never able to gain any power because if their labor was of the guild type and

had to be learned, the guild masters put them in subjection and organized them according to their interest. If their labor was not of this type but rather day labor, they never managed to organize themselves and remained unorganized rabble. The need for day labor in the towns created the rabble.

These towns were true "associations" created by a direct need to provide for protection of property, multiply the means of production, and defend the individual members. The rabble of these towns was deprived of all power. It was composed of individuals who were strange to one another, had arrived separately, were unorganized, and faced an organized power armed for war and jealously supervising them. In each craft journeymen and apprentices were organized as best suited their master's interest. Their patriarchal relationship with their masters gave the masters a double power, first because of their direct influence on all aspects of life of the journeymen and secondly because there was a real bond uniting the journeymen who worked for the same master, a bond separating them from journeymen working for other masters. And finally the journeymen were bound to the existing order by their interest in becoming masters themselves. While the rabble at least carried out some revolts against the whole municipal order, revolts that remained completely ineffective because of their impotence, the journeymen had only insignificant squabbles within their guild and such as pertain to the nature of the system. The great revolts of the Middle Ages all started in the country. They, too, remained totally ineffective because of the dispersal and resulting cruelty of the peasants.

Capital in these towns consisted of a house, tools of the craft, and natural hereditary customers; it was natural capital. Since it was unrealizable because of the primitive form of commerce and lack of circulation, it had to descend from father to son. Unlike modern capital which can be appraised monetarily and invested in this thing or that, this natural capital was directly tied up with the particular work of the owner, was inseparable from it, and was thus *estate* capital.

In the towns the division of labor between the various guilds was quite natural; in the guilds themselves it was not all carried out among the individual workers.

Every worker had to be well versed in a whole round of tasks and had to be able to make all things that could be made with his tools. The limited commerce and the lack of good communications between individual towns, the lack of population, and limited needs did not permit a higher division of labor. Every man who set out to become a master craftsman had to be proficient in the whole of his craft. The medieval craftsmen still exhibited an interest in their special work and their skill in it which could develop to a certain limited artistic talent. For that very reason, however, every medieval craftsman was completely absorbed in his work, had a contented slavish relationship to it, and was subjected to it to a far greater extent than is the modern worker for whom his work is a matter of indifference.

The next extension of the division of labor was the separation of production and commerce and the formation of a special class of merchants, a separation which had been handed down (as for example with the Jews) in established towns and soon appeared in new ones. With this there was the possibility of commerce transcending the immediate neighborhood, and the realization of this possibility depended on existing means of communication, the state of public safety in the countryside determined by political conditions (throughout the Middle Ages the merchants traveled in armed caravans, as is well known), and on the cruder or more developed needs of the area accessible to commerce as determined by the stage of culture. With commerce as the proper business of a particular class and extension of trade through the merchants beyond the immediate surroundings of the town, an immediate reciprocal action between production and commerce appeared. The towns entered into relations *with one another*. New tools were brought from one town into the other. The division between production and commerce soon created a new division of production among individual towns, each exploiting a predominant branch of industry. Earlier local restrictions gradually broke down.

It depends entirely on the extension of commerce whether the productive forces, especially inventions, in a locality are lost for later development or not. As long as there is no commerce beyond the immediate neighborhood, every invention must be separately made in each locality. Pure accidents such as eruptions of barbaric peoples and even ordinary wars are enough to cause a country with advanced productive forces and needs to start all over again from the beginning. In primitive history every invention had to be made anew, independently, every day and in each locality. That well-developed productive forces are not safe from complete destruction even with relatively extensive commerce is proved by the Phoenicians ⟨⟨and glass painting in the Middle Ages⟩⟩ whose inventions were largely lost for a long time through the displacement of this nation from commerce, its conquest by Alexander, and its consequent decline. Glass painting in the Middle Ages had a similar fate. Only when commerce has become worldwide and is based on large-scale industry, when all nations are drawn into the competitive struggle, will the permanence of the acquired productive forces be assured.

[*Manufacturing*] A direct consequence of the division of labor between the various towns was the rise of manufacturers, branches of production that had developed from the guild system. They first flourished in Italy and later in Flanders because of the historical condition of trade with foreign nations. In other countries, for example, England and France, manufacturing was at first confined to the domestic market. Besides the conditions already mentioned, manufacturing depends on an advanced concentration of population—particularly in the country—and of capital which began to accumulate in the hands of individuals, partly in the guilds despite their regulations, and partly among the merchants.

That kind of labor which from the beginning required a machine, even of the crudest kind, soon turned out to be most capable of development. Weaving, previously done by peasants in the country as a secondary job to provide clothing, was the first labor to receive an impetus and a further development through the extension of commerce. Weaving was the first and remained the main manufacturing. The rising demand for clothing materials from the growth of the population, the growing accumulation and mobilization of natural capital through accelerated circulation, the demand for luxuries caused by the accelerated circulation and generally facilitated by the gradual extension of commerce, gave weaving a quantitative and qualitative impetus which removed it from the prevailing form of production. Beside the peasants who continued, and still continue, to weave for their own use, a new class of weavers emerged in the towns whose fabrics were destined for the entire domestic market and usually also foreign markets. Weaving, a job usually requiring little skill, soon branched out into various kinds of jobs and resisted the restrictions of a guild. For this reason weaving was done mostly in villages and marketplaces, without guild organization. Villages grew into towns, and indeed the most flourishing ones in each country.

With guild-free manufacturing, property relations changed rapidly. The first advance beyond natural-estate capital was provided by the emergence of merchants whose capital was from the start movable, capital in the modern sense as far as we can speak of it in considering the circumstances of those times. The second advance came with manufacturing which again mobilized a great deal of natural capital and altogether increased the mass of movable capital as compared to that of natural capital. At the same time manufacturing became a refuge of the peasants from the guilds which excluded them or paid them poorly, just as earlier the guild towns had served as a refuge for the peasants from the landlords.

With the beginning of manufacturing there was immediately a period of vagrancy caused by the abolition of feudal retainers, the disbanding of armies which had served the kings against their vassals, the improvement of agriculture, and the transformation of large strips of arable land into pasture land. It is clear from this alone how this vagrancy coincides with the disintegration of the feudal system. Isolated epochs of this kind occurred as early as the thirteenth century. Only at the end of the fifteenth and beginning of the sixteenth centuries is it generally present and for quite some duration. These vagabonds were so numerous that, to give one example, Henry VIII of England had 72,000 of them hanged. They could be put to work only with the greatest difficulty and through most extreme destitution, and then after long resistance. The

rapid rise of manufacturing, particularly in England, gradually absorbed them.

With the rise of manufacturing, the various nations entered into a competitive relationship, the fight for trade, which was fought out in wars, protective duties, and prohibitions, while the nations formerly had carried on an inoffensive exchange if they were in contact at all. From then on trade assumed political significance.

The relationship between worker and employer also changed. In the guilds the patriarchal relationship between journeyman and master continued to exist; in manufacturing the monetary relation between worker and capitalist took its place, a relationship which retained a patriarchal tinge in the country and the small towns but quite early lost almost all patriarchal coloration in the larger, the real manufacturing towns.

Manufacturing and the movement of production in general received an enormous stimulus through the extension of commerce with the discovery of America and a sea route to the East Indies. The new products imported from America and the Indies and particularly the large quantities of gold and silver which came into circulation completely changed the position of classes toward each other and dealt a hard blow to feudal landed property and laborers. The expeditions of adventurers, colonization, and above all the extension of markets into a world market, now possible and becoming more and more a fact with each day, called forth a new phase of historical development which we cannot further discuss here. Through the colonization of newly discovered lands, the commercial struggle of nations against one another received new fuel and thus became bigger and more bitter.

Expansion of trade and manufacturing accelerated the accumulation of movable capital while natural capital in the guilds remained stable or even decreased without any stimulus for increased production. Trade and manufacturing created the big bourgeoisie; the petty bourgeoisie was concentrated in the guilds, no longer a prevailing power in the cities but bowing to the power of big merchants and manufacturers. ⟨⟨[vertically] The petty bourgeois—Middle class—Big bourgeoisie⟩⟩ As soon as the guilds came into contact with manufacturing, they declined.

During the epoch under discussion the relationships of the nations to one another took on two different forms. In the beginning the small quantity of gold and silver in circulation brought about the ban on the export of these metals. Industry, mostly imported from abroad and needed to employ the increasing urban population, required those privileges which could be granted not only against competition at home but mainly against foreign competition. In the original prohibitions the local guild privilege was extended over the whole nation. Customs duties originated from levies which feudal lords exacted as protection money from merchants passing through their territories and from levies later imposed by towns as the most convenient method of raising money for their treasury. The appearance of American gold and silver on the European markets, the gradual development of industry, the rapid expansion of trade, and the consequent rise of the non-guild bourgeoisie and of money gave these measures a different significance. Being from day to day less able to do without money, the state now upheld the ban on the export of gold and silver for fiscal reasons. The bourgeois for whom these masses of money on the market became the chief object of speculation were thoroughly pleased. Privileges became a source of income for the government and were sold for money. In customs legislation export duties appeared which had a purely fiscal aim and were only a hindrance to industry.

The second period began in the middle of the seventeenth century and lasted almost to the end of the eighteenth. Commerce and navigation had expanded more rapidly than manufacturing which played a secondary role. Colonies were becoming important customers. After long struggles the individual nations shared the opening world market. This period begins with the Navigation Laws and colonial monopolies. Competition of the nations among themselves was excluded so far as possible by tariffs, prohibitions, and treaties. In the last resort the competitive struggle was carried out and decided in wars (particularly in naval wars). The most powerful maritime nation, the English, held preeminence in trade and manufacturing. Here we already have concentration in one country.

Manufacturing was constantly protected at home by tariffs, in the colonial market by monopolies, and abroad as much as possible by differential duties. The processing of domestic raw materials was encouraged (wool and linen in England, silk in France); the export of raw materials was forbidden (wool in England); and the processing of important material was neglected or suppressed (cotton in England). The nation ruling in sea trade and colonial power naturally secured for itself also the greatest quantitative and qualitative expansion of manufacturing. Manufacturing could not do without protection. Through the slightest change taking place in other countries, it could lose its market and be ruined. It can be easily introduced into a country under reasonably favorable conditions and for this reason can be easily destroyed. Through the mode in which manufacturing was carried on particularly in rural areas of the eighteenth century, it was so much interwoven with the vital relationships of a great mass of individuals that no country dared jeopardize its existence by permitting free competition. When a country manages to export, this depends entirely on the extension or restriction of commerce and exercises a relatively small effect. [Corner of manuscript damaged.] Hence the secondary [importance] and influence of [the merchants] in the eighteenth century. More than anyone else the merchants and especially the shippers insisted on protection and monopolies. The manufacturers also demanded and received protection but were inferior in political importance at all times. The commercial towns, particularly the maritime towns, became to some degree civilized and bigbourgeois, but an extreme petty bourgeois outlook persisted in the factory towns. See Aikin [*Description of the Country from Thirty to Forty Miles round Manchester*, London, 1795], etc. The eighteenth century was a century of trade. Pinto says this expressly [*Traité de la circulation et du crédit*, Amsterdam, 1771]: "Commerce is the rage of the century," and: "for some time now people have been talking only about commerce, navigation, and the navy."

The movement of capital, although significantly accelerated, remained relatively slow. The splitting of the world market into separate parts, each of which was exploited by a particular nation, the exclusion of nations' competition among themselves, the clumsiness of production itself, and the fact that the financial system was only developing from its early stages—all this greatly impeded circulation. The consequence was a haggling, shabby, petty spirit which still clung to all merchants and the whole mode of carrying on trade. Compared with manufacturers and particularly craftsmen, they were certainly big bourgeois; compared with the merchants and industrialists of the next period they remain petty bourgeois. Cf. Adam Smith [*The Wealth of Nations*].

This period is also characterized by the cancellation of bans on the export of gold and silver, and the beginning of trade in money; by banks, national debts, paper money, speculation in stocks and shares, and jobbing in all articles; by the development of finance in general. Capital again lost a great part of the national character which it had still possessed.

The concentration of trade and manufacturing in one country, England, developed irresistibly in the seventeenth century and gradually created for that country a relative world market and thus a demand for its manufactured products which could no longer be met by the prevailing industrial forces of production. The demand outgrew the productive forces and was the motive power to bring about the third period of private ownership since the Middle Ages by producing big industry—the application of elemental forces to industrial purposes, machinery, and a very extensive division of labor. There already existed in England the remaining conditions for this new phase: freedom of competition within the nation and the development of theoretical mechanics (as perfected by Newton, the most popular science in France and England in the eighteenth century). (Free competition within the nation itself everywhere had to be obtained by revolution—1640 and 1688 in England, 1789 in France.) Competition soon forced every country that wanted to retain its historical role to protect its manufacturers by renewed customs regulations (the old duties were of little help against big industry) and soon introduce big industry under protective duties. Big industry universalized competition (practical free trade; the protective duty is only a palliative, a measure of defense

within free trade) despite protective measures, established means of communication and the modern world market, subordinated trade to itself, transformed all capital into industrial capital, and thus produced the rapid circulation (development of finance) and centralization of capital funds. (By universal competition it forced all individuals to strain their energy to the extreme. So far as possible, big industry destroyed ideology, religion, morality, etc., and where it could not, made them into a plain lie.) It produced world history for the first time in that it made every civilized nation and every individual member of the nation dependent for the satisfaction of his wants on the whole world, thus destroying the former natural exclusiveness of separate nations. It subsumed natural science under capital and took from the division of labor the last semblance of its natural character. It destroyed natural growth in general, so far as this is possible in labor, and resolved all natural relationships into money relationships. In the place of naturally grown towns it created overnight modern, large industrial cities. Wherever big industry prevailed, it destroyed the crafts and all earlier stages of industry. It completed the victory [of the town] over the country. [Its premise] was the automatic systems. [Its development] resulted in a mass of productive forces for which private property became just as much a fetter as the guild had been for the manufacturer and the small rural shop for the developing craft. Under the system of private property these productive forces receive only a one-sided development and become destructive forces for the majority. A great multitude of such forces cannot find application at all under the system of private ownership. In general, big industry created everywhere the same relation between the classes of society and thus destroyed the particularity of each nationality. And finally, while the bourgeoisie of each nation still retained separate national interests, big industry created a class having the same interests in all nations and for which nationality is already destroyed; a class which is really rid of the entire old world and stands opposed to it. Big industry makes unbearable for the worker not only his relation to the capitalist but even labor itself.

It is clear that big industry does not develop equally in all districts of a country. However, this does not hinder the class movement of the proletariat, because the proletarians created by big industry assume leadership of this movement and carry the crowd with them, and because the workers excluded from big industry are put in a worse situation than the workers in big industry itself. Countries with big industries affect in a similar manner the more or less non-industrial countries, if the latter are swept by global commerce into universal competitive struggle. These different forms are only so many forms of the organization of labor and hence of property. In each period a unification of the existing productive forces takes place insofar as this has been made necessary by needs.

This contradiction between the productive forces and the form of commerce, which we observe occurring several times in past history without endangering the basis of history, had to burst out in a revolution each time, taking on at the same time various secondary forms, such as comprehensive collisions, collisions of various classes, contradictions of consciousness, battle of ideas, etc., political struggle, etc. From a narrow point of view one can isolate one of these secondary forms and consider it the basis of these revolutions. This is all the more easy as the individuals who started the revolutions had illusions about their own activity according to their degree of education and stage of historical development.

In our view all collisions in history have their origin in the contradiction between the productive forces and the form of interaction [*Verkehrsform*]. Incidentally, this contradiction does need to have reached its extreme in a particular country to lead to collisions in that country. Competition with industrially more developed countries brought about by expanded international commerce is sufficient to produce a similar contradiction in countries where industry is lagging behind (e.g. the latent proletariat in Germany brought out by the competition of English industry).

Competition isolates individuals, not only the bourgeois but even more the proletarians, despite the fact that it brings them together. It takes a long time before these individuals can unite, apart from the fact that for this union—if it is not to be merely local—big industry must first produce the necessary means, the big industrial cities and inexpensive, quick communica-

tions. Therefore, every organized power standing in opposition to these isolated individuals, who live in relationships daily reproducing this isolation, can be conquered only after long struggles. To demand the opposite would be tantamount to demanding that competition should not exist in this definite historical period, or that the individuals should banish from their minds relationships over which they, the isolated, have no control.

* * *

In big industry and competition all the conditions of existence, the determining factors, and the biases of individuals are fused together into the two simplest forms: private property and labor. With money every form of interaction, and interaction itself, is considered accidental for individuals. Money implies that all previous interaction was only commerce of individuals under particular conditions, not of individuals as individuals. These conditions are reduced to two: accumulated labor of private property, and actual labor. Even if only one of these ceases, interaction comes to a standstill. The modern economists themselves, for example, Sismondi, Cherbuliez, etc., juxtapose "association of individuals" and "association of capital." On the other hand, the individuals themselves are completely subsumed under the division of labor and brought into complete dependence on one another. Private property, insofar as it is opposed to labor within labor itself, evolves out of the necessity of accumulation and has at first the form of community. But in its further development it approaches more and more the modern form of private property. From the outset, the division of labor implies division of the *conditions of labor*, of tools and materials, and the splitting up of accumulated capital into the hands of various owners, and thus the division between capital and labor and different forms of capital itself. The further division of labor proceeds and the more accumulation grows, the more pronounced does the fragmentation become. Labor itself can exist only under the premise of this fragmentation.

Personal energy of the individuals of various nations —Germans and Americans—energy generated already through crossbreeding—hence the cretinism of the Germans—in France, England, etc., foreign peoples transplanted to a land already developed, in America to virgin land—in Germany the native population quietly remained in its locale.

Thus two facts become clear. First, the productive forces appear as a world by themselves independent of, removed from, and alongside individuals because the individuals whose forces they are, exist as split up and opposed to one another. On the other hand these forces are only real forces in the interaction and association of the individuals. Thus we have, on the one hand, a totality of productive forces which, so to speak, have assumed material form and are for the individuals no longer the forces of individuals but of private property—of individuals only insofar as they are owners of private property. Never before have the productive forces taken on a form so indifferent to the interaction of individuals *as* individuals, because their interaction was still restricted. On the other hand, opposing the productive forces, there is the majority of the individuals from whom these forces have been wrested away and who have become abstract individuals deprived of all real life content. Only through this fact, however, are they enabled to enter into relation with one another *as individuals*. The only connection still linking them with the productive forces and with their own existence, labor, has lost all semblance of self-activity and sustains their life only by stunting it. While in earlier periods self-activity and the production of material life were separated by the fact that they devolved on different persons and because the production of material life was considered a subordinate mode of self-activity due to the narrowness of the individuals themselves, they now diverge to such an extent that material life appears as the end, and labor, the producer of this material life (now the only possible but negative form of self-activity, as we see), appears as means.

Things have come to the point where individuals must appropriate the existing totality of productive forces not merely to achieve self-activity but to secure their very existence. This appropriation is determined by the object to be appropriated—the productive forces developed to a totality and existing only within

a universal interaction. From this aspect alone, this appropriation must have a universal character corresponding to the productive forces and interaction. The appropriation of these forces is itself nothing more than the development of individual capacities corresponding to the material instruments of production. For this very reason, the appropriation of a totality of instruments of production is the development of a totality of capabilities in the individuals themselves. It is further determined by the appropriating individuals. Only the proletarians of the present, completely deprived of any self-activity, can achieve a complete and unrestricted self-activity involving the appropriation of a totality of productive forces and consequently the development of a totality of capacities. All previous revolutionary appropriations were restricted. Individuals, whose self-activity was restricted by a crude instrument of production and limited interaction, appropriated this crude instrument of production and merely attained a new plateau of limitation. Their instrument of production became their property, but they themselves remained subject to the division of labor and their own instrument of production. In all appropriations up to now a mass of individuals remained subservient to a single instrument of production. In the appropriation by the proletarians, a mass of instruments of production must be subservient to each individual and the property of all. The only way for individuals to control modern universal interaction is to make it subject to the control of all.

The appropriation is further determined by the manner in which it must be carried through. It can only be accomplished by a union, universal because of the character of the proletariat itself, and through a revolution in which the power of the social organization and of earlier modes of production and interaction is overthrown and the proletariat's universal character and energy for the act of appropriation is developed. Furthermore, the proletariat must get rid of everything still clinging to it from its earlier position in society.

Not until this stage is reached will self-activity coincide with material life, will individuals become complete individuals. Only then will the shedding of all natural limitations be accomplished. The transformation of labor into self-activity corresponds to the transformation of the previous restricted interaction into the interaction of individuals as such. With the appropriation of the total productive forces through united individuals, private property ceases to exist. While in previous history a particular condition always appeared as accidental, now the isolation of individuals and the particular private gain of any individual have become accidental.

Individuals who are no longer subjected to the division of labor have been conceived by the philosophers as an ideal under the name of "Man." They have grasped the whole process described as the evolutionary process of "Man," so at every historical stage "Man" was substituted for individuals and presented as the motive force of history. The whole process was seen as a process of the self-alienation of "Man," essentially because the average individual of the later stage was always foisted on the earlier stage and the consciousness of a later period on the individuals of an earlier.

《《Self-alienation》》 Through this inversion, which from the beginning has been an abstraction of the actual conditions, it was possible to transform all history into an evolutionary process of consciousness.

Civil society comprises the entire material interaction among individuals at a particular evolutionary stage of the productive forces. It comprises the entire commercial and industrial life of a stage and hence transcends the state and the nation even though that life, on the other hand, is manifested in foreign affairs as nationality and organized within a state. The term "civil society" emerged in the eighteenth century when property relations had already evolved from the community of antiquity and medieval times. Civil society as such only develops with the bourgeoisie. The social organization, however, which evolves directly from production and commerce and in all ages forms the basis of the state and the rest of the idealistic superstructure, has always been designated by the same name.

Marx and Engels

The Communist Manifesto

A spectre is haunting Europe—the spectre of Communism. All the Powers of old Europe have entered into a holy alliance to exorcise this spectre: Pope and Czar, Metternich and Guizot, French Radicals and German police-spies.

Where is the party in opposition that has not been decried as Communistic by its opponents in power? Where the Opposition that has not hurled back the branding reproach of Communism, against the more advanced opposition parties, as well as against its reactionary adversaries?

Two things result from this fact:

I. Communism is already acknowledged by all European Powers to be itself a Power.

II. It is high time that Communists should openly, in the face of the whole world, publish their views, their aims, their tendencies, and meet this nursery tale of the Spectre of Communism with a Manifesto of the party itself.

To this end, Communists of various nationalities have assembled in London, and sketched the following Manifesto, to be published in the English, French, German, Italian, Flemish and Danish languages.

I

Bourgeois and Proletarians*

The history of all hitherto existing society† is the history of class struggles.

Freeman and slave, patrician and plebeian, lord and serf, guild-master‡ and journeyman, in a word, oppressor and oppressed, stood in constant opposition to one another, carried on an uninterrupted, now hidden, now open fight, a fight that each time ended, either in a revolutionary reconstitution of society at large, or in the common ruin of the contending classes.

In the earlier epochs of history, we find almost everywhere a complicated arrangement of society into various orders, a manifold gradation of social rank. In ancient Rome we have patricians, knights, plebeians, slaves; in the Middle Ages, feudal lords, vassals, guild-masters, journeymen, apprentices, serfs; in almost all of these classes, again, subordinate gradations.

The modern bourgeois society that has sprouted from the ruins of feudal society has not done away with class antagonisms. It has but established new classes,

---

The edition reprinted here is the standard English edition of 1888.

*By bourgeoisie is meant the class of modern Capitalists, owners of the means of social production and employers of wage-labour. By proletariat, the class of modern wage–labourers who, having no means of production of their own, are reduced to selling their labour-power in order to live. [*Note by Engels to the English edition of 1888.*]

†That is, all *written* history. In 1847, the pre-history of society, the social organisation existing previous to recorded history, was all but unknown. Since then, Haxthausen discovered common ownership of land in Russia. Mauer proved it to be the social foundation from which all Teutonic races started in history, and by and by village communities were found to be, or to have been the primitive form of society everywhere from India to Ireland. The inner organisation of this primitive Communistic society was laid bare, in its typical form, by Morgan's crowning discovery of the true nature of the *gens* and its relation to the *tribe*. With the dissolution of these primeval communities society begins to be differentiated into separate and finally antagonistic classes. I have attempted to retrace this process of dissolution in *Der Ursprung der Familie, des Privateigenthums und des Staats*, 2nd edition, Stuttgart, 1886. [*Note by Engels to the English edition of 1888, and—less the last sentence—to the German edition of 1890.*]

‡Guild-master, that is, a full member of a guild, a master within, not a head of a guild. [*Note by Engels to the English edition of 1888.*]

new conditions of oppression, new forms of struggle in place of the old ones.

Our epoch, the epoch of the bourgeoisie, possesses, however, this distinctive feature: it has simplified the class antagonisms. Society as a whole is more and more splitting up into two great hostile camps, into two great classes directly facing each other: Bourgeoisie and Proletariat.

From the serfs of the Middle Ages sprang the chartered burghers of the earliest towns. From these burgesses the first elements of the bourgeoisie were developed.

The discovery of America, the rounding of the Cape, opened up fresh ground for the rising bourgeoisie. The East-Indian and Chinese markets, the colonisation of America, trade with the colonies, the increase in the means of exchange and in commodities generally, gave to commerce, to navigation, to industry, an impulse never before known, and thereby, to the revolutionary element in the tottering feudal society, a rapid development.

The feudal system of industry, under which industrial production was monopolised by closed guilds, now no longer sufficed for the growing wants of the new markets. The manufacturing system took its place. The guild-masters were pushed on one side by the manufacturing middle class; division of labour between the different corporate guilds vanished in the face of division of labour in each single workshop.

Meantime the markets kept ever growing, the demand ever rising. Even manufacture no longer sufficed. Thereupon, steam and machinery revolutionised industrial production. The place of manufacture was taken by the giant, Modern Industry, the place of the industrial middle class, by industrial millionaires, the leaders of whole industrial armies, the modern bourgeois.

Modern industry has established the world market, for which the discovery of America paved the way. This market has given an immense development to commerce, to navigation, to communication by land. This development has, in its turn, reacted on the extension of industry; and in proportion as industry, commerce, navigation, railways extended, in the same proportion the bourgeoisie developed, increased its

capital, and pushed into the background every class handed down from the Middle Ages.

We see, therefore, how the modern bourgeoisie is itself the product of a long course of development, of a series of revolutions in the modes of production and of exchange.

Each step in the development of the bourgeoisie was accompanied by a corresponding political advance of that class. An oppressed class under the sway of the feudal nobility, an armed and self-governing association in the medieval commune;* here independent urban republic (as in Italy and Germany), there taxable "third estate" of the monarchy (as in France), afterwards, in the period of manufacture proper, serving either the semi-feudal or the absolute monarchy as a counterpoise against the nobility, and, in fact, cornerstone of the great monarchies in general, the bourgeoisie has at last, since the establishment of Modern Industry and of the world market, conquered for itself, in the modern representative State, exclusive political sway. The executive of the modern State is but a committee for managing the common affairs of the whole bourgeoisie.

The bourgeoisie, historically, has played a most revolutionary part.

The bourgeoisie, wherever it has got the upper hand, has put an end to all feudal, patriarchal, idyllic relations. It has pitilessly torn asunder the motley feudal ties that bound man to his "natural superiors," and has left remaining no other nexus between man and man than naked self-interest, than callous "cash payment." It has drowned the most heavenly ecstasies of religious fervour, of chivalrous enthusiasm, of philistine sentimentalism, in the icy water of egotistical

---

*"Commune" was the name taken, in France, by the nascent towns even before they had conquered from their feudal lords and masters local self-government and political rights as the "Third Estate." Generally speaking, for the economical development of the bourgeoisie, England is here taken as the typical country; for its political development, France. [*Note by Engels to the English edition of 1888.*]

This was the name given their urban communities by the townsmen of Italy and France, after they had purchased or wrested their initial rights of self-government from their feudal lords. [*Note by Engels to the German edition of 1890.*]

calculation. It has resolved personal worth into exchange value, and in place of the numberless indefeasible chartered freedoms, has set up that single, unconscionable freedom—Free Trade. In one word, for exploitation, veiled by religious and political illusions, it has substituted naked, shameless, direct, brutal exploitation.

The bourgeoisie has stripped of its halo every occupation hitherto honoured and looked up to with reverent awe. It has converted the physician, the lawyer, the priest, the poet, the man of science, into its paid wage-labourers.

The bourgeoisie has torn away from the family its sentimental veil, and has reduced the family relation to a mere money relation.

The bourgeoisie has disclosed how it came to pass that the brutal display of vigour in the Middle Ages, which Reactionists so much admire, found its fitting complement in the most slothful indolence. It has been the first to show what man's activity can bring about. It has accomplished wonders far surpassing Egyptian pyramids, Roman aqueducts, and Gothic cathedrals; it has conducted expeditions that put in the shade all former Exoduses of nations and crusades.

The bourgeoisie cannot exist without constantly revolutionising the instruments of production, and hereby the relations of production, and with them the whole relations of society. Conversation of the old modes of production in unaltered form, was, on the contrary, the first condition of existence for all earlier industrial classes. Constant revolutionising of production, uninterrupted disturbance of all social conditions, everlasting uncertainty and agitation distinguish the bourgeois epoch from all earlier ones. All fixed, fast-frozen relations, with their train of ancient and venerable prejudices and opinions, are swept away, all new-formed ones become antiquated before they can ossify. All that is solid melts into air, all that is holy is profaned, and man is at last compelled to face with sober senses, his real conditions of life, and his relations with his kind.

The need of a constantly expanding market for its products chases the bourgeoisie over the whole surface of the globe. It must nestle everywhere, settle everywhere, establish connexions everywhere.

The bourgeoisie has through its exploitation of the world market given a cosmopolitan character to production and consumption in every country. To the great chagrin of Reactionists, it has drawn from under the feet of industry the national ground on which it stood. All old-established national industries have been destroyed or are daily being destroyed. They are dislodged by new industries, whose introduction becomes a life and death question for all civilised nations, by industries that no longer work up indigenous raw material, but raw material drawn from the remotest zones; industries whose products are consumed, not only at home, but in every quarter of the globe. In place of the old wants, satisfied by the productions of the country, we find new wants, requiring for their satisfaction the products of distant lands and climes. In place of the old local and national seclusion and self-sufficiency, we have intercourse in every direction, universal interdependence of nations. And as in material, so also in intellectual production. The intellectual creations of individual nations become common property. National one-sidedness and narrow-mindedness become more and more impossible, and from the numerous national and local literatures, there arises a world literature.

The bourgeoisie, by the rapid improvement of all instruments of production, by the immensely facilitated means of communication, draws all, even the most barbarian, nations into civilisation. The cheap pieces of its commodities are the heavy artillery with which it batters down all Chinese walls, with which it forces the barbarians' intensely obstinate hatred of foreigners to capitulate. It compels all nations, on pain of extinction, to adopt the bourgeois mode of production; it compels them to introduce what it calls civilisation into their midst, i.e., to become bourgeois themselves. In one word, it creates a world after its own image.

The bourgeoisie has subjected the country to the rule of the towns. It has created enormous cities, has greatly increased the urban population as compared with the rural, and has thus rescued a considerable part of the population from the idiocy of rural life. Just as it has made the country dependent on the towns, so it has made barbarian and semibarbarian countries dependent on the civilised ones, nations of peasants on nations of bourgeois, the East on the West.

The bourgeoisie keeps more and more doing away with the scattered state of the population, of the means of production, and of property. It has agglomerated population, centralised means of production, and has concentrated property in a few hands. The necessary consequence of this was political centralisation. Independent, or but loosely connected provinces with separate interests, laws, governments and systems of taxation, became lumped together into one nation, with one government, one code of laws, one national class-interest, one frontier and one customs-tariff.

The bourgeoisie, during its rule of scarce one hundred years, has created more massive and more colossal productive forces than have all preceding generations together. Subjection of Nature's forces to man, machinery, application of chemistry to industry and agriculture, steam-navigation, railways, electric telegraphs, clearing of whole continents for cultivation, canalisation of rivers, whole populations conjured out of the ground—what earlier century had even a presentiment that such productive forces slumbered in the lap of social labour?

We see then: the means of production and of exchange, on whose foundation the bourgeoisie built itself up, were generated in feudal society. At a certain stage in the development of these means of production and of exchange, the conditions under which feudal society produced and exchanged, the feudal organisation of agriculture and manufacturing industry, in one word, the feudal relations of property became no longer compatible with the already developed productive forces; they became so many fetters. They had to be burst asunder; they were burst asunder.

Into their place stepped free competition, accompanied by a social and political constitution adapted to it, and by the economical and political sway of the bourgeois class.

A similar movement is going on before our own eyes. Modern bourgeois society with its relations of production, of exchange and of property, a society that has conjured up such gigantic means of production and of exchange, is like the sorcerer, who is no longer able to control the powers of the nether world whom he has called up by his spells. For many a decade past the history of industry and commerce is but the history of the revolt of modern productive forces against modern conditions of production, against the property relations that are the conditions for the existence of the bourgeoisie and of its rule. It is enough to mention the commercial crises that by their political return put on its trial, each time more threateningly, the existence of the entire bourgeois society. In these crises a great part not only of the existing products, but also of the previously created productive forces, are periodically destroyed. In these crises there breaks out an epidemic that, in all earlier epochs, would have seemed an absurdity—the epidemic of overproduction. Society suddenly finds itself put back into a state of momentary barbarism; it appears as if a famine, a universal war of devastation had cut off the supply of every means of subsistence; industry and commerce seem to be destroyed; and why? Because there is too much civilisation, too much means of subsistence, too much industry, too much commerce. The productive forces at the disposal of society no longer tend to further the development of the conditions of bourgeois property; on the contrary, they have become too powerful for these conditions, by which they are fettered, and so soon as they overcome these fetters, they bring disorder into the whole of bourgeois society, endanger the existence of bourgeois property. The conditions of bourgeois society are too narrow to comprise the wealth created by them. And how does the bourgeoisie get over these crises? On the one hand by enforced destruction of a mass of productive forces; on the other, by the conquest of new markets, and by the more thorough exploitation of the old ones. That is to say, by paving the way for more extensive and more destructive crises, and by diminishing the means whereby crises are prevented.

The weapons with which the bourgeoisie felled feudalism to the ground are now turned against the bourgeoisie itself.

But not only has the bourgeoisie forged the weapons that bring death to itself; it has also called into existence the men who are to wield those weapons—the modern working class—the proletarians.

In proportion as the bourgeoisie, *i.e.*, capital, is developed, in the same proportion is the proletariat, the modern working class, developed—a class of labourers, who live only so long as they find work, and who find work only so long as their labour increases capital. These labourers, who must sell themselves piecemeal, are a commodity, like every other article of commerce, and are consequently exposed to all the vicissitudes of competition, to all the fluctuations of the market.

Owing to the extensive use of machinery and to division of labour, the work of the proletarians has lost all individual character, and, consequently, all charm for the workman. He becomes an appendage of the machine, and it is only the most simple, most monotonous, and most easily acquired knack, that is required of him. Hence, the cost of production of a workman is restricted, almost entirely, to the means of subsistence that he requires for his maintenance, and for the propagation of his race. But the price of a commodity, and therefore also of labour, is equal to its cost of production. In proportion, therefore, as the repulsiveness of the work increases, the wage decreases. Nay more, in proportion as the use of machinery and division of labour increases, in the same proportion the burden of toil also increases, whether by prolongation of the working hours, by increase of the work exacted in a given time or by increased speed of the machinery, etc.

Modern industry has converted the little workshop of the patriarchal master into the great factory of the industrial capitalist. Masses of labourers, crowded into the factory, are organised like soldiers. As privates of the industrial army they are placed under the command of a perfect hierarchy of officers and sergeants. Not only are they slaves of the bourgeois class, and of the bourgeois State; they are daily and hourly enslaved by the machine, by the overlooker, and, above all, by the individual bourgeois manufacturer himself. The more openly this depotism proclaims gain to be its end and aim, the more petty, the more hateful and the more embittering it is.

The less the skill and exertion of strength implied in manual labour, in other words, the more modern industry becomes developed, the more is the labour of men superseded by that of women. Differences of age and sex have no longer any distinctive social validity for the working class. All are instruments of labour, more or less expensive to use, according to their age and sex.

No sooner is the exploitation of the labourer by the manufacturer, so far, at an end, and he receives his wages in cash, than he is set upon by the other portions of the bourgeoisie, the landlord, the shopkeeper, the pawnbroker, etc.

The lower strata of the middle class—the small tradespeople, shopkeepers, and retired tradesmen generally, the handicraftsmen and peasants—all these sink gradually into the proletariat, partly because their diminutive capital does not suffice for the scale on which Modern Industry is carried on, and is swamped in the competition with the large capitalists, partly because their specialised skill is rendered worthless by new methods of production. Thus the proletariat is recruited from all classes of the population.

The proletariat goes through various stages of development. With its birth begins its struggle with the bourgeoisie. At first the contest is carried on by individual labourers, then by the workpeople of a factory, then by the operatives of one trade, in one locality, against the individual bourgeois who directly exploits them. They direct their attacks not against the bourgeois conditions of production, but against the instruments of production themselves; they destroy imported wares that compete with their labour, they smash to pieces machinery, they set factories ablaze, they seek to restore by force the vanished status of the workman of the Middle Ages.

At this stage the labourers still form an incoherent mass scattered over the whole country, and broken up by their mutual competition. If anywhere they unite to form more compact bodies, this is not yet the consequence of their own active union, but of the union of the bourgeoisie, which class, in order to attain its own political ends, is compelled to set the whole proletariat in motion, and is moreover yet, for a time, able to do so. At this stage, therefore, the proletarians do not fight their enemies, but the enemies of their enemies, the remnants of absolute monarchy, the landowners, the non-industrial bourgeois, the petty bourgeoisie. Thus the whole historical movement is concentrated in the hands of the bourgeoisie; every victory so obtained is a victory for the bourgeoisie.

But with the development of industry the proletariat not only increases in number; it becomes concentrated in greater masses, its strength grows, and it feels that strength more. The various interests and conditions of life within the ranks of the proletariat are more and more equalised, in proportion as machinery obliterates all distinctions of labor, and nearly everywhere reduces wages to the same low level. The growing competition among the bourgeois, and the resulting commercial crises, make the wages of the workers ever more fluctuating. The unceasing improvement of machinery, ever more rapidly developing, makes their livelihood more and more precarious; the collisions between individual workmen and individual bourgeois take more and more the character of collisions between two classes. Thereupon the workers begin to form combinations (Trades' Unions) against the bourgeois; they club together in order to keep up the rate of wages; they found permanent associations in order to make provision beforehand for these occasional revolts. Here and there the contest breaks out into riots.

Now and then the workers are victorious, but only for a time. The real fruit of their battles lies, not in the immediate result, but in the ever-expanding union of the workers. This union is helped on by the improved means of communication that are created by modern industry and that place the workers of different localities in contact with one another. It was just this contact that was needed to centralise the numerous local struggles, all of the same character, into one national struggle between classes. But every class struggle is a political struggle. And that union, to attain which the burghers of the Middle Ages, with their miserable highways, required centuries, the modern proletarians, thanks to railways, achieve in a few years.

This organisation of the proletarians into a class, and consequently into a political party, is continually being upset again by the competition between the workers themselves. But it ever rises up again, stronger, firmer, mightier. It compels legislative recognition of particular interests of the workers, by taking advantage of the divisions among the bourgeoisie itself. Thus the ten-hours' bill in England was carried.

Altogether collisions between the classes of the old society further, in many ways, the course of development of the proletariat. The bourgeoisie finds itself in a constant battle. At first with the aristocracy; later on, with those portions of the bourgeoisie itself, whose interests have become antagonistic to the progress of industry; at all times, with the bourgeoisie of foreign countries. In all these battles it sees itself compelled to appeal to the proletariat, to ask for its help, and thus, to drag it into the political arena. The bourgeoisie itself, therefore, supplies the proletariat with its own elements of political and general education, in other words, it furnishes the proletariat with weapons for fighting the bourgeoisie.

Further, as we have already seen, entire sections of the ruling classes are, by the advance of industry, precipitated into the proletariat, or are at least threatened in their conditions of existence. These also supply the proletariat with fresh elements of enlightenment and progress.

Finally, in times when the class struggle nears the decisive hour, the process of dissolution going on within the ruling class, in fact within the whole range of old society, assumes such a violent, glaring character, that a small section of the ruling class cuts itself adrift, and joins the revolutionary class, the class that holds the future in its hands. Just as, therefore, at an earlier period, a section of the nobility went over to the bourgeoisie, so now a portion of the bourgeoisie goes over to the proletariat, and in particular, a portion of the bourgeois ideologists, who have raised themselves to the level of comprehending theoretically the historical movement as a whole.

Of all the classes that stand face to face with the bourgeoisie today, the proletariat alone is a really revolutionary class. The other classes decay and finally disappear in the face of Modern Industry; the proletariat is its special and essential product.

The lower middle class, the small manufacturer, the shopkeeper, the artisan, the peasant, all these fight against the bourgeoisie, to save from extinction their existence as fractions of the middle class. They are therefore not revolutionary, but conservative. Nay more, they are reactionary, for they try to roll back the wheel of history. If by chance they are revolutionary, they are so only in view of their impending transfer into the proletariat, they thus defend not their present, but their future interests, they desert their own standpoint to place themselves at that of the proletariat.

The "dangerous class," the social scum, that passively rotting mass thrown off by the lowest layers of old society may, here and there, be swept into the movement by a proletarian revolution; its conditions of life, however, prepare it far more for the part of a bribed tool of reactionary intrigue.

In the conditions of the proletariat, those of old society at large are already virtually swamped. The proletarian is without property; his relation to his wife and children has no longer anything in common with the bourgeois family relations; modern industrial labour, modern subjection to capital, the same in England as in France, in America as in Germany, has stripped him of every trace of national character. Law, morality, religion, are to him so many bourgeois prejudices, behind which lurk in ambush just as many bourgeois interests.

All the preceding classes that got the upper hand, sought to fortify their already acquired status by subjecting society at large to their conditions of appropriation. The proletarians cannot become masters of the productive forces of society, except by abolishing their own previous mode of appropriation, and thereby also every other previous mode of appropriation. They have nothing of their own to secure and to fortify; their mission is to destroy all previous securities for, and insurances of, individual property.

All previous historical movements were movements of minorities, or in the interest of minorities. The proletarian movement is the self-conscious, independent movement of the immense majority, in the interest of the immense majority. The proletariat, the lowest stratum of our present society, cannot stir, cannot raise itself up, without the whole superincumbent strata of official society being sprung into the air.

Though not in substance, yet in form, the struggle of the proletariat with the bourgeoisie is at first a national struggle. The proletariat of each country must, of course, first of all settle matters with its own bourgeoisie.

In depicting the most general phases of the development of the proletariat, we traced the more or less veiled civil war, raging within existing society, up to the point where that war breaks out into open revolution, and where the violent overthrow of the bourgeoisie lays the foundation for the sway of the proletariat.

Hitherto, every form of society has been based, as we have already seen, on the antagonism of oppressing and oppressed classes. But in order to oppress a class, certain conditions must be assured to it under which it can, at least, continue its slavish existence. The serf, in the period of serfdom, raised himself to membership in the commune, just as the petty bourgeois, under the yoke of feudal absolutism, managed to develop into a bourgeois. The modern labourer, on the contrary, instead of rising with the progress of industry, sinks deeper and deeper below the conditions of existence of his own class. He becomes a pauper, and pauperism develops more rapidly than population and wealth. And here it becomes evident, that the bourgeoisie is unfit any longer to be the ruling class in society, and to impose its conditions of existence upon society as an over-riding law. It is unfit to rule because it is incompetent to assure an existence to its slave within his slavery, because it cannot help letting him sink into such a state, that it has to feed him, instead of being fed by him. Society can no longer live under this bourgeoisie, in other words, its existence is no longer compatible with society.

The essential condition for the existence, and for the sway of the bourgeois class, is the formation and augmentation of capital; the condition for capital is wage-labour. Wage-labour rests exclusively on competition between the labourers. The advance of industry, whose involuntary promoter is the bourgeoisie, replaces the isolation of the labourers, due to competition, by their revolutionary combination, due to association. The development of Modern Industry, therefore, cuts from under its feet the very foundation on which the bourgeoisie produces and appropriates products. What the bourgeoisie, therefore, produces, above all, is its own grave-diggers. Its fall and the victory of the proletariat are equally inevitable.

II

Proletarians and Communists

In what relation do the Communists stand to the proletarians as a whole?

The Communists do not form a separate party opposed to other working-class parties.

They have no interests separate and apart from those of the proletariat as a whole.

They do not set up any sectarian principles of their own, by which to shape and mould the proletarian movement.

The Communists are distinguished from the other working-class parties by this only: 1. In the national struggles of the proletarians of the different countries, they point out and bring to the front the common interests of the entire proletariat, independently of all nationality. 2. In the various stages of development which the struggle of the working class against the bourgeoisie has to pass through, they always and everywhere represent the interests of the movement as a whole.

The Communists, therefore, are on the one hand, practically, the most advanced and resolute section of the working-class parties of every country, that section which pushes forward all others; on the other hand, theoretically, they have over the great mass of the proletariat the advantage of clearly understanding the line of march, the conditions, and the ultimate general results of the proletarian movement.

The immediate aim of the Communists is the same as that of all the other proletarian parties: formation of the proletariat into a class, overthrow of the bourgeois supremacy, conquest of political power by the proletariat.

The theoretical conclusions of the Communists are in no way based on ideas or principles that have been invented, or discovered by this or that would-be universal reformer.

They merely express, in general terms, actual relations springing from an existing class struggle, from a historical movement going on under our very eyes.

The abolition of existing property relations is not at all a distinctive feature of Communism.

All property relations in the past have continually been subject to historical change consequent upon the change in historical conditions.

The French Revolution, for example, abolished feudal property in favour of bourgeois property.

The distinguishing feature of Communism is not the abolition of property generally, but the abolition of bourgeois property. But modern bourgeois private property is the final and most complete expression of the system of producing and appropriating products, that is based on class antagonisms, on the exploitation of the many by the few.

In this sense, the theory of the Communists may be summed up in the single sentence: Abolition of private property.

We Communists have been reproached with the desire of abolishing the right of personally acquiring property as the fruit of a man's own labour, which property is alleged to be the groundwork of all personal freedom, activity and independence.

Hard-won, self-acquired, self-earned property! Do you mean the property of the petty artisan and of the small peasant, a form of property that preceded the bourgeois form? There is no need to abolish that; the development of industry has to a great extent already destroyed it, and is still destroying it daily.

Or do you mean modern bourgeois private property?

But does wage-labour create any property for the labourer? Not a bit. It creates capital, *i.e.*, that kind of property which exploits wage-labour, and which cannot increase except upon condition of begetting a new supply of wage-labour for fresh exploitation. Property, in its present form, is based on the antagonism of capital and wage-labour. Let us examine both sides of this antagonism.

To be a capitalist is to have not only a purely personal, but a social *status* in production. Capital is a collective product, and only by the united action of many members, nay, in the last resort, only by the united action of all members of society, can it be set in motion.

Capital is, therefore, not a personal, it is a social power.

When, therefore, capital is converted into common property, into the property of all members of society, personal property is not thereby transformed into social property. It is only the social character of the property that is changed. It loses its class character.

Let us now take wage-labour.

The average price of wage-labour is the minimum wage, *i.e.*, that quantum of the means of subsistence, which is absolutely requisite to keep the labourer in bare existence as a labourer. What, therefore, the wage-labourer appropriates by means of his labour, merely suffices to prolong and reproduce a bare existence. We by no means intend to abolish this personal appropriation of the products of labour, an appropriation that is made for the maintenance and reproduction of human life, and that leaves no surplus wherewith to command the labour of others. All that we want to do away with is the miserable character of this appropriation, under which the labourer lives merely to increase capital, and is allowed to live only in so far as the interest of the ruling class requires it.

In bourgeois society, living labour is but a means to increase accumulated labour. In Communist society, accumulated labour is but a means to widen, to enrich, to promote the existence of the labourer.

In bourgeois society, therefore, the past dominates the present; in Communist society, the present dominates the past. In bourgeois society capital is independent and has individuality, while the living person is dependent and has no individuality.

And the abolition of this state of things is called by the bourgeois abolition of individuality and freedom! And rightly so. The abolition of bourgeois individuality, bourgeois independence, and bourgeois freedom is undoubtedly aimed at.

By freedom is meant, under the present bourgeois conditions of production, free trade, free selling and buying.

But if selling and buying disappears, free selling and buying disappears also. This talk about free selling and buying, and all the other "brave words" of our bourgeoisie about freedom in general, have a meaning, if any, only in contrast with restricted selling and buying, with the fettered traders of the Middle Ages, but have no meaning when opposed to the Communistic abolition of buying and selling, of the bourgeois conditions of production, and of the bourgeoisie itself.

You are horrified at our intending to do away with private property. But in your existing society, private property is already done way with for nine-tenths of the population; its existence for the few is solely due to its non-existence in the hands of those nine-tenths. You reproach us, therefore, with intending to do away with a form of property, the necessary condition for whose existence is the non-existence of any property for the immense majority of society.

In one word, you reproach us with intending to do away with your property. Precisely so; that is just what we intend.

From the moment when labour can no longer be converted into capital, money, or rent, into a social power capable of being monopolised, *i.e.*, from the moment when individual property can no longer be transformed into bourgeois property, into capital, from that moment, you say, individuality vanishes.

You must, therefore, confess that by "individual" you mean no other person than the bourgeois, than the middle-class owner of property. This person must, indeed, be swept out of the way, and made impossible.

Communism deprives no man of the power to appropriate the products of society; all that it does is to deprive him of the power to subjugate the labours of others by means of such appropriation.

It has been objected that upon the abolition of private property all work will cease, and universal laziness will overtake us.

According to this, bourgeois society ought long ago to have gone to the dogs through sheer idleness; for those of its members who work, acquire nothing, and those who acquire anything, do not work. The whole of this objection is but another expression of the tautology: that there can no longer be any wage-labour when there is no longer any capital.

All objections urged against the Communistic mode of producing and appropriating material products, have, in the same way, been urged against the Communistic modes of producing and appropriating intellectual products. Just as, to the bourgeois, the disappearance of class property is the disappearance of production itself, so the disappearance of class culture is to him identical with the disappearance of all culture.

That culture, the loss of which he laments, is, for the enormous majority, a mere training to act as a machine.

But don't wrangle with us so long as you apply, to our intended abolition of bourgeois property, the standard of your bourgeois notions of freedom, culture, law, &c. Your very ideas are but the outgrowth of the conditions of your bourgeois production and bourgeois property, just as your jurisprudence is but the will of your class made into a law for all, a will, whose essential character and direction are determined by the economical conditions of existence of your class.

The selfish misconception that induces you to transform into eternal laws of nature and of reason, the social forms springing from your present mode of production and form of property—historical relations that rise and disappear in the progress of production—this misconception you share with every ruling class that has preceded you. What you see clearly in the case of ancient property, what you admit in the case of feudal property, you are of course forbidden to admit in the case of your own bourgeois form of property.

Abolition of the family! Even the most radical flare up at this infamous proposal of the Communists.

On what foundation is the present family, the bourgeois family, based? On capital, on private gain. In its completely developed form this family exists only among the bourgeoisie. But this state of things finds its complement in the practical absence of the family among the proletarians, and in public prostitution.

The bourgeois family will vanish as a matter of course when its complement vanishes, and both will vanish with the vanishing of capital.

Do you charge us with wanting to stop the exploitation of children by their parents? To this crime we plead guilty.

But, you will say, we destroy the most hallowed of relations, when we replace home education by social.

And your education! Is not that also social, and determined by the social conditions under which you educate, by the intervention, direct or indirect, of society, by means of schools, &c? The Communists have not invented the intervention of society in education; they do but seek to alter the character of that intervention, and to rescue education from the influence of the ruling class.

The bourgeois clap-trap about the family and education, about the hallowed co-relation of parent and child, becomes all the more disgusting, the more, by the action of Modern Industry, all family ties among the proletarians are torn asunder, and their children transformed into simple articles of commerce and instruments of labour.

But you Communists would introduce community of women, screams the whole bourgeoisie in chorus.

The bourgeois sees in his wife a mere instrument of production. He hears that the instruments of production are to be exploited in common, and, naturally, can come to no other conclusion than that the lot of being common to all will likewise fall to the women.

He has not even a suspicion that the real point aimed at is to do away with the status of women as mere instruments of production.

For the rest, nothing is more ridiculous than the virtuous indignation of the bourgeois at the community of women which, they pretend, is to be openly and officially established by the Communists. The Communists have no need to introduce community of women; it has existed almost from time immemorial.

Our bourgeois, not content with having the wives and daughters of their proletarians at their disposal, not to speak of common prostitutes, take the greatest pleasure in seducing each other's wives.

Bourgeois marriage is in reality a system of wives in common and thus, at the most, what the Communists might possibly be reproached with, is that they desire to introduce, in substitution for a hypocritically concealed, an openly legalised community of women. For the rest, it is self-evident that the abolition of the present system of production must bring with it the abolition of the community of women springing from that system, i.e., of prostitution both public and private.

The Communists are further reproached with desiring to abolish countries and nationality.

The working men have no country. We cannot take from them what they have not got. Since the proletariat must first of all acquire political supremacy, must rise to be the leading class of the nation, must constitute itself *the* nation, it is so far, itself national, though not in the bourgeois sense of the word.

National differences and antagonisms between peoples are daily more and more vanishing, owing to the development of the bourgeoisie, to freedom of commerce, to the world market, to uniformity in the mode of production and in the conditions of life corresponding thereto.

The supremacy of the proletariat will cause them to vanish still faster. United action, of the leading civilised countries at least, is one of the first conditions for the emancipation of the proletariat.

In proportion as the exploitation of one individual by another is put an end to, the exploitation of one nation by another will also be put an end to. In proportion as the antagonism between classes within the nation vanishes, the hostility of one nation to another will come to an end.

The charges against Communism made from a religious, a philosophical, and, generally, from an ideological standpoint, are not deserving of serious examination.

Does it require deep intuition to comprehend that man's ideas, views and conceptions, in one word, man's consciousness, changes with every change in the conditions of his material existence, in his social relations and in his social life?

What else does the history of ideas prove, than that intellectual production changes its character in proportion as material production is changed? The ruling ideas of such age have ever been the ideas of its ruling class.

When people speak of ideas that revolutionise society, they do but express the fact, that within the old society, the elements of a new one have been created, and that the dissolution of the old ideas keeps even pace with the dissolution of the old conditions of existence.

When the ancient world was in its last throes, the ancient religions were overcome by Christianity. When Christian ideas succumbed in the 18th century to rationalist ideas, feudal society fought its death battle with the then revolutionary bourgeoisie. The ideas of religious liberty and freedom of conscience merely gave expression to the sway of free competition within the domain of knowledge.

"Undoubtedly," it will be said, "religious, moral, philosophical and juridical ideas have been modified in the course of historical development. But religion, morality, philosophy, political science, and law, constantly survived this change.

"There are, besides, eternal truths, such as Freedom, Justice, etc., that are common to all states of society. But Communism abolishes eternal truths, it abolishes all religion and all morality, instead of constituting them on a new basis; it therefore acts in contradiction to all past historical experience."

What does this accusation reduce itself to? The history of all past society has consisted in the development of class antagonisms, antagonisms that assumed different forms at different epochs.

But whatever form they may have taken, one fact is common to all past ages, *viz.*, the exploitation of one part of society by the other. No wonder, then, that the social consciousness of past ages, despite all the multiplicity and variety it displays, moves within certain common forms, or general ideas, which cannot completely vanish except with the total disappearance of class antagonisms.

The Communist revolution is the most radical rupture with traditional property relations; no wonder that its development involves the most radical rupture with traditional ideas.

But let us have done with the bourgeois objections to Communism.

We have seen above, that the first step in the revolution by the working class is to raise the proletariat to the position of ruling class, to win the battle of democracy.

The proletariat will use its political supremacy to wrest, by degrees, all capital from the bourgeoisie, to centralise all instruments of production in the hands of the State, *i.e.*, of the proletariat organised as the ruling class; and to increase the total of productive forces as rapidly as possible.

Of course, in the beginning, this cannot be effected except by means of despotic inroads on the rights of property, and on the conditions of bourgeois production; by means of measures, therefore, which appear economically insufficient and untenable, but which, in the course of the movement, outstrip themselves, necessitate further inroads upon the old social order, and are unavoidable as a means of entirely revolutionising the mode of production.

These measures will of course be different in different countries.

Nevertheless in the most advanced countries, the following will be pretty generally applicable.

1. Abolition of property in land and application of all rents of land to public purposes.
2. A heavy progressive or graduated income tax.
3. Abolition of all right of inheritance.
4. Confiscation of the property of all emigrants and rebels.
5. Centralisation of credit in the hands of the State, by means of a national bank with State capital and an exclusive monopoly.
6. Centralisation of the means of communication and transport in the hands of the State.
7. Extension of factories and instruments of production owned by the State; the bringing into cultivation of waste-lands, and the improvement of the soil generally in accordance with a common plan.
8. Equal liability of all to labour. Establishment of industrial armies, especially for agriculture.
9. Combination of agriculture with manufacturing industries; gradual abolition of the distinction between town and country, by a more equable distribution of the population over the country.
10. Free education for all children in public schools. Abolition of children's factory labour in its present form. Combination of education with industrial production, &c, &c.

When, in the course of development, class distinctions have disappeared, and all production has been concentrated in the hands of a vast association of the whole nation, the public power will lose its political character. Political power, properly so called, is merely the organised power of one class for oppressing another. If the proletariat during its contest with the bourgeoisie is compelled, by the force of circumstances, to organise itself as a class, if, by means of a revolution, it makes itself the ruling class, and, as such, sweeps away by force the old conditions of production, then it will, along with these conditions, have swept away the conditions for the existence of class antagonisms and of classes generally, and will thereby have abolished its own supremacy as a class.

In place of the old bourgeois society, with its classes and class antagonisms, we shall have an association, in which the free development of each is the condition for the free development of all.

III

Socialist and Communist Literature

1. Reactionary Socialism

a. Feudal Socialism Owing to their historical position, it became the vocation of the aristocracies of France and England to write pamphlets against modern bourgeois society. In the French revolution of July 1830, and in the English reform agitation, these aristocracies again succumbed to the hateful upstart. Thenceforth, a serious political contest was altogether out of question. A literary battle alone remained possible. But even in the domain of literature the old cries of the restoration period* had become impossible.

In order to arouse sympathy, the aristocracy were obliged to lose sight, apparently, of their own interests, and to formulate their indictment against the bourgeoisie in the interest of the exploited working class alone. Thus the aristocracy took their revenge by singing lampoons on their new master, and whispering in his ears sinister prophecies of coming catastrophe.

In this way arose feudal Socialism; half lamentation, half lampoon; half echo of the past, half menace of the

*Not the English Restoration 1660 to 1689, but the French Restoration 1814 to 1830. [*Note by Engels to the English edition of 1888.*]

future; at times, by its bitter, witty and incisive criticism, striking the bourgeoisie to the very heart's core; but always ludicrous in its effect, through total incapacity to comprehend the march of modern history.

The aristocracy, in order to rally the people to them, waved the proletarian alms-bag in front for a banner. But the people, so often as it joined them, saw on their hindquarters the old feudal coats of arms, and deserted with loud and irreverent laughter.

One section of the French Legitimists and "Young England" exhibited this spectacle.

In pointing out that their mode of exploitation was different to that of the bourgeoisie, the feudalists forget that they exploited under circumstances and conditions that were quite different, and that are now antiquated. In showing that, under their rule, the modern proletariat never existed, they forget that the modern bourgeoisie is the necessary offspring of their own form of society.

For the rest, so little do they conceal the reactionary character of their criticism that their chief accusation against the bourgeoisie amounts to this, that under the bourgeoisie *régime* a class is being developed, which is destined to cut up root and branch the old order of society.

What they upbraid the bourgeoisie with is not so much that it creates a proletariat, as that it creates a *revolutionary* proletariat.

In political practice, therefore, they join in all coercive measures against the working class; and in ordinary life, despite their high-falutin phrases, they stoop to pick up the golden apples dropped from the tree of industry, and to barter truth, love, and honour for traffic in wool, beetroot-sugar, and potato spirits.*

---

*This applies chiefly to Germany where the landed aristocracy and squirearchy have large portions of their estates cultivated for their own account by stewards, and are, moreover, extensive beetroot-sugar manufacturers and distillers of potato spirits. The wealthier British aristocracy are, as yet, rather above that; but they, too, know how to make up for declining rents by lending their names to floaters of more or less shady joint-stock companies. [*Note by Engels to the English edition of 1888.*]

As the parson has ever gone hand in hand with the landlord, so has Clerical Socialism with Feudal Socialism.

Nothing is easier than to give Christian asceticism a Socialist tinge. Has not Christianity declaimed against private property, against marriage, against the State? Has it not preached in the place of these, charity and poverty, celibacy and mortification of the flesh, monastic life and Mother Church? Christian Socialism is but the holy water with which the priest consecrates the heart-burnings of the aristocrat.

b. Petty-Bourgeois Socialism The feudal aristocracy was not the only class that was ruined by the bourgeoisie, not the only class whose conditions of existence pined and perished in the atmosphere of modern bourgeois society. The medieval burgesses and the small peasant proprietors were the precursors of the modern bourgeoisie. In those countries which are but little developed, industrially and commercially, these two classes still vegetate side by side with the rising bourgeoisie.

In countries where modern civilisation has become fully developed, a new class of petty bourgeois has been formed, fluctuating between proletariat and bourgeoisie and ever renewing itself as a supplementary part of bourgeois society. The individual members of this class, however, are being constantly hurled down into the proletariat by the action of competition, and, as modern industry develops, they even see the moment approaching when they will completely disappear as an independent section of modern society, to be replaced, in manufactures, agriculture and commerce, by overlookers, bailiffs and shopmen.

In countries like France, where the peasants constitute far more than half of the population, it was natural that writers who sided with the proletariat against the bourgeoisie, should use, in their criticism of the bourgeois *régime*, the standard of the peasant and petty bourgeois, and from the standpoint of these intermediate classes should take up the cudgels for the working class. Thus arose petty-bourgeois Socialism. Sismondi was the head of this school, not only in France but also in England.

This school of Socialism dissected with great acuteness the contradictions in the conditions of modern production. It laid bare the hypocritical apologies of economists. It proved, incontrovertibly, the disastrous effects of machinery and division of labour, the concentration of capital and land in a few hands; overproduction and crises; it pointed out the inevitable ruin of the petty bourgeois and peasant, the misery of the proletariat, the anarchy in production, the crying inequalities in the distribution of wealth, the industrial war of extermination between nations, the dissolution of old moral bonds, of the old family relations, of the old nationalities.

In its positive aims, however, this form of Socialism aspires either to restoring the old means of production and of exchange, and with them the old property relations, and the old society, or to cramping the modern means of production and of exchange, within the framework of the old property relations that have been, and were bound to be, exploded by those means. In either case, it is both reactionary and Utopian.

Its last words are: corporate guilds for manufacture; patriarchal relations in agriculture.

Ultimately, when stubborn historical facts had dispersed all intoxicating effects of self-deception, this form of Socialism ended in a miserable fit of the blues.

c. *German, or "True," Socialism* The Socialist and Communist literature of France, a literature that originated under the pressure of a bourgeoisie in power, and that was the expression of the struggle against this power, was introduced into Germany at a time when the bourgeoisie, in that country, had just begun its contest with feudal absolutism.

German philosophers, would-be philosophers, and *beaux esprits*, eagerly seized on this literature, only forgetting, that when these writings immigrated from France into Germany, French social conditions had not immigrated along with them. In contact with German social conditions, this French literature lost all its immediate practical significance, and assumed a purely literary aspect. Thus, to the German philosophers of the Eighteenth Century, the demands of the first French Revolution were nothing more than the demands of "Practical Reason" in general, and the utterance of the will of the revolutionary French bourgeoisie signified in their eyes the laws of pure Will, of Will as it was bound to be, of true human Will generally.

The work of the German *literati* consisted solely in bringing the new French ideas into harmony with their ancient philosophical conscience, or rather, in annexing the French ideas without deserting their own philosophic point of view.

This annexation took place in the same way in which a foreign language is appropriated, namely, by translation.

It is well known how the monks wrote silly lives of Catholic Saints *over* the manuscripts on which the classical works of ancient heathendom had been written. The German *literati* reversed this process with the profane French literature. They wrote their philosophical nonsense beneath the French original. For instance, beneath the French criticism of the economic functions of money, they wrote "Alienation of Humanity," and beneath the French criticism of the bourgeois State they wrote, "Dethronement of the Category of the General," and so forth.

The introduction of these philosophical phrases at the back of the French historical criticisms they dubbed "Philosophy of Action," "True Socialism," "German Science of Socialism," "Philosophical Foundation of Socialism," and so on.

The French Socialist and Communist literature was thus completely emasculated. And, since it ceased in the hands of the German to express the struggle of one class with the other, he felt conscious of having overcome "French one-sidedness" and of representing, not true requirements, but the requirements of Truth; not the interests of the proletariat, but the interests of Human Nature, of Man in general, who belongs to no class, has no reality, who exists only in the misty realm of philosophical fantasy.

This German Socialism, which took its schoolboy task so seriously and solemnly, and extolled its poor stock-in-trade in such mountebank fashion, meanwhile gradually lost its pedantic innocence.

The fight of the German, and, especially, of the Prussian bourgeoisie, against feudal aristocracy and absolute monarchy, in other words, the liberal movement, became more earnest.

By this, the long wished-for opportunity was offered to "True" Socialism of confronting the political movement with the Socialist demands, of hurling the traditional anathemas against liberalism, against representative government, against bourgeois competition, bourgeois freedom of the press, bourgeois legislation, bourgeois liberty and equality, and of preaching to the masses that they had nothing to gain, and everything to lose, by this bourgeois movement. German Socialism forgot, in the nick of time, that the French criticism, whose silly echo it was, presupposed the existence of modern bourgeois society, with its corresponding economic conditions of existence, and the political constitution adapted thereto, the very thing whose attainment was the object of the pending struggle in Germany.

To the absolute governments, with their following of parsons, professors, country squires and officials, it served as a welcome scarecrow against the threatening bourgeoisie.

It was a sweet finish after the bitter pills of floggings and bullets with which these same governments, just at that time, dosed the German working-class risings.

While this "True" Socialism thus served the governments as a weapon for fighting the German bourgeoisie, it, at the same time, directly represented a reactionary interest, the interest of the German Philistines. In Germany, the *petty-bourgeois* class, a relic of the sixteenth century, and since then constantly cropping up again under various forms, is the real social basis of the existing state of things.

To preserve this class is to preserve the existing state of things in Germany. The industrial and political supremacy of the bourgeoisie threatens it with certain destruction; on the one hand, from the concentration of capital; on the other, from the rise of a revolutionary proletariat. "True" Socialism appeared to kill these two birds with one stone. It spread like an epidemic.

The robe of speculative cobwebs, embroidered with flowers of rhetoric, steeped in the dew of sickly sentiment, this transcendental robe in which the German Socialists wrapped their sorry "eternal truths," all skin

and bone, served to wonderfully increase the sale of their goods amongst such a public.

And on its part, German Socialism recognised, more and more, its own calling as the bombastic representative of the petty-bourgeois Philistine.

It proclaimed the German nation to be the model nation, and the German petty Philistine to be the typical man. To every villainous meanness of this model man it gave a hidden, higher, Socialistic interpretation, the exact contrary of its real character. It went to the extreme length of directly opposing the "brutally destructive" tendency of Communism, and of proclaiming its supreme and impartial contempt of all class struggles. With very few exceptions, all the so-called Socialist and Communist publications that now (1847) circulate in Germany belong to the domain of this foul and enervating literature.*

2. Conservative, or Bourgeois, Socialism

A part of the bourgeoisie is desirous of redressing social grievances, in order to secure the continued existence of bourgeois society.

To this section belong economists, philanthropists, humanitarians, improvers of the condition of the working class, organisers of charity, members of societies for the prevention of cruelty to animals, temperance fanatics, hole-and-corner reformers of every imaginable kind. This form of Socialism has, moreover, been worked out into complete systems.

We may cite Proudhon's *Philosophie de la Misère* as an example of this form.

The Socialistic bourgeois want all the advantages of modern social conditions without the struggles and dangers necessarily resulting therefrom. They desire the existing state of society minus its revolutionary and disintegrating elements. They wish for a bourgeoisie without a proletariat. The bourgeoisie naturally con-

---

*The revolutionary storm of 1848 swept away this whole shabby tendency and cured its protagonists of the desire to dabble further in Socialism. The chief representative and classical type of this tendency is Herr Karl Grün. [*Note by Engels to the German edition of 1890.*]

ceives the world in which it is supreme to be the best; and bourgeois Socialism develops this comfortable conception into various more or less complete systems. In requiring the proletariat to carry out such a system, and thereby to march straightway into the social New Jerusalem, it but requires in reality, that the proletariat should remain within the bounds of existing society, but should cast away all its hateful ideas concerning the bourgeoisie.

A second and more practical, but less systematic, form of this Socialism sought to depreciate every revolutionary movement in the eyes of the working class, by showing that no mere political reform, but only a change in the material conditions of existence, in economical relations, could be of any advantage to them. By changes in the material conditions of existence, this form of Socialism, however, by no means understands abolition of the bourgeois relations of production, an abolition that can be effected only by a revolution, but administrative reforms, based on the continued existence of these relations; reforms, therefore, that in no respect affect the relations between capital and labour, but, at the best, lessen the cost, and simplify the administrative work, of bourgeois government.

Bourgeois Socialism attains adequate expression, when, and only when, it becomes a mere figure of speech.

Free trade: for the benefit of the working class. Protective duties: for the benefit of the working class. Prison Reform: for the benefit of the working class. This is the last word and the only seriously meant word of bourgeois Socialism.

It is summed up in the phrase: the bourgeois is a bourgeois—for the benefit of the working class.

3. Critical-Utopian Socialism and Communism

We do not here refer to that literature which, in every great modern revolution, has always given voice to the demands of the proletariat, such as the writings of Babeuf and others.

The first direct attempts of the proletariat to attain its own ends, made in times of universal excitement, when feudal society was being overthrown, these attempts necessarily failed, owing to the then undeveloped state of the proletariat, as well as to the absence of the economic conditions for its emancipation, conditions that had yet to be produced, and could be produced by the impending bourgeois epoch alone. The revolutionary literature that accompanied these first movements of the proletariat had necessarily a reactionary character. It inculcated universal asceticism and social levelling in its crudest form.

The Socialist and Communist systems properly so called, those of Saint-Simon, Fourier, Owen and others, spring into existence in the early undeveloped period, described above, of the struggle between proletariat and bourgeoisie (see Section I. Bourgeois and Proletarians).

The founders of these systems see, indeed, the class antagonisms, as well as the action of the decomposing elements in the prevailing form of society. But the proletariat, as yet in its infancy, offers to them the spectacle of a class without any historical initiative or any independent political movement.

Since the development of class antagonism keeps even pace with the development of industry, the economic situation, as they find it, does not as yet offer to them the material conditions for the emancipation of the proletariat. They therefore search after a new social science, after new social laws, that are to create these conditions.

Historical action is to yield to their personal inventive action, historically created conditions of emancipation to fantastic ones, and the gradual, spontaneous class organisation of the proletariat to an organisation of society specially contrived by these inventors. Future history resolves itself, in their eyes, into the propaganda and the practical carrying out of their social plans.

In the formation of their plans they are conscious of caring chiefly for the interests of the working class, as being the most suffering class. Only from the point of view of being the most suffering class does the proletariat exist for them.

The undeveloped state of the class struggle, as well as their own surroundings, causes Socialists of this kind to consider themselves far superior to all class antagonisms. They want to improve the condition of every member of society, even that of the most favoured. Hence, they habitually appeal to society at large, without distinction of class; nay, by preference, to the ruling class. For how can people, when once they understand their system, fail to see in it the best possible plan of the best possible state of society?

Hence, they reject all political, and especially all revolutionary, action; they wish to attain their ends by peaceful means, and endeavour, by small experiments, necessarily doomed to failure, and by the force of example, to pave the way for the new social Gospel.

Such fantastic pictures of future society, painted at a time when the proletariat is still in a very undeveloped state and has but a fantastic conception of its own position, correspond with the first instinctive yearnings of that class for a general reconstruction of society.

But these Socialist and Communist publications contain also a critical element. They attack every principle of existing society. Hence they are full of the most valuable materials for the enlightenment of the working class. The practical measures proposed in them—such as the abolition of the distinction between town and country, of the family, of the carrying on of industries for the account of private individuals, and of the wage system, the proclamation of social harmony, the conversion of the functions of the State into a mere superintendence of production, all these proposals point solely to the disappearance of class antagonisms which were, at that time, only just cropping up, and which, in these publications, are recognised in their earliest indistinct and undefined forms only. These proposals, therefore, are of a purely Utopian character.

The significance of Critical-Utopian Socialism and Communism bears an inverse relation to historical development. In proportion as the modern class struggle develops and takes definite shape, this fantastic standing apart from the contest, these fantastic attacks on it, lose all practical value and all theoretical justification. Therefore, although the originators of these systems were, in many respects, revolutionary, their disciples have, in every case, formed mere reactionary sects.

They hold fast by the original views of their masters, in opposition to the progressive historical development of the proletariat. They, therefore, endeavour, and that consistently, to deaden the class struggle and to reconcile the class antagonisms. They still dream of experimental realisation of their social Utopias, of founding isolated "phalanstères," of establishing "Home Colonies," of setting up a "Little Icaria"* — duodecimo editions of the New Jerusalem—and to realise all these castles in the air, they are compelled to appeal to the feelings and purses of the bourgeois. By degrees they sink into the category of the reactionary [or] conservative Socialists depicted above, differing from these only by more systematic pedantry, and by their fanatical and superstitious belief in the miraculous effects of their social science.

They, therefore, violently oppose all political action on the part of the working class; such action, according to them, can only result from blind unbelief in the new Gospel.

The Owenites in England, and the Fourierists in France, respectively oppose the Chartists and the *Réformistes*.

IV

Position of the Communists in Relation to the Various Existing Opposition Parties

Section II has made clear the relations of the Communists to the existing working-class parties, such as the Chartists in England and the Agrarian Reformers in America.

Phalanstères were Socialist colonies on the plan of Charles Fourier; *Icaria* was the name given by Cabet to his Utopia and, later on, to his American Communist colony. [*Note by Engels to the English edition of 1888.*]

"Home Colonies" were what Owen called his Communist model societies. *Phalanstères* was the name of the public palaces planned by Fourier. *Icaria* was the name given to the Utopian land of fancy, whose Communist institutions Cabet portrayed. [*Note by Engels to the German edition of 1890.*]

The Communists fight for the attainment of the immediate aims, for the enforcement of the momentary interests of the working class; but in the movement of the present, they also represent and take care of the future of that movement. In France the Communists ally themselves with the Social-Democrats,† against the conservative and radical bourgeoisie, reserving, however, the right to take up a critical position in regard to phrases and illusions traditionally handed down from the great Revolution.

In Switzerland they support the Radicals, without losing sight of the fact that this party consists of antagonistic elements, partly of Democratic Socialists, in the French sense, partly of radical bourgeois.

In Poland they support the party that insists on an agrarian revolution as the prime condition for national emancipation, that party which fomented the insurrection of Cracow in 1846.

In Germany they fight with the bourgeoisie whenever it acts in a revolutionary way, against the absolute monarchy, the feudal squirearchy, and the petty bourgeoisie.

But they never cease, for a single instant, to instil into the working class the clearest possible recognition of the hostile antagonism between bourgeoisie and proletariat, in order that the German workers may straightway use, as so many weapons against the bourgeoisie, the social and political conditions that the bourgeoisie must necessarily introduce along with its supremacy, and in order that, after the fall of the reactionary class in Germany, the fight against the bourgeoisie itself may immediately begin.

The Communists turn their attention chiefly to Germany, because that country is on the eve of a bourgeois revolution that is bound to be carried out under more advanced conditions of European civilisation, and with a much more developed proletariat, than that of England was in the seventeenth, and of France in the eighteenth century, and because the bourgeois revolution in Germany will be but the prelude to an immediately following proletarian revolution.

In short, the Communists everywhere support every revolutionary movement against the existing social and political order of things.

In all these movements they bring to the front, as the leading question in each, the property question, no matter what its degree of development at the time.

Finally, they labour everywhere for the union and agreement of the democratic parties of all countries.

The Communists disdain to conceal their views and aims. They openly declare that their ends can be attained only by the forcible overthrow of all existing social conditions. Let the ruling classes tremble at a Communistic revolution. The proletarians have nothing to lose but their chains. They have a world to win.

WORKING MEN OF ALL COUNTRIES, UNITE!

---

†The party then represented in Parliament by Ledru-Rollin, in literature by Louis Blanc, in the daily press by the *Réforme*. The name of Social-Democracy signified, with these its inventors, a section of the Democratic or Republican party more or less tinged with Socialism. [*Note by Engels to the English edition of 1888.*]

The party in France which at that time called itself Socialist-Democratic was represented in political life by Ledru-Rollin and in literature by Louis Blanc; thus it differed immeasurably from present-day German Social-Democracy. [*Note by Engels to the German edition of 1890.*]

MARX

The Eighteenth Brumaire of Louis Bonaparte

I

Hegel remarks somewhere that all facts and person-ages of great importance in world history occur, as it were, twice. He forgot to add: the first time as tragedy, the second as farce. Caussidière for Danton, Louis Blanc for Robespierre, the Montagne of 1848 to 1851 for the Montagne of 1793 to 1795, the Nephew for the Uncle. And the same caricature occurs in the cir-cumstances attending the second edition of the eigh-teenth Brumaire!

Men make their own history, but they do not make it just as they please; they do not make it under cir-cumstances chosen by themselves, but under circum-stances directly encountered, given and transmitted from the past. The tradition of all the dead generations weighs like a nightmare on the brain of the living. And just when they seem engaged in revolutionising them-selves and things, in creating something that has never yet existed, precisely in such periods of revolutionary crisis they anxiously conjure up the spirits of the past to their service and borrow from them names, battle-cries and costumes in order to present the new scene of world history in this time-honoured disguise and this borrowed language. Thus Luther donned the mask of the Apostle Paul, the revolution of 1789 to 1814 draped itself alternately as the Roman Republic and the Roman Empire, and the revolution of 1848 knew nothing better to do than to parody, now 1789, now the revolutionary tradition of 1793 to 1795. In like manner a beginner who has learnt a new language always translates it back into his mother tongue, but he has assimilated the spirit of the new language and can freely express himself in it only when he finds his way in it without recalling the old and forgets his na-tive tongue in the use of the new.

Consideration of this world-historical necromancy reveals at once a salient difference. Camille Desmou-lins, Danton, Robespierre, Saint-Just, Napoleon, the heroes as well as the parties and the masses of the old French Revolution, performed the task of their time in Roman costume and with Roman phrases, the task of unchaining and setting up modern *bourgeois* soci-ety. The first ones knocked the feudal basis to pieces and mowed off the feudal heads which had grown on it. The other created inside France the considerations under which free competition could first be devel-oped, parcelled landed property exploited and the un-chained industrial productive forces of the nation employed; and beyond the French borders he every-where swept the feudal institutions away, so far as was necessary to furnish bourgeois society in France with a suitable up-to-date environment on the European Continent. The new social formation once estab-lished, the antediluvian Colossi disappeared and with them resurrected Romanity—the Brutuses, Gracchi, Publicolas, the tribunes, the senators, and Caesar him-self. Bourgeois society in its sober reality had begotten its true interpreters and mouthpieces in the Says, Cousins, Royer-Collards, Benjamin Constants and Guizots; its real commanders sat behind the counter, and the hogheaded Louis XVIII was its political chief. Wholly absorbed in the production of wealth and in peaceful competitive struggle, it no longer compre-hended that ghosts from the days of Rome had watched over its cradle. But unheroic as bourgeois so-ciety is, it nevertheless took heroism, sacrifice, terror, civil war and battles of peoples to bring it into being. And in the classically austere traditions of the Roman Republic its gladiators found the ideals and the art forms, the self-deceptions that they needed in order to conceal from themselves the bourgeois limitations of

Reprinted from *Karl Marx/Friedrich Engels: Collected Works* by permission of International Publishers.

816

the content of their struggles and to maintain their passion on the high plane of great historical tragedy. Similarly, at another stage of development, a century earlier, Cromwell and the English people had borrowed speech, passions and illusions from the Old Testament for their bourgeois revolution. When the real aim had been achieved, when the bourgeois transformation of English society had been accomplished, Locke supplanted Habakkuk.

Thus the resurrection of the dead in those revolutions served the purpose of glorifying the new struggles, not of parodying the old; of magnifying the given task in imagination, not of fleeing from its solution in reality; of finding once more the spirit of revolution, not of making its ghost walk about again.

From 1848 to 1851 only the ghost of the old revolution walked about, from Marrast, the *républicain en gants jaunes*, who disguised himself as the old Bailly, down to the adventurer who hides his commonplace repulsive features under the iron death mask of Napoleon. An entire people, which had imagined that by means of a revolution it had imparted to itself an accelerated power of motion, suddenly finds itself set back into a defunct epoch and, in order that no doubt as to the relapse may be possible, the old dates arise again, the old chronology, the old names, the old edicts, which had long become a subject of antiquarian erudition, and the old myrmidons of the law, who had seemed long decayed. The nation feels like that mad Englishman in Bedlam who fancies that he lives in the times of the ancient Pharaohs and daily bemoans the hard labour that he must perform in the Ethiopian mines as a gold digger, immured in this subterranean prison, a dimly burning lamp fastened to his head, the overseer of the slaves behind him with a long whip, and at the exits a confused welter of barbarian mercenaries, who understand neither the forced labourers in the mines nor one another, since they speak no common language. "And all this is expected of me," sighs the mad Englishman, "of me, a freeborn Briton, in order to make gold for the old Pharaohs." "In order to pay the debts of the Bonaparte family," sighs the French nation. The Englishman, so long as he was in his right mind, could not get rid of the fixed idea of making gold. The French, so long as they were en-

gaged in revolution, could not get rid of the memory of Napoleon, as the election of December 10 proved. They hankered to return from the perils of revolution to the fleshpots of Egypt, and December 2, 1851 was the answer. They have not only a caricature of the old Napoleon, they have the old Napoleon himself, caricatured as he must appear in the middle of the nineteenth century.

The social revolution of the nineteenth century cannot draw its poetry from the past, but only from the future. It cannot begin with itself before it has stripped off all superstition about the past. Earlier revolutions required recollections of past world history in order to dull themselves to their own content. In order to arrive at its own content, the revolution of the nineteenth century must let the dead bury their dead. There the words went beyond the content; here the content goes beyond the words.

The February revolution was a surprise attack, a *taking* of the old society *unawares*, and the people proclaimed this unexpected *coup de main* as a deed of historic importance, ushering in the new epoch. On December 2 the February revolution is conjured away by a cardsharper's trick, and what seems overthrown is no longer the monarchy but the liberal concessions that were wrung from it by centuries of struggle. Instead of *society* having conquered a new content for itself, it seems that the *state* only returned to its oldest form, to the shamelessly simple domination of the sabre and the cowl. This is the answer to the *coup de main* of February 1848, given by the *coup de tête* of December 1851. Easy come, easy go. Meanwhile the intervening time has not passed by unused. During the years 1848 to 1851 French society made up, and that by an abbreviated because revolutionary method, for the studies and experiences which, in a regular, so to speak, textbook course of development, would have had to precede the February revolution, if it was to be more than a ruffling of the surface. Society now seems to have fallen back behind its point of departure; it has in truth first to create for itself the revolutionary point of departure, the situation, the relations, the conditions under which alone modern revolution becomes serious.

Bourgeois revolutions, like those of the eighteenth century, storm swiftly from success to success, their dramatic effects outdo each other, men and things seem set in sparkling brilliants, ecstasy is the everyday spirit, but they are short-lived, soon they have attained their zenith, and a long crapulent depression seizes society before it learns soberly to assimilate the results of its storm-and-stress period. On the other hand, proletarian revolutions, like those of the nineteenth century, criticise themselves constantly, interrupt themselves continually in their own course, come back to the apparently accomplished in order to begin it afresh, deride with unmerciful thoroughness the inadequacies, weaknesses and paltrinesses of their first attempts, seem to throw down their adversary only in order that he may draw new strength from the earth and rise again, more gigantic, before them, and recoil again and again from the indefinite prodigiousness of their own aims, until a situation has been created which makes all turning back impossible, and the conditions themselves cry out:

Hic Rhodus, hic salta!
Here is the rose, here dance!

For the rest, every fairly competent observer, even if he had not followed the course of French development step by step, must have had a presentiment that an unheard-of fiasco was in store for the revolution. It was enough to hear the self-complacent howl of victory with which Messieurs the Democrats congratulated each other on the beneficial consequences of the second Sunday in May 1852. In their minds the second Sunday in May 1852 had become a fixed idea, a dogma, like the day on which Christ should reappear and the millennium begin, in the minds of the Chiliasts. As ever, weakness had taken refuge in a belief in miracles, fancied the enemy overcome when it had only conjured him away in imagination, and lost all understanding of the present in a passive glorification of the future in store for it and of the deeds it had *in petto* but which it merely did not want as yet to make public. Those heroes who seek to disprove their proven incapacity by offering each other their sympathy and getting together in a crowd had tied up their bundles, collected their laurel wreaths in advance and were just then engaged in discounting on the exchange market the republics *in partibus* for which they had already

providently organised the government personnel with all the calm of their unassuming disposition. December 2 struck them like a thunderbolt from a clear sky, and the peoples that in periods of pusillanimous depression gladly let their inward apprehension be drowned out by the loudest bawlers will have perhaps convinced themselves that the times are past when the cackle of geese could save the Capitol.

The Constitution, the National Assembly, the dynastic parties, the blue and the red republicans, the heroes of Africa, the thunder from the platform, the sheet lightning of the daily press, the entire literature, the political names and the intellectual reputations, the civil law and the penal code, the *liberté,égalité, fraternité* and the second Sunday in May 1852—all has vanished like a phantasmagoria before the spell of a man whom even his enemies do not make out to be a magician. Universal suffrage seems to have survived only for a moment, in order that with its own hand it may make its last will and testament before the eyes of all the world and declare in the name of the people itself: "All that comes to birth is fit for overthrow, as nothing worth."

It is not enough to say, as the French do, that their nation was taken unawares. A nation and a woman are not forgiven the unguarded hour in which the first adventurer that came along could violate them. The riddle is not solved by such turns of speech, but merely formulated differently. It remains to be explained how a nation of thirty-six million can be surprised and delivered unresisting into captivity by three swindlers.

Let us recapitulate into general outline the phases that the French Revolution went through from February 24, 1848 to December 1851.

Three main periods are unmistakable: *the February period*; May 4, 1848 to May 28, 1849: *the period of the constitution of the republic* or *of the Constituent National Assembly*; May 28, 1849 to December 2, 1851: *the period of the constitutional republic* or *of the Legislative National Assembly*.

The *first period*, from February 24, or the overthrow of Louis Philippe, to May 4, 1848, the meeting of the Constituent Assembly, the *February period* proper, may be described as the *prologue* to the revolution. Its character was officially expressed in the fact that the government improvised by it declared itself that it was *provisional* and, like the government, everything that was mooted, attempted or enunciated during this period proclaimed itself to be only *provisional*. Nothing and nobody ventured to lay claim to the right of existence and of real action. All the elements that had prepared or determined the revolution, the dynastic opposition, the republican bourgeoisie, the democratic-republican petty bourgeoisie and the Social-Democratic workers, provisionally found their place in the February *government*.

It could not be otherwise. The February days originally aimed at an electoral reform, by which the circle of the politically privileged among the possessing class itself was to be widened and the exclusive domination of the finance aristocracy overthrown. When it came to the actual conflict, however, when the people mounted the barricades, the National Guard maintained a passive attitude, the army offered no serious resistance and the monarchy ran away, the republic appeared to be a matter of course. Every part construed it in its own way. Having secured it arms in hand, the proletariat impressed its stamp upon it and proclaimed it to be a *social republic*. There was thus indicated the general content of the modern revolution, a content which was in most singular contradiction to everything that, with the material available, with the degree of education attained by the masses, under the given circumstances and relations, could be immediately realised in practice. On the other hand, the claims of all the remaining elements that had collaborated in the February revolution were recognised by the lion's share that they obtained in the government. In no period do we, therefore, find a more confused mixture of high-flown phrases and actual uncertainty and clumsiness, of more enthusiastic striving for innovation and more thorough domination of the old routine, of more apparent harmony of the whole of society and more profound estrangement of its elements. While the Paris proletariat still revelled in the vision of the wide prospects that had opened before it and indulged in earnest discussions on social problems, the old forces of society had grouped themselves, rallied, reflected and found unexpected support in the mass of the nation, the peasants and petty bourgeois,

who all at once stormed on to the political stage, after the barriers of the July monarchy had fallen.

The *second period*, from May 4, 1848 to the end of May 1849, is the period of the *constitution, the foundation, of the bourgeois republic*. Directly after the February days not only had the dynastic opposition been surprised by the republicans and the republicans by the Socialists, but all France by Paris. The National Assembly, which met on May 4, 1848, had emerged from the national elections and represented the nation. It was a living protest against the aspirations of the February days and was to reduce the results of the revolution to the bourgeois scale. In vain the Paris proletariat, which immediately grasped the character of this National Assembly, attempted on May 15, a few days after it met, forcibly to negate its existence, to dissolve it, to disintegrate again into its constituent parts the organic form in which the proletariat was threatened by the reacting spirit of the nation. As is known, May 15 had no other result save that of removing Blanqui and his comrades, that is, the real leaders of the proletarian party, from the public stage for the entire duration of the cycle we are considering.

The *bourgeois monarchy* of Louis Philippe can be followed only by a *bourgeois republic*, that is to say, whereas a limited section of the bourgeoisie ruled in the name of the king, the whole of the bourgeoisie will now rule on behalf of the people. The demands of the Paris proletariat are utopian nonsense, to which an end must be put. To this declaration of the Constituent National Assembly the Paris proletariat replied with the *June insurrection*, the most colossal event in the history of European civil wars. The bourgeois republic triumphed. On its side stood the finance aristocracy, the industrial bourgeoisie, the middle class, the petty bourgeois, the army, the lumpenproletariat organised as the Mobile Guard, the intellectuals, the clergy and the rural population. On the side of the Paris proletariat stood none but itself. More than 3,000 insurgents were butchered after the victory, and 15,000 were deported without trial. With this defeat the proletariat recedes into the *background* of the revolutionary stage. It attempts to press forward again on every occasion, as soon as the movement appears to make a fresh start, but with ever decreased expenditure of strength and always slighter results. As soon as one of the social strata situated above it gets into revolutionary ferment, the proletariat enters into an alliance with it and so shares all the defeats that the different parties suffer, one after another. But these subsequent blows become the weaker, the greater the surface of society over which they are distributed. The more important leaders of the proletariat in the Assembly and in the press successively fall victim to the courts, and ever more equivocal figures come to head it. In part it throws itself into *doctrinaire experiments, exchange banks and workers' associations, hence into a movement in which it renounces the revolutionising of the old world by means of the latter's own great, combined resources, and seeks, rather, to achieve its salvation behind society's back, in private fashion, within its limited conditions of existence, and hence necessarily suffers shipwreck.* It seems to be unable either to rediscover revolutionary greatness in itself or to win new energy from the connections newly entered into, until *all classes* with which it contended in June themselves lie prostrate beside it. But at least it succumbs with the honours of the great, world-historic struggle; not only France, but all Europe trembles at the June earthquake, while the ensuing defeats of the upper classes are so cheaply bought that they require barefaced exaggeration by the victorious party to be able to pass for events at all, and become the more ignominious the further the defeated party is from the proletarian party.

The defeat of the June insurgents, to be sure, had indeed prepared and levelled the ground on which the bourgeois republic could be founded and built up, but it had shown at the same time that in Europe the questions at issue are other than that of "republic or monarchy." It had revealed that here *bourgeois republic* signifies the unlimited despotism of one class over other classes. It had proved that in countries with an old civilisation, with a developed formation of classes, with modern conditions of production and with an intellectual consciousness in which all traditional ideas have been dissolved by the work of centuries, *the republic* signifies in *general only the political form of the revolutionising of bourgeois society* and not its *conservative form of life*, as, for example, in the United States

of North America, where, though classes already exist, they have not yet become fixed, but continually change and interchange their component elements in constant flux, where the modern means of production, instead of coinciding with a stagnant surplus population, rather compensate for the relative deficiency of heads and hands, and where, finally, the feverish, youthful movement of material production, which has to make a new world its own, has left neither time nor opportunity for abolishing the old spirit world.

During the June days all classes and parties had united in the *Party of Order* against the proletarian class as the *Party of Anarchy*, of socialism, of communism. They had "saved" society from "*the enemies of society.*" They had given out the watch-words of the old society, "*property, family, religion, order,*" to their army as passwords and had proclaimed to the counter-revolutionary crusaders: "By this sign thou shalt conquer!" From this moment, as soon as one of the numerous parties which had gathered under this sign against the June insurgents seeks to hold the revolutionary battlefield in its own class interest, it goes down before the cry: "Property, family, religion, order." Society is saved just as often as the circle of its rulers contracts, as a more exclusive interest is maintained against a wider one. Every demand of the simplest bourgeois financial reform, of the most ordinary liberalism, of the most formal republicanism, of the most shallow democracy, is simultaneously castigated as an "attempt on society" and stigmatised as "socialism." And, finally, the high priests of "religion and order" themselves are driven with kicks from their Pythian tripods, hauled out of their beds in the darkness of night, put in prison-vans, thrown into dungeons or sent into exile; their temple is razed to the ground, their mouths are sealed, their pens broken, their law torn to pieces in the name of religion, of property, of the family, of order. Bourgeois fanatics for order are shot down on their balconies by mobs of drunken soldiers, their domestic sanctuaries profaned, their houses bombarded for amusement—in the name of property, of the family, of religion and of order. Finally, the scum of bourgeois society forms the *holy phalanx of order* and the hero Krapülinski installs himself in the Tuileries as the "*savior of society.*"

VII

On the threshold of the February revolution, the *social republic* appeared as a phrase, as a prophecy. In the June days of 1848, it was drowned in the blood of the *Paris proletariat*, but it haunts the subsequent acts of the drama like a ghost. The *democratic republic* announces its arrival. On June 13, 1849 it is dissipated together with its *petty bourgeois*, who have taken to their heels, but in its flight it blows its own trumpet with redoubled boastfulness. The *parliamentary republic*, together with the bourgeoisie, takes possession of the entire stage; it enjoys its existence to the full, but December 2, 1851 buries it to the accompaniment of the anguished cry of the coalitioned royalists: "Long live the Republic!"

The French bourgeoisie balked at the power of the working proletariat; it has brought the lumpenproletariat to power, with the chief of the Society of December 10 at the head. The bourgeoisie kept France in breathless fear of the future terrors of red anarchy; Bonaparte discounted this future for it when, on December 4, he had the eminent bourgeois of the Boulevard Montmartre and the Boulevard des Italiens shot down at their windows by the liquor-inspired army of order. The bourgeoisie apotheosised the sword; the sword rules it. It destroyed the revolutionary press; its own press has been destroyed. It placed popular meetings under police supervision; its salons are under the supervision of the police. It disbanded the democratic National Guards; its own National Guard is disbanded. It imposed a state of siege; a state of siege is imposed upon it. It supplanted the juries by military commissions; its juries are supplanted by military commissions. It subjected public education to the sway of the priests; the priests subject it to their own education. It transported people without trial; it is being transported without trial. It repressed every stirring in society by means of the state power; every stirring in its society is suppressed by the state power. Out of enthusiasm for its purse, it rebelled against its own politicians and men of letters; its politicians and men of letters are swept aside, but its purse is being plundered now that its mouth has been gagged and its pen broken. The bourgeoisie never wearied of crying out to the revolution what Saint Arsenius cried out to the Christians: *"Fuge, tace, quiesce!* Flee, be silent, keep still!"

The French bourgeoisie had long ago found the solution to Napoleon's dilemma: *"Dans cinquante ans, l'Europe sera républicaine ou cosaque."* It had found the solution to it in the *"république cosaque."* No Circe, by means of black magic, has distorted that work of art, the bourgeois republic, into a monstrous shape. That republic has lost nothing but the semblance of respectability. Present-day France was contained in a finished state within the parliamentary republic. It only requires a bayonet thrust for the abcess to burst and the monster to spring forth before our eyes.

Why did the Paris proletariat not rise in revolt after December 2?

The overthrow of the bourgeoisie had as yet been only decreed: the decree had not been carried out. Any serious insurrection of the proletariat would at once have put fresh life into the bourgeoisie, would have reconciled it with the army and ensured a second June defeat for the workers.

On December 4 the proletariat was incited by bourgeois and *épicier* to fight. On the evening of that day several legions of the National Guard promised to appear, armed and uniformed, on the scene of battle. For the bourgeois and the *épicier* had got wind of the fact that in one of his decrees of December 2 Bonaparte abolished the secret ballot and enjoined them to record their "yes" or "no" in the official registers after their names. The resistance of December 4 intimidated Bonaparte. During the night he caused placards to be posted on all the street corners of Paris, announcing the restoration of the secret ballot. The bourgeois and the *épicier* believed that they had gained their end. Those who failed to appear next morning were the bourgeois and the *épicier*.

By a *coup de main* during the night of December 1 to 2, Bonaparte had robbed the Paris proletariat of its leaders, the barricade commanders. An army without officers, averse to fighting under the banner of the Montagnards because of the memories of June 1848 and 1849 and May 1850, it left to its vanguard, the secret societies, the task of saving the insurrectionary honour of Paris, which the bourgeoisie had so unresistingly surrendered to the soldiery that, later on, Bonaparte could sneeringly give as his motive for disarming the National Guard—his fear that its arms would be turned against itself by the anarchists!

"C'est le triomphe complet et définitif du socialisme!" Thus Guizot characterised December 2. But if the overthrow of the parliamentary republic contains within itself the germ of the triumph of the proletarian revolution, its immediate and palpable result was *the victory of Bonaparte over parliament, of the executive power over the legislative power, of force without words over the force of words.* In parliament the nation made its general will the law, that is, it made the law of the ruling class its general will. Before the executive power it renounces all will of its own and submits to the superior command of an alien will, to authority. The executive power, in contrast to the legislative power, expresses the heteronomy of a nation, in contrast to its autonomy. France, therefore, seems to have escaped the despotism of a class only to fall back beneath the despotism of an individual, and, what is more, beneath the authority of an individual without authority. The struggle seems to be settled in such a way that all classes, equally impotent and equally mute, fall on their knees before the rifle butt.

But the revolution is thorough. It is still journeying through purgatory. It does its work methodically. By December 2, 1851 it had completed one half of its preparatory work; it is now completing the other half. First it perfected the parliamentary power, in order to be able to overthrow it. Now that it has attained this, it perfects the *executive power*, reduces it to its purest expression, isolates it, sets it up against itself as the sole target, in order to concentrate all its forces of destruction against it. And when it has done this second half of its preliminary work, Europe will leap from its seat and exultantly exclaim: Well burrowed, old mole!

This executive power with its enormous bureaucratic and military organisation, with its extensive and artificial state machinery, with a host of officials numbering half a million, besides an army of another half million, this appalling parasitic body, which enmeshes the body of French society like a net and chokes all its pores, sprang up in the days of the absolute monarchy, with the decay of the feudal system, which it helped to hasten. The seignorial privileges of the landowners and towns became transformed into so many attributes of the state power, the feudal dignitaries into paid officials and the motley pattern of conflicting medieval plenary powers into the regulated plan of a state authority whose work is divided and centralised as in a factory. The first French Revolution, with its task of breaking all separate local, territorial, urban and provincial powers in order to create the civil unity of the nation, was bound to develop what the absolute monarchy had begun: the centralisation, but at the same time the extent, the attributes and the agents of governmental power. Napoleon perfected this state machinery. The Legitimist monarchy and the July monarchy added nothing but a greater division of labour, growing in the same measure as the division of labour within bourgeois society created new groups of interests, and, therefore, new material for state administration. Every *common* interest was straightway severed from society, counterposed to it as a higher, *general* interest, snatched from the activity of society's members themselves and made an object of government activity, whether it was a bridge, a schoolhouse and the communal property of a village community, or the railways, the national wealth and the national university of France. Finally, in its struggle against the revolution, the parliamentary republic found itself compelled to strengthen, along with the repressive measures, the resources and centralisation of governmental power. All revolutions perfected this machine instead of breaking it. The parties that contended in turn for domination regarded the possession of this huge state edifice as the principal spoils of the victor.

But under the absolute monarchy, during the first revolution, under Napoleon, bureaucracy was only the means of preparing the class rule of the bourgeoisie. Under the Restoration, under Louis Philippe, under the parliamentary republic, it was the instrument of the ruling class, however much it strove for power of its own.

Only under the second Bonaparte does the state seem to have made itself completely independent. As against civil society, the state machine has consolidated its position so thoroughly that the chief of the Society of December 10 suffices for its head, a casual adventurer from abroad, raised up as leader by a drunken soldiery, which he has bought with liquor and sausages, and which he must continually ply with more sausage. Hence the downcast despair, the feeling of most dreadful humiliation and degradation that oppresses the breast of France and makes her catch her breath. She feels dishonoured.

And yet the state power is not suspended in mid air. Bonaparte represents a class, and the most numerous class of French society at that, the *small-holding peasantry*.

Just as the Bourbons were the dynasty of big landed property and just as the Orleans were the dynasty of money, so the Bonapartes are the dynasty of the peasants, that is, the mass of the French people. Not the Bonaparte who submitted to the bourgeois parliament, but the Bonaparte who dispersed the bourgeois parliament is the chosen man of the peasantry. For three years the towns had succeeded in falsifying the meaning of the election of December 10 and in cheating the peasants out of the restoration of the empire. The election of December 10, 1848 has been consummated only by the coup d'état of December 2, 1851.

The small-holding peasants form a vast mass, the members of which live in similar conditions but without entering into manifold relations with one another. Their mode of production isolates them from one another instead of bringing them into mutual intercourse. The isolation is increased by France's bad means of communication and by the poverty of the peasants. Their field of production, the smallholding, admits of no division of labour in its cultivation, no application of science and, therefore, no diversity of development, no variety of talent, no wealth of social relationships. Each individual peasant family is almost self-sufficient; it itself directly produces the major part of its consumption and thus acquires its means of life more through exchange with nature than in intercourse with society. A smallholding, a peasant and his family; alongside them another smallholding, another peasant and another family. A few score of these made up a village, and a few score of villages make up a department. In this way, the great mass of the French nation is formed by simple addition of homologous magnitudes, much as potatoes in a sack form a sack of potatoes. Insofar as millions of families live under economic conditions of existence that separate their mode of life, their interests and their culture from those of the other classes, and put them in hostile opposition to the latter, they form a class. Insofar as there is merely a local interconnection among these small-holding peasants, and the identity of their interests begets no community, no national bond and no political organisation among them, they do not form a class. They are consequently incapable of enforcing their class interests in their own name, whether through a parliament or through a convention. They cannot represent themselves, they must be represented. Their representative must at the same time appear as their master, as an authority over them, as an unlimited governmental power that protects them against the other classes and sends them rain and sunshine from above. The political influence of the small-holding peasants, therefore, finds its final expression in the executive power subordinating society to itself.

Historical tradition gave rise to the belief of the French peasants in the miracle that a man named Napoleon would bring all the glory back to them. And an individual turned up who gives himself out as the man because he bears the name of Napoleon, as a result of the *Code Napoléon*, which lays down that *la recherche de la paternité est interdite*. After a vagabondage of twenty years and after a series of grotesque adventures, the legend finds fulfillment and the man becomes Emperor of the French. The fixed idea of the Nephew was realised, because it coincided with the fixed idea of the most numerous class of the French people.

But, it may be objected, what about the peasant risings in half of France, the raids on the peasants by the army, the mass incarceration and transportation of peasants?

Since Louis XIV, France has experienced no similar persecution of the peasants "for demagogic practices."

But let there be no misunderstanding. The Bonaparte dynasty represents not the revolutionary, but the conservative peasant; not the peasant that strikes out beyond the condition of his social existence, the smallholding, but rather the peasant who wants to consolidate this holding; not the country folk who, linked up with the towns, want to overthrow the old order through their own energies, but on the contrary those who, in stupefied seclusion within this old order, want to see themselves and their smallholdings saved and favoured by the ghost of the empire. It represents not the enlightenment, but the superstition of the peasant; not his judgment, but his prejudice; not his future, but his past; not his modern Cévennes, but his modern Vendée.

The three years' rigorous rule of the parliamentary republic had freed a part of the French peasants from the Napoleonic illusion and had revolutionised them, even if only superficially; but the bourgeoisie violently repressed them whenever they set themselves in motion. Under the parliamentary republic the modern and the traditional consciousness of the French peasant contended for mastery. This progress took the form of an incessant struggle between the schoolmasters and the priests. The bourgeoisie struck down the schoolmasters. For the first time the peasants made efforts to behave independently in the face of the activity of the government. This was shown in the continual conflict between the *maires* and the prefects. The bourgeoisie deposed the *maires*. Finally, during the period of the parliamentary republic, the peasants of different localities rose against their own offspring, the army. The bourgeoisie punished them with states of siege and punitive expeditions. And this same bourgeoisie now cries out about the stupidity of the masses, the *vile multitude*, that has betrayed it to Bonaparte. It has itself forcibly strengthened the imperial sentiments of the peasant class, it conserved the conditions that form the birthplace of this peasant religion. The bourgeoisie, to be sure, is bound to fear the stupidity of the masses as long as they remain conservative, and the insight of the masses as soon as they become revolutionary.

In the risings after the coup d'état, a part of the French peasants protested, arms in hand, against their own vote of December 10, 1848. The school they had gone through since 1848 had sharpened their wits. But they made themselves over to the underworld of history; history held them to their word, and the majority was still so prejudiced that in precisely the reddest departments the peasant population voted openly for Bonaparte. In its view, the National Assembly had hindered his progress. He had now merely broken the fetters that the towns had imposed on the will of the countryside. In some parts the peasants even entertained the grotesque notion of a convention side by side with Napoleon.

After the first revolution had transformed the peasants from semi-villains into freeholders, Napoleon confirmed and regulated the conditions on which they could exploit undisturbed the soil of France which had only just fallen to their lot and slake their youthful passion for property. But what is now causing the ruin of the French peasant is his smallholding itself, the division of the land, the form of property which Napoleon consolidated in France. It is precisely the material conditions which made the French feudal peasant a small-holding peasant and Napoleon an emperor. Two generations have sufficed to produce the inevitable result: progressive deterioration of agriculture, progressive indebtedness of the agriculturist. The "Napoleonic" form of property, which at the beginning of the nineteenth century was the condition for the liberation and enrichment of the French country folk, has developed in the course of this century into the law of their enslavement and pauperisation. And precisely this law is the first of the *"idées napoléoniennes"* which the second Bonaparte has to uphold. If he still shares with the peasants the illusion that the cause of their ruin is to be sought, not in this smallholding property itself, but outside it, in the influence of secondary circumstances, his experiments will burst like soap bubbles when they come in contact with the relations of production.

The economic development of small-holding property has radically changed the relation of the peasants to the other classes of society. Under Napoleon, the fragmentation of the land in the countryside supplemented free competition and the beginning of big industry in the towns. The peasant class was the ubiquitous protest against the landed aristocracy which had just been overthrown. The roots that smallholding property struck in French soil deprived feudalism of all nutriment. Its landmarks formed the natural fortifications of the bourgeoisie against any *coup de main* on the part of its old overlords. But in the course of the nineteenth century the feudal lords were replaced by urban usurers; the feudal obligation that went with the land was replaced by the mortgage; aristocratic landed property was replaced by bourgeois capital. The smallholding of the peasant is now only the pretext that allows the capitalist to draw profits, interest and rent from the soil, while leaving it to the tiller of the soil himself to see how he can extract his wages. The mortgage debt burdening the soil of France imposes on the French peasantry payment of an amount of interest equal to the annual interest on the entire British national debt. Small-holding property, in this enslavement by capital to which its development inevitably pushes forward, has transformed the mass of the French nation into troglodytes. Sixteen million peasants (including women and children) dwell in hovels, a large number of which have but one opening, others only two and the most favoured only three. And windows are to a house what the five senses are to the head. The bourgeois order, which at the beginning of the century set the state to stand guard over the newly arisen smallholding and manured it with laurels, has become a vampire that sucks out its blood and brains and throws them into the alchemist's cauldron of capital. The *Code Napoléon* is now nothing but a *codex* of distraints, forced sales and compulsory auctions. To the four million (including children, etc.) officially recognised paupers, vagabonds, criminals and prostitutes in France must be added five million who hover on the margin of existence and either have their haunts in the countryside itself or, with their rags and their children, continually desert the countryside for the towns and the towns for the countryside. The interests of the peasants, therefore, are no longer, as under Napoleon, in accord with, but in opposition to the interests of the bourgeoisie, to capital. Hence the peasants find their natural ally and leader in the *urban proletariat*, whose task is the overthrow of the bourgeois order. But *strong and unlimited government*—and this is the second "*idée napoléonienne*," which the second Napoleon has to carry out—is called upon to defend this "material" order by force. This *"ordre matériel"* also serves as the catchword in all of Bonaparte's proclamations against the rebellious peasants.

Besides the mortgage which capital imposes on it, the smallholding is burdened by *taxes*. Taxes are the source of life for the bureaucracy, the army, the priests and the court, in short, for the whole apparatus of the executive power. Strong government and heavy taxes are identical. By its very nature, small-holding property forms a suitable basis for an all-powerful and innumerable bureaucracy. It creates a uniform level of relationships and persons over the whole surface of the land. Hence it also permits of uniform action from a supreme centre on all points of this uniform mass. It annihilates the aristocratic intermediate grades between the mass of the people and the state power. On all sides, therefore, it calls forth the direct interference of this state power and the interposition of its immediate organs. Finally, it produces an unemployed surplus population for which there is no place either on the land or in the towns, and which accordingly reaches out for state offices as a sort of respectable alms, and provokes the creation of state posts. By the new markets which he opened at the point of the bayonet, by the plundering of the Continent, Napoleon repaid the compulsory taxes with interest. These taxes were a spur to the industry of the peasant, whereas now they rob his industry of its last resources and complete his inability to resist pauperism. And an enormous bureaucracy, well-braided and well-fed, is the "*idée napoléonienne*" which is most congenial of all to the second Bonaparte. How could it be otherwise, seeing that alongside the actual classes of society he is forced to create an artificial caste, for which the maintenance of his regime becomes a bread-and-butter question? Accordingly, one of his first financial operations was the raising of officials' salaries to their old level and the creation of new sinecures.

Another "*idée napoléonienne*" is the domination of the *priests* as an instrument of government. But while in its accord with society, in its dependence on natural forces and its submission to the authority which protected it from above, the smallholding that had newly come into being was naturally religious, the smallholding that is ruined by debts, at odds with society and authority, and driven beyond its own limitations naturally becomes irreligious. Heaven was quite a pleasing accession to the narrow strip of land just won, especially as it makes the weather; it becomes an insult as soon as it is thrust forward as substitute for the smallholding. The priest then appears as only the anointed bloodhound of the earthly police—another *"idée napoléonienne."* On the next occasion, the expedition against Rome will take place in France itself, but in a sense opposite to that of M. de Montalembert.

Lastly, the culminating point of the *"idées napoléoniennes"* is the preponderance of the *army.* The army was the *point d'honneur* of the smallholding peasants, it was they themselves transformed into heroes, defending their new possessions against the outer world, glorifying their recently won nationhood, plundering and revolutionising the world. The uniform was their own state dress; war was their poetry; the smallholding, extended and rounded off in imagination, was their fatherland, and patriotism the ideal form of their sense of property. But the enemies against whom the French peasant has now to defend his property are not the Cossacks; they are the *huissiers* and the tax collectors. The smallholding lies no longer in the so-called fatherland, but in the register of mortgages. The army itself is no longer the flower of the peasant youth; it is the swampflower of the peasant lumpenproletariat. It consists in large measure of *remplaçants,* of substitutes, just as the second Bonaparte is himself only a *remplaçant,* the substitute for Napoleon. It now performs its deeds of valour by hunting down the peasants like chamois, and in organised drives, by doing *gendarme* duty, and if the internal contradictions of his system chase the chief of the Society of December 10 over the French border, his army, after some acts of brigandage, will reap, not laurels, but thrashings.

One sees: *all "idées napoléoniennes" are ideas of the undeveloped smallholding in the freshness of its youth;* for the smallholding that has outlived its day they are an absurdity. They are only the hallucinations of its death struggle, words that are transformed into phrases, spirits transformed into ghosts. But the parody of the empire was necessary to free the mass of the French nation from the weight of tradition and to work out in pure form the opposition between the state power and society. With the progressive undermining of smallholding property, the state structure erected upon it collapses. The centralisation of the state that modern society requires arises only on the ruins of the military-bureaucratic government machinery which was forged in opposition to feudalism.

The condition of the French peasants provides us with the answer to the riddle of the *general elections of December 20 and 21,* which bore the second Bonaparte up Mount Sinai, not to receive laws, but to give them.

Manifestly, the bourgeoisie had now no choice but to elect Bonaparte. When the puritans at the Council of Constance complained of the dissolute lives of the popes and wailed about the necessity of moral reform, Cardinal Pierre d'Ailly thundered at them: "Only the devil in person can still save the Catholic Church, and you ask for angels." In like manner, after the coup d'état, the French bourgeoisie cried: Only the chief of the Society of December 10 can still save bourgeois society! Only theft can still save property; only perjury, religion; bastardy, the family; disorder, order!

As the executive authority which has made itself an independent power, Bonaparte feels it to be his mission to safeguard "bourgeois order." But the strength of this bourgeois order lies in the middle class. He looks on himself, therefore, as the representative of the middle class and issues decrees in this sense. Nevertheless, he is somebody solely due to the fact that he has broken the political power of this middle class and daily breaks it anew. Consequently, he looks on himself as the adversary of the political and literary power of the middle class. But by protecting its material power, he generates its political power anew. The cause must accordingly be kept alive; but the effect, where it manifests itself, must be done away with. But this cannot pass off without slight confusions of cause and effect, since in their interaction both lose their distinguishing features. New decrees that obliterate the border line. As against the bourgeoisie, Bonaparte looks on himself, at the same time, as the representative of the peasants and of the people in general, who wants to make the lower classes of the people happy within the framework of bourgeois society. New decrees that cheat the "true Socialists" of their statecraft in advance. But, above all, Bonaparte looks on himself as the chief of the Society of December 10, as the representative of the lumpenproletariat, to which he himself, his entourage, his government and his army belong, and whose prime consideration is to benefit it-self and draw California lottery prizes from the state treasury. And he vindicates his position as chief of the Society of December 10 with decrees, without decrees and despite decrees.

This contradictory task of the man explains the con-tradictions of his government, the confused, blind to-ing and fro-ing which seeks now to win, now to hu-miliate first one class and then another and arrays all of them uniformly against him, whose practical un-certainty forms a highly comical contrast to the impe-rious, categorical style of the government decrees, a style which is faithfully copied from the uncle.

Industry and trade, hence the business affairs of the middle class, are to prosper in hothouse fashion under the strong government. The grant of innumerable rail-way concessions. But the Bonapartist lumpenprole-tariat is to enrich itself. The initiated play *tripotage* on the *bourse* with the railway concessions. But no capi-tal is forthcoming for the railways. Obligation of the Bank to make advances on railways shares. But, at the same time, the Bank is to be exploited for personal ends and therefore must be cajoled. Release of the Bank from the obligation to publish its report weekly. Leonine agreement of the Bank with the government. The people are to be given employment. Initiation of public works. But the public works increase the obli-gations of the people in respect of taxes. Hence re-duction of the taxes by an onslaught on the *rentiers*, by conversion of the five per cent bonds to four-and-a-half per cent. But, once more, the middle class must receive a *douceur*. Therefore doubling of the wine tax for the people, who buy it *en détail*, and halving of the wine tax for the middle class, who drink it *en gros*. Dis-solution of the actual workers' associations, but prom-ises of miracles of association in the future. The peasants are to be helped. Mortgage banks that expe-dite their getting into debt and accelerate the concen-tration of property. But these banks are to be used to make money out of the confiscated estates of the House of Orleans. No capitalist wants to agree to this condition, which is not in the decree, and the mort-gage bank remains a mere decree, etc., etc.

Bonaparte would like to appear as the patriarchal benefactor of all classes. But he cannot give to one class without taking from another. Just as at the time of the Fronde it was said of the Duke of Guise that he was the most *obligeant* man in France because he had turned all his estates into his partisans' obligations to him, so Bonaparte would fain be the most *obligeant* man in France and turn all the property, all the labour of France into a personal obligation to himself. He would like to steal the whole of France in order to be able to make a present of her to France or, rather, in order to be able to buy France anew with French money, for as the chief of the Society of December 10 he must needs buy what ought to belong to him. And all the state institutions, the Senate, the Council of State, the legislative body, the Legion of Honour, the soldiers' medals, the wash-houses, the public works, the railways, the *état-major* of the National Guard ex-cluding privates, and the confiscated estates of the House of Orleans—all become parts of the institution of purchase. Every place in the army and in the gov-ernment machine becomes a means of purchase. But the most important feature of this process, whereby France is taken in order to be given back, is the per-centages that find their way into the pockets of the head and the members of the Society of December 10 during the transaction. The witticism with which Countess L., the mistress of M. de Morny, charac-terised the confiscation of the Orleans estates: *"C'est le premier vol* de l'aigle"* is applicable to every flight of this *eagle*, which is more like a *raven*. He himself and his adherents call out to one another daily like that Italian Carthusian admonishing the miser who, with boastful display, counted up the goods on which he could yet live for years to come: *"Tu fai conto sopra i beni bisogna prima far il conto sopra gli anni."*† Lest they make a mistake in the years, they count the min-utes. A gang of shady characters push their way forward to the court, into the ministries, to the head of the ad-ministration and the army, a crowd of the best of whom it must be said that no one knows whence he comes, a noisy, disreputable, rapacious *bohème* that crawls into braided coats with the same grotesque dig-

---

*Vol means flight and theft.
†"Thou countest thy goods, thou shouldst first count thy years."

nity as the high dignitaries of Soulouque. One can visualize clearly this upper stratum of the Society of December 10, if one reflects that *Véron-Crevel‡* is its preacher of morals and *Granier de Cassagnac* its thinker. When Guizot, at the time of his ministry, utilised this Granier on a hole-and-corner newspaper against the dynastic opposition, he used to boast of him with the quip: *"C'est le roi des drôles,"* "he is the king of buffoons." One would do wrong to recall the Regency or Louis XV in connection with Louis Bonaparte's court and clique. For "often already, France has experienced a government of mistresses; but never before a government of *hommes entretenus.*"§

‡In his novel *Cousine Bette*, Balzac delineates the thoroughly dissolute Parisian philistine in Crevel, a character based on Dr. Véron, owner of the *Constitutionnel*.
§The words quoted are those of Madame Girardin.

Driven by the contradictory demands of his situation and being at the same time, like a conjurer, under the necessity of keeping the public gaze fixed on himself, as Napoleon's substitute, by springing constant surprises, that is to say, under the necessity of executing a coup d'état *en miniature* every day, Bonaparte throws the entire bourgeois economy into confusion, violates everything that seemed inviolable to the revolution of 1848, makes some tolerant of revolution, others desirous of revolution, and produces actual anarchy in the name of order, while at the same time stripping its halo from the entire state machine, profanes it and makes it at once loathsome and ridiculous. The cult of the Holy Coat of Trier he duplicates in Paris with the cult of the Napoleonic imperial mantle. But when the imperial mantle finally falls on the shoulders of Louis Bonaparte, the bronze statue of Napoleon will crash from the top of the Vendôme Column.

MARX

Preface to *A Contribution to the Critique of Political Economy*

Preface

I examine the system of bourgeois economy in the following order: *capital, landed property, wage-labour; the State, foreign trade, world market*. The economic conditions of existence of the three great classes into which modern bourgeois society is divided are analyzed under the first three headings; the interconnection of the other three headings is self-evident. The first part of the first book, dealing with Capital, comprises the following chapters: 1. The commodity; 2. Money or simple circulation; 3. Capital in general. The present part consists of the first two chapters. The entire material lies before me in the form of monographs, which were written not for publication but for self-clarification at widely separated periods; their remoulding into an integrated whole according to the plan I have indicated will depend upon circumstances.

A general introduction, which I had drafted, is omitted, since on further consideration it seems to be confusing to anticipate results which still have to be substantiated, and the reader who really wishes to follow me will have to decide to advance from the particular to the general. A few brief remarks regarding the course of my study of political economy may, however, be appropriate here.

Although jurisprudence was my special study, I pursued it as a subject subordinated to philosophy and history. In the year 1842–43, as editor of the *Rheinische Zeitung*, I first found myself in the embarrassing position of having to discuss what is known as material interests. The deliberations of the Rhine Province As-

The translation is based on that of Salo Ryazanskaya and is taken from *Karl Marx/Friedrich Engels: Collected Works*, published by International Publishers. Reprinted with permission.

sembly in thefts of wood and the division of landed property; the official polemic started by Herr von Schaper, then Ober-präsident of the Rhine Province, against the *Rheinische Zeitung* about the condition of the Mosel peasantry, and finally the debates on free trade and protective tariffs caused me in the first instance to turn my attention to economic questions. On the one hand, at that time when good intentions "to push forward" often took the place of factual knowledge, an echo of French socialism and communism, slightly tinged by philosophy, was noticeable in the *Rheinische Zeitung*. I objected to this dilettantism, but at the same time frankly admitted in a controversy with the *Allgemeine Augsburger Zeitung* that my previous studies did not allow me to express any opinion on the content of the French theories. When the publishers of the *Rheinische Zeitung* conceived the illusion that by a more compliant policy on the part of the paper it might be possible to secure the abrogation of the death sentence passed upon it, I eagerly grasped the opportunity to withdraw from the public stage to my study.

The first work which I undertook to dispel the doubts assailing me was a critical reexamination of the Hegelian philosophy of law; the introduction to this work being published in the *Deutsch-Französische Jahrbücher* issue in Paris in 1844. My inquiry led me to the conclusion that neither legal relations nor political forms could be comprehended whether by themselves or on the basis of a so-called general development of the human mind, but that on the contrary they originate in the material conditions of life, the totality of which Hegel, following the example of English and French thinkers of the eighteenth century, embraces within the term "civil society"; that the anatomy of this civil society, however, has to be sought in political economy. The study of this, which I began in Paris, I continued in Brussels, where I moved owing to an expulsion order issued by M. Guizot. The general conclusion at which I arrived and which, once reached, became the guiding principle of my studies can be summarised as follows. In the social production of their existence, men inevitably enter into definite relations, which are independent of their will, namely relations of production appropriate to a given stage in the development of their material forces of production. The totality of these relations of production constitutes the economic structure of society, the real foundation, on which arises a legal and political superstructure and to which correspond definite forms of social consciousness. The mode of production of material life conditions the general process of social, political and intellectual life. It is not the consciousness of men that determines their existence, but their social existence that determines their consciousness. At a certain stage of development, the material productive forces of society come into conflict with the existing relations of production or—this merely expresses the same thing in legal terms—with the property relations within the framework of which they have operated hitherto. From forms of development of the productive forces these relations turn into their fetters. Then begins an era of social revolution. The changes in the economic foundation lead sooner or later to the transformation of the whole immense superstructure. In studying such transformations it is always necessary to distinguish between the material transformation of the economic conditions of production, which can be determined with the precision of natural science, and the legal, political, religious, artistic or philosophic—in short, ideological forms in which men become conscious of this conflict and fight it out. Just as one does not judge an individual by what he thinks about himself, so one cannot judge such a period of transformation by its consciousness, but, on the contrary, this consciousness must be explained from the contradictions of material life, from the conflict existing between the social forces of production and the relations of production. No social formation is ever destroyed before all the productive forces for which it is sufficient have been developed, and new superior relations of production never replace older ones before the material conditions for their existence have matured

within the framework of the old society. Mankind thus inevitably sets itself only such tasks as it is able to solve, since closer examination will always show that the problem itself arises only when the material conditions for its solution are already present or at least in the course of formation. In broad outline, the Asiatic, ancient, feudal and modern bourgeois modes of production may be designated as epochs marking progress in the economic development of society. The bourgeois relations of production are the last antagonistic form of the social process of production—antagonistic not in the sense of individuals' social conditions of existence—but the productive forces developing within bourgeois society create also the material conditions for a solution of this antagonism. The prehistory of human society accordingly closes with this social formation.

Friedrich Engels, with whom I maintained a constant exchange of ideas by correspondence since the publication of his brilliant essay on the critique of economic categories (printed in the *Deutsch-Französische Jahrbücher*), arrived by another road (compare his *Condition of the Working-Class in England*) at the same result as I, and when in the spring of 1845 he too came to live in Brussels, we decided to set forth together our conception as opposed to the ideological one of German philosophy, in fact to settle accounts with our former philosophical conscience. The intention was carried out in the form of a critique of post-Hegelian philosophy. The manuscript, two large octavo volumes, had long ago reached the publishers in Westphalia when we were informed that owing to changed circumstances it could not be printed. We abandoned the manuscript to the gnawing criticism of the mice all the more willingly since we have achieved our main purpose—self-clarification. Of the scattered works in which at that time we presented one or another aspect of our views to the public, I shall mention only the *Manifesto of the Communist Party*, jointly written by Engels and myself, and a *Speech on the Question of Free Trade*, which I myself published. The salient points of our conception were first outlined in an academic, although polemical, form in my *Poverty of Philosophy . . .*, this book which was aimed at Proudhon appeared in 1847. The publication of an essay on

Wage-Labour written in German in which I combined the lectures I had held on this subject at the German Workers' Society in Brussels, was interrupted by the February Revolution and my forcible removal from Belgium in consequence.

The publication of the *Neue Rheinische Zeitung* in 1848 and 1849 and subsequent events cut short my economic studies, which I could only resume in London in 1850. The enormous amount of material relating to the history of political economy assembled in the British Museum, the fact that London is a convenient vantage point for the observation of bourgeois society, and finally the new stage of development which this society seemed to have entered with the discovery of gold in California and Australia, induced me to start again from the very beginning and to work carefully through the new material. These studies led partly of their own accord to apparently quite remote subjects on which I had to spend a certain amount of time. But it was in particular the imperative necessity of earning my living which reduced the time at my disposal. My collaboration, continued now for eight years, with the *New York Tribune*, the leading Anglo-American newspaper, necessitated an excessive fragmentation of my studies, for I wrote only exceptionally newspaper correspondence in the strict sense. Since a considerable part of my contributions consisted of articles dealing with important economic events in Britain and on the continent, I was compelled to become conversant with practical details which, strictly speaking, lie outside the sphere of political economy.

This sketch of the course of my studies in the domain of political economy is intended merely to show that my views—no matter how they may be judged and how little they conform to the interested prejudices of the ruling classes—are the outcome of conscientious research carried on over many years. At the entrance to science, as at the entrance to hell, the demand must be made:

Qui si convien lasciare ogni sospetto
Ogni viltà convien che qui sia morta.[1]

Karl Marx
London, January 1859

[1] Here all mistrust must be abandoned, Here all cowardice must perish. (Dante, *The Divine Comedy*, 3013).

MARX
Capital

CHAPTER ONE, SECTION 4

4. The Fetishism of the Commodity and Its Secret

A commodity appears at first sight an extremely obvious, trivial thing. But its analysis brings out that it is a very strange thing, abounding in metaphysical subtleties and theological niceties. So far as it is a use-value, there is nothing mysterious about it, whether we consider it from the point of view that by its properties it satisfies human needs, or that it first takes on these properties as the product of human labour. It is absolutely clear that, by his activity, man changes the forms of the materials of nature in such a way as to make them useful to him. The form of wood, for instance, is altered if a table is made out of it. Nevertheless the table continues to be wood, an ordinary, sensuous thing. But as soon as it emerges as a commodity, it changes into a thing which transcends sensuousness. It not only stands with its feet on the ground, but, in relation to all other commodities, it stands on its head, and evolves out of its wooden brain grotesque ideas, far more wonderful than if it were to begin dancing of its own free will.[18]

The mystical character of the commodity does not therefore arise from its use-value. Just as little does it proceed from the nature of the determinants of value. For in the first place, however varied the useful kinds of labour, or productive activities, it is a physiological fact that they are functions of the human organism, and that each such function, whatever may be its nature or its form, is essentially the expenditure of hu-

man brain, nerves, muscles and sense organs. Secondly, with regard to the foundation of the quantitative determination of value, namely the duration of what expenditure or the quantity of labour, this is quite palpably different from its quality. In all situations, the labour-time it costs to produce the means of subsistence must necessarily concern mankind, although not to the same degree at different stages of development.[19] And finally, as soon as men start to work for each other in any way, their labour also assumes a social form.

Whence, then, arises the enigmatic character of the product of labour, as soon as it assumes the form of a commodity? Clearly, it arises from this form itself. The equality of the kinds of human labour takes on a physical form in the equal objectivity of the products of labour as values; the measure of the expenditure of human labour-power by its duration takes on the form of the magnitude of the value of the products of labour; and finally the relationships between the producers, within which the social characteristics of their labours are manifested, take on the form of a social relation between the products of labour.

The mysterious character of the commodity-form consists therefore simply in the fact that the commodity reflects the social characteristics of men's own labour as objective characteristics of the products of labour themselves, as the socio-natural properties of these things. Hence it also reflects the social relation of the producers to the sum total of labour as a social relation between objects, a relation which exists apart from and outside the producers. Through this substi-

Translated by Ben Fowkes.

[18] One may recall that China and the tables began to dance when the rest of the world appeared to be standing still— *pour encourager les autres.*

[19] Among the ancient Germans the size of a piece of land was measured according to the labour of a day; hence the acre was called *Tagwerk, Tagwanne (jurnale,* or *terra jurnalis,* or *diornalis), Mannwerk, Mannskraft, Mannsmaad, Mannshauet,* etc. See Georg Ludwig von Maurer, *Einleitung zur Geschichte der Mark-, Hof-, usw. Verfassung,* Munich, 1854, p. 129 ff.

tution, the products of labour become commodities, sensuous things which are at the same time supra-sensible or social. In the same way, the impression made by a thing on the optic nerve is perceived not as a subjective excitation of that nerve but as the objective form of a thing outside the eye. In the act of seeing, of course, light is really transmitted from one thing, the external object, to another thing, the eye. It is a physical relation between physical things. As against this, the commodity-form, and the value-relation of the products of labour within which it appears, have absolutely no connection with the physical nature of the commodity and the material [dinglich] relations arising out of this. It is nothing but the definite social relation between men themselves which assumes here, for them, the fantastic form of a relation between things. In order, therefore, to find an analogy we must take flight into the misty realm of religion. There the products of the human brain appear as autonomous figures endowed with a life of their own, which enter into relations both with each other and with the human race. So it is in the world of commodities with the products of men's hands. I call this the fetishism which attaches itself to the products of labour as soon as they are produced as commodities, and is therefore inseparable from the production of commodities.

As the foregoing analysis has already demonstrated, this fetishism of the world of commodities arises from the peculiar social character of the labour which produces them.

Objects of utility become commodities only because they are the products of the labour of private individuals who work independently of each other. The sum total of the labour of all these private individuals forms the aggregate labour of society. Since the producers do not come into social contact until they exchange the products of their labour, the specific social characteristics of their private labours appear only within this exchange. In other words, the labour of the private individual manifests itself as an element of the total labour of society only through the relations which the act of exchange establishes between the products, and, through their mediation, between the producers. To the producers, therefore, the social relations between their private labours appear as what they are, i.e.

they do not appear as direct social relations between persons in their work, but rather as material [dinglich] relations between persons and social relations between things.

It is only by being exchanged that the products of labour acquire a socially uniform objectivity as values, which is distinct from their sensuously varied objectivity as articles of utility. This division of the product of labour into a useful thing and a thing possessing value appears in practice only when exchange has already acquired a sufficient extension and importance to allow useful things to be produced for the purpose of being exchanged, so that their character as values has already to be taken into consideration during production. From this moment on, the labour of the individual producer acquires a twofold social character. On the one hand, it must, as a definite useful kind of labour, satisfy a definite social need, and thus maintain its position as an element of the total labour, as a branch of the social division of labour, which originally sprang up spontaneously. On the other hand, it can satisfy the manifold needs of the individual producer himself only in so far as every particular kind of useful private labour can be exchanged with, i.e. counts as the equal of, every other kind of useful private labour. Equality in the full sense between different kinds of labour can be arrived at only if we abstract from their real inequality, if we reduce them to the characteristic they have in common, that of being the expenditure of human labour-power, of human labour in the abstract. The private producer's brain reflects this twofold social character of his labour only in the forms which appear in practical intercourse, in the exchange of products. Hence, the socially useful character of his private labour is reflected in the form that the product of labour has to be useful to others, and the social character of the equality of the various kinds of labour is reflected in the form of the common character, as values, possessed by these materially different things, the products of labour.

Men do not therefore bring the products of their labour into relation with each other as values because they see these objects merely as the material integuments of homogeneous human labour. The reverse is true: by equating their different products to each other in exchange as values, they equate their different kinds of labour as human labour. They do this without being aware of it.[20] Value, therefore, does not have its description branded on its forehead; it rather transforms every product of labour into a social hieroglyphic. Later on, men try to decipher the hieroglyphic, to get behind the secret of their own social product: for the characteristic which objects of utility have of being values is as much men's social product as is their language. The belated scientific discovery that the products of labour, in so far as they are values, are merely the material expressions of the human labour expended to produce them, marks an epoch in the history of mankind's development, but by no means banishes the semblance of objectivity possessed by the social characteristics of labour. Something which is only valid for this particular form of production, the production of commodities, namely the fact that the specific social character of private labours carried on independently of each other consists in their equality as human labour, and, in the product, assumes the form of the existence of value, appears to those caught up in the relations of commodity production (and this is true both before and after the above-mentioned scientific discovery) to be just as ultimately valid as the fact that the scientific dissection of the air into its component parts left the atmosphere itself unaltered in its physical configuration.

What initially concerns producers in practice when they make an exchange is how much of some other product they get for their own; in what proportions can the products be exchanged? As soon as these proportions have attained a certain customary stability, they appear to result from the nature of the products, so that, for instance, one ton of iron and two ounces of gold appear to be equal in value, in the same way as a pound of gold and a pound of iron are equal in weight, despite their different physical and chemical proper-

ties. The value character of the products of labour becomes firmly established only when they act as magnitudes of value. These magnitudes vary continually, independently of the will, foreknowledge and actions of the exchangers. Their own movement within society has for them the form of a movement made by things, and these things, far from being under their control, in fact control them. The production of commodities must be fully developed before the scientific conviction emerges, from experience itself, that all the different kinds of private labour (which are carried on independently of each other, and yet, as spontaneously developed branches of the social division of labour, are in a situation of all-round dependence on each other) are continually being reduced to the quantitative proportions in which society requires them. The reason for this reduction is that in the midst of the accidental and ever-fluctuating exchange relations between the products, the labour-time socially necessary to produce them asserts itself as a regulative law of nature. In the same way, the law of gravity asserts itself when a person's house collapses on top of him.[21] The determination of the magnitude of value by labour-time is therefore a secret hidden under the apparent movements in the relative values of commodities. Its discovery destroys the semblance of the merely accidental determination of the magnitude of the value of the products of labour, but by no means abolishes that determination's material form.

Reflection on the forms of human life, hence also scientific analysis of those forms, takes a course directly opposite to their real development. Reflection begins *post festum*, and therefore with the results of the process of development ready to hand. The forms which stamp products as commodities and which are therefore the preliminary requirements for the circulation of commodities, already possess the fixed qual-

---

20 Therefore, when Galiani said: Value is a relation between persons ('*La Ricchezza è una ragione tra due persone*') he ought to have added: a relation concealed beneath a material shell. (Galiani, *Della Moneta*, p. 222, Vol. 3 of Custodi's collection entitled *Scrittori classici italiani di economia politica, Parte moderna*, Milan, 1803.)

21 'What are we to think of a law which can only assert itself through periodic crises? It is just a natural law which depends on the lack of awareness of the people who undergo it' (Friedrich Engels, *Umrisse zu einer Kritik der Nationalökonomie*, in the *Deutsch-Französische Jahrbücher*, edited by Arnold Ruge and Karl Marx, Paris, 1844) [English translation in Marx/Engels' *Collected Works*, Vol. 3, London, 1975, p. 433].

ity of natural forms of social life before man seeks to give an account, not of their historical character, for in his eyes they are immutable, but of their content and meaning. Consequently, it was solely the analysis of the prices of commodities which led to the determination of the magnitude of value, and solely the common expression of all commodities in money which led to the establishment of their character as values. It is however precisely this finished form of the world of commodities—the money form—which conceals the social character of private labour and the social relations between the individual workers, by making those relations appear as relations between material objects, instead of revealing them plainly. If I state that coats or boots stand in a relation to linen because the latter is the universal incarnation of abstract human labour, the absurdity of the statement is self-evident. Nevertheless, when the producers of coats and boots bring these commodities into a relation with linen, or with gold or silver (and this makes no difference here), as the universal equivalent, the relation between their own private labour and the collective labour of society appears to them in exactly this absurd form.

The categories of bourgeois economics consist precisely of forms of this kind. They are forms of thought which are socially valid, and therefore objective, for the relations of production belonging to this historically determined mode of social production, i.e. commodity production. The whole mystery of commodities, all the magic and necromancy that surrounds the products of labour on the basis of commodity production, vanishes therefore as soon as we come to other forms of production.

As political economists are fond of Robinson Crusoe stories,[22] let us first look at Robinson on his island.

Undemanding though he is by nature, he still has needs to satisfy, and must therefore perform useful labours of various kinds: he must make tools, knock together furniture, tame llamas, fish, hunt and so on. Of his prayers and the like, we take no account here, since our friend takes pleasure in them and sees them as recreation. Despite the diversity of his productive functions, he knows that they are only different forms of activity of one and the same Robinson, hence only different modes of human labour. Necessity itself compels him to divide his time with precision between his different functions. Whether one function occupies a greater space in his total activity than another depends on the magnitude of the difficulties to be overcome in attaining the useful effect aimed at. Our friend Robinson Crusoe learns this by experience, and having saved a watch, ledger, ink and pen from the shipwreck, he soon begins, like a good Englishman, to keep a set of books. His stock-book contains a catalogue of the useful objects he possesses, of the various operations necessary for their production, and finally of the labour-time that specific quantities of these products have on average cost him. All the relations between Robinson and these objects that form his self-created wealth are here so simple and transparent that even Mr Sedley Taylor could understand them. And yet those relations contain all the essential determinants of value.

Let us now transport ourselves from Robinson's island, bathed in light, to medieval Europe, shrouded in darkness. Here, instead of the independent man, we find everyone dependent—serfs and lords, vassals and suzerains, laymen and clerics. Personal dependence characterizes the social relations of material production as much as it does the other spheres of life based on that production. But precisely because relations of personal dependence form the given social foundation, there is no need for labour and its products to assume a fantastic form different from their reality. They take the shape, in the transactions of society, of services in kind and payments in kind. The

[22] Even Ricardo has his Robinson Crusoe stories. 'Ricardo makes his primitive fisherman and primitive hunter into owners of commodities who immediately exchange their fish and game in proportion to the labour-time which is materialized in these exchange-values. On this occasion he slips into the anachronism of allowing the primitive fisherman and hunter to calculate the value of their implements in accordance with the annuity tables used on the London Stock Exchange in 1817. Apart from bourgeois society, the "parallelograms of Mr Owen" seem to have been the only form of

society Ricardo was acquainted with' (Karl Marx, *Zur Kritik etc.*, pp. 38–9) [English translation, p. 60].

natural form of labour, its particularity—and not, as in a society based on commodity production, its universality—is here its immediate social form. The *corvée* can be measured by time just as well as the labour which produces commodities, but every serf knows that what he expends in the service of his lord is a specific quantity of his own personal labour-power. The tithe owed to the priest is more clearly apparent than his blessing. Whatever we may think, then, of the different roles in which men confront each other in such a society, the social relations between individuals in the performance of their labour appear at all events as their own personal relations, and are not disguised as social relations between things, between the products of labour.

For an example of labour in common, i.e. directly associated labour, we do not need to go back to the spontaneously developed form which we find at the threshold of the history of all civilized peoples.[23] We have one nearer to hand in the patriarchal rural industry of a peasant family which produces corn, cattle, yarn, linen and clothing for its own use. These things confront the family as so many products of its collective labour, but they do not confront each other as commodities. The different kinds of labour which create these products—such as tilling the fields, tending the cattle, spinning, weaving and making clothes— are already in their natural form social functions; for they are functions of the family, which, just as much as a society based on commodity production, possesses

its own spontaneously developed division of labour. The distinction of labour within the family and the labour-time expended by the individual members of the family, are regulated by differences of sex and age as well as by seasonal variations in the natural conditions of labour. The fact that the expenditure of the individual labour-powers is measured by duration appears here, by its very nature, as a social characteristic of labour itself, because the individual labour-powers, by their very nature, act only as instruments of the joint labour-power of the family.

Let us finally imagine, for a change, an association of free men, working with the means of production held in common, and expending their many different forms of labour-power in full self-awareness as one single social labour force. All the characteristics of Robinson's labour are repeated here, but with the difference that they are social instead of individual. All Robinson's products were exclusively the result of his own personal labour and they were therefore directly objects of utility for him personally. The total product of our imagined association is a social product. One part of this product serves as fresh means of production and remains social. But another part is consumed by the members of the association as means of subsistence. This part must therefore be divided amongst them. The way this division is made will vary with the particular kind of social organization of production and the corresponding level of social development attained by the producers. We shall assume, but only for the sake of a parallel with the production of commodities, that the share of each individual producer in the means of subsistence is determined by his labour-time. Labour-time would in that case play a double part. Its apportionment in accordance with a definite social plan maintains the correct proportion between the different functions of labour and the various needs of the associations. On the other hand, labour-time also serves as a measure of the part taken by each individual in the common labour, and of his share in the part of the total product destined for individual consumption. The social relations of the individual producers, both towards their labour and the products of their labour, are here transparent in their simplicity, in production as well as in distribution.

[23] 'A ridiculous notion has spread abroad recently that communal property in its natural, spontaneous form is specifically Slav, indeed exclusively Russian. In fact, it is the primitive form that we can prove to have existed among Romans, Teutons and Celts, and which indeed still exists to this day in India, in a whole range of diverse patterns, albeit sometimes only as remnants. A more exact study of the Asiatic, and specifically of the Indian form of communal property would indicate the way in which different forms of spontaneous, primitive communal property give rise to different forms of its dissolution. Thus the different original types of Roman and Germanic private property can be deduced from the different forms of Indian communal property' (Karl Marx, *Zur Kritik, etc.,* p. 10) [English translation, p. 33].

For a society of commodity producers, whose general social relation of production consists in the fact that they treat their products as commodities, hence as values, and in this material [*sachlich*] form bring their individual, private labours into relation with each other as homogeneous human labour, Christianity with its religious cult of man in the abstract, more particularly in its bourgeois development, i.e. in Protestantism, Deism, etc., is the most fitting form of religion. In the ancient Asiatic, Classical-antique, and other such modes of production, the transformation of the product into a commodity, and therefore men's existence as producers of commodities, plays a subordinate role, which however increases in importance as these communities approach nearer and nearer to the stage of their dissolution. Trading nations, properly so called, exist only in the interstices of the ancient world, like the gods of Epicurus in the *intermundia*, or Jews in the pores of Polish society. Those ancient social organisms of production are much more simple and transparent than those of bourgeois society. But they are founded either on the immaturity of man as an individual, when he has not yet torn himself loose from the umbilical cord of his natural species-connection with other men, or on direct relations of dominance and servitude. They are conditioned by a low stage of development of the productive powers of labour and corresponding limited relations between men within the process of creating and reproducing their material life, hence also limited relations between man and nature. These real limitations are reflected in the ancient worship of nature, and in other elements of tribal religions. The religious reflections of the real world can, in any case, vanish only when the practical relations of everyday life between man and man, and man and nature, generally present themselves to him in a transparent and rational form. The veil is not removed from the countenance of the social life-process, i.e. the process of material production, until it becomes production by freely associated men, and stands under their conscious and planned control. This, however, requires that society possess a material foundation, or a series of material conditions of existence, which in their turn are the natural and spontaneous product of a long and tormented historical development.

Political economy has indeed analysed value and its magnitude, however incompletely,[24] and has uncovered the content concealed within these forms. But it has never once asked the question why this content has assumed that particular form, that is to say, why labour is expressed in value, and why the measurement of labour by its duration is expressed in the mag-

24 The insufficiency of Ricardo's analysis of the magnitude of value—and his analysis is by far the best—will appear from the third and fourth books of this work. As regards value in general, classical political economy in fact nowhere distinguishes explicitly and with a clear awareness between labour as it appears in the value of a product, and the same labour as it appears in the product's use-value. Of course the distinction is made in practice, since labour is treated sometimes from its quantitative aspect, and at other times qualitatively. But it does not occur to the economist that a purely quantitative distinction between the kinds of labour presupposes their qualitative unity or equality, and therefore their reduction to abstract human labour. For instance, Ricardo declares that he agrees with Destutt de Tracy when the latter says: 'As it is certain that our physical and moral faculties are alone our original riches, the employment of those faculties, labour of some kind, is our original treasure, and it is always from this employment that all those things are created which we call riches ... It is certain too, that all those things only represent the labour which has created them, and if they have a value, or even two distinct values, they can only derive them from that' (the value) 'of the labour from which they emanate' (Ricardo, *The Principles of the Political Economy*, 3rd edn, London, 1821, p. 334). We would here only point out that Ricardo imposes his own more profound interpretation on the words of Destutt. Admittedly Destutt does say that all things which constitute wealth 'represent the labour which has created them,' but, on the other hand, he also says that they acquire their 'two different values' (use-value and exchange-value) from 'the value of labour.' He thus falls into the commonplace error of the vulgar economists, who assume the value of one commodity (here labour) in order in turn to use it to determine the values of other commodities. But Ricardo reads him as if he had said that labour (not the value of labour) is represented both in use-value and in exchange-value. Nevertheless, Ricardo himself makes so little of the dual character of the labour represented in this twofold way that he is forced to spend the whole of his chapter 'Value and Riches, their Distinctive Properties' on a laborious examination of the trivialities of a J. B. Say. And at the end he is therefore quite astonished to find that while

nitude of the value of the product.[25] These formulas, which bear the unmistakable stamp of belonging to a social formation in which the process of production has mastery over man, instead of the opposite, appear to the political economists' bourgeois consciousness to be as much a self-evident and nature-imposed necessity as productive labour itself. Hence the pre-bour-

geois forms of the social organization of production are treated by political economy in much the same way as the Fathers of the Church treated pre-Christian religions.[26]

Destutt agrees with him that labour is the source of value, he nevertheless also agrees with Say about the concept of value.

[25] It is one of the chief failings of classical political economy that it has never succeeded, by means of its analysis of commodities, and in particular of their value, in discovering the form of value which in fact turns value into exchange-value. Even its best representatives, Adam Smith and Ricardo, treat the form of value as something of indifference, something external to the nature of the commodity itself. The explanation for this is not simply that their attention is entirely absorbed by the analysis or the magnitude of value. It lies deeper. The value-form of the product of labour is the most abstract, but also the most universal form of the bourgeois mode of production; by that fact it stamps the bourgeois mode of production as a particular kind of social production of a historical and transitory character. If then we make the mistake of treating it as the eternal natural form of social production, we necessarily overlook the specificity of the value-form, and consequently of the commodity-form together with its further developments, the money form, the capital form, etc. We therefore find that economists who are entirely agreed that labour-time is the measure of the magnitude of value, have the strangest and most contradictory ideas about money, that is, about the universal equivalent in its finished form. This emerges sharply when they deal with banking, where the commonplace definitions of money will no longer hold water. Hence there has arisen in opposition to the classical economists a restored Mercantilist System (Ganilh etc.), which sees in value only the social form, or rather its insubstantial semblance. Let me point out once and for all that by classical, political economy I mean all the economists who, since the time of W. Petty, have investigated the real internal framework [Zusammenhang] of bourgeois relations of production, as opposed to the vulgar economists who only flounder around within the apparent framework of those relations, ceaselessly ruminate on the materials long since provided by scientific political economy, and seek there plausible explanations of the crudest phenomena for the domestic purposes of the bourgeoisie. Apart from this, the vulgar economists confine themselves to systematizing in a pedantic way, and proclaiming for everlasting truths, the banal and complacent

notions held by the bourgeois agents of production about their own world, which is to them the best possible one.

[26] 'The economists have a singular way of proceeding. For them, there are only two kinds of institutions, artificial and natural. The institutions of feudalism are artificial institutions, those of the bourgeoisie are natural institutions. In this they resemble the theologians, who likewise establish two kinds of religion. Every religion which is not theirs is an invention of men, while their own is an emanation of God . . . Thus there has been history, but there is no longer any' (Karl Marx, Misère de la philosophie. Réponse à la philosophie de la misère de M. Proudhon, 1847, p. 113). Truly comical is M. Bastiat, who imagines that the ancient Greeks and Romans lived by plunder alone. For if people live by plunder for centuries there must, after all, always be something there to plunder, in other words, the objects of plunder must be continually reproduced. It seems, therefore, that even the Greeks and the Romans had a process of production, hence an economy, which constituted the material basis of their world as much as the bourgeois economy constitutes that of the present-day world. Or perhaps Bastiat means that a mode of production based on the labour of slaves is based on a system of plunder? In that case he is on dangerous ground. If a giant thinker like Aristotle could err in his evaluation of slave-labour, why should a dwarf economist like Bastiat be right in his evaluation of wage-labour? I seize this opportunity of briefly refuting an objection made by a German-American publication to my work Zur Kritik der Politischen Ökonomie, 1859. My view is that each particular mode of production, and the relations of production corresponding to it at each given moment, in short 'the economic structure of society,' is 'the real foundation, on which arises a legal and political superstructure and to which correspond definite forms of social consciousness,' and that 'the mode of production of material life conditions the general process of social, political and intellectual life.' In the opinion of the German-American publication this is all very true for our own times, in which material interests are preponderant, but not for the Middle Ages, dominated by Catholicism, nor for Athens and Rome, dominated by politics. In the first place, it strikes us as odd that anyone should suppose that these well-worn phrases about the Middle Ages and the ancient world were unknown to anyone else. One thing is clear: the Middle Ages could not live on Catholicism, nor could the

The degree to which some economists are misled by the fetishism attached to the world of commodities, or by the objective appearance of the social characteristics of labour, is shown, among other things, by the dull and tedious dispute over the part played by nature in the formation of exchange-value. Since exchange-value is a definite social manner of expressing the labour bestowed on a thing, it can have no more natural content than has, for example, the rate of exchange.

As the commodity-form is the most general and the most undeveloped form of bourgeois production, it makes its appearance at an early date, though not in the same predominant and therefore characteristic manner as nowadays. Hence its fetish character is still relatively easy to penetrate. But when we come to more concrete forms, even this appearance of simplicity vanishes. Where did the illusions of the Monetary System come from? The adherents of the Monetary System did not see gold and silver as representing money as a social relation of production, but in the form of natural objects with peculiar social properties. And what of modern political economy, which looks down so disdainfully on the Monetary System? Does not its fetishism become quite palpable when it deals with capital? How long is it since the disappearance of the Physiocratic illusion that ground rent grows out of the soil, not out of society?

But, to avoid anticipating, we will content ourselves here with one more example relating to the commodity-form itself. If commodities could speak, they would say this: our use-value may interest men, but it does not belong to us as objects. What does belong to us as

objects, however, is our value. Our own intercourse as commodities proves it. We relate to each other merely as exchange-values. Now listen how those commodities speak through the mouth of the economist:

'Value (i.e. exchange-value) is a property of things, riches (i.e. use-value) of man. Value, in this sense, necessarily implies exchanges, riches do not.'[27]

'Riches (use-value) are the attribute of man, value is the attribute of commodities. A man or a community is rich, a pearl or a diamond is valuable . . . A pearl or a diamond is valuable as a pearl or diamond.'[28]

So far no chemist has ever discovered exchange-value either in a pearl or a diamond. The economists who have discovered this chemical substance, and who lay special claim to critical acumen, nevertheless find that the use-value of material objects belongs to them independently of their material properties, while their value on the other hand, forms a part of them as objects. What confirms them in this view is the peculiar circumstance that the use-value of a thing is realized without exchange, i.e. in the direct relation between the thing and man, while, inversely, its value is realized only in exchange, i.e. in a social process. Who would not call to mind at this point the advice given by the good Dogberry to the night-watchman Seacoal?

'To be a well-favoured man is the gift of fortune; but reading and writing comes by nature.'[29]

---

[27] *Observations on Some Verbal Disputes in Pol. Econ., Particularly Relating to Value, and to Supply and Demand*, London, 1821, p. 16.

[28] S. Bailey, op. cit., p. 165.

[29] Both the author of *Observations etc.*, and S. Bailey accuse Ricardo of converting exchange-value from something relative into something absolute. The reverse is true. He has reduced the apparent relativity which these things (diamonds, pearls, etc.) possess to the true relation hidden behind the appearance, namely their relativity as mere expressions of human labour. If the followers of Ricardo answer Bailey somewhat rudely, but by no means convincingly, this is because they are unable to find in Ricardo's own works any elucidation of the inner connection between value and the form of value, or exchange-value.

---

ancient world on politics. On the contrary, it is the manner in which they gained their livelihood which explains why in one case politics, in the other case Catholicism, played the chief part. For the rest, one needs no more than a slight acquaintance with, for example, the history of the Roman Republic, to be aware that its secret history is the history of landed property. And then there is Don Quixote, who long ago paid the penalty for wrongly imagining that knight errantry was compatible with all economic forms of society.

MARX

The Civil War in France

On the dawn of the 18th of March, Paris arose to the thunderburst of "Vive la Commune!" What is the Commune, that sphinx so tantalizing to the bourgeois mind?

"The proletarians of Paris," said the Central Committee in its manifesto of the 18th March, "amidst the failures and treasons of the ruling classes, have understood that the hour has struck for them to save the situation by taking into their own hands the direction of public affairs. . . . They have understood that it is their imperious duty and their absolute right to render themselves master of their own destinies, by seizing upon the governmental power."

But the working class cannot simply lay hold of the ready-made State machinery, and wield it for its own purposes.

The centralized State power, with its ubiquitous organs of standing army, police, bureaucracy, clergy, and judicature—organs wrought after the plan of a systematic and hierarchic division of labour—originates from the days of absolute monarchy, serving nascent middle-class society as a mighty weapon in its struggles against feudalism. Still, its development remained clogged by all manner of mediaeval rubbish, seignorial rights, local privileges, municipal and guild monopolies and provincial constitutions. The gigantic broom of the French Revolution of the eighteenth century swept away all these relics of bygone times, thus clearing simultaneously the social soil of its last hindrances to the superstructure of the modern State edifice raised under the First Empire, itself the offspring of the coalition wars of old semi-feudal Europe against modern France. During the subsequent *régimes* the Government, placed under parliamentary control—that is, under the direct control of the propertied classes—became not only a hotbed of huge national debts and crushing taxes; with its irresistible allurements of place, pelf, and patronage, it became not only the bone of contention between the rival factions and adventurers of the ruling classes; but its political character changed simultaneously with the economic changes of society. At the same pace at which the progress of modern industry developed, widened, intensified the class antagonism between capital and labour, the State power assumed more and more the character of the national power of capital over labour, of a public force organized for social enslavement, of an engine of class despotism. After every revolution marking a progressive phase in the class struggle, the purely repressive character of the State power stands out in bolder and bolder relief. The Revolution of 1830, resulting in the transfer of Government from the landlords to the capitalists, transferred it from the more remote to the more direct antagonists of the working men. The bourgeois Republicans, who, in the name of the Revolution of February, took the State power, used it for the June massacres, in order to convince the working class that "social" republic meant the republic ensuring their social subjection, and in order to convince the royalist bulk of the bourgeois and landlord class that they might safely leave the cares and emoluments of government to the bourgeois "Republicans." However, after their one heroic exploit of June, the bourgeois Republicans had, from the front, to fall back to the rear of the "Party of Order"—a combination formed by all the rival fractions and factions of the appropriating class in their now openly declared antagonism to the producing classes. The proper form of their joint-stock Government was the *Parliamentary Republic*, with Louis Bonaparte for its President. Theirs was a *régime* of avowed class terrorism and deliberate insult towards the "vile multitude." If the Parliamentary Republic, as M. Thiers said, "divided them (the different fractions of the ruling class) least," it opened an abyss between that class and the whole body of society outside their spare ranks. The restraints by which their own divisions had under former *régimes* still checked the State power, were removed by their union; and in view of the threatening upheaval of the proletariat, they now used that State power mercilessly and ostentatiously as the national war-engine of capital against labour. In their uninterrupted crusade against the producing masses they were, however, bound not only to invest the executive with continually increased powers of repression, but at the same time to divest their own parliamentary stronghold—the National Assembly—one by one, of all its own means of defence against the Executive. The Executive, in the person of Louis Bonaparte, turned them out. The natural offspring of the "Party-of-Order" Republic was the Second Empire.

The Empire, with the *coup d'état* for its certificate of birth, universal suffrage for its sanction, and the sword for its sceptre, professed to rest upon the peasantry, the large mass of producers not directly involved in the struggle of capital and labour. It professed to save the working class by breaking down Parliamentarism, and, with it, the undisguised subserviency of Government to the propertied classes. It professed to save the propertied classes by upholding their economic supremacy over the working class; and, finally, it professed to unite all classes by reviving for all the chimera of national glory. In reality, it was the only form of government possible at a time when the bourgeoisie had already lost, and the working class had not yet acquired, the faculty of ruling the nation. It was acclaimed throughout the world as the saviour of society. Under its sway, bourgeois society, freed from political cares, attained a development unexpected even by itself. Its industry and commerce expanded to colossal dimensions; financial swindling celebrated cosmopolitan orgies; the misery of the masses was set off by a shameless display of gorgeous, meretricious, and debased luxury. The State power, apparently soaring high above society, was at the same time itself the greatest scandal of that society and the very hotbed of all its corruptions. Its own rottenness, and the rottenness of the society it had saved, were laid bare by the bayonet of Prussia, herself eagerly bent upon transferring the supreme seat of the *régime* from Paris to Berlin. Imperialism is, at the same time, the most prostitute and the ultimate form of the State power which nascent middle-class society had commenced to elaborate as a means of its own emancipation from feudalism, and which full-grown bourgeois society had finally transformed into a means for the enslavement of labour by capital.

The direct antithesis to the Empire was the Commune. The cry of "Social Republic," with which the revolution of February was ushered in by the Paris proletariat, did but express a vague aspiration after a Republic that was not only to supersede the monarchical form of class-rule, but class-rule itself. The Commune was the positive form of that Republic.

Paris, the central seat of the old governmental power, and, at the same time, the social stronghold of the French working class, had risen in arms against the attempt of Thiers and the Rurals to restore and perpetuate that old governmental power bequeathed to them by the Empire. Paris could resist only because in consequence of the siege, it had got rid of the army, and replaced it by a National Guard, the bulk of which consisted of working men. This fact was now to be transformed into an institution. The first decree of the Commune, therefore, was the suppression of the standing army, and the substitution for it of the armed people.

The Commune was formed of the municipal councillors, chosen by universal suffrage in the various wards of the town, responsible and revocable at short terms. The majority of its members were naturally working men, or acknowledged representatives of the working class. The Commune was to be a working, not a parliamentary, body, executive and legislative at the same time. Instead of continuing to be the agent of the Central Government, the police was at once stripped of its political attributes, and turned into the responsible and at all times revocable agent of the Commune. So were the officials of all other branches of the Administration. From the members of the Commune downwards, the public service had to be done at *workmen's wages*. The vested interests and the representation allowances of the high dignitaries of State disappeared along with the high dignitaries themselves.

Public functions ceased to be the private property of the tools of the Central Government. Not only municipal administration, but the whole initiative hitherto exercised by the State was laid into the hands of the Commune.

Having once got rid of the standing army and the police, the physical force elements of the old Government, the Commune was anxious to break the spiritual force of repression, the "parson-power," by the disestablishment and disendowment of all churches as proprietary bodies. The priests were sent back to the recesses of private life, there to feed upon the alms of the faithful in imitation of their predecessors, the Apostles. The whole of the educational institutions were opened to the people gratuitously, and at the same time cleared of all interference of Church and State. Thus, not only was education made accessible to all, but science itself freed from the fetters which class prejudice and governmental force had imposed upon it.

The judicial functionaries were to be divested of that sham independence which had but served to mask their abject subserviency to all succeeding governments to which, in turn, they had taken, and broken, the oaths of allegiance. Like the rest of public servants, magistrates and judges were to be elective, responsible, and revocable.

The Paris Commune was, of course, to serve as a model to all the great industrial centres of France. The communal *régime* once established in Paris and the secondary centres, the old centralized Government would in the provinces, too, have to give way to the self-government of the producers. In a rough sketch of national organization which the Commune had no time to develop, it states clearly that the Commune was to be the political form of even the smallest country hamlet, and that in the rural districts the standing army was to be replaced by a national militia, with an extremely short term of service. The rural communes of every district were to administer their common affairs by an assembly of delegates in the central town, and these district assemblies were again to send deputies to the National Delegation in Paris, each delegate to be at any time revocable and bound by the *mandat impératif* (formal instructions) of his con-

stituents. The few but important functions which still would remain for a central government were not to be suppressed, as has been intentionally misstated, but were to be discharged by Communal, and therefore strictly responsible agents. The unity of the nation was not to be broken, but, on the contrary, to be organized by the Communal constitution, and to become a reality by the destruction of the State power which claimed to be the embodiment of that unity independent of, and superior to, the nation itself, from which it was but a parasitic excrescence. While the merely repressive organs of the old governmental power were to be amputated, its legitimate functions were to be wrested from an authority usurping pre-eminence over society itself, and restored to the responsible agents of society. Instead of deciding once in three or six years which member of the ruling class was to misrepresent the people in Parliament, universal suffrage was to serve the people, constituted in Communes, as individual suffrage serves every other employer in the search for the workmen and managers in his business. And it is well known that companies, like individuals, in matters of real business generally know how to put the right man in the right place, and if they for once make a mistake, to redress it promptly. On the other hand, nothing could be more foreign to the spirit of the Commune than to supersede universal suffrage by hierarchic investiture.

It is generally the fate of completely new historical creations to be mistaken for the counterpart of older and even defunct forms of social life, to which they may bear a certain likeness. Thus, this new Commune, which breaks the modern State power, has been mistaken for a reproduction of the mediaeval Communes, which first preceded, and afterwards became the substratum of, that very State power. — The communal constitution has been mistaken for an attempt to break up into a federation of small States, as dreamt of by Montesquieu and the Girondins, that unity of great nations, which, if originally brought about by political force, has now become a powerful coefficient of social production. — The antagonism of the Commune against the State power has been mistaken for an exaggerated form of the ancient struggle against over-centralization. Peculiar historical circumstances may have prevented the classical development, as in France, of the bourgeois form of government, and may have allowed, as in England, to complete the great central State organs by corrupt vestries, jobbing councillors, and ferocious poor-law guardians in the towns, and virtually hereditary magistrates in the counties. The Communal Constitution would have restored to the social body all the forces hitherto absorbed by the State parasite feeding upon, and clogging the free movement of, society. By this one act it would have initiated the regeneration of France.— The provincial French middle-class saw in the Commune an attempt to restore the sway their order had held over the country under Louis Philippe, and which, under Louis Napoleon, was supplanted by the pretended rule of the country over the towns. In reality, the Communal Constitution brought the rural producers under the intellectual lead of the central towns of their districts, and there secured to them, in the working men, the natural trustees of their interests.— The very existence of the Commune involved, as a matter of course, local municipal liberty, but no longer as a check upon the, now superseded, State power. It could only enter into the head of a Bismarck, who, when not engaged on his intrigues of blood and iron, always likes to resume his old trade, so befitting his mental calibre, of contributor to *Kladderadatsch* (the Berlin *Punch*), it could only enter into such a head, to ascribe to the Paris Commune aspirations after that caricature of the old French municipal organization of 1791, the Prussian municipal constitution which degrades the town governments to mere secondary wheels in the police-machinery of the Prussian State. The Commune made that catch-word of bourgeois revolutions, cheap government, a reality, by destroying the two greatest sources of expenditure—the standing army and State functionarism. Its very existence presupposed the non-existence of monarchy, which, in Europe at least, is the normal incumbrance and indispensable cloak of class-rule. It supplied the Republic with the basis of really democratic institutions. But neither cheap government nor the "true Republic" was its ultimate aim; they were its mere concomitants.

The multiplicity of interpretations to which the Commune has been subjected, and the multiplicity of interests which construed it in their favour, show that it was a thoroughly expansive political form, while all previous forms of government had been emphatically repressive. Its true secret was this. It was essentially a working-class government, the produce of the struggle of the producing against the appropriating class, the political form at last discovered under which to work out the economical emancipation of Labour.

Except on this last condition, the Communal Constitution would have been an impossibility and a delusion. The political rule of the producer cannot coexist with the perpetuation of his social slavery. The Commune was therefore to serve as a lever for uprooting the economical foundations upon which rests the existence of classes, and therefore of class rule. With labour emancipated, every man becomes a working man, and productive labour ceases to be a class attribute.

It is a strange fact. In spite of all the tall talk and all the immense literature, for the last sixty years, about Emancipation of Labour, no sooner do the working men anywhere take the subject into their own hands with a will, than uprises at once all the apologetic phraseology of the mouthpieces of present society with its two poles of Capital and Wage-slavery (the landlord now is but the sleeping partner of the capitalist), as if capitalist society was still in its purest state of virgin innocence, with its antagonisms still undeveloped, with its delusions still unexploded, with its prostitute realities not yet laid bare. The Commune, they exclaim, intends to abolish property, the basis of all civilization! Yes, gentlemen, the Commune intended to abolish that class-property which makes the labour of the many the wealth of the few. It aimed at the expropriation of the expropriators. It wanted to make individual property a truth by transforming the means of production, land and capital, now chiefly the means of enslaving and exploiting labour, into mere instruments of free and associated labour.—But this is Communism, "impossible" Communism! Why, those members of the ruling classes who are intelligent enough to perceive the impossibility of continuing the present system—and they are many—have become the obtrusive and full-mouthed apostles of cooperative production. If cooperative production is not to remain a sham and a snare; if it is to supersede the

Capitalist system; if united cooperative societies are to regulate national production upon a common plan, thus taking it under their own control, and putting an end to the constant anarchy and periodical convulsions which are the fatality of Capitalist production — what else, gentlemen, would it be but Communism, "possible" Communism?

The working class did not expect miracles from the Commune. They have no ready-made utopias to introduce *par décret du peuple*. They know that in order to work out their own emancipation, and along with it that higher form to which present society is irresistibly tending by its own economical agencies, they will have to pass through long struggles, through a series of historic processes, transforming circumstances and men. They have no ideals to realize, but to set free elements of the new society with which old collapsing bourgeois society itself is pregnant. In the full consciousness of their historic mission, and with the heroic resolve to act up to it, the working class can afford to smile at the coarse invective of the gentlemen's gentlemen with the pen and inkhorn, and at the didactic patronage of well-wishing bourgeois-doctrinaires, pouring forth their ignorant platitudes and sectarian crotchets in the oracular tone of scientific infallibility.

When the Paris Commune took the management of the revolution in its own hands; when plain working men for the first time dared to infringe upon the Governmental privilege of their "natural superiors," and, under circumstances of unexampled difficulty, performed their work modestly, conscientiously, and efficiently — performed it at salaries the highest of which barely amounted to one-fifth of what, according to high scientific authority, is the minimum required for a secretary to a certain metropolitan school-board, — the old world writhed in convulsions of rage at the sight of the Red Flag, the symbol of the Republic of Labour, floating over the Hôtel de Ville.

And yet, this was the first revolution in which the working class was openly acknowledged as the only class capable of social initiative, even by the great bulk of the Paris middle class — shopkeepers, tradesmen, merchants — the wealthy capitalists alone excepted. The Commune had saved them by a sagacious settlement of that ever-recurring cause of dispute among the middle classes themselves — the debtor and creditor accounts. The same portion of the middle class, after they had assisted in putting down the working men's insurrection of June, 1848, had been at once unceremoniously sacrificed to their creditors by the then Constituent Assembly. But this was not their motive for now rallying round the working class. They felt that there was but one alternative — the Commune, or the Empire — under whatever name it might reappear. The Empire had ruined them economically by the havoc it made of public wealth, by the wholesale financial swindling it fostered, by the props it lent to the artificially accelerated centralization of capital, and the concomitant expropriation of their ranks. It had suppressed them politically, it had shocked them morally by its orgies, it had insulted their Voltairianism by handing over the education of their children to the *frères Ignorantins*, it had revolted their national feeling as Frenchmen by precipitating them headlong into a war which left only one equivalent for the ruins it made — the disappearance of the Empire. In fact, after the exodus from Paris of the high Bonapartist and capitalist *Bohême*, the true middle-class Party of Order came out in the shape of the "Union Républicaine," enrolling themselves under the colours of the Commune and defending it against the wilful misconstruction of Thiers. Whether the gratitude of this great body of the middle class will stand the present severe trial, time must show.

The Commune was perfectly right in telling the peasants that "its victory was their only hope." Of all the lies hatched at Versailles and re-echoed by the glorious European penny-a-liner, one of the most tremendous was that the Rurals represented the French peasantry. Think only of the love of the French peasant for the men to whom, after 1815, he had to pay the milliard of indemnity! In the eyes of the French peasant, the very existence of a great landed proprietor is in itself an encroachment on his conquests of 1789. The bourgeois, in 1848, had burthened his plot of land with the additional tax of forty-five cents in the franc; but then he did so in the name of the revolution; while now he had fomented a civil war against the revolution, to shift on to the peasant's shoulders the chief load of the five milliards of indemnity to be paid to the Prussians. The Commune, on the other hand, in one of its first proclamations, declared that the true originators of the war would be made to pay its cost. The Commune would have delivered the peasant of the blood tax,—would have given him a cheap government,—transformed his present blood-suckers, the notary, advocate, executor, and other judicial vampires, into salaried communal agents, elected by, and responsible to, himself. It would have freed him of the tyranny of the *garde champêtre*, the gendarme, and the prefect, would have put enlightenment by the schoolmaster in the place of stuntification by the priest. And the French peasant is, above all, a man of reckoning. He would find it extremely reasonable that the pay of the priest, instead of being extorted by the tax-gatherer, should only depend upon the spontaneous action of the parishioners' religious instincts. Such were the great immediate boons which the rule of the Commune—and that rule alone—held out to the French peasantry. It is, therefore, quite superfluous here to expatiate upon the more complicated but vital problems which the Commune alone was able, and at the same time compelled, to solve in favour of the peasant, viz., the hypothecary debt, lying like an incubus upon his parcel of soil, the *prolétariat foncier* (the rural proletariat), daily growing upon it, and his expropriation from it enforced, at a more and more rapid rate, by the very development of modern agriculture and the competition of capitalist farming.

The French peasant had elected Louis Bonaparte president of the Republic; but the Party of Order created the Empire. What the French peasant really wants he commenced to show in 1849 and 1850, by opposing his maire to the Government's prefect, his schoolmaster to the Government's priest, and himself to the Government's gendarme. All the laws made by the Party of Order in January and February, 1850, were avowed measures of repression against the peasant. The peasant was a Bonapartist, because the great Revolution, with all its benefits to him, was, in his eyes, personified in Napoleon. This delusion, rapidly breaking down under the Second Empire (and in its very nature hostile to the Rurals), this prejudice of the past, how could it have withstood the appeal of the Commune to the living interests and urgent wants of the peasantry?

The Rurals—this was, in fact, their chief apprehension—knew that three months' free communication of Communal Paris with the provinces would bring about a general rising of the peasants, and hence their anxiety to establish a police blockade around Paris, so as to stop the spread of the rinderpest.

If the Commune was thus the true representative of all the healthy elements of French society, and therefore the truly national Government, it was, at the same time, as a working men's Government, as the bold champion of the emancipation of labour, emphatically international. Within sight of the Prussian army, that had annexed to Germany two French provinces, the Commune annexed to France the working people all over the world.

The Second Empire had been the jubilee of cosmopolitan black-leggism, the rakes of all countries rushing in at its call for a share in its orgies and in the plunder of the French people. Even at this moment the right hand of Thiers is Ganesco, the foul Wallachian, and his left hand is Markowski, the Russian spy. The Commune admitted all foreigners to the honour of dying for an immortal cause. Between the foreign war lost by their treason, and the civil war fomented by their conspiracy with the foreign invader, the bourgeoisie had found the time to display their patriotism by organizing police-hunts upon the Germans in France. The Commune made a German working-man its Minister of Labour. Thiers, the bourgeoisie, the Second Empire, had continually deluded Poland by loud professions of sympathy, while in reality betraying her to, and doing the dirty work of, Russia. The Commune honoured the heroic sons of Poland by placing them at the head of the defenders of Paris. And, to broadly mark the new era of history it was conscious of initiating, under the eyes of the conquering Prussians on the one side, and of the Bonapartist army, led by Bonapartist generals, on the other, the Commune pulled down that colossal symbol of martial glory, the Vendôme column.

The great social measure of the Commune was its own working existence. Its special measures could but betoken the tendency of a government of the people by the people. Such were the abolition of the night-work of journeymen bakers; the prohibition, under penalty, of the employers' practice to reduce wages by levying upon their workpeople fines under manifold pretexts,—a process in which the employer combines in his own person the parts of legislator, judge, and executor, and filches the money to boot. Another measure of this class was the surrender, to associations of workmen, under reserve of compensation, of all closed workshops and factories, no matter whether the respective capitalists had absconded or preferred to strike work.

The financial measures of the Commune, remarkable for their sagacity and moderation, could only be such as were compatible with the state of a besieged town. Considering the colossal robberies committed upon the city of Paris by the great financial companies and contractors, under the protection of Haussmann, the Commune would have had an incomparably better title to confiscate their property than Louis Napoleon had against the Orléans family. The Hohenzollern and the English oligarchs who both have derived a good deal of their estates from Church plunder, were, of course, greatly shocked at the Commune clearing but 8,000f. out of secularisation.

While the Versailles Government, as soon as it had recovered some spirit and strength, used the most violent means against the Commune; while it put down the free expression of opinion all over France, even to the forbidding of meetings of delegates from the large towns; while it subjected Versailles and the rest of France to an espionage far surpassing that of the Second Empire; while it burned by its gendarme inquisitors all papers printed at Paris, and sifted all correspondence from and to Paris; while in the National Assembly the most timid attempts to put in a word for Paris were howled down in a manner unknown even to the *Chambre introuvable* of 1816; with the savage warfare of Versailles outside, and its attempts at corruption and conspiracy inside Paris—would the Commune not have shamefully betrayed its trust by affecting to keep up all the decencies and appearances of liberalism as in a time of profound peace? Had the Government of the Commune been akin to that of M. Thiers, there would have been no more occasion to suppress Party-of-Order papers at Paris than there was to suppress Communal papers at Versailles.

It was irritating indeed to the Rurals that at the very same time they declared the return to the Church to be the only means of salvation for France, the infidel Commune unearthed the peculiar mysteries of the Picpus nunnery, and of the Church of Saint Laurent. It was a satire upon M. Thiers that, while he showered grand crosses upon the Bonapartist generals in acknowledgment of their mastery in losing battles, signing capitulations, and turning cigarettes at Wilhelmshöhe, the Commune dismissed and arrested its generals whenever they were suspected of neglecting their duties. The expulsion from, and arrest by, the Commune of one of its members who had slipped in under a false name, and had undergone at Lyons six days' imprisonment for simple bankruptcy, was it not a deliberate insult hurled at the forger, Jules Favre, then still the foreign minister of France, still selling France to Bismarck, and still dictating his orders to that paragon Government of Belgium? But indeed the Commune did not pretend to infallibility, the invariable attribute of all governments of the old stamp. It published its doings and sayings, it initiated the public into all its shortcomings.

In every revolution there intrude, at the side of its true agents, men of a different stamp; some of them survivors of and devotees to past revolutions, without insight into the present movement, but preserving popular influence by their known honesty and courage, or by the sheer force of tradition; others mere bawlers, who, by dint of repeating year after year the same set of stereotyped declarations against the Government of the day, have sneaked into the reputation of revolutionists of the first water. After the 18th of March, some such men did also turn up, and in some cases contrived to play preeminent parts. As far as their power went, they hampered the real action of the working class, exactly as men of that sort have hampered the full development of every previous revolution. They are an unavoidable evil; with time they are shaken off; but time was not allowed to the Commune.

Wonderful, indeed, was the change the Commune had wrought in Paris! No longer any trace of the meretricious Paris of the Second Empire. No longer was Paris the rendezvous of British landlords, Irish absentees, American ex-slaveholders and shoddy men,

Russian ex-serfowners, and Wallachian boyards. No more corpses at the Morgue, no nocturnal burglaries, scarcely any robberies, in fact, for the first time since the days of February, 1848, the streets of Paris were safe, and that without any police of any kind.

> "We," said a member of the Commune, "hear no longer of assassination, theft, and personal assault; it seems indeed as if the police had dragged along with it to Versailles all its Conservative friends."

The *cocottes* had refound the scent of their protectors—the absconding men of family, religion, and, above all, of property. In their stead, the real women of Paris showed again at the surface—heroic, noble, and devoted, like the women of antiquity. Working, thinking, fighting, bleeding Paris—almost forgetful, in its incubation of a new society, of the cannibals at its gates—radiant in the enthusiasm of its historic initiative!

Opposed to this new world at Paris, behold the old world at Versailles—that assembly of the ghouls of all defunct *régimes*, Legitimists and Orleanists, eager to feed upon the carcass of the nation,—with a tail of antediluvian Republicans, sanctioning, by their presence in the Assembly, the slaveholders' rebellion, relying for the maintenance of their Parliamentary Republic upon the vanity of the senile mountebank at its head, and caricaturing 1789 by holding their ghastly meetings in the *Jeu de Paume*.* There it was, this Assembly, the representative of everything dead in France, propped up to the semblance of life by nothing but the swords of the generals of Louis Bonaparte. Paris all truth, Versailles all lie; and that lie vented through the mouth of Thiers.

Thiers tells a deputation of the mayors of the Seine-et-Oise,—

> "You may rely upon my word, which I have *never* broken!"

He tells the Assembly itself that "it was the most freely elected and most Liberal Assembly France ever possessed"; he tells his motley soldiery that it was "the admiration of the world, and the finest army France every possessed"; he tells the provinces that the bombardment of Paris by him was a myth:

> "If some cannon-shots have been fired, it is not the deed of the army of Versailles, but of some insurgents trying to make believe that they are fighting, while they dare not show their faces."

He again tells the provinces that

> "the artillery of Versailles does not bombard Paris, but only cannonades it."

He tells the Archbishop of Paris that the pretended executions and reprisals (!) attributed to the Versailles troops were all moonshine. He tells Paris that he was only anxious "to free it from the hideous tyrants who oppress it," and that, in fact, the Paris of the Commune was "but a handful of criminals."

The Paris of M. Thiers was not the real Paris of the "vile multitude," but a phantom Paris, the Paris of the *francs-fileurs*, the Paris of the Boulevards, male and female—the rich, the capitalist, the gilded, the idle Paris, now thronging with its lackeys, its blacklegs, its literary *bohême*, and its *cocottes* at Versailles, Saint-Denis, Rueil, and Saint-Germain; considering the civil war but an agreeable diversion, eyeing the battle going on through telescopes, counting the rounds of cannon, and swearing by their own honour and that of their prostitutes, that the performance was far better got up than it used to be at the Porte St. Martin. The men who fell were really dead; the cries of the wounded were cries in good earnest; and, besides the whole thing was so intensely historical.

This is the Paris of M. Thiers, as the Emigration of Coblenz was the France of M. de Calonne.

Marx
Critique of the Gotha Program

I

1. "Labour is the source of all wealth and all culture, and *since* useful labour is possible only in society and through society, the proceeds of labour belong undiminished with equal right to all members of society."

First part of the paragraph: "Labour is the source of all wealth and all culture."

Labour is *not the source* of all wealth. *Nature* is just as much the source of use values (and it is surely of such that material wealth consists!) as labour, which itself is only the manifestation of a force of nature, human labour power. The above phrase is to be found in all children's primers and is correct insofar as it is *implied* that labour is performed with the pertinent objects and instruments. But a socialist programme cannot allow such bourgeois phrases to pass over in silence the *conditions* that alone give them meaning. And insofar as man from the outset behaves towards nature, the primary source of all instruments and objects of labour, as an owner, treats her as belonging to him, his labour becomes the source of use values, therefore also of wealth. The bourgeois have very good grounds for ascribing *supernatural creative power* to labour; since precisely from the fact that labour is determined by nature, it follows that the man who possesses no other property than his labour power must, in all conditions of society and culture, be the slave of other men who have made themselves the owners of the material conditions of labour. He can work only with their permission, hence live only with their permission.

Let us now leave the sentence as it stands, or rather limps. What would one have expected in conclusion? Obviously this:

"Since labour is the source of all wealth, no one in society can appropriate wealth except as the product of labour. Therefore, if he himself does not work, he lives by the labour of others and also acquires his culture at the expense of the labour of others."

Instead of this, by means of the verbal rivet "*and since*" a second proposition is added in order to draw a conclusion from this and not from the first one.

Second part of the paragraph: "Useful labour is possible only in society and through society."

According to the first proposition, labour was the source of all wealth and all culture; therefore no society is possible without labour. Now we learn, conversely, that no "useful" labour is possible without society.

One could just as well have said that only in society can useless and even socially harmful labour become a gainful occupation, that only in society can one live by being idle, etc., etc.—in short, one could just as well have copied the whole of Rousseau.

And what is "useful" labour? Surely only labour which produces the intended useful result. A savage— and man was a savage after he had ceased to be an ape —who kills an animal with a stone, who collects fruits, etc., performs "useful" labour.

Thirdly. The conclusion: "And since useful labour is possible only in society and through society, the proceeds of labour belong undiminished with equal right to all members of society."

A fine conclusion! If useful labour is possible only in society and through society, the proceeds of labour belong to society—and only so much therefrom accrues to the individual worker as is not required to maintain the "condition" of labour, society.

In fact, this proposition has at all times been made use of *by the champions of the state of society prevail-*

Reprinted from *Karl Marx/Friedrich Engels Collected Works*, by permission of International Publishers.

ing at any given time. First come the claims of the government and everything that sticks to it, since it is the social organ for the maintenance of the social order; then come the claims of the various kinds of private owners for the various kinds of private property are the foundations of society, etc. One sees that such hollow phrases can be twisted and turned as desired.

The first and second parts of the paragraph have some intelligible connection only in the following wording:

"Labour becomes the source of wealth and culture only as social labour," or, what is the same thing, "in and through society."

This proposition is incontestably correct, for although isolated labour (its material conditions presupposed) can create use values, it can create neither wealth nor culture.

But equally incontestable is the other proposition:

"In proportion as labour develops socially, and becomes thereby a source of wealth and culture, poverty and destitution develop among the workers, and wealth and culture among the non-workers."

This is the law of all history hitherto. What, therefore, had to be done here, instead of setting down general phrases about "*labour*" and "*society,*" was to prove concretely how in present capitalist society the material, etc., conditions have at last been created which enable and compel the workers to lift this historical curse.

In fact, however, the whole paragraph, bungled in style and content, is only there in order to inscribe the Lassallean catchword of the "undiminished proceeds of labour" as a slogan at the top of the party banner. I shall return later to the "proceeds of labour," "equal right," etc., since the same thing recurs in a somewhat different form further on.

2. "In present-day society, the means of labour are the monopoly of the capitalist class; the resulting dependence of the working class is the cause of misery and servitude in all their forms."

This sentence, borrowed from the Rules of the International, is incorrect in this "improved" edition.

In present-day society the means of labour are the monopoly of the landowners (the monopoly of land ownership is even the basis of the monopoly of capital) *and* the capitalists. In the passage in question, the Rules of the International mention neither the one nor the other class of monopolists. They speak of the "*monopoly of the means of labour, that is, the sources of life.*" The addition, "sources of life," makes it sufficiently clear that land is included in the means of labour.

The correction was introduced because Lassalle, for reasons now generally known, attacked *only* the capitalist class and not the landowners. In England, the capitalist is mostly not even the owner of the land on which his factory stands.

3. "The emancipation of labour demands the raising of the means of labour to the common property of society and the collective regulation of the total labour with a fair distribution of the proceeds of labour."

"The raising of the means of labour to common property"! Ought obviously to read their "conversion into common property." But this only in passing.

What are "*proceeds of labour*"? The product of labour or its value? And in the latter case, is it the total value of the product or only that part of the value which labour has newly added to the value of the means of production consumed?

"Proceeds of labour" is a loose notion which Lassalle has put in the place of definite economic concepts.

What is "fair" distribution?

Do not the bourgeois assert that present-day distribution is "fair"? And is it not, in fact, the only "fair" distribution on the basis of the present-day mode of production? Are economic relations regulated by legal concepts or do not, on the contrary, legal relations arise from economic ones? Have not also the socialist sectarians the most varied notions about "fair" distribution?

To understand what is implied in this connection by the phrase "fair distribution," we must take the first paragraph and this one together. The latter presupposes a society wherein "the means of labour are common property and the total labour is collectively regulated," and from the first paragraph we learn that "the proceeds of labour belong undiminished with equal right to all members of society."

"To all members of society"? To those who do not work as well? What remains then of "the undiminished proceeds of labour"? Only to those members of society who work? What remains then of "the equal right" of all members of society?

But "all members of society" and "equal right" are obviously mere phrases. The crucial point is this, that in this communist society every worker must receive his "undiminished" Lassallean "proceeds of labour."

Let us take first of all the words "proceeds of labour" in the sense of the product of labour; then the collective proceeds of labour are the *total social product*.

From this must now be deducted:

First, cover for replacement of the means of production used up.

Secondly, additional portion for expansion of production.

Thirdly, reserve or insurance funds to provide against accidents, disturbances caused by natural factors, etc.

These deductions from the "undiminished proceeds of labour" are an economic necessity and their magnitude is to be determined according to available means and forces, and partly by computation of probabilities, but they are in no way calculable by equity.

There remains the other part of the total product, intended to serve as means of consumption.

Before this is divided among the individuals, there has to be again deducted from it:

First, the general costs of administration not directly appertaining to production.

This part will, from the outset, be very considerably restricted in comparison with present-day society and it diminishes in proportion as the new society develops.

Secondly, that which is intended for the common satisfaction of needs, such as schools, health services, etc.

From the outset this part grows considerably in comparison with present-day society and it grows in proportion as the new society develops.

Thirdly, funds for those unable to work, etc., in short, for what is included under so-called official poor relief today.

Only now do we come to the "distribution" which the programme, under Lassallean influence, has alone in view in its narrow fashion, namely, to that part of the means of consumption which is divided among the individual producers of the collective.

The "undiminished proceeds of labour" have already unnoticeably become converted into the "diminished" proceeds, although what the producer is deprived of in his capacity as a private individual benefits him directly or indirectly in his capacity as a member of society.

Just as the phrase of the "undiminished proceeds of labour" has disappeared, so now does the phrase of the "proceeds of labour" disappear altogether.

Within the collective society based on common ownership of the means of production, the producers do not exchange their products; just as little does the labour employed on the products appear here *as the value* of these products, as a material quality possessed by them, since now, in contrast to capitalist society, individual labour no longer exists in an indirect fashion but directly as a component part of the total labour. The phrase "proceeds of labour," objectionable even today on account of its ambiguity, thus loses all meaning.

What we are dealing with here is a communist society, not as it has *developed* on its own foundations, but on the contrary, just as it *emerges* from capitalist society, which is thus in every respect, economically, morally and intellectually, still stamped with the birthmarks of the old society from whose womb it emerges. Accordingly, the individual producer receives back from society—after the deductions have been made—exactly what he gives to it. What he has given to it is his individual quantum of labour. For example, the social working day consists of the sum of the individual hours of work; the individual labour time of the individual producer is the part of the social working day contributed by him, his share in it. He receives a certificate from society that he has furnished such and such an amount of labour (after deducting his labour for the common funds), and with this certificate he draws from the social stock of means of consumption as much as the same amount of labour costs. The same amount of labour which he has given to society in one form he receives back in another.

Here obviously the same principle prevails as that which regulates the exchange of commodities, as far as this is the exchange of equal values. Content and form are changed, because under the altered circumstances no one can given anything except his labour, and because, on the other hand, nothing can pass to the ownership of individuals except individual means of consumption. But, as far as the distribution of the latter among the individual producers is concerned, the same principle prevails as in the exchange of commodity-equivalents: a given amount of labour in one form is exchanged for an equal amount of labour in another form.

Hence, *equal right* here is still in principle—*bourgeois right*, although principle and practice are no longer at loggerheads, while the exchange of equivalents in commodity exchange only exists *on the average* and not in the individual case.

In spite of this advance, this *equal right* is still constantly encumbered by a bourgeois limitation. The right of the producers is *proportional* to the labour they supply; the equality consists in the fact that measurement is made with an *equal standard*, labour. But one man is superior to another physically or mentally and so supplies more labour in the same time, or can work for a longer time; and labour, to serve as a measure, must be defined by its duration or intensity, otherwise it ceases to be a standard of measurement. This *equal* right is an unequal right for unequal labour. It recognizes no class distinctions, because everyone is only a worker like everyone else; but it tacitly recognizes the unequal individual endowment and thus productive capacity of the workers as natural privileges. *It is, therefore, a right of inequality, in its content, like every right.* Right by its nature can exist only as the application of an equal standard; but unequal individuals (and they would not be different individuals if they were not unequal) are measurable by an equal standard only insofar as they are made subject to an equal criterion, are taken from a *certain* side only, for instance, in the present case, are regarded *only as workers* and nothing more is seen in them, everything else being ignored. Besides, one worker is married, another not; one has more children than another, etc., etc. Thus, given an equal amount of work done, and

hence an equal share in the social consumption fund, one will in fact receive more than another, one will be richer than another, etc. To avoid all these defects, right would have to be unequal rather than equal.

But these defects are inevitable in the first phase of communist society as it is when it has just emerged after prolonged birth-pangs from capitalist society. Right can never be higher than the economic structure of society and its cultural development which this determines.

In a higher phase of communist society, after the enslaving subordination of the individual to the division of labour, and thereby also the antithesis between mental and physical labour, has vanished; after labour has become not only a means of life but life's prime want; after the productive forces have also increased with the all-round development of the individual, and all the springs of common wealth flow more abundantly—only then can the narrow horizon of bourgeois right be crossed in its entirety and society inscribe on its banners: From each according to his abilities, to each according to his needs!

I have dealt at greater length with the "undiminished proceeds of labour," on the one hand, and with "equal right" and "fair distribution," on the other, in order to show what a crime it is to attempt, on the one hand, to force on our Party again, as dogmas, ideas which in a certain period had some meaning but have now become obsolete verbal rubbish, while again perverting, on the other, the realistic outlook, which it cost so much effort to instil into the Party but which has now taken root in it, by means of ideological, legal and other trash so common among the Democrats and French Socialists.

Quite apart from the analysis so far given, it was in general a mistake to make a fuss about so-called *distribution* and put the principal stress on it.

Any distribution whatever of the means of consumption is only a consequence of the distribution of the conditions of production themselves. The latter distribution, however, is a feature of the mode of production itself. The capitalist mode of production, for example, rests on the fact that the material conditions of production are in the hands of non-workers in the form of capital and land ownership, while the masses are only owners of the personal condition of production, of labour power. If the elements of production are so distributed, then the present-day distribution of the means of consumption results automatically. If the material conditions of production are the collective property of the workers themselves, then there likewise results a distribution of the means of consumption different from the present one. The vulgar socialists (and from them in turn a section of the Democrats) have taken over from the bourgeois economists the consideration and treatment of distribution as independent of the mode of production and hence the presentation of socialism as turning principally on distribution. After the real relation has long been made clear, why retrogress again?

4. "The emancipation of labour must be the work of the working class, in relation to which all other classes are *only one reactionary mass*."

The main clause is taken from the introductory words of the Rules of the International, but "improved." There it is said: "The emancipation of the working classes must be conquered by the working classes themselves"; here, on the contrary, the "working class" has to emancipate—what? "Labour." Let him understand who can.

In compensation, the subordinate clause, on the other hand, is a Lassallean quotation of the first water: "in relation to which (the working class) all other classes are *only one reactionary mass*."

In the *Communist Manifesto* it is said: "Of all the classes that stand face to face with the bourgeoisie today, the proletariat alone is a *really revolutionary class*. The other classes decay and finally disappear in the face of Modern Industry; the proletariat is its special and essential product."

The bourgeoisie is here conceived as a revolutionary class—as the bearer of large-scale industry—in relation to the feudal lords and the middle estates, who desire to maintain all social positions that are the creation of obsolete modes of production. Thus they do not form *together with the bourgeoisie* only one reactionary mass.

On the other hand, the proletariat is revolutionary in relation to the bourgeoisie because, having itself grown up on the basis of large-scale industry, it strives to strip off from production the capitalist character that the bourgeoisie seeks to perpetuate. But the *Manifesto* adds that the "middle estates" are becoming revolutionary "in view of their impending transfer into the proletariat."

From this point of view, therefore, it is again nonsense to say that they, "together with the bourgeoisie," and with the feudal lords into the bargain, "form only one reactionary mass" in relation to the working class.

Did anyone proclaim to the artisans, small manufacturers, etc., and *peasants* during the last elections: In relation to us you, together with the bourgeoisie and feudal lords, form only one reactionary mass?

Lassalle knew the *Communist Manifesto* by heart, as his faithful followers know the gospels written by him. If, therefore, he has falsified it so grossly, this has occurred only to put a good colour on his alliance with absolutist and feudal opponents against the bourgeoisie.

In the above paragraph, moreover, his oracular saying is dragged in by the hair, without any connection with the botched quotation from the Rules of the International. Thus it is here simply an impertinence, and indeed not at all displeasing to Mr. Bismarck, one of those cheap pieces of insolence in which the Marat of Berlin deals.

5. "The working class strives for its emancipation first of all *within the framework of the present-day national state*, conscious that the necessary result of its efforts, which are common to the workers of all civilised countries, will be the international brotherhood of peoples."

Lassalle, in opposition to the *Communist Manifesto* and to all earlier socialism, conceived the workers' movement from the narrowest national standpoint. He is being followed in this—and that after the work of the International!

It is altogether self-evident that, to be able to fight at all, the working class must organise itself at home *as a class* and that its own country is the immediate arena of its struggle. To this extent its class struggle is national, not in substance, but, as the *Communist Manifesto* says, "in form." But the "framework of the present-day national state," for instance, the German Empire, is itself in its turn economically "within the framework of the world market," politically "within the framework of the system of states." Every businessman knows that German trade is at the same time foreign trade, and the greatness of Mr. Bismarck consists, to be sure, precisely in his pursuing his kind of *international* policy.

And to what does the German workers' party reduce its internationalism? To the consciousness that the result of its efforts "will be the *international brotherhood of peoples*"—a phrase borrowed from the bourgeois League of Peace and Freedom, which is intended to pass as equivalent to the international brotherhood of the working class in the joint struggle against the ruling classes and their governments. So not a word *about the international functions* of the German working class! And it is thus that it is to defy its own bourgeoisie—which is already linked up in brotherhood against it with the bourgeois of all other countries—and Mr. Bismarck's international policy of conspiracy!

In fact, the internationalism of the programme stands *even infinitely below* that of the Free Trade Party. The latter also asserts that the result of its efforts will be "the international brotherhood of peoples." But it also *does* something to make trade international and by no means contents itself with the consciousness—that all peoples are carrying on trade at home.

The international activity of the working classes does not in any way depend on the existence of the "*International Working Men's Association.*" This was only the first attempt to create a central organ for that activity; an attempt which was a lasting success on account of the impulse which it gave, but which was no longer realisable in *its first historical form* after the fall of the Paris Commune.

Bismarck's *Norddeutsche* was absolutely right when it announced, to the satisfaction of its master, that the German workers' party had forsworn internationalism in the new programme.

II

"Starting from these basic principles, the German workers' party strives by all legal means for the *free state—and—*socialist society; the abolition of the wage system *together with* the *iron law of wages—*and—exploitation in every form; the elimination of all social and political inequality."

I shall return to the "free" state later.

So, in future, the German workers' party has got to believe in Lassalle's "iron law of wages"! That this may not be lost, the nonsense is perpetrated of speaking of the "abolition of the wage system" (it should read: system of wage labour) "*together with* the iron law of wages." If I abolish wage labour, then naturally I abolish its laws too, whether they are of "iron" or sponge. But Lassalle's attack on wage labour turns almost solely on this so-called law. In order, therefore, to prove that the Lassallean sect has won, the "wage system" must be abolished "*together with* the iron law of wages" and not without it.

It is well known that nothing of the "iron law of wages" is Lassalle's except the word "iron" borrowed from Goethe's "eternal, iron, great laws." The word *iron* is a label by which the true believers recognize one another. But if I take the law with Lassalle's stamp on it and, consequently, in his sense, then I must also take it with his substantiation. And what is that? As Lange already showed, shortly after Lassalle's death, it is the Malthusian theory of population (preached by Lange himself). But if this theory is correct, then again I can*not* abolish the law even if I abolish wage labour a hundred time over, because the law then governs not only the system of wage labour but *every* social system. Basing themselves directly on this, the economists have been proving for fifty years and more that socialism cannot abolish destitution, *which has its basis in nature*, but can only make it *general*, distribute it simultaneously over the whole surface of society!

But all this is not the main thing. *Quite apart* from the *false* Lassallean formulation of the law, the truly outrageous retrogression consists in the following:

Since Lassalle's death there has asserted itself in *our* Party the scientific understanding that *wages* are not what they *appear* to be, namely the *value,* or *price, of labour,* but only a masked form for the *value,* or *price, of labour power.* Thereby the whole bourgeois conception of wages hitherto, as well as all the criticism hitherto directed against this conception, was thrown overboard once for all and it was made clear that the wage-worker has permission to work for his own subsistence, that is, *to live* only insofar as he works for a certain time gratis for the capitalist (and hence also for the latter's co-consumers of surplus value); that the whole capitalist system of production turns on increasing this gratis labour by extending the working day or by developing productivity, that is, increasing the intensity of labour power, etc.; that, consequently, the system of wage labour is a system of slavery, and indeed of a slavery which becomes more severe in proportion as the social productive forces of labour develop, whether the worker receives better or worse payment. And after this understanding has gained more and more ground in our Party, one returns to Lassalle's dogmas although one must have known that Lassalle *did not know* what wages were, but following in the wake of the bourgeois economists took the appearance for the essence of the matter.

It is as if, among slaves who have at last got behind the secret of slavery and broken out in rebellion, a slave still in thrall to obsolete notions were to inscribe on the programme of the rebellion: Slavery must be abolished because the feeding of slaves in the system of slavery cannot exceed a certain low maximum!

Does not the mere fact that the representatives of our Party were capable of perpetrating such a monstrous attack on the understanding that has spread among the mass of our Party prove by itself with what criminal levity and with what lack of conscience they set to work in drawing up this compromise programme!

Instead of the indefinite concluding phrase of the paragraph, "the elimination of all social and political inequality," is ought to have been said that with the abolition of class distinctions all social and political inequality arising from them would disappear of itself.

III

"The German workers' party, in order *to pave the way for the solution of the social question,* demands the establishment of producers' cooperative societies with *state aid under the democratic control of the working people.* The producers' cooperative societies *are to be called into being* for industry and agriculture on such a scale *that the socialist organisation of the total labour will arise from them.*"

After the Lassallean "iron law of wages," the panacea of the prophet. The way for it is "paved" in worthy fashion. In place of the existing class struggle appears a newspaper scribbler's phrase: "*the* social *question,*" for the "*solution*" of which one "paves the way." Instead of arising from the revolutionary process of the transformation of society, the "socialist organisation of the total labour" "arises" from the "state aid" that the state gives to the producers' cooperative societies which the *state,* not the worker, "*calls into being.*" It is worthy of Lassalle's imagination that with state loans one can build a new society just as well as a new railway!

From the remnants of a sense of shame, "state aid" has been put—"under the democratic control of the working people."

In the first place, the "working people" in Germany consist in their majority of peasants, and not of proletarians.

Secondly, "democratic" means in German "*volks-herrschaftlich*" ["by the rule of the people"]. But what does "control of the working people by the rule of the people" mean? And particularly in the case of working people who, through these demands that they put to the state, express their full consciousness that they neither rule nor are ripe for rule!

It would be superfluous to deal here with the criticism of the recipe prescribed by Buchez in the reign of Louis Philippe in *opposition* to the French Socialists and accepted by the reactionary workers of the *Atelier.* The chief offence does not lie in having inscribed this specific nostrum in the programme, but in taking a retrograde step at all from the standpoint of a class movement to that of a sectarian movement.

That the workers desire to establish the conditions for cooperative production on a social scale, and first of all on a national scale, in their own country, only means that they are working to transform the present conditions of production, and it has nothing in common with the foundation of cooperative societies with state aid. But as far as the present cooperative societies are concerned, they are of value *only* insofar as they are the independent creations of the workers and not protégés either of the governments or of the bourgeois.

IV

I come now to the democratic section.

A. *"The free basis of the state."*

First of all, according to II, the German workers' party strives for "the free state."

Free state—what is it?

It is by no means the purpose of the workers, who have got rid of the narrow mentality of humble subjects, to set the state "free." In the German Empire the "state" is almost as "free" as in Russia. Freedom consists in converting the state from an organ superimposed upon society into one completely subordinate to it, and even today forms of state are more free or less free to the extent that they restrict the "freedom of the state."

The German workers' party—at least if it adopts the programme—shows that its socialist ideas are not even skin-deep, in that, instead of treating existing society (and this holds good for any future one) as the *basis* of the existing *state* (or of the future state in the case of future society), it treats the state rather as an independent entity that possesses its own *"intellectual, ethical and libertarian bases."*

And what of the wild abuse which the programme makes of the words *"present-day state," "present-day society,"* and of the still more riotous misconception it creates in regard to the state to which it addresses its demands?

"Present-day society" is capitalist society, which exists in all civilised countries, more or less free from me-

dieval admixture, more or less modified by the particular historical development of each country, more or less developed. On the other hand, the "present-day state" changes with a country's frontier. It is different in the Prusso-German Empire from that in Switzerland, and different in England from that in the United States. "The *present-day* state" is, therefore, a fiction.

Nevertheless, the different states of the different civilised countries, in spite of their motley diversity of form, all have this in common that they are based on modern bourgeois society, more or less capitalistically developed. They have, therefore, also certain essential characteristics in common. In this sense it is possible to speak of the "present-day state," in contrast with the future, in which its present root, bourgeois society, will have died off.

The question then arises: what transformation will the state undergo in communist society? In other words, what social functions will remain in existence there that are analogous to present state functions? This question can only be answered scientifically, and one does not get a flea-hop nearer to the problem by a thousandfold combination of the word people with the word state.

Between capitalist and communist society lies the period of the revolutionary transformation of the one into the other. Corresponding to this is also a political transition period in which the state can be nothing but *the revolutionary dictatorship of the proletariat.*

Now the programme deals neither with this nor with the future state of communist society.

Its political demands contain nothing beyond the old democratic litany familiar to all: universal suffrage, direct legislation, popular rights, a people's militia, etc. They are a mere echo of the bourgeois People's Party, of the League of Peace and Freedom. They are all demands which, insofar as they are not exaggerated in fantastic presentation, have already been *implemented.* Only the state to which they belong does not lie within the borders of the German Empire, but in Switzerland, the United States, etc. This sort of "state of the future" is a *present-day state,* although existing outside the "framework" of the German Empire.

But one thing has been forgotten. Since the German worker's party expressly declares that it acts within "the present-day national state," hence within its own state, the Prusso-German Empire — its demands would indeed otherwise be largely meaningless, since one only demands what one has not yet got — it should not have forgotten the chief thing, namely that all those pretty little gewgaws rest on the recognition of what is called sovereignty of the people and hence are appropriate only in a *democratic republic*.

Since one has not the courage — and wisely so, for the circumstances demand caution — to demand the democratic republic, as the French workers' programmes under Louis Philippe and under Louis Napoleon did, one should not have resorted to the subterfuge, neither "honest" nor decent, of demanding things which have meaning only in a democratic republic from a state which is nothing but a police-guarded military despotism, embellished with parliamentary forms, alloyed with a feudal admixture and at the same time already influenced by the bourgeoisie, and bureaucratically carpentered, and then assuring this state into the bargain that one imagines one will be able to force such things upon it "by legal means."

Even vulgar democracy, which sees the millennium in the democratic republic and has no suspicion that it is precisely in this last form of state of bourgeois society that the class struggle has to be fought out to a conclusion — even it towers mountains above this kind of democratism which keeps within the limits of what is permitted by the police and not permitted by logic.

That, in fact, by the word "state" is meant the government machine or the state insofar as it forms a special organism separated from society through division of labour, is shown alone by the words

> "the German workers' party demands *as the economic basis of the state*: a single progressive income tax," etc.

Taxes are in the economic basis of the government machinery and of nothing else. In the state of the future existing in Switzerland, this demand has been pretty well fulfilled. Income tax presupposes various sources of income of the various social classes, and hence capitalist society. It is, therefore, nothing remarkable that the Liverpool FINANCIAL REFORM-ERS, bourgeois headed by Gladstone's brother, are putting forward the same demand as the programme.

B. "The German workers' party demands as the intellectual and ethical basis of the state:

1. "Universal and *equal education of the people* by the state. Universal compulsory school attendance. Free instruction."

Equal education of the people? What idea lies behind these words? Is it believed that in present-day society (and it is only with this that one is dealing) education can be *equal* for all classes? Or is it demanded that the upper classes also shall be compulsorily reduced to the modicum of education — the elementary school — that alone is compatible with the economic conditions not only of the wage labourers but of the peasants as well?

"Universal compulsory school attendance. Free instruction." The former exists even in Germany, the latter in Switzerland and in the United States in the case of elementary schools. If in some states of the latter country "upper" educational institutions are also "free," that only means in fact defraying the cost of the education of the upper classes from the general tax receipts. Incidentally, the same holds good for "free administration of justice" demanded under A, 5. The administration of criminal justice is to be had free everywhere; that of civil justice is concerned almost exclusively with conflicts over property and hence affects almost exclusively the propertied classes. Are they to carry on their litigation at the expense of the national coffers?

The paragraph on the schools should at least have demanded technical schools (theoretical and practical) in combination with the elementary school.

"Education of the people by the state" is altogether objectionable. Defining by a general law the expenditures on the elementary schools, the qualifications of the teaching staff, the subjects of instruction, etc., and, as is done in the United States, supervising the fulfilment of these legal specifications by state inspectors, is a very different thing from appointing the state as the educator of the people! Government and Church should rather be equally excluded from any influence on the school. Particularly, indeed, in the Prusso-Ger-

man Empire (and one should not take refuge in the rotten subterfuge that one is speaking of a "state of the future;" we have seen how matters stand in this respect) the state has need, on the contrary, of a very stern education by the people.

But the whole programme, for all its democratic clang, is tainted through and through by the Lassallean sect's servile belief in the state, or, what is no better, by a democratic belief in miracles, or rather it is a compromise between these two kinds of belief in miracles, both equally remote from socialism.

"Freedom of science" says a paragraph of the Prussian Constitution. Why, then, here?

"Freedom of conscience"! If one desired at this time of the *Kulturkampf* to remind liberalism of its old catchwords, it surely could have been done only in the following form: Everyone should be able to attend to his religious as well as his bodily needs without the police sticking their noses in. But the workers' party ought at any rate in this connection to have expressed its awareness of the fact that bourgeois "freedom of conscience" is nothing but the toleration of all possible kinds of *religious unfreedom of conscience*, and that for its part it endeavours rather to liberate the conscience from the witchery of religion. But one chooses not to transgress the "bourgeois" level.

8

NIETZSCHE FOR AND AGAINST

Modern political thought begins with Machiavelli; it ends (many would claim) with an admirer of his, Friedrich Nietzsche (1844–1900). The interpretation of Nietzsche, though, is far more problematic than that of Machiavelli. First, this is because we cannot read Nietzsche "innocently," for we cannot help being constantly reminded of the uses to which Nazism put his arguments. Second, disputes over his work form a key battleground in the raging conflict between those who see themselves as continuing the Enlightenment enterprise (the "moderns") and their opponents, who describe themselves as postmodernists and/or deconstructionists and who argue that all claims to "correct" interpretations of texts or to "accurate" representations of the world must be abandoned. Nietzsche's hostility to Enlightenment arguments makes it reasonable to think of him as the first of the "postmoderns," but, in fact, his views on knowledge and interpretation are far from being identical with those of the deconstructionists.

My casual use of the phrase 'in fact' betrays this as no impartial account of Nietzsche's views. In the few pages which follow I will present both a sympathetic exposition and a critique of Nietzsche, but the reading I propose is only one of many competing readings, and the importance of Nietzsche lies not only in what he says but also in the uses to which he can be put. Nietzsche, for example, was contemptuous of feminism, yet many feminists turn to him as the first theorist of "the other" and of "difference." Nietzsche hated democracy and liberalism, yet some democrats call for a post-Nietzschean liberalism. If these enterprises are misconceived (as I think they are) it is not primarily because they are based on misinterpretations of Nietzsche's work, but because they are based on misunderstandings of how a feminist or liberal argument needs to run.

Before we can proceed, we need to clear out of the way two misconceptions about Nietzsche. The first is that because he was admired by the Nazis he must have been an anti-Semite. On this question the record is clear. Nietzsche was consistently opposed to "this accursed anti-Semitism." He was hostile to German nationalism (describing himself as "a bad German") and favored European unification (calling himself "a very good European"). He thought that the Jews should be assimilated if they wished to be, and that "the anti-Semitic bawlers" should be banished from the country if this would help the development of a new "European" culture. Nietzsche's sister, Elisabeth Förster-Nietzsche, was a vicious anti-Semite, who, after his death, encouraged the Nazis to claim him as one of their own. And, if Nietzsche can be exonerated of the charge of anti-Semitism, some of his views were naturally attractive to fascism. He defended violence and even cruelty; he believed in inequality and even slavery. He had contempt for democracy. These are the real charges against him.

Second, Nietzsche did not hold that there were an infinite number of equally good interpretations either of nature or of any text. As a young man he wrote, "What then is truth? A mobile army of metaphors, metonymies, anthropomorphisms, a sum, in short, of human relationships which, rhetorically and poetically intensified, ornamented and transformed, come to be thought of, after long usage by a people, as fixed, binding, and canonical. Truths are illusions which we have forgotten are illusions, worn-out metaphors now impotent to stir the senses, coins which have lost their faces and are considered now as metal rather than currency." Throughout his life he was to hold to this view that truths, like coins, are artificial, not natural. He consistently dismissed the idea "that things possess a constitution in themselves quite apart from interpretation and subjectivity" as "a quite idle hypothesis." In other words, knowledge is always the result of a creative act, an act which is necessarily subjective and can never be impartial: Knowledge is always the result of an act of interpretation and is always knowledge from a certain point of view. This claim may not be compatible with the conviction that some interpretations of reality simply correspond to the facts, but it is entirely compatible with the claim that some points of view give one a clearer picture than others, that some currencies have greater purchasing power than others. Nietzsche is hostile to positivism, on the one hand, and to an unchecked scepticism or relativism, on the other. The position he adopts is unstable and ambiguous, his expressions varying depending on which enemy he is combatting, but it is clear that, even if he has his deconstructionist moments, he is no deconstructionist.

Where, then, to begin in seeking to interpret Nietzsche? A useful starting point is his rejection of the conviction that had been shared by Hobbes, Locke, Hume, and Mill: that human beings seek pleasure and flee pain. Out of this conviction it was easy to construct a morality which insisted that humans should help others in their quest for pleasure and avoid inflicting unnecessary pain. Nietzsche's response to this whole line of thought was simple and devastating: People enjoy inflicting pain and take pleasure in cruelty, so that pleasures cannot be harmonized. Indeed, people take satisfaction in deliberately inflicting pain on themselves (including through hard work, self-discipline, and chastity, through asceticism). Nietzsche insisted that it was impossible to make sense of human behavior by interpreting human beings as pleasure-seeking animals. Nor were humans self-mortifying merely because they were caught up in a struggle for survival which obliged them to exercise self-discipline, for why, then, would they take pleasure in inflicting pain on others?

The only viable explanation of human behavior, Nietzsche believed, was that there was a universal "will to power." The strong take pleasure in exercising power over others; the weak are reduced to taking pleasure in exercising power over themselves. How could one take pleasure in inflicting pain on oneself? For Nietzsche, as later for Freud, the idea that one takes pleasure in one's own pain is not an empty paradox, because there is no unitary self. The runner whose feet hurt takes pleasure in his own strength and chooses to ignore the fact that what he is actually experiencing is pain. The saint fasts so that he may be holier than others and regards the pangs of hunger as a small price to pay. Pleasure and pain can thus be interpreted only in the context of a more fundamental drive, a drive that transmutes pains into pleasures and pleasures into pains, and this drive is the will to power.

Nietzsche's reinterpretation of human behavior in terms of a will to power makes conventional morality untenable. It does not follow from his analysis that overt cruelty and violence are bound to be part of daily life, any more than Freud's account of the pervasiveness of sexual drives implies that promiscuity and adultery must be the norm. But just as Freud's analysis implies that, when people seem least interested in sex (when studying philosophy, for example), they must be sublimating a sexual drive, so Nietzsche's analysis implies that, when they are outwardly peaceable (when playing chess, to take an apposite example), they must be seeking to dominate others. What Nietzsche and Freud aim to transform, in their different ways, is our understanding of motive, and just as a Freudian will find the notion of a Platonic friendship inherently problematic, so a Nietzschean must find the idea of a society of equals superficial and misleading.

In Nietzsche's view, conventional morality, with its invocation, for example, to do unto others as you would be done by, could only be adopted in a world where people had lost touch with their real motives. Moreover, conventional morality depends on a series of concepts—the will, the soul—which cannot be shown to refer to anything in the real world. How, then, did morality arise? Nietzsche thinks it easy to explain how the categories of good and bad would have been used by people who loved power and pursued simple pleasures (including the pleasures of rape and rapine). But how did the fictitious categories of good and evil arise? This is Nietzsche's problem of the genealogy of morals. Like Mandeville, he believes that human beings are not naturally moral and that they have become domesticated over time. Indeed, he would claim that it is the capacity for moral behavior—the ability to make promises, to admit guilt—which makes human beings *human*. It follows, then, that human beings are not naturally human at all, but, insofar as they are animals, are subhuman or prehuman. If morality is the result of an historical process of domestication, who invented it? Nietzsche's answer is that the weak, the victims of rape and rapine, who were looking for whatever weapons they could find to use against the strong, were the inventors of morality.

In Nietzsche's view, it is the discovery of guilt (rather than tools or language) which makes human beings. Consequently, just as one can conceive of prehumans, one can imagine posthumans or, to use a more conventional translation, Overmen or, alternatively, Supermen. If human beings are the product of an historical process, then something, somebody, may come after us, and, if we are lucky, this new person will be someone freed from the illusion of morality (with its inevitable concomitants, shame, disgrace, guilt, and remorse), a posthuman, able to pursue power not with the feeble indirection of a moralist, but frankly and openly. Nietzsche's analysis of morality implies that it may be possible to go "beyond good and evil," to "revalue all values," to escape the confusion of moral codes which have concealed from men their biological nature, their will to power.

Nietzsche's genealogy of morals is thus an attempt to give a naturalistic explanation of how and why humans might have invented morality. It relies upon two interrelated presumptions. First, there is no human essence seeking to realize itself in history. Nietzsche turns his back on all teleologies which claim there is a purpose or direction to history. It is perfectly conceivable that humans might never have been domesticated, and the Overman may never develop. History has no in-built logic or justification. Second, Nietzsche takes it for granted that there is no divine sanction for morality and no afterlife in which the cruel will be punished and the meek will inherit the earth. In the Germany of his day, Christian belief was in sharp decline, and Nietzsche (himself the son and grandson of clergymen) thought it perfectly reasonable to presume the "death of God." In a Godless world there are no inherent moral values, only biological drives, and the puzzle is how these drives could cause people to invent God, morality, and the soul.

Christian morality, Nietzsche believed, was founded in a grotesque misunderstanding of the world. A religion designed to empower the feeble in their struggle with the strong, it had been all too successful, driving the will to power through tortuous and hypocritical detours. But, paradoxically, Christian claims to knowledge and Christian practices of self-discipline had opened the way to modern science, which had dissolved faith itself. Nietzsche believed that he lived in an age of nihilism, when the beliefs which had seemed to give meaning to existence had been irrevocably undermined, and human beings were left only with a series of shallow practices—self-discipline, the pursuit of knowledge, self-sacrifice—which no longer made sense. But his response was that human beings must embrace nihilism, not evade it. It was this that the ancient Greeks had understood: that it would be better not to have been born, and that, failing that, one should hope to die soon. Life involves suffering, and death offers neither meaning nor justification. How can one face these harsh truths? In Nietzsche's view, they cannot be moralized: It is morality's inability to face them honestly which shows the urgent need to go beyond good and evil. But what lies beyond good and evil? Both pleasure and power are transitory and are easily overwhelmed by pain and death. Nietzsche believes that there are two appropriate responses to this state of affairs, comedy and tragedy. We can laugh at disaster; we can face despair and transform it into a thing of beauty. Beyond morality, in Nietzsche's view, lies the world of art, and the greatest work of art is not a statue or a play, but a human life itself. Nietzsche thus believes in discipline, self-mastery, courage, gentleness, not because these are moral categories, but because they represent aesthetic accomplishments. To escape from the human, all too human, we must rediscover the idea that it is art, not morality, that makes sense of life. Hence Nietzsche preached what he termed "a gay science": true knowledge must lead one to laughter, not mere learning.

We have now touched on some of Nietzsche's characteristic doctrines—the will to power, the overman, the step beyond good and evil, the paradoxical rejection and embrace of nihilism. There remain three points to make. The first can be made by comparing Nietzsche with Hume. Hume, like Nietzsche, thought that much of morality was an artificial invention. Like Nietzsche he thought that we will never understand the "secret springs" of the world: Even the concept of causation was one invented by us and foisted on the world around us, not something that we had found in nature. Like Nietzsche, Hume wanted to rescue human beings from an ascetic morality which had led them to have contempt for physical pleasure and to seek a justification for existence outside the world of daily experience. Like Nietzsche, Hume denied there was any unitary self which could be held responsible or found guilty. In many respects Nietzsche simply presses home Hume's sceptical attack on Christianity, metaphysics, and teleology. But Hume believed that, given their natural capacities and needs, human beings, anywhere and everywhere, would be driven to invent property, promises, and responsibility. Nietzsche insists that ours is only one possible genealogy. In other cultures, other times, other places, quite different values and institutions might emerge. Moreover, Hume insists that property, promises, and responsibility were artificial constructs designed to serve a continuing purpose, while Nietzsche believes that to understand how a cultural practice came into existence may help explain why it exists today, but it does not follow that, because it once fulfilled a function, it still fulfills the same (or any) function.

Here we can glimpse the pervasive influence of Darwin on Nietzsche's thought. Just as lungs evolved from gills, hands from flippers, so contemporary practices may have had historical antecedents quite different in form and function and may give rise to unimaginable future social systems. Humans as they are now are no guide to posthumans as they may once be, nor is the good of humanity the ultimate standard, for humans, like Neanderthals, may be doomed to extinction, to be replaced by some species with a more effective will to power. Darwinism encourages Nietzsche to adopt a radical historical relativism (the end result of history is entirely unpredictable), while he interprets it as offering a standard of value which enables one to step back not only from the welfare of individuals but even from the welfare of the species (to think, not in terms of good and evil, or mere survival, but of the survival of those who best embody a universal will to power). Moreover, Darwin suggested a fundamental principle of interpretation. He had argued that what appeared to be aesthetic standards (embodied, for example, in the peacock's tail) were in fact tactics for reproduction, so for Nietzsche moral values could be reduced to a comparable biological drive, the will to power. Nietzsche was no simple Darwinist, for he thought Darwin had underestimated the "active" principle in biological adaptation, and he had sympathies with Lamarck, but Darwin's stress on competition and struggle seems to provide a basic reference point for much of his thought.

If Darwinism opens the way to a much more historical mode of thought than Hume had imagined possible, it (and much else in nineteenth-century thought) constantly invites Nietzsche to adopt biological and medical metaphors, in the belief that they are more than mere metaphors, are rather true perspectives on reality. Here is a distinguished Nietzsche scholar, Alexander Nehamas, tackling a central problem for any student of Nietzsche:

> Let us suppose (a considerable supposition!) that morality is an interpretation. What is it an interpretation of? Nietzsche's general answer is that it is an interpretation of the phenomenon to which he refers as "human suffering." His own attitude toward this phenomenon is very complex. In one mood, he debunks it. He attributes it not to a divine cause (as, we shall see, he claims that morality does), not even to anything serious, but to the lowest and crudest physiological causes. Such a cause, he writes, "may perhaps lie in some disease of the *nervus sympathicus,* or in an excessive secretion of bile, or in a deficiency in potassium sulphate and phosphate in the blood, or in an obstruction of the abdomen which impedes the blood circulation, or in degeneration of the ovaries and the like." For years, I considered this as one of those horribly embarrassing passages that Nietzsche's readers inevitably have to put up with in defensive silence. Then I realized that Nietzsche was actually making a joke. . . .

Nehamas goes on to explicate Nietzsche's amusing reference to "the (nonexistent) *nervus sympathicus,*" and to laugh at "ovarian degeneration (whatever that is)." Frankly, this is a bit like a commentator on Augustine talking of "the (nonexistent) soul" or "original sin (whatever that is)." Nietzsche (who was usually ill, and in pain) is perfectly serious about physiology, as should be apparent from his note at the end of the first essay of the *Genealogy.* Just as we prefer to read Freud as an interpreter of dreams rather than as a theorist of brain function, so we prefer to read Nietzsche as an interpreter of morals rather than as a theorist of the moral effects of disease, but if we are going to be Nietzscheans, if we are going to face squarely the origins of our beliefs, then we should not dismiss as a joke something that he intended perfectly seriously, even if this enables us to avoid embarrassment.

My title is "Nietzsche For and Against." For myself, I believe one can defend Nietzsche's epistemology, his radical historicism, even, under certain circumstances, his retreat from morality to aesthetics. His misconceived Darwinism and his crude biological determinism deserve to be understood, but they cannot be defended. In the end, though, there is one central defect in Nietzsche's politics. We can trace it in his attitude to tragedy, which he both admired (since it faced suffering without blinking) and rejected (because it was a public drama designed to entertain the common man). Or in his preference for aristocratic Sparta over democratic Athens. Martha Nussbaum finds it in his admiration for mercy, but contempt for pity. Best of all, Philippa Foot, in a classic essay on "Nietzsche's Immoralism" remarks: "Nietzsche says at one point that contempt is better than hatred, and of course he thinks the idea of equality utterly despicable. Now what I wonder is this: whether the practice of justice may not absolutely require a certain recognition of equality between human beings. . . ."

Nietzsche's commitment to inequality presents two problems. First, Nietzsche was hostile to any morality founded in what he terms *ressentiment,* yet, in any society in which inequality is prevalent and justice is denied, resentment will (quite properly) flourish. By seeking to reproduce a society of slaves and masters, by aiming to foster inequality in all its forms, he condemns human beings to experience yet again all the confusions and hypocrisies for which he has such contempt. Second, on Nietzsche's own analysis, human history since written records began has been marked by the progressive triumph of the weak over the strong, the apparently irreversible moralization of society. In a fragment written some six months after *On the Genealogy of Morality* (1887) and some eighteen months before he slipped into permanent madness, Nietzsche questioned whether Darwin had been right to assume that competition favors the strong, for in society at least the reverse principle seems to hold:

> The strongest and most fortunate are weak when opposed by organized herd instincts, by the timidity of the weak, by the vast majority. My general view of the world of values shows that it is not the lucky strokes, the select types, that have the upper hand in the supreme values that are today placed over mankind; rather it is the decadent types—perhaps there is nothing in the world more interesting than this *unwelcome* spectacle—. . . . If one translates reality into a morality, this morality is: The mediocre are worth more than the exceptions; the decadent forms more than the mediocre; the will to nothingness has the upper hand over the will to life. . . . I rebel against the translation of reality into a morality. . . . a reality that is the reverse of the struggle for existence as taught by Darwin's school. . . . I find the "cruelty of nature," of which so much is said, in another place: She is cruel towards her children of fortune, she spares and protects and loves the meek. . . . (*Will to Power,* 685, translated by Kaufmann and Hollingdale)

Machiavelli, whom Nietzsche admired, might have led him to address the same problem in slightly different terms: Popular governments are always stronger than tyrannies or aristocracies. If he accepts this argument, Nietzsche faces a serious dilemma. His values are based not on conventional morality, nor (like Machiavelli's) on practical reality, nor (like those of Freudians or social Darwinists) on an appeal to an irresistible natural principle. What, then, can they be based on? The answer (in the absence of religion) would seem to be an aesthetic preference for the strong and independent individual. But this is not, I think, his position in *On the Genealogy of Morality,* nor in another fragment from 1888 in which he insists that there must (despite appearances) be a "real world" to which he can appeal, and talks of the "restoration of nature" (401). Nietzsche believes he is arguing on the side, not only of beauty, but also of man's true nature, which is that of "the Darwinian beast." Take away his claim to ground his argument in nature, and it becomes easy to argue that the meek are entitled to inherit the earth. When Nietzsche argues against Darwin he destroys his own position.

Suggestions for Further Reading

A standard introduction is R. J. Hollingdale, *Nietzsche: The Man and His Philosophy* (Baton Rouge: Louisiana State University Press, 1965). For a survey of his political thought there is Keith Ansell-Pearson, *An Introduction to Nietzsche As Political Thinker* (Cambridge: Cambridge University Press, 1994). Invaluable is Richard Schacht (ed.), *Nietzsche, Genealogy, Morality: Essays on Nietzsche's*

"Genealogy of Morals" (Berkeley: University of California Press, 1994), since it reflects a diversity of points of view (for myself, I found the essays by Foot, Solomon, Nussbaum, MacIntyre, and Leiter particularly helpful). What appears to be missing from the Nietzsche literature is a book comparable to Richard Wollheim's *Sigmund Freud* (Cambridge: Cambridge University Press, 1990), which takes nineteenth-century physiology literally. On Nietzsche and Darwin, see Daniel C. Dennett, *Darwin's Dangerous Idea* (London: Allen Lane, 1995).

Three writers are of particular importance if one wants to trace Nietzsche's contemporary influence. Fundamental is Michel Foucault's *Discipline and Punish* (London: Allen Lane, 1977) and his "Nietzsche, Genealogy, and History," in Paul Rabinow (ed.), *The Foucault Reader* (New York: Pantheon Books, 1984). On Foucault see Gary Gutting (ed.), *The Cambridge Companion to Foucault* (Cambridge: Cambridge University Press, 1994). For a reading of Nietzsche influenced by Heidegger, see Jacques Derrida, *Spurs: Nietzsche's Styles,* trans. B. Harlow (Chicago: University of Chicago Press, 1979). And for attempts to reconcile some aspects of Nietzsche with some aspects of liberalism, see Richard Rorty, *Contingency, Irony, and Solidarity* (Cambridge: Cambridge University Press, 1989) and William Connolly, *Political Theory and Modernity* (Oxford: Blackwell, 1988).

Finally, for a study which carries many of the themes of this reader into the twentieth century, I recommend Stephen Holmes, *The Anatomy of Antiliberalism* (Cambridge Mass.: Harvard University Press, 1993).

NIETZSCHE

On the Genealogy of Morality

PREFACE

1

We are unknown to ourselves, we knowers: and for a good reason. We have never sought ourselves—how then should it happen that we *find* ourselves one day? It has rightly been said: "where your treasure is, there will your heart be also";[1] *our* treasure is where the beehives of our knowledge stand. We are forever underway toward them, as born winged animals and honey-gatherers of the spirit, concerned with all our heart about only one thing—"bringing home" something. As for the rest of life, the so-called "experiences"—who of us even has enough seriousness for them? Or enough time? In such matters I'm afraid we were never really "with it": we just don't have our heart there—or even our ear! Rather, much as a divinely distracted, self-absorbed person into whose ear the bell has just boomed its twelve strokes of noon suddenly awakens and wonders, "what did it actually toll just now?" so we rub our ears *afterwards* and ask, completely amazed, completely disconcerted, "what did we actually experience just now?" still more: "who *are* we actually?" and count up, afterwards, as stated, all twelve quavering bell-strokes of our experience, of our life, of our *being*—alas! and miscount in the process . . . We remain of necessity strangers to ourselves, we do not understand ourselves, we *must* mistake ourselves, for us the maxim reads to all eternity: "each is furthest from himself,"—with respect to ourselves we are not "knowers" . . .

From Nietzsche, *On the Genealogy of Morality*, translated by Maudemarie Clark and Alan J. Swensen copyright © 1998. Reprinted by permission of the publisher.
[1] [Matthew 6:21.]

2

—My thoughts on the *origins* of our moral prejudices—for that is what this polemic is about—found their first, economical, and preliminary expression in the collection of aphorisms that bears the title *Human, All Too Human: A Book for Free Spirits*, the writing of that was begun in Sorrento during a winter that permitted me to pause, as a traveler pauses, and look out over the broad and dangerous land through which my spirit had thus far traveled. This occurred in the winter of 1876–77; the thoughts themselves are older. In essentials they were already the same thoughts which I now take up again in the treatises at hand: let us hope that the long period in between has been good for them, that they have become more mature, brighter, stronger, more perfect! That I still hold fast to them today, that they themselves have, in the meantime, held to each other ever more firmly, indeed have grown into each other and become intermeshed, strengthens within me the cheerful confidence that they came about not singly, not arbitrarily, not sporadically, but rather from the beginning arose out of a common root, out of a *basic will* of knowledge which commands from deep within, speaking ever more precisely, demanding something ever more precise. For this alone is fitting for a philosopher. We have no right to be *single* in anything: we may neither err singly nor hit upon the truth singly. Rather, with the necessity with which a tree bears its fruit our thoughts grow out of us, our values, our yes's and no's and if's and whether's—the whole lot related and connected among themselves, witnesses to one will, one health, one earthly kingdom, one sun.—And do they taste good *to you*, these fruits of ours?—But of what concern is that to the trees! Of what concern is that *to us*, us philosophers! . . .

3

Given a skepticism that is characteristic of me, to which I reluctantly admit—for it is directed towards *morality*, towards everything on earth that has until now been celebrated as morality—a skepticism that first appeared so early in my life, so spontaneously, so irrepressibly, so much in contradiction to my environment, age, models, origins, that I almost have the right to call it my *"a priori"*—it was inevitable that early on my curiosity and my suspicion as well would stop at the question: *what*, in fact, is the *origin* of our good and evil? In fact, the problem of the origin of evil haunted me as a thirteen-year-old lad: at an age when one has "half child's play, half God in one's heart,"[2] I devoted my first literary child's play to it, my first philosophic writing exercise—and as to my "solution" to the problem back then, well, I gave the honor to God, as is fitting, and made him the *father* of evil. Was *this* what my *"a priori"*[3] wished of me? that new, immoral, at least immoralistic "a priori" and the, alas! so anti-Kantian, so mysterious "categorical imperative" speaking through it, to which I have since increasingly lent my ear, and not just my ear? . . . Fortunately I learned early on to distinguish theological from moral prejudice and no longer sought the origin of evil *behind* the world. A little historical and philological schooling, combined with an innate sense of discrimination in all psychological questions, soon transformed my problem into a different one: under what conditions did man invent those value judgments good and evil? *and what value do they themselves have?* Have they inhibited or furthered human flourishing up until now? Are they a sign of distress, of impoverishment, of the degeneration of life? Or, conversely, do they betray the fullness, the power, the will of life, its courage, its confidence, its future?—In response I found and ventured a number of answers; I distinguished ages, peoples, degrees of rank among individuals; I divided up my problem; out of the answers came new questions, in-

vestigations, conjectures, probabilities: until I finally had a land of my own, a ground of my own, an entire unspoken growing blossoming world, secret gardens as it were, of which no one was permitted even an inkling . . . O how we are *happy*, we knowers, provided we simply know how to be silent long enough! . . .

4

The first impetus to divulge something of my hypotheses on the origin of morality came to me from a clear, tidy, and smart, even overly smart little book in which for the first time I was clearly confronted by the reverse and perverse sort of genealogical hypotheses, the specifically *English* sort, and this book attracted me—with that power of attraction exerted by everything contrary, everything antipodal. The title of the little book was *The Origin of Moral Sensations*; its author, Dr. Paul Rée;[4] the year of its publication, 1877. I may never have read anything to which I so emphatically said "no" as I did to this book, proposition by proposition, conclusion by conclusion: and yet entirely without vexation or impatience. In the previously named volume on which I was then working, I made occasional and occasionally inopportune reference to the propositions of that book, not that I refuted them—what have I to do with refutations!—but rather, as befits a positive spirit, putting in place of the improbable the more probable, sometimes in place of one error another one. It was then, as mentioned, that I brought into the light of day those hypotheses concerning origins to which these treatises are devoted, clumsily, as I wish last of all to conceal from myself—still unfree, still without a language of my own for these

---

[2] [Lines 3781–82 of Goethe's *Faust, Part One* —M.C.]

[3] [Nonempirical or independent of experience; literally: from what is before.]

[4] [Dr. Paul Rée (1849–1901), doctor of law, philosopher, physician. N met Rée in 1873 and the two developed a close friendship. They shared a commitment to providing an explanation of morality in completely naturalistic terms, without reference to religious or metaphysical sources and taking account only of what can be known of human beings from a scientific point of view. Their relationship ended badly in the winter of 1882–83 due to complications within the "trinity" the two men had formed with a young Russian woman, Lou Andreas-Salomé.]

things of my own, and with many a relapse and wavering. In particular, compare what I say in *Human, All Too Human* 45, on the dual pre-history of good and evil (namely out of the sphere of the nobles and that of the slaves); likewise section 136, on the value and origins of ascetic morality; likewise 96, 99, and volume II, 89, on the "morality of custom," that much older and more original kind of morality that is removed *toto caelo*[5] from the altruistic manner of valuation (which Dr. Rée, like all English genealogists of morality, sees as the moral manner of valuation *in itself*); likewise volume I, 92; *Wanderer*, section 26; *Daybreak*, 112, on the origins of justice as a settlement between approximately equal powers (equilibrium as presupposition of all contracts, accordingly of all law); likewise *Wanderer* 22 and 33, on the origins of punishment, for which the purpose of terrorizing is neither essential nor present at the beginning (as Dr. Rée believes: —rather this was inserted into it, under specific circumstances, and always as something incidental, as something additional).

5

Actually there was something much more important on my mind just then than my own or anyone else's hypothesizing about the origin of morality (or, more precisely: the latter concerned me solely for the sake of an end to which it is one means among many). The issue for me was the *value* of morality—and over this I had to struggle almost solely with my great teacher Schopenhauer,[6] to whom that book, the passion and the secret contradiction of that book, is directed, as if to a contemporary (—for that book, too, was a "polemic"). In particular the issue was the value of the unegoistic, of the instincts of compassion, self-denial, self-sacrifice, precisely the instincts that Schopenhauer had

gilded, deified, and made otherworldly until finally they alone were left for him as the "values in themselves," on the basis of which he *said "no"* to life, also to himself. But against precisely *these* instincts there spoke from within me an ever more fundamental suspicion, an ever deeper-delving skepticism! Precisely here I saw the *great* danger to humanity, its most sublime lure and temptation—and into what? into nothingness?—precisely here I saw the beginning of the end, the standstill, the backward-glancing tiredness, the will turning *against* life, the last sickness gently and melancholically announcing itself: I understood the ever more widely spreading morality of compassion—which seized even the philosophers and made them sick—as the most uncanny symptom of our now uncanny European culture, as its detour to a new Buddhism? to a Buddhism for Europeans? to—*nihilism?* . . . For this preferential treatment and overestimation of compassion on the part of modern philosophers is something new: until this point philosophers had agreed precisely on the *worthlessness* of compassion. I name only Plato, Spinoza,[7] La Rochefoucauld,[8] and Kant, four spirits as different from each other as possible, but united on one point: their low regard for compassion. —

6

This problem of the *value* of compassion and of the morality of compassion (—I am an opponent of the disgraceful modern softening of feelings—) appears at first to be only an isolated matter, a lone question mark; whoever sticks here for once, however, and

---

[5] [By a tremendous distance; literally: by all of heaven.]

[6] [Arthur Schopenhauer (1788–1860), sometimes described as the "philosopher of pessimism." Largely ignored until very late in his life, he became the most widely read German philosopher in the English-speaking world during the second half of the nineteenth century.]

[7] [Baruch (Benedict) Spinoza (1632–1677), Dutch-Jewish philosopher, usually grouped with Descartes and Leibniz as one of the three most important modern rationalists; known especially for his attempt to overcome the dualism between mind and matter and for his "geometrical" method of presenting philosophy. Spinoza's major work, *Ethica*, was published by his friends shortly after his death.]

[8] [François VI, duc de La Rochefoucauld (1613–1680), French aristocrat and classical author. La Rochefoucauld's only major work, the *Maximes*, is a collection of maxims or aphorisms—a literary form that aims at expressing a truth in a brief and pointed and sometimes paradoxical form.]

learns to ask questions here, will fare as I have fared:—an immense new vista opens up to him, a possibility takes hold of him like a dizziness, every sort of mistrust, suspicion, fear springs forth, the belief in morality, in all morality totters,—finally a new challenge is heard. Let us speak it aloud, this *new challenge*: we need a *critique* of moral values, *for once the value of these values must itself be called into question*—and for this we need a knowledge of the conditions and circumstances out of which they have grown, under which they have developed and shifted (morality as consequence, as symptom, as mask, as Tartuffery, as sickness, as misunderstanding; but also morality as cause, as medicine, as stimulus, as inhibitor, as poison), knowledge of a kind that has neither existed up until now nor even been desired. One has taken the *value* of these "values" as given, as a fact, as beyond all calling-into-question; until now one has not had even the slightest doubt or hesitation in ranking "the good" as of higher value than "the evil," of higher value in the sense of its furtherance, usefulness, beneficiality—with respect to man *in general* (taking into account the future of man). What? if the opposite were true? What? if a symptom of regression also lay in the "good," likewise a danger, a temptation, a poison, a narcotic through which perhaps the present were living *at the expense of the future?* Perhaps more comfortably, less dangerously, but also in a reduced style, on a lower level? . . . So that precisely morality would be to blame if a *highest power and splendor* of the human type—in itself possible—were never attained? So that precisely morality were the danger of dangers? . . .

7

Suffice it to say that once this prospect opened up to me, I myself had reasons for looking about for learned, bold, and industrious comrades (I am still doing so today). It is a matter of traveling the vast, distant, and so concealed land of morality—of the morality which has really existed, really been lived—with a completely new set of questions and as it were with new eyes: and is this not virtually to *discover* this land for the first

time? . . . If in the process I thought of, among others, the above named Dr. Rée, this happened because I had no doubt that he would be pushed by the very nature of his questions to a more correct method of attaining answers. Did I deceive myself in this? My wish, in any case, was to turn so sharp and disinterested an eye in a better direction, the direction of the real *history of morality* and to warn him while there was still time against such English hypothesizing *into the blue*. It is of course obvious which color must be a hundred times more important to a genealogist of morality than blue: namely *gray*, which is to say, that which can be documented, which can really be ascertained, which has really existed, in short, the very long, difficult-to-decipher hieroglyphic writing of the human moral past! *This* was unknown to Dr. Rée; but he had read Darwin:[9]—and thus in his hypothesizing we have, in a manner that is at least entertaining, the Darwinian beast politely joining hands with the most modern, unassuming moral milquetoast who "no longer bites" —the latter with an expression of a certain good-natured and refined indolence on his face, into which is mixed even a grain of pessimism, of weariness: as if there weren't really any reward for taking all these things—the problems of morality—so seriously. To me it seems that, on the contrary, there are no things which would *reward* one more for taking them seriously; to which reward belongs, for example, that one might perhaps some day gain permission to take them *cheerfully*. For cheerfulness, or to say it in my language, *gay science*—is a reward: a reward for a long, brave, industrious, and subterranean seriousness that is admittedly not for everyone. On that day, however, when we say from a full heart: "Onward! even our old morality belongs *in comedy!*" we will have discovered a new complication and possibility for the Dionysian drama of the "Destiny of the Soul"—: and he will certainly make use of it, one can bet on that, he, the great old eternal comic poet of our existence! . . .

---

[9] [Charles Robert Darwin (1809–1882), English naturalist, author of *On the Origin of Species by Means of Natural Selection* (1859).]

8

—If this book is unintelligible to anyone and hard on the ears, the fault, as I see it, does not necessarily lie with me. It is clear enough, presupposing, as I do, that one has first read my earlier writings and has not spared some effort in the process: these are in fact not easily accessible. As far as my *Zarathustra* is concerned, for example, I count no one an authority on it who has not at sometime been deeply wounded and at sometime deeply delighted by each of its words: for only then may he enjoy the privilege of reverent participation in the halcyon element out of which the work was born, in its sunny brightness, distance, expanse, and certainty. In other cases the aphoristic form creates a difficulty—it lies in the fact that we don't attach *enough weight* to this form today. An aphorism honestly coined and cast has not been "deciphered" simply because it has been read through; rather its *interpretation* must now begin, and for this an art of interpretation is needed. In the third treatise of this book I have offered a sample of what I call "interpretation" in such a case:—an aphorism is placed before this treatise, the treatise itself is a commentary on it. Admittedly, to practice reading as an *art* in this way one thing above all is necessary, something which these days has been unlearned better than anything else— and it will therefore be a while before my writings are "readable"—something for which one must almost be a cow and in any case *not* a "modern man": *ruminating* . . .

Sils-Maria, Upper Engadine, in July 1887.

FIRST TREATISE: "GOOD AND EVIL," "GOOD AND BAD"

1

—These English psychologists whom we also have to thank for the only attempts so far to produce a history of the genesis of morality—they themselves are no small riddle for us; I confess, in fact, that precisely as riddles in the flesh they have something substantial over their books—*they themselves are interesting!* These English psychologists—what do they actually want? One finds them, whether voluntarily or involuntarily, always at the same task, namely of pushing the *partie honteuse*[10] of our inner world into the foreground and of seeking that which is actually effective, leading, decisive for our development, precisely where the intellectual pride of man would least of all *wish* to find it (for example in the *vis inertiae*[11] of habit or in forgetfulness or in a blind and accidental interlacing and mechanism of ideas or in anything purely passive, automatic, reflexive, molecular, and fundamentally mindless)—what is it actually that always drives these psychologists in precisely *this* direction? Is it a secret, malicious, base instinct to belittle mankind, one that perhaps cannot be acknowledged even to itself? Or, say, a pessimistic suspicion, the mistrust of disappointed, gloomy idealists who have become poisonous and green? Or a little subterranean animosity and rancor against Christianity (and Plato) that has perhaps not yet made it past the threshold of consciousness? Or even a lascivious taste for the disconcerting, for the painful-paradoxical, for the questionable and nonsensical aspects of existence? Or finally—a little of everything, a little meanness, a little gloominess, a little anti-Christianity, a little tickle and need for pepper? . . . But I am told that they are simply old, cold, boring frogs who creep and hop around on human beings, into human beings, as if they were really in their element there, namely in a *swamp*. I resist this, still more, I don't believe it; and if one is permitted to wish where one cannot know, then I wish from my heart that the reverse may be the case with them —that these explorers and microscopists of the soul are basically brave, magnanimous, and proud animals who know

---

[10] [Shameful part (in the plural, this expression is the equivalent of the English "private parts").]

[11] [Force of inactivity. In Newtonian physics, this term denotes the resistance offered by matter to any force tending to alter its state of rest or motion.]

how to keep a rein on their hearts as well as their pain and have trained themselves to sacrifice all desirability to truth, to *every* truth, even plain, harsh, ugly, unpleasant, unchristian, immoral truth . . . For there are such truths.—

2

Hats off then to whatever good spirits may be at work in these historians of morality! Unfortunately, however, it is certain that they lack the *historical spirit* itself, that they have been left in the lurch precisely by all the good spirits of history! As is simply the age-old practice among philosophers, they all think *essentially* ahistorically; of this there is no doubt. The ineptitude of their moral genealogy is exposed right at the beginning, where it is a matter of determining the origins of the concept and judgment "good." "Originally"— so they decree—"unegoistic actions were praised and called good from the perspective of those to whom they were rendered, hence for whom they were *useful*; later one *forgot* this origin of the praise and, simply because unegoistic actions were *as a matter of habit* always praised as good, one also felt them to be good— as if they were something good in themselves." One sees immediately: this first derivation already contains all the characteristic traits of the idiosyncrasy of English psychologists—we have "usefulness," "forgetting," "habit," and in the end "error," all as basis for a valuation of which the higher human being has until now been proud as if it were some kind of distinctive prerogative of humankind. This pride *must* be humbled, this valuation devalued: has this been achieved? . . . Now in the first place it is obvious to me that the actual genesis of the concept "good" is sought and fixed in the wrong place by this theory: the judgment "good" does *not* stem from those to whom "goodness" is rendered! Rather it was "the good" themselves, that is the noble, powerful, higher-ranking, and high-minded who felt and ranked themselves and their doings as good, which is to say, as of the first rank, in contrast to everything base, low-minded, common, and vulgar. Out of this *pathos of distance* they first took for themselves the right to create values, to coin names for values: what

did they care about usefulness! The viewpoint of utility is as foreign and inappropriate as possible, especially in relation to so hot an outpouring of highest rank-ordering, rank-distinguishing value judgments: for here feeling has arrived at an opposite of that low degree of warmth presupposed by every calculating prudence, every assessment of utility—and not just for once, for an hour of exception, but rather for the long run. As was stated, the pathos of nobility and distance, this lasting and dominant collective and basic feeling of a higher ruling nature in relation to a lower nature, to a "below"—*that* is the origin of the opposition "good" and "bad." (The right of lords to give names goes so far that we should allow ourselves to comprehend the origin of language itself as an expression of power on the part of those who rule: they say "this *is* such and such," they seal each thing and happening with a sound and thus, as it were, take possession of it.) It is because of this origin that from the outset the word "good" does *not* necessarily attach itself to "unegoistic" actions—as is the superstition of those genealogists of morality. On the contrary, only when aristocratic value judgments begin to *decline* does this entire opposition "egoistic" "unegoistic" impose itself more and more on the human conscience—to make use of my language, it is *the herd instinct* that finally finds a voice (also *words*) in this opposition. And even then it takes a long time until this instinct becomes dominant to such an extent that moral valuation in effect gets caught and stuck at that opposition (as is the case in present-day Europe: today the prejudice that takes "moral," "unegoistic," "*désintéressé*"[12] to be concepts of equal value already rules with the force of an "*idée fixe*"[13] and sickness in the head).

3

In the second place, however: quite apart from the historical untenability of that hypothesis concerning the origins of the value judgment "good," it suffers from an inherent psychological absurdity. The usefulness of

---

[12] [Disinterested, unselfish, selfless.]
[13] [Obsession; literally: a fixed idea.]

the unegoistic action is supposed to be the origin of its praise, and this origin is supposed to have been *forgotten:*—how is this forgetting even *possible?* Did the usefulness of such actions cease at some point? The opposite is the case: this usefulness has been the everyday experience in all ages, something therefore that was continually underscored anew; accordingly, instead of disappearing from consciousness, instead of becoming forgettable, it could not help but impress itself upon consciousness with ever greater clarity. How much more reasonable is that opposing theory (it is not therefore truer—) advocated for example by Herbert Spencer[14]—which ranks the concept "good" as essentially identical with the concept "useful," "purposive," so that in the judgments "good" and "bad" humanity has summed up and sanctioned its *unforgotten* and *unforgettable* experiences concerning what is useful-purposive, what is injurious-nonpurposive. Good, according to this theory, is whatever has proved itself as useful from time immemorial: it may thus claim validity as "valuable in the highest degree," as "valuable in itself." This path of explanation is also false, as noted above, but at least the explanation is in itself reasonable and psychologically tenable.

4

—The pointer to the *right* path was given to me by the question: what do the terms coined for "good" in the various languages actually mean from an etymological viewpoint? Here I found that they all lead back to the *same conceptual transformation*—that everywhere the basic concept is "noble," "aristocratic" in the sense of related to the estates, out of which "good" in the sense of "noble of soul," "high-natured of soul," "privileged of soul" necessarily develops: a development that always runs parallel to that other one which makes "common," "vulgar," "base" pass over finally into the concept "bad." The most eloquent example of the lat-

ter is the German word *"schlecht"* [bad] itself: which is identical with *"schlicht"* [plain, simple]—compare *"schlechtweg," "schlechterdings"* [simply or down-right] —and originally designated the plain, the common man, as yet without a suspecting sideward glance, simply in opposition to the noble one. Around the time of the Thirty-Years' War, in other words late enough, this sense shifts into the one now commonly used.— With respect to morality's genealogy this appears to me to be an *essential* insight; that it is only now being discovered is due to the inhibiting influence that democratic prejudice exercises in the modern world with regard to all questions of origins. And this influence extends all the way into that seemingly most objective realm of natural science and physiology, as I shall merely hint at here. But the nonsense that this prejudice—once unleashed to the point of hate—is able to inflict, especially on morality and history, is shown by Buckle's[15] notorious case; the *plebeianism* of the modern spirit, which is of English descent, sprang forth there once again on its native ground, vehemently like a muddy volcano and with that oversalted, overloud, common eloquence with which until now all volcanoes have spoken.—

5

With regard to *our* problem—which can for good reasons be called a *quiet* problem and which addresses itself selectively to but few ears—it is of no small interest to discover that often in those words and roots that designate "good" that main nuance still shimmers through with respect to which the nobles felt themselves to be humans of a higher rank. To be sure, they may name themselves in the most frequent cases simply after their superiority in power (as "the powerful," "the lords," "the commanders") or after the most visible distinguishing mark of this superiority, for example as "the

---

[14] [Herbert Spencer (1820–1903), English sociologist and philosopher. An early advocate of evolutionary theory, he is the father of Social Darwinism: Spencer coined the phrase "survival of the fittest."]

[15] [Henry Thomas Buckle (1821–1862), English historian. Holding in contempt the history of his day, which emphasized politics, war, and heroes, he aimed to make history scientific by discovering the fixed laws that govern the actions of men and therefore of societies.]

rich," "the possessors," (that is the sense of *arya*;[16] and likewise in Iranian and Slavic). But also after a *typical character trait*: and this is the case which concerns us here. They call themselves for example "the truthful"—led by the Greek nobility, whose mouthpiece is the Megarian poet Theognis.[17] The word coined for this, *esthlos*,[18] means according to its root one who *is*, who possesses reality, who is real, who is true; then, with a subjective turn, the true one as the truthful one: in this phase of the concept's transformation it becomes the by and catchword of the nobility and passes over completely into the sense of "aristocratic," as that which distinguishes from the *lying* common man as Theognis understands and depicts him—until finally, after the demise of the nobility, the word remains as the term for *noblesse* of soul and becomes as it were ripe and sweet. In the word *kakos*[19] as well as in *deilos*[20] (the plebeian in contrast to the *agathos*)[21] cowardliness is underscored: perhaps this gives a hint in which direction one should seek the etymological origins of *agathos*, which can be interpreted in many ways. In the Latin *malus*[22] (beside which I place *melas*),[23] the common man could be characterized as the dark-colored, above all as the black-haired ("*hic niger est*—"),[24] as the pre-Aryan occupant of Italian soil, who by his color stood out most clearly from the blonds who had become the rulers, namely the Aryan conqueror-race; at any rate Gaelic offered me an exactly corresponding case—*fin*[25] (for example in the name Fin-Gal), the distinguishing word of the nobility, in the end, the good, noble, pure one, originally the blond-headed one, in contrast to the dark, black-haired original inhabitants. The Celts, incidentally, were by all means a blond race; it is wrong to associate those

tracts of an essentially dark-haired population, which are noticeable on the more careful ethnographic maps of Germany, with any Celtic origins or blood mixtures, as even Virchow[26] does: rather it is the *pre-Aryan* population of Germany that comes to the fore in these places. (The same is true for almost all of Europe: in essence, the subjected race has in the end regained the upper hand there, in color, shortness of skull, perhaps even in intellectual and social instincts—who will guarantee us that modern democracy, the even more modern anarchism, and in particular that inclination toward the "commune," the most primitive form of society—an inclination now common to all of Europe's socialists—does not signify, on the whole, a tremendous *atavism*—and that the *race of lords* and conquerors, that of the Aryans, is not in the process of succumbing physiologically as well? . . .) I believe I may interpret the Latin *bonus*[27] as "the warrior": assuming that I am correct in tracing *bonus* back to an older *duonus*[28] (compare *bellum* = *duellum* = *duenlum*,[29] in which that *duonus* seems to me to be preserved). *Bonus* accordingly as man of strife, of division (*duo*), as man of war—one sees what it was about a man that constituted his "goodness" in ancient Rome. Our German "*gut*" [good] itself: wasn't it supposed to mean "the godly one," the man "of godly race"? And to be identical with the name for the nation (originally for the nobility) of the Goths? The reasons for this supposition do not belong here.—

6

To this rule that the concept of superiority in politics always resolves itself into a concept of superiority of soul, it is not immediately an exception (although it provides occasion for exceptions) when the highest caste is at the same time the *priestly* caste and hence prefers for its collective name a predicate that recalls its priestly function. Here, for example, "pure" and

---

[16] [Sanskrit: noble.]

[17] [Late 6th–early 5th century B.C.E.]

[18] [Good, brave, noble.]

[19] [Bad, ugly, ill-born, base, cowardly, ignoble.]

[20] [Cowardly, worthless, low-born, miserable, wretched.]

[21] [Good, well-born, noble, brave, capable.]

[22] [Bad, evil.]

[23] [Black, dark.]

[24] [He is black. Horace's Satires, I. 4, line 85.]

[25] [Gaelic: white, bright.]

[26] [Rudolf Virchow (1821–1902), physician, professor of medicine, and liberal politician.]

[27] [Good.]

[28] [Earlier form of *bonus*.]

[29] [War; the latter two are older, poetic forms.]

"impure" stand opposite each other for the first time as marks of distinction among the estates; and here, too, one later finds the development of a "good" and a "bad" in a sense no longer related to the estates. Incidentally, let one beware from the outset of taking these concepts "pure" and "impure" too seriously, too broadly, or even too symbolically: rather all of earlier humanity's concepts were initially understood in a coarse, crude, superficial, narrow, straightforward, and above all *unsymbolic* manner, to an extent that we can hardly imagine. The "pure one" is from the beginning simply a human being who washes himself, who forbids himself certain foods that bring about skin diseases, who doesn't sleep with the dirty women of the baser people, who abhors blood—nothing more, at least not much more! On the other hand the entire nature of an essentially priestly aristocracy admittedly makes clear why it was precisely here that the valuation opposites could so soon become internalized and heightened in a dangerous manner; and indeed through them gulfs were finally torn open between man and man across which even an Achilles of free-spiritedness will not be able to leap without shuddering. From the beginning there is something *unhealthy* in such priestly aristocracies and in the habits ruling there, ones turned away from action, partly brooding, partly emotionally explosive, habits that have as a consequence the intestinal disease and neurasthenia that almost unavoidably clings to the priests of all ages; but what they themselves invented as a medicine against this diseasedness of theirs—must we not say that in the end it has proved itself a hundred times more dangerous in its aftereffects than the disease from which it was to redeem them? Humanity itself still suffers from the aftereffects of these priestly cure naïvetés! Think, for example, of certain dietary forms (avoidance of meat), of fasting, of sexual abstinence, of the flight "into the wilderness" (Weir-Mitchellian isolation,[30]

admittedly without the ensuing fattening diet and over-feeding, which constitutes the most effective antidote for all the hysteria of the ascetic ideal): in addition, the whole anti-sensual metaphysics of priests, which makes lazy and overrefined, their self-hypnosis after the manner of the fakir and Brahmin—brahma used as glass pendant and *idée fixe*—and the final, only too understandable general satiety along with its radical cure, *nothingness* (or God—the longing for a *unio mystica*[31] with God is the longing of the Buddhist for nothingness, Nirvana—and nothing more!) With priests *everything* simply becomes more dangerous, not only curatives and healing arts, but also arrogance, revenge, acuity, excess, love, lust to rule, virtue, disease;—though with some fairness one could also add that it was on the soil of this *essentially dangerous* form of human existence, the priestly form, that man first became *an interesting animal*, that only here did the human soul acquire *depth* in a higher sense and become *evil*—and these are, after all, the two basic forms of the previous superiority of man over other creatures! . . .

7

—One will already have guessed how easily the priestly manner of valuation can branch off from the knightly-aristocratic and then develop into its opposite; this process is especially given an impetus every time the priestly caste and the warrior caste confront each other jealously and are unable to agree on a price. The knightly-aristocratic value judgments have as their presupposition a powerful physicality, a blossoming, rich, even overflowing health, together with that which is required for its preservation: war, adventure, the hunt, dance, athletic contests, and in general everything which includes strong, free, cheerful-hearted activity. The priestly-noble manner of valuation—as we have seen—has other presuppositions: too bad for it when it

---

[30] [Silas Weir Mitchell (1829–1914), Philadelphian physician and novelist who specialized in treating "nervous" disorders. He became widely known in America and Europe for his "rest cure" for such illnesses: patients were first isolated from the influence of hovering, over-careful family members and restricted to bed for four to six weeks, during which they

---

were not allowed to have visitors or to read or write. They were fed by a nurse and given massages to keep up strength and muscle tone. When they began to show improvement, patients were ordered to get up and take exercise.]

[31] [Mystical union.]

comes to war! Priests are, as is well known, the *most evil enemies*—why is that? Because they are the most powerless. Out of their powerlessness their hate grows into something enormous and uncanny, into something most spiritual and most poisonous. The truly great haters in the history of the world have always been priests, also the most ingenious haters:—compared with the spirit of priestly revenge all the rest of spirit taken together hardly merits consideration. Human history would be much too stupid an affair without the spirit that has entered into it through the powerless:—let us turn right to the greatest example. Of all that has been done on earth against "the noble," "the mighty," "the lords," "the power-holders," nothing is worthy of mention in comparison with that which the *Jews* have done against them: the Jews, that priestly people who in the end were only able to obtain satisfaction from their enemies and conquerors through a radical revaluation of their values, that is, through an act of *spiritual revenge*. This was the only way that suited a priestly people, the people of the most suppressed priestly desire for revenge. It was the Jews who in opposition to the aristocratic value equation (good = noble = powerful = beautiful = happy = beloved of God) dared its inversion, with fear-inspiring consistency, and held it fast with teeth of the most unfathomable hate (the hate of powerlessness), namely: "the miserable alone are the good; the poor, powerless, lowly alone are the good; the suffering, deprived, sick, ugly are also the only pious, the only blessed in God, for them alone is there blessedness,—whereas you, you noble and powerful ones, you are in all eternity the evil, the cruel, the lustful, the insatiable, the godless, you will eternally be the wretched, accursed, and damned!" . . . We know *who* inherited this Jewish revaluation . . . In connection with the enormous and immeasurably doom-laden initiative provided by the Jews with this most fundamental of all declarations of war, I call attention to the proposition which I arrived at on another occasion ("Beyond Good and Evil" section 195)—namely, that with the Jews *the slave revolt in morality* begins: that revolt which has a two-thousand-year history behind it and which has only moved out of our sight today because it—has been victorious . . .

8

—But you don't understand that? You don't have eyes for something that has taken two thousand years to achieve victory? . . . There is nothing to wonder at in this: all *lengthy* things are difficult to see, to see in their entirety. *This* however is what happened: out of the trunk of that tree of revenge and hate, Jewish hate—the deepest and most sublime hate, namely an ideal-creating, value-reshaping hate whose like has never before existed on earth—grew forth something just as incomparable, a *new love*, the deepest and most sublime of all kinds of love:—and from what other trunk could it have grown? . . . But by no means should one suppose it grew upwards as, say, the true negation of that thirst for revenge, as the opposite of Jewish hate! No, the reverse is the truth! This love grew forth out of it, as its crown, as the triumphant crown unfolding itself broadly and more broadly in purest light and sunny fullness, reaching out, as it were, in the realm of light and of height, for the goals of that hate—for victory, for booty, for seduction—with the same drive with which the roots of that hate sunk themselves ever more thoroughly and greedily down into everything that had depth and was evil. This Jesus of Nazareth, as the embodied Gospel of Love, this "Redeemer" bringing blessedness and victory to the poor, the sick, the sinners—was he not precisely seduction in its most uncanny and irresistible form, the seduction and detour to precisely those *Jewish* values and reshapings of the ideal? Has not Israel reached the final goal of its sublime desire for revenge precisely via the detour of this "Redeemer," this apparent adversary and dissolver of Israel? Does it not belong to the secret black art of a truly *great* politics of revenge, of a far-seeing, subterranean, slow-working and pre-calculating revenge, that Israel itself, before all the world, should deny as its mortal enemy and nail to the cross the actual tool of its revenge, so that "all the world," namely all the opponents of Israel, could take precisely this bait without thinking twice? And, out of all sophistication of the spirit, could one think up any more *dangerous* bait? Something that in its enticing, intoxicating, anesthetizing, destructive power might equal that symbol of the "holy cross," that gruesome paradox of a "god on the cross," that mystery of an inconceivable, final, extreme cruelty and self-crucifixion of God *for the salvation of man?* . . . What is certain, at least, is that *sub hoc signo*[32] Israel, with its revenge and revaluation of all values, has thus far again and again triumphed over all other ideals, over all *more noble* ideals.— —

9

—"But why are you still talking about *nobler* ideals! Let's submit to the facts: the people were victorious— or 'the slaves,' or 'the mob,' or 'the herd,' or whatever you like to call them—if this happened through the Jews, so be it! then never has a people had a more world-historic mission. 'The lords' are cast off; the morality of the common man has been victorious. One may take this victory to be at the same time a blood poisoning (it mixed the races together)—I won't contradict; in any event it is beyond doubt that this toxication *succeeded*. The 'redemption' of the human race (namely from 'the lords') is well under way; everything is jewifying or christifying or mobifying as we watch (what do the words matter!). The progress of this poisoning through the entire body of humanity appears unstoppable, from now on its tempo and step may even be slower, more refined, less audible, more thoughtful—one has time after all . . . Does the church today still have a *necessary* task in this scheme, still a right to existence at all? Or could one do without it? *Quaeritur.*[33] It seems more likely that it inhibits and holds back this progress instead of accelerating it? Well, even that could be its usefulness . . . By now it is certainly something coarse and peasant-like, which repels a more delicate intelligence, a truly modern taste. Shouldn't it at least become somewhat refined? . . . Today it alienates more than it seduces . . . Which of us indeed would be a free spirit if there were no church? The church, *not* its poison, repels us . . . Leav-

[32] [Under this sign.]
[33] [One asks, i.e., that is the question.]

ing the church aside, we, too, love the poison . . ."— This, the epilogue of a "free spirit" to my speech, an honest animal, as he has richly betrayed, moreover a democrat; he had listened to me up until then and couldn't stand to hear me be silent. For at this point I have much to be silent about.—

10

The slave revolt in morality begins when *ressentiment* itself becomes creative and gives birth to values: the *ressentiment* of beings denied the true reaction, that of the deed, who recover their losses only through an imaginary revenge. Whereas all noble morality grows out of a triumphant yes-saying to oneself, from the outset slave morality says "no" to an "outside," to a "different," to a "not-self": and *this* "no" is its creative deed. This reversal of the value-establishing glance—this *necessary* direction toward the outside instead of back onto oneself—belongs to the very nature of *ressentiment*: in order to come into being, slave-morality always needs an opposite and external world; it needs, psychologically speaking, external stimuli in order to be able to act at all,—its action is, from the ground up, reaction. The reverse is the case with the noble manner of valuation: it acts and grows spontaneously, it seeks out its opposite only in order to say "yes" to itself still more gratefully and more jubilantly—its negative concept "low" "common" "bad" is only an after-birth, a pale contrast-image in relation to its positive basic concept, saturated through and through with life and passion: "we noble ones, we good ones, we beautiful ones, we happy ones!" When the noble manner of valuation lays a hand on reality and sins against it, this occurs relative to the sphere with which it is *not* sufficiently acquainted, indeed against a real knowledge of which it rigidly defends itself: in some cases it forms a wrong idea of the sphere it holds in contempt, that of the common man, of the lower people; on the other hand, consider that the affect of contempt, of looking down on, of the superior glance—assuming that it does *falsify* the image of the one held in contempt— will in any case fall far short of the falsification with which the suppressed hate, the revenge of the power-less, lays a hand on its opponent—in effigy, of course. Indeed there is too much carelessness in contempt, too much taking-lightly, too much looking-away and impatience mixed in, even too much of a feeling of cheer in oneself, for it to be capable of transforming its object into a real caricature and monster. Do not fail to hear the almost benevolent nuances that, for example, the Greek nobility places in all words by which it distinguishes the lower people from itself; how they are mixed with and sugared by a kind of pity, considerateness, leniency to the point that almost all words that apply to the common man ultimately survive as expressions for "unhappy" "pitiful" (compare *deilos, deilaios, poneros, mochtheros,* the latter two actually designating the common man as work-slave and beast of burden)[34]—and how, on the other hand, to the Greek ear "bad" "low" "unhappy" have never ceased to end on the same note, with a tone color in which "un-happy" predominates: this as inheritance of the old, nobler aristocratic manner of valuation that does not deny itself even in its contempt (let philologists be reminded of the sense in which *oizyros, anolbos, tlemon, dystychein, xymphora* are used).[35] The "well-born" simply *felt* themselves to be the "happy"; they did not first have to construct their happiness artificially by looking at their enemies, to talk themselves into it, to *lie themselves into it* (as all human beings of *ressentiment* tend to do); and as full human beings, over-loaded with power and therefore *necessarily* active, they likewise did not know how to separate activity out from happiness,—for them being active is of necessity included in happiness (whence *eu prattein*[36] takes its origins)—all of this very much in opposition to "hap-piness" on the level of the powerless, oppressed, those festering with poisonous and hostile feelings, in whom it essentially appears as narcotic, anesthetic, calm, peace, "Sabbath," relaxation of mind and stretching of limbs, in short, *passively.* While the noble human being lives with himself in confidence and openness (*gennaios* "nobleborn" underscores the nuance "sincere" and probably also "naive") the human being of *ressentiment* is neither sincere, nor naive, nor honest and frank with himself. His soul *looks obliquely* at things; his spirit loves hiding places, secret passages and backdoors, everything hidden strikes him as *his* world, *his* security, *his* balm; he knows all about being silent, not forgetting, waiting, belittling oneself for the moment, humbling oneself. A race of such human beings of *ressentiment* in the end necessarily becomes *more prudent* than any noble race, it will also honor prudence in an entirely different measure: namely as a primary condition of existence. With noble human beings, in contrast, prudence is likely to have a refined aftertaste of luxury and sophistication about it:—here it is not nearly as essential as the complete functional reliability of the regulating *unconscious* instincts or even a certain imprudence, for example the gallant making-straight-for-it, be it toward danger, be it toward the enemy, or that impassioned suddenness of anger, love, reverence, gratitude, and revenge by which noble souls in all ages have recognized each other. For the *ressentiment* of the noble human being, when it appears in him, runs its course and exhausts itself in an immediate reaction, therefore it does not *poison*—on the other hand it does not appear at all in countless cases where it is unavoidable in all the weak and pow-erless. To be unable for any length of time to take his enemies, his accidents, his *misdeeds* themselves seri-ously—that is the sign of strong, full natures in which there is an excess of formative, reconstructive, healing power that also makes one forget (a good example of this from the modern world is Mirabeau,[37] who had no memory for insults and base deeds committed against him and who was only unable to forgive because he—forgot). Such a human is simply able to shake off with

---

[34] [*Deilos:* cowardly, worthless, low-born, miserable, wretched; *deilaios:* wretched, sorry, paltry; *poneros:* wretched, oppressed by toils, worthless, base, cowardly; *mochtheros:* wretched, suffering hardship, miserable, worthless, knavish.]

[35] [*Oizyros:* woeful, pitiable, miserable, sorry, poor; *anolbos:* unblest, wretched, luckless, poor; *tlemon:* suffering, enduring; hence: "steadfast, stouthearted," but also "wretched, miserable"; *dystychein:* to be unlucky, unhappy, unfortunate; *xymphora:* originally "chance," then usually in a bad sense, that is, "misfortune."]

[36] [To do well, to fare well, or to do good.]

[37] [Honoré Gabriel Riqueti, Comte de Mirabeau (1749–1791), French politician, orator, and writer.]

a single shrug a collection of worms that in others would dig itself in; here alone is also possible—assuming that it is at all possible on earth—the true *"love of one's enemies."* What great reverence for his enemies a noble human being has!—and such reverence is already a bridge to love . . . After all, he demands his enemy for himself, as his distinction; he can stand no other enemy than one in whom there is nothing to hold in contempt and *a very great deal* to honor! On the other hand, imagine "the enemy" as the human being of *ressentiment* conceives of him—and precisely here is his deed, his creation: he has conceived of "the evil enemy," *"the evil one,"* and this indeed as the basic concept, starting from which he now also thinks up, as reaction and counterpart, a "good one"—himself! . . .

11

Precisely the reverse, therefore, of the case of the noble one, who conceives the basic concept "good" in advance and spontaneously, starting from himself that is, and from there first creates for himself an idea of "bad"! This "bad" of noble origin and that "evil" out of the brewing cauldron of unsatiated hate—the first, an after-creation, something on the side, a complementary color; the second, in contrast, the original, the beginning, the true *deed* in the conception of a slave morality—how differently the two words "bad" and "evil" stand there, seemingly set in opposition to the same concept "good"! But it is *not* the same concept "good": on the contrary, just ask yourself *who* is actually "evil" in the sense of the morality of *ressentiment.* To answer in all strictness: *precisely* the "good one" of the other morality, precisely the noble, the powerful, the ruling one, only recolored, only reinterpreted, only reseen through the poisonous eye of *ressentiment.* There is one point we wish to deny least of all here: whoever encounters those "good ones" only as enemies encounters nothing but *evil enemies,* and the same humans who are kept so strictly within limits *inter pares,*[38] by mores, worship, custom, gratitude, still more by mutual surveillance, by jealousy,

and who on the other hand in their conduct towards each other prove themselves so inventive in consideration, self-control, tact, loyalty, pride, and friendship, —they are not much better than uncaged beasts of prey toward the outside world, where that which is foreign, the foreign world, begins. There they enjoy freedom from all social constraint; in the wilderness they recover the losses incured through the tension that comes from a long enclosure and fencing-in within the peace of the community; they step *back* into the innocence of the beast-of-prey conscience, as jubilant monsters, who perhaps walk away from a hideous succession of murder, arson, rape, torture with such high spirits and equanimity that it seems as if they have only played a student prank, convinced that for years to come the poets will again have something to sing and to praise. At the base of all these noble races one cannot fail to recognize the beast of prey, the splendid *blond beast* who roams about lusting after booty and victory; from time to time this hidden base needs to discharge itself, the animal must get out, must go back into the wilderness: Roman, Arab, Germanic, Japanese nobility, Homeric heroes, Scandinavian Vikings —in this need they are all alike. It is the noble races who have left the concept "barbarian" in all their tracks wherever they have gone; indeed from within their highest culture a consciousness of this betrays itself and even a pride in it (for example when Pericles says to his Athenians in that famous funeral oration, "to every land and sea our boldness has broken a path, everywhere setting up unperishing monuments in good *and bad*"). This "boldness" of noble races—mad, absurd, sudden in its expression; the unpredictable, in their enterprises even the improbable—Pericles singles out for distinction the *rhathymia*[39] of the Athenians— their indifference and contempt toward all security, body, life, comfort; their appalling light-heartedness and depth of desire in all destruction, in all the delights of victory and of cruelty—all was summed up for those who suffered from it in the image of the "barbarian," of the "evil enemy," for example the "Goth," the "Vandal." The deep, icy mistrust that the German

---

[38] [Among equals; here, "among themselves."]

[39] [Easiness of temper; indifference, rashness. Thucydides 2. 39.]

stirs up as soon as he comes into power, today once again—is still an atavism of that inextinguishable horror with which Europe has for centuries watched the raging of the blond Germanic beast (although there is hardly a conceptual, much less a blood-relationship between the ancient Teutons and us Germans). I once called attention to Hesiod's embarrassment as he was devising the succession of the cultural ages and attempted to express it in terms of gold, silver, bronze: he knew of no other way to cope with the contradiction posed by the glorious but likewise so gruesome, so violent world of Homer, than by making one age into two, which he now placed one after the other— first the age of the heroes and demigods of Troy and Thebes, as this world had remained in the memory of the noble dynasties who had their own ancestors there; then the bronze age, which was that same world as it appeared to the descendants of the downtrodden, plundered, mistreated, dragged-off, sold-off: an age of bronze, as stated—hard, cold, cruel, without feeling or conscience, crushing everything and covering it with blood. Assuming it were true, that which is now in any case believed as "truth," that the *meaning of all culture* is simply to breed a tame and civilized animal, a *domestic animal*, out of the beast of prey "man," then one would have to regard all those instincts of reaction and *ressentiment*, with the help of which the noble dynasties together with their ideals were finally brought to ruin and overwhelmed, as the actual *tools of culture*; which is admittedly not to say that the *bearers* of these instincts themselves at the same time also represent culture. On the contrary, the opposite would not simply be probable—no! today it is *obvious!* These bearers of the oppressing and retaliation-craving instincts, the descendants of all European and non-European slavery, of all pre-Aryan population in particular— they represent the *regression* of humankind! These "tools of culture" are a disgrace to humanity, and rather something that raises a suspicion, a counter-argument against "culture" in general! It may be entirely justifiable if one cannot escape one's fear of the blond beast at the base of all noble races and is on guard: but who would not a hundred times sooner fear if he might at the same time admire, than *not* fear but be unable to escape the disgusting sight of the deformed, reduced, atrophied, poisoned? And is that not

our doom? What causes *our* aversion to "man"?—for we *suffer* from man, there is no doubt.—*Not* fear; rather that we have nothing left to fear in man; that the worm "man" is in the foreground and teeming; that the "tame man," this hopelessly mediocre and uninspiring being, has already learned to feel himself as the goal and pinnacle, as the meaning of history, as "higher man"—indeed that he has a certain right to feel this way, insofar as he feels himself distanced from the profusion of the deformed, sickly, tired, worn-out of which Europe today is beginning to stink; hence as something that is at least relatively well-formed, at least still capable of living, that at least says "yes" to life . . .

12

—At this point I will not suppress a sigh and a final confidence. What is it that I in particular find utterly unbearable? That with which I cannot cope alone, that causes me to suffocate and languish? Bad air! Bad air! That something deformed comes near me; that I should have to smell the entrails of a deformed soul! . . . How much can one not otherwise bear of distress, deprivation, foul weather, infirmity, drudgery, isolation? Basically one deals with everything else, born as one is to a subterranean and fighting existence; again and again one reaches the light, again and again one experiences one's golden hour of victory,—and then one stands there as one was born, unbreakable, tensed, ready for something new, something still more difficult, more distant, like a bow that any distress simply pulls tauter still.—But from time to time grant me— assuming that there are heavenly patronesses beyond good and evil—a glimpse, grant me just one glimpse of something perfect, completely formed, happy, powerful, triumphant, in which there is still something to fear! Of a human being who justifies man *himself*; a human being who is a stroke of luck, completing and redeeming man, and for whose sake one may hold fast to *belief in man!* . . . For things stand thus: the reduction and equalization of the European human conceals *our* greatest danger, for this sight makes tired . . . We see today nothing that wishes to become greater, we sense that things are still going downhill, downhill

—into something thinner, more good-natured, more prudent, more comfortable, more mediocre, more apathetic, more Chinese, more Christian—man, there is no doubt, is becoming ever "better" . . . Precisely here lies Europe's doom—with the fear of man we have also forfeited the love of him, the reverence toward him, the hope for him, indeed the will to him. The sight of man now makes tired—what is nihilism today if it is not *that*? . . . We are tired of *man* . . .

13

—But let us come back: the problem of the *other* origin of "good," of the good one as conceived by the man of *ressentiment*, demands its conclusion.—That the lambs feel anger toward the great birds of prey does not strike us as odd: but that is no reason for holding it against the great birds of prey that they snatch up little lambs for themselves. And when the lambs say among themselves "these birds of prey are evil; and whoever is as little as possible a bird of prey but rather its opposite, a lamb,—isn't he good?" there is nothing to criticize in this setting up of an ideal, even if the birds of prey should look on this a little mockingly and perhaps say to themselves: "*we* do not feel any anger towards them, these good lambs, as a matter of fact, we love them: nothing is more tasty than a tender lamb." —To demand of strength that it *not* express itself as strength, that it *not* be a desire to overwhelm, a desire to cast down, a desire to become lord, a thirst for enemies and resistances and triumphs, is just as nonsensical as to demand of weakness that it express itself as strength. A quantum of power is just such a quantum of drive, will, effect—more precisely, it is nothing other than this very driving, willing, effecting, and only through the seduction of language (and the basic errors of reason petrified therein), which understands and misunderstands all effecting as conditioned by an effecting something, by a "subject," can it appear otherwise. For just as common people separate the lightning from its flash and take the latter as a *doing*, as an effect of a subject called lightning, so popular morality also separates strength from the expressions of strength as if there were behind the strong an indifferent substratum that is free to express strength—or not

to. But there is no such substratum; there is no "being" behind the doing, effecting, becoming; "the doer" is simply fabricated into the doing—the doing is everything. Common people basically double the doing when they have the lightning flash; this is a doing-doing: the same happening is posited first as cause and then once again as its effect. Natural scientists do no better when they say "force moves, force causes," and so on—our entire science, despite all its coolness, its freedom from affect, still stands under the seduction of language and has not gotten rid of the changelings slipped over on it, the "subjects" (the atom, for example, is such a changeling, likewise the Kantian "thing in itself"): small wonder if the suppressed, hiddenly glowing affects of revenge and hate exploit this belief and basically even uphold no other belief more ardently than this one, that *the strong one is free* to be weak, and the bird of prey to be a lamb:—they thereby gain for themselves the right to hold the bird of prey *accountable* for being a bird of prey . . . When out of the vengeful cunning of powerlessness the oppressed, downtrodden, violated say to themselves: "let us be different from the evil ones, namely good! And good is what everyone is who does not do violence, who injures no one, who doesn't attack, who doesn't retaliate, who leaves vengeance to God, who keeps himself concealed, as we do, who avoids all evil, and in general demands very little of life, like us, the patient, humble, righteous"—it means, when listened to coldly and without prejudice, actually nothing more than: "we weak ones are simply weak; it is good if we do nothing *for which we are not strong enough*"—but this harsh matter of fact, this prudence of the lowest order, which even insects have (presumably playing dead when in great danger in order not to do "too much"), has, thanks to that counterfeiting and self-deception of powerlessness, clothed itself in the pomp of renouncing, quiet, patiently waiting virtue, as if the very weakness of the weak—that is to say, his *essence*, his effecting, his whole unique, unavoidable, undetachable reality—were a voluntary achievement, something willed, something chosen, a *deed*, a *merit*. This kind of human *needs* the belief in a neutral "subject" with free choice, out of an instinct of self-preservation, self-affirmation, in which every lie tends to hallow itself. It is perhaps for this reason that the subject (or, to speak more popularly, the *soul*) has until now been the best article of faith on earth, because it made possible for the majority of mortals, the weak and oppressed of every kind, that sublime self-deception of interpreting weakness itself as freedom, of interpreting their being-such-and-such as a *merit*.

14

Would anyone like to go down and take a little look into the secret of how they *fabricate ideals* on earth? Who has the courage to do so? . . . Well then! The view into these dark workplaces is unobstructed here. Wait just a moment, Mr. Wanton-Curiosity and Daredevil: your eyes must first get used to this falsely shimmering light . . . So! Enough! Now speak! What's going on down there? Tell me what you see, man of the most dangerous curiosity—now *I* am the one listening.—

—"I don't see anything, but I hear all the more. There is a cautious malicious quiet whispering and muttering-together out of all corners and nooks. It seems to me that they are lying; a sugary mildness sticks to each sound. Weakness is to be lied into a *merit*, there is no doubt about it—it is just as you said."—

—Go on!

—"and the powerlessness that does not retaliate into kindness; fearful baseness into 'humility'; subjection to those whom one hates into 'obedience' (namely to one whom they say orders this subjection—they call him God). The inoffensiveness of the weak one, cowardice itself, which he possesses in abundance, his standing-at-the-door, his unavoidable having-to-wait, acquires good names here, such as 'patience,' it is even called virtue *itself*; not being able to avenge oneself is called not wanting to avenge oneself, perhaps even forgiveness ('for *they* know not what they do—we alone know what *they* do!'). They also talk of 'love of one's enemies'—and sweat while doing so."

—Go on!

—"They are miserable, there is no doubt, all of these whisperers and nook-and-cranny counterfeiters, even if they are crouching together warmly—but they tell me that their misery is a distinction and election from God, that one beats the dogs one loves the most; perhaps this misery is also a preparation, a test, a

schooling, perhaps it is still more—something for which there will one day be retribution, paid out with enormous interest in gold, no! in happiness. This they call 'blessedness.' "

—Go on!

—"Now they are giving me to understand that they are not only better than the powerful, the lords of the earth, whose saliva they must lick (*not* out of fear, not at all out of fear! but rather because God commands that they honor all authority)—that they are not only better, but that they are also 'better off,' at least will be better off one day. But enough! enough! I can't stand it anymore. Bad air! Bad air! This workplace where they *fabricate ideals*—it seems to me it stinks of sheer lies."

—No! A moment more! You haven't said anything about the masterpiece of these artists of black magic who produce white, milk, and innocence out of every black:—haven't you noticed what the height of their sophistication is, their boldest, finest, most ingenious, most mendacious artistic stroke? Pay attention! These cellar animals full of revenge and hate—what is it they make precisely out of this revenge and hate? Did you ever hear these words? Would you guess, if you trusted their words alone, that those around you are all humans of *ressentiment*? . . .

—"I understand, I'll open my ears once again (oh! oh! oh! and *close* my nose). Now for the first time I hear what they have said so often: 'We good ones—we *are the just*'—what they demand they call not retaliation but rather 'the triumph of *justice*'; what they hate is not their enemy, no! they hate '*injustice*,' 'ungodliness'; what they believe and hope for is not the hope for revenge, the drunkenness of sweet revenge (—already Homer called it 'sweeter than honey'), but rather the victory of God, of the *just* God over the ungodly; what is left on earth for them to love are not their brothers in hate but rather their 'brothers in love,' as they say, all the good and just on earth."

—And what do they call that which serves them as comfort against all the sufferings of life—their phantasmagoria of the anticipated future blessedness?

—"What? Did I hear right? They call that 'the last judgment,' the coming of *their* kingdom, of the 'kingdom of God'—*meanwhile*, however, they live 'in faith,' 'in love,' 'in hope.' "

—Enough! Enough!

15

In faith in what? In love of what? In hope of what?—These weak ones—someday *they* too want to be the strong ones, there is no doubt, someday *their* "kingdom" too shall come—among them it is called "the kingdom of God" pure and simple, as was noted: they are of course so humble in all things! Even to experience *that* they need to live long, beyond death—indeed they need eternal life so that in the 'kingdom of God' they can also recover eternally the losses incurred during that earth-life "in faith, in love, in hope." Recover their losses for what? Recover their losses through what? . . . It was a gross blunder on Dante's part, it seems to me, when, with terror-instilling ingenuousness, he placed over the gate to his hell the inscription "I, too, was created by eternal love":—in any case, over the gate of the Christian paradise and its "eternal blessedness" there would be better justification for allowing the inscription to stand "I, too, was created by eternal *hate*"—assuming that a truth may stand above the gate to a lie! For *what* is the blessedness of that paradise? . . . We would perhaps guess it already; but it is better that it is expressly documented for us by an authority not to be underestimated in such matters, Thomas Aquinas,[40] the great teacher and saint. "*Beati in regno coelestia,*" he says meekly as a lamb, "*videbunt poenas damnatorum, **ut beatitudo illis magis complaceat.***"[41] Or would you like to hear it in a stronger key, for instance from the mouth of a triumphant church father[42] who counseled his Christians against the cruel pleasures of the public spectacles—and why? "Faith offers us much more,"—he says, *De spectac. c. 29 ss.*—"*something much stronger*; thanks to salvation there are entirely different joys at our dis-

posal; in place of the athletes we have our martyrs; if we desire blood, well, we have the blood of Christ . . . But what awaits us above all on the day of his return, of his triumph!"—and now he continues, the enraptured visionary: "*At enim supersunt alia spectacula, ille ultimus et perpetuus judicii dies, ille nationibus insperatus, ille derisus, cum tanta saeculi vetustas et tot ejus nativitates uno igne haurientur. Quae tunc spectaculi latitudo! **Quid admirer! Quid rideam! Ubi gaudeam! Ubi exultem,** spectans tot et tantos reges, qui in coelum recepti nuntiabantur, cum ipso Jove et ipsis suis testibus in imis tenebris congemescentes! Item praesides* (the provincial governor) *persecutores dominici nominis saevioribus quam ipsi flammis saevierunt insultantibus contra Christianos liquescentes! Quos praeterea sapientes illos philosophos coram discipulis suis una conflagrantibus erubescentes, quibus nihil ad deum pertinere suadebant, quibus animas aut nullas aut non in pristina corpora redituras affirmabant! Etiam poetas non ad Rhadamanti nec ad Minois, sed ad inopinati Christi tribunal palpitantes! Tunc magis tragoedi audiendi, magis scilicet vocales* (in better voice, even more awful screamers) *in sua propria calamitate; tunc histriones cognoscendi, solutiores multo per ignem; tunc spectandus auriga in flammea rota totus rubens, tunc xystici contemplandi non in gymnasiis, sed in igne jaculati, nisi quod ne tunc quidem illos velim vivos, ut qui malim ad eos potius conspectum **insatiabilem** conferre, qui in dominum desaevierunt. 'Hic est ille, dicam, fabri aut quaestuariae filius* (as everything that follows shows, and in particular this well-known designation from the Talmud for the mother of Jesus, from here on Tertullian means the Jews), *sabbati destructor, Samarites et daemonium habens. Hic est, quem a Juda redemistis, hic est ille arundine et colaphis diverberatus, sputamentis dedecoratus, felle et aceto potatus. Hic est, quem clam discentes subripuerunt, ut resurrexisse dicatur vel hortulanus detraxit, ne lactucae suae frequentia commeantium laederentur.' Ut talia spectes, **ut talibus exultes,** quis tibi praetor aut consul aut quaestor aut sacerdos de sua liberalitate praestabit? Et tamen haec jam habemus quodammodo **per fidem** spiritu imaginante repraesentata. Ceterum qualia illa sunt, quae nec oculus vidit nec auris audivit nec in cor hominis ascenderunt? (1 Cor. 2:9) Credo circo et utraque cava* (first

---

[40] [Thomas Aquinas (1225–1274), Christian theologian and philosopher, canonized by Pope John XXII in 1323 and declared a Doctor of the Church by Pope Pius V in 1567.]

[41] ["The blessed in the kingdom of heaven will see the punishments of the damned, *in order that their bliss be more delightful to them.*" *Summa Theologica* III *Supplementum* Q. 94, Art. 1.]

[42] [Tertullian (ca. 155–after 220), important early Christian theologian, polemicist, and moralist from Carthage in North Africa.]

and fourth tiers, or, according to others, comic and tragic stages) *et omni stadio gratiora.*"[43] — **Per fidem:**[44] thus it is written.

Let us conclude. The two *opposed* values 'good and bad,' 'good and evil,' have fought a terrible millennia-long battle on earth; and as certainly as the second value has had the upper hand for a long time, even so there is still no shortage of places where the battle goes on, undecided. One could even say that it has in the meantime been borne up ever higher and precisely thereby become ever deeper, ever more spiritual: so that today there is perhaps no more decisive mark of the *"higher nature,"* of the more spiritual nature, than to be conflicted in that sense and still a real battle-ground for those opposites. The symbol of this battle, written in a script that has so far remained legible across all of human history, is "Rome against Judea, Judea against Rome": — so far there has been no greater event than *this* battle, *this* formulation of the problem, *this* mortally hostile contradiction. Rome sensed in the Jew something like anti-nature itself, its antipodal monstrosity as it were; in Rome the Jew was held to have been *"convicted* of hatred against the entire human race": rightly so, insofar as one has a right to tie the salvation and the future of the human race to the unconditional rule of aristocratic values, of Roman values. What the Jews on the other hand felt towards Rome? One can guess it from a thousand indications; but it will suffice to recall again the Johannine Apocalypse, that most immoderate of all written outbursts that revenge has on its conscience. (Do not underestimate, by the way, the profound consistency of the Christian instinct when it gave precisely this book of hate the name of the disciple of love, the same one to whom it attributed that enamored-rapturous gospel —: therein lies a piece of truth, however much literary counterfeiting may have been needed for this purpose.) The Romans were after all the strong and noble ones, such that none stronger and nobler have ever existed, ever even been dreamt of; everything that remains of them, every inscription thrills, supposing that one can guess *what* is doing the writing there. The Jews, conversely, were that priestly people of *ressentiment* par excellence, in whom there dwelt a popular-moral genius without parallel: just compare the peoples with related talents — for instance the Chi-

[43] ["But indeed there are still other sights, that last and eternal day of judgment, that day unlooked for by the nations, that day they laughed at, when the world so great with age and all its generations shall be consumed by one fire. What variety of sights then! *What should I admire! What should I laugh at! In which should I feel joy! In which should I exult,* seeing so many and great *kings* who were reported to have been received into heaven, now groaning in deepest darkness with Jove himself and those who testified of their reception into heaven! Likewise the praesides *(the provincial governor)*, persecutors of the name of the Lord, being liquefied by flames fiercer than those with which they themselves raged against the Christians! What wise men besides, those very philosophers reddening before their disciples as they blaze together, the disciples to whom they suggested that nothing was of any concern to God; to whom they asserted that our souls are either nothing or they will not return to their former bodies! And also the poets, trembling before the judgment seat, not of Rhadamanthys or Minos but of the Christ, whom they did not expect! Then the great tragedians will be heard, in great voice, no doubt *(in better voice, even more awful screamers)*, in their own calamities; then the actors will be recognized, made a great deal more limber by the fire; then the charioteer will be seen, all red on a flaming wheel; then the athletes will be observed, not in their gymnasiums but cast in the fire — were it not for the fact that not even then would I wish to see them since I would much rather bestow my *insatiable* gaze on those who raged against the Lord. 'This is he,' I shall say, 'the son of the carpenter or the prostitute *(as everything that follows shows, and in particular also this well-known designation from the Talmud for the mother of Jesus, from here on Tertullian means the Jews)*, the Sabbath-breaker, the Samaritan, the one possessed of a devil. This is he whom you bought from Judas, this is the one struck by reed and fist, defiled by spit, given gall and vinegar to drink. This is he whom the disciples secretly stole away that it might be said he had risen, or perhaps the gardener dragged him away so that his lettuce would not be damaged by the crowd of those coming and going.' That you may see such things, *that you may exult in such things* — what praetor or consul or quaestor or priest will, out of his generosity, see to this? And yet even now we have them in a way, *by faith*, represented through the imagining spirit. On the other hand, what are those things which eye hath not seen nor ear heard, nor have ever entered into the heart of man? *(1 Cor. 2:9)* I believe they are more pleasing than circus and both theaters *(first and fourth tiers, or, according to others, comic and tragic stages)* and any stadium."]

[44] [By (my) faith.]

nese or the Germans—with the Jews in order to feel what is first and what fifth rank. Which of them has been victorious in the meantime, Rome or Judea? But there is no doubt at all: just consider before whom one bows today in Rome itself as before the quintessence of all the highest values—and not only in Rome, but over almost half the earth, everywhere that man has become tame or wants to become tame,—before *three Jews*, as everyone knows, and *one Jewess* (before Jesus of Nazareth, the fisher Peter, the carpet-weaver Paul, and the mother of the aforementioned Jesus, called Mary). This is very remarkable: Rome has succumbed without any doubt. To be sure, in the Renaissance there was a brilliant-uncanny reawakening of the classical ideal, of the noble manner of valuing all things: Rome itself moved like one awakened from apparent death, under the pressure of the new Judaized Rome built above it, which presented the appearance of an ecumenical synagogue and was called "church": but immediately Judea triumphed again, thanks to that thoroughly mobbish (German and English) *ressentiment* movement called the Reformation, and that which had to follow from it, the restoration of the church—also the restoration of the old sepulchral sleep of classical Rome. In an even more decisive and more profound sense than before, Judea once again achieved a victory over the classical ideal with the French Revolution: the last political nobleness there was in Europe, that of the seventeenth and eighteenth *French* centuries, collapsed under the instincts of popular *ressentiment*—never on earth has a greater jubilation, a noisier enthusiasm been heard! It is true that in the midst of all this the most enormous, most unexpected thing occurred: the classical ideal itself stepped *bodily* and with unheard of splendor before the eyes and conscience of humanity—and once again, more strongly, more simply, more penetratingly than ever, the terrible and thrilling counter-slogan "the *privilege of the few*" resounded in the face of the old lie-slogan of *ressentiment*, "the privilege of the majority," in the face of the will to lowering, to debasement, to leveling, to the downward and evening-ward of man! Like a last sign pointing to the *other* path, Napoleon appeared, that most individual and late-born human being there ever was, and in him the incarnate problem of the *noble ideal in itself*—consider

well, *what* kind of problem it is: Napoleon, this synthesis of an *inhuman* and a *superhuman* . . .

17

—Was that the end of it? Was that greatest of all conflicts of ideals thus placed *ad acta*[45] for all time? Or just postponed, postponed for a long time? . . . Won't there have to be a still much more terrible, much more thoroughly prepared flaming up of the old fire someday? Still more: wouldn't precisely *this* be something to desire with all our might? even to will? even to promote? . . . Whoever starts at this point, like my readers, to ponder, to think further, will hardly come to an end any time soon—reason enough for me to come to an end myself, assuming that it has long since become sufficiently clear what I *want*, what I want precisely with that dangerous slogan that is so perfectly tailored to my last book: *"Beyond Good and Evil"* . . . At the very least this does *not* mean "Beyond Good and Bad."—

> *Note.* I take advantage of the opportunity that this treatise gives me to express publicly and formally a wish that until now I have expressed only in occasional conversations with scholars: namely that some philosophical faculty might do a great service for the promotion of *moral-historical* studies through a series of academic essay contests:—perhaps this book will serve to give a forceful impetus in just such a direction. With respect to a possibility of this sort let me suggest the following question: it merits the attention of philologists and historians as much as that of those who are actual scholars of philosophy by profession.
>
> *"What clues does the study of language, in particular etymological research, provide for the history of the development of moral concepts?"*

—On the other hand it is admittedly just as necessary to win the participation of physiologists and physicians

[45] [Shelved, filed away.]

for these problems (of the *value* of previous estimations of value): it may be left to the professional philosophers to act as advocates and mediators in this individual case as well, after they have succeeded in reshaping in general the relationship between philosophy, physiology, and medicine—originally so standoffish, so mistrustful—into the friendliest and most fruit-bearing exchange. Indeed every value table, every "thou shalt," of which history or ethnological research is aware, needs *physiological* illumination and interpretation first of all, in any case before the psychological; all of them likewise await a critique on the part of medical science. The question: what is the *value* of this or that value table or "morality"? demands to be raised from the most diverse perspectives; for this "value relative *to what end?*" cannot be analyzed too finely. Something, for example, that clearly had value with regard to the greatest possible longevity of a race (or to a heightening of its powers of adaptation to a specific climate, or to the preservation of the greatest number), would by no means have the same value if it were an issue of developing a stronger type. The welfare of the majority and the welfare of the few are opposing value viewpoints: to hold the former one to be of higher value already *in itself*, this we will leave to the naïveté of English biologists . . . *All* sciences are henceforth to do preparatory work for the philosopher's task of the future: understanding this task such that the philosopher is to solve the *problem of value*, that he is to determine the *order of rank among values*. —

SECOND TREATISE: "GUILT," "BAD CONSCIENCE," AND RELATED MATTERS

1

To breed an animal that *is permitted to promise*—isn't this precisely the paradoxical task nature has set for itself with regard to man? isn't this the true problem *of* man? . . . That this problem has been solved to a high degree must appear all the more amazing to one who can fully appreciate the force working in opposition,

that of *forgetfulness*. Forgetfulness is no mere *vis inertiae* as the superficial believe; rather, it is an active and in the strictest sense positive faculty of suppression, and is responsible for the fact that whatever we experience, learn, or take into ourselves enters just as little into our consciousness during the condition of digestion (one might call it "inanimation") as does the entire thousandfold process through which the nourishing of our body, so-called "incorporation," runs its course. To temporarily close the doors and windows of consciousness; to remain undisturbed by the noise and struggle with which our underworld of subservient organs works for and against each other; a little stillness, a little *tabula rasa* of consciousness so that there is again space for new things, above all for the nobler functions and functionaries, for ruling, foreseeing, predetermining (for our organism is set up oligarchically)— that is the use of this active forgetfulness, a doorkeeper as it were, an upholder of psychic order, of rest, of etiquette: from which one can immediately anticipate the degree to which there could be no happiness, no cheerfulness, no hope, no pride, no *present* without forgetfulness. The human being in whom this suppression apparatus is damaged and stops functioning is comparable to a dyspeptic (and not just comparable—) he can't "process" anything . . . Precisely this necessarily forgetful animal in whom forgetting represents a force, a form of *strong* health, has now bred in itself an opposite faculty, a memory, with whose help forgetfulness is disconnected for certain cases,— namely for those cases where a promise is to be made: it is thus by no means simply a passive no-longer-being-able-to-get-rid-of the impression once it has been inscribed, not simply indigestion from a once-pledged word over which one cannot regain control, but rather an active no-longer-wanting-to-get-rid-of, a willing on and on of something one has once willed, a true *memory of the will*: so that a world of new strange things, circumstances, even acts of the will may be placed without reservation between the original "I want," "I will do," and the actual discharge of the will, its *act*, without this long chain of the will breaking. But how much this presupposes! In order to have this kind of command over the future in advance, man must first have learned to separate the necessary from the acci-

dental occurrence, to think causally, to see and anticipate what is distant as if it were present, to fix with certainty what is end, what is means thereto, in general
to be able to reckon, to calculate, — for this, man himself must first of all have become *calculable, regular,
necessary,* in his own image of himself as well, in order to be able to vouch for himself *as future,* as one
who promises does!

2

Precisely this is the long history of the origins of *responsibility.* As we have already grasped, the task of
breeding an animal that is permitted to promise includes, as condition and preparation, the more specific task of first *making* man to a certain degree
necessary, uniform, like among like, regular, and accordingly predictable. The enormous work of what I
have called "morality of custom" (cf. *Daybreak* 9, 14,
16) — the true work of man on himself for the longest
part of the duration of the human race, his entire *prehistoric* work, has in this its meaning, its great justification — however much hardness, tyranny, mindlessness,
and idiocy may be inherent in it: with the help of the
morality of custom and the social straightjacket man
was *made* truly calculable. If, on the other hand, we
place ourselves at the end of the enormous process,
where the tree finally produces its fruit, where society
and its morality of custom finally brings to light that *to
which* it was only the means: then we will find as the
ripest fruit on its tree the *sovereign individual,* the individual resembling only himself, free again from the
morality of custom, autonomous and supermoral (for
"autonomous" and "moral" are mutually exclusive),
in short, the human being with his own independent
long will, the human being who *is permitted to promise* — and in him a proud consciousness, twitching in
all his muscles, of *what* has finally been achieved and
become flesh in him, a true consciousness of power and
becomeflesh in him, a true consciousness of power and
freedom, a feeling of the completion of man himself. This being who has become free, who is really
permitted to promise, this lord of the *free* will, this sovereign — how could he not know what superiority he
thus has over all else that is not permitted to promise

and vouch for itself, how much trust, how much fear,
how much reverence he awakens — he "*earns*" all
three — and how this mastery over himself also necessarily brings with it mastery over circumstances, over
nature and all lesser-willed and more unreliable creatures? The "free" human being, the possessor of a
long, unbreakable will, has in this possession his *standard of value* as well: looking from himself toward the
others, he honors or holds in contempt; and just as
necessarily as he honors the ones like him, the strong
and reliable (those who are *permitted* to promise), —
that is, everyone who promises like a sovereign,
weightily, seldom, slowly, who is stingy with his trust,
who *conveys a mark of distinction* when he trusts, who
gives his word as something on which one can rely because he knows himself to be strong enough to uphold
it even against accidents, even "against fate" —: just as
necessarily he will hold his kick in readiness for the
frail dogs who promise although they are not permitted to do so, and his switch for the liar who breaks his
word already the moment it leaves his mouth. The
proud knowledge of the extraordinary privilege of *responsibility,* the consciousness of this rare freedom,
this power over oneself and fate, has sunk into his lowest depth and has become instinct, the dominant instinct: — what will he call it, this dominant instinct,
assuming that he feels the need to have a word for it?
But there is no doubt: this sovereign human being
calls it his *conscience* . . .

3

His conscience? . . . One can guess in advance that
the concept "conscience," which we encounter here
in its highest, almost disconcerting form, already has
behind it a long history and metamorphosis. To be
permitted to vouch for oneself, and with pride, hence
to be *permitted to say* "*yes*" to oneself too — that is, as
noted, a ripe fruit, but also a *late* fruit: — how long this
fruit had to hang on the tree harsh and sour! And for
a still much longer time one could see nothing of such
a fruit, — no one could have promised it, however certainly everything on the tree was prepared and in the
process of growing towards it! — "How does one make

a memory for the human animal? How does one impress something onto this partly dull, partly scattered momentary understanding, this forgetfulness in the flesh, so that it remains present?" . . . As one can imagine, the answers and means used to solve this age-old problem were not exactly delicate; there is perhaps nothing more terrible and more uncanny in all of man's prehistory than his *mnemotechnique.* "One burns something in so that it remains in one's memory: only what does not cease *to give pain* remains in one's memory"—that is a first principle from the most ancient (unfortunately also longest) psychology on earth. One might even say that everywhere on earth where there is still solemnity, seriousness, secrecy, gloomy colors in the life of man and of a people, something of that terribleness *continues to be felt* with which everywhere on earth one formerly promised, pledged, vowed: the past, the longest deepest hardest past, breathes on us and wells up in us when we become "serious." Whenever man considered it necessary to make a memory for himself it was never done without blood, torment, sacrifice; the most gruesome sacrifices and pledges (to which sacrifices of firstborn belong), the most repulsive mutilations (castrations, for example), the cruelest ritual forms of all religious cults (and all religions are in their deepest foundations systems of cruelties)—all of this has its origin in that instinct that intuited in pain the most powerful aid of mnemonics. In a certain sense the entirety of asceticism belongs here: a few ideas are to be made indelible, omnipresent, unforgettable, "fixed," for the sake of hypnotizing the entire nervous and intellectual system with these "fixed ideas"—and the ascetic procedures and forms of life are means for taking these ideas out of competition with all other ideas in order to make them "unforgettable." The worse humanity was "at memory" the more terrible is the appearance of its practices; the harshness of penal laws in particular provides a measuring stick for the amount of effort it took to achieve victory over forgetfulness and to keep a few primitive requirements of social co-existence *present* for these slaves of momentary affect and desire. We Germans certainly do not regard ourselves as a particularly cruel and hard-hearted people, still less as particularly frivolous or living-for-the-day; but one need

only look at our old penal codes to discover what amount of effort it takes to breed a "people of thinkers" on earth (that is to say: *the* people of Europe, among whom one still finds even today the maximum of confidence, seriousness, tastelessness, and matter-of-factness, qualities which give it a right to breed every type of European mandarin). Using terrible means these Germans have made a memory for themselves in order to become master over their mobbish basic instincts and the brutal heavy-handedness of the same: think of the old German punishments, for example of stoning (—even legend has the millstone fall on the head of the guilty one), breaking on the wheel (the most characteristic invention and specialty of German genius in the realm of punishment!), casting stakes, having torn or trampled by horses ("quartering"), boiling the criminal in oil or wine (as late as the fourteenth and fifteenth centuries), the popular flaying (*"Riemenschneiden"*), cutting flesh from the breast; also, no doubt, that the evil-doer was smeared with honey and abandoned to the flies under a burning sun. With the help of such images and processes one finally retains in memory five, six "I will nots," in connection with which one has given one's *promise* in order to live within the advantages of society,—and truly! with the help of this kind of memory one finally came "to reason"!—Ah, reason, seriousness, mastery over the affects, this entire gloomy matter called reflection, all these prerogatives and showpieces of man: how dearly they have been paid for! how much blood and horror there is at the base of all "good things"! . . .

4

But how then did that other "gloomy thing," the consciousness of guilt, the entire "bad conscience" come into the world?—And thus we return to our genealogists of morality. To say it once more—or haven't I said it at all yet?—they aren't good for anything. Their own five-span-long, merely "modern" experience; no knowledge, no will to knowledge of the past; still less an instinct for history, a "second sight" necessary precisely here—and nonetheless doing history of morality: this must in all fairness end with results that stand in a relation to truth that is not even flirtatious. Have these previous genealogists of morality even remotely dreamt, for example, that that central moral concept "guilt" had its origins in the very material concept "debt"? Or that punishment as *retribution* developed completely apart from any presupposition concerning freedom or lack of freedom of the will?—and to such a degree that in fact a *high* level of humanization is always necessary before the animal "man" can begin to make those much more primitive distinctions "intentional," "negligent," "accidental," "accountable," and their opposites, and to take them into account when measuring out punishment. The thought, now so cheap and apparently so natural, so unavoidable, a thought that has even had to serve as an explanation of how the feeling of justice came into being at all on earth—"the criminal has earned his punishment *because* he could have acted otherwise"—is in fact a sophisticated form of human judging and inferring that was attained extremely late; whoever shifts it to the beginnings lays a hand on the psychology of older humanity in a particularly crude manner. Throughout the greatest part of human history punishment was definitely *not* imposed *because* one held the evil-doer responsible for his deed, that is, *not* under the presupposition that only the guilty one is to be punished:—rather, as parents even today punish their children, from anger over an injury suffered, which is vented on the agent of the injury—anger held within bounds, however, and modified through the idea that every injury has its *equivalent* in something and can really be paid off, even if only through the *pain* of its agent. Whence has this age-old, deeply-rooted, perhaps now no longer eradicable idea taken its power—the idea of an equivalence between injury and pain? I have already given it away: in the contractual relationship between *creditor* and *debtor*, which is as old as the existence of "legal subjects" and in turn points back to the basic forms of purchase, sale, exchange, trade, and commerce.

5

Calling to mind these contract relationships admittedly awakens various kinds of suspicion and resist-

ance toward the earlier humanity that created or permitted them, as is, after the preceding remarks, to be expected from the outset. Precisely here there are *promises* made; precisely here it is a matter of *making* a memory for the one who promises; precisely here, one may suspect, will be a place where one finds things that are hard, cruel, embarrassing. In order to instill trust in his promise of repayment, to provide a guarantee for the seriousness and the sacredness of his promise, to impress repayment on his conscience as a duty, as an obligation, the debtor—by virtue of a contract—pledges to the creditor in the case of non-payment something else that he "possesses," over which he still has power, for example his body or his wife or his freedom or even his life (or, under certain religious conditions, even his blessedness, the salvation of his soul, finally even his peace in the grave: as in Egypt where the corpse of the debtor found no rest from the creditor, even in the grave—and indeed there was something to this rest, precisely among the Egyptians.) Above all, however, the creditor could subject the body of the debtor to all manner of ignominy and torture, for example cutting as much from it as appeared commensurate to the magnitude of the debt: —and everywhere and early on there were exact assessments of value developed from this viewpoint—some going horribly into the smallest detail—*legally* established assessments of the individual limbs and areas on the body. I take it already as progress, as proof of a freer, more grandly calculating, *more Roman* conception of the law when the Twelve Tables legislation of Rome decreed it was of no consequence how much or how little the creditors cut off in such a case, *"si plus minusve secuerunt, ne fraude esto."*[46] Let us make clear to ourselves the logic of this whole form of compensation: it is foreign enough. The equivalence consists in this: that in place of an advantage that directly makes good for the injury (hence in place of a compensation in money, land, possession of any kind) the creditor is granted a certain *feeling of satisfaction* as repayment and compensation,—the feeling of satisfaction that comes from being permitted to vent his power without a second thought on one who is pow-

---

[46] [If they have secured more or less, let that be no crime.]

erless, the carnal delight "*de faire le mal pour le plaisir de le faire,*"[47] the enjoyment of doing violence: which enjoyment is valued all the higher the lower and baser the creditor's standing in the social order and can easily appear to him as a most delectable morsel, indeed as a foretaste of a higher status. Through his "punishment" of the debtor the creditor participates in a *right of lords:* finally he, too, for once attains the elevating feeling of being permitted to hold a being in contempt and maltreat it as something "beneath himself "—or at least, if the actual power of punishment, the execution of punishment has already passed over into the hands of the "authorities," of *seeing* it held in contempt and maltreated. The compensation thus consists in a directive and right to cruelty.—

6

In *this* sphere, in contract law that is, the moral conceptual world "guilt," "conscience," "duty," "sacredness of duty" has its genesis—its beginning, like the beginning of everything great on earth, was thoroughly and prolongedly drenched in blood. And might one not add that this world has in essence never again entirely lost a certain odor of blood and torture? (not even in old Kant: the categorical imperative smells of cruelty . . .) It was likewise here that that uncanny and perhaps now inextricable meshing of ideas, "guilt and suffering," was first knitted. Asking once again: to what extent can suffering be a compensation for "debts"? To the extent that *making*-suffer felt good, and in the highest degree; to the extent that the injured one exchanged for what was lost, including the displeasure over the loss, an extraordinary counter-pleasure: *making*-suffer,—a true *festival*, something that, as stated, stood that much higher in price, the more it contradicted the rank and social standing of the creditor. This stated as conjecture: for it is difficult to see to the bottom of such subterranean things, not to mention that it is embarrassing; and whoever clumsily throws the concept of "revenge" into the middle of it all has

covered and obscured his insight into the matter rather than making it easier (—revenge simply leads back to the same problem: "how can making-suffer be a satisfaction?"). It seems to me that it is repugnant to the delicacy, even more to the Tartuffery of tame domestic animals (which is to say modern humans, which is to say us) to imagine in all its force the degree to which *cruelty* constitutes the great festival joy of earlier humanity, indeed is an ingredient mixed in with almost all of their joys; how naïvely, on the other hand, how innocently its need for cruelty manifests itself, how universally they rank precisely "disinterested malice" (or, to speak with Spinoza, *sympathia malevolens*)[48] as a *normal* quality of man—: thus as something to which the conscience heartily says "*yes*"! Perhaps even today there is enough of this oldest and most pervasive festival joy of man for a more profound eye to perceive; in *Beyond Good and Evil* 229 (even earlier in *Daybreak* 18, 77, 113), I pointed with a cautious finger to the ever-growing spiritualization and "deification" of cruelty that runs though the entire history of higher culture (and in a significant sense even constitutes it). In any case it has not been all that long since one could not imagine royal marriages and folk festivals in the grandest style without executions, torturings, or perhaps an *auto-da-fé*, likewise no noble household without beings on whom one could vent one's malice and cruel teasing without a second thought (—think for example of Don Quixote at the court of the Duchess: today we read the entire *Don Quixote* with a bitter taste on our tongue, almost with anguish, and would as a result appear very strange, very puzzling to its author and his contemporaries—they read it with the very clearest conscience as the most lighthearted of books, they practically laughed themselves to death over it). Seeing-suffer feels good, making-suffer even more so—that is a hard proposition, but a central one, an old powerful human-all-too-human proposition, to which, by the way, even the apes might subscribe: for it is said that in thinking up bizarre cruelties they already abundantly herald and, as it were, "prelude" man. Without cruelty, no festival: thus teaches the

---

[47] [To do evil for the pleasure of doing it.]

[48] [Ill-willing sympathy.]

oldest, longest part of man's history—and in punishment too there is so much that is *festive!*—

7

—With these thoughts, incidentally, it is by no means my intent to help our pessimists to new grist for their discordant and creaking mills of life-weariness; on the contrary they are meant expressly to show that back then, when humanity was not yet ashamed of its cruelty, life on earth was more lighthearted than it is now that there are pessimists. The darkening of the heavens over man has always increased proportionally as man has grown ashamed *of man*. The tired pessimistic glance, the mistrust toward the riddle of life, the icy "no" of disgust at life—these are not the distinguishing marks of the *most evil* ages of the human race: rather, being the swamp plants they are, they first enter the light of day when the swamp to which they belong appears,—I mean the diseased softening and moralization by virtue of which the creature "man" finally learns to be ashamed of all of his instincts. Along the way to "angel" (to avoid using a harsher word here) man has bred for himself that upset stomach and coated tongue through which not only have the joy and innocence of the animal become repulsive but life itself has become unsavory:—so that he at times stands before himself holding his nose and, along with Pope Innocent the Third, disapprovingly catalogues his repulsive traits ("impure begetting, disgusting nourishment in the womb, vileness of the matter out of which man develops, revolting stench, excretion of saliva, urine, and feces"). Now, when suffering is always marshalled forth as the first among the arguments *against* existence, as its nastiest question mark, one would do well to remember the times when one made the reverse judgment because one did not wish to do without *making*-suffer and saw in it an enchantment of the first rank, an actual seductive lure *to* life. Perhaps back then—to the comfort of delicate souls—pain didn't yet hurt as much as it does today; at least such a conclusion will be permissible for a physician who has treated Negroes (taken as representatives of prehistorical man—) for cases of serious internal infection that would almost drive even the best constituted European to despair;—in Negroes they do *not* do this. (Indeed the curve of human capacity for feeling pain appears to sink extraordinarily and almost abruptly as soon as one gets beyond the upper ten thousand or ten million of the highest level of culture; and I, for my part, do not doubt that when held up against one painful night of a single hysterical educated female the combined suffering of all the animals thus far questioned with the knife to obtain scientific answers simply isn't worth considering.) Perhaps one may even be allowed to admit the possibility that this pleasure in cruelty needn't actually have died out: but, in the same proportion as the pain hurts more today, it would need a certain sublimation and subtilization, namely it would have to appear translated into the imaginative and inward, adorned with all kinds of names so harmless that they arouse no suspicion, not even in the most delicate, most hypocritical conscience ("tragic pity" is such a name; another is *les nostalgies de la croix*).[49] What actually arouses indignation against suffering is not suffering in itself, but rather the senselessness of suffering; but neither for the Christian, who has interpreted into suffering an entire secret salvation machinery, nor for the naive human of older times, who knew how to interpret all suffering in terms of spectators or agents of suffering, was there any such *meaningless* suffering at all. So that concealed, undiscovered, unwitnessed suffering could be banished from the world and honestly negated, one was almost compelled back then to invent gods and intermediate beings of all heights and depths, in short, something that also roams in secret, that also sees in the dark, and that does not easily let an interesting painful spectacle escape it. For with the help of such inventions life back then was expert at the trick at which it has always been expert, of justifying itself, of justifying its "evil"; today it would perhaps need other auxiliary inventions for this (for example life as riddle, life as epistemological problem). "Every evil is justified, the sight of which edifies a god": thus went the

---

[49] [The nostalgias of the cross.]

prehistoric logic of feeling—and, really, was it only the prehistoric? The gods, conceived of as friends of *cruel* spectacles—oh how far this age-old conception extends even into our humanized Europe! on this point one may consult with Calvin[50] and Luther[51] for instance. It is certain in any case that the *Greeks* still knew of no more pleasant offering with which to garnish the happiness of their gods than the joys of cruelty. With what sort of eyes then do you think Homer had his gods look down on the fates of humans? What was the ultimate meaning of Trojan wars and similar tragic horrors? There can be no doubt at all: they were meant as *festival games* for the gods: and, insofar as the poet is in this respect more "godlike" than other humans, probably also as festival games for the poets . . . The moral philosophers of Greece later imagined the eyes of the gods no differently, still glancing down at the moral struggle, at the heroism and the self-torture of the virtuous: the "Heracles of duty" was on a stage, he also knew he was on it; virtue without witnesses was something entirely inconceivable for this people of spectacles. Wasn't that philosophers' invention, so audacious, so fateful, which was first devised for Europe back then—that of "free will," of the absolute spontaneity of man in good and evil—devised above all in order to create a right to the idea that the interest of the gods in man, in human virtue, *could never be exhausted?* On this stage, the earth, there would never be a shortage of truly new things, of truly unheard-of tensions, complications, catastrophes: a world conceived as completely deterministic would have been predictable for the gods and accordingly soon tiring—reason enough for these *friends of the gods*, the philosophers, not to expect their gods to be able to deal with such a deterministic world! In antiquity all of humanity is full of tender considerations for "the spectator," as an essentially public, essentially visible world that could not imagine happiness without spectacles and festivals.—And, as already mentioned, in great *punishment* too there is so much that is festive! . . .

50 [John Calvin (1509–1564) Protestant Reformer and theologian.]
51 [Martin Luther (1483–1546), instigator of the 16th century Reformation and of Protestantism.]

8

The feeling of guilt, of personal obligation—to take up the train of our investigation again—had its origin, as we have seen, in the oldest and most primitive relationship among persons there is, in the relationship between buyer and seller, creditor and debtor: here for the first time person stepped up against person, here for the first time a person *measured himself* by another person. No degree of civilization however low has yet been discovered in which something of this relationship was not already noticeable. Making prices, gauging values, thinking out equivalents, exchanging— this preoccupied man's very first thinking to such an extent that it is in a certain sense thinking *itself:* here that oldest kind of acumen was bred, here likewise we may suspect the first beginnings of human pride, man's feeling of pre-eminence with respect to other creatures. Perhaps our word "man" (*manas*)[52] still expresses precisely something of this self-esteem: man designated himself as the being who measures values, who values and measures, as the "appraising animal in itself." Purchase and sale, together with their psychological accessories, are older than even the beginnings of any societal associations and organizational forms: it was out of the most rudimentary form of personal legal rights that the budding feeling of exchange, contract, guilt, right, obligation, compensation first *transferred* itself onto the coarsest and earliest communal complexes (in their relationship to similar complexes), together with the habit of comparing, measuring, and calculating power against power. The eye was simply set to this perspective: and with that clumsy consistency characteristic of earlier humanity's thinking— which has difficulty moving but then continues relentlessly in the same direction—one arrived straightaway at the grand generalization "every thing has its price; *everything* can be paid off"—at the oldest and most naive moral canon of *justice*, at the beginning of all "good-naturedness," all "fairness," all "good will," all "objectivity" on earth. Justice at this first stage is the good will among parties of approximately equal power

52 [Sanskrit: mind; understanding or the conscious will.]

to come to terms with one another, to reach an "understanding" again by means of a settlement—and in regard to less powerful parties, to *force* them to a settlement among themselves.—

9

Always measured by the standard of an earlier time (which earlier time is, by the way, at all times present or again possible): the community, too, thus stands to its members in that important basic relationship, that of the creditor to his debtor. One lives in a community, one enjoys the advantages of a community (oh what advantages! we sometimes underestimate this today), one lives protected, shielded, in peace and trust, free from care with regard to certain injuries and hostilities to which the human *outside*, the "outlaw," is exposed—a German understands what "Elend," *êlend*[53] originally means—, since one has pledged and obligated oneself to the community precisely in view of these injuries and hostilities. What happens *in the other case?* The community, the deceived creditor, will exact payment as best it can, one can count on that. Here it is least of all a matter of the direct injury inflicted by the injuring party; quite apart from this, the criminal is above all a "breaker," one who breaks his contract and word *with the whole*, in relation to all goods and conveniences of communal life in which he has until this point had a share. The criminal is a debtor who not only fails to pay back the advantages and advances rendered him, but also even lays a hand on his creditor: he therefore not only forfeits all of these goods and advantages from now on, as is fair,—he is also now reminded *how much there is to these goods*. The anger of the injured creditor, of the community, gives him back again to the wild and outlawed condition from which he was previously protected: it expels him from itself,—and now every kind of hostility may vent itself on him. At this level of civilization "punishment" is simply the copy, the *mimus* of normal behavior toward the hated, disarmed, defeated enemy, who has forfeited not only every right and protection, but also every mercy; in other words, the law of war and the victory celebration of *vae victis!*[54] in all their ruthlessness and cruelty:—which explains why war itself (including the warlike cult of sacrifice) has supplied all the *forms* in which punishment appears in history.

10

As its power grows, a community no longer takes the transgressions of the individual so seriously because they can no longer count as dangerous and subversive for the continued existence of the whole to the same extent as formerly: the evildoer is no longer "made an outlaw" and cast out; the general anger is no longer allowed to vent itself in the same unbridled manner as formerly—rather, from now on, the evildoer is carefully defended against this anger, particularly that of the ones directly injured, and taken under the protection of the whole. Compromise with the anger of the one immediately affected by the misdeed; a striving to localize the case and prevent a further or indeed general participation and unrest; attempts to find equivalents and to settle the entire affair (the *compositio*);[55] above all the increasingly more resolute will to understand every offense as in some sense *capable of being paid off*, hence, at least to a certain extent, to *isolate* the criminal and his deed from each other—these are the traits that are imprinted with increasing clarity onto the further development of penal law. If the power and the self-confidence of a community grow, the penal law also always becomes milder; every weakening and deeper endangering of the former brings the latter's harsher forms to light again. The "creditor" has always become more humane to the degree that he has become richer; finally the amount of injury he

---

[53] [The New High German *Elend* (misery) derives from the Old High German adjective *elilenti* (in another land or country; banished) via the shortened Middle High German *ellende* or *êlend* (foreign, miserable).]

[54] [Woe to the conquered! Livy, *Ab urbe condita*, Book V, 48, 9.]

[55] [Term from Roman law referring to the settlement in a case of injury or damage caused by an illegal act.]

can bear without suffering from it even becomes the *measure* of his wealth. It would not be impossible to imagine a *consciousness of power* in society such that society might allow itself the noblest luxury there is for it—to leave the one who injures it *unpunished*. "What concern are my parasites to me?" it might then say. "Let them live and prosper: I am strong enough for that!" . . . The justice that began with "everything can be paid off, everything must be paid off," ends by looking the other way and letting the one unable to pay go free,—it ends like every good thing on earth, by *cancelling itself*. This self-cancellation of justice: we know what pretty name it gives itself—*mercy* ; as goes without saying, it remains the privilege of the most powerful, better still, his beyond-the-law.

11

—Here a word in opposition to recent attempts to seek the origin of justice on an entirely different ground,—namely that of *ressentiment*. First, for the ears of psychologists, supposing they should have the desire to study *ressentiment* itself up close for once: this plant now blooms most beautifully among anarchists and anti-Semites—in secret, incidentally, as it has always bloomed, like the violet, albeit with a different scent. And as like must necessarily always proceed from like, so it will not surprise us to see proceeding again from just such circles attempts like those often made before—compare above, section 14—to hallow *revenge* under the name of *justice*—as if justice were basically only a further development of the feeling of being wounded—and retroactively to raise to honor along with revenge the *reactive* affects in general and without exception. At the latter I would least take offense: with respect to the entire biological problem (in relation to which the value of these affects has thus far been underestimated) it would even appear to me to be a *merit*. I call attention only to the circumstance that it is from the spirit of *ressentiment* itself that this new nuance of scientific fairness (in favor of hate, envy, ill will, suspicion, rancor, revenge) grows forth. For this "scientific fairness" immediately shuts down and makes room for accents of mortal hostility and

prejudice as soon as it is a matter of another group of affects that are, it seems to me, of still much higher biological value than those reactive ones, and accordingly deserve all the more to be *scientifically* appraised and esteemed: namely the truly *active* affects like desire to rule, greed, and the like. (E. Dühring,[56] *Value of Life*; *Course in Philosophy*; basically everywhere.) So much against this tendency in general: as for Dühring's particular proposition that the homeland of justice is to be sought on the ground of reactive feeling, one must, for love of the truth, pit against it in stark reversal this alternative proposition: the *last* ground conquered by the spirit of justice is the ground of reactive feeling! If it really happens that the just man remains just even toward those who injure him (and not merely cold, moderate, distant, indifferent: being just is always a *positive* way of behaving), if the high, clear objectivity—that sees as deeply as it does generously—of the just eye, the *judging* eye, does not cloud even under the assault of personal injury, derision, accusation, well, then that is a piece of perfection and highest mastery on earth—what is more, something one would be prudent not to expect here, in which one in any case should not all too easily *believe*. Even with the most righteous persons it is certain that a small dose of attack, malice, insinuation is, on the average, already enough to chase the blood into their eyes and the fairness *out*. The active, the attacking, encroaching human is still located a hundred paces nearer to justice than the reactive one; he simply has no need to appraise his object falsely and with prejudice as the reactive human does, must do. Therefore in all ages the aggressive human, as the stronger, more courageous, more noble one, has in fact also had the *freer* eye, the *better* conscience on his side: conversely one can already guess who actually has the invention of the "bad conscience" on his conscience,—the human being of *ressentiment*! Finally, just look around in history: in which sphere has the entire administration of justice, also the true need for justice,

---

[56] [Eugen Karl Dühring (1833–1921). Philosopher and political economist. In his autobiography (1882) he claims to have been the founder of anti-Semitism, and he was a major figure in the anti-Semitic movement in Germany.]

thus far been at home on earth? Perhaps in the sphere of the reactive human? Absolutely *not*: rather in that of the active, strong, spontaneous, aggressive. Considered historically, justice on earth represents—let it be said to the annoyance of the above-named agitator (who himself once confessed: "the doctrine of revenge runs through all my works and efforts as the red thread of justice")—precisely the battle *against* reactive feelings, the war against them on the part of active and aggressive powers that have used their strength in part to call a halt to and impose measure on the excess of reactive pathos and to force a settlement. Everywhere justice is practiced and upheld one sees a stronger power seeking means to put an end to the senseless raging of *ressentiment* among weaker parties subordinated to it (whether groups or individuals), in part by pulling the object of *ressentiment* out of the hands of revenge, in part by setting in the place of revenge the battle against the enemies of peace and order, in part by inventing, suggesting, in some cases imposing compensations, in part by raising certain equivalents for injuries to the status of a norm to which *ressentiment* is henceforth once and for all restricted. But the most decisive thing the highest power does and forces through against the predominance of counter- and after-feelings—which it always does as soon as it is in any way strong enough to do so—is the establishment of the *law*, the imperative declaration of what in general is to count in its eyes as permitted, as just, what as forbidden, as unjust: after it has established the law, it treats infringements and arbitrary actions of individuals or entire groups as wanton acts against the law, as rebellion against the highest power itself, thereby diverting the feeling of its subjects away from the most immediate injury caused by such wanton acts and thus achieving in the long run the opposite of what all revenge wants, which sees only the viewpoint of the injured one, allows only it to count—from now on the eye is trained for an ever *more impersonal* appraisal of deeds, even the eye of the injured one himself (although this last of all, as was mentioned at the start).— Accordingly, only once the law has been established do "justice" and "injustice" exist (and *not* as Dühring would have it, beginning with the act of injuring). To talk of justice and injustice *in themselves* is devoid of

all sense; *in itself* injuring, doing violence, pillaging, destroying naturally cannot be "unjust," insofar as life acts *essentially*—that is, in its basic functions—in an injuring, violating, pillaging, destroying manner and cannot be *thought* at all without this character. One must even admit to oneself something still more problematic: that, from the highest biological standpoint, conditions of justice can never be anything but *exceptional conditions*, as partial restrictions of the true will of life—which is out after power—and subordinating themselves as individual means to its overall end: that is, as means for creating *greater* units of power. A legal system conceived of as sovereign and universal, not as a means in the battle of power complexes, but rather as means *against* all battle generally, say in accordance with Dühring's communist cliché that every will must accept every other will as equal, would be a principle *hostile to life*, a destroyer and dissolver of man, an attempt to kill the future of man, a sign of weariness, a secret pathway to nothingness.—

12

Yet a word on the origin and purpose of punishment— two problems that fall out or ought to fall out separately: unfortunately they are usually lumped together. How do the previous genealogists of morality carry on in this case? Naively, as they have always carried on— they discover some "purpose" or other in punishment, for example revenge or deterrence, then innocently place this purpose at the beginning as *causa fiendi*[57] of punishment, and—are done. The "purpose in law," however, is the last thing that is usable for the history of the genesis of law: on the contrary, for history of every kind there is no more important proposition than that one which is gained with such effort but also really *ought to be* gained,—namely, that the cause of the genesis of a thing and its final usefulness, its actual employment and integration into a system of purposes, lie *toto caelo* apart; that something extant, something that has somehow or other come into being, is again and again interpreted according to new views, monop-

[57] [Cause of the coming into being.]

olized in a new way, transformed and rearranged for a new use by a power superior to it; that all happening in the organic world is an *overpowering, a becoming-lord-over*; and that, in turn, all overpowering and becoming-lord-over is a new interpreting, an arranging by means of which the previous "meaning" and "purpose" must of necessity become obscured or entirely extinguished. However well one has grasped the *utility* of some physiological organ (or of a legal institution, a social custom, a political practice, a form in the arts or in religious cult), one has still not comprehended anything regarding its genesis: as uncomfortable and unpleasant as this may sound to earlier ears, —for from time immemorial one had thought that in comprehending the demonstrable purpose, the usefulness of a thing, a form, an arrangement, one also comprehended the reason for its coming into being— the eye as made to see, the hand as made to grasp. Thus one also imagined punishment as invented for punishing. But all purposes, all utilities, are only *signs* that a will to power has become lord over something less powerful and has stamped its own functional meaning onto it; and in this manner the entire history of a "thing," an organ, a practice can be a continuous sign-chain of ever new interpretations and arrangements, whose causes need not be connected even among themselves—on the contrary, in some cases only accidentally follow and replace one another. The "development" of a thing, a practice, an organ is accordingly least of all its *progressus* toward a goal, still less a logical and shortest *progressus*, reached with the smallest expenditure of energy and cost,—but rather the succession of more or less profound, more or less independent processes of overpowering that play themselves out in it, including the resistances expended each time against these processes, the attempted changes of form for the purpose of defense and reaction, also the results of successful counter-actions. The form is fluid but the "meaning" is even more so . . . Even in the individual organism things are no different: with each essential growth of the whole the "meaning" of the individual organs shifts as well,—in some cases their partial destruction, their reduction in number (for example through destruction of the intermediate members), can be a sign of growing strength and perfection. I wanted to say: even the partial *loss of*

utility, atrophying and degenerating, the forfeiture of meaning and purposiveness, in short death, belongs to the conditions of true *progressus*: which always appears in the form of a will and way to *greater power* and is always pushed through at the expense of numerous smaller powers. The magnitude of a "progress" is even *measured* by the mass of all that had to be sacrificed for it; humanity as mass sacrificed for the flourishing of a single *stronger* species of human being—that *would be* progress . . .—I emphasize this main viewpoint of historical methodology all the more because it basically goes against the presently ruling instincts and taste of the times, which would rather learn to live with the absolute randomness, indeed the mechanistic senselessness of all happening than with the theory of a *power-will* playing itself out in all happening. The democratic idiosyncrasy against everything that rules and desires to rule, the modern *misarchism* (to create a bad word for a bad thing) has gradually transformed and disguised itself into something spiritual, most spiritual, to such an extent that today it is already penetrating, is *allowed* to penetrate, step by step into the most rigorous, apparently most objective sciences; indeed it appears to me already to have become lord over the whole of physiology and the doctrine of life— to its detriment, as goes without saying—by removing through sleight of hand one of its basic concepts, that of true *activity*. Under the pressure of that idiosyncrasy one instead places "adaptation" in the foreground, that is to say an activity of second rank, a mere reactivity; indeed life itself is defined as an ever more purposive inner adaptation to external circumstances (Herbert Spencer). In so doing, however, one mistakes the essence of life, its *will to power*; in so doing one overlooks the essential pre-eminence of the spontaneous, attacking, infringing, reinterpreting, reordering, and formative forces, upon whose effect the "adaptation" first follows; in so doing one denies the lordly role of the highest functionaries in the organism itself, in which the will of life appears active and form-giving. One recalls that for which Huxley[58] re-

---

[58] [T(homas) H(enry) Huxley (1825–1895), English biologist. He was one of Darwin's close associates and perhaps his chief defender in the public debates concerning the theory of evolution.]

proached Spencer—his "administrative nihilism": but it is a matter of *more* than just "administering" . . .

13

—To return to our topic, namely to *punishment*, one must then distinguish in it two sorts of things: first that which is relatively *permanent* in it, the practice, the act, the "drama," a certain strict sequence of procedures; on the other hand that which is *fluid* in it, the meaning, the purpose, the expectation tied to the execution of such procedures. It is presupposed here without further ado, per analogy, according to the main viewpoint of the historical methodology just developed, that the procedure itself will be something older, earlier than its use for punishment, that the latter was first placed into, interpreted into the procedure (which had long existed, but was practiced in another sense)—in short, that things are *not* as our naive genealogists of morality and law have thus far assumed, all of whom thought of the procedure as *invented* for the purpose of punishing, as one once thought of the hand as invented for the purpose of grasping. Now as for that other element in punishment—that which is fluid, its "meaning"—in a very late state of culture (for example in present-day Europe), the concept "punishment" in fact no longer represents a single meaning at all but rather an entire synthesis of "meanings": the previous history of punishment in general, the history of its exploitation for the most diverse purposes, finally crystallizes into a kind of unity that is difficult to dissolve, difficult to analyze and—one must emphasize—is completely and utterly *undefinable*. (Today it is impossible to say for sure why we actually punish: all concepts in which an entire process is semiotically summarized elude definition; only that which has no history is definable.) In an earlier stage, by contrast, that synthesis of "meanings" still appears more soluble, also more capable of shifts; one can still perceive in each individual case how the elements of the synthesis change their valence and rearrange themselves accordingly, so that now this, now that element comes to the fore and dominates at the expense of the remaining ones, indeed in some cases one element (say the purpose of deterrence) seems to cancel out all the

rest of the elements. To give at least some idea of how uncertain, how after-the-fact, how accidental "the meaning" of punishment is and how one and the same procedure can be used, interpreted, arranged with respect to fundamentally different intentions: I offer here the schema that offered itself to me on the basis of a relatively small and random body of material. Punishment as rendering-harmless, as prevention of further injury. Punishment as payment to the injured party for the injury, in any form (even in that of a compensating affect). Punishment as isolation of a disturbance of equilibrium in order to prevent a further spreading of the disturbance. Punishment as instilling fear of those who determine and execute the punishment. Punishment as a kind of compensation for the benefits the criminal has enjoyed up to that point (for example when he is made useful as a slave in the mines). Punishment as elimination of a degenerating element (in some cases of an entire branch, as according to Chinese law: thus as a means for preserving the purity of the race or for maintaining a social type). Punishment as festival, namely as mocking and doing violence to a finally defeated enemy. Punishment as making a memory, whether for the one who suffers the punishment—so-called "improvement"—or for the witnesses of the execution. Punishment as payment of an honorarium, stipulated on the part of the power that protects the evil-doer from the excesses of revenge. Punishment as compromise with the natural state of revenge, insofar as the latter is still upheld and claimed as a privilege by powerful clans. Punishment as declaration of war and war-time measure against an enemy of peace, of law, of order, of authority, whom one battles—with the means that war furnishes—as dangerous to the community, as in breach of contract with respect to its presuppositions, as a rebel, traitor, and breaker of the peace.—

14

This list is certainly not complete; obviously punishment is overladen with utilities of all kinds. All the more reason to subtract from it a *supposed* utility that admittedly counts in popular consciousness as its most essential one,—precisely the one in which belief in punishment, teetering today for several reasons, still finds its most forceful support. Punishment is supposed to have the value of awakening in the guilty one the *feeling of guilt*; one seeks in it the true *instrumentum* of that reaction of the soul called "bad conscience," "pang of conscience." But by so doing one lays a hand on reality and on psychology, even for today— and how much more for the longest part of the history of man, his prehistory! Precisely among criminals and prisoners the genuine pang of conscience is something extremely rare; the prisons, the penitentiaries are *not* the breeding places where this species of gnawing worm most loves to flourish:—on this there is agreement among all conscientious observers, who in many cases render a judgment of this sort reluctantly enough and against their most personal wishes. In general, punishment makes hard and cold; it concentrates; it sharpens the feeling of alienation; it strengthens the power of resistance. If it should happen that it breaks the vigor and brings about a pitiful prostration and self-abasement, such a result is surely even less pleasing than the average effect of punishment— which is characterized by a dry gloomy seriousness. But if we think, say, of those millennia *before* the history of man, then one may unhesitatingly judge that it is precisely through punishment that the development of the feeling of guilt has been most forcefully *held back*—at least with respect to the victims on whom the punishing force vented itself. For let us not underestimate the extent to which precisely the sight of the judicial and executive procedures prevents the criminal from feeling his deed, the nature of his action, as *in itself* reprehensible, for he sees the very same kind of actions committed in the service of justice and then approved, committed with a good conscience: thus spying, outwitting, bribery, entrapment, the whole tricky and cunning art of police and prosecutors; moreover—based on principle, without even the excuse of emotion—robbing, overpowering, slandering, taking captive, torturing, murdering as displayed in the various kinds of punishment—all of these thus actions his judges in no way reject and condemn *in themselves*, but rather only in a certain respect and practical application. The "bad conscience," this most uncanny and interesting plant of our earthly vegeta-

tion, did *not* grow on this ground,—indeed, in the consciousness of the ones judging, the ones punishing, there was for the longest time *nothing* expressed that suggested one was dealing with a "guilty one." But rather with an instigator of injury, with an irresponsible piece of fate. And the one himself upon whom the punishment afterwards fell, again like a piece of fate, had no other "inner pain" than he would have had at the sudden occurrence of something unanticipated, of a frightful natural event, of a plummeting, crushing boulder against which one can no longer fight.

15

This once entered Spinoza's consciousness in an ensnaring manner (to the vexation of his interpreters, who really *exert* themselves to misunderstand him at this point, for example Kuno Fischer)[59] when one afternoon, bothered by who knows what kind of memory, he dwelt on the question of what actually remained for him of the famous **morsus conscientiae**[60]—he who had sent good and evil into exile among the human illusions and had fiercely defended the honor of his "free" God against those blasphemers who claimed something to the effect that God works everything *sub ratione boni*[61] ("that, however, would be to subject God to fate and would in truth be the greatest of all absurdities"—). For Spinoza the world had stepped back again into that innocence in which it had lain before the invention of the bad conscience: what had become of the *morsus conscientiae* in the process? "The opposite of *gaudium*,"[62] he finally said to himself,—"a sadness, accompanied by the image of a past matter that has turned out in a manner contrary to all expectation." Eth. III propos. XVIII schol. I. II. For thousands of years instigators of evil overtaken by punishment have felt *no different than Spinoza* with regard to their "transgression": "something has unex-

[59] [Kuno Fischer (1824–1907), professor of philosophy at Heidelberg, author of the ten-volume *Geschichte der neuern Philosophie* (History of Modern Philosophy).]
[60] [Sting of conscience.]
[61] [For the sake of the good.]
[62] [Joy.]

pectedly gone wrong here," *not:* "I should not have done that"—they submitted themselves to the punishment as one submits to a sickness or a misfortune or to death, with that stouthearted fatalism without revolt by which the Russians, for example, even today have the advantage over us Westerners in dealing with life. If there was a critique of the deed back then, it was prudence that exercised this critique on the deed: without question we must seek the actual *effect* of punishment above all in a sharpening of prudence, in a lengthening of memory, in a will hereafter to proceed more cautiously, more mistrustfully, more secretively, in the insight that one is once and for all too weak for many things, in a kind of improvement in self-assessment. Generally what can be achieved among humans and animals through punishment is an increase of fear, a sharpening of prudence, mastery of the appetites: punishment thus *tames* man, but it does not make him "better"—one might with greater justification maintain the opposite. ("Injury makes prudent," say the common folk: insofar as it makes prudent, it also makes bad. Fortunately, it often enough makes stupid.)

16

At this point I can no longer avoid helping my own hypothesis on the origin of the "bad conscience" to a first, preliminary expression: it is not easy to present and needs to be considered, guarded, and slept over for a long time. I take bad conscience to be the deep sickness into which man had to fall under the pressure of that most fundamental of all changes he ever experienced—the change of finding himself enclosed once and for all within the sway of society and peace. Just as water animals must have fared when they were forced either to become land animals or to perish, so fared these half animals who were happily adapted to wilderness, war, roaming about, adventure—all at once all of their instincts were devalued and "disconnected." From now on they were to go on foot and "carry themselves" where they had previously been carried by the water: a horrible heaviness lay upon them. They felt awkward doing the simplest tasks; for this new, unfamiliar world they no longer had their old leaders, the

regulating drives that unconsciously guided them safely—they were reduced to thinking, inferring, calculating, connecting cause and effect, these unhappy ones, reduced to their "consciousness," to their poorest and most erring organ! I do not believe there has ever been such a feeling of misery on earth, such a leaden discomfort—and yet those old instincts had not all at once ceased to make their demands! It's just that it was difficult and seldom possible to yield to them: for the most part they had to seek new and as it were subterranean gratifications. All instincts that do not discharge themselves outwardly *turn themselves inwards*—this is what I call the *internalizing* of man: thus first grows in man that which he later calls his "soul." The entire inner world, originally thin as if inserted between two skins, has spread and unfolded, has taken on depth, breadth, height to the same extent that man's outward discharging has been *obstructed.* Those terrible bulwarks with which the organization of the state protects itself against the old instincts of freedom—punishments belong above all else to these bulwarks—brought it about that all those instincts of the wild free roaming human turned themselves backwards *against man himself.* Hostility, cruelty, pleasure in persecution, in assault, in change, in destruction— all of that turning itself against the possessors of such instincts: *that* is the origin of "bad conscience." The man who, for lack of external enemies and resistance, and wedged into an oppressive narrowness and regularity of custom, impatiently tore apart, persecuted, gnawed at, stirred up, maltreated himself; this animal that one wants to "tame" and that beats itself raw on the bars of its cage; this deprived one, consumed by homesickness for the desert, who had to create out of himself an adventure, a place of torture, an uncertain and dangerous wilderness—this fool, this longing and desperate prisoner became the inventor of "bad conscience." In him, however, the greatest and most uncanny of sicknesses was introduced, one from which man has not recovered to this day, the suffering of man *from man,* from *himself*—as the consequence of a forceful separation from his animal past, of a leap and plunge, as it were, into new situations and conditions of existence, of a declaration of war against the old instincts on which his energy, desire, and terribleness had thus far rested. Let us immediately add that, on the other hand, with the appearance on earth of an animal soul turned against itself, taking sides against itself, something so new, deep, unheard of, enigmatic, contradictory, *and full of future* had come into being that the appearance of the earth was thereby essentially changed. Indeed, divine spectators were necessary to appreciate the spectacle that thus began and whose end is still by no means in sight—a spectacle too refined, too wonderful, too paradoxical to be permitted to play itself out senselessly-unnoticed on some ridiculous star! Since that time man is *included* among the most unexpected and exciting lucky throws in the game played by the "big child" of Heraclitus, whether called Zeus or chance—he awakens for himself an interest, an anticipation, a hope, almost a certainty, as if with him something were announcing itself, something preparing itself, as if man were not a goal but only a path, an incident, a bridge, a great promise . . .

17

To the presupposition of this hypothesis on the origin of bad conscience belongs first, that this change was not gradual, not voluntary, and that it presented itself not as an organic growing into new conditions, but rather as a break, a leap, a compulsion, an inescapable doom, against which there was no struggle and not even any *ressentiment.* Second, however, that this fitting of a previously unrestrained and unformed population into a fixed form, given its beginning in an act of force, could be brought to its completion only by acts of force—that the oldest "state" accordingly made its appearance as a terrible tyranny, as a crushing and ruthless machinery, and continued to work until finally such a raw material of people and half-animals was not only thoroughly kneaded and pliable but also *formed.* I use the word "state": it goes without saying who is meant by this—some pack of blond beasts of prey, a race of conquerors and lords, which, organized in a warlike manner and with the power to organize, unhesitatingly lays its terrible paws on a population enormously superior in number perhaps, but still form-

less, still roaming about. It is in this manner, then, that the "state" begins on earth: I think the flight of fancy that had it beginning with a "contract" has been abandoned. Whoever can give orders, whoever is "lord" by nature, whoever steps forth violently, in deed and gesture—what does he have to do with contracts! With such beings one does not reckon, they come like fate, without basis, reason, consideration, pretext; they are there like lightning is there: too terrible, too sudden, too convincing, too "different" even to be so much as hated. Their work is an instinctive creating of forms, impressing of forms; they are the most involuntary, unconscious artists there are:—where they appear, in a short time something new stands there, a ruling structure that *lives,* in which parts and functions are delimited and related to one another, in which nothing at all finds a place that has not first had placed into it a "meaning" with respect to the whole. They do not know what guilt, what responsibility, what consideration is, these born organizers; in them that terrible artists' egoism rules, that has a gaze like bronze and that knows itself already justified to all eternity in its "work," like the mother in her child. *They* are not the ones among whom "bad conscience" grew, that is clear from the outset—but it would not have grown *without them,* this ugly growth, it would be missing, if an enormous quantity of freedom had not been banished from the world, at least from visibility, and made *latent* as it were, under the pressure of the blows of their hammers, of their artist's violence. This *instinct for freedom,* forcibly made latent—we have already grasped it—this instinct for freedom, driven back, suppressed, imprisoned within, and finally discharging and venting itself only on itself: this, only this, is *bad conscience* in its beginnings.

18

One should guard against forming a low opinion of this entire phenomenon just because it is ugly and painful from the outset. After all, the active force that is at work on a grander scale in those violence-artists and organizers and that builds states, is basically the same force that here—inwardly, on a smaller, pettier scale, in a backwards direction, in the "labyrinth of the breast," to use Goethe's words—creates for itself the bad conscience and builds negative ideals: namely that *instinct for freedom* (speaking in my language: the will to power). Only here the matter on which this force's formative and violating nature vents itself is precisely man himself, his entire animal old self—and *not*, as in that larger and more conspicuous phenomenon, the *other* human, the *other* humans. This secret self-violation, this artists' cruelty, this pleasure in giving oneself—as heavy resisting suffering matter—a form, in burning into oneself a will, a critique, a contradiction, a contempt, a "no"; this uncanny and horrifying-pleasurable work of a soul compliant-conflicted with itself, that makes itself suffer out of pleasure in making-suffer, this entire *active* "bad conscience," as the true womb of ideal and imaginative events, finally brought to light—one can guess it already—a wealth of new disconcerting beauty and affirmation and perhaps for the first time beauty *itself* . . . For what would be "beautiful" if contradiction had not first come to a consciousness of itself, if the ugly had not first said to itself "I am ugly"? . . . After this hint, that enigma will at the least be less enigmatic, namely, to what extent an ideal, a beauty can be suggested by contradictory concepts like *selflessness, self-denial, self-sacrifice*; and we know one thing henceforth, this I do not doubt—namely what kind of *pleasure* it is that the selfless, the self-denying, the self-sacrificing feel from the very start: this pleasure belongs to cruelty.—So much for the present on the origins of the "unegoistic" as a *moral* value and toward staking out the ground from which this value has grown: bad conscience, the will to self-maltreatment, first supplies the presupposition for the *value* of the unegoistic.—

19

It is a sickness, bad conscience—this admits of no doubt—but a sickness as pregnancy is a sickness. Let us seek out the conditions under which this sickness has come to its most terrible and most sublime pinnacle:—we shall see just what it was that thus first made its entry into the world. For this we need a long breath,—and to start off we must return once again to an earlier viewpoint. The civil-law relationship of the debtor to his creditor, of which I have already spoken at length, was once again—and indeed in a manner that is historically exceedingly curious and questionable—interpreted into a relationship in which it is for us modern humans perhaps at its most incomprehensible: namely the relationship of *those presently living* to their *ancestors*. Within the original clan association—we are speaking of primeval times—the living generation always acknowledges a juridical obligation to the earlier generation, and particularly to the earliest one, which founded the clan (and by no means a mere sentimental obligation: one might with good reason even deny the latter altogether for the longest part of the existence of the human race). Here the conviction holds sway that it is only through the sacrifices and achievements of the ancestors that the clan *exists* at all,—and that one has to *repay* them through sacrifices and achievements: one thereby acknowledges a *debt* that is continually growing, since these ancestors, in their continued existence as powerful spirits, do not cease to use their strength to bestow on the clan new benefits and advances. For nothing perhaps? But to those brutal and "soul-poor" ages there is no "for nothing." What can one give back to them? Sacrifices (initially only nourishment, in the coarsest sense), festivals, shrines, tributes, above all obedience—for all customs, as works of the ancestors, are also their statutes and commands—: does one ever give them enough? This suspicion remains and grows: from time to time it forces a great redemption, lock, stock, and barrel, some enormity of a counter-payment to the "creditor" (the notorious sacrifice of the firstborn, for example; blood, human blood in any case). The fear of the progenitor and his power, the consciousness of debts toward him necessarily increases, according to this kind of logic, to exactly the same degree that the power of the clan itself increases, that the clan itself stands ever more victorious, independent, honored, feared. By no means the other way around! Rather every step toward the atrophying of the clan, all miserable chance occurrences, all signs of degeneration, of approaching dissolution always *diminish* the fear of the spirit of the founder and give an ever more reduced notion of his shrewdness, his foresightedness, and his presence as power. If one imagines this brutal kind of logic carried through to its end: finally, through the imagination of growing fear the progenitors of the *most powerful* clans must have grown into enormous proportions and have been pushed back into the darkness of a divine uncanniness and unimaginability:—in the end the progenitor is necessarily transfigured into a *god*. This may even be the origin of the gods, an origin, that is, out of *fear!* . . . And those who think it necessary to add: "but also out of piety!" would hardly be right with regard to the longest period of the human race, its primeval period. All the more, admittedly, for the *middle* period in which the noble clans take shape:—who in fact returned, with interest, to their originators, the ancestors (heroes, gods) all of the qualities that had in the meantime become apparent in them, the *noble* qualities. Later we will take another look at the aristocratizing and ennobling of the gods (which is by no means their "hallowing"): for the present let us simply bring the course of this whole development of guilt consciousness to a conclusion.

20

As history teaches, the consciousness of having debts to the deity by no means came to an end even after the decline of the "community" organized according to blood-relationships; in the same way that it inherited the concepts "good and bad" from the clan nobility (together with its basic psychological propensity for establishing orders of rank), humanity also inherited, along with the deities of the clan and tribe, the pressure of the still unpaid debts and of the longing for the redemption of the same. (The transition is made by those broad slave and serf populations who adapted themselves to the cult of the gods practiced by their lords, whether through force or through submissiveness and mimicry: starting from them, this inheritance then overflows in all directions.) For several millennia the feeling of guilt toward the deity did not stop growing and indeed grew ever onward in the same proportion as the concept of god and the feeling

for god grew on earth and was borne up on high. (The whole history of ethnic fighting, triumphing, reconciling, merging—everything that precedes the final rank-ordering of all ethnic elements in every great racial synthesis—is reflected in the genealogical confusion of their gods, in the legends of their fights, triumphs, and reconciliations; development toward universal empires is also always development toward universal deities; despotism with its overpowering of the independent nobility also always prepares the way for some kind of monotheism.) The rise of the Christian god as the maximum god that has been attained thus far therefore also brought a maximum of feelings of guilt into appearance on earth. Assuming that we have by now entered into the *reverse* movement, one might with no little probability deduce from the unstoppable decline of faith in the Christian god that there would already be a considerable decline in human consciousness of guilt as well; indeed the prospect cannot be dismissed that the perfect and final victory of atheism might free humanity from this entire feeling of having debts to its beginnings, its *causa prima*.[63] Atheism and a kind of *second innocence* belong together. —

21

So much for the present, in short and roughly speaking, on the connection of the concepts "guilt," "duty" to religious presuppositions: I have until now intentionally left aside the actual moralization of these concepts (their being pushed back into conscience, more precisely the entanglement of *bad* conscience with the concept of god) and at the end of the previous section even spoke as if there were no such moralization, consequently, as if those concepts were now necessarily coming to an end now that their presupposition, the faith in our "creditor," in God, has fallen. The facts of the case diverge from this in a terrible manner. With the moralization of the concepts guilt and duty, with their being pushed back into *bad* conscience, we have

---

[63] [First cause.]

in actual fact the attempt to *reverse* the direction of the development just described, at least to bring its movement to a standstill: precisely the prospect of a conclusive redemption *shall* now pessimistically close itself off once and for all; the gaze *shall* now bleakly deflect off, deflect back from a brazen impossibility; those concepts "guilt" and "duty" *shall* now turn themselves backwards—and against whom? There can be no doubt: first against the "debtor," in whom bad conscience now fixes itself firmly, eats into him, spreads out, and grows like a polyp in every breadth and depth until finally, with the impossibility of discharging the debt, the impossibility of discharging penance is also conceived of, the idea that it cannot be paid off ("*eternal* punishment")—; finally, however, even against the "creditor," think here of the *causa prima* of man, of the beginning of the human race, of its progenitor, who is now burdened with a curse ("Adam," "Original Sin," "unfreedom of the will") or of nature, from whose womb man arises and into which the evil principle is now placed ("demonizing of nature") or of existence generally, which is left as *valueless in itself* (nihilistic turning away from it, longing into nothingness or longing into its "opposite," a being-other, Buddhism and related things)—until all at once we stand before the paradoxical and horrifying remedy in which tortured humanity found temporary relief, *Christianity's* stroke of genius: God sacrificing himself for the guilt of man, God himself exacting payment of himself, God as the only one who can redeem from man what has become irredeemable for man himself—the creditor sacrificing himself for his debtor, out of *love* (is that credible?—), out of love for his debtor! . . .

22

One will already have guessed *what* actually happened with all of this and *under* all of this: that will to self-torment, that suppressed cruelty of the animal-human who had been made inward, scared back into himself, of the one locked up in the "state" for the purpose of taming, who invented the bad conscience in order to cause himself pain after the *more natural* out-

let for this *desire to cause pain* was blocked,—this man of bad conscience has taken over the religious presupposition in order to drive his self-torture to its most gruesome severity and sharpness. Guilt before *God*: this thought becomes an instrument of torture for him. In "God" he captures the most extreme opposites he can find to his actual and inescapable animal instincts; he reinterprets these animal instincts themselves as guilt before God (as hostility, rebellion, insurrection against the "lord," the "father," the primal ancestor and beginning of the world); he harnesses himself into the contradiction "God" and "devil"; he takes all the "no" that he says to himself, to nature, naturalness, the facticity of his being and casts it out of himself as a "yes," as existing, corporeal, real, as God, as holiness of God, as judgeship of God, as executionership of God, as beyond, as eternity, as torture without end, as hell, as immeasurability of punishment and guilt. This is a kind of madness of the will in psychic cruelty that has absolutely no equal: the *will* of man to find himself guilty and reprehensible to the point that it cannot be atoned for; his *will* to imagine himself punished without the possibility of the punishment ever becoming equivalent to the guilt; his *will* to infect and make poisonous the deepest ground of things with the problem of punishment and guilt in order to cut off the way out of this labyrinth of "*idées fixes*" once and for all; his *will* to erect an ideal—that of the "holy God"—in order, in the face of the same, to be tangibly certain of his absolute unworthiness. Oh, this insane sad beast man! What ideas occur to it, what anti-nature, what paroxysms of nonsense; what *bestiality of idea* immediately breaks forth when it is hindered only a little from being a *beast of deed* !. . . All of this is interesting to the point of excess, but also of such black gloomy unnerving sadness that one must forcibly forbid oneself to look too long into these abysses. Here there is *sickness*, beyond all doubt, the most terrible sickness that has thus far raged in man:— and whoever is still capable of hearing (but one no longer has the ears for it today!—) how in this night of torture and absurdity the cry *love* resounded, the cry of the most longing delight, of redemption in *love*, will turn away, seized by an invincible horror . . . There is so much in man that is horrifying! . . . The earth has been a madhouse for too long! . . .

23

Let this suffice once and for all concerning the origins of the "holy God."—That *in itself* the conception of gods does not necessarily lead to this degradation of the imagination, which we could not spare ourselves from calling to mind for a moment, that there are *more noble* ways of making use of the fabrication of gods than for this self-crucifixion and self-defilement of man in which Europe's last millennia have had their mastery—this can fortunately be read from every glance one casts on the *Greek gods*, these reflections of noble and autocratic human beings in whom the *animal* in man felt itself deified and *did not* tear itself apart, *did not* rage against itself! For the longest time these Greeks used their gods precisely to keep "bad conscience" at arm's length, to be able to remain cheerful about their freedom of soul: that is, the reverse of the use which Christianity made of its god. They took this to *great lengths*, these splendid and lionhearted childish ones; and no lesser authority than that of the Homeric Zeus himself gives them to understand here and there that they make it too easy for themselves. "A wonder!" he says once—it concerns the case of Aegisthus, a *very* bad case—

> A wonder, how much the mortals complain
>   against the gods!
> *Only from us is there evil*, they think; but they
>   themselves
> Create their own misery through lack of
>   understanding, even counter to fate.

But one hears and sees at the same time that even this Olympian spectator and judge is far from being angry at them for this and from thinking evil of them: "how *foolish* they are!" so he thinks in the face of the misdeeds of the mortals,—and "foolishness," "lack of understanding," a little "disturbance in the head," this much even the Greeks of the strongest, bravest age *allowed* themselves as the reason for much that was bad and doom-laden:—foolishness, *not* sin! do you understand that? . . . But even this disturbance in the head was a problem—"indeed, how is it even possible? whence could it actually have come, given heads such as *we* have, we men of noble descent, of happiness, of optimal form, of the best society, of nobility, of virtue?"—thus the noble Greek wondered for centuries in the face of every incomprehensible atrocity and wanton act with which one of his equals had sullied himself. "A god must have beguiled him," he said to himself finally, shaking his head . . . This way out is *typical* of the Greeks . . . In this manner the gods served in those days to justify humans to a certain degree even in bad things, they served as causes of evil—in those days it was not the punishment they took upon themselves but rather, as is *more noble*, the guilt . . .

24

—I close with three question marks, as one can of course see. "Is an ideal actually being erected here or is one being demolished?" thus one might ask me . . . But have you ever asked yourselves enough how dearly the erection of *every* ideal on earth has exacted its payment? How much reality always had to be libeled and mistaken, how much lying sanctified, how much conscience disturbed, how much "god" had to be sacrificed each time? So that a sanctuary can be erected, *a sanctuary must be shattered*: that is the law—show me a case where it is not fulfilled! . . . We modern humans, we are the heirs of millennia of conscience-vivisection and cruelty to the animal-self: in this we have our longest practice, our artistry perhaps, in any case our sophistication, our overrefinement of taste. For all too long man has regarded his natural inclinations with an "evil eye," so that in him they have finally become wedded to "bad conscience." A reverse attempt would *in itself* be possible—but who is strong enough for it?—namely to wed to bad conscience the *unnatural* inclinations, all those aspirations to the beyond, to that which is contrary to the senses, contrary to the instincts, contrary to nature, contrary to the animal—in short the previous ideals which are all ideals hostile to life, ideals of those who libel the world. To whom to turn today with *such* hopes and demands? . . . In so doing one would have precisely the *good* human beings against oneself; and, in fairness, the comfortable, the reconciled, the vain, the enraptured, the tired . . . What is there that insults more deeply, that separates off so fundamentally, as letting others notice something of the strictness and height with which one treats oneself? And on the other hand—how accommodating, how full of love the whole world shows itself toward us as soon as we do like all the world and "let ourselves go" like all the world! . . . For this goal one would need a *different* kind of spirits than are probable in this of all ages: spirits strengthened by wars and victories, for whom conquering, adventure, danger, pain have even become a need; for this one would need acclimatization to sharp high air, to wintry journeys, to ice and mountain ranges in every sense; for this one would need a kind of sublime malice itself, an ultimate most self-assured mischievousness of knowledge, which belongs to great health; one would need, in brief and gravely enough, precisely this *great health!* . . . Is this even possible today? . . . But someday, in a stronger time than this decaying, self-doubting present, he really must come to us, the *redeeming* human of the great love and contempt, the creative spirit whose compelling strength again and again drives him out of any apart or beyond, whose loneliness is misunderstood by the people as if it were a flight *from* reality—: whereas it is only his submersion, burial, absorption *in* reality so that one day, when he again comes to light, he can bring home the *redemption* of this reality: its redemption from the curse that the previous ideal placed upon it. This human of the future who will redeem us from the previous ideal as much as from that *which had to grow out of it*, from the great disgust, from the will to nothingness; this bell-stroke of noon and of the great decision, that makes the will free again, that gives back to the earth its goal and to man his hope; this Anti-Christ and anti-nihilist; this conqueror of God and of nothingness—*he must one day come* . . .

25

—But what am I saying? Enough! Enough! At this point there is only one thing fitting for me, to be silent: otherwise I would be laying a hand on that which only a younger one is free to choose, a "more future one," a stronger one than I am—which only *Zarathustra* is free to choose, *Zarathustra the godless* . . .